SOMETHING ABOUT THE AUTHOR®

Something about
the Author *was named
an "Outstanding
Reference Source,"*
*the highest honor given
by the American
Library Association
Reference and Adult
Services Division.*

ISSN 0276-816X

sOmeTHING ABOUT THe AUTHOR®

Facts and Pictures about Authors and Illustrators of Books for Young People

volume 225

GALE
CENGAGE Learning

Detroit • New York • San Francisco • New Haven, Conn • Waterville, Maine • London

LSL
Ref
PN
451
.S6
v.225

Something about the Author, Volume 225

Project Editor: Lisa Kumar

Permissions: Leitha Etheridge-Sims

Imaging and Multimedia: Leitha Etheridge-Sims, John Watkins

Composition and Electronic Capture: Amy Darga

Manufacturing: Rhonda Dover

Product Manager: Mary Onorato

For product information and technology assistance, contact us at
Gale Customer Support, 1-800-877-4253.
For permission to use material from this text or product,
submit all requests online at **www.cengage.com/permissions.**
Further permissions questions can be emailed to
permissionrequest@cengage.com

Gale, Cengage Learning
27500 Drake Rd.
Farmington Hills, MI, 48331-3535

LIBRARY OF CONGRESS CATALOG CARD NUMBER 62-52046

ISBN-13: 978-1-4144-6128-1
ISBN-10: 1-4144-6128-3

ISSN 0276-816X

This title is also available as an e-book.
ISBN-13: 978-1-4144-6457-2
ISBN-10: 1-4144-6457-6
Contact your Gale, Cengage Learning sales representative for ordering information.

Printed in Mexico
1 2 3 4 5 6 7 15 14 13 12 11

Contents

Authors in Forthcoming Volumes vii

Introduction ix

SATA Product Advisory Board xi

Illustrations Index 205

Author Index 241

A

Adl, Shirin 1975- 1

Anderson, Stephanie 1976- 2

Axton, David
   See Koontz, Dean 105

B

Barnhouse, Rebecca 1961- 4

Beardshaw, Rosalind 1969- 6

Beauford, Jhenne Tyler
   See Beauford, Tyler 8

Beauford, Tyler 1990- 8

Beavers, Ethen 1971- 9

Bial, Raymond 1948- 10

Bragg, Georgia 16

Brown, Leo 17

Burningham, John 1936- 19

Butler, John 1952- 27

C

Cadnum, Michael 1949- 30

Carey, Janet Lee 1954- 36

Champlin, Susan 1961- 39

Chatterton, Martin 1961- 39

Christie, Gregory
   See Christie, R. Gregory 43

Christie, R. Gregory 1971- 43

Coffey, Brian
   See Koontz, Dean 105

Cohen, Lisa 1963- 48

Cooper, Melrose
   See Kroll, Virginia L. 113

Couloumbis, Akila 1932-2009 50

Crewe, Megan 1980- 51

D

De Pretto, Lorenzo 1966- 52

di Bartolo, Jim 52

Doyle, Eugenie 1952- 54

Dwyer, Deanna
   See Koontz, Dean 105

Dwyer, K.R.
   See Koontz, Dean 105

E

Ebbitt, Carolyn Q. 1974(?)- 57

F

Fleming, Candace 1962- 58

Fox, Louisa
   See Kroll, Virginia L. 113

Francis, Guy 63

Frazee, Marla 1958- 66

G

Gibson, Marley 1966- 73

Glaser, Linda 74

Goode, Diane 1949- 78

Goode, Diane Capuozzo
   See Goode, Diane 78

Graullera, Fabiola
   See Graullera Ramirez, Fabiola 85

Graullera Ramirez, Fabiola 85

Groth-Fleming, Candace
   See Fleming, Candace 58

H

Harmon, Kate
    See Gibson, Marley 73

Haverfield, Mary 86

Hill, Isabel 87

Hill, Isabel T.
    See Hill, Isabel 87

Hill, John
    See Koontz, Dean 105

Hobbie, Holly 1942- 88

Holgate, Doug 92

Hoppey, Tim 1958- 93

Huntley, Amy 94

I

Ibatoulline, Bagram 1965(?)- 96

J

Jessell, Tim 101

K

Kim, Dong-hwa 1950- 103

Koontz, Dean 1945- 105

Kroll, Virginia L. 1948- 113

L

Lavis, Steve 120

Law, Dr. Stephen
    See Law, Stephen 122

Law, Stephen 122

Lemaître, Pascal 1967- 123

Leung, Hilary 1975- 126

M

May, Katie 127

McAllister, Angela 129

McDonald, Candice Hartsough 1982- 133

McDonnell, Christine 1949- 134

Morales, Magaly 137

Morpurgo, Michael 1943- 138

N

Nichols, Leigh
    See Koontz, Dean 105

North, Anthony
    See Koontz, Dean 105

O

O'Hearn, Kate 148

P

Paige, Richard
    See Koontz, Dean . . . .

Parra, John 1972- 149

Phillips, Gary R. 151

Polenghi, Evan 1961- 152

R

Rex, Adam 153

Rim, Sujean 156

Robinson, Fiona 1965- 157

Roos, Maryn 159

Ross, Tony 1938- 160

Rubinger, Ami 1953- 171

S

Schrader, Dave 1967(?)- 173

Snir, Eleyor 174

Spillebeen, Geert 1956- 174

Spinelli, Eileen 1942- 176

Stamp, Jørgen 1969- 183

Stead, Philip C.
    See Stead, Philip Christian 184

Stead, Philip Christian 184

Stringer, Helen 186

Swain, Wilson 1976- 187

Swearingen, Greg 1976- 188

T

Taylor, Susan Champlin
    See Champlin, Susan 39

V

Vitale, Stefano 1958- 190

W

Warman, Jessica 1981- 194

West, Owen
    See Koontz, Dean 105

Whitley, David 1984- 195

Winter, Jonah 1962- 197

Z

Zulkey, Claire 1979- 203

Authors in Forthcoming Volumes

Below are some of the authors and illustrators that will be featured in upcoming volumes of *SATA*. These include new entries on the swiftly rising stars of the field, as well as completely revised and updated entries (indicated with *) on some of the most notable and best-loved creators of books for children.

*Hilari Bell ▮ A former librarian, Bell writes imaginatively plotted science-fiction and fantasy. Her novels include *The Prophecy, A Matter of Profit,* and *Trickster's Girl,* the books in her adventurous "Shield, Sword, and Crown," "Knight and Rogue," and "Goblin" series. In contrast to much genre fiction, Bell's stories are notable for their absence of clear heroes and villains; her characters and societies are drawn with distinct shades of gray and are often motivated by fealty and obligation rather than honor or duty.

Janet Cleland ▮ Cleland had her start as an artist with Hallmark Cards, and a move to the San Francisco Bay area inspired her to start her own illustration business. Her whimsical art has appeared in both editorial and advertising work, as well as on calendars, puzzles, and other products. Dog-loving readers young and old know Cleland's artwork through her collaboration with popular thriller author Dean Koontz: *Christmas Is Good!: Trixie Treats and Holiday Wisdom, I, Trixie Who Is Dog,* and *Trixie and Jinx.*

*Sharon Creech ▮ *Walk Two Moons* brought Creech instant celebrity when it won the 1995 Newbery Honor Medal. *Absolutely Normal Chaos,* her first novel for teens, established her rapport with young teens, and was followed by the Carnegie Medal-nominated *Heartbeat* as well as *Replay* and *The Unfinished Angel.* Creech has also won fans among the younger set through her picture books *Granny Torrelli Makes Soup* and *Who's That Baby?: New-Baby Songs.*

*Jean Craighead George ▮ Through animal studies, such as *Dipper of Copper Creek* and *Luck: The Story of a Sandhill Crane,* Newbery Medal-winning George established herself as young America's naturalist of record. As a fiction writer, *My Side of the Mountain, Julie of the Wolves,* and *Charlie's Raven* feature adventurous stories about young people learning to survive in the wilderness. Whether fact or fiction, her lyrical writing is distinguished by authentic detail and a blend of scientific curiosity, wonder, and concern for the natural environment.

*Charise Mericle Harper ▮ With their brightly colored artwork rendered in diverse styles, Harper's self-illustrated picture books range from the lighthearted to the factual, and her whimsical humor can be gleaned from their titles: *There Was a Bold Lady Who Wanted a Star, Cupcake: A Journey to Special, The Little Book of Not So, Flush!: The Scoop on Poop throughout the Ages,* and *The Power of Cute.* Her imaginative storytelling also finds an outlet in her "Fashion Kitty" graphic novel series, the middle-grade novel *Flashcards of My Life,* and the books in her "Just Grace" reader series.

*Gordon Korman ▮ Korman published his first book when he was fourteen years old, and he hasn't stopped since. From his "Macdonald Hall" series about a pair of rambunctious boarding-school students to his "Swindle" series featuring a crime-solving youngster, his slapstick humor, madcap plots, and high-spirited, rebellious characters have earned Korman fans throughout Canada and the United States. Additionally, he courts fans of fast-moving thrillers in his "Island" and "Dive" trilogies, as well as in his "On the Run" books.

Mario Lopez ▮ A veteran of television, film, and Broadway, Lopez's appearance on the popular *Dancing with the Stars* series revealed his likeable personality and led to increased visibility and numerous hosting opportunities. In addition to acting, Lopez is also a sports and fitness advocate and has co-authored *Mario Lopez's Knockout Fitness* as well as two cookbooks promoting healthy eating. In *Mud Tacos!,* a collaboration with his sister, Marissa Lopez Wong, he shares the humorous traditions of his close-knit Hispanic family.

Wilson Kimeli Naiyomah ▮ A member of the Wasinkishu clan of Kenya, Naiyomah has created a unique bridge between his African village and the United States through his skill as a storyteller. By explaining the tragedy suffered by Americans on September 11, 2001 he inspired village elders to give a generous gift of livestock that was acknowledged by the U.S. State Department and chronicled in the *New York Times.* Carmen Agra Deedy, a children's author, was inspired to contact Naiyomah after reading the newspaper's account, and the inspiring children's book *Fourteen Cows for America* was the result.

Dina Nayeri ▮ Iranian-born writer Nayeri collaborates with her brother, writer and editor Daniel Nayeri, on the novels *Another Faust, Another Pan,* and *Another Jeykll.* Geared for teen readers, novels in the Nayeris' "Another" series weave elements of leather-bound classics into the lives of hip students at an elite New York City prep school. In addition to being entertaining mysteries, the stories are liberally salted with literary references to writers ranging from James Barrie, Johann Wolfgang von Goethe, and Lord Byron to Nathaniel Hawthorne, Robert Louis Stevenson, and Laura Ingalls Wilder.

*Carole Boston Weatherford ▮ Weatherford's writing focuses on important moments in African-American history as well as the importance of perseverance, family ties, and closely held traditions. Among her award-winning titles for younger children are the picture books *The Sound That Jazz Makes, Moses: When Harriet Tubman Led Her People to Freedom,* and *Dear Mr. Rosenwald,* as well as *Becoming Billie Holiday,* which earned Weatherford a Coretta Scott King Author honor.

Introduction

Something about the Author (*SATA*) is an ongoing reference series that examines the lives and works of authors and illustrators of books for children. *SATA* includes not only well-known writers and artists but also less prominent individuals whose works are just coming to be recognized. This series is often the only readily available information source on emerging authors and illustrators. You'll find *SATA* informative and entertaining, whether you are a student, a librarian, an English teacher, a parent, or simply an adult who enjoys children's literature.

What's Inside *SATA*

SATA provides detailed information about authors and illustrators who span the full time range of children's literature, from early figures like John Newbery and L. Frank Baum to contemporary figures like Judy Blume and Richard Peck. Authors in the series represent primarily English-speaking countries, particularly the United States, Canada, and the United Kingdom. Also included, however, are authors from around the world whose works are available in English translation. The writings represented in *SATA* include those created intentionally for children and young adults as well as those written for a general audience and known to interest younger readers. These writings cover the entire spectrum of children's literature, including picture books, humor, folk and fairy tales, animal stories, mystery and adventure, science fiction and fantasy, historical fiction, poetry and nonsense verse, drama, biography, and nonfiction. Obituaries are also included in *SATA* and are intended not only as death notices but also as concise overviews of people's lives and work. Additionally, each edition features newly revised and updated entries for a selection of *SATA* listees who remain of interest to today's readers and who have been active enough to require extensive revisions of their earlier biographies.

Autobiography Feature

Beginning with Volume 103, many volumes of *SATA* feature one or more specially commissioned autobiographical essays. These unique essays, averaging about ten thousand words in length and illustrated with an abundance of personal photos, present an entertaining and informative first-person perspective on the lives and careers of prominent authors and illustrators profiled in *SATA*.

Two Convenient Indexes

In response to suggestions from librarians, *SATA* indexes no longer appear in every volume but are included in alternate (odd-numbered) volumes of the series, beginning with Volume 57.

SATA continues to include two indexes that cumulate with each alternate volume: the Illustrations Index, arranged by the name of the illustrator, gives the number of the volume and page where the illustrator's work appears in the current volume as well as all preceding volumes in the series; the Author Index gives the number of the volume in which a person's biographical sketch, autobiographical essay, or obituary appears in the current volume as well as all preceding volumes in the series.

These indexes also include references to authors and illustrators who appear in *Gale's Yesterday's Authors of Books for Children, Children's Literature Review,* and *Something about the Author Autobiography Series.*

Easy-to-Use Entry Format

Whether you're already familiar with the *SATA* series or just getting acquainted, you will want to be aware of the kind of information that an entry provides. In every *SATA* entry the editors attempt to give as complete a picture of the person's life and work as possible. A typical entry in *SATA* includes the following clearly labeled information sections:

PERSONAL: date and place of birth and death, parents' names and occupations, name of spouse, date of marriage, names of children, educational institutions attended, degrees received, religious and political affiliations, hobbies and other interests.

ADDRESSES: complete home, office, electronic mail, and agent addresses, whenever available.

CAREER: name of employer, position, and dates for each career post; art exhibitions; military service; memberships and offices held in professional and civic organizations.

MEMBER: professional, civic, and other association memberships and any official posts held.

AWARDS, HONORS: literary and professional awards received.

WRITINGS: title-by-title chronological bibliography of books written and/or illustrated, listed by genre when known; lists of other notable publications, such as plays, screenplays, and periodical contributions.

ADAPTATIONS: a list of films, television programs, plays, CD-ROMs, recordings, and other media presentations that have been adapted from the author's work.

WORK IN PROGRESS: description of projects in progress.

SIDELIGHTS: a biographical portrait of the author or illustrator's development, either directly from the biographee—and often written specifically for the *SATA* entry—or gathered from diaries, letters, interviews, or other published sources.

BIOGRAPHICAL AND CRITICAL SOURCES: cites sources quoted in "Sidelights" along with references for further reading.

EXTENSIVE ILLUSTRATIONS: photographs, movie stills, book illustrations, and other interesting visual materials supplement the text.

How a *SATA* Entry Is Compiled

SATA editors examine a wide variety of published sources to gather information for an entry. Biographical and bibliographic sources are consulted, as are book reviews, feature articles, published interviews, and material sometimes obtained from the biographee's family, publishers, agent, or other associates. Whenever possible, the author or illustrator is sent a copy of the entry to check for accuracy and completeness.

Entries that have not been verified by the biographees or their representatives are marked with an asterisk (*).

Contact the Editor

We encourage our readers to examine the entire *SATA* series. Please write and tell us if we can make *SATA* even more helpful to you. Give your comments and suggestions to the editor:

Editor
Something about the Author
Gale, Cengage Learning
27500 Drake Rd.
Farmington Hills MI 48331-3535

Toll-free: 800-877-GALE
Fax: 248-699-8070

Something about the Author Product Advisory Board

The editors of *Something about the Author* are dedicated to maintaining a high standard of excellence by publishing comprehensive, accurate, and highly readable entries on a wide array of writers for children and young adults. In addition to the quality of the content, the editors take pride in the graphic design of the series, which is intended to be orderly yet inviting, allowing readers to utilize the pages of *SATA* easily and with efficiency. Despite the longevity of the *SATA* print series, and the success of its format, we are mindful that the vitality of a literary reference product is dependent on its ability to serve its users over time. As literature, and attitudes about literature, constantly evolve, so do the reference needs of students, teachers, scholars, journalists, researchers, and book club members. To be certain that we continue to keep pace with the expectations of our customers, the editors of *SATA* listen carefully to their comments regarding the value, utility, and quality of the series. Librarians, who have firsthand knowledge of the needs of library users, are a valuable resource for us. The *Something about the Author* Product Advisory Board, made up of school, public, and academic librarians, is a forum to promote focused feedback about *SATA* on a regular basis. The nine-member advisory board includes the following individuals, whom the editors wish to thank for sharing their expertise:

Eva M. Davis
Director,
Canton Public Library,
Canton, Michigan

Joan B. Eisenberg
Lower School Librarian,
Milton Academy,
Milton, Massachusetts

Francisca Goldsmith
Teen Services Librarian,
Berkeley Public Library,
Berkeley, California

Susan Dove Lempke
Children's Services Supervisor,
Niles Public Library District,
Niles, Illinois

Robyn Lupa
Head of Children's Services,
Jefferson County Public Library,
Lakewood, Colorado

Victor L. Schill
Assistant Branch Librarian/Children's Librarian,
Harris County Public Library/Fairbanks Branch,
Houston, Texas

Caryn Sipos
Community Librarian,
Three Creeks Community Library,
Vancouver, Washington

Steven Weiner
Director,
Maynard Public Library,
Maynard, Massachusetts

something ABOUT the AUThOR

ADL, Shirin 1975-

Personal

Born 1975, in Harlow, England; daughter of Farokh (a writer) and Minoo (a homemaker) Saramad; married Kamyar Adl (a photographer); children: Dara. *Education:* Loughborough University, B.A. (first class honors).

Addresses

Home—Oxford, England. *E-mail*—shirin@shirinadl.co.uk.

Career

Illustrator and author. Presenter at workshops and schools. *Exhibitions:* Work included in New Designers Exhibition, London, England, 1999; at Coningsby Gallery, London, 1999; and at a National Geographic Society reception attended by Queen Elizabeth II and the duke of Edinburgh, 1999.

Awards, Honors

Talented Designer Award, Hallmark Cards Marketing & Sales Division, 1999; named British Booktrust Illustrator for Children's Book Week, 2010.

Writings

SELF-ILLUSTRATED

I Is for Iran, photographs by husband, Kamyar Adl, Frances Lincoln (London, England, 2011.

ILLUSTRATOR

Na'ima B. Robert, *Ramadan Moon,* Frances Lincoln (London, England), 2009.

Elizabeth Laird, *Pea Boy and Other Stories from Iran,* Frances Lincoln (London, England), 2009.

I'm Sad, Tango Books (London, England), 2011.

Debjani Chatterjee and Brian D'Arcy, editors, *Let's Celebrate: Festival Poems from around the World,* Frances Lincoln (London, England), 2011.

Contributor to online magazines and Web sites.

Sidelights

Born in England and raised in Iran, Shirin Adl has drawn on her childhood experiences to create artwork for picture books such as *Ramadan Moon* by Na'ima B. Robert and *Pea Boy and Other Stories from Iran* by Elizabeth Laird. In the former title, Robert follows the activities of a Muslim family during the holy month of Ramadan, an Islamic holiday of spiritual renewal that is celebrated worldwide and marked by religious rituals, fasting, and charitable deeds. *Ramadan Moon* garnered strong reviews, with several critics applauding the combination of Adl's mixed-media illustrations and Robert's free-verse narrative. In *Booklist* Gillian Engberg stated that the "poetic words and playful, patterned collage artwork capture both the solemnity and joy" of the holiday. Fawzia Gilani-Williams, writing in *School Library Journal,* similarly noted that Robert's "poetic style is captivating and [is] enhanced by Adl's appealing and colorful multimedia illustrations."

Shirin Adl's illustration projects include creating the artwork for Na'
ima B. Robert's picture book **Ramadan Moon.** (Frances Lincoln Ltd., 2009.
Illustration copyright © 2009 by Shirin Adl. Reproduced by permission.)

Laird collects seven traditional folktales in *Pea Boy and
Other Stories from Iran,* "a vivid combination of the
strange and the familiar," as George Hunt commented
in *Books for Keeps.* This anthology includes stories
such as "Kayvan the Brave," which recalls the British
fairytale "Jack the Giant Killer," as well as "The Spar-
row's Quest," about a tiny bird's search for the most
powerful substance in the world. Adl again drew praise
for her collage illustrations, *School Library Journal*
contributor Donna Cardon noting that the artist "often
uses cloth with patterns characteristic of the region in
her compositions." Adl's mixed-media pictures, done
"in bright watercolor, colored pencil, photos, and fab-
rics extend the fun with delicate detail and lively
scenes," wrote Hazel Rochman in her *Booklist* review
of *Pea Boy and Other Stories from Iran.*

"The most important things in life as I'm sure we can
all agree are health, happiness and being surrounded by
people we love," Adl told *SATA.* "I also think having a
job that you enjoy is very important. When I tell people
what I do for a living, they usually reply with, 'You are
so lucky' and I have to agree! I love being an illustrator. Sometimes I even feel sad when I have to take time
off work!

"When I was young I loved listening to the stories that
my parents and grandparents told. I would often draw
pictures for them later. But I didn't always know that I

wanted to become an illustrator. For a while I wanted to
become a pilot then an astronaut. I studied biology and
I wanted to become an explorer in the Amazon rainfor-
est and discover new insects. It wasn't until my last
year at school that I remembered how much I loved art.

"I like all different kinds of illustration but working on
picture books is my favourite. I enjoy every part of the
process from reading a story for the first time to coming up with ideas to finishing the final artwork. I like
putting a lot of detail in my work and I love drawing
big scenes with lots of people or animals doing different things."

Biographical and Critical Sources

PERIODICALS

Booklist, November 15, 2009, Gillian Engberg, review of
    Ramadan Moon, p. 47; September 15, 2010, Hazel
    Rochman, review of *Pea Boy and Other Stories from
    Iran,* p. 62.
Books for Keeps, November, 2009, Khalida Alvi, review
    of *Ramadan Moon;* March, 2010, George Hunt, re-
    view of *Pea Boy and Other Stories from Iran.*
Kirkus Reviews, October 1, 2009, review of *Ramadan
    Moon.*
School Library Journal, December, 2009, Fawzia Gilani-
    Williams, review of *Ramadan Moon,* p. 90; Novem-
    ber, 2010, Donna Cardon, review of *Pea Boy and
    Other Stories from Iran,* p. 140.

ONLINE

Fuse #8 Production Web log, http://blog.schoollibrary
    journal.com/ (July 10, 2010), Elizabeth Bird, review
    of *Pea Boy and Other Stories from Iran.*
Shirin Adl Home Page, http://www.shirinadl.co.uk (Janu-
    ary 20, 2011).
Shirin Adl Web log, http://shirinadl.blogspot.com (January
    20, 2011).

*   *   *

ANDERSON, Stephanie 1976-

Personal

Born 1976. *Education:* Rhode Island School of Design,
B.F.A., 1999.

Addresses

Home—Pittsfield, MA.

Career

Painter and children's book illustrator. *Exhibitions:*
Work exhibited at Attleboro Museum, Attleboro, MA;
Academy of Art University, San Francisco, CA; and
Gallery on the Green, Pawling, NY.

Awards, Honors

Marion Vannett Ridgway Award, 2004, for *Weaving the Rainbow* by George Ella Lyon; Cooperative Children's Book Center Choices selection, Best Books of the Year selection, Bank Street College of Education, Jane Addams Children's Book Award Honor Book designation, and Notable Social Studies Trade Book selection, Children's Book Council/National Council for the Social Studies, all c. 2009, all for *You and Me and Home Sweet Home* by Lyon.

Illustrator

Marc Aronson, *Witch-Hunt: Mysteries of the Salem Witch Trials,* Simon & Schuster (New York, NY), 2003.

George Ella Lyon, *Weaving the Rainbow,* Atheneum Books for Young Readers (New York, NY), 2004.

Polly Kanevsky, *Sleepy Boy,* Atheneum Books for Young Readers (New York, NY), 2006.

George Ella Lyon, *You and Me and Home Sweet Home,* Atheneum Books for Young Readers (New York, NY), 2009.

Sidelights

An accomplished watercolorist, Stephanie Anderson has provided the artwork for several children's books, among them *Sleepy Boy* by Polly Kanevsky. A bedtime

Stephanie Anderson's illustration projects include capturing George Ella Lyon's family-centered story in You and Me and Home Sweet Home. (Illustration copyright © 2009 by Stephanie Anderson. Reprinted with permission of Atheneum Books for Young Readers, an imprint of Simon & Schuster Children's Publishing Division.)

tale, Kanevsky's story focuses on a fidgety youngster who has trouble falling asleep one night. As his father cuddles up next to him, soothing the boy with comforting words, the child recalls his trip to the zoo earlier that day, where he witnessed a lioness caring for her cub. "Readers see what the boy sees in his mind's eye," remarked a *Kirkus Reviews* critic, who further noted that Anderson's illustrations depict "a shadowed, shared tenderness between both parent/child dyads." A contributor in *Publishers Weekly* also offered praise for Anderson's artwork, stating that the "watercolor and charcoal paintings bring to mind [nineteenth-century French impressionist] Mary Cassatt's portraits of children, but they are suffused with a remarkable golden Renaissance light."

Anderson has collaborated with award-winning author George Ella Lyon on the picture books *Weaving the Rainbow* and *You and Me and Home Sweet Home.* In *Weaving the Rainbow* Lyon depicts the life of an unusual artist, one who raises her own flock of sheep, shears and spins the wool, dyes it by hand, and finally weaves it into a wondrous, multi-hued tapestry. "Anderson's soft-focus watercolors capture the beauty and serenity of the artist's pastoral surroundings," Jennifer Mattson commented in *Booklist,* and *School Library Journal* reviewer Liza Graybill applauded the combination of Lyon's text and Anderson's art in *Weaving the Rainbow,* observing that they "complement each other in evoking the essence of creating art and in portraying the lush countryside."

Lyon's volunteer work with nonprofit homebuilder Habitat for Humanity informs *You and Me and Home Sweet Home,* which centers on the construction of a new house for a youngster and her mother. Here "Anderson's watercolor-and-pastel-pencil illustrations burst off the page with energy and life," according to a contributor in *Kirkus Reviews.*

Biographical and Critical Sources

PERIODICALS

Booklist, February 15, 2004, Jennifer Mattson, review of *Weaving the Rainbow,* p. 1063; April 15, 2006, Hazel Rochman, review of *Sleepy Boy,* p. 52.

Kirkus Reviews, February 1, 2004, review of *Weaving the Rainbow,* p. 136; April 1, 2006, review of *Sleepy Boy,* p. 350; September 15, 2009, review of *You and Me and Home Sweet Home.*

Publishers Weekly, February 16, 2004, review of *Weaving the Rainbow,* p. 170; April 3, 2006, review of *Sleepy Boy,* p. 71.

School Library Journal, February, 2004, Liza Graybill, review of *Weaving the Rainbow,* p. 118; May, 2006, Martha Topol, review of *Sleepy Boy,* p. 90; November, 2009, Wendy Lukehart, review of *You and Me and Home Sweet Home,* p. 83.

Watercolor, winter, 2008, John A. Parks, "In the Moment" (profile of Anderson).

ONLINE

Gallery on the Green Web site, http://gotgpawling.com/ (February 1, 2011), "Stephanie Anderson."*

* * *

AXTON, David
See KOONTZ, Dean

* * *

BARNHOUSE, Rebecca 1961-

Personal
Born 1961, in Vero Beach, FL. *Education:* Florida State University, B.A.; University of North Carolina at Chapel Hill, M.A., Ph.D.

Addresses
Home—OH. *Office*—English Department, Youngstown State University, One University Plaza, Youngstown, OH 44555. *Agent*—Anna Webman, Curtis Brown, Ltd., 10 Astor Pl., New York, NY 10003. *E-mail*—rabarnhouse@gmail.com.

Career
Author and educator. Youngstown State University, Youngstown, OH, professor of English. Also taught high school.

Awards, Honors
Named Distinguished Professor in Teaching, and Distinguished Professor in Scholarship, both Youngstown State University; Northeast Ohio Council on Higher Education Award for Teaching Excellence.

Writings

FICTION

The Book of the Maidservant, Random House (New York, NY), 2009.
The Coming of the Dragon, Random House (New York, NY), 2010.
Peaceweaver, Random House (New York, NY), 2012.

NONFICTION

Recasting the Past: The Middle Ages in Young Adult Literature, Boynton/Cook Publishers (Portsmouth, NH), 2000.

Rebecca Barnhouse (Photograph by Carl Yeet. Reproduced by permission.)

(With Benjamin C. Withers) *The Old English Hexateuch: Aspects and Approaches,* Medieval Institute Publications (Kalamazoo, MI), 2000.
The Middle Ages in Literature for Youth: A Guide and Resource Book, Scarecrow Press (Lanham, MD), 2004.
The Book of the Knight of the Tower: Manners for Young Medieval Women (monograph), Palgrave Macmillan (New York, NY), 2006.

Former editor of *Lyre Review.* Contributor to periodicals, including *ALAN Review, Lion and the Unicorn,* and *Literature and Medicine.*

Adaptations
The Book of the Maidservant and *The Coming of the Dragon* were adapted as audiobooks.

Sidelights
Rebecca Barnhouse, a professor of English who specializes in medieval literature, is also the author of the young-adult novels *The Book of the Maidservant,* a work of historical fiction, and *The Coming of the Dragon,* a fantasy tale. In addition to her fictional works, Barnhouse has also published several scholarly titles, including the monograph *The Book of the Knight of the Tower: Manners for Young Medieval Women.*

Barnhouse developed an early love of literature. An avid reader as a child, she was particularly drawn to the "Little House" books by Laura Ingalls Wilder, as well as to the "Alfred Hitchcock and the Three Investigators" mystery series. Her interests then turned to fantasy and science fiction, such as tales by such notable authors as J.R.R. Tolkien, Arthur C. Clarke, and Ursula K. LeGuin. As a teenager, Barnhouse also practiced calligraphy, a hobby that introduced her to the beauty of hand-lettered manuscripts and served as a catalyst for her studies of medieval literature and culture. "There's nothing more thrilling to me than holding a thousand-year-old book and looking at the ways the scribe worked, seeing where he re-inked his pen or decorated a hole in the parchment, or where another scribe took over, sometimes mid-sentence," Barnhouse remarked to Ellen Booraem in an *Enchanted Inkpot* online interview.

The Book of the Maidservant, Barnhouse's debut work of fiction, is based on *The Book of Margery Kempe,* a work from the early 1400s that is regarded as the earliest surviving autobiography written in English. The tale focuses on Johanna, an oft-criticized serving girl in the household of Dame Margery, who must accompany her reverent but emotionally exhausting mistress on a pilgrimage from England to Rome. During the backbreaking journey, Margery engages in a heated confrontation with her fellow travelers and eventually abandons the group, leaving Johanna stranded in Europe. "Maidservant Johanna is an engaging lass, hardworking and ingenious," a critic noted in *Kirkus Reviews,* and Connie C. Rockman observed in *School Library Journal* that Barnhouse's tale "constantly points out the vulnerability of a peasant girl whose survival depends in equal parts on luck, wit, and exhausting labor." "Filled with vivid descriptions of medieval life, engagingly written, and superbly researched," according to *Horn Book* contributor Monica Edinger, "*The Book of the Maidservant* is a compelling read."

In writing *The Coming of the Dragon* Barnhouse drew on her knowledge of the Old English epic poem *Beowulf* to tell the story of Rune, a young villager who stands beside his aging king when their land is invaded by a terrifying dragon. "I've always loved the end of *Beowulf,* the section with the dragon, and I've always wanted to know more than the poem tells us—but from an emotional perspective, not a scholarly one," the author remarked to Booraem. "Why did those warriors act the way they did? What would it have been like to encounter that dragon?" Writing in *Booklist,* Cindy Welch observed of *The Coming of the Dragon* that Barnhouse "weaves an absorbing tale of a young man finding his courage," while *School Library Journal* reviewer Mandy Lawrence asserted that Rune's "innocence and perseverance make him a sympathetic and unlikely hero."

"Reading and writing have always been big parts of my life," Barnhouse told *SATA,* "and they've also been closely linked with friendship. When I was a teenager,

my best friend and I shared books all the time. We also wrote stories for (and about) each other. A story written by my friend, starring the two of us, was a treasured gift. We even wrote a novel together; I'd write one chapter and she would write the next. It wasn't very good, but when we finished, we were proud of our accomplishment. As adults, we still share books: the ones we're reading and the ones we're writing."

Biographical and Critical Sources

PERIODICALS

Booklist, October 15, 2010, Cindy Welch, review of *The Coming of the Dragon,* p. 52.

Horn Book, November-December, 2009, Monica Edinger, review of *The Book of the Maidservant,* p. 663.

Journal of Adolescent and Adult Literacy, November, 2001, Jeanne M. McGlinn, review of *Recasting the Past: The Middle Ages in Young Adult Literature,* p. 248.

Cover of Barnhouse's young-adult novel **The Book of the Maidservant,** *featuring artwork by Grady McFerrin.* (Jacket art copyright © 2009 by Random House Children's Books. Used by permission of Random House Children's Books, a division of Random House, Inc.)

Kirkus Reviews, September 15, 2009, review of *The Book of the Maidservant.*

Medium Aevum, fall, 2001, Rohini Jayatilaka, review of *The Old English Hexateuch: Aspects and Approaches,* p. 367.

School Library Journal, July, 2005, Julie Webb, review of *The Middle Ages in Literature for Youth: A Guide and Resource Book,* p. 135; November, 2009, Connie C. Rockman, review of *The Book of the Maidservant,* p. 100; November, 2010, Mandy Lawrence, review of *The Coming of the Dragon,* p. 102.

Voice of Youth Advocates, April, 2005, Mary Arnold, review of *The Middle Ages in Literature for Youth,* p. 80; October, 2009, Laura Woodruff, review of *The Book of the Maidservant,* p. 310.

ONLINE

Enchanted Inkpot Web log, http://community.livejournal. com/enchantedinkpot/ (December 8, 2010), Ellen Booraem, interview with Barnhouse.

Rebecca Barnhouse Home Page, http://www.rebeccabarn house.com (January 20, 2011).

*   *   *

BEARDSHAW, Rosalind 1969-

Personal

Born 1969, in England. *Education:* Manchester Polytechnic, B.A. (illustration), 1992.

Addresses

Home and office—York, England. *Agent*—Heather Richards, 9 Somerville Lea, Aldeburgh, Suffolk IP15 5LH, England.

Career

Illustrator. Volunteer with learning-disabled adults.

Writings

SELF-ILLUSTRATED

Grandma's Beach, Bloomsbury (London, England), 2001, Bloomsbury Children's Books (New York, NY), 2004.

Grandpa's Surprise, Bloomsbury Children's Books (New York, NY), 2004.

My Fairy Mobile Book (interactive book), Campbell (London, England), 2005.

ILLUSTRATOR

Kate Ruttle and Richard Brown, *Hickory, Dickory, Dock,* Cambridge University Press (Cambridge, England), 1996.

Kate Ruttle and Richard Brown, adaptors, *Over in the Meadow,* Cambridge University Press (Cambridge, England), 1996.

Kate Ruttle and Richard Brown, *Afloat in a Boat,* Cambridge University Press (Cambridge, England), 1996.

Susan Price, reteller, *Goldilocks and the Three Bears,* Cambridge University Press (Cambridge, England), 1999.

Lisa Bruce, *Fran's Flower,* Bloomsbury (London, England), 1999, HarperCollins (New York, NY), 2000.

Sally Grindley, *Who Is It?,* Peachtree (Atlanta, GA), 2000.

Gillian Lobel, *Does Anybody Love Me?,* Good Books (Intercourse, PA), 2002.

Laura Dollin, *Christmas Angel,* Candlewick Press (Cambridge, MA), 2002.

Lisa Bruce, *Fran's Friend,* Bloomsbury Children's Books (New York, NY), 2003.

Laura Dollin, *Santa Claus,* Candlewick Press (Cambridge, MA), 2003.

Pennie Kidd, *Oops!,* Lion (Oxford, England), 2004.

Tony Bonning, *Snog the Frog,* Barron's (Hauppauge, NY), 2005.

Tom Barber, *A Tale of Two Goats,* Barron's (Hauppauge, NY), 2005.

Catherine Shoolbred, *Merry Christmas!,* Egmont (London, England), 2005.

Anna McQuinn, *Lola at the Library,* Charlesbridge (Watertown, MA), 2006.

Lynne Rickards, *Jack's Bed,* Crabtree Pub. Co. (New York, NY), 2006.

Cristin Ditchfield, *Cowlick!,* Random House (New York, NY), 2006.

Gillian Lobel's story of an industrious young toddler is brought to life in Beardshaw's art for **Does Anybody Love Me?** (Good Books, 2002. Illustration copyright © 2002 by Rosalind Beardshaw. All rights reserved. Reproduced by permission.)

Anna McQuinn, *Lulu Loves the Library,* Alanna Books (London, England), 2006, published as *Lola at the Library,* Charlesbridge (Watertown, MA), 2009.

Diana Kimpton, *The Lamb-a-roo,* Gingham Dog Press (Columbus, OH), 2006.

Janet Bingham, *My Little Star,* Scholastic U.K. (London, England), 2007, published as *Mommy's Little Star,* Scholastic (New York, NY), 2008.

Janet Bingham, *New Home for Little Fox,* Scholastic UK (London, England), 2008, published as *Daddy's Little Scout,* Cartwheel (New York, NY), 2010.

David Algrim, *Oops-a-Daisy!,* Golden Books (New York, NY), 2009.

Christin Ditchfield, *Shwatsit!: No One Knows Just What It Means,* Golden Books (New York, NY), 2009.

Anna McQuinn, *Lulu Loves Stories,* Alanna Books (London, England), 2009, published as *Lola Loves Stories,* Charlesbridge (Watertown, MA), 2010.

Books featuring Beardshaw's art have been published in French, Chinese, Greek, Danish, Korean, Slovenian, Basque, Spanish, and Italian.

Sidelights

British illustrator Rosalind Beardshaw knew she wanted to be an artist as a young girl. Since graduating from college in the early 1990s, she has focused her talents on illustrating children's books, particularly stories that feature animal characters. Reviewing her artwork for Christin Ditchfield's lighthearted *Cowlick!,* a porquoi story that links the persistent curl in a boy's hair to a nighttime visit from a loving bovine, a *Publishers Weekly* contributor cited "Beardshaw's . . . cheery, close-perspective acrylic paintings," and Stephanie Zvirin wrote in *Booklist* that her "thickly brushed" and colorful paintings "include many close-ups that make the book ideal for group sharing." Also noting the artist's ability to create pictures that can captivate large audiences, *School Library Journal* critic Be Astengo wrote that in Tony Bonning's *Snog the Frog* "Beardshaw makes excellent use of the page layout to create large images that will be seen from the back of the storytime room."

Both *Lola and the Library* and *Lola Loves Stories* are tales by Anna McQuinn that focus on a young black girl and her love of books. In *Lola and the Library* readers can follow Lola as she makes the rounds on library day, listening to storytelling, participating in a singalong, and checking out a week's worth of books with her library card. "Beardshaw's vividly colored acrylic paintings" are "charged with a child's vibrant enthusiasm," wrote a *Kirkus Reviews* writer, and in *School Library Journal* Sally R. Dow predicted that the book is "perfect for instilling a love of libraries . . . in the youngest patrons." Daily storytelling between parents and child is the focus of *Lola Loves Stories,* and here "McQuinn and Beardshaw keep their young African-American heroine firmly rooted in the real world," according to a *Publishers Weekly* contributor.

Beardshaw creates the images that bring to life Christin Ditchfield's whimsical porquois tale in **Cowlick!** (Illustration copyright © 2007 by Rosalind Beardshaw. Used by permission of Golden Books, an imprint of Random House Children's Books, a division of Random House, Inc.)

In addition to her collaborations with McQuinn, Beardshaw's colorful and child-friendly artwork has also appeared in stories by Sally Grindley, Lobel, Bonning, and Lisa Bruce. According to a *Kirkus Reviews* writer, the artist's "rich, colorful illustrations add a charming element" to Lobel's reassuring story in *Does Anybody Love Me?,* and in *Publishers Weekly* a critic concluded that Beardshaw's acrylic paintings for Lobel's child-centered tale "exude a gung-ho cheeriness."

Beardshaw's original picture books, *Grandma's Beach* and *Grandpa's Surprise,* were inspired by her memories of her fun-loving grandparents. In *Grandma's Beach* Emily and her mother are excited about their upcoming day at the seashore, but when Mom has to go to work instead, Grandma finds a way to make a day spent at home just as exciting. In *Grandpa's Surprise* a little boy named Stanley feels bad when a neighbor gets a shiny new bike, but when Grandpa finds out, he puts his engineering and scavenging skills to work on a new go-cart for Stanley that quickly becomes the envy of the neighborhood. Citing Beardshaw's colorful illustrations, a *Kirkus Reviews* critic praised the multigenerational picture books for featuring "subtle and positively uplifting" stories designed to "help any child through those inevitable crestfallen moments in life." "Using thick strokes and a melange of summer fruit-colored paints, Beardshaw zooms in on her characters," observed Ilene Cooper in her *Booklist* review of *Grand-*

ma's Beach and *Grandpa's Surprise,* and *School Library Journal* critic Catherine Threadgill deemed the images "bright, glossy, and scaled to draw the attention of tiny eyes."

Biographical and Critical Sources

PERIODICALS

Booklist, August, 2004, Ilene Cooper, review of *Grandma's Beach,* p. 1940; January 1, 2007, Stephanie Zvirin, review of *Cowlick!,* p. 113.

Kirkus Reviews, September 15, 2002, review of *Does Anybody Love Me?,* p. 1394; February 1, 2003, review of *Fran's Friend,* p. 226; April 1, 2004, review of *Grandma's Beach,* p. 324; January 1, 2005, review of *Snog the Frog,* p. 48; June 15, 2006, review of *Lola at the Library,* p. 636; December 1, 2006, review of *Cowlick!,* p. 1218; February 15, 2009, review of *Mole's in Love;* August 15, 2009, review of *Shwatsit!: No One Knows Just What It Means.*

Publishers Weekly, October 7, 2002, review of *Does Anybody Love Me?,* p. 72; May 22, 2006, review of *The Lamb-a-Roo,* p. 50; January 1, 2007, review of *Cowlick!,* p. 48; June 28, 2010, review of *Lola Loves Stories,* p. 126.

School Library Journal, August, 2004, Catherine Threadgill, review of *Grandma's Beach,* p. 83; August, 2005, Be Astengo, review of *Snog the Frog,* p. 85; July,

2006, Sally R. Dow, review of *Lola at the Library,* p. 83; January, 2007, Julie Roach, review of *Cowlick!,* p. 90; March, 2009, Margaret R. Tassia, review of *Mole's in Love,* p. 106; November, 2009, Debbie S. Hoskins, review of *Shwatsit!,* p. 76; July, 2010, Sara Figueroa, review of *Lola Loves Stories,* p. 66.

ONLINE

Rosalind Beardshaw Home Page, http://www.rosalind beardshaw.com (January 15, 2011).*

*   *   *

BEAUFORD, Jhenne Tyler
See BEAUFORD, Tyler

*   *   *

BEAUFORD, Tyler 1990-
(Jhenne Tyler Beauford)

Personal

Born 1990, in MD. *Ethnicity:* African American. *Education:* Attended Solano Community College.

Addresses

Home—Vallejo, CA. *E-mail*—Jhenne.Tyler@gmail.com.

Career

Student, freelance journalist, voice actress, and illustrator. Teezer's Tees (mother-daughter fashion line), cofounder and illustrator, beginning 2007; Sickled Pink ("Spooky Chic" fashion line), founder, owner, and illustrator/designer, beginning 2009. Freelance editor and writer for online media, beginning 2008; Racebending.com, staff writer, beginning 2009; *Lip Gloss* (teen magazine), staff artist and features editor, beginning 2010. Web designer.

Awards, Honors

Winner, NewMoonGirls.com Illustration Contest, 2008; Certificate of Special Congressional Recognition for outstanding and invaluable service to the community and journalistic initiative, 2008.

Illustrator

Cheryl Dellasega, *Sistrsic92 (Meg)* ("Bloggrls" series), Marshall Cavendish (Tarrytown, NY), 2009.

Contributor to *Teen Voices,* 2007-09, and *Teen Scene,* beginning 2010.

Biographical and Critical Sources

PERIODICALS

Booklist, October 1, 2009, Lynn Rutan, review of *Sistrsic92 (Meg),* p. 38.

One of several collaborations with Christin Ditchfield, the humorous picture book Shwatsit! features artwork by Beardshaw. (Illustration copyright © 2009 by Rosalind Beardshaw. Used by permission of Golden Books, an imprint of Random House Children's Books, a division of Random House, Inc.)

School Library Journal, January, 2010, Carol A. Edwards, review of *Sistrsic92 (Meg),* p. 100.

ONLINE

Tyler Beauford Portfolio Home Page, http://jhennetyler. cleanfolio.com (December 13, 2010).

*   *   *

BEAVERS, Ethen 1971-

Personal

Born 1971, in Grants Pass, OR; married. *Hobbies and other interests:* Drawing, flyfishing.

Addresses

Home—Modesto, CA.

Career

Illustrator and animator. Freelance cartoonist, beginning 2003; created storyboards for Warner Brothers animated television program *Justice League Unlimited.*

Illustrator

Michael Buckley, *NERDS: National Espionage, Rescue, and Defense Society,* Amulet Books (New York, NY), 2009.
Michael Buckley, *NERDS 2!: M Is for Mama's Boy,* Amulet Books (New York, NY), 2010.
Irene Trimble, adaptor, *The Call of Kur,* Random House (New York, NY), 2010.

Contributor to comic-book series, including "Mutation," "Six," "Justice League Unlimited," "Star Wars: Clone Wars," "Titans Go!," "Samurai Jack," "Indiana Jones Adventures," and "Buffy the Vampire Slayer."

Sidelights

An artist whose work ranges from children's books to comic books and animation, Ethen Beavers has contributed to several popular comics series from DC Comics and Dark Horse Comics. Beavers' stylized, energetic illustrations have also appeared in Michael Buckley's *NERDS: National Espionage, Rescue, and Defense Society* and *NERDS 2!: M Is for Mama's Boy,* as well as in Irene Trimble's *The Call of Kur.*

In *NERDS* Buckley presents what *School Library Journal* contributor Travis Jonker described as "an action-packed, tongue-in-cheek take" on the comic-book battle between arch villains and superheroes. In the story, a group of preteen misfits turn their various deformities to superpowers that can benefit all of mankind, and Beavers' "angular, black-and-white illustrations high-

light main characters and pivotal moments," according to the critic. A "fun adventure [that] is sure to attract followers," *NERDS* gains "further appeal" from Beavers' "comic-strip style illustrations," according to Todd Morning in *Booklist.*

Biographical and Critical Sources

PERIODICALS

Booklist, October 15, 2009, Todd Morning, review of *NERDS: National Espionage, Rescue, and Defense Society,* p. 53.
Kirkus Reviews, August 15, 2009, review of *NERDS.*
Publishers Weekly, August 31, 2009, review of *NERDS,* p. 59.
School Library Journal, December, 2009, Travis Jonker, review of *NERDS,* p. 107.

***Ethen Beavers contributes the cartoon artwork to Michael Buckley's middle-grade thriller* NERDS: National Espionage, Rescue, and Defense Society.** (Amulet Books, 2010. Illustration copyright © 2010 by Ethan Beavers. Reproduced by permission.)

ONLINE

Ethen Beavers Web log, http://cretineb.deviantart.com
(January 15, 2011).*

*   *   *

BIAL, Raymond 1948-

Raymond Bial (Reproduced by permission.)

Personal

Born November 5, 1948, in Danville, IL; son of Marion
(a U.S. Air Force officer) and Catherine (a medical secretary) Bial; married Linda LaPuma (a librarian), August 25, 1979; children: Anna, Sarah, Luke. *Education:*
University of Illinois, B.S. (with honors), 1970, M.S.,
1979. *Politics:* "Independent." *Religion:* Roman Catholic. *Hobbies and other interests:* Gardening, fishing,
hiking, travel.

Addresses

Home—Urbana, IL. *Home and office*—First Light Photography, P.O. Box 593, Urbana, IL 61801. *E-mail*—
ray@raybial.com.

Career

Photographer, librarian, and writer. Librarian at public
schools, colleges, and universities for over thirty years,
including at Parkland College Library, Champaign, IL,
beginning 1980. University of Illinois, Urbana, teacher.

Member

Author's Guild, Society of Children's Book Writers and
Illustrators, Society of Midland Authors, University of
Illinois Alumni Association.

Awards, Honors

Best Publicity commendation, Library Public Relations
Council, 1984, 1986; Historian of the Year, Champaign
County, IL, 1984; Award of Superior Achievement, Illi-
nois State Historical Society, 1985; staff development
award, Parkland College, 1985, 1990; Certificate of
Commendation, American Association for State and Local History, 1986; Writer's Choice selection, National
Endowment for the Arts/Pushcart Foundation, 1986, for
First Frost; Outstanding Science Trade Book for Children designation, 1991, for *Corn Belt Harvest;* Parents'
Choice Foundation Choice designation, and American
Library Association Notable Children's Book designation, both 1994, both for *Amish Home;* Ohio Farm Bureau Children's Literature Award, 1995, for *Portrait of
a Family Farm;* Black History Month 25 Top Picks in-
cludee, 1996, for *The Underground Railroad;* Orbis
Pictus honor books for nonfiction, 1996, for *With Needle
and Thread,* and 2002, for *Tenement;* Society of School
Librarians International Book Award Honor designation, 1998, for *Where Lincoln Walked;* Spur Award se-

lections for Best Children's Books about the American
West, 2000, for *The Pueblo,* and 2001, for *Ghost Towns
of the American West;* John Burroughs Award for best
environmental books for children, and Orbis Pictus
Award for Best Nonfiction, both 2000, both for *A Handful of Dirt;* numerous selections as Notable Social Studies Trade Book for Young People, Children's Book
Council.

Writings

FICTION; FOR CHILDREN

The Fresh Grave and Other Ghostly Stories, illustrated by
    daughter, Anna Bial, Face to Face Books, 1997.
The Ghost of Honeymoon Creek, illustrated by Anna Bial,
    Face to Face Books, 1999.
Shadow Island (novel), Face to Face Books, 2000, pub-
    lished as *Shadow Island: A Tale of Lake Superior,*
    Blue Horse Books (Milwaukee, WI), 2006.

NONFICTION FOR CHILDREN; AND PHOTOGRAPHER

Corn Belt Harvest, Houghton (Boston, MA), 1991.
County Fair, Houghton (Boston, MA), 1992.
Amish Home, Houghton (Boston, MA), 1993.
Frontier Home, Houghton (Boston, MA), 1993.
Shaker Home, Houghton (Boston, MA), 1994, revised as
    The Shaker Village, University Press of Kentucky
    (Lexington, KY), 2008.
Portrait of a Farm Family, Houghton (Boston, MA), 1995.
The Underground Railroad, Houghton (Boston, MA),
    1995.
With Needle and Thread: A Book about Quilts, Houghton
    (Boston, MA), 1996.

Mist over the Mountains: Appalachia and Its People, Houghton (Boston, MA), 1997.

The Strength of These Arms: Life in the Slave Quarters, Houghton (Boston, MA), 1997.

Where Lincoln Walked, Walker Books (New York, NY), 1997.

Cajun Home, Houghton (Boston, MA), 1998.

One-Room School, Houghton (Boston, MA), 1999.

A Handful of Dirt, Walker (New York, NY), 2000.

Ghost Towns of the American West, Houghton (Boston, MA), 2001.

A Book Comes Together: From Idea to Library, Bound to Stay Bound Books (Jacksonville, IL), 2002.

Tenement: Immigrant Life on the Lower East Side, Houghton (Boston, MA), 2002.

The Long Walk: The Story of Navajo Captivity, Benchmark Books (New York, NY), 2003.

Where Washington Walked, Walker (New York, NY), 2004.

Nauvoo: Mormon City on the Mississippi River, Houghton Mifflin (Boston, MA), 2006.

The Super Soybean, Albert Whitman (Morton Grove, IL), 2007.

Champaign, Arcadia Pub. (Charleston, SC), 2008.

Ellis Island: Coming to the Land of Liberty, Houghton Mifflin Books for Children (Boston, MA), 2009.

Rescuing Rover: A Book about Saving Our Dogs, Houghton Mifflin (New York, NY), 2011.

NONFICTION; "LIFEWAYS" SERIES

The Navajo, Benchmark Books (New York, NY), 1999.

The Cherokee, Benchmark Books (New York, NY), 1999.

The Iroquois, Benchmark Books (New York, NY), 1999.

The Sioux, Benchmark Books (New York, NY), 1999.

The Ojibwe, Benchmark Books (New York, NY), 2000.

The Pueblo, Benchmark Books (New York, NY), 2000.

The Seminole, Benchmark Books (New York, NY), 2000.

The Comanche, Benchmark Books (New York, NY), 2000.

The Apache, Benchmark Books (New York, NY), 2001.

The Huron, Benchmark Books (New York, NY), 2001.

The Haida, Benchmark Books (New York, NY), 2001.

The Cheyenne, Benchmark Books (New York, NY), 2001.

The Inuit, Benchmark Books (New York, NY), 2002.

The Shoshone, Benchmark Books (New York, NY), 2002.

The Powhatan, Benchmark Books (New York, NY), 2002.

The Nez Perce, Benchmark Books (New York, NY), 2002.

The Blackfeet, Benchmark Books (New York, NY), 2003.

The Tlingit, Benchmark Books (New York, NY), 2003.

The Mandan, Benchmark Books (New York, NY), 2003.

The Choctaw, Benchmark Books (New York, NY), 2003.

The Delaware, Benchmark Books (New York, NY), 2004.

The Chumash, Benchmark Books (New York, NY), 2004.

The Arapaho, Benchmark Books (New York, NY), 2004.

The Wampanoag, Benchmark Books (New York, NY), 2004.

The Shawnee, Benchmark Books (New York, NY), 2004.

The Menominee, Benchmark Books (New York, NY), 2005.

The Crow, Benchmark Books (New York, NY), 2005.

The Cree, Benchmark Books (New York, NY), 2005.

The Delaware, Marshall Cavendish Benchmark (New York, NY), 2005.

NONFICTION; "BUILDING AMERICA" SERIES

The Mills, Benchmark Books (New York, NY), 2002.

The Houses, Benchmark Books (New York, NY), 2002.

The Forts, Benchmark Books (New York, NY), 2002.

The Farms, Benchmark Books (New York, NY), 2002.

The Canals, Benchmark Books (New York, NY), 2002.

NONFICTION; "AMERICAN COMMUNITY" SERIES

Missions and Presidios, Children's Press (New York, NY), 2004.

Longhouses, Children's Press (New York, NY), 2004.

Frontier Settlements, Children's Press (New York, NY), 2004.

Early American Villages, Children's Press (New York, NY), 2004.

Cow Towns, Children's Press (New York, NY), 2004.

OTHER

Ivesdale: A Photographic Essay, Champaign County Historical Archives, 1982.

(Photographer and calligrapher) *Upon a Quiet Landscape: The Photographs of Frank Sadorus,* Champaign County Historical Museum, 1983.

(Editor) *In All My Years: Portraits of Older Blacks in Champaign-Urbana,* Champaign County Historical Museum, 1983, revised edition, 1986.

There Is a Season, Champaign County Nursing Home, 1984.

(With Kathryn Kerr) *First Frost,* Stormline Press, 1985.

Common Ground: Photographs of Rural and Small Town Life, Stormline Press, 1986.

Stopping By: Portraits from Small Towns, University of Illinois Press, 1988.

(With wife, Linda LaPuma Bial) *The Carnegie Library in Illinois,* University of Illinois Press, 1988.

(Author of introduction) Gary Irving, photographer, *Beneath an Open Sky,* University of Illinois Press (Champaign, IL), 1990.

From the Heart of the Country: Photographs of the Midwestern Sky, Sagamore Publishing, 1991.

Looking Good: A Guide to Photographing Your Library, American Library Association, 1991.

Champaign: A Pictorial History, Bradley Publishing, 1993.

(Photographer) *Marcia Adams Heirloom Recipes,* Clarkson Potter (New York, NY, 1994.

Visit to Amish Country, Phoenix Publishing, 1995.

Zoom Lens Photography, Amherst Media, 1996.

Contributor of photo-essay to *Townships,* University of Iowa Press, 1992. Contributor of photographers to periodicals.

Sidelights

Raymond Bial has blended a love of photography and writing with a special feeling for rural and small-town America to create numerous illustrated books looking at subjects from harvesting corn and soybeans to rural architecture to one-room schools. His books on the many cultures of America—from Cajun to Native American to Appalachian—also introduce young readers to a type of living history that makes dry facts come alive. Other texts by Bial present historical topics, such as slavery, tenement life, colonial-era-technology, the growth of the Shaker community, the treatment of Native Americans, and the life of U.S. presidents George Washington and Abraham Lincoln. His contributions to the "Building America" series, which include such titles as *The Canals, The Mills,* and *The Forts,* were cited by *Booklist* contributor Susan Dove Lempke for their "strong research, clear writing, good organization," and Bial's "handsome color photographs." In addition, Bial has produced several works of juvenile fiction, among them *The Fresh Grave and Other Ghostly Stories* and the novel *Shadow Island: A Tale of Lake Superior.*

Born in Illinois, Bial grew up in the same rural, small-town community he portrays in books such as *Corn Belt Harvest, Cow Towns,* and *Early American Villages.*

As the author/photographer once told *SATA:* "When I was growing up in the 1950s I spent several of the most joyous years of my young life in a small town in Indiana. With my friends, I bicycled around the neighborhood, went swimming at the municipal pool, stopped for ice cream at the local hotspot, and frequently visited our Carnegie public library. Some people might think that such memories are simply nostalgic, but I know that our little town was pleasant, comfortable, and safe—and I will always cherish those years.

"Later, our family moved to a farm in southern Michigan. Although I missed my old friends, as well as the charming atmosphere of my old 'hometown,' I enjoyed taking care of our livestock and running free through the woods, marsh, and fields around our new home. The moment I walked out of the house, I was truly outside. The marsh, in particular, was bursting forth with wildlife—turtles, frogs, muskrats, ducks—and I delighted in my explorations and discoveries." While his family had the usual ups and downs, as Bial recalled, "I

Bial captures a self-sufficient way of life in his photographs for **Portrait of a Farm Family.** (Copyright © 1995 by Raymond Bial. Reproduced by permission of Houghton Mifflin Harcourt Publishing Company.)

was simply thrilled to be alive, directly experiencing the world around me, especially when I could be out of doors in the light and weather."

During childhood, Bial was also interested in social and cultural history, and he continued this interest in college. After training as a librarian, he worked in that field for over three decades; his wife, Linda, is a professor of library science, and the couple has produced several volumes of local history. Although Bial knew as a child that he wanted to become an author, during his twenties he discovered photography. "I never consciously decided to become a photographer," he once explained; "I simply loved the experience of making photographs. I've never received any formal training or education in the art form. Rather, I have relied upon my own instincts in making photographs which matter to me personally." While developing his skills in 35mm and large-format photography, in 1991 Bial fulfilled his childhood dream, combining his talents in writing and photography in his first book for children, *Corn Belt Harvest.*

Blending photographs and a straightforward, sometimes lyrical, text, *Corn Belt Harvest* describes the planting, harvesting, storage, and marketing methods of Midwest corn growers. Well received by critics, the book also received an Outstanding Science Trade Book for Children citation. Reviewing the title in *Booklist,* Hazel Rochman called *Corn Belt Harvest* an "informative photoessay" that features "clear color photographs" depicting the corn-growing and-harvesting process. The author/photographer "communicates a sense of process and connection in machines and nature," concluded Rochman, while a *Kirkus Reviews* critic noted that both text and photos are "commendably clear and informative." Writing in *School Library Journal,* Joyce Adams Burner cited the book's "big, beautiful color photographs," and further remarked that "Bial writes in a smooth, precise manner, yet conveys his love for the region." Burner concluded: "Overall, this is a jewel of a book, well suited for reports."

Other photo essays by Bial include *County Fair, Portrait of a Farm Family,* and *A Handful of Dirt. County Fair* traces a fair from set-up through opening day to the break-down of the tents. Here "Bial captures the sense of anticipation that swirls around a fair, as well as offering an insightful look at what goes on behind the scenes," noted *Booklist* contributor Ilene Cooper. Focusing on everything from livestock barns to homemade pies to and rides and other amusements, the book features "attractive color photos [that] . . . stand out on the pages," according to Cooper.

Dairy farming is the subject of *Portrait of a Farm Family.* Mary Harris Veeder noted in her *Booklist* review of this work that Bial's profile of the "everyday world" of the Steidinger family "fits its subject neatly into an excellent discussion of family-farm based agriculture in the U.S. economy." *Horn Book* contributor Elizabeth S. Watson also praised the work, noting that Bial's "fine

photo-essay radiates the warmth of a close ten-member family engaged in hard work toward a common goal—the survival of the family farm." Moving from the farm directly down to the land itself, *A Handful of Dirt* introduces readers to the many creatures—from bacteria to bugs and worms to shakes and gophers—that live on and in the soil. Noting the inclusion of photographs taken with an electron microscope, *Book* contributor Kathleen Odean predicted that Bial's "fine photo-essay will change how children view everyday dirt."

With *Amish Home* Bial struck on a winning formula: introducing America's diverse culture through domestic artifacts. His focus on things rather than people was a necessity in his first book of this type; the Amish people do not wish to be photographed. In more recent volumes, however, such as *Frontier Home* and *Cajun Home,* artifacts take on almost totemic values by introducing readers to the language, culture, food, and even history of the groups they represent. *Frontier Home* conjures up a bygone life through photos taken at pioneer villages and sites, pairing these images with the letters of actual pioneers, while in *Cajun Home* Bial profiles the ethnic group which emigrated from France, settled in Canada, and later moved on to Louisiana.

Reviewing *Amish Home* for *Booklist,* Kay Weisman praised the work as "haunting" and noted that Bial's work "will be welcomed by libraries everywhere." Alexandra Marris, reviewing *Amish Home* for *School Library Journal,* called the book "attractive and compelling," adding that "Bial clearly demonstrates his deep respect for these people and their complex system of values." In *Booklist* Carolyn Phelan commented of *Frontier Homes* that "Bial's photography gives the book a look of integrity as well as a window into the lives of the pioneers," while Judith Constantinides, reviewing *Cajun Home* in *School Library Journal,* remarked on Bial's "stunning full-color pictures of little things" by means of which he "meticulously builds a portrait of a fascinating people."

Tenement: Immigrant Life on the Lower East Side stands in contrast to much of Bial's works because, while it presents a look backward to a historic time and place, it takes readers far from its author's rural roots. Inspired by the author's visit to New York City's Lower East Side Tenement Museum and the writings and photographs of turn-of-the-twentieth-century social reformer Jacob Riis, *Tenement* weaves together many threads, including what *School Library Journal* reviewer Diane S. Marton praised as a "finely written, spare text" and the author's "beautifully composed, stunning" photographs, to depict a harsh life of cramped, unsanitary living conditions, brutal poverty, and debilitating work. Praising the book as a "substantial historic overview," a *Kirkus Reviews* critic noted that Bial's "out-of-towner" perspective enriches his work: "his picture is a clearer one, especially for non-New Yorkers," than other books on the subject, the critic explained. With an eye toward the book's audience, *Booklist* reviewer Cooper wrote that *Tenement* "will certainly be an eye-opener to many young people who are used to their own space."

The people of Appalachia receive the Bial treatment in *Mist over the Mountains: Appalachia and Its People.* As much a culture as a place, this region of small farms and folk arts is rich in culture and history, both of which Bial illuminates in text and photos. A *Kirkus Reviews* contributor called Bial's book a "superb photo-essay," while *Booklist* writer Phelan concluded that "this handsome book casts its beam of light with care and respect." A popular American handicraft forms the focus of *With Needle and Thread: A Book about Quilts,* a survey of patch-fabric stitchery from pioneer days through the era of the AIDS quilt. "With quiet prose and clear, lovely full-color photographs, Bial has stitched together a 'sampler' about people and the quilts they sew," commented *Booklist* contributor Hazel Rochman in her review of this title.

Migration is a focus of two books by Bial, both of which take readers back to the nineteenth century. In *Nauvoo: Mormon City on the Mississippi* he focuses on the Mormon migration of 1839, during which a Mormon community led by Joseph Smith fled New York and fled west to avoid religious persecution. Crossing the Mississippi to Illinois, they established the city of Nauvoo, but intolerance toward them continued. After Smith's murder, Nauvoo's Mormon population fled west once more, eventually settling in Utah. Bial tells his story in a mix of "period portraits and clear, well-composed photographs," according to Phelan, producing what the critic praised as a "well-written account" that "sheds light on nineteenth-century American religious intolerance." Praising *Nauvoo* as an "effectively written account [that] provides a sympathetic but balanced introduction to Mormon beliefs," Deanna Romriell added in her *School Library Journal* review that Bial presents his photographic history whith his characteristic "sensitivity and respect."

Focusing on one of the great symbols of America as the land of immigrants, *Ellis Island: Coming to the Land of Liberty* transports readers back in time to the island that would become the first step to a new life for almost 12,000 men, women, and children from around the world. Known as Oyster Island when it was farmed by

Bial turns his lens to America's most famous port of entry in **Ellis Island: Coming to the Land of Liberty.** (Photograph courtesy of New York Public Library.)

colonists, the island was acquired by the U.S. government in the late 1800s and served as the country's largest immigration station until it closed in the mid-1950s. In addition to presenting many contemporary and original images of the island, Bial also describes the motivations for the waves of immigrants that arrived on U.S. shores from Great Britain, Europe, and elsewhere. Restored by the U.S. Parks Service, Ellis Island continues to welcome visitors from around the world in its incarnation as a museum. "Primary-source quotes and period photos pair eloquently with the modern narrative voice and color photographs of the museum exhibits," wrote Rebecca Dash in her *School Library Journal* review of *Ellis Island,* and Bial's "measured account" is "enriched by frequent quotes from those who passed through its doors," according to a *Kirkus Reviews* writer.

The lives of American presidents have also come into clearer focus through Bial's work. *Where Lincoln Walked* traces the career of the man who guided the nation through a civil war from his humble log-cabin beginnings to his years in Washington, DC. Interspersed with the text are photos of places associated with Abraham Lincoln, including his homes and offices, as well as contemporary mid-nineteenth-century images such as paintings and engravings. Eunice Weech, writing in *School Library Journal,* called this book "another of Bial's beautifully executed photo-essays," while a *Kirkus Reviews* writer dubbed *Where Lincoln Walked* an "extraordinarily honest, if brief, pictorial portrayal."

Where Washington Walked is a similar work that follows the revolutionary general and first president on his path through the country's early history, pairing what *School Library Journal* contributor Elaine Fort Weischedel described as an "interesting" text with prints, paintings, and Bial's photographs of historic landmarks in Washington's life. From the first president's boyhood home of Ferry Farm to Mount Vernon and the sites now contained in Colonial Williamsburg, Bial's "sharply focused, well-composed" color photographs were cited by Phelan, along with the book's "clearly written biographical account." *Where Washington Walked* comprises a "unusually vivid photographic record" of its subject's life and accomplishments, concluded Phelan.

Beginning his well-illustrated "Lifeways" series in 1999, Bial has compiled fact-based histories of over two dozen Native American tribes, profiling "the history, culture, and social traditions" of each people "in clear, respectful language," according to Linda Greengrass in her *School Library Journal* review of *The Inuit.* Each volume contains an example of tribal folklore as well as a discussion of the ceremonies, geography, language, history, way of life, crafts, and community organization that make each group unique. Not surprisingly, these histories also have a special feature: what *School Library Journal* reviewer Sue Morgan characterized as "elegant full-color photography" of both tribal landmarks and existing artifacts. Also containing the author's photographs, a related volume, *The Long Walk:*

The Story of Navajo Captivity, focuses on the 300-mile march endured by the Navajo to a U.S. government reservation in southeastern New Mexico during the late 1800s, an imprisonment policy that was later overturned. Bial also includes an overview of Navajo history in this well-illustrated work.

Biographical and Critical Sources

PERIODICALS

Book, March, 2001, Kathleen Odean, review of *A Handful of Dirt,* p. 86.

Booklist, December 15, 1991, Hazel Rochman, review of *Corn Belt Harvest,* p. 761; February 1, 1992, Ilene Cooper, review of *County Fair,* p. 1023; February 15, 1993, Kay Weisman, review of *Amish Home,* p. 1055; November 1, 1993, Carolyn Phelan, review of *Frontier Home,* p. 516; April 1, 1995, Hazel Rochman, review of *The Underground Railroad,* p. 1390; September 1, 1995, Mary Harris Veeder, review of *Portrait of a Farm Family,* p. 73; March 1, 1996, Hazel Rochman, review of *With Needle and Thread: A Book about Quilts,* p. 1175; March 1, 1997, Carolyn Phelan, review of *Mist over the Mountains: Appalachia and Its People,* p. 1156; March 15, 1998, Ilene Cooper, review of *Cajun Home,* p. 1236; March 1, 2002, Susan Dove Lempke, reviews of *The Canals* and *The Houses,* both p. 1132; October 15, 2002, Ilene Cooper, review of *Tenement: Immigrant Life on the Lower East Side,* p. 406; December 15, 2004, Carolyn Phelan, review of *Where Washington Walked,* p. 739; November 1, 2006, Carolyn Phelan, review of *Nauvoo: Mormon City on the Mississippi River,* p. 47; September 1, 2007, John Peters, review of *The Super Soybean,* p. 112; August 1, 2009, Linda Perkins, review of *Ellis Island: Coming to the Land of Liberty,* p. 62.

Horn Book, May-June, 1994, Ellen Fader, review of *Shaker Home,* p. 332; November-December, 1995, Elizabeth S. Watson, review of *Portrait of a Farm Family,* pp. 759-760; November-December, 2002, Susan P. Bloom, review of *Tenement,* p. 773.

Kirkus Reviews, December 1, 1991, review of *Corn Belt Harvest,* p. 1529; February 1, 1993, review of *Amish Home,* p. 142; February 15, 1997, review of *Mist over the Mountains,* p. 297; November 15, 1997, review of *Where Lincoln Walked,* p. 1704; July 1, 2002, review of *Tenement,* p. 949; December 15, 2004, review of *Where Washington Walked,* p. 1198; August 15, 2007, review of *The Super Soybean;* May 1, 2009, review of *Ellis Island.*

Publishers Weekly, January 16, 1995, review of *The Underground Railroad,* p. 455; July 20, 2002, review of *Tenement,* p. 73.

School Library Journal, February, 1992, Joyce Adams Burner, review of *Corn Belt Harvest,* p. 92; May, 1993, Alexandra Marris, review of *Amish Home,* p. 112; February, 1998, Eunice Weech, review of *Where Lincoln Walked,* p. 94; May, 1998, Judith Constantinides, review of *Cajun Home,* p. 150; February,

2002, Marlene Gawron, review of *The Canals,* p. 140; April, 2002, Linda Greengrass, review of *The Inuit,* p. 163; September, 2002, Diane S. Marton, review of *Tenement,* p. 240; March, 2003, Ginny Gustin, review of *The Long Walk,* p. 246; June, 2003, S.K. Joiner, review of *The Mandan,* p. 155; May, 2004, Sue Morgan, reviews of *The Chumash* and *The Wampanoag,* both p. 162; January, 2005, Joyce Adams Burner, review of *Cow Towns,* p. 107; February, 2005, Elaine Fort Weischedel, review of *Where Washington Walked,* p. 114; June, 2006, Marlette Grant-Jackson, review of *The Delaware,* p. 169; December, 2006, Deanna Romriell, review of *Nauvoo,* p. 160; January, 2007, Kathryn Kosiorek, review of *Shadow Island,* p. 123; October, 2007, Frances E. Millhouser, review of *The Super Soybean,* p. 170; January, 2009, Rebecca Dash, review of *Ellis Island,* p. 140.

ONLINE

Raymond Bial Home Page, http://www.raybial.com (January 15, 2011).*

* * *

BRAGG, Georgia

Personal

Daughter of Charles Bragg (an artist) and Jennie Tomao (an artist); married Harvey Rosenfield (an attorney and consumer advocate); children: two.

Addresses

Home—Los Angeles, CA. *Agent*—Edward Necarsulmer IV, McIntosh & Otis, Inc., 353 Lexington Ave., New York, NY 10016. *E-mail*—georgia@georgiabragg.com.

Career

Artist and writer. Painter and printmaker; worked as a storyboard artist for commercials and movies.

Writings

Matisse on the Loose (novel), Delacorte Press (New York, NY), 2009.
How They Croaked: The Awful Ends of the Awfully Famous, illustrated by Kevin O'Malley, Walker & Company (New York, NY), 2011.

Sidelights

In *Matisse on the Loose,* her debut novel for young readers, Georgia Bragg draws on her experiences as a printmaker, painter, and storyboard artist to craft the tale of a mischievous aspiring artist. In addition to her elementary-grade novel, Bragg has also turned to younger children as author of the picture book *How They Croaked: The Awful Ends of the Awfully Famous,* a humorous story which features artwork by Kevin O'Malley.

Matisse on the Loose centers on Matisse Jones, an eleven year old from a most eccentric family: his father parades his portable, homemade barbeque around the neighborhood; his older sister, Frida, has an unhealthy obsession with the color purple; and his younger sibling, Man Ray, also sports the name of a famous artist. Matisse spends much of his free time copying the works of the great masters at the Geraldine Emmett Art Museum, where his mother serves as the head of security. During an exhibition of works by his namesake, nineteenth-century French painter Henri Matisse, the youngster spots an opportunity to display his own work, and with the security system turned off, he replaces a Matisse original with his very convincing copy. Unfortunately, when the preteen is unable to return the true portrait to its frame, he finds himself on the run as an unlikely art thief.

"The writing is fast paced and Matisse's observations provide some laugh-out-loud amusement," Richelle Roth commented in her *School Library Journal* con-

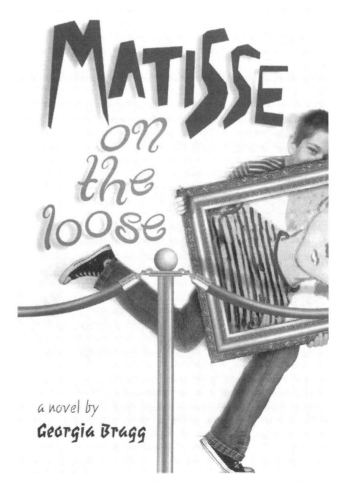

Cover of Georgia Bragg's middle-grade novel Matisse on the Loose, *featuring artwork by Philip Booker.* (Jacket art copyright © 2009 by Philip Booker. Reproduced by permission of Dell Publishing, a division of Random House, Inc.)

tributor of *Matisse on the Loose.* A *Kirkus Reviews* critic also praised Bragg's novel, describing the work as "by turns genuinely funny and self-consciously amusing."

Biographical and Critical Sources

PERIODICALS

Booklist, June 1, 2009, Shelle Rosenfeld, review of *Matisse on the Loose,* p. 56.
Kirkus Reviews, June 15, 2009, review of *Matisse on the Loose.*
School Library Journal, July, 2009, Richelle Roth, review of *Matisse on the Loose,* p. 79.

ONLINE

Georgia Bragg Home Page, http://georgiabragg.com (January 20, 2011).*

*   *   *

BROWN, Leo

Personal

Born in England; married; children.

Addresses

Home—England. *Agent*—Beehive Illustration Agency, 42a Cricklade St., Cirencester, Gloucestershire GL7 1JH, England. *E-mail*—leo@morpheusanimations.fsnet. co.uk.

Career

Illustrator, comics artist, sculptor, and animator. Freelance illustrator, beginning c. 1990; concept designer and animator for television and film.

Writings

SELF-ILLUSTRATED; "STARGAZERS" CHAPTER BOOKS

There Is Always Someone Watching, BookSurge (North Charleston, SC), 2006.

ILLUSTRATOR

Alan Gibbons, *Lifelines: Charles Darwin,* Kingfisher (New York, NY), 2008.
Steve Augarde, *Leonardo da Vinci,* Kingfisher (New York, NY), 2009.

Also creator of sketchbooks, including *Wings and Things, Claws and Tails,* and *Snigs and Snails and Faerie Tales.*

Sidelights

In addition to working as a storyboard artist and character developer for television and film animation, British artist Leo Brown has also contributed his artwork to children's books, both as an artist and an author. Melding traditional skills with technology, Brown works in watercolor, acrylic, and oils, then enhances his images digitally. His detailed, animation-style art is a feature of fictional journals based on the lives of Renaissance artist Leonardo da Vinci and nineteenth-century biologist Charles Darwin. It is also paired with Brown's original fantasy story about a gnome named Elmore in *There Is Always Someone Watching,* the first volume in his "Stargazers" chapter-book series.

In *Lifelines: Charles Darwin* author Alan Gibbons creates a fictional diary of James Kincaid, a cabin boy on the HMS *Beagle* during that ship's historic journey around South America during the mid-1830s. Charles Darwin, the *Beagle*'s naturalist, used the knowledge gained on this trip to develop his groundbreaking theory of evolution, and readers can follow his discoveries through Kincaid's entries and Brown's detailed scrapbook-like art. Published to coincide with the 200th anniversary of Darwin's birth, *Lifelines* contains "large, brightly colored line-and-wash pictures" that are mixed with photographs of actual objects dating to the time of the voyage, according to *Booklist* contributor Carolyn Phelan.

Teaming up with author Steve Augarde, Brown creates a similar journal effect in *Leonardo da Vinci,* which pairs the recollections of a ten-year-old painter's apprentice with Brown's colorful art, photographs and reproductions of da Vinci's drawings, as well as with interactive elements that make the volume "highly visual," according to *School Library Journal* contributor Jody Kopple. "Brown's artwork, peppered with da Vinci's distinctive designs, adds liveliness and color to the narrative," added Ian Chipman in his *Booklist* review, the critic noting that *Leonardo da Vinci* presents "a fascinating glimpse of da Vinci at the height of his inventive prowess . . . that's well supported by germane details of life in 1490s Italy."

Biographical and Critical Sources

PERIODICALS

Booklist, January 1, 2009, Carolyn Phelan, review of *Lifelines: Charles Darwin,* p. 68; November 1, 2009, Ian Chipman, review of *Leonardo da Vinci,* p. 57.
Kirkus Reviews, September 15, 2009, review of *Leonardo da Vinci.*

***Leo Brown's illustration projects include Alan Gibbons' illustrated biography* Lifelines: Charles Darwin.** (Kingfisher, 2008. Illustration copyright © 2008 by Leo Brown. Reproduced by permission.)

School Library Journal, January, 2010, Jody Kopple, review of *Leonardo da Vinci,* p. 117.

ONLINE

Leo Brown Home Page, http://www.leobrownstudios.com (January 12, 2011).*

*   *   *

BURNINGHAM, John 1936-

Personal

Born April 27, 1936, in Farnham, Surrey, England; son of Charles (a salesman) and Jessie Burningham; married Helen Gillian Oxenbury (a designer, author, and illustrator of children's books), August 15, 1964; children: Lucy, William Benedict, Emily. *Education:* Central School of Art (London, England), national diploma in design, 1959.

Addresses

Home—London, England. *Agent*—Conville & Walsh Ltd., 2 Ganton St., London W1F 7QL, England.

Career

Author, illustrator, and freelance designer. Worked at farming, slum-clearance, and forestry, in the Friend's Ambulance Unit, and at school building as an alternative to military service, 1953-55; freelance illustrator traveling through Italy, Yugoslavia, and Israel, 1953-55; worked for a year on set designs, models, and puppets for an animated puppet film in the Middle East, 1959-60; designed posters for London Transport and the British Transport Commission, early 1960s; author and illustrator of children's books, 1963—; freelance designer of murals, exhibitions, three-dimensional models, magazine illustrations and advertisements.

Awards, Honors

Kate Greenaway Medal for Illustration, British Library Association, 1963, for *Borka;* American Institute of Graphic Arts book of the year selection, 1967-68, for *The Extraordinary Tug-of-War;* Kate Greenaway Medal, 1970, Honorary Award, Biennale of Illustrations (Bratislava), *New York Times* Best Illustrated Children's Books of the Year designation, and Outstanding Book citations from *School Library Journal* all 1971, *Boston Globe/Horn Book* Award for Illustration, and Children's Book Showcase selection, both 1972, and American Library Association (ALA) Notable Book citation, all for *Mr. Gumpy's Outing;* Children's Book of the Year citations, Child Study Association of America, 1971, for both *Seasons* and *Mr. Gumpy's Outing,* and 1976, for *Mr. Gumpy's Motor Car; Horn Book* Honor designation, 1977, for *Come away from the Water, Shirley,* 1978, for *Time to Get out of the Bath, Shirley,* and 1988,

John Burningham (Photograph by Christina Gascoigne. Reproduced by permission.)

for *John Patrick Norman McHennessey, the Boy Who Was Always Late; New York Times* Best Illustrated Children's Books of the Year citations, and 1977, for *Come away from the Water, Shirley;* Deutscher Jugendliteraturpreis (German youth literature prize), West German Federal Ministry of the Interior, 1980, for *Would You Rather . . .;* Kurt Maschler/Emil Award runner-up, National Book League (Great Britain), 1983, for *The Wind in the Willows,* and 1986, for *Where's Julius?;* Kurt Maschler/Emil Award, 1984, and *New York Times* Best Illustrated Book Award, 1985, both for *Granpa;* Parents' Choice Picture Book Award, 1988, for *John Patrick Norman McHennessey, the Boy Who Was Always Late;* Parents' Choice Picture Book Award, 1990, and Books Can Develop Empathy award, 1991, both for *Hey! Get off Our Train!;* Nestlé Smarties Book Prize Bronze Award, 2000, for *Husherbye.*

Writings

SELF-ILLUSTRATED

Borka: The Adventures of a Goose with No Feathers, J. Cape (London, England), 1963, Random House (New York, NY), 1964.

(Illustrated with Leigh Taylor) *ABC,* J. Cape (London, England), 1964, Bobbs-Merrill (Indianapolis, IN), 1967.

Trubloff: The Mouse Who Wanted to Play the Balalaika, J. Cape (London, England), 1964, Random House (New York, NY), 1965.

Humbert, Mister Firkin, and the Lord Mayor of London, J. Cape (London, England), 1965, Bobbs-Merrill (Indianapolis, IN), 1967.

Cannonball Simp: The Story of a Dog Who Joins a Circus, J. Cape (London, England), 1966, Bobbs-Merrill (Indianapolis, IN), 1967.

Harquin: The Fox Who Went down to the Valley, J. Cape (London, England), 1967, Bobbs-Merrill (Indianapolis, IN), 1968.

Seasons, J. Cape (London, England), 1969, Bobbs-Merrill (Indianapolis, IN), 1971.

Mr. Gumpy's Outing, Holt (New York, NY), 1970.

(Adapter) *Around the World in Eighty Days,* J. Cape (London, England), 1972.

Mr. Gumpy's Motor Car, J. Cape (London, England), 1973, Macmillan (New York, NY), 1975.

Come away from the Water, Shirley, Crowell (New York, NY), 1977.

Time to Get out of the Bath, Shirley, Crowell (New York, NY), 1978.

Would You Rather . . ., Crowell (New York, NY), 1978.

The Shopping Basket, Crowell (New York, NY), 1980.

Avocado Baby, Crowell (New York, NY), 1982.

Granpa, J. Cape (London, England), 1984, Crown (New York, NY), 1985.

Where's Julius?, Crown (New York, NY), 1986.

John Patrick Norman McHennessey, the Boy Who Was Always Late, Crown (New York, NY), 1987, reprinted, Alfred Knopf (New York, NY), 2008.

Oi! Get off Our Train!, J. Cape (London, England), 1989, published as *Hey! Get off Our Train!,* Crown (New York, NY), 1990.

Aldo, Crown (New York, NY), 1991.

Harvey Slumfenburger's Christmas Present, Candlewick Press (Cambridge, MA), 1993.

Courtney, Crown (New York, NY), 1994.

First Steps: Letters, Numbers, Colors, Opposites, Candlewick (Cambridge, MA), 1994.

Cloudland, J. Cape (London, England), 1996.

Whadayamean?, Crown (New York, NY), 1999.

Hushabye, Knopf (New York, NY), 2000.

The Magic Bed, Knopf (New York, NY), 2003.

Edwardo: The Horriblest Boy in the Whole Wide World, Alfred A. Knopf (New York, NY), 2006.

It's a Secret, Candlewick Press (Somerville, MA), 2009.

There's Going to Be a Baby, Candlewick Press (Somerville, MA), 2010.

"LITTLE BOOK" SERIES; SELF-ILLUSTRATED

The Rabbit, J. Cape (London, England), 1974, Crowell (New York, NY), 1975.

The School, J. Cape (London, England), 1974, Crowell (New York, NY), 1975.

The Snow, J. Cape (London, England), 1974, Crowell (New York, NY), 1975.

The Baby, J. Cape (London, England), 1974, Crowell (New York, NY), 1975.

The Blanket, J. Cape (London, England), 1975, Crowell (New York, NY), 1976.

The Cupboard, J. Cape (London, England), 1975, Crowell (New York, NY), 1976.

The Dog, J. Cape (London, England), 1975, Crowell (New York, NY), 1976.

The Friend, J. Cape (London, England), 1975, Crowell (New York, NY), 1976.

"NUMBER PLAY" SERIES; SELF-ILLUSTRATED

Count Up: Learning Sets, Viking (New York, NY), 1983.

Five Down: Numbers as Signs, Viking (New York, NY), 1983.

Just Cats: Learning Groups, Viking (New York, NY), 1983.

Pigs Plus: Learning Addition, Viking (New York, NY), 1983.

Read One: Numbers as Words, Viking (New York, NY), 1983.

Ride Off: Learning Subtraction, Viking (New York, NY), 1983.

"FIRST WORDS"/ "NOISY WORDS" SERIES

Sniff Shout, Viking (New York, NY), 1984.

Skip Trip, Viking (New York, NY), 1984.

Wobble Pop, Viking (New York, NY), 1984.

Slam Bang!, Viking (New York, NY), 1985.

Cluck Baa, Viking (New York, NY), 1985.

Jangle Twang, Viking (New York, NY), 1985.

"PLAY AND LEARN" SERIES; SELF-ILLUSTRATED

John Burningham's ABC, Crown (New York, NY), 1985, published as *Alphabet Book,* Walker (London, England), 1987.

John Burningham's Colors, Crown (New York, NY), 1985.

John Burningham's 123, Crown (New York, NY), 1985.

John Burningham's Opposites, Crown (New York, NY), 1985.

Letters, Candlewick Press (Cambridge, MA), 2003.

Numbers, Candlewick Press (Cambridge, MA), 2003.

WALL FRIEZES

Birdland, Braziller (New York, NY), 1966.

Lionland, J. Cape (London, England), 1966, Braziller (New York, NY), 1967.

Storyland, J. Cape (London, England), 1966, Braziller (New York, NY), 1967.

Jungleland, J. Cape (London, England), 1968.

Wonderland, J. Cape (London, England), 1968.

Around the World, J. Cape (London, England), 1972.

OTHER

(Illustrator) Ian Fleming, *Chitty-Chitty-Bang-Bang: The Magical Car,* Random House (New York, NY), 1964, new edition, Puffin (London, England), 2008.

(Illustrator) Letta Schatz, editor, *The Extraordinary Tug-of-War,* Follett (New York, NY), 1968.

(Illustrator) Kenneth Grahame, *The Wind in the Willows,* Viking (New York, NY), 1983.

John Burningham's England (adult picture book), J. Cape (London, England), 1993.

John Burningham's France (adult picture book), DK Publications, 1998.

(Illustrator with others) Caroline Castle, *For Every Child: The UN Convention on the Rights of the Child in Words and Pictures,* Fogelman Books/UNICEF (New York, NY), 2001.

(Compiler) *When We Were Young,* research and interviews by Rose Foot, Bloomsbury (London, England), 2004.

John Burningham, foreword by Maurice Sendak, Candlewick Press (Somerville, MA), 2009.

Burningham's books have been published in Afrikaans, Danish, Dutch, Finnish, French, German, Irish, Japanese, Norwegian, Swedish, Spanish, Welsh, and Zulu.

Adaptations

Weston Woods has made filmstrips of *Mr. Gumpy's Outing,* *Come away from the Water, Shirley,* and *Mr. Gumpy's Motor Car* (filmstrip with cassette), 1982; Finehouse/Evergreen has made a filmstrip of *Cannonball.*

Sidelights

Dubbed "one of the most outstanding author-illustrators of children's books writing today" by Fionna Lafferty in the *St. James Guide to Children's Writers,* British writer John Burningham has dozens of books to his credit, including two Kate Greenaway-medal winners. During his long career, Burningham has created such memorable picture-book characters as the titular fowl in *Borka: The Adventures of a Goose with No Feathers,* an eccentric rustic in *Mr. Gumpy's Outing* and its sequel, *Mr. Gumpy's Motor Car,* a child of nervous parents in *Come away from the Water, Shirley* and *Time to Get out of the Bath, Shirley,* a girl and her beloved grandfather in *Granpa,* a balalaika-playing mouse in *Trubloff: The Mouse Who Wanted to Play the Balalaika,* and a cat with a wild nightlife in *It's a Secret.* In addition, he has shared his inspirations, his art, and his life in *John Burningham's England* and *John Burningham's France* as well as in the illustrated autobiography *John Burningham.*

Blending wry textual humor with equally humorous line drawings embellished with crayon, wash, and a wide assortment of other media, Burningham's signature style is one in which light-filled colors and nature's landscape predominate. "Fans of Burningham will delight in his witty, winsome pictures," noted *School Li-*

Burningham's amusing stories for children include his self-illustrated picture book **It's a Secret!** (Copyright © 2009 by John Burningham. Reproduced by permission of Candlewick Press, Somerville, MA on behalf of Walker Books, London.)

brary Journal contributor Kathy Krasniewicz, the critic describing the artist's work as "full of animation and expression." Chris Stephenson, writing in *Carousel,* called Burningham "one of that small band of innovative, adventurous illustrators who, through a combination of boldness of design and virtuosity of artwork, enhanced by texts which probed, explored, resonated and above all, entertained, completely transformed children's books."

Writing in the London *Guardian,* Joanna Carey attributed the continuing appeal of Burningham's picture books to his ability to see the world through a child's eyes: "Burningham understands and reflects the skewed logic and the strange, often urgent preoccupations that govern children's lives, and he recognises—with a mischievous, oblique humor—the gulf that lies between the child's and the adult's perceptions of the world," Carey noted.

Born on April 27, 1936, in Farnham, Surrey, Burningham was the youngest of three children. His father's work as a salesman took the family all over the country. As a child Burningham attended ten different schools and was forever trying to fit in as the new kid at school or in the neighborhood. Books and being read to, constants amid all the moving about, were an early delight for him.

At age twelve, Burningham was sent to the famous Summerhill School, an experiment in liberal teaching methods run by A.S. Neill. Here lessons were not compulsory and Burningham began drawing and painting, finding his own way rather than having his future dictated to him. Serving alternative service instead of enlisting in the British military, he spent two years working at forestry and social work, attending art classes in the evening. From 1956 to 1959 he attended London's Central School of Art and Craft, and it was there he met his future wife, children's-book illustrator Helen Oxenbury. Once out of school, Burningham had a variety of jobs in graphic arts, including designing stage sets and creating magazine cartoons, Christmas cards, cereal boxes, and posters for the London Transport system. He had no luck with publishers, however, taking his portfolio around London, but winning no commissions. Finally he determined to create his own book.

Published in 1963, Burningham's *Borka* tells the tale of a young hatchling who is rejected by other geese because she looks different; eventually Borka finds a home with birds who can accept her as she is. *Borka* earned its author the prestigious Kate Greenaway Medal for illustration and also launched Burningham's career as an author-illustrator, even though he had not planned on writing for children. "It is difficult to say why things happen," Burningham told Michele Field in *Publishers Weekly.* "If I had written a novel and it had won some kind of award, undoubtedly I'd still be writing novels." *Borka* also gained critical approval for its comical style and impressive pictures. "There is humor, boldness and

verve in the story," a *Sunday Herald Tribune Book Week* reviewer remarked, ". . . and in the well-drawn pictures, bright and childlike yet with original and interesting coloring." A reviewer for *Junior Bookshelf* similarly called *Borka* "exceedingly funny in conception" and praised it for its "consistent absurdity." The critic concluded: "So hilarious and lovely a book is a major contribution to the long and glorious history of the English picture book."

Burningham's next four books also feature animal characters behaving in human ways. In *Trubloff,* for instance, the author "gets a great deal of fun and a measure of beauty out of a charmingly absurd story of a mouse with musical aspirations," as a *Junior Bookshelf* writer commented. *Cannonball Simp* is about an ugly dog that goes from being unwanted to starring in a circus; its pictures "talk directly to young children," Robert Cohen wrote in *Young Readers Review. Harquin* tells the story of a foxhunt from the fox's point of view, while *Humbert, Mr. Firkin, and the Lord Mayor of London* finds a cart-horse saving the parade on the Lord Mayor's Show Day.

Some critics believe that the storylines of Burningham's early books are overshadowed by their illustrations. Richard Kluger, writing in the *Sunday Herald Tribune Book Week,* remarked that *Trubloff* "is strong as art, a bit flat as story," and Nancy Young Orr wrote in *School Library Journal* that the rich illustrations give *Harquin* "a verve and humor which the text alone fails to supply." Others found Burningham's stories to be skillfully written. In *Trubloff,* for instance, the author's pictures "are as fascinating as his story," Patience M. Daltry asserted in the *Christian Science Monitor,* and a *Publishers Weekly* writer stated in a review of *Cannonball Simp* that, "after looking at his wild and glorious creatures and reading the wild and glorious stories he writes about them . . . Burningham is now my favorite Englishman." As a *Junior Bookshelf* critic concluded in a review of *Humbert,* Burningham has "a remarkable gift for inventing very funny stories and putting them into brief, unobtrusively perfect words."

Seven years after his first book, Burningham produced another Greenaway winner in *Mr. Gumpy's Outing.* Mr. Gumpy travels along in his boat and picks up animals and children who promise not to cause trouble. The creatures cannot avoid breaking their promises, however, and the whole crew ends up in the water. Nevertheless, the tale ends happily with Mr. Gumpy serving tea to his now-soggy passengers. Dorothy Butler found the book to be a "classic example" of a story for young children; it is "beautifully paced, each character coming alive through his action and speech, with no need for description," the critic commented in *Signal. Mr. Gumpy's Outing* is "a blessing of a book," Joan Bodger Mercer likewise concluded in the *New York Times Book Review.* "Pored over, read aloud or acted out it should bring joy to the nursery." A sequel about an ill-fated car trip, *Mr. Gumpy's Motor Car,* was equally successful;

Virginia Haviland observed of this work in *Horn Book* that Burningham "is blessed with a gift for both verbal and visual storytelling; his flow of words describing the muddy crisis matches the charm of his watercolor scenes."

The tale of a boy who must outwit a series of animals on his way home from the store, *The Shopping Basket* "is the latest in a long line of marvelously humourous, idiosyncratic tales told by John Burningham," Jean Russell remarked in *Books for Your Children.* Lafferty similarly praised *The Shopping Basket* as "one of the best children's books ever conceived. Not only is it a nicely moralistic tale," the critic explained, but its use of vocabulary and repetition make it "a near perfect book for children beginning to read." "Sound psychology, beautifully exact and humorous drawing, a restrained and rhythmic text, it is all here, adding up to a picture book which falls only a little short of perfection," a *Junior Bookshelf* writer commented in an appraisal of *The Shopping Basket.*

In *Hushabye* kittens, baby bears, fish, and other creatures all grow tired and curl up to fall asleep, each in its own special place and manner. Told in what a *Publishers Weekly* critic called "a simple narrative featuring intermittent rhyme," Burningham's story "strikes a restful and dream-like chord, and provides a perfect invitation to sleep," according to Lauralyn Persson in *School Library Journal.* In *Booklist* Gillian Engberg praised "the irresistibly soothing sound, rhythm, and motion in the words." A *Horn Book* critic noted the "friendly collage artwork" with which Burningham illustrates his book, while a *Kirkus Reviews* writer predicted that the large type used for the text of *Hushabye* "will be visible in dim light," a definite plus for bedtime stories.

A cat's night out is Burningham's focus in *It's a Secret,* as the nocturnal ramblings of a family cat are discovered to be quite outlandish. Although Marie Elaine has been told that Malcolm the cat likes to be outside at night, she is in for an adventure when she meets up with Malcolm after dark and is invited to accompany him. The cat is dressed up and wearing a hat; with the little girl in tow, he goes on a journey that readers can follow in Burningham's color-enhanced art. *It's a Secret!* "is everything you want in a journey," asserted Daniel Handler in his *New York Times Book Review* appraisal: "a familiar face, a grave danger, tricky maneuvers, elegant delectables, some trail marks so you know you can find your way home and, yes, a wonderful secret" as the title promises. "Burningham's signature sketchy mixed-media illustrations are a good fit for the dreamlike story, as is the off-killer logic of the text," wrote Kathleen Kelly MacMillan in *School Library Journal,* while *Booklist* contributor Ilene Cooper cited the story's "fabulous art" as it brings to life the story's feline-filled and "special, secret world."

In the picture book *Aldo* a large imaginary rabbit named Aldo is the only friend of a lonely little girl, protecting her from bullies at school and reading to her by night.

Another caretaker animal is presented in *Courtney,* the story of children who badly want a dog. The pet they select during a trip to the dog pound is not quite the purebred animal their snobbish parents were hoping for, however. Fortunately, Courtney turns out to be a Mary Poppins in dog clothing, capable of cooking, juggling, and rescuing all in turn. Deborah Stevenson commented in *Bulletin of the Center for Children's Books* that such a talented dog "will charm quite a few viewers . . . as Burningham, with his usual ability to make silent animals personable and friendly, depicts Courtney as a walrus-ish yet debonair individual who never loses his air of mystery." Kate McClelland noted in a *School Library Journal* review of *Courtney* that this "is all typically assured Burningham at his ironic best," while in *Kirkus Reviews* a critic wrote that the artist's "familiar cartoon mode" is "poignantly expressive," and results in a book that is "witty, well told, and superbly illustrated."

Although his work involving animals has been very successful, Burningham has become "increasingly interested in the relationships between adults and children," as the author/illustrator told Field in *Publishers Weekly.* In the books *Come away from the Water, Shirley* and *Time to Get out of the Bath, Shirley,* he contrasts the imaginative adventures of a little girl with her parents' warnings to stay out of trouble. Both books feature brightly colored illustrations of Shirley's exploits that are paired with subdued portraits of her dreary parents. The result is "all too brief a masterpiece of humor and affection, with . . . unforgettable illustrations," according to David Anable in the *Christian Science Monitor.* As Margery Fisher concluded in *Growing Point,* Burningham's "Shirley" books provide readers with "a marvelously comical and inventive juxtaposition of everyday taps, toothpaste and domestic admonition with storybook cliches and uninhibited fun."

Although both his "Mr. Gumpy" and "Shirley" books have been popular enough to warrant further episodes, Burningham has deliberately avoided creating a long-running series. "I am very fond of Mr. Gumpy, but it would be awful to spend my life doing *just* Mr. Gumpy—or anything else," the author explained to Field. "The problem is that it is easier once you've established a character to keep it going. But I am always more interested in doing something I haven't done before."

In *Granpa* Burningham turns away from comic situations to portray a little girl's relationship with her grandfather ends with the man's passing. With just a brief story, the author "suggests a whole life story for Granpa and shows a small girl reacting to death," Pat Triggs wrote in *Books for Keeps.* While death is a difficult subject to introduce to children, Burningham treats it "gently [and] poetically," Andrew Clements commented in the *New Statesman,* citing the book's "spare, immensely evocative" illustrations. Despite its sober ending, *Granpa* has humor in its "funny drawings"; Burn-

Burningham's engaging illustrations pair with a gentle nighttime story in **The Magic Bed.** (Copyright © 2003 by John Burningham. Used by permission of Random House Group, Ltd., and by permission of Alfred A. Knopf, an imprint of Random House Children's Books, a division of Random House, Inc.)

ingham "has not been more amusing, more wise," Marcus Crouch remarked in *Junior Bookshelf.* As William Feaver stated in the London *Observer,* in *Granpa* "Burningham has succeeded in dealing with what, since Victorian times, has been the impossible in picture-book terms: real-life death."

Father Christmas gets the Burningham treatment in *Harvey Slumfenburger's Christmas Present,* in which Santa, exhausted after delivering presents all night, discovers one deliveray that he has overlooked. Because poor little Harvey Slumfenburger is unlikely to get any other gifts this Christmas, Santa sets out on foot to deliver it, having already tucked his reindeer into bed for the night. Along the way, Santa utilizes several modes of transportation and meets other travelers in a book that could become "a classic," according to Keith Barker in *School Librarian.* Sheila Moxley called *Harvey Slumfenburger's Christmas Present* "poignant" and "lightly funny" in her review for *School Library Journal,* and in *Booklist* Carolyn Phelan drew special attention to Burn-

ingham's "signature ink drawings with watercolor washes" which she predicted "will keep children rapt."

In the books *Cloudland* and *Whadayamean?* Burningham experiments with mixed-media illustrations, blending photographic images with his own artwork. In *Cloudland* young Albert is out hiking in the mountains with his parents when he tumbles off a cliff. Happily, he lands on a cloud, caught by cloud children who introduce him to all manner of lovely pastimes including swimming, painting, dancing, and making music. Seeing the lights of the city below, Albert finally remembers his family and desires to go home. Without question or approbation, his parents welcome the missing child home and tuck him into bed, as much a part of the fantasy as Albert himself. *Booklist* critic Julie Corsaro commented that in *Cloudland* "Burningham explores a common childhood fantasy in an impressively illustrated picture book" that employs photographic images of clouds with sketchy figures overlaid to create a three-dimensional effect. A reviewer for *Junior Book-*

shelf dubbed *Cloudland* "a sumptuous example of John Burningham's skill in marrying the magic of the simple story with the splendid page after page of illustrations which will appeal to both reader and listener," and in *Books for Keeps* George Hunt found it to be a "visually striking and entertaining book."

Even more stylistically innovative is Burningham's environmental story *Whadayamean?,* which mixes satellite photography, paintings, and soft-focus photos with pastels, pen and ink, and various other collage features. In the story, God wakes up one day and decides to visit Earth, the paradise he/she once created. Accompanied by two earthling children found picnicking under a tree, God discovers that things have gone terribly wrong on the planet, with pollution, killing, and starvation to be found in abundance. God entrusts the children with the task of talking to benighted adults and getting them on the right path, which they do in this eco-fantasy. Rosemary Stones called *Whadayamean?* a "fable for our times" in *Books for Keeps,* noting that the "impact is wrenching as the small figures are dwarfed by the scale of our planet's destruction." Joan Zahnleiter remarked in *Magpies* that Burningham "has given the creation story an ecological turn in this spectacular picture book." Athough there is a mixed bag of media in the artwork, the critic continued, "Burningham's consummate skill as an illustrator has brought them all into an harmonious whole which flows through the book along with the text."

Burningham creates a different sort of bedtime story in *The Magic Bed,* which finds young Georgie too big for the crib he has been sleeping in. His father buys him an old bed from a used furniture store that is said to have magical abilities. If Georgie says the correct secret word out loud, the bed will take him on adventures in faraway places. When he discovers the magic word, the boy does indeed visit those distant places . . . in his dreams. When Georgie's grandmother eventually gets rid of the old bed and buys him a brand new one that does not have magical powers, the boy has one last dream-time adventure. Gillian Engberg, writing in *Booklist,* predicted that "Burningham's simple, sly sentences and whimsical mixed-media art will immediately transport children on their own imagined departures," and Amy Lilien-Harper wrote in *School Library Journal* that, "with simple, word-perfect prose, Burningham captures a child's imagination." A *Kirkus Reviews* critic concluded of *The Magic Bed* that "Burningham's whimsical illustrations are a perfect match for his experienced, well-paced prose."

Described by a *Kirkus Reviews* writer as a picture-book "take on the effects of positive and negative reinforcement," *Edwardo: The Horriblest Boy in the Whole Wide World* shows what happens when a boy's verbal environment is transformed. Edwardo is a typical boy: sometimes clumsy, sometimes goofy, sometimes loud, and sometimes feisty. His parents respond to their son's missteps with denigrating comments that convince the boy to take on a bad-boy attitude. Then he accidentally does something right, and gets praise, which changes his world. Illustrated in Burningham's characteristic "minimalist" line-and-water-color images, *Edwardo* encourages readers to "imagine themselves as naughty, guilty, and nice," according to *Booklist* contributor Hazel Rochman, while a *Kirkus Reviews* writer described the book as "a cautionary tale that children may want to bring to their parents." A reviewer in *Publishers Weekly* deemed *Edwardo* a "delightfully inverted cautionary tale," adding that "Burningham's spare, whimsical watercolors amplify the wry humor" of his text.

Burningham believes that maintaining his interest in his work contributes to its quality and broad appeal. Really great children's books, he wrote in *Junior Bookshelf,* "contain as much for adults as for children because the person who made them was concerned to satisfy himself as well as his readers. This is an attitude which anyone who embarks on creative work must have if he is to achieve anything."

"I enjoy making children's books—and I use the word 'making' rather than writing because I think of my books as a series of drawings held together by a thread of text," Burningham also noted in *Junior Bookshelf.* "I enjoy it because it allows me to work with the maximum freedom and to carry out my own ideas." The author wants his readers to have freedom as well, he continued: "I try not to make my own drawings too formal and finished so that the child who is reading or looking can have the maximum freedom to imagine for himself. The sense of finding something out is as important in pictures as it is in words."

In a statement posted on the British Council for the Arts Web site, Burningham noted: "With each new book I think, can I do it again? Can I pull it off again? There are terrible moments when I feel I have lost it, and I have no ability. But then it all gets back on course. Drawing is like playing the piano, . . . you have to practise constantly to keep it fluent. Even after forty years it doesn't get any easier."

According to *New York Times Book Review* contributor Vicki Weissman, Burningham has succeeded in using his "tremendous craft" to give his books an open, imaginative feeling. The critic remarked: "Burningham has long since grasped that all children need is a trigger and their imaginations will do the rest. What is more, he is content to leave it to them." In addition, his books excel because "he has the ability to capture in his simple drawings the essence and spirit of his characters—whether animals or people and portray them in a way that little children respond to," Russell wrote. "Burningham," concluded Stephenson in his *Carousel* profile, "is a quiet man who has a deep respect for the value of words and chooses them carefully; who thinks deeply and cares passionately about the planet; and who, like many serious people, maintains a constant, warm underglow of humour."

Biographical and Critical Sources

BOOKS

Burningham, John, *John Burningham*, foreword by Maurice Sendak, Candlewick Press (Somerville, MA), 2009.

Children's Books and Their Creators, edited by Anita Silvey, Houghton Mifflin (Boston, MA), 1995.

Children's Literature Review, Volume 9, Gale (Detroit, MI), 1985.

Egoff, Sheila A., *Thursday's Child: Trends and Patterns in Contemporary Children's Literature*, American Library Association, 1981, p. 268.

St. James Guide to Children's Writers, St. James Press (Detroit, MI), 1999.

PERIODICALS

Booklist, October 15, 1993, Carolyn Phelan, review of *Harvey Slumfenburger's Christmas Present*, p. 450; December 15, 1996, Julie Corsaro, review of *Cloudland*, p. 731; September 1, 1999, Shelley Townsend-Hudson, review of *Whadayamean?*, p. 138; April 1, 2001, Gillian Engberg, review of *Mr. Gumpy's Outing*, p. 1477; October 1, 2001, Gillian Engberg, review of *Hushabye*, p. 323; November 15, 2003, Gillian Engberg, review of *The Magic Bed*, p. 598; January 1, 2007, Hazel Rochman, review of *Edwardo: The Horriblest Boy in the Whole Wide World*, p. 112; June 1, 2009, Ilene Cooper, review of *It's a Secret!*, p. 65.

Books for Keeps, November, 1984, Pat Triggs, review of *Granpa*, p. 4; March, 1997, George Hunt, review of *Cloudland*, p. 20; May, 1999, Rosemary Stones, review of *Whadayamean?*, p. 23.

Books for Your Children, spring, 1981, Jean Russell, "Cover Artist: John Burningham," pp. 6-7.

Bulletin of the Center for Children's Books, December, 1994, Deborah Stevenson, review of *Courtney*, p. 123.

Carousel, spring, 1999, Chris Stephenson, "Out of This World: John Burningham," pp. 20-21.

Christian Science Monitor, November 4, 1965, Patience M. Daltry, "Imagination Needs No Visa," p. B1; November 2, 1977, David Anable, "Shirley Battles Pirates in Deep-Sea Daydreams," p. B2.

Growing Point, July, 1978, Margery Fisher, review of *Time to Get out of the Bath, Shirley*, p. 3369.

Guardian (London, England), September 2, 2000, Clare Bayley, "Indulging the Urge to Muck About"; March 8, 2003, Joanna Carey, reviews of *The Magic Bed* and *Borka: The Adventures of a Goose with No Feathers*; July 26, 2009, Kate Kellaway, review of *John Burningham*.

Horn Book, August, 1976, Virginia Haviland, review of *Mr. Gumpy's Motor Car*, p. 385; November-December, 2001, review of *Hushabye*, p. 732.

Independent (London, England), April 18, 2009, Deborah Orr, interview with Burningham.

Junior Bookshelf, December, 1963, review of *Borka*, p. 335; July, 1964, John Burningham, "Drawing for Children," pp. 139-141; November, 1964, review of *Trubloff: The Mouse Who Wanted to Play the Balalaika*, p. 288; February, 1966, review of *Humbert, Mr. Firkin, and the Lord Mayor of London*, pp. 27-28; February, 1981, review of *The Shopping Basket*, p. 11; February, 1985, Marcus Crouch, review of *Granpa*, p. 12; October, 1996, review of *Cloudland*, p. 182.

Kirkus Reviews, July 15, 1994, review of *Courtney*, p. 979; September 1, 2001, review of *Hushabye*, p. 1286; August 1, 2003, review of *The Magic Bed*, p. 1013; January 15, 2007, review of *Edwardo*, p. 70; May 1, 2009, review of *It's a Secret!*

Magpies, May, 1999, Joan Zahnleiter, review of *Whadayamean?*, p. 22.

New Statesman, December 7, 1984, Clements, Andrew, "A Serious Business," p. 30.

New York Times Book Review, November 7, 1971, Joan Bodger Mercer, review of *Mr. Gumpy's Outing*, p. 46; May 8, 1988, Vicki Weissman, "The Gorilla Was on His Side," p. 32; December 6, 2009, Daniel Handler, review of *It's a Secret!*, p. 52.

Observer (London, England), November 25, 1984, William Feaver, "Bumps in the Night," p. 27.

Publishers Weekly, August 7, 1967, review of *Cannonball Simp*, p. 54; July 24, 1987, Michele Field, interview with Burningham and Helen Oxenbury, pp. 168-169; July 26, 1999, review of *Whadayamean?*, p. 83; October 1, 2001, review of *Hushabye*, p. 60; January 27, 2003, review of *Would You Rather*, p. 262; September 20, 2003, review of *The Magic Bed*, p. 64; January 15, 2007, review of *Edwardo*, p. 50; June 8, 2009, review of *It's a Secret!*, p. 42.

School Librarian, November, 1993, Keith Barker, review of *Harvey Slumfenburger's Christmas Present*, p. 147.

School Library Journal, November, 1968, Nancy Young Orr, review of *Harquin*, p. 75; October, 1993, Sheila Moxley, review of *Harvey Slumfenburger's Christmas Present*, p. 42; September, 1994, Kate McClelland, review of *Courtney*, p. 180; December, 2001, Lauralyn Persson, review of *Hushabye*, p. 91; October, 2003, Amy Lilien-Harper, review of *The Magic Bed*, p. 114; February, 2007, Kathy Krasniewicz, review of *Edwardo*, p. 85; March, 2007, Rick Margolis, interview with Burningham, p. 39; June, 2009, Kathleen Kelly MacMillan, review of *It's a Secret!*, p. 80.

Signal, January, 1977, Dorothy Butler, "Cushla and Her Books," pp. 3-37.

Sunday Herald Tribune Book Week, May 10, 1964, review of *Borka*, pp. 34-35; September 12, 1965, Richard Kluger, "The Glottis Got Us," p. 28.

Young Readers Review, December, 1967, Robert Cohen, review of *Cannonball Simp*, p. 16.

ONLINE

British Council for the Arts Web site, http://magicpencil.britishcouncil.org/ (April 29, 2005), "John Burningham."*

BUTLER, John 1952-

Personal

Born 1952; married; children: two daughters.

Addresses

Home—Kent, England. *E-mail*—john@johnbutlerart. com.

Career

Author and illustrator.

Awards, Honors

British Petroleum Conservation Award, 1995; Sheffield Children's Book Award shortlist, and Federation of Children's Book Groups Awards shortlist, both 1997, both for *Little Elephant Thunderfoot;* Norfolk Libraries Children's Book Award, 1998; Best Children's Books of the Year selection, Bank Street College of Education, 2002, for *Pi-shu, the Little Panda;* Best Children's Books of the Year selection, Bank Street College of Education, 2004, for *Can You Cuddle like a Koala?;* British Booktrust Early Years Awards shortlist for Best Baby Book, 2004, for *Hush Little Ones;* Southampton Best Book to Share selection, 2004.

Writings

SELF-ILLUSTRATED

While You Were Sleeping, Peachtree Publishers (Atlanta, GA), 1999.

Pi-shu, the Little Panda, Peachtree Publishers (Atlanta, GA), 2001.

Whose Baby Am I?, Viking (New York, NY), 2001.

If You See a Kitten, Peachtree Publishers (Atlanta, GA), 2002.

Hush Little Ones, Peachtree Publishers (Atlanta, GA), 2002.

Can You Cuddle like a Koala?, Peachtree Publishers (Atlanta, GA), 2003.

Who Says Woof?, Viking (New York, NY), 2003.

Whose Nose and Toes?, Viking (New York, NY), 2004.

Ten in the Den, Peachtree Publishers (Atlanta, GA), 2005.

Ten in the Meadow, Peachtree Publishers (Atlanta, GA), 2006.

Can You Growl like a Bear?, Peachtree Publishers (Atlanta, GA), 2007.

It Was Bedtime in the Jungle, Puffin (London, England), 2009, published as *Bedtime in the Jungle,* Peachtree Publishers (Atlanta, GA), 2009.

ILLUSTRATOR

(With Gwen Fulton and Sheila Smith) Gill Gould, compiler, *Disappearing Animals of Europe,* W. & R. Chambers (Edinburgh, Scotland), 1978.

(With Alan R. Thomson and Sheila Smith) Gill Gould, compiler, *Disappearing Animals of the Forests of Africa,* W. & R. Chambers (Edinburgh, Scotland), 1980.

(With Alan R. Thomson and Stephen Adams) Gill Gould, compiler, *Disappearing Animals of the Seas,* W. & R. Chambers (Edinburgh, Scotland), 1980.

Margaret Lane, *The Stickleback,* Methuen/Walker (London, England), 1981, published as *The Fish: The Story of the Stickleback,* Dial (New York, NY), 1981.

Alfred Leutscher, *Earth,* Dial (New York, NY), 1983.

Derek Hall, *Otter Swims,* Knopf (New York, NY), 1984, published as *Kylee the Otter,* Walker (London, England), 1989.

Derek Hall, *Panda Climbs,* Knopf (New York, NY), 1984, published as *Chi-li the Panda,* Walker (London, England), 1988.

Derek Hall, *Tiger Runs,* Knopf (New York, NY), 1984, published as *Khana the Tiger,* Walker (London, England), 1989.

Derek Hall, *Elephant Bathes,* Knopf (New York, NY), 1985, published as *Balego the Elephant,* Walker (London, England), 1989.

Derek Hall, *Gorilla Builds,* Knopf (New York, NY), 1985, published as *Simbi the Gorilla,* Walker (London, England), 1988.

Derek Hall, *Polar Bear Leaps,* Knopf (New York, NY), 1985, published as *Laska the Polar Bear,* Walker (London, England), 1988.

Anne Carter, *Ruff Leaves Home,* Crown (New York, NY), 1986.

Anne Carter, *Bella's Secret Garden,* Crown (New York, NY), 1987.

Anne Carter, *Molly in Danger,* Crown (New York, NY), 1987.

Anne Carter, *Scurry's Treasure,* Crown (New York, NY), 1987.

Beth Spanjian, *Baby Grizzly,* Western Publishing (Racine, WI), 1988.

Beth Spanjian, *Baby Lamb,* Western Publishing (Racine, WI), 1988.

Beth Spanjian, *Baby Triceratops,* Western Publishing (Racine, WI), 1988.

(With Peter Barrett) Jenny Wood, *My First Book of Animals,* Warner Juvenile Books (New York, NY), 1989.

William F. Russell, editor, *Animal Families of the Wild: Animal Stories,* Crown (New York, NY), 1990.

Alexander McCall Smith, *Akimbo and the Elephants,* Mammoth (London, England), 1990.

(With Brian McIntryre) Michael Chinery, *Grassland and Prairies,* Kingfisher Books (London, England), 1991, published as *Grassland Animals,* Random House (New York, NY), 1992.

Derek Hall, *Baby Animals: Five Stories of Endangered Species,* Candlewick Press (Cambridge, MA), 1992.

Anita Ganeri, *The Giant Book of Animal Worlds,* Lodestar Books (New York, NY), 1992.

(With Brian McIntyre) Michael Chinery, *Polar Lands,* Kingfisher Books (London, England), 1992, published as *Questions and Answers about Polar Animals,* Kingfisher Books (New York, NY), 1994.

Tess Lemmon, *Apes,* Ticknor & Fields (New York, NY), 1993.

Theresa Radcliffe, *Shadow the Deer,* Viking (New York, NY), 1993.

Philip Steele, *The Giant Panda,* Kingfisher Books (New York, NY), 1994.

Theresa Radcliffe, *The Snow Leopard,* Viking (New York, NY), 1994.

Theresa Radcliffe, *Cimru the Seal,* Viking (New York, NY), 1996.

Sally Grindley, *Little Elephant Thunderfoot,* Orchard (London, England), 1996, Peachtree Publishers (Atlanta, GA), 1999.

Janine Amos, *Animals,* World Book/Two-Can (Chicago, IL), 1997.

Theresa Radcliffe, *Bashi, Elephant Baby,* Viking (New York, NY), 1997.

Sally Grindley, *Polar Star,* Orchard (London, England), 1997, Peachtree Publishers (Atlanta, GA), 1998.

Sally Grindley, *Little Tang,* Orchard (London, England), 1998.

Sally Grindley, *Little Sibu: An Orangutan Tale,* Peachtree Publishers (Atlanta, GA), 1999.

Theresa Radcliffe, *Maya, Tiger Cub,* Viking (New York, NY), 1999.

Theresa Radcliffe, *Nanu, Penguin Chick,* Viking (New York, NY), 2000.

(With Keith Furnival) Alastair Smith, *Night-time,* Scholastic (New York, NY), 2002.

Dianna Hutts Aston, *Bless This Mouse,* Handprint Books (Brooklyn, NY), 2004.

Christine Morton-Shaw and Greg Shaw, *Wake up, Sleepy Bear!,* Viking (New York, NY), 2006.

Marion Dane Bauer, *A Mummy for Owen,* Simon & Schuster (London, England), 2007, published as *A Mama for Owen,* Simon & Schuster (New York, NY), 2007.

Nancy Markham Alberts, *Just One More?,* Handprint Books (Brooklyn, NY), 2007.

Lauren Thompson, *Wee Little Chick,* Simon & Schuster (New York, NY), 2008.

Lauren Thompson, *Wee Little Lamb,* Simon & Schuster (New York, NY), 2009.

Lauren Thompson, *Wee Little Bunny,* Simon & Schuster (New York, NY), 2010.

Also illustrator of book covers.

Sidelights

British author and illustrator John Butler has earned recognition for his warm, intricate portraits of animals. Done primarily in acrylics and colored pencil, his work has graced the pages of numerous picture books, including his self-illustrated *While You Were Sleeping, Ten in the Den,* and *Bedtime in the Jungle.* "I have always been fascinated by wildlife and that's why my books are mostly about animals and where they live," Butler remarked on his home page. "I think we can learn a lot from nature."

Butler began his career illustrating works for other authors. In *Shadow the Deer,* a story by Theresa Radcliffe, a fawn becomes prey for a hungry fox when its mother steals away for a drink. "Butler's lifelike illustrations, worked with gouache, watercolors and air brush, capture uncanny details," a critic noted in *Publishers Weekly.* Radcliffe and Butler also join forces to create *Bashi, Elephant Baby,* a tale of survival on the African plains. Here "Butler's realistic paintings of the animals heighten the drama," Lauren Adams remarked in her *Horn Book* review of the work.

In Sally Grindley's *Little Sibu: An Orangutan Tale* the author examines a young orangutan's growing need for independence. In his artwork, a *Publishers Weekly* contributor stated, "Butler sets naturalistic details against impressionistic backgrounds." Based on a true story, Marion Dane Bauer's *A Mama for Owen* looks at the unlikely relationship between a baby hippo and a giant tortoise. "Butler's acrylics-and-colored-pencil pictures are awash in pale and shadowy or rosy and golden tones," according to a critic reviewing *A Mama for Owen* in *Kirkus Reviews.*

Butler has also enjoyed a successful collaboration with writer Lauren Thompson. In *Wee Little Chick* a diminutive barnyard creature proves just as capable of climbing, running, and loudly peeping as her larger siblings. According to *School Library Journal* reviewer Kristen Frey, Butler's illustrations for Thompson's text artistically "portray the story's springtime mood and warm-hearted tone." A shy animal learns to explore the world with the help of his woodland friends in *Wee Little Lamb,* another story by Thompson in which Butler's brightly colored pictures "seem to pop off the page," as Linda Staskus noted in *School Library Journal.* The playful adventures of a tiny rabbit are at the heart of *Wee Little Bunny.* Here "Butler crafts an idyllic . . . setting, all bright blue sky and soft green grasses," according to a contributor in *Kirkus Reviews.*

While You Were Sleeping, Butler's first self-illustrated picture book, is a counting book for young readers. A *Publishers Weekly* critic declared that the artist's "animals portraits are the stuff of wide-eyed wonder," and Hazel Rochman wrote in *Booklist* that his mix of "words and pictures have the soothing rhythm of a lullaby." A newborn discovers the beauties and dangers of the jungle in *Pi-shu, the Little Panda,* and here Butler's "pictures are gorgeous, with panoramic views of the valleys and mountains at dusk," according to *School Library Journal* critic Holly Belli. Toddlers are introduced to a host of animal offspring in *Whose Baby Am I?,* another original story featuring illustrations that "realistically capture . . . achingly adorable animals," a contributor observed in *Publishers Weekly.*

A counting book told in verse, Butler's *Ten in the Den* focuses on a group of cuddly animals that squeezes together for the night in a small den. "Sweet, softly colored illustrations make this a perfect bedtime book," remarked a *Kirkus Reviews* critic, and Jane Marino reported in *School Library Journal* that the "repetition and sound words invite participation." In a companion tale, *Ten in the Meadow,* the animal friends gather for an exuberant game of hide-and-seek. According to Robin L. Gibson in *School Library Journal,* "Butler's soft, wide-eyed animals will appeal to children."

Butler has also earned praise for several of his bedtime tales. *Hush Little Ones* portrays a variety of animal parents as they prepare their infants for a night of slumber. In the words of *Booklist* critic Ilene Cooper, "the love that's portrayed . . . is palpable," and a *Kirkus Reviews* contributor noted of Butler's artwork that "the snoozers are rendered in astonishingly lifelike close-ups." Inspired by the familiar children's song "Over in the Meadow," *Bedtime in the Jungle* depicts the efforts of a mother leopard, crocodile, and rhino, among others, to lull their young ones to sleep. "Nicely paired with the soporific text are Butler's realistic acrylic-and-colored-pencil illustrations," remarked a critic in *Kirkus Reviews,* and in *Booklist* Bina Williams observed of *Bedtime in the Jungle* that the book's "dreamy and dusky landscapes [are] certain to soothe the wildest of human beasts."

Biographical and Critical Sources

PERIODICALS

Booklist, December 1, 1999, Hazel Rochman, review of *While You Were Sleeping,* p. 708; March 15, 2001, Ellen Mandel, review of *Pi-Shu, the Little Panda,* p. 1402; June 1, 2001, Denise Wilms, review of *Whose Baby Am I?,* p. 1885; October 15, 2001, Cynthia Turnquest, review of *While You Were Sleeping,* p. 399; November 15, 2002, Ilene Cooper, review of *Hush, Little Ones,* p. 608; March 1, 2003, Todd Morning, review of *If You See a Kitten,* p. 1201; September 1, 2007, Carolyn Phelan, review of *Can You Growl like a Bear?,* p. 124; May 15, 2008, Abby Nolan, review of *Wee Little Chick,* p. 50; September 15, 2009, Bina Williams, review of *Bedtime in the Jungle,* p. 62; January 1, 2010, Hazel Rochman, review of *Wee Little Bunny,* p. 96.

Horn Book, January-February, 1998, Lauren Adams, review of *Bashi, Elephant Baby,* p. 67.

Kirkus Reviews, August 15, 2002, review of *Hush, Little Ones,* p. 1219; February 15, 2003, review of *If You See a Kitten,* p. 301; August 15, 2005, review of *Ten in the Den,* p. 910; March 1, 2007, review of *A Mama for Owen,* p. 216; November 15, 2008, review of *Wee Little Lamb;* August 15, 2009, review of *Bedtime in the Jungle;* December 1, 2009, review of *Wee Little Bunny.*

Publishers Weekly, June 14, 1993, review of *Shadow the Deer,* p. 68; July 26, 1993, review of *Apes,* p. 73; December 8, 1997, review of *Bashi, Elephant Baby,* p. 71; January 18, 1999, review of *Little Sibu: An Orangutan Tale,* p. 338; December 6, 1999, review of *While You Were Sleeping,* p. 76; January 29, 2001, review of *Pi-Shu, the Little Panda,* p. 89; April 16, 2001, review of *Whose Baby Am I?,* p. 63; February 3, 2003, review of *If You See a Kitten,* p. 74; October 1, 2007, review of *Can You Growl like a Bear?,* p. 55; December 10, 2007, review of *Wee Little Chick,* p. 54.

School Library Journal, March, 2000, Sue Sherif, review of *Maya, Tiger Cub,* p. 211; June, 2001, Holly Belli, review of *Pi-shu, The Little Panda,* p. 104; August, 2001, Margaret Bush, review of *Nanu, Penguin Chick,* p. 158; September, 2005, Jane Marino, review of *Ten in the Den,* p. 190; September, 2006, Robin L. Gibson, review of *Ten in the Meadow,* p. 160; November, 2006, DeAnn Okamura, review of *Wake up, Sleepy Bear!,* p. 107; February, 2007, Wendy Lukehart, review of *A Mama for Owen,* p. 84; September, 2007, Jayne Damron, review of *Can You Growl like a Bear?,* p. 158; January, 2008, Kristen Frey, review of *Wee Little Chick,* p. 98; May, 2008, Blair Christolon, review of *Just One More?,* p. 92; July, 2009, Linda Staskus, review of *Wee Little Lamb,* p. 68; September, 2009, C.J. Connor, review of *Bedtime in the Jungle,* p. 118; February, 2010, Susan Weitz, review of *Wee Little Bunny,* p. 96.

ONLINE

John Butler Home Page, http://www.johnbutlerart.com (January 20, 2011).

C

CADNUM, Michael 1949-

Personal

Born May 3, 1949, in Orange, CA; married; wife's name Sherina. *Education:* Attended University of California, Berkeley, and San Francisco State University.

Addresses

Home—Albany, CA. *E-mail*—michael@michaelcadnum. com.

Career

Novelist and poet. Worked for a suicide prevention help line.

Awards, Honors

Creative writing fellowship, National Endowment for the Arts; Helen Bullis Prize, *Poetry Northwest;* Edgar Allan Poe Award nomination, Mystery Writers of America, 1991, for *Calling Home,* 1992, for *Breaking the Fall;* Owl Creek Book Award finalist; *Los Angeles Times* Book Award finalist, and National Book Award finalist, both 2000, both for *The Book of the Lion;* Quick Picks for Reluctant Young-Adult Readers designation, American Library Association (ALA), 2000, for *Rundown;* Best Books for Young Adults designation, ALA, 2010, for *Flash.*

Writings

NOVELS

Nightlight, St. Martin's Press (New York, NY), 1990.
Sleepwalker, St. Martin's Press (New York, NY), 1991.
Saint Peter's Wolf, Carroll & Graf (New York, NY), 1991.
Calling Home, Viking (New York, NY), 1991.
Breaking the Fall, Viking (New York, NY), 1992.

Michael Cadnum (Photograph by Richard Mewton. Reproduced by permission.)

Ghostwright, Carroll & Graf (New York, NY), 1992.
The Horses of the Night, Carroll & Graf (New York, NY), 1993.
Skyscape, Carroll & Graf (New York, NY), 1994.
Taking It, Viking (New York, NY), 1995.
The Judas Glass, Carroll & Graf (New York, NY), 1996.

Zero at the Bone, Viking (New York, NY), 1996.
Edge, Viking (New York, NY), 1997.
In a Dark Wood, Orchard (New York, NY), 1998.
Heat, Viking (New York, NY), 1998.
Rundown, Viking (New York, NY), 1999.
Redhanded, Viking (New York, NY), 2000.
Raven of the Waves, Orchard (New York, NY), 2000.
The Book of the Lion, Viking (New York, NY), 2000.
Forbidden Forest: The Story of Little John and Robin Hood, Orchard (New York, NY), 2002.
The Leopard Sword (sequel to *The Book of the Lion*), Viking (New York, NY) 2002.
Daughter of the Wind, Orchard (New York, NY), 2003.
Ship of Fire, Viking (New York, NY), 2003.
Starfall: Phaeton and the Chariot of the Sun, Orchard (New York, NY), 2004.
Blood Gold, Viking (New York, NY), 2004.
The Dragon Throne (sequel to *The Leopard Sword*), Viking (New York, NY), 2005.
Nightsong: The Legend of Orpheus and Eurydice, Orchard Books/Scholastic (New York, NY), 2006.
The King's Arrow, Viking (New York, NY), 2008.
Peril on the Sea, Farrar, Straus & Giroux (New York, NY), 2009.
Flash, Farrar, Straus & Giroux (New York, NY), 2010.

FOR CHILDREN

The Lost and Found House, illustrated by Steve Johnson and Lou Fancher, Viking (New York, NY), 1997.

POETRY

The Morning of the Massacre (chapbook), Bieler Press, 1982.
Wrecking the Cactus (chapbook), Salt Lick Press, 1985.
Invisible Mirror (chapbook), Ommation Press, 1986.
Foreign Springs (chapbook), Amelia Press (Bakersfield, CA), 1987.
By Evening, Owl Creek Press (Seattle, WA), 1992.
The Cities We Will Never See, Singular Speech Press (Canton, CT), 1993.
The Woman Who Discovered Math, Red Booth Chapbooks, 2001.
Illicit (chapbook), Frank Cat Press, 2001.
Day by Day (e-book), Mudlark, 2003.

OTHER

Ella and the Canary Prince (fiction chapbook), Subterranean Press, 1999.
Together Again: The True Story of Humpty Dumpty (fiction chapbook), Subterranean Press, 2001.
Can't Catch Me and Other Twice-told Tales (short stories), Tachyon Publications, 2006.

Contributor to numerous anthologies edited by Ellen Datlow and Terri Windling, as well as to *Mystery Writer's Annual, Mystery Scene, Poet and Critic,* and *Second Sight: Stories for a New Millennium,* Putnam, 1999.

Contributor to periodicals, including *America, Antioch Review, Beloit Fiction Journal, Beloit Poetry Journal, Commonweal,* and *Rolling Stone.* Contributor to "Read This" (column), *New York Review of Science Fiction.*

Sidelights

A popular and versatile writer, Michael Cadnum has earned praise for his evocative poetry volumes, suspense novels, contemporary fiction, and stories based on history, myth, and legend. Horror and suspense novels such as *Sleepwalker* and *The Judas Glass* have a broad appeal to adults and teens who enjoy stories featuring ghosts, werewolves, and vampires, while Cadnum's psychological thrillers, such as *Flash,* address many of the serious problems experienced by adolescents. Discussing his interest in working in a variety of genres, Cadnum stated to Lisa Graff in an interview posted on his home page: "Try thinking of historical fiction as stories about a future that you can visit. You can look at tailors' books of clothing, and practice fenc-

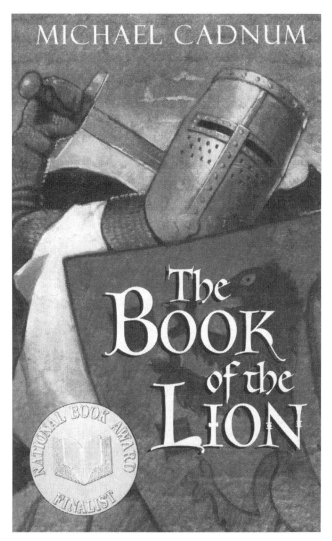

Cover of Cadnum's **The Book of the Lion,** *featuring artwork by Gregg Thorkelson.* (Illustration copyright © 2000 by Gregg Thorkelson. All rights reserved. Used by permission of Viking Children's Books, a division of Penguin Putnam Young Readers Group, a member of Penguin Group (USA) Inc., 345 Hudson Street, New York, NY 11014.)

ing and read love letters from the absent era. As though the future endowed us with artifacts! Similarly, think of a contemporary novel as being about the very near future—the events have not yet happened, but can. In this way, all writing is about an imaginative future—one with secrets that you can discover."

What binds all of Cadnum's fictional efforts is his ability to populate the pages of his books with realistic individuals. "I try to discover my characters and to see through their eyes—and feel what they feel," the author told Wes Adams in an interview posted on his home page. "So I don't see myself describing characters—I know them." His National Book Award finalist *The Book of the Lion,* as well as the novels *The King's Arrow* and *Peril on the Sea,* present new twists on traditional stories by featuring exciting storylines, compelling characters, and realistic settings that bring to life everything from the twelfth-century Crusades to the California Gold Rush. Reviewing *Ship of Fire,* a story about Sir Francis Drake's raid on Spanish ships at Cadiz in 1597, *Booklist* critic John Peters cited Cadnum's reputation "for rousing historical adventures set against gruesomely naturalistic backdrops." In a contrast that shows the author's versatility, his retelling of portions of Ovid's ancient tales in *Starfall: Phaeton and the Chariot of the Sun* was praised by a *Publishers Weekly* contributor as "a trilogy of enchanting tales" in which the storyteller succeeds in "humanizing classical figures and transforming lofty language into accessible, lyrical prose."

Cadnum grew up near the beaches of Southern California, and while he enjoyed watching television like most teens, he derived even greater pleasure from reading. "I have always felt our lives are too small, too thin and insubstantial," he explained in an interview with *Authors and Artists for Young Adults* (*AAYA*). "When we watch television—and I have always watched a lot of television—we are powerfully distracted from our routines, but only through reading are we really nourished." A voracious reader, he dipped into everything from pulp fiction to philosophy, and in books he discovered much about the world. "Books, unlike so much else in the real world, give, and ask nothing in return," Cadnum explained.

After graduating from high school, Cadnum attended college, taking classes at both the University of California at Berkeley and San Francisco State University, and earning a National Endowment for the Arts fellowship for his poetry. His first published book, *The Morning of the Massacre,* was released in 1982 and was followed by several other verse collections. While poetry continued to be his main focus through the 1980s, Cadnum began dabbling with prose in the 1970s, and he soon started his copious research on the historical novel that would be published, decades later, as *Ship of Fire.*

In addition to his writing, Cadnum also worked for a suicide help-line, which brought him into contact with people overwhelmed by life, from successful profes-

Cover of Cadnum's adventure novel The Dragon Throne, *featuring artwork by Gregg Thorkelson.* (Illustration copyright © by 2005 Gregg Thorkelson. All rights reserved. Used by permission of Viking Children's Books, a division of Penguin Putnam Young Readers Group, a member of Penguin Group (USA) Inc., 345 Hudson Street, New York, NY 11014.)

sionals harboring unfulfilled desires or hidden demons to troubled teenagers coping with dysfunctional families. His first published novel, 1990's *Nightlight,* features a man who is haunted by a recurring nightmare that ultimately morphs into real-life terror during his search for a missing relative. An archaeologist who is haunted by dreams of his dead wife finds his own tendency to sleepwalk shared by an eighth-century Norse corpse that he and his crew discover while excavating a Yorkshire bog in *Sleepwalker,* while in *Saint Peter's Wolf* a San Francisco psychologist and art collector confronted by with marital problems becomes obsessed by werewolves after discovering a set of antique silver fangs. *Saint Peter's Wolf,* which was Cadnum's first book to attract a young-adult audience, retells the werewolf myth with a twist: after the psychologist begins to morph into a violent beast, he finds the freedom and power of his creature-self attractive and ultimately attempts to cast off his human side. Writing in *Voice of Youth Advocates,* Delia A. Culberson praised *Saint Peter's Wolf* as "a spellbinding *tour de force* in a rare blend of fantasy, horror, adventure, suspense, and passionate love" as well as "a superb, fascinating book that subtly evokes that ancient, primal yearning in all living, breathing things for total, exhilarating freedom."

Although Cadnum had an adult audience in mind when he wrote it, *Calling Home* was marketed to young adults. The novel focuses on Peter, a teenaged alcoholic who accidentally kills his best friend, Mead, in a moment of drunken anger. To cover up the act, Peter impersonates Mead in phone calls to the boy's worried parents, making them think that Mead has run away. Ultimately, his guilt overcomes his alcoholic haze, and Peter confesses to another friend.

Reviewing *Calling Home* for the *Wilson Library Journal,* Cathi Dunn MacRae noted that Cadnum "skillfully shapes suspense through masterful control of language," taking readers "so completely inside this disconnected boy, . . . they will never forget the experience." *Horn Book* critic Patty Campbell dubbed the novel an "exquisitely crafted work, a prose poem of devastating impact," adding that, "not since the debut of Robert Cormier with *The Chocolate War . . .* has such a major talent emerged in adolescent literature." Roger Sutton observed in the *Bulletin of the Children's Center for Books* that *Calling Home* offers "probably the truest portrait of a teenaged alcoholic we've had in YA fiction."

Like *Calling Home, Breaking the Fall* focuses on a troubled teenager. In this case, high school sophomore Stanley North has difficulty coping with his parents' crumbling marriage and his grades are suffering. While his savvy girlfriend Sky encourages him to turn to sports as a way of dealing with his stress, Stanley's self-destructive friend Jared has a stronger lure: the thrill of breaking into houses. Praising the author's engrossing, suspenseful plot and his ability to create sympathetic characters, *Horn Book* contributor Maeve Visser Knoth wrote that in *Breaking the Fall* Cadnum "writes truthfully about the seductive nature of power and friendships, recognizing the lengths to which young people will go in order to prove themselves." Susan L. Rogers noted as a caveat in *School Library Journal* that "some readers may be disturbed by this story, although mature teens may find it a more realistic reflection of a troubled world."

Other teen thrillers have followed, including *Taking It, Zero to the Bone,* and *Edge.* In *Taking It* Cadnum traces the psychological deterioration of Anna Charles, a seventeen-year-old kleptomaniac and the daughter of wealthy, divorced parents, as her compulsion to shoplift causes her to withdraw from family and friends and ultimately put herself in danger. Praising Cadnum's "tight, beautiful prose" and his "finesse" in handling Anna's problems, *Booklist* reviewer Merri Monks concluded that *Taking It* "should not be missed." A *Publishers Weekly* commentator was similarly impressed, declaring that Cadnum writes with "subtlety and tremendous insight" and "keeps readers on the edge of their seats with this taut psychological portrait."

Zero at the Bone is narrated by Cray Buchanan, a high-school senior whose sister, Anita, has disappeared, sending the Buchanan family into an emotional tailspin. Family tragedy is also the subject of *Edge,* which focuses on high-school dropout Zachary Madison. After his successful father, a writer, is permanently paralyzed by a car-jacker, Zach decides to seek justice when the man accused of attacking his father is set free.

Inspired by Cadnum's eyewitness account of a bungled robbery, *Flash,* a contemporary drama for young adult audiences, centers on five individuals whose lives are forever altered by a desperate act. "What happened was that, through through terrorism and economic failure, our own era became an intriguing period of history—riddled with tension, and peopled with individuals with powerful grievances," the author remarked to Adams. "I knew that I had to respond to the high and low crimes I was seeing all around me—and *Flash* was the result." "Superb writing, with . . . meticulous care given to plotting and characterization, makes this an outstanding commentary on our times," according to a contributor in *Kirkus Reviews.* wrote. *Flash* is "rich with literary devices including doubling, irony, and metaphor," *Horn*

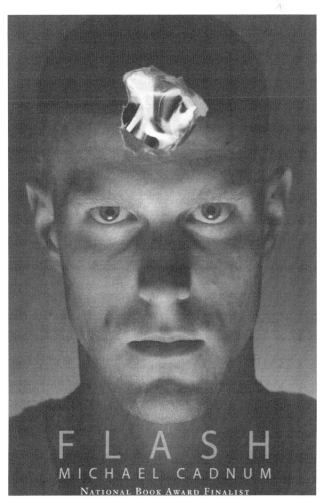

***Cover of Cadnum's futuristic young-adult novel* Flash.** (Farrar, Straus & Giroux, 2010. Reproduced by permission of Farrar, Straus & Giroux, LLC.)

Book critic Patty Campbell similarly remarked, and the novel "reminds us why Cadnum warrants comparisons with Robert Cormier."

In the late 1990s Cadnum broadened his storytelling focus, expanding from contemporary suspense to both historical and fantasy fiction. An interest in the Robin Hood legend inspired *In a Dark Wood* and *Forbidden Forest: The Story of Little John and Robin Hood.* "I did a tremendous amount of research for *In a Dark Wood,*" Cadnum recalled, "but I didn't know I was doing research. I thought I was reading about Robin Hood and traveling to Crusader castles in the Middle East and monasteries in France. I was just doing what I loved, and I turned out to know enough after a while to write a novel." The classic story in *In a Dark Wood* is told from the point of view of the Sheriff of Nottingham, the man traditionally cast as the villain of the piece. In Cadnum's version, the sheriff and his teenaged assistant must deal with the chaos caused by the wily thief known only as Robin Hood. In *Forbidden Forest* the story of Robin's slow-witted sidekick Little John is recounted, from the man's flight into the woods to avoid the wrath of a vicious nobleman to his efforts to right a wrong done to a beautiful young woman who has won his heart. "Cadnum succeeds admirably in capturing the squalor and casual brutality of the times," noted a *Kirkus Reviews* critic in reviewing *Forbidden Forest,* while in *Kliatt* Paula Rohrlick deemed the novel a "stirring story that imaginatively elaborates on the legend of the forest outlaws."

Continuing his focus on medieval history, Cadnum spins a three-part story of the Crusades in *The Book of the Lion, The Leopard Sword,* and *The Dragon Throne.* As the trilogy opens, Edmund finds himself fleeing for his life after his master, a moneyer who mints coins for the king, is found to be dishonest. Captured and imprisoned, the boy is taken on as squire to Sir Nigel, a knight on his way to Rome to fight for the cross in the Third Crusade. The pair meets up with Sir Rannulf and his squire, Hubert. Traveling together, they join the armies of King Richard and other Christian kings to fight in the bloody Siege of Acre, during which Muslim commander Saladin and his army manage to withstand the crusading armies for almost two years before surrendering.

Narrated by eighteen-year-old Hubert, *The Leopard Sword* finds the knights and their retinue surviving shipwrecks, storms, and Roman thieves while making the treacherous journey back to England. Once at home, the war-weary group encounters a kingdom in tatters due to Prince John's efforts to usurp the throne from his brother, Richard, as well as more-personal difficulties. While noting the violence throughout the series, Rorhlick wrote in *Kliatt* that Cadnum's novels "offer . . . a new perspective on knights and the Crusades." Praising *The Leopard Sword,* in particular, Rohrlick dubbed the novel a "stirring, violent tale of life in the Middle Ages" in which "Cadnum continues his explora-

tion of 'the call that war has on young people.'" In *School Library Journal* Renee Steinberg noted the book's "exciting climax," asserting that Cadnum has "skillfully woven" a wealth of historical facts into his fictional tale.

An act of courage on the part of Hubert results in knighthood for both squires, and in *The Dragon Throne* Edmund and Hubert once again find themselves on the road to Rome. While hunted by Prince John due to their continued allegiance to King Richard, the pair is also escorting Ester de Laci on a pilgrimage to the holy city so that she can pray for her injured father. "During this journey through Europe, the dangers and unrest of the time period come alive," Denise Moore noted in *School Library Journal,* describing the third volume in the series. A *Kirkus Reviews* critic predicted that *The Dragon Throne* will, "like its predecessors, . . . leave readers pondering . . . 'the terrible paradox—that caring, responsible individuals can engage in acts of brutality.'"

As in *Starfall,* Cadnum draws on mythology for *Nightsong: The Legend of Orpheus and Eurydice,* a novel that "brings new meaning to an ancient romance," as a *Publishers Weekly* critic stated. Cadnum retells the classic tale of the great musician and poet Orpheus, who wins the undying love of Princess Eurydice. On their wedding day, however, Eurydice suffers a fatal snakebite, and Orpheus descends into the underworld to rescue his bride. By playing Apollo's lyre, he convinces Pluto and Persephone to let him return Eurydice to the land of the living. In exchange, he agrees not to gaze at her on the journey, but his pledge has tragic consequences. "The story is a powerful one, delivered in comprehensible yet elevated language," Nancy Menaldi-Scanlan remarked in *School Library Journal,* and *Booklist,* critic Gillian Engberg applauded "the well-paced story's messages about art's enduring, healing power."

In *The King's Arrow* a work of historical fiction, Cadnum ponders a centuries-old mystery: Was England's King William II killed accidentally or murdered? Set in the year 1100, the work centers on eighteen-year-old Simon, the son of a Norman father and an English mother, who joins the king's hunting party as a guide to Walter Tirel, a Norman lord. When Tirel's arrow—intended for Ronald, William's fierce guardian—fatally wounds the king, Simon and Tirel must flee the country, hotly pursued by the revenge-minded Roland. In *Booklist,* Carolyn Phelan remarked that the "story is rich in details that lend credibility to the period setting," and Caitlin Augusta noted in *School Library Journal* that "Cadnum's elegiac style gracefully complements his tale of a time when honor and right speaking could cost or save a man's life." Praising *The King's Arrow* in *Kliatt,* Rohrlick noted that "this fast-moving, realistically brutal adventure will be welcomed by fans of the genre."

One of the most famous naval battles in history, the English defeat of the Spanish Armada in 1588, forms the backdrop for Cadnum's *Peril on the Sea.* "Because this particular novel follows a genuine, violent ten-day period of bloodshed and stormy weather," the author remarked to Graff, "I was freed to depict actual events—I didn't have to make up this sweeping calamity. It really happened. But as to the creation of the novel, and the hopes and fears of my characters—I had faith in them, and I knew that they would tell their stories through me if I let them." In the work, after young Sherwin Morris is saved from drowning by privateer Brandon Fletcher, he agrees to record the piratical exploits of the captain, who hopes to bolster his rivalry with Sir Francis Drake. When Fletcher's ship is drafted to help combat the Spanish threat, Sherwin finds himself in the middle of a bloody ship-versus-ship encounter. "Cadnum's prose is vivid and evocative, brilliantly re-creating life at sea in the Elizabethan era," a contributor noted in *Kirkus Reviews,* and Ian Chipman maintained in *Booklist* that the author "focuses his attention on the excitement and intrigue of a major event in the history of naval warfare."

"I grew up in a Southern California landscape that was a swath of dwellings and freeways, punctuated—carved out—with empty canyons," Cadnum explained to *SATA,* referencing a talk he gave at the University of Ghent in 2011. "As very little children we were forbidden to visit these places.

"With good reason. The canyons occupied our neighborhood, a widening emptiness cloaked with ice plants and ivy, ground cover intended to slow erosion and mute the advance of the precarious emptiness. The legend was alive how one of our own climbed down into the abyss, twisted an ankle and died yelling, his voice muffled by the embrace of an erosion fold in the pebbled sandstone.

"I lived a place called Costa Mesa, and this was a town that thoroughly valued sports: baseball, soccer, and basketball. I did my best to play these sports and I tried to enjoy them. But what I learned best in participating in such contests was how to assess the reports and opinions of my teammates.

"One day I was sitting next to a friend when he explained to me in that offhand, assertive tone even young men use with each other, 'I have a job at the race track.' He added, 'They have me using a shovel.

"I knew this race track, out by the Orange County Airport. The racetrack was a place where they had drag races—stock cars would go as fast as they could. The races were short and loud. What was the shovel for?, I asked—already feeling uneasy.

"My friend told me his job was to scrape up the squashed bodies of people who had been run over. That was his job—he scraped. And he told his story so well that at the time I believed him.

"I was appalled and disgusted by what he said. I had no way to mistrust him, no way to peel off the truth from

what was not true—I had at that time no insight. I was too new to storytelling. His outrageous invention seemed true to me.

"I have giving a great deal of thought to the question of how we determine what is true in a story. Whether the story is about a bank robbery I actually witnessed, as in my novel *Flash,* or a massacre of prisoners ordered by King Richard Lionheart, as in *The Book of the Lion,* I want to know as much of the truth as I can. Even when I write about the gods, as I do in a novel like *Starfall,* I want to know what a god's voice sounds like, what sort of weight his presence has. I want to truly know, and to have that as a part of my experience as a human being.

"This is why I never think of myself as writing for an adult, or for a child, or for a young-adult reader. I don't write for a reader at all. I write so I can be more alive. And I know as a result of this single-mindedness, readers can come to my books and enjoy my discoveries."

Biographical and Critical Sources

BOOKS

Authors and Artists for Young Adults, Volume 23, Gale (Detroit, MI), 1998.
St. James Guide to Young-Adult Writers, 2nd edition, St. James Press (Detroit, MI), 1999.

PERIODICALS

Booklist, July, 1995, Merri Monks, review of *Taking It,* p. 1879; August, 2002, Carolyn Phelan, review of *The Leopard Sword,* p. 1945; September 15, 2003, John Peters, review of *Ship of Fire,* p. 229; November 15, 2003, Linda Perkins, review of *Daughter of the Wind,* p. 591; January 1, 2004, Patricia Austin, review of *The Book of the Lion,* p. 892; May 15, 2004, Ed Sullivan, review of *Blood Gold,* p. 1628; October 1, 2004, Gillian Engberg, review of *Starfall: Phaeton and the Chariot of the Sun,* p. 321; December 15, 2006, Gillian Engberg, review of *Nightsong,* p. 41; December 15, 2007, Carolyn Phelan, review of *The King's Arrow,* p. 43; April 15, 2009, Ian Chipman, review of *Peril on the Sea,* p. 50; May 1, 2010, Daniel Kraus, review of *Flash,* p. 49.
Bulletin of the Center for Children's Books, May, 1991, Roger Sutton, review of *Calling Home,* p. 212; July-August, 1997, Deborah Stevenson, review of *Edge.*
Childhood Education, fall, 2002, John McAndrew, review of *Forbidden Forest,* p. 51.
Horn Book, November-December, 1992, Maeve Visser Knoth, review of *Breaking the Fall,* p. 726; March-April, 1994, Patrick Jones, "People Are Talking about . . . Michael Cadnum," pp. 177-180; May-June, 1994, Patty Campbell, review of *Calling Home;* July-August, 1997, Amy E. Chamberlain, review of *Edge,* p. 452; July-August, 2002, Joanna Rudge Long, re-

view of *Forbidden Forest,* p. 453; July-August, 2004, Betty Carter, review of *Blood Gold,* p. 448; March-April, 2008, Anita L. Burkam, review of *The King's Arrow,* p. 213; July-August, 2010, Patty Campbell, review of *Flash,* p. 101.

Kirkus Reviews, June 1, 1993, review of *Horses of the Night,* p. 674; May 1, 2002, review of *Forbidden Forest,* p. 650; August 15, 2002, review of *The Leopard Sword,* p. 1219; April 2, 2004, review of *Blood Gold,* p. 325; September 1, 2004, review of *Starfall,* p. 861; April 15, 2005, review of *The Dragon Throne,* p. 469; October 15, 2006, review of *Nightsong,* p. 1067; December 15, 2007, review of *The King's Arrow;* May 1, 2009, review of *Peril on the Sea;* May 1, 2010, review of *Flash.*

Kliatt, March, 1994, Larry W. Prater, review of *Ghostwright,* p. 14; March, 2002, Paula Rohrlick, review of *Forbidden Forest,* p. 6, and *The Book of the Lion,* p. 14; September, 2002, Paula Rohrlick, review of *The Leopard Sword,* p. 8; September, 2003, Paula Rohrlick, review of *Ship of Fire,* p. 6; November, 2003, Claire Rosser, review of *Daughter of the Wind,* p. 5; January, 2004, Sherri F. Ginsberg, review of *The Book of the Lion,* p. 44; May, 2004, Paula Rohrlick, review of *Blood Gold,* p. 6, and Janet Julian, review of *The Leopard Stone,* p. 52; September, 2004, Paula Rohrlick, review of *Starfall,* p. 6; May, 2005, Paula Rohrlick, review of *The Dragon Throne,* p. 8; November, 2006, Paula Rohrlick, review of *Nightsong,* p. 6; January, 2008, Paula Rohrlick, review of *The King's Arrow,* p. 5.

Library Journal, February 15, 1991, Eric W. Johnson, review of *Sleepwalker,* p. 219; July, 1992, Marylaine Block, review of *Ghostwright,* pp. 119-120; September 1, 1994, Robert C. Moore, review of *Skyscape,* p. 213.

Locus, June, 1990, Edward Bryant, review of *Nightlight,* p. 23, and Scott Winnett, review of *Nightlight,* p. 31; July, 1993, Scott Winnett, review of *Horses of the Night,* p. 33.

Los Angeles Times Book Review, July 21, 1991, Don G. Campbell, review of *Saint Peter's Wolf,* p. 6.

New York Times Book Review, March 31, 1991, Ed Weiner, review of *Sleepwalker,* p. 16.

Publishers Weekly, June 1, 1992, review of *Ghostwright;* August 22, 1994, review of *Skyscape,* p. 43; July 10, 1995, review of *Taking It,* p. 59; January 8, 1996, review of *The Judas Glass,* p. 59; June 17, 1996, review of *Zero at the Bone,* p. 66; July 14, 2003, review of *Daughter of the Wind,* p. 78; October 18, 2004, review of *Starfall,* p. 64; March 27, 2006, review of *Can't Catch Me and Other Twice-told Tales,* p. 63; December 4, 2006, review of *Nightsong,* p. 58; July 12, 2010, review of *Flash,* p. 48.

School Library Journal, September, 1992, Susan L. Rogers, review of *Breaking the Fall,* p. 274; June, 2002, Starr E. Smith, review of *Forbidden Forest,* p. 130; October, 2002, Renee Steinberg, review of *The Leopard Sword,* p. 160; October, 2003, Karen T. Bilton, review of *Ship of Fire,* p. 162; December, 2003, Barbara Scotto, review of *Daughter of the Wind,* p. 144; June, 2004, Kimberly Monaghan, review of *Blood*

Gold, p. 136; October, 2004, Patricia D. Lothrop, review of *Starfall,* p. 158; June, 2005, Denise Moore, review of *The Dragon Throne,* p. 152; April, 2007, Nancy Menaldi-Scanlan, review of *Nightsong,* p. 128; March, 2008, Caitlin Augusta, review of *The King's Arrow,* p. 196; June, 2010, Jake Pettit, review of *Flash,* p. 96.

Voice of Youth Advocates, October, 1990, Mary Lee Tiernan, review of *Nightlight,* p. 225; August, 1991, Jane Chandra, review of *Calling Home,* p. 168; December, 1991, Delia A. Culberson, review of *Saint Peter's Wolf;* February, 1996, Becky Kornman, review of *Taking It,* pp. 368-369; December, 1996, Rachelle M. Blitz, review of *The Judas Glass,* p. 276; February, 1997, Carla A. Tripp, review of *Zero at the Bone,* p. 326.

Wilson Library Journal, April, 1992, Cathi Dunn MacRae, review of *Calling Home,* p. 98.

ONLINE

Michael Cadnum Home Page, http://www.michaelcadnum. com (January 20, 2011).

*   *   *

CAREY, Janet Lee 1954-

Personal

Born 1954, in NY; married; children: three sons. *Hobbies and other interests:* Hiking, reading, family, meditation, yoga, music.

Addresses

Home—Western WA. *E-mail*—janetleecarey@hotmail. com.

Career

Writer and educator. Teacher at writing workshops; presenter at schools.

Awards, Honors

Georgia State Best Children's Book nomination, 2002, for *Molly's Fire;* William Allen White Award nomination, Georgia State Best Children's Book nomination, Washington State Book Award nomination, and Mark Twain Award, all 2005, all for *Wenny Has Wings;* American Library Association Best Books for Young Adults selection, 2008, for *Dragon's Keep;* Gold Star Award, *Teen Reads Too* Web site, 2011, for *The Dragons of Noor.*

Writings

YOUNG-ADULT NOVELS

Molly's Fire, Atheneum Books for Young Readers (New York, NY), 2000.

Janet Lee Carey (Photograph by Heidi Pettit/Litartphotography. Reproduced by permission.)

Wenny Has Wings, Atheneum Books (New York, NY), 2002.

The Double Life of Zoe Flynn, Atheneum Books for Young Readers (New York, NY), 2004.

The Beast of Noor, Atheneum Books for Young Readers (New York, NY), 2006.

Dragon's Keep, Harcourt (Orlando, FL), 2007.

Stealing Death, Egmont USA (New York, NY), 2009.

Dragons of Noor, Egmont USA (New York, NY), 2010.

Adaptations

Wenny Has Wings was adapted as a feature film in Japan, 2008.

Sidelights

Janet Lee Carey began writing as a young girl and has since produced books for both children and young adults. Her stories range across genres, from the historical novel *Molly's Fire* to the contemporary stories in *Wenny Has Wings* and *The Double Life of Zoe Flynn*. Carey also spins entertaining middle-grade fantasies in the companion volumes *The Beasts of Noor* and *Dragons of Noor,* as well as producing *Stealing Death* and *Dragon's Keep,* the latter which *Kliatt* contributor Cara Chancellor described as an "enjoyable, fast paced, and easy to read" story that "projects a [timely] theme of embracing one's differences." "I think most of the stories wait down inside a person, like a secret storyteller," Carey noted, discussing her inspiration on her home page. "Things that happen in the outside world awaken the storyteller, and suddenly she begins to speak. So it's not so much a matter of making the stories up, as learning how to sit very still, and listen."

In her first novel, *Molly's Fire,* Carey introduces thirteen-year-old Molly, who refuses to believe that her father was shot down over Holland during World War II. Molly forms a friendship with Jane, who is half-Japanese, and along with Jane and another friend, Peter,

she sets out to discover if her father is alive. The children's investigation leads them to visit a nearby German prisoner-of-war camp. A *Publishers Weekly* contributor noted in a review of *Molly's Fire* that "the details about food ration coupons, victory gardens and Japanese internment camps breathe life into an important period of history."

Wenny Has Wings finds young Will writing letters to his dead sister Wenny, who was killed when both siblings were hit by a truck. Will's near-death experience is mixed with a story of a family struggling to survive after a tragedy. Ilene Cooper, writing in *Booklist*, commended Carey's story for illustrating "sibling relationship" as well as "its unique capturing of the phenomenon of heading into the light." In a review for *School Library Journal*, B. Allison Gray called the work "a useful meditation on death and guilt," and a *Kirkus Reviews* contributor referred to *Wenny Has Wings* as "a gentle epistolary novel requiring at least three hankies."

In *The Double Life of Zoe Flynn* Carey introduces Zoe, a girl who comes to terms with homelessness after her dad loses both his teaching job and his bookstore. As the family flounders economically, with both parents only able to get part-time work, Zoe finds herself living out of a van with her parents and attending a new school 500 miles away from the beloved California town she once called home. A *Kirkus Reviews* contributor called *The Double Life of Zoe Flynn* "thought-provoking," while Hazel Rochman commented in *Booklist* that "there's plenty of drama in the hardship of the middle-class kid." For Miriam Lang Budin, writing in *School Library Journal,* "the struggles of this middle-class family to keep their heads above water are realistically and sympathetically presented" in Carey's story.

The Beast of Noor tells the adventure story of fifteen-year-old Miles Ferrell and his thirteen-year-old sister Hanna. The Ferrell family has long been shunned by the locals due to a legend that asserts that they brought a monster dog called the Shriker to the area when they arrived 300 years before. As the teens set out to break the family curse, they soon find themselves in the Otherworld, trying to capture the Shriker. Sally Estes, writing in *Booklist,* noted that in *The Beast of Noor* Carey "delivers an eerie, atmospheric tale, full of terror and courage." *School Library Journal* contributor Saleena L. Davidson wrote that *The Beast of Noor* "reads almost like a fairy tale, with the same rhythms and the same etiquette," and a *Kirkus Reviews* contributor referred to the novel as "an engaging tale, with just the right touch of terror to make a good story."

The adventures of Miles and Hanna continue in *Dragons of Noor,* as the dragons that have been exiled from their home land of Oth are about to return after 700 years. The cautious truce between the humans of Noor and their dragon guests is threatened now that several small children have disappeared. When the youngest Farrell goes missing, Miles and Hanna are determined to solve the mystery, a mystery that involves the magical and ancient forest of waytrees that is fast losing its ability to connect the worlds of Noor and Oth. Calling Miles and Hanna "realistic teens," Mara Alpert added in *School Library Journal* that Carey's "world building and tone [in *Dragons of Noor*] are just right, and the themes of friendship, loyalty, responsibility, and protection of the planet are never intrusive."

A standalone fantasy, *Stealing Death* focuses on seventeen-year-old Kipp, who lives with his immigrant parents in a rural region that is suffering from drought. Returning one day from hunting for wild horses, Kipp finds his home afire. He saves his little sister from the blaze, but the Death Catcher, known as the Gwali, takes the rest of his family in the devastating fire. With his ability to see spirits, Kipp realizes that the Gwali captures human souls and he resolves to stop the Death Catcher from taking more souls. When the Gwali returns, this time to take the soul of the young man's beloved Zalika, Kipp steals the sack in which the creature's souls are collected and rides away on the Gwali's fast-moving horse. In *School Library Journal* Eric

Cover of Carey's teen novel Stealing Death, *featuring artwork by Paul Young.* (Egmont USA, 2010. Illustration copyright © 2010 by Paul Young. Reproduced by permission.)

Norton dubbed *Stealing Death* "truly a unique work," "original, beautiful, amazing, and deeply moving." In *Kirkus Reviews* a contributor noted that Carey spins her magic through the creation of "a lightly sketched spiritual system" which is "conveyed through song and pourquoi tales." "This extensive story of connections, details, and final plot twists will engage fantasy fans," concluded Andrew Medlar in *Booklist,* while a *Publishers Weekly* critic wrote that "fairy tale elements and poetic descriptions lend a mythic quality" to the story.

On her home page, Carey offered encouragement for young writers, framing it around a single word of advice: "Persevere." "Don't let rejection stop you from writing the story you really want to write," she maintained. "Rejection doesn't mean your work's not good enough. Keep writing, and keep revising. Listen to the story hidden deep inside you and write that. When you've polished your work, send it out. Make friends with other writers and encourage one another. The single word my former editor, Jon Lanman, sent to me when he left Atheneum was persevere. I remember that when I'm feeling overwhelmed or hopeless over a rejection or a bad review."

Carey carefully chooses a charitable organization to donate to as a part of each new book launch. By connecting story themes with various charities, she hopes to raise reader awareness and provide a way for young people to make a difference in the world. For example, the release of *The Dragons of Noor* was dedicated to the Nature Conservancy's Plant a Billion Trees program.

Biographical and Critical Sources

PERIODICALS

Booklist, July, 2002, Ilene Cooper, review of *Wenny Has Wings,* p. 1841; September 1, 2004, Hazel Rochman, review of *The Double Life of Zoe Flynn,* p. 120; August 1, 2006, Sally Estes, review of *The Beast of Noor,* p. 65; February 1, 2007, Diana Tixier Herald, review of *Dragon's Keep,* p. 46; September 15, 2009, Andrew Medlar, review of *Stealing Death,* p. 52; December 15, 2010, Cindy Welch, review of *The Dragons of Noor,* p. 54.

Bulletin of the Center for Children's Books, October, 2006, Karen Coats, review of *The Beast of Noor,* p. 62; May, 2007, Katrina Bromann, review of *Dragon's Keep,* p. 362.

Journal of Adolescent & Adult Literacy, November, 2008, Traci Avalos, review of *Dragon's Keep,* p. 256.

Kirkus Reviews, June 1, 2002, review of *Wenny Has Wings,* p. 801; June 1, 2004, review of *The Double Life of Zoe Flynn,* p. 534; June 15, 2006, review of *The Beast of Noor,* p. 632; March 15, 2007, review of *Dragon's Keep;* August 15, 2009, review of *Stealing Death.*

Kliatt, May, 2007, Cara Chancellor, review of *Dragon's Keep,* p. 8.

Library Journal, April, 2007, Cheri Dobbs, review of *Dragon's Keep,* p. 128.

Magazine of Fantasy and Science Fiction, February, 2007, Charles de Lint, review of *The Beast of Noor,* p. 35.

Publishers Weekly, May 29, 2000, review of *Molly's Fire,* p. 83; July 15, 2002, review of *Wenny Has Wings,* p. 74; May 7, 2007, review of *Dragon's Keep,* p. 61; October 5, 2009, review of *Stealing Death,* p. 52.

School Library Journal, May, 2000, Faith Brautigan, review of *Molly's Fire,* p. 170; July, 2002, B. Allison Gray, review of *Wenny Has Wings,* p. 114; August, 2004, Miriam Lang Budin, review of *The Double Life of Zoe Flynn,* p. 116; November, 2006, Saleena L. Davidson, review of *The Beast of Noor,* p. 130; September, 2009, Eric Norton, review of *Stealing Death,* p. 152; November, 2010, Mara Alpert, review of *The Dragons of Noor,* p. 106.

Voice of Youth Advocates, April, 2007, Dawn Talbot, review of *Dragon's Keep,* p. 62; October, 2009, Ann Welton, review of *Stealing Death,* p. 326.

ONLINE

Janet Lee Carey Home Page, http://www.janetleecarey. com (January 15, 2011).

Janet Lee Carey Web log, http://Dreamwalks.blogspot.com (January 15, 2011).

LibraryLionsRoar Web log, http://LibraryLionsRoar.blog spot.com/ (January 15, 2011), interview with Carey.

SimonSays.com, http://www.simonsays.com/ (February 20, 2007), interview with Carey.

*   *   *

CHAMPLIN, Susan 1961-
(Susan Champlin Taylor)

Personal

Born 1961, in Los Angeles, CA; married (divorced); married Stan Mack (a cartoonist), April, 2010; children: one daughter. *Education:* Stanford University, B.A. (English).

Addresses

Home—New York, NY.

Career

Author, editor, and journalist. *People* (magazine), L.A. Bureau correspondent, 1983-86; *Modern Maturity* (magazine), associate editor, 1987-89, senior editor, 1989-95, and managing editor, 1995-97; *Bon Appétit* (magazine), managing editor, 2000-01; freelance editor and writer.

Member

Phil Beta Kappa.

Writings

(With Joseph Champlin, under name Susan Champlin Taylor) *A Thoughtful Word, a Healing Touch: A Guide for Visiting the Sick,* Twenty-third Publications (New London, CT), 1995.

(With husband Stan Mack) *Road to Revolution!* ("Cartoon Chronicles of America" series), illustrated by Mack, Bloomsbury (New York, NY), 2009.

Contributor to periodicals, including *Bon Appétit, Modern Maturity,* and *National Wildlife.* Editor of cookbooks, including *The Bon Appétit Cookbook,* 2006, *The Bon Appétit Fast Easy Fresh Cookbook,* 2008, and *Bon Appétit Desserts,* 2010.

Biographical and Critical Sources

PERIODICALS

Booklist, June 1, 2009, Jesse Karp, review of *Road to Revolution!,* p. 56.

School Library Journal, July, 2009, Lisa Goldstein, review of *Road to Revolution!,* p. 104.

ONLINE

Susan Champlin Web log, http://wwkhd.blogspot.com (January 15, 2011).*

*   *   *

CHATTERTON, Martin 1961-

Personal

Born 1961, in Liverpool, England; married Annie Carroll (an illustrator); children: Sophie, Danny. *Education:* Attended Hugh Baird College, 1979-80; Kingston University London, B.A. (graphic design; with honours), 1983. *Hobbies and other interests:* Soccer, skiing, sailing, traveling, cooking.

Addresses

Home—Byron Bay, New South Wales, Australia. *Agent*—Tara Wynne, Curtis Brown, Sydney, New South Wales, Australia. *E-mail*—martin@bboomerang.com.

Career

Illustrator and author. Former graphic designer; The Point (now Forepoint; graphic design firm), London, England, cofounder with Simon Bailey and creative director until 1998. Lecturer at University of Central Lancashire, 1987-91; guest lecturer at schools, including Birmingham School of Art, Cumbria School of Art,

York School of Art, Maidstone College of Art, Manchester Metropolitan University, and Kingston University. Presenter at schools. Member, Walker Books Authors and Illustrators Trust. *Exhibitions:* Work included in Association of Illustrators exhibits, 1991, 1993.

Member

British Society of Authors, Society of Children's Book Writers and Illustrators, Northern Rivers Writers Centre.

Awards, Honors

B & H Illustration Award, 1984, 1985, 1987; Design & Art Direction gold award, 1990, 1991, 1992; Experian Big Book Award, and Nottinghamshire Book Award for illustration, both 2000, both for *Big Bad Raps* by Tony Mitton; Angus Book Award shortlist, and Salford Children's Book Award shortlist, both 2005, both for *Michigan Moorcroft;* New South Wales Premier's Literary Award shortlist, 2008, for *The Brain Finds a Leg.*

Writings

SELF-ILLUSTRATED

Silly Circus, Walker Books (London, England), 1993.
Roxy's Street, Walker Books (London, England), 1994.
Martin Chatterton's Weird World of Pop, Hodder (London, England), 1995.
Martin Chatterton's Weird World of TV, Hodder (London, England), 1995.
Holidaze!, Egmont (London, England), 2003.
Spooks!, Egmont (London, England), 2003.
Puters!, Egmont (London, England), 2003.
Skool!, Egmont (London, England), 2003.
Michigan Moorcroft, Scholastic (London, England), 2003.
Stunt Monkeys, Stripes Publishing, 2007.
The Brain Finds a Leg (young-adult novel), Little Hare (London, England), 2007, Peachtree Publishers (Atlanta, GA), 2009.
The Brain Full of Holes (young-adult novel), Little Hare (London, England), 2008, Peachtree Publishers (Atlanta, GA), 2010.

"UTTERLY NUTTY" SERIES; SELF-ILLUSTRATED

The Nutty Footy Book, Puffin (London, England), 1994, published as *The Utterly Nutty History of Footy,* 1997.
The Euro Nutty Footy Book, Puffin (London, England), 1996.
Utterly Nutty World Cup Footy, Puffin (London, England), 1998.
The Utterly Nutty World of Animals, Puffin (London, England), 1998.
The Utterly Nutty World of Sport, Puffin (London, England), 1998.
The Utterly Nutty World of the Movies, Puffin (London, England), 1999.

The Utterly Nutty World of the Future, Puffin (London, England), 1999.
The Utterly Nutty A-Z of Footy, Puffin (London, England), 1999.

"BAD DOG" SERIES; SELF-ILLUSTRATED

Bad Dog and That Hollywood Hoohah, Scholastic (London, England), 2002, Scholastic, Inc. (New York, NY), 2005.
Bad Dog and Those Crazy Martians, Scholastic (London, England), 2002, Scholastic, Inc. (New York, NY), 2005.
Bad Dog and the Curse of the President's Knee, Scholastic (London, England), 2002, Scholastic, Inc. (New York, NY), 2005.
Bad Dog Rockin' up a Phat On in da House, Scholastic (London, England), 2003.
Bad Dog Goes Barktastic, Baby!, Scholastic (London, England), 2004, published as *Bad Dog Goes Barktastic!,* Scholastic, Inc. (New York, NY), 2005.

Author's books have been translated into Chinese, Dutch, Finnish, French, and Spanish.

"WILLY WAGGLEDAGGER" SERIES; SELF-ILLUSTRATED

By the Picking of My Nose, Little Hare (London, England), 2009.
A Belt around My Bum, Little Hare (London, England), 2010.
Chew Bee or Not Chew Bee, Little Hare (London, England), 2011.

ILLUSTRATOR

Mary Hoffman, *Cyril MC,* Puffin (London, England), 1988.
Roger McGough, *Helen Highwater,* Puffin (London, England), 1989.
Tony Bradman, *Tommy Niner and the Planet of Danger,* Puffin (London, England), 1991.
Paul Shipton, *Zargon Zoo,* Heinemann (London, England), 1991.
Jon Blake, *The Likely Stories,* Viking (London, England), 1991.
C.J. Moore, *Jack and His Computer,* Heinemann (London, England), 1992.
Tony Bradman, *Tommy Niner and the Mystery Spaceship,* Puffin (London, England), 1993.
George Beal, *The Kingfisher First Thesaurus,* Kingfisher Books (New York, NY), 1993.
Richard Johnson, *Look at Me in Funny Clothes!,* Candlewick Press (Cambridge, MA), 1994.
Richard Johnson, *Look at Me in a Funny Hat!,* Candlewick Press (Cambridge, MA), 1994.
Laurence Anholt, *How to Be a Superkid,* Walker Books (London, England), 1994.
Can Dogs Fly?: Fido's Book of Pop-up Transportation Surprises, Dial Books for Young Readers (New York, NY), 1995.

Jon Blake, *Little Stupendo,* Walker Books (London, England), 1995.

Alexander McCall Smith, *Billy Rubbish,* Methuen (London, England), 1995.

Tony Bradman, *Tommy Niner and the Moon of Doom,* Puffin (London, England), 1996.

Richard Brown, *Nonsense!,* Cambridge University Press (Cambridge, England), 1996.

Richard Brown, *Big Bad Raps,* Orchard (London, England), 1996.

Tony Mitton, *Royal Raps,* Orchard (London, England), 1996.

Tony Mitton, *Alien on the 99th Floor,* Heinemann (London, England), 1996.

Kate Ruttle, *Five Little Monkeys,* Cambridge University Press (Cambridge, England), 1996.

Kate Ruttle, *Spider McDrew,* Collins (London, England), 1996.

Alan Durant, *Happy Birthday Spider McDrew,* Collins (London, England), 1997.

Tony Bradman, *The Magnificent Mummies,* Puffin (London, England), 1997, Crabtree (New York, NY), 2002.

Tony Bradman, *Midnight in Memphis,* Puffin (London, England), 1998, Crabtree (New York, NY), 2002.

Tony Bradman, *Kristel Dimond, Timecop,* Walker Books (London, England), 1998.

Nick Storme, *Derek Dungbeetle in Paradise,* Mammoth (London, England), 1998.

Nick Storme, *Derek Dungbeetle Gets the Blues,* Mammoth (London, England), 1998.

Tony Mitton, *Fangtastic Raps,* Orchard (London, England), 1998.

Tony Mitton, *Hop on Top,* Cambridge University Press (Cambridge, England), 1998.

Tony Mitton, *Ham and Jam,* Cambridge University Press (Cambridge, England), 1999.

Tony Mitton, *Jump and Bump,* Cambridge University Press (Cambridge, England), 1999.

Tony Bradman, *The Thing That Came from Jason's Nose,* Mammoth (London, England), 1999.

Jon Blake, *Little Stupendo Rides Again,* Walker Books (London, England), 1999.

Tony Mitton, *Monster Raps,* Orchard (London, England), 1999.

Tony Mitton, *Scary Raps,* Orchard (London, England), 1999.

Tony Mitton, *Robin Hood Raps,* Orchard (London, England), 1999.

(With Ann Chatterton) Sam McBratney, *Stranger from Somewhere in Time,* Mammoth (London, England), 2000, Crabtree (New York, NY), 2002.

Tony Mitton, *Groovy Greek Hero Raps,* Orchard (London, England), 2000.

Tony Mitton, *Mega Greek Myth Raps,* Orchard (London, England), 2000.

(With Ann Chatterton) Simon Puttock, *"Here I Am!" Said Smedley,* Mammoth (London, England), 2000, Crabtree (New York, NY), 2002.

Brenda Parkes, *The Runaway Pizza,* Rigby (London, England), 2000.

Brenda Parkes, *Little Stupendo Flies High,* Walker Books (London, England), 2001.

Brenda Parkes, *Great Greek Myth Raps,* Orchard (London, England), 2001.

Brenda Parkes, *Charlie Chimpanzee,* Cambridge University Press (Cambridge, England), 2001.

Maoliosa Kelly, *Elvis and the Scooter,* Harcourt (London, England), 2003.

Tony Bradman, *Voodoo Child,* Egmont (London, England), 2004.

Tony Bradman, *Final Cut,* Egmont (London, England), 2004.

Tony Bradman, *Deadly Game,* Egmont (London, England), 2004.

Yuck! The Grossest Joke Book Ever!, Kingfisher (Boston, MA), 2004.

Tony Bradman, *The Surprise Party,* Crabtree (New York, NY), 2005.

What a Hoot!: Over 150 Hilarious Animal Jokes, Kingfisher (Boston, MA), 2005.

Boo!: Over 150 Spooky Jokes!, Kingfisher (Boston, MA), 2006.

Susie Gibbs, collector, *Scary Poems to Make You Shiver,* Oxford University Press (New York, NY), 2006.

Tony Bradman, *Mummies Find Fame,* Egmont (London, England), 2006, published as *The Mummy Family Find Fame,* Crabtree (New York, NY), 2006.

(With Tony Trimmer) *Sidesplitters: A Joke a Day: 365 Guaranteed Giggles,* Kingfisher (Boston, MA), 2007.

Geoffrey McSkimming, *Ogre in a Toga,* Scholastic (London, England), 2007.

Nigel Crowle, *Incredible Creatures,* Puffin (London, England), 2007.

Nigel Crowle, *Mighty Egyptians,* Puffin (London, England), 2007.

Nigel Crowle, *Heroic Greeks,* Puffin (London, England), 2007.

Nigel Crowle, *Amazing Space,* Puffin (London, England), 2007.

Nigel Crowle, *Freaky Football,* Puffin (London, England), 2007.

Susan Gates, under pen name W.C. Flushing, *King Tut's Golden Toilet,* Puffin (London, England), 2007.

Susan Gates, under pen name W.C. Flushing, *Hadrian's Lucky Latrine,* Puffin (London, England), 2007.

Susan Gates, under pen name W.C. Flushing, *Henry VIII's Privy,* Puffin (London, England), 2007.

Susan Gates, under pen name W.C. Flushing, *Queen Victoria's Potty,* Puffin (London, England), 2007.

Also illustrator of "Little Horrors" series. Contributor to periodicals, including *Daily Express,* London *Guardian, New Woman, Observer, Punch, She, Sunday Express,* and *That's Life.*

Sidelights

Since his first illustration project was published in 1988, British artist Martin Chatterton has created art for dozens of stories for a range of writers, among them Tony Bradman, Roger McGough, Nick Storme, Tony Mitton, Sam McBratney, Brenda Parkes, Kate Ruttle, and Nigel Crowle. While Chatterton's cartoon art captures his offbeat humor, so do his original self-illustrated stories,

Martin Chatterton's illustration projects include capturing the humor of Tony Bradman's story in the easy reader Midnight in Memphis. (Illustration copyright © 1998 by Martin Chatterton. Reproduced by permission of Egmont Books Limited, London.)

which include *Martin Chatterton's Weird World of Pop, Michigan Moorcroft, The Brain Finds a Leg,* and *Bad Dog and That Hollywood Hoohah.* Praising Chatterton's cartoon art for *Derek Dungbeetle in Paradise*, a graphic novel with a text by Storme, London *Guardian* contributor Philip Pullman wrote that "every page is alive with witty drawings" that make the book "appeal to readers' intelligence as well as sense of fun."

Born in Liverpool in 1961, Chatterton completed his degree in graphic design in 1983 and moved into a career in London. He joined Simon Bailey to create a successful graphic-design firm, but he turned to book illustration full time in the late 1990s. His animated artwork has frequently been paired with stories designed to attract reluctant readers, among them Bradman's *Midnight in Memphis, The Surprise Party, The Mummy Family Finds Fame,* and *The Magnificent Mummies,* all which chronicle the quirky adventures of a family of fun-loving mummies. Part of a series designed to help transition beginning readers into chapter books, *The Magnificent Mummies* benefits from Chatterton's cartoon art, which helps "make sense of the twisted plot and mixed historical references," according to *School Library Journal* contributor Laura Scott. In her review of *The Surprise Party* for *Canadian Review of Materials,* Caitlin Fralick wrote that the "dynamic" illustrations "are the book's strength" and Chatterton's use of "bright colour and busy backgrounds will appeal to young readers."

Chatterton pairs his humorous artwork with an original story in his young-adult novels *The Brain Finds a Leg* and *The Brain Full of Holes,* two books that focus on the exploits of a young gumshoe named Theophilus Brain, who boasts that he is the world's greatest detective. In *The Brain Finds a Leg* Theo works with his assistant Sheldon to track down the owner of a disembodied leg found floating in a river. Moving the action to Switzerland, *The Brain Full of Holes* continue Theo's adventures in a fast-moving and chaotic tale that mixes parallel universes, airborne bovines, and miniaturized physicists. Describing *The Brain Finds a Leg* as "one wild comedy," a *Kirkus Reviews* writer added that "Chatterton has a ball trying to make his story as outrageous as possible, and young readers who crave literary insanity will love reading it."

Other original novels by Chatterton include the "Bad Dogs" and "Willy Waggledagger" novels, the latter which purports to chronicle the adventures of a preteen William Shakespeare, Willy, after he escapes from his boring parents and joins the touring musical group the Black Skulls. In the series, Chatterton sets the stage for children who will be introduced to the works of Shakes-

Cover of Chatterton's middle-grade novel The Brain Finds a Leg, *featuring artwork by Maureen Withee.* (Little Hare, 2007; Peachtree, 2009. Reproduced by permission.)

peare in future years, introducing characters such as Queen Elizabeth and capturing the life and habits of Elizabethan England. *Bad Dog and All That Hollywood Hoo-Hah, Bad Dog and Those Crazee Martians,* and *Bad Dog and the Curse of the President's Knee* focus on a canine hero that stays one step away from a cage at the local animal shelter by taking advantage of a bizarre range of travel opportunities, from an acting stint based in Hollywood to a space-ship trip to Mars.

Biographical and Critical Sources

PERIODICALS

Booklist, January 1, 1994, review of *The Kingfisher First Thesaurus,* p. 851; May 1, 2002, John Peters, review of *Midnight in Memphis* p. 1531; May 1, 2010, Todd Morning, review of *The Brain Full of Holes,* p. 55.

Guardian (London, England), June 16, 1998, Philip Pullman, review of *Derek Dungbeetle in Paradise,* p. 2.

Kirkus Reviews, September 1, 2009, review of *The Brain Finds a Leg.*

Library Journal, August, 2002, Kathleen Simonetta, review of *Midnight in Memphis,* p. 146.

Publishers Weekly, September 11, 1995, review of *Can Dogs Fly? Fido's Book of Pop-up Transportation Surprises,* p. 84.

Resource Links, December, 2005, Adriane Pettit, review of *The Surprise Party,* p. 14; December, 2006, Claire Hazzard, *The Mummy Family Finds Fame,* p. 22.

School Library Journal, July, 2002, Laura Scott, review of *The Magnificent Mummies,* p. 83.

ONLINE

Canadian Review of Materials Online, http://www.umanitoba/ca/cm/ (December 15, 2010), Catherine Hoyt, review of *Stranger from Somewhere in Time;* Caitlin Fralick, review of *The Surprise Party;* Robert Groberman, review of *The Mummy Family Finds Fame,* p. 48.

Martin Chatterton Home Page, http://www.worldofchatterton.com (December 13, 2010).*

*   *   *

CHRISTIE, Gregory
See CHRISTIE, R. Gregory

*   *   *

CHRISTIE, R. Gregory 1971-
(Gregory Christie)

Personal

Born July 26, 1971; son of Gerard A. (a pharmacist) and Ludria V. (a dietician) Christie. *Education:* School

R. Gregory Christie. (Photograph by Gary Spector. Reproduced by permission.)

of Visual Arts (New York, NY), B.F.A. (media arts), 1993. *Hobbies and other interests:* Handmade and archival-quality bookmaking.

Addresses

Office—Gas-Art Studios, 320 7th Ave., Brooklyn, NY 11215. *E-mail*—christie@gas-art.com.

Career

Illustrator and muralist. Commercial Art Supply, Plainfield, NJ, worked in sales and stock, 1985-89; *Newark Star Ledger,* Newark, NJ, intern/spot illustrator, 1989; Solomon R. Guggenheim Museum, New York, NY, worked in stock and book store sales, 1989, security, 1991-98. Freelance illustrator, beginning 1993; work included on covers of numerous jazz recordings. Lecturer to schools; mentor to art students. *Exhibitions:* Work included in Original Art Show, Society of Illustrators, New York, NY, 1996, and as part of numerous group exhibitions. Solo exhibitions staged at Maryland Institute College of Art, Baltimore, 2006; Ensworth School Gallery, Nashville, TN, 2007; Brooklyn Public Library, Brooklyn, NY, 2007; Kinokuniya Bookstore, Kuala Lumpur, Malaysia, 2009; Rahway Public Library, Rahway, NJ; and Children's Museum of Manhattan, New York, NY, 2010.

Awards, Honors

Coretta Scott King Illustrator Honor Book designation, American Library Association (ALA), 1997, for *The Palm of My Heart; New York Times* Ten Best-Illustrated Children's Books selection, and New York Public Library One-Hundred Recommended Book Titles selection, both 2000, and Coretta Scott King Illustrator Honor Book designation, ALA, 2001, all for *Only Passing Through* by Anne F. Rockwell; *New York Times* Best Illustrated Children's Book, 2002, for *Stars in the Darkness* by Barbara M. Joossee; Ezra Jack Keats Award, Ezra Jack Keats Foundation, and Claudia Lewis Award, both 2003, both for *Yesterday I Had the Blues* by Jeron Ashford Frame; Best of the Best listee, Chicago Public Library, 2005, and Best Children's Books of the Year selection, Bank Street College of Education, 2006, both *The Sun's Daughter* by Pat Sherman; Notable Children's Book selection, ALA, and Coretta Scott King Illustrator Honor Book designation, both 2006, both for *Brothers in Hope* by Mary Williams; Amelia Bloomer Project listee, ALA, and Parents' Choice Silver honor, both 2006, both for *Keep Climbing, Girls* by Beah E. Richards; Schneider Family Book Award, 2007, for *The Deaf Musicians* by Pete Seeger and Paul DuBois Jacobs; Cooperative Children's Book Center (CCBC) Choices listee, ALA Notable Children's Book selection, and Theodor Seuss Geisel Award, all 2008, all for *Jazz Baby* by Lisa Wheeler; Simon Wiesenthal Center Children's Book Award, New Mexico Book Award, Western Writers of America Spur Award, and CCBC Choices selection, all 2009, all for *Bad News for Outlaws* by Vaunda Micheaux Nelson; CCBC Choices selection, 2010, for *Make Way for Dyamonde Diamond* by Nikki Grimes; Best of the Best listee, Chicago Public Library, 2010, for *Rich* by Grimes.

Illustrator

America, My Land, Your Land, Lee & Low Books (New York, NY), 1996.

(Under name Gregory Christie) Davida Adedjouma, editor, *The Palm of My Heart: Poetry by African-American Children,* introduction by Lucille Clifton, Lee & Low Books (New York, NY), 1996.

William Miller, *Richard Wright and the Library Card,* Lee & Low Books (New York, NY), 1997.

Anne F. Rockwell, *Only Passing Through: The Story of Sojourner Truth,* Knopf (New York, NY), 2000.

Barbara M. Joosse, *Stars in the Darkness,* Chronicle Books (San Francisco, CA), 2001.

Tony Medina, *DeShawn Days,* Lee & Low Books (New York, NY), 2001.

Tonya Bolden, *Rock of Ages: A Tribute to the Black Church,* Knopf (New York, NY), 2001.

Tony Medina, *Love to Langston,* Lee & Low Books (New York, NY), 2002.

Rukhsana Khan, *Ruler of the Courtyard,* Viking (New York, NY), 2003.

Jeron Ashford Frame, *Yesterday I Had the Blues,* Tricycle Press (Berkeley, CA), 2003.

Lisa Wheeler, *Jazz Baby,* Harcourt (Orlando, FL), 2004.

Barbara M. Joosse, *Hot City,* Philomel Books (New York, NY), 2004.

Tonya Bolden, *The Champ: The Story of Muhammad Ali,* Knopf (New York, NY), 2004.

Pat Sherman, *The Sun's Daughter,* Clarion Books (New York, NY), 2005.

Steve Seskin and Allen Shamblin, *A Chance to Shine,* Tricycle Press (Berkeley, CA), 2005.

Mary Williams, *Brothers in Hope: The Story of the Lost Boys of Sudan,* Lee & Low (New York, NY), 2005.

Pete Seeger and Paul DuBois, *The Deaf Musicians,* Putnam's (New York, NY), 2006.

Carole Boston Weatherford, *Dear Mr. Rosenwald,* Scholastic (New York, NY), 2006.

Beah E. Richards, *Keep Climbing, Girls,* Simon & Schuster (New York, NY), 2006.

Lisa Wheeler, *Jazz Baby,* Harcourt (Orlando, FL), 2007.

Muriel Harris Weinstein, *When Louis Armstrong Taught Me Scat,* Chronicle Books (San Francisco, CA), 2008.

Vaunda Micheaux Nelson, *Bad News for Outlaws: The Remarkable Life of Bass Reeves, Deputy U.S. Marshal,* Carolrhoda Books (Minneapolis, MN), 2009.

Anne Rockwell, *Open the Door to Liberty!: A Biography of Toussaint L'Ouverture,* Houghton Mifflin Harcourt (Boston, MA), 2009.

Erica Silverman, *Pettina and the Wind-rope,* Farrar, Straus & Giroux (New York, NY), 2009.

Dinah Johnson, *Black Magic,* Henry Holt (New York, NY), 2010.

Arnold Adoff, *Roots and Blues: A Celebration,* Clarion Books (New York, NY), 2010.

Contributor to periodicals, including *New Yorker, Village Voice, Madison, Travel & Leisure, Parenting, Los Angeles, Rolling Stone, Parenting, Golf, Vibe, Cigar Aficionado, Teaching Tolerance, Atlantic Monthly,* and *Philadelphia Inquirer.*

ILLUSTRATOR; "DYAMONDE DANIEL" SERIES

Nikki Grimes, *Make Way for Dyamonde Daniel,* Putnam's (New York, NY), 2009.

Nikki Grimes, *Rich,* Putnam's (New York, NY), 2009.

Nikki Grimes, *Almost Zero,* Putnam's (New York, NY), 2010.

Sidelights

A three-time recipient of the prestigious Coretta Scott King Honor Book designation, R. Gregory Christie has earned recognition for his bold, evocative illustrations—primarily done in acrylics and gouache—that have graced the pages of a number of highly regarded children's books. Christie's intensely colored paintings, which have appeared in the *New Yorker, Village Voice, Rolling Stone,* and other periodicals, feature the elongated figures that are considered a hallmark of his work. The artist varies his approach to illustration depending on his audience, telling a *Seven Impossible Things before Breakfast* online interviewer: "I decided on more approachable images for younger children's books. I do

Christie captures the rural southern setting of generations past in his artwork for Anne Rockwell's picture book **Only Passing Through.** (Illustration copyright © 2000 by R. Gregory Christie. Used by permission of Alfred A. Knopf, an imprint of Random House Children's Books, a division of Random House, Inc.)

this with color and form but keep myself challenged by abstracting each figure's proportion. In chapter books for older readers, I tend to use darker earth colors and make images that can easily be hung in any contemporary art show and hold its own."

In *DeShawn Days,* a collection of poems by Tony Medina that focuses on life from the perspective of a ten-year-old African-American boy, Christie provides illustrations that are suffused with the warmth and joy of a close-knit family scene, and are alternately "bleak and sophisticated," according to a *Publishers Weekly* reviewer. Wanda Meyers-Hines also praised Christie's work in *School Library Journal,* writing that the artist's acrylic and gouache paintings "beautifully capture the cultural and artistic aspects" of a young boy's home life in the pages of *Yesterday I Had the Blues,* by Jeron Ashford Frame. Reflecting the sultry mood of Barbara M. Joosse's summertime story in *Hot City,* Christie cools his palette of hot pinks, reds, and bright oranges with clear yellows to create "quirky acrylic paintings [that] take playful liberties with perspective and scale," according to a *Publishers Weekly* reviewer. His "viva-

cious, artfully distorted" images for the book "sizzle along with the rhythmic, smooth-as-melted-butter" text, according to a *Kirkus Reviews* writer.

Anne F. Rockwell's *Only Passing Through: The Story of Sojourner Truth,* a biography of the African-American abolitionist, orator, and freedom fighter, is expressively illustrated by Christie, his choice of hues and his manipulation of the human figure working together to give "a powerful sense of Sojourner Truth's . . . compelling personality," in the opinion of *Book* critic Kathleen Odean. Another biography, Tonya Bolden's *The Champ: The Story of Muhammad Ali,* was described by a *Kirkus Reviews* writer as "picture-book biography at its best" due in part to Christie's "strongly hued" and "eye-catching" illustrations.

In his work for *Ruler of the Courtyard* Christie exhibits his versatility by drawing on images from a Middle Eastern aesthetic. Set in Pakistan, Rukhsana Khan's story focuses on a young girl who is terrorized by the chickens running wild outside her family's rural home. Christie's "vigorous and slightly naive" art warms the story with what *School Library Journal* reviewer Dona

Ratterree described as "hot bright backgrounds" and "attentive detail." While his art "provide[s] the balance between ambiguity and realism that the text requires," Christie also astutely captures the girl's "feelings through her facial expressions and body language," a *Kirkus Reviews* writer observed of *Ruler of the Courtyard.* Another multicultural picture book, Pat Sherman's *The Sun's Daughter,* features a Native-American porquoi story that is enhanced by dramatic illustrations by Christie that "intensify the sense of abstraction from reality common to folklore," according to *Booklist* contributor Jennifer Mattson.

Returning to his own culture, Christie contributes what a *Publishers Weekly* contributor deemed "stylized, boldly hued gouache and colored pencil art" to Carole Boston Weatherford's *Dear Mr. Rosenwald.* Based on the true story of the way one man's vision and the aspirations of a poor rural community combined to create a school for black children during the 1920s, *Dear Mr. Rosenwald* presents "a heartening sliver of American history," according to the *Publishers Weekly* critic. In *Booklist* Hazel Rochman wrote that Christie's "exuberant gouache and colored-pencil illustrations" bring to life the "vibrant family and community" at the center of Weatherford's tale, and *School Library Journal* reviewer

Carole Boston Weatherford's story of a dedicated teacher is brought to life in Christie's naïf-styled paintings for **Dear Mr. Rosenwald.** (Illustration copyright © 2006 by R. Gregory Christie. Reproduced by permission of Scholastic, Inc.)

Catherine Threadgill deemed the book's art a "good complement" to the "rough-around-the-edges" account of its young narrator.

Christie has provided the artwork for a number of books that celebrate the joys of music. A jazz drummer who adjusts to a new playing style after experiencing hearing loss is the focus of *The Deaf Musicians,* a picture-book collaboration between Paul DuBois and legendary folk singer Pete Seeger. "Christie's snazzy style matches perfectly with the book's vivacity," Genevieve Gallagher remarked in *School Library Journal.* In Lisa Wheeler's *Jazz Baby,* a household full of adults and children, including an enraptured infant, groove to the beat of a energetic recording. A contributor in *Kirkus Reviews* offered praise for Christie's vibrant paintings here, writing that they "locate this colorfully garbed, expressively hip family within an equally vibrant community." *When Louis Armstrong Taught Me Scat,* Muriel Harris Weinstein's tribute to the great jazz trumpeter and singer, centers on a young girl who learns to be-bop when "Satchmo" visits her dreams. "Christie's vibrant acrylics offer a pleasing, surreal fluidity," a reviewer stated in a *Publishers Weekly* appraisal of Weinstein's story.

An encouraging, uplifting poem by African-American actress and writer Beah E. Richards, first published in 1951, gets new life in the picture book *Keep Climbing, Girls,* featuring gouache illustrations by Christie. "Bold brush strokes create a landscape simplified to its essence," Carolyn Phelan remarked in *Booklist.* The illustrator's distinctive brushstrokes also bring to life Dinah Johnson's *Black Magic,* in which a youngster contemplates the sensations and emotions associated with the color black. "Christie's artwork takes the words and imaginatively whirls them in stylized, riotously colored pictures," *Booklist* critic Ilene Cooper maintained of this work.

A nineteenth-century African-American lawman is the subject of *Bad News for Outlaws: The Remarkable Life of Bass Reeves, Deputy U.S. Marshal,* an award-winning picture-book biography by Vaunda Micheaux Nelson. An escaped slave who served as a federal marshal in Indian Territory (now Oklahoma), Reeves was credited with more than 3,000 arrests during his career. "Christie's memorable paintings convey Reeves's determination and caring," Lisa Glasscock remarked in *School Library Journal,* and a *Kirkus Reviews* contributor believed that the illustrations "echo the heroic spirit" of the text. "An exciting subject [is] captured with narrative panache and visual swagger," concluded Ian Chipman in his *Booklist* review of Nelson's story. Similar in tone, Rockwell's *Open the Door to Liberty!: A Biography of Toussaint L'Ouverture* examines the life of the freed slave who led the fight for Haitian independence. In the words of *School Library Journal* critic Rebecca Donnelly, here "Christie's bold, naive gouache illustrations invoke Haiti's beauty, and savage history."

Christie has also enjoyed a successful collaboration with Nikki Grimes, serving as the illustrator for her

Christie focuses on the Wild Wild West in his paintings for Vaunda Micheaux Nelson's true-to-life story in **Bad News for Outlaws.** (Illustration copyright © 2009 by R. Gregory Christie. Reproduced by permission of Carolrhoda Books, a division of Lerner Publishing Group. No part of this excerpt may be used or reproduced in any manner whatsoever without the prior written permission of Lerner Publishing Group, Inc.)

chapter books about a feisty third-grader in New York City who is struggling to cope with the many changes in her life. In *Make Way for Dyamonde Daniel,* the debut work in the series, the title character confronts a schoolmate about his rude behavior, earning a new friend in the process. "Gregory's familiar black-and-white sketches add a hip, urban feel to the tale," wrote a contributor in *Kirkus Reviews.* In a follow-up, *Almost Zero,* the youngster learns a valuable lesson after complaining about her wardrobe. According to Alyson Low in *School Library Journal,* "Christie's sketches in thick lines of black ink add to the book's appeal."

With dozens of books and a host of awards to his credit, Christie refuses to rest on his laurels. "I'm drawn to projects that will challenge me and give me a little bit of fear because I have no idea how I will approach it," he remarked to Yuko Shimizu in an *Illustration Friday* online interview. "I'm not the type of illustrator to stick to one aesthetic or keep a visual consistency from one project to the next." Christie further noted, "I also choose my projects to right the wrongs I see in the American educational system if not in American society. There are so many enriching stories about brown people's history and America has often neglected these amazing tales. I never learned about the heroes that I've

found today through reading and I want the society to have a balance when it comes to learning about every culture's historical achievements."

Biographical and Critical Sources

PERIODICALS

Book, May, 2001, Kathleen Odean, review of *Only Passing Through: The Story of Sojourner Truth,* p. 80.

Booklist, October 1, 2001, Hazel Rochman, review of *Rock of Ages: The Story of the Lost Boys of Sudan,* p. 334; November 1, 2003, Jennifer Mattson, review of *Yesterday I Had the Blues,* p. 500; March 15, 2005, Jennifer Mattson, review of *The Sun's Daughter,* p. 1292; May 1, 2005, Hazel Rochman, review of *Brother in Hope: The Story of the Lost Boys of Sudan,* p. 1584; February 1, 2006, Carolyn Phelan, review of *Keep Climbing, Girls,* p. 70; October 1, 2006, Hazel Rochman, review of *Dear Mr. Rosenwald,* p. 61; February 1, 2009, Daniel Kraus, review of *Open the Door to Liberty: A Biography of Toussaint L' Ouverture,* p. 52; February 1, 2009, Ian Chipman, review of *When Louis Armstrong Taught Me Scat,* p. 58; May 1, 2009, Carolyn Phelan, review of *Make Way for Dyamonde Daniel,* p. 78; October 1, 2009, Ian Chipman, review of *Bad News for Outlaws: The Remarkable Life of Bass Reeves, Deputy U.S. Marshal,* p. 39; November 1, 2009, Carolyn Phelan, review of *Rich,* p. 45; February 1, 2010, Ilene Cooper, review of *Black Magic,* p. 61.

Christian Parenting Today, March, 2001, review of *Only Passing Through,* p. 62.

Horn Book, March-April, 2003, Susan P. Bloom, review of *Ruler of the Courtyard,* p. 204; January-February, 2004, Susan Dove Lempke, review of *Yesterday I Had the Blues,* p. 69; January-February, 2005, Kathleen Isaacs, review of *The Champ: The Story of Muhammad Ali,* p. 106; November-December, 2009, Betty Carter, review of *Bad News for Outlaws,* p. 698.

Kirkus Reviews, December 15, 2002, review of *Ruler of the Courtyard,* p. 1851; August 15, 2003, review of *Yesterday I Had the Blues,* p. 1072; May 15, 2004, review of *Hot City,* p. 493; March 1, 2005, review of *The Sun's Daughter,* p. 295; December 15, 2004, review of *The Champ,* p. 1198; December 1, 2005, Beah E. Richards, review of *Keep Climbing, Girls,* p. 1279; August 15, 2006, review of *Dear Mr. Rosenwald,* p. 853; October 15, 2007, review of *Jazz Baby;* April 15, 2009, review of *Make Way for Dyamonde Daniel;* October 15, 2009, review of *Bad News for Outlaws.*

New York Times Book Review, November 19, 2000, Linda Villarosa, "Serving No Master but the Truth," p. 61.

Print, January, 2001, Ariana Donalds, "Home and Away," p. 104.

Publishers Weekly, May 21, 2001, review of *DeShawn Days,* p. 107; January 6, 2003, review of *Ruler of the Courtyard,* p. 59; July 12, 2004, review of *Hot City,* p. 63; March 21, 2005, review of *The Sun's Daughter,* p. 51; October 23, 2006, review of *Dear Mr. Rosen-*

wald, p. 51; March 2, 2009, review of *When Louis Armstrong Taught Me Scat,* p. 62; November 2, 2009, review of *Bad News for Outlaws,* p. 52; January 11, 2010, review of *Black Magic,* p. 48.

School Library Journal, July, 2001, Patti Gonzales, review of *DeShawn Days,* p. 96; February, 2003, Dona Ratterree, review of *Ruler of the Courtyard,* p. 114; October, 2003, Wanda Meyers-Hines, review of *Yesterday I Had the Blues,* p. 119; June, 2005, Mary N. Oluonye, review of *Brothers in Hope,* p. 131, and Cris Riedel, review of *The Sun's Daughter,* p. 144; February, 2006, Julie Roach, review of *Keep Climbing, Girls,* p. 124; October, 2006, Catherine Threadgill, review of *Dear Mr. Rosenwald,* p. 129; November, 2006, Genevieve Gallagher, review of *The Deaf Musicians,* p. 112; March, 2009, Rebecca Donnelly, review of *Open the Door to Liberty!,* p. 168; July, 2009, Jackie Partch, review of *Make Way for Dyamonde Daniel,* p. 64; November, 2009, Lisa Glasscock, review of *Bad News for Outlaws,* p. 134; February, 2010, Mary Landrum, review of *Black Magic,* p. 88; January, 2011, Alyson Low, review of *Almost Zero,* p. 76.

ONLINE

Illustration Friday Web site, http://illustrationfriday.com/ (January 6, 2010), Yuko Shimizu, "IF Interview with R. Gregory Christie."

R. Gregory Christie Home Page, http://www.gas-art.com (January 20, 2011).

Seven Impossible Things before Breakfast Web log, http://blaine.org/sevenimpossiblethings/ (January 13, 2009), interview with Christie.

*　　*　　*

COFFEY, Brian
See KOONTZ, Dean

*　　*　　*

COHEN, Lisa 1963-

Personal

Born 1963, in Cape Town, South Africa; married; children: one daughter.

Addresses

Home—New Orleans, LA.

Career

Artist and children's book illustrator.

Awards, Honors

Best Books of 2001 selection, *Los Angeles Times,* for *The Blues Singers* by Julius Lester.

Writings

Libba Moore Gray, *Little Lil and the Swing-singing Sax,* Simon & Schuster (New York, NY), 1996.

Julius Lester, *The Blues Singers: Ten Who Rocked the World,* Hyperion Books for Children (New York, NY), 2001.

Kim L. Siegelson, *Dancing the Ring Shout!,* Hyperion Books for Children (New York, NY), 2003.

Quincy Troupe, *Little Stevie Wonder* (includes music CD), Houghton Mifflin (Boston, MA), 2005.

Dimitrea Tokunbo, *The Sound of Kwanzaa,* Scholastic Press (New York, NY), 2009.

Sidelights

A native of South Africa who is now based in New Orleans, Louisiana, Lisa Cohen is a self-taught artist who has provided the illustrations for picture books that include Kim L. Siegelson's *Dancing the Ring Shout!* and Quincy Troupe's *Little Stevie Wonder.* Cohen, who moved to the United States in the early 1980s, made her picture-book debut in 1996 with the release of *Little Lil and the Swing-singing Sax,* a poignant tale by Libba Moore Gray.

Set during the Christmas season, *Little Lil and the Swing-singing Sax* centers on a young girl's efforts to retrieve a saxophone belonging to her uncle, a musician who pawned the instrument so that he could purchase medicine for the girl's mother. According to *Booklist* reviewer Bill Ott, "Cohen's primitive-style illustrations employ blocks of bold colors to suggest a wide range of emotions," and a *Publishers Weekly* critic also praised Cohen's artwork, noting that "the characters and their surroundings are pressed into the paintings as if into a modern stained glass window."

Siegelson draws on an African-American ritual for *Dancing the Ring Shout!,* "a warm celebration of an uplifting tradition," according to a contributor in *Publishers Weekly.* As the annual harvest draws to an end, young Toby is invited for the first time to join his family's "ring shout," a joyous circle dance featuring song and prayer. Asked to bring something to play that demonstrates his appreciation, Toby grows confused until he finds a simple but effective way to participate in the celebration. "Cohen's boldly colored, flat illustrations swirl across the pages," a *Kirkus Reviews* critic observed, and in *School Library Journal* Mary N. Oluonye described the art for *Dancing the Ring Shout!* as "vibrant and eye-catching."

In *The Blues Singers: Ten Who Rocked the World* Julius Lester presents profiles of Bessie Smith, Muddy Waters, Ray Charles, and other legendary recording artists. In the words of a *Publishers Weekly* reviewer, Cohen's "chunky, stylized portraits of each singer capture some of the performers' signature looks," and *Black Issues Book Review* contributor Khafre Abif reported that "Cohen's paintings invoke the spirit and soul of each blues

Lisa Cohen's colorful stylized art captures the ethnic inspiration underlying Dimitrea Tokunbo's picture-book text for **The Sound of Kwanzaa.** (Illustration copyright © 2009 by Lisa Cohen. Reproduced by permission of Scholastic, Inc.)

great." Another musical genius is the focus of *Little Stevie Wonder,* Troupe's picture-book biography of the Grammy Award-winning artist known for such hit songs as "You Are the Sunshine of My Life," "Higher Ground," and "Living for the City." "Cohen's paintings convey a celebratory joyfulness," a contributor wrote in *Publishers Weekly,* and Ilene Cooper maintained in *Booklist* that Cohen's "acrylic artwork . . . is as dynamic as Wonder's music." *School Library Journal* reviewer Mary Elam declared that the illustrations in *Little Stevie Wonder* "perfectly match the joyful nature of the narrative."

Dimitrea Tokunbo offers young readers an introduction to an African-American holiday in *The Sound of Kwanzaa.* Focusing on the holiday's seven guiding principles, the author uses direct language to depict a host of festive activities, including the lighting of candles. "Cohen's equally simple illustrations complement the text," a critic in *Kirkus Reviews* noted, and *Booklist* contributor Linda Perkins cited the illustrator's "effective use of shape, silhouette, and bold color" as a highlight of the work.

Biographical and Critical Sources

PERIODICALS

Black Issues Book Review, September, 2001, Khafre Abif, review of *The Blues Singers: Ten Who Rocked the World,* p. 76.

Booklist, September 1, 1996, Bill Ott, review of *Little Lil and the Swing-singing Sax,* p. 142; June 1, 2001, Stephanie Zvirin, review of *The Blues Singers,* p. 1870; December 1, 2003, Terry Glover, review of *Dancing the Ring Shout!,* p. 685; February 1, 2005, Ilene Cooper, review of *Little Stevie Wonder,* p. 976; November 1, 2009, Linda Perkins, review of *The Sound of Kwanzaa,* p. 51.

Kirkus Reviews, September 1, 2003, review of *Dancing the Ring Shout!,* p. 1131; April 1, 2005, review of *Little Stevie Wonder,* p. 427; September 15, 2009, review of *The Sound of Kwanzaa.*

Publishers Weekly, October 14, 1996, review of *Little Lil and the Swing-singing Sax,* p. 83; May 14, 2001, review of *The Blues Singers,* p. 81; October 27, 2003, review of *Dancing the Ring Shout!,* p. 68; May 30, 2005, review of *Little Stevie Wonder,* p. 60.

School Library Journal, June, 2001, Tim Wadham, review of *The Blues Singers,* p. 138; September, 2003, Grace Oliff, review of *Little Lil and the Swing-singing Sax,* p. 84; December, 2003, Mary N. Oluonye, review of *Dancing the Ring Shout!,* p. 126; December, 2004, Ginny Gustin, review of *The Blues Singers,* p. 61; June, 2005, Mary Elam, review of *Little Stevie Wonder,* p. 146; October, 2009, Madeline J. Bryant, review of *The Sound of Kwanzaa,* p. 84.

ONLINE

Houghton Mifflin Web site, http://www.houghtonmifflin books.com/ (February 1, 2011), interview with Cohen.*

COOPER, Melrose
See KROLL, Virginia L.

*   *   *

COULOUMBIS, Akila 1932-2009

Personal

Born 1932, in Utica, NY; died February 14, 2009, in Gainesville, FL; son of Fotty and Nicky Couloumbis; married Audrey Peyton (an author); children: Nikki, Zachary. *Politics:* Democrat.

Career

Actor and director. Theater for the Forgotten, New York, NY, founder and director. *Military service:* Served in U.S. Air Force.

Member

Screen Actors Guild, Actors Equity.

Writings

(With wife, Audrey Couloumbis) *War Games,* Random House (New York, NY), 2009.

Sidelights

The husband of award-winning children's author Audrey Couloumbis, actor and theatre director Akila Couloumbis collaborated with his wife on the middle-grade novel *War Games.* Set in a small town in Greece during World War II, *War Games* is based on Couloumbis's own childhood. Praised by *New York Times Book Review* contributor Julie Just as a "richly detailed" story inspired by "family memories of the period," *War Games* was published in 2009, the year of Akila Couloumbis's death.

The year is 1941 when twelve-year-old Petros and his teen brother Zola begin to experience World War II first hand. German troops have finally invaded Italy, and now Italian soldiers must make way for German soldiers on the streets of their town. German commanding officers also take their place within the community, and a Nazi officer is soon garrisoned in the boys' family home. Now the brothers live with fear, worried that the officer will discover that their older cousin, Landros, is fighting for the underground. Petros adn Zola also fear that the German will discover their U.S. citizenship and detect their own ongoing efforts to aid the Italian resistance. "A gripping story that's also a fine introduction to a complex time," according to *Horn Book* critic Joanna Rudge Long, *War Games* features an "easily read narrative" that is "lively with dialogue." Kathleen Isaacs praised the Couloumbiss' story in *School Library*

Journal, dubbing the novel "a grand read: an adventure full of the particulars of boys' play, and an unusual perspective on World War II lives." In *Booklist* Ian Chipman called *War Games* an "interesting addition to World War II fiction that ventures into a relatively unexplored corner of Greece," and a *Publishers Weekly* critic deemed the novel a "poignant and plainspoken account of the everyday impacts of a vast war and the importance of small victories."

Biographical and Critical Sources

PERIODICALS

Booklist, October 1, 2009, Ian Chipman, review of *War Games,* p. 38.

Horn Book, November-December, 2009, Joanna Rudge Long, review of *War Games,* p. 665.

New York Times Book Review, January 17, 2010, Julie Just, review of *War Games,* p. 13.

Publishers Weekly, October 26, 2009, review of *War Games,* p. 58.

School Library Journal, October, 2009, Kathleen Isaacs, review of *War Games,* p. 124.

Cover of Audrey and Akila Coluloumbis' novel War Games, *which is based on Akila's childhood during World War II.* (Jacket copyright © 2009 by Random House Children's Books. Used by permission of Random House Children's Books, a division of Random House, Inc.)

Obituaries

ONLINE

Clay Today Online, http://www.claytoday.biz/ (January 15, 2011).*

* * *

CREWE, Megan 1980-

Personal

Born 1980, in Toronto, Ontario, Canada; married. *Education:* York University, B.A. (psychology). *Hobbies and other interests:* Martial arts, travel.

Addresses

Home—Toronto, Ontario, Canada. *E-mail*—megan@ megancrewe.com.

Career

Author. Tutor to children and adolescents with special needs; presenter at schools.

Megan Crewe (Photograph by Chris Blanchenot. Reproduced by permission.)

Writings

Give up the Ghost, Henry Holt (New York, NY), 2009.

Contributor to print and online periodicals, including *In 2 Print.*

Sidelights

Although Megan Crewe completed her first book-length work of fiction when she was fourteen years old, she never considered locating a publisher, and she ultimately ended up earning a college degree in psychology. Crewe's interest in writing necessarily took a back seat to her studies at York University, but she still managed to have several stories published in magazines as well as online. When she once again focused her energies on writing, the Canadian-based Crewe finally found success, and in 2009 she made her publishing debut in *Give up the Ghost.*

In *Give up the Ghost* readers meet sixteen-year-old Cassandra McKenna, a girl with a special gift. Cass has the ability to see ghosts, including the spectral visitation of her recently drowned sister Paige. Because she is not popular with the living students in her high school, Cass spends most of her time with the teen ghosts that roam the school's halls, and as revenge for a bullying incident in middle school she uses ghostly gossip to give her snobbish classmates a comeuppance. When Tim, a fellow student, learns the truth, he asks Cass to help him talk to his recently passed mom.

Through their friendship Cass begins to reconsider her long-held grudge against the living. Citing the "mysterious plot elements" and the innocent teen romance in the novel, Lindsay Cesari wrote in *School Library Journal* that *Give up the Ghost* "will quickly engage reluctant readers." In *Kirkus Reviews* a critic noted that in the fictional Cass Crewe creates "a poignant character study of a deeply wounded girl moving toward a nuanced, forgiving view of humanity," and a *Publishers Weekly* contributor praised *Give up the Ghost* as both "realistic and honest in its portrayal of an angry, struggling teen-age girl."

Biographical and Critical Sources

PERIODICALS

Bulletin of the Center for Children's Books, October, 2009, Deborah Stevenson, review of *Give up the Ghost,* p. 63.
Kirkus Reviews, August 15, 2009, review of *Give up the Ghost.*
Publishers Weekly, September 21, 2009, review of *Give up the Ghost,* p. 60.
School Library Journal, October, 2009, Lindsay Cesari, review of *Give up the Ghost,* p. 124.

ONLINE

Megan Crewe Home Page, http://www.megancrewe.com (December 13, 2010).

D

DE PRETTO, Lorenzo 1966-

Personal

Born 1966, in Vicenza, Italy. *Education:* Istituto d'arte di Cittadella, degree, 1986.

Addresses

Home—Piovene Rocchette, Vicenza, Italy.

Career

Illustrator, graphic designer, animator, and author. Affiliated with Breganze Comics, c. late 1970s; graphic designer for advertising, beginning c. 1989; Gardaland (amusement park), designer of licensed products for "Prezzemolo" character and animator of animated television series, beginning 1993; creator of characters and comic-book series for advertising.

Writings

(With Giuseppe Ferrario) *Prezzemolo: Le storie più belle* (anthology; originally published in comic-book form), Pavesio (Turin, Italy), 2001.

Elisabetta Dami, writing as Geronimo Stilton, *Geronimo Stilton alla scoperta dell'America* ("Geronimo Stilton" series), 2007, translated by Nanette McGuiness as *The Discovery of America*, NBM/Papercutz (New York, NY), 2009.

Creator of or contributor to comic series, including "Ennio e di Jacopo the Punk," "Lupo Alberto va in città," "Bruky," and "Geronimo Stilton."

Biographical and Critical Sources

PERIODICALS

Booklist, October 1, 2009, Kat Kan, review of *The Discovery of America,* p. 41.

Kirkus Reviews, September 1, 2009, review of *The Discovery of America.*

Publishers Weekly, August 31, 2009, review of *The Discovery of America,* p. 42.

ONLINE

FanoFunny Web site, http://www.fanofunny.com/ (January 15, 2011), "Lorenzo De Pretto."*

*   *   *

di BARTOLO, Jim

Personal

Married Laini Taylor (an author and artist), June, 2001; children: Clementine. *Education:* College degree; California College of the Arts, B.F.A., 2000. *Hobbies and other interests:* Writing, music, travel.

Addresses

Home—Portland, OR. *Agent*—Jane Putch, Eyebait Licensing and Management, janeputch@aol.com. *E-mail*—jimdibartolo@comcast.net.

Career

Illustrator for books, comic books, and role-playing game manuals.

Awards, Honors

(With Laini Taylor) National Book Award finalist in Young People's category, and YALSA Top-Ten Best Books for Young Adults selection, both 2009, both for *Lips Touch: Three Times.*

Illustrator

Laini Taylor, *The Drowned* (graphic novel), Image Comics, 2004.

Laini Taylor, *Blackbringer* ("Dreamdark" fantasy series), Putnam (New York, NY), 2007.

Laini Taylor, *Lips Touch: Three Times,* Arthur A. Levine Books (New York, NY), 2009.

Laini Taylor, *Silksinger* ("Dreamdark" fantasy series), G.P. Putnam's Sons (New York, NY), 2009.

Contributor to anthologies, including *Fractured Fables,* Image Comics, 2010. Contributor to comic-book series, including "Rex Mundi" by Arvad Nelson, Dark Horse Comics, 2007, and to role-playing-game manuals published by White Wolf Publishing, beginning 2002.

Sidelights

Since graduating from the California College of the Arts, Jim di Bartolo has worked as an illustrator, and his color-washed pencil and ink drawings can be found in comic books, graphic novels, and RPG manuals, as well as on the covers of trade books. Di Bartolo's most creative ventures have been those done with his wife, artist and author Laini Taylor, whose illustrated fantasy

novel *Lips Touch: Three Times* earned the couple both critical acclaim and the honor of ranking as National Book Award finalists in the Young People's Literature category.

The idea for *Lips Touch* grew out of di Bartolo and Taylor's years at California College of the Arts, where they met and shared their enthusiasm for the heavily illustrated adult novels of the late nineteenth century. Containing two short stories and a novella, the book also features forty-one pages of two-color art. In Taylor's stories, romance melds with the supernatural and the pivotal kiss in each story sets in motion a chain of events that may compromise a human soul. Serving as what a *Publishers Weekly* critic described as "tantalizing visual preludes to each tale," di Bartolo's images capture the same mix of visual beauty and emotional aloofness that characterized the work of Pre-Raphaelite artists such as Dante Gabriel Rossetti. As *Horn Book* reviewer Deirdre F. Baker noted, they "display comics' conventions of feminine beauty, set in a realm of a sin-

Jim di Bartolo's illustration projects include creating the art work for wife Laini Taylor's fantasy story collection Lips Touch: Three Times. (Illustration copyright © 2009 by Jim di Bartolo. Reproduced by permission of Scholastic, Inc.)

ister, shadowy atmosphere all red and gray." Praising Taylor's "beautiful fantasy writing" as "reminiscent of [stories by] Charles de Lint and Neil Gaiman," Debbi Carton also admired di Bartolo's illustrations in *Booklist,* writing that they serve as "a fine match for the lyrical, romantic text" in *Lips Touch.*

In creating his art, di Bartolo begins with a strong foundation grounded in his skilled drawing abilities. After a pencil sketch on smooth Bristol board, he then applies watercolor and sometimes ink. Digital enhancing comes last, as colors are filtered or otherwise altered and other visual elements added. In addition to *Lips Touch* and his collaboration with Taylor on the graphic novel *The Drowned,* he has contributed cover art and interior images to the novels *Blackbringer* and *Silksinger,* which are part of Taylor's "Dreamdark" fantasy series. Other collaborative work includes a retelling of "Pinocchio" for the comic anthology *Fractured Fables,* while his solo work has included contributing illustrations to Arvad Nelson's ongoing "Rex Mundi" comics saga.

Biographical and Critical Sources

PERIODICALS

Booklist, October 1, 2009, Debbie Carton, review of *Lips Touch: Three Times,* p. 42.
Bulletin of the Center for Children's Books, November, 2009, April Spisak, review of *Lips Touch,* p. 130.
Horn Book, January-February, 2010, Deirdre F. Baker, review of *Lips Touch,* p. 94.
Kirkus Reviews, September 15, 2009, review of *Lips Touch.*
Publishers Weekly, October 18, 2004, review of *The Drowned,* p. 50; September 21, 2009, review of *Lips Touch,* p. 59.
School Library Journal, November, 2009, Ginny Gustin, review of *Lips Touch,* p. 123.
Voice of Youth Advocates, December, 2009, Rebecca C. Moore, review of *Lips Touch,* p. 425.

ONLINE

Jim di Bartolo Home Page, http://www.jimdibartolo.com (December 13, 2010).
Jim di Bartolo Web log, http://jimdibartolo.blogspot.com (January 22, 2011).*

*   *   *

DOYLE, Eugenie 1952-

Personal

Born 1952; daughter of Joseph (an attorney) and Eugenie (a professor of pediatrics) Doyle; married Sam Burr (a farmer and former state legislative counselor),

Eugenie Doyle (Photograph by Trent Campbell. Reproduced by permission.)

July 7, 1984; children: Nora, Silas and Caleb (twins). *Education:* Harvard College, B.A. (English), 1974; Vermont College, M.F.A. (writing), 1995. *Hobbies and other interests:* Dance, yoga, dragonboating.

Addresses

Home—Monkton Ridge, VT. *Office*—Last Resort Farm, 2246 Tyler Bridge Rd., Monkton, VT 05443. *E-mail*—edoyle@madriver.com.

Career

Writer and farmer. Last Resort Farm, Monkton, VT, co-owner and operator. New England Young Writers Conference, Breadloaf VT, instructor; Farming in Monkton (annual writing contest), sponsor; presenter at schools and libraries.

Awards, Honors

Honor Book designation, Society of School Librarians International, 2010, for *According to Kit.*

Writings

FICTION

Stray Voltage, Front Street (Asheville, NC), 2002.
According to Kit, Front Street (Honesdale, PA), 2009.

Contributor of short stories to periodicals, including *Glimmer Train, StoryQuarterly,* and *Rush Hour.*

Sidelights

Eugenie Doyle enjoys an unconventional lifestyle, working as a farmer for six months of the year and writing for the other six. The author of the young-adult novels *Stray Voltage* and *According to Kit,* Doyle owns and operates the Last Resort Farm, an organic produce and hay operation in Vermont, together with her husband, Sam Burr. Assisted frequently by their three grown children, Doyle and Burr grow organic strawberries, peas, currants, garlic, gooseberries, and pumpkins, among other crops, which they sell locally at farmer's markets, a farm stand, co-op groceries, restaurants, and through farmshares.

Doyle, a graduate of Radcliffe College and the Vermont College M.F.A. writing program, used her agricultural experiences to craft *Stray Voltage,* a "distinguished first novel," according to B. Allison Gray in *School Library Journal.* The work focuses on Ian Daley, an eleven year old who is struggling to cope with his mother's abrupt decision to leave the family's Vermont dairy farm and move—alone—to California. With little support from his taciturn older brother and stern father, whose livelihood is threatened by random electric bursts from damaged power lines, Ian finds an outlet for his suffering through his relationship with a kindly teacher who encourages the youngster to voice his feelings in a series of writing assignments. "Doyle has written a sparely eloquent, deeply moving family story that is enriched by its wonderfully realized rural setting," Michael Cart noted in his review of the novel for *Booklist,* and a *Publishers Weekly* critic similarly observed that the author's "prose gracefully metes out the rhythms of farm life, capturing the silence and the beauty as well as the unrest lurking beneath the surface." A contributor in *Kirkus Reviews* stated that, although the novel may hold more appeal for adults than teens, "for those younger readers who identify with Ian, it is sure to strike a deep chord."

In her award-winning novel *According to Kit* Doyle again looks at rural life, this time through the eyes of a frustrated teenager. After fifteen-year-old Kit witnesses a knifing incident at her school and her ballet teacher falls seriously ill, the teen's mother decides to home-school her child, forcing Kit to endure long days of stifling routine on the family's dairy farm. To escape her dour mother's constant negativity, Kit dreams of a career as a professional dancer and practices her routines

alone in the barn. When a team of new dance instructors arrives in town and encourages the teen to apply to a special school in Montreal, Kit's dream of attending predictably meets with her mother's disapproval. *Booklist* reviewer Frances Bradburn found much to praise in *According to Kit,* commenting that Doyle's "characters are complicated and authentic, if not universally likeable." A number of critics remarked that the author accurately captures the protagonist's desire to perfect her skills; a *Kirkus Reviews* contributor, for example, wrote that the scenes in which Kit "performs ballet steps will strike a chord with those who love dance."

Biographical and Critical Sources

PERIODICALS

Booklist, January 1, 2003, Michael Cart, review of *Stray Voltage,* p. 880; November 1, 2009, Frances Bradburn, review of *According to Kit,* p. 56.

Bulletin of the Center for Children's Books, January, 2003, review of *Stray Voltage,* p. 195.

Kirkus Reviews, November 1, 2002, review of *Stray Voltage,* p. 1610; August 15, 2009, review of *According to Kit.*

Cover of Doyle's young-adult novel According to Kit. (Front Street, 2009. Jacket photographs copyright © 2009 by JupiterImages Corporation. Reproduced by permission.)

Publishers Weekly, November 4, 2002, review of *Stray Voltage,* p. 84.

School Library Journal, October, 2002, B. Allison Gray, review of *Stray Voltage,* p. 161; December, 2009, Eliza Langhans, review of *According to Kit,* p. 114.

Voice of Youth Advocates, February, 2003, review of *Stray Voltage,* p. 472.

ONLINE

Boyds Mills Press Web site, http://www.boydsmillspress. com/ (January 21, 2011), "Eugenie Doyle."

Last Resort Farm Web site, http://www.lastresortfarm.com/ (January 21, 2011).

Skidmore College Web site, http://cms.skidmore.edu/ (spring, 2006), Barbara Melville, "Meet the Parents," profile of Doyle.

*   *   *

DWYER, Deanna
See KOONTZ, Dean

*   *   *

DWYER, K.R.
See KOONTZ, Dean

E-F

EBBITT, Carolyn Q. 1974(?)-

Personal

Born c. 1974; daughter of Marilyn S. (a preparatory school headmistress) and Kenneth C. (a business executive) Ebbitt; married Robert Russo III (an attorney), June, 2009. *Education:* Vanderbilt University, B.A. (special education and elementary education; Columbia University, M.F.A. (writing). *Hobbies and other interests:* Photography, swimming, skiing, tennis, painting, baking, reading.

Addresses

Home—New York, NY. *E-mail*—carolyn@carolynqebbitt.com.

Career

Author and educator. Private tutor to learning-disabled and gifted children.

Writings

The Extra-Ordinary Princess, Bloomsbury (New York, NY), 2009.

Sidelights

Carolyn Q. Ebbitt's writing career began before she ever put pen to paper. Shortly after graduating from college, Ebbitts was teaching a group of fifth graders. "Even before I began writing *The Extra-Ordinary Princess,*" she explained on her home page, "I knew there would be a smart character with a learning disability in it. . . . I was teaching my 5th grade reading group and I spent a lot of time looking for a book with a dyslexic hero or heroine, and it was hard to find. We all felt that there should be more books featuring different styles of learning!"

In *The Extra-Ordinary Princess* Ebbitt takes readers to the fantasy kingdom of Gossling where they meet Amelia, the youngest of four sisters in a royal household. While each of her older sisters has a special grace or talent that make them very princess-like, Amelia seems pretty ordinary and has no illusions that she will ever become queen. However, the twelve year old's future seems less certain when a deadly plague is unleashed as the result of an ancient curse and Gossling's king and queen both die. When her magician uncle takes in power and shows his evil intent by transforming her older sisters into trees and swans, Amelia learns that she has a talent of her own when she joins her friend Henry to save her country. "Amelia is a sympathetic character with whom tweens waiting to come into their own can identify," wrote a *Kirkus Reviews* writer in appraising *The Extra-Ordinary Princess,* and *School Library Journal* critic Nancy P. Reeder noted that the story "gathers momentum with [its] many twists and turns." Appealing to middle graders due to its mix of "fairy-tale traditions" and modern culture, Ebbitt's novel also benefits from what *Booklist* critic Kara Dean described as "moments of genuine intrigue and compelling drama."

Biographical and Critical Sources

PERIODICALS

Booklist, May 15, 2009, Kara Dean, review of *The Extra-Ordinary Princess,* p. 55.
Kirkus Reviews, July 1, 2009, review of *The Extra-Ordinary Princess.*
School Library Journal, September, 2009, Nancy P. Reeder, review of *The Extra-Ordinary Princess,* p. 156.

ONLINE

Carolyn Q. Ebbitt Home Page, http://www.carolynqebbitt.com (December 13, 2010).*

FLEMING, Candace 1962-
(Candace Groth-Fleming)

Personal

Born May 24, 1962; daughter of Charles (a superintendent) and Carol (a homemaker) Groth; married Scott Fleming (in commercial real estate), November 9, 1985; children: Scott, Michael. *Education:* Eastern Illinois University, B.A., 1985. *Religion:* Lutheran. *Hobbies and other interests:* Reading, collecting antiquarian books, camping, hiking, travel.

Addresses

Home—Oak Park, IL. *E-mail*—candymfleming@aol.com.

Career

Author. Harper College, Palatine, IL, adjunct professor of liberal arts, 1997—.

Member

Authors Guild Midwest.

Awards, Honors

Highlights for Children History Feature of the Year citation, 1995, and Patriotic Feature of the Year, 1996; Best Juvenile Trade Book of the Year designation, Chicago Women in Publishing, 1996, for *Women of the Lights;* Notable Book citation, American Library Association (ALA), and Parents' Choice Silver Honor designation, both 1997, both for *Gabriella's Song;* Notable Children's Book in the Language Arts citation, National Council of Teachers of English, 1997, for *Gabriella's Song,* and 1998, for *The Hatmaker's Sign; Parenting* Best Book of the Year designation, American Folklore Society Aesop Award, and International Reading Association/*Storytelling World* Award, all 1998, and State of New York's Charlotte Book Award, 2000, all for *The Hatmaker's Sign;* One Hundred Books for Reading and Sharing designation, New York Public Library, 1999, and CCBC Choices selection, 2000, both for *When Agnes Caws;* CCBC Choices selection, and Best Children's Book citation, Bank Street College of Education, both 2000, both for *A Big Cheese for the White House;* Capitol Choices selection, and New York Public Library Best Books for Reading and Sharing selection, both 2002, Children's Notable Book selection, ALA, 2004, and several children's choice nominations and awards, all for *Muncha! Muncha! Muncha!;* ALA Notable Book citation, Best Book for Young Adults selection, YALSA, and James Madison Honor Book selection, all c. 2003, all for *Ben Franklin's Almanack;* ALA Notable Book citation, and Best Book for Young Adults selection, YALSA, both c. 2005, both for *Our Eleanor; Boston Globe/Horn Book* Award for Nonfiction, Orbis Pictus Honor Book selection, Flora Steiglits Straus Award for Nonfiction, Bank Street College of

Candace Fleming (Reproduced by permission.)

Education, Los Angeles Literary Book Prize, and ALA Best Books selection, all c. 2008, all for *The Lincolns;* Best Children's Book selection, Bank Street College of Education, and CCBC Choice selection, both 2008, and several state award nominations, all for *Fabled Fourth Graders of Aesop Elementary School;* Chicago Public Library Best of the Best selection, 2010, for *The Fabled Fifth Graders of Aesop Elementary School;* Parents' Choice Recommended designation, and *Booklist* Editor's Choice selection, both 2010, both for *Clever Jack Takes the Cake;* Best Book designation, and YALSA Award for Excellence in Nonfiction for Young Adults nomination, both ALA, and One Hundred Books for Reading and Sharing selection, New York Public Library, all 2010, all for *The Great and Only Barnum.*

Writings

PICTURE BOOKS

(Under name Candace Groth-Fleming) *Professor Fergus Fahrenheit and His Wonderful Weather Machine,* illustrated by Don Weller, Simon & Schuster (New York, NY), 1994.

Women of the Lights, illustrated by James Watling, Albert Whitman (Morton Grove, IL), 1995.

Madame LaGrande and Her So High, to the Sky, Uproarious Pompadour, illustrated by S.D. Schindler, Alfred A. Knopf (New York, NY), 1996.

Gabriella's Song, illustrated by Giselle Potter, Atheneum (New York, NY), 1997.

Westward Ho, Carlotta!, illustrated by David Catrow, Atheneum (New York, NY), 1998.

The Hatmaker's Sign: A Story by Benjamin Franklin, illustrated by Robert Andrew Parker, Orchard Books (New York, NY), 1998.

A Big Cheese for the White House: The True Tale of a Tremendous Cheddar, illustrated by S.D. Schindler, D.K. Ink (New York, NY), 1999.

Who Invited You?, illustrated by George Booth, Atheneum (New York, NY), 2000.

Muncha! Muncha! Muncha!, illustrated by G. Brian Karas, Atheneum (New York, NY), 2001.

When Agnes Caws, Atheneum (New York, NY), 2002.

Boxes for Katje, illustrated by Stacey Dressen-McQueen, Farrar, Straus (New York, NY), 2003.

This Is the Baby, illustrated by Maggie Smith, Farrar, Straus (New York, NY), 2003.

Gator Gumbo: A Spicy-Hot Southern Tale, illustrated by Sally Ann Lambert, Farrar, Straus (New York, NY), 2004.

Smile, Lily!, illustrated by Yumi Heo, Athenum (New York, NY), 2004.

Sunny Boy!: The Life and Times of a Tortoise, illustrated by Anne Wilsdorf, Farrar, Straus (New York, NY), 2005.

Tippy-Tippy-Tippy-Hide!, illustrated by G. Brian Karas, Atheneum (New York, NY), 2007.

Imogene's Last Stand, illustrated by Nancy Carpenter, Schwartz & Wade (New York, NY), 2009.

Clever Jack Takes the Cake, illustrated by G. Brian Karas, Schwartz & Wade (New York, NY), 2010.

Seven Hungry Babies, illustrated by Eugene Yelchin, Atheneum Books for Young Readers (New York, NY), 2010.

Oh, No!, illustrated by Eric Rohmann, Schwartz & Wade (New York, NY), 2011.

BIOGRAPHIES

Ben Franklin's Almanack: Being a True Account of the Good Gentleman's Life, Atheneum (New York, NY), 2003.

Our Eleanor: A Scrapbook Look at Eleanor Roosevelt's Remarkable Life, Atheneum (New York, NY), 2005.

The Lincolns: A Scrapbook Look at Abraham and Mary, Schwartz & Wade Books (New York, NY), 2008.

The Great and Only Barnum: The Tremendous, Stupendous Life of Showman P.T. Barnum, illustrated by Ray Fenwick, Schwartz & Wade (New York, NY), 2009.

Amelia Lost: The Life and Disappearance of Amelia Earhart, Schwartz & Wade (New York, NY), 2011.

OTHER

Lowji Discovers America (elementary-grade novel), Atheneum (New York, NY), 2005.

The Fabled Fourth Graders of Aesop Elementary School (elementary-grade novel), Schwartz & Wade Books (New York, NY), 2007.

The Fabled Fifth Graders of Aesop Elementary School (elementary-grade novel), Schwartz & Wade (New York, NY), 2010.

Contributor to magazines, including *Boys' Life* and *American Baby.*

Sidelights

In some of her picture books for young children, Candace Fleming sometimes weaves elements of history and tradition in an engaging illustrated story, while others feature whimsical humor and likeable animal characters. A girl on a trip down the bayou finds her tiny boat full to brimming after several critters climb aboard in Fleming's counting book *Who Invited You?,* while in *Seven Hungry Babies* a mother bird becomes overwhelmed while caring for seven insistent young hatchlings. An enthusiastic *Publishers Weekly* contributor praised *Who Invited You?* as a "clever cumulative counting caper," while in *School Library Journal* Marge Loch-Wouters dubbed *Seven Hungry Babies* a "bouncy, onomatopoeic tale" featuring a rhythmic and "playful text." Also praising *Seven Hungry Babies,* a *Kirkus Reviews* critic concluded that "Fleming's minimal text is perfectly pitched to a very young audience," and in *Booklist* Daniel Kraus warned adults that the humorous story is "just the thing to turn a large-group read-aloud into a frenzied chicken coop."

Cover of Fleming's humorous chapter book The Fabled Fourth Graders of Aesop Elementary School. *(Schwartz & Wade Books, 2007. Used by permission of Schwartz & Wade Books, an imprint of Random House Children's Books, a division of Random House, Inc.)*

Featuring artwork by G. Brian Karas, *Muncha! Muncha! Muncha!* echoes Beatrix Potter's classic childhood story *Peter Rabbit* in its tale of three rabbits. In Fleming's version, the bunnies are poised to raid the garden of Mr. McGreely, a man whose efforts to preserve his beautifully maintained vegetable garden may all be for naught. In a sequel, *Tippy-Tippy-Tippy-Hide!,* the battle between gardener and hungry bunnies continues as the floppy-eared creatures infiltrate Mr. McGreely's property and cause the frustrated farmer to lock himself inside his own house. In *School Library Journal* Lisa Gangemi Kropp dubbed *Muncha! Muncha! Muncha!* "a hilarious hop through the garden," while in *Booklist* Gillian Engberg praised the story as a "delightful offering" complete with "hilarious, slapdash problem solving and irresistible sounds." The "irresistible rhyme and onomatopoeia" in *Tippy-Tippy-Tippy-Hide!* "will read-aloud well to a rowdy crowd," predicted Engberg, while in *School Library Journal* Martha Topol concluded that, with its "lighthearted conflict, lively language, and those mischievous, childlike bunnies," Fleming's "sassy sequel will please fans of the first book."

Fleming and Karas team up again with humorous results in *Clever Jack Takes the Cake,* as Jack's lack of ready money prompts him to bake a cake as a gift to his friend the princess on her tenth birthday. He trades his tools for cake ingredients and whips up a beautiful cake, but his adventures while transporting the cake to the party wind up being the real gift for the story-loving birthday girl. Praising Karas's colored pencil and gouache illustrations for *Clever Jack Takes the Cake,* Engberg added that "Fleming writes with rhythmic repetition and delicious word choices that lend themselves perfectly to dramatic narration." "The creators of *Muncha! Muncha! Muncha!* celebrate storytelling with a sparkling specimen of that very thing," exclaimed a *Publishers Weekly* contributor, and in *School Library Journal* Heidi Estrin recommended Fleming's tale to story-hour organizers looking for an "entertaining adventure . . . packed with action."

Imogene's Last Stand, a picture book illustrated by Nancy Carpenter, focuses on a young girl who is fascinated by history. Imogene lives in New Hampshire, where old buildings and other relics of history can be found all around her town. When she learns that an old building in town is going to be torn down, she unsuccessfully petitions the mayor to preserve the building and make it a history museum. When the determined young girl discovers a letter dating from America's revolutionary era, she accomplishes her goal and also adds another layer to her own town's history. In *Booklist,* Ieva Bates recommended *Imogene's Last Stand* as "a jumping off place for some early elementary history lessons," and a *Kirkus Reviews* writer noted that Fleming's technique of including "famous quotes . . . add a layer of historical depth to the story." In *Booklist* Daniel Kraus wrote that the author's "sense of small-town space is impeccable" and predicted that her inclusion of "historical facts and quotes . . . are just the thing to get new Imogenes fired up."

Giselle Potter creates the whimsical art that pairs up with Fleming's story in the picture book **Gabriella's Song.** (Aladdin, 1997. Illustration copyright © 1997 by Giselle Potter. Reprinted with permission of Atheneum Books for Young Readers, an imprint of Simon & Schuster Children's Publishing Division.)

Turning once again to history, Fleming's award-winning picture book *The Hatmaker's Sign: A Story by Benjamin Franklin* retells a story first related by the eighteenth-century inventor and statesman, while *The Lincolns: A Scrapbook Look at Abraham and Mary* focuses on the private life of one of the best-known presidents of the United States. In *A Big Cheese for the White House: The True Tale of a Tremendous Cheddar* the author mines U.S. history again, this time coming up with a humorous tale based on an actual 1801 newspaper headline from Cheshire, Massachusetts in which a 1,235-pound wheel of cheese took a trip south to Washington, DC, as a gift for President Thomas Jefferson. Fleming gets creative with the life of one of the most famous women of the early twentieth century in *Our Eleanor: A Scrapbook Look at Eleanor Roosevelt's Remarkable Life* by creating a fictional memoir comprised of phonographs and other ephemera capturing the life of America's first lady. Noting that Roosevelt is the focus of several books for younger readers, *Booklist* critic John Peters ranked *Our Eleanor* as "something special," and fellow *Booklist* critic Jennifer Mattson deemed Fleming's biography an "intimate, unvarnished, and ultimately deeply moving portrait." A similar profile is presented in *The Lincolns,* which returns readers to the mid-nineteenth century and the president whose life was taken during the U.S. Civil War.

Another amazing career is profiled by Fleming in the illustrated biography *The Great and Only Barnum: The*

Tremendous, Stupendous Life of Showman P.T. Barnum, which follows the career of the man who founded the Barnum & Bailey Circus. As the pages turn, readers can experience the excitement felt by children of the mid-1800s as the circus came to town and they could see bearded ladies and the dwarf Tom Thumb, as well as exotic animals, tight-rope walkers, jugglers, clowns, and the famous showman himself. Illustrated by Ray Fenwick with images that are inspired by nineteenth-century poster and advertising art, the story also explores Barnum's life and describes the museum of oddities that he took on the road and ultimately transformed into the "Greatest Show on Earth." The man's darker side is also brought into focus, including his alcoholism, his questionable marriages, and his poor treatment of several of the individuals whose physical misfortunes attracted paying audiences. Praising *The Great and Only Barnum* as a "sweeping yet cohesive biography," Kraus added in *Booklist* that "Fleming's vivacious prose . . . and copious source notes" combine to produce "a full picture of one of the [forbears] . . . of modern celebrity." In his review for the *New York Time Book Review,* James Hynes described Fleming's subject as "a canny businessman who was just a little luckier, more energetic and more imaginative than his competitors," adding that her "lively and well-researched biography . . . takes an evenhanded approach" in a book that "manages to be both honest and fun." "Audiences will step right up to this illuminating and thorough portrait of an entertainment legend," predicted a *Publishers Weekly* critic.

In addition to picture books, Fleming has also written chapter books for upper-elementary-grade readers. In both *The Fabled Fourth Graders of Aesop Elementary School* and *The Fabled Fifth Graders of Aesop Elementary School* she combines well-known fables salted with word play into the saga of an unruly class of students, producing what a *Kirkus Reviews* critic dubbed "a winner." In *The Fabled Fourth Graders of Aesop Elementary School* readers meet a group of energetic children and their inventive teacher Mr. Jupiter. The antics of Calvin Tallywong, Amisha Spelwadi, Ashley Z., and Bernadette Braggadoccio continue through the following year and their antics play out in the pages of *The Fabled Fifth Graders of Aesop Elementary School.* In *School Library Journal* Amanda Raklovits described the first collection of elementary-grade adventures as "humorous and occasionally bizarre," adding that Fleming's stories "would make for interesting comparisons with the well-known animal fables." A *Publishers Weekly* critic noted of *The Fabled Fourth Graders of Aesop Elementary School* that "there's plenty to laugh at and even to ponder," and Abby Nolan wrote of the sequel in *Booklist* that it "won't disappoint fans" of Fleming's school stories.

In *Lowji Discovers America* Fleming introduces a nine-year-old boy who moves with his family from Bombay, India, to small-town Illinois. Living in a small apartment and with few friends during the summer before he starts school, Lowji decides to adopt a pet. Much to the surprise of his landlady, Mrs. Crisp, the boy's interpretation of "pet" is neither conventional nor singular, and soon apartment tenants are sharing space with a dog, cat, goats, and even a pig named Blossom. Full of information about East Indian culture as well as the Zoroastrian religion, *Lowji Discovers America* was praised by *School Library Journal* critic Lauralyn Persson as "a refreshingly light novel" that "opens a window to what may be an unfamiliar culture to many readers." In *Booklist* Engberg cited Fleming's "brisk, lively" prose and recommended the book as "a gentle, effective story about the loneliness and bewilderment" of a transplanted child.

"I remember the day I discovered the music and magic of words," Fleming once commented. "It was the day my second-grade teacher, Miss Johnson, held up a horn-shaped basket filled with papier-mâché pumpkins and asked the class to repeat the word 'cornucopia.' It sounded good. I said it again, and again, and I decided I loved that word. I loved its rhythm and cadence. I loved the way it felt on my tongue and fell on my ears. I skipped all the way home from school that day chanting 'Cornucopia! Cornucopia!' From then on, I really began listening to words—to the sounds they made, and the way they were used, and how they made me feel. I longed to put them together in ways that were beautiful, and yet told a story.

"Now, my family and close friends will tell you that I have always made up stories. My mother loves to tell of the time I regaled our next-door neighbor with tales of our family trip to Paris, France. So vivid were my descriptions of that romantic city that my neighbor believed every word I said. I can only imagine his chagrin when he learned I had never been beyond my home state of Indiana.

"I told many stories like this. My classmates heard the saga of my three-legged dog Tiger. My Sunday school teacher listened, wide-eyed, as I told the tale of the ghost in our attic. Lots of people heard my tall tales. Lots of people believed them.

"Technically, I suppose you could call this lying. Fortunately, I had parents who understood the difference between imagination and lies. They encouraged me to make up stories, but they strongly suggested that I not claim these stories as truth. Eventually, I took their advice.

"The result? My love of language and my need to tell a good story merged, and I became a writer. I filled notebook after notebook with my stories, poems, and plays. I couldn't stop the flow of words and ideas that rushed from my pencil, and I didn't try. Often, I arrived home from school, closed my bedroom door, and wrote for hours on end. When I wasn't writing, I was reading, and if something I read sparked my imagination, I would start writing all over again.

Fleming tells a fanciful story in* Clever Jack Takes the Cake, *and G. Brian Karas brings it to life in his colorful art. (Illustration copyright © 2010 by G. Brian Karas. Used by permission of Schwartz & Wade, an imprint of Random House Children's Books, a division of Random House, Inc.)

"I still have many of those notebooks today. I cherish them. They are a record of my writing life, from second grade to the present. In them I can see my struggle to tell a good and believable story. I can see my struggle to use musical language. I can't help but recognize that these are the same struggles I have as a writer today. They are also my goals. I want to tell you a good story. I want to tell it in a believable way. And I want to tell it with language that opens your ears to the music and magic of words."

Biographical and Critical Sources

PERIODICALS

Booklist, May 1, 1998, Helen Rosenberg, review of *Westward Ho, Carlotta!,* p. 1520; February 15, 1999, Stephanie Zvirin, review of *When Agnes Caws,* p. 95; November 1, 1999, Hazel Rochman, review of *A Big Cheese for the White House: The True Tale of a Tremendous Cheddar,* p. 538; October 15, 2001, Shelley Townsend-Hudson, review of *Who Invited You?,* p. 400; January 1, 2002, Gillian Engberg, review of *Muncha! Muncha! Muncha!,* p. 851; March 15, 2005, Gillian Engberg, review of *Lowji Discovers America,* p. 1292; August, 2005, Julie Cummins, review of *Sunny Boy!: The Life and Times of a Tortoise,* p. 2034; September 1, 2005, Jennifer Mattson, review of *Our Eleanor: A Scrapbook Look at Eleanor Roosevelt's Remarkable Life,* p. 108; December 15, 2006, Gillian Engberg, review of *Tippy-Tippy-Tippy, Hide!,* p. 51; July 1, 2007, Kathleen Isaacs, review of *The Fabled Fourth Graders of Aesop Elementary School,* p. 59; June 1, 2009, Daniel Kraus, review of *The Great and Only Barnum: The Tremendous, Stupendous Life of Showman P.T. Barnum,* p. 87; July 1, 2009, Daniel Kraus, review of *Imogene's Last Stand,* p. 66; January 1, 2010, Daniel Kraus, review of *Seven Hungry Babies,* p. 98; July 1, 2010, Gillian Engberg, review of *Clever Jack Takes the Cake,* p. 62; September 1, 2010, Abby Nolan, review of *The Fabled Fifth Graders of Aesop Elementary School,* p. 101.

Horn Book, March-April, 1998, Mary M. Burns, review of *The Hatmaker's Sign: A Story by Benjamin Franklin,* p. 212; March, 1999, Susan P. Bloom, review of *When Agnes Caws,* p. 188; September, 1999, Mary M. Burns, review of *A Big Cheese for the White House,* p. 594; November-December, 2008, Jonathan Hunt, review of *The Lincolns,* p. 722; September-October, 2009, Jonathan Hunt, review of *The Great and Only Barnum,* p. 581; November-December, 2009, Betty Carter, review of *Imogene's Last Stand,* p. 652.

Kirkus Reviews, September 1, 2005, review of *Our Eleanor,* p. 972; July 1, 2007, review of *The Fabled Fourth Graders of Aesop Elementary School;* September 1, 2008, review of *The Lincolns;* August 15, 1009, review of *The Great and Only Barnum;* September 1, 2009, review of *Imogene's Last Stand;* February 15, 2010, review of *Seven Hungry Babies.*

Publishers Weekly, May 25, 1998, review of *Westward Ho, Carlotta!,* p. 88; December 21, 1998, review of *When Agnes Caws,* p. 67; September 27, 1999, review of *A Big Cheese for the White House,* p. 105; October 1, 2001, review of *Who Invited You?,* p. 61; December 10, 2001, review of *Muncha! Muncha! Muncha!,* p. 69; September 19, 2005, review of *Our Eleanor,* p. 68; October 10, 2005, review of *Sunny Boy!,* p. 61; December 18, 2006, review of *Tippy-Tippy-Tippy, Hide!,* p. 62; August 13, 2007, review of *The Fabled Fourth Graders of Aesop Elementary School,* p. 67; October 5, 2009, Ieva Bates, review of *Imogene's Last Stand,* p. 90; July 19, 2010, review of *Clever Jack Takes the Cake,* p. 127; January 17, 2011, review of *Amelia Lost: The Life and Disappearance of Amelia Earhart,* p. 51.

New York Times Book Review, November 9, 2008, Andrew Holleran, review of *The Lincolns,* p. 26; December 6, 2009, James Hynes, review of *The Great and Only Barnum,* p. 48.

School Library Journal, April, 1998, Jack Hechtopf, review of *The Hatmaker's Sign,* p. 98; July, 1998, Steven Engelfried, review of *Westward Ho, Carlotta!,* p. 74; February, 1999, Luann Toth, review of *When Agnes Caws,* p. 84; August, 1999, Amy Lilien-Harper, review of *A Big Cheese for the White House,* p. 134; October, 2001, Linda Ludke, review of *Who Invited You?,* p. 114; February, 2002, Lisa Gangemi Kropp, review of *Muncha! Muncha! Muncha!,* p. 100; August, 2005, Rosalyn Pierini, review of *Sunny Boy!,* p. 94; October, 2005, Lauralyn Persson, review of *Lowji Discovers America,* p. 41; November, 2005, Andrew Medlar, review of *Our Eleanor,* p. 158; March, 2006, John Peters, review of *Our Eleanor,* p. 90; January, 2007, Martha Topol, review of *Tippy-Tippy-Tippy, Hide!,* p. 92; October, 2007, Amanda Raklovits, review of *The Fabled Fourth Graders of Aesop Elementary School,* p. 114; October, 2008, Janet S. Thompson, review of *The Lincolns,* p. 168; September, 2009, Mary Mueller, review of *The Great and Only Barnum,* p. 181; February, 2010, Marge Loch-Wouters, review of *Seven Hungry Babies,* p. 82; July, 2010, Heidi Estrin, review of *Clever Jack Takes the Cake,* p. 59.

ONLINE

Candace Fleming Home Page, http://www.candacefleming.com (January 15, 2010).

*   *   *

FOX, Louisa
See KROLL, Virginia L.

*   *   *

FRANCIS, Guy

Personal

Born in Provo, UT; married; wife's name Lorien; children: Calvin, Samantha, Madeline, Max. *Education:* Attended Brigham Young University. *Hobbies and other interests:* Model trains, flying remote-controlled airplanes, fixing old cars, camping, rock climbing.

Addresses

Home and office—Provo, UT. *Agent*—Shannon Associates, 630 9th Ave., Ste. 707, New York, NY 10036. *E-mail*—web@guyfrancis.com.

Career

Illustrator.

Member

Society of Children's Book Writers and Illustrators, Utah Children's Writers and Illustrators.

Illustrator

Pat Bagley, *Showdown in Slickrock,* Buckaroo Books (Carson City, NV), 1995.

Diane McAffee, *The Amazing Incredible Sulk,* Bookcraft (Salt Lake City, UT), 1998.

Diane McAffee, *Kaylee, Clean Your Room,* Bookcraft (Salt Lake City, UT), 1999.

Jackie Glassman, *The Cherry Pie,* Scholastic (New York, NY), 2001.

Margie Palatini, *Mary Had a Little Ham,* Hyperion Books for Children (New York, NY), 2003.

Dona Smith, *Wingin' It with the Wright Brothers,* Scholastic (New York, NY), 2003.

Dona Smith, *Cross-country with Lewis and Clark,* Scholastic (New York, NY), 2004.

Garen Eileen Thomas, *Santa's Kwanzaa,* Hyperion Books for Children (New York, NY), 2004.

Kelly DiPucchio, *Mrs. McBloom, Clean up Your Classroom!,* Hyperion Books For Children (New York, NY), 2005.

Margie Palatini, *Shelly,* Dutton Children's Books (New York, NY), 2006.

Joanne Ryder, *Dance by the Light of the Moon,* Hyperion Books for Children (New York, NY), 2007.

Phyllis J. Perry, *The Alien, the Giant, and Rocketman,* Mondo Publishing (New York, NY), 2007.

Elizabeth Rusch, *The Planet Hunter: How Astronomer Mike Brown's Search for the Tenth Planet Shook up the Solar System,* Rising Moon (Flagstaff, AZ), 2007, published as *The Planet Hunter: The Story behind What Happened to Pluto,* 2008.

(With Mike Wohnoutka) Tim Kehoe, *The Unusual Mind of Vincent Shadow,* Little, Brown (New York, NY), 2009.

Erin Soderberg, *Monkey See, Monkey Zoo,* Bloomsbury (New York, NY), 2010.

Jeff Corwin, *The Great Alaska Adventure!,* Puffin Books (New York, NY), 2010.

Chris Kurtz, *The Pup Who Cried Wolf,* Bloomsbury (New York, NY), 2010.

Tim Kehoe, *The Unusual Mind of Vincent Shadow: The Whizzer Wishbook,* Little, Brown (New York, NY), 2010.

Linda Phillips Teitel, *Angus MacMouse Brings down the House,* Bloomsbury (New York, NY), 2010.

"ADAM SHARP" SERIES BY GEORGE EDWARD STANLEY

Adam Sharp, the Spy Who Barked, Golden Books (New York, NY), 2002, published as *The Spy Who Barked,* Random House (New York, NY), 2003.

Adam Sharp, London Calling, Golden Books (New York, NY), 2002, published as *London Calling,* Random House (New York, NY), 2003.

Swimming with Sharks, Random House (New York, NY), 2003.

Operation Spy School, Random House (New York, NY), 2003.

Moose Master, Random House (New York, NY), 2004.

Code Word Kangaroo, Random House (New York, NY), 2004.

"GHOSTVILLE ELEMENTARY" SERIES BY MARCIA THORNTON JONES AND DEBBIE DADEY

Happy Boo-day to You!, Scholastic (New York, NY), 2004.

Ghosts Be Gone!, Scholastic (New York, NY), 2004.

Beware of the Blabbermouth!, Scholastic (New York, NY), 2004.

Class Trip to the Haunted House, Scholastic (New York, NY), 2005.

The Treasure Haunt, Scholastic (New York, NY), 2005.

Frights! Camera! Action!, Scholastic (New York, NY), 2005.

Frighting like Cats and Dogs, Scholastic (New York, NY), 2006.

Guys and Ghouls, Scholastic (New York, NY), 2006.

Red, White, and Boo!, Scholastic (New York, NY), 2007.

No Haunting Zone!, Scholastic (New York, NY), 2007.

Sidelights

An illustrator based in Utah, Guy Francis has provided the artwork for dozens of children's books, among them *Mary Had a Little Ham* by Margie Palatini, *Dance by the Light of the Moon* by Joanne Ryder, and *The Pup Who Cried Wolf* by Chris Kurtz. Francis is known for crafting energetic, cartoon-like illustrations that add an element of humor to the text. In addition to his literary endeavors, he does a variety of editorial and commercial work, as well as animation. "I am thrilled to be making a living doing what I love," Francis noted on his home page.

In *Mary Had a Little Ham* Palatini chronicles the story of Stanley Snoutowski, a multi-talented piglet who dreams of making it big on Broadway. Once he arrives in New York City, though, Stanley finds it difficult to land a gig, but with encouragement from his former teacher, Mary, he finally triumphs in a number of stage productions, including *Pigmalion* and *Hamlet.* "Francis's cheerfully goofy illustrations extend the jokes," a *Kirkus Reviews* critic noted. "Francis' artwork is a hoot," wrote *Booklist* critic Jennifer Mattson, and a contributor in *Publishers Weekly* maintained that the illustrator's depiction of "cute, anthropomorphic Stanley has plenty of, er, animal magnetism." Francis and Palatini also joined forces on *Shelly,* the tale of an introverted duckling who prefers to stay in his shell while his three high-powered sisters explore the world. "Francis' colorful, amusingly detailed illustrations of the animated bird characters extend the emotion and comedy" of the narrative, Gillian Engberg remarked in *Booklist.* Robin L. Gibson also praised Francis's pictures in *School Library Journal,* commenting that, "humorous, playful, and tender, they are a good match to the witty text."

Told in rhyming couplets, Garen Eileen Thomas's *Santa's Kwanzaa* focuses on the holiday celebrations of "Santa Kwaz," an African-American version of Kris Kringle. According to *Booklist* reviewer Terry Glover, "Francis' rich artwork puts a fine point on this cultural tale, right down to the kente-cloth-patterned endpapers." A teacher on the verge of retirement employs a student's clever plan to reduce clutter in *Mrs. McBloom, Clean up Your Classroom!* After fifty years at Knickerbocker Elementary, Mrs. McBloom has collected a mountain of supplies, books, and misplaced clothes, and now she desperately needs to clear space for her replacement. Young Georgia Peachpit has the perfect solution, one that not only eliminates the mess but also provides a poignant tribute to the beloved teacher. "The

comic pictures are packed with all kinds of objects," Hazel Rochman reported in *Booklist,* and *School Library Journal* reviewer Jane Barrer observed that "the wealth of strange objects to be discovered on every page will engage readers' interest."

Inspired by the nineteenth-century American song "Buffalo Gals," *Dance by the Light of the Moon* centers on a glamorous barnyard gala. "The cartoon illustrations playfully depict the gals and guys 'puttin' on the ritz' with visual puns," a contributor stated in *Kirkus Reviews,* and *School Library Journal* critic Kathleen Whalin also praised Francis's art, noting that his "moonlit landscapes are filled with animal characters that seem to leap from the pages." In *The Pup Who Cried Wolf* by Chris Kurtz, a feisty Chihuahua longs to join a wolf pack. It ventures from New York City to Yellowstone National Park, where it encounters a host of complications. According to *Booklist* contributor Todd Morning, Francis's pictures for *The Pup Who Cried Wolf* "extend the action and fun" of Kurtz's entertaining tale.

Biographical and Critical Sources

PERIODICALS

Booklist, December 15, 2003, Jennifer Mattson, review of *Mary Had a Little Ham,* p. 754; September 15, 2004, Terry Glover, review of *Santa's Kwanzaa,* p. 254; August, 2005, Hazel Rochman, review of *Mrs. McBloom, Clean up Your Classroom!,* p. 2038; February 1, 2006, Gillian Engberg, review of *Shelly,* p. 56; January 1, 2007, Shelle Rosenfeld, review of *Dance by the Light of the Moon,* p. 116; October 15, 2009, Ian Chipman, review of *The Unusual Mind of Vincent Shadow,* p. 65; May 15, 2010, Todd Morning, review of *The Pup Who Cried Wolf,* p. 42.

Kirkus Reviews, September 15, 2003, review of *Mary Had a Little Ham,* p. 1180; November 1, 2004, review of *Santa's Kwanzaa,* p. 1054; August 1, 2005, review of *Mrs. McBloom, Clean up Your Classroom!,* p. 846; December 15, 2005, review of *Shelly,* p. 1326; December 1, 2006, review of *Dance by the Light of the Moon,* p. 1226; October 1, 2009, review of *The Unusual Mind of Vincent Shadow.*

Publishers Weekly, October 6, 2003, review of *Mary Had a Little Ham,* p. 84; September 27, 2004, review of *Santa's Kwanzaa,* p. 61; February 13, 2006, review of *Shelly,* p. 89; November 2, 2009, review of *The Unusual Mind of Vincent Shadow,* p. 52.

School Library Journal, November, 2003, Ellen A. Greever, review of *Mary Had a Little Ham,* p. 112; September, 2005, Jane Barrer, review of *Mrs. McBloom, Clean up Your Classroom!,* p. 169; February, 2006, Robin L. Gibson, review of *Shelly,* p. 108; January, 2007, Kathleen Whalin, review of *Dance by the Light of the Moon,* p. 108; January, 2008, John Peters, review of *The Planet Hunter: The Story behind What Happened to Pluto,* p. 110; December,

Guy Francis's illustration projects include creating the art for Tim Kehoe's middle-grade novel The Unusual Mind of Vincent Shadow. (Little, Brown & Company, 2009. Copyright © 2009 by Vincent Shadow, Inc. Reproduced by permission.)

2009, Jeffrey Hastings, review of *The Unusual Mind of Vincent Shadow,* p. 122; June, 2010, Terrie Dorio, review of *Angus MacMouse Brings down the House,* p. 85.

ONLINE

Guy Francis Home Page, http://www.guyfrancis.com (January 21, 2011).
Guy Francis Web log, http://kactiguy.blogspot.com (January 21, 2011).
Shannon Associates Web site, http://www.shannon associates.com/ (January 21, 2011), "Guy Francis."
Utah Children's Writers and Illustrators Web site, http://www.ucwi.org/ (May, 2004), interview with Francis.*

* * *

FRAZEE, Marla 1958-

Personal

Born January 16, 1958, in Los Angeles, CA; daughter of Gerald W. (in business) and Nancy (a teacher) Frazee; married Tim Bradley (a freelance photographer), May 29, 1982; children: Graham, Reed, James. *Education:* Art Center College of Design, B.F.A., 1981.

Addresses

Home—Pasadena, CA. *Agent*—Steven Malk, Writer's House, 21 W. 26th St., New York, NY 10010. *E-mail*—Marla@marlafrazee.com.

Career

Illustrator and educator. Freelance illustrator, 1981—; commercial work includes designing team characters for National Football League, Happy Meal boxes for McDonald's, and toy design for Mattel, Milton Bradley, and Parker Brothers. Art Center College of Design, Pasadena, CA, teacher of children's book illustration, beginning 1990.

Member

Society of Children's Book Writers and Illustrators, Children's Literature Council of Southern California.

Awards, Honors

Notable Book selection, American Library Association (ALA), 1995, for *That Kookoory!* by Margaret Walden Froehlich; Pick of the Lists selection, American Booksellers Association, 1997, for *The Seven Silly Eaters* by Mary Ann Hoberman, 1998, for *On the Morn of Mayfest* by Erica Silverman, and 2000, for *Harriet, You'll Drive Me Wild!* by Mem Fox; Excellence in Illustration Award, Southern California Council on Literature for Children and Young People, 1998, for *The Seven Silly Eaters; Horn Book* Fanfare citation, and ALA Notable

Marla Frazee (Reproduced by permission.)

Book selection, both 1999, both for *Hush, Little Baby,* and 2001, for *Everywhere Babies* by Susan Meyers; Parents' Choice Award, 2000, for *Harriet, You'll Drive Me Wild!;* Best Book of the Year citation, *School Library Journal,* Reading Magic Award, *Parenting* magazine, and Best Children's Books Award, *Child* magazine, all for *Everywhere Babies;* Borders' Original Voices Award in picture-book category, Golden Kite Award, Society of Children's Book Writers and Illustrators, and Parents' Choice Award, all 2002, all for *Mrs. Biddlebox* by Linda Smith; 100 Books for Reading and Sharing selection, New York Public Library, ALA Notable Book selection, and Parent's Choice Gold Award, all 2003, all for *Roller Coaster;* 100 Books for Reading and Sharing selection, and Quill Award nominee, both 2005, both for *New Baby Train* by Woody Guthrie; International Reading Association/Children's Book Council Children's Choice selection, and Oppenheim Toy Portfolio Platinum Award, both 2006, both for *Santa Claus;* Parent's Choice Silver Honor, and New York Book Show award, 2007, both for *Walk On!;* Josette Frank Award, Bank Street College of Education Book Committee, ALA Notable Book selection, Quill Book Award finalist, and *Boston Globe/Horn Book* Honor Book designation, all 2007, all for *Clementine* by Sara Pennypacker; *Boston Globe/Horn Book* Honor Book designation, and ABC Best Book for Children selection, both 2008, and Caldecott Honor Book designation, 2009, all for *A Couple of Boys Have the Best Week Ever;* Caldecott Honor Book designation, 2010, for *All the World* by Liz Garton Scanlon.

Writings

SELF-ILLUSTRATED

(Adapter) *Hush Little Baby: A Folksong with Pictures,* Browndeer Press (San Diego, CA), 1999.
Roller Coaster, Harcourt (San Diego, CA), 2003.
Santa Claus: The World's Number-One Toy Expert, Harcourt (Orlando, FL), 2005.
(With others) *Why Did the Chicken Cross the Road?,* Dial Books (New York, NY), 2006.
Walk On!: A Guide for Babies of All Ages, Harcourt (Orlando, FL), 2006.
Hush, Little Baby: A Folk Song with Pictures, Harcourt (Orlando, FL), 2007.
A Couple of Boys Have the Best Week Ever, Harcourt (Orlando, FL), 2008.
The Boss Baby, Beach Lane Books (New York, NY), 2011.

ILLUSTRATOR

Sue Alexander, *World Famous Muriel and the Magic Mystery,* Crowell (New York, NY), 1990.
Margaret Walden Froehlich, *That Kookoory!,* Browndeer Press (San Diego, CA), 1995.
Mary Ann Hoberman, *The Seven Silly Eaters,* Browndeer Press (San Diego, CA), 1997.
Erica Silverman, *On the Morn of Mayfest,* Simon & Schuster (New York, NY), 1998.
Mem Fox, *Harriet, You'll Drive Me Wild!,* Harcourt (San Diego, CA), 2000.
Susan Meyers, *Everywhere Babies,* Harcourt (San Diego, CA), 2001.
Linda Smith, *Mrs. Biddlebox,* HarperCollins (New York, NY), 2002.
Woody Guthrie, *New Baby Train,* Little, Brown (Boston, MA), 2004.
Liz Garton Scanlon, *All the World,* Beach Lane Books (New York, NY), 2009.

ILLUSTRATOR; "CLEMENTINE" CHAPTER-BOOK SERIES BY SARA PENNYPACKER

Clementine, Hyperion (New York, NY), 2006.
The Talented Clementine, Hyperion Books (New York, NY), 2007.
Clementine's Letter, Hyperion Books for Children (New York, NY), 2008.
Clementine, Friend of the Week, Disney-Hyperion Books (New York, NY), 2010.

Sidelights

A talented artist who also shares her knowledge as a teacher, Marla Frazee has provided the illustrations for a number of award-winning books for children, in addition to writing self-illustrated stories such as *Roller Coaster, Santa Claus: The World's Number-One Toy Expert, Walk On!: A Guide for Babies of All Ages, A Couple of Boys Have the Best Week Ever,* and *The Boss*

Baby. Noting Frazee's ability to tell visual stories, Leonard S. Marcus also touched upon another factor that distinguishes the illustrator's success in his *Horn Book* appraisal of her career. "What a reader first notices about one of her books is how well Frazee draws," Marcus noted. In an age where digital technology proliferates, "not all illustration students still believe that learning to draw even matters, let alone that drawing remains a foundational skill," he added "Frazee's books make the case, as eloquently as any being published today, that practiced, inspired draftsmanship has as much to communicate as ever."

In 2009 Frazee was awarded one of the highest commendations in her field when her artwork for *A Couple of Boys Have the Best Week Ever* earned a Caldecott Honor Book designation; a second Honor designation came a year later acknowledging her illustrations for Liz Garton Scanlon's *All the World,* a picture book that moves young readers from their everyday world to considerations of the cosmos. Frazee's watercolor-and-pencil art for Scanlon's book was described by a *Publishers Weekly* contributor as "blithesome," while in *School Library Journal* Maryann H. Owen asserted that the "charming illustrations and lyrical rhyming couplets" in *All the World* "speak volumes in celebration of the world and humankind."

Illustrating children's books was a childhood career goal," Frazee once told *SATA.* "I have wanted to be a children's book illustrator for a very long time," and "a host of crayoned and stapled childhood efforts attest to that fact. I was first 'published' in the third grade, when my best friend . . . wrote a story called 'The Friendship Circle' and I illustrated it. It won an award in a state competition, so we were asked to make a duplicate copy for our elementary school library. It was made out of construction paper and held together with brass fasteners, but it sat in the library for years. I remember sneaking peeks at the shelf as our class filed in for library time and seeing it keeping company with *real* books. I felt as if I'd arrived!"

Other inspirations included *Where the Wild Things Are* by Maurice Sendak, and Robert McCloskey's self-illustrated *Blueberries for Sal.* "I spent countless hours studying those wonderful endpapers of Sal and her mother canning blueberries in their cozy kitchen. I wondered how an illustrator could draw a room that somehow included me, the viewer. I don't remember talking to anyone about these issues, but my fifth-grade teacher, Mrs. Holcomb, made some predictions about what some of her students would grow up to be. She said I would illustrate children's books, painting outdoors in a sunlit meadow. So far, no meadow."

After much training and effort, Frazee was given the chance to illustrate her first picture book, Sue Alexander's *World Famous Muriel and the Magic Mystery.* Published in 1990, the book was the third in Alexander's series about the clever junior detective, certainly no easy shoes for an illustrator to step into. Yet Bessie Egan, writing in *School Library Journal,* praised the art as "full of vitality and humorous detail."

Frazee's pen-and-ink drawings for *That Kookoory!* by Margaret Walden Froehlich garnered rave reviews. According to critics, their vintage feel complements Froehlich's tale of an indomitable rooster that is so excited by the local fair that he wakens before his barn friends and sets off alone, only to be stalked on the road by a hungry weasel. A *Publishers Weekly* contributor praised the way Frazee conveys the shifts of time over the course of Kookoory's long and event-filled day, writing that the illustrator's "bucolic scenes" evoke "the rural America of a more relaxed era." Ann A. Flowers, writing for *Horn Book,* termed *That Kookoory!* "a gentle and affectionate story with illustrations to match."

Another book with an old-fashioned air is *Mrs. Biddlebox* by Linda Smith. The title character wakes up on the wrong side of the bed, with a growling stomach and looking out on a dreary, gray day. Instead of moping about, she sweeps the fog and gloom into a bowl, mixes it with some sun, and bakes up a delicious cake. "Frazee depicts the feisty little lady's energetic transformation from beleaguered grouch to jubilant cook with all the vigor it deserves," Joanna Rudge Long concluded of the work in *Horn Book.*

Frazee, a mother of three herself, tackles every parent's biggest dinnertime nightmare in her illustrations for Mary Ann Hoberman's *The Seven Silly Eaters.* As she once admitted to *SATA,* the story's nine characters "were inspired by my own children, nieces, nephews, and neighbors—each one a very specific person, with a very specific set of quirks and endearments. . . . I built the Peters' family home out of foamcore, so that I knew the floor plan as well as I do the house I live in. Anything I can do to make the book come alive for me, in the most tangible sense, will make it that much more believable to my readers." In Hoberman's humorous tale, the Peters family membership demands that their harried, cellist mother prepare a separate dish for each of them. As the family grows larger, the woman grows more frantic and her days more arduous. "The limber lines and cartoon-like animation . . . handily match the energy

Frazee's illustrations add energy and humor to Erica Silverman's picture book **On the Morning of Mayfest.** (Illustration copyright © 1998 Marla Frazee. Reprinted with the permission of Simon & Schuster Books for Young Readers, an imprint of Simon & Schuster Children's Publishing Division.)

and wit of the text's quatrain couplets," noted a *Publishers Weekly* reviewer of the work. Several critics also praised the inviting and cheerily chaotic household Frazee creates in *The Seven Silly Eaters;* as *New York Times Book Review* contributor Jon Agee commented, the illustrator's "busy, animated pictures cleverly elaborate the story's growing disorder."

Another frazzled mother is the star of *Harriet, You'll Drive Me Wild!* by Mem Fox. Preschooler Harriet is always making messes, even though she does not mean to be difficult and is always sorry. Harriet's mother does not mean to get angry and yell when Harriet is naughty, and when she is pushed over the edge after Harriet rips open her feather pillow at naptime, the woman quickly apologizes too. "Extending the text," Kate McClelland wrote in *School Library Journal,* are Frazee's "expressive illustrations done in pencil and transparent drawing inks." These "handsome domestic vignettes" are "realistic and reassuring," wrote a *Publishers Weekly* reviewer.

Among Frazee's traditional-themed illustration projects is *New Baby Train,* a Woody Guthrie folksong-turned-picture book. In the tale, a guitar-strumming narrator hops aboard a crowded train and helps deliver infants to loving families. "As a tribute to Guthrie's role as the Okie balladeer, Frazee conjures a romanticized Dust Bowl-era setting," noted a contributor in *Publishers Weekly,* and *Horn Book* reviewer Martha V. Parravano applauded the work's "gouache illustrations of a flat, sere landscape reinforced by speckled-brown-paper backgrounds and endpapers that look like corrugated cardboard."

Frazee's collaboration with author Sara Pennypacker on the "Clementine" chapter books has also attracted positive reviews. In series opener *Clementine* readers meet the titular kindhearted but often misunderstood third grader. Here she earns a scolding from her teacher after becoming distracted during the Pledge of Allegiance by the janitor's romantic rendezvous with the lunch lady. Clementine then earns the ire of several adults when she creates a new hair style for her best friend using plastic scissors and permanent markers. The rambunctious protagonist also vies for a role in the school talent show in *The Talented Clementine,* while in *Clementine's Letter* problems arise when the girl's third-grade teacher leaves for a week of training and the substitute changes the classroom rules.

"Frazee's abundant pen-and-ink illustrations bounce along the pages with the same energy as the story," remarked *Horn Book* reviewer Maeve Visser Knoth in a review of *Clementine,* and in *Booklist* Carolyn Phelan stated that the artist "capture[s] every nuance of the characters' emotions, from bemusement to anger to dejection." "Frazee's polished, warm-spirited line drawings" for *The Talented Clementine* reflect "the endearing idiosyncrasies of its heroine," according to *Booklist* critic Jennifer Mattson. Describing the "vibrant spirit"

Frazee's line drawings, with their good-natured humor, say more than her simple text in the picture-book **Walk On!** (Copyright © 2006 by Marla Frazee. Reprinted by permission of Harcourt, Inc. This material may not be reproduced in any form or by any means without the prior written permission of the publisher.)

of Pennypacker's young character, Terrie Dorio concluded in her *School Library Journal* review of *Clementine's Letter* that "Frazee's pen-and-ink drawings perfectly capture Clementine's personality and her world."

"The most rewarding aspect of my work [as a book illustrator] is telling stories with my pictures," Frazee once explained to *SATA.* "Often, the story I'm telling in the illustrations is different from the story that is being told in the words. Of course, the word-story and the picture-story should work together to create a seamless whole. That is the unique challenge of the picture book, and the reason it gives me such pleasure to illustrate them.

"Creating the pictures for my books generally takes me a year. I usually start by visualizing the characters, because once I know who my characters are, I can then imagine where they live and how they act. As I'm defining the characters and the setting, I am trying to visualize the entire book as an object. What size should it be? Is it horizontal or vertical? At what point in the text will the page turns be? Where is the type and where is the image? I work out the answers to these questions by doing tiny thumbnail sketches of the entire book on one piece of paper. Sometimes I work on thumbnail sketches for months."

Frazee's work visualizing a text is made easier when she illustrates her own stories. In *Roller Coaster,* for ex-

Frazee's illustration projects include creating artwork for Liz Garton Scanlon's picture book **All the World.** (Illustration copyright © 2009 by Marla Frazee. Reprinted with the permission of Beach Lane Books, an imprint of Simon & Schuster Children's Publishing Division.)

ample, she follows a young girl as she nervously stands in line to go on her first ever ride on the big roller coaster along with scores of other soon-to-be riders. Frazee captures the heart of the book—the nearly wordless spreads depicting the speeding roller coaster and the reactions of each rider—"with consummate skill," according to a *Kirkus Reviews* contributor. Humor comes from the unexpected expressions on various riders' faces at pivotal points in the ride—a little old lady throws her hands up in the air in joy, for example, while behind her two strapping young men grip their car with white knuckles. The many faces provide "a marvelous showcase for Frazee's expressive watercolors," commented a *Publishers Weekly* critic.

Frazee tackles a most imposing subject in *Santa Claus,* another self-illustrated work. "Initially, I was intimidated by the idea of a Santa book," the artist admitted on the Harcourt Trade Publishers Web site. "So many stories have been told about Santa—his workshop, the elves, the reindeer, the sleigh, and all the distracting trappings of the North Pole. Instead, I wanted to focus

on how hard Santa's job is. Can you imagine running that entire operation?" Frazee's Santa, adorned in red high-top sneakers and patterned boxer shorts, works tirelessly yet gleefully, whether he is doing research on his computer or testing the bounciness of pogo sticks. *Horn Book* reviewer Bridget T. McCaffrey complimented Frazee's "effortlessly clever, detailed illustrations," and *Booklist* critic Gillian Engberg wrote that the author/illustrator creates "a strong sense of motion in her winsome scenes."

Inspired by her own grown son's preparations to leave home for college, Frazee offers encouraging advice to infants ready to take their first steps in the self-illustrated instructional manual *Walk On!: A Guide for Babies of All Age.* The infant star of *The Boss Baby* needs no instructions or encouragement, however: this youngster takes charge of everyone in the family from day one. Filled with cartoon illustrations inspired by mid-twentieth-century art, Frazee's story for *The Boss Baby* casts a humourous light on a household where a clever baby's earsplitting demands for food, attention, and other necessities give way to verbal cuteness as he learns new ways to control the family. A critic in *Publishers Weekly* described *Walk On!* as "a hilarious how-to" that "is as handsome as it is funny, with page after page of elegantly drafted spot illustrations," while another reviewer for the same periodical recommended *The Boss Baby* as "the perfect pick-me-up for both older siblings and bleary-eyed new parents."

Like *The Boss Baby, A Couple of Boys Have the Best Week Ever* showcases Frazee's arch humor by featuring "another riotous story that plays deadpan words off of sly, subversive pictures," according to Engberg. While visiting Eamon's grandparents in Malibu, best friends James and Eamon attend a local day camp where they are introduced to the flora and fauna of the state's coastal regions. While the educational opportunities that Frazee recounts in the book's text appear to be many, her cartoon illustrations tell a different story: from the perspective of the two boys the vacation's stand-outs include watching unrestricted amounts of television and playing video games, building tents out of mattresses and bedding, eating banana waffles and Hawaiian food, and walking around with stylish sunglasses. The story was inspired by the author's own son James and his good friend, and has its roots in a "Thank You" card created for Eamon's real-life grandparents that was designed as a book and decorated with the help of the two boys. Engberg recommended *A Couple of Boys Have the Best Week Ever* for capturing "the close friendship of two boys," and Blair Christolon observed in *School Library Journal* that the book's "artful illustrations" allow "readers [to] catch glimpses of just how savvy and creative these kids can be." A *Publishers Weekly* contributor cited Frazee's focus on "casual extended-family affection, with a knowing wink at the friends' dismissal of their elders' best-laid plans." Together with her "deadpan text," the author/illustrator's "hilarious round-headed cartoons romp across the page in snort-inducing counterpoint," wrote a *Kirkus Reviews* writer, and in *Horn Book* Kitty Flynn maintained that the "energetic illustrations and sound-bite speech balloons provide a boys'-eye view" of what many young readers will agree IS the perfect kid vacation.

Frazee continues to find her work for children to be both challenging and rewarding. "The picture book audience is often pre-literate, so they 'read' the pictures as the words are being read to them," Frazee once explained to *SATA*. "Consequently, these young children notice every detail, follow every sequential action, pick up on every clue, and will carefully go back into the book after it has been read and find things they may have missed the first, second, or third time around. There isn't anything I've ever put into a book that a child hasn't, at one time or another, noticed. I can't say the same for adults. It is a rare grown-up that catches anything but the broad action. Also, there isn't any guessing when it comes to how much or if a child likes a given book. If a book bores them, they will get up and find something else to do. And if it's a book they like, they will hold onto it for dear life. When children's book authors and illustrators visit classrooms and bookstores, they are often the recipient of real big hugs. These are hugs of thanks, really, for the gift of a story.

"It is wonderful to work for an audience of children. I hope I am lucky enough to be a children's book illustrator for a very long time."

Biographical and Critical Sources

PERIODICALS

Booklist, April 15, 1995, Mary Harris Veeder, review of *That Kookoory!,* p. 1505; March 1, 1997, Hazel Rochman, review of *The Seven Silly Eaters,* p. 1172; May 15, 1998, Kay Weisman, review of *On the Moon of Mayfest,* p. 1633; March 1, 2000, Hazel Rochman, review of *Harriet, You'll Drive Me Wild!,* p. 1250; November 15, 2002, GraceAnne A. DeCandido, review of *Mrs. Biddlebox,* p. 612; November 1, 2005, Gillian Engberg, review of *Santa Claus: The World's Number-One Toy Expert,* p. 40; April 1, 2006, Jennifer Mattson, review of *Walk On!: A Guide for Babies of All Ages,* p. 45; October 15, 2006, Carolyn Phelan, review of *Clementine,* p. 55; March 15, 2007, Jennifer Mattson, review of *The Talented Clementine,* p. 54; March 1, 2008, Gillian Engberg, review of *A Couple of Boys Have the Best Week Ever,* p. 72; April 1, 2008, Ilene Cooper, review of *Clementine's Letter,* p. 44; July 1, 2009, Daniel Kraus, review of *All the World,* p. 64.

Bulletin of the Center for Children's Books, March, 2008, review of *A Couple of Boys Have the Best Week Ever,* p. 279; October, 2009, Elizabeth Bush, review of *All the World,* p. 81; September, 2010, Deborah Stevenson, review of *The Boss Baby,* p. 17.

Horn Book, July-August, 1995, Ann A. Flowers, review of *That Kookoory!,* p. 449; May-June, 1997, Ann A. Flowers, review of *The Seven Silly Eaters,* p. 308; November, 1999, Martha V. Parravano, review of *Hush, Little Baby,* p. 752; March, 2000, review of *Harriet, You'll Drive Me Wild!,* p. 184; May, 2001, review of *Everywhere Babies,* p. 312; November-December, 2002, Joanna Rudge Long, review of *Mrs. Biddlebox,* pp. 739-740; May-June, 2003, Christine M. Heppermann, review of *Roller Coaster,* pp. 328-329; September-October, 2004, Martha V. Parravano, review of *New Baby Train,* p. 566; November-December, 2005, Bridget T. McCaffrey, review of *Santa Claus,* p. 693; May-June, 2006, Jennifer M. Brabander, review of *Walk On!,* p. 295; January-February, 2007, Maeve Visser Knoth, review of *Clementine,* p. 71; May-June, 2007, Robin Smith, review of *The Talented Clementine,* p. 287; January-February, 2008, Julie Roach, review of *Clementine,* p. 26; March-April, 2008, Kitty Flynn, review of *A Couple of Boys Have the Best Week Ever,* p. 202; July-August, 2008, Susan Dove Lempke, review of *Clementine's*

Letter, p. 455; January-February, 2009, Lolly Robinson, review of *A Couple of Boys Have the Best Week Ever,* p. 14; September-October, 2009, Jennifer M. Brabander, review of *All the World,* p. 546; July-August, 2010, Leonard S. Marcus, "Something Old, Something New," p. 140.

Kirkus Reviews, August 1, 2002, review of *Mrs. Biddlebox,* p. 1144; May 1, 2003, review of *Roller Coaster,* p. 676; November 1, 2005, review of *Santa Claus,* p. 1193; July 15, 2006, review of *Clementine,* p. 728; March 1, 2007, review of *The Talented Clementine,* p. 230; February 1, 2008, review of *A Couple of Boys Have the Best Week Ever;* March 15, 2008, review of *Clementine's Letter;* August 15, 2009, review of *All the World.*

Newsweek, December 1, 1997, Malcolm Jones, Jr., review of *The Seven Silly Eaters,* p. 78.

New York Times Book Review, October 22, 1995, Jane Langton, review of *That Kookoory!,* p. 41; July 6, 1997, Jon Agee, review of *The Seven Silly Eaters,* p. 16; August 10, 2003, Jeanne B. Pinder, review of *Roller Coaster,* p. 18; November 8, 2009, Andrew Bast, review of *All the World,* p. 19.

Publishers Weekly, April 3, 1995, review of *That Kookoory!,* p. 62; February 3, 1997, review of *The Seven Silly Eaters,* p. 106; May 18, 1998, review of *On the Morn of Mayfest,* p. 78; August 30, 1999, review of *Hush, Little Baby,* p. 82; March 20, 2000, review of *Harriet, You'll Drive Me Wild!,* p. 91; September 4, 2000, review of *The Seven Silly Eaters,* p. 110; March 19, 2001, review of *Everywhere Babies,* p. 98; July 15, 2002, review of *Mrs. Biddlebox,* p. 73; April 21, 2003, review of *Roller Coaster,* p. 61; June 9, 2003, review of *Harriet, You'll Drive Me Wild!,* p. 54; September 8, 2003, review of *Hush, Little Baby,* p. 79; August 2, 2004, review of *New Baby Train,* p. 69; February 6, 2006, review of *Walk On!,* p. 68; February 18, 2008, review of *A Couple of Boys Have the*

Best Week Ever, p. 153; August 24, 2009, review of *All the World,* p. 59; July 5, 2010, review of *The Boss Baby,* p. 41.

School Library Journal, July, 1990, Bessie Egan, review of *World Famous Muriel and the Magic Mystery,* p. 55; May, 1995, Martha Topol, review of *That Kookoory!,* p. 84; June, 1998, Carol Ann Wilson, review of *On the Morn of Mayfest,* p. 122; October, 1999, Ginny Gustin, review of *Hush, Little Baby,* p. 138; April, 2000, Kate McClelland, review of *Harriet, You'll Drive Me Wild!,* p. 104; October, 2002, Mary Ann Carcich, review of *Mrs. Biddlebox,* p. 132; July, 2003, Shelley B. Sutherland, review of *Roller Coaster,* p. 96; October, 2004, Jane Marino, review of *New Baby Train,* p. 142; October, 2006, Cheryl Ashton, review of *Clementine,* p. 123, and Carolyn Janssen, review of *Why Did the Chicken Cross the Road?,* p. 132; April, 2007, Mary Jean Smith, review of *The Talented Clementine,* p. 114; March, 2008, Blair Christolon, review of *A Couple of Boys Have the Best Week Ever,* p. 162; July, 2008, Terrie Dorio, review of *Clementine's Letter,* p. 79; August, 2009, Maryann H. Owen, review of *All the World,* p. 92.

ONLINE

California Readers Web site, http://www.californiareaders. org/ (February 1, 2008), Ann Stalcup, "Meet Marla Frazee."

Cynsations Web site, http://cynthialeitichsmith.blogspot. com/ (September 20, 2007), Cynthia Leitich Smith, interview with Frazee.

Harcourt Trade Publishers Web site, http://www.harcourt books.com/ (February 1, 2008), interview with Frazee.

Marla Frazee Home Page, http://www.marlafrazee.com (January 11, 2011).

G

GIBSON, Marley 1966-
(Kate Harmon)

Personal

Born 1966, in Boston, MA; partner of Patrick Burns. *Education:* University of Alabama, B.A. *Hobbies and other interests:* Cooking, writing, listening to music, SCUBA diving, travel.

Addresses

Home—Boston, MA. *Agent*—Deidre Knight, Knight Agency, 570 East Ave., Madison, GA 30650; deidre. knightknightagency.net. *E-mail*—marley@excite-lite. com.

Career

Author and paranormal investigator. U.S. Congressional liaison in Washington, DC, and Austin, TX, until 1993; meeting planner and marketing-events coordinator in medical, higher education, financial, and technology sectors, Boston, MA; writer, 2001—; paranormal investigator, 2007—. Television appearances include *My Ghost Story,* Biography Channel.

Member

Meeting Planners International, Romance Writers of America, Society of Children's Books Writers and Illustrators, Chick Lit Writers of America (founder).

Writings

(With Cecil Murphey) *Christmas Miracles,* St. Martin's Press (New York, NY), 2009.
(With Patrick Burns and Dave Schrader) *The Other Side: A Teen's Guide to Ghost Hunting and the Paranormal,* Houghton Mifflin Harcourt (Boston, MA), 2009.

"GHOST HUNTRESS" SERIES

The Awakening, Houghton Mifflin Harcourt (Boston, MA), 2009.
The Guidance, Graphia (Boston, MA), 2009.

The Reason, Houghton Mifflin Harcourt (Boston, MA), 2010.
The Counseling, Graphia (Boston, MA), 2010.

"SORORITY 101" SERIES

(As Kate Harmon) *The Formal,* Speak (New York, NY), 2008.
(As Kate Harmon) *The New Sisters,* Speak (New York, NY), 2008.
(As Kate Harmon) *Zeta or Omega!,* Speak (New York, NY), 2008.

Sidelights

In *The Awakening* and other works in her popular "Ghost Huntress" series of young-adult novels, Boston-based author Marley Gibson depicts the adventures of a team of paranormal investigators led by high school student Kendall Moorehead, a teen with psychic abilities. Interestingly, Gibson shares a passion for ghost hunting with her fictional protagonists, having investigated numerous sites across the United States, including the Sprague Mansion, a former governor's residence in Cranston, Rhode Island, and the Stanley Hotel in Estes Park, Colorado, the last which inspired Stephen King's horror novel *The Shining.* Discussing the origins of the series on her home page, Gibson recalled: "I was at the New England Romance Writers Conference and went to a session on 'Ghost Hunting 101' by the New England Ghost Project. They showed evidence from their ghost hunts and played sound files they'd recorded. It totally blew me away. I had no idea people went ghost hunting. Sitting right there, the whole story of *The Awakening* came to me like a movie and I knew I had to write about teenaged ghost hunters."

Gibson began creating stories as a young child with encouragement from her grandmother, who was herself an author. "She said that our imaginations could take us to far away worlds and we could be anyone we wanted to be," the author recalled on her home page. A voracious reader, she discovered romance novels at the age of twelve, devouring the works of Doreen Owens Malik and Elaine Harper and even penning a fifty-page story of her own. Gibson excelled in her English classes at school, and she eventually earned a bachelor's degree in communications from the University of Alabama. After working for her parents' congressman in Washington, DC, and another congressman in Texas, Gibson moved to Boston, Massachusetts, where she began a career as a meeting planner and marketing-events coordinator. Writing has always been essential to Gibson's professional life; she noted on her home page that "in my first job, I was writing press releases, constituent letters, and then later marketing pieces, collaterals, Web sites, advertisements, newsletters and client mailings. Grammar and I have been good friends for a while."

In 2001 Gibson decided that a career change was in order. After trying her hand at romance novels and releasing a number of young-adult works under the pseudonym Kate Harper, she began the "Ghost Huntress" series. In *The Awakening* Gibson introduces Kendall, a sixteen year old who, after moving to a small Georgia town, discovers that she has the ability to communicate with "trapped" spirits. Enlisting the help of some new friends, Kendall attempts to save her father from a malicious ghost inhabiting his workplace. Gibson "manages to maintain a realistic feel" in the novel, observed

a *Publishers Weekly* critic, and *The Awakening* "reads like a good episode of your favorite ghost-hunting show."

Kendall and her team of ghost hunters return in *The Guidance,* in which a catty cheerleader who claims to be telepathic finds herself possessed by the vengeful spirit of a U.S. Civil War soldier. *School Library Journal* contributor Jake Pettit applauded the "thrilling story," predicting that "teens will love this one." Kendall has a premonition of her own death and looks into the strange goings-on at her town's mayoral mansion in *The Reason,* "a wild ride on the paranormal train," according to Amanda Moss Struckmeyer in *School Library Journal.*

In addition to writing fiction, Gibson has also coauthored the nonfiction work *The Other Side: A Teen's Guide to Ghost Hunting and the Paranormal.* Gibson, along with Patrick Burns and Dave Schrader, offers helpful advice to budding paranormal investigators, placing a strong emphasis on preparation and safety. The information "is presented in a chatty style," wrote a *Kirkus Reviews* critic, and in *School Library Journal* Misti Tidman similarly observed that the "authors take a light, conversational tone even when discussing technical aspects of ghost hunting."

Biographical and Critical Sources

PERIODICALS

Booklist, May 15, 2009, review of *The Awakening,* p. 48; September 1, 2009, review of *The Guidance,* p. 86.
Kirkus Reviews, August 15, 2009, review of *The Other Side: A Teen's Guide to Ghost Hunting and the Paranormal.*
School Library Journal, June, 2009, Misti Tidman, review of *The Awakening,* p. 124; November, 2009, Jake Pettit, review of *The Guidance,* p. 106; March, 2010, Misti Tidman, review of *The Other Side,* p. 176; July, 2010, Amanda Moss Struckmeyer, review of *The Reason,* p. 88.

ONLINE

Marley Gibson Home Page, http://marleygibson.com (February 1, 2011).
Young Adult Books Central Web site, http://www.yabookscentral.com/ (February 1, 2011), Myra McEntire, interview with Gibson.*

*   *   *

GLASER, Linda

Personal

Born May 10, in NY; married; children: daughters.

Addresses

Home—Duluth, MN. *E-mail*—lglaser@cpinternet.com.

Cover of Marley Gibson's coauthored ghost-hunting guidebook The Other Side, *which mixes fun with practical advice.* (Cover photos copyright © 2009 by VEER. Reproduced by permission of Houghton Mifflin Harcourt Publishing Company.)

Career

Author and educator. Writing teacher and consultant.

Member

Society of Children's Book Writers and Illustrators, Children's Literature Network.

Awards, Honors

Outstanding Science Trade Book designation, National Science Teachers Association/Children's Book Council (NSTA/CBC), 1992, for *Wonderful Worms*, 1998, for *Spectacular Spiders*, 2003, for *Brilliant Bees;* Notable Book selection, American Jewish Library, and Book of the Year selection, *Smithsonian* magazine, both 1997, both for *The Borrowed Hanukkah Latkes;* Neumann College Outstanding Merit Award, and Outstanding Science Trade Book designation, NSTA/CBC, both for *Our Big Home;* Oppenheim Toy Portfolio Gold Seal Award, and Sydney Taylor Notable Book selection, Association of Jewish Libraries, both 2004, both for *Mrs. Greenberg's Messy Hanukkah;* Best Children's Book of the Year selection, Bank Street College of Education, Sydney Taylor Notable Book designation, Minnesota Book Award finalist, and Jeannette Fair Award, all 2005, all for *Bridge to America;* Best Children's Book of the Year selection, Bank Street College of Education, 2006, for *Hello, Squirrels!;* Sydney Taylor Honor Book designation, Oppenheim Toy Portfolio Gold Seal Award, and Minnesota Book Award finalist, all 2010, all for *Emma's Poem;* Best of the Best selection, Chicago Public Library, and International Honor Book designation, Society of School Librarians, both 2010, both for *Garbage Helps Our Garden Grow.*

Writings

Keep Your Socks on, Albert!, illustrated by Sally G. Ward, Dutton Children's Books (New York, NY), 1992.

Wonderful Worms, illustrated by Linda Krupinski, Millbrook Press (Brookfield, CT), 1992.

Stop That Garbage Truck!, illustrated by Karen Lee Schmidt, Albert Whitman (Morton Grove, IL), 1993.

Tanya's Big Green Dream, illustrated by Susan McGinnis, Macmillan (New York, NY), 1994.

Rosie's Birthday Rat, illustrated by Nancy Poydar, Delacorte Press (New York, NY), 1996.

Compost!: Growing Gardens from Your Garbage, illustrated with photographs by Anca Hariton, Millbrook Press (Brookfield, CT), 1996.

Beautiful Bats, illustrated by Sharon Lane Holm, Millbrook Press (Brookfield, CT), 1997.

The Borrowed Hanukkah Latkes, illustrated by Nancy Cote, Albert Whitman (Morton Grove, IL), 1997.

Spectacular Spiders, illustrated by Gay W. Holland, Millbrook Press (Brookfield, CT), 1998.

Fabulous Frogs, illustrated by Loretta Krupinski, Millbrook Press (Brookfield, CT), 1999.

Magnificent Monarchs, illustrated by Gay Holland, Millbrook Press (Brookfield, CT), 2000.

Our Big Home: An Earth Poem, illustrated by Elisa Kleven, Millbrook Press (Brookfield, CT), 2000.

It's Fall! ("Celebrate the Seasons" series), illustrated by Susan Swan, Millbrook Press (Brookfield, CT), 2001.

It's Spring! ("Celebrate the Seasons" series), illustrated by Susan Swan, Millbrook Press (Brookfield, CT), 2002.

It's Winter! ("Celebrate the Seasons" series), illustrated by Susan Swan, Millbrook Press (Brookfield, CT), 2002.

It's Summer! ("Celebrate the Seasons" series), illustrated by Susan Swan, Millbrook Press (Brookfield CT), 2003.

Brilliant Bees, illustrated by Gay W. Holland, Millbrook Press (Brookfield CT), 2003.

Mrs. Greenberg's Messy Hanukkah, illustrated by Nancy Cote, Albert Whitman (Morton Grove, IL), 2004.

Bridge to America: Based on a True Story (novel), Houghton Mifflin (Boston, MA), 2005.

Hello, Squirrels!: Scampering through the Seasons, illustrated by Gay W. Holland, Millbrook Press (Minneapolis, MN), 2006.

Dazzling Dragonflies: A Life Cycle Story, illustrated by Mia Posada, Millbrook Press (Minneapolis, MN), 2008.

Hoppy Hanukkah!, illustrated by Daniel Howarth, Albert Whitman (Morton Grove, IL), 2009.

Singing Crickets, illustrated by Tess Feltes, Millbrook Press (Minneapolis, MN), 2009.

Emma's Poem: The Voice of the Statue of Liberty, illustrated by Claire A. Nivola, Houghton Mifflin Books for Children (Boston, MA), 2010.

Garbage Helps Our Garden Grow: A Compost Story, illustrated with photographs by Shelley Rotner, Millbrook Press (Minneapolis, MN), 2010.

Hoppy Passover!, illustrated by Daniel Howarth, Albert Whitman (Chicago, IL), 2011.

Hannah's Way, illustrated by Adam Gustavson, Kar-Ben Publishing (Minneapolis, MN), 2012.

Several of Glaser's works have been translated into Japanese, Korean, and Chinese.

Sidelights

An award-winning author of both fiction and nonfiction for children, Linda Glaser has enjoyed a lifelong fascination with literature. Though she struggled to learn how to read, not mastering the skill until she was in third grade, Glaser enjoyed being read to by her mother, who introduced her to the works of Eleanor Estes, author of *The Moffats* and *The Hundred Dresses.* As Glaser stated on her home page, "now I not only love reading children's books, I also love writing them."

Glaser made her literary debut in 1991 with the release of *Keep Your Socks on, Albert!,* an easy reader about a frustrated opossum's mission to locate a favorite article of clothing, a search that is complicated by Albert's gabby sister. According to a critic in *Publishers Weekly,* "Glaser depicts sibling antics and interaction with dead-on accuracy and wit." In *Tanya's Big Green Dream* a youngster meets a host of obstacles as she plans a tree-planting ceremony for Earth Day. "Readers will rejoice in Tanya's sense of accomplishment," Frances Bradburn remarked in *Booklist.* Another work that celebrates the joys of nature, *Our Big Home: An Earth Poem,* features Glaser's "lyrical" free verse, observed *Booklist* reviewer John Peters. The author's "appreciation of the interconnectedness of all living things forms the heart of this celebratory picture book," commented a contributor in *Publishers Weekly,* and Rosie Peasley wrote in *School Library Journal* that *Our Big Home* "serves as a breezy introduction to ecological interdependence."

Glaser examines the habits and behaviors of insects in such works as *Brilliant Bees* and *Magnificent Monarchs.* The former title centers on a young girl's observations of honeybee life, including their ability to gather nectar and construct a hive. Glaser's "narrative is logically organized and clearly written," as *School Library Journal* reviewer Karey Wehner noted. In *Dazzling Dragonflies: A Life Cycle Story,* the author follows the growth of this aerial insect from egg to nymph to adult. Patricia Manning described the work in *School Library Journal* as "basic, attractive, and easy to read." Glaser also examines the wonders of the natural world in her "Celebrate the Seasons" series. In series installment *It's Spring!* she "uses simple language to convey the changes brought by spring," as a *Kirkus Reviews* contributor reported. In *School Library Journal* Meghan R. Malone called *It's Winter!* "an exemplary exploration of a season."

Linda Glaser focuses on one of the most magical creatures of nature in **Magnificent Monarchs,** *a picture book illustrated by Gay Holland.* (Illustration copyright © 2000 by Gay Holland. Reproduced in the U.S. by permission of The Millbrook Press, Inc, a division of Lerner Publishing Group. No part of this excerpt may be used or reproduced in any manner whatsoever without the prior written permission of Lerner Publishing Group, Inc., and in the rest of the world by permission of Gay Holland.)

The Jewish holiday known as the Festival of Lights is the focus of a number of Glaser's picture books. In *The Borrowed Hanukkah Latkes,* a "well-told, well-illustrated, and entertaining . . . story," according to *Booklist* reviewer Carolyn Phelan, a little girl convinces a stubborn neighbor to join her family for a special dinner. *Mrs. Greenberg's Messy Hanukkah,* a companion tale, follows the misadventures of the endearing youngster and her elderly neighbor as they prepare latkes. "Kids will be shaking their heads in . . . amusement," a *Kirkus Reviews* critic predicted in reviewing Glaser's tale. A family of bunnies enjoys the holiday by lighting candles and spinning the dreidel in *Hoppy Hanukkah!,* a "gentle introduction to the rituals of a traditional celebration," according to a *Kirkus Reviews* contributor.

Bridge to America: Based on a True Story, Glaser's debut novel, centers on Fivel, a youngster who endures the hardships of a Polish shtetl before venturing to America to begin a new life. "Glaser offers a compelling historical novel here," Jennifer Mattson declared in *Booklist,* and *School Library Journal* critic Barbara Auerbach called the work a "riveting account and sensitive portrayal of what it means to be an immigrant." In *Emma's Poem: The Voice of the Statue of Liberty* Glaser presents a picture-book biography of Emma Lazarus, the writer and activist whose sonnet "The New Colossus" is engraved at the base of the iconic statue in New York Harbor. A *Publishers Weekly* contributor applauded Glaser's "concise narration, reminiscent of blank verse," and Grace Oliff maintained in *School Library Journal* that the author's "text illuminates the woman."

"I send a big thank you to teachers, librarians, booksellers and parents who share their passion for books with children," Glaser commented to *SATA.* "I will be forever grateful to my mother for reading aloud and opening the world of books to me. I continue to love being read to!"

Biographical and Critical Sources

PERIODICALS

Booklist, May 15, 1994, Frances Bradburn, review of *Tanya's Big Green Dream,* p. 1680; February 15, 1996, Carolyn Phelan, review of *Compost! Growing Gardens from Your Garbage,* p. 1024; September 1, 1997, Carolyn Phelan, review of *The Borrowed Hanukkah Latkes,* p. 139; January 1, 1999, Kay Weisman, review of *Spectacular Spiders,* p. 882; May 15, 2000, John Peters, review of *Our Big Home: An Earth Poem,* p. 1748; February 15, 2001, Connie Fletcher, review of *It's Fall!,* p. 231; May 15, 2002, Carolyn Phelan, review of *It's Spring!,* p. 1600; January 1, 2003, Diane Foote, review of *It's Winter!,* p. 906; November 1, 2003, Carolyn Phelan, review of *Brilliant Bees,* p. 498; September 15, 2004, Stephanie Zvirin, review of

Glaser teams up with artist Daniel Howarth to introduce young readers to an important Jewish holiday in **Hoppy Hunukkah!** (Albert Whitman & Company, 2009. Illustration copyright © 2009 by Daniel Howarth. Reproduced by permission.)

Mrs. Greenberg's Messy Hanukkah, p. 249; August, 2005, Jennifer Mattson, review of *Bridge to America,* p. 1966; April 15, 2006, Kathy Broderick, review of *Hello Squirrels! Scampering through the Seasons,* p. 49; December 1, 2007, Carolyn Phelan, review of *Dazzling Dragonflies: A Life Cycle Story,* p. 54; February 1, 2010, Hazel Rochman, review of *Emma's Poem: The Voice of the Statue of Liberty,* p. 46; April 15, 2010, Carolyn Phelan, review of *Garbage Helps Our Garden Grow: A Compost Story,* p. 47.

Horn Book, November-December, 2004, Jeannine M. Chapman, review of *Mrs. Greenberg's Messy Hanukkah,* p. 659; November-December, 2009, Claire E. Gross, review of *Hoppy Hanukkah!,* p. 640; May-June, 2010, Joanna Rudge Long, review of *Emma's Poem,* p. 106.

Kirkus Reviews, August 1, 2001, review of *It's Fall!,* p. 1122; February 15, 2002, review of *It's Spring!,* p. 256; September 1, 2002, review of *It's Winter!,* p. 1309; November 1, 2004, review of *Mrs. Greenberg's Messy Hanukkah,* p. 1049; October 15, 2005, review of *Bridge to America,* p. 1138; September 15, 2009, review of *Hoppy Hanukkah!;* March 1, 2010, review of *Emma's Poem.*

Publishers Weekly, December 13, 1991, review of *Keep Your Socks on, Albert!,* p. 55; October 6, 1997, review

of *The Borrowed Hanukkah Latkes,* p. 52; May 1, 2000, review of *Our Big Home,* p. 70; March 15, 2010, review of *Emma's Poem,* p. 51.

School Library Journal, April, 2000, Rosie Peasley, review of *Our Big Home,* p. 104; January, 2001, Patricia Manning, review of *Magnificent Monarchs,* p. 117; October, 2001, Linda M. Kenton, review of *It's Fall!,* p. 118; March, 2002, Alison Kastner, review of *It's Spring!,* p. 187; November, 2002, Meghan R. Malone, review of *It's Winter!,* p. 123; January, 2004, Karey Wehner, review of *Brilliant Bees,* p. 116; November, 2005, Barbara Auerbach, review of *Bridge to America,* p. 134; August, 2008, Patricia Manning, review of *Dazzling Dragonflies,* p. 110; October, 2009, Teri Markson, review of *Hoppy Hanukkah!,* p. 79; March, 2010, Grace Oliff, review of *Emma's Poem,* p. 118.

ONLINE

Children's Literature Network, http://www.childrenslitera turenetwork.org/ (June 22, 2010), interview with Glaser.

Linda Glaser Home Page, http://www.lindaglaserauthor. com (January 21, 2011).

Linda Glaser Web log, http://lindaglaserauthor.blogspot. com (January 21, 2011).

GOODE, Diane 1949-
(Diane Capuozzo Goode)

Personal

Born September 14, 1949, in Brooklyn, NY; daughter of Armand R. and Paule Capuozzo; married David A. Goode (an author and professor), May 26, 1973; children: Peter. *Education:* Attended École des Beaux Arts, Aix-en-Provence, France, 1971-72; Queens College of the City University of New York, B.F.A., 1972.

Addresses

Home—Watchung, NJ. *Agent*—Steve Malk, Writers House, 21 W. 26th St., New York, NY 10010. *E-mail*—dianegoode@mac.com.

Career

Author and illustrator. Substitute teacher in New York, NY, public schools, 1972-73; children's book illustrator and writer, 1975—. University of California, Los Angeles, teacher of studio workshops on children's book illustration, 1976-79. Chair, Original Art Show, New York, NY, 2007. *Exhibitions:* Work exhibited at museums, colleges, and libraries, including Metropolitan Museum of Art, New York, NY, 1982; Denver Public Library, Denver, CO, 1985; Krasl Art Center, St. Joseph, MI, 1987; Mount Holyoke College Art Museum, South Hadley, MA, 1991-92; Cedar Rapids Museum of Art, Cedar Rapids, IA, 1998-2001; Keene State College Gallery, Keene, NH; Simmons College Art Gallery, Boston, MA; Dromkeen Children's Literature Collection, Riddells Creek, Victoria, Australia; Pelham Art Center, Pelham, NY; University of Southern Maine, Portland; and the University of Wisconsin at Eau Claire.

Member

Society of Illustrators, New York, NY.

Awards, Honors

Notable Book designation, American Library Association (ALA), 1976, for *Tattercoats* by Flora Annie Steele; Southern California Council on Literature for Children and Young People award for illustration, 1976, for both *The Selchie's Seed* by Shulamith Levey Oppenheim and *Little Pieces of the West Wind* by Christian Garrison, and 1979, for *The Dream Eater* by Garrison; Children's Choice citation, International Reading Association/Children's Book Council (CBC), 1982, for *The Unicorn and the Plow* by Louise Moeri; Caldecott Honor Book designation, and Notable Book designation, both ALA, Library of Congress Children's Book of the Year designation, Notable Children's Trade Books in the Field of Social Studies designation, National Council for Social Studies (NCSS)/CBC, and Teachers' Choice award, National Council of Teachers of English (NCTE), all 1983, all for *When I Was Young in the Mountains* by Cynthia Rylant; Notable Children's Trade Books in the Field of

Social Studies designation, NCSS/CBC, Notable Book designation, ALA, *Redbook* Top-Ten Children's Picture Books designation, Teachers' Choice award, NCTE, and Parents' Choice Award, all 1985, all for *Watch the Stars Come Out* by Riki Levinson; Pick of the List selection, American Bookseller, and Parents' Choice Award, both 1986, both for *I Go with My Family to Grandma's* by Levinson; Notable Children's Trade Books in the Field of Social Studies designation, NCSS/CBC, Pick of the List selection, American Bookseller, and Best Children's Books of the Year designation, Child Study Children's Book Committee, all 1987,all for *I Go with My Family to Grandma's;* Best Children's Books of the Year designation, Child Study Children's Book Committee, 1989, for *I Hear a Noise;* Notable Children's Trade Books in the Field of Social Studies designation, NCSS/CBC, and Pick of the List selection, American Bookseller, both 1989, both for *The Diane Goode Book of American Folk Tales and Songs;* Pick of the List selection, American Bookseller, 1990, for *Diane Goode's American Christmas,* and 1991, for *Where's Our Mama?; Storytelling World* Award, 1998, for *Diane Goode's Book of Giants and Little People;* Society of Illustrators Certificate of Merit; named English-speaking Union Ambassador of Honor; Parents' Choice Silver Honor selection, 2007, for *Alligator Boy* by Rylant; *Storytelling World* Award, 2008, for *President Pennybaker* by Kate Feiffer.

Writings

SELF-ILLUSTRATED

(Reteller) Julian Hawthorne, *Rumpty-Dudget's Tower,* Knopf (New York, NY), 1987.
I Hear a Noise, Dutton (New York, NY), 1988.
Where's Our Mama?, Dutton (New York, NY), 1991.
Mama's Perfect Present, Dutton (New York, NY), 1996.
The Dinosaur's New Clothes, Blue Sky (New York, NY), 1999.
(Reteller) *Cinderella: The Dog and Her Little Glass Slipper,* Blue Sky (New York, NY), 2000.
Tiger Trouble!, Blue Sky (New York, NY), 2001.
Monkey Mo Goes to Sea, Blue Sky (New York, NY), 2002.
Thanksgiving Is Here!, HarperCollins (New York, NY), 2003.
Mind Your Manners!, Farrar, Straus & Giroux (New York, NY), 2005.
The Most Perfect Spot, HarperCollins (New York, NY), 2006.

Authors's work has been translated into Spanish, French, German, Dutch, Danish, Greek, Japanese, Korean, and Chinese and has been published in South Africa.

Work included in permanent collection at Kerlan Collection, University of Minnesota.

ANTHOLOGIES; SELF-ILLUSTRATED

Diane Goode's Little Library of Christmas Classics, Random House (New York, NY), 1983.

The Diane Goode Book of American Folk Tales and Songs, compiled by Ann Durell, Dutton (New York, NY), 1989.

Diane Goode's American Christmas, Dutton (New York, NY), 1990.

Diane Goode's Book of Silly Stories and Songs, Dutton (New York, NY), 1992.

Diane Goode's Christmas Magic: Poems and Carols, Random House (New York, NY), 1992.

The Little Books of Nursery Animals (contains *The Little Book of Cats, The Little Book of Farm Friends, The Little Book of Mice,* and *The Little Book of Pigs*), Dutton (New York, NY), 1993.

Diane Goode's Book of Scary Stories and Songs, Dutton (New York, NY), 1994.

Diane Goode's Book of Giants and Little People, Dutton (New York, NY), 1997.

ILLUSTRATOR

Christian Garrison, *Little Pieces of the West Wind,* Bradbury (New York, NY), 1975.

Shulamith Levey Oppenheim, *The Selchie's Seed,* Bradbury (New York, NY), 1975, revised edition, Harcourt (New York, NY), 1996.

Christian Garrison, *Flim and Flam and the Big Cheese,* Bradbury (New York, NY), 1976.

Flora Annie Steele, *Tattercoats: An Old English Tale,* Bradbury (New York, NY), 1976.

(And translator) Madame de Beaumont, *Beauty and the Beast,* Bradbury (New York, NY), 1978.

Christian Garrison, *The Dream Eater,* Bradbury (New York, NY), 1978.

Emoeke de Papp Severo, translator, *The Good-hearted Youngest Brother* (translation of the Hungarian folktale "A josivu legenyke"), Bradbury (New York, NY), 1981.

Louise Moeri, *The Unicorn and the Plow,* Dutton (New York, NY), 1982.

Cynthia Rylant, *When I Was Young in the Mountains,* Dutton (New York, NY), 1982.

J.M. Barrie, *Peter Pan,* retold by Josette Frank, Random House (New York, NY), 1983.

Carlo Collodi, *The Adventures of Pinocchio,* Random House (New York, NY), 1983.

Amy Ehrlich, adapter, *The Random House Book of Fairy Tales,* Random House (New York, NY), 1985.

Riki Levinson, *Watch the Stars Come Out,* Dutton (New York, NY), 1985.

Deborah Hautzig, *The Story of the Nutcracker Ballet,* Random House (New York, NY), 1986.

Riki Levinson, *I Go with My Family to Grandma's,* Dutton (New York, NY), 1986.

(And translator) Charles Perrault, *Cinderella,* Knopf (New York, NY), 1988.

Noel Streatfeild, *Ballet Shoes,* Random House (New York, NY), 1991.

Noel Streatfeild, *Theater Shoes,* Random House (New York, NY), 1994.

Lloyd Alexander, *The House Gobbaleen,* Dutton (New York, NY), 1995.

Robert Louis Stevenson, *A Child's Garden of Verses,* Morrow (New York, NY), 1998.

Cynthia Rylant, *Christmas in the Country,* Blue Sky (New York, NY), 2002.

Margaret Wise Brown, *Christmas in the Barn,* HarperCollins (New York, NY), 2004.

Cynthia Rylant, *Alligator Boy,* Harcourt (Orlando, FL), 2007.

Cynthia Rylant, *Baby Face: A Book of Love for Baby,* Simon & Schuster (New York, NY), 2008.

Kate Feiffer, *President Pennybaker,* Simon & Schuster Books for Young Readers (New York, NY), 2008.

Elise Primavera, *Louise the Big Cheese: Divine Diva,* Simon & Schuster Books for Young Readers (New York, NY), 2009.

Kate Feiffer, *My Mom Is Trying to Ruin My Life,* Simon & Schuster Books for Young Readers (New York, NY), 2009.

Kate Feiffer, *But I Wanted a Baby Brother!,* Simon & Schuster Books for Young Readers (New York, NY), 2010.

Elise Primavera, *Louise the Big Cheese and the La-di-dah Shoes,* Simon & Schuster Books for Young Readers (New York, NY), 2010.

Stephanie Barden, *Cinderella Smith,* Harper (New York, NY), 2011.

Elise Primavera, *Louise the Big Cheese and the Big Smarty-Pants,* Simon & Schuster Books for Young Readers (New York, NY), 2011.

Elise Primavera, *Louise the Big Cheese and the Ooh-la-la Charm School,* Simon & Schuster Books for Young Readers (New York, NY), 2011.

Sidelights

Diane Goode is an celebrated author and illustrator who is noted for her whimsical picture books as well as for her illustrated anthologies of folk tales and songs. Goode's original tales, such as *Where's Our Mama?, Mind Your Manners!,* and *The Most Perfect Spot,* have earned praise for their sly narratives and expressive artwork, while others, such as *Cinderella: The Dog and Her Little Glass Slipper* and *The Dinosaur's New Clothes,* recast traditional stories in a fresh and humorous setting. The versatile Goode has also paired her illustrations with the writings of other authors to create works such as the Caldecott honor book *When I Was Young in the Mountains* by Cynthia Rylant, Kate Feiffer's *President Pennybaker,* and Stephanie Barden's *Cinderella Smith* as well as beautifully illustrated renditions of such classics as *Peter Pan* and *A Child's Garden of Verses.*

"When I was a child I loved books and art," Goode once told *SATA.* "Reading allowed me to escape into the reality of others, and drawing let me create my own. My father was of Italian descent, and my mother was French. My brother and I enjoyed the richness of both cultures. We traveled to Europe every summer from the time we were infants, visiting family and the great cathedrals and museums of the world. These early impressions helped shape my appreciation for life and art. I was bedazzled by Michelangelo's *Pieta.* Could marble be warm and luminous? Could monumental forms be at once tender and powerful? Man's creative ability seemed staggering. I saw the works of Da Vinci, Rembrandt, Botticelli, Lautrec, Monet, Manet, Cezanne, and all the great artists. I was awestruck. I was in love with art!

"I have been drawing ever since I can remember, but my formal education began at Queens College in art history. I soon switched to fine arts, where I tried my hand at everything: drawing, painting, sculpture, etching, and color theory. I took a year off to study at the École des Beaux Arts in Aix-en-Provence. It was an artist's dream.

"After graduating, I taught high school for a year, putting together a portfolio at night. In my blissful ignorance of publishing, I had decided to illustrate children's books. It was just as well that I was so naive, or else I would have been too afraid to try. As luck would have it, I was contracted to illustrate my first picture

Diane Goode conjures up all manner of almost-scary creatures in the art for her self-illustrated **Diane Goode's Book of Scary Stories and Songs.** (Illustration copyright © 1994 by Diane Goode. Used by permission of Dutton Children's Books, a division of Penguin Putnam Young Readers Group, a member of Penguin Group (USA) Inc., 345 Hudson Street, New York, NY 11014.)

book in 1973. I was twenty-four then and knew nothing at all about commercial art. Since I was living in California, my New York publisher taught me color separation over the phone!"

Goode's first illustration project was *The Selchie's Seed,* a story by Shulamith Oppenheim, and her success here provided her with the opportunity to create artwork for texts by other authors. Moving to more classic works, she began to illustrate anthologies of traditional tales, such as *Diane Goode's Little Library of Christmas Classics,* which contains such popular Christmas tales as "The Fir Tree," "The Night before Christmas," and "The Nutcracker," as well as several well-known Christmas carols. "This small, gaily decorated slipcase holds four books that Goode has illustrated in extremely pretty, full-color, animated holiday scenes," noted a reviewer for *Publishers Weekly.* George A. Woods observed in the *New York Times* that the "star of this package . . . is Diane Goode, whose illustrations lend just the right accompanying note to each book."

Goode's illustrated retellings of oft-told tales and verses won the admiration of critics and readers alike. Her retelling of Julian Hawthorne's *Rumpty-Dudget's Tower* brought praise from Jeanne Marie Clancy in *School Library Journal:* "Goode's colorful cross-hatched illustrations for her adaptation enhance the story and capture the spirit of the characters, especially the mischievous Rumpty-Dudget." A *Booklist* reviewer commented that the "beauty and wit of Goode's well-composed artwork will draw readers into the rather old-fashioned tale," while *Horn Book* critic Margaret A. Bush concluded that Goode's "fine execution of both text and illustration breathes new life into the old story, making it freshly accessible as an old-fashioned fairy tale, eminently suited for reading aloud." Goode's illustrations have also been credited with attractively interpreting Robert Louis Stevenson's collection *A Child's Garden of Verses. School Library Journal* critic Robin L. Gibson asserted of this work that the artist "applies her characteristically charming illustrations to Stevenson's poems with appealing results." Gibson went on to observe that Goode "captures the exuberance of childhood in many pictures."

Much of Goode's creative energy has focused on anthologies. In *Diane Goode's Book of Scary Stories and Songs* she collects tales featuring ghosts and goblins from around the world. *Horn Book* contributor Nancy Vasilakis dubbed the book a "welcome addition to the Halloween or storytelling shelves." A *Publishers Weekly* reviewer, noting that the stories "are rather tame," assured apprehensive readers that *Diane Goode's Book of Scary Stories and Songs* "will be appreciated more for its rich multicultural flavor than for its fright value." With *Diane Goode's Book of Giants and Little People* the author/illustrator deals with the theme of the "triumph of a small but clever hero over a gigantic adversary," according to *Booklist* reviewer Julie Corsaro.

A mother deals with her rambunctious brood in Goode's self-illustrated story in **Mama's Perfect Present.** (Puffin Books, 1996. Copyright © 1996 by Diane Goode. Used by permission of Dutton, a division of Penguin Putnam Young Readers Group, a member of Penguin Group (USA) Inc., 345 Hudson Street, New York, NY 11014.)

Working once again with tall tales and folktales from around the world, Goode puts together a smorgasbord of stories. Corsaro went on to note that "Goode's elegant watercolors bring it all together, her appealing cartoon-style art displaying a penchant for the compelling contrast between big and small." A *Publishers Weekly* critic wrote of *Diane Goode's Book of Giants and Little People* that these stories add to Goode's "stable of stellar collections." "With this blithely spirited book," concluded the reviewer, "Goode has done it again . . . and that's no exaggeration."

Goode expanded her role from illustrator and reteller to author/illustrator of original stories in 1988 with *I Hear a Noise*. A reviewer for *Junior Bookshelf* deemed Goode's authorial debut "a joyously funny book," adding that, "in its high spirits, its high humour, the book is entirely original." *I Hear a Noise* is a story without narrative; it employs only dialogue and art to address the familiar childhood fear of bedtime fiends. Like many little boys, the hero, lying in bed, complains that he hears a noise. While his mother tries to comfort him, a green dragon swoops in, snatches, and flies off with mother and son in tow. Back at its castle, the monster's siblings argue over these human trophies, until the

mother dragon stops the squabbling by insisting that the captives be returned to their home. Goode "puts an amusing new twist on the well-worn subject of monsters at bedtime," declared a *Kirkus Reviews* critic. A reviewer for *Booklist* called *I Hear a Noise* a "gloriously spine-tingling thriller," adding that the author/illustrator's "engagingly expressive creatures . . . will leave youngsters clamoring for yet one more read of this soft-edged, bedtime chiller."

Goode's French heritage and travels have inspired her popular picture books *Where's Our Mama?* and *Mama's Perfect Present*. In the first, two children become separated from their mother at the Gare d'Orsay train station in Paris. Aided by a kindly French gendarme, the brother and sister set out to find their beautiful mother, trekking from one place to the next. All the while, the illustrations reveal the "lost" mother in one corner of the crowded page; finally the two children see her as well. Set early in the twentieth century, *Where's Our Mama?* was written in tribute to Goode's own mother. A writer for *Kirkus Reviews* observed that the book is reminiscent of a Russian folktale and called it "a charming transformation of a story that deftly dramatizes the child's-eye view of a most important person." *Horn Book* reviewer Mary M. Burns concluded her enthusiastic review by calling *Where's Our Mama?* "as gallic as a shrug, as logical as Pascal, and as winning as a song by Maurice Chevalier."

"Mayhem? Mais oui! The rosy-cheeked children who searched Paris high and low in *Where's Our Mama?* are back," celebrated a *Publishers Weekly* reviewer in announcing the arrival of Goode's sequel, *Mama's Perfect Present.* Now accompanied by their dachshund, Zaza, who leaves path of destruction in its wake, the two siblings are searching for the perfect birthday gift for their beloved mother. Not surprisingly, each place they visit is also visited with chaos as a result of their rambunctious dog. A *Publishers Weekly* critic promised that this sequel "will leave young readers chuckling at Zaza's exploits and everyone else chuckling an appreciative ooh-la-la." Mary M. Burns asserted in *Horn Book:* "This is a true picture story, with the understated text serving as a straight-faced, innocent commentary on the action, which is visualized through careful manipulation of line, deft shading, and delicate hatching." In a *Booklist* review, Ilene Cooper commented that "the story is clever and full of fun, but it is really the pictures that make this come alive."

Goode's illustration projects for other writers include a new edition of **Ballet Shoes** *by noted British children's author Noel Streatfeild.* (Illustration © 1991 by Diane Goode. Used by permission of Random House Children's Books, a division of Random House, Inc.)

Other picture books by Goode include *Tiger Trouble!,* which finds a boy and his pet tiger, Lily, threatened with eviction from their city apartment after their new cat-hating landlord moves in upstairs. Fortunately, Lily proves her worth when robbers appear, giving an upbeat ending to what a *Kirkus Reviews* writer called a "fanciful and cheerily outlandish tale." Praising the story's nostalgic 1930s setting, *School Library Journal* contributor Bina Williams noted that "Goode's fetching watercolors" for *Tiger Trouble!* "are delightful and luminous," while in *Booklist* Ilene Cooper wrote that the story's "multiethnic cast of kids is endearing, [and] the New York setting bristles with activity."

Set in a similar era, *Monkey Mo Goes to Sea* finds a boy paired with another unusual pet, this time a monkey. Visiting his grandfather for lunch on a luxurious ocean liner docked nearby, Bertie and his pet Mo do their best to behave, with humorous results. The impish Mo "will endear himself to youngsters as they will recognize . . . much of themselves in his well-intentioned" antics, predicted Rosalyn Pierini in *School Library Journal,* while Cooper wrote that Goode's "well-structured book has a sly story that's as strong as the illustrations."

Goode shows that she is not afraid to give tradition a friendly tug with books such as *The Dinosaur's New Clothes* and *Cinderella: The Dog and Her Little Glass Slipper.* With *The Dinosaur's New Clothes* she provides Hans Christian Andersen's classic story with "a prehistoric makeover," according to a *Publishers Weekly* critic. Goode recasts the royals of the original version as a gaggle of pompadoured dinosaurs holding court at the French palace of Versailles, while a Tyrannosaurus rex—king of all dinosaurs—stars as the fashion-conscious emperor. "It's all good silly fun," concluded the critic, "a light parody of Andersen's send-up of gullibility and greed." A pack of hounds step into key roles in Goode's revisionist "Cinderella," and "silly images abound," according to a *Publishers Weekly* writer. Scruffy canines with powdered wigs fill the royal ballroom, dresses are patterned with paw prints, and "Goode works dog motifs into her luminous paintings with amusing frequency."

Based on an 1802 school primer outlining the rules for proper dinner-table behavior, Goode's self-illustrated *Mind Your Manners!* showcases her humor and sense of fun as she transforms dour pronouncements such as "Stuff not thy mouth so as to fill thy cheeks" into what *Booklist* critic Jennifer Mattson deemed a "comic, pictorial narrative" showing an elegantly dressed family of the times gleefully engaging in "precisely the opposite of everything the text prescribes," to the disgust and dismay of their captive dinner guests. In *The Most Perfect Spot,* a little boy invites his mother to join him on a picnic in the park, only to find that every location where they choose to sit has its drawbacks. Goode's "animated line and watercolor illustrations capture the comic events of this memorable day," a contributor stated in

Cynthia Rylant's nostalgic story in **When I Was Young in the Mountains** *is a perfect match for Goode's detailed and evocative art.* (Illustration copyright © 1982 by Diane Goode. All rights reserved. Used by permission of Dutton Children's Books, a division of Penguin Putnam Young Readers Group, a member of Penguin Group (USA) Inc., 345 Hudson Street, New York, NY 11014.)

Kirkus Reviews, and Maryann H. Owen, reviewing the work in *School Library Journal,* commented that the pictures "depict an affable multihued cast of characters and a warm parent/child relationship while exuding a pleasant, old-fashioned flavor."

Goode has illustrated a number of titles by famed children's author Rylant. Told in rhyming text, *Alligator Boy* centers on a youngster who decides to recreate his persona after spotting a stuffed gator at a natural history museum. With the help of a specially tailored costume that fits him head to toe, the youngster gains the courage to confront his nemesis, the classroom bully. Writing in *School Library Journal,* Marianne Saccardi applauded Goode's illustrations "in which she evokes a former time." Rylant collects six poems that celebrate triumphal moments in a child's life in *Baby Face: A Book of Love for Baby,* and here "Goode's watercolor, pencil and gouache pictures . . . gambol on white backgrounds," as a contributor in *Kirkus Reviews* stated. A *Publishers Weekly* critic noted of the same book that the illustrator "employs a looser line and simpler figures than usual," augmenting the text "with buoyant, energetic vignettes."

Goode has also enjoyed a successful collaboration with Feiffer, providing the artwork for such humorous works as *President Pennybaker.* This story centers on an exas-

perated youngster who, tired of his parents' seemingly endless list of rules, decides to run for the highest office in the nation. Once in office, however, the lad realizes that his constituents want more than unlimited cake and ice cream, and he hands his responsibilities to an unlikely candidate. Feiffer's narrative is "underscored by Goode's artfully composed, old-timey illustrations," a critic in *Kirkus Reviews* wrote, and Steven Engelfried maintained in *School Library Journal* that "Goode's breezy watercolors set just the right tone." Similar in tone, Feiffer's *My Mom Is Trying to Ruin My Life* concerns a girl's desperate plan to escape her meddling parents. Here "Goode's watercolor illustrations adeptly convey the wry tone of the tale," remarked a *Kirkus Reviews* contributor. A frustrated boy's efforts to exchange his infant sister for another newborn is the focus on *But I Wanted a Baby Brother!,* another humorous story by Feiffer, and here "Goode's sense of comic detailing is faultless," in the words of a *Publishers Weekly* reviewer.

Goode and Elise Primavera have combined talents for a series of picture books about a spunky young dancer named Louise who dreams of success on the big stage. In the debut work, *Louise the Big Cheese: Divine Diva,* the lively protagonist spots an opportunity to step into the limelight when her teacher announces a class production of "Cinderella." Unfortunately, Louise's best friend lands the plum role and when Louise is relegated to playing a mouse it creates tension between the girls. Goode's "playful watercolors with whimsical and expressive black outlines capture Louise's mercurial personality," a *Publishers Weekly* contributor remarked. *Louise the Big Cheese and the La-di-dah Shoes,* a sequel, follows the youngster's attempts to exchange her drab brown footwear for something far more fashionable. According to Linda Staskus in *School Library Journal,* Goode's "bright, expressive illustrations, filled with splashes of hot pinks and dialogue balloons, capture her personality to the fullest."

As Goode once explained of her work to *SATA,* "When you depend on pure line for expression, the slightest variation in length or thickness of the line of the mouth, the angle of an eyebrow, the sweep of a tail, the pose of a foot, changes the mood of the entire illustration. I often do the same small character over and over until the line is right, until I can just dash it off and it seems to come alive. My theme for this new approach is 'less is more.'

"In a successful picture book, illustration and text should move together like perfectly attuned partners in a dance. The illustrations not only support, but can serve as a counterpoint to the text. If I've done it right, the effort should not be evident, it should look easy and natural. It's an exciting process.

"Working in the field of children's literature has been a great joy," the author/illustrator once noted. "How lucky to be able to do the work I love and also contribute in

Elise Primavera's humorous story in Louise the Big Cheese and the La-di-da Shoes *gains extra impact from Goode's engaging illustrations.* (Illustration copyright © 2010 by Diane Goode. Reprinted with permission of Simon & Schuster Books for Young Readers, an imprint of Simon & Schuster Children's Publishing Division.)

some small way to the lives of our children. How lucky to find in my work the two things I've cherished since childhood: art and books."

Biographical and Critical Sources

BOOKS

Cummins, Julie, editor, *Children's Book Illustration and Design*, PBC International, 1992.

PERIODICALS

Booklist, January 15, 1988, review of *Rumpty-Dudget's Tower*, p. 862; December 1, 1988, review of *I Hear a Noise*, pp. 647-648; July, 1996, Ilene Cooper, review of *Mama's Perfect Present*, p. 1824; September 15, 1997, Julie Corsaro, review of *Diane Goode's Book of Giants and Little People*, p. 237; November 1, 2000, GraceAnne A. DeCandido, review of *Cinderella: The Dog and Her Little Glass Slipper*, p. 543; October 1, 2001, Ilene Cooper, review of *Tiger Trouble!*, p. 325; March 15, 2002, Ilene Cooper, review of *Monkey Mo Goes to Sea*, p. 1256; October 15, 2003, Ilene Cooper, review of *Thanksgiving Is Here!*, p. 418; November 15, 2005, Jennifer Mattson, review of *Mind Your Manners!*, p. 49; May 15, 2007, Randall Enos, review of *Alligator Boy*, p. 48; March 15, 2009, Courtney Jones, review of *My Mom Is Trying to Ruin My Life*, p. 66; April 15, 2010, Patricia Austin, review of *But I Wanted a Baby Brother!*, p. 50.

Horn Book, March-April, 1988, Margaret A. Bush, review of *Rumpty-Dudget's Tower*, pp. 199-200; November-December, 1991, Mary M. Burns, review of *Where's Our Mama?*, pp. 727-728; January-February, 1995, Nancy Vasilakis, review of *Diane Goode's Book of Scary Stories and Songs*, p. 75; November-December, 1996, Mary M. Burns, review of *Mama's Perfect Present*, pp. 723-724; March-April, 2002, Mary M. Burns, review of *Monkey Mo Goes to Sea*, p. 202; November-December, 2002, Mary M. Burns, review of *Christmas in the Country*, p. 738.

Junior Bookshelf, April, 1989, review of *I Hear a Noise*, p. 61.

Kirkus Reviews, July 1, 1988, review of *I Hear a Noise*, p. 973; August 1, 1991, review of *Where's Our Mama?*, p. 1010; September 1, 2001, review of *Tiger Trouble!*, p. 1290; November 1, 2002, review of *Christmas in the Country*, p. 1625; August 1, 2003, review of *Thanksgiving Is Here!*, p. 1017; October 15, 2005, review of *Mind Your Manners!*, p. 1138; April 1, 2006, review of *The Most Perfect Spot*, p. 347; January 15, 2008, review of *Baby Face: A Book of Love for Baby*; July 1, 2008, review of *President Pennybaker*; February 15, 2009, review of *My Mom Is Trying to Ruin My Life*; February 15, 2010, review of *Louise the Big Cheese and the La-di-da Shoes*.

New York Times, December 4, 1983, George A. Woods, review of *Diane Goode's Little Library of Christmas Classics*, pp. 77-79.

New York Times Book Review, February 12, 2006, Julie Just, review of *Mind Your Manners!*, p. 17; October 12, 2008, review of *President Pennybaker*, p. 23.

Publishers Weekly, September 2, 1983, review of *Diane Goode's Little Library of Christmas Classics*, p. 80; July 4, 1994, review of *Diane Goode's Book of Scary Stories and Songs*, p. 60; September 2, 1996, review of *Mama's Perfect Present*, p. 129; July 28, 1997, review of *Diane Goode's Book of Giants and Little People*, p. 73; June 28, 1999, review of *The Dinosaur's New Clothes*, p. 78; August 7, 2000, review of *Cinderella*, p. 95; February 25, 2002, review of *Monkey Mo Goes to Sea*, p. 66; September 22, 2003, review of *Thanksgiving Is Here!*, p. 65; May 8, 2006, review of *The Most Perfect Spot*, p. 65; February 18, 2008, review of *Baby Face*, p. 152; July 21, 2008, review of *President Pennybaker*, p. 158; September 14, 2009, review of *Louise the Big Cheese: Divine Diva*, p. 47; April 19, 2010, review of *But I Wanted a Baby Brother!*, p. 51.

School Library Journal, January, 1988, Jeanne Marie Clancy, review of *Rumpty-Dudget's Tower*, p. 66; January, 1999, Robin L. Gibson, review of *A Child's Garden of Verses*, p. 121; September, 2000, Margaret A. Chang, review of *Cinderella*, p. 216; December, 2001, Bina Williams, review of *Tiger Trouble!*, p. 102; March, 2002, Rosalyn Pierini, review of *Monkey Mo Goes to Sea*, p. 187; September, 2003, Andrea Tarr, review of *Thanksgiving Is Here!*, p. 178; November, 2005, Grace Oliff, review of *Mind Your Manners!*, p. 92; May, 2006, Maryann H. Owen, review of *The Most Perfect Spot*, p. 88; June, 2007, Marianne Saccardi, review of *Alligator Boy*, p. 123; August,

2008, Steven Engelfried, reviews of *President Penny-baker,* p. 88, and Amelia Jenkins, review of *Baby Face,* p. 101; September, 2009, Ieva Bates, review of *Louise the Big Cheese,* p. 131; February, 2010, Linda Staskus, review of *Louise the Big Cheese and the La-di-da Shoes,* p. 92; June, 2010, Anne Beier, review of *But I Wanted a Baby Brother!,* p. 70.

ONLINE

Diane Goode Home Page, http://www.dianegoode.com (January 21, 2011).

Scholastic Web site, http://www2.scholastic.com/ (January 21, 2011), interview with Goode.

Simon & Schuster Web site, http://www.simonandschuster. com/ (January 21, 2011), "Diane Goode."*

*   *   *

GOODE, Diane Capuozzo
See GOODE, Diane

*   *   *

GRAULLERA, Fabiola
See GRAULLERA RAMIREZ, Fabiola

*   *   *

GRAULLERA RAMIREZ, Fabiola
(Fabiola Graullera)

Personal

Born in Mexico City, Mexico. *Education:* Universidad Nacional Autónoma de México/Escuela Nacional de Artes Plásticas, degree (graphic communication).

Addresses

Home—Mexico City, Mexico. *E-mail*—fabiolagrau@ aol.com.

Career

Illustrator and artist. *Tané* (periodical), illustrator, 1997-99; freelance illustrator. *Exhibitions:* Work included in exhibitions in Mexico and Spain.

Awards, Honors

Tejas Star Book Award finalist, 2009, for *I Am René, the Boy/Soy René, el niño;* Américas Award Commended designation, Consortium of Latin American Studies Programs, and *Skipping Stones* Honor Award, both 2010, both for *René Has Two Last Names/René tiene dos apellidos.*

Illustrator

René Colato Laínez, *I Am René, the Boy/Soy René, el niño,* Piñata Books (Houston, TX), 2005

René Colato Laínez, *René Has Two Last Names/René tiene dos apellidos,* Piñata Books (Houston, TX), 2009

Illustrator of other books published in Mexico, including bilingual dictionaries in the *Diccionario Escolar Enfocado/In Focus School Dictionary* series.

Biographical and Critical Sources

PERIODICALS

Kirkus Reviews, April 15, 2005, review of *I Am René, the Boy/Soy René, el niño,* p. 476.

School Library Journal, October, 2009, Diana Borrego Martinez, review of *René Has Two Last Names/René tiene dos apellidos,* p. 116.

ONLINE

Ilustradores en México Web site, http://www.ilustracion mexico.org/ (January 15, 2010), "Fabiolo Graullera."*

*   *   *

GROTH-FLEMING, Candace
See FLEMING, Candace

H-I

HARMON, Kate
See GIBSON, Marley

*   *   *

HAVERFIELD, Mary

Personal

Married Pat Haverfield (an advertising photographer and director); children: Graham. *Education:* Attended Philadelphia College of Art, University of Houston, and Art Center School of Design.

Addresses

Home—Dallas, TX. *E-mail*—mary@maryhaverfield. com.

Career

Illustrator and author of children's books, beginning c. 1990. Presenter at schools.

Member

Picture Book Artists Association.

Writings

SELF-ILLUSTRATED

Harriett the Homeless Raccoon, Bright Sky Press (Albany, TX), 2005.

ILLUSTRATOR

Evelyn Oppenheimer, *Tilli Comes to Texas,* Hendrick-Long (Dallas, TX), 1986.

Sue Kassirer, adaptor, *The Adventures of Pinocchio* (based on the story by Carlo Collodi), Random House (New York, NY), 1992.
Jean Monrad Thomas, *A Child's Book of Hope,* Random House (New York, NY), 1999.
Celeste Ryan, *The Dream Quilt,* WaterBrook Press (Colorado Springs, CO), 1999.
Jane Roberts Wood, *Mocha: The Real Doctor,* Bright Sky Press (Albany, TX), 2003.
Jane Kurtz, *Johnny Appleseed,* Aladdin (New York, NY), 2004.
Jane Kurtz, *Mister Bones: Dinosaur Hunter,* Aladdin (New York, NY), 2004.
Gayle Byrne, *Sometimes It's Grandmas and Grandpas, Not Mommies and Daddies,* Abbeville Kids (New York, NY), 2009.

Contributor to periodicals.

Sidelights

Working primarily in colored pencil, water color, and gouache, Mary Haverfield is an illustrator whose light-filled images have brought to life picture-book texts by a range of authors that include Evelyn Oppenheimer, Celeste Ryan, Jane Kurtz, and Gayle Burne. After studying at the Philadelphia College of Art, the University of Houston, and the prestigious Art Center School of Design in Pasadena, California, Haverfield established herself as a professional illustrator, creating images for advertisements, greeting cards, and educational publications. Her first picture-book assignment, Oppenheimer's *Tilli Comes to Texas,* was published in 1986, while Sue Kassirer's retelling of Carlo Collodi's *Pinocchio* marked Haverfield's debut with a mainstream trade-book publisher.

Sometimes It's Grandmas and Grandpas, not Mommies and Daddies pairs Haverfield's illustrations with a story by Byrne in which a little girl shares her experiences growing up in the home of her loving grandparents. As the text explores the positive aspects of the girl's situation, the artist's "realistic watercolor illustrations rein-

Mary Haverfield's illustrations for Gayle Byrne's picture book **Sometimes It's Grandmas and Grandpas, Not Mommies and Daddies** *shines a fresh light on extended families.* (Illustration copyright © 2009 by Mary Haverfield. Compilation copyright © 2009 by Abbeville Press. Reproduced by permission.)

force the reassuring mood of the story," according to *School Library Journal* contributor Martha Simpson, and in *Booklist* Ilene Cooper cited Haverfield's ability to "extend the feeling of normalcy and security" in her paintings. In a *Publishers Weekly* review, a critic also praised *Sometimes It's Grandmas and Grandpas, Not Mommies and Daddies,* writing that "Haverfield's . . . homey watercolors reinforce the bond between the girl and her grandmother and grandfather." Mary Anne Hannibal also praised the book in *Childhood Education,* describing it as "a welcome addition to children's literature addressing diversity in family structure."

In addition to illustrating stories by other authors, Haverfield has also created the original picture book *Harriett the Homeless Raccoon,* which was inspired by an uninvited houseguest that shared the Haverfields' home one summer. Brought to life in engaging watercolor images, her story follows a young raccoon that sets out from her family den to find a less-crowded home. The creature's attempts to settle in the attic of a warm and cozy house are discouraged, but when she is trapped and relocated temporarily to the studio shed behind the house, Harriett liberates herself, explores the art supplies, and shows her creative side. In addition to her story, Haverfield also includes facts about raccoons in the wild and relates several other stories about the amazingly determined and agile creatures.

Biographical and Critical Sources

PERIODICALS

Booklist, November 15, 2009, Ilene Cooper, review of *Sometimes It's Grandmas and Grandpas, Not Mommies and Daddies,* p. 43.

Childhood Education, winter, 2009, Mary Anne Hannibal, review of *Sometimes It's Grandmas and Grandpas, Not Mommies and Daddies,* p. 116.

Kirkus Reviews, August 15, 2004, review of *Johnny Appleseed,* p. 808; October 1, 2009, review of *Sometimes It's Grandmas and Grandpas, Not Mommies and Daddies.*

Publishers Weekly, November 2, 2009, review of *Sometimes It's Grandmas and Grandpas, Not Mommies and Daddies,* p. 50.

School Library Journal, December, 1986, Marilyn Burrington, review of *Tilli Comes to Texas,* p. 93; December, 2004, Laura Scott, review of *Johnny Appleseed,* p. 134; January, 2010, Martha Simpson, review of *Sometimes It's Grandmas and Grandpas, Not Mommies and Daddies,* p. 69.

ONLINE

Mary Haverfield Home Page, http://www.maryhaverfield. com (January 13, 2011).

Mary Haverfield Web log, http://maryhaverfield.blogspot. com (January 13, 2011).*

*   *   *

HILL, Isabel
(Isabel T. Hill)

Personal

Born in AL. *Education:* M.A.

Addresses

Home—Brooklyn, NY. *Office*—53 Prospect Park W., Brooklyn, NY 11215. *E-mail*—info@isabelhill.com.

Career

Architectural historian, urban planner, photographer and filmmaker, and author. Former grant reviewer, State of New York; urban planner in Brooklyn, NY. Filmmaker, beginning c. 1994; Building History Productions, co-founder and producer of documentary films *Made in Brooklyn* and *Brooklyn Matters.* Presenter at schools, libraries, and museums.

Awards, Honors

Eliot Willensky Award, and Best in Category Award, Birmingham Educational Film Festival, both for *Made in Brooklyn.*

Isabel Hill (Photograph by Jackie Weisburg. Reproduced by permission.)

Writings

(And photographer) *Urban Animals,* Star Bright Books (New York, NY), 2009.

Contributor to journals and to periodicals, including the *New York Times.*

Sidelights

In the 1970s Isabel Hill began her career as an architectural historian, a vocation that has allowed her to study a range of cities and also expand her work into the areas of urban planning, photographer, and documentary filmmaker. As the founder of Building History Associates, she has produced two highly regarded films focusing on specific urban issues in Brooklyn, New York, and their implications for other U.S. cities. In hopes of preserving historic neighborhoods for future generations, Hill is also passionate about and focused on making the built environment a compelling topic for school-aged children. To jumpstart this mission, she completed *Urban Animals,* a book of photographs and rhyming text, to teach children about architecture. "It is really amazing to see how a child's attention to her/his own neighborhood sharpens just by looking at buildings," she observed on her home page. "They begin to develop enthusiasm and concern about their own neighborhoods and to notice what makes their streets unique and special. They start to feel good about their community and care about making it cleaner, safer, and more beautiful."

In *Urban Animals* Hill's goal is to instill in children an appreciation for the mix of small shops, nineteenth-century row-houses, and manufacturing/loft buildings that make up many older city neighborhoods. Her photographs reveal the animal images that can be found decorating older structures—from horses, geese, and dogs to donkeys, snakes, and alligators—be they made of terra cotta, stone, or metal. In addition to her simple rhyming text, Hill includes a glossary that defines relevant architectural terms. In *Kirkus Reviews* a contributor praised *Urban Animals,* writing that its "engaging tour" of architectural New York City will inspire children to "go out immediately on animal quests of their own." Barbara Moon asserted in *Time Out Kids—New York* that readers of Hill's "wonderful little gem" of a book will "enjoy identifying a menagerie of sculptured creatures," and her inclusion of a "glossary and directory of animal locations make the book complete."

Biographical and Critical Sources

PERIODICALS

Kirkus Reviews, September 15, 2009, review of *Urban Animals.*
Time Out Kids—New York, November, 2009, Barbara Moon, review of *Urban Animals.*

ONLINE

Isabel Hill Home Page, http://www.isabelhill.com (December 22, 2010).
New Day Films Web site, http://www.newday.com/ (January 10, 2011), "Isabel Hill."

*   *   *

HILL, Isabel T.
See HILL, Isabel

*   *   *

HILL, John
See KOONTZ, Dean

*   *   *

HOBBIE, Holly 1942-

Personal

Born Denise Holly Ulinskas, 1942; married W. Douglas Hobbie (a writer), 1964; children: Brett (deceased), Jocelyn, Nathaniel. *Education:* Attended Pratt Institute (art education) and Boston University (painting).

Addresses

Home—Conway, MA.

Career

Author, illustrator, and graphic artist.

Awards, Honors

ABBY Honor Book selection, American Booksellers Association, c. 1997, for *Toot and Puddle.*

Writings

SELF-ILLUSTRATED

Friendship Grows like a Garden, Little Simon (New York, NY), 2006.
Happiness Comes from the Heart, Little Simon (New York, NY), 2006.
Fanny, Little, Brown (New York, NY), 2008.
Fanny and Annabelle, Little, Brown Books for Young Readers (New York, NY), 2009.
Everything but the Horse, Little, Brown (New York, NY), 2010.

SELF-ILLUSTRATED; "TOOT AND PUDDLE" SERIES

Toot and Puddle, Little, Brown (Boston, MA), 1997.
A Present for Toot, Little, Brown (Boston, MA), 1998.
You Are My Sunshine, Little, Brown (Boston, MA), 1999.
Puddle's ABC, Little, Brown (Boston, MA), 2000.
Welcome to Woodcock Pocket, Little, Brown (Boston, MA), 2001.
I'll Be Home for Christmas, Little, Brown (Boston, MA), 2001.
Top of the World, Little, Brown (Boston, MA), 2002.
Charming Opal, Little, Brown (Boston, MA), 2003.
The New Friend, Little, Brown (Boston, MA), 2004.
Wish You Were Here, Little, Brown (Boston, MA), 2005.
The One and Only, Little, Brown (Boston, MA), 2006.
Let It Snow, Little, Brown (New York, NY), 2007.

ILLUSTRATOR

Clement C. Moore, *The Night before Christmas,* Platt & Munk (New York, NY), 1976.
W.D. Hobbie, *Bloodroot,* Crown Publishers (New York, NY), 1991.

Illustrations collected in several books, including *A Treasury of Holly Hobbie,* Rand-McNally, 1979.

Adaptations

Hobbie's "Holly Hobbie" character was licensed by American Greetings, Mattel, Paramount, and Simon & Schuster. The "Toot and Puddle" characters were adapted for use on board games, cards, and stuffed toys; "Toot and Puddle" books were adapted as a television series produced by Mercury Filmworks, 2008-09, as well as a series of picture-book adaptations published by National Geographic.

Sidelights

In the 1960s a talented watercolor artist named Holly Hobbie was a young mother at home raising three children with her husband. Her sale of a drawing featuring a little girl in a homespun dress and large blue bonnet to the American Greetings card company in 1967 ultimately changed Hobbie's life and made her name known throughout the world. Hobbie's reputation for creating nostalgic, innocent images of children and their pets, inspired by her memories of growing up in rural New England, was one she carried with her for many years. She continued to add to her "Holly Hobbie" drawings, often using her growing children as models, and by 1970 the brand that bears her name was a top-seller in the United States. In 1974 Knickerbocker Toys began producing a line of "Holly Hobbie" rag dolls, with the result that by 1980 "Holly Hobbie" merchandise accounted for more than one billion dollars in sales. Reintroduced in the late 1980s to a new generation of children, "Holly Hobbie" entered into her third incarnation in the mid-2000s when American Greeting capitalized on the many mothers who, remembering the character from their own childhoods, wanted to share "Holly Hobbie" with their own children.

While the flesh-and-blood Holly Hobbie might have been somewhat upstaged by her rag-doll alter-ego—many "Holly Hobbie" fans do not even realize that there is an actual Holly Hobbie—in the mid-1990s she reclaimed her famous name, albeit with the help of a pair of appealing pigs named Toot and Puddle. As author and illustrator of the popular "Toot and Puddle" picture books, Hobbie has won herself a new generation of fans and her characters even starred in their very own television series in 2008.

In *Toot and Puddle* the spunky Toot decides to travel around the globe, and he shares his adventures with home-happy Puddle in a series of postcards addressed to the home in Woodcock Pocket. *A Present for Toot* finds a perplexed Puddle trying to find the perfect birthday present for his friend, with Tulip the parrot ultimately deemed the perfect choice. Toot feels down in the dumps in *You Are My Sunshine,* and *Puddle's ABC* gives young listeners a review of the alphabet while describing how Puddle teaches Otto the turtle how to read. The "Toot and Puddle" series celebrates the holiday season in *I'll Be Home for Christmas,* as the globe-trotting Toot heads off to Scotland to join the 100th birthday celebration of his Great-Great-Aunt Peg the pig. Fortunately, Toot catches a ride on Santa's sleigh and returns home in time to share Christmas Day with his best friend. Through Puddle's worries over Toot's absence, "Hobbie effectively injects some mild, preschooler-friendly tension into the plot," noted Heather Vogel Frederick in her *New York Times Book Review* appraisal of *I'll Be Home for Christmas,* the critic adding that Hobbie's "effervescent watercolors" bring to life the cozy interior of Puddle's home through contrasts with "the chilly winter landscape."

In *Charming Opal* Hobbie introduces Puddle's young cousin Opal, a piglet who is excited about her loose tooth. Anticipating the inevitable visit from the Tooth Fairy turns quickly to concern when it is discovered that the tooth is no longer in the happy piglet's mouth: it is at the bottom of Pocket Pond! Opal returns, with best friend Daphne in tow, in *The New Friend,* but the friendship is tested when Daphne reveals herself to be a prima donna. Hobbie's "absolutely adorable watercolor illustrations" for *Charming Opal* "add emotion to the simple text," noted a *Kirkus Reviews* writer, while in *School Library Journal* Mary Elam wrote that the author/illustrator's engaging characters, depicted in "humorous and expressive" images, "are perfectly tuned-in to her audience." In *The New Friend* Hobbie shares what *School Library Journal* reviewer Maryann H. Owen called "a gentle, entertaining lesson showing that everyone is special."

The travel-happy Toot strays again in both *Top of the World* and *Wish You Were Here,* the latter which find the piglet limping home from the jungles of Borneo and into the caring arms of Puddle and Opal. *Let It Snow* captures the joy of the first snowstorm of winter, as it is shared by true-blue friends. A *Kirkus Reviews* writer noted of *Wish You Were Here* that Hobbie brings to life the friends' adventures by paying "exquisite attention to detail in her peerless watercolors." *Let It Snow* treats readers to a "loving paean to friendship and gift-giving," according to *School Library Journal* contributor Lisa Falk, while a *Publishers Weekly* critic dubbed the same book "another merry and bright visit to Woodcock Pocket." "Every new Toot & Puddle adventure is an eagerly awaited event," exclaimed a *Kirkus Reviews* contributor in a review of *Top of the World.*

Holly Hobbie introduces young children to a spunky and likeable young piglet in her picture-book series that starts with **Charming Opal.** (Little, Brown & Company, 2003. Copyright © 2003 by Holly Hobbie and Douglas Hobbie. Reproduced by permission.)

In *Fanny* and *Fanny and Annabelle* Hobbie introduces a young girl who loves to play with her doll Annabelle. Annabelle is handmade by Fanny, and when friends come to play and bring their glamorous fashion dolls Fanny worries that her beloved rag doll may be lacking. However, the girl eventually reconsiders and Annabelle has a prominent part in Fanny's next play-date, complete with a tiny new handmade doll of her very own. *Fanny and Annabelle* finds Fanny creating a picture-book about her beloved doll, and Hobbie alternates her story of Fanny's project with pages from the young girl's own story. In *Booklist* Carolyn Phelan wrote that Hobbie's "beautifully painted scenes. . ." in *Fanny* "are wonderfully evocative," while a *Publishers Weekly* critic enjoyed the book's cartoon-style art, rendered in "a palette of bright pastels punctuated by lively orange." Phelan described *Fanny and Annabelle* as a "highly appealing, original picture book" and Piper Nyman wrote in *School Library Journal* that its pen-and-ink and water-color illustrations "capture an almost country charm but retain an urban sophistication." In *School Library Journal* Linda Staskus described Hobbie's young heroine as "an independent thinker" who demonstrates to readers that "not following the crowd can have unexpectedly wonderful results."

Discussing the origins of her "second" career as an author and illustrator, Hobbie explained to *Publishers Weekly* interviewer Shannon Maughan that the inspiration to do piglets "started with . . . postcards my daughter had sent us from San Francisco. The cards had pictures of real pigs on them and they really [cheered] . . . us up. Around the same time, I visited a friend's farm in Vermont and saw a sow with her piglets. I knew then that I wanted to draw pigs." "Toot and Puddle couldn't be more different than what I was doing before," Hobbie added to Maughan, referencing her years drawing "Holly Hobbie" scenes. "I wanted to disconnect and start fresh." While she has indeed started fresh, Hobbie brings the same talent and warmth to her "Toot and Puddle" picture books. As Frederick explained in her *New York Times Book Review* appraisal, "The heart and soul of Hobbie's books are her characters," and she captures the duo's "innate pigness, with winning results. Their friendship is utterly loyal, . . . reflecting for children the fact that there are as many ways of embracing life as there are individuals, that it's equally acceptable to be bold and adventurous or content with quieter joys."

Biographical and Critical Sources

BOOKS

The Art of Holly Hobbie: Drawing on Affection, Random House (New York, NY), 1986.

PERIODICALS

Booklist, September 15, 2000, Lauren Peterson, review of *Puddle's ABC,* p. 248; September 15, 2001, Ilene Coo-

Hobbie reveals the imaginary world dolls conjure for young girls in her self-illustrated story **Fanny.** (Little, Brown & Company, 2008. Copyright © 2003 by Holly Hobbie and Douglas Hobbie. Reproduced by permission.)

per, review of *I'll Be Home for Christmas,* p. 235; October 1, 2002, Marta Segal Block, review of *Top of the World,* p. 336; November 15, 2008, Carolyn Phelan, review of *Fanny,* p. 50; September 15, 2009, Carolyn Phelan, review of *Fanny and Annabelle,* p. 64.

Bulletin of the Center for Children's Books, December, 2000, review of *Puddle's ABC,* p. 147; November, 2001, review of *I'll Be Home for Christmas,* p. 104; October, 2002, review of *Top of the World,* p. 60.

Good Housekeeping, May, 1990, "At Home with Holly Hobbie," p. 168.

Horn Book, November-December, 2007, Martha V. Parravano, review of *Let It Snow,* p. 630.

Kirkus Reviews, July 15, 2002, review of *Top of the World,* p. 1033; August 1, 2003, review of *Charming Opal,* p. 1017; July 15, 2004, review of *The New Friend,* p. 687; August 1, 2005, review of *Wish You Were Here,* p. 849; August 1, 2006, review of *The One and Only,* p. 788; August 15, 2009, review of *Fanny and Annabelle.*

New York Times Book Review, December 16, 2001, Heather Vogel Frederick, review of *I'll Be Home for Christmas,* p. 20; October 19, 2003, review of *Charming Opal,* p. 26.

Publishers Weekly, September 15, 1997, review of *Toot and Puddle,* p. 76; August, 28, 2000, review of *Puddle's ABC,* p. 82; September 24, 2001, review of *I'll Be Home for Christmas,* p. 248; June 24, 2002, review of *Top of the World,* p. 56; January 20, 2003, review of *Travels with Toot and Puddle,* p. 84; July 21, 2003, review of *Charming Opal,* p. 194; October 22, 2007, review of *Let It Snow,* p. 54; June 30, 2008, review of *Fanny,* p. 183; September 14, 2009, review of *Fanny and Annabelle,* p. 48.

School Library Journal, November, 2000, Hennie Vaandrager, review of *Puddle's ABC,* p. 122; June, 1991, Susan L. Rogers, review of *Bloodroot,* p. 106; October, 2001, review of *I'll Be Home for Christmas,* p. 66; December, 2003, Mary Elam, review of *Charming Opal,* p. 114; October, 2004, Maryann H. Owen, review of *The New Friend,* p. 115; October, 2005, Linda L. Walkins, review of *Wish You Were Here,* p. 116; October, 2007, Lisa Falk, review of *Let It Snow,* p. 99; October, 2008, Linda Staskus, review of *Fanny,* p. 110; December, 2009, Piper Nyman, review of *Fanny and Annabelle,* p. 84.

Tribune Books (Chicago, IL), review of *Charming Opal,* p. 5.*

*   *   *

HOLGATE, Doug

Personal

Born in Australia. *Education:* University degree (plant and wildlife illustration).

Addresses

Home—Melbourne, Victoria, Australia. *Agent*—Shannon Associates, 630 9th Ave., Ste. 707, New York, NY 10036.

Career

Illustrator and cartoonist. Presenter at comic-book conventions.

Illustrator

GRAPHIC NOVELS

Brian Anderson, *The Adventures of Commander Zack Proton and the Red Giant,* Aladdin Paperbacks (New York, NY), 2006.

Kevin Patrick, *Prehistoric Australia,* Random House Australia (North Sydney, New South Wales, Australia), 2007.

Adam Taor, *There's a Worm on My Eyeball: The Alien Zoo of Germs, Worms, and Lurgies That Could Be Living inside You,* Random House Australia (North Sydney, New South Wales, Australia), 2007.

Brian Anderson, *The Adventures of Commander Zack Proton and the Warlords of Nibblecheese,* Aladdin Paperbacks (New York, NY), 2007.

Brian Anderson, *The Adventures of Commander Zack Proton and the Wrong Planet,* Aladdin Paperbacks (New York, NY), 2007.

Kevin Patrick, *Airborne Australia,* Random House Australia (North Sydney, New South Wales, Australia), 2008.

Sarah Weeks, *Oggie Cooder, Party Animal,* Scholastic Press (New York, NY), 2009.

Donald Lemke, *Revealed!,* Stone Arch Books (Minneapolis, MN), 2009.

Donald Lemke, *Super Zero,* Stone Arch Books (Mankato, MN), 2009.

Donald Lemke, *Zinc Alloy vs. Frankenstein,* Stone Arch Books (Minneapolis, MN), 2009.

Donald Lemke, *Coldfinger,* Stone Arch Books (Minneapolis, MN), 2010.

Josh Lewis, *Super Chicken Nugget Boy and the Furious Fry,* Hyperion/Disney (New York, NY), 2010.

Josh Lewis, *Super Chicken Nugget Boy and the Pizza Planet People,* Hyperion/Disney (New York, NY), 2010.

Donald Lemke, *Wheelies of Justice,* Stone Arch Books (Mankato, MN), 2010.

Karl Kruszelnicki, *Dinosaurs Aren't Dead,* Pan Macmillan (Sydney, New South Wales, Australia), 2010.

Donald Lemke, *Spokes on the Water,* Stone Arch Books (Mankato, MN), 2011.

Steven Kroll, *Superdragon,* Marshall Cavendish Children's (New York, NY), 2011.

Contributor to comic-book series, including "Zinc Ally," "The Adventures of Dermott the Cute Gay Nerd!," and "Super Chicken Nugget Boy." Contributor to magazines, including *New Yorker* and *Mad,* and to the *Flight* journal series.

"HORROR HIGH" GRAPHIC-NOVEL SERIES BY PAUL STAFFORD

The 101 Damnations, Random House Australia (Melbourne, Victoria, Australia), 2006.

The Interghouls Cricket Cup, Random House Australia (Melbourne, Victoria, Australia), 2006.

The Great Brain Robbery, Random House Australia (Melbourne, Victoria, Australia), 2006.

The Feral Peril Random House Australia (Melbourne, Victoria, Australia), 2006.

Biographical and Critical Sources

PERIODICALS

School Library Journal, January, 2009, Carrie Rogers-Whitehead, review of *Super Zero,* p. 133; September, 2009, Lisa Gieskes, review of *Zink Alloy vs. Frankenstein,* p. 188; March, 2010, S. McClendon, review of *There's a Worm on My Eyeball!: The Alien Zoo of Germs, Worms and Lurgies That Could Be Living inside You,* p. 181; June, 2010, Jane Cronkhite, review of *Super Chicken Nugget Boy and the Furious Fry,* p. 78.

ONLINE

Doug Holgate Home Page, http://www.skullduggery.com.au (January 15, 2011).

Doug Holgate Web log, http://douglasbot.livejournal.com (January 15, 2011).

Pulp Faction Web site, http://www.pulpfaction.net/ (April, 2005), Christian Read, interview with Holgate.*

*   *   *

HOPPEY, Tim 1958-

Personal

Born 1958, in New York, NY; married; wife's name Ellen; children: three. *Education:* Hobart College, B.A. (English and history).

Addresses

Home—Shoreham, NY.

Career

Firefighter and writer. Firefighter in East Harlem, NY, for more than twenty-five years.

Writings

FOR CHILDREN

Tito, the Firefighter/Tito, el bombero, illustrated by Kimberly Hoffman, translation by Eida de la Vega, Raven Tree Press (Green Bay, WI), 2004.

(With Rafael Rivera, Jr.) *Baseball on Mars/Béisbol en Marte,* illustrated by Christina Rodriguez, translation by Gabriela Baeza Ventura, Piñata Books (Houston, TX), 2009.

Jungle Scout: A Vietnam War Story, illustrated by Ramon Espinoza, Stone Arch Books (Mankato, MN), 2009.

The Good Fire Helmet, illustrated by Lori McElrath-Eslick, Alma Little (St. Paul, MN), 2010.

OTHER

Subterranean Angels (poetry), Everett Press (St. James, NY), 1983.

Author of *Where There's Smoke* (poetry), Argonne House Press. Contributor of poetry to periodicals, including *Chelsea, Mudfish,* and *Wisconsin Review.*

Sidelights

In addition to his work as an author, Tim Hoppey is a firefighter stationed in the predominately Hispanic New York City neighborhood of East Harlem. Hoppey's picture books for children, which feature bilingual texts, include *Tito, the Firefighter/Tito, el bombero* and *Baseball on Mars/Béisbol en Marte,* the latter a bilingual tale coauthored by Rafael Rivera, Jr. In addition to his work for children, Hoppey has also penned *Jungle Scout: A Vietnam War Story,* a graphic novel for teens, as well as two works of poetry for adults.

Born in New York City, Hoppey earned a bachelor's degree in English and history from Hobart College. His picture-book debut, *Tito, the Firefighter/Tito, el bombero,* draws on his own life in its focus on a boy's budding friendship with a neighborhood firefighter. Tito, a resident of East Harlem, dreams of riding on a fire truck and during his frequent visits to the station he often strikes up a conversation with Richie, a kindly firefighter. When a Spanish-speaking neighbor comes to the firehouse, the bilingual Tito is able to translate his urgent message and the youngster earns a special reward for his efforts. Ann Welton, writing in *School Library Journal,* called *Tito, the Firefighter/Tito, el bombero* "a refreshing slice of life." Noting that Hoppey incorporates Spanish words and phrases into his narrative, a *Kirkus Reviews* critic assured that the story "has the benefit of suggesting the value of bilingualism."

In *Baseball on Mars/Béisbol en Marte* a father learns to appreciate his son's creativity and love of imaginative play. Told in English and Spanish, the work centers on Roberto, a youngster who uses his father's favorite chair as the pilot seat for his homemade spaceship. Roberto's father had planned to relax in the comforting chair while watching an important baseball game. However, when he sees his son's backyard project, the man undergoes a change of heart and ultimately joins Roberto on a "voyage" to outer space. Reviewing *Baseball on Mars/Béisbol en Marte* for *School Library Journal,* Michael Shapiro observed that Hoppey shows how "a simple game of catch between father and son can become an event of cosmic proportions."

Tim Hoppey teams up with Rafael Rivera, Jr., to write Baseball on Mars, *a bilingual picture book illustrated by Christina Rodriguez.* (Piñata Books, 2009. Illustration copyright © 2009 by Christina Rodriguez. Reproduced by permission.)

Biographical and Critical Sources

PERIODICALS

Kirkus Reviews, June 1, 2005, review of *Tito, the Firefighter/Tito, el bombero,* p. 637.
Library Media Connection, May-June, 2009, Audrey Irene Daigneault, review of *Jungle Scout: A Vietnam War Story,* p. 76.
School Library Journal, October, 2005, Ann Welton, review of *Tito, the Firefighter/Tito, el bombero,* p. 149; October, 2009, Michael Shapiro, review of *Baseball on Mars/Béisbol en Marte,* p. 118.

ONLINE

Delta Publishing Company Web site, http://www.delta publishing.com/ (February 1, 2011), "Tim Hoppey."
Elva Resa Publishing Web site, http://www.elvaresa.com/ (February 1, 2011), "Tim Hoppey."*

*   *   *

HUNTLEY, Amy

Personal

Children: one daughter. *Education:* B.A. (English); M.A. (English). *Hobbies and other interests:* Reading attending the theatre, playing the piano.

Addresses

Home—East Lansing, MI. *E-mail*—Amy@amyhuntley. com.

Career

Author and educator. Teacher of high-school and middle-school English and history beginning 1989.

Member

Society of Children's Book Writers and Illustrators.

Awards, Honors

Morris Award nomination, YALSA/American Library Association, 2010, for *The Everafter.*

Writings

The Everafter, Balzer & Bray (New York, NY), 2009.

Author's work has been translated into Portuguese.

Adaptations

The Everafter was adapted for audiobook, narrated by Tavia Gilbert, Brilliance Audio, 2010.

Sidelights

A lifelong reader whose literary tastes range from Victorian novels to modern thrillers to children's books, Amy Huntley found the perfect career fit when she began teaching high-school English in the late 1980s. With *The Everafter* Huntley also fulfilled a dream she had held since her childhood years: to write the kind of novel she loved to discover as a teen reader.

When readers first meet Madison Stanton, the narrator of *The Everafter,* the seventeen year old is coming to the realization that she is no longer among the living. Floating weightlessly in an endless darkness, Maddy does not remember how she died and cannot discern any meaning in the life she led. Then objects begin to appear, sporadically, and when Maddy touches each one she is reconnected at the point in her past where she possessed that particular object and then lost it. From a pair of socks and her boyfriend's sweatshirt to the keys to the family car, each object returns the girl to a particular moment in time and provides her with a small part of the answer to her central question: how did she die? Only when she comes to realize that her boyfriend and another schoolmate also inhabit the dreamlike nothingness does Maddy begin to put the pieces of her last few moments of life together in a novel that Laura Amos praised in *School Library Journal* as a "fresh take on a teen's journey of self-exploration." In *Kirkus Reviews* a contributor found *The Everafter* to be "cleverly constructed and compelling," adding that Huntley's knack for capturing the nuances of a teen's "relationships, choices and consequences" makes her story "intriguing and thought-provoking" as well. Noting the narrator's "bouncy, 'ohmygod' voice," *Booklist* contributor Daniel Kraus deemed *The Everafter* "catnip for those who like their romances draped in tragedy," and in *Publishers Weekly* a critic deemed Maddy "an engaging protagonist" and her creator "an author worth watching."

"When I look back at the process of writing *The Everafter,* I can see how different aspects of my life became incorporated into the themes of the novel," Huntley told *SATA.* "Coping with change is probably the biggest theme of the story, and much of how I allowed that theme to shape its plot and characters came from my experiences as a teacher. I work with high-school kids, and it seems like we are forever threatening teenagers with change. In middle school we talk about how different it will be in high school. In high school, we start telling them to prepare for college. In college, the job market. All these changes occur inside of relatively short (when compared to the span of other time periods of our lives) intervals of two to four years. I see a lot of stress in high school kids related to all this change.

"Another theme in the book, mother-daughter relationships, was heavily influenced by my daughter—who was four when I began the novel. Ironically enough, I wasn't even aware of how influential that theme was in the book until a teenage reader told her mother to read the book. I couldn't at first figure out why she was recommending it to her mother instead of her friends! Twelve hours later, the role of mothers and daughters in the book finally surfaced in my conscious. I realized

Cover of Amy Huntley's fantasy novel The Everafter, *about a teen in limbo who must discover how and why she died.* (Balzer & Bray, 2009. Cover photographs copyright © 2009 by Al Richards and Michael Dunning. Reproduced by permission.)

how fascinated I had been, before I even began the novel, with the way my daughter could be—all at once in my memories—so many different ages, so many different people. Knowing and loving these different versions of her led to me craft Maddy's plot using vignettes that covered disparate points in time during her life.

"Dead teenage narrators are quite popular these days. I'm sure that impacted the way I explored the afterlife in this novel, but the strongest influence on that was an interest I've had all my life in understanding the universe and an individual person's place within it. I think our memories haunt us, for both better and worse, and it was that idea that I took into the novel when I was shaping notions about ghosts and the afterlife. Rather than giving Maddy the opportunity to haunt other people's lives, I gave her the opportunity to haunt her own. After all, that's an opportunity we all have in the here and now. We don't need to wait for the afterlife to have that chance. I hoped to reach readers with that realization."

Biographical and Critical Sources

PERIODICALS

Booklist, August 1, 2009, Daniel Kraus, review of *The Everafter,* p. 55.
Kirkus Reviews, September 15, 2009, review of *The Everafter.*
Publishers Weekly, October 26, 2009, review of *The Everafter,* p. 59.
School Library Journal, December, 2009, Laura Amos, review of *The Everafter,* p. 122.
Voice of Youth Advocates, December, 2009, Beth Karpas, review of *The Everafter,* p. 420.

ONLINE

Amy Huntley Home Page, http://amyhuntley.com (January 22, 2011).
Amy Huntley Web log, http://www.everafterwords.blogspot. com (January 22, 2011).
HarperCollins Web site, http://www.harpercollinschildrens. com/ (January 22, 2011).*

*   *   *

IBATOULLINE, Bagram 1965(?)-

Personal

Surname pronounced "E-bat-too-LEEN"; born c. 1965, in Omsk, USSR (now Russia); immigrated to United States, 1991. *Education:* Art College of Kazan, degree; State Academic Institute of Arts (Moscow, USSR), degree.

Addresses

Home—Chichester, NY.

Career

Illustrator.

Awards, Honors

Boston Globe/Horn Book Award for Fiction, 2006, for *The Miraculous Journey of Edward Tulane* by Kate DiCamillo; New York Public Library 100 Best Books for Reading and Sharing designation, 2006, for *The Adventures of Marco Polo* by Russell Freedman.

Illustrator

Philip E. Booth, *Crossing,* Candlewick Press (Cambridge, MA), 2001.
Michele Benoit Slawson, *Signs for Sale,* Viking (New York, NY), 2002.
Stephen Mitchell, reteller, *The Nightingale* (based on the story by Hans Christian Andersen), Candlewick Press (Cambridge, MA), 2002.
Paul Fleischman, *The Animal Hedge,* Candlewick Press (Cambridge, MA), 2003.
Celeste Davidson Mannis, *The Queen's Progress: An Elizabethan Alphabet,* Viking (New York, NY), 2003.
James Giblin, *Secrets of the Sphinx,* Scholastic Press (New York, NY), 2004.
Deborah Noyes, *Hana in the Time of the Tulips,* Candlewick Press (Cambridge, MA), 2004.
M.T. Anderson, *The Serpent Came to Gloucester,* Candlewick Press (Cambridge, MA), 2005.
Paul Fleischman, *Graven Images: Three Stories,* Candlewick Press (Cambridge, MA), 2006.
Kate DiCamillo, *The Miraculous Journey of Edward Tulane,* Candlewick Press (Cambridge, MA), 2006.
Stephen Mitchell, adaptor, *The Tinderbox* (based on the story by Hans Christian Andersen), Candlewick Press (Cambridge, MA), 2006.
Diane Stanley, *Bella at Midnight: The Thimble, the Ring, and the Slippers of Glass,* HarperCollins (New York, NY), 2006.
Elizabeth Winthrop, *The First Christmas Stocking,* Random House Children's Books (New York, NY), 2006.
Russell Freedman, *The Adventures of Marco Polo,* Arthur Levine Books (New York, NY), 2006.
Kate DiCamillo, *Great Joy,* Candlewick Press (Cambridge, MA), 2007.
Staton Rabin, *Mr. Lincoln's Boys: Being the Mostly True Adventures of Abraham Lincoln's Trouble-making Sons Tad and Willie,* Viking (New York, NY), 2008.
Lois Lowry, *Crow Call,* Scholastic Press (New York, NY), 2009.
Jane Yolen, *The Scarecrow's Dance,* Simon & Schuster Books for Young Readers (New York, NY), 2009.
L.G. Bass, *There Was a Little Gnome,* Atheneum Books for Young Readers (New York, NY), 2009.
Hans Christian Andersen, *Thumbelina,* retold by Brian Alderson, Candlewick Press (Somerville, MA), 2009.
L.G. Bass, *Boom Boom Go Away!,* Atheneum Books for Young Readers (New York, NY), 2010.

Rosemary Wells, *On the Blue Comet,* Candlewick Press (Somerville, MA), 2010.

Linda Sue Park, *The Third Gift,* Clarion (New York, NY), 2011.

Sidelights

As an illustrator inspired by classical art and the works of the Old Masters, Russian-born artist Bagram Ibatoulline is recognized for his ability to work in a variety of styles, making each of his illustration projects—which range from Celeste Davidson Mannis's *The Queen's Progress: An Elizabethan Alphabet* and Stanton Rabin's *Mr. Lincoln's Boys: Being the Mostly True Adventures of Abraham Lincoln's Troublemaking Sons Tad and Willie* to Lois Lowry's family-centered *Crow Call* and Rosemary Wells' dream-time fantasy *On the Blue Comet*—an unexpected delight. Characteristic of the artist's work, *Mr. Lincoln's Boys* features what *Booklist* critic John Peters described as "finely detailed, sepia-tone period scenes" peopled with "excellent likenesses of Lincoln and other historical figures." In *School Library Journal* Lee Bock cited Ibatoulline's "masterful illustrations" of Lincoln and his family as "evocative and detailed," adding that "they fill the pages" of Rabin's story "with visual information and emotion."

As far back as he can remember Ibatoulline has been actively exploring different artistic styles and mediums. Beginning his training at a children's art school in the then-Soviet Union, he subsequently attended the Art College of Kazan, where he studied for four years. After graduation, Ibatoulline moved to Moscow to attend the State Art Institute. "I enjoy any style—it is never my intention to copy a particular look or aesthetic," the artist noted in an online interview for *Bookbrowse.* "Instead I do a lot of groundwork and extensive research on the time period in order to come up with my own approach."

Among Ibatoulline's illustration projects are several classical stories of childhood, and each benefits from his unique revisioning. In Stephen Mitchell's retelling of *The Nightingale,* a classic story by Hans Christian Andersen, the artist crafts a Chinese setting by placing his images in detailed, scroll-like panels painted in vibrant jewel tones. As Gillian Engberg wrote in *Booklist,* Ibatoulline's contribution to *The Nightingale* is "stunning," and a *Publishers Weekly* wrote that the illustrator's "elaborate, harmonious watercolors pay homage to the flat style of Chinese brush paintings with iconic fidelity." Another Andersen classic, *The Tinderbox,* is also presented in Mitchell's retelling, and its story of a soldier who manages to retain a cache of gold with the help of three magical creatures comes to life in ink-and-watercolor images that take on the quality of eighteenth-century lithographs. Ibatoulline's choice of a northern Europe backdrop presents what *Horn Book* contributor Joanna Rudge Long described as "a sumptuous setting for this strange, profoundly provocative classic," and

Margaret Bush wrote in *School Library Journal* that the artist's "finely hatched pen drawings" "have an appropriately old-fashioned look."

In his work for *The Queen's Progress,* Ibatoulline once again demonstrates his penchant for detail by capturing the stylistic nuances of the Elizabethan era in "handsome illustrations evoking the period," according to Carolyn Phelan in *Booklist.* Nancy Menaldi-Scanlan had similar praise in her *School Library Journal* review, commenting that "Ibatoulline's acrylic paintings are superb in their elegance and fascinating in their detail." The queen's "ornate gowns and her courtly accoutrements are delightfully offset by her servants' plain garb and earnest expressions," Menaldi-Scanlan added, noting the illustrator's insertion of humor into his complex images. Deeming *The Queen's Progress* "dense, erudite, and absorbing," a *Publishers Weekly* contributor cited Ibatoulline's use of "period touches, whether . . . outfitting the courtiers in brocade or depicting a maze of hedgerows."

As a *Kirkus Reviews* writer noted, Ibatoulline "exhibits chameleon-like adaptability with his chapter-introducing illustrations" to Russell Freedman's *The Adventures of Marco Polo,* "varying style from Western to Eastern to suit the subject." An exploration of the many versions of the noted explorer's *The Description of the World,* a book first published in the thirteenth century, Freedman's text retraces Polo's trip through the Middle and Far East, lacing the explorer's own words into a compelling original narrative. As a *Publishers Weekly* contributor noted, Ibatoulline works in a similar fashion, creating "accomplished paintings [that] reflect the artistic conventions of the cultures Marco encountered . . . and act as a visual bridge between the events of the text" and archival images. Calling the book "as beautiful as many of the sights the explorer observed," Ilene Cooper added in her *Booklist* review that *The Adventures of Marco Polo* stands as another example of Ibatoulline's versatility, as well as "a glorious piece of bookmaking [that] readers will find it a pleasure to explore."

In *The Miraculous Journey of Edward Tulane* Ibatoulline joins award-winning author Kate DiCamillo to draw readers into the world of a china rabbit who feels so self-important that the love of his child owner inspires no gratitude in return. When Edward the rabbit becomes lost and goes on a journey similar to the wooden doll in Rachel Fielding's *Hitty,* the toy's heart eventually grows. In the pages of this novel-length work, Ibatoulline contributes "haunting color plates and sepia illustrations at the beginning of each chapter [that] evoke the era of Andrew Wyeth, Howard Pyle and Maxfield Parrish," according to *New York Times Book Review* contributor Michael Patrick Hearn. Another collaboration with DiCamillo, *Great Joy,* finds a young girl worried about the welfare of an organ grinder and his monkey when she sees them sleeping in the cold one night just before Christmas. Enhancing a story that

Bagram Ibatoulline's detailed art has appeared in many picture books, among them The Animal Hedge *by Paul Fleischman.* (Illustrations copyright © 2003 by Bagram Ibatoulline. Reproduced by permission of Candlewick Press, Inc., Somerville, MA.)

School Library Journal contributor Eva Mitnick characterized as "simplicity itself," Ibatoulline's evocative gouache paintings are "reminiscent of Norman Rockwell's work in their warmth and realism" and their ability "to enrich and expand" DiCamillo's simple holiday tale.

Like the Old Masters, Ibatoulline has shown himself to be equally adept at capturing sumptuous luxury and the simplicity of rural life. In *Crow Call,* for example, Lowry's story describes a girl's effort to build a new relationship with her father, a man recently returned from fighting in World War II, while also enjoying the simple activities and rituals of their family farm. In earth-toned watercolor-and-gouache images that evoke the paintings of American artist Andrew Wyeth in their detail, Ibatoulline presents "each frame of the story . . . like an old-time movie," according to *Booklist* contributor Cooper. Capturing Lowry's "nostalgic story," the "remarkable, atmospheric illustrations" in *Crow Call* contribute to what *School Library Journal* critic Maryann H. Owen recommended as a tale about "a treasured day spent with a special person [that] will resonate with readers everywhere." Jane Yolen's poetic picture book *The Scarecrow's Dance* also benefits from Ibatoulline's art, which Engberg described in *Booklist* as "beautiful, spooky, dimly lit images" that "show the slender straw man floating and dancing."

Ibatoulline teams up with Brian Anderson to bring to life a beloved fairy tale in **Thumbelina.** (Illustration copyright © 2009 by Bagram Ibatoulline. Reproduced by permission of Candlewick Press, Somerville, MA.)

Biographical and Critical Sources

PERIODICALS

Booklist, August, 2002, Denise Wilms, review of *Signs for Sale,* p. 1976; November 1, 2002, Gillian Engberg, review of *The Nightingale,* p. 488; April 1, 2003, Carolyn Phelan, review of *The Queen's Progress: An Elizabethan Alphabet,* p. 1394; November 1, 2004, Gillian Engberg, review of *Hana in the Time of the Tulips,* p. 498; September 15, 2004, Hazel Rochman, review of *Secrets of the Sphinx,* p. 240; June 1, 2005, Jennifer Mattson, review of *The Serpent Came to Gloucester,* p. 1805; February 1, 2006, Ilene Cooper, review of *Bella at Midnight: The Thimble, the Ring, and the Slippers of Glass,* p. 49; January 1, 2006, Ilene Cooper, review of *The Miraculous Journey of Edward Tulane,* p. 112; October 6, 2006, Ilene Cooper, review of *The Adventures of Marco Polo,* p. 46; November 15, 2006, Ilene Cooper, review of *The First Christmas Stocking,* p. 56; October 15, 2007, Ilene Cooper, review of *Great Joy,* p. 46; July 1, 2008, John Peters, review of *Mr. Lincoln's Boys: Being the Mostly True Adventures of Abraham Lincoln's Troublemaking Sons Tad and Willie,* p. 59; July 1, 2009, Gillian Engberg, review of *The Scarecrow's Dance,* p. 69; October 15, 2009, Ilene Cooper, review of *Crow Call,* p. 50; December 15, 2009, Andrew Medlar, review of *Boom Boom Go Away!,* p. 43; July 1, 2010, Daniel Kraus, review of *On the Blue Comet,* p. 61.

Horn Book, November-December, 2004, Betty Carter, review of *Secrets of the Sphinx,* p. 727; March-April, 2006, Susan Dove Lempke, review of *The Miraculous Journey of Edward Tulane,* p. 184; April, 2006, Susan Dove Lempke, review of *Bella at Midnight,* p. 194; May-June, 2007, Joanna Rudge Long, review of *The Tinderbox,* p. 261.

Kirkus Reviews, September 15, 2001, review of *Crossing,* p. 1354; April 15, 2002, review of *Signs for Sale,* p. 579; September 15, 2004, review of *Hana in the Time of the Tulips,* p. 197; June 1, 2005, review of *The Serpent Came to Gloucester,* p. 632; January 15, 2006, review of *The Miraculous Journey of Edward Tulane,* p. 83; September 15, 2006, review of *The Adventures of Marco Polo;* November 1, 2006, review of *The First Christmas Stocking;* February 1, 2007, review of *The Tinderbox,* p. 119; August 1, 2008, review of *Mr. Lincoln's Boys;* July 15, 2009, review of *The Scarecrow's Dance.*

New York Times Book Review, May 14, 2006, Michael Patrick Hearn, review of *The Miraculous Journey of Edward Tulane,* p. 116; December 16, 2007, Sarah Ellis, review of *Great Joy,* p. 20; April 11, 2010, Emily Jenkins, review of *Thumbelina,* p. 14.

Publishers Weekly, October 8, 2001, review of *Crossing,* p. 64; April 22, 2002, review of *Signs for Sale,* p. 69; October 14, 2002, review of *The Nightingale,* p. 84; April 28, 2003, review of *The Queen's Progress,* p. 69; September 8, 2003, review of *The Animal Hedge,* p. 76; November 22, 2004, review of *Hana in the Time of the Tulips,* p. 60; May 16, 2005, review of *The Serpent Came to Gloucester,* p. 62; December 12,

2005, Katherine Paterson, review of *The Miraculous Journey of Edward Tulane,* p. 67; October 2, 2006, review of *The Adventures of Marco Polo,* p. 65; October 22, 2007, review of *Great Joy,* p. 55; September 28, 2009, review of *Crow Call,* p. 64; January 18, 2010, review of *Boom Boom Go Away!,* p. 45.

School Arts, January, 2005, Ken Marantz, review of *Hana in the Time of the Tulips,* p. 67.

School Library Journal, November, 2001, Wanda Meyers-Hines, review of *Crossing,* p. 140; July, 2002, Carol Schene, review of *Signs for Sale,* p. 99; November, 2002, Heide Piehler, review of *The Nightingale,* p. 110; May, 2003, Nancy Menaldi-Scanlan, review of *The Queen's Progress,* p. 138; October, 2004, Kathy Krasniewicz, review of *Hana in the Time of the Tulips,* p. 126; November, 2004, Daryl Grabarek, review of *Secrets of the Sphinx,* p. 163; June, 2005, Margaret Bush, review of *The Serpent Came to Gloucester,* p. 51; March, 2006, Kathleen Isaacs, review of *Bella at Midnight,* p. 230; March, 2007, Margaret Bush, review of *The Tinderbox,* p. 150; October, 2007, Eva Mitnick, review of *Great Joy,* p. 97; September, 2008, Lee Bock, review of *Mr. Lincoln's Boys,* p. 167; July, 2009, Wendy Lukehart, review of *The Scarecrow's Dance,* p. 69; October, 2009, Maryann H. Owen, review of *Crow Call,* p. 98; January, 2010, Marianne Saccardi, review of *Boom Boom Go Away!,* p. 74.

ONLINE

BookBrowse, http://www.bookbrowse.com/ (October 10, 2006), interview with Ibatoulline.

Candlewick Press Web site, http://www.candlewickportals. com/ (January 15, 2011), "Bagram Ibatoulline."*

J-K

JESSELL, Tim

Personal

Married; wife's name Ragan; children: Abby, Ben, Molly. *Education:* University of Tulsa, B.F.A. (commercial design; cum laude). *Hobbies and other interests:* Falconry, coaching his children's sports teams.

Addresses

Home—Stillwater, OK. *Office*—Tim Jessell Illustration, 7906 N. Perkins Rd., Stillwater, OK 74075. *Agent*—Suzanne Craig, Suzanne Craig Represents, Inc., 4015 E. 53rd St., Tulsa, OK 74135; suzanne@suzannecraig.com. *E-mail*—tim@timjessell.com.

Career

Commercial artist and illustrator. Freelance illustrator, beginning 1992. *Exhibitions:* Work has been shown at Society of Illustrators Annual Exhibitions, New York, NY.

Awards, Honors

Society of Illustrators Gold Medal Award; Addy, *Print,* Graphex, and other illustration awards; *AdWeek* magazine illustrator-of-the-year designation; inducted into Hall of Distinction at Terre Haute South Vigo High School.

Writings

SELF-ILLUSTRATED

Amorak, Creative Education (Mankato, MN), 1994.
Paper Tiger, Harcourt (San Diego, CA), 1997.
Falcon, Random House (New York, NY), 2011.

ILLUSTRATOR

Stan Lee, *Stan Lee's Superhero Christmas,* Katherine Tegan Books (New York, NY), 2004.

Paul Haven, *Two Hot Dogs with Everything,* Random House (New York, NY), 2006.
Alan Armstrong, *Raleigh's Page,* Random House (New York, NY), 2007.
Alan Armstrong, *Looking for Marco Polo,* Random House (New York, NY), 2009.
David A. Kelly, *Babe Ruth and the Baseball Curse,* Random House (New York, NY), 2009.
Kristin Kladstrup, *A Night in Santa's Great Big Bag,* Viking (New York, NY), 2010.

Contributor of illustrations to periodicals, including *Boy's Life, Time,* and *Texas Monthly.*

ILLUSTRATOR; "SECRETS OF DROON" SERIES BY TONY ABBOTT

The Hidden Stairs and the Magic Carpet, Scholastic (New York, NY), 1999.
Journey to the Volcano Palace, Scholastic (New York, NY), 1999.
The Mysterious Island, Scholastic (New York, NY), 1999.
City in the Clouds, Scholastic (New York, NY), 1999.
The Great Ice Battle, Scholastic (New York, NY), 2000.
The Sleeping Giant of Goll, Scholastic (New York, NY), 2000.
Into the Land of the Lost Secrets, Scholastic (New York, NY), 2000.
The Golden Wasp, Scholastic (New York, NY), 2000.
Tower of the Elf King, Scholastic (New York, NY), 2000.
Quest for the Queen, Scholastic (New York, NY), 2000.
The Hawk Bandits of Tarkoom, Scholastic (New York, NY), 2001.
Under the Serpent Sea, Scholastic (New York, NY), 2001.
The Mask of Maliban, Scholastic (New York, NY), 2001.
Voyage of the Jaffa Wind, Scholastic (New York, NY), 2002.
The Moon Scroll, Scholastic (New York, NY), 2002.
The Knights of Silversnow, Scholastic (New York, NY), 2002.
Search for the Dragon Ship, Scholastic (New York, NY), 2003.
The Coiled Viper, Scholastic (New York, NY), 2003.

Also illustrator of other titles in the "Secrets of Droon" series.

Sidelights

Award-winning commercial artist Tim Jessell has worked for a wide variety of clients, from Apple Computer and Nike to Anheuser-Busch and Dr. Pepper. However appreciative those clients may be of Jessell's versatile yet realistic style, his biggest fans are likely to be the countless children who have enjoyed his original self-illustrated picture books *Amorak* and *Paper Tiger* as well as the artwork he has contributed to books by writers such as Paul Haven, Tony Abbott, and Alan Armstrong.

Raised in Indiana, Jessell studied art in high school, where his teacher gave him a strong grounding in the basics. He earned a football scholarship to the University of Tulsa, and there he earned a B.F.A. in commercial design. Jessell's realistic style was a perfect match with the needs of advertisers, and he was able to build a successful career as a commercial artist after going freelance in 1992. He has moved from sketching and working with pastel and other artistic media to creating his images digitally, retaining the traditional approach that has caused his work to be dubbed "tradigital."

In 1994 Jessell created his first original picture book, *Amorak*. Featuring compelling and detailed art, the book transports readers to the far north, where a wolf's distant howl is heard as an elderly man tucks his grandson into bed. To reassure the boy, the man tells an Inuit Creation story in which the Great Being brings all manner of creature forth to inhabit an empty world. When sick and weak creatures begin to gain prominence, taking an increasing share of scarce resources, the Great Being creates Amorak. Father of all wolves, Amorak performs an important service by culling the herds and allowing healthy creatures to thrive. Praising Jessell's picture-book debut, a *Publishers Weekly* contributor wrote that the author/illustrator's "suggestively lit paintings, rich with nocturnal blues and golden firelight, sustain the intensity and wonder of his tale."

In addition to creating illustrations for Abbott's multivolume "Secrets of Droon" middle-grade novel series, Jessell joined Marvel Comics writer Stan Lee to create *Stan Lee's Superhero Christmas*. Lee's first book for children, *Stan Lee's Superhero Christmas* features the yuletide adventures of the Protector, as the musclebound hero attempts to rescue Santa from the evil trolls who have trapped him in an icy kingdom. Calling the project "one of those cases where a book's text is completely overshadowed by the illustrations," Dave Jenkinson wrote in the *Canadian Review of Materials* that in *Stan Lee's Superhero Christmas* Jessell's dramatic, high-energy "pastel and mixed media illustrations are visually engrossing."

Jessell's work for Haven's *Two Hot Dogs with Everything,* a novel about an eleven-year-old baseball fan who hopes that superstition can prop up the score of his

Jessell draws on research of the past in his artwork for Alan Armstrong's **Looking for Marco Polo.** (Illustration copyright © 2009 by Tim Jessell. Used by permission of Random House Children's Books, a division of Random House, Inc.)

favorite team, inspired a *Kirkus Reviews* contributor to call the work "magical and delightful." Jessell also provided the artwork for *Raleigh's Page,* an historical novel by Alan Armstrong. Set in late-sixteenth-century England, *Raleigh's Page* centers on Andrew Saintleger, an adventurous eleven year old who gains a position as a page to legendary explorer Sir Walter Raleigh. Andrew quickly gains his employer's confidence and embarks on a series of dangerous missions, including a journey to France to steal an important map of the New World and a trip to America that ends in a hostile confrontation with Native Americans. In *Booklist,* Carolyn Phelan applauded Jessell's "expressive pencil drawings," and Kim Dare, writing in *School Library Journal,* praised the combination of text and art, stating that "Armstrong's meticulous research, combined with Jessell's lively black-and-white illustrations, bring to life the people who shaped our nation's earliest history." Jessell and Armstrong have also teamed up on *Looking for Marco Polo,* an "entertaining blend of contemporary and historical adventure," according to *Booklist* critic Todd Morning.

In *A Night in Santa's Great Big Bag,* a picture book by Kristin Kladstrup, a stuffed animal takes an improbable journey on Christmas Eve. After Louis tells his favorite toy, Lamb, about the magic of Santa Claus, the curious creature quietly climbs into Santa's sack when the Christmas-night visitor stops at Louis's home. Once aloft, Lamb makes new friends with the soon-to-be-delivered toys, but at night's end he finds himself alone, worried that he will not be able to rejoin his owner. Fortunately, the jolly old elf has no intention of separating the pair and plans a return visit to Louis's house. Linda Israelson, reviewing *A Night in Santa's Great Big Bag* in *School Library Journal,* observed that Jessell's "colorful, festive illustrations" are a highlight of the work.

Biographical and Critical Sources

PERIODICALS

Booklist, August, 2007, Carolyn Phelan, review of *Raleigh's Page,* p. 77; January 1, 2009, Todd Morning, review of *Babe Ruth and the Baseball Curse,* p. 74; August 1, 2009, Todd Morning, review of *Looking for Marco Polo,* p. 70.

Bulletin of the Center for Children's Books, November, 2004, Krista Hutley, review of *Stan Lee's Superhero Christmas,* p. 131; May, 2006, Elizabeth Bush, review of *Two Hot Dogs with Everything,* p. 403.

Canadian Review of Materials, February 15, 2005, Dave Jenkinson, review of *Stan Lee's Superhero Christmas.*

Horn Book, November-December, 2007, Susan Dove Lempke, review of *Raleigh's Page,* p. 673.

Kirkus Reviews, April 1, 2006, review of *Two Hot Dogs with Everything,* p. 348; September 1, 2007, review of *Raleigh's Page;* January 15, 2009, review of *Babe Ruth and the Baseball Curse;* July 1, 2009, review of *Looking for Marco Polo.*

Publishers Weekly, June 27, 1994, review of *Amorak,* p. 76; April 17, 2006, review of *Two Hot Dogs with Everything,* p. 188.

School Library Journal, May, 2006, Marilyn Taniguchi, review of *Two Hot Dogs with Everything,* p. 348; November, 2007, Kim Dare, Kim. review of *Raleigh's Page,* p. 116; September, 2009, Kathleen Meulen, review of *Babe Ruth and the Baseball Curse,* p. 183; December, 2009, Caroline Tesauro, review of *Looking for Marco Polo,* p. 105; October, 2010, Linda Israelson, review of *A Night in Santa's Great Big Bag,* p. 74.

Texas Monthly, January, 1991, "Texas Desperado: Award-winning Western Illustrator Tim Jessell," p. 74.

Tulsa World (Tulsa, OK), December 29, 2010, Bill Haisten, "Oklahoma Artist's Works Used by Alamo Bowl."

ONLINE

Directory of Illustration Web site, http://www.directory ofillustration.com/ (January 21, 2011), "Tim Jessell."

Tim Jessell Home Page, http://www.timjessell.com (January 21, 2011).*

* * *

KIM, Dong-hwa 1950-

Personal

Born November 10, 1950, in Seoul, South Korea.

Addresses

Home—South Korea (Republic of Korea).

Career

Illustrator and author; creator of comics beginning 1975.

Awards, Honors

YALSA Great Graphic Novel for Teens selection, American Library Association, 2009, for "The Color of Earth" series.

Writings

"STORY OF LIFE ON THE GOLDEN PLAINS" GRAPHIC NOVEL SERIES; SELF-ILLUSTRATED

The Color of Earth, (originally serialized in *Twenty Seven* magazine), translated by Lauren Na, First Second (New York, NY), 2009.

The Color of Water, (originally serialized in *Twenty Seven* magazine), translated by Lauren Na, First Second (New York, NY), 2009.

The Color of Heaven, (originally serialized in *Twenty Seven* magazine), translated by Lauren Na, First Second (New York, NY), 2009.

OTHER

Creator of "My Sky," published in *Daily Hanguk* beginning 1975. Author of other comic series, with titles translated as "Spring Rain," "A Story of Kisaeng," "Ugly," "Bug Boy," and "A Yellow Story."

Sidelights

Well known in his native Korea, Kim Dong-hwa is an acclaimed author and illustrator in the field of "manhwa," or comics. The unique perspective Kim brings to the genre through his thoughtful and evocative story arcs and his brilliantly colored art were the province of Korean readers for over three decades, until his "Story of Life on the Golden Plains" series was translated into English and published in the graphic-novel trilogy that includes *The Color of Earth, The Color of Water,* and *The Color of Heaven.*

Born in 1950, Kim began his career creating "sunjung," a comics genre for girls that features light, sweet stories and cute images. His first series, "My Sky," ran in Korea's well-known newspaper the *Daily Hanguk,* beginning in 1975. His experiences in creating stories for female readers, as well as his mastery of the sunjung style, with its contrast between cartoon characters and detailed drawings of nature and landscape, made his work unique, and with his "Story of Life on the Golden Plains" Kim broke ground in adult comics in his native country. First serialized in the magazine *Twenty Seven,* the series ran for three years and was then released in five volumes by a Korean publisher. "Since I was very young, I've been interested expressing the growth and change (mentally and physically) of a girl in manhwa form," Kim told Newsarama.com interviewer Michael Lorah in discussing the genesis of the series. "I consider the process of a girl becoming a woman one of the biggest mysteries and wonders of life. And one day when my mother was sleeping in her sickbed, I looked down at her wrinkled face and suddenly realized that she must had been young and beautiful once. Then I started imagining her childhood and youth. What would she have looked like in her 60s, 50s, 40s and etc.? These thoughts inspired me to put my hand to the plow. Ehwa is the result of tracing back my mother's youth."

Ehwa, the pivotal character in the "Story of Life on the Golden Plains," is first introduced to readers in *The Color of Earth,* where she helps her widowed mother run a tavern in their small rural village. A preteen, the girl is becoming aware of sexual differences between herself and the village boys. When her mother begins a romantic relationship with a traveling picture salesman, Ehwa begins to understand more fully the passive role that is expected of a woman in early twentieth-century Korean society.

Somewhat outcast from their neighbors because of the older woman's unmarried status, Ehwa and her mother develop a close emotional bond that lasts throughout both their lives. *The Color of Water* focuses on Ehwa's budding romance with Duksam, a champion wrestler who she deeply loves. The attempt of Duksam's teacher, Master Cho, to break off the relationship and gain Ehwa for himself causes great pain for the young lovers, but in *The Color of Heaven* the enduring patience of seventeen-year-old Ehwa and the support of her loving mother allow love to win out.

Reviewing *The Color of Earth* in *Publishers Weekly,* a critic described Kim's series as "a moving and evocative look at love as seen through the eyes of one feeling it for the first time and another who longs to savor it once more." In *Booklist,* Francisca Goldsmith called the series opener "beautifully scripted and drawn," and its story "richly literate and imaginative." Kim "uses flowers in many of the vignettes to explain aspects of love or to represent his characters and their relationships," Alana Abbott observed in her *School Library Journal* review of *The Color of Earth,* referencing a characteristic element of the author/illustrator's unique manhwa style. "A Korean village is a far cry from the environment of most American teens, but the romantic themes will keep even modern girls pining for more," wrote Andrea Lipinski in her review of *The Color of Water,* and Goldsmith remarked on the "stately and symbol-laden pace" of the second volume of the trilogy. Kim's sunjung-style images are "simple at first glance but on closer examination . . . amazing in their detail," wrote *School Library Journal* critic Andrea Lipinski in her review of *The Color of Heaven,* and a *Kirkus Reviews* writer concluded that the final volume of the trilogy "blends achingly beautiful artwork with a well-paced story." "Intimate in its scope but epic in its execution," according to *World Literature Today* critic Rob Vollmar, Kim's "Story of Life on the Golden Plains" "benefits from the visual ebullience of Eastern narrative art traditions."

Discussing how cultural differences may limit English-language readers from appreciating his story in "The Color of Earth," Kim was optimistic, telling Lorah: "The United States is a combination of diverse cultures and races, and American readers are not only well educated but also open-minded to something new and fresh. The Korean emotions and cultural background from the book will be unfamiliar and exotic, but Americans are equipped with sufficient knowledge and willingness to read and learn. In addition, no matter where and when a life takes place, there are similar things happening all over the world. I know American readers will come to see this."

Biographical and Critical Sources

PERIODICALS

Booklist, June 1, 2009, Francisca Goldsmith, review of *The Color of Earth,* p. 64; September 1, 2009, Francisca Goldsmith, review of *The Color of Water,* p. 90; October 15, 2009, Francisca Goldsmith, review of *The Color of Heaven,* p. 44.
Kirkus Reviews, June 1, 2009, review of *The Color of Water;* September 15, 2009, review of *The Color of Heaven.*
Publishers Weekly, April 20, 2009, review of *The Color of Earth,* p. 38; September 28, 2009, review of *The Color of Heaven,* p. 50.
School Library Journal, September, 2009, Andrea Lipinski, review of *The Color of Water,* and Alana Abbott, review of *The Color of Earth,* both p. 192; November, 2009, Andrea Lipinski, review of *The Color of Heaven,* p. 143.
World Literature Today, January-February, 2010, Rob Vollmar, "Three Korean Graphic Novelists Reimagine the Genre," p. 56.

ONLINE

Newsarama Web site, http://www.newsarama.com/ (April 15, 2009), Michael C. Lorah, interview with Kim.*

KOONTZ, Dean 1945-

(David Axton, Brian Coffey, Deanna Dwyer, K.R. Dwyer, John Hill, Leigh Nichols, Anthony North, Richard Paige, Owen West)

Personal

Born July 9, 1945, in Everett, PA; son of Ray and Florence Koontz; married Gerda Ann Cerra, October 15, 1966.

Addresses

Home—Newport Beach, CA. *Agent*—Robert Gottlieb, Trident Media Group, 488 Madison Ave., 17th Fl., New York, NY 10022. *E-mail*—dean@deankoontz.com.

Career

Author. Teacher-counselor with Appalachian Poverty Program, 1966-67; high-school English teacher, 1967-69; writer, 1969—.

Awards, Honors

Atlantic Monthly college creative writing award, 1966, for story "The Kittens"; Hugo Award nomination, World Science Fiction Convention, 1971, for novella *Beastchild;* Litt.D., Shippensburg State College, 1989.

Writings

FOR CHILDREN

Oddkins: A Fable for All Ages, illustrated by Phil Parks, Warner (New York, NY), 1988.
Santa's Twin, illustrated by Phil Parks, HarperPrism (New York, NY), 1996.
The Paper Doorway: Funny Verse and Nothing Worse, illustrated by Phil Parks, HarperCollins (New York, NY), 2001.
Every Day's a Holiday, illustrated by Phil Parks, HarperCollins (New York, NY), 2003.
Robot Santa: The Further Adventures of Santa's Twin, HarperCollins (New York, NY), 2004.
I, Trixie Who Is Dog, illustrated by Janet Cleland, G.P. Putnam's Sons (New York, NY), 2009.
Trixie and Jinx, illustrated by Janet Cleland, G.P. Putnam's Sons (New York, NY), 2010.

"FRANKENSTEIN" NOVEL SERIES

(With Kevin J. Anderson) *Prodigal Son,* Bantam Books (New York, NY), 2005.
(With Ed Gorman) *City of Night,* Bantam Books (New York, NY), 2005.
Dead and Alive, Bantam Books (New York, NY), 2009.

Dean Koontz (AP Images. Reproduced by permission.)

Lost Souls, Bantam Books (New York, NY), 2010.

NOVELS

Star Quest, Ace Books (New York, NY), 1968.
The Fall of the Dream Machine, Ace Books (New York, NY), 1969.
Fear That Man, Ace Books (New York, NY), 1969.
Anti-Man, Paperback Library (New York, NY), 1970.
Beastchild, Lancer Books (New York, NY), 1970.
Dark of the Woods, Ace Books (New York, NY), 1970.
The Dark Symphony, Lancer Books (New York, NY), 1970.
Hell's Gate, Lancer Books (New York, NY), 1970.
The Crimson Witch, Curtis Books (New York, NY), 1971.
A Darkness in My Soul, DAW Books (New York, NY), 1972.
The Flesh in the Furnace, Bantam (New York, NY), 1972.
Starblood, Lancer Books (New York, NY), 1972.
Time Thieves, Ace Books (New York, NY), 1972.
Warlock, Lancer Books (New York, NY), 1972.
A Werewolf among Us, Ballantine (New York, NY), 1973.
Hanging On, M. Evans (New York, NY), 1973.
The Haunted Earth, Lancer Books (New York, NY), 1973.
Demon Seed, Bantam (New York, NY), 1973.
(Under pseudonym Anthony North) *Strike Deep,* Dial (New York, NY), 1974.
After the Last Race, Atheneum (New York, NY), 1974.
Nightmare Journey, Putnam (New York, NY), 1975.

(Under pseudonym John Hill) *The Long Sleep,* Popular Library (New York, NY), 1975.

Night Chills, Atheneum (New York, NY), 1976.

(Under pseudonym David Axton) *Prison of Ice,* Lippincott (Philadelphia, PA), 1976, revised edition published under name Dean R. Koontz as *Icebound* (also see below), Ballantine (New York, NY), 1995.

Whispers (also see below), Putnam (New York, NY), 1980.

Phantoms (also see below), Putnam (New York, NY), 1983.

Darkfall (also see below), Berkley (New York, NY), 1984, published as *Darkness Comes,* W.H. Allen (London, England), 1984.

Twilight Eyes, Land of Enchantment (Westland, MI), 1985.

(Under pseudonym Richard Paige) *The Door to December,* New American Library (New York, NY), 1985.

The Vision (also see below), Putnam (New York, NY), 1986.

Strangers (also see below), Putnam (New York, NY), 1986.

Watchers (also see below), Putnam (New York, NY), 1987, reprinted, Berkley Books (New York, NY), 2003.

Lightning (also see below), Putnam (New York, NY), 1988, reprinted, Berkley Books (New York, NY), 2003.

Midnight, Putnam (New York, NY), 1989, reprinted, Berkley Books (New York, NY), 2004.

The Bad Place (also see below), Putnam (New York, NY), 1990, with a new afterword, 2004.

Cold Fire (also see below), Putnam (New York, NY), 1991, with a new afterword, 2004.

Three Complete Novels: The Servants of Twilight; Darkfall; Phantoms, Wings Books (New York, NY), 1991.

Hideaway (also see below), Putnam (New York, NY), 1992.

Dragon Tears (also see below), Berkley (New York, NY), 1992, published in a limited edition, Putnam (New York, NY), 1993.

Dean R. Koontz: A New Collection (contains *Watchers, Whispers,* and *Shattered* [originally published under pseudonym K.R. Dwyer; also see below]), Wings Books (New York, NY), 1992.

Mr. Murder (also see below), Putnam (New York, NY), 1993.

Winter Moon, Ballantine (New York, NY), 1993.

Three Complete Novels: Lightning; The Face of Fear; The Vision (*The Face of Fear* originally published under pseudonym Brian Coffey), Putnam (New York, NY), 1993.

Three Complete Novels: Strangers; The Voice of the Night; The Mask (*The Voice of the Night* originally published under pseudonym Brian Coffey; *The Mask* originally published under pseudonym Owen West), Putnam (New York, NY), 1994.

Dark Rivers of the Heart (also see below), Knopf (New York, NY), 1994.

Strange Highways (also see below), Warner Books (New York, NY), 1995.

Intensity (also see below), Knopf (New York, NY), 1995.

TickTock, Ballantine (New York, NY), 1996.

Three Complete Novels (contains *The House of Thunder, Shadowfires,* and *Midnight*), Putnam (New York, NY), 1996.

Sole Survivor, Ballantine (New York, NY), 1997.

Fear Nothing, Bantam (New York, NY), 1998.

Seize the Night (sequel to *Fear Nothing),* Bantam Doubleday Dell (New York, NY), 1999.

False Memory, Bantam (New York, NY), 2000.

From the Corner of His Eye, Bantam (New York, NY), 2000.

The Book of Counted Sorrows (e-book), bn.com, 2001, limited edition, Charnel House, 2001, hardcover edition, Dogged Press, 2009.

One Door away from Heaven, Bantam (New York, NY), 2002.

By the Light of the Moon, Bantam (New York, NY), 2003.

The Face, Bantam (New York, NY), 2003.

The Taking, Bantam (New York, NY), 2004.

Life Expectancy, Bantam (New York, NY), 2004.

Velocity, Bantam (New York, NY), 2005.

The Husband, Bantam Books (New York, NY), 2006.

The Darkest Evening of the Year, Bantam Books (New York, NY), 2007.

The Good Guy, Bantam Books (New York, NY), 2007.

Your Heart Belongs to Me, Bantam Books (New York, NY), 2008.

Breathless, Bantam Books (New York, NY), 2009.

Relentless, Bantam Books (New York, NY), 2009.

Shadowfires, Berkley Books (New York, NY), 2010.

Twilight Eyes, Berkley Books (New York, NY), 2010.

What the Night Knows, Bantam Books (New York, NY), 2011.

"ODD" NOVEL SERIES

Odd Thomas, Bantam (New York, NY), 2004.

Forever Odd, Bantam Books (New York, NY), 2005.

Brother Odd, Bantam Books (New York, NY), 2006.

Odd Thomas, Bantam Books (New York, NY), 2006.

In Odd We Trust (graphic novel), illustrated by Queenie Chan, Del Ray/Ballantine Books (New York, NY), 2008.

Odd Hours, Bantam Books (New York, NY), 2008.

UNDER PSEUDONYM BRIAN COFFEY

Blood Risk, Bobbs-Merrill (Indianapolis, IN), 1973.

Surrounded, Bobbs-Merrill (Indianapolis, IN), 1974.

The Wall of Masks, Bobbs-Merrill Indianapolis, IN), 1975.

The Face of Fear, Bobbs-Merrill (Indianapolis, IN), 1977.

The Voice of the Night, Doubleday (New York, NY), 1981.

Also author of script for *CHiPS* television series, 1978.

UNDER PSEUDONYM DEANNA DWYER

The Demon Child, Lancer Books (New York, NY), 1971.

Legacy of Terror, Lancer Books (New York, NY), 1971.

Children of the Storm, Lancer Books (New York, NY), 1972.

The Dark of Summer, Lancer Books (New York, NY), 1972.

Dance with the Devil, Lancer Books (New York, NY), 1973.

UNDER PSEUDONYM K.R. DWYER

Chase, Random House (New York, NY), 1972.
Shattered, Random House (New York, NY), 1973.
Dragonfly, Random House (New York, NY), 1975.

UNDER PSEUDONYM LEIGH NICHOLS

The Key to Midnight, Pocket Books (New York, NY), 1979.
The Eyes of Darkness, Pocket Books (New York, NY), 1981.
The House of Thunder, Pocket Books (New York, NY), 1982.
Twilight, Pocket Books (New York, NY), 1984, revised edition published under name Dean R. Koontz as *The Servants of Twilight*, Berkley (New York, NY), 1990.
Shadowfires, Avon (New York, NY), 1987.

UNDER PSEUDONYM OWEN WEST

(With wife, Gerda Koontz) *The Pig Society* (nonfiction), Aware Press (Granada Hills, CA), 1970.
(With Gerda Koontz) *The Underground Lifestyles Handbook*, Aware Press (Granada Hills, CA), 1970.
Soft Come the Dragons (story collection), Ace Books (New York, NY), 1970.
Writing Popular Fiction, Writer's Digest (Cincinnati, OH), 1973.
The Funhouse (novelization of screenplay), Jove (New York, NY), 1980.
The Mask, Jove (New York, NY), 1981.
How to Write Best-selling Fiction, Writer's Digest (Cincinnati, OH), 1981.

OTHER

(Author of text) David Robinson, *Beautiful Death: Art of the Cemetery,* Penguin Studio (New York, NY), 1996.
("Editor") *Life Is Good!: Lessons in Joyful Living, by Trixie Koontz, Dog,* Yorkville Press (New York, NY), 2004.
Christmas Is Good!: Trixie Treats and Holiday Wisdom, illustrated by Janet Cleland, Yorkville Press (New York, NY), 2005, revised edition published as *Christmas Is Good: Trixie's Guide to a Happy Holiday,* Hyperion (New York, NY), 2009.
Bliss to You: Trixie's Guide to a Happy Life, Hyperion (New York, NY), 2008.
A Big Little Life: A Memoir of a Joyful Dog, Hyperion (New York, NY), 2009.

Contributor to books, including *Infinity 3,* edited by Robert Haskins, Lancer Books, 1972; *Again, Dangerous Visions,* edited by Harlan Ellison, Doubleday, 1972; *Final Stage,* edited by Edward L. Ferman and Barry N. Malzberg, Charterhouse, 1974; *Night Visions IV,* Dark Harvest, 1987; *Stalkers: All New Tales of Terror and Suspense,* edited by Ed Gorman and Martin H. Greenberg, illustrated by Paul Sonju, Dark Harvest, 1989; and *Night Visions VI: The Bone Yard,* Berkley, 1991.

Adaptations

Demon Seed was filmed by Metro-Goldwyn-Mayer/Warner Bros., 1977; *Shattered* was filmed by Warner Bros., 1977; *Watchers* was filmed by Universal, 1988; *Hideaway,* starring Jeff Goldblum, was filmed by Tri-Star, 1994; *Mr. Murder* was filmed by Patchett Kaufman Entertainment/Elephant Walk Entertainment, 1999. Many of Koontz's works have been adapted for audiobook, including *Cold Fire, Hideaway,* and *The Bad Place,* Reader's Chair (Hollister, CA), 1991; *Mr. Murder* and *Dragon Tears,* Simon & Schuster Audio; *Dark Rivers of the Heart, Icebound,* and *Intensity,* Random House Audio; *Strange Highways* and *Chase,* Warner Audio; *Phantoms, Lightning,* and *Winter Moon,* Brilliance Audio, 2007; and *Bliss to You: Trixie's Guide to a Happy Life, Shadowfires,* and *Darkfall,* Brilliance Audio, 2008. Koontz's novel *Prodigal Son* was adapted as a graphic novel written by Chuck Dixon and illustrated by Brett Booth, Del Rey (New York, NY), 2008.

Sidelights

Popular among both adult and teen readers around the world, Dean Koontz is an acknowledged master of a

Cover of Koontz's suspense-filled thriller Velocity, *a story about a mass murderer's crazed game with life that features coverart by Ashton Franklin.* (Jacket art © Ashton Franklin. Used by permission of Bantam Books, a division of Random House, Inc.)

hybrid class of books that combines the genres of romance, thriller, horror, and science fiction. His many novels have sold in the millions and several have been adapted for successful films. Although known primarily as a horror novelist, Koontz himself rejects such labels and views his plots as optimistic tales showing hard-fought battles between good and evil. A favorite Koontz theme is the conflict between emotion and reason, and the emotional level of his books—a step beyond the genre's standard fare—has gained him the respect of many critics. According to Charles de Lint, writing in the *Magazine of Fantasy and Science Fiction,* Koontz consistently succeeds at "telling a harrowing, highly suspenseful story featuring quick-witted protagonists who face the world with a positive attitude and exchange rapid-fire dialogue." "I have attempted, book by book, to speak to the reader's intellect and emotions as well as to his desire for a 'good read'," the author himself once stated. "I believe the best fiction does three things well: tells an involving story, makes the reader think, and makes the reader feel."

An only child, Koontz grew up in Bedford, Pennsylvania. "I began writing when I was a child," he once explained, noting that "reading and writing provided much needed escape from the poverty in which we lived and from my father's frequent fits of alcohol-induced violence." While still in college, he started publishing his short stories and won an *Atlantic Monthly* fiction contest. Marrying his fiancée, Gerda, and graduating from Shippensburg State College in 1966, Koontz taught for a while in the Appalachian Poverty Program and in Pennsylvania schools, while also continuing to write and sell stories. In 1968 his first novel, *Star Quest,* was published, and Koontz quickly followed it with a second science-fiction novel.

In the early 1970s, determined to make a try at full-time writing, Koontz was aided by his wife, who agreed to support the family for five years while her husband followed his dream. He adopted an assortment of pseudonyms and tackled various genres, including science fiction, mystery, and thrillers. "The curse lies in the fact that much of the early work is of lower quality that what came after," Koontz remarked, "both because I was so young and unself-critical and because the low earnings from each book forced me to write a lot of them in order to keep financially afloat." Koontz marks *Chase,* a suspense novel written under the pseudonym K.R. Dwyer that describes the after-effects of the Vietnam War on a veteran as "the beginning of my *real* career as a writer." He moved from science fiction to suspense with that book, and never looked back.

Writing in several genres aided Koontz in developing his own unique form of dark suspense, and his addition of humor, romance, and occult elements have created a distinctive body of work. Considered his breakthrough novel, 1980's *Whispers* is a dark and violent story of childhood cruelty, rape, and murder. Hilary Thomas is a survivor of abusive alcoholic parents who has become a successful screenwriter; she is attacked by millionaire Bruno Frye, whom she subsequently stabs to death. When Bruno returns from the grave to stalk her, it is left to Hilary's police officer boyfriend to help her unravel the twisted tale of Bruno's childhood and reveal the powers at work in this "slick tale of horror," as Rex E. Klett described the book in *Library Journal.* A *Publishers Weekly* reviewer noted that the "psychological portrait of the sick, sick Bruno makes skin crawl."

Strangers, which was published in 1988, is characteristic Koontz: it tells the story of a group of people connected only by a weekend each spent at a motel in Nevada two years prior—a weekend none of them remember. As the characters begin to experience nightmares, intense fears, and even the effects of supernormal powers, they are driven to uncover the mystery and conspiracy that binds them. Deborah Kirk, writing in the *New York Times Book Review,* found some characters unconvincing but concluded that *Strangers* is "an engaging, often chilling, book." In *Library Journal* Eric W. Johnson dubbed the novel an "almost unbearably suspenseful page-turner," while a *Booklist* reviewer

deemed Koontz a "true master" and found *Strangers* to be "a rich brew of gothic horror and science fiction, filled with delectable turns of the imagination."

The misuse of science is at the heart of *Watchers,* which was chosen one of the American Library Association's best books for young adults in 1987. Recombinant DNA experiments go wrong at a government lab, and suddenly two mutants—one with human intelligence to be used for spying and the other a killer—are on the loose in Southern California. The intelligent mutant, a golden retriever, is pursued by the killer mutant, a blend of ape and dog that is named Outsider. Soon two humans, Travis and Nora, become involved helping the dog, nicknamed Einstein, escape the wrath of Outsider. While Audrey B. Eaglen described *Watchers* in a review for *School Library Journal* as "about as horrifying as warm milk toast," others disagreed; *New York Times Book Review* contributor Katherine Weber had special praise for Einstein, whom she described as "the most richly drawn character in the book."

Koontz's vivid imagination enriches his storys' plot and setting, and he also demonstrates a consistent affinity for creating likeable protagonists. In *Intensity* he introduces Chyna Shepherd, a psychology student who must combat Edgler Vess, a killer obsessed with intensity of sensation, be it pleasure or pain. Mixing murder with humor, *Relentless* finds psychopathic literary critic Shearman Waxx bent on making mincemeat of Cubby Greenwich's writing career in a story that showcases Koontz's "exquisite crafting of the thrilling, the unexplainable, and the personal," according to *Library Journal* contributor Julie Kane. A *Publishers Weekly* reviewer found *Intensity* "masterful, if ultimately predictable," and lauded Koontz's racing narrative, calling it a contender for the most "viscerally exciting thriller of the year." A companion novel, *Velocity* finds

novelist/bartender Billy Wiles facing a brutal killer in a game where an innocent victim loses his or her life due to Billy's inaction and inability to play by the rules. Soon, the game extends beyond Billy's control and he may become its next victim in a novel that a *Kirkus Reviews* critic cited for its "brilliant plotting" and suspense. In *Publishers Weekly* a critic wrote that the "graphic, fast-paced action, well-developed characters and relentless, nail-biting scenes" in *Velocity* "show Koontz at the top of his game."

Taking place in the coastal town of Moonlight Bay, California, *Fear Nothing* and *Seize the Night* also share the same protagonist: poet-surfer Christopher Snow, a man possessing a genetic mutation that makes him sensitive to light. In *Fear Nothing* the body of Snow's recently deceased father has vanished and been replaced by that of a murdered hitchhiker. Along with his Labrador-mix dog Orson, surfer-friend Bobby, and local disc jockey Sasha, Snow attempts to recover his father's corpse. Seven children abducted from their homes

serve as the central mystery in *Seize the Night,* and Snow follows the trail of the kidnappers, joined by Orson, Bobby, Sasha, a mind-reading cat, and a biker. The chase leads to a supposedly abandoned military base, Fort Wyvern, where genetic experiments are actually being conducted. Among the strange, mutated creatures Snow and his companions uncover are wormlike beings that can devour almost anything; in addition, Snow becomes trapped by a malfunctioning "temporal locator" and goes on time-travel journeys into both the future and the past.

Commenting on *Fear Nothing* in the *New York Times Book Review,* Maggie Garb characterized the novel as an "overwrought narrative," maintaining that Koontz's detective trio "seem more like the stuff of adolescent fantasy than fully believable sleuths." Garb also criticized Koontz's "surfer lingo and literary pretension" as detrimental to the suspense of the book. An *Entertainment Weekly* critic described *Seize the Night* as "that holy-cow kind of novel—park your brains, don't ask why, [and] tighten your seat belt." In the *New York Times Book Review,* David Walton characterized the same novel as "a bros-and-brew backslapper in which characters refer to Coleridge and T.S. Eliot as often as to genetic mutation."

In *False Memory* Koontz focuses on a woman who suffers from the mental disorder autophobia, or fear of self. Marty Rhodes, successful at work and in her marriage, takes her agoraphobic friend Susan to therapy sessions with psychiatrist Mark Ahriman twice each week. Suddenly, Marty begins to develop a fear that she will inflict harm upon herself or her loved ones. Meanwhile, Marty's husband, Dusty, a painting contractor, courageously saves his half-brother Skeet from taking a suicidal leap off a rooftop. After Dusty places Skeet in rehab, he returns home to find that Marty has removed all the sharp objects from the house. Soon Dusty begins to develop signs of paranoia, a clue that the troubles of all four disturbed protagonists are somehow linked. Ray Olsen, writing in *Booklist,* called *False Memory* "remarkably engaging, despite having so many pages and so little plot." While noting that the book "could have been trimmed by 200 pages and not lost any impact," David Olsen wrote in *Library Journal* that Koontz's "characters are rich, and the main story compelling." A *Publishers Weekly* reviewer comments that with "the amazing fertility of its prose, the novel feels like one of Koontz's earlier tales, with a simple core plot, strong everyman heroes (plus one deliciously malevolent villain) and pacing that starts at a gallop and gets only faster."

In *The Taking* Koontz draws on his science-fiction roots and weaves a "gripping, blood-curdling, thought-provoking parable," according to Ray Olson in *Booklist.* At the home of novelist Molly Sloan and her husband Neil in California's San Bernardino Mountains, it seems like everything is suddenly starting to come apart. In addition to a mysterious, glowing acid rain, the power appears to be off, but somehow appliances run and soon clocks start spinning out of control. Before long the couple realizes their true dilemma: the nation is under attack by a malevolent alien race. "Mixing a hair-raising plot with masterly story telling and a subtle network of well-placed literary allusions, this deservedly popular author has written a tour de force," stated Nancy McNicol in *Library Journal,* while a reviewer for *Publishers Weekly* commented that "Koontz remains one of the most fascinating of contemporary popular novelists."

Koontz based his novel *Prodigal Son* on *Frankenstein,* the horror classic by eighteenth-century writer Mary Shelley. In Koontz's update—written with Kevin J. Anderson as part of a multi-volume series—two centuries have passed and the perennially forty-something Dr. Victor Frankenstein is now living under the assumed name of Helios in pre-Hurricane Katrina New Orleans. Continuing his macabre experiments, Helios spawns pod-grown creatures, members of a "New Race" of perfect humans, to live as humans within the city, his ultimate intention to eventually replace all actual humans. Meanwhile, Deucalion, the doctor's original "monster," is also still living in seclusion at a remote Tibetian monastery. When he learns of Helios's existence and discovers that one of the doctor's perfect beings has become a serial murderer, the "monstrous" Deucalion becomes a force for good in Koontz's characteristic battle of good against evil. Noting the novel's "cliffhanger" ending, a *Publishers Weekly* reviewer wrote of *Prodigal Son* that Koontz's "odd juxtaposition of a police procedural with a neo-gothic, mad scientist plot gives the novel a wickedly unusual and intriguing feel."

Koontz continues his "Frankenstein" series in *City of Night,* coauthored with Ed Gorman, as well as *Dead and Alive,* both which follow Victor's multiple efforts to create the perfect wife and also cultivate his race of human replicants even as Mother Nature attempts to destroy his efforts in Hurricane Katrina. The saga continues in *Lost Souls,* as Victor turns up in Rainbow Falls, Montana, much to the chagrin of wife-prototype-in-hiding Erica Five. Meanwhile, Deucalion realizes that replicants are beginning their take-over of the human race and seeks help from two savvy San Francisco detectives. Noting the novel's mix of "grisly suspense, wry dialogue, . . . and cultural criticism," Olson added that in *Lost Souls* "Koontz does his [fictional] dance . . . more adroitly than almost ever before." Adding to their appeal to teen readers, the "Frankenstein" novels have also been adapted as graphic novels.

Koontz turns to supernatural thrillers in his "Odd Thomas" series. Set in Pico Mundo, California, and following the adventures of twenty-year-old fry cook Odd and his girlfriend Stormy, *Odd Thomas* finds the young man attempting to harness a new talent: his ability to see ghosts and other destructive spirits as well as sense a person's penchant or murder through a condition called psychic magnetism syndrome. When an unpleasant cus-

tomer at Odd's workplace seems to attract a collection of sinister spirits, the young cook is forced to turn sleuth in a novel that *Booklist* critic Ray Olson dubbed a "corker of a new thriller" that "employs dry, goofy humor" and a compelling mix of "tension and horror." "The rapid pace, eerie circumstances, and bizarre characters will keep readers turning pages," predicted Katherine Fitch in her *School Library Journal* review of *Odd Thomas,* adding that Koontz's concluding "chapters are so powerful and heartrending that they should be read several times."

Forever Odd finds Odd a year older and still mourning Stormy's death when his young friend Danny goes missing and his stepfather is found murdered. As Odd begins the chase and the mystery deepens, the fry cook learns that he has been the ultimate goal all along. In *Brother Odd* the young man hopes to find peace in St. Bartholomew's Abbey until evil tracks him to his desert sanctuary. A chance meeting with a pregnant young woman in *Odd Hours* propels Odd into yet another supernatural tangle involving three gun-toting street punks, a dunk in the Pacific Ocean, celebrity ghosts, and a conniving small-town minister. Reviewing *Forever Odd* in *Booklist,* Olson described the second "Odd Thomas" novel as "more suspenseful but less piquant" than the series opener, while the young man's narrative in *Brother Odd* features what *Magazine of Fantasy and Science Fiction* writer Charles de Lint described as a degree of "warmth" and "humor" that "echo[es]" Odd's character while also alleviating some of the grim elements" in Koontz's suspenseful tale. A *Publishers Weekly* critic also praised the third "Odd Thomas" installment, citing the author's "irresistibly offbeat mix of supernatural horror and laugh-out-loud humor," while Olson wrote that *Odd Hours* "starts with a bang and goes like a house afire straight through" to its surprising conclusion. According to de Lint, "what really makes [the 'Odd Thomas'] . . . series so readable is Odd's first person voice, a mix of the matter-of-fact with sometimes wry, sometimes hilarious observations of the world at large," and a *Publishers Weekly* contributor noted of *Odd Hours* that Koontz's "quirky humor" and his "sensitive portrayals of minor characters . . . are a plus."

A graphic-novel prequel to the first "Odd Thomas" novel, *In Odd We Trust* pairs manga-styled cartoon art by Queenie Chan with Koontz's story about nineteen-year-old Odd's efforts to deal with his special ability, track down a murderous stalker, and build a relationship with Stormy. "Filled with plenty of creepy moments," according to *School Library Journal* contributor Matthem L. Moffett, *In Odd We Trust* attracts teen readers with Chan's cartoon art, "a nice visual match for the difficult balance of humor and terror in the story," according to the critic.

In addition to his adult and young-adult fiction, Koontz has also aimed several books specifically at the juvenile market. In *Oddkins: A Fable for All Ages* magical toys have been created for the children who, for many reasons, need a special secret friend. Called Oddkins, these toys can come alive and possess the power of speech although they look and feel like ordinary stuffed toys; when the child no longer needs emotional support, the caretaking toy returns to its inanimate state. When evil toys are created by an equally evil toymaker and escape from the cellar of their toy factory, the Oddkins must stop them. Once again, Koontz sends an optimistic message in this clearly told battle of good against evil. A *Publishers Weekly* commentator noted that *Oddkins* has "enough excitement and humor to hold a child's attention."

Koontz's picture books for very young children include *Every Day's a Holiday.* Borrowing the "unbirthday" concept from Lewis Carroll's *Alice in Wonderland,* the book introduces a host of humorous holidays, both real and imagined. Illustrations by Phil Parks bring to life "Lost-Tooth Day," "Cinco de Mayo," and "Up-Is-Down Day," among others, creating a story that *Childhood Education* reviewer Angela Pitamber called "funny, easy to read, and informative." Another picture book, *Santa's Twin,* presents the story of Father Christmas as he tries to save the holiday season from his evil double.

Also illustrated by artist Parks and containing Koontz's lighthearted verse, *Robot Santa* finds Santa's brother Bob caught up in another series of problematic activities. *Robot Santa* was described by de Lint in the *Magazine of Fantasy and Science Fiction* as "light-hearted and fun."

In honor of Koontz's beloved dog, the author produced *I, Trixie, Who Is Dog* and *A Big Little Life: A Memoir of a Joyful Dog.* A golden retriever who ended her career as a trained service dog for Canine Companions for Independence at age three due to injury, Trixie joined the Koontz family in 1998, and she inspired the author with her doggy energy and joie de vivre. Narrated from the canine's perspective, *I, Trixie, Who Is Dog* pairs Janet Cleland's watercolor illustrations with Koontz's free-verse text. In *A Big Little Life* the author focuses on the time he shared with Trixie before she died in 2007. "Before Trixie I wasn't looking for the brightness in daily life like I used to," Koontz told *USA Today* interviewer Carol Memmott. "I started thinking about the wonder of the world again. She changed me by the example of her exuberance and her innocence." Noting the intellectual musings that are woven into Koontz's memoir, which include thoughts on love and loyalty,

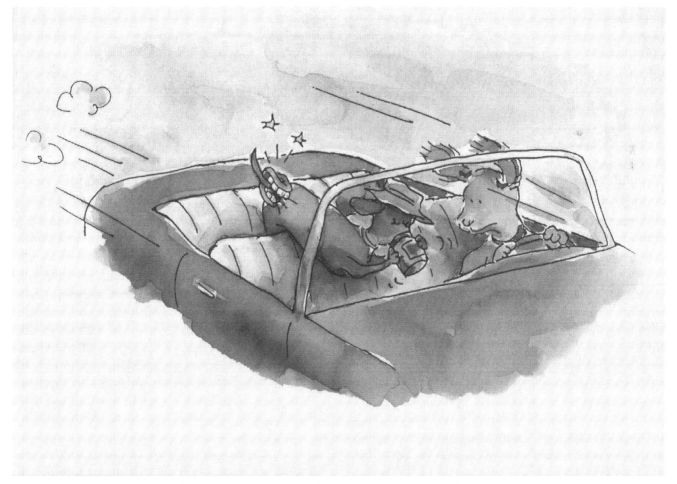

Koontz teams up with artist Janet Cleland to tell an engaging story based on the antics of his own beloved pet in **I, Trixie, Who Is Dog.** (Illustration copyright © 2009 by Janet Cleland. Used by permission of G.P. Putnam's Sons, a division of Penguin Young Readers Group, a member of Penguin Group (USA) Inc., 345 Hudson Street, New York, NY 10014. In the UK and British Commonwealth by Broadthink.)

types of consciousness, and animals' unfettering ignorance of mortality, *A Big Little Life* mixes "self-
deprecating humor and Trixie's comic élan to make this
one dog book that everyone . . . will deeply enjoy," according to *Booklist* critic Ray Olson. Liberated by his
affection for his beloved pet, "the media-shy author
opens up about childhood poverty, love for his wife and
his spiritual beliefs," asserted a *Kirkus Reviews* writer,
the critic adding that Koontz's affectionate memoir "also
provides plenty of laughs, borne more of his self-
effacing humor and mastery of language than doggie
antics."

While much of his fiction surveys the darker regions of
life—from serial killers to out-of-control technology
and social decay—Koontz also "gives readers bright
hope in a dark world," according to a *Publishers Weekly*
critic. As Edward Bryant noted in *Locus,* the author
"successfully does what most editors warn their writers
not to do. He crosses genre boundaries with impu-
nity. . . . He simply does pretty much what he wants,
and the novels are then categorized as 'Dean R. Koontz
books.'" Koontz also admittedly peppers his books with
upbeat messages. As he once remarked, he finds "the
human species—and Western culture—to be primarily
noble, honorable, and admirable. In an age when doom-
sayers are to be heard in every corner of the land, I find
great hope in our species and in the future we will
surely make for ourselves. . . . I think we live in a
time of marvels, not a time of disaster, and I believe we
can solve every problem that confronts us if we keep
our perspectives and our freedom."

Biographical and Critical Sources

BOOKS

Koontz, Dean, *A Big Little Life: A Memoir of a Joyful
Life,* Hyperion (New York, NY), 2010.
Munster, Bill, editor, *Sudden Fear: The Horror and Dark
Suspense Fiction of Dean R. Koontz,* Starmont House,
1988.
Munster, Bill, *Discovering Dean Koontz: Essays on Ameri-
ca's Best-selling Writer of Suspense and Horror Fic-
tion,* Borgo Press (San Bernardino, CA), 1998.
Ramsland, Katherine M., *Dean Koontz: A Writer's Biogra-
phy,* HarperPrism (New York, NY), 1997.
St. James Guide to Young-Adult Writers, St. James Press
(Detroit, MI), 1999.

PERIODICALS

Booklist, September 15, 1994, Ray Olson, review of *Dark
Rivers of the Heart,* p. 84; December 15, 1999, Ray
Olsen, review of *False Memory,* p. 739; December 15,
2003, Ray Olson, review of *Odd Thomas,* p. 707; May
1, 2004, Ray Olson, review of *The Taking,* p. 1483;
November 1, 2004, Ray Olson, review of *Life Expect-*
ancy, p. 444; January 1, 2005, Ray Olson, review of
Prodigal Son, p. 784; November 15, 2005, Ray Olson,
review of *Forever Odd,* p. 6; November 15, 2006,
Ray Olson, review of *Brother Odd,* p. 6; May 1, 2007,
Ray Olson, review of *The Good Guy,* p. 32; November 1, 2007, Ray Olson, review of *The Darkest
Evening of the Year,* p. 5; May 1, 2008, Ray Olson,
review of *Odd Hours,* p. 6; May 15, 2009, Ray Olson,
review of *Relentless,* p. 5; July 1, 2009, Ray Olson,
review of *A Big Little Life,* p. 5; May 1, 2010, Ray
Olson, review of *Lost Souls,* p. 6.
Bulletin of the Center for Children's Books, October, 2009,
Deborah Stevenson, review of *I, Trixie, Who Is Dog,*
p. 70.
Childhood Education, winter, 2004, Angela Pitamber, review of *Every Day's a Holiday,* p. 108.
Entertainment Weekly, January 15, 1999, "'Night' Stalker,"
p. 56.
Kirkus Reviews, November 1, 1992, review of *Dragon
Tears,* p. 1327; May 1, 2004, review of *The Taking,* p.
416; November 15, 2004, review of *Life Expectancy,*
p. 1063; May 1, 2005, review of *Velocity,* p. 498; May
15, 2007, review of *The Good Guy;* July 1, 2009, review of *A Big Little Life;* September 1, 2009, review
of *I, Trixie, Who Is Dog.*
Library Journal, May 15, 1980, Rex E. Klett, review of
Whispers, p. 1187; January, 2000, Jeff Ayers, review
of *False Memory,* p. 160; April 15, 2004, Kristen L.
Smith, review of *The Face,* p. 146; June 15, 2004,
Nancy McNicol, review of *The Taking,* p. 58; December 1, 2004, Nancy McNicol, review of *Life Expect-*
ancy, p. 101; February 1, 2005, Jeff Ayers, review of
Prodigal Son, p. 68; November, 2008, Matthew L.
Moffett, review of *In Odd We Trust,* p. 154; May 15,
2009, Julie Kane, review of *Relentless,* p. 62; July,
2009, Shannon Peterson, review of *Prodigal Son,* p.
106.
Locus, March, 1990, Edward Bryant, review of *The Bad
Place,* pp. 67-68.
Los Angeles Times Book Review, January 31, 1988, Dick
Lochte, "The Perils of Little Laura," p. 8; March 8,
1987, Paul Wilner, review of *Watchers,* p. 6; January
21, 1990, Don G. Campbell, review of *The Bad Place,*
p. 12.
Magazine of Fantasy and Science Fiction, June, 2004, p.
Charles de Lint, review of *Odd Thomas,* p. 33; June,
2005, Charles de Lint, reviews of *Life Expectancy,* p.
29, *The Taking,* p. 30, and *Robot Santa,* p. 32; May,
2007, Charles de Lint, review of *Brother Odd,* p. 55;
October-November, 2008, Charles de Lint, review of
Odd Hours, p. 34; December, 2008, Charles de Lint,
review of *In the Small,* p. 41; August-September, 2009,
Charles de Lint, review of *Prodigal Son,* p. 35;
January-February, 2010, Charles de Lint, review of
Relentless, p. 28.
New York Times Book Review, March 15, 1987, Katherine
Weber, review of *Watchers,* p. 16; November 13, 1994,
Jay E. Rosen, review of *Dark Rivers of the Heart,* p.
58; April 20, 1997, Charles Salzberg, review of *Sole
Survivor;* February 8, 1998, Maggie Garb, review of
Fear Nothing; February 7, 1999, David Walton, re-
view of *Seize the Night;* November 22, 2007, Janet
Maslin, review of *The Darkest Evening of the Year,* p.
E14.

People, January 19, 2004, Rob Taub, review of *Odd Thomas,* p. 45.

Publishers Weekly, September 10, 1973, review of *Hanging On,* p. 41; April 4, 1980, review of *Whispers,* p. 61; September 2, 1988, review of *Oddkins: A Fable for All Ages,* pp. 87-88; January 10, 1994, review of *Winter Moon,* pp. 56-57; December 13, 1999, review of *False Memory,* p. 67; December 22, 2003, review of *Odd Thomas,* p. 13; May 10, 2004, review of *The Taking,* p. 37; November 15, 2004, review of *Life Expectancy,* p. 41; January 17, 2005, review of *Prodigal Son,* p. 40; April 25, 2005, review of *Velocity,* p. 39; October 30, 2006, review of *Brother Odd,* p. 39; October 29, 2007, review of *The Darkest Evening of the Year,* p. 33; April 21, 2008, review of *Odd Hours,* p. 36; May 31, 2010, review of *Lost Souls,* p. 23.

School Library Journal, May, 2004, Katherine Fitch, review of *Odd Thomas,* p. 175; April, 2010, Meg Smith, review of *I, Trixie, Who Is Dog,* p. 132.

USA Today, June 9, 2009, Carol Memmott, "The House of Koontz," p. D1.

Voice of Youth Advocates, October, 1993, Christy Tyson, review of *Dragon's Tears,* p. 230.

Writer's Digest, November, 1989, Stanley Wiater, interview with Koontz, pp. 34-38.

ONLINE

Bookreporter.com, http://www.bookreporter.com/ (March 2, 2001), "Dean Koontz."

Dean Koontz Home Page, www.deankoontz.com (January 10, 2011).*

*   *   *

KROLL, Virginia L. 1948-
(Melrose Cooper, Louisa Fox)

Personal

Born April 28, 1948, in Buffalo, NY; daughter of Lester H. (a U.S. immigration inspector) and Helen (a registered nurse and model) Kroll; married David Haeick (in construction); children: Sara, Seth, Joshua, Hannah, Katya, Noah. *Education:* Attended State University of New York at Buffalo and Canisius College. *Religion:* Roman Catholic. *Hobbies and other interests:* Reading, crafts, friends, pets.

Addresses

Home—Hamburg, NY.

Career

Author and educator. Fifth-grade teacher in Buffalo, NY, area, 1968-69, 1980-81; Hamburg Memorial Youth Center, Hamburg, NY, recreation assistant, 1978-80. Medaille College, Buffalo, college instructor in writing for children course, 1993; Institute of Children's Literature, instructor, 1999—; presenter at schools.

Virginia Kroll (Photograph by Katya Kroll-Heick. Reproduced by permission.)

Awards, Honors

American Book Award, Before Columbus Foundation, 1991, for *Wood-Hoopoe Willie;* American Bookseller Pick of the Lists selection, 1992, for *Masai and I;* Children's Choice selection, International Reading Association (IRA), 2004, for *Busy, Busy Mouse;* Best Children's Book selection, Bank Street College of Education, 2004, for both *Especially Heroes* and *Busy, Busy Mouse;* Notable Book for a Global Society designation, IRA, 2007, for *Selvakumar Knew Better.*

Writings

Helen the Fish, illustrated by Teri Weidner, Albert Whitman (Morton Grove, IL), 1992.

My Sister, Then and Now, illustrated by Mary Worcester, Carolrhoda (Minneapolis, MN), 1992.

Masai and I, illustrated by Nancy Carpenter, Four Winds Press/Macmillan (New York, NY), 1992.

Naomi Knows It's Springtime, illustrated by Jill Kastner, Boyds Mills Press (Honesdale, PA), 1993.

Wood-Hoopoe Willie, illustrated by Katherine Roundtree, Charlesbridge (Watertown, MA), 1993.

Africa Brothers and Sisters, illustrated by Vanessa French, Four Winds Press/Macmillan (New York, NY), 1993.

A Carp for Kimiko, illustrated by Katherine Roundtree, Charlesbridge (Watertown, MA), 1993.

When Will We Be Sisters?, Scholastic (New York, NY), 1993.

I Wanted to Know All about God, illustrated by Debra Reid-Jenkins, Eerdmans (Grand Rapids, MI), 1994.

Beginnings: How Families Come to Be, illustrated by Stacey Schuett, Albert Whitman (Morton Grove, IL), 1994.

Pink Paper Swans, illustrated by Nancy Clouse, Eerdmans (Grand Rapids, MI), 1994.

Sweet Magnolia, illustrated by Laura Jakes, Charlesbridge (Watertown, MA), 1994.

Jaha and Jamil Went down the Hill: An African Mother Goose, illustrated by Katherine Roundtree, Charlesbridge (Watertown, MA), 1994.

The Seasons and Someone, illustrated by Tatsuro Kiuchi, Harcourt Brace (New York, NY), 1994.

New Friends, True Friends, Stuck-like-Glue Friends, illustrated by Rose Rosely, Eerdmans (Grand Rapids, MI), 1994.

Fireflies, Peach Pies, and Lullabies, illustrated by Nancy Cote, Simon & Schuster (New York, NY), 1995.

Hats off to Hair!, illustrated by Kay Life, Charlesbridge (Watertown, MA), 1995.

Shelter Folks, illustrated by Jan Naimo Jones, Eerdmans (Grand Rapids, MI), 1995.

(Under pseudonym Louisa Fox) *Every Monday in the Mailbox,* illustrated by Jan Naimo Jones, Eerdmans (Grand Rapids, MI), 1995.

Can You Dance, Dalila?, illustrated by Nancy Carpenter, Simon & Schuster (New York, NY), 1996.

Christmas Cow, Players Press (Studio City, CA), 1996.

Butterfly Boy, illustrated by Gerardo Suzán, Boyds Mills Press (Honesdale, PA), 1997.

Hands!, illustrated by Cathryn Falwell, Boyds Mills Press (Honesdale, PA), 1997.

The Making of Angels, illustrated by Victoria Lisi, Spindle Press (Denver, CO), 1997.

With Love, to Earth's Endangered Peoples, illustrated by Roberta Collier-Morales, Dawn (Nevada City, CA), 1998.

Motherlove, illustrated by Lucia Washburn, Dawn (Nevada City, CA), 1998.

Faraway Drums, illustrated by Floyd Cooper, Little, Brown (New York, NY), 1998.

When God Made the Tree, illustrated by Roberta Collier-Morales, Dawn (Nevada City, CA), 1999.

Cat!, illustrated by K. Dyble Thompson, Dawn (Nevada City, CA), 1999.

She Is Born: A Celebration of Daughters, Beyond Words (Hillsboro, OH), 2000.

Flurry's Frozen Tundra, illustrated by Michael S. Maydak, Bear & Co. (Gettysburg, PA), 2001.

Bluffy's Mighty Mountain, illustrated by Michael S. Maydak, Bear & Co. (Gettysburg, PA), 2001.

Kingston's Flowering Forest, illustrated by Michael S. Maydak, Bear & Co. (Gettysburg, PA), 2001.

Girl, You're Amazing!, illustrated by Mélisande Potter, Albert Whitman (Morton Grove, IL), 2001.

Especially Heroes, illustrated by Tim Ladwig, Eerdmans (Grand Rapids, MI), 2003.

Busy, Busy Mouse, illustrated by Fumi Kosaka, Viking (New York, NY), 2003.

Boy, You're Amazing!, illustrated by Sachiko Yoshikawa, Albert Whitman (Morton Grove, IL), 2004.

Brianna Breathes Easy: A Story about Asthma, illustrated by Jayoung Cho, Whitman (Morton Grove, IL), 2005.

Marta and the Manger Straw: A Christmas Tradition from Poland, Zonderkidz (Grand Rapids, MI), 2005.

Equal, Shmequal, illustrated by Philomena O'Neill, Charlesbridge (Watertown, MA), 2005.

Really Rabbits, illustrated by Philomena O'Neill, Charlesbridge (Watertown, MA), 2006.

On the Way to Kindergarten, illustrated by Elisabeth Schlossberg, Putnam (New York, NY), 2006.

Let There Be Llamas!, illustrated by Irina Lombardo, Pauline Books & Media (Boston, MA), 2006.

Uno dos tres posada: Let's Celebrate Christmas, illustrated by Loretta Lopez, Viking (New York, NY), 2006.

Selvakumar Knew Better, illustrated by Xiaojun Li, Shen's Books (Fremont, CA), 2006.

Easter Eggs for Anya: A Ukrainian Celebration of New Life in Christ, illustrated by Sally Wern Comport, Zonderkidz (Grand Rapids, MI), 2007.

Everybody Has a Teddy Bear, illustrated by Sophie Allsopp, Sterling (New York, NY), 2007.

The Thanksgiving Bowl, illustrated by Philomena O'Neill, Pelican Publishing (Gretna, LA), 2007.

Saying Grace: A Prayer of Thanksgiving, illustrated by Timothy Ladwig, Zonderkidz (Grand Rapids, MI), 2009.

Luisa's Christmas Piñata: A Celebration of the Journey to Bethlehem, Zonderkidz (Grand Rapids, MI), 2010.

Contributor of hundreds of articles to periodicals.

"THE WAY I ACT" BEGINNING-READER SERIES

Forgiving a Friend, illustrated by Paige Billin-Frye, Albert Whitman (Morton Grove, IL), 2005.

Jason Takes Responsibility, illustrated by Nancy Cote, Albert Whitman (Morton Grove, IL), 2005.

Honest Ashley, illustrated by Nancy Cote, Albert Whitman (Morton Grove, IL), 2006.

Ryan Respects, illustrated by Paige Billin-Frye, Albert Whitman (Morton Grove, IL), 2006.

Cristina Keeps a Promise, illustrated by Enrique O. Sanchez, Albert Whitman (Morton Grove, IL), 2006.

Good Neighbor Nicholas, illustrated by Nancy Cote, Albert Whitman (Morton Grove, IL), 2006.

Good Citizen Sarah, illustrated by Nancy Cote, Albert Whitman (Morton Grove, IL), 2007.

Makayla Cares about Others, illustrated by Nancy Cote, Albert Whitman (Morton Grove, IL), 2007.

UNDER PSEUDONYM MELROSE COOPER

I Got a Family, illustrated by Dale Gottlieb, Henry Holt (New York, NY), 1993.

Life Riddles (chapter book), Henry Holt (New York, NY), 1994.

I Got Community, illustrated by Dale Gottlieb, Henry Holt (New York, NY), 1995.

Life Magic (chapter book), Henry Holt (New York, NY), 1996.

Pets!, illustrated by Yumi Heo, Henry Holt (New York, NY), 1998.

Gettin' through Thursday, illustrated by Nneka Bennett, Lee & Low (New York, NY), 1998.

Sidelights

Virginia L. Kroll, the author of dozens of picture books for young readers as well as over 1,500 magazine articles, has established herself as a versatile and prolific writer since beginning her career in 1992. So plentiful is Kroll's imagination and output that she writes under two pseudonyms as a way of diffusing concern over her immense productivity. Her subject matter ranges from domestic tales of sisters to multiracial and multicultural topics to behavioral choices in her "The Way I Act" series to the environment and religion. Unafraid to take chances in her work, Kroll writes from the point of view of young African Americans in *Masai and I, Woodhoopoe Willie, Pink Paper Swans,* and *Faraway Drums* and from the point of view of a blind girl in *Naomi Knows It's Springtime,* a Japanese girl in *A Carp for Kimiko,* an Hispanic youth in *Butterfly Boy,* and even an East Indian family's dog in *Selvakumar Knew Better.* In books published under the pseudonym Melrose Cooper, Kroll has also penned inspirational stories of family life and children overcoming the effects of illness.

As Kroll once told *SATA,* "All I ever wanted to be is an author. And now that I am one, all I ever want to be is an author. In between the desire and the realized dream, I became a mother. Good thing. My six children and one grandchild give me stories every day. So do the children I visit in schools. There is a story in everyone I meet, everything I encounter, because they induce wonder."

Kroll might be considered an inspiration for many writers since most of her early books were accepted from the so-called "slush pile" of unsolicited manuscripts. Despite the positive response from editors, Kroll has had several negative responses which bothered her. One has been the prejudice of some editors against white authors writing about other cultures. In Kroll's view, it is foolish to believe a white person is not capable of writing "black material"—another's term, not hers. She does not want to write about a suburban middle-class white woman's world. So she writes whatever she has a desire to write.

On topic that has interested Kroll has been the African-American experience. "*Masai and I* began as a discussion with my former fifth graders about each other's heritage," the author once explained. In the book, a young African-American girl learns about the Masai culture in school. Each day she goes home and compares herself to the East African child she is studying. She wonders where a Masai girl would sleep, what she would do in her free time, and what she would wear and eat. Readers learn that while the everyday lives of Americans are different than the everyday lives of the Masai, children are still children, no matter where they live. In a *School Library Journal* review, Martha Topol called *Masai and I* "an interesting, richly blended book that connects two different worlds . . . pointing out similarities and differences."

Woodhoopoe Willie also deals with African heritage, this time by looking at the music of that continent. Willie, a young African-American boy who simply cannot sit still, shows a great but undeveloped talent for playing the drums. His continual percussive music-making brings to mind the drums of Africa that his grandfather heard on a trip to his ancestral homeland. Willie finally gets a chance to play these handmade native instruments during a Kwanzaa festival. A *Publishers Weekly* reviewer concluded of the book that "Kroll's melodic tale conveys the warmth among Willie's loving family as well as the musical legacy of several African peoples." In *Kirkus Reviews* a critic noted that in *Woodhoopoe Willie* Kroll presents an "effective interweaving of wholesome family dynamics and African heritage in the context of observance of Kwanzaa."

In Kroll's story for *Africa Brothers and Sisters* an only child complains to his father about not having any brothers or sisters, and his dad responds that he has hundreds of them in Africa. The father and son go on to talk about all these "relatives," providing readers with a basic primer of Africa's diverse cultures. Writing in *Booklist,* Quraysh Ali noted that it is "refreshing" to have the often absent black father very present in this title. *Africa Brothers and Sisters* "might unlock the door for many children in search of African heritage and identity, African American or not," the critic added. Although noticing that "information about the tribes is sometimes sketchy and obtrusive," Roger Sutton wrote in his *Bulletin of the Center for Children's Books* review that Kroll's story presents "a cozy slice-of-life."

Featuring Sachiko Yoshikawa's art, Kroll's **Boy, You're Amazing!** *celebrates the possibilities open to boys everywhere.* (Albert Whitman & Company, 2004. Illustration copyright © 2004 by Sachiko Yoshikawa. Reproduced by permission.)

Kroll addresses a child's curiosity about the wheres and whys of life in I Wanted to Know All about God, *a picture book illustrated by Debra Reid Jenkins.* (Illustration copyright © 1994 by Debra Reid Jenkins. Reproduced by permission of Eerdmans Books for Young Readers, an imprint of William B. Eerdmans Publishing Co.)

Other books dealing with African Americans and presenting a multicultural message include *Pink Paper Swans* and *Faraway Drums.* In the former title, Janetta, a young black girl, is fascinated by the origami her neighbor, Mrs. Tsujimoto, crafts to sell in shops. When the neighbor gets arthritis and her livelihood is endangered, Janetta becomes the fingers that create new folded-art paper. Sutton wrote in the *Bulletin of the Center for Children's Books* that although the text is somewhat long, "kids will enjoy the conversations of these coworkers, an ebullient girl and a gentle elderly woman, as well as the fanciful products of their cooperative occupation." A *Publishers Weekly* reviewer also praised *Pink Paper Swans*, describing it as both "gentle and affecting."

In *Faraway Drums* Kroll writes about Jamila Jefferson and her younger sister, Zakiya, as they stay home alone for the first time. Noises abound in their urban landscape, frightening the girls until Jamila remembers a game played by her great-grandmother and turns the scary sounds of the city and apartment house into those of the friendly drums and handmade musical instruments of Africa. Dawn Amsberry noted in *School Library Journal* that "images of Africa are subtly woven into the realistic backdrop of the girls' apartment," and recommended *Faraway Drums* to parents "in search of picture books about moving to a new home."

More multicultural fare is served up in *A Carp for Kimiko, Butterfly Boy,* and *Selvakumar Knew Better.* In the first story Kimiko wants a carp kite to fly on Children's Day, just like the one her brother has, but Japanese tradition dictates that only boys can fly these colorful kites. Kimiko's parents are understanding, however, and the day after the festival the little girl awakens to find a real carp swimming in the fish tank in her room. Janice Del Negro commented in *Booklist* that Kroll's story "succeeds" in "relaying its information with a minimum of didacticism and more than a little charm." Susan Middleton, writing in *School Library Journal,* called *A Carp for Kimiko* a "straightforward story that focuses on a Japanese holiday," while a *Kirkus Reviews* contributor dubbed it "a gentle story distinguished by unusual warmth and subtlety."

In *Butterfly Boy* Kroll introduces readers to an extremely sympathetic and caring Hispanic boy. Emilio takes care of his wheelchair-bound grandfather and reads to the elderly man about butterflies, even though others in the family believe Grandfather can no longer understand. Del Negro observed in her review of *Butterfly Boy* for the *Bulletin of the Center for Children's Books* that "Kroll's text is touching but crisp as she skillfully balances on the line between sweet and saccharine." Lisa S. Murphy, writing in *School Library Journal,* called the same book a "tender story about a loving Hispanic family," concluding that the "close relationship between grandfather and grandson shines through brightly."

Another close-knit family is at the center of *Selvakumar Knew Better,* as the story of young Dinakaran's escape from a violent tsunami in India comes to life in evocative art by Xioujun Li that Jill Heritage Maza described in *School Library Journal* as "breathtaking." Inspired by a true story set during the 2004 tsunami, Kroll's story was awarded the Notable Book for a Global Society designation from the International Reading Association.

A potpourri of families is presented in *Beginnings: How Families Come to Be,* with various tales of how six children began their life on Earth. There is a single parent, a Korean family, and an adopted child from South America. "Each vignette features a conversation between children and parents that has a realistic feel," noted *Booklist* reviewer Ilene Cooper. According to Cooper, "the multicultural families represented here show that love has no borders." Another family-centered story by Kroll, *Saying Grace: A Prayer of Thanksgiving,* also focuses on history as it follows a family's efforts to prepare for a harsh winter in colonial New England. As depicted in autumn-toned artwork by Tim Ladwig, daughter Grace decides to give thanks before each evening meal, thereby beginning the titular tradition in a story that a *Kirkus Reviews* writer predicted "will appeal to its target audience."

Kroll explores relationships from a Christian standpoint in *I Wanted to Know All about God*, a book that emphasizes "nature and human relationships," according to Julie Corsaro in *Booklist.* In the story, a multiracial cast of children plays together on snowy hills and at the beach, finding the answers to their questions about God in nature. A contributor to *Publishers Weekly* complained that the book is "somewhat treacly," but suggested that it "may appeal to those looking for short, inspirational bedtime reading."

Using the gender-neutral pen name Melrose Cooper, Kroll has written several groups of companion books, including *I Got a Family* and *I Got Community,* as well as *Life Riddles* and *Life Magic.* The latter two books, novels for middle-grade readers, feature members of the same family but focus on different characters in each title. In *Life Riddles,* for example, twelve-year-old Janelle wants to be a writer, but family poverty and an absent father prove obstacles to her goal. In *Voice of Youth Advocates,* Civia Tuteur called the book a "light, easy to read up-beat novel full of hope, support, and encouragement." Janelle's younger sister, Crystal, takes stage center in *Life Magic,* as she deals with the death of her beloved Uncle Joe from AIDS.

Lighter in tone is the rhyming text of the picture book *Pets!,* in which a young child searches for a pet at the circus. Equally lighthearted, *Busy, Busy Mouse* compares the life of a young rodent to the life of a pre-

schooler: the young girl wakes in the morning as the little mouse is going to bed, and when the little girl goes to bed the mouseling begins its busy "day." A critic in *Publishers Weekly* dubbed *Pets!* a "whimsical paean" to household critters, and a *Kirkus Reviews* contributor wrote that Kroll's "joyful" text even contains a mystery. Another *Kirkus Reviews* critic praised *Busy, Busy Mouse* for creating "a pleasant comforting mood with just the right mild, mischievous spirit," while Be Astengo noted in *School Library Journal* that "Kroll's staccato rhyming phrases keep the action moving along."

In *Girl, You're Amazing!* Kroll celebrates the qualities and potential of modern girls, while in *Boy, You're Amazing!* she gives the same upbeat treatment to boys. Although these stories are intended for young readers, a *Publishers Weekly* critic observed in a review of *Girl, You're Amazing!* that "this whimsical appreciation might address elementary-schoolers, big sisters, and mothers alike." Carolyn Janssen, in *School Library Journal,* deemed the same book "a joyous celebration of today's female" that is filled with "affirmation and encouragement," and *Booklist* contributor Linda Perkins cited the book's "snappy, upbeat rhymes." Of *Boy, You're Amazing!,* *School Library Journal* reviewer Shelley B. Sutherland noted that "Kroll celebrates the talents, accomplishments, and potential of boys," all in "joyful rhymes." *Booklist* contributor Terry Glover called the work a "confidence-boosting bounty of a book," while a *Kirkus Reviews* contributor recommended *Boy, You're Amazing!* as "a great gift for any young boy."

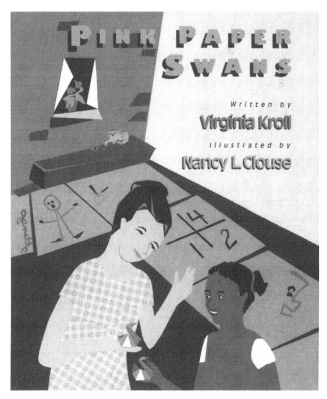

Nancy L. Clouse creates the Japanese-inspired art in Kroll's multigenerational story **Pink Paper Swans.** (William B. Eerdmans Publishing Co., 1994. Illustration copyright © 1994 by Nancy L. Clouse. Reproduced by permission.)

In her novel *Ordinary Heroes* Kroll sets the action in the 1960s and relates the story of a young girl who comes face to face with violent racism against a neighbor. As her father confronts their neighbor's tormentors, the girl realizes that being a hero is about staying true to and acting on your ideals. "*Especially Heroes* was an account of incidents that occurred in my life," Kroll explained in an interview on the Eerdmans Books Web site. "I guess I'd have to say that it is easier in many ways to tell a 'true' story than a purely fictional one because most of the material is already there, so you need only to add a bit here, subtract there, and change small details. True-to-life stories, for me, virtually write themselves." Karen Land, reviewing the novel in *School Library Journal*, wrote of *Especially Heroes* that "this is an excellent story for these troubled times, to help children understand the importance of standing up for one's beliefs, ideals, and freedom."

Brianna Breathes Easy: A Story about Asthma is a book about a common childhood illness. In the story, young Brianna has been cast as the lead in the Thanksgiving play at school. When she develops asthma she is taken to the hospital and the doctor explains how she can avoid "triggering" another asthma attack. "Newcomers to the condition will feel less alone," wrote Jennifer Mattson in *Booklist*, noting that asthma is the leading chronic illness among American children. Susan Weitz wrote that in *Brianna Breathes Easy* the illness is explained by Kroll "in an engagingly upbeat and not overly technical manner."

In *Equal Schmequal* Kroll introduces the concept of equality through an assortment of animal characters. In her story Mouse and several animal friends try to divide into teams for a game of tug-of-war, first by numbers, then by size, but in each case they find that it is hard to create truly equal teams. Once they think they finally have the solution, one team becomes distracted and the other easily wins. Ultimately, the characters realize that teams are not equal unless they put in equal effort. "Kroll gives the four definitions of equal from the viewpoints of math, art, the law, and team sports," explained Elaine Lesh Morgan in *School Library Journal*, while a *Kirkus Reviews* contributor described *Equal Schmequal* as "a cute look at what can be a difficult concept." Kroll also uses animal characters to introduce the difficulty of going to school for the first time in *On the Way to Kindergarten*, and she features a pair of extremely intelligent rabbits that learn to work together on household chores in *Really Rabbits*.

In *Forgiving a Friend* and *Jason Takes Responsibility*, the first volumes in her "The Way I Act" beginning readers, Kroll deals with experiences common to many young children. Jacob and Seth get into a fight after Jacob accidentally breaks one of Seth's toys in *Forgiving a Friend*. When Seth has a similar accident, he realizes that he needs to forgive his friend. "The 'do unto others' aspect of the story comes across loud and clear," noted Ilene Cooper in *Booklist*. In *Jason Takes Respon-*

sibility a boy accidentally loses an invitation to his grandmother's birthday party; in order for the party to go well, it is up to him to make sure that, despite the loss, everyone arrives. Sandra Welzenbach predicted of both titles that "young readers will relate to the simple plots."

The "Way I Act" series continues in several more easy-reading stories. A girl contemplates cheating on a school assignment in *Honest Ashley*, while in *Ryan Respects* a boy learns first hand about the pain caused by teasing. A choice between supporting others and enjoying oneself is the focus of *Cristina Keeps a Promise*, while in *Good Neighbor Nicholas* a boy learns to be compassionate about his elderly neighbor. Another community-centered story plays out in *Good Citizen Sarah*, while in *Makayla Cares about Others* a helpful young girl discovers that self-sacrifice is often part of helping other people.

In her *Booklist* review of *Honest Ashley* Kathy Broderick praised Kroll's "realistic story," while Maura Bresnahan predicted in *School Library Journal* that "young readers will identify with the realistic situations and believable characters" in the "Way I Act" books. "Kroll's smooth text tells a strong story of children developing important social skills and then watching them pay off," explained Kathy Broderick, discussing the "Way I Act" books in *Booklist*. Serving the goal of Kroll's series, *Makayla Cares about Others* features what Welzenbach described in *School Library Journal* as "an enjoyable story" that will also be "useful for discussing concern for others," and *Good Neighbor Nicholas* was described by a *Kirkus Reviews* writer as "a spoonful of sugar pleasantly offered."

Many people have told Kroll how wonderful it is that she has a gift she can get paid for. "This is true, but talent needs work," the writer explained. "A gift can sit there and look beautiful, but it is worth nothing at all until it is unwrapped and used properly." In her interview on the Eerdmans Books Web site, Kroll noted that the writing life is not always easy. "Rejections are a part of any writer's life and experience," she explained. "We have to learn to accept them and move forward. Writers also need self-discipline. Writing tends to be an isolating profession, and we have to push ourselves to get things done." Her advice for young writers? "Read all you can and try to write something every day. Believe in yourself, and look at your writing as a craft. The old adage, 'Practice makes perfect,' applies. The more you write, the better you'll become. That's no secret; it's just a fact."

Biographical and Critical Sources

PERIODICALS

Booklist, February 15, 1993, Quraysh Ali, review of *Africa Brothers and Sisters,* p. 1068; December 1, 1993, Janice Del Negro, review of *A Carp for Kimiko,* pp. 698-

699; February 15, 1994, Julie Corsaro, review of *I Wanted to Know All about God,* p. 1086; March 15, 1994, Ilene Cooper, review of *Beginnings: How Families Come to Be,* p. 1374; April 1, 2001, Linda Perkins, review of *Girl, You're Amazing!,* p. 1479; April 15, 2004, Terry Glover, review of *Boy, You're Amazing!,* p. 1446; March 1, 2005, Jennifer Mattson, review of *Brianna Breathes Easy: A Story about Asthma,* p. 1204; October 1, 2005, Ilene Cooper, review of *Forgiving a Friend,* p. 63; February 15, 2006, Julie Cummins, review of *On the Way to Kindergarten,* p. 103; April 15, 2006, Kathy Broderick, review of *Ryan Respects,* p. 52; June 1, 2006, Kathy Broderick, review of *Honest Ashley,* p. 87; July 1, 2006, Gillian Engberg, review of *Really Rabbits,* p. 66; March 15, 2007, Gillian Engberg, review of *Everybody Has a Teddy,* p. 53; October 1, 2007, Hazel Rochman, review of *The Thanksgiving Bowl,* p. 67.

Bulletin of the Center for Children's Books, April, 1993, Roger Sutton, review of *Africa Brothers and Sisters,* p. 255; October, 1994, Roger Sutton, review of *Pink Paper Swans,* pp. 52-53; September, 1997, Janice Del Negro, review of *Butterfly Boy,* p. 16.

Childhood Education, fall, 2003, Deborah Bitler, review of *Especially Heroes,* p. 39.

Kirkus Reviews, February 1, 1993, review of *Woodhoopoe Willie,* p. 149; August 1, 1993, review of *A Carp for Kimiko,* p. 1004; February 15, 1998, review of *Pets!,* p. 265; May 15, 2003, review of *Busy, Busy Mouse,* p. 752; February 15, 2004, review of *Boy, You're Amazing!,* p. 181; July 1, 2005, review of *Equal Shmequal,* p. 737; March 1, 2006, review of *On the Way to Kindergarten,* p. 233; August 15, 2006, review of *Good Neighbor Nicholas,* p. 846; January 15, 2007, review of *Makayla Cares about Others,* p. 75; August 15, 2009, review of *Saying Grace.*

Publishers Weekly, February 15, 1993, review of *Woodhoopoe Willie,* p. 236; January 3, 1994, review of *I Wanted to Know All about God,* p. 81; June 13, 1994, review of *Pink Paper Swans,* p. 63; January 19, 1998, review of *Pets!,* p. 377; February 12, 2001, review of *Girl, You're Amazing!,* p. 212; May 5, 2003, review of *Busy, Busy Mouse,* p. 219; July 1, 2005, review of *Equal Shmequal,* p. 737.

School Library Journal, October, 1992, Martha Topol, review of *Masai and I,* p. 91; March, 1994, Susan Middleton, review of *A Carp for Kimiko,* p. 202; June, 1997, Lisa S. Murphy, review of *Butterfly Boy,* pp. 95-96; May, 1998, Dawn Amsberry, review of *Faraway Drums,* p. 119; April, 2001, Carolyn Janssen, review of *Girl, You're Amazing!,* p. 114; April, 2003, Karen Land, review of *Especially Heroes,* p. 130; August, 2003, Be Astengo, review of *Busy, Busy Mouse,* p. 135; May, 2004, Shelley B. Sutherland, review of *Boy, You're Amazing!,* p. 116; July, 2005, Susan Weitz, review of *Brianna Breathes Easy,* p. 76; September, 2005, Elaine Lesh Morgan, review of *Equal Shmequal,* p. 176; January, 2006, Sandra Welzenbach, reviews of *Forgiving a Friend* and *Jason Takes Responsibility,* both p. 104; March, 2006, Maura Bresnahan, review of *Honest Ashley,* p. 194, and Martha Topol, review of *On the Way to Kindergarten,* p. 195; August, 2006, Rachel G. Payne, review of *Really Rabbits,* p. 91; September, 2006, Jill Heritage Maza, review of *Selvakumar Knew Better,* p. 177; March, 2007, Sandra Welzenbach, review of *Makayla Cares about Others,* p. 174; May, 2007, Linda Ludke, review of *Everybody Has a Teddy,* p. 102; January, 2008, Judy Chichinski, review of *Good Citizen Sarah,* p. 90.

Voice of Youth Advocates, August, 1994, Civia Tuteur, review of *Life Riddles,* p. 144.

ONLINE

Eerdmans Books Web site, http://www.eerdmans.com/ (August, 2003), interview with Kroll.*

L

LAVIS, Steve

Personal
Born in Hampshire, England; children: two sons. *Education:* Attended art college in England.

Addresses
Home—St Ives, Cornwall, England. *E-mail*—steve@stevelavis.co.uk.

Career
Author and illustrator of children's books. Also worked as a commercial illustrator.

Writings

SELF-ILLUSTRATED

Cock-a-doodle-doo: A Farmyard Counting Book, Ragged Bears (Andover, England), 1996, Dutton (New York, NY), 1997.
Jump!, Ragged Bears (Andover, England), 1997.
Jake and the Rabbit Chase, Ragged Bears (Sherborne, England), 1999.
Toby the Runaway Tractor, Ragged Bears (Sherborne, England), 1999.
Martha and the Picnic Party, Ragged Bears (Sherborne, England), 2000.
Little Mouse Has a Friend, Ragged Bears (Brooklyn, NY), 2000.
Little Mouse Has an Adventure, Ragged Bears (Brooklyn, NY), 2000.
Little Mouse Has a Busy Day, Ragged Bears (Brooklyn, NY), 2000.
Little Mouse Has a Party, Ragged Bears (Brooklyn, NY), 2000.
Noisy Wild Animals, Ragged Bears (Brooklyn, NY), 2000.
Noisy Farm Animals, Ragged Bears (Brooklyn, NY), 2000.

In the Jungle, Ragged Bears (Brooklyn, NY), 2001.
On the Farm, Ragged Bears (Brooklyn, NY), 2001.

Author and illustrator of *Racing Bears* and *In the Arctic.*

ILLUSTRATOR

Chris Powling, *Daredevils or Scaredycats,* Abelard (London, England), 1979.
Chris Powling, *Mog and the Rectifier,* Abelard (London, England), 1980.
Helen Hoke, editor, *Giants! Giants! Giants!,* Franklin Watts (London, England), 1980.
E. Nesbit, *Belinda and Bellament,* Macdonald & Company (London, England), 1982.
Geraldine McCaughrean, *One Thousand and One Arabian Nights,* Oxford University Press (Oxford, England), 1982.
Jan Mark, *Hairs in the Palm of the Hand,* Puffin (Harmondsworth, England), 1983.
Frances Hodgson Burnett, *The Secret Garden,* Puffin (Harmondsworth, England), 1983.
Steve Jackson, *The Tasks of Tantalon: A Puzzlequest Book,* Oxford University Press (Oxford, England), 1985.
Chris Powling, *Stuntkid,* Abelard (London, England), 1985.
Pat O'Shea, *Finn MacCool and the Small Men of Deeds,* Oxford University Press (Oxford, England), 1987.
Pat O'Shea, *The Magic Bottle,* Hippo (London, England), 1999.
Martin Waddell, *Two Brown Bears,* Oxford University Press (Oxford, England), 2002.
Dug Steer, *Nursery Tales: Five Interactive Pop-up Stories to Perform,* Templar (Dorking, England), 2004.
Shen Roddie, *You're Too Small!,* Tiger Tales (Wilton, CT), 2004.
David Bedford, *Max and Sadie,* Oxford University Press (Oxford, England), 2005.
Sally Symes, *Who's Been Walking on My Floor?!,* Barron's Educational Series (Hauppauge, NY), 2005.
Carol Roth, *All Aboard to Work—Choo-Choo!,* Albert Whitman (Park Ridge, IL), 2009.

Also illustrator of *Number Farm, Puzzle Train,* and *Where's Alfie? . . . In the Town,* Cat's Pyjamas (Middlesex, England).

Sidelights

A respected British author and illustrator, Steve Lavis has produced such well-received titles as *Cock-a-doodle-doo: A Farmyard Counting Book* and *Little Mouse Has a Friend.* After attending art college in England, Lavis made his mark in the literary world as an illustrator of numerous book covers, including the fantasy tales of Alan Garner and C.S. Lewis, before trying his hand at illustrating children's books. One such work, Shen Roddie's *You're Too Small!,* focuses on a clever and energetic mouse named Tad who, despite his willingness to help around the farm, is dismissed by the other animals because of his diminutive stature. When dinnertime arrives and the creatures find themselves locked out of the barn, however, they realize that only one of them is tiny enough to slip through a crack and open the door. According to a *Publishers Weekly* critic, Lavis "works in warm oranges and reds, employing a generous sense of scale to draw readers into the action." Sheilah Kosco, writing in *School Library Journal,* applauded Lavis's portrayal of Tad, noting that the illustrations "effectively demonstrate that he is not the smallest creature in the world even though he may feel like he is."

Lavis has also contributed the pictures to *All Aboard to Work—Choo-Choo!,* a tale by Carol Roth. Told in verse, the story follows a host of busy parents, including a professorial hen, a business-minded newt, and a fire-fighting feline, as they head to the train station to begin their commutes to work. "Lavis's kindly animals are outfitted and equipped for easy identification with their professions," remarked a contributor in *Kirkus Reviews,*

and Lynn K. Vanca wrote in *School Library Journal* that "Lavis's lighthearted, cheerful full-color artwork has plenty of detail tucked into the spreads."

Cock-a-doodle-doo, Lavis's self-illustrated debut, describes the playful activities of ten lively, noisy animals, including a group of squeaking mice that hope to pilfer grain from the barn. The title earned solid reviews: a contributor in *Publishers Weekly* hope that "the animals' energy and joyful cacophony of sounds make this a lively counting book," while *Booklist* critic Stephanie Zvirin applauded the "delightfully cacophonous collection of words for animal noises" that are arrayed in the book's final double-page illustration.

In his popular "Little Mouse" series for beginning readers, Lavis uses simple sentences and easy-to-follow plots to introduce such concepts as colors, prepositions, and the days of the week. "The text is just right for toddlers," Susan Marie Pitard remarked in her *School Library Journal* review of *Little Mouse Has a Friend* and *Little Mouse Has a Party.* Wendy S. Carroll, another *School Library Journal* critic, described Lavis's artwork in both *Little Mouse Has an Adventure* and *Little Mouse Has a Busy Day* as "bright, colorful, and appealing."

Biographical and Critical Sources

PERIODICALS

Booklist, November 15, 1996, Stephanie Zvirin, review of *Cock-a-doodle-doo: A Farmyard Counting Book,* p. 592; January 1, 1998, Hazel Rochman, review of *Jump,* p. 824.
Bookseller, February 20, 2004, Sarah Amond, review of *You're Too Small!,* p. 31.

Steve Lavis's illustration projects include creating the humorous art for Carol Roth's story in **All Aboard to Work—Choo-Choo!** (Albert Whitman & Company, 2009. Illustration copyright © 2009 by Steven Lavis. Reproduced by permission.)

Kirkus Reviews, February 15, 2004, review of *You're Too Small!,* p. 184; August 15, 2009, review of *All Aboard to Work—Choo-Choo!*

Publishers Weekly, December 16, 1996, review of *Cock-a-doodle-doo,* p. 58; November 6, 2000, "Introducing Little Mouse," p. 93; December 4, 2000, reviews of *Noisy Wild Animals* and *Noisy Farm Animals,* both p. 74; April 23, 2001, reviews of *On the Farm* and *In the Jungle,* both p. 80; March 15, 2004, review of *You're Too Small!,* p. 74; October 31, 2005, review of *Who's Been Walking on My Floor?!,* p. 59.

School Library Journal, January, 2001, Wendy S. Carroll, reviews of *Little Mouse Has a Busy Day* and *Little Mouse Has an Adventure,* both p. 103; June, 2001, Susan Marie Pitard, reviews of *Little Mouse Has a Friend* and *Little Mouse Has a Party,* both p. 122; June, 2004, Sheilah Kosco, review of *You're Too Small!,* p. 118; November, 2009, Lynn K. Vanca, review of *All Aboard to Work—Choo-Choo!,* p. 87.

ONLINE

Steve Lavis Home Page, http://www.stevelavis.com (January 21, 2011).*

*   *   *

LAW, Dr. Stephen
See LAW, Stephen

*   *   *

LAW, Stephen
(Dr. Stephen Law)

Personal

Children: two daughters. *Education:* Attended City University London; Trinity College Oxford, B.Phil; Queen's College Oxford, D.Phil.

Addresses

Office—Heythrop College, University of London, Kensington Sq., London W8 5HN, England. *E-mail*—think@royalinstitutephilosophy.org; s.law@heythrop.ac.uk.

Career

Educator, writer, and editor. Heythrop College London, London, England, senior lecturer in philosophy. Centre for Inquiry London, provost, 2008—. Also worked as a sand-blaster and damp-proofer, and as a postman in Girton, England, for four years.

Member

Royal Society of Arts.

Awards, Honors

Junior research fellowship, Queen's College Oxford; Prospect Millennium essay prize (joint winner), Economic and Social Research Council, 2000; Mindleheim Philosophy Prize, 2009, for German translation of *The Philosophy Gym.*

Writings

FOR CHILDREN

The Philosophy Files, illustrated by Daniel Postgate, Dolphin (London, England), 2000, published as *Philosophy Rocks!,* Volo (New York, NY), 2002.

The Outer Limits, illustrated by Daniel Postgate, Dolphin (London, England), 2003, published as *The Philosophy Files Two,* Orion (London, England), 2006.

(As Dr. Stephen Law) *Really, Really Big Questions about Life, the Universe, and Everything,* illustrated by Nishant Choksi, Kingfisher (New York, NY), 2009.

FOR ADULTS

The Philosophy Gym: Twenty-five Short Adventures in Thinking, illustrated by Daniel Postgate, St. Martin's Press (New York, NY), 2003.

The Xmas Files: The Philosophy of Christmas, Weidenfeld & Nicolson (London, England), 2003.

(Editor, with Elizabeth Burns) *Philosophy for AS and A2,* Routledge (New York, NY), 2004.

The War for Children's Minds, Routledge (New York, NY), 2006.

Philosophy, DK Publishing (New York, NY), 2007.

The Great Philosophers: The Lives and Ideas of History's Greatest Thinkers, Quercus (London, England), 2007.

(With Jessica Wilson) *A Brief Guide to Global Warming,* Robinson (London, England), 2007.

(Editor) *Israel, Palestine, and Terror,* Continuum (New York, NY), 2008.

Also editor of *THINK: Philosophy for Everyone.* Contributor to scholarly journals, including *Faith and Philosophy, Religious Studies, Journal of Consciousness Studies,* and *Journal of Philosophy of Education.*

Sidelights

A senior lecturer at Heythrop College in London, England, Stephen Law has written a number of well-received philosophy books for children. His book *Really, Really Big Questions about Life, the Universe, and Everything* was described as a "breezy mind-expander" by a critic in *Kirkus Reviews.* In his works for young readers, Law examines a variety of ethical, metaphysical, and scientific issues, including the origin of the universe, the reliability of knowledge, and the existence of a higher power. "I've always been struck by how philosophically minded children are," Law told Mel Steel in a London *Guardian* interview. "They ask questions and they get an answer, and behind that answer they find another question to ask, and it doesn't take long before they're starting to question some of our most basic and fundamental beliefs. If you repeatedly ask 'Why?', it's not long before you're really hitting philosophical bedrock."

Law developed an early interest in philosophical matters. "I had loads of great conversations with my parents at the dinner table when I was a teenager," he recalled to *Guardian* contributor Melissa Benn. "It was no-holds-barred on religion and politics. I got a lot of my education from sitting at that table, arguing about stuff." Although he possesses what Steel characterized as a "maverick combination of passion, rigour, patience and sedition," Law took a most indirect route to academic success. Growing up in Cambridge, England, he tackled A-level courses two different times: officials at his first school tired of his laziness and asked him to leave, while Law chose to end his scholastic pursuits at another college because of his displeasure with the syllabus, which required little of him other than to regurgitate material. After working for a time as a manual laborer, Law spent four years as a postman in Girton, England in the early 1980s. During this time, he read voraciously, primarily on the subject of philosophy. "One book led to another," he revealed to Benn. "Only then did it occur to me that I could go to university and look at these issues in depth." Law eventually entered City University London and ultimately a bachelor of philosophy degree at Trinity College Oxford. After completing a junior research fellowship at Queen's College, where he earned his doctorate, he landed a teaching position at Heythrop.

In his first work for young audiences, *The Philosophy Files* (published in the United States as *Philosophy Rocks!*), Law tackles a number of weighty subjects in an accessible manner. In chapters titled "What Is Real?," "Should I Eat Meat?," and "Where Do Right and Wrong Come From?" he "goes straight to the heart of some of the most vexed questions there are to ask," as Steel commented. Joel Shoemaker, writing in *School Library Journal*, maintained that Law "is successful in presenting . . . ideas objectively, balancing every argument with counterarguments and problems that they may raise."

In *Really, Really Big Questions about Life, the Universe, and Everything* Law again dissects complex issues "in an engaging style that avoids leading readers to any preconceived answers," as Brian Odom commented in *School Library Journal*. The work addresses dozens of intriguing topics, such as intelligent design, consciousness, the nature of evil, astrology, and the possibility of time travel. "This thought-provoking book poses challenging questions," a reviewer in *Publishers Weekly* noted, and Daniel Kraus warned in *Booklist*: "Kids, prepare to have your minds blown."

Biographical and Critical Sources

PERIODICALS

Booklist, December 15, 2009, Daniel Kraus, review of *Really, Really Big Questions about Life, the Universe, and Everything*, p. 37.
Guardian (London, England), July 22, 2000, Mel Steel, review of *The Philosophy Files*, p. 11; June 3, 2006, Melissa Benn, "Philosopher Stephen Law Is on the Warpath," p. 3.
Kirkus Reviews, September 15, 2009, review of *Really, Really Big Questions about Life, the Universe, and Everything*.
Library Journal, December, 2003, Francisca Goldsmith, review of *The Philosophy Gym: Twenty-five Short Adventures in Thinking*, p. 124.
Publishers Weekly, November 2, 2009, review of *Really, Really Big Questions about Life, the Universe, and Everything*, p. 53.
School Library Journal, October, 2002, Joel Shoemaker, review of *Philosophy Rocks!*, p. 187; January, 2010, Brian Odom, review of *Really, Really Big Questions about Life, the Universe, and Everything*, p. 123.

ONLINE

Heythrop College Web site, http://www.heythrop.ac.uk/ (January 21, 2011), "Stephen Law."
Stephen Law Web log, http://stephenlaw.blogspot.com (January 21, 2011).

*   *   *

LEMAÎTRE, Pascal 1967-

Personal

Born 1967, in Belgium; married; wife's name Manou; children: Maelle. *Education:* Attended La Cambre (Belgian school of visual arts).

Addresses

Home—Brussels, Belgium; Brooklyn, NY. *Agent*—Pippin Properties, 155 E. 38th St., Ste. 2H, New York, NY 10016.

Career

Author and illustrator. La Cambre, Brussels, Belgium, instructor. *Exhibitions:* Work included in Original Art Show, Society of Illustrators, New York, NY, 2002.

Writings

SELF-ILLUSTRATED

Elvire la girafe, Le Seuil (Paris, France), 1991, published as *Emily the Giraffe*, Hyperion Books for Children (New York, NY), 1993.
Zelda's Secret, Bridgewater Books (Mahwah, NJ), 1994.

ILLUSTRATOR

Toni Morrison and Slade Morrison, *The Book of Mean People,* Hyperion Books for Children (New York, NY), 2002.

Kate McMullan, *Supercat,* Workman Publishing (New York, NY), 2002.

Toni Morrison and Slade Morrison, *Who's Got Game? The Lion or the Mouse?* (also see below), Scribner (New York, NY), 2003.

Toni Morrison and Slade Morrison, *Who's Got Game? Poppy or the Snake?* (also see below), Scribner (New York, NY), 2003.

Toni Morrison and Slade Morrison, *Who's Got Game? The Ant or the Grasshopper?* (also see below), Scribner (New York, NY), 2003.

Kate McMullan, *Supercat to the Rescue,* Workman Publishing (New York, NY), 2003.

Kate McMullan, *Baby Goose,* Hyperion Books for Children (New York, NY), 2004.

Toni Morrison and Slade Morrison, *Who's Got Game?: Three Fables* (includes *The Ant or the Grasshopper?, The Lion or the Mouse?,* and *Poppy or the Snake?*), Scribner (New York, NY), 2005.

Michaela Muntean, *Do Not Open This Book!,* Scholastic (New York, NY), 2006.

Andrea Beaty, *Doctor Ted,* Simon & Schuster (New York, NY), 2007.

Alison McGhee, *Always,* Simon & Schuster Books for Young Readers (New York, NY), 2009.

Andrea Beaty, *Firefighter Ted,* Margaret K. McElderry Books (New York, NY), 2009.

Andrea Beaty, *Hush, Baby Ghostling,* Margaret K. McElderry Books (New York, NY), 2009.

Kate McMullan, *Bulldog's Big Day,* Orchard Books (New York, NY), 2011.

Andrea Beaty, *Artist Ted,* Margaret K. McElderry Books (New York, NY), 2012.

Illustrations have appeared in numerous periodicals, including *Astrapi, Aventuriers, Bonjour, Dauphin, Le Ligueur, Le Monde, Liberation, Libre Belgique, Marie-France, Maxime, New Yorker, New York Times, New York Times Book Review, Notre Temps, Phosphore,* and *Time,* as well as in art annuals.

Sidelights

Belgian-born artist Pascal Lemaître has illustrated books by children's authors that include Kate McMullan, Michaela Muntean, Alison McGhee, Andrea Beaty, and the mother-son writing team of Toni and Slade Morrison. Frequently compared by critics to the work of such well-known illustrators as William Steig, Shel Silverstein, and James Stevenson, Lemaître's pen-and-ink drawings also appear in alongside his original stories in *Elvire la girafe* and *Zelda's Secret.* His editorial illustrations can also be found in the pages of periodicals such as *Time, Print, Fortune, 3x3,* the *New York Times Book Review, New Yorker, New York Times,* and the *Wall Street Journal;* internationally, his artwork and photog-

Kate McMullan's **Baby Goose** *features several rhymes by the great Mother Goose, each brought to life in Pascal Lemaître's graphite-and-watercolor art.* (Hyperion Books for Children, 2004. Illustration © 2004 by Pascal Lemaître. All rights reserved. Reproduced by Hyperion Books for Children.)

Lemaître's illustration projects include creating the expressive art for Andrea Beaty's picture book Firefighter Ted. (Illustration copyright © 2009 by Pascal Lemaître. Reprinted with permission of Margaret K. McElderry Books, an imprint of Simon & Schuster Children's Publishing Division.)

raphy have appeared in the widely read *Le Monde, Marie-France, Magazine Litteraire, Le Liguer,* and *Notre Temps.* Reviewing Lemaître's work for McGhee's *Always,* a picture book that brings to life the grandiose plans of a puppy intending to take his job as a child's guardian seriously, Judith Constantinides noted in *School Library Journal* that Lemaître's pencil-and-pastel "artwork . . . provides a perfect match for the whimsical text" and captures "the love between the two friends beautifully."

As an illustrator for children, Lemaître is noted for creating "whimsical, cartoon-style, pen-and-ink drawings," as Marie Orlando noted in a *School Library Journal* review of McMullan's *Baby Goose.* "The best part is the action," *Booklist* contributor Hazel Rochman wrote in her review of Lemaître's work for the Morrisons' *Who's Got Game? The Lion or the Mouse?* Praising the artist's contributions to another book by the mother-and-son team, Steven Engelfried wrote in *School Library Journal* that "Lemaître's cartoons help with the story's pace" in *Who's Got Game? The Ant or the Grasshopper?;* his decision to "switch from small panels to full-page scenes effectively accentuates dramatic moments" in the Morrisons' story.

Lemaître's humorous approach to illustration is apparent in his work for Muntean's *Do Not Open This Book!,* which centers on a swine scribe who interacts with readers by demanding that they leave him alone so that

he can pen another awarding-winning novel. The comedy of Muntean's text is enhanced by Lemaître's art, which details the swine's frustration with writer's block and the unfolding of his unusual creative process. According to *School Library Journal* reviewer Joy Fleishhacker, Lemaître's artwork parallels the dry, comedic tone of Muntean's text through "loose-lined, messy-looking cartoons in glossy, bold colors." Sparking additional fun, the artist incorporates "tiny sidekicks—a round brown spider and violet-blue fly—who mimic [the pig's] gestures and imply that he's harmless," noted a *Publishers Weekly* reviewer.

Working with Beaty, Lemaître has created art for her picture book *Hush, Baby Ghostling,* as well as for her companion volumes *Doctor Ted, Firefighter Ted,* and *Artist Ted.* In *Hush, Baby Ghostling,* Beaty's story about a mother ghost's attemps to get her young ghost child to quiet down for the night, the artist contributes colored-ink drawings that erase all things scary from the tale. A bear named Ted, the young star of Beaty's three connected stories, shows his self-reliance when he hurts his knee in *Doctor Ted,* tracks down the source of smoke in *Firefighter Ted,* and vies for a place among the Old Masters in *Artist Ted.* In every case, the bear's good-intentioned efforts are not matched by training and ability, resulting in a series of humorous misunderstandings. "Lemaître's bright backgrounds and varied compositions" in *Doctor Ted* range "from vignette clusters to close-ups [and] keep interest," according to

School Library Journal contributor Gay Lynn Van Vleck, The "poignant facial expressions" the artist gives to the story's "cartoonish creatures provide a good visual counterpoint to Beaty's sweet, matter-of-fact sense of humor," wrote *Booklist* critic Abby Nolan, and a *Publishers Weekly* contributor asserted of *Doctor Ted* that the artist's mix of "chunky ink lines and almost neon-like digital colors give[s] every page plenty of punch."

Biographical and Critical Sources

PERIODICALS

Booklist, October 15, 2002, Hazel Rochman, review of *The Book of Mean People,* p. 412; May 15, 2003, Francisca Goldsmith, review of *Who's Got Game? The Ant or the Grasshopper?,* p. 1660; November 15, 2003, Hazel Rochman, review of *Who's Got Game? The Lion or the Mouse?,* p. 598; February 15, 2004, Francisca Goldsmith, review of *Who's Got Game? Poppy or the Snake?,* p. 1077; November 15, 2004, Hazel Rochman, review of *Baby Goose,* p. 588; March 15, 2006, Jennifer Mattson, review of *Do Not Open This Book!,* p. 53; June 1, 2008, Abby Nolan, review of *Doctor Ted,* p. 86; August 1, 2009, Hazel Rochman, review of *Always,* p. 75; October 1, 2009, Shelle Rosenfeld, review of *Firefighter Ted,* p. 50.

Bulletin of the Center for Children's Books, January, 2003, review of *The Book of Mean People,* p. 206; April, 2004, Elizabeth Bush, review of *Who's Got Game? Poppy or the Snake?,* p. 344; March, 2006, Elizabeth Bush, review of *Do Not Open This Book!,* p. 321.

Horn Book, May-June, 2008, Christine M. Heppermann, review of *Doctor Ted,* p. 292; September-October, 2009, Christine M. Heppermann, review of *Firefighter Ted,* p. 537.

Kirkus Reviews, October 15, 2004, review of *Baby Goose,* p. 1010; February 15, 2006, review of *Do Not Open This Book!,* p. 188; March 1, 2008, review of *Doctor Ted;* July 15, 2009, review of *Hush, Baby Ghostling;* May 15, 2009, review of *Always;* August 15, 2009, review of *Firefighter Ted.*

Publishers Weekly, September 9, 2002, review of *The Book of Mean People,* p. 68; June 2, 2003, review of *Who's Got Game? The Ant or the Grasshopper?,* p. 50; November 1, 2004, review of *Baby Goose,* p. 60; January 9, 2006, review of *Do Not Open This Book!,* p. 52; March 3, 2008, review of *Doctor Ted,* p. 45; June 8, 2009, review of *Always,* p. 43; September 14, 2009, review of *Firefighter Ted,* p. 48.

School Library Journal, November, 2002, Maryann H. Owen, review of *Supercat,* p. 130, and Judith Constantinides, review of *The Book of Mean People,* p. 132; September, 2003, Steven Englefried, review of *Who's Got Game? The Ant or the Grasshopper?,* p. 204; December, 2003, John Peters, review of *Who's Got Game? The Lion or the Mouse?,* p. 138; November, 2004, Marie Orlando, review of *Baby Goose,* p. 128; April, 2006, Joy Fleishhacker, review of *Do Not Open This Book!,* p. 114; April, 2008, Gay Lynn Van Vleck, review of *Doctor Ted,* p. 102; May, 2009, Judith Constantinides, review of *Always,* p. 83; July, 2009, Ieva Bates, review of *Hush, Baby Ghostling,* p. 60; September, 2009, Susan E. Murray, review of *Firefighter Ted,* p. 115.

Voice of Youth Advocates, June, 2004, Tim Brennan, review of *Who's Got Game? Poppy or the Snake?,* p. 145.

ONLINE

Pascal Lemaître Home Page, http://www.pascallemaitre. com (January 15, 2011).

Pippin Properties Web site, http://www.pippinproperties. com/ (January 15, 2011), "Pascal Lemaître."

Richochet-Jeunes Web site, http://www.ricochet-jeunes.org/ (January 10, 2007), "Pascal Lemaître."*

*   *   *

LEUNG, Hilary 1975-

Personal

Born 1975, in Hamilton, Ontario, Canada. *Education:* Sheridan College, degree, 1998 (illustration); graduate study at New Media Design.

Addresses

Home—Toronto, Ontario, Canada. *E-mail*—hilary@ ninjacowboybear.com.

Career

Graphic artist and illustrator. Presenter at schools.

Illustrator

David Bruins, *The Legend of Ninja Cowboy Bear* (originally self-published), Kids Can Press (Toronto, Ontario, Canada), 2009.

David Bruins, *Ninja Cowboy Bear Presents the Way of the Ninja,* Kids Can Press (Toronto, Ontario, Canada), 2010.

Biographical and Critical Sources

PERIODICALS

Kirkus Reviews, September 1, 2009, review of *The Legend of Ninja Cowboy Bear.*

School Library Journal, December, 2009, Laura Butler, review of *The Legend of Ninja Cowboy Bear,* p. 78.

ONLINE

Canadian Children's Book Centre Web site, http://www. bookcentre.ca/ (January 15, 2011), "Hilary Leung."

Hilary Leung Home Page, http://www.ninja-cowboy-bear. com (December 22, 2010).*

M-N

MAY, Katie

Personal
Born in England. *Education:* Attended art school. *Hobbies and other interests:* Photography, travel, reading, swimming.

Addresses
Home—Fethiye, Turkey; England. *E-mail*—katie@katie may.me.uk; katiemaygreen@hotmail.com.

Career
Illustrator and graphic artist. Designer of cards and stationary for Hallmark.

Illustrator
Liz Kessler, *Philippa Fisher's Fairy Godsister,* Orion Children's (London, England), 2007, Candlewick Press (Somerville, MA), 2009.

Darcey Bussell, *Delphie and the Magic Ballet Shoes* ("Magic Ballerina" series), HarperCollins Children's (London, England), 2008, published as *The Magic Ballet Shoes,* HarperCollins (New York, NY), 2009.

Darcey Bussell, *Delphie and the Magic Spell* ("Magic Ballerina" series), HarperCollins Children's (London, England), 2008, published as *The Magic Spell,* HarperCollins Children's (New York, NY), 2009.

Darcey Bussell, *Delphie and the Masked Ball* ("Magic Ballerina" series), HarperCollins Children's (London, England), 2008.

Darcey Bussell, *Delphie and the Glass Slippers* ("Magic Ballerina" series), HarperCollins Children's (London, England), 2008.

Darcey Bussell, *Delphie and the Fairy Godmother* ("Magic Ballerina" series), HarperCollins Children's (London, England), 2008.

Darcey Bussell, *Delphie and the Birdthday Show* ("Magic Ballerina" series), HarperCollins Children's (London, England), 2008.

Liz Kessler, *Philippa Fisher and the Dream-maker's Daughter,* Candlewick Press (Somerville, MA), 2009.

Liz Kessler, *Philippa Fisher and the Stone Fairy's Promise,* Orion Children's (London, England), 2010, published as *Philippa Fisher and the Fairy's Promise,* Candlewick Press (Somerville, MA), 2010.

Illustrator of interactive books, including *Deck the Halls* (sticker book), 2009.

Books featuring May's illustrations have been translated into French and German.

Sidelights
Katie May is a British illustrator whose pastel-toned images have appeared on greeting cards and stationary, in fashion and editorial illustrations, and in the pages of girl-focused novels by Darcey Bussell and Liz Kessler. Her first book-illustration project, Kessler's *Philippa Fisher's Fairy Godsister,* was published in 2007 and led to May's choice as illustrator for Bussell's popular "Magic Ballerina" series.

The "Magic Ballerina" books are inspired by the real-life experiences of their author, Bussell, who began her career as a prima ballerina in her early teens. In series opener *Delphie and the Magic Ballet Shoes,* which was published in the United States as *The Magic Ballet Shoes,* Delphie Durand dreams of attending Madame Zarakova's School of Ballet, and her dreams come through when Madame herself takes the talented girl under her wing. Bringing to life what *Booklist* critic Gillian Engberg described as a story "as substantial as cotton candy," May's "whimsical line drawings" will appeal to "young balletomanes," according to the critic. May and Bussell continue their collaboration in several other books, among them *Delphine and the Magic Secret, Delphine and the Glass Slippers,* and *Delphine and the Birthday Show.*

May also brings her characteristic lighthearted flair to her illustrations for Kessler's novels about a preteen who looks for magic in her life and finds it. In *Philippa Fisher's Fairy Godsister* eleven-year-old Philippa first meets Daisy, a youthful fairy guardian who helps the girl deal with family problems while also deciding how to use the three wishes that she has been is given. *Philippa Fisher and the Dream-maker's Daughter,* in which Daisy helps Philippa narrate the story of her magical adventures in the world of Ravenleigh Woods, continues Kessler's focus on discovering one's uniqueness, a theme that "will resonate with girls going through their own emotional awakenings," according to *School Library Journal* contributor Robyn Gioia. In reviewing *Philippa Fisher's Fairy Godsister, Horn Book* critic Susan Dove Lempke noted the book's appeal to tween readers and praised it as "a realistic school story with a magical twist."

Biographical and Critical Sources

PERIODICALS

Booklist, October 15, 2008, Kay Weisman, review of *Philippa Fisher's Fairy Godsister,* p. 42; May 15, 2009, Gillian Engberg, review of *The Magic Ballet Shoes,* p. 56.

Horn Book, November-December, 2008, Susan Dove Lempke, review of *Philippa Fisher's Fairy Godsister,* p. 707.

Kirkus Reviews, August 1, 2008, review of *Philippa Fisher's Fairy Godsister.*

School Library Journal, November, 2008, Robyn Gioia, review of *Philippa Fisher's Fairy Godsister,* p. 124; November, 2009, Maria B. Salvadore, review of *Philippa Fisher and the Dream-Maker's Daughter,* p. 112.

Katie May created the detailed illustrations that bring to life Darcey Bussell's fanciful story in **The Magic Ballet Shoes.** (Illustration copyright © 2009 by Katie May. Used by permission of HarperCollins Children's Books, a division of HarperCollins Publishers.)

ONLINE

Katie May Home Page, http://www.katiemay.me.uk (December 22, 2010).*

*   *   *

McALLISTER, Angela

Personal

Born in Windsor, England; married; children: two. *Hobbies and other interests:* Archaeology.

Addresses

Home—Hampshire, England.

Career

Children's book author and illustrator. Also worked as a nanny in Holland, Portugal, and Windsor and London, England.

Writings

FOR CHILDREN

The King Who Sneezed, illustrated by Simon Henwood, Morrow (New York, NY), 1988.

Snail's Birthday Problem, illustrated by Susie Jenkin-Pearce, Viking (New York, NY), 1989.

(Self-illustrated) *Nothing to Do,* Bodley Head (London, England), 1989.

(Self-illustrated) *Nothing to Cook,* Bodley Head (London, England), 1989.

The Whales' Tale, illustrated by Michaela Bloomfield, Aurum (London, England), 1990, published as *When the Ark Was Full,* Dutton (New York, NY), 1990.

Nesta, the Little Witch, illustrated by Susie Jenkin-Pearce, Viking (New York, NY), 1990.

The Enchanted Flute, illustrated by Margaret Chamberlain, Aurum (London, England), 1990.

The Acorn Sailor, illustrated by Alex Ayliffe, Aurum (London, England), 1990.

The Christmas Wish, illustrated by Susie Jenkin-Pearce, Aurum (London, England), 1990, Viking (New York, NY), 1991.

Matepo, illustrated by Jill Newton, Aurum (London, England), 1990, Dial (New York, NY), 1991.

(Self-illustrated) *The Battle of Sir Cob and Sir Filbert,* Clarkson N. Potter (New York, NY), 1991.

Mungo Moonbats, Dent (London, England), 1991.

Paradise Park, illustrated by Martin Pierce, Bodley Head (London, England), 1991.

One Breeze-scented, Sun-sparkling Morning, illustrated by Susie Jenkin-Pearce, Hutchinson (London, England), 1992.

Dinny's Diplodocus, Bodley Head (London, England), 1992.

Jessie's Journey, illustrated by Anne Magill, Macmillan (New York, NY), 1992.

The Babies of Cockle Bay, illustrated by Susie Jenkin-Pearce, Hutchinson (London, England), 1993, Barron's (Hauppauge, NY), 1994.

The Snow Angel, illustrated by Claire Fletcher, Lothrop, Lee & Shepard (New York, NY), 1993.

Sleepy Ella, illustrated by Susan Winter, Dent (London, England), 1993, Doubleday (New York, NY), 1994.

Felix and the Dragon, illustrated by Jane Tattersfield, Dent (London, England), 1993, illustrated by Mary Claire Smith, Orion (London, England), 2005.

Midnight at the Oasis, illustrated by Frances Lloyd, Bodley Head (London, England), 1994.

Daniel's Train, illustrated by Alan Curless, Hutchinson (London, England), 1994.

The Wind Garden, illustrated by Claire Fletcher, Bodley Head (London, England), 1994, Lothrop, Lee & Shepard (New York, NY), 1995.

The Ice Palace, illustrated by Angela Barrett, Putnam (New York, NY), 1994.

Scaredy Ghosts, illustrated by Susie Jenkin-Pearce, Hippo (London, England), 1998.

The Clever Cowboy, illustrated by Katherine Lodge, DK Publishing (New York, NY), 1998.

Jack and Lily, illustrated by Phillida Gili, Orion (London, England), 2001.

(Reteller) *The Tortoise and the Hare: An Aesop's Fable,* illustrated by Jonathan Heale, Frances Lincoln (London, England), 2001.

Be Good Gordon, illustrated by Tim Archbold, Bloomsbury (London, England), 2001.

The Baddies' Goodies, illustrated by Sally Anne Lambert, Bloomsbury (London, England), 2002, published as *Barkus, Sly, and the Golden Egg,* Bloomsbury (New York, NY), 2002.

Blue Rabbit, illustrated by Jason Cockcroft, Bloomsbury (London, England), 2003, published as *The Little Blue Rabbit,* Bloomsbury (New York, NY), 2003.

Harry's Box, illustrated by Jenny Jones, Bloomsbury (New York, NY), 2003.

Night-night, Little One, illustrated by Maggie Kneen, Random House (New York, NY), 2003.

Found You, Little Wombat!, illustrated by Charles Fuge, Gullane (London, England), 2003.

Little Jack Rabbit, illustrated by Sue Porter, Gullane (London, England), 2003.

Elephant in a Rowboat, illustrated by Holly Swain, Gullane (London, England), 2004.

Brave Bitsy and the Bear, illustrated by Tiphanie Beeke, Macmillan (London, England), 2004, Clarion (New York, NY), 2006.

Jasmine's Lion, illustrated by Marie-Louise Fitzpatrick, Doubleday (London, England), 2005.

Big Yang and Little Yin, illustrated by Eleanor Taylor, Gullane (London, England), 2005.

Monster Pet, illustrated by Charlotte Middleton, Margaret K. McElderry Books (New York, NY), 2005.

Trust Me, Mom!, illustrated by Ross Collins, Bloomsbury (New York, NY), 2005.

The Tide Turner, Orion (London, England), 2006.

Ruby and Little Joe, illustrated by Terry Milne, Simon & Schuster (London, England), 2006, published as *Mama and Little Joe,* Margaret K. McElderry Books (New York, NY), 2007.

Just like Sisters, illustrated by Sophie Fatus, Atheneum (New York, NY), 2006.

Digory the Dragon Slayer, illustrated by Ian Beck, Bloomsbury (New York, NY), 2006.

A Pocketful of Kisses, illustrated by Sue Hellard, Bloomsbury (London, England), 2006, published as *Take a Kiss to School,* Bloomsbury (New York, NY), 2006.

Digory and the Lost King, illustrated by Ian Beck, Bloomsbury (London, England), 2006, Bloomsbury (New York, NY), 2007.

A Place for Middle, illustrated by Nick Maland, Hodder (London, England), 2007.

Little Fallow, illustrated by Tina Macnaughton, Gullane (London, England), 2007.

Santa's Little Helper, illustrated by Daniel Howarth, Orchard Books (New York, NY), 2008.

Leon and the Place Between, illustrated by Grahame Baker-Smith, Templar Books (Somerville, MA), 2009.

Cover of Angela McAllister's novel Digory the Dragon Slayer, *featuring artwork by Ian Beck.* (Illustration © 2006 by Ian Beck. Reprinted by permission of Bloomsbury USA.)

Salty and Button, illustrated by Tiphanie Beeke, Macmillan (London, England), 2009.

The Runaway, illustrated by Peter Bailey, Orion (London, England), 2009.

Yuck! That's Not a Monster!, illustrated by Alison Edgson, Good Books (Intercourse, PA), 2010.

Little Mist, illustrated by Sarah Fox-Davies, Alfred A. Knopf (New York, NY), 2011.

Author's works have been translated into Welsh.

OTHER

(Illustrator) Margaret Greaves, *Magic from the Ground,* Dent (London, England), 1992.

Adaptations

Digory the Dragon Slayer was adapted as an audiobook by BBC Audiobooks America, 2006.

Sidelights

Angela McAllister is a prolific British author of picture books and chapter books. Since the late 1980s McAllister has produced more than fifty works for young readers, entertaining children in the United States as well as her native England with stories such as *Harry's Box, Digory the Dragon Slayer, Leon and the Place Between,* and *Yuck! That's Not a Monster!* Citing the author's "nimble prose" in *Harry's Box* for bringing to life a story about the power of imagination, a *Publishers Weekly* contributor added that in her repetitive text McAllister "echo[es] . . . the ambitions of imaginative kids everywhere."

While usually working with other illustrators, such as Katherine Lodge, Angela Barrett, Sue Hellard, and frequent collaborator Susie Jenkin-Pearce, McAllister also dons the illustrator cap for *The Battle of Sir Cob and Sir Filbert.* Reviewing this story, which finds two knights engaged in a fight during which they ultimately destroy the very things they are both fighting for, a *Publishers Weekly* reviewer wrote that McAllister's pen-and-ink art "displays her humor in yet another medium and brings new dimension to her talent." As McAllister noted in an interview on the Little Tiger Press Web site, "I love the interaction of images and words in a picture book—the way the words spark the visual narrative, which then contributes something unexpected and unique to create the whole work. I started my publishing career as an illustrator so I have great admiration for the skill of the illustrators I work with now."

McAllister honed her storytelling talents while growing up in a large family, and she well knows the value of humorous nonsense and wordplay, as well as upbeat endings, among young readers. Her first published book, *The King Who Sneezed,* introduces the aptly named King Parsimonious, a monarch who is so foolish that he does not realize that his own stinginess has caused his castle to become damp and uncomfortable. The

Artist Sophie Fatus teams up with McAllister to tell a story of two unusual friends in **Just like Sisters.** (Illustration copyright © 2005 by Sophie Fatus. Reprinted with permission of Atheneum Books for Young Readers, an imprint of Simon & Schuster Children's Publishing Division.)

Yippeeville Pancake Tossin' Contest brings together a host of quirky characters in *The Clever Cowboy,* as a group of spatula-wielding buckaroos attempt to out-toss each other and wind up blanketing the sun with a poorly aimed flapjack, while a young mole finds the second day of school easier to deal with when armed with a pocketful of kisses in *Take a Kiss to School.* Reviewing *The Clever Cowboy* in *Publishers Weekly,* a critic cited the "spirited mood" carried by McAllister's "western vernacular," while a *Kirkus Reviews* contributor deemed *Take a Kiss to School* "heartwarming" and "a sweet take on an old theme."

Long-distance pen pals Nancy and Ally finally meet in *Just like Sisters* and realize that their friendship is just as strong in real life—even though Nancy is a human child and Ally is an alligator. Calling *Just like Sisters* a "fresh, but odd spin on pen pals," a *Kirkus Reviews* writer added that artist Sophie Fatus's inclusion of "coy details" in her "colorful illustrations add understated humor" to McAllister's story. "A strong intertwining of text and illustration" makes *Just like Sisters* "a charming celebration of friendship," concluded Elaine Lesh Morgan in *School Library Journal.*

In the chapter book *Digory the Dragon Slayer* McAllister introduces readers to a young boy who enjoys nothing better than spending time alone in the forest near his village playing his lute and making up songs. One day Digory finds a strange object in the woods. When the object is discovered to be a dragon's tooth, the boy is hailed as a dragon slayer. Forced to leave off writing songs, Digory soon finds himself mounted on an old, deaf horse named Barkley and clad in a suit of home-

made armor. Reluctantly setting off to slay dragons, rescue distressed damsels, and eventually marry a beautiful princess, the boy ultimately meets his destiny at the castle of King Widget, where both a fun-loving princess named Enid and a fearsome dragon live. Digory's adventures continue in *Digory and the Lost King* as the young knight follows the trail of the missing King Widget and the monarch's long-missing twin brother. The boy finds that even more is expected of him, however, when he is mistaken for a powerful wizard. McAllister's "lighthearted plot and the strong underlying message about courage and individuality" in *Digory the Dragon Slayer* makes the book "a good choice for fantasy fans," according to *School Library Journal* contributor Elaine E. Knight. Discussing the sequel, Knight cited the "amusing" pen-and-ink art by Ian Beck for contributing to *Digory and the Lost King,* the critic adding that McAllister's "lighthearted fantasy spoof is filled with mock heroic dialogue and derring-do."

Ruby and Little Joe—published in the United States as *Mama and Little Joe*—centers on a pair of stuffed animals who find it difficult to adjust to unfamiliar surroundings. When Mama Ruby, a toy kangaroo, and her baby, Little Joe, arrive at their new home, they are shunned by the shinier, brighter toys, despite Mama's best efforts to make friends. When Little Joe is accidentally carted off to the trash, however, his mother finds help from unexpected sources. Writing in *Booklist,* Ilene Cooper offered praise for *Mama and Little Joe,* remarking that "what McAllister does well is show the characters' evolution from stuck-up stuffies to caring friends."

A stuffed animal is also the focus of *Brave Bitsy and the Bear.* When a young girl loses track of her lilac-furred stuffed bunny, Bitsy, while playing in the woods, the toy encounters a kindly brown bear that offers to help Bitsy find her way home. Unfortunately, the bruin is preparing to hibernate and falls asleep before reaching his den, prompting Bitsy and the other woodland creatures to shelter him when it begins to snow. A contributor in *Kirkus Reviews* described *Brave Bitsy and the Bear* as a "charming tale of an unlikely friendship," and Linda Staskus commented in *School Library Journal* that McAllister's "plot is fresh and original, the smoothly flowing narrative has sparks of suspense, and Bitsy is an irresistible heroine."

In McAllister's *Leon and the Place Between* a youngster visits a wondrous otherworld through the power of magic. While attending a performance by Abdul Kazam, an incredible stage magician, Leon is called upon to assist with the disappearing act. Suddenly, the boy is transported to the "place between," a dazzling limbo that exists to hold people and props before they reappear before the audience. "McAllister's descriptive text provides powerful emphasis through taut dialogue," Meg Smith commented in *School Library Journal.*

A fluffy, good-natured creature comes to the rescue of his gruesome siblings in *Yuck! That's Not a Monster!,* a

***Grahame Baker-Smith creates the dynamic artwork for McAllister's over-the-top story in* Leon and the Place Between.** (Illustration copyright © 2008 by Grahame Baker-Smith. Reproduced by permission of Candlewick Press, Somerville, MA.)

"cute fable about kindness," according to a contributor in *Kirkus Reviews.* When their triplets hatch, Mr. and Mrs. Monster are greeted by spiky, green-skinned Frightful; his snarling, purple-toned sister Horrid; and, much to their surprise, a pink, furry creature they name Little Shock. Despite their best efforts to encourage Little Shock's monstrous tendencies, he remains sweet and generous, traits that come in handy when Frightful and Horrid disturb a nightmarish creature in the woods. McAllister's "message about celebrating differences comes through," a *Publishers Weekly* critic stated, and Gay Lynn Van Vleck wrote in her *School Library Journal* review of *Yuck!* felt that young readers "exploring irony will be fans of this story."

Biographical and Critical Sources

PERIODICALS

Booklist, March 15, 1992, Julie Corsaro, review of *The Battle of Sir Cob and Sir Filbert,* p. 1389; September 1, 1992, Hazel Rochman, review of *Jessie's Journey,* p. 67; October 1, 1993, Janice Del Negro, review of *The Show Angel,* p. 353; October 15, 1994, Mary Harris Veeder, review of *The Ice Palace,* p. 437; March 15, 1995, Julie Corsaro, review of *The Wind Garden,* p. 1335; October 1, 1998, GraceAnne A. DeCandido, review of *The Clever Cowboy,* p. 336; June 1, 2003, Lauren Peterson, review of *The Little Blue Rabbit,* p. 1787; August, 2003, John Peters, review of *Harry's Box,* p. 1989; August 1, 2006, Hazel Rochman, review of *Take a Kiss to School,* p. 95; April 1, 2007, Ilene Cooper, review of *Mama and Little Joe,* p. 58.

Bulletin of the Center for Children's Books, January, 1989, review of *The King Who Sneezed,* p. 129; May, 1990, review of *When the Ark Was Full,* p. 221; January, 1992, review of *The Enchanted Flute,* p. 133; December, 1998, review of *The Clever Cowboy,* p. 137; April, 2004, Janice Del Negro, review of *The Tortoise and the Hare: An Aesop's Fable,* p. 339.

Kirkus Reviews, June 1, 2002, review of *Barkus, Sly, and the Golden Egg,* p. 807; October 15, 2002, review of *Be Good, Gordon,* p. 1534; February 15, 2003, review of *Night-night, Little One,* p. 312; June 15, 2003, review of *Harry's Box,* p. 861; October 15, 2005, review of *Trust Me, Mom!,* p. 1143; May 1, 2006, review of *Digory the Dragon Slayer,* p. 463; May 15, 2006, review of *Just like Sisters,* p. 521; June 15, 2006, review of *Take a Kiss to School,* p. 635; July 1, 2006, review of *Felix and the Blue Dragon,* p. 679; October 1, 2006, review of *Brave Bitsy and the Bear,* p. 1020; March 1, 2007, review of *Mama and Little Joe,* p. 227; May 1, 2007, review of *Digory and the Lost King;* December 15, 2007, review of *A Place for Middle;* July 1, 2009, review of *Leon and the Place Between;* May 1, 2010, review of *Yuck! That's Not a Monster!*

Publishers Weekly, December 14, 1990, review of *Matepo,* p. 66; January 13, 1992, review of *The Battle of Sir Cob and Sir Filbert;* October 24, 1994, review of *The

Ice Palace,* p. 61; November 9, 1998, review of *The Clever Cowboy,* p. 75; December 9, 2002, review of *Night-night, Little One,* p. 81; May 26, 2003, review of *The Little Blue Rabbit,* p. 68; July 7, 2003, review of *Harry's Box,* p. 71; June 12, 2006, review of *Take a Kiss to School,* p. 51; August 3, 2009, review of *"Leon and the Place Between,* p. 44; July 5, 2010, review of *Yuck! That's Not a Monster!,* p. 42.

School Library Journal, February, 1989, Kathy Piehl, review of *The King Who Sneezed,* p. 72; April, 1990, Susan H. Patron, review of *Snail's Birthday Problem,* p. 93; September, 1990, Kathy Piehl, review of *When the Ark Was Full,* p. 206; March, 1991, Lisa S. Murphy, review of *Nesta, the Little Witch,* p. 175; June, 1991, Susan Scheps, review of *Matepo,* p. 85; December, 1991, Susan L. Rogers, review of *The Enchanted Flute,* p. 96; June, 1992, Lauralyn Persson, review of *The Battle of Sir Cob and Sir Filbert,* p. 98; January, 1993, Elizabeth Hanson, review of *Jessie's Journey,* p. 81; November, 1993, Shirley Wilton, review of *The Snow Angel,* p. 86; July, 1994, Alexandra Marris, review of *Sleepy Ella,* p. 85; October, 1994, Patricia Lothrop Green, review of *The Ice Palace,* p. 125; April, 1995, Patricia Pearl Dole, review of *The Wind Garden,* p. 104; October, 1998, Roxanne Burg, review of *The Clever Cowboy,* p. 107; September, 202, Marie Orlando, review of *Barkus, Sly, and the Golden Egg,* p. 200; January, 2003, Bina Williams, review of *Be Good, Gordon,* p. 105; March, 2003, Carolyn Janssen, review of *Night-night, Little One,* p. 198; July, 2003, Wendy Woodfill, review of *The Little Blue Rabbit,* p. 101; October, 2003, Kathleen Whalin, review of *Harry's Box,* p. 130; July, 2005, Shawn Brommer, review of *Monster Pet!,* p. 78; December, 2005, Robin L. Gibson, review of *Trust Me, Mom!,* p. 118; June, 2006, Elaine Lesh Morgan, review of *Just like Sisters,* p. 121; July, 2006, Lisa Gangemi Kropp, review of *Take a Kiss to School,* p. 82; August, 2006, Elaine E. Knight, review of *Digory the Dragon Slayer,* p. 92; October, 2006, Linda Staskus, review of *Brave Bitsy and the Bear,* p. 116; April, 2007, Amy Lilien-Harper, review of *Mama and Little Joe,* p. 112; July, 2007, Elaine E. Knight, review of *Digory and the Lost King,* p. 81; September, 2009, Meg Smith, review of *Leon and the Place Between,* p. 128; August, 2010, Gay Lynn Van Vleck, review of *Yuck! That's Not a Monster!,* p. 80.

ONLINE

Little Tiger Press Web site, http://www.littletigerpress.com/ (February 1, 2011), interview with McAllister.*

*   *   *

McDONALD, Candice Hartsough 1982-

Personal

Born 1982, in IN; married Brandon McDonald; children; Virginia. *Education:* Herron School of Art and Design, B.F.A. (illustration), 2005.

Addresses

Home—Indianapolis, IN. *E-mail*—candice@cordialkit ten.com.

Career

Illustrator, beginning 2007. *Exhibitions:* Work exhibited at Studio School and Gallery, Indianapolis, IN, 2007; Gallery j3mf, Hannover, Germany, 2007; and Lala Gallery, Lafayette, IN, 2009.

Awards, Honors

Society of School Librarians International award, 2010, for *Oliver at the Window* by Elizabeth Shreeve.

Illustrator

Elizabeth Shreeve, *Oliver at the Window,* Front Street (Honesdale, PA), 2009.

Mary Rand Hess, *The Day I Met the Nuts,* Story Pie Press (Loudon County, VA), 2010.

Biographical and Critical Sources

PERIODICALS

Booklist, November 1, 2009, Randall Enos, review of *Oliver at the Window,* p. 52.

Kirkus Reviews, September 15, 2009, review of *Oliver at the Window.*

Library Journal, October, 2009, Maryann H. Owen, review of *Oliver at the Window,* p. 105.

ONLINE

Candice Hartsough McDonald Home Page, http://www. cordialkitten.com (December 22, 2010).

Candice Hartsough McDonald Web log, http://cordialkit ten.blogspot.com (December 22, 2010).

*   *   *

McDONNELL, Christine 1949-

Personal

Born July 3, 1949, in Southampton, NY; daughter of Peter Joseph (in public relations) and Margaret McDonnell; married Terry Shaneyfelt (an artist and baker), December 8, 1979; children: Garth (stepson), Soo Ae, Joseph Doo Wook. *Education:* Barnard College, B.A., 1972; Columbia University, M.L.S., 1973; graduate study at Simmons College, 1979-81.

Addresses

Home—Jamaica Plain, MA. *Office*—Jerry Kaplan Library, Devotion School, 345 Harvard St., Brookline, MA 02446. *E-mail*—chris_mcdonnell@brookline.k12. ma.us.

Career

Writer and educator. New York Public Library, New York, NY, children's librarian, 1972-75; junior-high-school librarian in Arlington, MA, 1976-79; Simmons College, Boston, MA, assistant professor of education, 1979-82, director of community programs at Center for the Study of Children's Literature, 1979-80, acting director, 1981; Pierce School, Brookline, MA, teacher, beginning 1982; Devotion School, Brookline, currently librarian.

Awards, Honors

Two Brookline Education Foundation grants.

Writings

Don't Be Mad, Ivy, illustrated by Diane de Groat, Dial (New York, NY), 1981.

Toad Food and Measle Soup, illustrated by Diane de Groat, Dial (New York, NY), 1982, illustrated by G. Brian Karas, Viking (New York, NY), 2001.

Lucky Charms and Birthday Wishes, illustrated by Diane de Groat, Viking (New York, NY), 1984.

Count Me In (novel), Viking (New York, NY), 1986.

Just for the Summer, illustrated by Diane de Groat, Viking (New York, NY), 1987.

Friends First, illustrated by Diane de Groat, Viking (New York, NY), 1990.

It's a Deal, Dogboy, illustrated by G. Brian Karas, Viking (New York, NY), 1998.

Ballet Bug, illustrated by Martha Doty, Viking (New York, NY), 2001.

Dog Wants to Play, illustrated by Jeff Mack, Viking (New York, NY), 2009.

Goyangi Means Cat, illustrated by Steve Johnson and Lou Fancher, Viking (New York, NY), 2011.

Contributor of articles and reviews to periodicals, including *Horn Book.*

Author's work has been translated into Spanish.

Sidelights

In her works for young readers, including *Toad Food and Measle Soup, Ballet Bug,* and *Dog Wants to Play,* Christine McDonnell explores universal childhood experiences. "I am interested in the importance of little events in children's lives—birthday parties, new pets, spelling bees, and special toys," McDonnell once told *SATA.* "To children these are not insignificant: they are the stuff of real life. I look for the drama in everyday happenings. I am interested in the issues that concern children at different ages: the need for independence, self-respect, friends, security. I also like dualities— simple but complex, serious but funny."

McDonnell's books have been consistently praised for their realistic plots and characters. As Karen Jameson commented in *Horn Book,* her "quiet stories reflect the

Christine McDonnell's humorous story is paired with Jeff Mack's colorful digitized art in the picture book **Dog Wants to Play.** (Illustration copyright © 2009 by Jeff Mack. Used by permission of Viking Children's Books, a division of Penguin Young Readers Group, a member of Penguin Group (USA) Inc., 345 Hudson Street, New York, NY 10014.)

author's sense of the working of young minds and her ability to write sensitively about everyday events." Ellen D. Warwick, reviewing the author's picture book *Just for the Summer* in *School Library Journal,* concluded of the work that, "Once again, McDonnell displays her special gift for authentic dialogue and warm family relationships."

Born in Southampton, New York, in 1949, McDonnell grew up around books and enthusiastic readers with wide-ranging literary tastes. The volumes that influenced her most as a child included E.B. White's novels *Charlotte's Web* and *Stuart Little* as well as works by nineteenth-century writers Louisa May Alcott and Edith Nesbit. She began writing after earning her degree in library science at Columbia University and starting work in a junior-high-school library. Although she first wrote book reviews and short fiction for adult readers, her exposure to children soon inspired McDonnell to shift her focus to younger audiences. Most of her book-length fiction has been crafted for beginning readers and incorporates short chapters and simple vocabulary within an engaging plot.

In her first published book, *Don't Be Mad, Ivy,* McDonnell introduces readers to six-year-old Ivy Adams. Ivy is a typical young girl whose life is punctuated by numerous activities, many involving best friends Emily Mott, Lydia, and eight-year-old Leo Nolan. McDonnell's story entertains beginning readers with six short episodes in Ivy's life. While the majority of them—" The Birthday Present," "The Swimming Pool," and "The Borrowed Bear," among them—are based on the author's childhood, others were inspired by McDonnell's stepson, Garth. Describing Ivy as "independent and ingenious," *Horn Book* contributor Mary M. Burns added that the young protagonist's "triumphs and trials are appropriately scaled to younger readers" in a story that is "warm and reassuring."

Other books by McDonnell feature easy-to-relate-to situations encountered by Ivy, Emily, Lydia, Leo, and their other friends. In *Just for the Summer* Lydia visits Ivy and Emily's neighborhood, staying with aunts May and Connie while her father recovers from a serious illness at a hospital back home. Although worried about her father, Lydia also finds time to make new friends in summer camp, start a toddler day-care business, and brave the local swimming hole to learn a new skill. A *Publishers Weekly* reviewer called *Just for the Summer* "a gem of a story" and "a well-written and fully-faceted reflection of one young girl's life."

In *Lucky Charms and Birthday Wishes* McDonnell presented five stories in which readers follow Emily through what turns out to be a fantastic school year. At first nervous about whether she will fit in or not, Emily ultimately discovers her ability to cope with the changes the year brings as she comes to terms with the school bully, supports friend Lydia in dealing with Lydia's father's continued illness, and is able to appreciate a birthday gift that holds special significance.

Leo returns to entertain eager readers in *Toad Food and Measle Soup* as he rescues a lost puppy, survives his mother's attempts to turn the family into tofu-eaters, and presents an amazing book report in front of his class. Describing Leo as "gentle, imaginative, [and] cheerful . . . [as well as] a daydreamer," Elizabeth Holtze added in her *School Library Journal* review of *Toad Food and Measle Soup* that McDonnell "presents a very human boy, beset by the insecurities of youth . . . [and] does so with clever, gentle humor."

It's a Deal, Dogboy also features Leo—dubbed "Dogboy" by his older sister. Leo is not-so-eagerly awaiting the beginning of fourth grade and he spends his summer playing baseball with his best buddy Johnny and several—ick!—girls. Other activities include outfitting a newly acquired tree house, getting a new dog, and putting up with annoyingly "punked-out" older sister Eleanor and whiny younger cousin Tim. "Leo and his misadventures are lively and credible," noted *Horn Book* reviewer Nancy Vasilakis, the critic adding that "fans of the series—as well as new friends—should find [*It's a Deal, Dogboy*] a briskly engaging diversion." Calling the chapter book a "springboard into summer" for beginning readers, *School Library Journal* reviewer Janet M. Bair added that "the stories [in *It's a Deal, Dogboy*] could be used to start some lively classroom discussions."

While several of McDonnell's books deal with the same popular cast of characters, she has also written standalone novels with young-adult readers in mind. *Friends First* finds Miranda confused about her changing feelings toward Gus, a neighbor and classmate who has been her best buddy since they were both toddlers. A frightening encounter with a local street gang further deters Miranda from a blossoming adolescent love affair with her best friend until she learns to deal with her changing feelings and her initial fear of men. *Count Me In* finds thirteen-year-old Katie confronting the possibility that she might no longer be the sole apple of her mother's eye after her newly remarried mom and stepdad Steve let slip the news that they are expecting a baby. While fantasizing that she will find a secure home with her divorced father, Katie is disappointed to find the man distracted and emotionally unavailable due to

the hectic pace of his job and his preoccupation with a new girlfriend. *Count Me In* "is a book about new shapes of families," McDonnell once told *SATA*, "and the struggle that all of us have in finding a place for ourselves within our family." Praising *Count Me In* as "a very human story with an underlying warmth that is extremely appealing," *Horn Book* contributor Elizabeth S. Watson added that "the gradual growth of Katie's role within each of her families is skillfully drawn and believable." In reviewing the book for *Publishers Weekly*, a critic also deemed *Count Me In* "sensitive" and "satisfying," adding that McDonnell "handles a familiar subject well, with characters real enough to make the point" that people create their own definitions of family.

Ballet Bug, a novel for middle-grade readers, centers on a hockey player who decides to expand her horizons by taking dance lessons. While attending a slumber party, young Bea is introduced to the joys of ballet by her friend Rebecca, a dance enthusiast. After convincing her mother that she can handle both activities, Bea splits her time between hockey and ballet and she eventually earns a role in her troupe's performance of *The Nutcracker*. Bea also comes to the aid of her new friend, Margaret, a talented African-American dancer, when the girl becomes the target of a pair of jealous, conniving rivals. "This is a fast, fun read with a feisty main character and some interesting subplots," Carol Schene remarked of *Ballet Bug* in *School Library Journal*.

Praised as a "charming and simply told story" by *School Library Journal* critic Lisa Gangemi Kropp, McDonnell's picture book *Dog Wants to Play* concerns a puppy's efforts to find a suitable playmate. As it roams the barnyard, Dog encounters a host of other animals, including a lamb, chick, and pig, all of whom decline its invitation to play ball. Just when it appears that Dog has exhausted its options, the pup finds a willing partner in a little boy who hopes for a diversion from his own busy schedule. "Preschoolers will understand Dog's dilemma," Julie Cummins stated in *Booklist*, and a contributor in *Kirkus Reviews* noted that McDonnell's "repetitive phrases and rhyming couplets . . . are a good match for the youngest listeners."

McDonnell, who works as a librarian in Brookline, Massachusetts, has described her chapter-book fiction as "episodic." As she once explained to *SATA*: "I enjoy the unfolding of character through separate events. I think such a style is well suited to the needs of younger readers, who may have difficulty following a continuous long story.

"I believe in strong characters, straightforward stories, and clean, simple, evocative writing," McDonnell added. "The children's authors I admire most are E.B. White, Eleanor Estes, Paula Fox, and Katherine Paterson."

Biographical and Critical Sources

PERIODICALS

Booklist, November 1, 1998, Helen Rosenberg, review of *It's a Deal, Dogboy,* p. 493; November 1, 2009, Julie Cummins, review of *Dog Wants to Play,* p. 52.

Horn Book, April, 1982, Mary M. Burns, review of *Don't Be Mad, Ivy,* p. 167; June, 1984, Karen Jameson, review of *Lucky Charms and Birthday Wishes,* p. 331; July-August, 1986, Elizabeth S. Watson, review of *Count Me In,* pp. 449-450; November-December, 1998, Nancy Vasilakis, review of *It's a Deal, Dogboy,* pp. 735-736.

Kirkus Reviews, August 15, 2009, review of *Dog Wants to Play.*

Publishers Weekly, June 27, 1986, review of *Count Me In,* p. 94; October 9, 1987, review of *Just for the Summer,* p. 88; May 11, 1990, review of *Friends First,* p. 261.

School Library Journal, October, 1982, Elizabeth Holtze, review of *Toad Food and Measle Soup,* p. 143; October, 1987, Ellen D. Warwick, review of *Just for the Summer,* p. 127; November, 1998, Janet M. Bair, review of *It's a Deal, Dogboy,* p. 90; September, 2001, Carol Schene, review of *Ballet Bug,* p. 193; September, 2009, Lisa Gangemi Kropp, review of *Dog Wants to Play,* p. 129.*

*   *   *

MORALES, Magaly

Personal

Born in Veracruz, Mexico; married; husband's name Isael; children: Rodrigo, Quetzally. *Education:* Attended Gestalt School of Design; M.A. (Gestalt psychotherapy). *Hobbies and other interests:* Swimming.

Addresses

Home—Mexico. *Agent*—Charlotte Sheedy Literary Agency, 65 Bleecker St., New York, NY 10012. *E-mail*—magymorales735@hotmail.com.

Career

Illustrator and educator. Freelance designer; teacher of physical education.

Awards, Honors

Cañon del Sumidero (swimming marathon), winner, 1991, 1993.

Illustrator

Pat Mora, *A Piñata in a Pine Tree: A Latino Twelve Days of Christmas,* Clarion (New York, NY), 2009.

Carmen Tafolla, *What Can You Do with a Paleta?/¿Qué puedes hacer con una paleta?,* Tricycle Press (Berkeley, CA), 2009.

Monica Brown, *Chavela and the Magic Bubble,* Clarion Books (Boston, MA), 2010.

Sidelights

A teacher and designer, Mexican artist Magaly Morales has contributed her colorful acrylic images to picture books that include Pat Mora's *A Piñata in a Pine Tree: A Latino Twelve Days of Christmas, What Can You Do with a Paleta?/¿Qué puedes hacer con una paleta?* by Carmen Tafolla, and Monica Brown's *Chavela and the Magic Bubble.* Reviewing her work for *What Can You Do with a Paleta?,* Rebecca Hickman noted in *School Library Journal* that Morales's "broad, curvy brushstrokes of contrasting bright and fruity colors . . . capture the look of Mexican folk art." In *Booklist* Linda Perkins dubbed the same picture book "an appealing introduction to a yummy aspect of Latino culture."

The sister of award-winning Mexican artist Yuyi Morales, Magaly Morales focused on her two passions—competitive sports and art—while growing up. In college, while studying graphic design, she also competed in swimming competitions, winning a fifteen-kilometer swimming marathon twice during the early 1990s. Since earning a master's degree in Gestalt psychotherapy and starting her own family, Morales has continued to pursue her two passions through her career as a physical education teacher as well as by her work as a freelance designer and illustrator.

In *A Piñata in a Pine Tree* Mora adapts the traditional English Christmas carol, giving it a Latin-American fla-

Magaly Morales's illustration work is the highlight of Pat Mora's Latin-themed version of a traditional Christmas song, A Piñata in a Pine Tree. (Illustration copyright © 2009 by Magaly Morales. Reproduced by permission of Clarion Books, an imprint of Houghton Mifflin Harcourt Publishing Company.)

vor by including tamalitos, colorful sugar candies, spinning tops, and luminarias in a young girl's holiday-themed gift countdown. In *Booklist,* Andrew Medlar cited the "colorful and vibrant style" of Morales's acrylic paintings, which feature endearing round-headed children and blended tones of pink, green, blue, and orange. A *Publishers Weekly* critic also praised the folk-art-inspired illustrations in *A Piñata in a Pine Tree,* writing that they "glow with warm, festive colors, evoking lantern light," while in *School Library Journal* Diane Olivo-Posner called Morales' art "pleasing to the eye." Describing Mora's story as a "zippy spin on 'The Twelve Days of Christmas,'" Chelsey Philpot added in *Horn Book* that the "candy-colored acrylic paintings" that chronicle the tale "play with space and . . . exude the girl's contagious holiday joy."

Sugary sweets are also served up in Morales's artwork for *Chavela and the Magic Bubble,* which features what a *Publishers Weekly* critic described as "luminous" paintings "infuse[d] . . . with a homespun magic." In Brown's story an imaginative and gum-loving young girl is carried away on a giant bubble to the region in Mexico where the sap of sapodilla trees—the chicle that is used in traditional chewing gum—is cultivated. Crafted in chewing-gum tones, the illustrations in *Chavela and the Magic Bubble* "underscore the child's Mexican-American heritage" and capture "the story's joyful tone," according to *School Library Journal* contributor Mary Landrum. Praising Brown's story for taking readers on an "exciting, magical journey," Hazel Rochman recommended *Chavela and the Magic Bubble* as "handsomely illustrated in brilliantly colored double-page spreads."

Biographical and Critical Sources

PERIODICALS

Booklist, May 15, 2009, Linda Perkins, review of *What Can You Do with a Paleta?/¿Qué puedes hacer con una paleta?,* p. 47; November 1, 2009, Andrew Medlar, review of *A Piñata in a Pine Tree: A Latino Twelve Days of Christmas,* p. 51; April 1, 2010, Hazel Rochman, review of *Chavela and the Magic Bubble,* p. 45.

Horn Book, November-December, 2009, Chelsey Philpot, review of *A Piñata in a Pine Tree,* p. 646.

Kirkus Reviews, September 15, 2009, review of *A Piñata in a Pine Tree.*

Publishers Weekly, October 26, 2009, review of *A Piñata in a Pine Tree,* p. 54; March 15, 2010, review of *Chavela and the Magic Bubble,* p. 52.

School Library Journal, July, 2009, Rebecca Hickman, review of *What Can You Do with a Paleta?,* p. 77; October, 2009, Diane Olivo-Posner, review of *A Piñata in a Pine Tree,* p. 82; April, 2010, Mary Landrum, review of *Chavela and the Magic Bubble,* p. 120.

ONLINE

Magaly Morales Home Page, http://magalymorales.com (December 22, 2010).*

MORPURGO, Michael 1943-

Personal

Born October 5, 1943, in St. Albans, England; son of Tony Valentine Bridge and Catherine Noel Kippe; stepson of Jake Eric Morpurgo; married Clare Allen, 1963; children: three. *Education:* King's College London, B.A., 1967.

Addresses

Home—Devon, England. *Agent*—David Higham Associates, 5-8 Lower John St., Golden Square, London W1R 4HA, England.

Career

Writer and educator. Primary school teacher, 1967-75. Joint founder and director, Farms for City Children, 1976—; opened Nethercourt House farm, 1976, Treginnis Isaf, 1989, and Wick Court, 1998.

Awards, Honors

Whitbread Award runner up, 1982, for *War Horse;* Carnegie Medal shortlist inclusion, 1988, for *King of the Cloud Forests,* 1991, for *Waiting for Anya,* 1995, for *Arthur, King of Britain,* and 1996, for *The Wreck of the Zanzibar;* London *Guardian* Children's Fiction Prize runner up, 1991, for *Waiting for Anya;* Silver Pencil Award (Holland); Prix Sorcières (France), 1993, for *King of the Cloud Forests,* 1999, for *Wombat Goes Walkabout,* and 2001, for *Kensuke's Kingdom;* Best Books selection, *School Library Journal,* 1995, and Top of the List selection for Youth Fiction, *Booklist,* 1995, both for *The War of Jenkins' Ear;* Circle of Gold Award; Whitbread Award, 1995, for *The Wreck of the Zanzibar;* Nestlé Smarties Gold Medal, 1997, for *The Butterfly Lion;* Editor's Choice, *Books for Keeps,* 1999, for *Cockadoodle-Doo, Mr. Sultana!;* named member, Order of the British Empire, 1999, for creating Farms for City Children; Nestlé Smarties Bronze Award, 2002, for *The Last Wolf;* named children's laureate of England, 2003-05; named children's laureate of Scotland, c. 2004; Carnegie Medal shortlist, Whitbread Children's Book Award shortlist, and *Guardian* Children's Fiction Prize long-list inclusion, all 2004, Hampshire Book Award, Red House Children's Book Award, and Blue Peter Book Award, all 2005, and California Young Readers Medal, 2007, all for *Private Peaceful;* Blue Peter Award shortlist, 2006, for *The Amazing Story of Adolphus Tips;* created chevalier des Arts et des Lettres (France).

Writings

FICTION; FOR CHILDREN

It Never Rained: Five Stories, illustrated by Isabelle Hutchins, Macmillan (London, England), 1974.

Michael Morpurgo (Photograph by James Ravilious. Reproduced by permission of the Estate of James Ravilious.)

Thatcher Jones, illustrated by Trevor Ridley, Macmillan (London, England), 1975.

Long Way Home, Macmillan (London, England), 1975.

(Compiler with Graham Barrett) *The Story-Teller,* Ward Lock (London, England), 1976.

Friend or Foe, illustrated by Trevor Stubley, Macmillan (London, England), 1977.

What Shall We Do with It?, illustrated by Priscilla Lamont, Ward Lock (London, England), 1978.

Do All You Dare, photographs by Bob Cathmoir, Ward Lock (London, England), 1978.

(Editor) *All around the Year,* photographs by James Ravilious, drawings by Robin Ravilious, new poems by Ted Hughes, J. Murray (London, England), 1979.

The Day I Took the Bull by the Horn, Ward Lock (London, England), 1979.

The Ghost-Fish, Ward Lock (London, England), 1979.

Love at First Sight, Ward Lock (London, England), 1979.

That's How, Ward Lock (London, England), 1979.

The Marble Crusher, and Other Stories (also see below), illustrated by Trevor Stubley, Macmillan (London, England), 1980.

The Nine Lives of Montezuma, illustrated by Margery Gill, Kaye & Ward (Kingswood, England), 1980.

Miss Wirtle's Revenge, illustrated by Graham Clarke, Kaye & Ward (Kingswood, England), 1981.

The White Horse of Zennor, and Other Stories from below the Eagle's Nest, Kaye & Ward (Kingswood, England), 1982.

The War Horse, Kaye & Ward (Kingswood, England), 1982, Greenwillow (New York, NY), 1983, reprinted, Scholastic (New York, NY), 2007.

Twist of Gold, Kaye & Ward (Kingswood, England), 1983, Viking (New York, NY), 1993, reprinted, Egmont (London, England), 2007.

Little Foxes, illustrated by Gareth Floyd, Kaye & Ward (Kingswood, England), 1984, reprinted, Egmont (London, England), 2008.

Why the Whales Came, Scholastic (New York, NY), 1985.

Tom's Sausage Lion, illustrated by Robina Green, A. & C. Black (London, England), 1986, reprinted, BBC Consumer Publishing (London, England), 2003.

Jo-Jo, the Melon Donkey (also see below), illustrated by Chris Molan, Simon & Schuster (New York, NY), 1987, illustrated by Tony Kerins, Heinemann (London, England), 1995.

King of the Cloud Forests, Viking (New York, NY), 1988.

My Friend Walter, Heinemann (London, England), 1988.

Mr. Nobody's Eyes, Heinemann (London, England), 1989, Viking (New York, NY), 1990, reprinted, Egmont (London, England), 2007.

Conker (also see below), illustrated by Alasdair Bright, Heinemann (London, England), 1989.

Waiting for Anya, Heinemann (London, England), 1990, Viking (New York, NY), 1991, reprinted, Egmont (London, England), 2007.

Colly's Barn (also see below), illustrated by Alasdair Bright, Heinemann (London, England), 1991.

The Sandman and the Turtles, Heinemann (London, England), 1991, Philomel (New York, NY), 1994.

The War of Jenkins' Ear, Heinemann (London, England), 1993, Philomel (New York, NY), 1995, reprinted, Egmont (London, England), 2007.

Snakes and Ladders, Heinemann (London, England), 1994.

(Editor) *Ghostly Haunts,* illustrated by Nilesh Mistry, Pavilion (London, England), 1994.

Arthur, High King of Britain, illustrated by Michael Foreman, Pavilion (London, England), 1994, Harcourt (San Diego, CA), 1995.

The Dancing Bear, illustrated by Christian Birmingham, Young Lion (London, England), 1994, Houghton (Boston, MA), 1996.

(Editor) *Muck and Magic: Tales from the Countryside,* forward by HRH the Princess Royal, Heinemann (London, England), 1995.

The Wreck of the Zanzibar, illustrated by Christian Birmingham, Viking (New York, NY), 1995.

Blodin the Beast, illustrated by Christina Balit, Fulcrum (Golden, CO), 1995.

Sam's Duck, illustrated by Keith Bowen, Collins (London, England), 1996.

The King in the Forest, illustrated by T. Kerins, Simon & Schuster (New York, NY), 1996, reprinted, Wayland (London, England), 2008.

The Butterfly Lion, illustrated by Christian Birmingham, Collins (London, England), 1996.

The Ghost of Grania O'Malley, Viking (New York, NY), 1996.

Robin of Sherwood, illustrated by Michael Foreman, Harcourt (San Diego, CA), 1996.

(Editor) *Beyond the Rainbow Warrior,* Pavilion (London, England), 1996.

The Marble Crusher (includes *The Marble Crusher, Colly's Barn,* and *Conker*), Mammoth (London, England), 1997.

Farm Boy, illustrated by Michael Foreman, Pavilion (London, England), 1997.

Red Eyes at Night, illustrated by Tony Ross, Hodder (London, England), 1997.

Wartman, illustrated by Joanna Carey, Barrington Stoke (Edinburgh, Scotland), 1998.

Escape from Shangri-La, Philomel Books (New York, NY), 1998.

Cockadoodle-Doo, Mr. Santana!, illustrated by Michael Foreman, Scholastic (New York, NY), 1998, published as *Cockadoodle-Doo, Mr Sultana!,* illustrated by Holly Swain, Scholastic (London, England), 1998.

(Reteller) *Joan of Arc of Domremy,* illustrated by Michael Foreman, Harcourt Brace (San Diego, CA), 1999.

(Compiler) *Animal Stories,* illustrated by Andrew Davidson, Kingfisher (New York, NY), 1999.

Kensuke's Kingdom, illustrated by Michael Foreman, Heinemann (London, England), 1999, Scholastic (New York, NY), 2003.

The Rainbow Bear, illustrated by Michael Foreman, Doubleday (London, England), 1999.

Billy the Kid, illustrated by Michael Foreman, Pavilion (London, England), 2000.

Black Queen, Corgi Juvenile (London, England), 2000.

(Compiler) *The Kingfisher Book of Great Boy Stories: A Treasury of Classics from Children's Literature,* Kingfisher (New York, NY), 2000.

Wombat Goes Walkabout, illustrated by Christian Birmingham, Candlewick Press (Cambridge, MA), 2000.

The Silver Swan, illustrated by Christian Birmingham, Phyllis Fogelman Books (New York, NY), 2000.

From Hereabout Hill, Mammoth (London, England), 2000.

Who's a Big Bully Then?, illustrated by Joanna Carey, Barrington Stoke (Edinburgh, Scotland), 2000.

Mister Skip, Roaring Good Reads, 2000.

The King in the Forest, Hodder (London England), 2001.

Toro! Toro!, illustrated by Michael Foreman, Collins (London, England), 2002.

Out of the Ashes, illustrated by Michael Foreman, Macmillan (London, England), 2002.

Cool!, illustrated by Michael Foreman, Collins (London, England), 2002.

Because a Fire Was in My Head, Faber & Faber (London, England), 2002.

Beastman of Ballyloch, HarperCollins Canada (Toronto, Ontario, Canada), 2002.

Jim Davis: A High-Sea Adventure, Scholastic (New York, NY), 2002.

The Last Wolf, illustrated by Michael Foreman, Doubleday (London, England), 2002.

Sleeping Sword, Egmont (London, England), 2003.

Gentle Giant, illustrated by Michael Foreman, Collins (London, England), 2003.

Mairi's Mermaid, illustrated by Lucy Richards, Crabtree Publishing (New York, NY), 2003.

Cool as a Cucumber, illustrated by Tor Freeman, Walker (London, England), 2003.

Private Peaceful, Walker (London, England), 2003, Scholastic (New York, NY), 2006.

(Reteller) *Sir Gawain and the Green Knight,* illustrated by Michael Foreman, Candlewick Press (Cambridge, MA), 2004.

Little Albatross, illustrated by Michael Foreman, Doubleday (London, England), 2004.

Dolphin Boy, illustrated by Michael Forman, Anderson (London, England), 2004.

(Reteller) *The Orchard Book of Aesop's Fables,* illustrated by Emma Chichester Clark, Orchard (London, England), 2004, published as *The McElderry Book of Aesop's Fables,* Margaret K. McElderry Books (New York, NY), 2005.

I Believe in Unicorns, illustrated by Gary Blythe, Walker (London, England), 2005, Candlewick Press (Cambridge, MA), 2006.

(Reteller) *Beowulf,* illustrated by Michael Foreman, Candlewick Press (Cambridge, MA), 2006.

The Amazing Story of Adolphus Tips, Scholastic (New York, NY), 2006.

Alone on a Wide Sea, HarperCollins (London, England), 2006.

On Angel Wings, illustrated by Quentin Blake, Egmont (London, England), 2006, Candlewick Press (Cambridge, MA), 2007.

It's a Dog's Life, illustrated by Judith Allibone, Farrar, Straus & Giroux (New York, NY), 2007, illustrated by Patrick Benson, Egmont (London, England), 2010.

Born to Run, illustrated by Michael Foreman, HarperCollins Children's (London, England), 2007.

The Mozart Question, illustrated by Michael Foreman, Walker (London, England), 2007, Candlewick Press (Cambridge, MA), 2008.

Animal Tales: Three Stories in One (contains *Jo-Jo the Melon Donkey, Conker,* and *Colly's Barn*), Egmont (London, England), 2008.

Kaspar, Prince of Cats, illustrated by Michael Foreman, HarperCollins Children's (London, England), 2008.

This Morning I Met a Whale, illustrated by Christian Birmingham, Walker (London, England), 2008.

(Reteller) *Hansel and Gretel,* illustrated by Emma Chichester Clark, Candlewick Press (Cambridge, MA), 2008.

Running Wild, illustrated by Sarah Young, HarperCollins Children (London, England), 2009.

The Kites Are Flying, illustrated by Laura Carlin, Walker (London, England), 2009.

Not Bad for a Bad Lad, illustrated by Michael Foreman, HarperCollins Children's (London, England), 2010.

An Elephant in the Garden, HarperCollins Children's (London, England), 2010.

Shadow, HarperCollins Children's (London, England), 2010.

Some of Morpurgo's books have been translated into Gaelic and Welsh.

"MUDPUDDLE FARM" SERIES; ILLUSTRATED BY SHOO RAYNER

Mossop's Last Chance (also see below), A. & C. Black (London, England), 1988.

Albertine, Goose Queen (also see below), A. & C. Black (London, England), 1989.

Jigger's Day Off (also see below), A. & C. Black (London, England), 1990.

And Pigs Might Fly! (also see below), A. & C. Black (London, England), 1991.

Martians at Mudpuddle Farm (also see below), A. & C. Black (London, England), 1992.

Mum's the Word, A. & C. Black (London, England), 1995.

Stories from Mudpuddle Farm (includes *And Pigs Might Fly!, Martians at Mudpuddle Farm,* and *Jigger's Day Off*), A. & C. Black (London, England), 1995.

Cock-a-Doodle-Do (includes *Mossop's Last Chance* and *Albertine, Goose Queen*), HarperCollins Children's (London, England), 2008.

Pigs Might Fly! (includes *And Pigs Might Fly* and *Jigger's Day Off*), HarperCollins Children's (London, England), 2008.

Alien Invasion (includes *Martians at Mudpuddle Farm* and *Mum's the Word*), HarperCollins Children's (London, England), 2008.

Mudpuddle Farm: Six Animal Adventures, HarperCollins Children's (London, England), 2009.

OTHER

(Compiler with Clifford Simmons) *Living Poets,* J. Murray (London, England), 1974.

(Librettist) *Words of Songs,* music by Phyllis Tate, Oxford University Press (Oxford, England), 1985.

The Voices of Children, resource materials by Michael Goron, Collins (London, England), 2007.

(Editor with Quentin Blake) *The Birthday Book,* foreword by His Royal Highness the Prince of Wales, Jonathan Cape (London, England), 2008.

(With Peter Bailey) *Singing for Mrs. Pettigrew: A Story-Maker's Journey,* Heinemann (Harlow, England), 2008, published as *Singing for Mrs. Pettigrew: Stories and Essays from a Writing Life,* Candlewick Press (Somerville, MA), 2009.

Adaptations

Why the Whales Came was adapted as a film titled *When the Whales Came,* 1989, by Golden Swan Films; *My Friend Walter* was adapted as a television film by Portobello Films for Thames Television/WonderWorks, 1993; *Out of the Ashes* was adapted as a television film; *Billy the Kid* was adapted as a play, produced in Southwark, England, 2007. Several of Morpurgo's books have been adapted as audiobooks, including *Kensuke's Kingdom,* 2001; and *Private Peaceful,* read by Jeff Woodman, Recorded Books, 2005. *War Horse* was adapted as a play by Nick Stafford, produced at the National Theater, London, England, 2007, published by Oxford University Press (Oxford, England), 2009. *War Horse* was adapted for film, directed by Steven Spielberg, planned for release in 2011. *Rainbow Bear* was adapted as a musical, music by Stephen Barlow, and was performed as a ballet by National Youth Ballet of Great Britain, 2010.

Sidelights

The recipient of many of his country's top literary honors, British author Michael Morpurgo has contributed original children's literature in the genres of historical fiction, animal stories, fantasies, picture books, easy readers, and retellings of legend and myth. Although his books are generally uplifting and teach ethical lessons, Morpurgo is never preachy; his ability to spin an engaging tale is what has made stories told in *Why the Whales Came, The War of Jenkins' Ear, The Wreck of the Zanzibar, Escape from Shangri-La, Out of the Ashes, The Amazing Story of Adolphus Tips,* and *The Mozart Question* so popular. Throughout his career, he has worked with a number of talented artists, such as Michael Foreman, Christian Birmingham, Gary Blythe, Tony Ross, Sarah Young, Quentin Blake, and Judith Allibone. Often praised for the simple elegance of his prose, Morpurgo is frequently lauded for creating books that are "heartwarming and sensitive," according to Jennifer Taylor in her essay for the *St. James Guide to Young-Adult Writers.* Morpurgo's books are also enduring; many of them continue to remain in print decades after their initial publication.

Morpurgo was born in 1943, in St. Albans, England, into a country that had been at war with Nazi Germany for over four years. At the age of seven he went away to a grammar school in Sussex where he was introduced to "class war," as he once recalled to *Booklist* contributor Ilene Cooper. "The schoolboys and the village boys had fights and difficulties; walking along cow paths, we'd hurl insults at each other. It was an indication that there were people out there who didn't like you because of the way you spoke, and we didn't like them either. And while things have changed since the 1950s, class still seems to me to be a cancer that riddles our society." As a young schoolboy Morpurgo was viewed by his friends as "good at rugby and a bit stupid," as he admitted in his *Young Writer* interview. It was not until years later that he gained his love of reading, especially the novels of Robert Louis Stevenson, Paul Gallico, and Ernest Hemingway and the poetry of Ted Hughes, a poet laureate of England and a close friend of Morpurgo's.

At age fourteen Morpurgo entered Kings School in Canterbury, graduating in 1962. The following year he married Clare Allen, daughter of the publisher of Penguin books, and the couple eventually raised two sons and one daughter. Meanwhile, he completed his degree at King's College London in 1967, began working as a teacher, and also completed his compulsory service in the British Army. Teaching turned his interest to writing. "I had a notion I could tell a tale when the children I was teaching really seemed to want to listen to the tales I told them," Morpurgo noted in *Young Writer.* Reading Hughes's *Poetry in the Making* influenced the young teacher to think that he, too, could string words together rhythmically, and the book literally got him writing. "No better invitation to write was ever written and I accepted," Morpurgo remarked in *Young Writer.* "I love the sound of words, the rhythm of a sentence."

Morpurgo's early work includes both short novels for ten to twelve year olds and picture books for younger readers. By producing books such as *Miss Wirtle's Revenge,* a tale about a little girl who competes successfully against a class full of boys, Morpurgo established a writing career "successfully outside the mainstream," in the opinion of *Times Literary Supplement* reviewer

Cover of Morpurgo's young-adult novel The War of Jenkins' Ear, *featuring artwork by Toby Gowing.* (Illustration © 1995 by Toby Gowing. Reproduced by permission of Philomel, a division of Penguin Putnam Young Readers Group, a member of Penguin Group (USA) Inc., 345 Hudson Street, New York, NY 11014.)

Josephine Karavasil. His short novel *Nine Lives of Montezuma,* published in 1980, details nine narrow-escape adventures of a farmyard cat named Montezuma. Told from the cat's point of view, the book also follows the farming year as a background story. When Montezuma is about to die, it is secure in the knowledge that there is a descendant to take its place in the scheme of things on the farm. In *Junior Bookshelf* D.A. Young noted that Morpurgo's story "is told without sentimentality, though not without sentiment," and recommended *Nine Lives of Montezuma* "with confidence to cat-lovers of any age."

Animals play a starring role in Morpurgo's first book to be published in the United States. Based on a true story, *War Horse* describes World War I as seen through the eyes of Joey, a farm horse commandeered by the British Cavalry in 1914. At that time, mounted troops stood little chance against the mechanized horrors of modern warfare, and Joey endures bombardment and capture by the Germans. He is set to work pulling ambulances and guns while worked by different masters, but he never forgets young Albert, the kind son of his original owner back in England. In the end, persistence and courage pay off as Joey and Albert are reunited. Kate M. Flanagan, writing in *Horn Book,* noted that "the courage of the horse and his undying devotion to the boy" permeate this book, which she maintained is written with "elegant, old-fashioned grace." In *Voice of Youth Advocates* Diane G. Yates commented that Morpurgo's "message about the futility and carnage of war comes across loud and clear." Highlighting similarities between *War Horse* and Anna Sewell's classic *Black Beauty,* Margery Fisher concluded in *Growing Point* that Morpurgo's book "is a most accomplished piece of story-telling, full of sympathy for an animal manipulated by man but preserving its dignity." Warmly received on both sides of the Atlantic, *War Horse* helped win an international audience for Morpurgo.

As with *War Horse, Twist of Gold* draws on history, this time taking readers back to 1840s Ireland. When famine hits, Sean and Annie O'Brien set off for North America to find their father, an adventurous journey that takes them across the ocean and then across a continent via wagon train and river boat. A saga of a challenging childhood, *Twist of Gold* was described by Fisher as a "touching and inventive adventure story."

More attention came Morpurgo's way with the 1985 publication of *Why the Whales Came,* a novel that was subsequently adapted for film. Set in 1914 on Bryher in the Scilly Islands off England's southwest coast, *Why the Whales Came* introduces siblings Gracie and Daniel. Forbidden to associate with the Birdman, a strange old man who lives on the far side of the island, the children realize that the deaf old man is actually lonely, not evil. Ultimately, the three become fast friends as World War II hovers ominously in the background. On Bryher there is another, parallel war: one between the islanders and the ceaseless barrage of sea and weather. When a whale washes ashore, Gracie, Daniel, and the Birdman must convince residents to return the creature to the sea rather than butcher it and risk calling forth an ancient curse. "The success of Morpurgo's novel comes . . . from its portrait of the two children and from its exploration of the blend of superstition and communal spirit existing in an isolated settlement," noted Crouch in his review of *Why the Whales Came.* Cindy Darling Codell, writing in *School Library Journal,* commented that the author's language "is lean, yet lyrical," and that his descriptive paragraphs "let readers taste the salt of the sea and feel the grit of the islander's lives." In *Growing Point* Fisher dubbed *Why the Whales Came* "a forceful and exciting narrative."

The Scilly Islands also provide a setting for Morpurgo's Whitbread Award-winning novel *Wreck of the Zanzibar.* The book describes a childhood on Bryher Island as told through the diary of Laura, whose secret treasure is Zanzibar, a carved wooden tortoise. Laura's narrative is the record of a harsh life, of adversity and the will to overcome. Crouch commented that *The Wreck of the*

Zanzibar, while a short book, is "by no means a slight one," and praised the "beautiful timing throughout." A further tale with an island setting is recounted in *Ghost of Grania O'Malley,* a story set off the coast of Ireland and involving young Jessie, her American cousin Jack, and the ghost of the female pirate Grania O'Malley as they battle to prevent the ecological destruction of the island.

Morpurgo's picture books are often cited for their artwork; while some illustrators are selected by his publisher, the author often teams up with artists whose work he admires. One such artist is Birmingham, with whom Morpurgo created the picture books *The Dancing Bear, Wombat Goes Walkabout, The Butterfly Lion,* and *This Morning I Met a Whale. The Dancing Bear* tells the story of young singer Roxanne and the orphaned bear cub she has raised. When a film crew comes to her remote village to make a video, Roxanne is lured by stories of fame and fortune. Her decision to leave with the group ultimately results in a poignant tragedy. Featuring a happier ending, *This Morning I Met a Whale* carries an environmental message in its story about a whale that becomes beached on the shore of the Thames. Asking for help from young Michael, the creature also warns that Earth will face tragic consequences unless humans work to heal nature's wounds. Enjoying the poignant story in *The Dancing Bear, School Library Journal* contributor Kathy East predicted that Morpurgo's lesson is "likely to appeal more to adults, who will relate to the [story's] elderly narrator."

Blake's distinctive art is a highlight of *On Angel Wings,* a holiday-themed story. As Morpurgo's narrator makes plain, now that he is all grown up he no longer believes the story told each Christmas by his grandpa, who claimed that, as a young shepherd boy, he was among the first to see the newborn baby Jesus. Grandpa's tale is a detailed one that evokes the cold of a winter's night, the appearance of the angel Gabriel, and the brilliance of the shining star that leads him to Bethlehem and the manger. "Morpurgo's tone blends reverence with wit," noted a *Publishers Weekly* contributor, the reviewer adding that this same attitude is captured in "Blake's pen-and-ink and watercolor cartoons." Paired with the author's "exhilarating version of the Nativity story," the artist's characteristic loosely drawn illustrations "can rise to glorious heights," asserted Martha V. Parravano in *Horn Book,* and in *Booklist* Cooper concluded of *On Angel Wings* that Morpurgo's "detailed" retelling "is matched by pictures that . . . strike the right note between reverence and exuberance."

One of several collaborations with Foreman, Morpurgo's *The Rainbow Bear* presents a story about a polar bear that decides to hunt rainbows rather than seals. The book is "a fable about the folly of trying to become something that you naturally are not," according to London *Observer* critic Kate Kellaway. As the reviewer further noted, Morpurgo's story is "gracefully told and elegantly concluded." Other picture-book collaborations

between Morpurgo and Foreman include *Cockadoodle-Doo, Mr. Sultana!, Gentle Giant, Little Albatross,* and *Dolphin Boy.* A retelling of a traditional story about a rooster that refuses to be cheated out of a button it finds, *Cockadoodle-Doo, Mr. Sultana!* wascommended by *School Librarian* critic Mary Medlicott as "rumbustiously full of life," with language "as rich as a plum pudding." *Dolphin Boy,* in which an impoverished seaside town is entertained by a group of dolphins, was praised by a *Kirkus Reviews* critic as "a happy tale" that "celebrates a collective act of kindness."

Also featuring artwork by Foreman, Morpurgo's chapter book *The Mozart Question* is set against the backdrop of 1960s Venice. Paulo Levi is a famous violinist who has just turned fifty when he grants an interview with a young journalist named Lesley. Although Paulo has never agreed to speak about his one idiosyncrasy—that he refuses to perform works by Mozart—Lesley naively puts this question to him and Levi answers it. In his answer, he describes how he learned to play the violin in secret, taught by a street musician named Benjamin because his father refused to either teach him or play himself. The reasons stretch back to a Nazi concentration camp, where Paulo's parents and Benjamin first met and where they were forced to play music by Mozart to calm the Jewish prisoners exiting the transport trains and entering the camp on the way to a likely death. Although Hazel Rochmen noted in her *Booklist* review of *The Mozart Question* that Morpurgo's "view of the survivors is a little too glowing," she also cited his "honest" and "unsensational" approach to a tragic time in history. In a story told with "compassion and honesty," Morpurgo and Foreman present "another view of the Holocaust and music's potential to heal," noted Renee Steinberg in her *School Library Journal* review of the novel.

Animals figure in many of Morpurgo's stories, both in his picture books and his longer fiction. Published in two different illustrated versions, *It's a Dog's Life* follows a dog on its busy day on a family farm as it herds sheep, teases the farm cat, and waits for the farmer's daughter to return home from school. *Little Foxes* finds young Billy attracted to the wildlife living near a ruined church; the mythic Yeti save a lost boy in *King of the Cloud Forests;* a donkey helps to save sixteenth-century Venice from a flood and becomes a hero in *Jo-Jo, the Melon Donkey;* an abandoned cat leads a young hotel bell-boy on an adventure-filled trip around the world in *Kaspar, Prince of Cats; Farm Boy* details the animal-filled memories of four generations of an English farming family; and in *Toro! Toro!* a man recalls his love for a bull in his native Spain. Reviewing *King of the Cloud Forests,* Jacqueline Simms wrote in the *Times Literary Supplement* that Morpurgo's "marvelous adventure story . . . will surely become a perennial favourite," and *Bulletin of the Center for Children's Books* contributor Roger Sutton predicted that the "brief and dramatic novel . . . may woo reluctant readers back to the fold." "Morpurgo's storytelling style is unhurried," noted

School Library Journal critic Lee Bock in a review of *Farm Boy,* while a *Kirkus Reviews* contributor called the same book "a small gem" and an "expertly crafted reminder that stories can link generations." Amy Spaulding, writing in *School Library Journal,* noted of *Jo-Jo, the Melon Donkey* that Morpurgo's "writing style follows that of the literary fairy tale, being at once simple and elegant," while a *Kirkus Reviews* critic cited the story's "nice blend of humor and sadness" as well as its ability to capture "the vibrancy of 16th-century Venice." In *School Library Journal,* Shawn Brommer described *Toro! Toro!* as "ideal for reluctant readers" in its focus "on the loss and grief that grows out of times of war."

Like *Toro! Toro!,* many of Morpurgo's novels are set during wartime and focus on the repercussions of political aggression. *Waiting for Anya* addresses the plight of Jewish children in France during World War II, while in *Escape from Shangri-La* an old man's memories of rescuing British forces from Dunkirk are rekindled by a granddaughter's affection. Another old man reflects on his life from boyhood to his years of soccer-playing as a youth, and then his capture by enemy troops during World War II in *Billy the Kid,* and in *The Kites Are Flying!* a child living in modern-day Palestine sails homemade kites over the wall to Israel as a way of dealing with the death of his brother as a result of age-old hostilities.

Waiting for Anya is set in the Pyrenees just after the surrender of the French forces. Jo, a young shepherd,

becomes involved in a scheme to save the local children when he discovers that a man named Benjamin has been hiding them at a farm near the village of Lescun. Benjamin smuggles groups of these children across the border into Spain; he is also waiting for his own daughter, Anya, to make her way to his safe house from Paris. Jo begins delivering supplies to the farm, a job that becomes far riskier after the Nazis occupy Lescun and threaten to kill anyone aiding fugitives. Soon, however, the entire town is aiding the effort to smuggle the children across the border. Although Benjamin is ultimately captured and sent to Auschwitz, Anya's fate is more heartening in Morpurgo's "gripping, clearly written story," as Ellen Fader described it in *Horn Book.* Crouch, reviewing the novel in *Junior Bookshelf,* called *Waiting for Anya* "an intensely exciting story guaranteed to keep a sensitive reader on the edge of his chair." Morpurgo's tale is "rich in the qualities which make for critical approval," Crouch added, concluding that while "there have been many Second World War stories for the young, none . . . deals more convincingly with its perils and dilemmas."

In *Escape from Shangri-La* an old tramp named Popsicle turns out to be Cessie's long-lost grandfather. When the old man has a stroke, he is admitted to the Shangri-La nursing home, but his health quickly declines. Finally Cessie finds her grandfather's real home: an old lifeboat that has been used to help in the evacuation of British forces from Dunkirk during World War II. From a photograph and news clippings, Cessie learns

Morpurgo explores an interesting story based in World War II history in his book **The Mozart Question,** *featuring illustrations by Michael Foreman.*
(Illustration copyright © 2007 by Michael Foreman. Reproduced by permission of Candlewick Press, Somerville, MA on behalf of Walker Books, London.)

that her grandfather took part in this heroic effort. After a faded photo of the Frenchwoman who hid him from the Germans after he fell overboard during the rescue effort makes Popsicle recall the past, Cessie helps her grandfather and other unhappy residents of the home make a break for it. Together they head to France to track down this woman, only to discover that she never returned from German arrest in 1940. "Readers will enjoy the climactic adventure and respond on a deeper level to the friendship between a spirited child and a lifelong loner," wrote John Peters in a *Booklist* review of *Escape from Shangri-La.*

Returning to World War I, *Private Peaceful* follows the recollections of fourteen-year-old Thomas Peaceful who, by lying about his age, followed his older brother Charlie from the family's farm into the British Army and, ultimately, into the trenches at the war's front lines in France. In Morpurgo's highly lauded novel, "exquisitely written vignettes explore bonds of brotherhood that cannot be broken by the physical and psychological horrors" of World War I, according to *Horn Book* contributor Peter D. Sieruta. In what *Booklist* critic Hazel Rochman described as a "terse and beautiful narrative," Thomas recalls his life from the cold depth of a trench, realizing that he will likely not survive the battle to be waged the following day. "Using first-person narration, Morpurgo draws readers into this young man's life, relating memories that are idyllic, sobering, and poignant," wrote *School Library Journal* contributor Delia Fritz. The plot builds through the tragedy of Charlie's mental illness, Thomas's frustrated love, the indignities of poverty, and his father's death. In praise of the novel, Rochman added that Morpurgo's suspenseful ending is "shocking, honest, and unforgettable."

Morpurgo adopts a lighter tone in *The Amazing Story of Adolphus Tips,* which introduces a spirited preteen girl through the pages of a decades-old diary. The diary is given by Lily Tregenza to her grandson, Boowie, and through it Boowie gets to know a new side of the older woman he knows only as Grandma. Lily, a spirited young girl, watches her father leave to fight in World War II when she is twelve years old. When the family is forced to leave their Devon farmhouse on the English coast while U.S. Army troops use the area to rehearse for the invasion of France at Normandy, Lily's beloved cat Tips goes missing. Worried about her cat, as well as about her father's safety, Lily learns to deal with both through her friendship with an African-American soldier named Adolphus. Lily's "personal story of anger and love is as gripping as the war drama" within her tale is set, according to Rochman, while in *Kirkus Reviews* a critic praised the girl's narration as "clear and believable."

Turning to his memories of his own school years, Morpurgo sets *The War of Jenkins' Ear* in an English boarding school. Here young Toby Jenkins meets a remarkable boy named Christopher who claims to be the reincarnation of Jesus Christ. Although Christopher be-

gins to develop a following among the students, he is betrayed by one of his friends and expelled from the school for blasphemy. *Quill & Quire* contributor Joanne Schott commented of the novel that "a strict school of 40 years ago makes a credible setting and gives scope for the complex relationships Morpurgo uses to examine questions of belief and credulity, deception and self-deception, loyalty and the pressure of doubt." Tim Rausch, writing in *School Library Journal,* called *The War of Jenkins' Ear* a book that "tackles provocative themes, dealing with the issues of hate, revenge, prejudice, and especially faith in an intelligent and fresh manner."

Many of Morpurgo's novels for children feature young characters who show their resilience when they are challenged by life. In one such novel, *Kensuke's Kingdom,* he transports readers to an exotic setting. Here a young boy, who fell overboard from his family's boat, makes his way to a remote island. On his own except for a dog he befriends, the boy meets a mysterious old Japanese man—the Kensuke of the title—who slowly allows the youngster into his heart. *Kensuke's Kingdom* "must be ranked alongside Morpurgo's best," declared Linda Newbery in a *School Librarian* review, the critic adding that, "like several of his most successful stories, [the novel] has the feel of a fable."

Illustrated by Sarah Young, *Running Wild* focuses on another young boy who must learn to survive on his own. For Will, life has been difficult since his father was killed in the Iraq War. A trip to Indonesia along with his mother helps the ten year old forget his sadness. Then, a morning ride along the beach on an elephant named Oona becines a race against death as Oona attempts to outrun a giant tsunami wave. Safe on a jungle hilltop, Will surveys the tragic destruction below and realizes that his mother must have been killed. He is now truly alone, and only by building a bond with Oona will he have any chance of surviving. Comparing *Running Wild* to Rudyard Kipling's *The Jungle Book,* Marzena Currie noted in her *School Librarian* review that Morpurgo's tale "is a brilliant adventure story with some strong environmental issues." With its "lively and engaging story," the critic added, the elementary-grade novel "will appeal particularly to boy readers."

In addition to creating original texts, Morpurgo has also breathed new life into old stories, from the tales of the Brothers Grimm and Aesop to the legends about Beowulf, Robin Hood, and King Arthur. *Arthur, High King of Britain,* which Morpurgo reshapes as a time-travel adventure, was dubbed "the real thing—darkness and all," by Heather McCammond-Watts in her *Bulletin of the Center for Children's Books* review. With *Robin of Sherwood* added twists such as an albino Marion help to create an "outstanding new version of the Robin Hood legend," according to Nancy Zachary in *Voice of Youth Advocates.* Morpurgo's retelling of the classic *Sir Gawain and the Green Knight* is introduced to new generations through what Connie C. Rockman described in *School Library Journal* as "the vibrant and compelling voice of a storyteller," and a *Kirkus Reviews* writer praised the same work as a "handsomely packaged" and "fluid translation of the 14th-century tale." Turning to fairy tales, Morpurgo's version of *Hansel and Gretel,* featuring illustrations by Emma Chichester Clark, is enriched with complex passions and a confrontation with black magic wherein "strong familial bonds allow the innocent brother and sister to overcome evil," according to *School Library Journal* contributor Susan Scheps.

On his home page, Morpurgo discussed his writing process, and how long it takes him to write a book. "It depends on how well I'm writing," he explained, "how well it's flowing. But I usually spend several months dreaming it up in my head—I call it my 'dreamtime', the most important part of my story inventing when I try to weave the story together, do my research, and find the right voice for the story. Once I begin writing," he added, "I write very fast and will finish a book in two or three months. Then revising it might take another month. So, on average, a novel takes upwards of six months to write."

Living in the countryside for much of a career spent writing and working with children, Morpurgo recognized the importance to city-born-and-bred kids that they be introduced to the wonders of nature. To that end, he and his wife started Farms for City Children in the 1970s. Under this program, urban chidlren stay at Morpurgo's farm and work and take care of animals for several weeks. The program became so popular that the Morpurgos soon operated three farms where more than 2,000 children per year were given the opportunity to get in touch with nature and themselves. In 1999, Morpurgo and his wife were honored with the Order of the British Empire for their work with Farms for City Children.

Biographical and Critical Sources

BOOKS

Children's Literature Review, Volume 51, Gale (Detroit, MI), 1999, pp. 116-151.
Hobson, Margaret, Jennifer Madden, and Ray Pryterch, *Children's Fiction Sourcebook: A Survey of Children's Books for 6-13 Year Olds,* Ashgate Publishing (Aldershot, Hampshire, England), 1992, pp. 154-155.
St. James Guide to Young-Adult Writers, 2nd edition, edited by Tom Pendergast and Sara Pendergast, St. James Press (Detroit, MI), 1999, pp. 603-605.

PERIODICALS

Booklist, January 1, 1996, Ilene Cooper, interview with Morpurgo, p. 816; October 1, 1996, Carolyn Phelan, review of *Robin of Sherwood,* p. 350; June 1, 1997,

Kathleen Squires, review of *The Butterfly Lion,* p. 1704; September 15, 1998, John Peters, review of *Escape from Shangri-La,* p. 231; February 15, 2004, Todd Morning, review of *Toro! Toro!,* p. 1060; April 15, 2004, Connie Fletcher, review of *Gentle Giant,* p. 1447; October 1, 2004, Hazel Rochman, review of *Private Peaceful,* p. 326; November 1, 2004, Carolyn Phelan, review of *Sir Gawain and the Green Knight,* p. 480; May 1, 2005, Hazel Rochman, review of *The McElderry Book of Aesop's Fables,* p. 1588; April 15, 2006, Hazel Rochman, review of *The Amazing Story of Adolphus Tips,* p. 59; December 1, 2006, Ilene Cooper, review of *I Believe in Unicorns,* p. 47; March 1, 2007, Linda Perkins, review of *Beowulf,* p. 74; October 15, 2007, Ilene Cooper, review of *On Angel Wings,* p. 52; March 15, 2008, Hazel Rochman, review of *The Mozart Question,* p. 48; August 1, 2009, Michael Cart, review of *Singing for Mrs. Pettigrew: Stories and Essays from a Writing Life,* p. 61.

Books for Keeps, September, 1997, Clive Barnes, review of *Sam's Duck,* p. 23; May, 1998, Gwynneth Bailey, review of *Red Eyes at Night,* p. 24; March, 1999, Rosemary Stores, review of *Cockadoodle-Doo, Mr Sultana!,* p. 21; May, 1999, review of *The Rainbow Bear,* p. 6; January, 2002, George Hunt, review of *Out of the Ashes,* p. 23; March, 2002, George Hunt, review of *Toro! Toro!,* p. 22.

Bulletin of the Center for Children's Books, July-August, 1988, Roger Sutton, review of *King of the Cloud Forests,* pp. 234-235; May, 1995, Heather McCammond-Watts, review of *Arthur, High King of Britain,* p. 317; December, 2004, Deborah Stevenson, review of *Private Peaceful,* p. 177.

Growing Point, November, 1980, Margery Fisher, review of *The Nine Lives of Montezuma,* p. 3776; November, 1982, Margery Fisher, review of *War Horse,* p. 3989; January, 1984, Margery Fisher, review of *Twist of Gold,* pp. 4183-4184; January, 1987, Margery Fisher, review of *Why the Whales Came,* p. 4749.

Horn Book, December, 1983, Kate M. Flanagan, review of *War Horse,* pp. 711-712; July-August, 1991, Ellen Fader, review of *Waiting for Anya,* p. 458; March-April, 1996, Elizabeth S. Watson, review of *The Wreck of the Zanzibar,* p. 198; November-December, 2004, Peter D. Sieruta, review of *Private Peaceful,* p. 713; November-December, 2007, Martha V. Parravano, review of *On Angel Wings,* p. 634.

Junior Bookshelf, December, 1980, D.A. Young, review of *The Nine Lives of Montezuma,* p. 294; December, 1985, Marcus Crouch, review of *Why the Whales Came,* p. 279; February, 1991, Marcus Crouch, review of *Waiting for Anya,* pp. 35-36; August, 1995, Marcus Crouch, review of *The Wreck of the Zanzibar,* p. 148.

Kirkus Reviews, December 1, 1987, review of *Jo-Jo, the Melon Donkey,* p. 1677; April 15, 1997, review of *The Butterfly Lion,* p. 645; December 15, 1998, review of *Farm Boy;* September 15, 2004, review of *Private Peaceful,* p. 916; October 15, 2004, review of *Sir Gawain and the Green Knight,* p. 1011; January 1, 2005, review of *Dolphin Boy,* p. 55; June 1, 2005, review of *The McElderry Book of Aesop's Fables,* p. 641; April 1, 2006, review of *The Amazing Story of*

Adolphus Tips, p. 352; October 15, 2006, reviews of *I Believe in Unicorns* and *Beowulf,* both p. 1075; September 1, 2008, review of *Hansel and Gretel*; September 1, 2009, review of *Singing for Mrs. Pettigrew.*

Magpies, November, 1999, Catherine McClellan, review of *Wombat Goes Walkabout,* p. 6.

Observer (London, England), October 24, 1999, review of *Wombat Goes Walkabout,* and Kate Kellaway, review of *The Rainbow Bear,* both p. 13.

Publishers Weekly, February 12, 1999, review of *Joan of Arc of Domremy,* p. 95; December 6, 2004, review of *Private Peaceful,* p. 60; October 22, 2007, review of *On Angel Wings,* p. 53; February 11, 2008, review of *The Mozart Question,* p. 70.

Quill & Quire, July, 1993, Joanne Schott, review of *The War of Jenkins' Ear,* p. 59.

School Librarian, autumn, 1998, Norton Hodges, review of *Escape from Shangri-La,* p. 147; spring, 1999, Jam Cooper, review of *Joan of Arc of Domremy,* pp. 40-41; summer, 1999, Mary Medlicott, review of *Cockadoodle-Doo, Mr Sultana!,* p. 79; winter, 1999, Linda Newbery, review of *Kensuke's Kingdom,* p. 192; spring, 2001, Chris Brown, review of *Billy the Kid,* pp. 47-48; summer, 2001, Nikki Gamble, review of *The Silver Swan,* p. 90; autumn, 2001, Chris Brown, review of *Out of the Ashes,* pp. 158-159; spring, 2010, Robin Barlow, review of *The Kites Are Flying,* p. 36, and Marzena Currie, review of *Running Wild,* p. 37.

School Library Journal, February, 1987, Cindy Darling Codell, review of *Why the Whales Came,* p. 82; April, 1988, Amy Spaulding, review of *Jo-Jo, the Melon Donkey,* p. 87; July, 1995, Helen Gregory, review of *Arthur, High King of Britain,* p. 89; September, 1995, Tim Rausch, review of *The War of Jenkins' Ear,* p. 219; May, 1996, Kathy East, review of *The Dancing Bear,* p. 114; August, 1997, Gebregeorgis Yohannes, review of *The Butterfly Lion,* p. 158; March, 1999, Lee Bock, review of *Farm Boy,* p. 212; May, 1999, Shirley Wilton, review of *Joan of Arc of Domremy,* p. 128; April, 2001, Edith Ching, review of *The Kingfisher Book of Great Boy Stories: A Treasury of Classics from Children's Literature,* p. 146; March, 2004, Kathy Krasniewicz, review of *Gentle Giant,* p. 120; May, 2004, Shawn Brommer, review of *Toro! Toro!,* p. 154; October, 2004, Connie C. Rockman, review of *Sir Gawain and the Green Knight,* p. 172; November, 2004, Delia Fritz, review of *Private Peaceful,* p. 150;

June, 2005, review of *The McElderry Book of Aesop's Fables,* p. 140; August, 2006, Jane G. Connor, review of *The Amazing Story of Adolphus Tips,* p. 126; December, 2006, Susan Helper, review of *I Believe in Unicorns,* p. 110; October, 2007, Anne Connor, review of *On Angel Wings,* p. 102; May, 2008, Renee Steinberg, review of *The Mozart Question,* p. 134; January 2009, Susan Scheps, review of *Hansel and Gretel,* p. 93; November, 2009, Miriam Lang Budin, review of *Singing for Mrs. Pettigrew,* p. 114.

Times Educational Supplement, February 8, 2002, reviews of *The Last Wolf, Toro! Toro!,* and *Out of the Ashes,* all pp. 20-21; November 5, 2004, Geraldine Brennan, "Dear Mr Morpingo: Inside the World of Michael Morpurgo," p. 19.

Times Literary Supplement, March 26, 1982, Josephine Karavasil, "Matters of Rhythm and Register," p. 347; February 19, 1988, Jacqueline Simms, "Magic Man," p. 200.

Voice of Youth Advocates, April, 1984, Diane G. Yates, review of *War Horse,* p. 32; February, 1997, Nancy Zachary, review of *Robin of Sherwood,* p. 330; June, 1998, Kathleen Beck, review of *The War of Jenkins' Ear,* pp. 103-104.

ONLINE

Achuka Web site, http://www.achuka.com/ (April 20, 2003), "Michael Morpurgo."

Michael Morpurgo Home Page, http://www.michaelmorpurgo.com (January 15, 2011).

Young Writer Online, http://www.mystworld.com/youngwriter/ (February 12, 2003), "Michael Morpurgo."*

* * *

NICHOLS, Leigh
See KOONTZ, Dean

* * *

NORTH, Anthony
See KOONTZ, Dean

O-P

O'HEARN, Kate

Personal

Born in Canada.

Addresses

Home—Hastings, England.

Career

Author.

Writings

Pegasus and the Flame, Hodder Children's Books (London, England), 2011.

Contributor to fiction anthology *Wow 366: Speedy Stories in Just 366 Words,* Scholastic UK (London, England), 2008.

"SHADOW OF THE DRAGON" NOVEL SERIES

Kira, Hodder Children's Books (London, England), 2008, Kane Miller (Tulsa, OK), 2009.
Elspeth, Hodder Children's (London, England), 2009.

Sidelights

Although Kate O'Hearn was born in Canada, her family spent time in New York City as well as in cities in Californian, Florida, Illinois, and Texas before crossing the Atlantic and establishing a new home in England. These travels "added to my love of reading and the fantastic stories my parents told us on our long journeys," O'Hearn noted on her home page. "It wasn't long after that I was making up my own stories filled with strange and wonderful characters that I came to care deeply

for." After pursuing other jobs as an adult, O'Hearn eventually rekindled her love of storytelling in her novels *Kira* and *Elspeth,* which are part of her "Shadow of the Dragon" series.

In *Kira* O'Hearn introduces her twelve-year-old heroine, a feisty girl who longs to live the life of her father, a former knight and dragon slayer. Unfortunately, Kira's kingdom is not an enlightened one as far as women's rights are concerned, and the girl's destiny is to be married by age thirteen. When reigning Lord Dorcon declares war and calls his people to his side, unmarried girls like Kira are imprisoned to keep them out of the way. Together with younger sister Elspeth, Kira escapes and finds protection in the Rogue Mountains, aided by brother Dane, a wizard named Paradon, and a young dragon. In retaliation, Dorcon unleashes all his forces to track her down and end her life. With its mix of history and fantasy, *Kira* features "plenty of exciting action sequences" and "will appeal to girls clamoring for a hearty heroine," predicted *Booklist* contributor Kimberly Garnick. O'Hearn's tale "is exciting and fast paced," according to *School Library Journal* contributor Saleena Davidson, the critic also calling the story's characters "well rounded and believable."

The adventures of Kira and sister Elspeth continue in *Elspeth,* as they continue their lives as outlaws hunted by the vicious Lord Dorcon. Still hoping to rescue their third sister, Kahrin, the girls are also determined to break the equally unjust King Argon's hold on his kingdom and its people. With the help of the wizard Paradon, the older sisters are eventually sent into the future to further their aims, while Elspeth is separated by time and finds herself alone in the past, with no way to return to her own time. As Kira works to find a way to rescue Elspeth, she also hopes to dismantle the First Law that prevents females from reading or remaining unmarried.

Praising O'Hearn's follow-up novel as "more complex and . . . less predictable" than *Kira,* a *Kirkus Reviews* writer described *Elspeth* as "an exciting read and a good entry-level introduction to high fantasy." The author "does a great job of creating an action-packed adventure filled with suspense and even a little romance," wrote Kira Moody in her *School Library Journal* of O'Hearn's novel, the critic also ranking the storytelling as "fast-paced and entertaining."

Biographical and Critical Sources

PERIODICALS

Booklist, October 15, 2009, Kimberly Garnick, review of *Kira,* p. 65.
Kirkus Reviews, August 15, 2009, review of *Kira;* February 15, 2010, review of *Elspeth.*
School Library Journal, October, 2009, Saleena L. Davidson, review of *Kira,* p. 134; June, 2010, Kira Moody, review of *Elspeth,* p. 115.
Voice of Youth Advocates, October, 2009, Julie Watkins, review of *Kira,* p. 334; June, 2010, Julie Watkins, review of *Elspeth,* p. 168.

ONLINE

Kate O'Hearn Home Page, http://www.kateohearn.com (December 22, 2010).*

* * *

PAIGE, Richard
See KOONTZ, Dean

* * *

PARRA, John 1972-

Personal

Born 1972, in Santa Barbara, CA; married; wife's name Maria. *Education:* Art Center College of Design, B.F.A. (with honors).

Addresses

Home—Jamaica, NY. *Agent*—Vicki Prentice Associates, Inc., 630 5th Ave., 20th Fl., Rockefeller Center, New York, NY 10111. *E-mail*—john@johnparraart.com.

Career

Illustrator and graphic designer. Teacher and lecturer at schools and colleges. *Exhibitions:* Work exhibited in galleries in New York, NY, Los Angeles, CA, and elsewhere throughout the United States, and included in private collections.

Awards, Honors

Golden Kite award for Picture-Book Illustration, Society of Children's Book Writers and Illustrators, American Library Association Pura Belpré Award Honor des-

John Parra (Photograph by Maria Parra. Reproduced by permission.)

ignation and Notable Children's Book designation, and Cooperative Children's Book Center Choices selection, all 2010, all for *Gracias/Thanks* by Pat Mora; honors from Society of Illustrators, New York, NY, Latino Literacy Now, and other organizations.

Illustrator

Monica Brown, *My Name Is Gabriela: The Life of Gabriela Mistral/Me llamo Gabriela: la vida de Gabriela Mistral,* Luna Rising (Flagstaff, AZ), 2005.
Tony Johnston, *P Is for Piñata: A Mexico Alphabet,* Sleeping Bear Press (Chelsea, MI), 2008.
Pat Mora, *Gracias/Thanks,* Spanish translation by Adriana Dominguez, Lee & Low (New York, NY), 2009.
Monica Brown, *Waiting for the BiblioBurro,* Tricycle Press (Berkeley, CA), 2011.

Contributor to periodicals, including *L.A. Weekly, Minneapolis/St. Paul Magazine,* and *Print.*

Sidelights

Beginning his career illustrating Monica Brown's bilingual picture-book biography *My Name Is Gabriela: The Life of Gabriela Mistral/Me llamo Gabriela: la vida de Gabriela Mistral,* John Parra creates unique images that capture traditional elements of Mexican folk art. Praising *My Name Is Gabriela* as a "lyrical homage to the Chilean Nobel Prize winner," Maria Otero-Boisvert added in her *School Library Journal* review that Parra's "naïve-style illustrations" allow readers "a view into a softly colored world of people, places, and creatures."

Raised in Southern California in a close-knit Hispanic family, Parra exhibited a creative talent that eventually earned him a full scholarship to Pasadena's prestigious Art Center College of Design. After earning his B.F.A. with honors, he relocated to New York City and established himself as a freelance illustrator and graphic artist, where his clients have included music and book publishers, magazines, and various corporations. Since illustrating his first picture book, Parra has quickly distinguished himself in the field, earning several awards for his colorful folk-art-inspired contribution to Pat Mora's text in the bilingual book *Gracias/Thanks.*

In his work for *Gracias/Thanks* Parra captures the events in a young boy's day as he expresses gratitude for the things both large and small that bring him joy. Cast with a multi-racial family, the book's "vivid acrylic illustrations have the feel of folk-art woodcuts and whimsically portray . . . the boy's world," according to *Booklist* contributor Linda Perkins. Mora's "poetic writing . . . carries a sense of happiness," wrote Shannon Dye Gemberling, the *School Library Journal* contributor adding that Parra's "brightly colored acrylic illustrations are full of fun details and add depth" to the optimistic read-aloud. "The lines and imperfections" in Parra's images create "a worn, homey appearance that matches the . . . old-fashioned feel" of Mora's story, wrote *Horn Book* reviewer Jennifer M. Brabander, and a *Kirkus Reviews* writer dubbed *Gracias/Thanks* a "graceful celebration" in which the artist's use of "flat perspectives and bright colors skillfully complement[s] the . . . voice" of Mora's young narrator.

Another illustration project, *P Is for Piñata: A Mexico Alphabet,* features "texutral folk art paintings [that] visually exude Mexico," according to a *Publishers Weekly* contributor. Tony Johnston's text for the book travels from A to Z via highlights of Mexico's culture and geography, and while Sandra Welzenbach wrote in *School Library Journal* that English-language readers may require assistance with some Spanish pronunciation, Parra's "vividly colored illustrations" clearly "reflect Mexico's traditions and cultures." The artist's use of "folk-art elements, sound composition, and imaginative touches" transform *P Is for Piñata* into what Carolyn Phelan described in *Booklist* as a "colorful" story-hour trip for imaginative young travelers.

Biographical and Critical Sources

PERIODICALS

Booklist, December 15, 2008, Carolyn Phelan, review of *P Is for Piñata: A Mexico Alphabet,* p. 42; November 1, 2009, Linda Perkins, review of *Gracias/Thanks,* p. 35.

Horn Book, January-February, 2010, Jennifer M. Brabander, review of *Gracias/Thanks,* p. 77.

Kirkus Reviews, October 1, 2009, review of *Gracias/ Thanks.*

Publishers Weekly, November 3, 2008, review of *P Is for Piñata,* p. 58.

School Library Journal, February, 2006, Maria Otero-Boisvert, review of *My Name Is Gabriela: The Life of Gabriela Mistral/Me llamo Gabriela: la vida de Gab-*

Parra teams up with well-known author Pat Mora to create the upbeat bilingual picture book Gracias/Thanks. (Illustration copyright © 2009 by John Parra. Reproduced by permission of Lee & Low Books, Inc.)

riela Mistral, p. 126; January, 2009, Sandra Welzenbach, review of *P Is for Piñata,* p. 92; December,
2009, Shannon Dye Gemberling, review of *Gracias/
Thanks,* p. 103.

ONLINE

John Parra Home Page, http://www.johnparraart.com (December 22, 2010).

                    *   *   *

PHILLIPS, Gary R.

Personal

Married; children: two daughters. *Hobbies and other interests:* Camping, tennis, painting out in nature, drawing.

Addresses

Home—Montgomery County, PA. *Office*—Gary Phillips
Studio, 9018 Independence Dr., Green Lane, PA 18054.
E-mail—GaryPhillipsStudio@verizon.net.

Career

Illustrator.

Awards, Honors

Verse Page Illustrator of the Year, *Highlights for Children* magazine, 2003; named Outstanding Pennsylvania
Illustrator, Pennsylvania School Librarians Association,
2010; five other awards from *Highlights for Children*
magazine; Mom's Choice Award, 2010, for *Ocean Hide
and Seek* by Jennifer Evans Kramer.

Illustrator

Melinda R. Boroson, *Eighty-six Years: The Legend of the
Boston Red Sox,* Brown House Books (Waltham, MA),
2005.
Charlotte Blessing, *New Old Shoes,* Pleasant St. Press
(Raynham, MA), 2008.
Suzanne Slade, *Animals Are Sleeping,* Sylvan Dell (Mount
Pleasant, SC), 2008.
Jennifer Evans Kramer, *Ocean Hide and Seek,* Sylvan Dell
(Mount Pleasant, SC), 2009.

Also illustrator of *The Naptime Book, Tiny Little En-
gine,* and *Santa's Little Sleigh.* Contributor to periodicals, including *Highlights for Children, Ranger Rick,*
and *Runner's World.*

Sidelights

A freelance illustrator based in Pennsylvania, Gary R.
Phillips has provided the artwork for a number of children's books, including *New Old Shoes* by Charlotte

Gary R. Phillips (Reproduced by permission.)

Blessing and *Ocean Hide and Seek* by Jennifer Evans
Kramer. In the former title, which is narrated by a pair
of red sneakers, Blessing explores the success of the
Soles4Souls program, which recycles used shoes to
people in need of them across the globe. The work follows the red sneakers as they are purchased for their
original owner, a young boy living in the United States,
and eventually make their way to Africa, where they
are worn by a soccer-loving youngster and ultimately
used to decorate a scarecrow. "Phillips's jewel-toned
artwork . . . closely zooms in on the sneakers," remarked a critic in *Kirkus Reviews,* and Kate Neff wrote
in *School Library Journal* that the artist's "color-
saturated illustrations provide a vibrant background to
this touching story."

Phillips has also contributed the illustrations to Suzanne
Slade's *Animals Are Sleeping,* a bedtime tale. In this, a
host of mother animals, including a giraffe, sloth, and
clown fish, gently lull their respective infants to rest.
"The lush full-color illustrations continue the soothing
effect of the text," observed *School Library Journal* reviewer Lisa Gangemi Kropp. In *Ocean Hide and Seek*
Kramer examines the various ways that sea creatures
can use camouflage to protect themselves from predators. Carolyn Phelan, reviewing the illustrated work in
Booklist, maintained that patient readers will be "rewarded as shadowy sea creatures gradually come into
view" in Phillips's detailed, nature-themed art.

Biographical and Critical Sources

PERIODICALS

Booklist, March 15, 2009, Carolyn Phelan, review of *Ocean Hide and Seek,* p. 63; September 1, 2009, Carolyn Phelan, review of *New Old Shoes,* p. 100.
Kirkus Reviews, August 15, 2009, review of *New Old Shoes.*
School Library Journal, June, 2008, Lisa Gangemi Kropp, review of *Animals Are Sleeping,* p. 131; June, 2009, Ellen Heath, review of *Ocean Hide and Seek,* p. 110; August, 2009, Kate Neff, review of *New Old Shoes,* p. 70.

ONLINE

Gary R. Phillips Home Page, http://garyphillipsstudio.com (January 21, 2011).
Sylvan Dell Publishing Web site, http://www.sylvandellpublishing.com/ (January 21, 2011), "Gary R. Phillips."

*   *   *

POLENGHI, Evan 1961-

Personal

Born 1961, in New York, NY. *Education:* Pratt Institute, B.F.A. (art), 1983.

Addresses

Home—New York, NY. *Office*—Polenghi Studio, 60 W. 76th St., Ste. 6H, New York, NY 10023. *E-mail*—evan@evanpolenghi.com.

Career

Illustrator and fine artist. Learning Maestros, art directory, 1999-2010; Evan Polenghi Studio, New York, NY, founder and owner, beginning 1996; commercial clients include Museum of Modern Art, Toshiba, and World Financial Center. *Exhibitions:* Work included in exhibitions and in private collections around the world.

Illustrator

Marilyn Singer, *I'm Your Bus,* Scholastic Press (New York, NY), 2009.

Contributor to periodicals, including *Boston Globe, Metropolitan Life, Ms., New York Times, Oracle, Oregonian, Profit,* and *Upside.*

Biographical and Critical Sources

PERIODICALS

Booklist, July 1, 2009, Gillian Engberg, review of *I'm Your Bus,* p. 66.
Chicago Tribune, June 27, 2009, Mary Harris Russell, review of *I'm Your Bus,* p. 15.
Kirkus Reviews, June 15, 2009, review of *I'm Your Bus.*
School Library Journal, September, 2009, Barbara Elleman, review of *I'm Your Bus,* p. 134.

ONLINE

Evan Polenghi Home Page, http://www.evanpolenghi.com (December 22, 2010).*

R

REX, Adam

Personal

Married; wife's name Marie (an astrophysicist). *Education:* University of Arizona, B.F.A. (illustration).

Addresses

Home—Tucson, AZ. *Agent*—Steve Malk, Writers House, 21 W. 26th St., New York, NY 10010. *E-mail*—adam rex@earthlink.net.

Career

Author and illustrator. Creator of greeting-card art.

Awards, Honors

Golden Kite Award, Society of Children's Book Writers and Illustrators, Parents' Choice Gold Medal, and International Reading Association (IRA) Notable Book selection, all 2004, all for *The Dirty Cowboy* by Amy Timberlake; Jack Gaughan Award for Best Emerging Artist, 2005; IRA Notable Book selection, 2006, for *Ste-e-e-e-eamboat A-comin'!* by Jill Esbaum; American Library Association Best Books for Teens selection, 2010, for *Fat Vampire.*

Writings

SELF-ILLUSTRATED

Frankenstein Makes a Sandwich, and Other Stories You're Sure to Like, Because They're All about Monsters, and Some of Them Are Also about Food. You Like Food, Don't You? Well, All Right, Harcourt (Orlando, FL), 2006.
Tree Ring Circus, Harcourt (Orlando, FL), 2006.
Pssst!, Harcourt (Orlando, FL), 2007.
The True Meaning of Smekday (novel), Hyperion (New York, NY), 2007.

Adam Rex (Photograph by Sonya Sones. Reproduced by permission.)

Frankenstein Takes the Cake, Harcourt (Orlando, FL), 2008.
Fat Vampire: A Never-Coming-of-Age Story, Balzer & Bray (New York, NY), 2010.

Contributor of illustrated short fiction to anthology *Guys Read: Funny Business,* edited by Jon Scieszka, Harper Collins (New York, NY), 2011.

ILLUSTRATOR

Amy Timberlake, *The Dirty Cowboy,* Farrar, Straus & Giroux (New York, NY), 2003.
Katy Kelly, *Lucy Rose: Here's the Thing about Me,* Delacorte (New York, NY), 2004.
Jill Esbaum, *Ste-e-e-e-eamboat A-comin'!,* Farrar, Straus & Giroux (New York, NY), 2005.
Katy Kelly, *Lucy Rose: Big on Plans,* Delacorte (New York, NY), 2005.
Katy Kelly, *Lucy Rose: Busy like You Can't Believe,* Delacorte (New York, NY), 2006.
Elvira Woodruff, *Small Beauties: The Journey of Darcy Heart O'Hara,* Knopf (New York, NY), 2006.
Mac Barnett, *Billy Twitters and His Blue Whale Problem,* Disney/Hyperion Books (New York, NY), 2009.

Mac Barnett, *The Case of the Case of Mistaken Identity* ("Brixton Brothers" series), Simon & Schuster Books for Young Readers (New York, NY), 2009.

Mac Barnett, *Guess Again!,* Simon & Schuster Books for Young Readers (New York, NY), 2009.

Mac Barnett, *The Ghostwriter Secret* ("Brixton Brothers" series), Simon & Schuster Books for Young Readers (New York, NY), 2010.

Contributor of illustrations to books, including *Manners Mash-Up,* and to periodicals, including *Amazing Stories, Cricket,* and *Spider.* Illustrator of books used in role-playing games *Dungeons & Dragons, Forgotten Realms,* and *Magic: The Gathering.*

Adaptations

The True Meaning of Smeckday was adapted as an audiobook read by Bahni Turpin, Listening Library, 2010.

Sidelights

Adam Rex is an award-winning illustrator whose art is featured in children's books such as *The Dirty Cowboy* by Amy Timberlake and *Small Beauties: The Journey of Darcy Heart O'Hara* by Elvira Woodruff. Apart from his illustration projects, Rex has also created several humorous, self-illustrated books, including *Pssst!,* which chronicles a youngster's visit to an unusual zoo. Rex turns to longer fiction in *The True Meaning of Smekday,* a middle-grade novel about the alien conquest of Earth, and *Fat Vampire: A Never-Coming-of-Age Story,* a tale for older teens. "I think I write first and foremost for myself," Rex admitted to an interviewer for the *Seven Impossible Things before Breakfast* Web log. "I just kind of trust that if I write something that I find compelling or funny, and it's appropriate for kids in tone and language, that some kids will find it compelling or funny, too."

Raised in Arizona, Rex developed an interest in children's literature while working at a bookstore during his teen years. "I was hearing about Lane Smith, William Joyce, Steve Johnson and Lou Fancher, and so forth," he told Kelly R. Fineman on the *Writing and Ruminating* Web site. "The market seemed so utterly different from the books I remembered from my childhood. These were very vibrant, painterly, irreverent . . . . So at sixteen or seventeen I decided picture books might be a way to reconcile my love of making pictures and inventing stories."

Rex made his children's book debut in 2003, providing the illustrations for Timberlake's *The Dirty Cowboy.* In the work, a filthy cowpoke heads to the river for his annual bath, leaving his faithful dog to guard his clothes. When the canine does not recognize his sweet-swelling owner upon the man's return, however, a raucous battle for the scruffy duds ensues. "Rex's rich paintings add sparkle to the story's dramatic telling," noted *Booklist* contributor Todd Morning, and a *Publishers Weekly* reviewer applauded the artist's "farcical golden-and copper-toned illustrations, which call to mind the tall-tale humor of Andrew Glass."

Woodruff's picture book *Small Beauties* concerns Darcy Heart O'Hara, an Irish lass who immigrates to North America with her family after their potato crop fails. Rex's illustrations have "are strongly designed, with good use of the golden light of mist, memory and longing," noted a contributor in *Kirkus Reviews.* "Rich in detail of the Irish landscape," commented Lee Bock in *School Library Journal,* "the art gives a deeper understanding of this powerful story." The illustrator takes a more humorous slant in Mac Barnett's whimsically titled *Billy Twitters and His Blue Whale Problem,* and here his "goofy illustrations blend the realistic with the fantastic," according to *School Library Journal* contributor Kathleen Kelly MacMillan. In *Publishers Weekly* a reviewer cited Rex's "*Mad* magazine-style artwork" as "realistic enough to drive home the humor and full of clever touches," while a *Kirkus Reviews* writer dubbed *Billy Twitters and His Blue Whale Problem* "definitely funny and slyly subversive."

Rex's first self-illustrated work, *Frankenstein Makes a Sandwich,* collects poems that spoof famous Hollywood monsters such as the Creature from the Black Lagoon and Count Dracula. "Rex demonstrates a dizzying yet fitting variety of artistic styles, layouts and lettering," a *Publishers Weekly* critic stated of the work. "Some of the styles were chosen because they just seemed natural

Cover of Rex's highly animated, self-illustrated picture book **Tree Ring Circus.** (Copyright © 2006 by Adam Rex. Reproduced by permission of Harcourt, Inc. This material may not be reproduced in any form or by any means without the prior written permission of the publisher.)

for the poem in question," the illustrator remarked on the Harcourt Books Web site. "'Dr. Jekyll and Mr. Henderson,' for example, takes place largely at a society ball, so I tried my best to imitate the look of turn-of-the-[twentieth-]century fashion and society artists like Charles Dana Gibson." According to Bock, *Frankenstein Makes a Sandwich* "is fresh, creative, and funny, with just enough gory detail to cause a few gasps." In a sequel, *Frankenstein Takes the Cake*, Rex "delivers spot-on rhymes about B-movie monsters," and his "eclectic imagery and freewheeling verse will have readers going back for seconds," according to a *Publishers Weekly* critic.

In the cumulative rhyming tale *Tree Ring Circus*, a fast-growing tree provides shelter for a bevy of forest creatures and escaped circus animals. Debbie Stewart Hoskins, writing in *School Library Journal,* described Rex's self-illustrated story as "carefully designed, humorously detailed, and appropriately silly." A young girl receives a host of strange requests from the residents of her local zoo in *Pssst!,* another orginal work by Rex that a *Kirkus Reviews* contributor characterized as a "gleefully postmodern romp." A reviewer in *Publishers Weekly* stated that in *Pssst!* Rex "conveys [the animals'] personalities with an astringent attitude and a refreshing brake on the cuteness" and deemed the work "a very funny excursion."

In Rex's illustrated middle-grade novel *The True Meaning of Smekday,* eleven-year-old Gratuity Tucci joins forces with renegade alien J. Lo to rescue the youngster's mother from the Boov, a race of extraterrestrials hoping to force all humans to live on reservations in Florida. *School Library Journal* critic Jane Henriksen Baird praised Rex's "imaginative, wacky, hilarious sci-fi story," and Lisa Von Drasek, writing in the *New York Times Book Review,* predicted that the tale "will captivate fans of the wordplay and characters in Terry Pratchett's 'Discworld' [series] and of the outrageously entertaining satire of Douglas Adams's *Hitchhiker's Guide to the Galaxy.*"

In *Fat Vampire* Rex introduces fifteen-year-old Doug Lee, a vampire victim who is doubly cursed: in addition to being a bloodthirsty immortal, he is also cursed to remain a chubby adolescent forever. Because Doug does not have the classic charisma of the vampires of popular fiction, he must resort to more desperate measures to feed his bloodlust; meanwhile, his efforts to impress a pretty East Indian exchange student named Sejal are threatened by the relentless pursuit of the star of a new reality television show, *Vampire Hunters*. In *Booklist* Debbie Carton dubbed *Fat Vampire* an "indulgent and delightfully macabre spoof on the . . . vampire craze" spawned by Stephenie Meyers' "Twilight" novels. Rex's text includes "freshly worded observations on modern life and teen angst," wrote Christine M. Heppermann, the *Horn Book* critic praising *Fat Vampire* as a "funny, biting foray into vampire lit."

Biographical and Critical Sources

PERIODICALS

Booklist, September 1, 2003, Todd Morning, review of *The Dirty Cowboy,* p. 131; November 1, 2004, Ilene Cooper, review of *Lucy Rose: Here's the Thing about Me,* p. 485; October 15, 2006, Kay Weisman, review of *Lucy Rose: Busy like You Can't Believe,* p. 44; October 1, 2007, Jennifer Hubert, review of *The True Meaning of Smekday,* p. 59; October 15, 2009, Carolyn Phelan, review of *The Case of the Mistaken Identity,* p. 63; May 15, 2010, Debbie Carton, review of *Fat Vampire: A Never-Coming-of-Age Story,* p. 47.

Horn Book, November-December, 2007, Tanya D. Auger, review of *The True Meaning of Smekday,* p. 685; July-August, 2010, Christine M. Heppermann, review of *Fat Vampire,* p. 120.

Kirkus Reviews, June 15, 2003, review of *The Dirty Cowboy,* p. 865; March 15, 2005, review of *Ste-e-e-eamboat A-comin'!,* p. 350; June 1, 2005, review of *Lucy Rose: Big on Plans,* p. 638; June 1, 2006, review of *Tree Ring Circus,* p. 579; August 1, 2006, review of *Frankenstein Makes a Sandwich,* p. 795; August 15, 2006, review of *Small Beauties: The Journey of Darcy Heart O'Hara,* p. 854; August 1, 2007, review of *Pssst!;* August 15, 2008, review of *Frankenstein Takes the Cake;* May 1, 2009, review of *Billy Twitters and His Blue Whale Problem;* August 1, 2009, review of *Guess Again!;* September 1, 2009, review of *The Case of the Case of Mistaken Identity.*

New York Times Book Review, November 11, 2007, Lisa Von Drasek, review of *The True Meaning of Smekday;* October 12, 2008, "Monster Management," p. 25.

Publishers Weekly, July 14, 2003, review of *The Dirty Cowboy,* p. 75; July 10, 2006, review of *Tree Ring Circus,* p. 80; August 28, 2006, review of *Frankenstein Makes a Sandwich,* p. 53; September 10, 2007, review of *Pssst!,* p. 59; October 1, 2007, review of *The True Meaning of Smekday,* p. 57; July 14, 2008, review of *Frankenstein Takes the Cake,* p. 66; May 18, 2009, review of *Billy Twitters and His Blue Whale Problem,* p. 52; August 31, 2009, review of *Guess Again!,* p. 58; April 26, 2010, review of *The Clock without a Face,* p. 108; June 28, 2010, review of *Fat Vampire,* p. 131.

School Library Journal, March, 2005, Nancy Menaldi-Scanlan, review of *Ste-e-e-eamboat A-comin'!',* p. 170; September, 2006, Lee Bock, review of *Small Beauties,* p. 188, and review of *Frankenstein Makes a Sandwich,* p. 196; October, 2006, Shawn Brommer, review of *Lucy Rose: Busy like You Can't Believe,* p. 114, and Debbie Stewart Hoskins, review of *Tree Ring Circus,* p. 124; November, 2007, Rick Margolis, "Adam Rex, Space Cadet," p. 37, and Jane Henriksen Baird, review of *The True Meaning of Smekday,* p. 135; September, 2008, Wendy Lukehart, review of *Frankenstein Takes the Cake,* p. 168; August, 2009, Laura Butler, review of *Guess Again!,* p. 69; August, 2009, Kathleen Kelly MacMillan, review of *Billy Twitters and His Blue Whale Problem,* p. 69; March, 2010,

Mairead McInnes, review of *The Case of the Case of Mistaken Identity,* p. 151; July, 2010, Donna Rosenblum, review of *Fat Vampire,* p. 96.

ONLINE

Adam Rex Home Page, http://www.adamrex.com (January 10, 2011).
Adam Rex Web log, http://www.adamrex.blogspot.com (January 10, 2011).
Harcourt Book Web site, http://www.harcourtbooks.com/ (December 20, 2007), interview with Rex.
Seven Impossible Things before Breakfast Web site, http://blaine.org/sevenimpossiblethings/ (September 6, 2007), Eisha and Julie Danielson, interview with Rex.
Writing and Ruminating Web site, http://kellyrfineman.blogspot.com/ (March 1, 2007), Kelly R. Fineman, interview with Rex.*

*   *   *

RIM, Sujean

Personal

Born in Brooklyn, NY. *Education:* Parsons School of Design, degree (fashion design).

Addresses

Home—New York, NY. *E-mail*—sujean@sujeanrim.com.

Career

Illustrator and designer. Former fashion accessories and shoe designer; freelance designer and illustrator beginning 1995.

Writings

SELF-ILLUSTRATED

Birdie's Big-Girl Shoes, Little, Brown Books for Young Readers (New York, NY), 2009.
Birdie's Big-Girl Dress, Little, Brown Books for Young Readers (New York, NY), 2011.

ILLUSTRATOR

Susan Waggoner, *Litle Cakes: Classic Recipes for Any Occasion,* Universe Publishing, 2004.
Rebecca Heller, *Surf like a Girl,* Three Rivers Press, 2006.
Veronica Chambers, *The Joy of Doing Things Badly,* Broadway Books (New York, NY), 2006.
DailyCandy A to Z: An Insider's Guide to the Sweet Life, Hyperion (New York, NY), 2006.

Sujean Rim (Photograph by Bob Bianchini. Reproduced by permission.)

Peter York and Olivia Stewart Liberty, *Cooler, Faster, More Expensive,* Atlantic (London, England), 2007.
Paopla Jacobbi, *I Want Those Shoes,* Scribner (New York, NY), 2007.
Laura Schaefer, *The Teashop Girls,* Simon & Schuster Books for Young Readers (New York, NY), 2008.
The DailyCandy Lexicon: Words That Don't' Exist but Should, Virgin Books (New York, NY), 2010.

Illustrator for fashion-themed Web site DailyCandy.com.

ILLUSTRATOR; "FASHION-FORWARD ADVENTURES OF IMOGENE" SERIES BY LISA BARHAM

A Girl like Moi, Simon Pulse (New York, NY), 2006.
Project Paris, Simon Pulse (New York, NY), 2007.
Accidentally Fabulous, Simon Pulse (New York, NY), 2008.

Sidelights

Sujean Rim's whimsical and colorful water-color images have been commissioned by clients that include Almay, Target, Tiffany & Company, and Barney's as well as on the popular DailyCandy Web site. Beginning in the mid-2000s Rim also created art for several children's books, among them Lisa Barham's multi-volume "Fashion-forward Adventures of Imogene" series, Laura Schaefer's middle-grade novel *The Teashop Girls,* and her own picture-book story, *Birdie's Big-Girl Shoes.*

A New York City native, Rim started her creative career after graduating from the Parsons School of Design, where she majored in fashion design. Although she had success designing shoes and handbags for several firms, Rim's fashion illustrations were too engaging to be consigned to the design room only. In addition to creating the upbeat yet lighthearted spot art that has helped fuel the popularity of the woman-focused DailyCandy.com, Rim has also created advertising art for retailers ranging from Target to Tiffany & Company. Her focus on cutting-edge fashion for urban woman made her the perfect choice to illustrate Barham's young-adult novels, which chronicle the adventures of a resourceful teen fashionista in *A Girl like Moi, Project Paris,* and *Accidentally Fabulous.*

Described by *Booklist* contributor Karen Cruze as "a light confection about a little girl who covets her mother's high heels," *Birdie's Big-Girl Shoes* pairs Rim's artfully tinted water-color illustrations with her story about a girl who loves helping her mother chose the outfit she will wear to work each morning. When Mom finally allows the girl to play with her shoes, five-year old Birdie's cautious steps in a sequence of oversized stilettos, flats, and strappy sandals help her to realize that childhood is by far the most comfortable place to be. In *School Library Journal* Kathleen Finn noted the "bold, stylized watercolor and collage" art that pairs with Rim's "simple text," and a *Kirkus Reviews* writer maintained that the author/artist's "retro-styled water-color collages" effectively reflect Birdie's attempt to navigate a grown-up-sized world, while the inclusion of "textured accents provide spunk." *Birdie's Big-Girl Shoes* treats young readers to "some fashionable fun," concluded the *Kirkus Reviews* contributor, and Cruze dubbed Rim's picture-book debut "refreshing."

Biographical and Critical Sources

PERIODICALS

Booklist, December 1, 2008, Carolyn Phelan, review of *The Teashop Girls,* p. 52; November 1, 2009, Karen Cruze, review of *Birdie's Big-Girl Shoes,* p. 51.

Bulletin of the Center for Children's Books, October, 2009, Deborah Stevenson, review of *Birdie's Big-Girl Shoes,* p. 80.

Kirkus Reviews, November 15, 2008, review of *The Teashop Girls;* August 1, 2009, review of *Birdie's Big-Girl Shoes.*

Kliatt, July, 2007, Olivia Durant, review of *A Girl like Moi,* p. 22.

New York Times Book Review, December 20, 2009, Lucinda Rosenfeld, review of *Birdie's Big-Girl Shoes,* p. 13.

Publishers Weekly, November 24, 2008, review of *The Teashop Girls,* p. 58.

School Library Journal, July, 2007, Rhona Campbell, review of *Project Pads: The Fashion-Forward Adventures of Imogene,* p. 96; July, 2007, Erin Schirota, review of *A Girl like Moi,* p. 96; September, 2009, Kathleen Finn, review of *Birdie's Big-Girl Shoes,* p. 132.

ONLINE

Sujean Rim Home Page, http://www.sujeanrim.com (December 22, 2010).*

*   *   *

ROBINSON, Fiona 1965-

Personal

Born 1965, in England; immigrated to United States. *Education:* Attended art school.

Addresses

Home—Brooklyn, NY.

Career

Author and illustrator of children's books. *Exhibitions:* Works have been exhibited in galleries in London, England.

Awards, Honors

Honors from Royal Academy of Arts.

Writings

SELF-ILLUSTRATED

The Useful Moose: A Truthful, Moose-full Tale, Harry N. Abrams (New York, NY), 2004.

The 3-2-3 Detective Agency In: The Disappearance of Dave Warthog, Amulet Books (New York, NY), 2009.

ILLUSTRATOR

Nancy Raines Day, *Flamingo's First Christmas,* Harry N. Abrams (New York, NY), 2005.

Rim takes a break from fashion illustration to create her original self-illustrated picture book Birdie's Big-Girl Shoes.. (Little, Brown & Company Books for Young Readers, 2009. Illustration copyright © 2009 by Sujean Rim. Reproduced by permission.)

Contributor to periodicals, including the *Wall Street Journal.*

Sidelights

Born in England but now living in Brooklyn, New York, Fiona Robinson has had her work exhibited in London galleries as well as in the pages of the *Wall Street Journal.* Robinson focuses on younger audiences in her first book for children, the whimsical, self-illustrated *The Useful Moose: A Truthful, Moose-full Tale,* which finds a young moose lover traveling to Alaska only to find that all the moose there have left gone south on vacation. Robinson's illustrations also appear in her easy reader *The 3-2-3 Detective Agency In: The Disappearance of Dave Warthog* as well as in Nancy Raines Day's *Flamingo's First Christmas.* "All the good-natured silliness of the book's scenario" is captured in Robinson's "tall oil paintings," according to a *Publishers Weekly* contributor, reviewing Day's whimsical tale.

Molly, the young narrator of *The Useful Moose,* loves everything about moose, and she is very disappointed to arrive in a moose-less Alaska on a family vacation. Return to her home in the lower forty-eight, Molly discovers three young moose living in her family's apart-

ment building and soon the antlered creatures are helping out with cooking, dishwashing, and the laundry. Ultimately the moose return to their northern home, but the friendship stays strong in Robinson's entertaining tale. In *Publishers Weekly* a critic wrote that Robinson's cartoon pictures of "gangly moose . . . using their antlers as a clothes-drying device" add to the story's "silliness and warmth," while Jessi Platt noted in her *School Library Journal* review that the humorous illustrations in *The Useful Moose* "reinforce the mood and action of the story" and make it "an excellent choice for individual or group readings."

In *The Disappearance of Dave Warthog* Robinson introduces five unusual sleuths: a sloth names Slingshot, Bluebell the rat, Roger the dung beetle, Priscilla the penguin, and Jessica the donkey, all which join together to form the 3-2-3 Detective Agency. The team goes to work when critters living in Whiska City begin disappearing. Fans of "funny mysteries will adore it," Paula Willey predicted of Robinson's story in *School Library Journal,* and a *Publishers Weekly* contributor cited the "fresh and honest sense of humor" with which she portrays "values of friendship and kindness." Cast with characters featuring "unique personalities and skills,"

Fiona Robinson pairs her quirky cartoon art with a suitably humorous tale of mystery in **The 323 Detective Agency In: The Disappearance of Dave Warthog.** (Amulet Books, 2009. Illustration copyright © 2009 by Fiona Robinson. Reproduced by permission.)

Robinson's "loose, colorful, and cartoony comic-book panels invite readers right into" the pages of *The Disappearance of Dave Warthog,* concluded *Booklist* contributor Kat Kan.

Biographical and Critical Sources

PERIODICALS

Booklist, July 1, 2009, Kat Kan, review of *The 3-2-3 Detective Agency In: The Disappearance of Dave Warthog,* p. 59.

Kirkus Reviews, July 1, 2009, review of *The Disappearance of Dave Warthog.*

Publishers Weekly, October 25, 2004, review of *The Useful Moose: A Truthful, Moose-full Tale,* p. 47; September 26, 2005, review of *Flamingo's First Christmas,* p. 87; August 24, 2009, review of *The Disappearance of Dave Warthog,* p. 49.

School Library Journal, January, 2005, Jessi Platt, review of *The Useful Moose,* p. 97; September, 2009, Paula Willey, review of *The Disappearance of Dave Warthog,* p. 190.*

*   *   *

ROOS, Maryn

Personal

Born in CA. *Education:* Brigham Young University, B.F.A. (illustration; magna cum laude), 1995.

Addresses

Home—Provo, UT. *Agent*—Shannon Associates, 333 W. 57th St., Ste. 810, New York, NY 10019. *E-mail*—maryn@marynroos.com.

Career

Illustrator and animator. Waterford Institute (educational software developer), UT, former illustrator and developer of interactive games; Lucas Learning, Ltd. (educational software developer), northern CA, former lead artist; Image Learning (educational publisher), Provo, UT, illustrator.

Illustrator

Lea Gillespie Grant, *Never Say Goodbye,* Tommy Nelson (Nashville, TN), 2003.

Tricia Goyer, *Ten Minutes to Showtime!,* Tommy Nelson (Nashville, TN), 2004.

Rory Zuckerman, *Colorful Sleepy Sheep,* Castle Pacific Pub. (Seattle, WA), 2004.

Rory Zuckerman, *Counting Sleepy Sheep,* Castle Pacific Pub. (Seattle, WA), 2004.

Rory Zuckerman, *Shapely Sleepy Sheep,* Castle Pacific Pub. (Seattle, WA), 2004.

Karen Hill, *Ava, the One and Only,* Little Simon Inspirations (New York, NY), 2005.

God Made the World, Jump at the Sun/Hyperion Books for Children (New York, NY), 2006.

Noah Builds an Ark, Jump at the Sun/Hyperion Books for Children (New York, NY), 2006.

Mary Schulte, *Who Do I Look Like?,* Children's Press (New York, NY), 2006.

Rory Zuckerman, *Alphabetical Sleepy Sheep,* Castle Pacific (Seattle, WA), 2007.

Mario Lopez and Marissa Lopez Wong, *Mud Tacos!,* Celebra Children's Books (New York, NY), 2009.

Whoopi Goldberg with Deborah Underwood, *Terrible Terrel,* Disney/Jump at the Sun (New York, NY), 2010.

"WILLIMENA RULES!" BEGINNING CHAPTER-BOOK SERIES BY VALERIE WILSON WESLEY

How to Lose Your Class Pet, Jump at the Sun/Hyperion Paperbacks for Children (New York, NY), 2003.

How to Fish for Trouble, Jump at the Sun (New York, NY), 2004.

How to Lose Your Cookie Money, Jump at the Sun (New York, NY), 2004.

23 Ways to Mess up Valentine's Day, Jump at the Sun/ Hyperion Books for Children (New York, NY), 2005.

How to (Almost) Ruin Your School Play, Jump at the Sun/ Hyperion Books for Children (New York, NY), 2005.

"SHANNA'S FIRST READERS" SERIES BY JEAN MARZOLLO

Shanna's Animal Riddles, Jump at the Sun/Hyperion Books for Children (New York, NY), 2004.

Shanna's Bear Hunt, Jump at the Sun/Hyperion Books for Children (New York, NY), 2004.

Shanna's Hip, Hop, Hooray!, Jump at the Sun/Hyperion Books for Children (New York, NY), 2004.

Shanna's Lost Shoe, Jump at the Sun/Hyperion Books for Children (New York, NY), 2004.

Shanna's Party Suprise, Jump at the Sun/Hyperion Books for Children (New York, NY), 2004.

Shanna's Pizza Parlor, Jump at the Sun/Hyperion Books for Children (New York, NY), 2004.

"SUGAR PLUM BALLERINAS" CHAPTER-BOOK SERIES BY WHOOPI GOLDBERG WITH DEBORAH UNDERWOOD

Plum Fantastic, Disney/Jump at the Sun Books (New York, NY), 2008.

Toeshoe Trouble, Disney/Jump at the Sun Books (New York, NY), 2009.

Perfectly Prima, Disney/Jump at the Sun Books (New York, NY), 2010.

Sidelights

In addition to her career designing and illustrating educational materials for software publishers, Maryn Roos has contributed artwork to many stories for young children, among them Mary Schulte's *Who Do I Look Like?* and Mario Lopez's humorous picture book *Mud Tacos!*

Maryn Roos teams up with celebrity author Mario Lopez and his sister Marissa Lopez Wong to create the Latino-themed picture book **Mud Tacos!.** (Illustration copyright © 2009 by Via Mar Productions, Inc. All rights reserved. Used by permission of Celebra Children's Books, a division of Penguin Young Readers Group, a member of Penguin Group (USA) Inc., 345 Hudson Street, New York, NY 10014.)

Based in Utah, Roos specializes in attracting beginning readers, crafting colorful digitalized cartoon images featuring engaging characters. Reviewing *Mud Tacos!* for *Kirkus Reviews,* a contributor cited the story's "cartoon-style illustrations" for featuring elements that will "make children of Latino background feel culturally connected" to Lopez's story, while in *School Library Journal* Eve Ottenberg Stone noted of *Who Do I Look Like?* that Schulte's question-and-answer format illuminates family relationships while Roos's "bold and humorous" images "show a racially diverse family."

Many of Roos's illustration projects include series fiction, such as the stories in both Valerie Wilson Wesley's "Willimena Rules!" chapter-book series and the "Sugar Plum Ballerinas" chapter-book series, the last in which actor Whoopi Goldberg teams up with Deborah Underwood to recount the dance-themed adventures of several preteen friends. In *How to Fish for Trouble,* which finds Wesley's young heroine attempting to steal attention from her visiting cousin Teddy during a family fishing trip, the artist's "quirky, cartoon illustrations will keep the pages turning," as *School Library Journal* contributor Ajoke' T.I. Kokodoko predicted. Willimena moves to third grade in *How to Lose Your Class Pet,* and here Roos's pencil drawings "convey the oftentimes-humorous tone" of Wesley's story, according to Elaine Lesh Morgan in the same periodical.

Roos's "inviting full-color illustrations" for Jean Marzollo's "Shanna's First Readers" series capture the activities of a friendly young girl and result in stories that *Booklist* critic Karen Hutt anticipated "will draw in early readers." Reviewing series installments *Shanna's Hip, Hop, Hooray!, Shanna's Party Surprise,* and *Shan-*

na's Bear Hunt in *School Library Journal,* Deborah Rothaug concluded that Roos's "large, brightly colored and sharply outlined cartoon characters are sure to attract children's attention."

Biographical and Critical Sources

PERIODICALS

Black Issues Book Review, July-August, 2004, Suzanne Rust, review of *How to Fish for Trouble,* p. 60.
Booklist, August, 2004, Karen Hutt, review of *Shanna's Bear Hunt,* p. 1943; January 1, 2009, Bina Williams, review of *Sugar Plum Ballerinas,* p. 84.
Kirkus Reviews, September 1, 2008, review of *Sugar Plum Ballerinas;* October 1, 2009, review of *Mud Tacos!*
Publishers Weekly, December 1, 2003, review of *How to Lose Your Class Pet,* p. 58; September 29, 2008, review of *Plum Fantastic,* p. 82.
School Library Journal, January, 2004, Elaine Lesh Morgan, review of *How to Lose Your Class Pet,* p. 107; October, 2004, Ajoke' T.I. Kokodoko, review of *How to Fish for Trouble,* p. 135; October, 2004, Deborah Rothaug, review of *Shanna's Bear Hunt,* p. 123; June, 2006, Eve Ottenberg Stone, review of *Who Do I Look Like?,* p. 119; December, 2008, Bethany A. Lafferty, review of *Plum Fantastic,* p. 90; October, 2009, Amanda Moss Struckmeyer, review of *Toeshoe Trouble,* p. 92.

ONLINE

Maryn Roos Home Page, http://www.marynroos.com (December 28, 2010).
Maryn Roos Web log, http://baroness.blogspot.com (January 15, 2011).*

* * *

ROSS, Tony 1938-

Personal

Born August 10, 1938, in London, England; son of Eric Turle Lee (a businessman and magician) and Effie Ross; married Carole Jean D'Arcy (divorced); married; second wife's name Joan (divorced); married 1979; third wife's name Zoe; children: (first marriage) Philippa (adopted); (second marriage) George (stepson), Alexandra; (third marriage) Katherine. *Education:* Liverpool College of Art, diplomas, 1960, 1961. *Religion:* Methodist. *Hobbies and other interests:* Sailing small boats, cats, the monarchy, collecting toy soldiers, lamb cutlets.

Addresses

Home and office—Nottingham, England.

Career

Author and illustrator of children's books. Smith, Kline & French Laboratories, graphic designer, 1962-64; Brunnings Advertising, art director, 1964-65; Manchester Polytechnic, Manchester, England, lecturer, 1965-72, senior lecturer in illustration, 1972-85; full-time writer and illustrator, beginning 1985. Consultant in graphic design.

Member

Society of Industrial Artists and Designers.

Awards, Honors

Children's Choice selection, International Reading Association (IRA)/Children's Book Center (CBC), and Best Children's Picture Book of the Year designation, *Redbook,* both 1985, both for *I'm Coming to Get You!*; Kate Greenaway Medal commendation, 1986, for *I Want My Potty,* and shortlist, 1990, for *Dr Xargle's Book of Earth Tiggers* by Jeanne Willis; Deutscher Jugendliteratur Preis (West Germany), 1986; National Art Library Illustration Award shortlist, 1998, for *Sloth's Shoes* by Willis, 1999, for *Why?* by Lindsay Camp, 2000, for *The Boy Who Lost his Bellybutton* by Willis; Nestlé Smarties Book Prize Silver Award, 2003, for *Tadpole's Promise* by Willis; two Silver Pencil awards and two Silver Paintbrush awards (Netherlands); Schonste Bucher aus aller Welt award (East Germany); Parents' Choice Award, 2002, for *I Want to Be a Cowgirl* by Willis; Children's Choices selection, IRA/CBC, 2005, for *Dear Max* by Sally Grindley; Cooperative Children's Book Council (CCBC) Choices selection, and Charlotte Zolotow Award Honor Book designation, both 2006, both for *Gorilla! Gorilla!* by Willis; CCBC Choices selection, 2006, for *Notso Hotso* by Anne Fine.

Writings

SELF-ILLUSTRATED CHILDREN'S BOOKS

Tales from Mr Toffy's Circus, six volumes, W.J. Thurman (London, England), 1973.

(Reteller) *Goldilocks and the Three Bears,* Andersen Press (London, England), 1976, Overlook Press (Woodstock, NY), 1992.

Hugo and the Wicked Winter, Sidgwick & Jackson (London, England), 1977.

Hugo and the Man Who Stole Colors, Follett (New York, NY), 1977.

(Reteller) *The Pied Piper of Hamelin,* Andersen Press (London, England), 1977.

Norman and Flop Meet the Toy Bandit, W.J. Thurman (London, England), 1977.

(Reteller) *Little Red Riding Hood,* Andersen Press (London, England), 1978.

Hugo and Oddsock, Andersen Press (London, England), 1978.

(Reteller) *The True Story of Mother Goose and Her Son Jack,* Andersen Press (London, England), 1979, Rourke (Windermere, FL), 1982.

The Greedy Little Cobbler, Andersen Press (London, England), 1979, Barrons (Woodbury, NY), 1980.

Hugo and the Ministry of Holidays, Andersen Press (London, England), 1980, David & Charles (North Pomfret, VT), 1987.

Jack and the Beanstalk, Andersen Press (London, England), 1980, Delacorte (New York, NY), 1981.

Puss in Boots: The Story of a Sneaky Cat, Delacorte (New York, NY), 1981.

Naughty Nigel, Andersen Press (London, England), 1982, reprinted, 2009, published as *Naughty Nicky,* Holt (New York, NY), 1983.

(Reteller) *The Enchanted Pig: An Old Rumanian Tale,* Andersen Press (London, England), 1982.

(Reteller) *The Three Pigs,* Pantheon (New York, NY), 1983.

(Reteller) *Jack the Giantkiller,* Andersen Press (London, England), 1983, Dial (New York, NY), 1987.

The Boy Who Cried Wolf, Dial (New York, NY), 1985.

Lazy Jack, Andersen Press (London, England), 1985, Dial (New York, NY), 1986.

(Reteller) *Foxy Fables,* Dial (New York, NY), 1986.

(Reteller) *Stone Soup,* Dial (New York, NY), 1987.

Oscar Got the Blame, Andersen Press (London, England), 1987, Dial (New York, NY), 1988.

Super Dooper Jezebel, Farrar, Straus (New York, NY), 1988.

Hansel and Gretel, Andersen (London, England), 1989, David & Charles (North Pomfret, VT), 1990.

I Want a Cat, Farrar, Straus (New York, NY), 1989.

Treasure of Cozy Cove, Andersen Press (London, England), 1989, Farrar, Straus (New York, NY), 1990.

Mrs Goat and Her Seven Little Kids, Atheneum (London, England), 1990.

This Old Man: A Musical Counting Book, Aladdin (New York, NY), 1990, published as *This Old Man: A Musical Counting Book,* Collins (London, England), 1990.

Going Green: A Kid's Handbook to Saving the Planet, Puffin Books (New York, NY), 1990.

Happy Blanket, Farrar, Straus (New York, NY), 1990.

(Reteller) *Five Favorite Tales,* Andersen Press (London, England), 1990.

A Fairy Tale, Little, Brown (Boston, MA), 1991.

Don't Do That!, Crown (New York, NY), 1991.

Big, Bad Barney Bear, Andersen Press (London, England), 1992.

(Abridger) Lewis Carroll, *Alice's Adventures in Wonderland,* Andersen Press (London, England), 1992.

I Want to Be, Kane/Miller (Brooklyn, NY), 1993.

Eventful Years: A Tribute to the Royal Air Force, 1918-1993, Wingham Aviation Books (Elmstone, Kent, England), 1993.

(Abridger) Lewis Carroll, *Through the Looking-Glass and What Alice Found There,* Maxwell Macmillan (New York, NY), 1993.

Weather, Harcourt Brace (New York, NY), 1994.

Pets, Harcourt Brace (New York, NY), 1994.

Bedtime, Harcourt (New York, NY), 1995.

Shapes, Red Wagon Books (New York, NY), 1995.

Furry Tales: A Bumper Book of Ten Favourite Animal Tales, Andersen Press (London, England), 1999.

Centipede's 100 Shoes, Andersen Press (London, England), 2002, Henry Holt (New York, NY), 2003.

Is It Because?, Andersen Press (London, England), 2004, Barrons Educational Series (Hauppauge, NY), 2005.

Say Please!, Kane/Miller (La Jolla, CA), 2006.

(Compiler) *Three Little Kittens and Other Favorite Nursery Rhymes,* Andersen Press (London, England), 2007, Henry Holt (New York, NY), 2009, published as *My Favorite Nursery Rhymes,* Andersen Press, 2008.

(Compiler) *My First Nursery Stories,* Andersen Press (London, England), 2008.

"TOWSER" SERIES; SELF-ILLUSTRATED

I'm Coming to Get You!, Dial (New York, NY), 1984.

Towser and Sadie's Birthday, Pantheon (New York, NY), 1984.

Towser and the Terrible Thing, Pantheon (New York, NY), 1984.

Towser and the Water Rats, Pantheon (New York, NY), 1984.

Towser and the Haunted House, Andersen Press (London, England), 1985, David & Charles (North Pomfret, VT), 1987.

Towser and the Funny Face, David & Charles (North Pomfret, VT), 1987.

Towser and the Magic Apple, David & Charles (North Pomfret, VT), 1987.

"LITTLE PRINCESS" SERIES; SELF-ILLUSTRATED

I Want My Potty, Kane/Miller (Brooklyn, NY), 1986, new edition, Andersen Press (London, England), 2005.

I Want My Dinner, Andersen Press (London, England), 1995.

I Want a Sister, Andersen Press (London, England), 1999.

I Don't Want to Go to Hospital, Andersen Press (London, England), 2000.

Wash Your Hands!, Kane/Miller (New York, NY), 2000, published as *I Don't Want to Wash My Hands,* Collins (London, England), 2003.

I Want My Dummy, Andersen Press (London, England), 2001, published as *I Want My Pacifier,* Kane/Miller (La Jolla, CA), 2004.

I Want My Tooth, Andersen Press (London, England), 2002, Kane/Miller (La Jolla, CA), 2005.

I Don't Want to Go to Bed!, Andersen Press (London, England), 2003, Kane/Miller (La Jolla, CA), 2004.

I Want My Mum!, Andersen Press (London, England), 2004.

I Want a Friend, Andersen Press (London, England), 2005.

I Want My Present, Andersen Press (London, England), 2005.

Say Please!, Andersen Press (London, England), 2005.

I Want to Go Home!, Andersen Press (London, England), 2006.

I Want My Light On!, Andersen Press (London, England), 2007.

I Want My Tent!, Andersen Press (London, England), 2007.

I Don't Want a Cold!, Andersen Press (London, England), 2007.

I Want a Trumpet!, Andersen Press (London, England), 2007.

I Want a Sledge!, Andersen Press (London, England), 2007.

I Want My New Shoes!, Andersen Press (London, England), 2007.

Can I Keep It?, Andersen Press (London, England), 2007.

I Want to Be Tall!, Andersen Press (London, England), 2008.

I Want My Puppets!, Andersen Press (London, England), 2008.

I Want to Go to the Fair!, Andersen Press (London, England), 2008.

I Don't Like Salad!, Andersen Press (London, England), 2008.

I Want to Be a Cavegirl!, Andersen Press (London, England), 2008.

I Don't Want to Comb My Hair!, Andersen Press (London, England), 2008.

I Want a Shop!, Andersen Press (London, England), 2008.

I Want to Be a Pirate!, Andersen Press (London, England), 2008.

I Want Two Birthdays!, Andersen Press (London, England), 2008, Lerner (Minneapolis, MN), 2010.

I Want a Story!, Andersen Press (London, England), 2009.

ILLUSTRATOR

Iris Grender, *Did I Ever Tell You . . .?,* Hutchinson (London, England), 1977.

Iris Grender, *The Second Did I Ever Tell You . . .? Book,* Hutchinson (London, England), 1978.

Patricia Gray and David Mackay, *Two Monkey Tales,* Longman (London, England), 1979.

Bernard Stone, *The Charge of the Mouse Brigade,* Andersen Press (London, England), 1979.

Jean Russell, editor, *The Magnet Book of Strange Tales,* Methuen (London, England), 1980.

Philip Curtis, *Mr Browser Meets the Burrowers,* Andersen Press (London, England), 1980, published as *Invasion from below the Earth,* Knopf (New York, NY), 1981.

Bernard Stone, *The Tale of Admiral Mouse,* Andersen Press (London, England), 1981.

Iris Grender, *Did I Ever Tell You about My Irish Great Grandmother?,* Hutchinson (London, England), 1981.

Naomi Lewis, *Hare and Badger Go to Town,* Andersen Press (London, England), 1981.

Iris Grender, *But That's Another Story,* Knight (London, England), 1982.

Eric Morecambe, *The Reluctant Vampire,* Methuen (London, England), 1982.

Philip Curtis, *The Revenge of the Brain Sharpeners,* Andersen (London, England), 1982.

J.K. Hooper, *Kaspar and the Iron Poodle,* Andersen Press (London, England), 1982.

Jean Russell, editor, *The Methuen Book of Sinister Stories,* Methuen (London, England), 1982.

Philip Curtis, *Mr Browser and the Mini-Meteorites,* Andersen Press (London, England), 1983, published as *Invasion of the Comet People,* Knopf (New York, NY), 1983.

Philip Curtis, *Mr Browser and the Brain Sharpeners,* Andersen Press (London, England), 1983.

Hazel Townson, *The Shrieking Face,* Andersen Press (London, England), 1984.

Alan Sillitoe, *Marmalade Jim and the Fox,* Robson (London, England), 1984.

Roger Collinson, *Paper Flags and Penny Ices,* Andersen Press (London, England), 1984.

Michael Palin, *Limericks,* Red Fox (London, England), 1985.

W.J. Corbett, *The End of the Tale,* Methuen (London, England), 1985.

Philip Curtis, *Mr Browser in the Space Museum,* Andersen Press (London, England), 1985.

Hazel Townson, *Terrible Tuesday,* Andersen Press (London, England), 1985, Morrow (New York, NY), 1986.

Philip Curtis, *The Quest of the Quidnuncs,* Andersen Press (London, England), 1986.

Andrew Davies, *Alfonzo Bonzo,* Methuen (London, England), 1986, Scholastic (London, England), 2006.

Hiayam Oram, *Jenna and the Troublemaker,* Holt (New York, NY), 1986.

Adrian Henri, *The Phantom Lollipop Lady, and Other Poems,* Methuen (London, England), 1986.

Andrew Matthews, *Dixie's Demon,* Methuen (London, England), 1987.

Songs from Play School, A. & C. Black (London, England), 1987.

Iris Grender, *The Third Did I Ever Tell You . . .?,* David & Charles (North Pomfret, VT), 1987.

Iris Grender, *Did I Ever Tell You . . . What the Children Told Me?,* David & Charles (North Pomfret, VT), 1987.

Pat Thomson, *The Treasure Sock,* Delacorte (New York, NY), 1987.

Trinka Hakes Noble, *Meanwhile Back at the Ranch,* Dial Books for the Young (New York, NY), 1987.

Heather Eyles, *Well I Never!,* Stoddart (London, England), 1988.

Hywin Oram, *Anyone Seen Harry Lately?,* Andersen Press (London, England), 1988, David & Charles (North Pomfret, VT), 1989.

Ian Whybrow, *Sniff,* Bodley Head (London, England), 1989.

Naughty Stories, Arrow (London, England), 1989.

Adrian Henri, *Rhinestone Rhino, and Other Poems,* Methuen (London, England), 1989.

Jeanne Willis, *Earthlets, as Explained by Professor Xargle,* Dutton (New York, NY), 1989, published as *Dr Xargle's Book of Earthlets,* Andersen Press (London, England), 1989.

Barbara S. Hazen, *The Knight Who Was Afraid of the Dark,* Dial Books for Young Readers (New York, NY), 1989.

The Pop-up Book of Nonsense Verse, Random House (New York, NY), 1989.

Ian Whybrow, *Sniff the Wonderdog,* Bodley Head (London, England), 1990.

Ian Whybrow, *Sniff Bounces Back,* Bodley Head (London, England), 1990.

Jack Elkington and Julia Heiles, *The Young Green Consumer Guide,* Victor Gollancz (London, England), 1990.

Andrew Matthews, *Dr Monsoon Taggart's Amazing Finishing Academy,* Mammoth (London, England), 1990.

Hazel Townson, *Victor's Party,* Andersen Press (London, England), 1990.

Vernon Scannell, *Love Shouts and Whispers,* Trafalgar (London, England), 1990.

Adèle Geras, *The Fantora Family Files,* Collins (London, England), 1990.

Alexander McCall Smith, *The Joke Machine,* Piccolo (London, England), 1990.

W.J. Corbett, *Toby's Iceberg,* Methuen (London, England), 1990.

Andrew Matthews, *Mistress Moonwater,* Mammoth (London, England), 1990.

Philip Curtis, *Pen Friend from Another Planet,* Andersen Press (London, England), 1990.

Jeanne Willis, *Dr Xargle's Book of Earth Tiggers,* Andersen Press (London, England), 1990, published as *Earth Tigerlets, as Explained by Professor Xargle,* Dutton (New York, NY), 1991.

Jeanne Willis, *Dr Xargle's Book of Earth Mobiles,* Andersen Press (London, England), 1991.

Margaret Mahy, *Bubble Trouble,* Hamish Hamilton (London, England), 1991.

Hazel Townson, *Snakes Alive!, and Other Stories,* Andersen Press (London, England), 1991.

Even Naughtier Stories, Red Fox (London, England), 1991.

Vernon Scannell, *Travelling Light: Poems,* Bodley Head (London, England), 1991.

Terence Blacker, *The Great Denture Adventure,* Macmillan (London, England), 1991.

Simon Brett, *How to Be a Little Sod,* Gollancz (London, England), 1992.

Michael Rosen, *Reckless Ruby,* Andersen Press (London, England), 1992.

Michael Rosen, *Burping Bertha,* Andersen Press (London, England), 1993.

Roald Dahl, *Fantastic Mr Fox,* Viking (London, England), 1993.

Tim Healey, *It Came through the Wall,* Hutchinson (London, England), 1993, Mondo-Tronics (San Rafael, CA), 1996.

Roald Dahl, *The Magic Finger,* Viking (London, England), 1993.

Claude Delafosse, *Animals,* Moonlight (London, England), 1994, Scholastic, Inc. (New York, NY), 1995.

Silly Stories, Orion (London, England), 1994.

Willis Hall, *The Vampire's Christmas,* Red Fox (London, England), 1994.

Hywin Oram, *The Second Princess,* Artists & Writers Guild, 1994.

Ian Whybrow, *Nice One, Sniff,* Bodley Head (London, England), 1994.

Claude Delafosse, *Paintings,* Moonlight (London, England), 1994, published as *Portraits,* Scholastic, Inc. (New York, NY), 1995.

Sally Pomme Clayton, *Tales of Amazing Maidens,* Orchard (London, England), 1995, published as *The Girl Who Went to the Underworld; The Girl Who Loved Food,* 1998.

Karen Wallace, *Ace Ghosts: A Spooky Tale from Creakie Hall,* Hamish Hamilton (London, England), 1996.

Karen Wallace, *Ghouls Rule: A Spooky Tale from Creakie Hall,* Hamish Hamilton (London, England), 1996.

Lynne Reid Banks, *Harry the Poisonous Centipede's Big Adventure,* Collins (London, England), 1996, Harper-Collins (New York, NY), 2001.

Allan Ahlberg, *Miss Dirt the Dustman's Daughter,* Viking (London, England), 1996.

Lindsay Camp, *The Midnight Feast,* Andersen Press (London, England), 1996.

Willis Hall, *Vampire Park,* Bodley Head (London, England), 1996.

Michael Rosen, *Norma's Notebook,* Sundance Publishing (Littleton, MA), 1997.

Polly, the Most Poetic Person, Orchard (London, England), 1997.

Adrian Mitchell, *Balloon Lagoon and the Magic Islands of Poetry,* Orchard (London, England), 1997.

Geraldine McCaughrean, *The Wooden Horse; Pandora's Box,* Orchard (London, England), 1997.

Geraldine McCaughrean, *Theseus and the Minotaur; Orpheus and Eurydice; Apollo and Daphne,* Orchard (London, England), 1997.

Jeanne Willis, *Sloth's Shoes,* Andersen Press (London, England), 1997, Kane/Miller (La Jolla, CA), 1998.

Michael Morpurgo, *Red Eyes at Night,* Hodder (London, England), 1998.

Jeanne Willis, *The Wind in the Wallows,* Andersen Press (London, England), 1998.

Lindsay Camp, *Why?,* Putnam (New York, NY), 1998.

Tony Bradman, selector, *The Kingfisher Treasury of Pirate Stories,* Kingfisher (Boston, MA), 1999.

Tony Robinson, *Tony Robinson's Kings and Queens,* Red Fox (London, England), 1999.

Jeanne Willis, *The Boy Who Lost His Bellybutton,* Andersen Press (London, England), 1999, Dorling Kindersley (New York, NY), 2000.

Jeanne Willis, *Susan Laughs,* Andersen Press (London, England), 1999, Henry Holt (New York, NY), 2000.

June Crebbin, *Tarquin, the Wonder Horse,* Walker (London, England), 2000.

Jeanne Willis, *What Did I Look like When I Was a Baby?,* G.P. Putnam (New York, NY), 2000.

Laurence Anholt, *Micky the Muckiest Boy,* Orchard (London, England), 2000.

Ian Whybrow, *There's a Spell up My Nose,* Hodder (London, England), 2000.

Ian Whybrow, *Robin Hood's Best Shot,* Hodder (London, England), 2000.

Ian Whybrow, *The Boy Who Had (Nearly) Everything,* Hodder (London, England), 2000.

Adèle Geras, *The Cats of Cuckoo Square: Two Stories,* Delacorte Press (New York, NY), 2001.

Barbara Eupan Todd, *Worzel Gummidge,* new edition, Oxford University Press (Oxford, England), 2001.

Anna Perera, *Skew Whiff,* Oxford University Press (Oxford, England), 2001.

Jan Page, *It's Not Funny,* Corgi Pups (London, England), 2001.

Astrid Lindgren, *Pippi Goes Aboard,* new edition, Oxford University Press (Oxford, England), 2001.

Astrid Lindgren, *Pippi in the South Seas,* new edition, Oxford University Press (Oxford, England), 2001.

Oscar Wilde, *The Picture of Dorian Gray,* new edition, Viking (New York, NY), 2001.

Richmal Crompton, *William and the Bomb, and Other Stories,* adapted by Martin Jarvis, Macmillan (London, England), 2001.

Richmal Crompton, *William the Great Actor, and Other Stories,* adapted by Martin Jarvis, Macmillan (London, England), 2001.

Jon Blake, *One Girl School,* Oxford University Press (Oxford, England), 2001.

Andrew Matthews, reteller, *The Orchard Book of Shakespeare Stories,* Orchard (London, England), 2001, published in eight volumes, 2002–2003.

Jeanne Willis, *Mankey Monkey,* Andersen Press (London, England), 2002.

Jeanne Willis, *Don't Let Go!,* Andersen Press (London, England), 2002, G.P. Putnam (New York, NY), 2003.

Jeanne Willis, *Mark Two,* Andersen Press (London, England), 2002.

Hazel Townson, *The Invisible Boy,* Andersen Press (London, England), 2002.

Paul Stewart, *The Were-Pig,* Corgi Pups (London, England), 2002.

Anne Fine, *How to Cross the Road and Not Turn into a Pizza,* Walker (London, England), 2002.

Charles Causley, *Jack the Treacle-Eater, and Other Poems,* Macmillan (London, England), 2002.

Charles Causley, *Figgie Hobbin, and Other Poems,* Macmillan (London, England), 2002.

Tony Bradman, *The Two Jacks,* Barrington Stoke (Edinburgh, Scotland), 2002.

Jeanne Willis, *I Want to Be a Cowgirl,* Henry Holt (New York, NY), 2002.

Ian Whybrow, *Young Robin's Hood,* Mondo (New York, NY), 2002.

Barbara Mitchelhill, *The Case of the Popstar's Wedding,* Andersen Press (London, England), 2002, Stone Arch Books (Minneapolis, MN), 2007.

Berlie Doherty, *Tilly Mint Tales,* new edition, Young Corgi (London, England), 2003.

Berlie Doherty, *Tricky Nelly's Birthday Treat,* Walker (London, England), 2003.

Margaret Mahy, *The Gargling Gorilla, and Other Stories,* Collins (London, England), 2003.

Jeanne Willis, *Tadpole's Promise,* Andersen Press (London, England), 2003, Atheneum (New York, NY), 2005.

Charles Causley, *The Young Man of Cury, and Other Poems,* new edition, Macmillan (London, England), 2003.

Helen Cresswell, *Lizzie Dripping,* new edition, Oxford University Press (Oxford, England), 2003.

Charles Causley, *All Day Saturday, and Other Poems,* new edition, Macmillan (London, England), 2003.

Adèle Geras, *The Cats of Cuckoo Square: Callie's Kitten,* Dell Yearling Books (New York, NY), 2003.

Adèle Geras, *The Fabulous Fantora Photographs,* Oxford University Press (Oxford, England), 2003.

Adèle Geras, *The Fabulous Fantora Files,* Oxford University Press (Oxford, England), 2003.

Astrid Lindgren, *The Best of Pippi Longstocking,* new edition, Oxford University Press (Oxford, England), 2003.

Tony Bradman, *Ali Baba and the Stolen Treasure,* Orchard (London, England), 2003.

Adélè Geras, *The Cats of Cuckoo Square: Geejay the Hero,* Dell Yearling Books (New York, NY), 2003.

Francesca Simon, *Helping Hercules,* Dolphin (London, England), 2003.

Jeanne Willis, *I Hate School,* Andersen Press (London, England), 2003, Atheneum Books for Young Readers (New York, NY), 2004.

Carol Diggory Shields, *English Fresh Squeezed!: Forty Thirst-for-Knowledge-quenching Poems,* Handprint Books (New York, NY), 2004.

Adrian Mitchell, *Daft as a Doughnut,* Orchard (London, England), 2004.

Barbara Mitchelhill, *How to Be a Detective,* Andersen Press (London, England), 2004, Stone Arch Books (Minneapolis, MN), 2007.

John Foster, compiler, *The Flying Trapeze, and Other Puzzle Poems,* Oxford University Press (Oxford, England), 2004.

Eoin Colfer, *The Legend of Spud Murphy,* Puffin (London, England), 2004.

Tony Bradman, *Robin Hood and the Silver Arrow,* Orchard (London, England), 2004.

Tony Bradman, *William Tell and the Apple for Freedom,* Orchard (London, England), 2004.

Tony Bradman, *Aladdin and the Fabulous Genie,* Orchard (London, England), 2004.

Tony Bradman, *Arthur and the King's Sword,* Orchard (London, England), 2004.

Tony Bradman, *Jason and the Voyage to the Edge of the World,* Orchard (London, England), 2004.

Jeanne Willis, *Shhh!,* Hyperion Books for Children (New York, NY), 2004.

D.J. Lucas (pen name of Sally Grindley), *Dear Max,* Orchard (London, England), 2004, Margaret K. McElderry Books (New York, NY), 2006.

Giles Andrae, *Luke Lancelot and the Treasure of the Kings!,* Puffin (London, England), 2005.

Francesca Simon, *Don't Cook Cinderella,* Dolphin (London, England), 2005.

Eric Brown, *Space Ace,* Barington Stoke (Edinburgh, Scotland), 2005.

John Foster, *The Universal Vacuum Cleaner, and Other Riddle Poems,* Oxford University Press (Oxford, England), 2005.

D.J. Lucas (pen name of Sally Grindley), *Bravo Max,* Orchard (London, England), 2005, Margaret K. McElderry Books (New York, NY), 2007.

Jan Mark, *Robin Hood All at Sea,* Barrington Stoke (Edinburgh, Scotland), 2005.

Jeanne Willis, *Misery Moo,* Henry Holt (New York, NY), 2005.

Jeanne Willis, *Mayfly Day,* Andersen Press (London, England), 2006.

Ian Whybrow, *The Knights of the Brown Table,* Hodder (London, England), 2006.

Ian Whybrow, *The Secret Superhero,* Hodder (London, England), 2006.

Martin Waddell, *The Orchard Book of Goblins, Ghouls, and Ghosts and Other Magical Stories,* Orchard (London, England), 2006.

Eoin Colfer, *The Legend of Captain Crow's Teeth,* Puffin (London, England), 2006.

Lynne Reid Banks, *Harry the Poisonous Centipede Goes to Sea,* HarperCollins (New York, NY), 2006.

Andrew Matthews, reteller, *Much Ado about Nothing: A Shakespeare Story,* Orchard (London, England), 2006.

Andrew Matthews, reteller, *Othello: A Shakespeare Story,* Orchard (London, England), 2006.

Andrew Matthews, reteller, *Richard III: A Shakespeare Story,* Orchard (London, England), 2006.

Jan Mark, *King John and the Abbot,* Barrington Stoke (Edinburgh, Scotland), 2006.

Anne Cassidy, *Sammy and the Starman,* Barrington Stoke (Edinburgh, Scotland), 2006.

Ian Whybrow, *Through the Cat-flap,* Hodder (London, England), 2006.

Ian Whybrow, *Alex, the Walking Accident,* Hodder (London, England), 2006.

Anne Fine, *Notso Hotso,* Farrar, Straus (New York, NY), 2006.

Paul Steward, *Dogbird, and Other Mixed-up Tales,* Corgi Pups (London, England), 2006.

Jeanne Willis, *Gorilla! Gorilla!,* Atheneum (New York, NY), 2006.

Jeanne Willis, *Daft Bat,* Andersen (London, England), 2006, Sterling (New York, NY), 2008.

Jeanne Willis, *The Really Rude Rhino,* Andersen (London, England), 2006.

Barbara Mitchelhill, *Spycatcher,* Andersen Press (London, England), 2006, Stone Arch Books (Minneapolis, MN), 2007.

Zoë Ross, *Nicky,* Andersen Press (London, England), 2007.

Kes Gray, *Nelly the Monstersitter,* Picture Window Books (Minneapolis, MN), 2007.

Barbara Mitchelhill, *The Case of the Disappearing Daughter,* Stone Arch Books (Minneapolis, MN), 2007.

Jeanne Willis, *Grill Pan Eddy,* Andersen Press (London, England), 2007.

Jeanne Willis, *Cottonwool Colin,* Andersen Press (London, England), 2007, published as *Cottonball Colin,* Eerdmans Books for Young Readers (Grand Rapids, MI), 2008.

Barbara Mitchelhill, *Serious Graffiti,* Andersen Press (London, England), 2007, published as *The Graffiti Mystery,* Stone Arch Books (Mankato, MN), 2009.

Jeanne Willis, *Old Dog,* Andersen Press (London, England), 2008.

Jeanne Willis, *Mammoth Pie,* Andersen Press (London, England), 2008.

Hazel Townson, *Deathwood Damian Strikes Again,* Andersen Press (London, England), 2008.

Astrid Lindgren, *Emil's Clever Pig,* new edition, Oxford University Press (Oxford, England), 2008.

Astrid Lindgren, *Emil and the Great Escape,* new edition, Oxford University Press (Oxford, England), 2008.

Astrid Lindgren, *Emil and the Sneaky Rat,* new edition, Oxford University Press (Oxford, England), 2008.

Astrid Lindgren, *Karlson on the Roof,* new edition, Oxford University Press (Oxford, England), 2008.

Astrid Lindgren, *Lotta Makes a Mess!,* new edition, Oxford University Press (Oxford, England), 2008.

Richmal Crompton, *Meet Just William,* adapted by Martin Jarvis, Macmillan (London, England), 2008.

June Crebbin, *Invasion,* Walker (London, England), 2008.

Tony Bradford, *The Orchard Book of Heroes and Villains,* Walker (London, England), 2008.

Jeanne Willis, *Big Bad Bun,* Andersen Press (London, England), 2009.

Jeanne Willis, *Flabby Cat and Slobby Dog,* Lerner (Minneapolis, MN), 2009.

Andrew Matthews, reteller, *Julius Caesar: A Shakespeare Story,* Orchard (London, England), 2009.

Andrew Matthews, reteller, *King Lear: A Shakespeare Story,* Orchard (London, England), 2009.

Andrew Matthews, reteller, *The Merchant of Venice: A Shakespeare Story,* Orchard (London, England), 2009.

Andrew Matthews, reteller, *The Taming of the Shrew: A Shakespeare Story,* Orchard (London, England), 2009.

Astrid Lindgren, *Karlson Flies Again,* new edition, Oxford University Press (Oxford, England), 2009.

Tony Bradman, *Michael,* Andersen Press (London, England), 2009.

Richmal Crompton, *Meet Just William Again,* adapted by Martin Jarvis, Macmillan (London, England), 2009.

Barbara Mitchelhill, *The Mystery of the Missing Mutts,* Stone Arch Books (Mankato, MN), 2009.

Barbara Mitchelhill, *Under Cover,* Andersen Press (London, England), 2009, Stone Arch Books (Mankato, MN), 2011.

Barbara Mitchelhill, *Gruesome Ghosts,* Andersen Press (London, England), 2009, Stone Arch Books (Mankato, MN), 2011.

David Walliams, *Billionaire Boy,* HarperCollins Children's (London, England), 2010.

ILLUSTRATOR; "AMBER BROWN" SERIES BY PAULA DANZIGER

Amber Brown Is Not a Crayon, Putnam (New York, NY), 1994.

Forever Amber Brown, Putnam (New York, NY), 1996.

You Can't Eat Your Chicken Pox, Amber Brown, Putnam (New York, NY), 1996.

Amber Brown Sees Red, Putnam (New York, NY), 1997.

Amber Brown Goes Fourth, Putnam (New York, NY), 1997.

Amber Brown Wants Extra Credit, Putnam (New York, NY), 1997.

Amber Brown Is Feeling Blue, Putnam (New York, NY), 1998.

I, Amber Brown, Putnam (New York, NY), 1999.

It's Justin Time, Amber Brown, Putnam (New York, NY), 2001.

What a Trip, Amber Brown, Putnam (New York, NY), 2001.

Get Ready for Second Grade, Amber Brown, Putnam (New York, NY), 2002.

It's a Fair Day, Amber Brown, Putnam (New York, NY), 2002.

Amber Brown Is Green with Envy, Putnam (New York, NY), 2003.

Second Grade Rules, Amber Brown, Putnam (New York, NY), 2004.

Orange You Glad It's Halloween, Amber Brown?, Putnam (New York, NY), 2005.

ILLUSTRATOR; "MS WIZ" SERIES BY TERENCE BLACKER

In Control, Ms Wiz?, Macmillan (London, England), 1996, Marshall Cavendish (Tarrytown, NY), 2009.

Ms Wiz Spells Trouble, Macmillan (London, England), 1996, Marshall Cavendish (Tarrytown, NY), 2008.

You're Kidding, Ms Wiz, Macmillan (London, England), 1996.

In Stitches with Ms Wiz, Macmillan (London, England), 1996, Marshall Cavendish (Tarrytown, NY), 2008.

Power-Crazy Ms Wiz, Macmillan (London, England), 1997.

Ms Wiz Banned!, Macmillan (London, England), 1997.

Ms Wiz Loves Dracula, Macmillan (London, England), 1997.

Ms Wiz, Supermodel, Macmillan (London, England), 1997.

Ms Wiz Smells a Rat, Macmillan (London, England), 1998.

Ms Wiz and the Sister of Doom, Macmillan (London, England), 1999.

Ms Wiz Goes to Hollywood, Macmillan (London, England), 2000.

Ms Wiz, Millionaire, Macmillan (London, England), 2001.

The Secret Life of Ms Wiz, Macmillan (London, England), 2002.

Ms Wiz Magic (omnibus edition), Macmillan (London, England), 2003.

The Amazing Adventures of Ms Wiz (omnibus edition), Macmillan (London, England), 2003.

Ms Wiz Superstar (omnibus edition), Macmillan (London, England), 2004.

The Crazy World of Ms Wiz (omnibus edition), Macmillan (London, England), 2004.

Ms Wiz Mayhem (omnibus edition), Macmillan (London, England), 2006.

Totally Spaced, Ms Wiz (omnibus edition), Andersen Press (London, England), 2008.

Fangtastic, Ms Wiz (omnibus edition), Andersen Press (London, England), 2008.

Ms Wiz Rocks, Andersen Press (London, England), 2009.

Out of Control, Ms Wiz (omnibus edition), Andersen Press (London, England), 2009.

In Jail, Ms Wiz?, Marshall Cavendish (New York, NY), 2009.

ILLUSTRATOR; "HORRID HENRY" SERIES BY FRANCESCA SIMON

Horrid Henry, Orion Children's Books (London, England), 1994, Sourcebooks Jabberwocky (Naperville, IL), 2009.

Horrid Henry and the Secret Club, Orion Children's (London, England), 1995.

Horrid Henry Tricks the Tooth Fairy, Orion Children's (London, England), 1996, Sourcebooks Jabberwocky (Naperville, IL), 2009.

Horrid Henry's Nits, Orion (London, England), 1997, published as *Horrid Henry's Head Lice,* Hyperion Books for Children (New York, NY), 2000.

Horrid Henry Strikes It Rich, Orion Children's (London, England), 1998, published as *Horrid Henry Gets Rich Quick,* Hyperion Books for Children (New York, NY), 2000.

Horrid Henry's Haunted House, Orion (London, England), 1999.

Horrid Henry's Revenge, Hyperion Books for Children (New York, NY), 2001.

Horrid Henry and the Bogey Babysitter, Dolphin (London, England), 2002.

Horrid Henry's Stinkbomb, Dolphin (London, England), 2002, Sourcebooks Jabberwocky (Naperville, IL), 2009.

A Triple Treat of Horrid Henry, Dolphin (London, England), 2003.

Horrid Henry and the Mummy's Curse, Dolphin (London, England), 2003, Sourcebooks Jabberwocky (Naperville, IL), 2009.

Horrid Henry's Joke Book, Orion Children's (London, England), 2004.

Horrid Henry Meets the Queen (includes audiotape), Dolphin (London, England), 2004.

Horrid Henry's Big Bad Book, Dolphin (London, England), 2004.

Horrid Henry's Wicked Ways, Dolphin (London, England), 2005.

Horrid Henry and the Mega-Mean Time Machine, Dolphin (London, England), 2005, Sourcebooks Jabberwocky (Naperville, IL), 2009.

Horrid Henry's Evil Enemies, Orion (London, England), 2006.

Horrid Henry's Christmas Cracker, Orion (London, England), 2006, published as *Horrid Henry's Christmas,* Sourcebooks Jabberwocky (Naperville, IL), 2009.

A Giant Slice of Horrid Henry (omnibus edition), Orion (London, England), 2006.

Horrid Henry and the Football Fiend, Orion (London, England), 2006, published as *Horrid Henry and the Soccer Fiend,* Sourcebooks Jabberwocky (Naperville, IL), 2009.

Horrid Henry and the Abominable Snowman, Orion (London, England), 2007.

Horrid Henry Rules the World, Orion (London, England), 2007.

A Hat Trick of Horrid Henry (omnibus edition), Orion (London, England), 2007.

Horrid Henry's Jolly Joke Book, Orion (London, England), 2007.

Horrid Henry's Mighty Joke Book, Orion (London, England), 2008.

Horrid Henry Robs the Bank, Orion (London, England), 2008.

Horrid Henry's House of Horrors, Orion (London, England), 2008.

Don't Be Horrid, Henry, Orion (London, England), 2008.

Horrid Henry's Birthday Party, Orion (London, England), 2009.

Horrid Henry vs. Moody Margaret, Orion (London, England), 2009.

Horrid Henry's Holiday, Orion (London, England), 2009.

Horrid Henry and the Scary Sitter, Sourcebooks Jabberwocky (Naperville, IL), 2009.

Horrid Henry's Underpants, Sourcebooks (Naperville, IL), 2009.

ILLUSTRATOR; "LITTLE WOLF" SERIES BY IAN WHYBROW

Little Wolf's Haunted Hall for Small Horrors, Collins (London, England), 1998, Carolrhoda Books (Minneapolis, MN), 2000.

Little Wolf's Book of Badness: A Little Wolf and Smellybreff Adventure, Carolrhoda Books (Minneapolis, MN), 1999.

Little Wolf's Diary of Daring Deeds, Carolrhoda Books (Minneapolis, MN), 2000.

Little Wolf, Forest Detective, Andersen Press (London, England), 2000, Carolrhoda Books (Minneapolis, MN), 2001.

Little Wolf's Big Book of Spooks and Clues, Omnibus (London, England), 2000.

Dear Little Wolf, First Avenue Editions (Minneapolis, MN), 2002.

Little Wolf's Handy Book of Poems, First Avenue Editions (Minneapolis, MN), 2002.

Little Wolf, Pack Leader, Carolrhoda Books (Minneapolis, MN), 2002.

Little Wolf, Terror of the Shivery Sea, Carolrhoda Books (Minneapolis, MN), 2004.

Badness for Beginners: A Little Wolf and Smellybreff Adventure, Carolrhoda Books (Minneapolis, MN), 2005.

What's the Time, Little Wolf?, Carolrhoda Books (Minneapolis, MN), 2006.

ILLUSTRATOR; "SIR GADABOUT" SERIES BY MARTYN BEARDSLEY

Sir Gadabout Does His Best, Dolphin (London, England), 2001.

Sir Gadabout and the Little Horror, Dolphin (London, England), 2002.

Sir Gadabout Goes Overboard, Dolphin (London, England), 2004.

Sir Gadabout Goes Barking Mad, Dolphin (London, England), 2005.

Sir Gadabout, Orion Children's Books (London, England), 2006.

Sir Gadabout Gets Worse, Orion Children's Books (London, England), 2006.

Sir Gadabout Goes to Knight School, Orion Children's Books (London, England), 2006.

Sir Gadabout Out of Time, Orion (London, England), 2007.

Sir Gadabout: Three Books in One (omnibus edition), Orion (London, England), 2007.

Sir Gadabout and the Camelot Calamity, Orion (London, England), 2008.

OTHER

Author of animated television films, including *What's in a Name?, King of All the Birds, Oscar Buys the Biscuits, Muddy Milly,* and *Spacemare.* Contributor of cartoons to magazines, including *Punch* and *Town.*

Adaptations

I'm Coming to Get You! was adapted as a filmstrip; King Rollo Films and Abbey Home Entertainment produced several videos based on Ross's work, including *I Want a Cat;* several of Ross's books have been adapted for television; the "Little Princess" books were adapted as an animated television series, broadcast on England's Channel 5 beginning 2006.

Sidelights

The work of award-winning British author and illustrator Tony Ross is well known to both young children and their parents. As exhibited in the books *I'm Coming to Get You!, Centipede's 100 Shoes,* and *I Want Two Birthdays!,* Ross's whimsical watercolor and pen-and-ink art appeals to bookworms from infancy to pre-teen, and his popular self-illustrated "Little Princess" stories inspired an animated television series broadcast in his native England. A large part of his success, Ross noted in a HarperCollins Canada Web site interview, is due to the respect he shows his audience. "Very young children I feel are very perceptive, I don't think it works to be too condescending with them so one or two difficult words are quite good and one or two difficult concepts are quite good," he remarked. "I don't write down to children; I try to understand their world and write up to it."

When he first hit the picture-book scene in the mid-1970s, Ross's unique illustration style attracted critical attention. He earned his first major award, a prestigious Kate Greenaway medal commendation, in 1986, for *I'm Coming to Get You.* "Ross's literary tale-telling favours a deadpan humour and aims to establish intimacy with the reader," observed Jane Doonan in her essay for *Twentieth-Century Children's Writers.* "His visual style varies considerably, but whatever he does, he always

Tony Ross captures an imperious young lady who practices giving orders like a grownup in his humorous self-illustrated **Wash Your Hands!** (Kane-Miller, 2000. Reproduced by permission.)

displays a strong sense of page design, and a masterly control of his media. Deceptively sketchy at times, his pen romps along, in the tradition of English narrative illustration. However whiskery fine, feathery light, frothy, bold, or meticulously incised, the line has unquenchable vitality."

Ross was born in London but grew up near Liverpool. He more or less drifted into art school at age eighteen, abandoning his early dream of working with horses. While in college, he sold drawings to magazines such as _New Statesman_ and _Punch,_ but rather than pursuing art after graduation he found more lucrative work in advertising and publicity firms. Ross made his entrance into the world of book illustration while teaching advertising part time at Manchester Polytechnic. Recalling that period in a British Council Web site interview with Kristina Hedderly, Ross explained: "I went into advertising and disliked it so much that I would spend my time writing a children's book while my boss wasn't looking. There was free paper, pencils and colours at the agency and I used all of those and wrote my first book there." The result, the six-volume _Tales from Mr Toffy's Circus,_ was released in 1973.

Within a decade Ross was able to support himself and his family by writing and drawing. As he was quoted as saying in _Twentieth-Century Children's Writers,_ "the motivation, of course, is the enjoyment a pen and a sheet of blank paper brings—certainly to me, every time, hopefully to others."

Since beginning his career, Ross has developed a distinctive drawing style which involves the black lines and transparent blocks of vivid color characteristic of graphic art. In _I'm Coming to Get You!,_ for instance, his "illustrations are in colors as loud as a yell, rendered in a scratchy fashion that intensifies the speedy effects," as a _Publishers Weekly_ reviewer commented. The net effect of Ross's animated line and "strong contrasts of light and dark and big and little" is, according to _Wilson Library Bulletin_ critics Donnarae MacCann and Olga Richard, a "sly, ebullient humor."

Ross shares this "sly, ebullient humor" with readers through both original stories and retellings or adaptations of traditional tales. _Super Dooper Jezebel,_ for instance, "is typical Ross from the zany cartoon-style watercolors to the ironic biting humor," as Heide Pilcher declared in _School Library Journal._ In _Lazy Jack_ the illustrator's "spacious watercolors add narrative twists of their own to this traditional tale," as a critic noted in the _Bulletin of the Center for Children's Books._ _Lazy Jack_ "is tongue-in-cheek, the art absurd, [and] the overall effect a super-silly read aloud," the critic added. In _Three Little Kittens and Other Favorite Nursery Rhymes_ Ross collects forty-nine childhood classics, including "There Was a Crooked Man" and "Little Miss Muffet." He "illustrates the rhymes with . . . an underlying sense of droll humor that suits them well," Carolyn Phelan noted in her _Booklist_ review of the work.

Ross's "Little Princess" books find an impatient but lovable young girl dealing with common childhood experiences. In _I Want Two Birthdays!_ the Little Princess learns that sometimes less is more after she convinces everyone in the kingdom to celebrate her birthday 365 days a year. "Ross's zany cartoon-style illustrations capture the princess' impulsive, egocentric nature," _Booklist_ critic Linda Perkins reported. In _School Library Journal_ Rachel Kamin applauded "the eccentric and memorable characters" found in _I Want My Light On!,_ a tale about overcoming fears. The "Little Princess" series also earned plaudits from Linda Staskus, who wrote in her _School Library Journal_ review of _I Want My Tooth_ that Ross's "lighthearted text" and softly colored pen-and-ink drawings present youngsters with "a good-humored and different take on a common childhood experience."

Ross's willingness to sometimes break with tradition gives his work a uniquely funny viewpoint. However, it is the combination of pictures and words that makes his books so enjoyable, according to a _Horn Book_ reviewer. The artist's illustrations "add much to the humor," the critic asserted, "interacting with the text in a lively interchange that enriches and extends both." Ross's work is distinguished by his "comic imagination and a superb sense of theater," MacCann and Richard stated. As a result, they concluded, "it is hard to think of many cartoonists in recent years who have developed as rapidly as Ross with both a comic touch and a serious design interest."

His particular strengths as an illustrator have allowed Ross to develop winning collaborations with a number of popular children's-book writers, among them Paula Danziger, Lynne Reid Banks, Francesca Simon, Jeanne Willis, and Ian Whybrow. Perhaps most well known to American readers is his work for Danziger's popular "Amber Brown" series. Amber Brown is a typical third grader whose joys and troubles reflect the issues pertinent to her age group. Ross's illustrations reveal a freckled, gangly, and sometimes scruffy Amber as well as her pals and her surroundings. _Horn Book_ correspondent Maeve Visser Knoth observed that both the text and drawings in _Amber Brown Is Not a Crayon_ are "well suited to the audience," while in _Booklist_ Hazel Rochman concluded: "Ross's cartoon-style illustrations capture Amber's vital classroom—the fun and the fights, as well as the empty place when a friend moves away." As Amber makes the move to fourth grade in _Amber Brown Is Green with Envy,_ Michele Shaw wrote in _School Library Journal_ that Ross intrigues readers with the girl's attempts to deal with changes in her life. His "black-and-white drawings show Amber's humorous facial expressions" as she grapples with her mother's upcoming remarriage, the possibility of moving to a new house, and the frustration of being left behind when her mom and aunt take a trip to Disneyland.

Ross's "imaginative drawings" in Reid Banks's multi-volume "Harry the Poisonous Centipede" saga, featur-

Ross's illustration work includes a collaboration with writer Jeanne Willis on the picture book **Flabby Cat and Slobby Dog.** (Andersen Press, 2009. Illustration copyright © 2009 by Tony Ross. Reproduced by permission.)

ing the adventures of a teenaged centipede, "enhance" the author's verbal hijinks, including her ability to tell her tale from a "limited, centipede linguistic perspective," as Kay Weisman noted in *Booklist.* Simon's "Horrid Henry" books center on a child "whose general meanness goes entirely unchecked," according to *School Library Journal* critic Pat Leach. In this series "Ross's hyperbolic line art will engage even the most reluctant readers," predicted a contributor in *Publishers Weekly,* and Jackie Partch, writing in *School Library Journal,* stated of the series that the "cartoon drawings are a perfect match for the protagonist's mischievous personality."

In such books as Whybrow's *Little Wolf's Book of Badness: A Little Wolf and Smellybreff Adventure* and *Little Wolf's Diary of Daring Deeds* "Ross's colorful line drawings are hysterically appealing, adding to the humor" of Whybrow's "lively and irreverent" storyline, according to Robyn Walker's *School Library Journal* appraisal of the former title. Ross has also contributed the illustrations to Terence Blacker's popular "Ms Wiz" series, about a curiously effective teacher who magically transforms a group of troublemakers into star pupils. Elaine E. Knight, writing in *School Library Journal,* noted that the "angular black-and-white drawings" in the "Ms Wiz" books "complement the sometimes wacky plotlines."

Ross and Willis have paired their talents on more than two dozen works, among them *Gorilla! Gorilla!,* a humorous tale about a case of mistaken identity involving a frightened mouse and the gorilla that frantically pursues her. In the words of *School Library Journal* reviewer Kathleen Kelly MacMillan, "Ross's bright pastel illustrations capture the mouse's fear and the gorilla's determination with verve." An overprotective mother wraps her youngest like a mummy to keep him safe from bumps and bruises, only to see her plan backfire in spectacular fashion, in *Cottonball Colin,* another title by Willis. Here Ross's watercolor paintings "take Colin from domestic comedy to thrilling action-adventure without a hitch," as a critic noted in *Publishers Weekly.* In *Flabby Cat and Slobby Dog* a pair of overweight couch potatoes embarks on several misadventures after they outgrow their lodgings. Ross's illustrations display their "customary energy and wry wit," according to a *Publishers Weekly* contributor.

In an interview posted on the HarperCollins Canada Web site, Ross discussed the philosophy that guides his illustration work. "I'm aware of the fact that with a picture book, a simple book, once the child has read it, I like them to be able to read it again and find something else that wasn't evident the first time," he explained. "I think it's important that a book can be read over and over again, and not give up everything on the first reading. So in a child-like attempt to make this happen I put little sub-plots, little bits of detail and little things that are really quite obscure, which may emerge in time."

Biographical and Critical Sources

BOOKS

Twentieth-Century Children's Writers, 4th edition, St. James (Detroit, MI), 1995, pp. 827-829.

PERIODICALS

Booklist, April 15, 1994, Hazel Rochman, review of *Amber Brown Is Not a Crayon,* p. 1533; October 15, 1994, Ilene Cooper, review of *The Second Princess,* p. 438; January 1, 1996, Carolyn Phelan, review of *Animals,* p. 838; June 1, 1998, Annie Ayres, review of *Sloth's Shoes,* p. 1785; May 15, 2001, Roger Leslie, review of *The Picture of Dorian Gray,* p. 1746; August 1, 2006, Kay Weisman, review of *Dear Max,* p. 86; October 15, 2006, Kay Weisman, review of *Harry the Poisonous Centipede Goes to Sea,* p. 44; February 1, 2009, Carolyn Phelan, review of *Three Little Kittens and Other Favorite Nursery Rhymes,* p. 45; May 15, 2009, Ilene Cooper, review of *Horrid Henry,* p. 46; February 1, 2010, Linda Perkins, review of *I Want Two Birthdays!,* p. 50.
Bulletin of the Center for Children's Books, July-August, 1986, review of *Lazy Jack,* p. 217.
Horn Book, July-August, 1994, Maeve Visser Knoth, review of *Amber Brown Is Not a Crayon,* p. 447; September-October, 2006, Susan Dove Lempke, review of *Gorilla! Gorilla!,* p. 573.
Kirkus Reviews, March 1, 2003, review of *Centipede's 100 Shoes,* p. 397; June 15, 2004, review of *I Hate School,* p. 583; May 15, 2005, review of *Tadpole's Promise,* p. 597; February 15, 2006, review of *Notso Hotso,* p. 182; May 1, 2006, review of *Gorilla! Gorilla!,* p. 470; March 1, 2007, review of *Bravo, Max!,* p. 222; July 15, 2008, review of *Ms Wiz;* March 1, 2009, review of *Three Little Kittens and Other Favorite Nursery Rhymes.*
Publishers Weekly, October 26, 1984, review of *I'm Coming to Get You!,* p. 104; February 24, 2003, review of *Centipede's 100 Shoes,* p. 70; August 7, 2006, review of *Dear Max,* p. 59; November 27, 2006, review of *Dogbird, and Other Mixed-up Tales,* p. 51; September 12, 2005, review of *Badness for Beginners: A Little Wolf and Smellybreff Adventure,* p. 68; August 7, 2006, review of *Dear Max,* p. 59; January 21, 2008, review of *Cottonball Colin,* p. 169; February 18, 2008, review of *Sir Gadabout,* p. 155; March 9, 2009, review of *Horrid Henry,* p. 47; March 16, 2009, review of *Three Little Kittens and Other Favorite Nursery Rhymes,* p. 60; August 31, 2009, review of *Flabby Cat and Slobby Dog,* p. 58.
School Library Journal, December, 1988, Heide Pieler, review of *Super Dooper Jezebel,* p. 92; March, 2001, Pat Leach, review of *Horrid Henry's Head Lice,* p.

220; May, 2001, Carrie Schadle, review of *Harry the Poisonous Centipede's Big Adventure,* p. 108; July, 2002, Ruth Semrau, review of *I Want to Be a Cowgirl,* p. 102; May, 2003, Pat Leach, review of *Little Wolf, Pack Leader,* p. 132; September, 2003, Michele Shaw, review of *Amber Brown Is Green with Envy,* p. 176; August, 2004, Marian Creamer, review of *I Hate School,* p. 104; September, 2005, Robyn Walker, review of *Badness for Beginners,* p. 188; October, 2005, Linda Staskus, review of *I Want My Tooth,* p. 127; March, 2006, Catherine Threadgill, review of *Notso Hotso,* p. 187; July, 2006, Kathleen Kelly MacMillan, review of *Gorilla! Gorilla!,* p. 90; September, 2006, Alison Grant, review of *Harry the Poisonous Centipede Goes to Sea,* p. 158; May, 2005, Joy Fleishhacker, review of *Tadpole's Promise,* p. 104; August, 2006, Nicki Clausen-Grace, review of *Dear Max,* p. 88; April, 2007, Cheryl Ashton, review of *Bravo, Max!,* p. 106; April, 2008, Linda Ludke, review of *Cottonball Colin,* p. 126; December, 2008, Elaine E. Knight, reviews of *In Stitches with Ms Wiz* and *Ms Wiz Spells Trouble,* both p. 84; April, 2009, Terrie Dorio, reviews of *Horrid Henry* and *Horrid Henry and the Mega-Mean Time Machine,* both p. 116, and Jackie Partch, reviews of *Horrid Henry Tricks the Tooth Fairy* and *Horrid Henry's Stinkbomb,* both p. 116; October, 2009, Maureen Wade, review of *Horrid Henry's Christmas,* p. 83, and Susan E. Murray, review of *Flabby Cat and Slobby Dog,* p. 108; March, 2010, Maryann H. Owen, review of *I Want Two Birthdays!,* p. 130; August, 2010, Rachel Kamin, review of *I Want My Light On!,* p. 85.
Wilson Library Bulletin, January, 1979, Donnarae MacCann and Olga Richard, review of *Hugo and Oddsock,* p. 378.

ONLINE

Andersen Press Web site, http://www.andersenpress.co.uk/ (February 1, 2011), "Tony Ross."
British Council Web site, http://www.britishcouncil.org/ (autumn, 2006), Kristina Hedderly, interview with Ross.
Contemporary Writers Web site, http://www.contemporary writer.com/ (February 1, 2011), "Tony Ross."
HarperCollins Web site, http://www.harpercollinschildrens books.co.uk/ (February 1, 2011), "Tony Ross."
HarperCollins Canada Web site, http://www.harpercollins. ca/ (February 1, 2011), interview with Ross.
Horrid Henry Web site, http://www.horridhenry.co.uk/ (February 1, 2011).*

*   *   *

RUBINGER, Ami 1953-

Personal

Born 1953, in Israel.

Addresses

Home—Tel-Aviv, Israel.

Career

Illustrator and author of children's books. *Haaretz* (daily newspaper), Tel Aviv, Israel, former staff illustrator; *Yedioth Ahronoth* (daily newspaper), Tel Aviv, Israel, former illustrator and editorial cartoonist; freelance illustrator and author.

Writings

SELF-ILLUSTRATED

Hatul gadol, hatul katan, Keter (Jerusalem, Israel), 2007, translated from the Hebrew by Ray Baitner as *Big Cat, Small Cat,* Abbeville Kids (New York, NY), 2008.

Pilim bhol hazvaim, Keter (Jerusalem, Israel), 2009, translated from the Hebrew by Ray Baitner as *I Dream of an Elephant,* Abbeville Kids (New York, NY), 2010.

Dog Number One, Dog Number 10, Abbeville Kids (New York, NY), 2011.

Also author/illustrator of picture book *Bobbie bo Bobbie Lech.*

OTHER

Illustrator of books by Shaharitah Yehudai, Beni Cohen, No'ah Blas, Rimonah Di-Nur, Amnon Shiloh, Shelomoh Abas, Chava Chavushi, Nirah Ruso, Dorit Orgad, David Sela, Yoram Afek, Yif'at Golan, Micha Shagrir, and Semadar Shir, all published in Hebrew.

Biographical and Critical Sources

PERIODICALS

Booklist, September 15, 2009, Ilene Cooper, review of *Big Cat, Small Cat,* p. 62.

Kirkus Reviews, July 1, 2009, review of *Big Cat, Small Cat.*

Publishers Weekly, August 24, 2009, review of *Big Cat, Small Cat,* p. 60.

School Library Journal, November, 2009, Gay Lynn van Vleck, review of *Big Cat, Small Cat,* p. 87; June, 2010, Judith Constantinides, review of *I Dream of an Elephant,* p. 82.*

S

SCHRADER, Dave 1967(?)-

Personal

Born c. 1967, in IL; married; children: seven. *Education:* Winona State College, degree.

Addresses

Home—Blaine, MN. *E-mail*—dave@darknessradio.com.

Career

Media personality, ghost hunter, and author. KLTK FM, Minneapolis, MN, co-host, with Tim Dennis, of "Darkness on the Edge of Town" (radio program), beginning 2006, and host of paranormal weekend retreats. Co-host of Web event *Ghost Adventures Live,* 2009; speaker at paranormal conferences.

Writings

(With Marley Gibson and Patrick Burns) *The Other Side: A Teen's Guide to Ghost Hunting and the Paranormal,* Houghton Mifflin Harcourt (Boston, MA), 2009.

Contributor to *TAPS Paramagazine.*

Sidelights

Best known as host of the paranormal radio program "Darkness on the Edge of Town," which is produced weekly and accessible online, Dave Schrader admits to witnessing ghostly apparitions, hearing disembodied voices, and seeing a mysterious airborne creature in the skies over an area know for its U.F.O. sightings. In addition to their work on radio, Schrader and his co-host, Tim Dennis, host paranormal retreats to sites of well-known hauntings throughout the United States. He also shares his knowledge of the paranormal in *The Other Side: A Teen's Guide to Ghost Hunting and the Paranormal,* which was coauthored by Marley Gibson and Patrick Burns.

Raised in Illinois, Schrader relocated to Minnesota as a student at Winona State College and stayed. His interest in the spirit world began much earlier, however: a spectral visit from his late grandmother remains one of his most vivid childhood memories. Grandmother returned again when Schrader was an adult: during the birth of his first son, he saw her assisting at the childbirth. He teamed up with Dennis, a Minnesota native, due to their shared interest in the supernatural and paranormal, and in the fall of 2006 "Darkness on the Edge of Town" went on the air. With celebrity guests who speak on topics ranging from grey aliens and serial killers to horror movies, automatic writing, and satanic infiltration, Schrader's radio program taps a widely held and growing fascination with the paranormal and has earned a wide audience.

Benefitting from Schrader's expertise, *The Other Side* takes a pragmatic approach to its topic, outlining the dos and don'ts of ghost hunting. Although the book features a lighthearted tone, the coauthors encourage readers to gain permission to enter private property, bring an adult along when stalking spirits, and always inform

Dave Schrader and his coauthors explore such amazing feats as a woman who can transport objects with her mind in the paranormal guidebook **The Other Side.** (Houghton Mifflin Harcourt, 2009. Photograph by Fred Shannon courtesy of Columbus Dispatch. Reproduced by permission.)

parents of their intended whereabouts. They also include a multicultural perspective, noting the death traditions and beliefs regarding the afterlife that are held by a variety of faith traditions. Reviewing *The Other Side,* Misti Tidman praised the work as a "succinct introduction," adding in her *School Library Journal* review that "the authors take a light, conversational tone even when discussing technical aspects of ghost hunting."

Biographical and Critical Sources

PERIODICALS

School Library Journal, March, 2010, Misti Tidman, review of *The Other Side: A Teen's Guide to Ghost Hunting and the Paranormal,* p. 176.
Star Tribune (Minneapolis, MN), December 6, 2006, David La Vaque, "Signals from Another World," p. N1; October 9, 2009, Tom Horgen, interview with Schrader, p. E3.

ONLINE

30oddminutes Web log, http://www.30oddminutes.com/ (June 9, 2010), "Kids and the Paranormal with Dave Schrader" (video interview).
Darkness on the Edge of Town Web site, http://www.darknessradio.com (January 15, 2011), "Dave Schrader."*

*   *   *

SNIR, Eleyor

Personal

Born in Israel; daughter of Israel and Mirik (a children's author) Snir; married; husband's name Yaron; children: Sol, Eliana, Gala. *Education:* Bachelor's degree (graphic design and illustration), 1999.

Addresses

Home—Hibat Zion, Israel. *E-mail*—info@petel-design. com.

Career

Clothing designer and illustrator. Petel Kids Clothing, Israel, owner and designer.

Member

Society of Children's Book Writers and Illustrators.

Awards, Honors

Gold Award, National Parenting Publications Awards, 2009, for *When I First Held You* by Mirik Snir.

Illustrator

Mirik Snir, *When I First Held You: A Lullaby from Israel,* translated from the Hebrew by Mary Jane Shubow, Kar-Ben Publishing (Minneapolis, MN), 2009.

Biographical and Critical Sources

PERIODICALS

Kirkus Reviews, August 15, 2009, review of *When I First Held You: A Lullaby from Israel.*
Publishers Weekly, October 5, 2009, review of *When I First Held You,* p. 46.
School Library Journal, November, 2009, Heidi Estrin, review of *When I First Held You,* p. 89.

ONLINE

Eleyor Snir Home Page, http://www.eleyor.com (December 28, 2010).*

*   *   *

SPILLEBEEN, Geert 1956-

Personal

Born 1956, in Belgium. *Education:* College degree.

Addresses

Home—Izegem, Belgium. *E-mail*—geert.spillebeen@ euronet.be.

Career

Journalist and author. Former high-school teacher of Dutch, economics, and English; Radio 1, Brussels, Belgium, radio host for eleven years, then journalist.

Awards, Honors

Best Book for Young Adults designation, American Library Association and Young Adult Library Services Association, and Outstanding International Book designation, U.S. Board on Books for Young People/Children's Book Council, all 2006, all for *Kipling's Choice.*

Writings

Zomer in Passendale, Altiora (Averbode, Belgium), 1998.
Age 14, Altiora (Averbode, Belgium), 2000, translated by Terese Edelstein, Houghton Mifflin Harcourt (Boston, MA), 2009.
Kiplings Keuze, Uitgeverij Altiora (Averbode, Belgium), 2002, translated by Terese Edelstein as *Kipling's Choice,* Houghton Mifflin (Boston, MA), 2005.

Man tegen de muur (adult novel), Davidsfons (Leuven, Belgium), 2005.
Abdous oorlog, Davidsfonds (Leuven, Belgium), 2006.

Also author of *Brownsea Boy Scouts in Flanders Fields: De eerste scouts ter wereld,* 2007.

Sidelights

Geert Spillebeen is well known in his native Belgium for his work on Radio 1, a Brussels-based station for which he has been both a morning news broadcaster and journalist. As a reporter covering world events, Spillebeen traveled throughout the globe and often found himself in war-torn areas such as the African Sudan and Sierra Leone. In addition to experiencing the horrors of modern warfare first hand through his travels, he grew up in Flanders, an area of Belgium that experienced brutal combat during World War I and where the battlefields and trenches, as well as the graves of the fallen, are a continuing reminder of the violence of the "War to End All Wars." "World War I and its traces . . . can still teach us some interesting lessons about the uselessness of any war nowadays," Spillebeen noted on his home page. Drawing on his historical knowledge and his gift for narrative, he shares these lessons in his books for children, two of which have been translated into English as *Age 14* and *Kipling's Choice.*

Raised in Ireland, Patrick Condon, the young hero of *Age 14*, dreams only of escape, and for him a post in the military seems like the only way to escape Ireland's poverty. Twelve years old in 1913, but tall for his age, Patrick enlists in the British Army by impersonating his seventeen-year-old brother, John. Patrick does not look the part of a teenager, but his enthusiasm for army life prompts his supervisors to ignore the fact that he is underage. When war breaks out the following year and Great Britain finds herself battling the Germans, Patrick suddenly finds himself in another situation where there is no escape. His regiment is sent to Belgium to fight in the trenches of Ypres, a city in the Dutch region of Flanders, which borders France, and where thousands of young men would lose their lives in the battles of Ypres, Passchendaele, and the Lys. Praised by *Booklist* contributor Hazel Rochman as a "spare, powerful novel," *Age 14* brings to life Patrick's "shocking loss of innocence when confronted with horrific slaughter." In "unadorned prose" Spillebeen "expresses unsettling truths in straightforward, clear terms," wrote a *Publishers Weekly* critic, and in *School Library Journal* Kristin Anderson praised *Age 14* as "a fine historical novel" in which the depiction of the "brutality and boredom of life as a soldier" is enhanced by painstaking research. Describing Spillebeen's middle-grade novel as "riveting," a *Kirkus Reviews* writer was equally laudatory, noting that *Age 14* "reminds readers of the world's many child soldiers as it sledgehammers the notion of glorifying war."

Published in its original Dutch as *Kiplings Keuze, Kipling's Choice* is based on the true story of British au-

Cover of Geert Spillebeen's World War I-era novel **Age 14**, *which focus on a young teen's experiences in the trenches in Europe.* (Jacket art copyright © 2009 by Richard Tuschman. Reproduced by permission of Houghton Mifflin Harcourt Publishing Company.)

thor Rudyard Kipling and his son John. For Kipling, a military life was the pinnacle of manly success, and when it was denied him due to his poor eyesight, he sought it for his son. In 1914, as war erupted throughout Europe, John courted his father's approval by applying for the army. Tragically, the son's nearsightedness was as bad as the father's, but through Rudyard's influence the eighteen year old was awarded a commission as a second lieutenant in an Irish regiment. "More reflective than suspenseful," according to a *Publishers Weekly* contributor, John's narrative in *Kipling's Choice* "subtly conveys the complexities and ironies of the father/son relationship" in addition to focusing on life at the front lines during World War I. Comparing the work to Michael Morpurgo's award-winning novel *Private Peaceful,* Rochman noted in *Booklist* that "the power of this story is in the contrast between the war and the home front." "A riveting account of World War I, *Kipling's Choice* could become the next great war novel," concluded Pat Bender in *School Library Journal,* and a *Kirkus Reviews* critic asserted that Spillibeen's "powerful anti-war novel deserves a place beside [Erich-Maria Remarque's] *All Quiet on the Western Front.*"

Biographical and Critical Sources

PERIODICALS

Booklist, May 15, 2005, Hazel Rochman, review of *Kipling's Choice,* p. 1671; September 1, 2009, Hazel Rochman, review of *Age 14,* p. 79.

Kirkus Reviews, May 1, 2005, review of *Kipling's Choice;* September 15, 2009, review of *Age 14.*

Publishers Weekly, April 18, 2005, review of *Kipling's Choice,* p. 64; October 19, 2009, review of *Age 14,* p. 55.

School Library Journal, June, 2005, Pat Bender, review of *Kipling's Choice,* p. 170; November, 2009, Kristin Anderson, review of *Age 14,* p. 122.

ONLINE

Geert Spillebeen Home Page, http://users.telenet.be/geert. spillebeen1 (January 15, 2011).*

*   *   *

SPINELLI, Eileen 1942-

Personal

Born August 16, 1942, in Philadelphia, PA; daughter of Joseph Patrick (an engineer) and Angela Marie Mesi; married Jerry Spinelli (a writer), May 21, 1977; children: six. *Religion:* Christian. *Hobbies and other interests:* Travel, herb gardening, old movies, anything to do with tea: tea parties, afternoon tea, collecting teapots.

Addresses

Home and office—Wayne, PA. *E-mail*—eileen@eileen-spinelli.com.

Career

Writer, 1960—. Teacher of creative writing; formerly worked as a secretary, waitress, and telephone receptionist.

Member

Authors Guild, Authors League, Society of Children's Book Writers and Illustrators.

Awards, Honors

Children's Choices designation, International Reading Association/Children's Book Council (IRA/CBC), Carolyn W. Field Award Honor designation, Pennsylvania Library Association, and Christopher Award, all 1990, all for *Somebody Loves You, Mr. Hatch;* Pick of the Lists selection, American Booksellers Association, 1998, for *Sophie's Masterpiece;* Oppenheim Toy Portfolio Platinum Award, 1999, for *When Mama Comes Home Tonight;* North Carolina Children's Book Award nomination, 2001, for *Lizzie Logan, Second Banana;* Bank Street College of Education Best Children's Books of the Year award, 2001, for *In My New Yellow Shirt,* 2003, for *Here Comes the Year; Storytelling World* Award, 2002, for *Sophie's Masterpiece;* Cooperative Children's Book Center Choice designation, 2003, for *Wanda's Monster;* Best Children's Books of the Year selection, Bank Street College of Education, 2003, for *Here Comes the Year;* Carolyn W. Field Award, Pennsylvania Library Association, 2004, for *Do You Have a Hat?;* Children's Choices designation, IRA/CBC, and Our Choice designation, Canadian Children's Book Centre, both 2005, both for *Something to Tell the Grandcows;* Best Children's Books of the Year, Bank Street College of Education, 2005, for *Now It Is Winter.*

Writings

The Giggle and Cry Book, illustrated by Lisa Atherton, Stemmer House (Owings Mills, MD), 1981.

Thanksgiving at the Tappletons', illustrated by Maryann Cocca-Leffler, Addison-Wesley (Reading, MA), 1982, new edition illustrated by Megan Lloyd, HarperCollins (New York, NY), 2003.

Animals of the North, illustrated by Laura D'Argo, New Seasons, 1990.

Teddy Bear and His Friends, illustrated by Mike Muir, New Seasons, 1990.

Somebody Loves You, Mr. Hatch, illustrated by Paul Yalowitz, Bradbury Press (New York, NY), 1991, reprinted, 2006.

Boy, Can He Dance!, illustrated by Paul Yalowitz, Four Winds Press (New York, NY), 1993.

If You Want to Find Golden, illustrated by Stacey Schuett, Albert Whitman (Morton Grove, IL), 1993.

Lizzie Logan Wears Purple Sunglasses, illustrated by Melanie Hope Greenberg, Simon & Schuster (New York, NY), 1995.

Naptime, Laptime, illustrated by Melissa Sweet, Cartwheel Books (New York, NY), 1995.

Where Is the Night Train Going?: Bedtime Poems, Boyds Mills Press (Honesdale, PA), 1996.

Lizzie Logan Gets Married, Simon & Schuster (New York, NY), 1997.

Lizzie Logan, Second Banana, Simon & Schuster (New York, NY), 1998.

Sophie's Masterpiece: A Spider's Tale, illustrated by Jane Dyer, Simon & Schuster (New York, NY), 1998.

Sadie Plays House: A Really Messy Sticker Book!, illustrated by Margeaux Lucas, Little Simon (New York, NY), 1998.

When Mama Comes Home Tonight, illustrated by Jane Dyer, Simon & Schuster (New York, NY), 1998.

Coming through the Blizzard: A Christmas Story, Simon & Schuster (New York, NY), 1999.

Tea Party Today: Poems to Sip and Savor, illustrated by Karen Dugan, Boyds Mills Press (Honesdale, PA), 1999.

Night Shift Daddy, illustrated by Melissa Iwai, Hyperion Books for Children (New York, NY), 2000.

Song for the Whooping Crane, illustrated by Elsa Warnick, Eerdmans (Grand Rapids, MI), 2000.

Six Hogs on a Scooter, Orchard Books (New York, NY), 2000.

In My New Yellow Shirt, illustrated by Hideko Takahashi, Henry Holt (New York, NY), 2001.

A Safe Place Called Home, illustrated by Christy Hale, Marshall Cavendish (New York, NY), 2001.

Kittycat Lullaby, illustrated by Anne Mortimer, Hyperion Books for Children (New York, NY), 2001.

Summerbath, Winterbath, illustrated by Elsa Warnick, Eerdmans (Grand Rapids, MI), 2001.

Summerhouse Time, illustrated by Emily Lisker, Simon & Schuster (New York, NY), 2001, illustrated by Joanne Lew-Vriethoff, Knopf (New York, NY), 2007.

Here Comes the Year, illustrated by Keiko Narahashi, Henry Holt (New York, NY), 2002.

Inside Out Day, illustrated by Michael Chesworth, Orchard Books (New York, NY), 2002.

Rise the Moon, illustrated by Raúl Colón, Dial Books (New York, NY), 2002.

Wanda's Monster, illustrated by Nancy Hayashi, Albert Whitman (New York, NY), 2002.

Bath Time, illustrated by Janet Pederson, Marshall Cavendish (New York, NY), 2003.

The Perfect Thanksgiving, illustrated by JoAnn Adinolfi, Henry Holt (New York, NY), 2003.

Moe McTooth: An Alley Cat's Tale, illustrated by Linda Bronson, Clarion Books (New York, NY), 2003.

What Do Angels Wear?, illustrated by Emily Arnold McCully, HarperCollins (New York, NY), 2003.

Three Pebbles and a Song, illustrated by S.D. Schindler, Dial Books (New York, NY), 2003.

City Angel, illustrated by Kyrsten Brooker, Dial Books (New York, NY), 2004.

Feathers: Poems about Birds, illustrated by Lisa McCue, Henry Holt (New York, NY), 2004.

I Know It's Autumn, illustrated by Nancy Hayashi, HarperCollins (New York, NY), 2004.

In Our Backyard Garden, illustrated by Marcy Ramsey, Simon & Schuster (New York, NY), 2004.

Something to Tell the Grandcows, illustrated by Bill Slavin, Eerdmans (Grand Rapids, MI), 2004.

While You Were Away, illustrated by Renée Graef, Hyperion Books for Children (New York, NY), 2004.

Do You Have a Hat?, illustrated by Geraldo Valério, Simon & Schuster (New York, NY), 2004.

Now It Is Winter, illustrated by Mary Newell DePalma, Eerdmans (Grand Rapids, MI), 2004.

The Best Time of the Day, illustrated by Bryan Langdo, Harcourt, Brace (Orlando, FL), 2005.

When You Are Happy, illustrated by Geraldo Valério, Simon & Schuster (New York, NY), 2006.

When Christmas Came, illustrated by Wayne Parmenter, Ideals Children's (Nashville, TN), 2006.

I Like Noisy, Mom Likes Quiet, illustrated by Lydia Halverson, Ideals Children's (Nashville, TN), 2006.

Hero Cat, illustrated by Jo Ellen McAllister Stammen, Marshall Cavendish (New York, NY), 2006.

Someday, illustrated by Rosie Winstead, Dial Books (New York, NY), 2007.

Where I Live, illustrated by Matt Phelan, Dial Books (New York, NY), 2007.

Polar Bear, Arctic Hare: Poems of the Frozen North, illustrated by Eugenie Fernandex, Wordsong (Honesdale, PA), 2007.

Heat Wave, illustrated by Betsy Lewin, Harcourt (New York, NY), 2007.

Callie Cat, Ice Skater, Albert Whitman (Morton Grove, IL), 2007.

Baby Loves You So Much!, illustrated by David Wenzel, Ideals Children's (Nashville, TN), 2007.

Hug a Bug, illustrated by Dan Andreasen, HarperCollins (New York, NY), 2008.

The Best Story, illustrated by Anne Wilsdorf, Dial Books (New York, NY), 2008.

How to Clean Your Room, illustrated by David Leonard, Ideals Children's Books (Nashville, TN), 2009.

Miss Fox's Class Goes Green, illustrated by Anne Kennedy, Albert Whitman (Morton Grove, IL), 2009.

Peace Week in Miss Fox's Class, illustrated by Anne Kennedy, Albert Whitman (Morton Grove, IL), 2009.

Princess Pig, illustrated by Tim Bowers, Knopf (New York, NY), 2009.

Silly Tilly, illustrated by David Slonim, Marshall Cavendish (New York, NY), 2009.

(With Jerry Spinelli) *Today I Will: A Year of Quotes, Notes, and Promises to Myself,* illustrated by Julia Rothman, Knopf (New York, NY), 2009.

Two to Cuddle, illustrated by Laura Logan, CandyCane Press (Nashville, TN), 2009.

When Papa Comes Home Tonight, illustrated by David McPhail, Simon & Schuster (New York, NY), 2009.

Buzz, illustrated by Vincent Nguyen, Simon & Schuster (New York, NY), 2010.

Do You Have a Cat?, illustrated by Geraldo Valério, Eerdmans (Grand Rapids MI), 2010.

Miss Fox's Class Earns a Field Trip, illustrated by Anne Kennedy, Albert Whitman (Chicago, IL), 2010.

The Dancing Pancake, illustrated by Joanne Lew-Vriethoff, Knopf (New York, NY), 2010.

Miss Fox's Class Shapes Up, illustrated by Anne Kennedy, Albert Whitman (Chicago, IL), 2011.

Now It Is Summer, illustrated by Mary Newell DePalma, Eerdmans (Grand Rapids, MI), 2011.

Poetry included in anthology *Animal Friends,* edited by Michael Hague, Holt (New York, NY), 2007. Contributor of hundreds of poems to periodicals.

Author's work has been translated into Spanish.

Sidelights

A poet and teacher of creative writing, Eileen Spinelli has produced numerous books for young children that combine the author's love of rhyme with her understanding of how young people view the world. Among her own picture-book contributions are *Somebody Loves You, Mr. Hatch, Silly Tilly,* and *Miss Fox's Class Earns a Field Trip,* and her poetry collections include *The*

Giggle and Cry Book and *Polar Bear, Arctic Hare: Poems of the Frozen North*. Additionally, the author has crafted a host of free-verse novels for older readers, such as *The Dancing Pancake*. The versatile Spinelli, who has dozens of works to her credit, finds inspiration most everywhere, as she remarked on her home page. "I go into a pet shop. I see a cute heap of kittens. I get an idea. I read the newspaper—an article about the whooping crane. I get an idea. I look at old family photos. I get an idea. Ideas have a way of presenting themselves as I go about my life."

Spinelli was born in Philadelphia, Pennsylvania, in 1942, and grew up in Secane, a nearby suburb. Always an enthusiastic reader, she counted among her favorite authors Marguerite de Angeli. Publishing her first work of poetry in 1960, when she was eighteen, Spinelli continued to write poetry for adults during her few free hours while raising her six children. "Teachers and our public library played a big part in my growing interest in books and writing," Spinelli once told *SATA*.

Spinelli began writing for a younger audience in 1979, after her children had grown old enough to allow her some free time. Her first work, a rhyming list book, was published two years later as *The Giggle and Cry Book* and was followed by two other books of poetry: *Naptime, Laptime* and *Where Is the Night Train Going?* In *Naptime, Laptime* Spinelli portrays a variety of animals indulging in a mid-day snooze, from field mice to Arctic seals to a young child's own stuffed animal. In *Booklist,* Carolyn Phelan praised Spinelli's text for being "simple enough to suit a toddler's attention span" while also containing enough humor to keep older listeners interested. *School Library Journal* critic Rosanne Cerny dubbed the book a "poetic paean to the perfect spot" to take an afternoon nap. Sleep also serves as the focus of *Where Is the Night Train Going?,* in which Spinelli collects poems about dozing. Calling the author's verse "consistently sweet and gentle, rather than distinguished or splashy," Liza Bliss commented in her *School Library Journal* review of *Where Is the Night Train Going?* that the book's words and pictures are perfectly matched in their "mild sense of humor" and ability to recognize "young children's sensibilities."

Spinelli's first prose work for children, *Thanksgiving at the Tappletons',* reached bookstore shelves in 1982. In an offbeat portrayal of the uniquely American tradition, the Tappletons start the day hungry and watch as, one by one, each course of their greatly anticipated evening meal sidesteps the dining-room table. The salad has been fed to the school rabbits; the baker is out of pies by the time Mr. Tappleton has a chance to stop by, and the Thanksgiving turkey winds up floating in a pond in the backyard. "For a Thanksgiving book without pilgrims and Indians, this one just might 'talk turkey,'" quipped *School Library Journal* contributor Betty Craig Campbell of Spinelli's humorous story, while *Booklist* reviewer Ilene Cooper deemed it "appetizing fare." *Thanksgiving at the Tappletons'* was re-issued with new illustrations by Megan Lloyd that depict the Tappletons as a family of wolves.

Spinelli has also revisited the holiday in a second picture book, *The Perfect Thanksgiving,* in which two families share the perfect holiday feast in very different ways, one with a formal, well-mannered feast and another with a relaxing and casual dinner. "The jovial celebration of a national feast day" in *The Perfect Thanksgiving* "highlights the common thread of loving kinship" woven through Spinelli's story, according to a *Kirkus Reviews* writer.

Spinelli's manypicture books range widely in theme, from humorous stories such as *Something to Tell the Grandcows* that are based on animal characters to rhyming bedtime lullabies designed to soothe the most fractious youngster. Featuring an all-critter cast, *Three Pebbles and a Song* re-tells the traditional "ant and grasshopper" fable but finds mice in the title roles. Although he is encouraged to help his family gather food and nesting materials for the coming winter, Moses the mouse decides to sing and dance instead. During the colder winter months that follow, Moses profits from his family's industry, and they, in turn, are entertained by his singing and dancing. A *Publishers Weekly* reviewer wrote that Spinelli's story celebrates "art's power to invigorate and to sustain."

Cats frequently appear as central characters in Spinelli's books. In *Moe McTooth: An Alley Cat's Tale,* for example, Moe enjoys prowling the city streets until the cold weather sends him in search of a warm home. Adopted by a friendly human, the cat enjoys a cozy

Eileen Spinelli teams up with artist Linda Bronson to create the jazz-flavored picture book **Moe McTooth: An Alley Cat's Tale.** (Illustration copyright © 2003 by Linda Bronson. Reprinted by permission of Clarion Books, an imprint of Houghton Mifflin Harcourt Publishing Company.)

Spinelli shows her talent for capturing a child's viewpoint in her story What Do Angels Wear?, *featuring artwork by Emily Arnold McCully.* (Illustration copyright © 2003 by Emily Arnold McCully. Reproduced by permission of HarperCollins Children's Books, a division of HarperCollins Publishers.)

apartment during the winter months, but when spring rolls around Moe must chose between returning to his street life or losing his new friend. Another wild cat is the focus of *Hero Cat,* in which a mother cat finds a safe, cozy spot in an abandoned building and there gives birth to five kittens. When the building is devastated by fire, she manages to save her litter, aided by some caring firemen. Felines are again Spinelli's focus in *Callie Cat, Ice Skater,* as a young kitten pursues her passion even though it is not shared by her two best friends, and In *Booklist* Kathleen Odean called *Moe McTooth* "a special treat for cat lovers," while Phelan wrote in the same periodical that *Callie Cat, Ice Skater* is "a rewarding picture book" with a "gently delivered message." "Spinelli's simple, short sentences" bring to life the drama of *Hero Cat,* noted Gillian Engberg, the *Booklist* critic adding that younger children concerned over the tiny kittens "will be reassured by the story of a parent's fiercely protective unconditional love."

Other animals and insects take center stage in works such as *Princess Pig* and *Buzz.* The former title centers on an easily confused hog that awakens to find herself draped in a beauty's queen sash that blew away from a county fair. Convinced she is royalty, the pig struts around the farm until she discovers that the other creatures are not easily impressed. Barbara Elleman, writing in *School Library Journal,* applauded "Spinelli's smoothly told story" about being true to oneself. A barnyard cut-up pushes a joke too far in *Silly Tilly,* a story in verse about a comedic goose. Though Tilly's antics keep the other animals in stitches, they become upset when she sits on Rooster's birthday cake and insist that she change her behavior, until the farmyard becomes eerily quiet. The author's "humorous triads" contribute much to this "surefire hit for storytime and shared reading sessions," a critic noted in a *Kirkus Reviews* appraisal of *Silly Tilly.*

Spinelli introduces young readers to reatures from the frozen northmdash;from beluga whales to musk oxen to snow fleas—in *Polar Bear, Arctic Hare.* Hazel Rochman, reviewing the work for *Booklist,* commented that the author's "rhythmic poems . . . combine simple wordplay with exciting biological fact," and a *Kirkus Reviews* contributor maintained that Spinelli's "light, inventive, easy-to-understand poetry is worth reading, either alone or aloud." A bumblebee that suffers a crisis of confidence after perusing the newspaper learns that you cannot believe everything you read in *Buzz.* "This is a honey of a story with the simple message: be(e) who you are," Julie Cummins wrote of this humorous story in *Booklist.*

A wise and gentle teacher is at the heart of Spinelli's "Miss Fox's Class" series of picture books. In the debut title, *Peace Week in Miss Fox's Class,* the students pledge to behave and do charitable works for each other after their classroom squabbles get out of hand. According to Rochman, the familiar schoolyard situations "make this a fun story that will open discussions with bullies, victims, and bystanders." The students become environmentally conscious in *Miss Fox's Class Goes Green,* while *Miss Fox's Class Earns a Field Trip* finds them banding together to raise money for an outing to a theme park. Phelan, in her review of the latter work, maintained that young readers will appreciate "the buoyant humor as the story unfolds in well-chosen words."

Some of Spinelli's books are designed for bedtime sharing. In *When Mama Comes Home Tonight* a toddler anticipates a reunion with a working parent and all the fun they will have in the hours spend between dinner and bedtime. Inevitably, of course, the rhyming book ends with lullabies. *Booklist* contributor Stephanie Zvirin called the story "tender" and recommended it as "the perfect book for lap sharing." A companion volume, *When Papa Comes Home Tonight,* "has the same quiet warmth and sweetness" as its predecessor, Rochman observed. *Night Shift Daddy* puts a different spin on bedtime as Dad tucks his daughter in and then goes out the door to work. In the morning he returns and listens to *his* bedtime story before the girl leaves home for a day of activities. In *Rise the Moon* Spinelli's poems celebrate people and creatures who welcome the soothing light of the moon as it rises and bathes the world in its own special glow. A *Publishers Weekly* critic praised this bedtime story as a "poetic tribute to the moon and the many magical and mysterious ways it influences and inspires," and Engberg deemed *Rise the Moon* "a beautiful, reassuring celebration of night."

Other picture books by Spinelli include *Heat Wave,* which opens a nostalgic window on to how people survived the heat of summer in the days before air conditioning. In *Somebody Loves You, Mr. Hatch* a retiring bachelor seems to lead a monotonous life until he receives a Valentine box filled with candy from a mysterious admirer. A contributor to *Kirkus Reviews* called *Somebody Loves You, Mr. Hatch* "charming," adding that it contains "a real plot" and an "amiable tone" that should appeal to young listeners. In *If You Want to Find Golden* a young boy and his mother spend a day together in the city where they live and discover a rainbow of color mixed in with their everyday activities. "From the white sugar-frosted doughnut at the diner to plump purple grapes at the grocery store, . . . young readers will enjoy this dawn to dusk catalogue of colors," claimed Lisa Dennis in a *School Library Journal* review.

Described by *Booklist* contributor Jennifer Mattson as a "reassuring urban lullaby," Spinelli's *City Angel* was the author's response to the September 11, 2001 tragedy and celebrates a human ecosystem: the many cultures and traditions that coexist within New York City. Brought to life in paintings by Kyrsten Brooker, Spinelli's text for *City Angel* personifies the compassion and caring of city residents in the form of a winged black woman clad in white who "offer[s] . . . quiet acts of kindness in the form of smiles, hugs or an unseen helping hand," as a *Publishers Weekly* observed.

Spinelli has also authored a series of books for older readers that features a spunky young protagonist named Lizzie Logan. Lizzie is introduced in the middle-grade novel *Lizzie Logan Wears Purple Sunglasses.* A ten year old with a formidable imagination, Lizzie proves to be a loyal friend to neighborhood newcomer Heather, despite the incredible lies she sometimes tells. While noting that Spinelli's chapter book is not a true-to-life portrait of young people, a *Kirkus Reviews* critic wrote that *Lizzie Logan Wears Purple Sunglasses* "buoyantly addresses the 'problem' of a great imagination in someone who is sensitive." In her *Horn Book* review, Nancy Vasilakis predicted that the book will "provide newly fluent readers with plenty of chuckles and a few anxious moments." Spinelli continues Lizzie's imaginative adventures in two more books: *Lizzie Logan Gets Married* and *Lizzie Logan, Second Banana.*

Spinelli explores how children cope with life's unexpected moments in *Summertime House,* as an eleven-year-old deals with her first crush, a withdrawn cousin, a runaway cat, and a reticent father during a family vacation. "Writing in short free verse chapters entirely from Sophie's perspective," as Nancy Brown explained in *School Library Journal,* "Spinelli has nonetheless created well-developed characters." In *Where I Live,* another novel told in free verse, Diana learns that her family will be moving to a new town now that her father has lost his job. According to *School Library Journal* critic Marilyn Taniguchi, "young readers facing similar circumstances will find their experiences and emotions echoed in Diana's thoughtful musings." Similar in theme and format, *The Dancing Pancake* centers on a preteen whose life is thrown into turmoil when her parents separate. A *Publishers Weekly* reviewer applauded the protagonist's "fresh, unadorned voice that is always believable and sympathetic," and Shawn Brommer, writing in *School Library Journal,* commented that in *The Dancing Pancake* Spinelli "succeeds in capturing the child's voice and deepest feelings."

Spinelli teams up with artist Joanne Lew-Vriethoff to create the family-themed picture book **The Dancing Pancake.** (Illustration copyright © 2010 by Joanne Lew-Vriethoff. Used by permission of Random House Children's Books, a division of Random House, Inc.)

Spinelli's proficiency in a variety of genres is a key to her literary success. "Every book has a different voice and calls for a different mode of writing," she told *BookPage* online interviewer Linda M. Castellitto. "I don't set out to do one or the other, it's more, how am I going to do this particular idea? The more you do it, the more you have a feel for what works."

Biographical and Critical Sources

PERIODICALS

Booklist, December 15, 1982, Ilene Cooper, review of *Thanksgiving at the Tappletons',* p. 569; December 1, 1995, Carolyn Phelan, review of *Naptime, Laptime,* p. 641; July, 1998, Stephanie Zvirin, review of *When Mama Comes Home Tonight,* p. 1879; January 1, 2003, Gillian Engberg, review of *Rise the Moon,* p. 88; April 15, 2003, Kathleen Odean, review of *Moe McTooth: An Alley Cat's Tale,* p. 1479; September 15, 2003, Kay Weisman, review of *Three Pebbles and a Song,* p. 249; November 1, 2003, Gillian Engberg, review of *What Do Angels Wear?,* p. 506; March 1, 2004, Gillian Engberg, review of *In Our Backyard Garden,* p. 1186; April 1, 2004, Terry Glover, review of *Something to Tell the Grandcows,* p. 1370; August, 2004, Carolyn Phelan, review of *I Know It's Autumn,* p. 1944; October 15, 2004, Julie Cummins, review of *Now It Is Winter,* p. 411; January 1, 2005, Jennifer Mattson, review of *City Angel,* p. 875; October 15, 2005, Shelle Rosenfeld, review of *The Best Time of Day,* p. 60; March 1, 2006, Julie Cummins, review of *When You Are Happy,* and Gillian Engberg, review of *Hero Cat,* both p. 101; April 15, 2007, Hazel Rochman, review of *Polar Bear, Arctic Hare: Poems of the Frozen North,* p. 48; May 1, 2007, Ilene Cooper, review of *Heat Wave,* p. 101; August, 2007, Jennifer Mattson, review of *Where I Live,* p. 78; October 15, 2007, Carolyn Phelan, review of *Callie Cat, Ice Skater,* p. 50; November 15, 2008, Daniel Kraus, review of *Hug a Bug,* p. 50; March 15, 2009, Julie Cummins, review of *Silly Tilly,* p. 67; April 1, 2009, Hazel Rochman, review of *When Papa Comes Home Tonight,* p. 45; April 15, 2009, Hazel Rochman, review of *Peace Week in Miss Fox's Class,* p. 47; May 1, 2009, Patricia Austin, review of *Princess Pig,* p. 89; August 1, 2009, Ilene Cooper, review of *Miss Fox's Class Goes Green,* p. 78; April 15, 2010, Carolyn Phelan, review of *Miss Fox's Class Earns a Field Trip,* p. 51; June 1, 2010, Julie Cummins, review of *Buzz,* p. 90.

Bulletin of the Center for Children's Books, June, 2003, review of *Moe McTooth,* p. 423; November, 2003, Karen Coats, review of *The Perfect Thanksgiving,* p. 125; March, 2004, Deborah Stevenson, review of *Something to Tell the Grandcows,* p. 296.

Horn Book, September-October, 1995, Nancy Vasilakis, review of *Lizzie Logan Wears Purple Sunglasses,* p. 605; November-December, 2007, Nell Beram, review of *Heat Wave,* p. 668.

Kirkus Reviews, December 15, 1991, review of *Somebody Loves You, Mr. Hatch,* p. 1985; June 1, 1995, review of *Lizzie Logan Wears Purple Sunglasses,* p. 787; Au-

gust 15, 2003, review of *The Perfect Thanksgiving,* p. 1079; January 1, 2004, review of *Something to Tell the Grandcows,* p. 41; March 1, 2004, review of *While You Are Away,* p. 230; August 15, 2004, review of *Now It Is Winter,* p. 813; September 15, 2005, review of *The Best Time of Day,* p. 1034; March 15, 2006, review of *When You Are Happy,* p. 301; February 15, 2007, review of *Polar Bear, Arctic Hare;* April 15, 2007, review of *Someday;* May 1, 2007, review of *Summerhouse Time;* May 1, 2007, review of *Summerhouse Time;* May 15, 2007, review of *Where I Live;* June 15, 2007, review of *Heat Wave;* September 15, 2007, review of *Callie Cat, Ice Skater;* May 1, 2008, review of *The Best Story;* February 1, 2009, review of *Silly Tilly;* June 15, 2009, review of *Miss Fox's Class Goes Green;* September 1, 2009, review of *Today I Will: A Year of Quotes, Notes, and Promises to Myself.*

Publishers Weekly, May 8, 2000, review of *Night Shift Daddy,* p. 221; December 16, 2002, review of *Rise the Moon,* p. 66; August 23, 2003, review of *Three Pebbles and a Song,* p. 63; September 22, 2003, review of *The Perfect Thanksgiving,* p. 65; January 17, 2005, review of *City Angel,* p. 55; July 9, 2007, review of *Heat Wave,* p. 52; May 17, 2010, review of *The Dancing Pancake,* p. 49; June 28, 2010, review of *Buzz,* p. 127.

School Library Journal, March, 1983, Betty Craig Campbell, review of *Thanksgiving at the Tappletons',* p. 167; January, 1994, Lisa Dennis, review of *If You Want to Find Golden,* pp. 99-100; February, 1996, Rosanne Cerny, review of *Naptime, Laptime,* p. 90; April, 1996, Liza Bliss, review of *Where Is the Night Train Going?,* pp. 130-131; April, 2003, Marge Loch-Wouters, review of *Moe McTooth,* p. 138; September, 2004, Kathleen Kelly MacMillan, review of *Now It Is Winter,* p. 181; February, 2005, Martha Topol, review of *City Angel,* p. 110; January, 2006, Lisa S. Schindler, review of *The Best Time of Day,* p. 114; April, 2006, Carol L. MacKay, review of *Hero Cat,* p. 118; May, 2007, June Wolfe, review of *Someday,* p. 108, Teresa Pfeifer, review of *Polar Bear, Arctic Hare,* p. 125, and Nancy Brown, review of *Summerhouse Time,* p. 144; June, 2007, Judy Chichinski, review of *Heat Wave,* p. 125; July, 2007, Marilyn Taniguchi, review of *Where I Live,* p. 85; August, 2008, Barbara Elleman, review of *The Best Story,* p. 102; December, 2008, Julie Roach, review of *Hug a Bug,* p. 104; April, 2009, Laura Stanfield, review of *When Papa Comes Home Tonight,* p. 116; May, 2009, Grace Oliff, review of *Peace Week in Miss Fox's Class,* p. 89; June, 2009, Barbara Elleman, review of *Princess Pig,* p. 100; October, 2009, Kristen Oravec, review of *Today I Will,* p. 154; April, 2010, Mary Hazelton, review of *Miss Fox's Class Earns a Field Trip,* p. 140; May, 2010, Shawn Brommer, review of *The Dancing Pancake,* p. 124.

ONLINE

BookPage.com, http://www.bookpage.com/ (January 21, 2011), Linda M. Castellitto, interview with Spinelli.

Eerdmans Books for Young Readers Web site, http://www. eerdmans.com/youngreaders/ (December, 2004), interview with Spinelli.

Eileen Spinelli Home Page, http://www.eileenspinelli.com (January 21, 2011).

Embracing the Child Web site, http://www.embracingthe child.org/ (April, 2006), interview with Spinelli.

*   *   *

STAMP, Jørgen 1969-

Personal

Born 1969, in Denmark. *Education:* Designskolen Kolding, degree (graphic design), 1996.

Addresses

Home—Denmark. *E-mail*—jstamp@webspeed.dk.

Career

Illustrator, author, and cartoonist. *Politiken* (newspaper), Copenhagen, Denmark, graphic designer, 1998-2003; freelance illustrator and graphic artist.

Writings

SELF-ILLUSTRATED

Dragens halsbrand, Carlsen (Copenhagen, Denmark), 2001.

(With Anne Misfeldt) *Kvæk,* Carlsen (Copenhagen, Denmark), 2002.

Højt at flyve, Carlsen (Copenhagen, Denmark), 2002, translated as *Flying High,* Enchanted Lion Books (New York, NY), 2009.

(With Anne Misfeldt) *Kør!,* Carlsen (Copenhagen, Denmark), 2006.

(With Anne Misfeldt) *Flyv!,* Carlsen (Copenhagen, Denmark), 2006.

(With Anne Misfeldt) *Vov,* Carlsen (Copenhagen, Denmark), 2006.

(With Anne Misfeldt) *Hvad nu hvis,* Turbine (Denmark), 2009.

(With Anne Misfeldt) *Tæl med mus,* Turbine (Denmark), 2009.

Hjulen på bussen, Carlsen (Copenhagen, Denmark), 2009.

Ti små cyklister, Carlsen (Copenhagen, Denmark), 2009.

Mons i regnvejr, Carlsen (Copenhagen, Denmark), 2010.

Mons i blæsevejr, Carlsen (Copenhagen, Denmark), 2010.

Creator, with Anne Misfeldt, of comic strip "Spirerne," beginning 2009. Also illustrator of educational readers published by Gyldendal.

SELF-ILLUSTRATED; "KALLE" SERIES

Super-Kalle, Carlsen (Copenhagen, Denmark), 2005.

Kalle og Giraf bygger en bil, Carlsen (Copenhagen, Denmark), 2005.

Kalles nye cykel, Carlsen (Copenhagen, Denmark), 2005.

Kalles bold, Carlsen (Copenhagen, Denmark), 2007.

Kalles båd, Carlsen (Copenhagen, Denmark), 2007.

Kalle og Giraf bygger hule, Carlsen (Copenhagen, Denmark), 2007.

ILLUSTRATOR

Anne M. Hansen and Lotte Toft, *Hvorfor ryger Nille?,* Projekt Unge & Rygning, 2000.

Terje Nordberg, *Din vej—psykologi og selværd,* photographs by Leif Zacho, [Denmark], 2000.

Lotte Salling, *1.b,* Carlsen (Copenhagen, Denmark), 2002.

Peter Bejder and Kim Boye Holt, *EU som en landsby, læ om EU,* Manana (Skødstrup, Denmark), 2004.

Bo Skjoldborg, *Vild ferie,* Forum (Copenhagen, Denmark), 2004.

Poul Larsen, *Storebjørn,* Følfod (Blokhus, Denmark), 2004.

Tomas Lagermand Lundme, *Umulige Jannik,* Carlsen (Copenhagen, Denmark), 2004.

Tomas Lagermand Lundme, *Helge Elg,* Carlsen (Copenhagen, Denmark), 2004.

Erik Bjerre and Pernille Pind, *Læs selv om korttricks,* Manana (Skødstrup, Denmark), 2005.

Erik Bjerre and Pernille Pind, *Læs selv om uendelighed,* Manana (Skødstrup, Denmark), 2005.

Erik Bjerre and Pernille Pind, *Læs selv om landkort,* Manana (Skødstrup, Denmark), 2005.

Erik Bjerre and Pernille Pind, *Læs selv om logik,* Manana (Skødstrup, Denmark), 2005.

Erik Bjerre and Pernille Pind, *Læs selv om mål,* Manana (Skødstrup, Denmark), 2005.

Erik Bjerre and Pernille Pind, *Læs selv om labyrinter,* Manana (Skødstrup, Denmark), 2005.

Lotte Salling, *1.b i byen,* Carlsen (Copenhagen, Denmark), 2005.

Birgitta Gärtner, *Prinsessen der selv ville børste tænder om torsdagen,* Carlsen (Copenhagen, Denmark), 2005.

Peter Mouritzen, *Øv!,* Høst & Søn (Copenhagen, Denmark), 2005.

Ulla Raben, *Johan og det sorte hul,* Forum (Copenhagen, Denmark), 2005.

Ulla Raben, *Johan og dragen,* Forum (Copenhagen, Denmark), 2005.

Charlotte Fleischer, *Det skal du få betalt!,* 2006.

Ulla Raben, *Johan og skatten,* Forum (Copenhagen, Denmark), 2006.

Ulla Raben, *Johan og de vilde dyr,* Forum (Copenhagen, Denmark), 2006.

Lotte Toft, *Hvorfor ryder Nille?,* 2007.

Peter Bejder and Kim Boye Holt, *En om EU,* Manana (Skødstrup, Denmark), 2007.

Bo Skjoldborg, *Vild panik,* 2007.

Mette Egelund Olsen, *Min morfars skattekiste,* Høst & Søn (Copenhagen, Denmark), 2009.

Sidelights

Jørgen Stamp is a Danish illustrator and cartoonist. Working in both acrylics and pen and ink, Stamp brings to life his own children's-book texts in addition to illustrating the stories of authors such as Bo Skjoldborg, Lotte Salling, Erik Bjerre and Pernille Pind, Ulla Raben, and Poul Larsen. Collaborating with fellow illustrator and textile designer Anne Misfeldt, he has also created the picture books *Vov, Kvæk, Kør!, Flyv!,* and *Hvad nu hvis,* as well as producing the weekly comic strip "Spirerne."

After graduating with a design degree in 1996, Stamp joined the staff of the Copenhagen-based newspaper *Politiken,* where he worked as an editorial illustrator until beginning work as a freelance artist. His first self-illustrated children's book, *Dragens halsbrand,* was published in 2001, and began Stamp's prolific illustration career. His "Kalle" books, which feature original stories that focus on a childlike giraffe and its friends, include *Super-Kalle, Kalle og Giraf bygger en bil, Kalles båd,* and *Kalles ny cykel.* The "Kalle" series has been popular with Danish children since installments began appearing in 2005.

Originally published in Danish as *Højt at flyve,* Stamp's self-illustrated picture book *Flying High* introduces a giraffe cartoon character that preceded Kalle by three years. Long-nosed and long-necked, Walter is determined to achieve his dream of flying. While the single-minded giraffe busies himself studying airplane plans and a how-to-build-an-airplane construction manual, his enthusiasm attracts Sonny the turtle, who asks if he can join Walter on his first flight. Although the giraffe rejects the turtle's request to be copilot because a turtle is too slow, he is proven wrong when a sudden storm causes his new red airplane to crash on its very its first flight. Stamp's "colorful cartoon illustrations convey the fast pace of" his story in *Flying High,* according to *School Library Journal* contributor Lisa Gangemi Kropp, and a *Children's Bookwatch* critic praised the author/illustrator for crafting "a fine fable about learning to value the contributions of others." Noting Stamp's skill at "telling visual jokes" in his cartoon art, a *Kirkus Reviews* writer maintained of *Flying High* that "it's hard not to warm to the sight of the goggled Walter in his little red plane."

Biographical and Critical Sources

PERIODICALS

Children's Bookwatch, July, 2009, review of *Flying High.*
Kirkus Reviews, September 1, 2009, review of *Flying High.*
School Library Journal, September, 2009, Lisa Gangemi Kropp, review of *Flying High,* p. 135.

ONLINE

Jørgen Stamp Home Page, http://www.jstamp.dk (December 28, 2010).*

* * *

Jørgen Stamp creates the fanciful illustrations that bring to life his uplifting story in **Flying High.** (Enchanted Lion Books, 2009. Illustration copyright © 2002 by Jorgen Stamp. Reproduced by permission.)

STEAD, Philip C.
See STEAD, Philip Christian

* * *

STEAD, Philip Christian
(Philip C. Stead)

Personal

Married; wife's name Erin E. (an illustrator). *Education:* University of Michigan, B.F.A.

Addresses

Home—Ann Arbor, MI.

Career

Author and illustrator of children's books.

Philip Stead (Photograph by Erin Stead. Reproduced by permission.)

Awards, Honors

Caldecott Medal, Chicago Public Library Best of the Best designation, New York Public Library Book for Reading and Sharing selection, and Best Illustrated Books selection, *New York Times,* all 2010, all for *A Sick Day for Amos McGee* illustrated by Erin E. Stead.

Writings

(Self-illustrated) *Creamed Tuna Fish and Peas on Toast,* Roaring Brook Press (New York, NY), 2009.
(As Philip C. Stead) *A Sick Day for Amos McGee,* illustrated by wife Erin E. Stead, Roaring Brook Press (New York, NY), 2010.
(Self-illustrated) *Jonathan and the Big Blue Boat,* Roaring Brook Press (New York, NY), 2011.

Sidelights

An author and illustrator of original picture books such as *Creamed Tuna Fish and Peas on Toast* and *Jonathan and the Big Blue Boat,* Philip Christian Stead has also collaborated with his wife, artist Erin E. Stead, on the award-winning *A Sick Day for Amos McGee.* Described by *School Library Journal* contributor Mary Jean Smith as a "quiet tale of good deeds rewarded," *A Sick Day for Amos McGee* was honored in 2010 with the prestigious Caldecott Medal.

After acquiring an interest in art during high school, Stead earned a fine-arts degree at the University of Michigan's School of Art and Design. A move to New York City led him to a job illustrating and designing publications and displays for the Brooklyn Children's Museum. After several years on the east coast, Stead returned to Michigan, and he and his wife now pursue their freelance careers from their home in Ann Arbor.

Stead's first original self-illustrated book, *Creamed Tuna Fish and Peas on Toast,* took over eighteen months to complete and is based on a family story. "In the 1950's my Grandpa Jack took his least favorite meal (creamed tuna fish and peas on toast) out to the yard, dug a hole, buried the casserole, and carved a headstone to memorialize the ill-fated dish," the author/illustrator explained to an interviewer for the Pizza Hut BOOK IT! Reading Program Web site. "All of the characters in *Creamed Tuna Fish and Peas on Toast* are my real family members—my grandparents, aunts, uncle and father. I took some artistic license as I recrafted the story to better fit a picture book format, but the essential details are all factual."

In Stead's fictional version, Grandpa Jack becomes Wild Man Jack, and his children thrill at his dinner-table stories about his least-favorite meal. Although his wife, Mama Jane, should consider herself forewarned, she plans Friday dinner around the detested tuna fish-and-peas concoction. The humorous results of her choice play out in Stead's collage illustrations and a call-and-response tale that is designed for interactive story times. For *School Library Journal* contributor Susan Weitz, the book's "charm is mainly in the pictures," which she described as "multilayered collages/paintings/ink drawings" highlighted by "gorgeous blotches of color." An "homage to Americana," in the opinion of a *Kirkus Reviews* writer, *Creamed Tuna Fish and Peas on Toast* finds Stead "proudly reclaiming the rhythms of old stories and craftsmanship not so common in the digital age."

Brought to life in Erin E. Stead's wood-block prints and pencil, *A Sick Day for Amos McGee* focuses on a zookeeper who treats each of his exotic charges like a friend. He enjoys a game with the elephant, chats with the penguin, reads soothing bedtime stories to the owl, and boosts the tortoise's self-confidence by challenging it to a race and letting it win. When Amos comes down with a cold that prevents him from traveling to work, the animals decide to visit him at home and care for him as he has cared for them. Stead's gentle story features a fresh take on "the familiar pet-bonding theme [that] will have great appeal," predicted Hazel Rochman in her *Booklist* review, and a *Publishers Weekly* cited the "quiet affection" in *A Sick Day for Amos McGee.* The illustrator's "elegant" images are "breathtaking in their delicacy," the critic added, while in *Horn Book* Kitty Flynn asserted that "Erin Stead's "attentively detailed . . . illustrations reveal character and enhance the cozy mood of Philip Stead's gentle text."

Biographical and Critical Sources

PERIODICALS

Booklist, May 1, 2010, Hazel Rochman review of *A Sick Day for Amos McGee,* p. 92.
Horn Book, May-June, 2010, Kitty Flynn, review of *A Sick Day for Amos McGee,* p. 72.
Kirkus Reviews, September 1, 2009, review of *Creamed Tuna Fish and Peas on Toast;* April 15, 2010, Philip C. Stead, review of *A Sick Day for Amos McGee.*
Publishers Weekly, May 10, 2010, review of *A Sick Day for Amos McGee,* p. 41.
School Library Journal, November, 2009, Susan Weitz, review of *Creamed Tuna Fish and Peas on Toast,* p. 89; May, 2010, Mary Jean Smith, review of *A Sick Day for Amos McGee,* p. 92.

ONLINE

Philip Stead Home Page, http://www.philipstead.com (December 28, 2010).
Pizza Hut BOOK IT! Reading Program Web site, http://www.bookitprogram.com/ (January 15, 2011), interview with Stead.

*   *   *

STRINGER, Helen

Personal

Born in Liverpool, England; immigrated to United States. *Education:* Attended film school. *Hobbies and other interests:* Cooking, entertaining, music, antiquarian books and periodicals.

Addresses

Home—Los Angeles, CA.

Career

Writer. Croxteth Hall, Liverpool, England, researcher; former television production company executive in charge of development; worked at an entertainment law firm. American Film Institute Center for Advanced Film and Television Studies, directing fellow. Presenter at schools and workshops.

Writings

The Last Ghost, Macmillan Children's (London, England), 2009, published as *Spellbinder,* Feiwel & Friends (New York, NY), 2009.

The Midnight Gate, Feiwel & Friends (New York, NY), 2011.

Adaptations

Spellbinder was adapted as an audiobook, narrated by Stringer, Random House Audio, 2010.

Sidelights

Helen Stringer has always been fascinated by history as well as by storytelling, but after graduating from film school she spent several years working in the motion-picture industry. She became inspired to write her first novel, *Spellbinder,* after discovering a manuscript from her past. "I came across a story I had written years ago in a box of junk and thought that perhaps I should write some more stories about the people in the same town," Stringer noted in an interview for the Macmillan Books Web site. "The first thing that I thought of was a girl with lank black hair sitting on a table tomb in an overgrown graveyard and she sort of took over from there."

Published in England as *The Last Ghost, Spellbinder* focuses on twelve-year-old Belladonna Johnson, a girl who has inherited the ability to see ghosts. After Belladonna's parents die in a car accident, their ghosts resume their old habits around the house, until one night when they join every other ghost on Earth in a mysterious disappearance. As one of the only people to notice the spiritual absence—she has lost not only her dearly departed parents but also many new ghostly friends—Belladonna teams up with Steve, a classmate with a knack for spying, and discovers a parallel world that holds the key to the ghosts' disappearance. In *The Midnight Gate* Stringer continues Belladonna's story as she is put in the care of foster parents who may or may not look out for the teen's best interests.

"Stringer's charming ghost story defies classification," noted Debbie Carton in her *Booklist* review of *Spellbinder,* the critic adding that the author's "fast-paced plot" is enhanced by "delightful touches." A *Publishers Weekly* contributor described the book as "adventurous" and "darkly humorous" and recommended the middle-grade novel to fans of "unusual ghost stories without the usual horror." "Magical creatures, amulets, and verses are all a part of this delightful tale," wrote Nancy D. Tolson in her *School Library Journal* review of *Spellbinder,* while a *Kirkus Reviews* writer concluded of Stringer's story that Belladonna's "wry wit and derring-do add up to a great read."

Biographical and Critical Sources

PERIODICALS

Booklist, October 15, 2009, Debbie Carton, review of *Spellbinder,* p. 65.

Bulletin of the Center for Children's Books, December, 2009, Deborah Stevenson, review of *Spellbinder,* p. 169.

Kirkus Reviews, August 1, 2009, review of *Spellbinder.*

Publishers Weekly, October 26, 2009, review of *Spellbinder,* p. 58.

School Library Journal, October, 2009, Nancy D. Tolson, review of *Spellbinder,* p. 138.

Voice of Youth Advocates, February, 2010, Jennifer McConnel, review of *Spellbinder,* p. 513.

ONLINE

Helen Stringer Home Page, http://www.helenstringer.net (December 28, 2010).

Macmillan Books Web site, http://us.macmillan.com/ (January 15, 2011), interview with Stringer.*

*   *   *

SWAIN, Wilson 1976-

Personal

Born 1976, in IL. *Education:* University of Indianapolis, B.F.A. (graphic design), 1998; Art Center College of Design, B.F.A. (illustration), 2003.

Addresses

Home—Glendale, CA. *E-mail*—contact@WilsonSwain.com.

Career

Illustrator, graphic designer, and artist. *Exhibitions:* Work exhibited at Nucleus Gallery, Alhambra, CA.

Illustrator

Ray Marshall, *The Castaway Pirates: A Pop-up Tale of Bad Luck, Sharp Teeth, and Stinky Toes,* Chronicle Books (San Francisco, CA), 2008.

Ralph Covert and G. Riley Mills, *A Nutty Nutcracker Christmas* (with music CD), Chronicle Books (San Francisco, CA), 2009.

Contributor to educational comic books, including "The Misfits," volume 10, by Kimber MacDonald.

Sidelights

Raised in Illinois and now living in Southern California, Wilson Swain is an artist and illustrator whose surreal, pastel-toned illustrations feature soft lines, skewed perspectives, and off-kilter graphical elements. Swain's illustration projects include creating the artwork for both Ray Marshall's *The Castaway Pirates: A Pop-up Tale of Bad Luck, Sharp Teeth, and Stinky Toes* and *A Nutty Nutcracker Christmas,* the latter a quirky retelling of a holiday favorite based on a musical performance by children's songwriter Ralph Covert.

After earning a degree in graphic design from the University of Indianapolis, Swain moved to the west coast, where he was accepted into the illustration program at Pasadena's prestigious Art Center College of Design. His first picture-book assignment came on the strength of his portfolio, which included artwork for educational comics. In *The Castaway Pirates* Swain worked closely with author Ray Marshall to adapt Marshall's humorous story about a shipload of unlucky pirates who hope to patch a leak in their rowboat before they become the snack of a hungry shark. A paper engineer, Marshall hoped to transform the story's two-dimensional art into pop-up images, and when Swain was assigned as illustrator the real work began. "Wilson was a wonderful choice for the book and provided some great suggestions . . . ," Marshall recalled on his home page. "I don't think he had any idea what he was letting himself in for! Illustrating for a pop-up book means having to understand how all the separate pop-up pieces fit together, and then draw them all separated—FOR BOTH the front and back of each piece! Wilson did an amazing job of being thrown in at the deep end of this process."

Swain's second illustration project, *A Nutty Nutcracker Christmas,* was also challenging, although its comics-style images remained confined to two dimensions during the production process. The story is based on a 2009 musical composed by Covert and Chicago playwright G. Riley Mills in which Tchaikovsky's well-known ballet *The Nutcracker* is re-visioned as a modern tale set in a twenty-first-century American household. In the story Clara's nutcracker is broken by brother Fritz, and the boy's punishment is a harsh one: his parents pull the plug on his favorite video game, Mouse Hunter 5000. When Fritz tracks down the prohibited computer game and boots it up, the evil Mouse King character escapes from his hard drive and into the family home, intent on ruining everyone's Christmas fun. As the story progresses, Fritz sets out on a quest to stop the Mouse King, aided by a living nutcracker named Marie who guides him to the land of living toys. Reviewing *A Nutty Nutcracker Christmas* in *Publishers Weekly,* a critic noted that "Swain's kinetic visuals complement the clever concept" behind Covert and Mills' story, and Virginia Walter wrote in *School Library Journal* that the artist's "heavily stylized acrylic, oil, and colored-pencil cartoons are appropriate to the [animated] text."

Biographical and Critical Sources

PERIODICALS

Kirkus Reviews, September 15, 2009, review of *A Nutty Nutcracker Christmas.*

Publishers Weekly, October 26, 2009, review of *A Nutty Nutcracker Christmas,* p. 55.

School Library Journal, November, 2006, Sadie Mattox, review of *The Misfits,* p. 167; October, 2009, Virginia Walter, review of *A Nutty Nutcracker Christmas,* p. 79.

USA Today, December 3, 2009, Bob Minzesheimer, review of *A Nutty Nutcracker Christmas,* p. 9.

ONLINE

Ray Marshall Web site, http://raymarshall.com/ (January 10, 2011), "The Castaway Pirates."

Wilson Swain Home Page, http://www.wilsonswain.com (December 28, 2010).

Wilson Swain Web log, http://wilsonswainnews.blogspot. com (January 10, 2011).

*   *   *

SWEARINGEN, Greg 1976-

Personal

Born 1976; married. *Education:* Columbus College of Art and Design, B.F.A., 1998. *Hobbies and other interests:* Music, reading, traveling, hiking.

Addresses

Home—CA. *E-mail*—gregswearingen@yahoo.com.

Career

Illustrator. Visiting lecturer at schools and colleges; member of exhibition juries; Fashion Institute of Technology, New York, NY, professional mentor. *Exhibitions:* Work included in exhibitions at Powerhouse Gallery, Cleveland, OH; Palo Alto Art Center, Palo Alto, CA; Quirk Gallery, Richmond, VA; Gallery One, Cleveland; Springville Museum of Art, Springville, UT; Museum of American Illustration, New York, NY; Grand Central Art Center Gallery, Santa Ana, CA; Saddleback College Art Gallery, Mission Viejo, CA; Baum Gallery, Conway, AR; Communication Arts Technologies Gallery, Rockville, MD; Spokane Falls Community College Fine Arts Gallery, Spokane, WA; Ettinger Gallery, Laguna, CA; and Gallery Nucleus, Alhambra, CA; and in shows staged by Society of Illustrators, New York, NY.

Awards, Honors

Norman Rockwell Museum at Stockbridge Award, Society of Illustrators, New York, NY, c. 1998; named Artist of the Month, American Greetings, July, 1998; Silver Medal, *Spectrum 11,* 2005; Power Artist designation, *Fantasy* magazine (Beijing, China), 2005; Award of Excellence, *Communication Arts,* 2006, 2007; Society of Illustrators Silver Medal, 2007, and certificates of merit.

Illustrator

Holly L. Niner, *Mr. Worry: A Story about OCD,* Albert Whitman (Morton Grove, IL), 2004.

Julia Donaldson, *The Giants and the Joneses,* Henry Holt (New York, NY), 2005.

Kelly Easton, *The Outlandish Adventures of Liberty Aimes,* Random House (New York, NY), 2009.

Deborah Beale and Tad Williams, *The Dragons of Ordinary Farm,* HarperCollins (New York, NY), 2009.

Glenn Dakin, *The Society of Unrelenting Vigilance,* Egmont (New York, NY), 2009.

"MAXIMUM BOY" SERIES BY DAN GREENBURG

Maximum Boy, Starring in Invasion from the Planet of the Cows, Scholastic (New York, NY), 2001.

Maximum Boy, Starring in Superhero—or Super Thief?, Scholastic (New York, NY), 2001.

Maximum Boy, Starring in The Day Everything Tasted like Broccoli, Scholastic (New York, NY), 2001.

Maximum Boy, Starring in The Hijacking of Manhattan, Scholastic (New York, NY), 2001.

Maximum Boy, Starring in Attack of the Soggy Underwater People, Scholastic (New York, NY), 2002.

Greg Swearingen's illustration projects include creating the artwork for Kelly Easton's middle-grade novel in **The Outlandish Adventures of Liberty Aimes.** (Wendy Lamb Books, 2009. Illustration copyright © 2009 by Greg Swearingen. Reproduced by permission of the illustrator.)

Maximum Boy, Starring in Maximum Girl Unmasked, Scholastic (New York, NY), 2002.

Maximum Boy, Starring in The Worst Bully in the Entire Universe, Scholastic (New York, NY), 2003.

Sidelights

The detailed illustrations of California artist and illustrator Greg Swearingen can be found on numerous book covers as well as in the pages of several books for children. In addition to illustrating Dan Greenburg's "Maximum Boy" chapter-book series, Swearingen has also contributed art to books that include *The Giants and the Joneses,* a humorous story by author Julia Donaldson, and Kelly Easton's quirky elementary-grade novel *The Outlandish Adventures of Liberty Aimes.* Reviewing the latter work, a *Kirkus Reviews* writer praised its "expressive, comical pencil illustrations" while in *School Library Journal* Eva Mitnick asserted that Swearingen's "charming illustrations . . . add immense appeal to this warm, delightfully odd fantasy."

Swearingen developed a talent for drawing during his teen years, which he spent primarily in the Midwest, and his style was influenced by "Golden Age" illustrators such as Edmund Dulac, N.C. Wyeth, and Jessie Willcox Smith. In 1994 he enrolled at Ohio's Columbus College of Art and Design, earning his B.F.A. four years later. A move to Cleveland and a job at American Greetings came next, but the positive response to his art encouraged Swearingen to begin his career as a freelance artist and illustrator. His first illustration assignment, Holly L. Niner's *Mr. Worry: A Story about OCD,* earned him positive reviews, *School Library Journal* contributor Erlene Bishop Killeen writing that Swearingen's "soft, soothing artwork" "add[s] whimsy and interest" to Niner's tale.

Years of experimentation with different artistic media resulted in Swearingen's highly detailed style of illustration, which incorporates acrylics, colored pencil, and translucent water color. On his home page, he discussed the process by which he creates the cover illustrations for which he has become well known and which can be crucial to a book's publishing success. "I begin by familiarizing myself with the book and its audience," he explained. "While reading the manuscript, I make small rough sketches. I refine my best sketches with pencil and ink. The art director presents my sketches to the editors, marketing department, and occasionally the author before choosing one for the cover.

"To create the final drawing, I research everything in the image, sculpt small models, and hire friends to pose for photo reference. I use all this visual information to tighten my drawing. I then do both a value and color study digitally, and complete the final artwork by hand on watercolor paper using acrylic, watercolor, and colored pencils."

Biographical and Critical Sources

PERIODICALS

Booklist, August 1, 2009, Ilene Cooper, review of *The Outlandish Adventures of Liberty Aimes,* p. 72.

Horn Book, July-August, 2009, Elissa Gershowitz, review of *The Outlandish Adventures of Liberty Aimes,* p. 420.

Kirkus Reviews, August 15, 2005, review of *The Giants and the Joneses,* p. 912; May 15, 2009, review of *The Dragons of Ordinary Farm;* May 15, 2009, review of *The Outlandish Adventures of Liberty Aimes.*

Publishers Weekly, June 8, 2009, review of *The Outlandish Adventures of Liberty Aimes,* p. 43.

School Library Journal, April, 2004, Erlene Bishop Killeen, review of *Mr. Worry: A Story about OCD,* p. 120; October, 2005, Elaine E. Knight, review of *The Giants and the Joneses,* p. 112; August, 2009, Beth L. Meister, review of *The Dragons of Ordinary Farm,* p. 117; August, 2009, Eva Mitnick, review of *The Outlandish Adventures of Liberty Aimes,* p. 102.

ONLINE

Greg Swearingen Home Page, http://www.gregswearingen. com (December 28, 2010).

T-Z

TAYLOR, Susan Champlin
See CHAMPLIN, Susan

* * *

VITALE, Stefano 1958-

Personal

Born August 27, 1958, in Padua, Italy; son of Guido Morassutti-Vitale (a landowner) and Carla Vitale (a homemaker); married Pamela Berry (an art director), May 28, 1988; children: Gianmarco, Anna. *Education:* Attended Bell School of Languages (Norwich, England), 1978, University of Venice, 1979, University of Verona, 1980-82, and University of California, Los Angeles, 1982-83; University of Southern California, B.S. (economics), 1984; Art Center College of Design (Pasadena, CA), B.F.A., 1987.

Addresses

Home—Venice, Italy. *Agent*—Lindgren & Smith, 250 W. 57th St., New York, NY 10107. *E-mail*—stefano@ stefanovitale.com.

Career

Freelance illustrator. Advertising clients have included Absolut Vodka, Mercedes-Benz, Xerox, Marriott Hotels, and New York University. *Exhibitions:* Work has been exhibited at galleries and museums, including Ursitti, MacGuiness Gallery, Washington, DC, 1988; Art Director's Club, New York, NY, 1993; Chrysler Museum of Art, Norfolk, VA, 1996; New York Public Library, 1997; Delaware Museum of Art, Wilmington, 1997; Schloss Maretsch, Bolzano, Italy, 1998; Cedar Rapids Museum of Art, Cedar Rapids, IA, 1998; Galleria Civica, Padova, Italy, 1999; Children's Art Museum, New York, NY, 2006; XYZ Gallery, Treviso, Italy, 2008; Biblioteca Europea, Rome, Italy, 2009; and by the Society of Illustrators, New York, NY.

Awards, Honors

Three-dimensional Illustration Award, 1992; Society of Publication Designers Spot Competition awards, 1993, 1994, 1998; Children's Book of Distinction designation, *Hungry Mind Review,* 1993, for *The World in 1492* by Jean Fritz; certificate of merit, Society of Illustrators, 1993; Society of Newspaper Design award, 1994; Notable Book designation, American Library Association, 1995, 1997; Parent's Choice Picture-Book Silver Honor, 1996; Aesop Prize, American Folklore Society/Library of Congress, 1996; *Storytelling World* Award Honor Book selection, 1998; gold award, National Parenting Publications, 1998; Reading Magic Award, *Parenting* magazine, 1999; One Hundred Titles for Reading and Sharing selection, New York Public Library, 2007, for *Why War Is Never a Good Idea* by Alice Walker; seven *American Illustration* awards.

Illustrator

Jim Aylesworth, *The Folks in the Valley: A Pennsylvania Dutch ABC,* HarperCollins (New York, NY), 1992.

Jean Fritz, Patricia McKissack, and others, *The World in 1492,* Henry Holt (New York, NY), 1992.

Nancy Jewell, *Christmas Lullaby,* Clarion (New York, NY), 1994.

Angela Shelf Medearis, *Too Much Talk,* Candlewick Press (New York, NY), 1995.

Charlotte Zolotow, *When the Wind Stops* (originally published 1962), new edition, HarperCollins (New York, NY), 1995.

Judy Sierra, adaptor, *Nursery Tales around the World,* Clarion (New York, NY), 1996.

Valiska Gregory, *When Stories Fell like Shooting Stars,* Simon & Schuster (New York, NY), 1996.

Aileen Fisher, *The Story of Easter,* HarperCollins (New York, NY), 1997.

David Kherdian, *The Rose's Smile: Farizad of the Arabian Nights,* Holt (New York, NY), 1997.

Edward Field, *Magic Words* (poetry), Harcourt (New York, NY), 1998.

Nancy Jewell, *Sailor's Song,* Clarion (New York, NY), 1999.

Charlotte Zolotow, *Sleepy Book* (originally published 1958), new edition, HarperCollins (New York, NY), 2001.

Judy Sierra, adaptor, *Can You Guess My Name?: Traditional Tales around the World,* Clarion (New York, NY), 2002.

Charlotte Zolotow, *If You Listen,* Running Press (Philadelphia, PA), 2002.

Alice Walker, *There Is a Flower at the Tip of My Nose Smelling Me,* HarperCollins (New York, NY), 2006.

Alice Walker, *Why War Is Never a Good Idea,* HarperCollins (New York, NY), 2007.

James Bruchac and Joseph Bruchac, retellers, *The Girl Who Helped Thunder, and Other Native American Folktales,* Sterling Pub. Co. (New York, NY), 2008.

Page McBrier, *Once There Was and Was Not: A Modern-Day Folktale from Armenia,* Heifer International/Verve Marketing (Chadds Ford, PA), 2008.

Betsy Franco, *Pond Circle,* Margaret K. McElderry Books (New York, NY), 2009.

Teri Sloat, *There Was an Old Man Who Painted the Sky,* Henry Holt (New York, NY), 2009.

Illustrator of *The Creation Creation* (video), music by Bela Fleck, narrated by Amy Grant, Rabbit Ears. Contributor, with others, to *Children of God Storybook Bible,* by Archbishop Desmond Tutu, [Cape Town, South Africa], 2010. Contributor to periodicals, including *Hemispheres, Time, Newsweek, Business Week, Town & Country, Reader's Digest, Glamour,* and *Metropolitan Home.*

Sidelights

Stefano Vitale is known for creating folk-art-style paintings that, in addition to earned him numerous awards, have successfully brought to life stories by a variety of children's book authors. Beginning his career as a fine-art painter of large canvases, Vitale moved to a smaller format when he refined his characteristic style: a primitive look that echoes the folk art of Mexico and the American Southwest and incorporates wood-grain texture and flat, saturated colors. In addition to his commercial design projects, Vitale's art has appeared in numerous picture books, among them Jim Aylesworth's *The Folks in the Valley: A Pennsylvania Dutch ABC,* David Kherdian's *The Rose's Smile: Farizad of the Arabian Nights,* and several stories by award-winning author Charlotte Zolotow as well as accompanying stories and poems by writers such as Alice Walker, Betsy Franco, and James and Joseph Bruchac.

Born in Italy in 1958, Vitale began his college education in the social sciences, graduating from the University of Southern California with a bachelor's degree in economics in 1984. Within the next three years he had refocused his interest, and in 1987 he received his B.F.A. from Pasadena, California's prestigious Art Center College of Design. Married the following year, Vitale marketed his artistic talents to advertisers, creating designs used in selling everything from hotels to motorcars. In his free time, he channeled his creative energy into the large-scale oil paintings that allowed him true

Stefano Vitale creates intricate folk-style images to pair with Nancy Jewell's text for **Sailor's Song.** (Illustration copyright © 1999 by Stefano Vitale. Reproduced by permission Clarion Books, an imprint of Houghton Mifflin Harcourt Publishing Company.)

Vitale's collaborations with author Jewell have included the holiday-themed picture book **Christmas Lullaby.** (Illustration copyright © 1994 by Stefano Vitale. Reproduced by permission Clarion Books, an imprint of Houghton Mifflin Harcourt Publishing Company.)

artistic expression. After living in New York City for several years, he returned to his native Italy and now makes his home in Venice.

"I began my illustrating career to finance my large-scale paintings," Vitale once told *SATA*. His first published illustration project, *Folks in the Valley*, appeared on bookstore shelves in 1992. Featuring a rhyming text, the book is "illustrated . . . with wit and naive charm," according to *Booklist* contributor Carolyn Phelan, her opinion reflecting the reception to Vitale's work among both critics and writers.

Focusing on the cyclical characteristics of the natural world, *When the Wind Stops* is one of several stories by Zolotow that Vitale has re-envisioned for a new generation of young children. His update of the 1962 original features "exquisite" full-color illustrations that "gloriously depict heaven and earth and give concrete meaning to abstract concepts," according to *Booklist* contributor Lauren Peterson. Using deep-hued oil paints to reprise Zolotow's 1958 picture book *Sleepy Book,* the illustrator uses similarly detailed paintings in warm, muted tones to evoke the text's dusky, lullaby feel. Commenting on the visual references to Old Masters painters Vincent van Gogh and Marc Chagall that distinguish the illustrator's paintings for *When the Wind Stops, School Library Journal* contributor Virginia Golodetz also cited that artwork for its "interesting detail."

Walker's *There Is a Flower at the Tip of My Nose Smelling Me* focuses on a young girl who is pondering the interrelationships that exist in the natural world. Hailed as "poetic in its appeal" and "artistically stunning" by *School Library Journal* contributor Mary Elam, the book was also described by a *Publishers Weekly* critic as "an illuminated prayer" on the strength of Vitale's inspirational images. Another book by Walker, *War Is Never a Good Idea,* teams "spare, eloquent" pacifist verses with what *Booklist* contributor Hazel Rochman described as "naive-style paintings in neon-bright colors [that] celebrate forest diversity and urban communities across the globe." Another natural cycle is described by poet Betsy Franco in *Pond Circle,* a picture book for young children that follows the food chain from lake water and algae up the ladder to fly, bullfrog, and several larger predators. Calling Vitale's paintings "creative and highly effective," *Horn Book* contributor Danielle J. Ford added that he "transforms the wood grain into the ripples on the pond surface or clouds floating in the evening sky." These "rich, colorful oil-on-wood illustrations are as poetic as the text in their depiction of the natural world," wrote *School Library Journal* contributor Kathleen Kelly MacMillan, and in *Booklist* Engberg predicted that Vitale's "close-up images of specific animals will delight the youngest kids."

Discussing Vitale's artistic contribution to Sierra's *Nursery Tales around the World,* Mary M. Burns noted in *Horn Book* that his "folk-art style done in oil paint on wood panels, illuminates the collection's multicultural roots; intricately designed borders incorporate motifs" drawn from the cultures represented in Sierra's selections. Another anthology by Sierra, *Can You Guess My Name?: Traditional Tales from around the World,* also benefits from the Vitale touch. The fifteen tales included in this book are divided among q12five traditional motifs embodied in "The Three Pigs," "The Bremen Town Musicians," "Hansel and Gretel," "The Frog Prince," and "Rumpelstiltskin." Discussing Vitale's contribution to the book, John Peters wrote in *Booklist* that "Vitale paints on rough wood to add visual effect," enhancing each image with unique painted borders and "scenes of stylized but easily recognizable figures." The "vibrant and detailed" borders for these images serve as "a strong component" of the book, according to a *Kirkus Reviews* writer. "Beautiful to look at, [and] appealing in tone," *Can You Guess My Name?* stands as "an outstanding example of what folklore collections for children can and should be," concluded Burns.

Deeming Vitale's illustrations "enchanting," *School Library Journal* critic Judith Constantinides also praised the artist's contribution to *The Rose's Smile,* Kherdian's reworking of the classic Arabian Nights saga for young people. Vitale's evocation of Persian miniatures and his use of "lush colors" also elicited Constantinides' approval; as the reviewer noted, "each page is elaborately framed and, as with medieval and Eastern art, sometimes depicts more than one scene from the story—a nice touch." "The story moves quickly," agreed Karen Morgan in *Booklist,* the critic going on to write of *The Rose's Smile* that "its appeal [is] magnified by Vitale's rich illustrations, which are lushly imbued with details of street and palace life and splendid gardens."

Vitale's painted illustrations continue to find a welcome place in collections of folk tales and legends. In Angela Shelf Medearis's *Too Much Talk* his paintings bring to life a West African tale about a group of local neighbors that are surprised when the animals and vegetables around them have been given the gift of gab. Praising the illustrations in *Two Much Talk, Booklist* contributor Julie Corsaro noted that Vitale's "subtly colored spreads . . . and flowing lines . . . echo the cadence of [Medearis's] text," while a *Publishers Weekly* reviewer asserted that, "even with lively, kid-pleasing narration, Vitale's . . . glowing, oil-on-wood paintings steal the show in this animated tale."

Focusing on Native American culture, the Bruchacs' *The Girl Who Helped Thunder, and Other Native American Folklore* features several stories collected from tribes throughout North America. Another folk-tale retelling, Teri Sloat's *There Was an Old Man Who Painted the Sky* also takes readers back in time in its focus on prehistoric cave paintings. Together with the "concise" stories retold by the Bruchacs, Vitale's characteristic oil-on-wood images in tones of red and blue "vividly reveal the colorful spirit of the tales," according to *School Library Journal* critic Jeff Meyer in his review of *The Girl Who Helped Thunder, and Other Native American Folklore.* Susan Scheps asserted in the same periodical that the "glorious mixed-media illustrations . . . , bursting with beautifully toned colors and an array of eye-catching patterns and stylized figures, are clearly the focus" of Sloat's picture book. Calling *There Was an Old Man Who Painted the Sky* an "intriguing creation story inspired by a real event," a *Kirkus Reviews* writer also cited "Vitale's psychedelic, mixed-media illustrations," and *Booklist* critic Andrew Medlar predicted that the book's "vibrant" art will appeal to "families wishing to impart diverse beliefs about earth's beginnings to their children."

Alice Walker's pacifist picture book Why War Is Never a Good Idea *is enriched by Vitale's unique illustrations.* (Illustration copyright © 2007 by Stefano Vitale. Used by permission of HarperCollins Children's Books, a division of HarperCollins Publishers.)

"Through the books I illustrate, I try to convey the images that the text suggests to me," Vitale once explained to *SATA*. "My working habits are like a nine-to-five job, interrupted by an occasional walk in the woods where I feel at peace." His advice to aspiring young illustrators? "Write your own stories and try to ignore this obsessive desire to be recognized."

Biographical and Critical Sources

PERIODICALS

Booklist, May 1, 1992, Carolyn Phelan, review of *The Folks in the Valley: A Pennsylvania Dutch ABC,* p. 1598; October 1, 1994, Carolyn Phelan, review of *Christmas Lullaby,* p. 333; July, 1995, Lauren Peterson, review of *When the Wind Stops,* p. 1879; January 1-15, 1996, Julie Corsaro, review of *Too Much Talk,* pp. 840-841; September 1, 1997, Karen Morgan, review of *The Rose's Smile: Farizad of the Arabian Nights,* p. 114; November 1, 2001, Hazel Rochman, review of *Sleepy Book,* p. 480; November 15, 2002, John Peters, review of *Can You Guess My Name?: Traditional Tales around the World,* p. 599; April 1, 2006, Hazel Rochman, review of *There Is a Flower at the Tip of My Nose Smelling Me,* p. 47; August, 2007, Hazel Rochman, review of *Why War Is Never a Good Idea,* p. 89; May 15, 2009, Andrew Medlar, review of *There Was an Old Man Who Painted the Sky,* p. 43; June 1, 2009, Gillian Engberg, review of *Pond Circle,* p. 76.

Bulletin of the Center for Children's Books, January, 2003, review of *Can You Guess My Name?,* p. 211.

Horn Book, May-June, 1996, Mary M. Burns, review of *Nursery Tales around the World,* pp. 343-344; January, 2002, review of *Sleepy Book,* p. 49; January-February, 2003, Mary M. Burns, review of *Can You Guess My Name?,* p. 87; January-February, 2008, Henrietta M. Smith, review of *Why War Is Never a Good Idea,* p. 103; July-August, 2009, Danielle J. Ford, review of *Pond Circle,* p. 407; 2009, Barbara Bader, review of *The Girl Who Helped Thunder, and Other Native American Folktales,* p. 106.

Kirkus Reviews, July 1, 2001, review of *Sleepy Book,* p. 950; October 15, 2002, review of *Can You Guess My Name?,* p. 1538; April 15, 2006, review of *There Is a Flower at the Tip of My Nose Smelling Me,* p. 418; August 15, 2007, review of *Why War Is Never a Good Idea;* May 15, 2009, review of *Pond Circle;* June 1, 2009, review of *There Was an Old Man Who Painted the Sky.*

New York Times Book Review, December 18, 1994, Cynthia Zarin, review of *Christmas Lullaby.*

Publishers Weekly, October 23, 1995, review of *Too Much Talk,* p. 67; September 3, 2001, review of *Sleepy Book,* p. 90; May 8, 2006, review of *There Is a Flower at the Tip of My Nose Smelling Me,* p. 64; October 8, 2007, review of *Why War Is Never a Good Idea,* p. 52; June 22, 2009, review of *Pond Circle,* p. 45.

School Library Journal, August, 1995, Virginia Golodetz, review of *When the Wind Stops,* p. 131; November, 1997, Judith Constantinides, review of *The Rose's Smile,* p. 109; August, 2001, Gay Lynn Van Vleck, review of *Sleepy Book,* p. 174; November, 2002, Lee Bock, review of *Can You Guess My Name?,* p. 148; May, 2006, Mary Elam, review of *There Is a Flower at the Tip of My Nose Smelling Me,* p. 118; October, 2007, Marie Orlando, review of *Why War Is Never a Good Idea,* p. 164; December, 2008, Jeff Meyer, review of *The Girl Who Helped Thunder, and Other Native American Folktales,* p. 144; May, 2009, Kathleen Kelly MacMillan, review of *Pond Circle,* p. 78; September, 2009, Susan Scheps, review of *There Was an Old Man Who Painted the Sky,* p. 148.

ONLINE

Lindgren & Smith Web site, http://www.lindgrensmith.com/ (January 10, 2011), "Stefano Vitale."

Stefano Vitale Home Page, http://www.stefanovitale.com (January 10, 2011).*

* * *

WARMAN, Jessica 1981-

Personal

Born 1981; married; husband's name Colin; children: two daughters. *Education:* Indiana University of Pennsylvania, B.A. (English; with honors), 2003; Seton Hall University, M.A. (creative writing). *Hobbies and other interests:* Distance running.

Addresses

Home—Murrysville, PA. *Agent*—Andrea Somberg, Harvey Klinger Agency, 300 W. 55th St., Ste. 11V, New York, NY 10019. *E-mail*—jkwarman@hotmail.com.

Career

Novelist.

Awards, Honors

Best Book for Young Adults designation, YALSA/American Library Association, for *Breathless.*

Writings

Breathless, Walker (New York, NY), 2009.
Where the Truth Lies, Walker Books for Young Readers (New York, NY), 2010.

Also author of poetry chapbook *How We Spend Our Days,* 2004. Contributor of poetry and short fiction to journals, including *Stickman Review, Penguin Political,* and *Redivider.*

Sidelights

Jessica Warman wrote the first draft of her debut novel, *Breathless,* at age eighteen, during the summer after she graduated from the Linsly School, a boarding school located in West Virginia. During the decade between the novel's completion and its publication, Warman completed her M.A. in creative writing and began her own family, revisiting and revising her manuscript as she gained additional insights into her craft as well as into life. Although *Breathless* shares its prep-school setting with Warman's second novel, *Where the Truth Lies,* it is openly autobiographical in its story of a teenager who is removed from her family and enrolled in boarding school while her parents cope with an emotionally troubled older brother.

Warman's determination to become a writer directed much of her education both in high school and in college. A summer course in creative writing at Yale University inspired her to enter the honors English program at Indiana University of Pennsylvania, and she published several stories and poems before completing her bachelor's degree. At Seton Hill University Warman's graduate studies included classes on the business side of writing, and it was here that she developed the perseverance required of those intent on pursuing publication in a competitive market. In Warman's case, she was able to combine that perseverance with talent, and she had an agent working to find a publisher for *Breathless* by the time she graduated.

Katie Kittrell is the narrator in *Breathless.* When readers first meet her at age fifteen she is passionate about her dreams of swimming in the Olympics, but less than enthusiastic about being sent away to Woodsdale boarding school. Although her parents believe it best that she leave home and avoid her schizophrenic older brother, Will, who is now suicidal, to Katie it feels like rejection, especially because she and Will are so close. At Woodsdale, she avoids the hurt by telling her new friends that her brother is dead. Apart from swimming, partying with the popular clique and spending time with a new boyfriend also help Katie hide from her feelings about her family. Fortunately, Katie's roommate, Mazzie, knows the truth and this young woman becomes a surprising but loyal confidante when Will's situation takes a tragic downturn. The "achingly realistic scenes and characters transcend cliché," wrote Gillian Engberg in a *Booklist* review of *Breathless,* the critic commending Warman's narrative for its "rare, refreshing honesty and flashes of wry humor." Noting that the novel portrays Will's descent into mental illness "with stark honesty," *School Library Journal* contributor Roxanne Myers Spencer praised the novel for providing readers with "an important look at an extremely difficult illness and its effects on a family," while a *Kirkus Reviews* writer commended Warman for depicting "Katie's emotions and her complex life and family with immediacy."

For seventeen-year-old Emily Meckler, the narrator of *Where the Truth Lies,* life at Connecticut's Stonybrook Academy is particularly challenging because her father is the headmaster. Although she seems happy and at ease, the teen is secretly haunted by fearful nightmares.

Unable to tell her parents or her best friends, Emily hopes to find safety in her romantic relationship with a handsome new student named Del Sugar. When Del is expelled from Stonybrook, leaving a trail of lies and a pregnant Emily in his wake, the young woman is forced to question many aspects of her life, including the source of her elemental fears. Calling *Where the Truth Lies* a "wrenching, episodic story," Engberg also praised Warman for capturing "the sibling-like tensions and intimacy of boarding-school friendships" in Emily's narration. In *School Library Journal,* Heather Miller Cover described Emily as "particularly insightful," and predicted that the novel "will be popular with fans of Sarah Dessen and Lurlene McDaniel."

Biographical and Critical Sources

PERIODICALS

Booklist, September 1, 2009, Gillian Engberg, review of *Breathless,* p. 105; November 1, 2010, Gillian Engberg, review of *Where the Truth Lies,* p. 66.
Bulletin of the Center for Children's Books, November, 2009, Deborah Stevenson, review of *Breathless,* p. 99; November, 2010, Deborah Stevenson, review of *Where the Truth Lies,* p. 154.
Kirkus Reviews, August 15, 2009, review of *Breathless.*
School Library Journal, November, 2009, Roxanne Myers Spencer, review of *Breathless,* p. 124; December, 2010, Heather Miller Cover, review of *Where the Truth Lies,* p. 130.

ONLINE

Embracing the Child Web site, http://www.embracingthe child.org/ (September, 2009), interview with Warman.
Jessica Warman Home Page, http://jessicawarman.com (December 28, 2010).

*   *   *

WEST, Owen
See KOONTZ, Dean

*   *   *

WHITLEY, David 1984-

Personal

Born 1984, in England. *Education:* Oxford University, degree (English), c. 2006.

Addresses

Home—Cheshire, England. *E-mail*—david.m.whitley@ gmail.com.

David Whitley (Photograph by Gordon Ward. Reproduced by permission.)

Career

Author. Presenter at schools and libraries. Vocalist with opera companies.

Awards, Honors

Kathleen Fidler Award shortlist, 2001; Cheshire Prize for Literature, 2004; Carnegie Award long-list inclusion, and Bradford Boase Award long-list inclusion, both 2009, and Audies Awards finalist, 2010, all for *The Midnight Charter.*

Writings

The Midnight Charter, Roaring Brook Press (New York, NY), 2009.
The Children of the Lost, Roaring Brook Press (New York, NY), 2011.

Author's books have been translated into twelve languages.

Adaptations

The Midnight Charter was adapted for audiobook, read by Simon Vance, Chiver's Children's Audio Books, 2009.

Sidelights

David Whitley began to earn plaudits for his writing ability while a student at Oxford University, where one of his children's stories was awarded the Cheshire Prize

for Literature. Fortunately, fame did not sideline Whitley's efforts to pursue his education; he returned to writing full time only after graduating with a degree in English. He allotted himself time to complete a children's novel and planned to continue his academic studies while his manuscript made the round of British publishers. However, "things moved a little swifter than that," as Whitley reflected on his home page. "I had just been accepted to study for a Master's Degree back at Oxford when I heard from my agent that Puffin wanted my book!" Published in 2009, *The Midnight Charter* once again put Whitley's name before the literary public when it appeared on the long list of both the Carnegie and Bradford Boase awards.

In *The Midnight Charter* Whitley takes readers back in time to the eighteenth century and the age of the Enlightenment where the thoughts of philosophers from Voltaire and Rousseau to Adam Smith shaped the scientific viewpoint that would characterize the Modern era. "It's a glorious period," he noted on his home page; "a flowering of thought and ideas. What if, amongst their great philosophical notions, the Enlightenment thinkers had conceived of a city without money, but which was ruled by the laws of the market, where everything and everyone was for sale? How would it work, what would life be like, and where would the power lie?"

Whitley imagines such a place in *The Midnight Charter* as he draws readers to the fortified city-state of Agora, where children under age twelve are a commodity that can be traded away by their parents. For Lily, an orphan, the marketplace sends her into the service of Count Stelli, an astrologer, where she meets Mark, a fellow orphan who is now the property of Stelli's son, Doctor Theophilus. When both children gain their independence, they find themselves governed by opposing values while still remaining friends. Rejecting the Agoran economy, Lily dedicates herself to helping those people who have nothing that society values. Meanwhile, Mark successfully markets his talent as a fortune teller and gains social and economic prominence. Meanwhile, a shadow looms over Agora as written in the Midnight Charter, a document that predicts the rise of two opposing powers—Protagonist and Antagonist—and the possible end of the Agoran way of life. Suspected as the dual sources of these two opposing forces, Lily and Mark are ultimately banished from Agora.

"Charity, greed, freedom, fate and political scheming are all woven through [the novel's] . . . richly conceived world," wrote a *Publishers Weekly* contributor in a review of Whitley's dystopian fiction debut, while a *Kirkus Reviews* critic praised *The Midnight Charter* as "refreshing in its classic approach." *School Library Journal* critic Sue Giffard dubbed the novel "exciting and gripping from the first heart-stopping line," as the story's "memorable" cast play out each part within a fictional "utopia closing in on itself, and a morality that is at the extreme edge of reason." Within Whitley's "intertwining plots" are "mysteries, politics and a tremendous amount of detailed world building," noted *Canadian Review of Materials* contributor Betsy Fraser, the critic predicting that *The Midnight Charter* "will appeal to both science fiction and fantasy readers." Reviewing *The Midnight Charter* in *Booklist*, Ian Chipman described Whitley's debut as both "ambitious" and "operatic," adding that the story's dramatic and surprising "crescendo will captivate thoughtful readers."

The Midnight Charter marked the beginning of Whitley's "Agora Trilogy" and was followed in 2001 with *The Children of the Lost*. In this volume, Mark and Lily remain living outside the walls of the city of Agora, finding a new home with the members of a forest commune where there is no private property. While attempting to decipher the meaning of an ancient document that appears to name them as integral to a yet-unidentified battle, the preteens also realize that, like Agora, other forms of economic human society can be fraught with problems. Reviewing the sequel in *Booklist*, Chipman wrote that *The Children of the Lost* "explores tantalizing new territory" and establishes Whitley's "Agora" saga "as one of the more literarily ambitious and complex fantasies going."

"One of the more unexpected joys of life as a children's author has been the opportunity to visit schools, libraries and book clubs, and talk directly to my readers," Whitley told *SATA*. "I'm no stranger to performance. As a classically trained bass-baritone I have sung under the baton of the late Richard Hickox, musical director of Opera Australia, and been a member of Bryn Terfel's touring chorus in Paris. But since becoming a working author, I have channeled my urge to climb onto a stage into a series of lively interactive Author Events designed to engage young readers in participating in creative fiction. And I love it!

"The children are extraordinary. I'm constantly bowled over by how clever they are, how willing to take an idea and make it their own. I've had questions of such insight from eleven year olds that it has taken me five minutes and a verbal essay to answer. I've had invitations to read their own work, which is almost always skilful, witty, and alarmingly dark.

"I do school events in person whenever I can, but nowadays, as more and more schools invite authors to appear via Skype, I can be in a classroom or library at the click of a mouse—and I never fail to go away with new energy and delight."

Biographical and Critical Sources

PERIODICALS

Booklist, August 1, 2009, Ian Chipman, review of *The Midnight Charter*, p. 58; February 1, 2011, Ian Chipman, review of *The Children of the Lost*, p. 76.

Bulletin of the Center for Children's Books, October, 2009, Karen Coats, review of *The Midnight Charter*, p. 89.

Canadian Review of Materials, November 20, 2009, Betsy Fraser, review of *The Midnight Charter*.

Kirkus Reviews, August 15, 2009, review of *The Midnight Charter*.

Publishers Weekly, August 3, 2009, review of *The Midnight Charter*, p. 45.

School Library Journal, October, 2009, Sue Giffard, review of *The Midnight Charter*, p. 140.

Voice of Youth Advocates, October, 2009, Rollie Welch, review of *The Midnight Charter*, p. 336.

ONLINE

David Whitley Home Page, http://www.davidwhitley.co.uk (December 28, 2010).

*   *   *

WINTER, Jonah 1962-

Personal

Born 1962, in Fort Worth, TX; son of Jeanette Winter (a writer and illustrator).

Addresses

Home and office—Pittsburgh, PA.

Career

Author, illustrator, musician, and poet. Worked variously as a llama rancher, a flower deliverer, and a children's book editor; George Mason University, VA, former instructor. Performer in musical band Ed's Redeeming Qualities.

Awards, Honors

Cohen Award, *Ploughshares* magazine, 2000, for "Sestina: Bob"; Slope Editions Book Prize, 2001, for *Maine: Poems*; Parent's Choice Gold Medal, 2002, for *Frida*; *Kirkus Reviews* Best Children's Books citation, 2006, and *Booklist* Top-Ten Black History Books for Youth selection, 2007, both for *Dizzy*; Capitol Choices selection, and Rainbow List selection, American Library Association, both 2009, both for *Gertrude Is Gertrude Is Gertrude*; Américas Award commended designation, 2009, for *Sonia Sotomayor*.

Writings

Diego, illustrated by mother, Jeanette Winter, Knopf (New York, NY), 1991.

Wyatt Earp and the Showdown at Tombstone, Disney Press (New York, NY), 1995.

(Self-illustrated) *Fair Ball!: Fourteen Great Stars from Baseball's Negro Leagues,* Scholastic (New York, NY), 1999.

Once upon a Time in Chicago: The Story of Benny Goodman, illustrated by Jeanette Winter, Hyperion (New York, NY), 2000.

Béisbol!: Latino Baseball Pioneers and Legends, introduction by Bruce Markusen Rodríguez, Lee & Low (New York, NY), 2001.

Wild Women of the Wild West, illustrated by Mary Morgan, Holiday House (New York, NY), 2002, illustrated by Susan Guevara, Holiday House (New York, NY), 2011.

Frida, illustrated by Ana Juan, Arthur A. Levine (New York, NY), 2002.

Paul Revere and the Bell Ringers, Aladdin (New York, NY), 2003.

Roberto Clemente: Pride of the Pittsburgh Pirates, illustrated by Raul Colón, Atheneum (New York, NY), 2005.

The 39 Apartments of Ludwig van Beethoven, illustrated by Barry Blitt, Schwartz & Wade (New York, NY), 2006.

Dizzy, illustrated by Sean Qualls, Arthur A. Levine (New York, NY), 2006.

Jonah Winter introduces readers to the life of an eccentric but very famous composer in **The 39 Apartments of Ludwig van Beethoven,** *a picture book with art by Barry Blitt.* (Illustration copyright © 2006 by Barry Blitt. Used by permission of Schwartz & Wade Books, an imprint of Random House Children's Books, a division of Random House, Inc.)

The Secret World of Hildegard, illustrated by Jeanette Winter, Arthur A. Levine (New York, NY), 2007.

Muhammad Ali: Champion of the World, illustrated by François Roca, Schwartz & Wade (New York, NY), 2008.

Steel Town, illustrated by Terry Widener, Atheneum (New York, NY), 2008.

Barack, illustrated by A.G. Ford, Katherine Tegen Books (New York, NY), 2008.

Gertrude Is Gertrude Is Gertrude Is Gertrude, illustrated by Calef Brown, Atheneum Books for Young Readers (New York, NY), 2009.

Peaceful Heroes, illustrated by Sean Addy, Arthur A. Levine Books (New York, NY), 2009.

The Fabulous Feud of Gilbert and Sullivan, illustrated by Richard Egielski, Arthur A. Levine Books (New York, NY), 2009.

Sonia Sotomayor: A Judge Grows in the Bronx/La juez que creció en el Bronx, illustrated by Edel Rodriguez, Spanish translation by Argentina Palacios Ziegler, Atheneum (New York, NY), 2009.

You Never Heard of Sandy Koufax?!, illustrated by André Carrilho, Schwartz & Wade Books (New York, NY), 2009.

Here Comes the Garbage Barge!, illustrated by Red Nose Studio, Schwartz & Wade Books (New York, NY), 2010.

Born and Bred in the Great Depression, illustrated by Kimberly Root, Schwartz & Wade Books (New York, NY), 2011.

POETRY FOR ADULTS

Maine: Poems, selected by David Lehman, Slope Editions (Raymond, NH), 2002.

Amnesia (poetry), Oberlin College Press (Oberlin, OH), 2004.

Contributor of poetry to periodicals, including *Ploughshares, Prairie Schooner,* and *Literary Review.*

Authors works have been translated into Spanish.

Adaptations

Barack was adapted as a sound recording, Recorded Books (Prince Frederick, MD), 2009.

Sidelights

In addition to writing poetry for adults, Jonah Winter has become well known to children through his many picture books for young readers. From jazz musicians to baseball players to artists, Winter introduces young readers to important people from history in biographies such as *Diego,* which recounts the childhood of Mexican muralist Diego Rivera, *Dizzy,* which focuses on jazz-music great Dizzy Gillespie, *The Secret World of Hildegard,* which introduces twelfth-century German mystic Hildegard von Bingen, and *Barack,* a picture-book profile of U.S. president Barack Obama. While other biographical profiles include legendary baseball players, expatriate poets and U.S. Supreme Court justices, and a firebrand of the American revolution, Winter also humorously chronicles the true story of a barge full of garbage that sailed the Atlantic coast without being allowed to dock in *Here Comes the Garbage Barge.* In *Steel Town* his free-verse ode to an early-twentieth-century manufacturing city ultimately "reveal[s] the quiet resilience of the human spirit," according to *Booklist* critic Thom Barthelmess. "As a nonfiction children's book writer," Winter explained to *Pittsburgh Post-Gazette* reporter Monessa Tinsley, "I see it as my job to educate children about historical figures who are either under-reported in the curriculum or . . . were mavericks in standing up to a racist culture and carving a path for other members of their respective cultures. If I can make a difference in raising the tolerance and knowledge levels of today's children, then I feel as if I'm doing my job."

Born and raised in Texas, Winter began his career as a poet, publishing his work in adult magazines as early as the age of seven. After graduating from college, however, he found the market for his poetry more competitive. Persisting in his efforts, Winter was ultimately rewarded for his stick-to-itiveness when he received a Pushcart prize for a ten-year-old poem that had been rejected by a number of periodicals. While working as a children's book editor, he wrote the text for his first published children's book *Diego,* at the request of his mother, illustrator and author Jeanette Winters. That book's success convinced Winter to focus his own efforts on writing for children and *Diego* became the first of several collaborations with his mother.

Featuring a bilingual text, *Diego* pairs a "crisp text" and "dynamic illustrations [that] successfully convey the spirit of the man and his work," according to a *Publishers Weekly* contributor. Winter continues his focus on the lives of Mexican artists in *Frida,* which gives readers an introduction to Frida Kahlo, the wife of Rivera and an artist in her own right. A *Publishers Weekly* contributor described *Frida* as "an outstanding introduction to an influential artist," and Nell D. Beram wrote in *Horn Book* that "Winter consistently manages to convey much" about his subject's life "with a few well-chosen words." Jane P. Marshall, reviewing *Frida* in New York's *Albany Times Union,* cited the "poetic sparseness" of Winter's text.

Winter's long interest in baseball began as a child, when he collected baseball cards, and he shares his love of the game and its history in several of his biographies. For his self-illustrated *Fair Ball!: Fourteen Great Stars from Baseball's Negro Leagues* he creates nostalgic paintings that mimic these old-time sports collectibles. "Winter's distinctive, painterly illustrations make the strongest statements in the book," Carolyn Phelan wrote in a favorable *Booklist* review of the book. Along with providing the history of fourteen major stars of the historical Negro Leagues, "Winter also slips amusing lore into his conversational text," explained a *Publishers Weekly* contributor.

The drama behind the composition of engaging light opera comes to life in Richard Egielski's art for Winter's picture book **The Fabulous Feud of Gilbert and Sullivan.** (Illustration copyright © 2009 by Richard Egielski. Reproduced by permission of Scholastic, Inc.)

Béisbol!: Latino Baseball Pioneers and Legends finds Winter pursuing a similar theme to *Fair Ball!*, focusing on fourteen legendary Latino baseball players in a work that Blair Christolon described in *School Library Journal* "will be a welcome addition to any baseball collection." In *Roberto Clemente: Pride of the Pittsburgh Pirates* he takes a narrower view by providing what a *Kirkus Reviews* contributor dubbed "a well-constructed introduction to a compassionate, dignified, multitalented sports hero." Featuring artwork by André Carrilho, *You Never Heard of Sandy Koufax?!* introduces readers to a left-handed pitcher who started his career with the Brooklyn Dodgers while battling the anti-Semitism of the time. In 1961, three years after moving with the team to Los Angeles, Koufax found his groove and shut out a long line of batters before retiring five years later at the peak of his career. Praising Carrilho's "breathtakingly dramatic and dynamic" art, a *Kirkus Reviews* writer added that *You Never Heard of Sandy Koufax?!* serves up "great baseball stuff," and a *Publishers Weekly* critic praised the book's "fans-in-the-stands-style prose" while dubbing it "a grand slam."

In a departure from his fact-based titles, Winter creates a picture book in the style of a "mockumentary" in *The 39 Apartments of Ludwig van Beethoven*. Salted with fact-based trivia that includes the number of legless pianos the German classical composer owned and the large number of apartments in which the tempestuous—and transient—musician resided, Winter imagines how

Beethoven might have moved those pianos from one place to another. "Older readers will enjoy its tongue-in-cheek lampoon of portentous documentaries," wrote a *Publishers Weekly* contributor, the critic concluding that "this irreverent account of a brilliant musician is full of satiric pleasures." Of Winter's characterization of Beethoven, a *Kirkus Reviews* contributor wrote: "through it all, Beethoven looms larger than life, as well he should."

Moving from classical music to jazz, Winter presents a picture-book biography of a twentieth-century American jazz legend in *Dizzy*. As a *Kirkus Reviews* contributor noted, his prose here "breaks into ecstatic scat," providing "syncopated rhythms of bebop [that] form the backbeat" of the biography. According to *School Library Journal* contributor Lee Bock, "through a powerful marriage of rhythmic text and hip and surprising illustrations, the unorthodox creator of Bebop comes to life" in *Dizzy*, aided by Sean Qualls' colorful art. *School Library Journal* contributor Ilene Cooper noted that, by inspiring an interest in "trumpet revolutionary Dizzy Gillespie," Winter inspires readers "to learn more about his music."

Beloved by their many fans for whom *The Mikado, The Pirates of Penzance,* and *H.M.S. Pinafore* rival the greatest classical operas, librettist W.S. Gilbert and musical composer Arthur Sullivan had a creative collaboration that lasted from 1871 to 1896. In *The Fabulous Feud of Gilbert and Sullivan* Winter describes life behind the curtain of Mr. D'Oyly Carte's theatre as Sullivan rejects Gilbert's idea of a play with supernatural elements as trite and forces the playwright to invent a better storyline for his next musical satire of British politics. Gilbert found his medium in Japan, and the light opera *The Mikado* proved to be the duo's most celebrated work. Brought to life in artwork by Richard Egielski that features what Lolly Robinson described in *Horn Book* as "crisp black outlines and a deep Victorian palette," Winter's entertaining story is such that "even G&S purists should applaud his attention to detail and recent scholarship," according to the critic. In *School Library Journal* Wendy Lukehart dubbed *The Fabulous Feud of Gilbert and Sullivan* "a class act," adding that both author and illustrator "succeed admirably in making the relationship between a Victorian librettist and a composer of comic operas accessible to children." Concluded *Booklist* critic Carolyn Phelan: "If the artists' quarrel seems an unlikely topic for a picture book, its resolution is a hopeful one for any audience."

Winter takes readers to turn-of-the-twentieth-century Paris in *Gertrude Is Gertrude Is Gertrude Is Gertrude,* a picture-book tribute to poet and larger-than-life personality Gertrude Stein. His text—"with a wink to Stein's own looping, playful, repetitive narrative style," according to Barthelmess in *Booklist*—is illustrated by Calef Brown in boldly colored acrylic paintings that evoke the modernist work of Matisse. In addition to capturing the creative energy of Stein's household, which she shared with life partner Alice B. Toklas and into which were welcomed many great artists of her day, Winter's book "mimes Stein's mischievous voice and cultivates its own literary audience," according to a *Publishers Weekly* critic.

In line with the author's goals of highlighting the contribution of history's mavericks—the men and women who broke with tradition in their ideas or actions—*Peaceful Heroes* includes fourteen individuals who Winter considers heroes, even though their battles were won through determination rather than aggression. Paired with portraits by artist Sean Addy, the book features fourteen short biographical essays that capture the lives of individuals both well known—Jesus, Mahatma Gandhi, Sojourner Truth, Clara Barton, and Martin Luther King, Jr.—and lesser known but still influential—Paul Rusesabagina, who kept over 1,200 Tutsis and mixed-race Hutus from being murdered by Rwanda's Hutu Interahamwe forces in 1994; San Salvadorian Archbishop Oscar Romero, who advocated for human rights until his assassination in 1980; Corrie ten Boom, who during World War II hid Jews in her native Netherlands until she was arrested and sent to a concentration camp; and Afghani feminist and activist Meena Keshwar Kamal, who gave voice to Muslim women until her

A larger-than-life literary figure is introduced to new generations in Winter's Gertrude Is Gertrude Is Gertrude, *a picture book featuring artwork by Calef Brown.* (Illustration copyright © 2009 by Calef Brown. Reprinted with permission of Atheneum Books for Young Readers, an imprint of Simon & Schuster Children's Publishing Division.)

assassination in 1987. "As a signpost to a richer understanding of peace, the collection has genuine value," wrote a *Publishers Weekly* contributor in appraising Winter's work, while in *School Library Journal* Grace Oliff cited Winter's "eclectic group" of essay subjects. While Oliff maintained that the author sometimes misrepresents history by "offering opinions as facts," she nonetheless recognized the book as "well-intentioned," and a *Kirkus Reviews* writer concluded of *Peaceful Heroes* that readers searching for "role models will be hard put to find more courageous, selfless examples."

Biographical and Critical Sources

PERIODICALS

Albany Times Union (Albany, NY), Jane P. Marshall, "Life Stories Make Great Tales for Children to Read," p. J5.

Booklist, April 15, 1999, Carolyn Phelan, review of *Fair Ball!: Fourteen Great Stars from Baseball's Negro Leagues,* p. 1528; September 1, 1999, Sally Estes, review of *Fair Ball!,* p. 132; October 1, 2001, Annie Ayres, review of *Béisbol!: Latino Baseball Pioneers and Legends,* p. 317; March 1, 2002, Hazel Rochman, review of *Frida,* p. 1148; February 15, 2005, Bill Ott, review of *Roberto Clemente: Pride of the Pittsburgh Pirates,* p. 1082; August 1, 2006, Hazel Rochman, review of *The 39 Apartments of Ludwig van Beethoven,* p. 79; November 1, 2006, Ilene Cooper, review of *Dizzy,* p. 63; October 1, 2007, Ilene Cooper, review of *The Secret World of Hildegard,* p. 72; April 1, 2008, Thom Barthelmess, review of *Steel Town,* p. 59; December 15, 2008, Ian Chipman, review of *You Never Heard of Sandy Koufax?!,* p. 51; January 1, 2009, Thom Barthelmess, review of *Is Gertrude Is Gertrude Is Gertrude,* p. 75; April 1, 2009, Carolyn Phelan, review of *The Fabulous Feud of Gilbert and Sullivan,* p. 38; October 1, 2009, Sonja Cole, interview with Winter, p. 522; December 15, 2009. Hazel Rochman, review of *Sonia Sotomayor: A Judge Grows in the Bronx,* p. 43.

Children's Bookwatch, December, 2006, review of *The 39 Apartments of Ludwig van Beethoven.*

Christian Century, December 4, 2002, review of *Frida,* p. 34.

Horn Book, March-April, 2002, Nell D. Beram, review of *Frida,* p. 233; November-December, 2006, Lolly Robinson, review of *Dizzy,* p. 738; September-October, 2007, Lauren Adams, review of *The Secret World of Hildegard,* p. 600; March-April, 2008, Tanya D. Auger, review of *Muhammad Ali: Champion of the World,* p. 231; July-August, 2008, Betty Carter, review of *Steel Town,* p. 436; March-April, 2009, Jonathan Hunt, review of *You Never Heard of Sandy Koufax?!,* p. 216; May-June, 2009, Lolly Robinson, review of *The Fabulous Feud of Gilbert and Sullivan,* p. 329.

Kirkus Reviews, December 1, 2001, review of *Frida,* p. 1691; February 15, 2005, review of *Roberto Clemente,* p. 238; August 15, 2006, review of *The 39 Apart-ments of Ludwig van Beethoven,* p. 854; September 15, 2006, review of *Dizzy,* p. 970; December 1, 2007, review of *Muhammad Ali;* May 1, 2008, review of *Steel Town;* October 1, 2008, review of *Barack;* January 1, 2009, review of *Is Gertrude Is Gertrude Is Gertrude;* January 15, 2009, review of *You Never Heard of Sandy Koufax?!;* August 15, 2009, review of *Peaceful Heroes;* January 15, 2010, review of *Here Comes the Garbage Barge!*

New York Times Book Review, May 11, 2008, Robert Lipsyte, review of *Muhammad Ali,* p. 16; October 12, 2008, review of *Barack,* p. 22.

Pittsburgh Post-Gazette, February 5, 2008, Monessa Tinsley, "Jonah Winter's Work Focuses on Famous People of Color."

Publishers Weekly, August 9, 1991, review of *Diego,* p. 57; May 10, 1999, review of *Fair Ball!,* p. 68; December 10, 2001, review of *Frida,* p. 69; April 21, 2003, review of *Maine,* p. 58; July 17, 2006, review of *The 39 Apartments of Ludwig van Beethoven,* p. 157; August 27, 2007, review of *The Secret World of Hildegard,* p. 94; December 24, 2007, review of *Muhammad Ali,* p. 55; September 15, 2008, review of *Barack,* p. 65; December 15, 2008, review of *Is Gertrude Is Gertrude Is Gertrude,* p. 52; January 5, 2009, review of *You Never Heard of Sandy Koufax?!,* p. 49; August 31, 2009, review of *Peaceful Heroes,* p. 58; November 23, 2009, review of *Sonia Sotomayor,* p. 55; January 11, 2010, review of *Here Comes the Garbage Barge!,* p. 47.

School Library Journal, July, 2001, Blair Christolon, review of *Beisbol!,* p. 101; March, 2002, Nancy Menaldi-Scanlan, review of *Frida,* p. 224; February, 2004, Gina Powell, review of *Paul Revere and the Bell Ringers,* p. 136; February 7, 2005, review of *Roberto Clemente,* p. 59; May, 2005, Marilyn Taniguchi, review of *Roberto Clemente,* p. 116; July, 2005, Coop Renner, review of *Frida,* p. 44; October, 2006, Joy Fleishhacker, review of *The 39 Apartments of Ludwig van Beethoven,* p. 130; October, 2006, Lee Bock, review of *Dizzy,* p. 143; October, 2007, Kathy Piehl, review of *The Secret World of Hildegard,* p. 140; January, 2008, Marilyn Taniguchi, review of *Muhammad Ali,* p. 112; May, 2008, Joan Kindig, review of *Steel Town,* p. 112; December, 2008, Kathy Piehl, review of *Barack,* p. 117; June, 2009, Wendy Lukehart, review of *The Fabulous Feud of Gilbert and Sullivan,* p. 113; December, 2009, Grace Oliff, review of *Peaceful Heroes,* p. 101; January, 2010, Ieva Bates, review of *Here Comes the Garbage Barge!,* p. 84.

ONLINE

Arthur A. Levine Web site, http://www.arthuralevinebooks. com/ (May 18, 2007), "Jonah Winter."

Oberlin College Web site, http://www.oberlin.edu/alum mag/ (winter, 2003), Katie Hubbard, "Winning Words."*

ZULKEY, Claire 1979-

Personal

Born April 15, 1979; daughter of Edward and Janice Zulkey; married Steve Delahoyde, October 11, 2008. *Education:* Georgetown University, B.A., 2001; Northwestern University, M.F.A. (creative writing).

Addresses

Home—Chicago, IL. *E-mail*—clairezulkey@zulkey.com.

Career

Journalist and author. Blogger, beginning 2003; freelance writer and editorial assistant.

Writings

Girls! Girls! Girls! (short stories), So New Media, 2004.
An Off Year, Dutton (New York, NY), 2009.

Contributor to books, including *Inventory: Sixteen Films Featuring Manic Pixie Dream Girls, Ten Great Songs Nearly Ruined by Saxophone, and One Hundred More Obsessively Specific Pop-Culture Lists,* Scribner (New York, NY), 2009. Contributor to periodicals, including the *Chicago Tribune, Elegant Bride, Los Angeles Times, Modern Bride, Time Out Chicago, Wall Street Journal* online, *Huffington Post,* and *ElleGirl,* and to Web logs, including Onion A.V. Club, The Frisky, The Back Table, RedEye, MBToolbox, and Flak Mag.

Sidelights

Claire Zulkey began writing her first novel, *An Off Year,* while she was a sophomore at Georgetown University. Coming off the heels of a high-school experience that was dominated by doing what was required to gain acceptance at her number-one college choice, Zulkey found her own freshman year confusing to say the least. In addition to translating her own experiences into a humorous narrative, she also wrote for her school newspaper. Since graduation, Zulkey has continued to share her engaging humor with readers, both in her Web log, zulkey.com, as well as through other online and print media, where she has published numerous articles and essays. Sixteen of these works—among them essays, lists, an interview, and short fiction—are collected in *Girls! Girls! Girls!,* which *Booklist* contributor Leon Wagner noted for its "wry wit" as well as for the "zany fictional worlds" Zulkey creates in her "more narrative stories."

In *An Off Year* readers meet Cecily Powell in August, as she and her parents arrive at her Midwestern college for the start of her freshman year. Cecily enters her dormitory, but at the door of her assigned room she panics, does an about-face, and requests to be driven back home. After a few weeks of down time, the teen begins to process the college experience, something she had not been able to do while trying to make the grades and achieve the SAT scores necessary to win a place in the freshman class. Talks with friends and counselors are helpful, and Cecily's thoughtful nature keeps her focused on the larger life goals that sometimes got lost amid the rigorous academics. Through Cecily's experiences, "Zulkey addresses the anticipation and trepidation that accompany leaving home in a funny and frank way," according to Kimberly Monaghan, the *School Library Journal* contributor also praising the novel's "honest and refreshing" narration. Reviewing *An Off Year* in *Booklist,* Heather Booth predicted that Zulkey's novel "could likely be more helpful to prospective college-goers than the student handbook."

Biographical and Critical Sources

PERIODICALS

Booklist, January 1, 2004, Leon Wagner, review of *Girls! Girls! Girls!,* p. 829; August 1, 2009, Heather Booth, review of *An Off Year,* p. 58.

Cover of Claire Zulkey's young-adult novel **An Off Year,** *which focuses on a college freshman's insecurities about what she wants for her future.* (Dutton, 2009. Jacket photograph copyright © 2009 by Bob Krasner. Used by permission of Penguin Group (USA) Inc.)

Bulletin of the Center for Children's Books, November, 2009, Deborah Stevenson, review of *An Off Year,* p. 135.

Kirkus Reviews, August 1, 2009, review of *An Off Year.*

School Library Journal, November, 2009, Kimberly Monaghan, review of *An Off Year,* p. 126.

ONLINE

Claire Zulkey Home Page, http://www.zulkey.com (December 28, 2010).

Word Riot Web log, http://www.wordriot.org/ (January 15, 2011), Ryan Robert Mullen, interview with Zulkey.

Illustrations Index

(In the following index, the number of the *volume* in which an illustrator's work appears is given *before* the colon, and the *page number* on which it appears is given *after* the colon. For example, a drawing by Adams, Adrienne appears in Volume 2 on page 6, another drawing by her appears in Volume 3 on page 80, another drawing in Volume 8 on page 1, and so on and so on. . . .)

YABC

Index references to *YABC* refer to listings appearing in the two-volume *Yesterday's Authors of Books for Children,* also published by Gale, Cengage Learning. *YABC* covers prominent authors and illustrators who died prior to 1960.

A

Aas, Ulf *5:* 174
Abbe, S. van
    See van Abbe, S.
Abel, Raymond *6:* 122; *7:* 195; *12:* 3; *21:* 86; *25:* 119
Abelliera, Aldo *71:* 120
Abolafia, Yossi *60:* 2; *93:* 163; *152:* 202
Abrahams, Hilary *26:* 205; *29:* 24, 25; *53:* 61
Abrams, Kathie *36:* 170
Abrams, Lester *49:* 26
Abulafia, Yossi *154:* 67; *177:* 3
Accardo, Anthony *191:* 3, 8
Accornero, Franco *184:* 8
Accorsi, William *11:* 198
Acs, Laszlo *14:* 156; *42:* 22
Acuna, Ed *198:* 79
Adams, Adrienne *2:* 6; *3:* 80; *8:* 1; *15:* 107; *16:* 180; *20:* 65; *22:* 134, 135; *33:* 75; *36:* 103, 112; *39:* 74; *86:* 54; *90:* 2, 3
Adams, Connie J. *129:* 68
Adams, John Wolcott *17:* 162
Adams, Kathryn *224:* 1
Adams, Lynn *96:* 44
Adams, Norman *55:* 82
Adams, Pam *112:* 1, 2
Adams, Sarah *98:* 126; *164:* 180
Adams, Steve *209:* 64
Adamson, George *30:* 23, 24; *69:* 64
Addams, Charles *55:* 5
Addison, Kenneth *192:* 173
Addy, Sean *180:* 8; *222:* 31
Ade, Rene *76:* 198; *195:* 162
Adinolfi, JoAnn *115:* 42; *176:* 2; *217:* 79
Adkins, Alta *22:* 250
Adkins, Jan *8:* 3; *69:* 4; *144:* 2, 3, 4; *210:* 11, 17, 18, 19
Adl, Shirin *225:* 2
Adler, Kelynn *195:* 47
Adler, Peggy *22:* 6; *29:* 31
Adler, Ruth *29:* 29
Adlerman, Daniel *163:* 2
Adragna, Robert *47:* 145
Agard, Nadema *18:* 1
Agee, Jon *116:* 8, 9, 10; *157:* 4; *196:* 3, 4, 5, 6, 7, 8
Agre, Patricia *47:* 195
Aguirre, Alfredo *152:* 218
Ahl, Anna Maria *32:* 24

Ahlberg, Allan *68:* 6, 7, 9; *165:* 5; *214:* 9
Ahlberg, Janet *68:* 6, 7, 9; *214:* 9
Aicher-Scholl, Inge *63:* 127
Aichinger, Helga *4:* 5, 45
Aitken, Amy *31:* 34
Ajhar, Brian *207:* 126; *220:* 2
Akaba, Suekichi *46:* 23; *53:* 127
Akasaka, Miyoshi *YABC 2:* 261
Akib, Jamel *181:* 13; *182:* 99; *220:* 74
Akino, Fuku *6:* 144
Alain *40:* 41
Alajalov *2:* 226
Albert, Chris *200:* 64
Alborough, Jez *86:* 1, 2, 3; *149:* 3
Albrecht, Jan *37:* 176
Albright, Donn *1:* 91
Alcala, Alfredo *91:* 128
Alcantará, Felipe Ugalde *171:* 186
Alcorn, John *3:* 159; *7:* 165; *31:* 22; *44:* 127; *46:* 23, 170
Alcorn, Stephen *110:* 4; *125:* 106; *128:* 172; *150:* 97; *160:* 188; *165:* 48; *201:* 113; *203:* 39; *207:* 3
Alcott, May *100:* 3
Alda, Arlene *44:* 24; *158:* 2
Alden, Albert *11:* 103
Aldridge, Andy *27:* 131
Aldridge, George *105:* 125
Aldridge, Sheila *192:* 4
Alejandro, Cliff *176:* 75
Alex, Ben *45:* 25, 26
Alexander, Ellen *91:* 3
Alexander, Lloyd *49:* 34
Alexander, Martha *3:* 206; *11:* 103; *13:* 109; *25:* 100; *36:* 131; *70:* 6, 7; *136:* 3, 4, 5; *169:* 120
Alexander, Paul *85:* 57; *90:* 9
Alexeieff, Alexander *14:* 6; *26:* 199
Alfano, Wayne *80:* 69
Aliki
    See Brandenberg, Aliki
Alko, Selina *218:* 2
Allamand, Pascale *12:* 9
Allan, Judith *38:* 166
Alland, Alexandra *16:* 255
Allen, Gertrude *9:* 6
Allen, Graham *31:* 145
Allen, Jonathan *131:* 3, 4; *177:* 8, 9, 10
Allen, Joy *168:* 185; *217:* 6, 7
Allen, Pamela *50:* 25, 26, 27, 28; *81:* 9, 10; *123:* 4, 5

Allen, Raul *207:* 94
Allen, Rowena *47:* 75
Allen, Thomas B. *81:* 101; *82:* 248; *89:* 37; *104:* 9
Allen, Tom *85:* 176
Allender, David *73:* 223
Alley, R.W. *80:* 183; *95:* 187; *156:* 100, 153; *169:* 4, 5; *179:* 17
Allison, Linda *43:* 27
Allon, Jeffrey *119:* 174
Allport, Mike *71:* 55
Almquist, Don *11:* 8; *12:* 128; *17:* 46; *22:* 110
Aloise, Frank *5:* 38; *10:* 133; *30:* 92
Alsenas, Linas *186:* 2
Alter, Ann *206:* 4, 5
Althea
    See Braithwaite, Althea
Altschuler, Franz *11:* 185; *23:* 141; *40:* 48; *45:* 29; *57:* 181
Alvin, John *117:* 5
Ambrus, Victor G. *1:* 6, 7, 194; *3:* 69; *5:* 15; *6:* 44; *7:* 36; *8:* 210; *12:* 227; *14:* 213; *15:* 213; *22:* 209; *24:* 36; *28:* 179; *30:* 178; *32:* 44, 46; *38:* 143; *41:* 25, 26, 27, 28, 29, 30, 31, 32; *42:* 87; *44:* 190; *55:* 172; *62:* 30, 144, 145, 148; *86:* 99, 100, 101; *87:* 66, 137; *89:* 162; *134:* 160
Ames, Lee J. *3:* 12; *9:* 130; *10:* 69; *17:* 214; *22:* 124; *151:* 13; *223:* 69
Amini, Mehrdokht *211:* 119
Amon, Aline *9:* 9
Amoss, Berthe *5:* 5
Amstutz, André *152:* 102; *214:* 11, 16; *223:* 99
Amundsen, Dick *7:* 77
Amundsen, Richard E. *5:* 10; *24:* 122
Ancona, George *12:* 11; *55:* 144; *145:* 7; *208:* 13
Anderson, Alasdair *18:* 122
Andersen, Bethanne *116:* 167; *162:* 189; *175:* 17; *191:* 4, 5; *218:* 20
Anderson, Bob *139:* 16
Anderson, Brad *33:* 28
Anderson, Brian *211:* 8
Anderson, C.W. *11:* 10
Anderson, Carl *7:* 4
Anderson, Catherine Corley *72:* 2
Anderson, Cecil *127:* 152
Anderson, David Lee *118:* 176
Anderson, Derek *169:* 9; *174:* 180
Anderson, Doug *40:* 111

Anderson, Erica 23: 65
Anderson, G.E. 223: 181
Anderson, Laurie 12: 153, 155
Anderson, Lena 99: 26
Anderson, Peggy Perry 179: 2
Anderson, Sara 173: 3
Anderson, Scoular 138: 13; 201: 6
Anderson, Stephanie 225: 3
Anderson, Susan 90: 12
Anderson, Tara 188: 132; 211: 115
Anderson, Wayne 23: 119; 41: 239; 56: 7; 62: 26; 147: 6; 202: 4, 5
Andreasen, Daniel 86: 157; 87: 104; 103: 201, 202; 159: 75; 167: 106, 107; 168: 184; 180: 247; 186: 9; 212: 101; 220: 110, 111; 221: 56
Andrew, Ian 111: 37; 116: 12; 166: 2
Andrew, John 22: 4
Andrews, Benny 14: 251; 31: 24; 57: 6, 7; 183: 8
Andrews, Vaughn 166: 28
Anelay, Henry 57: 173
Angel, Marie 47: 22
Angelo, Valenti 14: 8; 18: 100; 20: 232; 32: 70
Anglund, Joan Walsh 2: 7, 250, 251; 37: 198, 199, 200
Anholt, Catherine 74: 8; 131: 7; 141: 5
Anholt, Laurence 141: 4
Anno, Mitsumasa 5: 7; 38: 25, 26, 27, 28, 29, 30, 31, 32; 77: 3, 4; 157: 10, 11
Antal, Andrew 1: 124; 30: 145
Antram, David 152: 133
Apostolou, Christy Hale
See Hale, Christy
Apple, Margot 33: 25; 35: 206; 46: 81; 53: 8; 61: 109; 64: 21, 22, 24, 25, 27; 71: 176; 77: 53; 82: 245; 92: 39; 94: 180; 96: 107; 152: 4, 5; 162: 192, 194; 173: 44; 214: 21, 22, 23, 24
Appleyard, Dev 2: 192
Aragones, Sergio 48: 23, 24, 25, 26, 27
Araneus 40: 29
Arbo, Cris 103: 4; 220: 4, 5
Archambault, Matt 85: 173; 138: 19, 20; 143: 33; 145: 144; 179: 103; 187: 7; 219: 2
Archer, Janet 16: 69; 178: 156
Ardizzone, Edward 1: 11, 12; 2: 105; 3: 258; 4: 78; 7: 79; 10: 100; 15: 232; 20: 69,178; 23: 223; 24: 125; 28: 25, 26, 27, 28, 29, 30, 31,33, 34, 35, 36, 37; 31: 192, 193; 34: 215, 217; 60: 173; 64: 145; 87: 176; YABC 2: 25
Arena, Jill 176: 49
Arenella, Roy 14: 9
Argemi, David 197: 2
Argent, Kerry 103: 56; 138: 17; 158: 134
Arihara, Shino 201: 98
Arisman, Marshall 162: 50
Armer, Austin 13: 3
Armer, Laura Adams 13: 3
Armer, Sidney 13: 3
Armitage, David 47: 23; 99: 5; 155: 4
Armitage, Eileen 4: 16
Armstrong, George 10: 6; 21: 72
Armstrong, Shelagh 102: 114; 224: 4
Armstrong-Ellis, Carey 185: 196
Arno, Enrico 1: 217; 2: 22, 210; 4: 9; 5: 43; 6: 52; 29: 217, 219; 33: 152; 35: 99; 43: 31, 32, 33; 45: 212, 213, 214; 72: 72; 74: 166; 100: 169
Arnold, Alli 187: 40, 41
Arnold, Andrew 219: 155; 221: 155
Arnold, Caroline 174: 5
Arnold, Emily 76: 7, 9, 10
Arnold, Katya 115: 11; 168: 2, 3
Arnold, Tedd 116: 14; 133: 152; 160: 5; 208: 24, 25, 26, 176
Arnosky, Jim 22: 20; 70: 9, 10, 11; 118: 3, 5; 160: 8, 10; 189: 5, 7, 8, 9, 10; 217: 11, 12, 13, 14
Arnsteen, Katy Keck 105: 97; 116: 145

Arsenault, Isabelle 207: 7
Arrowood, Clinton 12: 193; 19: 11; 65: 210
Artell, Mike 89: 8
Arting, Fred J. 41: 63
Artzybasheff, Boris 13: 143; 14: 15; 40: 152, 155
Aruego, Ariane 6: 4
Aruego, José 4: 140; 6: 4; 7: 64; 33: 195; 35: 208; 68: 16, 17; 75: 46; 93: 91, 92; 94: 197; 109: 65, 67; 125: 2, 3, 4, 5; 127: 188; 143: 25; 178: 17, 19, 74; 188: 166; 202: 164
Arzoumanian, Alik 177: 12; 194: 115
Asare, Meshack 86: 9; 139: 19
Ascensios, Natalie 105: 139
Asch, Frank 5: 9; 66: 2, 4, 6, 7, 9, 10; 102: 18, 19,21; 154: 12
Ashby, Gail 11: 135
Ashby, Gil 146: 4
Ashby, Gwynneth 44: 26
Ashley, C.W. 19: 197
Ashmead, Hal 8: 70
Ashton, Tim 211: 204
Aska, Warabe 56: 10
Assel, Steven 44: 153; 77: 22, 97
Astrop, John 32: 56
Atene, Ann 12: 18
Atherton, Lisa 38: 198
Atkinson, Allen 60: 5
Atkinson, J. Priestman 17: 275
Atkinson, Janet 86: 147; 103: 138
Atkinson, Mike 127: 74
Atkinson, Wayne 40: 46
Attard, Karl 196: 22, 23
Attebery, Charles 38: 170
Atwell, Debby 150: 6
Atwood, Ann 7: 9
Aubrey, Meg Kelleher 77: 159
Auch, Herm 173: 7, 8
Auch, Mary Jane 173: 7
Augarde, Steve 25: 22; 159: 7; 210: 43, 44
Austerman, Miriam 23: 107
Austin, Margot 11: 16
Austin, Robert 3: 44
Austin, Virginia 81: 205; 127: 221
Auth, Tony 51: 5; 192: 18
Avendano, Dolores 158: 74
Avedon, Richard 57: 140
Averill, Esther 1: 17; 28: 39, 40, 41
Avilés, Martha 218: 6
Axeman, Lois 2: 32; 11: 84; 13: 165; 22: 8; 23: 49; 61: 116; 101: 124
Axtel, David 155: 110
Ayer, Jacqueline 13: 7
Ayer, Margaret 15: 12; 50: 120
Ayers, Alan 91: 58; 107: 169
Ayliffe, Alex 95: 164
Ayto, Russell 111: 5; 112: 54; 206: 7, 8; 213: 56
Azarian, Mary 112: 9, 10; 114: 129; 117: 171; 137: 163; 171: 4, 5; 181: 161; 188: 128

B

B.T.B.
See Blackwell, Basil T.
Baasansuren, Bolormaa 216: 40
Babbitt, Bradford 33: 158
Babbitt, Natalie 6: 6; 8: 220; 68: 20; 70: 242, 243; 194: 8, 9
Baca, Maria 104: 5
Bacchus, Andy 94: 87
Bacha, Andy 109: 169
Bachelet, Gilles 196: 18
Bachem, Paul 48: 180; 67: 65; 144: 206
Back, Adam 63: 125
Back, George 31: 161
Backes, Nick 190: 72
Backhouse, Colin 78: 142
Bacon, Bruce 4: 74

Bacon, Paul 7: 155; 8: 121; 31: 55; 50: 42; 56: 175; 62: 82, 84
Bacon, Peggy 2: 11, 228; 46: 44
Baek, Matthew J. 169: 95; 202: 8
Baer, Julie 161: 2
Baicker-McKee, Carol 177: 15; 180: 215
Bailey, Peter 58: 174; 87: 221; 194: 12
Bailey, Sheila 155: 11
Baker, Alan 22: 22; 61: 134; 93: 11, 12; 146: 6, 7, 10
Baker, Charlotte 2: 12
Baker, Garin 89: 65
Baker, Jeannie 23: 4; 88: 18, 19, 20
Baker, Jim 22: 24
Baker, Joe 82: 188; 111: 55; 124: 70; 197: 73
Baker, Keith 179: 6, 7; 222: 36
Baker, Leslie 112: 214; 132: 103, 246; 180: 74, 246
Baker-Smith, Grahame 223: 10; 225: 132
Baldacci, Rudy 184: 9
Baldridge, Cyrus LeRoy 19: 69; 44: 50
Baldus, Jackie 216: 81
Baldus, Zachary 152: 231; 187: 60
Balet, Jan 11: 22
Balian, Lorna 9: 16; 91: 16
Balit, Christina 102: 24; 159: 9; 162: 118, 119; 212: 2, 3
Ballantyne, R.M. 24: 34
Ballis, George 14: 199
Balouch, Kristen 176: 11
Baltzer, Hans 40: 30
Banbery, Fred 58: 15
Bancroft, Bronwyn 216: 42
Banfill, A. Scott 98: 7; 112: 59
Bang, Molly 24: 37, 38; 69: 8, 9, 10; 111: 7,9, 10, 11; 140: 11; 158: 37, 38, 39; 195: 3; 215: 11, 12, 13, 14
Banik, Yvette Santiago 21: 136
Banks, Erin Bennett 211: 12
Banner, Angela
See Maddison, Angela Mary
Bannerman, Helen 19: 13, 14
Banning, Greg 202: 98
Bannon, Laura 6: 10; 23: 8
Bantock, Nick 74: 229; 95: 6
Banyai, Istvan 185: 209; 193: 14, 16; 209: 155; 223: 166, 167
Baptist, Michael 37: 208
Baracca, Sal 135: 206
Baranaski, Marcin 182: 113
Barasch, Lynne 126: 16; 186: 15
Barbarin, Lucien C., Jr. 89: 88
Barbour, Karen 96: 5; 74: 209; 170: 16
Bare, Arnold Edwin 16: 31
Bare, Colleen Stanley 32: 33
Barger, Jan 147: 11
Bargery, Geoffrey 14: 258
Barkat, Jonathan 149: 177; 164: 254; 181: 106; 184: 186; 196: 11; 198: 148
Barker, Carol 31: 27
Barker, Cicely Mary 49: 50, 51
Barkley, James 4: 13; 6: 11; 13: 112
Barks, Carl 37: 27, 28, 29, 30, 31, 32, 33, 34
Barling, Joy 62: 148
Barling, Tom 9: 23
Barlow, Gillian 62: 20
Barlow, Perry 35: 28
Barlowe, Dot 30: 223
Barlowe, Wayne 37: 72; 84: 43; 105: 5
Barnard, Bryn 88: 53; 13: 55; 169: 13; 193: 194
Barneda, David 206: 11
Barner, Bob 29: 37; 128: 33; 136: 19, 20; 177: 27
Barnes, Hiram P. 20: 28
Barnes, Tim 137: 28
Barnes-Murphy, Rowan 88: 22
Barnett, Charles II 175: 150
Barnett, Ivan 70: 14
Barnett, Moneta 16: 89; 19: 142; 31: 102; 33: 30, 31, 32; 41: 153; 61: 94, 97

Barney, Maginel Wright *39:* 32, 33, 34; *YABC 2:* 306

Barnum, Jay Hyde *11:* 224; *20:* 5; *37:* 189, 190

Baron, Alan *80:* 3; *89:* 123

Barr, George *60:* 74; *69:* 64

Barragán, Paula S. *134:* 116; *186:* 158; *216:* 43, 44, 197

Barrall, Tim *115:* 152

Barraud, Martin *189:* 38

Barrauds *33:* 114

Barrer-Russell, Gertrude *9:* 65; *27:* 31

Barret, Robert *85:* 134

Barrett, Angela *40:* 136, 137; *62:* 74; *75:* 10; *76:* 142; *144:* 137; *145:* 14; *223:* 14

Barrett, Jennifer *58:* 149

Barrett, John E. *43:* 119

Barrett, Moneta *74:* 10

Barrett, Peter *55:* 169; *86:* 111

Barrett, Robert *62:* 145; *77:* 146; *82:* 35

Barrett, Ron *14:* 24; *26:* 35

Barron, John N. *3:* 261; *5:* 101; *14:* 220

Barrow, Ann *136:* 27

Barrows, Walter *14:* 268

Barry, Ethelred B. *37:* 79; *YABC 1:* 229

Barry, James *14:* 25

Barry, Katharina *2:* 159; *4:* 22

Barry, Robert E. *6:* 12

Barry, Scott *32:* 35

Barshaw, Ruth McNally *203:* 9

Bartenbach, Jean *40:* 31

Barth, Ernest Kurt *2:* 172; *3:* 160; *8:* 26; *10:* 31

Bartholomew, Caty *208:* 153

Bartholomew, Marie *200:* 66

Bartlett, Alison *101:* 65; *93:* 209; *51:* 209

Barton, Byron *8:* 207; *9:* 18; *23:* 66; *80:* 181; *90:* 18, 19, 20, 21; *126:* 29, 30

Barton, Harriett *30:* 71

Barton, Jill *129:* 108; *135:* 120; *145:* 185, 189; *184:* 177; *224:* 142, 143

Bartram, Robert *10:* 42

Bartram, Simon *218:* 8

Bartsch, Jochen *8:* 105; *39:* 38

Bascove, Barbara *45:* 73

Base, Graeme *101:* 15, 16, 17, 18; *162:* 8, 10, 12

Baseman, Gary *174:* 12

Bash, Barbara *132:* 9

Baskin, Leonard *30:* 42, 43, 46, 47; *49:* 125, 126, 128, 129,133; *173:* 120

Bass, Saul *49:* 192

Bassett, Jeni *40:* 99; *64:* 30

Basso, Bill *99:* 139; *189:* 134

Batchelor, Joy *29:* 41, 47, 48

Bate, Norman *5:* 16

Bates, Amy June *188:* 170; *189:* 27, 28

Bates, Leo *24:* 35

Batet, Carmen *39:* 134

Batherman, Muriel *31:* 79; *45:* 185

Battaglia, Aurelius *50:* 44

Batten, John D. *25:* 161, 162

Batten, Mary *162:* 14, 15

Battles, Asa *32:* 94, 95

Bauer, Carla *193:* 6

Bauer, Jutta *150:* 32

Bauernschmidt, Marjorie *15:* 15

Baum, Allyn *20:* 10

Baum, Willi *4:* 24, 25; *7:* 173

Bauman, Leslie *61:* 121

Baumann, Jill *34:* 170

Baumhauer, Hans *11:* 218; *15:* 163, 165, 167

Baxter, Glen *57:* 100

Baxter, Leon *59:* 102

Baxter, Robert *87:* 129

Bayer, Herbert *181:* 16

Bayley, Dorothy *37:* 195

Bayley, Nicola *40:* 104; *41:* 34, 35; *69:* 15; *129:* 33, 34, 35

Baylin, Mark *158:* 233

Baynes, Pauline *2:* 244; *3:* 149; *13:* 133, 135,137, 141; *19:* 18, 19, 20; *32:* 208, 213, 214; *36:* 105, 108; *59:* 12, 13, 14, 16, 17, 18, 20; *100:* 158, 159, 243; *133:* 3, 4

Beach, Lou *150:* 150; *207:* 117, 118

Beame, Rona *12:* 40

Bean, Jonathan *196:* 102

Bear's Heart *73:* 215

Beard, Alex *222:* 40

Beard, Dan *22:* 31, 32

Beard, J.H. *YABC 1:* 158

Bearden, Romare *9:* 7; *22:* 35

Beardshaw, Rosalind *169:* 22; *190:* 22; *224:* 12; *225:* 6, 7, 8

Beardsley, Aubrey *17:* 14; *23:* 181; *59:* 130, 131

Bearman, Jane *29:* 38

Beaton, Cecil *24:* 208

Beaton, Clare *125:* 28; *208:* 67; *220:* 10, 11, 12

Beauce, J.A. *18:* 103

Beaujard, Sophie *81:* 54

Beavers, Ethen *225:* 9

Beccia, Carlyn *189:* 29

Bechtold, Lisze *208:* 29

Beck, Charles *11:* 169; *51:* 173

Beck, Ian *138:* 27; *182:* 150; *190:* 25; *225:* 130

Beck, Melinda *203:* 112

Beck, Ruth *13:* 11

Becker, Harriet *12:* 211

Beckerman, Jonathan *208:* 194

Beckett, Sheilah *25:* 5; *33:* 37, 38

Beckhoff, Harry *1:* 78; *5:* 163

Beckhorn, Susan Williams *189:* 32

Beckman, Kaj *45:* 38, 39, 40, 41

Beckman, Per *45:* 42, 43

Beddows, Eric *72:* 70

Bedford, F.D. *20:* 118, 122; *33:* 170; *41:* 220, 221,230, 233

Bee, Joyce *19:* 62

Bee, William *188:* 6

Beeby, Betty *25:* 36

Beech, Carol *9:* 149

Beech, Mark *192:* 122

Beek *25:* 51, 55, 59

Beeke, Tiphanie *177:* 127; *204:* 140; *212:* 178; *218:* 102

Beekman, Doug *125:* 146, 148

Beerbohm, Max *24:* 208

Beeson, Bob *108:* 57

Begin, Mary Jane *82:* 13; *206:* 13

Beha, Philippe *172:* 85

Behr, Joyce *15:* 15; *21:* 132; *23:* 161

Behrens, Hans *5:* 97

Beier, Ellen *135:* 170; *139:* 47; *183:* 164; *221:* 177; *222:* 151

Beingessner, Laura *220:* 14

Beinicke, Steve *69:* 18

Beisner, Monika *46:* 128, 131; *112:* 127

Belden, Charles J. *12:* 182

Belina, Renate *39:* 132

Bell, Corydon *3:* 20

Bell, Graham *54:* 48

Bell, Julia *151:* 214

Bell, Julie *159:* 172; *165:* 18

Bell, Thomas P. *76:* 182

Bellamy, Glen *127:* 15

Beltran, Alberto *43:* 37

Bemelmans, Ludwig *15:* 19, 21; *100:* 27

Ben-Ami, Doron *75:* 96; *84:* 107; *108:* 132; *110:* 63; *159:* 157; *197:* 142

Bendall-Brunello, John *150:* 4; *157:* 163; *185:* 3, 4; *203:* 5

Benda, Wladyslaw T. *15:* 256; *30:* 76, 77; *44:* 182

Bender, Robert *77:* 162; *79:* 13; *160:* 23

Bendick, Jeanne *2:* 24; *68:* 27, 28

Benioff, Carol *121:* 42; *175:* 23

Benner, Cheryl *80:* 11

Bennett, Charles H. *64:* 6

Bennett, Erin Susanne *165:* 216

Bennett, F.I. *YABC 1:* 134

Bennett, James *146:* 240

Bennett, Jill *26:* 61; *41:* 38, 39; *45:* 54

Bennett, Rainey *15:* 26; *23:* 53

Bennett, Richard *15:* 45; *21:* 11, 12, 13; *25:* 175

Bennett, Susan *5:* 55

Benny, Mike *142:* 78; *203:* 13, 14; *207:* 85

Benoit, Elise *77:* 74

Benson, Linda *60:* 130; *62:* 91; *75:* 101; *79:* 156; *134:* 129

Benson, Patrick *68:* 162; *147:* 17, 18, 19, 20

Bentley, Carolyn *46:* 153

Bentley, James *149:* 30

Bentley, Roy *30:* 162

Benton, Jim *172:* 22

Benton, Thomas Hart *2:* 99

Berelson, Howard *5:* 20; *16:* 58; *31:* 50

Berenstain, Jan *12:* 47; *64:* 33, 34, 36, 37, 38, 40, 42, 44; *135:* 25, 28, 31, 35

Berenstain, Stan *12:* 47; *64:* 33, 34, 36, 37, 38, 40, 42, 44; *135:* 25, 28, 31, 35

Berenzy, Alix *65:* 13; *73:* 6; *78:* 115

Berg, Joan *1:* 115; *3:* 156; *6:* 26, 58

Berg, Ron *36:* 48, 49; *48:* 37, 38; *67:* 72

Bergen, David *115:* 44; *207:* 34

Berger, Barbara *77:* 14

Berger, Carin *185:* 6

Berger, Joe *221:* 9

Berger, William M. *14:* 143; *YABC 1:* 204

Bergherr, Mary *74:* 170; *151:* 123

Bergin, Mark *114:* 8, 9; *143:* 95; *160:* 26, 27

Bergstreser, Douglas *69:* 76

Bergum, Constance R. *121:* 14, 15; *208:* 31, 32, 33; *209:* 176

Bering, Claus *13:* 14

Berkeley, Jon *139:* 218

Berkowitz, Jeanette *3:* 249

Berman, Paul *66:* 14

Berman, Rachel *217:* 26

Bernal, Richard *154:* 176

Bernadette

   See Watts, Bernadette

Bernard, Gary *216:* 71

Bernardin, James *112:* 24; *167:* 94

Bernasconi, Pablo *183:* 10, 11

Bernath, Stefen *32:* 76

Berner, Rotraut Susanne *214:* 32

Bernhard, Durga *80:* 13

Bernstein, Michel J. *51:* 71

Bernstein, Ted *38:* 183; *50:* 131

Bernstein, Zena *23:* 46

Berridge, Celia *86:* 63

Berrill, Jacquelyn *12:* 50

Berry, Erick

   See Best, Allena

Berry, Holly *205:* 116; *210:* 49, 50

Berry, William D. *14:* 29; *19:* 48

Berry, William A. *6:* 219

Berson, Harold *2:* 17, 18; *4:* 28, 29, 220; *9:* 10; *12:* 19; *17:* 45; *18:* 193; *22:* 85; *34:* 172; *44:* 120; *46:* 42; *80:* 240

Bertholf, Bret *187:* 9; *189:* 32, 33

Berton, Patsy *99:* 16

Bertschmann, Harry *16:* 1

Besco, Don *70:* 99

Beskow, Elsa *20:* 13, 14, 15

Bess, Clayton *63:* 94

Best, Allena *2:* 26; *34:* 76

Betera, Carol *74:* 68

Bethell, Thomas N. *61:* 169

Bethers, Ray *6:* 22

Betteridge, Deirdre *214:* 34

Bettina

   See Ehrlich, Bettina

Betts, Ethel Franklin *17:* 161, 164, 165; *YABC 2:* 47

Betz, Rudolf *59:* 161

Bewick, Thomas *16:* 40, 41, 43, 44, 45, 47; *54:* 150; *YABC 1:* 107

Beyer, Paul J. III *74:* 24
Bezencon, Jacqueline *48:* 40
Biamonte, Daniel *40:* 90
Bianchi, John *91:* 19
Bianco, Pamela *15:* 31; *28:* 44, 45, 46
Bible, Charles *13:* 15
Bice, Clare *22:* 40
Biedrzycki, David *186:* 170; *219:* 7
Bierman, Don *57:* 184
Biggers, John *2:* 123
Biggs, Brian *192:* 38; *196:* 15; *207:* 170
Bikadoroff, Roxanna *201:* 74
Bileck, Marvin *3:* 102; *40:* 36, 37
Bilibin, Ivan *61:* 8, 9, 12, 13, 14, 15, 151, 152,
   154, 162
Billington, Patrick *98:* 71
Billout, Guy *144:* 38, 39
Bimen, Levent *5:* 179
Binch, Caroline *81:* 18; *140:* 15, 16; *144:* 115;
   211: 82
Binder, Hannes *169:* 163
Bing, Christopher *126:* 34
Binger, Bill *121:* 46
Binks, Robert *25:* 150
Binzen, Bill *24:* 47
Birch, Reginald *15:* 150; *19:* 33, 34, 35, 36;
   37: 196,197; *44:* 182; *46:* 176; *YABC 1:* 84;
   2: 34, 39
Birch, Wendy *223:* 70
Birchall, Mark *123:* 188
Bird, Esther Brock *1:* 36; *25:* 66
Birdsong, Keith *167:* 85; *219:* 105
Birkett, Georgie *204:* 121
Birkett, Rachel *78:* 206
Birling, Paul *109:* 30
Birmingham, Christian *132:* 243; *143:* 114;
   209: 58; *220:* 20
Birmingham, Lloyd P. *12:* 51; *83:* 13
Biro, Val *1:* 26; *41:* 42; *60:* 178; *67:* 23, 24;
   84: 242, 243
Bischoff, Ilse *44:* 51
Bishop, Don *199:* 133
Bishop, Gavin *97:* 17, 18; *144:* 42, 44; *216:*
   52, 55, 56, 57
Bishop, Kathleen Wong *115:* 67
Bishop, Rich *56:* 43
Bite, I. *60:* 14
Bittinger, Ned *93:* 117; *205:* 115
Bjorklund, Lorence *3:* 188, 252; *7:* 100; *9:*
   113; *10:* 66; *19:* 178; *33:* 122, 123; *35:* 36,
   37, 38, 39,41, 42, 43; *36:* 185; *38:* 93; *47:*
   106; *66:* 194; *YABC 1:* 242
Björkman, Steve *91:* 199; *160:* 110; *198:* 18;
   218: 188; *223:* 20, 21
Blabey, Aaron *214:* 35
Black Sheep *164:* 100
Blackburn, Loren H. *63:* 10
Blackall, Sophie *194:* 140; *209:* 157
Blackford, John *137:* 105; *180:* 36
Blackwell, Basil T. *YABC 1:* 68, 69
Blackwood, Freya *199:* 9
Blackwood, Gary L. *118:* 17
Blades, Ann *16:* 52; *37:* 213; *50:* 41; *69:* 21;
   99: 215
Blair, Jay *45:* 46; *46:* 155
Blaisdell, Elinore *1:* 121; *3:* 134; *35:* 63
Blake, Anne Catharine *189:* 71
Blake, Francis *198:* 4
Blake, Quentin *3:* 170; *10:* 48; *13:* 38; *21:*
   180; *26:* 60; *28:* 228; *30:* 29, 31; *40:* 108;
   45: 219; *46:* 165, 168; *48:* 196; *52:* 10, 11,
   12,13, 14, 15, 16, 17; *73:* 41, 43; *78:* 84, 86;
   80: 250, 251; *84:* 210, 211, 212; *87:* 177;
   96: 24, 26, 28; *124:* 79; *125:* 32, 34; *181:*
   139; *211:* 26, 27
Blake, Robert J. *37:* 90; *53:* 67; *54:* 23; *160:*
   28, 29
Blake, William *30:* 54, 56, 57, 58, 59, 60
Blakeslee, Lys *218:* 11, 105
Blanchard, N. Taylor *82:* 140
Blass, Jacqueline *8:* 215

Blazek, Scott R. *91:* 71
Bleck, Cathie *118:* 116
Bleck, Linda *204:* 124
Blegvad, Erik *2:* 59; *3:* 98; *5:* 117; *7:* 131; *11:*
   149; *14:* 34, 35; *18:* 237; *32:* 219; *60:* 106;
   66: 16, 17, 18, 19; *70:* 233; *76:* 18; *82:* 106;
   87: 45; *100:* 188; *129:* 125; *132:* 17, 18, 19,
   20; *176:* 14; *200:* 100; *YABC 1:* 201
Blessen, Karen *93:* 126
Bliss, Corinne Demas *37:* 38
Bliss, Harry *196:* 27, 28, 29
Blitt, Barry *179:* 199; *187:* 13; *225:* 198
Bloch, Lucienne *10:* 12
Blondon, Herve *129:* 48; *183:* 22
Bloom, Lloyd *35:* 180; *36:* 149; *47:* 99; *62:*
   117; *68:* 231; *72:* 136; *75:* 185; *83:* 99; *108:*
   19
Bloom, Suzanne *172:* 23, 24
Blossom, Dave *34:* 29
Blumenschein, E.L. *YABC 1:* 113, 115
Blumer, Patt *29:* 214
Blundell, Kim *29:* 36
Bluthenthal, Diana Cain *93:* 32; *104:* 106;
   177: 26
Blythe, Benjamin *128:* 7
Blythe, Gary *112:* 52; *181:* 166; *182:* 64; *185:*
   7; *186:* 116, 117
Boake, Kathy *176:* 185
Board, Perry *171:* 99
Boardman, Gwenn *12:* 60
Boase, Susan *224:* 53
Boatwright, Phil *211:* 195
Bober, Richard *125:* 145; *132:* 40
Bobri *30:* 138; *47:* 27
Bock, Vera *1:* 187; *21:* 41
Bock, William Sauts *8:* 7; *14:* 37; *16:* 120; *21:*
   141; *36:* 177; *62:* 203
Bodecker, N(iels) M(ogens) *8:* 13; *14:* 2; *17:*
   55, 56, 57; *73:* 22, 23, 24
Boehm, Linda *40:* 31
Bogacki, Tomek *138:* 31, 32; *144:* 123; *202:*
   13
Bogan, Paulette *197:* 152; *201:* 17
Bogdan, Florentina *107:* 43
Bohdal, Susi *22:* 44; *101:* 20
Bohlen, Nina *58:* 13
Boies, Alex *96:* 53
Bok, Chip *205:* 16
Bolam, Emily *101:* 216; *159:* 12; *205:* 59
Bolian, Polly *3:* 270; *4:* 30; *13:* 77; *29:* 197
Bolle, Frank *87:* 100; *208:* 101
Bollen, Roger *79:* 186; *83:* 16
Bolling, Vickey *114:* 44
Bollinger, Peter *101:* 7; *128:* 198; *172:* 26
Bolognese, Don *2:* 147, 231; *4:* 176; *7:* 146;
   17: 43; *23:* 192; *24:* 50; *34:* 108; *36:* 133;
   71: 24, 25; *103:* 131; *129:* 39, 40
Bolster, Rob *186:* 169
Bolton, A.T. *57:* 158
Bond, Arnold *18:* 116
Bond, Barbara Higgins *21:* 102
Bond, Bruce *52:* 97
Bond, Felicia *38:* 197; *49:* 55, 56; *89:* 170;
   90: 171; *126:* 37
Bond, Higgins *177:* 22, 23; *209:* 175; *220:* 22,
   23, 24
Bonn, Pat *43:* 40
Bonner, Hannah *197:* 13, 14
Bonners, Susan *41:* 40; *85:* 36; *94:* 99, 100;
   151: 105, 106
Bono, Mary *184:* 73
Bonsall, Crosby *23:* 6
Booker, Philip *225:* 16
Boon, Debbie *103:* 6; *144:* 188
Boon, Emilie *86:* 23, 24
Boone, Debbie *165:* 77
Boore, Sara *60:* 73
Bootman, Colin *155:* 13; *159:* 35; *174:* 192;
   222: 128
Booth, Franklin *YABC 2:* 76
Booth, George *191:* 13

Booth, Graham *32:* 193; *37:* 41, 42
Borda, Juliette *102:* 188
Bordier, Georgette *16:* 54
Boren, Tinka *27:* 128
Borges, Jose Francisco *119:* 62
Borja, Robert *22:* 48
Born, Adolf *49:* 63
Bornstein, Ruth *14:* 44; *88:* 45, 46; *107:* 30
Borten, Helen *3:* 54; *5:* 24
Bosin, Blackbear *69:* 104
Bossom, Naomi *35:* 48
Bostock, Mike *83:* 221; *114:* 14; *188:* 205
Boston, Peter *19:* 42
Bosustow, Stephen *34:* 202
Boszko, Ron *75:* 47
Bottner, Barbara *14:* 46
Boucher, Joelle *41:* 138
Boulat, Pierre *44:* 40
Boulet, Susan Seddon *50:* 47
Bouma, Paddy *118:* 25; *128:* 16
Bour, Daniele *66:* 145
Bourke-White, Margaret *15:* 286, 287; *57:* 102
Boutavant, Marc *200:* 136
Boutet de Monvel, M. *30:* 61, 62, 63, 65
Bowen, Betsy *105:* 222
Bowen, Richard *42:* 134
Bowen, Ruth *31:* 188
Bower, Ron *29:* 33
Bowers, David *95:* 38; *115:* 20; *127:* 169, 170;
   165: 57; *207:* 11
Bowers, Tim *185:* 35; *201:* 41; *218:* 13
Bowman, Claire *174:* 177
Bowman, Eric *151:* 23
Bowman, Leslie *85:* 203; *105:* 108; *116:* 76;
   128: 234; *182:* 24, 25
Bowman, Peter *146:* 214, 215; *150:* 115
Bowser, Carolyn Ewing *22:* 253
Boxall, Ed *178:* 28
Boyd, Aaron *158:* 242
Boyd, Patti *45:* 31
Boyle, Eleanor Vere *28:* 50, 51
Boynton, Sandra *57:* 13, 14, 15; *107:* 36, 37;
   152: 12, 13, 14
Bozzo, Frank *4:* 154
Brabbs, Derry *55:* 170
Brace, Eric *132:* 193, 194; *152:* 71; *184:* 195;
   197: 6; *201:* 54
Brackers de Hugo, Pierre *115:* 21
Bradford, June *158:* 138
Bradford, Ron *7:* 157
Bradley, David P. *69:* 105
Bradley, Richard D. *26:* 182
Bradley, William *5:* 164
Brady, Irene *4:* 31; *42:* 37; *68:* 191
Bragg, Michael *32:* 78; *46:* 31
Bragg, Ruth Gembicki *77:* 18
Brainerd, John W. *65:* 19
Braithwaite, Althea *23:* 12, 13; *119:* 16
Brak, Syd *146:* 187
Bralds, Braldt *90:* 28; *91:* 151
Bram, Elizabeth *30:* 67
Bramley, Peter *4:* 3
Brandenberg, Aliki *2:* 36, 37; *24:* 222; *35:* 49,
   50, 51,52, 53, 54, 56, 57; *75:* 15, 17; *92:*
   205; *113:* 18, 19, 20; *157:* 28; *156:* 111
Brandenburg, Alexa *75:* 19
Brandenburg, Jim *47:* 58; *150:* 212
Brandi, Lillian *31:* 158
Brandon, Brumsic, Jr. *9:* 25
Brannen, Sarah S. *202:* 15; *216:* 199
Bransom, Paul *17:* 121; *43:* 44
Braren, Loretta Trezzo *87:* 193
Brassard, France *186:* 22
Braun, Wendy *80:* 17, 18; *213:* 14
Brautigam, Don *115:* 175, 176; *225:* 109
Brazell, Derek *75:* 105; *79:* 9
Breathed, Berkeley *86:* 27, 28, 29; *161:* 13, 14
Breckenreid, Julia *192:* 209
Breen, Steve *186:* 23
Brennan, Steve *83:* 230; *101:* 184
Brenner, Fred *22:* 85; *36:* 34; *42:* 34

Brett, Bernard 22: 54
Brett, Harold M. 26: 98, 99, 100
Brett, Jan 30: 135; 42: 39; 71: 31, 32; 130: 23, 24, 25, 26, 27; 171: 15, 16
Brewer, Paul 106: 115; 145: 202
Brewer, Sally King 33: 44
Brewster, Patience 40: 68; 45: 22, 183; 51: 20; 66: 144; 89: 4; 97: 30, 31; 212: 99
Brick, John 10: 15
Brickman, Robin D. 131: 88; 142: 150; 155: 18; 178: 109; 184: 32
Bridge, David R. 45: 28
Bridgman, L.J. 37: 77
Bridwell, Norman 4: 37; 138: 36, 37, 40
Brierley, Louise 91: 22; 96: 165; 183: 51
Briggs, Harry 172: 187
Briggs, Raymond 10: 168; 23: 20, 21; 66: 29, 31, 32; 131: 28, 29; 184: 15, 16
Brigham, Grace A. 37: 148
Bright, Robert 24: 55
Brighton, Catherine 107: 39; 206: 23
Brinckloe, Julie 13: 18; 24: 79, 115; 29: 35; 63: 140; 81: 131
Brion 47: 116
Brisley, Joyce L. 22: 57
Brisson, James F. 110: 60
Brittingham, Geoffrey 88: 37
Brix-Henker, Silke 81: 194
Broadway, Hannah 208: 104
Brock, Charles E. 15: 97; 19: 247, 249; 23: 224, 225; 36: 88; 42: 41, 42, 43, 44, 45; 100: 189; YABC 1: 194, 196, 203
Brock, Emma 7: 21
Brock, Henry Matthew 15: 81; 16: 141; 19: 71; 34: 115; 40: 164; 42: 47, 48, 49; 49: 66
Brocksopp, Arthur 57: 157
Broda, Ron 136: 180; 174: 123
Brodkin, Gwen 34: 135
Brodovitch, Alexi 52: 22
Bromhall, Winifred 5: 11; 26: 38
Bromley, Lizzy 159: 179
Bronson, Linda 150: 210; 174: 133; 203: 16, 17; 225: 178
Brooke, L. Leslie 16: 181, 182, 183, 186; 17: 15, 16, 17; 18: 194
Brooker, Christopher 15: 251
Brooker, Kyrsten 111: 94; 140: 28; 162: 111; 175: 108; 186: 42, 225; 199: 12; 201: 30; 219: 98
Brooks, Erik 166: 52; 182: 30
Brooks, Karen Stormer 186: 110; 220: 65
Brooks, Maya Itzna 92: 153
Brooks, Ron 94: 15; 197: 188; 212: 6, 7, 8, 9
Brooks, S.G. 178: 127
Broomfield, Maurice 40: 141
Brotman, Adolph E. 5: 21
Brown, Buck 45: 48
Brown, Calef 179: 18; 210: 206; 217: 30, 31; 225: 201
Brown, Christopher 62: 124, 125, 127, 128
Brown, Craig 73: 28; 84: 65; 224: 18
Brown, Dan 61: 167; 115: 183, 184; 116: 28, 29; 193: 190; 200: 21, 23
Brown, David 7: 47; 48: 52
Brown, Denise 11: 213
Brown, Don 172: 29
Brown, Elbrite 195: 39; 198: 5
Brown, Ford Madox 48: 74
Brown, Gayle 224: 184
Brown, Hunter 191: 111, 112
Brown, Judith Gwyn 1: 45; 7: 5; 8: 167; 9: 182, 190; 20: 16, 17, 18; 23: 142; 29: 117; 33: 97; 36: 23, 26; 43: 184; 48: 201, 223; 49: 69; 86: 227; 110: 188; 153: 7
Brown, Kathryn 98: 26
Brown, Lisa 187: 175
Brown, Laurie Krasny 99: 30
Brown, Leo 225: 18

Brown, Marc (Tolon) 10: 17, 197; 14: 263; 51: 18; 53: 11, 12, 13, 15, 16, 17; 75: 58; 80: 24, 25, 26; 82: 261; 99: 29; 145: 22, 23, 25, 27; 162: 198; 224: 198
Brown, Marcia 7: 30; 25: 203; 47: 31, 32, 33, 34, 35,36, 37, 38, 39, 40, 42, 43, 44; YABC 1: 27
Brown, Margery W. 5: 32, 33; 10: 3
Brown, Martin 101: 43
Brown, Mary Barrett 97: 74
Brown, Palmer 36: 40
Brown, Paul 25: 26; 26: 107
Brown, Richard 61: 18; 67: 30
Brown, Rick 78: 71; 150: 154; 224: 16
Brown, Robert S. 85: 33
Brown, Rod 157: 142
Brown, Ruth 55: 165; 86: 112, 113; 105: 16, 17, 18; 171: 178
Brown, Trevor 99: 160; 139: 247; 189: 206
Browne, Anthony 45: 50, 51, 52; 61: 21, 22, 23, 24, 25; 105: 21, 22, 23, 25
Browne, Dik 8: 212; 67: 32, 33, 35, 37, 39
Browne, Gordon 16: 97; 64: 114, 116, 117, 119, 121
Browne, Hablot K. 15: 65, 80; 21: 14, 15, 16, 17, 18, 19,20; 24: 25
Browne, Jane 165: 222
Browning, Coleen 4: 132
Browning, Mary Eleanor 24: 84
Bruce, Robert 23: 23
Brude, Dick 48: 215
Bruel, Nick 166: 41; 205: 17, 18
Brule, Al 3: 135
Brumbeau, Jeff 157: 29
Bruna, Dick 43: 48, 49, 50; 76: 27, 28
Brundage, Frances 19: 244
Brunhoff, Jean de 24: 57, 58
Brunhoff, Laurent de 24: 60; 71: 35, 36, 37
Brunkus, Denise 84: 50; 123: 117; 178: 209; 193: 99; 204: 10, 11, 12; 209: 202
Brunson, Bob 43: 135
Bryan, Ashley 31: 44; 72: 27, 28, 29; 107: 92; 116: 192; 132: 24; 178: 33, 34, 35; 208: 83
Bryant, Laura J. 176: 36; 183: 168; 214: 141; 222: 49, 152
Bryant, Michael 93: 74
Brychta, Alex 21: 21
Bryer, Diana 107: 121
Bryson, Bernarda 3: 88, 146; 39: 26; 44: 185; 131: 40
Buba, Joy 12: 83; 30: 226; 44: 56
Buchanan, George 166: 198
Buchanan, Lilian 13: 16
Buchanan, Rachel 171: 71
Bucholtz-Ross, Linda 44: 137
Buchs, Thomas 40: 38
Buck, Margaret Waring 3: 30
Buckhardt, Marc 172: 59
Buckley, Mike 166: 180
Budwine, Greg 175: 172
Buehner, Mark 104: 12, 15; 105: 160; 119: 98; 157: 188; 159: 39, 40, 43; 192: 111; 219: 13, 14, 15, 16; 221: 17, 18, 19
Buehr, Walter 3: 31
Buell, Carl 222: 68
Buff, Conrad 19: 52, 53, 54
Buff, Mary 19: 52, 53
Bull, Charles Livingston 18: 207; 88: 175, 176
Bullen, Anne 3: 166, 167
Buller, Jon 205: 21
Bullock, Kathleen 77: 24
Bumgarner-Kirby, Claudia 77: 194
Burbank, Addison 37: 43
Burchard, Peter Duncan 3: 197; 5: 35; 6: 158, 218; 143: 17
Burckhardt, Marc 94: 48; 110: 89; 196: 41; 199: 116
Burger, Carl 3: 33; 45: 160, 162
Burgeson, Marjorie 19: 31
Burgess, Anne 76: 252
Burgess, Gelett 32: 39, 42

Burgess, Mark 157: 31
Burke, Jim 179: 19; 185: 63
Burke, Phillip 95: 117
Burkert, Nancy Ekholm 18: 186; 22: 140; 24: 62, 63,64, 65; 26: 53; 29: 60, 61; 46: 171; YABC 1: 46
Burkhardt, Bruce 142: 86
Burkhardt, Melissa A. 142: 86
Burleson, Joe 104: 35; 172: 139
Burn, Doris 6: 172
Burn, Jeffrey 89: 125; 152: 132
Burn, Ted
See Burn, Thomas E.
Burn, Thomas E. 151: 41
Burnard, Damon 115: 23
Burnett, Lindy 210: 59
Burnett, Virgil 44: 42
Burningham, John 9: 68; 16: 60, 61; 59: 28, 29, 30,31, 32, 33, 35; 111: 18, 19, 21; 160: 37; 225: 21, 24
Burns, Howard M. 12: 173
Burns, Jim 47: 70; 86: 32; 91: 197; 123: 16
Burns, M.F. 26: 69
Burns, Raymond 9: 29
Burns, Robert 24: 106
Burr, Dan 65: 28; 108: 134; 164: 203; 182: 68
Burr, Dane 12: 2
Burra, Edward YABC 2: 68
Burrell, Galen 56: 76
Burri, Rene 41: 143; 54: 166
Burridge, Marge Opitz 14: 42
Burris, Burmah 4: 81
Burroughs, John Coleman 41: 64
Burroughs, Studley O. 41: 65
Burton, Marilee Robin 46: 33
Burton, Virginia Lee 2: 43; 44: 49, 51; 100: 46, 47; YABC 1: 24; 147: 56
Busoni, Rafaello 1: 186; 3: 224; 6: 126; 14: 5; 16: 62, 63
Butchkes, Sidney 50: 58
Butler, Geoff 94: 20
Butler, Ralph 116: 212
Butterfield, Ned 1: 153; 27: 128; 79: 63
Butterworth, Ian 184: 48, 49
Butterworth, Nick 106: 43, 44; 149: 34
Buxton, John 123: 12
Buzelli, Christopher 105: 149
Buzonas, Gail 29: 88
Buzzell, Russ W. 12: 177
Byard, Carole 39: 44; 57: 18, 19, 20; 60: 60; 61: 93, 96; 69: 210; 78: 246; 79: 227
Byars, Betsy 46: 35
Byfield, Barbara Ninde 8: 18
Byfield, Graham 32: 29
Bynum, Janie 176: 50
Byrd, Robert 13: 218; 33: 46; 158: 70; 212: 100
Byrd, Samuel 123: 104

C

Cabat, Erni 74: 38
Cabban, Vanessa 138: 73; 176: 39; 185: 65
Cabrera, Jane 103: 24; 152: 27; 182: 33, 34
Caceres, Ana Palmero 198: 106
Caddy, Alice 6: 41
Cady, Harrison 17: 21, 23; 19: 57, 58
Caffrey, Aileen 72: 223; 141: 154
Cairns, Julia 177: 37
Caldecott, Randolph 16: 98, 103; 17: 32, 33, 36, 38, 39; 26: 90; 100: 49, 50; YABC 2: 172
Calder, Alexander 18: 168
Calderón, Gloria 179: 5
Calderon, W. Frank 25: 160
Caldwell, Ben 105: 75; 149: 60; 195: 61
Caldwell, Clyde 98: 100; 116: 39; 208: 145
Caldwell, Doreen 23: 77; 71: 41
Caldwell, John 46: 225

Call, Greg *126:* 135; *165:* 49; *182:* 105, 163; *197:* 18, 19; *200:* 159; *209:* 166; *212:* 161
Callahan, Kevin *22:* 42
Callahan, Philip S. *25:* 77
Callan, Jamie *59:* 37
Calvert, Rosemary *218:* 96
Calvin, James *61:* 92
Camburn-Bracalente, Carol A. *118:* 22
Cameron, Chad *190:* 144
Cameron, Julia Margaret *19:* 203
Cameron, Scott *99:* 18
Camm, Martin *140:* 208, 209, 210
Campbell, Ann *11:* 43; *123:* 182; *183:* 68
Campbell, Bill *89:* 39
Campbell, Ken *126:* 143; *205:* 162
Campbell, Robert *55:* 120
Campbell, Rod *51:* 27; *98:* 34
Campbell, Walter M. *YABC 2:* 158
Camps, Luis *28:* 120, 121; *66:* 35
Canga, C.B. *187:* 165
Caniglia, Jeremy *201:* 89
Cann, Helen *124:* 50; *141:* 78; *170:* 138; *179:* 22, 23
Cannell, Jon *196:* 43
Cannon, Janell *78:* 25; *128:* 40
Canright, David *36:* 162
Cantone, AnnaLaura *182:* 146; *196:* 80
Canty, Thomas *85:* 161; *92:* 47; *113:* 192; *134:* 60; *185:* 117
Canyon, Christopher *150:* 44; *151:* 112
Caparo, Antonio Javier *204:* 128; *218:* 88; *220:* 114; *221:* 167
Caporale, Wende *70:* 42
Capp, Al *61:* 28, 30, 31, 40, 41, 43, 44
Cappon, Manuela *154:* 64; *218:* 149
Caras, Peter *36:* 64
Caraway, Caren *57:* 22
Caraway, James *3:* 200, 201
Carbe, Nino *29:* 183
Cares, Linda *67:* 176
Carigiet, Alois *24:* 67
Carle, Eric *4:* 42; *11:* 121; *12:* 29; *65:* 32,33, 34, 36; *73:* 63, 65; *163:* 55, 56
Carling, Amelia Lau *164:* 46
Carlino, Angela *168:* 43; *188:* 20
Carlson, Nancy L. *41:* 116; *56:* 25; *90:* 45; *144:* 48, 50; *213:* 24, 25, 26
Carluccio, Maria *175:* 129; *221:* 119
Carmi, Giora *79:* 35; *149:* 40; *208:* 126
Carpenter, Nancy *76:* 128; *86:* 173; *89:* 171; *131:* 186; *134:* 8; *138:* 215; *153:* 204; *159:* 93; *165:* 232; *211:* 134; *216:* 113
Carr, Archie *37:* 225
Carrick, Donald *5:* 194; *39:* 97; *49:* 70; *53:* 156; *63:* 15, 16, 17, 18, 19, 21; *80:* 131; *86:* 151; *118:* 24
Carrick, Malcolm *28:* 59, 60
Carrick, Paul *118:* 26; *194:* 28
Carrick, Valery *21:* 47
Carrier, Lark *71:* 43
Carroll, Jim *88:* 211; *140:* 177; *153:* 99; *195:* 75
Carroll, Lewis
See Dodgson, Charles L.
Carroll, Michael *72:* 5
Carroll, Pamela *84:* 68; *128:* 214; *199:* 130
Carroll, Ruth *7:* 41; *10:* 68
Carter, Abby *81:* 32; *97:* 121; *102:* 61; *163:* 139; *164:* 125; *184:* 22, 23; *191:* 85; *222:* 51
Carter, Barbara *47:* 167, 169
Carter, David A. *114:* 24, 25; *170:* 42, 43
Carter, Don *124:* 54; *184:* 100; *192:* 43, 44, 45
Carter, Harry *22:* 179
Carter, Helene *15:* 38; *22:* 202, 203; *YABC 2:* 220, 221
Carter, Penny *173:* 91
Cartlidge, Michelle *49:* 65; *96:* 50, 51
Cartwright, Reg *63:* 61, 62; *78:* 26; *143:* 4
Cartwright, Shannon *176:* 81
Carty, Leo *4:* 196; *7:* 163; *58:* 131
Cary *4:* 133; *9:* 32; *20:* 2; *21:* 143

Cary, Page *12:* 41
Casale, Paul *71:* 63; *109:* 122; *136:* 28
Case, Chris *209:* 23
Case, Sandra E. *16:* 2
Caseley, Judith *87:* 36; *159:* 47, 48, 49
Casilla, Robert *78:* 7; *167:* 124; *211:* 41; *212:* 165
Casino, Steve *85:* 193
Cassel, Lili
See Wronker, Lili Cassel
Cassel-Wronker, Lili
See Wronker, Lili Cassel
Cassels, Jean *8:* 50; *150:* 119; *173:* 37; *186:* 182
Cassen, Melody *140:* 51
Cassity, Don *104:* 24
Cassler, Carl *75:* 137, 138; *82:* 162
Casson, Hugh *65:* 38, 40, 42, 43
Castellon, Federico *48:* 45, 46, 47, 48
Castle, Jane *4:* 80
Castro, Antonio *84:* 71
Casu, Danny "casroc" *201:* 10
Catalano, Dominic *94:* 79; *163:* 60, 61; *162:* 54
Catalanotto, Peter *63:* 170; *70:* 23; *71:* 182; *72:* 96; *74:* 114; *76:* 194, 195; *77:* 7; *79:* 157; *80:* 28, 67; *83:* 157; *85:* 27; *108:* 11; *113:* 30, 31, 33, 34, 36; *114:* 27, 28, 29; *117:* 53; *124:* 168; *159:* 54, 55; *195:* 19, 20, 21, 22, 24, 174; *200:* 156; *207:* 103; *209:* 184
Catania, Tom *68:* 82
Cather, Carolyn *3:* 83; *15:* 203; *34:* 216
Catlin, George *214:* 172
Catrow, David *117:* 179; *152:* 31, 33; *173:* 24; *206:* 29
Catusanu, Mircea *222:* 53
Cauley, Lorinda Bryan *44:* 135; *46:* 49
Cayard, Bruce *38:* 67
Cazet, Denys *52:* 27; *99:* 39, 40; *163:* 65, 66; *191:* 25, 27, 28
Ceccoli, Nicoletta *181:* 39; *188:* 99; *199:* 118; *209:* 6
Cecil, Randy *127:* 132, 133; *187:* 16, 17; *191:* 168; *209:* 5; *223:* 37, 38; *224:* 83
Cellini, Joseph *2:* 73; *3:* 35; *16:* 116; *47:* 103
Cepeda, Joe *90:* 62; *109:* 91; *134:* 172; *159:* 57, 58, 164; *197:* 157; *203:* 69, 95; *215:* 38, 39, 40
Chabrian, Debbi *45:* 55
Chabrian, Deborah *51:* 182; *53:* 124; *63:* 107; *75:* 84; *79:* 85; *82:* 247; *89:* 93; *101:* 197; *212:* 13
Chagnon, Mary *37:* 158
Chalmers, Mary *3:* 145; *13:* 148; *33:* 125; *66:* 214
Chamberlain, Christopher *45:* 57
Chamberlain, Margaret *46:* 51; *106:* 89; *188:* 193; *212:* 16, 17; *224:* 181
Chamberlain, Nigel *78:* 140
Chambers, C.E. *17:* 230
Chambers, Dave *12:* 151
Chambers, Jill *134:* 110
Chambers, Mary *4:* 188
Chambliss, Maxie *42:* 186; *56:* 159; *93:* 163, 164; *103:* 178; *186:* 33, 34; *196:* 39; *223:* 182
Champlin, Dale *136:* 124
Chan, Harvey *96:* 236; *99:* 153; *143:* 218; *179:* 144; *211:* 219
Chan, Peter *207:* 21; *221:* 39
Chandler, David P. *28:* 62
Chaney, Howard *139:* 27
Chang, Warren *101:* 209
Chapel, Jody *68:* 20
Chapman, C.H. *13:* 83, 85, 87
Chapman, Frederick T. *6:* 27; *44:* 28
Chapman, Gaye *203:* 133
Chapman, Gaynor *32:* 52, 53

Chapman, Jane *145:* 186; *150:* 56; *166:* 220; *174:* 202; *176:* 43, 44; *179:* 131; *202:* 189; *212:* 20, 21, 22; *216:* 123, 225; *221:* 181, 182
Chapman, Lynne *175:* 31; *197:* 25; *208:* 44
Chapman-Crane, Jeff *220:* 101
Chappell, Warren *3:* 172; *21:* 56; *27:* 125
Charles, Donald *30:* 154, 155
Charlip, Remy *4:* 48; *34:* 138; *68:* 53, 54; *119:* 29, 30; *210:* 63, 64
Charlot, Jean *1:* 137, 138; *8:* 23; *14:* 31; *48:* 151; *56:* 21
Charlot, Martin *64:* 72
Charlton, Michael *34:* 50; *37:* 39
Charmatz, Bill *7:* 45
Chartier, Normand *9:* 36; *52:* 49; *66:* 40; *74:* 220; *145:* 169; *168:* 91; *177:* 108
Chase, Lynwood M. *14:* 4
Chast, Roz *97:* 39, 40; *212:* 25
Chastain, Madye Lee *4:* 50
Chateron, Ann *152:* 19
Chatterton, Martin *68:* 102; *152:* 19; *225:* 42
Chau, Tungwai *140:* 35
Chauncy, Francis *24:* 158
Chayka, Doug *145:* 97; *177:* 150; *196:* 46; *212:* 58
Chee, Cheng-Khee *79:* 42; *81:* 224; *180:* 245
Chen, Chih-sien *90:* 226
Chen, Tony *6:* 45; *19:* 131; *29:* 126; *34:* 160
Chen, Wendy *221:* 76
Chen, Yong *183:* 34
Cheney, T.A. *11:* 47
Cheng, Andrea *205:* 28
Cheng, Judith *36:* 45; *51:* 16
Chermayeff, Ivan *47:* 53
Cherry, David *93:* 40
Cherry, Lynne *34:* 52; *65:* 184; *87:* 111; *99:* 46, 47
Chesak, Lina *135:* 118
Chess, Victoria *12:* 6; *33:* 42, 48, 49; *40:* 194; *41:* 145; *69:* 80; *72:* 100; *92:* 33, 34; *104:* 167
Chessare, Michele *41:* 50; *56:* 48; *69:* 145
Chesterton, G.K. *27:* 43, 44, 45, 47
Chestnutt, David *47:* 217
Chesworth, Michael *75:* 24, 152; *88:* 136; *94:* 25; *98:* 155; *160:* 42; *207:* 23, 24, 25; *214:* 145
Chetham, Celia *134:* 34
Chetwin, Grace *86:* 40
Cheung, Irving *158:* 96
Chevalier, Christa *35:* 66
Chew, Ruth *7:* 46; *132:* 147
Chewning, Randy *92:* 206
Chichester Clark, Emma *72:* 121; *77:* 212; *78:* 209; *87:* 143; *117:* 37, 39, 40; *144:* 138; *156:* 24, 25; *209:* 26
Chifflart *47:* 113, 127
Child, Lauren *119:* 32; *183:* 30, 31
Chin, Alex *28:* 54
Chitwood, Susan Tanner *163:* 16
Cho, Shinta *8:* 126
Chodos-Irvine, Margaret *52:* 102, 103, 107; *152:* 44
Choi, Yangsook *171:* 134; *173:* 135; *178:* 38, 39, 40
Choksi, Nishant *222:* 54
Chollat, Emilie *170:* 203
Chollick, Jay *25:* 175
Choma, Christina *99:* 169
Chomey, Steve *188:* 53
Chorao, Kay *7:* 200, 201; *8:* 25; *11:* 234; *33:* 187; *35:* 239; *69:* 35; *70:* 235; *123:* 174; *193:* 179; *215:* 43, 44, 45, 46
Chorney, Steve *221:* 63
Chow, Frances J. Soo Ping *206:* 36
Chowdhury, Subrata *62:* 130; *162:* 22, 23
Christelow, Eileen *38:* 44; *83:* 198, 199; *90:* 57, 58; *184:* 26
Christensen, Bonnie *93:* 100; *153:* 67; *213:* 29, 30

Christensen, Gardell Dano *1:* 57
Christensen, James C. *140:* 226
Christiana, David *90:* 64; *135:* 13; *171:* 7; *195:* 26, 27
Christiansen, Per *40:* 24
Christie, R. Gregory *116:* 107; *127:* 20, 21; *162:* 179; *164:* 114; *165:* 137; *174:* 157; *179:* 172; *185:* 17, 18, 19; *200:* 2; *204:* 85; *215:* 207; *218:* 57; *220:* 80, 130; *225:* 45, 46, 47
Christy, Howard Chandler *17:* 163, 164, 165, 168, 169; *19:* 186, 187; *21:* 22, 23, 24, 25
Christy, Jana *194:* 21
Chronister, Robert *23:* 138; *63:* 27; *69:* 167
Church, Caroline Jayne *179:* 27; *219:* 28, 29
Church, Frederick *YABC 1:* 155
Chute, Marchette *1:* 59
Chwast, Jacqueline *1:* 63; *2:* 275; *6:* 46, 47; *11:* 125; *12:* 202; *14:* 235
Chwast, Seymour *3:* 128, 129; *18:* 43; *27:* 152; *92:* 79; *96:* 56, 57, 58; *146:* 32, 33; *197:* 99
Cieslawksi, Steve *101:* 142; *127:* 116; *158:* 169, 171; *190:* 174; *212:* 85
Cinelli, Lisa *146:* 253
Cirlin, Edgard *2:* 168
Clairin, Georges *53:* 109
Clapp, John *105:* 66; *109:* 58; *126:* 7; *129:* 148; *130:* 165; *195:* 48; *220:* 102
Clark, Brenda *119:* 85; *153:* 55
Clark, David *77:* 164; *134:* 144, 145; *216:* 66, 67
Clark, Emma Chichester
   See Chichester Clark, Emma
Clark, Victoria *35:* 159
Clarke, Greg *169:* 134; *215:* 47, 115
Clarke, Gus *72:* 226; *134:* 31
Clarke, Harry *23:* 172, 173
Clarke, Peter *75:* 102
Claverie, Jean *38:* 46; *88:* 29
Clavis, Philippe Goossens *182:* 167
Clay, Wil *203:* 29
Clayton, Elaine *159:* 60; *209:* 32
Clayton, Robert *9:* 181
Cleary, Brian P. *186:* 37
Cleaver, Elizabeth *8:* 204; *23:* 36
Cleland, Janet *225:* 111
Cleland, T.M. *26:* 92
Clemens, Peter *61:* 125
Clement, Charles *20:* 38
Clement, Gary *186:* 79; *191:* 32
Clement, Janet *182:* 50
Clement, Nathan *200:* 30
Clement, Rod *97:* 42
Clement, Stephen *88:* 3
Clementson, John *84:* 213
Clemesha, David *192:* 49, 50
Cleminson, Kate *221:* 26
Clevin, Jorgen *7:* 50
Clifford, Judy *34:* 163; *45:* 198
Clokey, Art *59:* 44
Clouse, Dennis *187:* 158
Clouse, James *84:* 15
Clouse, Nancy L. *78:* 31; *114:* 90; *225:* 117
Clover, Peter *152:* 45
Cneut, Carll *156:* 166; *165:* 67; *197:* 26
Coalson, Glo *9:* 72, 85; *25:* 155; *26:* 42; *35:* 212; *53:* 31; *56:* 154; *94:* 37, 38, 193
Cober, Alan E. *17:* 158; *32:* 77; *49:* 127
Cober-Gentry, Leslie *92:* 111
Cocca-Leffler, Maryann *80:* 46; *136:* 60; *139:* 193; *194:* 31, 33, 34
Cochran, Bobbye *11:* 52
Cochran, Josh *221:* 27
CoConis, Ted *4:* 41; *46:* 41; *51:* 104
Cocozza, Chris *87:* 18; *110:* 173; *111:* 149
Cockroft, Jason *152:* 20
Coerr, Eleanor *1:* 64; *67:* 52
Coes, Peter *35:* 172
Cogancherry, Helen *52:* 143; *69:* 131; *77:* 93; *78:* 220; *109:* 204; *110:* 129; *203:* 92

Coggins, Jack *2:* 69
Cohen, Alix *7:* 53
Cohen, Lisa *225:* 49
Cohen, Miriam *155:* 23, 24
Cohen, Nancy R. *165:* 35
Cohen, Santiago *164:* 26; *215:* 52, 199
Cohen, Sheldon *105:* 33, 34; *166:* 46, 47
Cohen, Vincent O. *19:* 243
Cohen, Vivien *11:* 112
Coker, Paul *51:* 172
Colbert, Anthony *15:* 41; *20:* 193
Colby, C.B. *3:* 47
Cole, Babette *58:* 172; *96:* 63, 64; *155:* 29
Cole, Brock *68:* 223; *72:* 36, 37, 38, 192; *127:* 23; *136:* 64, 65; *197:*
Cole, Gwen *87:* 185
Cole, Henry *178:* 120; *181:* 42, 43; *189:* 60; *213:* 35, 36; *222:* 139
Cole, Herbert *28:* 104
Cole, Michael *59:* 46
Cole, Olivia H.H. *1:* 134; *3:* 223; *9:* 111; *38:* 104
Cole, Rachael *209:* 39
Colin, Paul *102:* 59; *123:* 118; *126:* 152; *192:* 129
Colley, Jacqui *202:* 20
Collicott, Sharleen *98:* 39; *143:* 29, 30
Collier, Bryan *126:* 54; *151:* 166; *174:* 16, 17, 18; *204:* 18, 19; *208:* 84; *211:* 143
Collier, David *13:* 127
Collier, John *27:* 179; *208:* 154
Collier, Steven *50:* 52
Collier-Morales, Roberta *168:* 61
Collins, Heather *66:* 84; *67:* 68; *81:* 40; *98:* 192, 193; *129:* 95, 96, 98
Collins, Matt *167:* 90
Collins, Ross *140:* 23, 24; *200:* 36, 37; *209:* 54
Colman, Audrey *146:* 161
Colón, Raul *108:* 112; *113:* 5; *117:* 167; *134:* 112; *146:* 23; *159:* 92; *166:* 73; *180:* 107; *186:* 156; *190:* 6; *193:* 24, 205; *202:* 21, 22, 23; *217:* 68; *220:* 126, 157
Colonna, Bernard *21:* 50; *28:* 103; *34:* 140; *43:* 180; *78:* 150
Comport, Sally Wern *117:* 169; *169:* 104; *190:* 42; *207:* 50
Conahan, Carolyn *215:* 17
Conde, J.M. *100:* 120
Condon, Grattan *54:* 85 Condon, Ken *161:* 44; *195:* 28, 29
Cone, Ferne Geller *39:* 49
Cone, J. Morton *39:* 49
Conklin, Paul *43:* 62
Connelly, Gwen *212:* 30
Connelly, James *198:* 12
Connolly, Howard *67:* 88
Connolly, Jerome P. *4:* 128; *28:* 52
Connolly, Peter *47:* 60
Conoly, Walle *110:* 224
Conover, Chris *31:* 52; *40:* 184; *41:* 51; *44:* 79; *213:* 39
Constantin, Pascale *207:* 159
Contreras, Gerry *72:* 9
Converse, James *38:* 70
Conway *62:* 62
Conway, Michael *69:* 12; *81:* 3; *92:* 108
Cook, Ande *188:* 135
Cook, G.R. *29:* 165
Cook, Joel *108:* 160
Cookburn, W.V. *29:* 204
Cooke, Donald E. *2:* 77
Cooke, Tom *52:* 118
Coomaraswamy, A.K. *50:* 100
Coombs, Charles *43:* 65
Coombs, Deborah *139:* 175
Coombs, Patricia *2:* 82; *3:* 52; *22:* 119; *51:* 32, 33, 34, 35, 36, 37, 38, 39, 40, 42, 43

Cooney, Barbara *6:* 16, 17, 50; *12:* 42; *13:* 92; *15:* 145; *16:* 74, 111; *18:* 189; *23:* 38, 89, 93; *32:* 138; *38:* 105; *59:* 48, 49, 51, 52, 53; *74:* 222; *81:* 100; *91:* 25; *96:* 71, 72, 74; *100:* 149; *YABC2:* 10
Cooper, Elisha *157:* 38, 39
Cooper, Floyd *79:* 95; *81:* 45; *84:* 82; *85:* 74; *91:* 118; *96:* 77, 78; *103:* 149; *144:* 54; *145:* 151; *159:* 198; *176:* 133, 134; *187:* 26, 27, 28, 29; *188:* 22; *199:* 175; *219:* 66
Cooper, Heather *50:* 39
Cooper, Helen *102:* 42, 43, 44
Cooper, Mario *24:* 107
Cooper, Marjorie *7:* 112
Cope, Jane *61:* 201; *108* 52
Copeland, Mark *180:* 12
Copelman, Evelyn *8:* 61; *18:* 25
Copley, Heather *30:* 86; *45:* 57
Corace, Jen *208:* 48
Corbett, Grahame *30:* 114; *43:* 67
Corbino, John *19:* 248
Corcos, Lucille *2:* 223; *10:* 27; *34:* 66
Cordell, Matthew *197:* 93; *199:* 20, 21
Córdova, Amy *220:* 194
Corey, Robert *9:* 34
Corlass, Heather *10:* 7
Cornell, James *27:* 60
Cornell, Jeff *11:* 58
Cornell, Laura *94:* 179; *95:* 25
Corr, Christopher *204:* 98
Corral, Ridrigs *212:* 87
Corrigan, Barbara *8:* 37
Corrigan, Patrick *145:* 149
Corwin, Judith Hoffman *10:* 28
Corwin, Oliver *191:* 119
Cory, Fanny Y. *20:* 113; *48:* 29
Cosentino, Ralph *169:* 32
Cosgrove, Margaret *3:* 100; *47:* 63; *82:* 133
Costabel, Eva Deutsch *45:* 66, 67
Costanza, John *58:* 7, 8, 9
Costello, Chris *86:* 78
Costello, David F. *23:* 55
Côté, Geneviéve *184:* 37, 39; *210:* 256; *211:* 151
Cote, Nancy *126:* 139; *156:* 101; *174:* 101; *182:* 53, 54, 55; *222:* 49
Cottenden, Jeff *190:* 45
Couch, Greg *94:* 124; *110:* 13; *162:* 31; *168:* 149; *199:* 22; *216:* 144
Councell, Ruth Tietjen *79:* 29
Courtney, Cathy *58:* 69, 144; *59:* 15; *61:* 20, 87
Courtney, R. *35:* 110
Counihan, Claire *133:* 106
Cousineau, Normand *89:* 180; *112:* 76
Cousins, Lucy *172:* 53, 54; *205:* 34, 35
Couture, Christin *41:* 209
Covarrubias, Miguel *35:* 118, 119, 123, 124, 125
Coville, Katherine *32:* 57; *36:* 167; *92:* 38
Covington, Neverne *113:* 87
Cowdrey, Richard *169:* 170; *178:* 205; *204:* 22, 23; *215:* 31
Cowell, Cressida *140:* 39
Cowell, Lucinda *77:* 54
Cowles, Rose *203:* 164, 167
Cox *43:* 93
Cox, Charles *8:* 20
Cox, David *56:* 37; *90:* 63; *119:* 38
Cox, Palmer *24:* 76, 77
Cox, Steve *140:* 96
Coxe, Molly *69:* 44
Coxon, Michele *158:* 80
Crabb, Gordon *70:* 39
Crabtree, Judith *98:* 42
Craft, Kinuko *22:* 182; *36:* 220; *53:* 122, 123, 148,149; *74:* 12; *81:* 129; *86:* 31; *89:* 139; *127:* 27, 28, 29; *132:* 142; *139:* 38
Craig, Daniel *177:* 67; *180:* 11; *185:* 203; *211:* 212; *224:* 27
Craig, David *136:* 198; *205:* 37

Craig, Helen *49:* 76; *62:* 70, 71, 72; *69:* 141; *94:* 42, 43, 44; *112:* 53; *135:* 101, 102; *213:* 45, 46, 47, 55, 81, 82
Crane, Alan H. *1:* 217
Crane, H.M. *13:* 111
Crane, Jack *43:* 183
Crane, Jordan *174:* 21
Crane, Walter *18:* 46, 47, 48, 49, 53, 54, 56, 57, 59, 60, 61; *22:* 128; *24:* 210, 217; *100:* 70, 71
Cravath, Lynne Avril *98:* 45; *182:* 58, 59; *216:* 48; *219:* 61; *220:* 124; *224:* 183
Crawford, Allen *212:* 181
Crawford, Denise *137:* 213
Crawford, Will *43:* 77
Credle, Ellis *1:* 69
Czekaj, Jef *217:* 44; *218:* 77
Czernecki, Stefan *154:* 104; *178:* 68, 69
Crespi, Francesca *87:* 90
Cressy, Michael *124:* 55; *203:* 132
Crews, Donald *32:* 59, 60; *76:* 42, 43, 44
Crews, Nina *97:* 49
Crichlow, Ernest *74:* 88; *83:* 203
Crilley, Mark *210:* 71
Croft, James *150:* 57
Crofut, Bob *80:* 87; *81:* 47
Crofut, Susan *23:* 61
Croll, Carolyn *80:* 137; *102:* 52
Cross, Peter *56:* 78; *63:* 60, 65
Crossman, David A. *219:* 38
Crowe, Elizabeth *88:* 144
Crowell, Pers *3:* 125
Cruikshank, George *15:* 76, 83; *22:* 74, 75, 76, 77, 78, 79,80, 81, 82, 84, 137; *24:* 22, 23
Crump, Fred H. *11:* 62
Cruz, Ray *6:* 55; *70:* 234; *123:* 173; *172:* 192
Csatari, Joe *44:* 82; *55:* 152; *63:* 25, 28; *102:* 58
Cuetara, Mittie *158:* 85
Cuffari, Richard *4:* 75; *5:* 98; *6:* 56; *7:* 13,84, 153; *8:* 148, 155; *9:* 89; *11:* 19; *12:* 55, 96,114; *15:* 51, 202; *18:* 5; *20:* 139; *21:* 197; *22:* 14, 192; *23:* 15, 106; *25:* 97; *27:* 133; *28:* 196; *29:* 54; *30:* 85; *31:* 35; *36:* 101; *38:* 171; *42:* 97; *44:* 92, 192; *45:* 212, 213; *46:* 36, 198; *50:* 164; *54:* 80, 136, 137, 145; *56:* 17; *60:* 63; *66:* 49, 50; *70:* 41; *71:* 132; *77:* 157; *78:* 58, 149; *79:* 120; *85:* 2, 152
Cugat, Xavier *19:* 120
Cumings, Art *35:* 160
Cummings, Chris *29:* 167
Cummings, Michael *159:* 142
Cummings, Pat *42:* 61; *61:* 99; *69:* 205; *71:* 57,58; *78:* 24, 25; *93:* 75; *107:* 49, 50; *164:* 259; *203:* 45, 46
Cummings, Richard *24:* 119
Cunette, Lou *20:* 93; *22:* 125
Cunningham, Aline *25:* 180
Cunningham, David *11:* 13
Cunningham, Imogene *16:* 122, 127
Cunningham, Kelley *176:* 159
Cupples, Pat *107:* 12; *126:* 109; *182:* 13; *198:* 68; *217:* 21, 22
Curlee, Lynn *98:* 48; *141:* 39; *190:* 48
Currey, Anna *190:* 145; *202:* 130, 132
Curry, John Steuart *2:* 5; *19:* 84; *34:* 36; *144:* 126
Curry, Tom *127:* 131; *185:* 25, 26
Curtis, Bruce *23:* 96; *30:* 88; *36:* 22
Curtis, Neil *167:* 30
Curtis, Stacy *205:* 38
Cusack, Margaret *58:* 49, 50, 51
Cushman, Doug *65:* 57; *101:* 39, 40; *133:* 179; *157:* 45; *186:* 157; *210:* 76, 77
Cutting, Ann *196:* 194
Cyrus, Kurt *132:* 39; *179:* 36, 37
Czechowski, Alicia *95:* 21; *171:* 37
Czernecki, Stefan *117:* 173

D

Dabcovich, Lydia *25:* 105; *40:* 114; *99:* 75, 76
Dacey, Bob *82:* 175; *152:* 65
d'Achille, Gino *127:* 175, 176
Daily, Don *78:* 197; *220:* 154
Dain, Martin J. *35:* 75
Dale, Penny *127:* 224; *151:* 57; *160:* 89; *197:* 75
Dale, Rae *72:* 197
Daley, Joann *50:* 22
Dalton, Anne *40:* 62; *63:* 119
Daly, Deborah M. *74:* 213
Daly, Jim *103:* 60; *150:* 48
Daly, Jude *138:* 118, 119; *213:* 41; *222:* 56, 57
Daly, Nicholas *37:* 53; *76:* 48, 49
Daly, Niki *107:* 15; *114:* 38, 39, 40; *164:* 86; *192:* 53; *198:* 26, 27
Daly, Paul *97:* 205
Dalziel, Brothers *33:* 113
D'Amato, Alex *9:* 48; *20:* 25
D'Amato, Janet *9:* 48; *20:* 25; *26:* 118
D'Amico, Steve *170:* 52
Danalis, Johnny *167:* 27
D'Andrea, Domenick *183:* 108
Daniel, Alan *23:* 59; *29:* 110; *76:* 50, 53, 55, 56; *153:* 76 *115:* 74; *134:* 70
Daniel, Lea *76:* 53, 55; *153:* 76
Daniel, Lewis C. *20:* 216
Daniels, Beau *73:* 4
Daniels, Steve *22:* 16
Daniels, Stewart *56:* 12
Dann, Bonnie *31:* 83
Dann, Penny *82:* 128
Danska, Herbert *24:* 219
Danyell, Alice *20:* 27
Darbyshire, Kristen *218:* 41
Dardik, Helen *208:* 200
Darley, F.O.C. *16:* 145; *19:* 79, 86, 88, 185; *21:* 28,36; *35:* 76, 77, 78, 79, 80, 81; *YABC 2:* 175
Darling, Lois *3:* 59; *23:* 30, 31
Darling, Louis *1:* 40, 41; *2:* 63; *3:* 59; *23:* 30,31; *43:* 54, 57, 59; *121:* 53
Darnell, K.L. *210:* 247
Darrow, David R. *84:* 101
Darrow, Whitney, Jr. *13:* 25; *38:* 220, 221
Darwin, Beatrice *43:* 54
Darwin, Len *24:* 82
Dastolfo, Frank *33:* 179
Dauber, Liz *1:* 22; *3:* 266; *30:* 49
Daugherty, James *3:* 66; *8:* 178; *13:* 27, 28, 161; *18:* 101; *19:* 72; *29:* 108; *32:* 156; *42:* 84; *YABC 1:* 256; *2:* 174
d'Aulaire, Edgar Parin *5:* 51; *66:* 53
d'Aulaire, Ingri Parin *5:* 51; *66:* 53
Davalos, Felipe *99:* 197; *159:* 66; *174:* 163
Davenier, Christine *125:* 88; *127:* 32; *128:* 152; *179:* 39, 40; *216:* 84, 85, 86, 87; *218:* 62, 63; *224:* 73
Davick, Linda *151:* 124; *208:* 187
David, Jacques-Louis *193:* 22
David, Jonathan *19:* 37
Davidson, Kevin *28:* 154
Davidson, Raymond *32:* 61
Davie, Helen K. *77:* 48, 49
Davies, Andy Robert *205:* 169
Davies, Lottie *214:* 69
Davis, Allen *20:* 11; *22:* 45; *27:* 222; *29:* 157; *41:* 99; *47:* 99; *50:* 84; *52:* 105
Davis, Bette J. *15:* 53; *23:* 95
Davis, Dimitris *45:* 95
Davis, Eleanor *209:* 33
Davis, Hendon *151:* 122
Davis, Jack E. *145:* 139; *175:* 84, 85; *208:* 102; *210:* 81, 82; *213:* 151
Davis, Jim *32:* 63, 64
Davis, Katie *152:* 52, 53, 54; *208:* 52
Davis, Lambert *110:* 23, 24; *176:* 58

Davis, Marguerite *31:* 38; *34:* 69, 70; *100:* 34; *YABC 1:* 126, 230
Davis, Nelle *69:* 191
Davis, Paul *78:* 214
Davis, Rich *206:* 38
Davis, Stuart *211:* 69
Davis, Yvonne LeBrun *94:* 144
Davisson, Virginia H. *44:* 178
DaVolls, Andy *85:* 53
Dawson, Diane *24:* 127; *42:* 126; *52:* 130; *68:* 104
Dawson, Janine *215:* 198
Dawson, Willow *208:* 54; *216:* 119
Day, Alexandra *67:* 59; *97:* 54; *166:* 65; *169:* 40; *197:* 50, 51, 52, 54
Day, Larry *169:* 88; *185:* 59
Day, Rob *94:* 110; *127:* 24; *197:* 32
Dean, Bob *19:* 211
Dean, David *192:* 55
de Angeli, Marguerite *1:* 77; *27:* 62, 65, 66, 67, 69, 70, 72; *100:* 75, 76; *YABC 1:* 166
DeArmond, Dale *70:* 47
Deas, Michael *27:* 219, 221; *30:* 156; *67:* 134; *72:* 24; *75:* 155; *84:* 206; *88:* 124
Deas, Rich *191:* 87; *193:* 10; *212:* 79
deBarros, Jim *196:* 60
Debon, Nicolas *151:* 60; *177:* 46
de Bosschere, Jean *19:* 252; *21:* 4; *186:* 44, 45
De Bruyn, M(onica) G. *13:* 30, 31
Decker, C.B. *172:* 120; *215:* 94
De Cuir, John F. *1:* 28, 29
Deeter, Catherine *74:* 110; *103:* 150; *137:* 50
Degen, Bruce *40:* 227, 229; *57:* 28, 29; *56:* 156; *75:* 229; *76:* 19; *81:* 36, 37; *92:* 26; *93:* 199; *97:* 56, 58, 59; *124:* 40; *147:* 39, 40, 41; *168:* 23; *205:* 45, 46
De Grazia *14:* 59; *39:* 56, 57
DeGrazio, George *88:* 40
deGroat, Diane *9:* 39; *18:* 7; *23:* 123; *28:* 200, 201; *31:* 58, 59; *34:* 151; *41:* 152; *43:* 88; *46:* 40, 200; *49:* 163; *50:* 89; *52:* 30, 34; *54:* 43; *63:* 5; *70:* 136; *71:* 99; *73:* 117,156; *77:* 34; *85:* 48; *86:* 201; *87:* 142; *90:* 72, 73, 143; *95:* 182; *111:* 123; *118:* 160; *126:* 8; *130:* 130; *138:* 93, 94; *169:* 46, 47
de Groot, Lee *6:* 21
Deines, Brian *110:* 139; *220:* 36, 37
DeJohn, Marie *89:* 78
Dekhteryov, B. *61:* 158
de Kiefte, Kees *94:* 107
Delacre, Lulu *36:* 66; *156:* 35; *202:* 10, 53; *209:* 36
Delaney, A. *21:* 78
Delaney, Michael *180:* 16
Delaney, Molly *80:* 43
Delaney, Ned *28:* 68; *56:* 80; *102:* 11
DeLapine, Jim *79:* 21
De La Roche Saint Andre, Anne *75:* 37
de Larrea, Victoria *6:* 119, 204; *29:* 103; *72:* 203; *87:* 199
Delehanty, Joan W. *223:* 165
DeLeon, Melanie *210:* 43
Delessert, Étienne *7:* 140; *46:* 61, 62, 63, 65, 67, 68; *130:* 38, 39, 40, 41, 42; *179:* 46, 47, 48, 49; *YABC 2:* 209
Delezenne, Christine *186:* 126
Del Negro, Janice *196:* 161
Delon, Melanie *216:* 30
DeLorenzo, Christopher *154:* 149
Delulio, John *15:* 54
DeLuna, Tony *88:* 95
Demarest, Chris L. *45:* 68, 69, 70; *73:* 172, 173, 176; *78:* 106; *82:* 48, 49; *89:* 212; *92:* 86; *128:* 57, 58; *175:* 46, 48
De Mejo, Oscar *40:* 67
De Muth, Roger *205:* 184; *221:* 35
Demi *11:* 135; *15:* 245; *66:* 129, 130; *89:* 216; *102:* 66, 67, 68; *210:* 86, 87, 89
Denetsosie, Hoke *13:* 126; *82:* 34
Denise, Christopher *147:* 43, 44; *176:* 101; *193:* 35, 36, 37; *201:* 37

Dennis, Morgan *18:* 68, 69; *64:* 89
Dennis, Wesley *2:* 87; *3:* 111; *11:* 132; *18:* 71, 72, 73, 74; *22:* 9; *24:* 196, 200; *46:* 178; *69:* 94, 96; *129:* 62
Denos, Julia *202:* 26
Denslow, W.W. *16:* 84, 85, 86, 87; *18:* 19, 20, 24; *29:* 211; *100:* 21
Denton, Kady MacDonald *110:* 82; *130:* 70; *181:* 54, 55, 56; *192:* 75
Denton, Phil *220:* 6
Denton, Terry *72:* 163; *174:* 26; *186:* 52; *196:* 83, 84
DePalma, Mary Newell *132:* 114; *139:* 75; *185:* 30, 31; *186:* 121; *213:* 62
dePaola, Tomie *8:* 95; *9:* 93; *11:* 69; 25; 103; *28:* 157; *29:* 80; *39:* 52, 53; *40:* 226; *46:* 187; *59:* 61, 62, 63, 64, 65, 66, 67, 68, 69, 71, 72, 74; *62:* 19; *108:* 63, 67, 68, 70; *155:* 62, 64, 66; *180:* 105; *200:* 47, 48, 49, 50
Deraney, Michael J. *77:* 35; *78:* 148
deRosa, Dee *70:* 48; *71:* 210; *91:* 78
Dervaux, Isabelle *111:* 117
DeSaix, Deborah Durland *180:* 15; *188:* 24
De Saulles, Tony *119:* 39
de Sève, Peter *146:* 261; *207:* 78; *219:* 42
Deshaprabhu, Meera Dayal *86:* 192
Desimini, Lisa *86:* 68; *94:* 47; *96:* 7; *104:* 107; *125:* 194; *131:* 180; *172:* 56; *216:* 89, 90
de St. Menin, Charles *70:* 17
Detmold, Edward J. *22:* 104, 105, 106, 107; *35:* 120; *64:* 5; *YABC 2:* 203
Detrich, Susan *20:* 133
Deutermann, Diana *77:* 175
DeVelasco, Joseph E. *21:* 51
de Veyrac, Robert *YABC 2:* 19
DeVille, Edward A. *4:* 235
de Visser, John *55:* 119
Devito, Bert *12:* 164
Devlin, Harry *11:* 74; *74:* 63, 65; *136:* 77, 78
Dewan, Ted *108:* 73; *157:* 55; *165:* 129
Dewar, Nick *133:* 122
Dewdney, Anna *184:* 43, 44
Dewey, Ariane *7:* 64; *33:* 195; *35:* 208; *68:* 16,17; *75:* 46; *93:* 91; *94:* 197; *109:* 65, 66, 67; *125:* 2, 3, 4, 5; *127:* 188; *143:* 25; *178:* 17, 19, 74; *188:* 166; *202:* 164
Dewey, Jennifer (Owings) *58:* 54; *64:* 214; *65:* 207; *88:* 169; *103:* 45
Dewey, Kenneth *39:* 62; *51:* 23; *56:* 163
de Zanger, Arie *30:* 40
Diakité, Baba Wagué *174:* 28
Diamond, Donna *21:* 200; *23:* 63; *26:* 142; *35:* 83, 84, 85, 86, 87, 88, 89; *38:* 78; *40:* 147; *44:* 152; *50:* 144; *53:* 126; *69:* 46, 47, 48, 201; *71:* 133; *123:* 19
Dias, Ron *71:* 67
Diaz, David *80:* 213; *96:* 83, 84; *108:* 228; *110:* 29; *149:* 106; *150:* 63; *179:* 160; *184:* 95, 97; *189:* 51, 52, 53; *221:* 86
di Bartolo, Jim *225:* 53
Dibley, Glin *138:* 83; *141:* 128; *211:* 162; *221:* 61
DiCesare, Joe *70:* 38; *71:* 63, 106; *79:* 214; *93:* 147; *116:* 217; *143:* 111; *166:* 57
Dick, John Henry *8:* 181
Dickens, Frank *34:* 131
Dickey, Robert L. *15:* 279
Dickson, Mora *84:* 21
Didier, Sam *166:* 114
Dietz, James *128:* 223; *193:* 136
di Fate, Vincent *37:* 70; *90:* 11; *93:* 60; *109:* 219, 220
Di Fiori, Lawrence *10:* 51; *12:* 190; *27:* 97; *40:* 219; *93:* 57; *130:* 45
Digby, Desmond *97:* 180
Dignan, James *196:* 143
Di Grazia, Thomas *32:* 66; *35:* 241
Dillard, Annie *10:* 32
Dillard, Sarah *136:* 186; *217:* 53
Dillon, Corinne B. *1:* 139

Dillon, Diane *4:* 104, 167; *6:* 23; *13:* 29; *15:* 99; *26:* 148; *27:* 136, 201; *51:* 29, 48, 51, 52, 53, 54,55, 56, 57, 58, 59, 60, 61, 62; *54:* 155; *56:* 69; *58:* 127,128; *61:* 95; *62:* 27; *64:* 46; *68:* 3; *69:* 209; *74:* 89; *79:* 92; *86:* 89; *92:* 28, 177; *93:* 7, 210; *94:* 239, 240; *97:* 167; *106:* 58, 59,61, 64; *107:* 3; *139:* 246; *167:* 77; *189:* 202; *191:* 191; *194:* 45, 46, 48, 49
Dillon, Leo *4:* 104, 167; *6:* 23; *13:* 29; *15:* 99; *26:* 148; *27:* 136, 201; *51:* 29, 48, 51, 52, 53, 54,55, 56, 57, 58, 59, 60, 61, 62; *54:* 155; *56:* 69; *58:* 127,128; *61:* 95; *62:* 27; *64:* 46; *68:* 3; *69:* 209; *74:* 89; *79:* 92; *86:* 89; *92:* 28, 177; *93:* 7, 210; *94:* 239, 240; *97:* 167; *106:* 58, 59,61, 64; *107:* 3; *139:* 246; *167:* 77; *189:* 202; *191:* 191; *194:* 45, 46, 48, 49
Dillon, Sharon Saseen *59:* 179, 188
DiMaccio, Gerald *121:* 80
DiMaggio, Joe *36:* 22
DiMassi, Gina *169:* 17
Dinan, Carol *25:* 169; *59:* 75
Dines, Glen *7:* 66, 67
Dinesen, Thomas *44:* 37
Dinh, Pham Viet *167:* 184
Dinnerstein, Harvey *42:* 63, 64, 65, 66, 67, 68; *50:* 146
Dinsdale, Mary *10:* 65; *11:* 171
Dinyer, Eric *86:* 148; *109:* 163; *110:* 239; *124:* 11; *150:* 69; *170:* 4; *171:* 30
Dion, Nathalie *170:* 124; *213:* 52
DiRocco, Carl *181:* 23
DiSalvo-Ryan, DyAnne *59:* 77; *62:* 185; *117:* 46; *144:* 64; *150:* 153; *186:* 162
Disney, Walt *28:* 71, 72, 73, 76, 77, 78, 79, 80, 81, 87, 88, 89,90, 91, 94
DiTerlizzi, Tony *105:* 7; *147:* 22; *154:* 31, 32, 33; *214:* 74
Divito, Anna *83:* 159
Dixon, Don *74:* 17; *109:* 196
Dixon, Larry *127:* 125
Dixon, Maynard *20:* 165
Doares, Robert G. *20:* 39
Dob, Bob *205:* 14
Dobias, Frank *22:* 162
Dobrin, Arnold *4:* 68
Dobson, Steven Gaston *102:* 103
Docherty, Thomas *218:* 45, 46
Dockray, Tracy *139:* 77
Docktor, Irv *43:* 70
Dodd, Ed *4:* 69
Dodd, Emma *203:* 57
Dodd, Julie *74:* 73
Dodd, Lynley *35:* 92; *86:* 71; *132:* 45, 46, 47
Dodge, Bill *96:* 36; *118:* 7, 8, 9; *133:* 135
Dodgson, Charles L. *20:* 148; *33:* 146; *YABC 2:* 98
Dodson, Bert *9:* 138; *14:* 195; *42:* 55; *54:* 8; *60:* 49; *101:* 125
Dodson, Liz Brenner *105:* 117; *111:* 15
Dohanos, Stevan *16:* 10
Dolce, J. Ellen *74:* 147; *75:* 41
Dolch, Marguerite P. *50:* 64
Dolesch, Susanne *34:* 49
Dollar, Diane *57:* 32
Dolobowsky, Mena *81:* 54
Dolson, Hildegarde *5:* 57
Domanska, Janina *6:* 66, 67; *YABC 1:* 166
Domi *134:* 113
Dominguez, El *53:* 94
Domjan, Joseph *25:* 93
Domm, Jeffrey C. *84:* 69; *135:* 70
Donahey, William *68:* 209
Donahue, Dorothy *76:* 170
Donahue, Vic *2:* 93; *3:* 190; *9:* 44
Donald, Elizabeth *4:* 18
Donalty, Alison *149:* 195, 196, 197
Donato *85:* 59; *149:* 204; *191:* 19
Donato, Michael A. *200:* 143
Doner, Kim *208:* 57

Doney, Todd L.W. *87:* 12; *93:* 112; *98:* 135; *101:* 57; *104:* 40; *118:* 163; *135:* 162, 163; *151:* 18
Donna, Natalie *9:* 52
Donohue, Dorothy *95:* 2; *132:* 30; *176:* 54, 55; *178:* 77, 78, 79
Dooling, Michael *82:* 19; *105:* 55; *106:* 224; *125:* 135; *171:* 46; *172:* 12; *176:* 120; *197:* 89; *220:* 39, 40
Doran, Ben-Ami *128:* 189
Doran, Colleen *211:* 48
Dore, Gustave *18:* 169, 172, 175; *19:* 93, 94, 95, 96, 97, 98,99, 100, 101, 102, 103, 104, 105; *23:* 188; *25:* 197, 199
Doremus, Robert *6:* 62; *13:* 90; *30:* 95, 96, 97; *38:* 97
Dorfman, Ronald *11:* 128
Doriau *86:* 59; *91:* 152
Dorman, Brandon *197:* 35; *204:* 6; *210:* 104; *212:* 95; *216:* 156; *222:* 133
Dormer, Frank W. *200:* 55; *222:* 48
Dorros, Arthur *78:* 42, 43; *91:* 28
Doruyter, Karel *165:* 105
dos Santos, Joyce Audy *57:* 187, 189
Doty, Roy *28:* 98; *31:* 32; *32:* 224; *46:* 157; *82:* 71; *142:* 7
Doucet, Bob *132:* 238; *169:* 159
Dougherty, Charles *16:* 204; *18:* 74
Doughty, Rebecca *177:* 174; *222:* 159
Doughty, Thomas *118:* 31; *140:* 60
Douglas, Aaron *31:* 103
Douglas, Allen *223:* 53
Douglas, Carole Nelson *73:* 48
Douglas, Goray *13:* 151
Dow, Brian *150:* 92
Dowd, Jason *132:* 51, 52; *164:* 244
Dowd, Vic *3:* 244; *10:* 97
Dowden, Anne Ophelia *7:* 70, 71; *13:* 120
Dowdy, Mrs. Regera *29:* 100
Downard, Barry *202:* 32
Downes, Belinda *180:* 29
Downing, Julie *60:* 140; *81:* 50; *86:* 200; *99:* 129
Doyle, Janet *56:* 31
Doyle, Richard *21:* 31, 32, 33; *23:* 231; *24:* 177; *31:* 87
Draper, Angie *43:* 84
Drath, Bill *26:* 34
Drawson, Blair *17:* 53; *126:* 65
Dray, Matt *177:* 47
Drescher, Henrik *105:* 60, 62, 63; *172:* 72
Drescher, Joan *30:* 100, 101; *35:* 245; *52:* 168; *137:* 52
Dressell, Peggy *186:* 41
Drew, Janet *201:* 177
Drew, Patricia *15:* 100
Dronzek, Laura *199:* 28, 29; *207:* 69
Drummond, Allan *209:* 41
Drummond, V.H. *6:* 70
Drury, Christian Potter *105:* 97; *186:* 224
Dubanevich, Arlene *56:* 44
Dubin, Jill *205:* 56; *217:* 25
Dubois, Claude K. *196:* 2
Dubois, Gerard *182:* 9
DuBurke, Randy *187:* 89; *222:* 136; *224:* 35
Ducak, Danilo *99:* 130; *108:* 214
Duchesne, Janet *6:* 162; *79:* 8
Duda, Jana *102:* 155; *209:* 134
Dudash, C. Michael *32:* 122; *77:* 134; *82:* 149; *212:* 93, 94
Duer, Douglas *34:* 177
Duewell, Kristina *195:* 76
Duffy, Daniel Mark *76:* 37; *101:* 196; *108:* 147, 148
Duffy, Joseph *38:* 203
Duffy, Pat *28:* 153
Dugan, Karen *181:* 26; *202:* 35
Dugin, Andrej *77:* 60
Dugina, Olga *77:* 60
Duke, Chris *8:* 195; *139:* 164

Duke, Kate 87: 186; 90: 78, 79, 80, 81; 192: 21, 59, 60, 61, 63
Duke, Marion 165: 87
Dulac, Edmund 19: 108, 109, 110, 111, 112, 113, 114, 115, 117; 23: 187; 25: 152; YABC 1: 37; 2: 147
Dulac, Jean 13: 64
Dumas, Philippe 52: 36, 37, 38, 39, 40, 41, 42, 43, 45; 119: 40, 41, 42
Dunaway, Nancy 108: 161
Dunbar, James 76: 63
Dunbar, Polly 181: 60, 61; 211: 51, 52, 53; 212: 42
Duncan, Beverly 72: 92
Duncan, John 116: 94
Dunn, H.T. 62: 196
Dunn, Harvey 34: 78, 79, 80, 81
Dunn, Iris 5: 175
Dunn, Phoebe 5: 175
Dunne, Jeanette 72: 57, 173, 222
Dunnick, Regan 176: 51; 178: 83, 84; 219: 36; 224: 144
Dunnington, Tom 3: 36; 18: 281; 25: 61; 31: 159; 35: 168; 48: 195; 79: 144; 82: 230
Dunn-Ramsey, Marcy 117: 131
Dunrea, Olivier 59: 81; 118: 53, 54; 124: 43
Duntze, Dorothee 88: 28; 160: 76
Dupasquier, Philippe 86: 75; 104: 76; 151: 63
duPont, Lindsay Harper 207: 39
DuQuette, Keith 90: 83; 155: 73, 74
Durand, Delphine 200: 56
Durham, Sarah 192: 248
Durney, Ryan 208: 122
Duroussy, Nathalie 146: 150
Durrell, Julie 82: 62; 94: 62
Dusíková, Maja 223: 49
Dutz 6: 59
Duvoisin, Roger 2: 95; 6: 76, 77; 7: 197; 28: 125; 30: 101, 102, 103, 104, 105, 107; 47: 205; 84: 254
Dyer, Dale 141: 71
Dyer, Jane 75: 219; 129: 28; 147: 49, 50, 51; 168: 121; 190: 4; 191: 57, 59, 60; 203: 4
Dyer, Sarah 212: 40
Dypold, Pat 15: 37

E

E.V.B.
See Boyle, Eleanor Vere (Gordon)
Eachus, Jennifer 29: 74; 82: 201; 164: 153
Eadie, Bob 63: 36
Eagle, Bruce 95: 119
Eagle, Ellen 82: 121; 89: 3
Eagle, Jeremy 141: 71
Eagle, Michael 11: 86; 20: 9; 23: 18; 27: 122; 28: 57; 34: 201; 44: 189; 73: 9; 78: 235; 85: 43
Earl-Bridges, Michele 159: 128
Earle, Edwin 56: 27
Earle, Olive L. 7: 75
Earle, Vana 27: 99
Earley, Lori 132: 2; 186: 4; 195: 8
Early, Margaret 72: 59
East, Jacqueline 218: 198; 224: 38
East, Stella 131: 223
Eastman, P.D. 33: 57
Easton, Reginald 29: 181
Eaton, Tom 4: 62; 6: 64; 22: 99; 24: 124
Eaves, Edward 224: 13
Ebbeler, Jeffrey 193: 62; 206: 45
Ebel, Alex 11: 89
Eberbach, Andrea 192: 115
Ebert, Len 9: 191; 44: 47
Echevarria, Abe 37: 69
Echo Hawk, Bunky 187: 192
Eckersley, Maureen 48: 62
Eckert, Horst 72: 62
Ede, Janina 33: 59

Edens, Cooper 49: 81, 82, 83, 84, 85; 112: 58
Edens, John 109: 115
Edgar, Sarah E. 41: 97
Edgerton, Perky 195: 144
Edliq, Emily S. 131: 107
Edrien 11: 53
Edwards, Freya 45: 102
Edwards, George Wharton 31: 155
Edwards, Gunvor 2: 71; 25: 47; 32: 71; 54: 106
Edwards, Jeanne 29: 257
Edwards, Linda Strauss 21: 134; 39: 123; 49: 88, 89
Edwards, Michelle 152: 62, 63
Edwards, Wallace 170: 55
Egan, Tim 155: 76, 77, 78
Egge, David 102: 71
Eggenhofer, Nicholas 2: 81
Eggleton, Bob 74: 40; 81: 190, 191; 105: 6; 121: 183; 149: 203; 166: 215
Egielski, Richard 11: 90; 16: 208; 33: 236; 38: 35; 49: 91, 92, 93, 95, 212, 213, 214, 216; 79: 122; 106: 67, 68, 69; 134: 135; 144: 244; 163: 82, 84; 207: 125; 225: 200
Ehlert, Lois 35: 97; 69: 51; 112: 7; 113: 208; 128: 63, 64, 65; 172: 77, 79, 80; 220: 43, 44, 45, 46, 47, 48
Ehrlich, Bettina 1: 83
Eitan, Ora 160: 165
Eichenberg, Fritz 1: 79; 9: 54; 19: 248; 23: 170; 24: 200; 26: 208; 50: 67, 68, 69, 70, 71, 72, 73,74, 75, 77, 79, 80, 81; 60: 165; 100: 137; YABC 1: 104, 105; 2: 213
Einsel, Naiad 10: 35; 29: 136
Einsel, Walter 10: 37
Einzig, Susan 3: 77; 43: 78; 67: 155; 129: 154
Eisner, Will 165: 82, 83
Eitzen, Allan 9: 56; 12: 212; 14: 226; 21: 194; 38: 162; 76: 218
Eldridge, H. 54: 109
Eldridge, Harold 43: 83
Elgaard, Greta 19: 241
Elgin, Kathleen 9: 188; 39: 69
Ellacott, S.E. 19: 118
Elliot, David 192: 26; 208: 62, 63
Elliott, Mark 93: 69; 105: 108; 107: 123; 140: 53; 165: 189; 173: 67; 195: 95; 203: 67; 210: 99; 221: 57, 70
Elliott, Sarah M. 14: 58
Ellis, Carson 216: 210
Ellis, Dianne 130: 208
Ellis, Jan Davey 88: 50; 115: 80
Ellis, Richard 130: 47, 48
Ellison, Chris 196: 66; 199: 131; 207: 193
Ellison, Pauline 55: 21
Ellwand, David 213: 60
Elmer, Richard 78: 5
Elmore, Larry 90: 8
Elschner, Géraldine 183: 38
Elwell, Peter 195: 150
Elwell, Tristan 110: 39; 121: 182; 127: 46; 137: 144; 141: 173; 151: 236; 158: 264; 167: 119, 120, 121; 169: 20; 190: 12; 202: 16
Elzbieta 88: 80, 81
Ember, Kathi 214: 147
Emberley, Ed 8: 53; 70: 53, 54; 146: 65, 69, 70; 218: 50
Emberley, Rebecca 218: 50
Emberley, Michael 34: 83; 80: 72; 119: 47, 48; 147: 100; 158: 115; 189: 62, 64; 203: 87, 89
Emerling, Dorothy 104: 27
Emery, Leslie 49: 187
Emmett, Bruce 49: 147; 80: 175; 101: 206; 220: 200
Emry-Perrott, Jennifer 61: 57
Emshwiller, Ed 174: 45
Endle, Kate 191: 167; 207: 41
Engel, Diana 70: 57
Engle, Mort 38: 64

Englebert, Victor 8: 54
English, Mark 101: 207; 220: 201
Enik, Ted 142: 39
Enos, Randall 20: 183
Enright, Maginel Wright 19: 240, 243; 39: 31, 35, 36
Enrique, Romeo 34: 135
Ensor, Barbara 180: 30
Epstein, Stephen 50: 142, 148
Erdogan, Buket 174: 179
Erdrich, Louise 141: 62
Erhard, Walter 1: 152
Erickson, Jim 196: 190
Erickson, Phoebe 11: 83; 59: 85
Erikson, Mel 31: 69
Eriksson, Eva 63: 88, 90, 92, 93; 203: 99; 207: 44
Ering, Timothy Basil 131: 100; 176: 63, 64; 202: 29; 204: 8
Erlbruch, Wolf 181: 66
Ernst, Lisa Campbell 47: 147; 95: 47; 154: 46, 47, 48; 164: 88; 212: 45
Esco, Jo 61: 103
Escourido, Joseph 4: 81
Escrivá, Viví 119: 51; 181: 36
Essakalli, Julie Klear 200: 58
Este, Kirk 33: 111
Estep, David 73: 57
Estes, Eleanor 91: 66
Estoril, Jean 32: 27
Estrada, Pau 74: 76
Estrada, Ric 5: 52, 146; 13: 174
Etchemendy, Teje 38: 68
Etheredges, the 73: 12
Etienne, Kirk-Albert 145: 184
Ets, Marie Hall 2: 102
Ettlinger, Doris 171: 98; 186: 106; 197: 126; 214: 125
Eulalie YABC 2: 315
Eustace, David 224: 24
Evangelista, Theresa M. 213: 67
Evans, Greg 73: 54, 55, 56; 143: 40, 41
Evans, Katherine 5: 64
Evans, Leslie 144: 227; 207: 57; 214: 88; 221: 28
Evans, Shane W. 159: 142; 160: 190; 168: 39; 188: 88; 189: 66, 67, 68
Everitt, Betsy 151: 110
Ewart, Claire 76: 69; 145: 59, 60
Ewing, Carolyn 66: 143; 79: 52
Ewing, Juliana Horatia 16: 92
Eyolfson, Norman 98: 154

F

Fabian, Limbert 136: 114
Facklam, Paul 132: 62
Falconer, Ian 125: 66; 179: 59
Falconer, Pearl 34: 23
Falkenstern, Lisa 70: 34; 76: 133; 78: 171; 127: 16; 191: 151
Falls, C.B. 1: 19; 38: 71, 72, 73, 74
Falter, John 40: 169, 170
Falwell, Cathryn 118: 77; 137: 185; 196: 71, 72
Fancher, Lou 138: 219; 141: 64; 144: 199; 177: 51; 214: 95; 221: 63
Fanelli, Sara 89: 63; 126: 69
Faria, Rosana 150: 143
Faricy, Patrick 185: 182; 212: 61
Farooqi, Musharraf Ali 207: 46
Farmer, Andrew 49: 102
Farmer, Peter 24: 108; 38: 75
Farnsworth, Bill 93: 189; 116: 147; 124: 8; 135: 52; 146: 242, 243, 244; 182: 176; 186: 31, 83, 84, 85; 191: 197; 222: 2
Farquharson, Alexander 46: 75
Farrell, David 40: 135
Farrell, Russell 196: 38

Farris, David *74:* 42
Fasolino, Teresa *118:* 145
Fatigati, Evelyn *24:* 112
Fatus, Sophie *182:* 74; *190:* 218; *225:* 131
Faul-Jansen, Regina *22:* 117
Faulkner, Jack *6:* 169
Faulkner, Matt *161:* 174; *167:* 75
Fava, Rita *2:* 29
Fax, Elton C. *1:* 101; *4:* 2; *12:* 77; *25:* 107
Fay *43:* 93
Fearing, Mark *223:* 142; *224:* 39, 40
Fearnley, Jan *153:* 82, 83; *205:* 63, 64, 65
Fearrington, Ann *146:* 80
Federspiel, Marian *33:* 51
Fedorov, Nickolai Ivanovich *110:* 102
Feelings, Tom *5:* 22; *8:* 56; *12:* 153; *16:* 105; *30:* 196; *49:* 37; *61:* 101; *69:* 56, 57; *93:* 74; *105:* 88
Fehr, Terrence *21:* 87
Feiffer, Jules *3:* 91; *8:* 58; *61:* 66, 67, 70, 74, 76,77, 78; *111:* 47, 48, 49, 50; *132:* 122; *157:* 62; *201:* 48, 49, 50
Feigeles, Neil *41:* 242
Feldman, Elyse *86:* 7
Feller, Gene *33:* 130
Fellows, Muriel H. *10:* 42
Felstead, Cathie *116:* 85
Felts, Shirley *33:* 71; *48:* 59
Fennell, Tracy *171:* 69
Fennelli, Maureen *38:* 181
Fenton, Carroll Lane *5:* 66; *21:* 39
Fenton, Mildred Adams *5:* 66; *21:* 39
Ferguson, Peter *177:* 30, 31; *181:* 154; *197:* 4; *199:* 40; *215:* 104; *221:* 66
Ferguson, Walter W. *34:* 86
Fernandes, Eugenie *77:* 67; *205:* 68
Fernandes, Stanislaw *70:* 28
Fernandez, Fernando *77:* 57
Fernandez, Laura *77:* 153; *101:* 117; *131:* 222; *170:* 119; *175:* 182
Ferrari, Alex *188:* 121
Ferrington, Susan *172:* 22
Fetz, Ingrid *11:* 67; *12:* 52; *16:* 205; *17:* 59; *29:* 105; *30:* 108, 109; *32:* 149; *43:* 142; *56:* 29; *60:* 34; *85:* 48; *87:* 146
Fiammenghi, Gioia *9:* 66; *11:* 44; *12:* 206; *13:* 57, 59; *52:* 126, 129; *66:* 64; *85:* 83; *91:* 161; *166:* 169
Fiedler, Joseph Daniel *96:* 42; *113:* 173; *129:* 164; *146:* 17; *159:* 68; *162:* 104
Field, Rachel *15:* 113
Fielding, David *70:* 124
Fieser, Stephen *152:* 36
Fine, Howard *145:* 159; *159:* 64; *165:* 134; *174:* 129; *181:* 68
Fine, Peter K. *43:* 210
Finger, Helen *42:* 81
Fink, Sam *18:* 119
Finlay, Winifred *23:* 72
Finney, Pat *79:* 215
Fiore, Peter *99:* 196; *125:* 139; *144:* 225; *160:* 169; *180:* 72; *212:* 103
Fiorentino, Al *3:* 240
Firehammer, Karla *174:* 202; *221:* 183
Firmin, Charlotte *29:* 75; *48:* 70
Firmin, Peter *58:* 63, 64, 65, 67, 68, 70, 71
Firth, Barbara *81:* 208; *127:* 218; *179:* 62
Fischel, Lillian *40:* 204
Fischer, Hans *25:* 202
Fischer, Scott M. *207:* 37; *217:* 29
Fischer-Nagel, Andreas *56:* 50
Fischer-Nagel, Heiderose *56:* 50
Fisher, Carolyn *154:* 50
Fisher, Chris *79:* 62; *158:* 248; *188:* 195
Fisher, Cynthia *117:* 45; *137:* 118; *195:* 40
Fisher, Jeffrey *142:* 80

Fisher, Leonard Everett *3:* 6; *4:* 72, 86; *6:* 197; *9:* 59; *16:* 151, 153; *23:* 44; *27:* 134; *29:* 26; *34:* 87, 89, 90, 91, 93, 94, 95, 96; *40:* 206; *50:* 150; *60:* 158; *73:* 68, 70, 71, 72, 73; *176:* 71, 72, 73; *208:* 131; *YABC 2:* 169
Fisher, Lois *20:* 62; *21:* 7
Fisher, Valorie *177:* 55; *214:* 92
Fisk, Nicholas *25:* 112
Fitschen, Marilyn *2:* 20, 21; *20:* 48
Fitz-Maurice, Jeff *175:* 2
Fitzgerald, F.A. *15:* 116; *25:* 86, 87
Fitzgerald, Joanne *157:* 153, 154; *198:* 34, 35
Fitzgerald, Royce *205:* 5
Fitzhugh, Louise *1:* 94; *9:* 163; *45:* 75, 78
Fitzhugh, Susie *11:* 117
Fitzpatrick, Jim *109:* 130
Fitzpatrick, Marie-Louise *125:* 69, 70; *189:* 72, 73
Fitzsimmons, Arthur *14:* 128
Fix, Philippe *26:* 102
Flack, Marjorie *21:* 67; *100:* 93; *YABC 2:* 122
Flagg, James Montgomery *17:* 227
Flavin, Teresa *132:* 115; *186:* 119
Flax, Zeona *2:* 245
Fleetwood, Tony *171:* 51
Fleishman, Seymour *14:* 232; *24:* 87
Fleming, Denise *71:* 179; *81:* 58; *126:* 71, 72, 73; *173:* 52, 53
Fleming, Guy *18:* 41
Flesher, Vivienne *85:* 55
Fletcher, Claire *80:* 106; *157:* 159
Flint, Russ *74:* 80
Floate, Helen *111:* 163
Floca, Brian *155:* 88, 89; *190:* 10, 66, 67
Floethe, Richard *3:* 131; *4:* 90
Floherty, John J., Jr. *5:* 68
Flook, Helen *160:* 81
Flora, James *1:* 96; *30:* 111, 112
Florczak, Robert *166:* 51
Florian, Douglas *19:* 122; *83:* 64, 65; *125:* 71, 72, 74, 76; *128:* 130; *177:* 58, 60
Flory, Jane *22:* 111
Flower, Renee *125:* 109
Floyd, Gareth *1:* 74; *17:* 245; *48:* 63; *62:* 35,36, 37, 39, 40, 41; *74:* 245; *79:* 56
Fluchere, Henri A. *40:* 79
Flynn, Alice *183:* 2
Flynn, Barbara *7:* 31; *9:* 70
Fogarty, Thomas *15:* 89
Foley, Greg *190:* 69
Folger, Joseph *9:* 100
Folkard, Charles *22:* 132; *29:* 128, 257, 258
Foott, Jeff *42:* 202
Forberg, Ati *12:* 71, 205; *14:* 1; *22:* 113; *26:* 22; *48:* 64, 65
Ford, George *24:* 120; *31:* 70, 177; *58:* 126; *81:* 103; *107:* 91; *136:* 100; *194:* 47; *208:* 81; *218:* 56
Ford, Gilbert *199:* 10
Ford, H.J. *16:* 185, 186
Ford, Jason *174:* 119
Ford, Pamela Baldwin *27:* 104
Fordham, John *168:* 160, 161
Foreman, Michael *2:* 110, 111; *67:* 99; *73:* 78, 79, 80,81, 82; *93:* 146; *135:* 55, 56, 57; *184:* 58, 59; *216:* 100, 101, 102, 103; *225:* 144
Forrester, Victoria *40:* 83
Forsey, Chris *140:* 210
Fortnum, Peggy *6:* 29; *20:* 179; *24:* 211; *26:* 76, 77, 78; *39:* 78; *58:* 19, 21, 23, 27; *YABC 1:* 148
Fortune, Eric *191:* 52
Foster, Brad W. *34:* 99
Foster, Genevieve *2:* 112
Foster, Gerald L. *7:* 78; *198:* 40
Foster, Jon *146:* 18; *198:* 7
Foster, Laura Louise *6:* 79
Foster, Marian Curtis *23:* 74; *40:* 42
Foster, Sally *58:* 73, 74
Fotheringham, Edwin *219:* 32

Foucher, Adele *47:* 118
Foust, Mitch *168:* 50
Fowler, Jim *184:* 190
Fowler, Mel *36:* 127
Fowler, Richard *87:* 219
Fowles, Shelley *165:* 127; *205:* 72
Fox, Charles Phillip *12:* 84
Fox, Christyan *188:* 36
Fox, Jim *6:* 187
Fox, Nathan *208:* 64
Fox-Davies, Sarah *76:* 150; *182:* 63; *199:* 42, 43
Frace, Charles *15:* 118
Frailey, Joy *72:* 108
Frame, Paul *2:* 45, 145; *9:* 153; *10:* 124; *21:* 71; *23:* 62; *24:* 123; *27:* 106; *31:* 48; *32:* 159; *34:* 195; *38:* 136; *42:* 55; *44:* 139; *60:* 39, 40, 41, 42, 43, 44, 46; *73:* 183
Frampton, David *85:* 72; *102:* 33; *139:* 182; *152:* 37; *189:* 171
Francis, Guy *198:* 164; *224:* 91; *225:* 65
Francois, Andre *25:* 117
Francoise
    See Seignobosc, Francoise
Frank, Lola Edick *2:* 199
Frank, Mary *4:* 54; *34:* 100
Franke, Phil *45:* 91
Frankel, Alona *66:* 70
Frankel, Julie *40:* 84, 85, 202
Frankenberg, Robert *22:* 116; *30:* 50; *38:* 92, 94, 95; *68:* 111
Frankfeldt, Gwen *84:* 223; *110:* 92
Frankland, David *169:* 137; *182:* 164; *201:* 159; *224:* 7
Franklin, Ashton *165:* 144; *225:* 107
Franklin, John *24:* 22
Franson, Leanne R. *111:* 57, 58; *151:* 7; *223:* 63, 64, 158
Frascino, Edward *9:* 133; *29:* 229; *33:* 190; *48:* 80, 81, 82, 83, 84, 85, 86
Frasconi, Antonio *6:* 80; *27:* 208; *53:* 41, 43, 45, 47,48; *68:* 145; *73:* 226; *131:* 68
Fraser, Betty *2:* 212; *6:* 185; *8:* 103; *31:* 72,73; *43:* 136; *111:* 76
Fraser, Eric *38:* 78; *41:* 149, 151
Fraser, F.A. *22:* 234
Fraser, James *171:* 68
Fraser, Mary Ann *137:* 63; *214:* 98
Frasier, Debra *69:* 60; *112:* 67; *182:* 81, 82, 83
Fraustino, Lisa Rowe *146:* 87
Frazee, Marla *72:* 98; *105:* 79, 80; *151:* 67, 68; *164:* 165; *171:* 190, 191; *187:* 53, 54, 55, 56, 143; *222:* 173; *225:* 68, 69, 70
Frazetta, Frank *41:* 72; *58:* 77, 78, 79, 80, 81, 82, 83
Frazier, Craig *177:* 63; *221:* 47
Freas, John *25:* 207
Fredrickson, Mark *103:* 33
Freeland, Michael J. *118:* 115
Freeman, Don *2:* 15; *13:* 249; *17:* 62, 63, 65, 67, 68; *18:* 243; *20:* 195; *23:* 213, 217; *32:* 155; *55:* 129
Freeman, Irving *67:* 150
Freeman, Laura *144:* 111; *200:* 62, 63
Freeman, Pietri *140:* 223
Freeman, Tom *167:* 118
Freeman, Tor *164:* 93
Fregosi, Claudia *24:* 117
Fremaux, Charlotte Murray *138:* 29; *141:* 95
French, Fiona *6:* 82, 83; *75:* 61; *109:* 170; *132:* 79, 80, 81, 82
French, Martin *163:* 4
French, S. Terrell *216:* 106
Frendak, Rodney *126:* 97, 98
Freschet, Gina *175:* 73
Freynet, Gilbert *72:* 221
Fried, Janice *202:* 121
Frieden, Sarajo *213:* 119
Friedman, Judith *43:* 197; *131:* 221
Friedman, Marvin *19:* 59; *42:* 86
Frinta, Dagmar *36:* 42

Frith, Michael K. *15:* 138; *18:* 120
Fritz, Ronald *46:* 73; *82:* 124
Fromm, Lilo *29:* 85; *40:* 197
Frost, A.B. *17:* 6, 7; *19:* 123, 124, 125, 126, 127, 128, 129,130; *100:* 119; *YABC 1:* 156, 157, 160; *2:* 107
Frost, Helen *183:* 51
Frost, Kristi *118:* 113
Frost, Michael *151:* 209; *209:* 44; *212:* 70
Froud, Brian *150:* 82, 83
Froud, Wendy *151:* 237
Fry, Guy *2:* 224
Fry, Rosalie *3:* 72; *YABC 2:* 180, 181
Fry, Rosalind *21:* 153, 168
Fryer, Elmer *34:* 115
Fuchs, Bernie *110:* 10; *162:* 46
Fuchs, Erich *6:* 84
Fuchshuber, Annegert *43:* 96
Fucile, Tony *221:* 48
Fufuka, Mahiri *32:* 146
Fuge, Charles *144:* 91, 93
Fujikawa, Gyo *39:* 75, 76; *76:* 72, 73, 74
Fulford, Deborah *23:* 159
Fuller, Margaret *25:* 189
Fulweiler, John *93:* 99
Funai, Mamoru *38:* 105
Funfhausen, Christian *196:* 30
Funk, Tom *7:* 17, 99
Furchgott, Terry *29:* 86
Furness, William Henry, Jr. *94:* 18
Furukawa, Mel *25:* 42
Fusari, Erika *164:* 227

G

Gaadt, David *78:* 212; *121:* 166; *201:* 171
Gaadt, George *71:* 9
Gaber, Susan *99:* 33; *115:* 57, 58; *164:* 195; *169:* 61, 62, 63; *185:* 50, 51; *188:* 124
Gaberell, J. *19:* 236
Gable, Brian *195:* 68, 69
Gabler, Mirko *99:* 71; *195:* 32
Gabor, Tim *216:* 61
Gackenbach, Dick *19:* 168; *41:* 81; *48:* 89, 90, 91, 92,93, 94; *54:* 105; *79:* 75, 76, 77
Gad, Victor *87:* 161
Gaetano, Nicholas *23:* 209
Gaffney-Kessell, Walter *94:* 219; *174:* 188
Gag, Flavia *17:* 49, 52
Gag, Wanda *100:* 101, 102; *YABC 1:* 135, 137, 138, 141, 143
Gagnon, Cecile *11:* 77; *58:* 87
Gaillard, Jason *200:* 69; *204:* 74
Gal, Laszlo *14:* 127; *52:* 54, 55, 56; *65:* 142; *68:* 150; *81:* 185; *96:* 104, 105
Galazinski, Tom *55:* 13
Galbraith, Ben *200:* 70
Galdone, Paul *1:* 156, 181, 206; *2:* 40, 241; *3:* 42,144; *4:* 141; *10:* 109, 158; *11:* 21; *12:* 118, 210; *14:* 12; *16:* 36, 37; *17:* 70, 71, 72, 73, 74; *18:* 111, 230; *19:* 183; *21:* 154; *22:* 150, 245; *33:* 126; *39:* 136, 137; *42:* 57; *51:* 169; *55:* 110; *66:* 80, 82, 139; *72:* 73; *100:* 84
Gale, Cathy *140:* 22; *143:* 52; *213:* 166
Gall, Chris *176:* 79, 80
Gallagher, Jack *187:* 100
Gallagher, S. Saelig *105:* 154; *198:* 91
Gallagher, Sears *20:* 112Gallagher-Cole, Mernie *206:* 56
Galloway, Ewing *51:* 154
Galouchka, Annouchka Gravel *95:* 55; *182:* 40
Galster, Robert *1:* 66
Galsworthy, Gay John *35:* 232
Galvez, Daniel *125:* 182
Gamble, Kim *112:* 64, 65; *124:* 77; *183:* 40, 42, 43, 56, 57; *187:* 170

Gammell, Stephen *7:* 48; *13:* 149; *29:* 82; *33:* 209; *41:* 88; *50:* 185, 186, 187; *53:* 51, 52, 53, 54, 55, 56,57, 58; *54:* 24, 25; *56:* 147, 148, 150; *57:* 27, 66; *81:* 62, 63; *87:* 88; *89:* 10; *106:* 223; *126:* 2; *128:* 71, 73, 74, 77; *154:* 34; *211:* 210
Gamper, Ruth *84:* 198
Gampert, John *58:* 94
Ganly, Helen *56:* 56
Gannett, Ruth Chrisman *3:* 74; *18:* 254; *33:* 77, 78
Gannon, Ned *205:* 6
Gantschev, Ivan *45:* 32
Garafano, Marie *73:* 33
Garbot, Dave *131:* 106
Garbutt, Bernard *23:* 68
Garcia *37:* 71
Garcia, Geronimo *222:* 73
Garcia, Manuel *74:* 145
Garcia-Franco, Rebecca *173:* 46
Gardiner, Lindsey *178:* 128; *186:* 137
Gardner, Earle *45:* 167
Gardner, Joan *40:* 87
Gardner, Joel *40:* 87, 92
Gardner, John *40:* 87
Gardner, Lucy *40:* 87
Gardner, Richard
 See Cummings, Richard
Gardner, Sally *171:* 177; *177:* 66, 68
Gargiulo, Frank *84:* 158
Garland, Michael *36:* 29; *38:* 83; *44:* 168; *48:* 78, 221, 222; *49:* 161; *60:* 139; *71:* 6, 11; *72:* 229; *74:* 142; *89:* 187; *93:* 183; *104:* 110; *131:* 55; *139:* 209; *168:* 56; *208:* 72, 73, 75
Garland, Peggy *60:* 139
Garland, Sarah *62:* 45; *135:* 67, 68; *171:* 118
Garn, Aimee *75:* 47
Garneray, Ambroise Louis *59:* 140
Garnett, Eve *3:* 75
Garnett, Gary *39:* 184
Garns, Allen *80:* 125; *84:* 39; *165:* 231; *209:* 44
Garófoli, Viviana *186:* 123
Garraty, Gail *4:* 142; *52:* 106
Garrett, Agnes *46:* 110; *47:* 157
Garrett, Edmund H. *20:* 29
Garrett, Tom *107:* 194; *215:* 179
Garrick, Jacqueline *67:* 42, 43; *77:* 94
Garrison, Barbara *19:* 133; *104:* 146; *109:* 87
Garro, Mark *108:* 131; *128:* 210
Garvey, Robert *98:* 222
Garza, Carmen Lomas *80:* 211; *182:* 86
Garza, Xavier *184:* 64
Gates, Frieda *26:* 80
Gaughan, Jack *26:* 79; *43:* 185
Gaver, Becky *20:* 61
Gavril, David *211:* 196
Gawing, Toby *72:* 52
Gay, Marie-Louise *68:* 76, 77, 78; *102:* 136; *126:* 76, 78, 81, 83; *127:* 55, 56; *179:* 70, 72, 73, 74; *224:* 81
Gay, Zhenya *19:* 135, 136
Gaydos, Tim *62:* 201
Gazsi, Ed *80:* 48
Gazso, Gabriel *73:* 85
Geary, Clifford N. *1:* 122; *9:* 104; *51:* 74
Geary, Rick *142:* 44, 46
Gee, Frank *33:* 26
Geehan, Wayne *157:* 181
Geer, Charles *1:* 91; *3:* 179; *4:* 201; *6:* 168; *7:* 96; *9:* 58; *10:* 72; *12:* 127; *39:* 156,157, 158, 159, 160; *42:* 88, 89, 90, 91; *55:* 111, 116
Geerinck, Manuel *173:* 128
Gehm, Charlie *36:* 65; *57:* 117; *62:* 60, 138
Geis, Alissa Imre *189:* 77
Geisel, Theodor Seuss *1:* 104, 105, 106; *28:* 108, 109, 110,111, 112, 113; *75:* 67, 68, 69, 70, 71; *89:* 127, 128; *100:* 106, 107, 108

Geisert, Arthur *92:* 67, 68; *133:* 72, 73, 74; *165:* 97, 98; *171:* 64, 65
Geldart, William *15:* 121; *21:* 202
Genia *4:* 84
Gentry, Cyrille R. *12:* 66
Genzo, John Paul *136:* 74
George, Jean *2:* 113
George, Lindsay Barrett *95:* 57; *155:* 97, 98
Geraghty, Paul *130:* 60, 61
Gerard, Jean Ignace *45:* 80
Gerard, Rolf *27:* 147, 150
Gerber, Mark *61:* 105
Gerber, Mary Jane *112:* 124; *171:* 56
Gerber, Stephanie *71:* 195
Gerdstein, Mordecai *169:* 105
Gergely, Tibor *54:* 15, 16
Geritz, Franz *17:* 135
Gerlach, Geff *42:* 58
Gerrard, Roy *47:* 78; *90:* 96, 97, 98, 99
Gerritsen, Paula *177:* 69; *217:* 166
Gershinowitz, George *36:* 27
Gerstein, Mordicai *31:* 117; *47:* 80, 81, 82, 83, 84, 85, 86; *51:* 173; *69:* 134; *107:* 122; *142:* 49, 52; *165:* 209; *176:* 119; *178:* 95, 97, 99; *215:* 173; *222:* 76
Gervase *12:* 27
Geter, Tyrone *146:* 249; *150:* 86
Getz, Arthur *32:* 148
Gévry, Claudine *188:* 47
Gewirtz, Bina *61:* 81
Giancola, Donato *95:* 146; *164:* 226
Gibala-Broxholm, Scott *205:* 76; *219:* 186
Gibbons, Gail *23:* 78; *72:* 77, 78, 79; *82:* 182; *104:* 65; *160:* 99, 100; *201:* 59, 60, 62
Gibbs, Tony *40:* 95
Gibran, Kahlil *32:* 116
Gibson, Barbara Leonard *205:* 77; *212:* 151
Gider, Iskender *81:* 193
Giebfried, Rosemary *170:* 135
Giesen, Rosemary *34:* 192, 193
Giffard, Hannah *83:* 70
Giguere, George *20:* 111
Gilbert, John *19:* 184; *54:* 115; *YABC 2:* 287
Gilbert, W.S. *36:* 83, 85, 96
Gilbert, Yvonne *116:* 70; *128:* 84; *149:* 119; *185:* 69; *192:* 25; *195:* 81
Gilchrist, Jan Spivey *72:* 82, 83, 84, 85, 87; *77:* 90; *105:* 89, 91; *130:* 63, 64; *155:* 105, 107; *182:* 67
Giles, Will *41:* 218
Gili, Phillida *70:* 73
Gill, Margery *4:* 57; *7:* 7; *22:* 122; *25:* 166; *26:* 146, 147
Gillen, Denver *28:* 216
Gillette, Henry J. *23:* 237
Gilliam, Stan *39:* 64, 81
Gillies, Chuck *62:* 31
Gillette, Jillian *87:* 58
Gillman, Alec *98:* 105
Gilman, Esther *15:* 124
Gilman, Phoebe *104:* 70, 71
Gilpin, Stephen *213:* 68
Ginsberg, Sari *111:* 184
Ginsburg, Max *62:* 59; *68:* 194 *Girard, Roge 161:* 30
Girouard, Patrick *155:* 100; *218:* 165
Giovanopoulos, Paul *7:* 104; *60:* 36
Giovine, Sergio *79:* 12; *93:* 118; *139:* 118; *205:* 114
Gist, E.M. *206:* 60
Githens, Elizabeth M. *5:* 47
Gladden, Scott *99:* 108; *103:* 160; *193:* 46, 47
Gladstone, Gary *12:* 89; *13:* 190
Gladstone, Lise *15:* 273
Glanzman, Louis S. *2:* 177; *3:* 182; *36:* 97, 98; *38:* 120, 122; *52:* 141, 144; *71:* 191; *91:* 54, 56
Glaser, Byron *154:* 59, 60
Glaser, Milton *3:* 5; *5:* 156; *11:* 107; *30:* 26; *36:* 112; *54:* 141; *151:* 70

Glass, Andrew *36:* 38; *44:* 133; *48:* 205; *65:* 3; *68:* 43, 45; *90:* 104, 105; *150:* 89; *223:* 73, 74
Glass, Marvin *9:* 174
Glasser, Judy *41:* 156; *56:* 140; *69:* 79; *72:* 101
Glattauer, Ned *5:* 84; *13:* 224; *14:* 26
Glauber, Uta *17:* 76
Gleeson, J.M. *YABC 2:* 207
Glegg, Creina *36:* 100
Glienke, Amelie *63:* 150
Gliewe, Unada *3:* 78, 79; *21:* 73; *30:* 220
Gliori, Debi *72:* 91; *138:* 82; *162:* 37; *189:* 79, 81, 82
Glovach, Linda *7:* 105
Gobbato, Imero *3:* 180, 181; *6:* 213; *7:* 58; *9:* 150; *18:* 39; *21:* 167; *39:* 82, 83; *41:* 137, 251; *59:* 177
Goble, Paul *25:* 121; *26:* 86; *33:* 65; *69:* 68, 69; *131:* 79, 80
Goble, Warwick *46:* 78, 79; *194:* 143
Godal, Eric *36:* 93
Godbey, Cory *221:* 154
Godkin, Celia *145:* 84, 86
Godfrey, Michael *17:* 279
Godon, Ingrid *166:* 163; *186:* 99
Goede, Irene *208:* 87
Goembel, Ponder *42:* 124
Goffe, Toni *61:* 83, 84, 85; *89:* 11; *90:* 124; *178:* 118
Goffstein, M.B. *8:* 71; *70:* 75, 76, 77
Golbin, Andre *15:* 125
Gold, Robert *166:* 151, 152
Goldfeder, Cheryl *11:* 191
Goldfinger, Jennifer P. *185:* 71
Goldman, Todd H. *221:* 50, 51
Goldsborough, June *5:* 154, 155; *8:* 92, *14:* 226; *19:* 139; *54:* 165
Goldsmith, Robert *110:* 77
Goldstein, Barry *198:* 147
Goldstein, Leslie *5:* 8; *6:* 60; *10:* 106
Goldstein, Nathan *1:* 175; *2:* 79; *11:* 41, 232; *16:* 55
Goldstrom, Robert *98:* 36; *145:* 51, 52
Golembe, Carla *79:* 80, 81; *136:* 91; *144:* 113; *193:* 53
Golin, Carlo *74:* 112
Gomez, Elena *188:* 122; *191:* 72
Gomez, Elizabeth *127:* 70; *133:* 76
Gomi, Taro *64:* 102; *103:* 74, 76
Gon, Adriano *101:* 112
Gonsalves, Ron *178:* 213; *212:* 196
Gonzalez, Maya Christina *104:* 3; *136:* 92; *215:* 4, 5
Gonzalez, Yolanda *212:* 65
Good, Karen Hillard *212:* 143; *214:* 103
Goodall, John S. *4:* 92, 93; *10:* 132; *66:* 92, 93; *YABC 1:* 198
Goode, Diane *15:* 126; *50:* 183; *52:* 114, 115; *76:* 195; *84:* 94; *99:* 141; *114:* 76, 77, 78; *170:* 99, 101; *225:* 80, 81, 82, 83, 84
Goodelman, Aaron *40:* 203
Goodenow, Earle *40:* 97
Goodfellow, Peter *62:* 95; *94:* 202
Goodman, Joan Elizabeth *50:* 86
Goodman, Vivienne *82:* 251; *146:* 181, 182
Goodnow, Patti *117:* 33
Goodrich, Carter *221:* 52, 53
Goodwin, Harold *13:* 74
Goodwin, Philip R. *18:* 206
Goor, Nancy *39:* 85, 86
Goor, Ron *39:* 85, 86
Goossens, Philippe *195:* 71
Gorbachev, Valeri *89:* 96; *112:* 97; *143:* 63, 64; *184:* 66, 67, 68, 101; *222:* 84, 85, 86, 87
Gordon, David *216:* 159
Gordon, Gwen *12:* 151
Gordon, Margaret *4:* 147; *5:* 48, 49; *9:* 79
Gordon, Mike *101:* 62, 63, 64
Gordon, Russell *136:* 204; *137:* 214
Gordon, Walter *138:* 9

Gore, Leonid *89:* 51; *94:* 74; *136:* 8; *158:* 117; *166:* 136; *168:* 36; *170:* 107; *181:* 94; *185:* 73; *222:* 89, 90, 91, 92
Gorecka-Egan, Erica *18:* 35
Gorey, Edward *1:* 60, 61; *13:* 169; *18:* 192; *20:* 201; *29:* 90, 91, 92, 93, 94, 95, 96, 97, 98, 99, 100; *30:* 129; *32:* 90; *34:* 200, *65:* 48; *68:* 24, 25; *69:* 79; *70:* 80, 82, 83, 84; *85:* 136; *127:* 62
Gorman, Mike *222:* 167
Gorsline, Douglas *1:* 98; *6:* 13; *11:* 113; *13:* 104; *15:* 14; *28:* 117, 118; *YABC 1:* 15
Gorton, Julia *108:* 94; *178:* 81, 82
Gosfield, Josh *118:* 165, 166; *149:* 67
Gosner, Kenneth *5:* 135
Gosney, Joy *167:* 142
Gotlieb, Jules *6:* 127
Goto, Scott *115:* 86; *136:* 69; *203:* 77, 78
Gott, Barry *197:* 95; *212:* 102
Gottlieb, Dale *67:* 162; *107:* 16; *149:* 6
Goudey, Ray *97:* 86
Gough, Alan *91:* 57
Gough, Philip *23:* 47; *45:* 90
Gould, Chester *49:* 112, 113, 114, 116, 117, 118
Gould, Jason *151:* 232
Gourbault, Martine *177:* 159
Govern, Elaine R. *26:* 94
Gower, Teri *102:* 184
Gowing, Toby *60:* 25; *63:* 33; *78:* 70, 252; *83:* 228; *86:* 187; *93:* 145; *108:* 133; *110:* 217; *184:* 125; *225:* 142
Grabianski *20:* 144
Grabianski, Janusz *39:* 92, 93, 94, 95
Graboff, Abner *35:* 103, 104
Graef, Renée *61:* 188; *72:* 207; *204:* 45; *210:* 249
Grafe, Max *156:* 173; *178:* 237; *192:* 240; *198:* 51
Graham, A.B. *11:* 61
Graham, Bob *101:* 66, 67, 68; *151:* 74, 75; *187:* 65, 67, 68, 70
Graham, Georgia *188:* 3; *190:* 75
Graham, L. *7:* 108
Graham, Margaret Bloy *11:* 120; *18:* 305, 307
Graham, Mark *88:* 208; *159:* 153; *182:* 3
Grahame-Johnstone, Janet *13:* 61
Grahame-Johnstone, Anne *13:* 61
Grainger, Sam *42:* 95
Gralley, Jean *166:* 86
Gramatky, Hardie *1:* 107; *30:* 116, 119, 120, 122, 123
Gran, Julie *168:* 118
Granahan, Julie *84:* 84
GrandPré, Mary *84:* 131; *109:* 199; *118:* 76; *180:* 65; *184:* 70, 71, 180; *192:* 87; *215:* 24
Grandström, Brita *176:* 139
Grandville, J.J. *45:* 81, 82, 83, 84, 85, 86, 87, 88; *47:* 125; *64:* 10
Granger, Paul *39:* 153
Granström, Brita *162:* 35; *167:* 46; *224:* 56, 57
Grant, (Alice) Leigh *10:* 52; *15:* 131; *20:* 20; *26:* 119; *48:* 202
Grant, Gordon *17:* 230, 234; *25:* 123, 124, 125, 126; *52:* 69; *YABC 1:* 164
Grant, Melvyn *159:* 186, 187; *170:* 48, 49; *213:* 168, 169
Grant, Michelle *210:* 95
Grant, Renee *77:* 40
Grant, Shirley *109:* 45
Graves, Elizabeth *45:* 101
Graves, Keith *167:* 89; *191:* 74; *216:* 34; *223:* 103
Gray, Harold *33:* 87, 88
Gray, Les *82:* 76; *83:* 232
Gray, Reginald *6:* 69
Greco, Tony *184:* 6
Greder, Armin *76:* 235
Green, Ann Canevari *62:* 48
Green, Eileen *6:* 97
Green, Elizabeth Shippen *139:* 109

Green, Jonathan *86:* 135; *105:* 109; *221:* 73
Green, Ken *111:* 68
Green, Michael *32:* 216
Green, Robina *87:* 138
Green, Jonathan *157:* 105
Greene, Jeffrey *117:* 93
Greenaway, Kate *17:* 275; *24:* 180; *26:* 107; *41:* 222, 232; *100:* 115, 116; *YABC 1:* 88, 89; *2:* 131, 133, 136,138, 139, 141
Greenberg, Melanie Hope *72:* 93; *80:* 125; *101:* 174; *133:* 180; *186:* 189; *214:* 105
Greenseid, Diane *178:* 106, 107
Greenstein, Elaine *150:* 100
Greenwald, Sheila *1:* 34; *3:* 99; *8:* 72
Greger, Carol *76:* 86
Gregorian, Joyce Ballou *30:* 125
Gregory, Emilian *177:* 146; *187:* 10
Gregory, Fran *130:* 4; *140:* 93
Gregory, Frank M. *29:* 107
Greiffenhagen, Maurice *16:* 137; *27:* 57; *YABC 2:* 288
Greiner, Robert *6:* 86
Gretter, J. Clemens *31:* 134
Gretz, Susanna *7:* 114
Gretzer, John *1:* 54; *3:* 26; *4:* 162; *7:* 125; *16:* 247; *18:* 117; *28:* 66; *30:* 85, 211; *33:* 235; *56:* 16
Grey, Mini *166:* 90; *192:* 71
Grey Owl *24:* 41
Gri *25:* 90
Grieder, Walter *9:* 84
Griesbach/Martucci *59:* 3
Grifalconi, Ann *2:* 126; *3:* 248; *11:* 18; *13:* 182; *46:* 38; *50:* 145; *66:* 99, 100, 101, 104, 106; *69:* 38; *70:* 64; *87:* 128; *90:* 53; *93:* 49; *128:* 48; *133:* 79, 81; *210:* 111
Griffin, Gillett Good *26:* 96
Griffin, James *30:* 166
Griffin, John Howard *59:* 186
Griffin, Rachel *131:* 23
Griffith, Gershom *94:* 214
Griffiths, Dave *29:* 76
Griffiths, Dean *168:* 180; *169:* 182
Grimly, Gris *186:* 102; *192:* 112; *197:* 86; *219:* 34
Grimsdell, Jeremy *83:* 75
Grimwood, Brian *82:* 89
Gringhuis, Dirk *6:* 98; *9:* 196
Gripe, Harald *2:* 127; *74:* 98
Grisha *3:* 71
Grobler, Piet *201:* 100
Grohmann, Susan *84:* 97
Gropper, William *27:* 93; *37:* 193
Gros *60:* 199
Grose, Helen Mason *YABC 1:* 260; *2:* 150
Grossman, Nancy *24:* 130; *29:* 101
Grossman, Robert *11:* 124; *46:* 39
Groth, John *15:* 79; *21:* 53, 54; *83:* 230
Grover, Lorie Ann *168:* 59
Grubb, Lisa *160:* 116
Grue, Lisa *187:* 193
Gruelle, Johnny *35:* 107
Gschwind, William *11:* 72
Guarnaccia, Steven *201:* 170, 173
Guay-Mitchell, Rebecca *110:* 95, 96; *135:* 240; *180:* 76; *181:* 71, 73; *216:* 77
Guback, Georgia *88:* 102
Gudeon, Karla *212:* 67
Guerguerion, Claudine *105:* 73
Guevara, Susan *97:* 87; *167:* 49; *194:* 54
Guggenheim, Hans *2:* 10; *3:* 37; *8:* 136
Guhathaakurta, Ajanta *183:* 199
Guida, Lisa Chauncy *172:* 188
Guilbeau, Honore *22:* 69
Guillette, Joseph *137:* 37
Guisewite, Cathy *57:* 52, 53, 54, 56, 57
Gukova, Julia *95:* 104; *154:* 103; *168:* 195
Gundersheimer, Karen *35:* 240; *82:* 100
Gunderson, Nick *57:* 120
Gunnella *192:* 144
Gurney, James *76:* 97; *86:* 32

Gurney, John Steven *75:* 39, 82; *110:* 175; *143:* 67, 68; *169:* 172; *217:* 50, 88
Gusman, Annie *38:* 62
Gustafson, Scott *34:* 111; *43:* 40
Gustavson, Adam *104:* 10; *171:* 183; *176:* 87; *197:* 94; *204:* 35; *219:* 187
Guthridge, Bettina *108:* 79; *186:* 92
Guthrie, R. Dale *64:* 143
Guthrie, Robin *20:* 122
Gutierrez, Akemi *172:* 87; *205:* 135
Gutierrez, Alan *136:* 31, 32
Gutierrez, Rudy *97:* 162; *203:* 79; *216:* 158
Gutmann, Bessie Pease *73:* 93, 94
Gwynne, Fred *41:* 94, 95
Gyberg, Bo-Erik *38:* 131

H

Haas, Irene *17:* 77; *87:* 46; *96:* 117
Hack, Konrad *51:* 127
Hader, Berta H. *16:* 126
Hader, Elmer S. *16:* 126
Haeffele, Deborah *76:* 99
Haemer, Alan *62:* 109
Hafner, Marylin *22:* 196, 216; *24:* 44; *30:* 51; *35:* 95; *51:* 25, 160, 164; *86:* 16; *105:* 196; *121:* 93, 94; *149:* 208, 209; *179:* 82, 83, 84, 115; *190:* 200; *201:* 29; *217:* 91
Hagerty, Sean *62:* 181
Hague, Michael *32:* 128; *48:* 98, 99, 100, 101, 103, 105,106, 107, 108, 109, 110; *49:* 121; *51:* 105; *64:* 14, 15; *79:* 134; *80:* 91, 92; *83:* 135; *100:* 241; *102:* 29; *129:* 101, 103, 104; *185:* 80, 81, 82; *215:* 89
Hair, Jonathan *115:* 135
Halas, John *29:* 41, 47, 48
Haldane, Roger *13:* 76; *14:* 202
Hale, Bruce *203:* 83
Hale, Christy *79:* 124; *84:* 200; *114:* 201; *128:* 2, 3; *146:* 203; *158:* 243; *167:* 99; *179:* 87
Hale, Irina *26:* 97
Hale, James Graham *88:* 207
Hale, Kathleen *17:* 79; *66:* 114, 116, 118
Hale, Nathan *210:* 115, 116; *214:* 179
Haley, Amanda *205:* 82, 83
Haley, Gail E. *43:* 102, 103, 104, 105; *78:* 65, 67; *136:* 106, 107
Hall, Amanda *96:* 110
Hall, Angus *224:* 192
Hall, August N. *217:* 74
Hall, Chuck *30:* 189
Hall, Douglas *15:* 184; *43:* 106, 107; *86:* 100; *87:* 82; *129:* 72
Hall, H. Tom *1:* 227; *30:* 210
Hall, Melanie *116:* 48, 49; *169:* 77, 78; *219:* 170
Hall, Sydney P. *31:* 89
Hall, Tim *164:* 196; *202:* 41
Hall, Vicki *20:* 24
Hallinan, P.K. *39:* 98
Hallman, Tom *98:* 166
Hally, Greg *101:* 200; *151:* 224
Halperin, Wendy Anderson *96:* 151; *125:* 96, 97, 98, 99; *139:* 22; *140:* 84; *200:* 77, 78; *210:* 157; *215:* 65
Halpern, Joan *10:* 25
Halpern, Shari *174:* 172
Halsey, Megan *96:* 172; *114:* 185; *180:* 8; *185:* 85
Halstead, Virginia *125:* 105
Halverson, Janet *49:* 38, 42, 44
Hallensleben, Georg *134:* 5, 6; *172:* 17
Hallett, Mark *220:* 63
Hamanaka, Sheila *71:* 100
Hamann, Brad *78:* 151
Hamann, Sigune *104:* 115
Hamberger, John *6:* 8; *8:* 32; *14:* 79; *34:* 136; *88:* 78
Hamil, Tom *14:* 80; *43:* 163

Hamilton, Bill and Associates *26:* 215
Hamilton, Helen S. *2:* 238
Hamilton, J. *19:* 83, 85, 87
Hamilton, Laurie *116:* 210
Hamilton, Todd Cameron *84:* 15
Hamlin, Janet *97:* 136; *124:* 90; *137:* 157; *182:* 117
Hamlin, Louise *71:* 135
Hammill, Matt *206:* 65
Hammond, Chris *21:* 37
Hammond, Elizabeth *5:* 36, 203
Hampshire, Michael *5:* 187; *7:* 110, 111; *48:* 150; *51:* 129
Hampson, Denman *10:* 155; *15:* 130
Hampton, Blake *41:* 244
Handford, Martin *64:* 105, 106, 107, 109
Handforth, Thomas *42:* 100, 101, 102, 103, 104, 105, 107
Handville, Robert *1:* 89; *38:* 76; *45:* 108, 109
Hane, Roger *17:* 239; *44:* 54
Haney, Elizabeth Mathieu *34:* 84
Hanke, Ted *71:* 10
Hankinson, Phil *181:* 164
Hanley, Catherine *8:* 161
Hann, Jacquie *19:* 144
Hanna, Cheryl *91:* 133
Hanna, Wayne A. *67:* 145
Hannon, Mark *38:* 37
Hanrahan, Kelly-Anne *203:* 142
Hansen, Gaby *159:* 11; *186:* 25; *224:* 11
Hansen, Mia *149:* 76
Hanson, Joan *8:* 76; *11:* 139
Hanson, Peter E. *52:* 47; *54:* 99, 100; *73:* 21; *84:* 79; *116:* 144
Hansson, Gunilla *64:* 111, 112
Harbour, Elizabeth *221:* 68
Hardcastle, Nick *121:* 82; *175:* 185; *222:* 135
Hardy, David A. *9:* 96; *119:* 74
Hardy, Paul *YABC 2:* 245
Hargis, Wes *219:* 70 Haring, Keith *145:* 65
Harlan, Jerry *3:* 96
Harlin, Greg *89:* 194; *103:* 82; *118:* 161; *121:* 167; *182:* 76; *201:* 172; *215:* 76
Harman, Dominic *206:* 48
Harness, Cheryl *106:* 80; *131:* 87; *178:* 111; *200:* 39
Harnischfeger *18:* 121
Harper, Arthur *YABC 2:* 121
Harper, Betty *126:* 90
Harper, Jamie *174:* 71; *214:* 212
Harper, Piers *79:* 27; *105:* 102; *161:* 67
Harrington, Glenn *82:* 18; *94:* 66, 68; *185:* 118
Harrington, Jack *83:* 162
Harrington, Richard *5:* 81
Harris, Andrew N. *191:* 78
Harris, Jim *127:* 130; *183:* 4
Harris, John *83:* 25
Harris, Nick *86:* 177
Harris, Susan Yard *42:* 121
Harrison, Florence *20:* 150, 152
Harrison, Harry *4:* 103
Harrison, Jack *28:* 149
Harrison, Mark *105:* 157; *165:* 190
Harrison, Ted *56:* 73
Harsh, Fred *72:* 107
Harston, Jerry *105:* 143
Hart, Lewis *98:* 115
Hart, Thomas *181:* 165
Hart, William *13:* 72
Hartland, Jessie *171:* 80, 81; *186:* 165; *223:* 58
Hartung, Susan Kathleen *150:* 107, 108; *173:* 106; *175:* 106; *192:* 78; *211:* 19
Hartelius, Margaret *10:* 24
Hartshorn, Ruth *5:* 115; *11:* 129
Harvey, Amanda *145:* 44
Harvey, Bob *48:* 219
Harvey, Gerry *7:* 180
Harvey, Lisa *97:* 21
Harvey, Paul *88:* 74

Harvey, Roland *71:* 88; *123:* 63; *179:* 94; *218:* 94; *219:* 74
Haskamp, Steve *195:* 36
Hassall, Joan *43:* 108, 109
Hassell, Hilton *YABC 1:* 187
Hassett, John *162:* 59
Hasselriis, Else *18:* 87; *YABC 1:* 96
Hastings, Glenn *89:* 183
Hastings, Ian *62:* 67
Hauman, Doris *2:* 184; *29:* 58, 59; *32:* 85, 86, 87
Hauman, George *2:* 184; *29:* 58, 59; *32:* 85, 86, 87
Hausherr, Rosmarie *15:* 29
Haverfield, Mary *225:* 87
Hawkes, Kevin *78:* 72; *104:* 198; *105:* 197; *112:* 109; *126:* 87; *144:* 88; *149:* 210; *150:* 110, 135; *156:* 94; *164:* 35; *186:* 18; *190:* 197; *198:* 152; *201:* 70, 71, 72; *220:* 99; *221:* 90, 92, 93
Hawkins, Jacqui *112:* 86; *162:* 64
Hawkinson, John *4:* 109; *7:* 83; *21:* 64
Hawkinson, Lucy *21:* 64
Hawthorne, Mike *140:* 228
Haxton, Elaine *28:* 131
Haydock, Robert *4:* 95
Hayes, Geoffrey *26:* 111; *44:* 133; *91:* 85; *207:* 63
Hayes, Karel *207:* 65
Haynes, Max *72:* 107
Hays, Michael *73:* 207; *83:* 93; *139:* 197; *146:* 202, 250; *202:* 47
Haywood, Carolyn *1:* 112; *29:* 104
Heale, Jonathan *104:* 117
Healy, Daty *12:* 143
Healy, Deborah *58:* 181, 182; *101:* 111
Heap, Sue *102:* 207; *150:* 113, 114; *187:* 84, 85, 87
Hearn, Diane Dawson *79:* 99; *113:* 13; *209:* 71, 72; *211:* 106
Hearon, Dorothy *34:* 69
Heaslip, William *57:* 24, 25
Hechtkopf, H. *11:* 110
Heck, Ed *173:* 81
Hector, Julian *205:* 85
Hedderwick, Mairi *30:* 127; *32:* 47; *36:* 104; *77:* 86; *145:* 91, 93, 95
Heffernan, Phil *146:* 197; *195:* 172; *218:* 123
Hefter, Richard *28:* 170; *31:* 81, 82; *33:* 183
Hehenberger, Shelly *126:* 91
Heigh, James *22:* 98
Heighway, Richard *25:* 160; *64:* 4
Heighway-Bury, Robin *159:* 89
Heine, Helme *67:* 86; *135:* 91, 92
Heinly, John *45:* 113
Hellard, Susan *81:* 21; *204:* 82; *209:* 92
Hellebrand, Nancy *26:* 57
Heller, Linda *46:* 86
Heller, Ruth M. *66:* 125; *77:* 30, 32
Hellmuth, Jim *38:* 164
Helms, Georgeann *33:* 62
Helquist, Brett *142:* 203; *146:* 133, 134; *156:* 10; *173:* 25; *180:* 106; *187:* 90, 91; *193:* 12; *224:* 186
Helweg, Hans *41:* 118; *50:* 93; *58:* 22, 26
Hemingway, Edward *212:* 71
Hemphill, Helen *179:* 95
Henba, Bobbie *90:* 195
Henderling, Lisa *214:* 65
Henderson, Dave *73:* 76; *75:* 191, 192, 193, 194; *82:* 4
Henderson, D.F. *216:* 77
Henderson, Douglas *103:* 68
Henderson, Kathy *55:* 32; *155:* 118
Henderson, Keith *35:* 122
Henderson, Meryl *127:* 58, 60; *169:* 81
Hendrix, John *187:* 133; *208:* 106, 107, 108; *216:* 115
Hendry, Linda *80:* 104; *83:* 83; *164:* 216
Hengeveld, Dennis *142:* 86
Henkes, Kevin *43:* 111; *108:* 106, 107, 108

Henneberger, Robert *1:* 42; *2:* 237; *25:* 83
Henriksen, Harold *35:* 26; *48:* 68
Henriquez, Celeste *103:* 137
Henriquez, Elsa *82:* 260
Henriquez, Emile F. *89:* 88; *211:* 56
Henry, Everett *29:* 191
Henry, Matthew *117:* 58
Henry, Paul *93:* 121; *194:* 125
Henry, Rohan *217:* 77
Henry, Thomas *5:* 102
Hensel *27:* 119
Henshaw, Jacqui *141:* 127
Henstra, Friso *8:* 80; *36:* 70; *40:* 222; *41:* 250; *73:* 100, 101
Henterly, Jamichael *93:* 4
Heo, Yumi *89:* 85, 86; *94:* 89, 90; *146:* 40, 137, 138; *163:* 227; *201:* 192
Hepple, Norman *28:* 198
Herbert, Helen *57:* 70
Herbert, Jennifer *189:* 47
Herbert, Wally *23:* 101
Herbster, Mary Lee *9:* 33
Herder, Edwin *182:* 104
Herge
  See Remi, Georges
Hermansen, Pal *133:* 113
Hermanson, Dennis *10:* 55
Hermes, Gertrude *54:* 161
Herr, Margo *57:* 191
Herr, Susan *83:* 163
Herriman, George *140:* 74, 75, 76, 77, 78
Herriman, Lisa *87:* 190
Herring, Michael *121:* 76; *182:* 103
Herrington, Roger *3:* 161
Herscovici, C. *165:* 240
Hescox, Richard *85:* 86; *90:* 30; *139:* 35
Heslop, Mike *38:* 60; *40:* 130
Hess, Lydia J. *85:* 17
Hess, Mark *111:* 146; *113:* 207
Hess, Paul *134:* 47; *166:* 133; *193:* 13
Hess, Richard *42:* 31
Hester, Ronnie *37:* 85
Heuser, Olga J. *121:* 116
Heusser, Sibylle *168:* 195
Heustis, Louise L. *20:* 28
Hewgill, Jodi *201:* 114
Hewitson, Jennifer *74:* 119; *124:* 167
Hewitt, Kathryn *80:* 126; *149:* 105; *184:* 93; *196:* 36
Hewitt, Margaret *84:* 112
Heyduck-Huth, Hilde *8:* 82
Heyer, Carol *74:* 122; *130:* 72, 73; *192:* 35; *203:* 78
Heyer, Hermann *20:* 114, 115
Heyer, Marilee *102:* 108
Heyman, Ken *8:* 33; *34:* 113
Heyne, Ulrike *146:* 151
Heywood, Karen *48:* 114
Hickling, P.B. *40:* 165
Hickman, Stephen *85:* 58; *136:* 33; *171:* 128
Hierstein, Judith *56:* 40; *162:* 168; *212:* 72
Higashi, Sandra *154:* 59, 60
Higginbottom, J. Winslow *8:* 170; *29:* 105, 106
Higgins, Chester *101:* 79
Higham, David *50:* 104
Hilb, Nora *176:* 8
Hild, Anja *215:* 194
Hildebrandt, Greg *8:* 191; *55:* 35, 36, 38, 39, 40, 42, 46; *172:* 110
Hildebrandt, Tim *8:* 191; *55:* 44, 45, 46
Hilder, Rowland *19:* 207
Hill, Eric *66:* 127, 128; *133:* 91
Hill, Gregory *35:* 190
Hill, Pat *49:* 120
Hillenbrand, Will *84:* 115; *92:* 76, 80; *93:* 131; *104:* 168; *128:* 137; *145:* 187; *146:* 184; *147:* 105, 106, 107; *152:* 59; *184:* 179; *195:* 34, 180; *196:* 125; *210:* 122, 123, 124; *217:* 62; *224:* 145
Hilliard, Richard *183:* 74

Hillier, Matthew *45:* 205
Hillman, Priscilla *48:* 115
Hills, Tad *113:* 4; *137:* 147; *173:* 83; *208:* 199
Himler, Ronald *6:* 114; *7:* 162; *8:* 17, 84, 125; *14:* 76; *19:* 145; *26:* 160; *31:* 43; *38:* 116; *41:* 44, 79; *43:* 52; *45:* 120; *46:* 43; *54:* 44, 83; *58:* 180; *59:* 38; *68:* 146; *69:* 231; *70:* 98; *71:* 177, 178; *77:* 219; *79:* 212; *83:* 62; *89:* 5; *91:* 160; *92:* 91, 92, 93; *94:* 93; *95:* 69, 174, 194; *99:* 99, 112; *113:* 92; *118:* 114; *137:* 73, 74, 77, 167; *163:* 99; *165:* 138; *178:* 9, 220; *183:* 77, 79, 80, 81; *184:* 80, 83; *215:* 151
Himmelman, John *47:* 109; *65:* 87; *94:* 96, 97; *159:* 85; *221:* 79, 80, 81, 82
Hinds, Bill *37:* 127, 130
Hines, Anna Grossnickle *51:* 90; *74:* 124; *95:* 78, 79,80, 81
Hines, Bob *135:* 149, 150
Hirao, Amiko *203:* 98
Hiroko *99:* 61
Hiroshige *25:* 71
Hirsh, Marilyn *7:* 126
Hiscock, Bruce *137:* 80, 81; *204:* 51, 53
Hissey, Jane *103:* 90; *130:* 81
Hitch, Jeff *99:* 206; *128:* 86
Hitz, Demi *11:* 135; *15:* 245; *66:* 129, 130; *152:* 94, 95
Hnizdovsky, Jacques *32:* 96; *76:* 187
Ho, Kwoncjan *15:* 132
Hoban, Lillian *1:* 114; *22:* 157; *26:* 72; *29:* 53; *40:* 105, 107, 195; *41:* 80; *69:* 107, 108; *71:* 98; *77:* 168; *106:* 50; *113:* 86; *136:* 118
Hoban, Tana *22:* 159; *104:* 82, 83, 85
Hobbie, Holly *225:* 90, 91
Hobbie, Jocelyn *190:* 78; *196:* 92
Hobbie, Nathaniel *196:* 92
Hobbs, Leigh *166:* 95
Hoberman, Norman *5:* 82
Hobson, Sally *77:* 185
Hockerman, Dennis *39:* 22; *56:* 23
Hodgell, P.C. *42:* 114
Hodges, C. Walter *2:* 139; *11:* 15; *12:* 25; *23:* 34; *25:* 96; *38:* 165; *44:* 197; *45:* 95; *100:* 57; *YABC 2:* 62, 63
Hodges, David *9:* 98
Hodgetts, Victoria *43:* 132
Hofbauer, Imre *2:* 162
Hoff, Syd *9:* 107; *10:* 128; *33:* 94; *72:* 115,116, 117, 118; *138:* 114, 115
Hoffman, Rosekrans *15:* 133; *50:* 219; *63:* 97
Hoffman, Sanford *38:* 208; *76:* 174; *88:* 160, 161; *151:* 156
Hoffmann, Felix *9:* 109
Hoffnung, Gerard *66:* 76, 77
Hofsinde, Robert *21:* 70
Hogan, Inez *2:* 141
Hogan, Jamie *192:* 94; *198:* 177
Hogarth, Burne *41:* 58; *63:* 46, 48, 49, 50, 52, 53, 54, 55,56
Hogarth, Paul *41:* 102, 103, 104; *YABC 1:* 16
Hogarth, William *42:* 33
Hogenbyl, Jan *1:* 35
Hogner, Nils *4:* 122; *25:* 144
Hogrogian, Nonny *3:* 221; *4:* 106, 107; *5:* 166; *7:* 129; *15:* 2; *16:* 176; *20:* 154; *22:* 146; *25:* 217; *27:* 206; *74:* 127, 128, 129, 149, 152; *127:* 99; *YABC 2:* 84, 94
Hokanson, Lars *93:* 111; *172:* 137; *212:* 88
Hokusai *25:* 71
Hol, Colby *126:* 96
Holberg, Richard *2:* 51
Holbrook, Kathy *107:* 114
Holdcroft, Tina *38:* 109
Holden, Caroline *55:* 159
Holder, Heidi *36:* 99; *64:* 9
Holder, Jim *204:* 163
Holder, Jimmy *151:* 224
Holderness, Grizelda *215:* 107
Hole, Stian *204:* 55
Holiday, Henry *YABC 2:* 107

Holl, F. *36:* 91
Holland, Brad *45:* 59, 159
Holland, Gay W. *128:* 105; *225:* 76
Holland, Janice *18:* 118
Holland, Marion *6:* 116
Holland, Richard *216:* 109, 124
Holldobler, Turid *26:* 120
Holliday, Keaf *144:* 236
Holling, Holling C. *15:* 136, 137
Hollinger, Deanne *12:* 116
Holm, Sharon Lane *114:* 84; *115:* 52
Holmes, B. *3:* 82
Holmes, Bea *7:* 74; *24:* 156; *31:* 93
Holmes, Dave *54:* 22
Holmes, Lesley *135:* 96
Holmgren, George Ellen *45:* 112
Holmlund, Heather D. *150:* 140
Holt, Norma *44:* 106
Holt, Pater *151:* 188
Holtan, Gene *32:* 192
Holub, Joan *149:* 72
Holyfield, John *149:* 231
Holz, Loretta *17:* 81
Hom, Nancy *79:* 195
Homar, Lorenzo *6:* 2
Homer, Winslow *128:* 8; *YABC 2:* 87
Honey, Elizabeth *112:* 95, 96; *137:* 93, 94
Honeywood, Varnette P. *110:* 68, 70
Hong, Lily Toy *76:* 104
Honigman, Marian *3:* 2
Honore, Paul *42:* 77, 79, 81, 82
Hood, Alun *69:* 145, 218; *72:* 41; *80:* 226; *87:* 4; *95:* 139
Hood, Susan *12:* 43
Hook, Christian *104:* 103
Hook, Frances *26:* 188; *27:* 127
Hook, Jeff *14:* 137; *103:* 105
Hook, Richard *26:* 188
Hooks *63:* 30
Hooper, Hadley *177:* 145
Hoover, Carol A. *21:* 77
Hoover, Russell *12:* 95; *17:* 2; *34:* 156
Hope, James *141:* 116
Hopkins, Chris *99:* 127
Hopkinson, Leigh *202:* 70
Hopman, Philip *178:* 184
Hoppe, Paul *209:* 85
Hoppin, Augustus *34:* 66
Horacek, Judy *211:* 86
Horacek, Petr *163:* 117; *214:* 113
Horder, Margaret *2:* 108; *73:* 75
Horen, Michael *45:* 121
Horne, Daniel *73:* 106; *91:* 153; *109:* 127; *110:* 232; *164:* 176
Horne, Richard *111:* 80
Horowitz, Dave *204:* 58
Horse, Harry *128:* 195; *169:* 86
Horstman, Lisa *219:* 79
Horton, Anthony *211:* 98
Horvat, Laurel *12:* 201
Horvath, David *192:* 95
Horvath, Ferdinand Kusati *24:* 176
Horvath, Maria *57:* 171
Horwitz, Richard *57:* 174
Hotchkiss, De Wolfe *20:* 49
Hough, Charlotte *9:* 112; *13:* 98; *17:* 83; *24:* 195
Houlihan, Ray *11:* 214
House, Caroline *183:* 121
Housman, Laurence *25:* 146, 147
Houston, James *13:* 107; *74:* 132, 134, 135
Hovland, Gary *88:* 172; *171:* 148
Hoyt, Eleanor *158:* 231
How, W.E. *20:* 47
Howard, Alan *16:* 80; *34:* 58; *45:* 114
Howard, Arthur *165:* 111, 112; *190:* 5
Howard, J.N. *15:* 234
Howard, John *33:* 179
Howard, Kim *116:* 71
Howard, Paul *142:* 126, 129; *144:* 187
Howard, Rob *40:* 161

Howarth, Daniel *170:* 34; *222:* 97, 98; *224:* 20; *225:* 77
Howe, John *79:* 101; *80:* 150; *115:* 47; *176:* 106; *207:* 32, 35
Howe, Phillip *79:* 117; *175:* 115
Howe, Stephen *1:* 232
Howell, Karen *119:* 123
Howell, Pat *15:* 139
Howell, Troy *23:* 24; *31:* 61; *36:* 158; *37:* 184; *41:* 76, 235; *48:* 112; *56:* 13; *57:* 3; *59:* 174; *63:* 5; *74:* 46; *89:* 188; *90:* 231; *95:* 97; *98:* 130; *99:* 189; *153:* 156, 157, 158; *176:* 104; *199:* 96, 98; *222:* 65
Howes, Charles *22:* 17
Hoyt, Ard *145:* 141; *190:* 82; *207:* 148
Hranilovich, Barbara *127:* 51
Hu, Ying-Hwa *116:* 107; *152:* 236; *173:* 171
Huang, Benrei *137:* 55
Huang, Zhong-Yang *117:* 30, 32; *213:* 18
Hubbard, Woodleigh Marx *98:* 67; *115:* 79; *160:* 138; *214:* 120
Hubbell, Patricia *222:* 31
Hubley, Faith *48:* 120, 121, 125, 130, 131, 132, 134
Hubley, John *48:* 125, 130, 131, 132, 134
Hudak, Michal *143:* 74
Hudnut, Robin *14:* 62
Huerta, Catherine *76:* 178; *77:* 44, 45; *90:* 182; *210:* 202
Huffaker, Sandy *10:* 56
Huffman, Joan *13:* 33
Huffman, Tom *13:* 180; *17:* 212; *21:* 116; *24:* 132; *33:* 154; *38:* 59; *42:* 147
Hughes, Arthur *20:* 148, 149, 150; *33:* 114, 148, 149
Hughes, Darren *95:* 44
Hughes, David *36:* 197
Hughes, Shirley *1:* 20, 21; *7:* 3; *12:* 217; *16:* 163; *29:* 154; *63:* 118; *70:* 102, 103, 104; *73:* 169; *88:* 70; *110:* 118, 119; *159:* 103
Hugo, Victor *47:* 112
Huliska-Beith, Laura *204:* 108; *220:* 137
Hull, Cathy *78:* 29
Hull, Richard *95:* 120; *123:* 175; *172:* 195
Hulsmann, Eva *16:* 166
Hume, Lachie *189:* 93
Hummel, Berta *43:* 137, 138, 139
Hummel, Lisl *29:* 109; *YABC 2:* 333, 334
Humphrey, Henry *16:* 167
Humphreys, Graham *25:* 168
Humphries, Tudor *76:* 66; *80:* 4; *124:* 4, 5
Huneck, Stephen *183:* 88, 89
Hunt, James *2:* 143
Hunt, Jonathan *84:* 120
Hunt, Paul *119:* 104; *129:* 135; *139:* 160; *173:* 112
Hunt, Robert *110:* 206, 235; *147:* 136, 137; *170:* 3; *211:* 76
Hunt, Scott *190:* 143
Hunter, Anne *133:* 190; *178:* 150
Huntington, Amy *180:* 99
Hurd, Clement *2:* 148, 149; *64:* 127, 128, 129, 131, 133, 134,135, 136; *100:* 37, 38
Hurd, Peter *24:* 30, 31,; *YABC 2:* 56
Hurd, Thacher *46:* 88, 89; *94:* 114, 115, 116; *123:* 81, 82, 84; *219:* 82
Hurlimann, Ruth *32:* 99
Hurst, Carol Otis *185:* 92
Hurst, Elise *221:* 98
Hurst, Philip *196:* 79
Hurst, Tracey *192:* 238
Hussar, Michael *114:* 113; *117:* 159
Hustler, Tom *6:* 105
Hutchins, Laurence *55:* 22
Hutchins, Pat *15:* 142; *70:* 106, 107, 108; *178:* 131, 132
Hutchinson, Sascha *95:* 211
Hutchinson, William M. *6:* 3, 138; *46:* 70
Hutchison, Paula *23:* 10
Hutton, Clarke *YABC 2:* 335
Hutton, Kathryn *35:* 155; *89:* 91

Hutton, Warwick *20:* 91
Huyette, Marcia *29:* 188
Hyatt, John *54:* 7
Hyatt, Mitch *178:* 162
Hyde, Maureen *82:* 17; *121:* 145, 146
Hyman, David *117:* 64
Hyman, Miles *210:* 132
Hyman, Trina Schart *1:* 204; *2:* 194; *5:* 153; *6:* 106; *7:* 138, 145; *8:* 22; *10:* 196; *13:* 96; *14:* 114; *15:* 204; *16:* 234; *20:* 82; *22:* 133; *24:* 151; *25:* 79, 82; *26:* 82; *29:* 83; *31:* 37, 39; *34:* 104; *38:* 84, 100, 128; *41:* 49; *43:* 146; *46:* 91, 92, 93, 95, 96, 97, 98, 99, 100, 101, 102, 103, 104, 105,108, 109, 111, 197; *48:* 60, 61; *52:* 32; *60:* 168; *66:* 38; *67:* 214; *72:* 74; *75:* 92; *79:* 57; *82:* 95, 238; *89:* 46; *95:* 91, 92, 93; *100:* 33, 199; *132:* 12; *147:* 33, 35, 36; *167:* 58, 60; *177:* 189, 190; *211:* 188

I

Ibarra, Rosa *147:* 91
Ibatoulline, Bagram *156:* 48; *174:* 33, 82; *202:* 30; *211:* 213; *224:* 84; *225:* 98, 99
Ichikawa, Satomi *29:* 152; *41:* 52; *47:* 133, 134,135, 136; *78:* 93, 94; *80:* 81; *146:* 143, 145, 146; *208:* 117, 118, 119
Ide, Jacqueline *YABC 1:* 39
Idle, Molly Schaar *223:* 95
Ilsley, Velma *3:* 1; *7:* 55; *12:* 109; *37:* 62; *38:* 184
Imai, Ayano *190:* 85, 86
in den Bosch, Nicole *150:* 204
Inga *1:* 142
Ingman, Bruce *134:* 50; *182:* 91, 92; *214:* 10
Ingpen, Robert *109:* 103, 104; *132:* 138; *137:* 177; *166:* 103; *181:* 140
Ingraham, Erick *21:* 177; *84:* 256; *103:* 66
Inkpen, Mick *99:* 104, 105; *106:* 44
Innerst, Stacy *149:* 104
Innocenti, Roberto *21:* 123; *96:* 122; *159:* 111, 197; *199:* 176
Inoue, Yosuke *24:* 118
Iofin, Michael *97:* 157
Iosa, Ann *63:* 189
Ipcar, Dahlov *1:* 124, 125; *49:* 137, 138, 139, 140, 141, 142,143, 144, 145; *147:* 122, 124, 126
Irvin, Fred *13:* 166; *15:* 143, 144; *27:* 175
Irving, Jay *45:* 72
Irving, Laurence *27:* 50
Isaac, Joanne *21:* 76
Isaacs, Gary *170:* 188
Isadora, Rachel *43:* 159, 160; *54:* 31; *79:* 106, 107,108; *121:* 100, 102; *165:* 116, 117; *204:* 61, 63, 64
Ishmael, Woodi *24:* 111; *31:* 99
Isol *220:* 73
Ives, Ruth *15:* 257
Iwai, Melissa *149:* 233; *183:* 92; *199:* 115
Iwamura, Kazuo *213:* 87

J

Jabar, Cynthia *101:* 201; *210:* 134, 135
Jackness, Andrew *94:* 237
Jackson, Julian *91:* 104, 106
Jackson, Michael *43:* 42
Jackson, Shelley *79:* 71; *99:* 109; *187:* 82
Jacob, Murv *89:* 30
Jacobi, Kathy *62:* 118
Jacobs, Barbara *9:* 136
Jacobs, Lou, Jr. *9:* 136; *15:* 128
Jacobsen, Laura *176:* 98; *177:* 85, 86
Jacobson, Rick *131:* 222; *170:* 119; *222:* 52

Jacobus, Tim *79:* 140; *109:* 126; *129:* 180
Jacques, Robin *1:* 70; *2:* 1; *8:* 46; *9:* 20; *15:* 187; *19:* 253; *32:* 102, 103, 104; *43:* 184; *73:* 135; *YABC 1:* 42
Jaeggi, Yoshiko *186:* 184
Jaffee, Al *66:* 131, 132
Jago *216:* 122
Jagr, Miloslav *13:* 197
Jahn-Clough, Lisa *88:* 114; *152:* 104; *193:* 70, 71
Jahnke, Robert *84:* 24
Jainschigg, Nicholas *80:* 64; *91:* 138; *95:* 63; *99:* 25; *108:* 50; *171:* 41
Jakesavic, Nenad *85:* 102
Jakobsen, Kathy *116:* 83
Jakubowski, Charles *14:* 192
Jambor, Louis *YABC 1:* 11
James, Ann *73:* 50; *82:* 113; *158:* 61; *183:* 44
James, Brian *140:* 91
James, Curtis E. *182:* 93
James, Derek *35:* 187; *44:* 91; *61:* 133; *74:* 2; *80:* 57; *86:* 88; *130:* 30; *179:* 29; *218:* 31
James, Gilbert *YABC 1:* 43
James, Gordon C. *195:* 89
James, Harold *2:* 151; *3:* 62; *8:* 79; *29:* 113; *51:* 195; *74:* 90
James, Kennon *126:* 211
James, Robin *50:* 106; *53:* 32, 34, 35
James, Simon *202:* 73, 74
James, Will *19:* 150, 152, 153, 155, 163
Janosch
    See Eckert, Horst
Janovitch, Marilyn *68:* 168
Janovitz, Marilyn *87:* 187; *130:* 198; *194:* 91
Jansons, Inese *48:* 117
Jansson, Alexander *216:* 59
Jansson, Tove *3:* 90; *41:* 106, 108, 109, 110, 111, 113, 114
Jaques, Faith *7:* 11, 132, 133; *21:* 83, 84; *69:* 114,116; *73:* 170
Jaques, Frances Lee *29:* 224
Jarka, Jeff *221:* 94
Jarrett, Clare *201:* 77
Jarrie, Martin *219:* 86
Jauss, Anne Marie *1:* 139; *3:* 34; *10:* 57, 119; *11:* 205; *23:* 194
Jay, Alison *158:* 97, 98; *183:* 126, 127; *196:* 95, 96, 97, 98; *200:* 72, 73, 74; *212:* 39
Jeffers, Oliver *175:* 111; *213:* 89
Jeffers, Susan *17:* 86, 87; *25:* 164, 165; *26:* 112; *50:* 132, 134, 135; *70:* 111, 112, 113; *137:* 107, 108, 109, 110, 111; *202:* 77, 78
Jefferson, Louise E. *4:* 160
Jenkin-Pearce, Susie *78:* 16
Jenkins, Debra Reid *85:* 202; *114:* 89; *173:* 134; *225:* 116
Jenkins, Jean *98:* 79, 102
Jenkins, Leonard *157:* 169; *167:* 128; *189:* 96, 97; *190:* 89
Jenkins, Patrick *72:* 126
Jenkins, Steve *124:* 177; *154:* 90, 91, 92, 93; *185:* 194; *188:* 81, 82, 83, 84, 85, 86; *218:* 67, 69, 70, 71, 72
Jenks, Aleta *73:* 117; *124:* 225
Jenkyns, Chris *51:* 97
Jensen, Bruce *95:* 39
Jensinius, Kirsten *56:* 58
Jeram, Anita *89:* 135; *102:* 122, 123; *129:* 112; *154:* 96, 97, 98; *164:* 154; *203:* 123, 124; *219:* 88, 89, 90, 91
Jernigan, E. Wesley *85:* 92
Jerome, Karen A. *72:* 194
Jeruchim, Simon *6:* 173; *15:* 250
Jeschke, Susan *20:* 89; *39:* 161; *41:* 84; *42:* 120
Jessel, Camilla *29:* 115
Jessell, Tim *159:* 3; *177:* 87; *181:* 95; *205:* 4; *213:* 74; *223:* 187; *225:* 102
Jeyaveeran, Ruth *182:* 100
Jiang, Cheng An *109:* 108
Jiang, Wei *109:* 108

Jimenez, Maria 77: 158; 93: 127
Jobling, Curtis 138: 74
Jocelyn, Marthe 118: 83; 137: 219; 163: 119,
    120; 198: 62
Joerns, Consuelo 38: 36; 44: 94
John, Diana 12: 209
John, Helen 1: 215; 28: 204
Johns, Elizabeth 127: 33
Johns, Jasper 61: 172
Johns, Jeanne 24: 114
Johnson, Adrian 143: 50
Johnson, Bruce 9: 47
Johnson, Cathy 92: 136; 218: 112
Johnson, Crockett
    See Leisk, David
Johnson, D. William 23: 104
Johnson, D.B. 183: 98, 139
Johnson, David A. 175: 18; 191: 91; 218: 19
Johnson, Gillian 119: 175; 164: 217; 215: 99
Johnson, Harper 1: 27; 2: 33; 18: 302; 19: 61;
    31: 181; 44: 46, 50, 95
Johnson, Ingrid 37: 118
Johnson, James Ralph 1: 23, 127
Johnson, James David 12: 195
Johnson, Jane 48: 136
Johnson, Joel Peter 98: 18; 128: 111; 201: 13;
    213: 189
Johnson, John E. 34: 133
Johnson, Kevin 72: 44
Johnson, Kevin Eugene 109: 215
Johnson, Larry 47: 56; 123: 107; 159: 203
Johnson, Layne 187: 94; 209: 63; 222: 100,
    101
Johnson, Margaret S. 35: 131
Johnson, Meredith Merrell 71: 181; 83: 158;
    89: 103; 104: 88
Johnson, Milton 1: 67; 2: 71; 26: 45; 31: 107;
    60: 112; 68: 96
Johnson, Pamela 16: 174; 52: 145; 62: 140;
    73: 116; 85: 64
Johnson, Paul Brett 83: 95; 132: 119
Johnson, Stephen T. 80: 15; 131: 35; 141: 96;
    145: 40; 164: 187; 175: 32; 189: 99, 100;
    208: 43
Johnson, Steve 138: 219; 141: 64; 144: 199;
    177: 51; 214: 95; 221: 63
Johnson, William R. 38: 91
Johnson-Petrov, Arden 115: 206
Johnston, David McCall 50: 131, 133
Johnston, Lynne 118: 85, 87, 89; 216: 127,
    128, 131
Johnstone, Anne 8: 120; 36: 89
Johnstone, Janet Grahame 8: 120; 36: 89
Jonas, Ann 50: 107, 108, 109; 135: 113
Jones, Bob 71: 5; 77: 199
Jones, Carol 5: 131; 72: 185, 186; 153: 111,
    112
Jones, Chuck 53: 70, 71
Jones, Curtis 211: 144
Jones, Davy 89: 176
Jones, Douglas B. 185: 192; 202: 82
Jones, Elizabeth Orton 18: 124, 126, 128, 129
Jones, Harold 14: 88; 52: 50
Jones, Holly 127: 3
Jones, Jeff 41: 64
Jones, Laurian 25: 24, 27
Jones, Margaret 74: 57
Jones, Noah Z. 182: 37; 203: 159
Jones, Randy 131: 104
Jones, Richard 127: 222
Jones, Robert 25: 67
Jones, Wilfred 35: 115; YABC 1: 163
Jordan, Charles 89: 58
Jordan, Jess 158: 136; 203: 111
Jordan, Martin George 84: 127
Jordan, Richard 84: 36
Jorgenson, Andrea 91: 111
Jorisch, Stéphane 153: 56, 193; 177: 29; 178:
    138, 139; 187: 23; 211: 182
Joseph, James 53: 88
Joudrey, Ken 64: 145; 78: 6

Joyce, William 72: 131, 132, 133, 134; 73:
    227; 145: 37
Joyner, Jerry 34: 138
Joyner, Loraine M. 209: 17
Joysmith, Brenda 210: 237
Juan, Ana 175: 38; 179: 111, 112; 213: 9
Jucker, Sita 5: 93
Judge, Lita 192: 99
Judkis, Jim 37: 38
Juhasz, Victor 31: 67
Jullian, Philippe 24: 206; 25: 203
Jung, Tom 91: 217
Junge, Alexandra 183: 37
Junge, Walter 67: 150
Jupo, Frank 7: 148, 149
Jurisch, Stephane 154: 105
Justice, Martin 34: 72

K

Kabatova-Taborska, Zdenka 107: 153
Kachik, John 165: 230
Kaczman, James 156: 98
Kadair, Deborah Ousley 184: 45, 89
Kahl, David 74: 95; 97: 35; 109: 174; 110:
    213; 198: 15
Kahl, M.P. 37: 83
Kahl, Virginia 48: 138
Kahn, Katherine Janus 90: 135; 211: 155; 218:
    75, 76; 220: 89,90
Kakimoo, Kozo 11: 148
Kalett, Jim 48: 159, 160, 161
Kalin, Victor 39: 186
Kalis, Jennifer 207: 82; 219: 62
Kalman, Maira 96: 131, 132; 137: 115
Kalmenoff, Matthew 22: 191
Kalow, Gisela 32: 105
Kamen, Gloria 1: 41; 9: 119; 10: 178; 35:
    157; 78: 236; 98: 82
Kaminsky, Jef 102: 153
Kandell, Alice 35: 133
Kane, Henry B. 14: 90; 18: 219, 220
Kane, Robert 18: 131
Kanfer, Larry 66: 141
Kangas, Juli 200: 88
Kappes, Alfred 28: 104
Karalus, Bob 41: 157
Karas, G. Brian 80: 60; 99: 179; 115: 41; 118:
    50; 136: 168; 145: 166; 149: 245; 159: 65;
    171: 192; 178: 142, 143; 202: 38; 209: 142;
    222: 106, 107, 108, 109; 225: 62
Karasz, Ilonka 128: 163
Karlin, Eugene 10: 63; 20: 131
Karlin, Nurit 63: 78; 103: 110
Karpinski, Tony 134: 160
Kasamatsu, Shiro 139: 155
Kasparavicius, Kestutis 139: 210
Kassian, Olena 64: 94
Kastner, Jill 79: 135; 117: 84, 85
Kasuya, Masahiro 41: 206, 207; 51: 100
Kasza, Keiko 191: 99, 100, 101, 102, 103
Katona, Robert 21: 85; 24: 126
Katz, Avi 199: 55
Katz, Karen 158: 123
Kauffer, E. McKnight 33: 103; 35: 127; 63: 67
Kaufman, Angelika 15: 156
Kaufman, Joe 33: 119
Kaufman, John 13: 158
Kaufman, Stuart 62: 64; 68: 226; 137: 44
Kaufmann, John 1: 174; 4: 159; 8: 43, 1; 10:
    102; 18: 133, 134; 22: 251
Kaye, Graham 1: 9; 67: 7, 8
Kaye, M.M. 62: 95
Kazalovski, Nata 40: 205
Keane, Bil 4: 135
Kearney, David 72: 47; 121: 83
Keating, Pamel T. 77: 37
Keats, Ezra Jack 3: 18, 105, 257; 14: 101,
    102; 33: 129; 57: 79, 80, 82, 83, 84, 87

Keegan, Charles 166: 211
Keegan, Marcia 9: 122; 32: 93
Keeler, Patricia A. 81: 56; 183: 102, 103
Keely, Jack 119: 95
Keely, John 26: 104; 48: 214
Keen, Eliot 25: 213
Keep, Richard C. 170: 122
Keeping, Charles 9: 124, 185; 15: 28, 134; 18:
    115; 44: 194, 196; 47: 25; 52: 3; 54: 156;
    69: 123, 124; 74: 56; 155: 9
Keeter, Susan 168: 46; 183: 192
Keith, Eros 4: 98; 5: 138; 31: 29; 43: 220; 52:
    91, 92, 93, 94; 56: 64, 66; 60: 37; 79: 93
Keleinikov, Andrei 65: 101, 102
Kelen, Emery 13: 115
Keller, A.J. 62: 198
Keller, Arthur I. 26: 106
Keller, Dick 36: 123, 125
Keller, Holly 45: 79; 76: 118, 119, 120, 121;
    108: 137, 138, 140; 157: 117, 118, 119; 216:
    136
Keller, Katie 79: 222; 93: 108
Keller, Laurie 196: 105, 106
Keller, Ronald 45: 208
Kelley, Gary 183: 105; 216: 78; 217: 95, 96,
    97
Kelley, Marty 211: 91
Kelley, True 41: 114, 115; 42: 137; 75: 35;
    92: 104, 105; 124: 62; 130: 100, 101; 179:
    120, 121, 122; 192: 251
Kellogg, Steven 8: 96; 11: 207; 14: 130; 20: ;
    201: 38 58; 29: 140, 141; 30: 35; 41: 141;
    57: 89, 90, 92,93, 94, 96; 59: 182; 73: 141;
    77: 129; 130: 105, 106; 177: 94, 95, 96, 97;
    199: 57; 217: 61; YABC 1: 65, 73
Kelly, Billy 158: 143
Kelly, Geoff 97: 196; 112: 25
Kelly, Irene 147: 134; 210: 144, 145
Kelly, John 194: 186
Kelly, Joseph 174: 94
Kelly, Kathleen M. 71: 109
Kelly, Laura 89: 217
Kelly, True 163: 87
Kelly, Walt 18: 136, 137, 138, 139, 140, 141,
    144, 145, 146, 148, 149
Kemble, E.W. 34: 75; 44: 178; YABC 2: 54,
    59
Kemly, Kathleen 209: 165
Kemp-Welsh, Lucy 24: 197; 100: 214
Kendall, Jane 150: 105; 186: 109
Kendall, Peter 152: 85
Kendrick, Dennis 79: 213
Kennaway, Adrienne 60: 55, 56; 171: 88, 89
Kennedy, Anne 212: 34
Kennedy, Doug 189: 104
Kennedy, Paul Edward 6: 190; 8: 132; 33: 120
Kennedy, Richard 3: 93; 12: 179; 44: 193;
    100: 15; YABC 1: 57
Kent, Jack 24: 136; 37: 37; 40: 81; 84: 89;
    86: 150; 88: 77
Kent, Rockwell 5: 166; 6: 129; 20: 225, 226,
    227,229; 59: 144
Kenyon, Tony 81: 201; 127: 74
Kepes, Juliet 13: 119
Kerins, Anthony 76: 84
Kerr, Judity 24: 137
Kerr, Phyllis Forbes 72: 141
Kessler, Leonard 1: 108; 7: 139; 14: 107, 227;
    22: 101; 44: 96; 67: 79; 82: 123
Kest, Kristin 168: 99; 173: 23
Kesteven, Peter 35: 189
Ketcham, Hank 28: 140, 141, 142
Kettelkamp, Larry 2: 164
Key, Alexander 8: 99
Khalsa, Dayal Kaur 62: 99
Kiakshuk 8: 59
Kid, Tom 207: 54
Kidd, Chip 94: 23
Kidd, Richard 152: 110
Kidd, Tom 64: 199; 81: 189; 185: 173

Kiddell-Monroe, Joan *19:* 201; *55:* 59, 60; *87:* 174; *121:* 112
Kidder, Harvey *9:* 105; *80:* 41
Kidwell, Carl *43:* 145
Kieffer, Christa *41:* 89
Kiesler, Kate *110:* 105; *136:* 142
Kiff, Ken *40:* 45
Kilaka, John *223:* 107
Kilbride, Robert *37:* 100
Kilby, Don *141:* 144
Kim, David *201:* 79; *202:* 97
Kim, Glenn *99:* 82
Kimball, Anton *78:* 114; *119:* 105
Kimball, Yeffe *23:* 116; *37:* 88
Kimber, Murray *171:* 91
Kimmel, Warren *176:* 112
Kincade, Orin *34:* 116
Kindersley, Barnabas *96:* 110
Kindred, Wendy *7:* 151
King, Colin *53:* 3
King, Robin *10:* 164, 165
King, Stephen Michael *141:* 31; *197:* 191; *218:* 81, 82
King, Tara Calahan *139:* 172
King, Tony *39:* 121
Kingman, Dong *16:* 287; *44:* 100, 102, 104
Kingsley, Charles *YABC 2:* 182
Kingston, Julie *147:* 14
Kingston, Maxine Hong *53:* 92
Kinney, Jeff *187:* 97
Kipling, John Lockwood *YABC 2:* 198
Kipling, Rudyard *YABC 2:* 196
Kipniss, Robert *29:* 59
Kirchherr, Astrid *55:* 23
Kirchhoff, Art *28:* 136
Kirk, Daniel *153:* 115, 116, 117; *173:* 101; *196:* 113, 114, 115, 116
Kirk, David *117:* 88, 89; *161:* 97, 98
Kirk, Ruth *5:* 96
Kirk, Steve *170:* 37
Kirk, Tim *32:* 209, 211; *72:* 89; *83:* 49
Kirmse, Marguerite *15:* 283; *18:* 153
Kirsch, Vincent X. *124:* 207
Kirschner, Ruth *22:* 154
Kirwan, Wednesday *198:* 73
Kish, Ely *73:* 119; *79:* 2
Kitamura, Satoshi *62:* 102; *98:* 91; *101:* 147; *138:* 2; *143:* 83, 85, 86; *201:* 83; *223:* 3, 4
Kiss, Andrew *168:* 115
Kitchel, JoAnn E. *133:* 32
Kitchen, Bert *70:* 126; *193:* 49
Kittelsen, Theodor *62:* 14
Kiuchi, Tatsuro *114:* 71
Kiwak, Barbara *172:* 135
Klahr, Susan *176:* 196
Klapholz, Mel *13:* 35
Klee, Jutte *209:* 136
Klein, Bill *89:* 105
Klein, Robert *55:* 77
Klein, Suzanna *63:* 104
Kleinman, Zalman *28:* 143
Kleven, Elisa *173:* 96, 97; *217:* 100, 102
Kliban, B. *35:* 137, 138
Kline, Michael *127:* 66
Klise, M. Sarah *180:* 117, 118; *181:* 97; *221:* 100, 102
Knabel, Lonnie *73:* 103; *75:* 187, 228; *194:* 216
Kneen, Maggie *140:* 139; *221:* 104, 105
Knight, Ann *34:* 143
Knight, Christopher *13:* 125
Knight, Hilary *1:* 233; *3:* 21; *15:* 92, 158, 159; *16:* 258, 259, 260; *18:* 235; *19:* 169; *35:* 242; *46:* 167; *52:* 116; *69:* 126, 127; *132:* 129; *YABC 1:* 168, 169, 172
Knorr, Laura *200:* 91
Knorr, Peter *126:* 92, 93
Knotts, Howard *20:* 4; *25:* 170; *36:* 163
Knutson, Barbara *112:* 134; *202:* 108
Knutson, Kimberley *115:* 90
Kobayashi, Ann *39:* 58

Kochalka, James *196:* 120, 121, 122
Kocsis, J.C.
  See Paul, James
Kodman, Stanislawa *201:* 85; *224:* 72
Koehler, Hanne Lore *176:* 203
Koehn, Ilse *34:* 198; *79:* 123
Koelsch, Michael *99:* 182; *107:* 164; *109:* 239; *138:* 142; *150:* 94; *176:* 105; *187:* 63; *198:* 63
Koering, Ursula *3:* 28; *4:* 14; *44:* 5; *64:* 140,141; *85:* 46
Koerner, Henry
  See Koerner, W.H.D.
Koerner, W.H.D. *14:* 216; *21:* 88, 89, 90, 91; *23:* 211
Koetsch, Mike *166:* 68
Koffler, Camilla *36:* 113
Kogan, Deborah Ray *161:* 101, 102
Koide, Yasuko *50:* 114
Kolado, Karen *102:* 228
Kolesova, Juliana *217:* 81; *222:* 185
Komoda, Kiyo *9:* 128; *13:* 214
Kompaneyets, Marc *169:* 92
Konashevich, Vladimir *61:* 160
Konashevicha, V. *YABC 1:* 26
Konigsburg, E.L. *4:* 138; *48:* 141, 142, 144, 145; *94:* 129, 130; *126:* 129, 130, 131; *194:* 95, 98
Kono, Erin Eitter *177:* 99
Kooiker, Leonie *48:* 148
Koonook, Simon *65:* 157
Koontz, Robin Michal *136:* 155
Koopmans, Loek *101:* 121
Kopelke, Lisa *154:* 107
Kopper, Lisa *72:* 152, 153; *105:* 135, 136
Korach, Mimi *1:* 128, 129; *2:* 52; *4:* 39; *5:* 159; *9:* 129; *10:* 21; *24:* 69
Koren, Edward *5:* 100; *65:* 65, 67
Kosaka, Fumi *164:* 130
Koscielniak, Bruce *99:* 122; *153:* 120, 121, 122
Koshkin, Alexander *92:* 180
Kossin, Sandy *10:* 71; *23:* 105
Kostin, Andrej *26:* 204
Kosturko, Bob *164:* 56
Kotzky, Brian *68:* 184
Kovacevic, Zivojin *13:* 247
Kovalski, Maryann *58:* 120; *84:* 88; *97:* 124, 125, 126; *158:* 3; *186:* 80
Kozjan, Drazen *209:* 99
Krahn, Fernando *2:* 257; *34:* 206; *49:* 152
Krall, Dan *218:* 84, 85
Kramer, Anthony *33:* 81
Kramer, David *96:* 162; *109:* 132; *150:* 220
Kramer, Frank *6:* 121
Krantz, Kathy *35:* 83
Kratter, Paul *139:* 65
Kraus, Robert *13:* 217; *65:* 113; *93:* 93, 94
Krause, Jon *176:* 62
Krauss, Trisha *174:* 10
Kredel, Fritz *6:* 35; *17:* 93, 94, 95, 96; *22:* 147; *24:* 175; *29:* 130; *35:* 77; *YABC 2:* 166, 300
Kreloff, Eliot *189:* 107, 108; *205:* 182
Krementz, Jill *17:* 98; *49:* 41
Krenina, Katya *117:* 106; *125:* 133; *176:* 117; *221:* 107
Kresin, Robert *23:* 19
Krieger, Salem *54:* 164
Kriegler, Lyn *73:* 29
Krinitz, Esther Nisenthal *193:* 196
Krommes, Beth *128:* 141; *149:* 136; *181:* 100, 101; *184:* 105; *188:* 125; *208:* 135; *209:* 185
Krone, Mike *101:* 71
Kronheimer, Ann *135:* 119
Krosoczka, Jarrett J. *155:* 142; *200:* 93, 94
Kruck, Gerald *88:* 181
Krudop, Walter Lyon *199:* 19
Krupinski, Loretta *67:* 104; *102:* 131; *161:* 105, 106
Krupp, Robin Rector *53:* 96, 98

Krush, Beth *1:* 51, 85; *2:* 233; *4:* 115; *9:* 61; *10:* 191; *11:* 196; *18:* 164, 165; *32:* 72; *37:* 203; *43:* 57; *60:* 102, 103, 107, 108, 109
Krush, Joe *2:* 233; *4:* 115; *9:* 61; *10:* 191; *11:* 196; *18:* 164, 165; *32:* 72, 91; *37:* 203; *43:* 57; *60:* 102, 103, 107, 108, 109
Krych, Duane *91:* 43
Krykorka, Vladyana *96:* 147; *143:* 90, 91; *168:* 14
Kubick, Dana *165:* 91; *212:* 104, 105, 212
Kubinyi, Laszlo *4:* 116; *6:* 113; *16:* 118; *17:* 100; *28:* 227; *30:* 172; *49:* 24, 28; *54:* 23; *167:* 149
Kubricht, Mary *73:* 118
Kucharik, Elena *139:* 31
Kuchera, Kathleen *84:* 5
Kuhn, Bob *17:* 91; *35:* 235
Kulikov, Boris *163:* 185; *185:* 23; *205:* 99, 100; *217:* 160
Kulka, Joe *188:* 110
Kukalis, Romas *90:* 27; *139:* 37
Kuklin, Susan *63:* 82, 83, 84
Kunhardt, Dorothy *53:* 101
Kunhardt, Edith *67:* 105, 106
Kunstler, Mort *10:* 73; *32:* 143
Kurchevsky, V. *34:* 61
Kurczok, Belinda *121:* 118
Kurelek, William *8:* 107
Kuriloff, Ron *13:* 19
Kurisu, Jane *160:* 120
Kuskin, Karla *2:* 170; *68:* 115, 116; *111:* 116
Kutzer, Ernst *19:* 249
Kuzma, Steve *57:* 8; *62:* 93
Kuznetsova, Berta *74:* 45
Kvasnosky, Laura McGee *93:* 103; *142:* 83; *182:* 108
Kwas, Susan Estelle *179:* 116; *217:* 90
Kyong, Yunmee *165:* 139

L

LaBlanc, Andre *24:* 146
Laboccetta, Mario *27:* 120
LaBrose, Darcie *157:* 134
Labrosse, Darcia *58:* 88; *108:* 77; *178:* 89
LaCava, Vince *95:* 118
Laceky, Adam *32:* 121
Lacis, Astra *85:* 117
Lacome, Julie *174:* 96, 97
La Croix *YABC 2:* 4
Ladd, London *206:* 50
Ladwig, Tim *98:* 212; *117:* 76; *215:* 32; *223:* 111, 112
La Farge, Margaret *47:* 141
LaFave, Kim *64:* 177; *72:* 39; *97:* 146; *99:* 172; *106:* 123; *149:* 126; *196:* 128, 129
Lafontaine, Roger *167:* 158
Lafrance, Marie *197:* 109
Lagarrigue, Jerome *136:* 102; *187:* 81
Laimgruber, Monika *11:* 153
Laio, Jimmy *213:* 57
Laite, Gordon *1:* 130, 131; *8:* 209; *31:* 113; *40:* 63; *46:* 117
Laliberté, Louise-Andrée *169:* 98
LaMarche, Jim *46:* 204; *61:* 56; *94:* 69; *114:* 22; *129:* 163; *162:* 78, 80
Lamb, Jim *10:* 117
Lambase, Barbara *101:* 185; *150:* 221; *166:* 234
Lambert, J.K. *38:* 129; *39:* 24
Lambert, Sally Anne *133:* 191
Lambert, Saul *23:* 112; *33:* 107; *54:* 136
Lambert, Stephen *109:* 33; *174:* 99
Lambo, Don *6:* 156; *35:* 115; *36:* 146
Lamontagne, Jacques *166:* 227
Lamut, Sonja *57:* 193
Lamut, Sonya *85:* 102
Landa, Peter *11:* 95; *13:* 177; *53:* 119
Landau, Jacob *38:* 111

Landis, Joan *104:* 23; *203:* 32
Landon, Lucinda *79:* 31
Landshoff, Ursula *13:* 124
Landström, Lena *146:* 165, 166
Landström, Olof *146:* 166, 168; *170:* 22
Lane, Daniel *112:* 60
Lane, John R. *8:* 145
Lane, John *15:* 176, 177; *30:* 146
Lane, Nancy *166:* 74
Lang, G.D. *48:* 56
Lang, Gary *73:* 75
Lang, Glenna *221:* 113
Lang, Jerry *18:* 295
Langdo, Bryan *186:* 187; *191:* 113, 114, 115
Lange, Dorothea *50:* 141
Langley, Jonathan *162:* 128
Langner, Nola *8:* 110; *42:* 36
Lanino, Deborah *105:* 148
Lantz, Paul *1:* 82, 102; *27:* 88; *34:* 102; *45:* 123
Larkin, Bob *84:* 225
Laroche, Giles *126:* 140; *146:* 81; *221:* 116, 117
LaRochelle, David *171:* 97
Larrecq, John *44:* 108; *68:* 56
Larsen, Suzanne *1:* 13
Larson, Gary *57:* 121, 122, 123, 124, 125, 126, 127
Larsson, Carl *35:* 144, 145, 146, 147, 148, 149, 150, 152, 153, 154
Larsson, Karl *19:* 177
Lartitegui, Ana G. *105:* 167
LaRue, Jenna *167:* 20
La Rue, Michael D. *13:* 215
Lasker, Joe *7:* 186, 187; *14:* 55; *38:* 115; *39:* 47; *83:* 113, 114, 115
Latham, Barbara *16:* 188, 189; *43:* 71
Lathrop, Dorothy *14:* 117, 118, 119; *15:* 109; *16:* 78, 79, 81; *32:* 201, 203; *33:* 112; *YABC 2:* 301
Lattimore, Eleanor Frances *7:* 156
Lauden, Claire *16:* 173
Lauden, George, Jr. *16:* 173
Laune, Paul *2:* 235; *34:* 31
Laure, Jason *49:* 53; *50:* 122
Lauter, Richard *63:* 29; *67:* 111; *77:* 198
Lavallee, Barbara *74:* 157; *92:* 154; *96:* 126; *145:* 193; *166:* 125, 126; *186:* 155; *192:* 172
Lave, Fitz Hugh *59:* 139
Lavis, Steve *43:* 143; *87:* 137, 164, 165; *222:* 161; *225:* 121
Layton, Neal *152:* 120, 121; *182:* 65; *187:* 103, 105, 106
Law, Jenny *201:* 31
Lawrason, June *168:* 30
Lawrence, John *25:* 131; *30:* 141; *44:* 198, 200; *214:* 7
Lawrence, Stephen *20:* 195
Lawson, Carol *6:* 38; *42:* 93, 131; *174:* 56; *189:* 89; *209:* 59
Lawson, George *17:* 280
Lawson, Robert *5:* 26; *6:* 94; *13:* 39; *16:* 11; *20:* 100, 102, 103; *54:* 3; *66:* 12; *100:* 144, 145; *YABC 2:* 222, 224, 225, 227, 228, 229, 230, 231, 232, 233, 234, 235, 237, 238, 239, 240, 241
Layfield, Kathie *60:* 194
Lazare, Jerry *44:* 109; *74:* 28
Lazarevich, Mila *17:* 118
Lazarus, Claire *103:* 30
Lazarus, Keo Felker *21:* 94
Lazzaro, Victor *11:* 126
Lea, Bob *166:* 208; *203:* 108
Lea, Tom *43:* 72, 74
Leacroft, Richard *6:* 140
Leaf, Munro *20:* 99
Leake, Donald *70:* 41
Leander, Patricia *23:* 27
Lear, Edward *18:* 183, 184, 185
Lear, Rebecca *149:* 46

Lebenson, Richard *6:* 209; *7:* 76; *23:* 145; *44:* 191; *87:* 153
Le Cain, Errol *6:* 141; *9:* 3; *22:* 142; *25:* 198; *28:* 173; *68:* 128, 129; *86:* 49
Lechon, Daniel *113:* 211
Leder, Dora *129:* 172
Ledger, Bill *181:* 58
Leduc, Bernard *102:* 36
Lee, Alan *62:* 25, 28
Lee, Bryce *99:* 60; *101:* 195; *196:* 53
Lee, Chinlun *181:* 138; *182:* 112
Lee, Declan *191:* 20
Lee, Dom *83:* 118, 120; *93:* 123; *121:* 121, 126; *146:* 174, 175, 206, 207; *174:* 204
Lee, Doris *13:* 246; *32:* 183; *44:* 111
Lee, Hector Viveros *115:* 96
Lee, Ho Baek *200:* 160
Lee, Huy Voun *217:* 106
Lee, Jeanne M. *158:* 56
Lee, Jared *93:* 200; *157:* 229; *215:* 113, 191, 192, 193
Lee, Jody *81:* 121; *82:* 225; *91:* 155; *100:* 182
Lee, Jody A. *127:* 124, 126, 127
See also Lee, Jody
Lee, Manning de V. *2:* 200; *17:* 12; *27:* 87; *37:* 102, 103, 104; *YABC 2:* 304
Lee, Margaret *213:* 179
Lee, Marie G. *138:* 157
Lee, Paul *97:* 100; *105:* 72, 209; *109:* 177; *128:* 113; *202:* 45
Lee, Robert J. *3:* 97; *67:* 124
Lee, Victor *96:* 228; *105:* 182; *140:* 196; *208:* 191
Lee, Virginia *208:* 139, 140; *218:* 28
Leech, Dorothy *98:* 76
Leech, John *15:* 59
Leedy, Loreen *84:* 142; *128:* 144, 145, 146; *175:* 125, 126, 127
Leeman, Michael *44:* 157
Leeming, Catherine *87:* 39
Lees, Harry *6:* 112
LeFever, Bill *88:* 220, 221
Legenisel *47:* 111
Legrand, Edy *18:* 89, 93
Lehman, Barbara *73:* 123; *170:* 130
Lehrman, Rosalie *2:* 180
Leichman, Seymour *5:* 107
Leick, Bonnie *205:* 104
Leighton, Clare *25:* 130; *33:* 168; *37:* 105, 106, 108, 109
Leisk, David *1:* 140, 141; *11:* 54; *30:* 137, 142, 143, 144
Leister, Bryan *89:* 45; *106:* 37; *114:* 67; *149:* 236; *222:* 181
Leloir, Maurice *18:* 77, 80, 83, 99
Lemaître, Pascal *144:* 175; *176:* 130; *189:* 135; *225:* 124, 125
Lemieux, Michele *100:* 148; *139:* 153
Lemke, Horst *14:* 98; *38:* 117, 118, 119
Lemke, R.W. *42:* 162
Lemon, David Gwynne *9:* 1
LeMoult, Adolph *82:* 116
Lenn, Michael *136:* 89
Lennon, John *114:* 100
Lennox, Elsie *95:* 163; *143:* 160
Lenski, Lois *1:* 144; *26:* 135, 137, 139, 141; *100:* 153, 154
Lent, Blair *1:* 116, 117; *2:* 174; *3:* 206, 207; *7:* 168, 169; *34:* 62; *68:* 217; *133:* 101; *183:* 60
Leonard, David *212:* 149
Leonard, Richard *91:* 128
Leonard, Tom *207:* 95; *219:* 55
Leone, Leonard *49:* 190
Lerner, Carol *86:* 140, 141, 142
Lerner, Judith *116:* 138
Lerner, Sharon *11:* 157; *22:* 56
Leroux-Hugon, Helene *132:* 139
Leslie, Cecil *19:* 244
Lessac, Frané *80:* 182, 207; *96:* 182; *202:* 58; *209:* 104

Lessing, Erich *167:* 52; *173:* 60
Lester, Alison *50:* 124; *90:* 147, 148; *129:* 130; *218:* 91, 93
Lester, Mike *208:* 50
Lethcoe, Jason *191:* 116, 117
Le Tord, Bijou *49:* 156; *95:* 112
Leutz, Emanuel *165:* 27
Levai, Blaise *39:* 130
Levert, Mireille *211:* 101
Levin, Ted *12:* 148
Levine, David *43:* 147, 149, 150, 151, 152; *64:* 11
Levine, Joe *71:* 88; *219:* 74
Levine, Marge *81:* 127
Levinson, David *178:* 232
Levit, Herschel *24:* 223
Levstek, Ljuba *131:* 192; *134:* 216; *149:* 65; *168:* 180
Levy, Jessica Ann *19:* 225; *39:* 191
Levy, Lina *117:* 126
Lewin, Betsy *32:* 114; *48:* 177; *90:* 151; *91:* 125; *92:* 85; *115:* 105; *169:* 110, 111; *178:* 47; *186:* 188; *194:* 201; *222:* 120
Lewin, Ted *4:* 77; *8:* 168; *20:* 110; *21:* 99,100; *27:* 110; *28:* 96, 97; *31:* 49; *45:* 55; *48:* 223; *60:* 20, 119, 120; *62:* 139; *66:* 108; *71:* 12; *72:* 21; *74:* 226; *76:* 139, 140; *77:* 82; *79:* 87; *85:* 49, 177; *86:* 55; *88:* 182; *93:* 28, 29; *94:* 34, 182, 194; *99:* 156; *104:* 8; *115:* 123; *118:* 74; *119:* 114, 116; *131:* 54; *145:* 99; *165:* 151; *177:* 75; *178:* 42; *190:* 30; *192:* 86; *195:* 101, 102; *203:* 52; *222:* 119
Lewis, Allen *15:* 112
Lewis, E.B. *88:* 143; *93:* 109; *119:* 79; *124:* 113; *128:* 49; *151:* 167; *168:* 110; *173:* 121; *174:* 66; *176:* 7; *184:* 150; *185:* 191; *211:* 108, 109, 110, 111; *223:* 17
Lewis, H.B. *170:* 124
Lewis, J. Patrick *162:* 83
Lewis, Jan *81:* 22
Lewis, Kim *136:* 165; *217:* 109, 111
Lewis, Richard W. *52:* 25
Lewis, Robin Baird *98:* 193
Lew-Vriethoff, Joanne *225:* 181
Leydon, Rita Floden *21:* 101
Li, Xiojun *187:* 172
Liao, Jimmy *202:* 100
Lichtenheld, Tom *152:* 125, 126; *222:* 160; *224:* 9
Lieblich, Irene *22:* 173; *27:* 209, 214
Lieder, Rick *108:* 197; *199:* 58, 59, 60
Lies, Brian *92:* 40; *141:* 101; *150:* 138; *190:* 97, 98, 99,
Liese, Charles *4:* 222
Liew, Sonny *219:* 108
Life, Kay *79:* 49
Lifton, Robert Jay *66:* 154
Lightburn, Ron *86:* 153; *91:* 122
Lightfoot, Norman R. *45:* 47
Lignell, Lois *37:* 114
Lill, Debra *121:* 70
Lilly, Charles *8:* 73; *20:* 127; *48:* 53; *72:* 9,16; *77:* 98; *102:* 94
Lilly, Ken *37:* 224
Lim, John *43:* 153
Limona, Mercedes *51:* 183
Lin, Grace *143:* 217; *162:* 86, 87; *174:* 185
Lincoln, Patricia Henderson *27:* 27; *78:* 127
Lindahn, Ron *84:* 17
Lindahn, Val *84:* 17
Lindberg, Howard *10:* 123; *16:* 190
Lindberg, Jeffrey *64:* 77; *77:* 71; *79:* 54; *80:* 149; *174:* 109; *179:* 52
Linden, Seymour *18:* 200, 201; *43:* 140
Lindenbaum, Pija *144:* 143; *183:* 113
Linder, Richard *27:* 119
Lindman, Maj *43:* 154
Lindsay, Norman *67:* 114
Lindsay, Vachel *40:* 118
Lindstrom, Jack *145:* 118
Line, Les *27:* 143

Linell
See Smith, Linell
Lionni, Leo *8:* 115; *72:* 159, 160, 161
Lipinsky, Lino *2:* 156; *22:* 175
Lippincott, Gary A. *70:* 35; *119:* 118; *220:* 105, 106, 107
Lippman, Peter *8:* 31; *31:* 119, 120, 160
Lisi, Victoria *89:* 145
Lisker, Emily *169:* 114
Lisker, Sonia O. *16:* 274; *31:* 31; *44:* 113, 114
Lisowski, Gabriel *47:* 144; *49:* 157
Lissim, Simon *17:* 138
Little, Ed *89:* 145; *151:* 53
Little, Harold *16:* 72
Little, Mary E. *28:* 146
Littlewood, Karen *165:* 126; *211:* 112
Litty, Julie *111:* 63
Litzinger, Rosanne *151:* 101; *176:* 118; *196:* 133, 134, 135; *208:* 129; *209:* 147
Liu, Lesley *143:* 72
Lively, Lorna *19:* 216
Livingston, Susan *95:* 22
Liwska, Renata *164:* 113; *199:* 25, 69; *220:* 79
Ljungkvist, Laura *180:* 120
Llerena, Carlos Antonio *19:* 181
Lloyd, Errol *11:* 39; *22:* 178
Lloyd, Megan *77:* 118; *80:* 113; *97:* 75; *117:* 94, 95; *189:* 121, 122; *208:* 128; *211:* 72
Lloyd, Sam *183:* 116, 117
Lo, Beth *165:* 154
Lo, Koon-chiu *7:* 134
Loates, Glen *63:* 76
Lobel, Anita *6:* 87; *9:* 141; *18:* 248; *55:* 85,86, 87, 88, 93, 104; *60:* 67; *78:* 263; *82:* 110; *96:* 157, 159; *101:* 84; *132:* 35; *162:* 93, 94
Lobel, Arnold *1:* 188, 189; *5:* 12; *6:* 147; *7:* 167, 209; *18:* 190, 191; *25:* 39, 43; *27:* 40; *29:* 174; *52:* 127; *55:* 89, 91, 94, 95, 97, 98, 99, 100, 101, 102,103, 105, 106; *60:* 18, 31; *66:* 181, 183; *75:* 57; *82:* 246; *136:* 146
Lobel, Gillian *190:* 21
Locker, Thomas *109:* 134
Lodge, Bernard *107:* 125, 126; *153:* 93
Loeb, Jeph *153:* 177
Lodge, Jo *112:* 119
Loefgren, Ulf *3:* 108
Loescher, Ann *20:* 108
Loescher, Gil *20:* 108
Loew, David *93:* 184; *171:* 120; *211:* 187
Lofting, Hugh *15:* 182, 183; *100:* 161, 162
Lofts, Pamela *60:* 188
Loh, George *38:* 88
Lomberg, Jon *58:* 160
Lonette, Reisie *11:* 211; *12:* 168; *13:* 56; *36:* 122; *43:* 155
Long, Ethan *168:* 146; *178:* 12; *182:* 120, 121; *196:* 124; *223:* 116, 117
Long, Laurel *162:* 135; *190:* 11; *203:* 113, 114
Long, Loren *99:* 176; *172:* 65; *182:* 78; *188:* 114, 115
Long, Melinda *152:* 128
Long, Miles *115:* 174
Long, Sally *42:* 184
Long, Sylvia *74:* 168; *132:* 63; *179:* 134
Longoni, Eduardo *73:* 85
Longtemps, Ken *17:* 123; *29:* 221; *69:* 82
Looser, Heinz *YABC 2:* 208
Lopez, Loretta *190:* 100
López, Rafael *197:* 160; *198:* 85
Lopshire, Robert *6:* 149; *21:* 117; *34:* 166; *73:* 13
Lord, John Vernon *21:* 104; *23:* 25; *51:* 22
Lorenz, Albert *40:* 146; *115:* 127
Loretta, Sister Mary *33:* 73
Lorraine, Walter H. *3:* 110; *4:* 123; *16:* 192; *103:* 119
Los, Marek *146:* 22; *193:* 23
Loss, Joan *11:* 163
Louderback, Walt *YABC 1:* 164
Loughridge, Stuart *214:* 131
Louis, Catherine *212:* 186

Lousada, Sandra *40:* 138
Louth, Jack *149:* 252; *151:* 191, 192
Love, Judy *173:* 43; *196:* 40
Lovelock, Brian *214:* 132, 197
Low, Joseph *14:* 124, 125; *18:* 68; *19:* 194; *31:* 166; *80:* 239
Low, William *62:* 175; *80:* 147; *112:* 194; *150:* 202; *169:* 175; *177:* 110; *192:* 27
Lowe, Vicky *177:* 130
Lowenheim, Alfred *13:* 65, 66
Lowenstein, Sallie *116:* 90, 91
Lowitz, Anson *17:* 124; *18:* 215
Lowrey, Jo *8:* 133
Lubach, Vanessa *142:* 152
Lubell, Winifred *1:* 207; *3:* 15; *6:* 151
Lubin, Leonard B. *19:* 224; *36:* 79, 80; *45:* 128, 129,131, 132, 133, 134, 135, 136, 137, 139, 140, 141; *70:* 95; *YABC2:* 96
Lucas, David *208:* 148
Lucht, Irmgard *82:* 145
Ludwig, Helen *33:* 144, 145
Luebs, Robin *212:* 109
Lufkin, Raymond *38:* 138; *44:* 48
Luhrs, Henry *7:* 123; *11:* 120
Lujan, Tonita *82:* 33
Lupo, Dom *4:* 204
Lustig, Loretta *30:* 186; *46:* 134, 135, 136, 137
Lutes, Jason *210:* 163
Luthardt, Kevin *172:* 125, 126; *217:* 2
Luxbacher, Irene *153:* 145; *219:* 112, 113
Luzak, Dennis *52:* 121; *99:* 142
Lydbury, Jane *82:* 98
Lydecker, Laura *21:* 113; *42:* 53
Lynch, Charles *16:* 33
Lynch, Marietta *29:* 137; *30:* 171
Lynch, P.J. *126:* 228; *129:* 110; *132:* 247; *183:* 64; *207:* 184; *213:* 100, 101, 102
Lyne, Alison Davis *188:* 118, 198
Lyon, Carol *102:* 26
Lyon, Elinor *6:* 154
Lyon, Fred *14:* 16
Lyon, Lea *212:* 110
Lyon, Tammie *175:* 170
Lyons, Oren *8:* 193
Lyster, Michael *26:* 41

M

Maas, Dorothy *6:* 175
Maas, Julie *47:* 61
Macaulay, David *46:* 139, 140, 141, 142, 143, 144, 145, 147, 149, 150; *72:* 167, 168, 169; *137:* 129, 130, 131, 132
MacCarthy, Patricia *69:* 141
Macdonald, Alister *21:* 55
Macdonald, Roberta *19:* 237; *52:* 164
MacDonald, Norman *13:* 99
MacDonald, Ross *201:* 103
MacDonald, Suse *54:* 41; *109* 138; *130:* 156; *193:* 106, 107, 109, 110
Mace, Varian *49:* 159
MacEachern, Stephen *206:* 2
Macguire, Robert Reid *18:* 67
Machetanz, Fredrick *34:* 147, 148
MacInnes, Ian *35:* 59
MacIntyre, Elisabeth *17:* 127, 128
Mack, Jeff *161:* 128; *194:* 119, 120; *219:* 67; *225:* 135
Mack, Stan *17:* 129; *96:* 33
Mackay, Donald *17:* 60
MacKaye, Arvia *32:* 119
Mackenzie, Robert *204:* 78
Mackenzie, Stuart *73:* 213
MacKenzie, Garry *33:* 159
Mackie, Clare *87:* 134
Mackinlay, Miguel *27:* 22
MacKinstry, Elizabeth *15:* 110; *42:* 139, 140, 141, 142, 143,144, 145

MacLeod, Lee *91:* 167
Maclise, Daniel *YABC 2:* 257
Macnaughton, Tina *182:* 145; *218:* 106, 107
MacRae, Tom *181:* 112
Madden, Don *3:* 112, 113; *4:* 33, 108, 155; *7:* 193; *78:* 12; *YABC 2:* 211
Maddison, Angela Mary *10:* 83
Madsen, Jim *146:* 259; *152:* 237; *184:* 106; *197:* 21; *202:* 103, 104
Maestro, Giulio *8:* 124; *12:* 17; *13:* 108; *25:* 182; *54:* 147; *59:* 114, 115, 116, 117, 118, 121, 123, 124, 125,126, 127; *68:* 37, 38; *106:* 129, 130, 131, 136, 137, 138
Maffia, Daniel *60:* 200
Maggio, Viqui *58:* 136, 181; *74:* 150; *75:* 90; *85:* 159; *90:* 158; *109:* 184; *193:* 113
Magnus, Erica *77:* 123
Magnuson, Diana *28:* 102; *34:* 190; *41:* 175
Magoon, Scott *181:* 104; *217:* 165; *222:* 126
Magovern, Peg *103:* 123; *218:* 164
Maguire, Sheila *41:* 100
Magurn, Susan *91:* 30
Mahony, Will *37:* 120
Mahony, Will *85:* 116
Mahood, Kenneth *24:* 141
Mahurin, Matt *164:* 225; *175:* 95; *189:* 37; *196:* 14; *209:* 163
Maik, Henri *9:* 102
Maione, Heather *106:* 5; *178:* 8; *189:* 126, 127; *193:* 58
Maisto, Carol *29:* 87
Maitland, Antony *1:* 100, 176; *8:* 41; *17:* 246; *24:* 46; *25:* 177, 178; *32:* 74; *60:* 65, 195; *67:* 156; *87:* 131; *101:* 110
Majewski, Dawn W. *169:* 95
Mak, Kam *72:* 25; *75:* 43; *87:* 186; *97:* 24; *102:* 154; *149:* 195; *186:* 28; *209:* 132
Makie, Pam *37:* 117
Maktima, Joe *116:* 191
Maland, Nick *99:* 77
Male, Alan *132:* 64
Malone, James Hiram *84:* 161
Malone, Nola Langner *82:* 239
Malone, Peter *191:* 121, 122, 123
Malsberg, Edward *51:* 175
Malvern, Corinne *2:* 13; *34:* 148, 149
Manchess, Gregory *165:* 241; *203:* 119
Mancusi, Stephen *63:* 198, 199
Mandelbaum, Ira *31:* 115
Manders, John *138:* 152, 155; *188:* 171; *190:* 92; *199:* 5; *217:* 52; *219:* 35; *219:* 115, 116, 117
Manet, Edouard *23:* 170
Mangiat, Jeff *173:* 127
Mangurian, David *14:* 133
Manham, Allan *42:* 109; *77:* 180; *80:* 227
Manley, Matt *103:* 167; *117:* 98; *172:* 49; *212:* 207
Manna, Giovanni *178:* 44
Manniche, Lise *31:* 121
Manning, Jane *96:* 203
Manning, Jo *63:* 154
Manning, Lawrence *191:* 153
Manning, Maurie J. *211:* 116
Manning, Mick *176:* 139; *224:* 57
Manning, Samuel F. *5:* 75
Mantel, Richard *57:* 73; *63:* 106; *82:* 255
Mantha, John *205:* 164; *217:* 117
Maraja *15:* 86; *YABC 1:* 28; *2:* 115
Marcellino, Fred *20:* 125; *34:* 222; *53:* 125; *58:* 205; *61:* 64, 121, 122; *68:* 154, 156, 157, 158, 159; *72:* 25; *86:* 184; *98:* 181; *118:* 129, 130, 131; *149:* 218; *194:* 7
Marchesi, Stephen *34:* 140; *46:* 72; *50:* 147; *66:* 239; *70:* 33; *73:* 18, 114, 163; *77:* 47, 76,147; *78:* 79; *80:* 30; *81:* 6; *89:* 66; *93:* 21,130; *94:* 94; *97:* 66; *98:* 96; *114:* 115, 116
Marchiori, Carlos *14:* 60
Marciano, John Bemelmans *118:* 133; *167:* 110, 111, 112

Marconi, Guilherme *220:* 143
Marcus, Barry David *139:* 248; *145:* 18
Maren, Julie *199:* 73
Margules, Gabriele *21:* 120
Mariana
    See Foster, Marian Curtis
Mariano, Michael *52:* 108
Marino, Dorothy *6:* 37; *14:* 135
Mario, Heide Stetson *101:* 202
Maris, Ron *71:* 123
Maritz, Nicolaas *85:* 123
Mark, Mona *65:* 105; *68:* 205; *116:* 213
Markham, R.L. *17:* 240
Marklew, Gilly *211:* 118
Marks, Alan *104:* 104; *109:* 182; *164:* 92;
    185: 134; *187:* 120, 121, 122; *218:* 114, 115
Marks, Cara *54:* 9
Marks, Colin *203:* 129
Marokvia, Artur *31:* 122
Marquez, Susan *108:* 121; *219:* 95
Marrella, Maria Pia *62:* 116
Marriott, Pat *30:* 30; *34:* 39; *35:* 164, 165,
    166; *44:* 170; *48:* 186, 187, 188, 189, 191,
    192, 193; *91:* 92
Mars, W.T. *1:* 161; *3:* 115; *4:* 208, 225; *5:* 92,
    105, 186; *8:* 214; *9:* 12; *13:* 121; *27:* 151;
    31: 180; *38:* 102; *48:* 66; *62:* 164, 165; *64:*
    62; *68:* 229; *79:* 55
Marschall, Ken *85:* 29
Marsh, Christine *3:* 164
Marsh, James *73:* 137
Marsh, Reginald *17:* 5; *19:* 89; *22:* 90, 96
Marshall, Anthony D. *18:* 216
Marshall, Felicia *170:* 190
Marshall, James *6:* 160; *40:* 221; *42:* 24, 25,
    29; *51:* 111, 112, 113, 114, 115, 116, 117,
    118, 119, 120, 121; *64:* 13; *75:* 126, 127,
    128, 129; *102:* 10, 12; *216:* 26, 28
Marshall, Janet *97:* 154
Marstall, Bob *55:* 145; *84:* 153, 170; *104:* 145;
    154: 166, 167, 168
Martchenko, Michael *50:* 129, 153, 155, 156,
    157; *83:* 144,145; *154:* 137, 138, 139
Marten, Ruth *129:* 52
Martin, Brad *199:* 186
Martin, Charles E. *70:* 144
Martin, Courtney A. *214:* 28
Martin, David Stone *24:* 232; *62:* 4
Martin, Fletcher *18:* 213; *23:* 151
Martin, Rene *7:* 144; *42:* 148, 149, 150
Martin, Richard E. *51:* 157; *131:* 203
Martin, Ron *32:* 81
Martin, Stefan *8:* 68; *32:* 124, 126; *56:* 33
Martin, Whitney *166:* 137
Martinez, Ed *58:* 192; *72:* 231; *77:* 33; *80:*
    214; *167:* 123
Martinez, John *6:* 113; *118:* 13; *139:* 143
Martinez, Sergio *158:* 190; *220:* 156
Martini, Angela *183:* 161
Martiniere, Stephan *171:* 130
Marton, Jirina *95:* 127, 128; *144:* 145
Martorell, Antonio *84:* 6; *97:* 161
Martucci, Griesbach *52:* 106
Marvin, Frederic *83:* 86
Marx, Robert F. *24:* 143
Marzollo, Jean *190:* 127
Masefield, Judith *19:* 208, 209
Masheris, Robert *78:* 51
Masiello, Ralph *186:* 171; *214:* 134
Mason, George F. *14:* 139
Mason, Robert *84:* 96
Masse, Josée *208:* 45; *217:* 19; *221:* 134
Massey, Barbara *68:* 142
Massie, Diane Redfield *16:* 194
Massie, Kim *31:* 43
Massini, Sarah *213:* 79
Mataya, David *121:* 66
Mathers, Petra *119:* 135; *163:* 104; *176:* 143,
    144; *187:* 142; *196:* 101
Mathewuse, James *51:* 143

Mathieu, Joseph *14:* 33; *39:* 206; *43:* 167; *56:*
    180; *79:* 126; *94:* 147; *185:* 140
Matje, Martin *169:* 177, 178; *172:* 180
Matsubara, Naoko *12:* 121
Matsuda, Shizu *13:* 167
Matsuoka, Mei *192:* 135; *214:* 84
Matte, L'Enc *22:* 183
Mattelson, Marvin *36:* 50, 51
Matteson, Jenny *180:* 132; *222:* 153
Matthews, Elizabeth *194:* 128; *223:* 35
Matthews, F. Leslie *4:* 216
Matthews, Tina *190:* 130
Mattingly, David *71:* 76, 77; *82:* 64; *91:* 216,
    217; *109:* 25
Matulay, Laszlo *5:* 18; *43:* 168
Matus, Greta *12:* 142
Maughan, Bill *181:* 31; *211:* 211
Mauldin, Bill *27:* 23
Mauterer, Erin Marie *119:* 5
Mawicke, Tran *9:* 137; *15:* 191; *47:* 100
Mawson, Matt *74:* 115
Max, Peter *45:* 146, 147, 148, 149, 150
Maxie, Betty *40:* 135
Maxwell, John Alan *1:* 148
May, Katie *225:* 128
May, Steve *204:* 30
Mayan, Earl *7:* 193
Maydak, Michael S. *220:* 117
Mayer, Bill *200:* 138
Mayer, Danuta *117:* 103
Mayer, Marianna *32:* 132
Mayer, Mercer *11:* 192; *16:* 195, 196; *20:* 55,
    57; *32:* 129, 130, 132, 133, 134; *41:* 144,
    248, 252; *58:* 186; *73:* 140, 142, 143; *137:*
    137, 138
Mayforth, Hal *166:* 77
Mayhew, James *85:* 121; *138:* 187; *149:* 140;
    204: 81
Mayhew, Richard *3:* 106
Mayo, Gretchen Will *38:* 81; *84:* 166
Mays, Victor *5:* 127; *8:* 45, 153; *14:* 245; *23:*
    50; *34:* 155; *40:* 79; *45:* 158; *54:* 91; *66:*
    240
Mazal, Chanan *49:* 104
Maze, Deborah *71:* 83
Mazellan, Ron *75:* 97, 98; *210:* 169
Mazetti, Alan *112:* 72
Mazille, Capucine *96:* 168
Mazza, Adriana Saviozzi *19:* 215
Mazzella, Mary Jo *82:* 165
Mazzetti, Alan *45:* 210
McAfee, Steve *135:* 146; *167:* 176; *191:* 84;
    210: 117; *218:* 34
McAlinden, Paul *112:* 128
McBride, Angus *28:* 49; *103:* 40
McBride, Will *30:* 110
McCaffery, Janet *38:* 145
McCall, Bruce *209:* 119
McCallum, Graham *78:* 78
McCallum, Stephen *141:* 143; *156:* 5; *166:*
    228
McCann, Gerald *3:* 50; *4:* 94; *7:* 54; *41:* 121
McCarthy, Dan *174:* 74
McCarthy, Linda *177:* 128; *218:* 104
McCarthy, Meghan *168:* 134; *199:* 74
McCauley, Adam *157:* 36; *184:* 199; *193:* 100;
    209: 122
McCay, Winsor *41:* 124, 126, 128, 129, 130,
    131; *134:* 77, 79
McClary, Nelson *1:* 111
McClements, George *196:* 146
McClennan, Connie *210:* 181
McClintock, Barbara *57:* 135; *95:* 130; *146:*
    190; *213:* 3, 5, 107, 108
McClintock, Theodore *14:* 141
McCloskey, Robert *1:* 184, 185; *2:* 186, 187;
    17: 209; *39:* 139, 140, 141, 142, 143, 146,
    147, 148; *85:* 150, 151; *100:* 172, 173, 174
McClung, Robert *2:* 189; *68:* 166, 167
McClure, Gillian *31:* 132; *150:* 53
McClure, Nikki *218:* 120

McConnel, Jerry *31:* 75, 187
McConnell, Mary *102:* 49
McCord, Kathleen Garry *78:* 236
McCormack, John *66:* 193
McCormick, A.D. *35:* 119
McCormick, Dell J. *19:* 216
McCoy, Glenn *212:* 132
McCrady, Lady *16:* 198; *39:* 127
McCrea, James *3:* 122; *33:* 216
McCrea, Ruth *3:* 122; *27:* 102; *33:* 216
McCue, Lisa *65:* 148, 149; *77:* 54; *80:* 132;
    175: 33; *177:* 133, 135; *212:* 136, 137, 138
McCully, Emily Arnold *2:* 89; *4:* 120, 121,
    146, 197; *5:* 2, 129; *7:* 191; *11:* 122; *15:*
    210; *33:* 23; *35:* 244; *37:* 122; *39:* 88; *40:*
    103; *50:* 30,31, 32, 33, 34, 35, 36, 37; *52:*
    89, 90; *57:* 6; *62:* 3; *70:* 195; *86:* 82; *96:*
    192; *97:* 93; *110:* 143,144; *117:* 47; *167:* 96;
    210: 175, 176; *225:* 179
McCurdy, Michael *13:* 153; *24:* 85; *81:* 160;
    82: 157, 158; *86:* 125; *97:* 92; *117:* 178;
    132: 6; *147:* 159, 160
McCusker, Paul *99:* 19
McDaniel, Jerry *132:* 135
McDaniel, Preston *160:* 206; *170:* 139
McDermott, Beverly Brodsky *11:* 180
McDermott, Gerald *16:* 201; *74:* 174, 175;
    163: 150, 151
McDermott, Mike *96:* 187
McDonald, Jill *13:* 155; *26:* 128
McDonald, Mercedes *169:* 118
McDonald, Ralph J. *5:* 123, 195
McDonnell, Flora *146:* 199, 200
McDonnell, Patrick *179:* 153, 154; *221:* 136,
    137, 138
McDonough, Don *10:* 163
McElligott, Matt *196:* 147
McElmurry, Jill *137:* 148; *163:* 141; *202:* 186
McElrath-Eslick, Lori *129:* 145; *142:* 21; *173:*
    123; *202:* 194; *204:* 88, 89
McEntee, Dorothy *37:* 124
McEwan, Keith *88:* 116; *165:* 122, 123
McEwen, Katharine *169:* 34
McFall, Christie *12:* 144
McFeely, Daniel *160:* 213
McGaw, Laurie *109:* 243; *143:* 216; *211:* 218
McGee, Barbara *6:* 165
McGee, Marni *163:* 153
McGillvray, Kim *158:* 171; *165:* 213; *186:*
    183; *190:* 175
McGinley-Nally, Sharon *131:* 19
McGinnis, Robert *110:* 113; *177:* 80
McGovern, Tara *98:* 171
McGraw, Sheila *83:* 146
McGregor, Barbara *200:* 155
McGregor, Malcolm *23:* 27
McGrory, Anik *193:* 120
McGuire, Robert *204:* 57; *209:* 86
McGuirk, Leslie *152:* 159
McHale, John *138:* 190
McHenry, E.B. *193:* 122
McHugh, Tom *23:* 64
McIntosh, Jon *42:* 56
McKay, Donald *2:* 118; *32:* 157; *45:* 151, 152
McKean, Dave *150:* 71; *174:* 156; *197:* 83,
    118
McKeating, Eileen *44:* 58
McKee, David *10:* 48; *21:* 9; *70:* 154, 155;
    107: 139, 140, 141; *134:* 218; *158:* 148, 149,
    150, 151
McKee, Diana *109:* 185
McKelvey, Patrick *164:* 141
McKendry, Joe *170:* 136
McKeveny, Tom *164:* 60; *173:* 79
McKie, Roy *7:* 44
McKie, Todd *205:* 181
McKillip, Kathy *30:* 153
McKinney, Ena *26:* 39
McKinnon, James *136:* 75
McKowen, Scott *172:* 63; *202:* 49
McLachlan, Edward *5:* 89

McLaren, Chesley *133:* 53; *213:* 112; *219:* 31
McLaren, Kirsty *123:* 99; *124:* 226
Mclean, Andrew *113:* 117, 118, 120, 121; *172:* 130, 131
Mclean, Janet *172:* 130
McLean, Meg *94:* 196
McLean, Sammis *32:* 197
McLean, Wilson *90:* 29; *113:* 195
McLoughlin, John C. *47:* 149
McLoughlin, Wayne *102:* 230; *134:* 178; *216:* 196
McMahon, Robert *36:* 155; *69:* 169
McManus, Shawn *85:* 71
McMenemy, Sarah *156:* 139; *211:* 93; *224:* 139
McMillan, Bruce *22:* 184
McMullan, James *40:* 33; *67:* 172; *87:* 142; *99:* 63, 64; *189:* 133; *196:* 51
McMullen, Nigel *146:* 177
McNeely, Tom *162:* 55
McNaught, Harry *12:* 80; *32:* 136
McNaughton, Colin *39:* 149; *40:* 108; *92:* 144, 145, 146; *134:* 104, 106; *211:* 122, 123, 124
McNicholas, Maureen *38:* 148
McNicholas, Shelagh *173:* 61; *191:* 125, 126
McPhail, David *14:* 105; *23:* 135; *37:* 217, 218, 220,221; *47:* 151, 152, 153, 154, 155, 156, 158, 159, 160, 162, 163, 164; *71:* 211; *81:* 139, 140, 142; *86:* 123; *132:* 150; *140:* 129, 131, 132; *183:* 134, 135, 137; *189:* 132; *219:* 121, 122, 123, 124, 125
McPhee, Richard B. *41:* 133
McPheeters, Neal *78:* 132; *86:* 90; *99:* 162; *111:* 141; *142:* 162
McQuade, Jacqueline *124:* 223
McQueen, Lucinda *28:* 149; *41:* 249; *46:* 206; *53:* 103
McQuillan, Mary *153:* 97; *200:* 140
McVay, Tracy *11:* 68
McVicker, Charles *39:* 150
McWilliam, Howard *219:* 135
Mead, Ben Carlton *43:* 75
Meade, Holly *90:* 102; *94:* 101; *149:* 8; *151:* 107
Mecray, John *33:* 62
Meddaugh, Susan *20:* 42; *29:* 143; *41:* 241; *77:* 50; *84:* 173, 174, 175, 176, 177, 178; *125:* 160, 161, 162; *176:* 148, 149, 150, 151
Meehan, Dennis B. *56:* 144
Meents, Len W. *73:* 147, 150
Meers, Tony *99:* 113
Meisel, Paul *98:* 137; *124:* 18; *162:* 180; *179:* 16; *181:* 62; *194:* 154; *221:* 5; *224:* 100, 101, 102, 133
Melanson, Luc *149:* 229; *198:* 97, 98; *221:* 166
Melendez, Francisco *72:* 180
Melling, David *202:* 199
Melnychuk, Monika *153:* 65
Melo, Esperança *196:* 90
Melo, John *16:* 285; *58:* 203
Meloni, Maria Teresa *98:* 62
Meltzer, Ericka
    See O'Rourke, Ericka
Menasco, Milton *43:* 85
Menchin, Scott *188:* 129
Mendelson, Steven T. *86:* 154
Mendelssohn, Felix *19:* 170
Mendola, Christopher *88:* 223
Meng, Heinz *13:* 158
Merian, Maria Sibylla *140:* 88
Mero, Lee *34:* 68
Merrell, David *205:* 3
Merrill, Frank T. *16:* 147; *19:* 71; *YABC 1:* 226, 229,273
Merriman, Rachel *98:* 108; *114:* 122; *149:* 142
Merveille, David *200:* 142
Meryman, Hope *27:* 41
Meryweather, Jack *10:* 179
Meseldzija, Petar *168:* 97
Meserve, Jessica *184:* 137; *211:* 127

Messick, Dale *64:* 150, 151, 152
Meth, Harold *24:* 203
Meyer, Herbert *19:* 189
Meyer, Renate *6:* 170
Meyers, Bob *11:* 136
Meyers, Nancy *172:* 124
Meynell, Louis *37:* 76
Micale, Albert *2:* 65; *22:* 185
Miccuci, Charles *82:* 163; *144:* 150
Micich, Paul *164:* 163
Middleton, Jeffrey *177:* 173; *222:* 157
Middleton, Joshua *208:* 146; *219:* 24
Middleton-Sandford, Betty *2:* 125
Mieke, Anne *45:* 74
Mighell, Patricia *43:* 134
Miglio, Paige *101:* 203; *151:* 223; *201:* 118, 119; *204:* 162
Mikec, Larry *204:* 125
Mikolaycak, Charles *9:* 144; *12:* 101; *13:* 212; *21:* 121; *22:* 168; *30:* 187; *34:* 103, 150; *37:* 183; *43:* 179; *44:* 90; *46:* 115, 118, 119; *49:* 25; *78:* 121, 122, 205, 207; *81:* 4
Milelli, Pascal *129:* 66; *135:* 153; *187:* 45
Miles, Elizabeth *117:* 77
Miles, Jennifer *17:* 278
Milgrim, David *158:* 157; *187:* 125, 126, 128; *223:* 124, 125, 126, 127
Milhous, Katherine *15:* 193; *17:* 51
Millais, John E. *22:* 230, 231
Millar, H.R. *YABC 1:* 194, 195, 203
Millard, C.E. *28:* 186
Millard, Kerry *105:* 124; *204:* 93, 94
Miller, Don *15:* 195; *16:* 71; *20:* 106; *31:* 178
Miller, Edna *29:* 148
Miller, Edward *115:* 64; *183:* 140, 141; *218:* 129, 130, 131
Miller, Frank J. *25:* 94
Miller, Grambs *18:* 38; *23:* 16
Miller, Ian *99:* 128
Miller, Jane *15:* 196
Miller, Marcia *13:* 233
Miller, Marilyn *1:* 87; *31:* 69; *33:* 157
Miller, Mitchell *28:* 183; *34:* 207
Miller, Phil *175:* 150
Miller, Shane *5:* 140
Miller, Virginia *81:* 206
Millman, Isaac *172:* 18
Mills, Elaine *72:* 181
Mills, Judith Christine *130:* 168, 169
Mills, Lauren *92:* 170
Mills, Yaroslava Surmach *35:* 169, 170; *46:* 114
Millsap, Darrel *51:* 102
Milone, Karen *89:* 169; *222:* 149
Milord, Susan *147:* 163, 164; *200:* 144
Milton, Debbie *162:* 161
Mims, Ashley *170:* 51
Min, Willemien *222:* 62
Miner, Julia *98:* 69
Minor, Wendell *39:* 188; *52:* 87; *56:* 171; *58:* 116; *62:* 56; *66:* 109; *74:* 93; *78:* 129; *94:* 67; *117:* 12, 13; *124:* 84, 86; *136:* 121; *164:* 168, 169; *170:* 71; *199:* 79, 80, 81, 82; *217:* 63; *223:* 149
Minter, Daniel *176:* 154; *179:* 177
Mirocha, Paul *81:* 133; *192:* 148; *194:* 36
Misako Rocks! *192:* 149, 150
Mitchell, Judith *109:* 117
Mitchell, Mark *91:* 208
Mitchell, Tracy *190:* 15
Mitgutsch, Ali *76:* 161
Mitsuhashi, Yoko *45:* 153
Miyake, Yoshi *38:* 141
Mizumura, Kazue *10:* 143; *18:* 223; *36:* 159
Mochi, Ugo *8:* 122; *38:* 150
Mock, Paul *55:* 83; *123:* 32
Modarressi, Mitra *90:* 236; *126:* 168; *173:* 165, 166; *200:* 147, 148
Modell, Frank *39:* 152
Mogenson, Jan *74:* 183
Mohn, Susan *89:* 224

Mohr, Mark *133:* 201
Mohr, Nicholasa *8:* 139; *113:* 127
Molan, Christine *60:* 177; *84:* 183
Moldon, Peter L. *49:* 168
Molk, Laurel *92:* 150
Mollica, Gene *197:* 11
Momaday, N. Scott *48:* 159
Mombourquette, Paul *112:* 91; *126:* 142
Monk, Julie *165:* 231; *191:* 96
Monks, Lydia *189:* 136, 137
Monroe, Chris *219:* 133
Monroy, Manuel *199:* 192
Montgomery, Lucy *150:* 126
Montgomery, Michael G. *208:* 159
Montgomery-Higham, Amanda *169:* 131
Monteiel, David *201:* 95
Montiel, David *69:* 106; *84:* 145
Montijo, Rhode *193:* 164
Montresor, Beni *2:* 91; *3:* 138; *38:* 152, 153, 154,155, 156, 157, 158, 159, 160; *68:* 63
Montserrat, Pep *128:* 135; *181:* 119; *184:* 53
Moon, Carl *25:* 183, 184, 185
Moon, Eliza *14:* 40
Moon, Ivan *22:* 39; *38:* 140
Moore, Adrienne *67:* 147
Moore, Agnes Kay Randall *43:* 187
Moore, Cyd *117:* 107, 108; *159:* 137, 138; *186:* 148, 149, 151; *203:* 15; *214:* 138, 139
Moore, Gustav *127:* 181, 182; *170:* 162, 163
Moore, Jackie *128:* 79
Moore, Janet *63:* 153
Moore, Margie *176:* 156; *221:* 125; *224:* 106, 107
Moore, Mary *29:* 160
Moore, Patrick *184:* 121
Moore, Yvette *101:* 11, 12; *154:* 141
Mora, Giovanni *179:* 127; *184:* 11
Mora, Raul Mina *20:* 41
Moraes, Odilon *102:* 144
Morales, Magaly *225:* 137
Morales, Yuyi *154:* 144
Moran, Rosslyn *111:* 26
Moran, Tom *60:* 100
Mordan, C.B. *193:* 115
Mordvinoff, Nicolas *15:* 179
Moreno, René King *169:* 59; *190:* 133, 209; *212:* 52
Morgan, Barbara *169:* 116
Morgan, Jacqui *58:* 57
Morgan, Mary *114:* 133, 134, 135; *123:* 11; *213:* 115, 116, 117
Morgan, Tom *42:* 157
Morgan, Pierr *173:* 148
Morgenstern, Michael *158:* 7, 57; *171:* 103; *174:* 60
Morice, Dave *93:* 142
Morin, Paul *73:* 132; *79:* 130; *88:* 140; *137:* 143
Moriuchi, Mique *177:* 203
Morozumi, Atsuko *110:* 155; *217:* 126, 127
Morrill, Leslie *18:* 218; *29:* 177; *33:* 84; *38:* 147; *42:* 127; *44:* 93; *48:* 164, 165, 167, 168, 169, 170,171; *49:* 162; *63:* 136, 180; *70:* 72; *71:* 70, 91,92; *72:* 228; *80:* 163, 164, 165; *90:* 121; *121:* 88; *178:* 117
Morrill, Rowena A. *84:* 16; *98:* 163
Morris, *47:* 91
Morris, Frank *55:* 133; *60:* 28; *76:* 2
Morris, Harry O. *119:* 138
Morris, Jackie *128:* 194; *144:* 119; *151:* 146; *202:* 126, 127; *204:* 83; *211:* 80; *214:* 163
Morris, Jennifer E. *179:* 157
Morris, Oradel Nolen *128:* 180
Morris, Tony *62:* 146; *70:* 97
Morrison, Bill *42:* 116; *66:* 170; *69:* 40
Morrison, Gordon *87:* 150; *113:* 93; *128:* 181, 182; *183:* 144, 145, 146
Morrison, Frank *169:* 162; *205:* 156; *224:* 121
Morrison, Taylor *159:* 144, 145; *187:* 131
Morrow, Gray *2:* 64; *5:* 200; *10:* 103, 114; *14:* 175

Morse, Scott *200:* 149, 150
Morton, Lee Jack *32:* 140
Morton, Marian *3:* 185
Mosberg, Hilary *117:* 195; *118:* 164; *149:* 55
Moser, Barry *56:* 68, 117, 118, 119, 120, 121, 122, 123, 124; *59:* 141; *60:* 160; *79:* 91, 147, 149, 151, 152; *82:* 81; *90:* 118; *91:* 35; *95:* 210; *97:* 91, 93; *102:* 152; *126:* 4; *128:* 175; *133:* 141; *138:* 167, 171, 174; *153:* 205; *174:* 130; *185:* 152, 154; *195:* 163; *204:* 115; *209:* 201
Moser, Cara *90:* 118; *138:* 167
Moses, Grandma *18:* 228
Moses, Will *178:* 170, 171
Moskof, Martin Stephen *27:* 152
Mosley, Francis *57:* 144
Moss, Donald *11:* 184
Moss, Geoffrey *32:* 198
Moss, Marissa *71:* 130; *104:* 127; *163:* 156; *216:* 164, 165, 166
Most, Bernard *48:* 173; *91:* 142, 143; *134:* 120
Mourning, Tuesday *205:* 25; *220:* 68; *221:* 42
Mowll, Joshua *188:* 133
Mowry, Carmen *50:* 62
Moxley, Sheila *96:* 174; *169:* 26; *206:* 16
Moyers, William *21:* 65
Moyler, Alan *36:* 142
Mozley, Charles *9:* 87; *20:* 176, 192, 193; *22:* 228; *25:* 205; *33:* 150; *43:* 170, 171, 172, 173, 174; *YABC2:* 89
Mueller, Hans Alexander *26:* 64; *27:* 52, 53
Mugnaini, Joseph *11:* 35; *27:* 52, 53; *35:* 62
Mujica, Rick *72:* 67; *88:* 95; *111:* 53; *180:* 185; *197:* 70
Mullen, Douglas *180:* 178
Muller, Robin *86:* 161
Muller, Steven *32:* 167
Muller, Jorg *35:* 215; *67:* 138, 139
Mulock, Julie *163:* 112
Mullins, Edward S. *10:* 101
Mullins, Patricia *51:* 68
Multer, Scott *80:* 108
Munari, Bruno *15:* 200
Munch, Edvard *140:* 143
Munowitz, Ken *14:* 148; *72:* 178, 179
Muñoz, Claudio *208:* 161
Munoz, William *42:* 160
Munro, Roxie *58:* 134; *136:* 177; *137:* 218; *184:* 133, 134; *223:* 130, 132, 133
Munsinger, Lynn *33:* 161; *46:* 126; *71:* 92; *82:* 80; *89:* 218; *92:* 125; *94:* 157, 158, 159, 160; *98:* 196; *103:* 198; *142:* 143; *145:* 133, 134, 136; *153:* 203; *176:* 162; *177:* 140, 141, 142; *189:* 113, 114, 116, 117; *201:* 42; *221:* 148, 149,150
Munson, Russell *13:* 9
Munster, Sebastian *166:* 107
Munzar, Barbara *149:* 75
Murdocca, Salvatore *73:* 212; *98:* 132; *111:* 168; *157:* 228; *164:* 257
Murphy, Bill *5:* 138; *130:* 170
Murphy, Jill *37:* 142; *70:* 166; *142:* 132, 134
Murphy, Kelly *130:* 212; *143:* 119; *176:* 158; *190:* 135
Murphy, Liz *210:* 183; *212:* 157
Murphy, Mary *196:* 158
Murphy, Tom *192:* 40
Murr, Karl *20:* 62
Murray, Joe *175:* 37
Murray, Ossie *43:* 176
Mussino, Attilio *29:* 131; *100:* 164
Mutchler, Dwight *1:* 25
Myers, Bernice *9:* 147; *36:* 75; *81:* 146, 147, 148
Muth, Jon J. *165:* 169; *167:* 109; *190:* 227; *193:* 59
Myers, Christopher *183:* 150; *193:* 139
Myers, Duane O. *99:* 145
Myers, Tim *147:* 168
Myers, V.G. *142:* 41
Myers, Lou *11:* 2

N

Nachreiner, Tom *29:* 182
Nacht, Merle *65:* 49
Nadler, Ellis *88:* 91
Nagle, Shane *180:* 223
Nagy, Ian *195:* 64
Najaka, Marlies *62:* 101
Nakai, Michael *30:* 217; *54:* 29
Nakata, Hiroe *157:* 156; *162:* 30; *205:* 124, 125
Nakatani, Chiyoko *12:* 124
Narahashi, Keiko *77:* 188; *82:* 213; *115:* 142, 143, 144
Nascimbene, Yan *133:* 128; *173:* 132, 133
Nash, Lesa *87:* 135
Nash, Linell *46:* 175
Nash, Scott *130:* 36; *188:* 196; *224:* 180
Naso, John *33:* 183
Nason, Thomas W. *14:* 68
Nasser, Muriel *48:* 74
Nast, Thomas *21:* 29; *28:* 23; *51:* 132, 133, 134, 135,136, 137, 138, 139, 141
Nasta, Vincent *78:* 185
Natale, Vincent *76:* 3; *78:* 125; *112:* 47; *166:* 81; *174:* 189; *185:* 212; *197:* 59; *218:* 35
Natchev, Alexi *96:* 177
Nathan, Charlott *125:* 151
Nathan, Cheryl *150:* 104; *186:* 112
Natti, Susanna *20:* 146; *32:* 141, 142; *35:* 178; *37:* 143; *71:* 49; *93:* 98; *125:* 166, 168; *126:* 228; *151:* 6; *178:* 8; *188:* 106
Navarra, Celeste Scala *8:* 142
Naylor, Penelope *10:* 104
Nazz, James *72:* 8
Nebel, M. *45:* 154
Neebe, William *7:* 93
Needham, Dave *196:* 85
Needler, Jerry *12:* 93
Neel, Alice *31:* 23
Neely, Beth *119:* 184
Neely, Keith R. *46:* 124
Neff, Leland *78:* 74
Negri, Rocco *3:* 213; *5:* 67; *6:* 91, 108; *12:* 159
Negrin, Fabian *174:* 125; *175:* 15; *223:* 91
Neidigh, Sherry *128:* 53; *204:* 101, 102, 103; *222:* 95
Neilan, Eujin Kim *180:* 241; *200:* 151, 152
Neill, John R. *18:* 8, 10, 11, 21, 30; *100:* 22
Neilsen, Cliff *158:* 131; *177:* 112, 121; *209:* 8; *215:* 150
Neilsen, Terese *116:* 74
Nelson, Craig *62:* 151; 153; *183:* 86
Nelson, Gail White *68:* 140
Nelson, Jennifer *129:* 152; *199:* 132
Nelson, Kadir *151:* 185; *154:* 146, 147; *157:* 189, 222; *181:* 122, 124; *197:* 155; *213:* 122, 123, 124
Nelson, Melissa *224:* 87
Nelson, S.D. *131:* 34; *181:* 126, 127
Ness, Evaline *1:* 164, 165; *2:* 39; *3:* 8; *10:* 147; *12:* 53; *26:* 150, 151, 152, 153; *49:* 30, 31, 32; *56:* 30; *60:* 113
Neubecker, Robert *170:* 143; *214:* 157
Neville, Vera *2:* 182
Nevins, Daniel *191:* 173
Nevwirth, Allan *79:* 168
Newberry, Clare Turlay *1:* 170
Newbold, Greg *108:* 125; *145:* 199; *151:* 23; *193:* 178; *197:* 10; *199:* 92, 93
Newfeld, Frank *14:* 121; *26:* 154
Newland, Gillian *220:* 132
Newman, Andy *149:* 61; *195:* 63
Newman, Ann *43:* 90
Newman, Barbara Johansen *191:* 137, 138
Newsham, Ian *143:* 162
Newsom, Carol *40:* 159; *44:* 60; *47:* 189; *65:* 29; *70:* 192; *80:* 36; *85:* 137, 138; *92:* 167; *191:* 82

Newsom, Tom *49:* 149; *71:* 13, 62; *75:* 156; *91:* 113
Newton, Jill *83:* 105; *200:* 154
Nez, John *218:* 136
Ng, Michael *29:* 171
Ng, Simon *167:* 7
Nguyen, Vincent *189:* 49
Nichols, Sandy *219:* 103
Nicholson, William *15:* 33, 34; *16:* 48
Nickens, Bessie *104:* 153
Nicklaus, Carol *45:* 194; *62:* 132, 133
Nickle, John *181:* 128
Nickless, Will *16:* 139
Nicholas, Corasue *154:* 20
Nicolas *17:* 130, 132, 133; *YABC 2:* 215
Niebrugge, Jane *6:* 118
Nielsen, Cliff *95:* 207, 208; *105:* 58; *114:* 112; *124:* 12; *125:* 91, 92; *132:* 224; *135:* 187; *136:* 40; *137:* 168; *145:* 54; *149:* 28; *158:* 129; *165:* 64, 158; *168:* 169; *170:* 6; *175:* 114, 116; *187:* 75, 76; *194:* 107; *197:* 172; *201:* 14; *208:* 192; *211:* 186; *216:* 215; *217:* 67; *224:* 61, 62
Nielsen, Jon *6:* 100; *24:* 202
Nielsen, Kay *15:* 7; *16:* 211, 212, 213, 215, 217; *22:* 143; *YABC 1:* 32, 33
Niemann, Christoph *191:* 141
Nikola-Lisa, W. *180:* 180
Niland, Deborah *25:* 191; *27:* 156; *135:* 50; *172:* 143
Niland, Kilmeny *25:* 191; *75:* 143
Nino, Alex *59:* 145
Ninon *1:* 5; *38:* 101, 103, 108
Nissen, Rie *44:* 35
Nithael, Mark *158:* 237
Nivola, Claire A. *78:* 126; *140:* 147; *208:* 164
Nixon, K. *14:* 152
Nobati, Eugenia *194:* 118
Noble, Louise *61:* 170
Noble, Marty *97:* 168; *125:* 171
Noble, Trinka Hakes *39:* 162; *84:* 157
Noda, Takayo *168:* 143
Noguchi, Yoshie *30:* 99
Nolan, Dennis *42:* 163; *67:* 163; *78:* 189; *82:* 225; *83:* 26; *92:* 169, 170; *103:* 166; *111:* 35; *112:* 213; *127:* 171; *166:* 161; *194:* 218
Noll, Sally *82:* 171
Nolte, Larry *121:* 63, 65
Nones, Eric Jon *61:* 111; *76:* 38; *77:* 177
Noonan, Daniel *100:* 224
Noonan, Julia *4:* 163; *7:* 207; *25:* 151; *91:* 29; *95:* 149
Norcia, Ernie *108:* 155; *140:* 47
Nordenskjold, Birgitta *2:* 208
Noreika, Robert *173:* 20; *217:* 24
Norling, Beth *149:* 153, 154; *209:* 77
Norman, Elaine *77:* 72, 176; *94:* 35; *136:* 63; *178:* 42
Norman, Mary *36:* 138, 147
Norman, Michael *12:* 117; *27:* 168
Northway, Jennifer *85:* 96
Nostlinger, Christiana *162:* 131
Novak, Linda *166:* 205
Novak, Matt *104:* 132, 133; *165:* 173, 174; *204:* 104, 106
Novelli, Luca *61:* 137
Novgorodoff, Danica *215:* 133
Nugent, Cynthia *106:* 189; *205:* 126, 127; *209:* 180
Numberman, Neil *220:* 133
Numeroff, Laura Joffe *28:* 161; *30:* 177
Nurse, Chris *164:* 91
Nussbaumer, Paul *16:* 219; *39:* 117
Nutt, Ken *72:* 69; *97:* 170
Nyce, Helene *19:* 219
Nygren, Tord *30:* 148; *127:* 164

O

Oakley, Graham *8:* 112; *30:* 164, 165; *84:* 188,189, 190, 191, 192
Oakley, Thornton *YABC 2:* 189
Oberheide, Heide *118:* 37
Obligado, Lilian *2:* 28, 66, 67; *6:* 30; *14:* 179; *15:* 103; *25:* 84; *61:* 138, 139, 140, 141, 143
Oblinski, Rafael *190:* 139
Obrant, Susan *11:* 186
O'Brien, Anne Sibley *53:* 116, 117; *155:* 115; *213:* 127; *224:* 71
O'Brien, John *41:* 253; *72:* 12; *89:* 59, 60; *98:* 16; *161:* 185; *169:* 16; *180:* 196
O'Brien, Patrick *193:* 142, 143, 144
O'Brien, Teresa *87:* 89
O'Brien, Tim *93:* 25; *136:* 94; *164:* 57; *169:* 57; *173:* 55; *175:* 86; *184:* 192; *191:* 134; *193:* 137; *210:* 159; *224:* 28, 29
O'Clair, Dennis *127:* 25
O'Connor, George *183:* 153
Odell, Carole *35:* 47
Odem, Mel *99:* 164; *167:* 84, 87
O'Donohue, Thomas *40:* 89
Oechsli, Kelly *5:* 144, 145; *7:* 115; *8:* 83, 183; *13:* 117; *20:* 94; *81:* 199
Ofer, Avi *208:* 143
Offen, Hilda *42:* 207
Ogden, Bill *42:* 59; *47:* 55
Ogg, Oscar *33:* 34
Ogle, Nancy Gray *163:* 144
Ohi, Ruth *90:* 175, 177; *131:* 63; *135:* 106; *175:* 107; *179:* 55
Ohlsson, Ib *4:* 152; *7:* 57; *10:* 20; *11:* 90; *19:* 217; *41:* 246; *82:* 106; *92:* 213
Ohtomo, Yasuo *37:* 146; *39:* 212, 213
O'Keefe, Jennifer *136:* 184
O'Kelley, Mattie Lou *36:* 150
Olbinski, Rafal *149:* 27; *158:* 77; *203:* 36
Oldland, Nicholas *223:* 136
O'Leary, Chris *208:* 166
Oleynikov, Igor *202:* 134
Oliver, Isaac *171:* 182
Oliver, Jenni *23:* 121; *35:* 112
Oliver, Narelle *152:* 192; *197:* 129, 130
Oller, Erika *128:* 186; *134:* 126
Olschewski, Alfred *7:* 172
Olsen, Ib Spang *6:* 178, 179; *81:* 164
Olson, Alan *77:* 229
Olson-Brown, Ellen *183:* 154
Olugebefola, Ademola *15:* 205
O'Malley, Kevin *94:* 180; *106:* 8; *113:* 108; *136:* 70; *157:* 193; *191:* 146; *203:* 78; *217:* 84
O'Neil, Dan IV *7:* 176
O'Neill, Catharine *72:* 113; *84:* 78; *134:* 153
O'Neill, Jean *22:* 146
O'Neill, Martin *187:* 39; *203:* 118
O'Neill, Michael J. *54:* 172
O'Neill, Rose *48:* 30, 31
O'Neill, Steve *21:* 118
Ono, Chiyo *7:* 97
Orbaan, Albert *2:* 31; *5:* 65, 171; *9:* 8; *14:* 241; *20:* 109
Orbach, Ruth *21:* 112
Orback, Craig *197:* 132
Orfe, Joan *20:* 81
Org, Ed *119:* 93
Ormai, Stella *72:* 129
Ormerod, Jan *55:* 124; *70:* 170, 171; *90:* 39; *132:* 172, 173, 174; *147:* 98
Ormsby, Virginia H. *11:* 187
O'Rourke, Ericka *108:* 216; *117:* 194; *111:* 142; *119:* 194; *137:* 152; *150:* 134; *167:* 64; *172:* 164; *188:* 163; *191:* 172; *201:* 15; *203:* 75; *209:* 130; *219:* 99
O'Rourke, Ericka Meltzer
   See O'Rourke, Ericka
Orozco, Jose Clemente *9:* 177
Orr, Forrest W. *23:* 9

Orr, N. *19:* 70
Ortiz, Vilma *88:* 158
Osborn, Kathy *152:* 232; *199:* 101, 102; *206:* 67
Osborn, Robert *65:* 49
Osborne, Billie Jean *35:* 209
Osmond, Edward *10:* 111
Ostow, David *223:* 138
O'Sullivan, Tom *3:* 176; *4:* 55; *78:* 195
Otani, June *124:* 42; *156:* 53
Otis, Rebecca *185:* 92
Ottley, Matt *147:* 221; *171:* 133
Otto, Svend *22:* 130, 141; *67:* 188, 189
Oudry, J.B. *18:* 167
Oughton, Taylor *5:* 23; *104:* 136
Overeng, Johannes *44:* 36
Overlie, George *11:* 156
Owens, Carl *2:* 35; *23:* 521
Owens, Gail *10:* 170; *12:* 157; *19:* 16; *22:* 70; *25:* 81; *28:* 203, 205; *32:* 221, 222; *36:* 132; *46:* 40; *47:* 57; *54:* 66, 67, 68, 69, 70, 71, 72, 73; *71:* 100; *73:* 64; *77:* 157; *80:* 32; *82:* 3; *99:* 226; *224:* 198
Owens, Mary Beth *113:* 202, 203; *191:* 148, 149
Owens, Nubia *84:* 74
Oxenbury, Helen *3:* 150, 151; *24:* 81; *68:* 174, 175,176; *81:* 209; *84:* 213, 245; *129:* 56; *149:* 159; *184:* 181; *224:* 147
Oz, Robin *88:* 167; *185:* 181

P

Padgett, Jim *12:* 165
Page, Gail *205:* 128
Page, Homer *14:* 145
Page, Mark *162:* 70
Paget, Sidney *24:* 90, 91, 93, 95, 97
Paget, Walter *64:* 122
Paillot, Jim *173:* 89
Pajouhesh, Noushin *160:* 121
Pak *12:* 76
Pak, Yu Cha *86:* 174
Paladino, Lance *134:* 30
Palazzo, Tony *3:* 152, 153
Palecek, Josef *56:* 136; *89:* 158
Palen, Debbie *135:* 88; *195:* 148, 149
Palencar, John Jude *84:* 12, 45; *85:* 87; *92:* 187; *99:* 128; *110:* 204; *150:* 122; *171:* 86; *207:* 36
Palin, Nicki *81:* 201; *89:* 161
Palladini, David *4:* 113; *40:* 176, 177, 178, 179, 181,224, 225; *50:* 138; *78:* 186
Pallarito, Don *43:* 36
Palmer, Carol *158:* 230; *195:* 187
Palmer, Heidi *15:* 207; *29:* 102
Palmer, Jan *42:* 153; *82:* 161
Palmer, Judd *153:* 160, 161
Palmer, Juliette *6:* 89; *15:* 208
Palmer, Kate Salley *104:* 143; *154:* 169
Palmer, Lemuel *17:* 25, 29
Palmisciano, Diane *110:* 62; *162:* 26; *202:* 138, 139
Palmquist, Eric *38:* 133
Pamintuan, Macky *214:* 160
Panesis, Nicholas *3:* 127
Panter, Gary *182:* 191
Panton, Doug *52:* 99
Paparone, Pamela *129:* 174
Papas, William *11:* 223; *50:* 160
Papin, Joseph *26:* 113
Papish, Robin Lloyd *10:* 80
Papp, Robert *198:* 41; *205:* 130; *219:* 53
Paradis, Susan *40:* 216
Paraquin, Charles H. *18:* 166
Pardo DeLange, Alex *179:* 128; *211:* 135, 136
Paris, Peter *31:* 127
Parisi, Elizabeth B. *141:* 82; *164:* 57
Park, Nick *113:* 143

Park, Seho *39:* 110
Park, W.B. *22:* 189
Parker, Ant *82:* 87, 88; *104:* 121
Parker, Lewis *2:* 179
Parker, Nancy Winslow *10:* 113; *22:* 164; *28:* 47, 144; *52:* 7; *69:* 153; *91:* 171, 174; *132:* 175
Parker, Robert *4:* 161; *5:* 74; *9:* 136; *29:* 39
Parker, Robert Andrew *11:* 81; *29:* 186; *39:* 165; *40:* 25; *41:* 78; *42:* 123; *43:* 144; *48:* 182; *54:* 140; *74:* 141; *91:* 24; *111:* 115; *151:* 201; *154:* 156; *200:* 163, 164; *211:* 67
Parker-Rees, Guy *149:* 145; *193:* 149, 150
Parkin, Trevor *140:* 151
Parkins, David *114:* 123; *146:* 176; *176:* 168; *192:* 107; *218:* 139, 140, 141, 148; *224:* 92
Parkinson, Kathy *71:* 143; *144:* 234
Parkinson, Keith *70:* 66
Parks, Gordon, Jr. *33:* 228
Parlato, Stephen *222:* 137
Parnall, Peter *5:* 137; *16:* 221; *24:* 70; *40:* 78; *51:* 130; *69:* 17, 155; *136:* 22, 23, 24
Parnall, Virginia *40:* 78
Paros, Jennifer *210:* 197
Parow, Lorraine *158:* 127
Parr, Todd *134:* 139, 140; *179:* 163, 164, 165
Parra, John *225:* 150
Parrish, Anne *27:* 159, 160
Parrish, Dillwyn *27:* 159
Parrish, Maxfield *14:* 160, 161, 164, 165; *16:* 109; *18:* 12, 13; *YABC 1:* 149, 152, 267; *2:* 146, 149
Parry, David *26:* 156
Parry, Marian *13:* 176; *19:* 179
Parsons, Garry *197:* 135
Partch, Virgil *45:* 163, 165
Pascal, David *14:* 174
Paschkis, Julie *177:* 153, 154; *220:* 140, 141
Pasquier, J.A. *16:* 91
Pastel, Elyse *201:* 123
Pasternak, Robert *119:* 53
Paterson, Diane *13:* 116; *39:* 163; *59:* 164, 165, 166,167; *72:* 51, 53; *129:* 175; *177:* 156, 157
Paterson, Helen *16:* 93
Patkau, Karen *112:* 123
Paton, Jane *15:* 271; *35:* 176
Patricelli, Leslie *207:* 129
Patrick, John *139:* 190
Patrick, Pamela *90:* 160; *93:* 211; *105:* 12
Patrick, Tom *190:* 103
Patterson, Geoffrey *54:* 75
Patterson, Robert *25:* 118
Patti, Joyce *187:* 145, 146
Patz, Nancy *111:* 40; *154:* 161; *214:* 80
Paul, James *4:* 130; *23:* 161
Paul, Korky *102:* 85
Paull, Grace *24:* 157; *87:* 127
Paulsen, Ruth Wright *79:* 160, 164; *189:* 146
Pavlov, Elena *80:* 49
Payne, Adam S. *135:* 166
Payne, C.F. *145:* 138, 140; *179:* 168
Payne, Joan Balfour *1:* 118
Payne, Tom *170:* 27
Payson, Dale *7:* 34; *9:* 151; *20:* 140; *37:* 22
Payzant, Charles *21:* 147
Peacock, Ralph *64:* 118
Peake, Mervyn *22:* 136, 149; *23:* 162, 163, 164; *YABC2:* 307
Pearson, Larry *38:* 225
Pearson, Tracey Campbell *64:* 163, 164, 167, 168, 169; *118:* 51; *156:* 169, 171, 172; *163:* 140; *219:* 140, 141, 142, 143
Peat, Fern B. *16:* 115
Peck, Anne Merriman *18:* 241; *24:* 155
Peck, Beth *66:* 242; *79:* 166; *80:* 136; *91:* 34; *95:* 9; *101:* 77; *164:* 197; *190:* 170
Peddicord, Jane Ann *199:* 106
Pedersen, Janet *193:* 152; *217:* 57; *218:* 15
Pedersen, Judy *66:* 217; *121:* 36; *172:* 67
Pedersen, Vilhelm *YABC 1:* 40

Pederson, Sharleen *12:* 92
Pedlar, Elaine *161:* 45
Peek, Merle *39:* 168
Peet, Bill *2:* 203; *41:* 159, 160, 161, 162, 163; *78:* 158, 159, 160, 161
Peguero, Adrian *116:* 133
Peguero, Gerard *116:* 133
Pels, Winslow Pinney *55:* 126
Peltier, Leslie C. *13:* 178
Peltzer, Marc *202:* 92
Penberthy, Mark *171:* 78
Pendle, Alexy *7:* 159; *13:* 34; *29:* 161; *33:* 215; *86:* 62
Pendola, Joanne *76:* 203; *81:* 125; *105:* 181; *178:* 152, 153
Pene du Bois, William *4:* 70; *10:* 122; *26:* 61; *27:* 145, 211; *35:* 243; *41:* 216; *68:* 180, 181; *73:* 45
Penfound, David *102:* 185
Pennington, Eunice *27:* 162
Peppe, Mark *28:* 142
Peppe, Rodney *4:* 164, 165; *74:* 187, 188, 189
Pepper, Hubert *64:* 143
Percy, Graham *63:* 2
Pericoli, Matteo *178:* 177
Perini, Ben *173:* 77
Perkins, David *60:* 68
Perkins, Lucy Fitch *72:* 199
Perkins, Lynne Rae *172:* 146; *212:* 153
Perl, Susan *2:* 98; *4:* 231; *5:* 44, 45, 118; *6:* 199; *8:* 137; *12:* 88; *22:* 193; *34:* 54, 55; *52:* 128; *YABC 1:* 176
Perlman, Janet *222:* 141
Perrone, Donna *78:* 166
Perry, Marie Fritz *165:* 180
Perry, Patricia *29:* 137; *30:* 171
Perry, Roger *27:* 163
Perske, Martha *46:* 83; *51:* 108, 147
Persson, Stina *175:* 166
Pesek, Ludek *15:* 237
Petach, Heidi *149:* 166; *200:* 207
Peters, David *72:* 205; *182:* 116
Petersen, Jeff *181:* 95
Petersham, Maud *17:* 108, 147, 148, 149, 150, 151, 152, 153
Petersham, Miska *17:* 108, 147, 148, 149, 150, 151, 152, 153
Peterson, Eric *109:* 125
Peterson, Nisse *99:* 27
Peterson, R.F. *7:* 101
Peterson, Russell *7:* 130
Petie, Haris *2:* 3; *10:* 41, 118; *11:* 227; *12:* 70
Petricic, Dusan *153:* 75, 76, 77; *170:* 12; *172:* 13; *176:* 170; *179:* 56
Petrides, Heidrun *19:* 223
Petrone, Valeria *159:* 160; *171:* 92; *186:* 173; *204:* 49; *216:* 208; *220:* 98
Petrosino, Tamara *177:* 40; *193:* 154, 155
Petruccio, Steven James *67:* 159; *127:* 5
Pettingill, Ondre *64:* 181; *70:* 64; *222:* 167, 168
Peyo *40:* 56, 57
Peyton, K.M. *15:* 212
Pfeifer, Herman *15:* 262
Pfister, Marcus *83:* 165, 166, 167; *146:* 152; *150:* 160; *207:* 132, 134, 135, 136
Pfloog, Jan *124:* 60
Pham, LeUyen *160:* 48; *175:* 154, 156; *179:* 149; *201:* 124, 125, 126, 127; *204:* 28; *208:* 206; *217:* 92
Phelan, Matt *182:* 160; *184:* 222; *215:* 140, 141; *221:* 157
Phillipps, J.C. *218:* 142
Phillips, Craig *70:* 151; *207:* 74; *221:* 159
Phillips, Douglas *1:* 19
Phillips, F.D. *6:* 202
Phillips, Gary R. *223:* 23
Phillips, Louise *133:* 67
Phillips, Matt *184:* 173
Phillips, Thomas *30:* 55
Philpot, Glyn *54:* 46

Phiz
    See Browne, Hablot K.
Piatti, Celestino *16:* 223
Pica, Steve *115:* 181
Picarella, Joseph *13:* 147
Picart, Gabriel *121:* 165; *201:* 169
Pichon, Liz *174:* 139
Pickard, Charles *12:* 38; *18:* 203; *36:* 152
Picken, George A. *23:* 150
Pickens, David *22:* 156
Pickering, Jimmy *195:* 152; *197:* 163
Pien, Lark *222:* 143, 144
Pienkowski, Jan *6:* 183; *30:* 32; *58:* 140, 141, 142,143, 146, 147; *73:* 3; *87:* 156, 157; *131:* 189
Pieper, Christiane *200:* 168
Pignataro, Anna *163:* 220; *223:* 143 Pile, Emma *218:* 156 Pileggi, Steve *145:* 122
Pilkey, Dav *68:* 186; *115:* 164, 166; *166:* 173, 174, 175
Pimlott, John *10:* 205
Pincus, Harriet *4:* 186; *8:* 179; *22:* 148; *27:* 164, 165; *66:* 202
Pini, Wendy *89:* 166
Pinkett, Neil *60:* 8
Pinkney, Brian *81:* 184, 185; *94:* 107; *113:* 146, 147; *117:* 121, 166; *132:* 145; *158:* 108, 191; *160:* 189; *200:* 8
Pinkney, Jerry *8:* 218; *10:* 40; *15:* 276; *20:* 66; *24:* 121; *33:* 109; *36:* 222; *38:* 200; *41:* 165, 166, 167, 168, 169, 170, 171, 173, 174; *44:* 198; *48:* 51; *53:* 20; *56:* 61, 68; *58:* 184; *60:* 59; *61:* 91; *71:* 146, 148, 149; *72:* 17; *73:* 149; *74:* 159,192; *75:* 45; *80:* 206; *81:* 44; *85:* 144; *95:* 50; *107:* 158, 159, 160; *108:* 164; *112:* 114, 115; *133:* 58; *195:* 140
Pinkwater, Daniel Manus *8:* 156; *46:* 180, 181, 182, 185, 188, 189, 190; *151:* 161 *76:* 178, 179, 180; *210:* 203
Pinkwater, Manus
    See Pinkwater, Daniel Manus
Pinkwater, Jill *114:* 160, 161; *158:* 179; *188:* 143, 145, 146
Pinto, Ralph *10:* 131; *45:* 93
Pinto, Sara *200:* 165
Pinon, Mark *74:* 22
Piven, Hanoch *173:* 142
Pistolesi *73:* 211
Pitcairn, Ansel *188:* 10
Pittman, Helena Clare *71:* 151
Pitz, Henry C. *4:* 168; *19:* 165; *35:* 128; *42:* 80; *YABC 2:* 95, 176
Pitzenberger, Lawrence J. *26:* 94
Pitzer, Susanna *181:* 131
Place, François *218:* 42
Plant, Andrew *214:* 166
Player, Stephen *82:* 190
Plecas, Jennifer *84:* 201; *106:* 124; *149:* 168; *205:* 180; *220:* 81
Ploog, Mike *180:* 19
Plowden, David *52:* 135, 136
Plume, Ilse *170:* 149
Plummer, William *32:* 31
Podevin, Jean François *184:* 185
Podwal, Mark *56:* 170, 173; *101:* 154, 155, 157; *149:* 176; *160:* 194; *224:* 127, 128, 129
Pogany, Willy *15:* 46, 49; *19:* 222, 256; *25:* 214; *44:* 142, 143, 144, 145, 146, 147, 148
Pohrt, Tom *67:* 116; *104:* 80; *152:* 199; *195:* 154; *199:* 85
Poirson, V.A. *26:* 89
Polacco, Patricia *74:* 195, 196, 197, 198; *123:* 121, 122, 123; *180:* 189, 190, 191, 193, 194; *212:* 168, 170, 171
Polgreen, John *21:* 44
Polhemus, Coleman *210:* 209
Politi, Leo *1:* 178; *4:* 53; *21:* 48; *47:* 173,174, 176, 178, 179, 180, 181
Pollack, Barbara *219:* 60
Pollema-Cahill, Phyllis *123:* 126
Pollen, Samson *64:* 80

Polonsky, Arthur *34:* 168
Polseno, Jo *1:* 53; *3:* 117; *5:* 114; *17:* 154; *20:* 87; *32:* 49; *41:* 245
Pomaska, Anna *117:* 148
Pons, Bernadette *184:* 100
Ponter, James *5:* 204
Poole, Colin *111:* 27
Poortvliet, Rien *6:* 212; *65:* 165, 166, 167
Pope, Kevin *183:* 158
Popp, Wendy *72:* 122; *158:* 68
Poppel, Hans *71:* 154, 155
Porfirio, Guy *76:* 134
Portal, Colette *6:* 186; *11:* 203
Porter, George *7:* 181
Porter, Janice Lee *136:* 175; *164:* 37
Porter, John *113:* 47
Porter, Pat Grant *84:* 112; *125:* 101
Porter, Sue *146:* 246, 247; *213:* 139, 140, 141; *221:* 91
Porter, Walter *124:* 175
Porto, James *221:* 14
Posada, Mia *187:* 151
Posen, Michael *175:* 82
Posthuma, Sieb *150:* 163
Postier, Jim *202:* 140; *204:* 25
Postma, Lidia *79:* 17
Potter, Beatrix *100:* 194, 195; *132:* 179, 180, 181, 182; *YABC 1:* 208, 209, 210, 212, 213
Potter, Giselle *117:* 123; *143:* 44; *144:* 170, 197; *149:* 7; *150:* 165; *187:* 152, 153; *190:* 198; *196:* 152; *200:* 12; *225:* 60
Potter, Katherine *104:* 147; *171:* 135; *173:* 136; *217:* 130, 131
Potter, Miriam Clark *3:* 162
Poulin, Stephane *98:* 140, 141
Poullis, Nick *146:* 210
Powell, Constance Buffington *174:* 141
Powell, Gary *151:* 208
Powell, Ivan *67:* 219
Power, Margaret *105:* 122
Powers, Daniel *161:* 173
Powers, Richard M. *1:* 230; *3:* 218; *7:* 194; *26:* 186
Powledge, Fred *37:* 154
Powzyk, Joyce *74:* 214
Poydar, Nancy *96:* 149; *190:* 180, 181, 182
Pracher, Richard *91:* 166
Prachaticka, Marketa *126:* 126
Prange, Beckie *181:* 169
Prap, Lila *177:* 165
Prater, John *103:* 142, 143, 144; *149:* 172
Pratt, Charles *23:* 29
Pratt, Christine Joy *214:* 167
Pratt, George *116:* 208; *212:* 37
Pratt, Pierre *150:* 73; *166:* 183; *168:* 172; *201:* 27; *208:* 171, 172, 173
Prebenna, David *73:* 174
Preiss-Glasser, Robin *123:* 176; *152* 40; *172:* 194
Press, Jenny *116:* 95
Preston, Mark *152:* 162
Pretro, Korinna *91:* 126
Prevost, Mikela *209:* 111
Price, Christine *2:* 247; *3:* 163, 253; *8:* 166
Price, Cynthia *118:* 156
Price, Edward *33:* 34
Price, Garrett *1:* 76; *2:* 42
Price, Hattie Longstreet *17:* 13
Price, Nick *216:* 173; *220:* 7
Price, Norman *YABC 1:* 129
Price, Willard *48:* 184
Priceman, Marjorie *81:* 171; *136:* 169; *156:* 200; *168:* 153, 154; *188:* 45
Priestley, Alice *168:* 33
Priestley, Chris *198:* 144
Primavera, Elise *26:* 95; *58:* 151; *73:* 37; *80:* 79; *86:* 156; *105:* 161; *213:* 157
Primrose, Jean *36:* 109
Prince, Alison *86:* 188, 189
Prince, Leonora E. *7:* 170
Pritchett, Shelley *116:* 148

Prittie, Edwin J. *YABC 1:* 120
Proimos, James *176:* 4; *217:* 132, 133, 134
Proimos, John *173:* 144
Prosmitsky, Jenya *132:* 33
Provensen, Alice *37:* 204, 215, 222; *70:* 176, 177, 178, 180; *71:* 213; *147:* 184; *191:* 190
Provensen, Martin *37:* 204, 215, 222; *70:* 176, 177, 178, 180; *71:* 213; *191:* 190
Pucci, Albert John *44:* 154
Pudlo *8:* 59
Puggaard, Ulla *196:* 25
Pullen, Zachary *211:* 161
Pulver, Harry, Jr. *129:* 159
Pulver, Robin *160:* 4
Punchatz, Don *99:* 57
Purdy, Susan *8:* 162
Pursell, Weimer *55:* 18
Purtscher, Alfons *97:* 6
Puskas, James *5:* 141
Pyk, Jan *7:* 26; *38:* 123
Pyle, Chuck *99:* 149; *191:* 83
Pyle, Howard *16:* 225, 226, 227, 228, 230, 231, 232, 235; *24:* 27; *34:* 124, 125, 127, 128; *59:* 132; *100:* 198

Q

Quackenbush, Robert *4:* 190; *6:* 166; *7:* 175, 178; *9:* 86; *11:* 65, 221; *41:* 154; *43:* 157; *70:* 185, 186; *71:* 137; *85:* 47; *92:* 148; *133:* 154, 164, 169
Qualls, Sean *177:* 167, 168; *193:* 43
Quennell, Marjorie (Courtney) *29:* 163, 164
Quidor, John *19:* 82
Quirk, John *62:* 170
Quirk, Thomas *12:* 81

R

Rackham, Arthur *15:* 32, 78, 214-227; *17:* 105, 115; *18:* 233; *19:* 254; *20:* 151; *22:* 129, 131, 132, 133; *23:* 175; *24:* 161, 181; *26:* 91; *32:* 118; *64:* 18; *100:* 9, 16, 203, 204; *YABC 1:* 25, 45, 55, 147; *2:* 103, 142, 173, 210
Racz, Michael *56:* 134
Raczka, Bob *191:* 155, 156
Radcliffe, Andrew *82:* 215
Rader, Laura *101:* 219; *197:* 147; *203:* 53
Radunsky, Vladimir *177:* 170; *192:* 30
Radzinski, Kandy *212:* 174
Rafilson, Sidney *11:* 172
Raglin, Tim *125:* 24
Raible, Alton *1:* 202, 203; *28:* 193; *35:* 181; *110:* 207
Raine, Patricia *82:* 74; *88:* 154
Ramá, Sue *173:* 45; *185:* 186; *190:* 184
Ramhorst, John *117:* 11
Ramirez, Gladys *177:* 19
Ramirez, Jose *207:* 27
Ramsey, James *16:* 41
Ramsey, Marcy Dunn *82:* 11; *180:* 186
Ramus, Michael *51:* 171
Rand, Paul *6:* 188
Rand, Ted *67:* 9, 10, 121, 123; *74:* 190; *84:* 170; *103:* 170; *112:* 6; *114:* 73; *139:* 168; *143:* 194; *156:* 154; *161:* 9, 10; *200:* 38; *204:* 7
Randazzo, Tony *81:* 98
Randell, William *55:* 54
Rane, Walter *93:* 144; *143:* 109; *184:* 126
Rankin, Joan *163:* 40; *212:* 176
Rankin, Laura *176:* 173, 174; *179:* 150
Ransome, Arthur *22:* 201

Ransome, James E. *74:* 137; *75:* 80; *84:* 181; *94:* 108; *117:* 115; *123:* 128, 129, 130; *158:* 101, 102; *159:* 205; *178:* 188, 189, 190; *216:* 114
Rantz, Don *119:* 184
Rao, Anthony *28:* 126
Raphael, Elaine *23:* 192; *71:* 24, 25
Rappaport, Eva *6:* 190
Raschka, Chris *80:* 187, 189, 190; *97:* 211; *115:* 210; *117:* 151, 152, 153, 154; *143:* 195; *145:* 153; *166:* 190, 191; *170:* 114; *207:* 140, 143, 144, 145; *208:* 82; *220:* 85
Rash, Andy *158:* 178; *162:* 172; *210:* 204; *219:* 145
Raskin, Ellen *2:* 208, 209; *4:* 142; *13:* 183; *22:* 68; *29:* 139; *36:* 134; *38:* 173, 174, 175, 176, 177, 178,179, 180, 181; *60:* 163; *86:* 81
Rathmann, Peggy *93:* 32; *94:* 168; *157:* 212, 214
Ratkus, Tony *77:* 133
Ratzkin, Lawrence *40:* 143
Rau, Margaret *9:* 157
Raverat, Gwen *YABC 1:* 152
Ravid, Joyce *61:* 73
Ravielli, Anthony *1:* 198; *3:* 168; *11:* 143
Ravilious, Robin *77:* 169
Rawlins, Donna *72:* 198; *73:* 15, 129
Rawlins, Janet *76:* 79
Rawlings, Steve *143:* 139; *151:* 54; *208:* 150
Rawlinson, Debbie *75:* 132
Ray, Deborah Kogan *8:* 164; *29:* 238; *50:* 112, 113; *62:* 119; *78:* 191; *203:* 149, 150, 151
Ray, Jane *96:* 166; *97:* 104; *152:* 208; *190:* 221; *196:* 165
Ray, Ralph *2:* 239; *5:* 73
Rayann, Omar *162:* 205; *186:* 29, 30
Rayevsky, Robert *64:* 17; *70:* 173; *80:* 204; *117:* 79; *190:* 187, 188
Raymond, Larry *31:* 108; *97:* 109
Rayner, Hugh *151:* 170
Rayner, Mary *22:* 207; *47:* 140; *72:* 191; *87:* 171, 172; *192:* 104
Rayner, Shoo
See Rayner, Hugh
Raynes, John *71:* 19
Raynor, Dorka *28:* 168
Raynor, Paul *24:* 73
Rayyan, Omar *110:* 222; *112:* 17; *125:* 131
Razzi, James *10:* 127
Read, Alexander D. *20:* 45
Reader, Dennis *71:* 157
Reasoner, Charles *53:* 33, 36, 37
Rebenschied, Shane *203:* 76; *215:* 124
Reczuch, Karen *115:* 132; *145:* 131
Redlich, Ben *163:* 221; *198:* 193
Reddy, Mike *203:* 67
Reed, Joseph *116:* 139
Reed, Lynn Rowe *115:* 173; *171:* 146; *208:* 177; *215:* 144, 145
Reed, Mike *211:* 147; *215:* 131
Reed, Tom *34:* 171
Reeder, Colin *74:* 202; *77:* 113
Rees, Mary *134:* 219
Reese, Bob *60:* 135
Reeve, Philip *171:* 50
Reeves, Eira B. *130:* 173, 174; *141:* 151
Reeves, Rick *181:* 179
Reeves, Rosie *202:* 200
Regan, Dana *117:* 116
Regan, Laura *103:* 198; *153:* 206
Reichert, Renée *169:* 127
Reid, Barbara *82:* 178; *92:* 17; *93:* 169, 170; *222:* 45
Reid, Stephen *19:* 213; *22:* 89
Reim, Melanie *104:* 151; *150:* 98
Reinert, Kirk *89:* 138; *195:* 129
Reinertson, Barbara *44:* 150; *62:* 103
Reiniger, Lotte *40:* 185
Reisberg, Mira *119:* 2
Reisch, Jesse *158:* 130
Reiser, Lynn *81:* 175; *138:* 184; *180:* 200

Reiss, John J. *23:* 193
Relf, Douglas *3:* 63
Relyea, C.M. *16:* 29; *31:* 153
Remi, Georges *13:* 184
Remington, Frederic *19:* 188; *41:* 178, 179, 180, 181, 183,184, 185, 186, 187, 188; *62:* 197
Remkiewicz, Frank *67:* 102; *77:* 171; *80:* 130; *113:* 107; *152:* 116; *152:* 211, 212; *157:* 148; *217:* 120, 138, 139, 140, 141
Rendon, Maria *116:* 141; *192:* *134:* 152
Renfro, Ed *79:* 176
Renier, Aaron *202:* 141; *207:* 119
Renlie, Frank *11:* 200
Reschofsky, Jean *7:* 118
Rethi *60:* 181
Rethi, Lili *2:* 153; *36:* 156
Reusswig, William *3:* 267
Revell, Cindy *195:* 93
Rex, Adam *156:* 172; *169:* 91; *186:* 178, 179; *215:* 103; *223:* 11; *225:* 154
Rex, Michael *157:* 147; *191:* 159, 160; *221:* 124
Rey, H.A. *1:* 182; *26:* 163, 164, 166, 167, 169; *69:* 172, 173, 174, 175; *86:* 195, 196, 197; *100:* 211; *YABC 2:* 17
Rey, Luis V. *201:* 162
Reynish, Jenny *222:* 155
Reynolds, Adrian *192:* 159, 160
Reynolds, Doris *5:* 71; *31:* 77
Reynolds, Peter H. *142:* 12; *179:* 175, 176; *202:* 113, 114
Rhead, Louis *31:* 91; *100:* 228
Rhodes, Andrew *38:* 204; *50:* 163; *54:* 76; *61:* 123, 124; *87:* 200
Ribbons, Ian *3:* 10; *37:* 161; *40:* 76
Ricci, Regolo *93:* 22; *164:* 148
Rice, Elizabeth *2:* 53, 214
Rice, Eve *34:* 174, 175; *91:* 172
Rice, James *22:* 210; *93:* 173
Rich, Anna *212:* 180
Rich, Martha *195:* 16
Richards, Chuck *170:* 154
Richards, George *40:* 116, 119, 121; *44:* 179
Richards, Henry *YABC 1:* 228, 231
Richardson, Ernest *2:* 144
Richardson, Frederick *18:* 27, 31
Richardson, John *110:* 88
Richman, Hilda *26:* 132
Richmond, George *24:* 179
Riddell, Chris *114:* 170, 195; *166:* 179; *199:* 164, 166, 167; *218:* 146, 148; *219:* 149, 150, 152, 153
Riddle, Tohby *74:* 204; *151:* 179; *223:* 154, 156
Riding, Peter *63:* 195
Rieniets, Judy King *14:* 28
Riger, Bob *2:* 166
Riggio, Anita *73:* 191; *85:* 63; *137:* 184; *172:* 165
Rigano, Giovanni *219:* 45
Riley, Jon *74:* 70
Riley, Kenneth *22:* 230
Riley, Terry *203:* 100
Riley-Webb, Charlotte *153:* 143
Rim, Sujean *225:* 157
Rinaldi, Angelo *165:* 60, 69
Ringgold, Faith *71:* 162; *114:* 173, 174, 176; *187:* 160, 161, 163
Ringi, Kjell *12:* 171
Rios, Tere
See Versace, Marie
Rioux, Jo *215:* 110
Ripper, Charles L. *3:* 175
Ripplinger, Henry *117:* 31
Ritchie, Scot *217:* 145
Ritchie, William *74:* 183
Ritter, John *175:* 14
Ritz, Karen *41:* 117; *72:* 239; *87:* 125; *102:* 7; *106:* 6
Rivas, Victor *209:* 193

Rivers, Ruth *178:* 193
Rivkin, Jay *15:* 230
Rivoche, Paul *45:* 125
Roach, Marilynne *9:* 158
Robbin, Jodi *44:* 156, 159
Robbins, Frank *42:* 167
Robbins, Ken *147:* 191, 192
Robbins, Ruth *52:* 102
Roberts, Cliff *4:* 126
Roberts, David *154:* 4, 6; *191:* 162; *196:* 184; *197:* 105; *210:* 257
Roberts, Doreen *4:* 230; *28:* 105
Roberts, Jim *22:* 166; *23:* 69; *31:* 110
Roberts, Tony *109:* 195, 214
Roberts, W. *22:* 2, 3
Robertson, M.P. *197:* 153
Robins, Arthur *137:* 172; *151:* 225; *204:* 161
Robinson, Aminah Brenda Lynn *86:* 205; *103:* 55; *159:* 175
Robinson, Charles [1870-1937] *17:* 157, 171, 172, 173, 175, 176; *24:* 207; *25:* 204; *YABC 2:* 308, 309, 310, 331
Robinson, Charles *3:* 53; *5:* 14; *6:* 193; *7:* 150; *7:* 183; *8:* 38; *9:* 81; *13:* 188; *14:* 248, 249; *23:* 149; *26:* 115; *27:* 48; *28:* 191; *32:* 28; *35:* 210; *36:* 37; *48:* 96; *52:* 33; *53:* 157; *56:* 15; *62:* 142; *77:* 41; *111:* 148
Robinson, Fiona *225:* 158
Robinson, Jerry *3:* 262
Robinson, Joan G. *7:* 184
Robinson, Lolly *90:* 227
Robinson, T.H. *17:* 179, 181, 182, 183; *29:* 254
Robinson, W. Heath *17:* 185, 187, 189, 191, 193, 195, 197, 199, 202; *23:* 167; *25:* 194; *29:* 150; *YABC 1:* 44; *2:* 183
Rocco, John *187:* 4; *188:* 151; *208:* 180, 181, 182; *213:* 94; *222:* 34
Roche, Christine *41:* 98
Roche, Denis *99:* 184; *180:* 32; *196:* 168
Roche, P.K. *57:* 151, 152
Rocker, Fermin *7:* 34; *13:* 21; *31:* 40; *40:* 190,191
Rocklen, Margot *101:* 181
Rockwell, Anne *5:* 147; *33:* 171, 173; *71:* 166, 167,168; *114:* 183, 184; *194:* 152, 155
Rockwell, Gail *7:* 186
Rockwell, Harlow *33:* 171, 173, 175
Rockwell, Lizzy *114:* 182; *162:* 182; *185:* 189
Rockwell, Norman *23:* 39, 196, 197, 199, 200, 203, 204, 207; *41:* 140, 143; *123:* 47; *YABC 2:* 60
Rockwood, Richard *119:* 75
Rodanas, Kristina *156:* 183, 184; *221:* 127
Rodegast, Roland *43:* 100
Rodgers, Frank *69:* 177
Rodriguez, Albert G. *182:* 50
Rodriguez, Christina *184:* 12; *225:* 94
Rodriguez, Edel *204:* 86
Rodriguez, Joel *16:* 65
Rodriguez, Robert *145:* 145; *212:* 33
Rodriguez-Howard, Pauline *177:* 18
Roe, Monika *210:* 94
Roeckelein, Katrina *134:* 223
Roennfeldt, Robert *66:* 243
Roever, J.M. *4:* 119; *26:* 170
Roffey, Maureen *33:* 142, 176, 177
Rogasky, Barbara *46:* 90
Rogé *173:* 160
Rogers, Carol *2:* 262; *6:* 164; *26:* 129
Rogers, Chris M. *150:* 59; *196:* 61
Rogers, Forest *87:* 160; *101:* 76
Rogers, Frances *10:* 130
Rogers, Gregory *104:* 76; *126:* 57; *171:* 26
Rogers, Jacqueline *78:* 249; *80:* 34; *86:* 54 *103:* 70; *115:* 72; *129:* 173; *131:* 57, 225; *143:* 211; *153:* 100; *193:* 186; *203:* 51; *213:* 144, 145, 146; *214:* 142
Rogers, Sherry *191:* 66
Rogers, Walter S. *31:* 135, 138; *67:* 65, 168; *100:* 81

Rogers, William A. *15:* 151, 153, 154; *33:* 35
Rogoff, Barbara *95:* 20
Rohmann, Eric *103:* 152; *198:* 151
Rojankovsky, Feodor *6:* 134, 136; *10:* 183; *21:* 128,129, 130; *25:* 110; *28:* 42; *68:* 120
Rolfsen, Alf *62:* 15
Rolston, Steve *209:* 154; *223:* 113
Romain, Trevor *134:* 157
Roman, Barbara J. *103:* 171
Romas *114:* 111; *165:* 63
Romero, Alejandro *187:* 185
Roos, Maryn *168:* 198; *225:* 160
Root, Barry *80:* 212; *90:* 196; *146:* 78; *156:* 165; *159:* 161; *182:* 18, 172
Root, Kimberly Bulcken *86:* 72; *98:* 21; *108:* 111; *127:* 114; *159:* 162; *176:* 134; *192:* 163
Roper, Bob *65:* 153
Roraback, Robin *111:* 156
Rorer, Abigail *43:* 222; *85:* 155
Rosales, Melodye *80:* 35
Rosamilia, Patricia *36:* 120
Rose, Carl *5:* 62
Rose, David S. *29:* 109; *70:* 120
Rose, Gerald *68:* 200, 201; *86:* 48
Rose, Ted *93:* 178
Rosen, Elizabeth *205:* 137
Rosenbaum, Jonathan *50:* 46
Rosenberg, Amye *74:* 207, 208
Rosenberry, Vera *87:* 22, 26; *144:* 212, 213; *158:* 120; *219:* 163, 164
Rosenblum, Richard *11:* 202; *18:* 18
Rosenstiehl, Agnès *203:* 153
Rosier, Lydia *16:* 236; *20:* 104; *21:* 109; *22:* 125; *30:* 151, 158; *42:* 128; *45:* 214; *77:* 227, 228
Rosing, Jens *85:* 142
Ross
See Thomson, Ross
Ross, Christine *83:* 172, 173
Ross, Clare Romano *3:* 123; *21:* 45; *48:* 199
Ross, Dave *32:* 152; *57:* 108
Ross, Graham *199:* 4
Ross, Herbert *37:* 78
Ross, John *3:* 123; *21:* 45
Ross, Johnny *32:* 190
Ross, Larry *47:* 168; *60:* 62
Ross, Ruth *109:* 233
Ross, Tony *17:* 204; *56:* 132; *65:* 176, 177, 179; *90:* 123; *123:* 186, 187, 190; *130:* 188, 190, 191, 192; *132:* 242; *174:* 159; *176:* 181, 182, 183; *202:* 198; *225:* 168, 170
Rossetti, Dante Gabriel *20:* 151, 153
Rostant, Larry *180:* 221; *194:* 108; *195:* 96; *197:* 12; *207:* 53; *210:* 189
Roth, Arnold *4:* 238; *21:* 133
Roth, Julie Jersild *180:* 206
Roth, Marci *135:* 223
Roth, R.G. *184:* 50
Roth, Rob *105:* 98; *146:* 41
Roth, Robert *176:* 159
Roth, Roger *61:* 128; *190:* 192
Roth, Ruby *216:* 185
Roth, Stephanie *136:* 171, 172
Roth, Susan L. *80:* 38; *93:* 78; *134:* 165, 166; *181:* 145, 146
Rothenberg, Joani Keller *162:* 190, 191
Rothman, Michael *139:* 62; *184:* 34 *Rotman, Jeffrey L. 145:* 30
Rotondo, Pat *32:* 158
Roughsey, Dick *35:* 186
Rouille, M. *11:* 96
Rounds, Glen *8:* 173; *9:* 171; *12:* 56; *32:* 194; *40:* 230; *51:* 161, 162, 166; *56:* 149; *70:* 198, 199; *YABC 1:* 1, 2, 3; *112:* 163
Roundtree, Katherine *114:* 88; *168:* 102
Rovetch, Lissa *201:* 164
Rowan, Evadne *52:* 51
Rowe, Eric *111:* 161
Rowe, Gavin *27:* 144; *72:* 47; *88:* 201
Rowe, John *132:* 70, 71; *180:* 126

Rowell, Kenneth *40:* 72
Rowen, Amy *52:* 143
Rowena *116:* 101
Rowland, Andrew *164:* 136
Rowland, Jada *83:* 73
Rowles, Daphne *58:* 24
Roy, Jeroo *27:* 229; *36:* 110
Royo *118:* 32; *144:* 105, 106, 108; *165:* 19; *166:* 166
Rubbino, Salvatore *220:* 147
Rubel, Nicole *18:* 255; *20:* 59; *81:* 66, 67; *95:* 169, 170; *119:* 60; *135:* 177, 179, 180; *169:* 68; *181:* 150
Rubel, Reina *33:* 217
Rud, Borghild *6:* 15
Ruddell, Gary *110:* 238; *116:* 207
Rudolph, Norman Guthrie *17:* 13
Rue, Leonard Lee III *37:* 164
Rueda, Claudia *183:* 170, 171
Ruelle, Karen Gray *126:* 193
Ruff, Donna *50:* 173; *72:* 203; *78:* 49; *80:* 120,121; *93:* 162; *164:* 121
Ruffins, Reynold *10:* 134, 135; *41:* 191, 192, 193, 194, 195, 196; *125:* 187, 188, 189; *162:* 197
Ruhlin, Roger *34:* 44
Rui, Paolo *217:* 115
Ruiz, Art *95:* 154; *110:* 91
Rumford, James *193:* 167
Runnerstroem, Bengt Arne *75:* 161
Ruse, Margaret *24:* 155
Rush, Ken *98:* 74
Rush, Peter *42:* 75
Russell, Charles M. *167:* 171
Russell, E.B. *18:* 177, 182
Russell, Jim *53:* 134
Russell, Natalie *218:* 170, 171
Russell, P. Craig *80:* 196; *146:* 102; *162:* 186
Russo, Marisabina *84:* 51; *106:* 164; *151:* 183; *188:* 153, 154, 155, 156
Russo, Susan *30:* 182; *36:* 144
Russon, Mary *87:* 145
Ruth, Greg *183:* 125
Ruth, Rod *9:* 161
Rutherford, Alexa *110:* 108
Rutherford, Jenny *78:* 5
Rutherford, Meg *25:* 174; *34:* 178, 179; *69:* 73; *72:* 31
Rutland, Jonathan *31:* 126
Ruurs, Margriet *147:* 195
Ruzzier, Sergio *159:* 176, 177; *163:* 184; *210:* 214, 216
Ryan, Amy *188:* 50
Ryan, Will *86:* 134
Ryden, Hope *8:* 176
Rylant, Cynthia *112:* 170, 172
Rymer, Alta M. *34:* 181
Ryniak, Christopher *178:* 11
Rystedt, Rex *49:* 80

S

Saaf, Chuck *49:* 179
Saaf, Donald *101:* 220; *124:* 180
Sabaka, Donna R. *21:* 172
Sabin, Robert *45:* 35; *60:* 30; *99:* 161; *223:* 29
Sabuda, Robert *170:* 166, 167, 168
Sacker, Amy *16:* 100
Saelig, S.M. *129:* 73; *173:* 59
Saffioti, Lino *36:* 176; *48:* 60; *223:* 26
Saflund, Birgitta *94:* 2
Sagsoorian, Paul *12:* 183; *22:* 154; *33:* 106; *87:* 152
Sahara, Tony *168:* 106; *177:* 181; *178:* 228; *186:* 132; *207:* 89
Sahlberg, Myron *57:* 165
Saidens, Amy *145:* 162; *191:* 131; *210:* 129
Saint Exupery, Antoine de *20:* 157

Saint James, Synthia *152:* 220; *188:* 90; *200:* 7

Sakai, Komako *213:* 148

Saldutti, Denise *39:* 186; *57:* 178

Sale, Morton *YABC 2:* 31

Sale, Tim *153:* 177

Salerno, Steven *150:* 79; *176:* 188; *202:* 39; *216:* 190

Salter, George *72:* 128, 130

Saltzberg, Barney *135:* 184, 185; *194:* 160

Saltzman, David *86:* 209

Salwowski, Mark *71:* 54

Salzman, Yuri *86:* 12

Sambourne, Linley *YABC 2:* 181

Sampson, Katherine *9:* 197

Samson, Anne S. *2:* 216

San Souci, Daniel *40:* 200; *96:* 199, 200; *113:* 171; *157:* 149; *170:* 69; *192:* 167, 168; *220:* 152; *221:* 126

Sancha, Sheila *38:* 185

Sanchez, Enrique O. *155:* 84

Sand, George X. *45:* 182

Sandberg, Lasse *15:* 239, 241

Sanders, Beryl *39:* 173

Sanderson, Ruth *21:* 126; *24:* 53; *28:* 63; *33:* 67; *41:* 48, 198, 199, 200, 201, 202, 203; *43:* 79; *46:* 36,44; *47:* 102; *49:* 58; *62:* 121, 122; *85:* 3; *109:* 207, 208, 209, 210; *172:* 157, 158; *223:* 85; *224:* 152, 153, 154

Sandia *119:* 74

Sandin, Joan *4:* 36; *6:* 194; *7:* 177; *12:* 145,185; *20:* 43; *21:* 74; *26:* 144; *27:* 142; *28:* 224, 225; *38:* 86; *41:* 46; *42:* 35; *59:* 6; *80:* 136; *94:* 188; *140:* 116; *153:* 179, 180; *197:* 168

Sandland, Reg *39:* 215

Sandoz, Edouard *26:* 45, 47

Sanford, John *66:* 96, 97

Sanger, Amy Wilson *205:* 140

Sankey, Tom *72:* 103

Sano, Kazuhiko *153:* 208; *195:* 171; *203:* 21; *221:* 71

Santat, Dan *188:* 160; *221:* 62; *223:* 163; *224:* 157, 158, 159

Santiago, Wilfred *210:* 48

Santore, Charles *54:* 139; *200:* 171, 172

Santoro, Christopher *74:* 215

Santos, Jesse J. *99:* 24

Sapieha, Christine *1:* 180

Saport, Linda *123:* 137, 138; *215:* 29

Sara

See De La Roche Saint Andre, Anne

Sarcone-Roach, Julia *215:* 158

Sardinha, Rick *175:* 151

Sarg, Tony *YABC 2:* 236

Sargent, Claudia *64:* 181

Sargent, Robert *2:* 217

Saris *1:* 33

Sarony *YABC 2:* 170

Saroff, Phyllis V. *202:* 160

Sasaki, Goro *170:* 46

Sasaki, Ellen Joy *216:* 49

Sasek, Miroslav *16:* 239, 240, 241, 242

Sassman, David *9:* 79

Sattler, Jennifer Gordon *218:* 175

Satty *29:* 203, 205

Sauber, Robert *40:* 183; *76:* 256; *78:* 154; *87:* 92

Saunders, Dave *85:* 163, 164, 165

Savadier, Elivia *84:* 50; *145:* 45; *164:* 206

Savage, Naomi *56:* 172

Savage, Steele *10:* 203; *20:* 77; *35:* 28

Savage, Stephen *174:* 182

Savio *76:* 4

Savitt, Sam *8:* 66, 182; *15:* 278; *20:* 96; *24:* 192; *28:* 98

Sawyer, Kem Knapp *84:* 228, 229

Say, Allen *28:* 178; *69:* 182, 183, 232; *110:* 194, 195,196; *161:* 154, 155

Sayles, Elizabeth *82:* 93; *105:* 155; *109:* 116; *180:* 64; *220:* 160, 161

Scabrini, Janet *13:* 191; *44:* 128

Scalora, Suza *224:* 160

Scanlan, Peter *83:* 27; *153:* 165; *187:* 149

Scanlon, Paul *83:* 87

Scannell, Reece *105:* 105

Scarry, Huck *35:* 204, 205

Scarry, Richard *2:* 220, 221; *18:* 20; *35:* 193, 194, 195,196, 197, 198, 199, 200, 201, 202; *75:* 165, 167, 168

Schachner, Judith Byron *88:* 180; *92:* 163; *93:* 102; *142:* 82; *178:* 199, 200; *190:* 140

Schade, Susan *205:* 21

Schaeffer, Mead *18:* 81, 94; *21:* 137, 138, 139; *47:* 128

Schaffer, Amanda *90:* 206

Schallau, Daniel *222:* 164

Schanzer, Rosalyn *138:* 192, 193

Scharl, Josef *20:* 132; *22:* 128

Scheel, Lita *11:* 230

Scheffler, Axel *180:* 23, 24

Scheib, Ida *29:* 28

Schermer, Judith *30:* 184

Schick, Eleanor *82:* 210, 211; *144:* 222

Schick, Joel *16:* 160; *17:* 167; *22:* 12; *27:* 176; *31:* 147, 148; *36:* 23; *38:* 64; *45:* 116, 117; *52:* 5, 85; *104:* 159

Schields, Gretchen *75:* 171, 203

Schindelman, Joseph *1:* 74; *4:* 101; *12:* 49; *26:* 51; *40:* 146; *56:* 158; *73:* 40

Schindler, Edith *7:* 22

Schindler, S.D. *38:* 107; *46:* 196; *74:* 162; *75:* 172, 173; *99:* 133; *112:* 177; *118:* 185, 186; *121:* 71; *136:* 159; *143:* 45; *149:* 120; *156:* 30; *169:* 135; *171:* 161, 162, 163; *172:* 9; *186:* 163; *194:* 109; *195:* 35; *198:* 170, 171, 172

Schlesinger, Bret *7:* 77

Schlossberg, Elisabeth *221:* 161

Schmid, Eleanore *12:* 188; *126:* 196, 197

Schmiderer, Dorothy *19:* 224

Schmidt, Bill *73:* 34; *76:* 220, 222, 224

Schmidt, Elizabeth *15:* 242

Schmidt, George Paul *132:* 122

Schmidt, Karen Lee *54:* 12; *71:* 174; *92:* 56; *94:* 190, 191; *127:* 103

Schmidt, Lynette *76:* 205

Schmitz, Tamara *207:* 147

Schneider, Christine M. *171:* 165

Schneider, Howie *181:* 159

Schneider, Rex *29:* 64; *44:* 171

Schnurr, Edward *170:* 62

Schoberle, Cecile *80:* 200; *92:* 134; *218:* 113

Schoenherr, Ian *32:* 83; *173:* 41

Schoenherr, John *1:* 146, 147, 173; *3:* 39, 139; *17:* 75; *29:* 72; *32:* 83; *37:* 168, 169, 170; *43:* 164, 165; *45:* 160, 162; *51:* 127; *66:* 196, 197, 198; *68:* 83; *72:* 240; *75:* 225; *88:* 176

Scholder, Fritz *69:* 103

Schomburg, Alex *13:* 23

Schongut, Emanuel *4:* 102; *15:* 186; *47:* 218, 219; *52:* 147, 148, 149, 150; *185:* 27

Schoonover, Frank *17:* 107; *19:* 81, 190, 233; *22:* 88,129; *24:* 189; *31:* 88; *41:* 69; *YABC 2:* 282, 316

Schories, Pat *164:* 210

Schottland, Miriam *22:* 172

Schramm, Ulrik *2:* 16; *14:* 112

Schreiber, Elizabeth Anne *13:* 193

Schreiber, Ralph W. *13:* 193

Schreiter, Rick *14:* 97; *23:* 171; *41:* 247; *49:* 131

Schroades, John *214:* 129

Schroeder, Binette *56:* 128, 129

Schroeder, E. Peter *12:* 112

Schroeder, Ted *11:* 160; *15:* 189; *30:* 91; *34:* 43

Schrotter, Gustav *22:* 212; *30:* 225

Schubert, Dieter *101:* 167, 168; *217:* 151, 152, 153, 155

Schubert, Ingrid *217:* 151, 152, 153, 155

Schubert-Gabrys, Ingrid *101:* 167, 168

Schucker, James *31:* 163

Schuett, Stacey *72:* 137; *208:* 204

Schulder, Lili *146:* 29

Schulke, Debra *57:* 167

Schulke, Flip *57:* 167

Schulz, Barbara *167:* 24

Schulz, Charles M. *10:* 137, 138, 139, 140, 141, 142; *118:* 192, 193, 194, 196, 199

Schutzer, Dena *109:* 32

Schwark, Mary Beth *51:* 155; *72:* 175

Schwartz, Amy *47:* 191; *82:* 100; *83:* 178, 179, 180,181; *129:* 107; *131:* 197, 198; *189:* 166, 168

Schwartz, Carol *124:* 41; *130:* 199

Schwartz, Charles *8:* 184

Schwartz, Daniel *46:* 37

Schwartz, Joanie *124:* 170

Schwartzberg, Joan *3:* 208

Schwarz, Viviane *204:* 132

Schweitzer, Iris *2:* 137; *6:* 207

Schweninger, Ann *29:* 172; *82:* 246; *159:* 202; *168:* 166; *211:* 193

Schwinger, Laurence *84:* 44; *91:* 61

Scofield, Penrod *61:* 107; *62:* 160

Scott, Anita Walker *7:* 38

Scott, Art *39:* 41

Scott, Frances Gruse *38:* 43

Scott, Julian *34:* 126

Scott, Roszel *33:* 238

Scott, Sally *87:* 27

Scott, Steve *166:* 230, 231; *171:* 93

Scott, Trudy *27:* 172

Scotton, Rob *214:* 183

Scrace, Carolyn *143:* 95, 96

Scrambly, Crab *198:* 196

Scribner, Joanne *14:* 236; *29:* 78; *33:* 185; *34:* 208; *78:* 75; *164:* 237; *203:* 73

Scrofani, Joseph *31:* 65; *74:* 225

Scroggs, Kirk *187:* 169

Seaman, Mary Lott *34:* 64

Searle, Ronald *24:* 98; *42:* 172, 173, 174, 176, 177, 179; *66:* 73, 74; *70:* 205, 206, 207

Searle, Townley *36:* 85

Sebree, Charles *18:* 65

Sedacca, Joseph M. *11:* 25; *22:* 36

Seder, Jason *108:* 102

Seeger, Laura Vaccaro *172:* 162

Seegmiller, Don *174:* 57

Seely, David *164:* 173

Seeley, Laura L. *97:* 105

Segal, John *178:* 202

Segar, E.C. *61:* 179, 181

Segur, Adrienne *27:* 121

Seibold, J. Otto *83:* 188, 190, 191; *149:* 212, 214, 215, 216; *196:* 177, 179; *215:* 204

Seignobosc, Francoise *21:* 145, 146

Sejima, Yoshimasa *8:* 187

Selig, Sylvie *13:* 199

Seltzer, Isadore *6:* 18; *133:* 59

Seltzer, Meyer *17:* 214

Selven, Maniam *144:* 133

Selway, Martina *169:* 157

Selznick, Brian *79:* 192; *104:* 25; *117:* 175; *126:* 156; *134:* 171; *158:* 76, 78; *169:* 70; *171:* 172, 173; *191:* 106; *192:* 130; *197:* 158; *203:* 35; *205:* 92; *210:* 219, 220, 221, 222

Sempe, Jean-Jacques *47:* 92; *YABC 2:* 109

Sendak, Maurice *1:* 135, 190; *3:* 204; *7:* 142; *15:* 199; *17:* 210; *27:* 181, 182, 183, 185, 186, 187, 189,190, 191, 192, 193, 194, 195, 197, 198, 199, 203; *28:* 181, 182; *32:* 108; *33:* 148, 149; *35:* 238; *44:* 180, 181; *45:* 97, 99; *46:* 174; *73:* 225; *91:* 10, 11 *YABC1:* 167; *113:* 163, 165, 167, 168; *118:* 153; *127:* 161

Senders, Marci *180:* 79

Sengler, Johanna *18:* 256

Senn, Steve *60:* 145

Seredy, Kate *1:* 192; *14:* 20, 21; *17:* 210

Sergeant, John 6: 74
Serra, Sebastía 212: 215
Servello, Joe 10: 144; 24: 139; 40: 91; 70: 130, 131; 146: 159
Seton, Ernest Thompson 18: 260-269, 271
Seuss, Dr.
  See Geisel, Theodor
Severin, John Powers 7: 62
Sewall, Marcia 15: 8; 22: 170; 37: 171, 172, 173; 39: 73; 45: 209; 62: 117; 69: 185, 186; 71: 212; 90: 232; 96: 127; 102: 101; 107: 129; 119: 176, 177, 178, 180
Seward, James 70: 35
Seward, Prudence 16: 243
Sewell, Helen 3: 186; 15: 308; 33: 102; 38: 189, 190, 191, 192
Seymour, Stephen 54: 21
Sfar, Joann 182: 183
Shachat, Andrew 82: 179
Shadbolt, Robert 203: 68
Shahn, Ben 39: 178; 46: 193
Shalansky, Len 38: 167
Shanks, Anne Zane 10: 149
Shannon, David 57: 137; 107: 184; 112: 216; 135: 12; 152: 223, 224, 225; 158: 192; 212: 159, 160, 163
Sharkey, Niamh 213: 152
Sharp, Paul 52: 60
Sharp, William 6: 131; 19: 241; 20: 112; 25: 141
Sharratt, Nick 102: 207, 208; 104: 163; 153: 198; 175: 176; 192: 208; 199: 141, 142, 143, 184, 187, 188
Shaw, Barclay 74: 14, 16; 118: 138
Shaw, Charles 21: 135; 38: 187; 47: 124; 126: 219
Shaw, Charles G. 13: 200
Shaw-Smith, Emma 144: 117
Shea, Edmund 56: 19
Shearer, Ted 43: 193, 194, 195, 196
Sheban, Chris 182: 185; 190: 102, 104; 202: 28; 204: 112, 114; 209: 150; 210: 107; 220: 103; 224: 185
Shecter, Ben 16: 244; 25: 109; 33: 188, 191; 41: 77
Shed, Greg 74: 94; 84: 204; 129: 149, 167: 91; 179: 192; 223: 104
Sheeban, Chris 144: 190; 158: 163
Shefcik, James 48: 221, 222; 60: 141
Shefelman, Karl 58: 168
Shefelman, Tom 204: 137
Shefts, Joelle 48: 210
Shein, Bob 139: 189
Sheinkin, Stephen 204: 139
Shekerjian, Haig 16: 245
Shekerjian, Regina 16: 245; 25: 73
Sheldon, David 184: 174; 185: 204; 211: 189
Shelley, John 186: 223
Shemie, Bonnie 96: 207
Shenton, Edward 45: 187, 188, 189; YABC 1: 218, 219, 221
Shepard, Ernest H. 3: 193; 4: 74; 16: 101; 17: 109; 25: 148; 33: 152, 199, 200, 201, 202, 203, 204, 205, 206,207; 46: 194; 98: 114; 100: 111, 178, 179, 217, 219, 220,221; YABC 1: 148, 153, 174, 176, 180, 181
Shepard, Mary 4: 210; 22: 205; 30: 132, 133; 54: 150, 152, 153, 157, 158; 59: 108, 109, 111; 100: 246
Shepherd, Amanda 198: 14
Shepherd, Irana 171: 112
Sheppard, Kate 195: 176
Shepperson, Rob 96: 153; 177: 163; 178: 204; 197: 34; 205: 108
Sheridan, Brian 196: 193
Sherman, Theresa 27: 167
Sherwan, Earl 3: 196
Shields, Charles 10: 150; 36: 63
Shields, Leonard 13: 83, 85, 87
Shiffman, Lena 139: 167; 168: 136
Shigley, Neil K. 66: 219

Shillabeer, Mary 35: 74
Shilston, Arthur 49: 61; 62: 58
Shimin, Symeon 1: 93; 2: 128, 129; 3: 202; 7: 85; 11: 177; 12: 139; 13: 202, 203; 27: 138; 28: 65; 35: 129; 36: 130; 48: 151; 49: 59; 56: 63, 65, 153
Shimizu, Yuko 215: 197
Shine, Andrea 104: 165; 128: 34
Shinn, Everett 16: 148; 18: 229; 21: 149, 150, 151; 24: 218
Shinn, Florence Scovel 63: 133, 135
Shore, Robert 27: 54; 39: 192, 193; YABC 2: 200
Shortall, Leonard 4: 144; 8: 196; 10: 166; 19: 227, 228, 229, 230; 25: 78; 28: 66, 167; 33: 127; 52: 125; 73: 12, 212
Shortt, T.M. 27: 36
Shpitalnik, Vladimir 83: 194
Shropshire, Sandy 170: 191
Shtainments, Leon 32: 161
Shulevitz, Uri 3: 198, 199; 17: 85; 22: 204; 27: 212; 28: 184; 50: 190, 191, 192, 193, 194, 195, 196,197, 198, 199, 201; 106: 181, 182, 183; 165: 203, 205; 166: 138
Shulman, Dee 180: 140
Shupe, Bobbi 139: 80, 81
Shute, A.B. 67: 196
Shute, Linda 46: 59; 74: 118
Siberell, Anne 29: 193
Sibley, Don 1: 39; 12: 196; 31: 47
Sibthorp, Fletcher 94: 111, 112
Sidjakov, Nicolas 18: 274
Siebel, Fritz 3: 120; 17: 145
Siebold, J. Otto 158: 227
Siegel, Hal 74: 246
Sieger, Ted 189: 172
Siegl, Helen 12: 166; 23: 216; 34: 185, 186
Silin-Palmer, Pamela 184: 102
Sill, John 140: 194; 141: 157; 221: 163; 222: 171
Sills, Joyce 5: 199
Silva, Simon 108: 122
Silver, Maggie 85: 210
Silveria, Gordon 96: 44
Silverstein, Alvin 8: 189
Silverstein, Shel 33: 211; 92: 209, 210
Silverstein, Virginia 8: 189
Silvey, Joe 135: 203
Simard, Rémy 95: 156; 221: 144
Siminovich, Laura 219: 172
Simmons, Elly 110: 2; 127: 69; 134: 181
Simon, Eric M. 7: 82
Simon, Hilda 28: 189
Simon, Howard 2: 175; 5: 132; 19: 199; 32: 163, 164, 165
Simont, Marc 2: 119; 4: 213; 9: 168; 13: 238,240; 14: 262; 16: 179; 18: 221; 26: 210; 33: 189, 194; 44: 132; 58: 122; 68: 117; 73: 204, 205, 206; 74: 221; 126: 199, 200; 133: 195; 163: 40; 164: 128; 223: 28
Sims, Agnes 54: 152
Sims, Blanche 44: 116; 57: 129; 75: 179, 180; 77: 92; 104: 192; 152: 117; 156: 160; 160: 70; 168: 174, 175; 198: 17
Singer, Edith G. 2: 30
Singer, Gloria 34: 56; 36: 43
Singer, Julia 28: 190
Singh, Jen 178: 146
Sinquette, Jaclyn 215: 83
Siomades, Lorianne 134: 45; 204: 48; 217: 157
Siracusa, Catherine 68: 135; 82: 218
Sís, Peter 67: 179, 181, 183, 184, 185; 96: 96, 98; 106: 193, 194, 195; 149: 224, 226; 180: 177; 192: 180, 182; 222: 64
Sivard, Robert 26: 124
Sivertson, Liz 116: 84
Skardinski, Stanley 23: 144; 32: 84; 66: 122; 84: 108
Slack, Michael 185: 108; 189: 173, 174
Slackman, Charles B. 12: 201

Slade, Christian 193: 187; 204: 134
Slade, Paul 61: 170
Slark, Albert 99: 212; 205: 161
Slater, Rod 25: 167
Slavin, Bill 182: 14, 15; 196: 90; 199: 148, 149, 150; 217: 20
Sloan, Joseph 16: 68
Sloane, Eric 21: 3; 52: 153, 154, 155, 156, 157, 158, 160
Sloat, Teri 164: 231
Slobodkin, Louis 1: 200; 3: 232; 5: 168; 13: 251; 15: 13, 88; 26: 173, 174, 175, 176, 178, 179; 60: 180
Slobodkina, Esphyr 1: 201
Slonim, David 166: 167, 168
Small, David 50: 204, 205; 79: 44; 95: 189, 190, 191; 126: 203, 204; 136: 119; 143: 201, 202, 203; 144: 246; 150: 5; 161: 176; 183: 181, 182, 183, 184; 200: 211; 212: 86; 216: 202, 203, 204
Small, W. 33: 113
Smalley, Janet 1: 154
Smath, Jerry 198: 179, 180
Smedley, William T. 34: 129
Smee, David 14: 78; 62: 30
Smee, Nicola 167: 156
Smith, A.G., Jr. 35: 182
Smith, Ali 204: 68
Smith, Alvin 1: 31, 229; 13: 187; 27: 216; 28: 226; 48: 149; 49: 60
Smith, Andy 188: 20; 207: 151
Smith, Anne 194: 147
Smith, Anne Warren 41: 212
Smith, Barry 75: 183
Smith, Brian 200: 183
Smith, Carl 36: 41
Smith, Cat Bowman 146: 39; 164: 219; 201: 55, 184
Smith, Craig 97: 197; 172: 175; 206: 40; 215: 19; 217: 129; 220: 145
Smith, Donald A. 178: 7
Smith, Doris Susan 41: 139
Smith, Douglas 189: 159; 213: 170
Smith, Duane 171: 152; 208: 97
Smith, E. Boyd 19: 70; 22: 89; 26: 63; YABC 1: 4, 5, 240, 248, 249
Smith, Edward J. 4: 224
Smith, Elwood H. 157: 231; 181: 79; 203: 160, 161, 162
Smith, Eunice Young 5: 170
Smith, Gary 113: 216
Smith, George 102: 169
Smith, Howard 19: 196
Smith, J. Gerard 95: 42
Smith, Jacqueline Bardner 27: 108; 39: 197
Smith, Jay J. 61: 119
Smith, Jeff 93: 191
Smith, Jessie Willcox 15: 91; 16: 95; 18: 231; 19: 57, 242; 21: 29, 156, 157, 158, 159, 160, 161; 34: 65; 100: 223; YABC 1: 6; 2: 180, 185, 191, 311, 325
Smith, Jos. A. 52: 131; 72: 120; 74: 151; 84: 147, 148; 85: 146; 87: 96; 94: 219; 96: 97; 104: 33; 108: 126, 127, 128; 111: 140; 136: 145; 181: 173; 200: 213; 201: 94
Smith, Kenneth R. 47: 182
Smith, Keri 216: 60
Smith, Kevin Warren 89: 112
Smith, Kristin 209: 197
Smith, L.H. 35: 174
Smith, Lane 76: 211, 213; 88: 115; 105: 202, 203,204, 205; 131: 207; 160: 217, 221; 179: 183, 184, 185, 186; 199: 122, 123, 124, 126; 224: 164
Smith, Lee 29: 32
Smith, Linell Nash 2: 195
Smith, Maggie Kaufman 13: 205; 35: 191; 110: 158; 178: 226; 190: 204; 209: 145
Smith, Mavis 101: 219
Smith, Moishe 33: 155
Smith, Philip 44: 134; 46: 203

Smith, Ralph Crosby *2:* 267; *49:* 203
Smith, Robert D. *5:* 63
Smith, Sally J. *84:* 55
Smith, Susan Carlton *12:* 208
Smith, Terry *12:* 106; *33:* 158
Smith, Virginia *3:* 157; *33:* 72
Smith, William A. *1:* 36; *10:* 154; *25:* 65
Smith-Moore, J.J. *98:* 147
Smolinski, Dick *84:* 217
Smoljan, Joe *112:* 201
Smollin, Mike *39:* 203
Smyth, Iain *105:* 207
Smyth, M. Jane *12:* 15
Smythe, Fiona *151:* 213
Smythe, Theresa *141:* 37
Snair, Andy *176:* 4
Sneed, Brad *125:* 25; *191:* 175, 176; *211:* 194
Snyder, Andrew A. *30:* 212
Snyder, Jerome *13:* 207; *30:* 173
Snyder, Joel *28:* 163
So, Meilo *162:* 201; *208:* 188
Soentpiet, Chris K. *97:* 208; *110:* 33; *159:* 184; *161:* 10; *163:* 130
Sofia *1:* 62; *5:* 90; *32:* 166; *86:* 43
Sofilas, Mark *93:* 157
Sogabe, Aki *207:* 153; *221:* 110
Sohn, Jiho *182:* 78
Sokol, Bill *37:* 178; *49:* 23
Sokolov, Kirill *34:* 188
Solbert, Ronni *1:* 159; *2:* 232; *5:* 121; *6:* 34; *17:* 249
Solomon, Michael *174:* 115
Solonevich, George *15:* 246; *17:* 47
Soloviov, Michael *223:* 122
Soma, Liana *81:* 118
Soman, David *90:* 122; *102:* 126; *140:* 120; *93*; *188:* 43, 89; *200:* 180, 181
Sommer, Robert *12:* 211
Song, Jae *203:* 27
Soo, Kean *201:* 185
Sorel, Edward *4:* 61; *36:* 82; *65:* 191, 193; *126:* 214
Sorensen, Henri *196:* 58
Sorensen, Henrik *62:* 16
Sorensen, Svend Otto *22:* 130, 141; *67:* 188, 189
Sorra, Kristin *155:* 80
Sosa, Hernan *198:* 66
Sostre, Maria *187:* 36
Sotomayor, Antonio *11:* 215
Souhami, Jessica *112:* 128; *176:* 193
Sousa, Natalie C. *209:* 89
Souza, Diana *71:* 139
Sovak, Jan *115:* 190
Sowards, Ben *215:* 62
Soyer, Moses *20:* 177
Spaenkuch, August *16:* 28
Spafford, Suzy *160:* 228
Spain, Valerie *105:* 76
Spain, Sunday Sahara *133:* 204
Spalenka, Greg *149:* 69; *151:* 228; *184:* 195; *191:* 21; *196:* 12; *198:* 181, 182, 201; *208:* 92
Spanfeller, James *1:* 72, 149; *2:* 183; *19:* 230, 231,232; *22:* 66; *36:* 160, 161; *40:* 75; *52:* 166; *76:* 37
Spangler, Brie *212:* 188
Sparks, Mary Walker *15:* 247
Spears, Rick *182:* 187; *220:* 67
Speidel, Sandra *78:* 233; *94:* 178; *134:* 180; *210:* 67
Speirs, John *67:* 178
Spence, Geraldine *21:* 163; *47:* 196
Spence, Jim *38:* 89; *50:* 102
Spencer, Laurie *113:* 12
Spencer, Mark *57:* 170
Spengler, Kenneth J. *146:* 256
Sperling, Andrea *133:* 182
Spiegel, Beth *184:* 203
Spiegel, Doris *29:* 111
Spiegelman, Art *109:* 227

Spier, Jo *10:* 30
Spier, Peter *3:* 155; *4:* 200; *7:* 61; *11:* 78; *38:* 106; *54:* 120, 121, 122, 123, 124, 125, 126, 127, 128, 129, 130,131, 132, 133, 134
Spilka, Arnold *5:* 120; *6:* 204; *8:* 131
Spirin, Gennady *95:* 196, 197; *113:* 172; *128:* 9; *129:* 49; *134:* 210; *153:* 9; *204:* 143, 144, 145; *220:* 153
Spiro, Ruth *208:* 197
Spivak, I. Howard *8:* 10; *13:* 172
Spohn, David *72:* 233
Spohn, Kate *87:* 195; *147:* 201, 202
Spollen, Christopher J. *12:* 214
Spooner, Malcolm *40:* 142
Spoor, Mike *220:* 92
Spowart, Robin *82:* 228; *92:* 149; *133:* 131; *176:* 163; *177:* 183, 184; *217:* 123, 124
Sprague, Kevin *150:* 60; *196:* 62
Spranger, Nina *201:* 199
Sprattler, Rob *12:* 176
Spring, Bob *5:* 60
Spring, Ira *5:* 60
Springer, Harriet *31:* 92
Spudvilas, Anne *110:* 74; *197:* 192; *199:* 154
Spurll, Barbara *78:* 199; *88:* 141, 142; *99:* 215
Spurrier, Steven *28:* 198
Spuvilas, Anne *85:* 114
Spy
    See Ward, Leslie
Squires, Stuart *127:* 74
St. Aubin, Bruno *179:* 54
St. John, J. Allen *41:* 62
Staake, Bob *209:* 168, 169
Stabin, Victor *101:* 131; *164:* 158
Stadler, John *62:* 33; *204:* 149
Stadnyk, Greg *212:* 55
Staffan, Alvin E. *11:* 56; *12:* 187
Stahl, Ben *5:* 181; *12:* 91; *49:* 122; *71:* 128; *87:* 206; *112:* 107
Stair, Gobin *35:* 214
Stallwood, Karen *73:* 126
Stamaty, Mark Alan *12:* 215
Stammen, JoEllen McAllister *113:* 14
Stamp, Jørgen *225:* 184
Stampnick, Ken *51:* 142
Stanbridge, Joanne *150:* 91
Stanley, Diane *3:* 45; *37:* 180; *80:* 217, 219
Stanley, Sanna *145:* 228
Star, Lindsay *219:* 39
Starcke, Helmut *86:* 217
Stark, Ken *197:* 102
Starr, Branka *73:* 25
Stasiak, Krystyna *49:* 181; *64:* 194
Staub, Leslie *103:* 54
Stauffer, Brian *220:* 123
Staunton, Ted *112:* 192
Stawicki, Matt *164:* 250
Stead, L. *55:* 51, 56
Steadman, Broeck *97:* 185, 186; *99:* 56; *121:* 48; *208:* 190
Steadman, Henry *211:* 130
Steadman, Ralph *32:* 180; *123:* 143, 145
Stearn, Nick *183:* 26
Stearn, Todd *218:* 179
Steckler, June *90:* 178
Steele, Robert Gantt *169:* 174
Steichen, Edward *30:* 79
Steig, William *18:* 275, 276; *70:* 215, 216, 217, 218; *111:* 173, 174, 175, 176, 177
Stein, David Ezra *211:* 168
Stein, Harve *1:* 109
Steinberg, Saul *47:* 193
Steinel, William *23:* 146
Steiner, Charlotte *45:* 196
Steiner, Joan *110:* 219; *199:* 160, 161
Steirnagel, Michael *80:* 56
Stemp, Eric *60:* 184
Stephens, Alice Barber *66:* 208, 209
Stephens, Charles H. *YABC 2:* 279
Stephens, Pam *198:* 69
Stephens, Pat *126:* 110; *128:* 101

Stephens, William M. *21:* 165
Stephenson, Kristina *224:* 169
Steptoe, Javaka *151:* 203, 204; *190:* 169; *213:* 163, 164
Steptoe, John *8:* 197; *57:* 9; *63:* 158, 159, 160, 161,163, 164, 165, 166, 167; *96:* 4; *105:* 87
Stern, Simon *15:* 249, 250; *17:* 58; *34:* 192, 193
Sterret, Jane *53:* 27
Stetsios, Debbie *165:* 108, 109
Steven, Kat *158:* 237
Stevens, David *62:* 44
Stevens, Helen *189:* 31; *207:* 83
Stevens, Janet *40:* 126; *57:* 10, 11; *80:* 112; *90:* 221, 222; *109:* 156; *130:* 34; *166:* 202; *176:* 53, 116; *193:* 199, 200, 202; *208:* 127; *212:* 182
Stevens, Mary *11:* 193; *13:* 129; *43:* 95
Stevenson, Harvey *66:* 143; *80:* 201, 221; *153:* 60; *191:* 166
Stevenson, James *42:* 182, 183; *51:* 163; *66:* 184; *71:* 185, 187, 188; *78:* 262; *87:* 97; *113:* 182, 183,184, 185; *161:* 182, 183
Stevenson, Sucie *92:* 27; *104:* 194, 195; *112:* 168; *160:* 202; *194:* 172, 173; *195:* 166
Stewart, April Blair *75:* 210
Stewart, Arvis *33:* 98; *36:* 69; *60:* 118; *75:* 91; *127:* 4
Stewart, Charles *2:* 205
Stewart, Joel *151:* 205; *211:* 170, 171
Stieg, William *172:* 58
Stiles, Fran *26:* 85; *78:* 56; *82:* 150
Stillman, Susan *44:* 130; *76:* 83
Stimpson, Tom *49:* 171
Stimson, James *208:* 46
Stinemetz, Morgan *40:* 151
Stinson, Paul *110:* 86
Stirnweis, Shannon *10:* 164
Stites, Joe *86:* 96
Stobbs, William *1:* 48, 49; *3:* 68; *6:* 20; *17:* 117, 217; *24:* 150; *29:* 250; *60:* 179; *87:* 204, 205,206
Stock, Catherine *37:* 55; *65:* 198; *72:* 7; *99:* 225; *114:* 197, 198, 199; *126:* 3; *145:* 161; *161:* 82; *173:* 149; *208:* 210; *214:* 192, 194; *224:* 196, 197
Stockman, Jack *113:* 24
Stoeke, Janet Morgan *90:* 225; *136:* 196; *202:* 182, 183
Stoerrle, Tom *55:* 147
Stolp, Jaap *49:* 98
Stolp, Todd *89:* 195
Stone, David L. *87:* 154
Stone, David *9:* 173
Stone, David K. *4:* 38; *6:* 124; *9:* 180; *43:* 182; *60:* 70
Stone, Helen V. *6:* 209
Stone, Helen *44:* 121, 122, 126
Stone, Kazuko G. *134:* 43
Stone, Kyle M. *202:* 185
Stone, Phoebe *86:* 212; *134:* 213; *162:* 188; *205:* 145
Stone, Steve *166:* 213; *208:* 185; *220:* 57,58; *224:* 124
Stone, Tony *150:* 34, 35
Storms, Patricia *217:* 163
Storrings, Michael *191:* 108; *216:* 217
Stoud, Virginia A. *89:* 31
Stover, Jill *82:* 234
Stower, Adam *217:* 89
Strachan, Bruce *205:* 146
Stratton, Helen *33:* 151
Stratton-Porter, Gene *15:* 254, 259, 263, 264, 268, 269
Straub, Matt *192:* 176
Straub, Phillip *197:* 22
Streano, Vince *20:* 173
Street, Janet Travell *84:* 235
Streeter, Clive *121:* 2
Strickland, Shadra *209:* 179

Stringer, Lauren *129:* 187; *154:* 172, 173; *161:* 127; *183:* 187, 188
Strodl, Daniel *47:* 95
Strogart, Alexander *63:* 139
Stromoski, Rick *111:* 179; *124:* 161, 190
Strong, Joseph D., Jr. *YABC 2:* 330
Stroyer, Poul *13:* 221
Strugnell, Ann *27:* 38
Struzan, Drew *117:* 6
Stubbs, William *73:* 196
Stubis, Talivaldis *5:* 182, 183; *10:* 45; *11:* 9; *18:* 304; *20:* 127
Stubley, Trevor *14:* 43; *22:* 219; *23:* 37; *28:* 61; *87:* 26
Stuck, Marion *104:* 44
Stuecklen, Karl W. *8:* 34, 65; *23:* 103
Stull, Betty *11:* 46
Stutzman, Mark *119:* 99
Stutzmann, Laura *73:* 185
Suarez, Maribel *162:* 208; *200:* 202
Suave, Gordon *209:* 66
Suba, Susanne *4:* 202, 203; *14:* 261; *23:* 134; *29:* 222; *32:* 30
Sue, Majella Lue *209:* 182; *212:* 146
Sueling, Barbara *98:* 185
Sueling, Gwenn *98:* 186
Sugarman, Tracy *3:* 76; *8:* 199; *37:* 181, 182
Sugimoto, Yugo *170:* 144; *223:* 137
Sugita, Yutaka *36:* 180, 181
Suh, John *80:* 157
Sullivan, Dorothy *89:* 113
Sullivan, Edmund J. *31:* 86
Sullivan, James F. *19:* 280; *20:* 192
Sully, Tom *104:* 199, 200; *182:* 77
Sumichrast, Jozef *14:* 253; *29:* 168, 213
Sumiko *46:* 57
Summers, Leo *1:* 177; *2:* 273; *13:* 22
Summers, Mark *118:* 144
Summers, Mike *190:* 176
Sutton, Judith *94:* 164
Svarez, Juan *56:* 113
Svendsen, Mark *181:* 176
Svolinsky, Karel *17:* 104
Swain, Carol *172:* 182
Swain, Su Zan Noguchi *21:* 170
Swan, Susan *22:* 220, 221; *37:* 66; *60:* 146; *145:* 205; *181:* 168
Swann, Susan *86:* 55
Swanson, Karl *79:* 65; *89:* 186
Swarner, Kristina *203:* 62; *215:* 184
Swayne, Sam *53:* 143, 145
Swayne, Zoa *53:* 143, 145
Swearingen, Greg *152:* 56; *165:* 135; *173:* 2; *224:* 32; *225:* 188
Sweat, Lynn *25:* 206; *57:* 176; *73:* 184; *168:* 178
Sweet, Darrell K. *60:* 9; *69:* 86; *74:* 15; *75:* 215; *76:* 130, 131; *81:* 96, 122; *82:* 253; *83:* 11; *84:* 14; *85:* 37; *89:* 140; *90:* 6; *91:* 137,139; *95:* 160, 161; *126:* 25; *185:* 175; *195:* 132
Sweet, Darrell K. *1:* 163; *4:* 136; *164:* 175
Sweet, Melissa *71:* 94; *72:* 172; *111:* 82; *139:* 53, 58; *141:* 88; *142:* 231; *155:* 121; *159:* 121, 122; *172:* 185; *188:* 127; *209:* 81; *211:* 174, 175; *218:* 21
Sweet, Ozzie *31:* 149, 151, 152
Sweetland, Robert *12:* 194
Swiatkowska, Gabi *132:* 43; *175:* 139; *180:* 218; *183:* 176
Swope, Martha *43:* 160; *56:* 86, 87, 89
Sylvada, Peter *154:* 174
Sylvester, Natalie G. *22:* 222
Szafran, Gene *24:* 144
Szasz, Susanne *13:* 55, 226; *14:* 48
Szekeres, Cyndy *2:* 218; *5:* 185; *8:* 85; *11:* 166; *14:* 19; *16:* 57, 159; *26:* 49, 214; *34:* 205; *60:* 150, 151, 152, 153, 154; *73:* 224; *74:* 218; *131:* 213, 215
Szpura, Beata *81:* 68; *119:* 65; *168:* 201
Szuc, Jeff *220:* 188

T

Taback, Simms *40:* 207; *52:* 120; *57:* 34; *80:* 241; *104:* 202, 203; *170:* 176, 177; *205:* 183
Taber, Patricia *75:* 124
Tabor, Nancy Maria Grande *89:* 210; *161:* 188
Taddei, Richard *112:* 13, 14
Tadgell, Nicole *150:* 77; *161:* 20; *177:* 186; *209:* 16; *220:* 190, 191
Tadiello, Ed *133:* 200
Tafuri, Nancy *39:* 210; *75:* 199, 200; *92:* 75; *130:* 215, 216, 217
Tailfeathers, Gerald *86:* 85
Tait, Douglas *12:* 220; *74:* 105, 106
Takabayashi, Mari *113:* 112; *130:* 22; *156:* 169
Takahashi, Hideko *136:* 160; *187:* 6; *209:* 152, 187
Takakjian, Portia *15:* 274
Takashima, Shizuye *13:* 228
Talarczyk, June *4:* 173
Talbott, Hudson *84:* 240; *163:* 100; *212:* 191, 192, 193
Tallarico, Tony *116:* 197
Tallec, Olivier *218:* 4
Tallon, Robert *2:* 228; *43:* 200, 201, 202, 203, 204, 205,206, 207, 209
Tamaki, Jillian *201:* 188
Tamas, Szecsko *29:* 135
Tamburine, Jean *12:* 222
Tanaka, Yoko *215:* 187
Tancredi, Sharon *215:* 127
Tandy, H.R. *13:* 69
Tandy, Russell H. *65:* 9; *100:* 30, 131
Tang, Charles *81:* 202; *90:* 192
Tang, Susan *80:* 174; *108:* 158
Tang, You-shan *63:* 100
Tankersley, Paul *69:* 206; *133:* 219
Tannenbaum, Robert *48:* 181
Tanner, Jane *87:* 13; *97:* 37
Tanner, Tim *72:* 192; *84:* 35
Tanobe, Miyuki *23:* 221
Tarabay, Sharif *110:* 149; *113:* 123; *169:* 83
Tarkington, Booth *17:* 224, 225
Tarlow, Phyllis *61:* 198
Tate, Don *159:* 141, 191; *183:* 69; *186:* 120
Tauss, Herbert *95:* 179
Tauss, Marc *117:* 160; *126:* 155; *178:* 221; *197:* 7; *223:* 168
Tavares, Matt *159:* 192, 193; *198:* 188, 189, 190; *199:* 86
Taylor, Ann *41:* 226
Taylor, Dahl *129:* 157
Taylor, Geoff *93:* 156; *197:* 173, 175; *204:* 151, 152
Taylor, Isaac *41:* 228
Taylor, Mike *143:* 99, 100
Teague, Mark *83:* 6; *139:* 241; *170:* 180, 181; *205:* 150, 151
Teale, Edwin Way *7:* 196
Teason, James *1:* 14
Teckentrup, Britta *200:* 191, 192
Teeple, Lyn *33:* 147
Tee-Van, Helen Damrosch *10:* 176; *11:* 182
Teevee, Ningeokuluk *223:* 173
Teicher, Dick *50:* 211
Teichman, Mary *77:* 220; *124:* 208; *127:* 22; *197:* 33
Temertey, Ludmilla *96:* 232; *104:* 43, 45; *109:* 244
Tempest, Margaret *3:* 237, 238; *88:* 200
Temple, Frances *85:* 185, 186, 187
Temple, Herbert *45:* 201
Templeton, Owen *11:* 77
ten Cate, Marijke *183:* 193
Tenggren, Gustaf *18:* 277, 278, 279; *19:* 15; *28:* 86; *YABC2:* 145
Tennent, Julie *81:* 105
Tenneson, Joyce *153:* 166
Tenney, Gordon *24:* 204

Tenniel, John *74:* 234, 235; *100:* 89; *YABC 2:* 99; *153:* 63
Tepper, Matt *116:* 80
Terkel, Ari *103:* 162
Terry, Michael *180:* 209
Terry, Will *131:* 73; *205:* 155; *223:* 105
Teskey, Donald *71:* 51
Tessler, Manya *200:* 193
Thacher, Mary M. *30:* 72
Thackeray, William Makepeace *23:* 224, 228
Thamer, Katie *42:* 187
Tharlet, Eve *146:* 149
Thelwell, Norman *14:* 201
Theobalds, Prue *40:* 23
Theurer, Marilyn Churchill *39:* 195
Thiesing, Lisa *89:* 134; *95:* 202; *156:* 190; *159:* 195
Thiewes, Sam *133:* 114
Thisdale, François *223:* 55
Thistlethwaite, Miles *12:* 224
Thollander, Earl *11:* 47; *18:* 112; *22:* 224
Thomas, Allan *22:* 13
Thomas, Art *48:* 217
Thomas, Eric *28:* 49
Thomas, Harold *20:* 98
Thomas, Jacqui *125:* 95
Thomas, Jan *197:* 180
Thomas, Mark *42:* 136
Thomas, Martin *14:* 255
Thomas, Middy *177:* 114
Thompson, Arthur *34:* 107
Thompson, Carol *85:* 189; *95:* 75; *102:* 86; *147:* 166; *189:* 179, 180, 181; *190:* 84; *207:* 18
Thompson, Colin *95:* 204
Thompson, Ellen *51:* 88, 151; *60:* 33; *67:* 42; *77:* 148; *78:* 75, 219; *79:* 122, 170; *84:* 219; *85:* 97; *87:* 37; *88:* 192, 194; *89:* 80; *93:* 37; *98:* 59; *132:* 14
Thompson, George W. *22:* 18; *28:* 150; *33:* 135
Thompson, John *58:* 201; *102:* 226; *124:* 154; *128:* 228; *129:* 157; *150:* 49; *185:* 160; *191:* 192; *224:* 110
Thompson, Julie *44:* 158
Thompson, Katherine *132:* 146
Thompson, K. Dyble *84:* 6
Thompson, Miles *152:* 77
Thompson, Sharon *74:* 113; *158:* 60; *165:* 87
Thomson, Arline K. *3:* 264
Thomson, Bill *186:* 160
Thomson, Hugh *26:* 88
Thomson, Ross *36:* 179
Thorkelson, Gregg *95:* 183, 184; *98:* 58; *165:* 30, 31; *225:* 31, 32
Thorn, Lori *189:* 119
Thornberg, Dan *104:* 125
Thornburgh, Rebecca McKillip *143:* 37
Thorne, Diana *25:* 212
Thornhill, Jan *77:* 213
Thorpe, Peter *58:* 109
Thorvall, Kerstin *13:* 235
Threadgall, Colin *77:* 215
Thurber, James *13:* 239, 242, 243, 245, 248, 249
Thurman, Mark *63:* 173; *168:* 116
Tibbles, Jean-Paul *115:* 200
Tibbles, Paul *45:* 23
Tibo, Gilles *67:* 207; *107:* 199, 201
Tichenor, Tom *14:* 207
Tichnor, Richard *90:* 218
Tiegreen, Alan *36:* 143; *43:* 55, 56, 58; *77:* 200; *94:* 216, 217; *121:* 54, 59
Tierney, Tom *113:* 198, 200, 201
Tildes, Phyllis Limbacher *210:* 240
Tilley, Debbie *102:* 134; *133:* 226; *137:* 101; *159:* 96; *190:* 211, 212; *213:* 51
Tillman, Nancy *211:* 129, 178
Tillotson, Katherine *224:* 175
Tilney, F.C. *22:* 231
Timbs, Gloria *36:* 90

Timmins, Harry *2:* 171
Timmons, Bonnie *194:* 189
Tinkelman, Murray *12:* 225; *35:* 44
Titherington, Jeanne *39:* 90; *58:* 138; *75:* 79; *135:* 161
Tjader, Ella *209:* 14
Tobin, Nancy *145:* 197
Toddy, Irving *172:* 144
Tokunbo, Dimitrea *181:* 183; *187:* 182, 183
Tolbert, Jeff *128:* 69
Toledo, Francisco *197:* 182; *198:* 199
Toledo, Natalia *197:* 182
Tolford, Joshua *1:* 221
Tolkien, J.R.R. *2:* 243; *32:* 215
Tolman, Marije *195:* 43
Tolmie, Ken *15:* 292
Tomei, Lorna *47:* 168, 171
Tomes, Jacqueline *2:* 117; *12:* 139
Tomes, Margot *1:* 224; *2:* 120, 121; *16:* 207; *18:* 250; *20:* 7; *25:* 62; *27:* 78, 79; *29:* 81, 199; *33:* 82; *36:* 186, 187, 188, 189, 190; *46:* 129; *56:* 71; *58:* 183; *70:* 228; *75:* 73, 75; *80:* 80; *83:* 97; *90:* 205
Tommaso, Rich *200:* 198
Tommorow, Tom *223:* 176
Toner, Raymond John *10:* 179
Tong, Gary *66:* 215
Tongier, Stephen *82:* 32
Tooke, Susan *173:* 162
Toothill, Harry *6:* 54; *7:* 49; *25:* 219; *42:* 192
Toothill, Ilse *6:* 54
Topaz, Ksenia *224:* 94
Topolski, Feliks *44:* 48
Torbert, Floyd James *22:* 226
Torgersen, Don *55:* 157
Torline, Kevin *169:* 171
Tormey, Bertram M. *75:* 3, 4
Torrecilla, Pablo *176:* 207
Torres, Leyla *156:* 199, 201
Torrey, Helen *87:* 41
Torrey, Marjorie *34:* 105
Torrey, Richard *189:* 182; *205:* 24
Toschik, Larry *6:* 102
Totten, Bob *13:* 93
Toy, Julie *128:* 112
Trachok, Cathy *131:* 16
Tracy, Libba *82:* 24
Trago, Keith *158:* 253
Trail, Lee *55:* 157
Trang, To Ngoc *167:* 180
Trang, Winson *89:* 151
Trapani, Iza *116:* 202; *214:* 203
Travers, Bob *49:* 100; *63:* 145
Treatner, Meryl *95:* 180
Tremain, Ruthven *17:* 238
Tresilian, Stuart *25:* 53; *40:* 212
Trezzo, Loretta *86:* 45
Trier, Walter *14:* 96
Trimby, Elisa *47:* 199
Trinkle, Sally *53:* 27
Triplett, Gina *182:* 193; *188:* 100; *198:* 38
Tripp, F.J. *24:* 167
Tripp, Wallace *2:* 48; *7:* 28; *8:* 94; *10:* 54,76; *11:* 92; *31:* 170, 171; *34:* 203; *42:* 57; *60:* 157; *73:* 182
Trivas, Irene *53:* 4; *54:* 168; *82:* 46, 101
Trnka, Jiri *22:* 151; *43:* 212, 213, 214, 215; *YABC 1:* 30, 31
Trondheim, Lewis *182:* 183
Troughton, Joanna *37:* 186; *48:* 72
Troyer, Johannes *3:* 16; *7:* 18
Trudeau, G.B. *35:* 220, 221, 222; *48:* 119, 123, 126, 127,128, 129, 133; *168:* 189
Trueman, Matthew *165:* 208; *183:* 191; *220:* 61; *222:* 174
Truesdell, Sue *55:* 142; *108:* 219, 220; *212:* 202; *220:* 78
Tryon, Leslie *84:* 7; *139:* 214; *143:* 10; *181:* 10

Tseng, Jean *72:* 195; *94:* 102; *119:* 126; *151:* 106; *173:* 138, 139; *200:* 158
Tseng, Mou-sien *72:* 195; *94:* 102; *119:* 126; *151:* 106; *173:* 138, 139; *200:* 158
Tsinajinie, Andy *2:* 62
Tsinganos, Jim *180:* 142
Tsugami, Kyuzo *18:* 198, 199
Tucker, Ezra *156:* 31
Tuckwell, Jennifer *17:* 205
Tudor, Bethany *7:* 103
Tudor, Tasha *18:* 227; *20:* 185, 186, 187; *36:* 111; *69:* 196, 198; *100:* 44; *YABC 2:* 46, 314; *160:* 234
Tuerk, Hanne *71:* 201
Tugeau, Jeremy *199:* 170; *203:* 96
Tulloch, Maurice *24:* 79
Tunis, Edwin *1:* 218, 219; *28:* 209, 210, 211, 212
Tunnicliffe, C.F. *62:* 176; *177;* 178, 179; 181
Turkle, Brinton *1:* 211, 213; *2:* 249; *3:* 226; *11:* 3; *16:* 209; *20:* 22; *50:* 23; *67:* 50; *68:* 65; *79:* 205, 206, 207; *128:* 47; *YABC 1:* 79
Turnbull, Christopher J. *143:* 99, 100
Turner, Gwenda *59:* 195
Turner, Helen *203:* 154
Turska, Krystyna *12:* 103; *31:* 173, 174, 175; *56:* 32,34; *100:* 66
Tusa, Tricia *72:* 242; *111:* 180, 181; *157:* 165; *164:* 186; *189:* 40; *201:* 9; *207:* 163, 164
Tusan, Stan *6:* 58; *22:* 236, 237
Tuschman, Richard *219:* 100; *224:* 188; *225:* 175
Tworkov, Jack *47:* 207
Tyers, Jenny *89:* 220
Tylden-Wright, Jenny *114:* 119
Tyrol, Adelaide Murphy *103:* 27
Tyrrell, Frances *107:* 204
Tzimoulis, Paul *12:* 104

U

Uchida, Yoshiko *1:* 220
Uderzo *47:* 88
Udovic, David *189:* 185; *195:* 201
Ueno, Noriko *59:* 155
Ugliano, Natascia *196:* 186
Ulm, Robert *17:* 238
Ulrich, George *73:* 15; *75:* 136, 139; *99:* 150
Ulriksen, Mark *101:* 58; *182:* 43; *210:* 243
Unada *84:* 67
    See Gliewe, Unada
Underhill, Liz *53:* 159
Underwood, Beck *192:* 36
Underwood, Clarence *40:* 166
Unger, Jim *67:* 208
Ungerer, Tomi *5:* 188; *9:* 40; *18:* 188; *29:* 175; *33:* 221, 222, 223, 225; *71:* 48; *106:* 209, 210, 211, 212
Unwin, Nora S. *3:* 65, 234, 235; *4:* 237; *44:* 173, 174; *YABC 1:* 59; *2:* 301
Upitis, Alvis *145:* 179
Urban, Helle *149:* 243
Urbanovic, Jackie *86:* 86; *189:* 186, 187
Urberuaga, Emilio *219:* 110, 175
U'ren, Andrea *213:* 177
Uris, Jill *49:* 188, 197
Ursell, Martin *50:* 51
Utpatel, Frank *18:* 114
Utz, Lois *5:* 190

V

Vagin, Vladimir *66:* 10; *142:* 215
Vaillancourt, Francois *107:* 199
Vainio, Pirkko *123:* 157, 158
Valério, Geraldo *180:* 225; *194:* 116

Vallejo, Boris *62:* 130; *72:* 212; *91:* 38; *93:* 61
Van Abbe, S. *16:* 142; *18:* 282; *31:* 90; *YABC 2:* 157, 161
Van Allsburg, Chris *37:* 205, 206; *53:* 161, 162, 163, 165,166, 167, 168, 169, 170, 171; *105:* 215, 216, 217, 218; *156:* 176, 177, 178
Vance, James *65:* 28
Van Der Linde, Henry *99:* 17
van der Meer, Ron *98:* 204, 205
van der Meer, Atie *98:* 204, 205
Vandivert, William *21:* 175
Van Dongen, H.R. *81:* 97
Van Dusen, Chris W. *173:* 169
Vane, Mitch *210:* 160; *218:* 152
Van Everen, Jay *13:* 160; *YABC 1:* 121
Van Fleet, John *165:* 12, 13
Van Frankenhuyzen, Gijsbert *145:* 230; *149:* 164; *184:* 151; *210:* 248
van Genechten, Guido *165:* 226
van Haeringen, Annemarie *193:* 206
Van Horn, William *43:* 218
van Hout, Mies *195:* 191; *207:* 58
van Kampen, Vlasta *194:* 217
van Lawick, Hugo *62:* 76, 79
Van Lieshout, Maria *201:* 196; *223:* 119
Van Loon, Hendrik Willem *18:* 285, 289, 291
van Munching, Paul *83:* 85
van Ommen, Sylvia *186:* 192
Van Patter, Bruce *183:* 195
Van Rynbach, Iris *102:* 192
Van Sciver, Ruth *37:* 162
VanSeveren, Joe *63:* 182
Van Stockum, Hilda *5:* 193
Van Vleet, John *213:* 180
Van Wassenhove, Sue *202:* 193
Van Wely, Babs *16:* 50; *79:* 16
Van Wright, Cornelius *72:* 18; *102:* 208; *116:* 107; *152:* 236; *173:* 170, 171; *199:* 185
Van Zyle, Jon *103:* 125; *160:* 181, 182; *176:* 199, 200; *221:* 128
Vardzigulyants, Ruben *90:* 54
Varga, Judy *29:* 196
Vargo, Kurt *79:* 224
Varley, Susan *61:* 199; *63:* 176, 177; *101:* 148; *134:* 220
Varon, Sara *195:* 208
Vasconcellos, Daniel *80:* 42
Vasiliu, Mircea *2:* 166, 253; *9:* 166; *13:* 58; *68:* 42
Vaughn, Frank *34:* 157
Vavra, Robert *8:* 206
Vawter, Will *17:* 163
Vayas, Diana *71:* 61
Vazquez, Carlos *125:* 184
Veeder, Larry *18:* 4
Velasquez, Eric *45:* 217; *61:* 45; *63:* 110, 111; *88:* 162; *90:* 34, 144; *94:* 213; *107:* 147; *132:* 192; *138:* 213; *159:* 126; *181:* 184; *184:* 96; *191:* 16; *192:* 234; *208:* 37; *214:* 81
Velasquez, Jose A. *63:* 73
Velez, Walter *71:* 75; *91:* 154; *121:* 181; *168:* 49; *207:* 52
Velthuijs, Max *110:* 228, 229
Vendrell, Carme Sole *42:* 205
Venezia, Mike *54:* 17
Venti, Anthony Bacon *124:* 103; *126:* 26
Venturo, Piero *61:* 194, 195
Ver Beck, Frank *18:* 16, 17
Verkaaik, Ben *110:* 209
Verling, John *71:* 27
Verney, John *14:* 225; *75:* 8
Vernon, Ursula *204:* 157
Verrier, Suzanne *5:* 20; *23:* 212
Verroken, Sarah *223:* 178
Versace, Marie *2:* 255
Verstraete, Randy *108:* 193
Vess, Charles *215:* 201
Vestal, H.B. *9:* 134; *11:* 101; *27:* 25; *34:* 158
Vestergaard, Hope *190:* 203
Vicatan *59:* 146

Vickrey, Robert *45:* 59, 64
Victor, Joan Berg *30:* 193
Vieceli, Emma *210:* 245
Viereck, Ellen *3:* 242; *14:* 229
Vigna, Judith *15:* 293; *102:* 194, 195, 196, 197
Vila, Laura *207:* 172
Vilato, Gaspar E. *5:* 41
Villiard, Paul *51:* 178
Vimnera, A. *23:* 154
Vincent, Eric *34:* 98
Vincent, Felix *41:* 237
Vincent, Gabrielle *121:* 175
Vip *45:* 164
Viskupic, Gary *83:* 48
Vitale, Stefano *109:* 71, 107; *114:* 219, 220; *123:* 106; *138:* 232; *180:* 228, 229; *212:* 38; *225:* 191, 192, 193
Vivas, Julie *51:* 67, 69; *96:* 225; *197:* 190; *199:* 71
Voake, Charlotte *114:* 221, 222; *180:* 232
Vo-Dinh, Mai *16:* 272; *60:* 191
Vogel, Ilse-Margret *14:* 230
Voigt, Erna *35:* 228
Vojnar, Kamil *95:* 31; *114:* 4; *115:* 62; *121:* 90; *124:* 72; *130:* 31; *141:* 81; *146:* 196; *150:* 123; *158:* 5, 6; *158:* 154; *171:* 119, 188; *179:* 15; *180:* 112; *203:* 74; *223:* 30
Vojtech, Anna *42:* 190; *108:* 222, 223; *150:* 203; *174:* 173
von Buhler, Cynthia *149:* 237; *162:* 177; *177:* 205; *180:* 77; *185:* 214, 215, 216
von Roehl, Angela *126:* 191
von Schmidt, Eric *8:* 62; *50:* 209, 210
von Schmidt, Harold *30:* 80
Vosburgh, Leonard *1:* 161; *7:* 32; *15:* 295, 296; *23:* 110; *30:* 214; *43:* 181
Voss, Tom *127:* 104
Voter, Thomas W. *19:* 3, 9
Vroman, Tom *10:* 29
Vulliamy, Clara *72:* 65

W

Waber, Bernard *47:* 209, 210, 211, 212, 213, 214; *95:* 215, 216, 217; *156:* 203, 205, 206, 207
Wachenje, Benjamin *194:* 170
Wack, Jeff *95:* 140; *110:* 90
Wagner, John *8:* 200; *52:* 104
Wagner, Ken *2:* 59
Wagner, Michael *211:* 159
Wahman, Wendy *218:* 186
Waide, Jan *29:* 225; *36:* 139
Wainwright, Jerry *14:* 85
Waites, Joan C. *171:* 2
Wakeen, Sandra *47:* 97
Wakiyama, Hanako *171:* 96; *192:* 236; *200:* 16
Waldherr, Kris *81:* 186
Waldman, Bruce *15:* 297; *43:* 178
Waldman, Neil *35:* 141; *50:* 163; *51:* 180; *54:* 78; *77:* 112; *79:* 162; *82:* 174; *84:* 5, 56, 106; *94:* 232, 233, 234; *96:* 41; *111:* 139; *113:* 9; *118:* 30; *142:* 220, 223; *203:* 173, 174
Waldrep, Richard *111:* 147; *198:* 202
Walker, Brian *144:* 128
Walker, Charles *1:* 46; *4:* 59; *5:* 177; *11:* 115; *19:* 45; *34:* 74; *62:* 168; *72:* 218
Walker, Dugald Stewart *15:* 47; *32:* 202; *33:* 112
Walker, Gil *8:* 49; *23:* 132; *34:* 42
Walker, Jeff *55:* 154; *123:* 116
Walker, Jim *10:* 94
Walker, Mort *8:* 213
Walker, Norman *41:* 37; *45:* 58
Walker, Stephen *12:* 229; *21:* 174
Wallace, Beverly Dobrin *19:* 259
Wallace, Cly *87:* 93

Wallace, Ian *53:* 176, 177; *56:* 165, 166; *58:* 4; *98:* 4; *101:* 191; *112:* 124; *141:* 197, 198, 199, 200; *151:* 212; *219:* 180, 182
Wallace, John *105:* 228
Wallace, Nancy Elizabeth *141:* 204; *186:* 195, 197, 199; *222:* 191, 192, 193, 194
Wallenta, Adam *123:* 180
Waller, S.E. *24:* 36
Wallner, Alexandra *15:* 120; *156:* 183
Wallner, John C. *9:* 77; *10:* 188; *11:* 28; *14:* 209; *31:* 56, 118; *37:* 64; *51:* 186, 187, 188, 189, 190, 191,192, 193, 194, 195; *52:* 96; *53:* 23, 26; *71:* 99; *73:* 158; *89:* 215; *141:* 9
Wallner, John *162:* 17
Wallower, Lucille *11:* 226
Walotsky, Ron *93:* 87
Walsh, Ellen Stoll *99:* 209; *147:* 219; *194:* 194, 195, 196
Walsh, Rebecca *158:* 193; *217:* 169, 170
Walsh, Vivian *149:* 215; *158:* 227
Walters, Anita *205:* 163
Walters, Audrey *18:* 294
Walther, Tom *31:* 179
Walton, Garry *69:* 149
Walton, Tony *11:* 164; *24:* 209; *153:* 8; *177:* 73
Waltrip, Lela *9:* 195
Waltrip, Mildred *3:* 209; *37:* 211
Waltrip, Rufus *9:* 195
Wan *12:* 76
Wan, Shelly *212:* 131
Wang, Lin *221:* 179
Wang, Shaoli *216:* 220
Wang, Suling *191:* 183; *213:* 194
Warburton, Sarah *154:* 187
Wappers, G. *121:* 40
Ward, Chad Michael *217:* 121
Ward, Fred *52:* 19
Ward, Helen *72:* 244; *144:* 240, 242
Ward, John *42:* 191; *96:* 54; *97:* 110; *123:* 105; *124:* 71; *173:* 66; *221:* 55
Ward, Keith *2:* 107; *132:* 69
Ward, Leslie *34:* 126; *36:* 87
Ward, Lynd *1:* 99, 132, 133, 150; *2:* 108, 158, 196, 259; *18:* 86; *27:* 56; *29:* 79, 187, 253, 255; *36:* 199,200, 201, 202, 203, 204, 205, 206, 207, 209; *43:* 34; *56:* 28; *60:* 116; *100:* 65
Ward, Peter *37:* 116
Waring, Geoff *172:* 84
Warhola, James *92:* 5; *115:* 85, 87; *118:* 174, 175, 177; *176:* 84; *187:* 189, 190; *223:* 102
Warner, Ben *159:* 171
Warner, Peter *14:* 87
Warner, Sally *214:* 210
Warnes, Tim *175:* 159; *202:* 188; *216:* 224
Warnick, Elsa *113:* 223
Warren, Betsy *2:* 101
Warren, Jim *85:* 81
Warren, Marion Cray *14:* 215
Warshaw, Jerry *30:* 197, 198; *42:* 165
Wasden, Kevin *102:* 162
Washington, Nevin *20:* 123
Washington, Phyllis *20:* 123
Wasserman, Amy L. *92:* 110; *209:* 95
Waterman, Stan *11:* 76
Watkins-Pitchford, D.J. *6:* 215, 217
Watling, James *67:* 210; *78:* 112; *101:* 81; *117:* 189, 190; *127:* 119, 120
Watson, Aldren A. *2:* 267; *5:* 94; *13:* 71; *19:* 253; *32:* 220; *42:* 193, 194, 195, 196, 197, 198, 199, 200, 201; *YABC 2:* 202
Watson, G. *83:* 162
Watson, Gary *19:* 147; *36:* 68; *41:* 122; *47:* 139
Watson, J.D. *22:* 86
Watson, Jesse Joshua *197:* 124; *199:* 181; *202:* 136
Watson, Karen *11:* 26
Watson, Mary *117:* 193
Watson, Richard Jesse *62:* 188, 189; *211:* 201

Watson, Wendy *5:* 197; *13:* 101; *33:* 116; *46:* 163; *64:* 12; *74:* 242, 243; *91:* 21; *142:* 228; *215:* 79
Watt, Mélanie *136:* 206; *193:* 211
Wattenberg, Jane *174:* 200; *185:* 46; *187:* 108
Watterson, Bill *66:* 223, 225, 226
Watts, Bernadette *4:* 227; *103:* 182, 183
Watts, James *59:* 197; *74:* 145; *86:* 124
Watts, John *37:* 149
Watts, Leslie Elizabeth *150:* 207; *165:* 106; *209:* 67
Watts, Stan *116:* 205
Weatherby, Mark Alan *77:* 141
Webb, Jennifer *110:* 79
Webb, Lanny *142:* 175
Webb, Sophie *135:* 214
Webber, Helen *3:* 141
Webber, Irma E. *14:* 238
Weber, Erik *56:* 19, 20
Weber, Florence *40:* 153
Weber, Jill *127:* 227, 228; *189:* 163; *208:* 157; *209:* 190, 191; *216:* 46
Weber, Roland *61:* 204
Weber, Sam *190:* 227
Weber, William J. *14:* 239
Webster, Jean *17:* 241
Weeks, Sarah *162:* 39
Wegman, William *78:* 243
Wegner, Fritz *14:* 250; *20:* 189; *44:* 165; *86:* 62
Weidenear, Reynold H. *21:* 122
Weigel, Jeff *170:* 193
Weihs, Erika *4:* 21; *15:* 299; *72:* 201; *107:* 207, 208
Weil, Lisl *7:* 203; *10:* 58; *21:* 95; *22:* 188,217; *33:* 193
Weiman, Jon *50:* 162, 165; *52:* 103; *54:* 78, 79, 81; *78:* 80; *82:* 107; *93:* 82; *97:* 69; *105:* 179; *193:* 65
Weiner, Greg *215:* 21
Weiner, Sandra *14:* 240
Weiner, Scott *55:* 27
Weinhaus, Karen Ann *53:* 90; *71:* 50; *86:* 124
Weinman, Brad *197:* 20
Weinstock, Robert *204:* 165, 166
Weisgard, Leonard *1:* 65; *2:* 191, 197, 204, 264, 265; *5:* 108; *21:* 42; *30:* 200, 201, 203, 204; *41:* 47; *44:* 125; *53:* 25; *85:* 196, 198, 200, 201; *100:* 139,207; *YABC 2:* 13
Weisman, David *173:* 47
Weiss, Ellen *44:* 202
Weiss, Emil *1:* 168; *7:* 60
Weiss, Harvey *1:* 145, 223; *27:* 224, 227; *68:* 214; *76:* 245, 246, 247
Weiss, Nicki *33:* 229
Weissman, Bari *49:* 72; *90:* 125; *139:* 142
Weitzman, David L. *172:* 199
Welch, Sheila Kelly *130:* 221
Welkes, Allen *68:* 218
Wellington, Monica *99:* 223; *157:* 259, 260, 261; *222:* 197, 198, 199, 200
Welliver, Norma *76:* 94
Wellner, Fred *127:* 53
Wells, Frances *1:* 183
Wells, H.G. *20:* 194, 200
Wells, Haru *53:* 120, 121
Wells, Robert E. *184:* 208
Wells, Rosemary *6:* 49; *18:* 297; *60:* 32; *66:* 203; *69:* 215, 216; *114:* 227; *118:* 149, 150; *156:* 188, 189, 190, 191; *207:* 180, 181, 182, 183
Wells, Rufus III *56:* 111, 113
Wells, Susan *22:* 43
Wendelin, Rudolph *23:* 234
Wengenroth, Stow *37:* 47
Weninger, Brigitte *189:* 192, 194
Werenskiold, Erik *15:* 6; *62:* 17
Werner, Honi *24:* 110; *33:* 41; *88:* 122
Werth, Kurt *7:* 122; *14:* 157; *20:* 214; *39:* 128
Wesson,
West, Harry A. *124:* 38

Westcott, Nadine Bernard *68:* 46; *84:* 49; *86:*
133; *106:* 199; *111:* 78; *113:* 111; *130:* 224;
139: 54; *158:* 256; *194:* 199
Westerberg, Christine *29:* 226
Westerduin, Anne *105:* 229
Westerman, Johanna *162:* 206
Weston, Martha *29:* 116; *30:* 213; *33:* 85, 100;
53: 181, 182, 183, 184; *77:* 95; *80:* 152;
119: 196,197, 198, 199; *127:* 189; *133:* 196;
209: 199
Wetherbee, Margaret *5:* 3
Wexler, Jerome *49:* 73; *150:* 129
Whalley, Peter *50:* 49
Whamond, Dave *222:* 203
Whatley, Bruce *186:* 93, 95; *207:* 127; *213:*
183, 184
Wheatley, Arabelle *11:* 231; *16:* 276
Wheeler, Cindy *49:* 205
Wheeler, Dora *44:* 179
Wheelright, Rowland *15:* 81; *YABC 2:* 286
Whelan, Michael *56:* 108; *70:* 27, 29, 67, 68,
148; *74:* 18; *84:* 14; *91:* 195, 196; *95:* 147;
98: 150, 151; *106:* 157; *113:* 218, 220; *116:*
99, 100
Whelan, Patrick *135:* 145
Whistler, Rex *16:* 75; *30:* 207, 208
White, Beth *216:* 139
White, Craig *110:* 130; *119:* 193; *130:* 33;
179: 31
White, David Omar *5:* 56; *18:* 6
White, Joan *83:* 225
White, Lee *221:* 176; *223:* 188, 189, 190
White, Martin *51:* 197; *85:* 127
Whitear *32:* 26
Whitehead, Beck *86:* 171
Whitehead, Jenny *221:* 16
Whitehead, S.B. *154:* 132
Whithorne, H.S. *7:* 49
Whitman, Candace *208:* 208
Whitney, George Gillett *3:* 24
Whitney, Jean *99:* 53
Whitson, Paul *102:* 161
Whittam, Geoffrey *30:* 191
Whyte, Mary *96:* 127
Wiberg, Harald *38:* 127; *93:* 215
Wick, Walter *77:* 128
Wickstrom, Sylvie *106:* 87; *169:* 180; *214:*
110
Wickstrom, Thor *200:* 205
Widener, Terry *105:* 230; *106:* 7; *163:* 23;
200: 17; *209:* 195
Wiese, Kurt *3:* 255; *4:* 206; *14:* 17; *17:* 18,
19; *19:* 47; *24:* 152; *25:* 212; *32:* 184; *36:*
211,213, 214, 215, 216, 217, 218; *45:* 161;
100: 92
Wiesner, David *33:* 47; *51:* 106; *57:* 67; *58:*
55; *64:* 78, 79, 81; *69:* 233; *72:* 247, 248,
249, 251,252, 253, 254; *83:* 134; *104:* 31;
117: 197, 199, 200, 202; *139:* 223, 224; *151:*
51; *181:* 189, 190
Wiesner, William *4:* 100; *5:* 200, 201; *14:* 262
Wight, Eric *218:* 190
Wiggins, George *6:* 133
Wijngaard, Juan *111:* 36; *114:* 124
Wikkelsoe, Otto *45:* 25, 26
Wikland, Ilon *5:* 113; *8:* 150; *38:* 124, 125,
130; *127:* 162
Wikler, Madeline *114:* 233
Wilbur, C. Keith, M.D. *27:* 228
Wilburn, Kathy *53:* 102; *68:* 234
Wilcox, Cathy *105:* 123
Wilcox, J.A.J. *34:* 122
Wilcox, Lydia *207:* 187
Wilcox, R. Turner *36:* 219
Wild, Jocelyn *46:* 220, 221, 222; *80:* 117
Wilde, George *7:* 139
Wildsmith, Brian *16:* 281, 282; *18:* 170, 171;
66: 25; *69:* 224, 225, 227; *77:* 103; *83:* 218;
124: 214,217, 219
Wildsmith, Mike *140:* 229

Wilhelm, Hans *58:* 189, 191; *73:* 157; *77:*
127; *135:* 229, 230, 233, 234; *196:* 209
Wilkin, Eloise *36:* 173; *49:* 208, 209, 210
Wilkinson, Barry *50:* 213
Wilkinson, Gerald *3:* 40
Wilkon, Jozef *31:* 183, 184; *71:* 206, 207, 209;
133: 222
Wilks, Mike *34:* 24; *44:* 203; *224:* 193
Willems, Mo *154:* 245, 246, 247; *180:* 236,
237, 239
Willey, Bee *103:* 129; *139:* 159; *173:* 115
Willhoite, Michael A. *71:* 214
William, Maria *168:* 51
Williams, Berkeley, Jr. *64:* 75
Williams, Ferelith Eccles *22:* 238
Williams, Garth *1:* 197; *2:* 49, 270; *4:* 205;
15: 198, 302, 304, 307; *16:* 34; *18:* 283,
298, 299, 300, 301; *29:* 177, 178, 179, 232,
233, 241, 242, 243, 244, 245, 248; *40:* 106;
66: 229, 230, 231, 233, 234; *71:* 192; *73:*
218, 219, 220; *78:* 261; *100:* 251, 252, 255;
136: 117; *YABC 2:* 15, 16, 19
Williams, J. Scott *48:* 28
Williams, Jennifer *102:* 201
Williams, Jenny *60:* 202; *81:* 21; *88:* 71
Williams, Kent *180:* 18
Williams, Kit *44:* 206, 207, 208, 209, 211, 212
Williams, Marcia *97:* 214; *159:* 208, 209
Williams, Maureen *12:* 238
Williams, Patrick *14:* 218
Williams, Richard *44:* 93; *72:* 229; *74:* 133;
78: 155, 237; *91:* 178; *110:* 212; *136:* 201,
202, 203; *152:* 115
Williams, Sam *124:* 222; *153:* 11; *177:* 201,
202; *180:* 34; *212:* 49
Williams, Sophy *135:* 236
Williams, Vera B. *53:* 186, 187, 188, 189; *102:*
201, 202, 203; *210:* 65
Williamson, Alex *177:* 180; *205:* 50
Williamson, Mel *60:* 9
Willingham, Fred *104:* 206; *154:* 157
Willis, Adam *181:* 75; *209:* 11
Willmore, J.T. *54:* 113, 114
Wilsdorf, Anne *180:* 122; *189:* 124; *191:* 195
Wilson, Anne *160:* 114; *224:* 199, 200
Wilson, Charles Banks *17:* 92; *43:* 73
Wilson, Connie *113:* 179
Wilson, Dagmar *10:* 47
Wilson, Dawn *67:* 161; *81:* 120; *113:* 158
Wilson, Edward A. *6:* 24; *16:* 149; *20:* 220,
221; *22:* 87; *26:* 67; *38:* 212, 214, 215, 216,
217
Wilson, Forrest *27:* 231
Wilson, Gahan *35:* 234; *41:* 136
Wilson, George *76:* 87
Wilson, Helen Miranda *140:* 61
Wilson, Jack *17:* 139
Wilson, Janet *77:* 154; *96:* 114; *99:* 219, 220;
153: 64 *106:* 122; *130:* 210; *145:* 178; *173:*
64
Wilson, John *22:* 240
Wilson, Maurice *46:* 224
Wilson, Patten *35:* 61
Wilson, Peggy *15:* 4; *84:* 20
Wilson, Phil *181:* 29
Wilson, Rowland B. *30:* 170
Wilson, Sarah *50:* 215
Wilson, Tom *33:* 232
Wilson, W.N. *22:* 26
Wilson-Max, Ken *170:* 196; *180:* 181
Wilton, Nicholas *103:* 52; *183:* 111
Wilwerding, Walter J. *9:* 32
Wimmer, Mike *63:* 6; *70:* 121; *75:* 186; *76:*
21,22, 23; *91:* 114; *97:* 45, 68; *98:* 28; *107:*
130; *146:* 21; *149:* 47; *173:* 126; *193:* 21,
25; *194:* 204, 205
Winborn, Marsha *78:* 34; *99:* 70; *192:* 20
Winch, John *165:* 233
Winchester, Linda *13:* 231
Wind, Betty *28:* 158
Windham, Kathryn Tucker *14:* 260

Windham, Sophie *184:* 212
Winfield, Alison *115:* 78; *214:* 121
Winfield, Wayne *72:* 23
Wing, Gary *64:* 147
Wing, Ron *50:* 85
Wingerter, Linda S. *132:* 199; *174:* 181; *200:*
196
Winick, Judd *124:* 227, 228, 229
Winn-Lederer, Ilene *202:* 91
Winnick, Karen B. *211:* 207
Winslow, Will *21:* 124
Winstead, Rosie *180:* 243
Winsten, Melanie Willa *41:* 41
Winter, Jeanette *151:* 240, 241, 242; *184:* 215,
217, 218, 219
Winter, Milo *15:* 97; *19:* 221; *21:* 181, 203,
204, 205; *64:* 19; *YABC 2:* 144
Winter, Paula *48:* 227
Winter, Susan *163:* 177; *182:* 201
Winters, Greg *70:* 117
Winters, Nina *62:* 194
Wise, Louis *13:* 68
Wiseman, Ann *31:* 187
Wiseman, B. *4:* 233
Wishnefsky, Phillip *3:* 14
Wiskur, Darrell *5:* 72; *10:* 50; *18:* 246
Wisniewski, David *95:* 220, 221
Wisniewski, Robert *95:* 10; *119:* 192
Withee, Maureen *225:* 42
Witschonke, Alan *153:* 149, 150
Witt, Dick *80:* 244
Wittmann, Patrick *162:* 204
Wittman, Sally *30:* 219
Wittner, Dale *99:* 43
Wittwer, Hala *158:* 267; *195:* 80
Woehr, Lois *12:* 5
Wohlberg, Meg *12:* 100; *14:* 197; *41:* 255
Wohnoutka, Mike *137:* 68; *190:* 199; *195:*
218; *205:* 132; *221:* 6
Wojtowycz, David *167:* 168
Woldin, Beth Weiner *34:* 211
Wolf, Elizabeth *133:* 151; *208:* 175
Wolf, J. *16:* 91
Wolf, Janet *78:* 254
Wolf, Linda *33:* 163
Wolfe, Corey *72:* 213
Wolfe, Frances *216:* 227
Wolfe, Gillian *199:* 193
Wolff, Ashley *50:* 217; *81:* 216; *156:* 216,
217; *170:* 57; *174:* 174; *184:* 72; *203:* 181,
182, 183, 184
Wolff, Glenn *178:* 230
Wolff, Jason *213:* 186
Wolfsgruber, Linda *166:* 61
Wondriska, William *6:* 220
Wong, Janet S. *98:* 225; *152:* 43
Wong, Ken *224:* 23
Wong, Nicole *174:* 13; *214:* 216; *215:* 25
Wonsetler, John C. *5:* 168
Wood, Audrey *50:* 221, 222, 223; *81:* 219,
221; *198:* 206
Wood, Don *50:* 220, 225, 226, 228, 229; *81:*
218, 220; *139:* 239, 240
Wood, Grant *19:* 198
Wood, Heather *133:* 108
Wood, Ivor *58:* 17
Wood, Jakki *211:* 209
Wood, Muriel *36:* 119; *77:* 167; *171:* 55; *187:*
46
Wood, Myron *6:* 220
Wood, Owen *18:* 187; *64:* 202, 204, 205, 206,
208, 210
Wood, Rob *193:* 48
Wood, Ruth *8:* 11
Woodbridge, Curtis *133:* 138; *204:* 113
Wooding, Sharon L. *66:* 237
Woodruff, Liza *132:* 239; *182:* 46, 204
Woodruff, Thomas *171:* 73
Woods, John, Jr. *109:* 142
Woodson, Jack *10:* 201
Woodson, Jacqueline *94:* 242

Woodward, Alice *26:* 89; *36:* 81
Wool, David *26:* 27
Woolley, Janet *112:* 75
Woolman, Steven *106:* 47; *163:* 73
Wooten, Vernon *23:* 70; *51:* 170
Worboys, Evelyn *1:* 166, 167
Word, Reagan *103:* 204
Wormell, Christopher *154:* 251; *202:* 206
Worth, Jo *34:* 143
Worth, Wendy *4:* 133
Wosmek, Frances *29:* 251
Wrenn, Charles L. *38:* 96; *YABC 1:* 20, 21
Wright, Barbara Mullarney *98:* 161
Wright, Cliff *168:* 203
Wright, Dare *21:* 206
Wright-Frierson, Virginia *58:* 194; *110:* 246
Wright, George *YABC 1:* 268
Wright, Joseph *30:* 160
Wronker, Lili Cassel *3:* 247; *10:* 204; *21:* 10
Wu, Donald *200:* 18
Wummer, Amy *154:* 181; *168:* 150; *176:* 85; *201:* 202, 203; *218:* 154
Wyant, Alexander Helwig *110:* 19
Wyatt, David *97:* 9; *101:* 44; *114:* 194; *140:* 20; *167:* 13; *188:* 48
Wyatt, Stanley *46:* 210
Wyeth, Andrew *13:* 40; *YABC 1:* 133, 134
Wyeth, Jamie *41:* 257
Wyeth, N.C. *13:* 41; *17:* 252, 253, 254, 255, 256, 257, 258, 259, 264, 265, 266, 267, 268; *18:* 181; *19:* 80, 191, 200; *21:* 57, 183; *22:* 91; *23:* 152; *24:* 28, 99; *35:* 61; *41:* 65; *100:* 206; *YABC1:* 133, 223; *2:* 53, 75, 171, 187, 317
Wyman, Cherie R. *91:* 42
Wynne, Patricia J. *210:* 260; *223:* 184

X

Xuan, YongSheng *119:* 202, 207, 208; *140:* 36; *187:* 21

Y

Yaccarino, Dan *141:* 208, 209; *147:* 171; *192:* 244, 245; *207:* 168
Yakovetic, Joe *59:* 202; *75:* 85
Yalowitz, Paul *93:* 33; *211:* 92
Yamaguchi, Marianne *85:* 118
Yamasaki, James *167:* 93
Yang, Belle *170:* 198
Yang, Jay *1:* 8; *12:* 239
Yap, Weda *6:* 176

Yaroslava
   See Mills, Yaroslava Surmach
Yashima, Taro *14:* 84
Yates, John *74:* 249, 250
Yates, Kelly *208:* 214
Yayo *178:* 88
Yeatts, Tabatha *215:* 210
Yee, Cora *166:* 233
Yee, Wong Herbert *115:* 216, 217; *172:* 204, 205; *194:* 59
Yelchin, Eugene *204:* 4
Yeo, Brad *135:* 121; *192:* 106
Yerxa, Leo *181:* 195
Yezerski, Thomas F. *162:* 29
Ylla
   See Koffler, Camilla
Yohn, F.C. *23:* 128; *YABC 1:* 269
Yoo, Taeeun *191:* 198
Yorinks, Adrienne *144:* 248; *200:* 214
Yorke, David *80:* 178
Yoshida, Toshi *77:* 231
Yoshikawa, Sachiko *168:* 104; *177:* 28; *181:* 196, 197; *225:* 115
Youll, Paul *91:* 218
Youll, Stephen *92:* 227; *118:* 136, 137; *164:* 248; *202:* 92
Young, Amy L. *185:* 218; *190:* 46
Young, Cybéle *167:* 9
Young, Ed *7:* 205; *10:* 206; *40:* 124; *63:* 142; *74:* 250, 251, 252, 253; *75:* 227; *81:* 159; *83:* 98; *94:* 154; *115:* 160; *137:* 162; *YABC 2:* 242; *173:* 174, 175, 176; *205:* 29; *212:* 82; *221:* 72
Young, Mary O'Keefe *77:* 95; *80:* 247; *134:* 214; *140:* 213; *211:* 223, 225
Young, Noela *8:* 221; *89:* 231; *97:* 195
Young, Paul *190:* 222; *225:* 38
Young, Selina *153:* 12; *201:* 204, 205
Yuen, Sammy *223:* 46
Yum, Hyewon *211:* 228
Yun, Cheng Mung *60:* 143
Yung, Jennifer *220:* 136

Z

Zacharow, Christopher *88:* 98
Zacks, Lewis *10:* 161
Zadig *50:* 58
Zaffo, George *42:* 208
Zagwyn, Deborah Turney *138:* 227
Zahares, Wade *193:* 219
Zaid, Barry *50:* 127; *51:* 201
Zaidenberg, Arthur *34:* 218, 219, 220
Zalben, Jane Breskin *7:* 211; *79:* 230, 231, 233; *170:* 202

Zallinger, Jean *4:* 192; *8:* 8, 129; *14:* 273; *68:* 36; *80:* 254; *115:* 219, 220, 222
Zallinger, Rudolph F. *3:* 245
Zakrajsek, Molly *177:* 146
Zappa, Ahmet *180:* 250
Zebot, George *83:* 214
Zecca, Katherine *207:* 195
Zeck, Gerry *40:* 232
Zeff, Joe *181:* 98; *221:* 101
Zeifert, Harriet *154:* 265, 267
Zeiring, Bob *42:* 130
Zeldich, Arieh *49:* 124; *62:* 120
Zeldis, Malcah *86:* 239; *94:* 198; *146:* 265, 266
Zelinsky, Paul O. *14:* 269; *43:* 56; *49:* 218-223; *53:* 111; *68:* 195; *102:* 219, 222, 221, 222; *154:* 255, 256, 257; *171:* 141; *185:* 96
Zelvin, Diana *72:* 190; *76:* 101; *93:* 207
Zemach, Kaethe *149:* 250
Zemach, Margot *3:* 270; *8:* 201; *21:* 210, 211; *27:* 204, 205, 210; *28:* 185; *49:* 22, 183, 224; *53:* 151; *56:* 146; *70:* 245, 246; *92:* 74
Zeman, Ludmila *153* 212
Zemsky, Jessica *10:* 62
Zepelinsky, Paul *35:* 93
Zerbetz, Evon *127:* 34; *158:* 109
Zezejl, Daniel *197:* 74
Zhang, Ange *101:* 190; *172:* 41
Zhang, Son Nang *163:* 113; *170:* 206
Ziegler, Jack *84:* 134
Zimdars, Berta *129:* 155
Zimet, Jay *147:* 94; *152:* 74; *196:* 75
Zimic, Tricia *72:* 95
Zimmer, Dirk *38:* 195; *49:* 71; *56:* 151; *65:* 214; *84:* 159; *89:* 26; *147:* 224
Zimmer, Tracie Vaughn *169:* 183
Zimmerman, Andrea *192:* 49, 50
Zimmermann, H. Werner *101:* 223; *112:* 197
Zimnik, Reiner *36:* 224
Zingone, Robin *180:* 134
Zinkeisen, Anna *13:* 106
Zinn, David *97:* 97
Zoellick, Scott *33:* 231
Zollars, Jaime *190:* 190
Zonia, Dhimitri *20:* 234, 235
Zorn, Peter A., Jr. *142:* 157
Zudeck, Darryl *58:* 129; *63:* 98; *80:* 52
Zug, Mark *88:* 131; *204:* 169
Zulewski, Tim *164:* 95
Zuma *99:* 36
Zvorykin, Boris *61:* 155
Zweifel, Francis *14:* 274; *28:* 187
Zwerger, Lisbeth *54:* 176, 178; *66:* 246, 247, 248; *130:* 230, 231, 232, 233; *181:* 92; *194:* 224, 225, 226
Zwinger, Herman H. *46:* 227
Zwolak, Paul *67:* 69, 71, 73, 74

Author Index

The following index gives the number of the volume in which an author's biographical sketch, Autobiography Feature, Brief Entry, or Obituary appears.

This index includes references to all entries in the following series, which are also published by The Gale Group.

YABC—*Yesterday's Authors of Books for Children: Facts and Pictures about Authors and Illustrators of Books for Young People from Early Times to 1960*
CLR—*Children's Literature Review: Excerpts from Reviews, Criticism, and Commentary on Books for Children*
SAAS—*Something about the Author Autobiography Series*

A

Aardema, Verna 1911-2000 107
    Obituary 119
    Earlier sketches in SATA :4, 68
    See also CLR 17
    See also SAAS 8
Aaron, Chester 1923- 216
    Autobiography Feature 216
    Earlier sketches in SATA 9, 74
    See also SAAS 12
Aaseng, Nate
    See Aaseng, Nathan
Aaseng, Nathan 1953- 172
    Brief entry 38
    Earlier sketches in SATA 51, 88
    See also CLR 54
    See also SAAS 12
Abadzis, Nick 1965- 193
Abalos, Rafael 1956-
    See Abalos, Rafael
Abalos, Rafael 1956- 197
Abbas, Jailan 1952- 91
Abbey, Lynn
    See Abbey, Marilyn Lorraine
Abbey, Marilyn Lorraine 1948- 156
Abbott, Alice
    See Borland, Kathryn Kilby
    and Speicher, Helen Ross S(mith)
Abbott, Jacob 1803-1879 22
Abbott, Manager Henry
    See Stratemeyer, Edward L.
Abbott, R(obert) Tucker 1919-1995 61
    Obituary 87
Abbott, Sarah
    See Zolotow, Charlotte
Abbott, Tony 1952- 205
    Earlier sketch in SATA 159
Abdelsayed, Cindy 1962- 123
Abdul, Raoul 1929- 12
Abeele, Veronique van den 196
Abel, Raymond 1911- 12
Abell, Kathleen 1938- 9
Abelove, Joan 110
Abels, Harriette S(heffer) 1926- 50
Abercrombie, Barbara 1939- 182
    Earlier sketch in SATA 16
Abercrombie, Barbara Mattes
    See Abercrombie, Barbara

Abercrombie, Lynn
    See Sorrells, Walter
Abernethy, Robert G(ordon) 1927- 5
Abisch, Roslyn Kroop 1927- 9
Abisch, Roz
    See Abisch, Roslyn Kroop
Ablow, Gail 1962- 198
Abodaher, David J. (Naiph) 1919- 17
Abolafia, Yossi 1944-
    See Abulafia, Yossi
Abolivier, Aurelie 219
Abouzeid, Chris 175
Abrahall, Clare Hoskyns
    See Hoskyns-Abrahall, Clare (Constance Drury)
Abrahams, Hilary (Ruth) 1938- 29
Abrahams, Peter 1947- 194
Abrahams, Robert David 1905-1998 4
Abramovitz, Anita (Zeltner Brooks) 1914- 5
Abrams, Joy 1941- 16
Abrams, Lawrence F. 58
    Brief entry 47
Abrashkin, Raymond 1911-1960 50
Abulafia, Yossi 1944- 177
    Brief entry 46
    Earlier sketch in SATA 60
Acampora, Paul 175
Accardo, Anthony 191
Acer, David 206
Achebe, Albert Chinualumogu
    See Achebe, Chinua
Achebe, Chinua 1930- 40
    Brief entry 38
    Earlier sketch in SATA 38
    See also CLR 156
Acheson, Alison 1964- 222
Ackerman, Diane 1948- 102
Ackerman, Eugene (Francis) 1888-1974 10
Ackerman, Karen 1951- 126
Ackerman, Susan Yoder 1945- 92
Ackison, Wendy Wassink 1956- 103
Ackley, Peggy Jo 1955- 58
Ackroyd, Peter 1949- 153
Acorn, John (Harrison) 1958- 79
Acredolo, Linda (Potter) 1947- 159
Acs, Laszlo (Bela) 1931- 42
    Brief entry 32
Acuff, Selma Boyd 1924- 45

Ada, Alma Flor 1938- 222
    Autobiography Feature 222
    Earlier sketches in SATA 43, 84, 143, 181
    See also CLR 62
Adair, Gilbert 1944- 98
Adair, Ian 1942- 53
Adair, Margaret Weeks (?)-1971 10
Adam, Cornel
    See Lengyel, Cornel Adam
Adam, Mark
    See Alexander, Marc
Adam, Robert 1948- 93
Adams, Adrienne 1906- 90
    Earlier sketch in SATA 8
    See also CLR 73
Adams, Andy 1859-1935
    See YABC 1
Adams, Barbara Johnston 1943- 60
Adams, Bruin
    See Ellis, Edward S.
Adams, Captain Bruin
    See Ellis, Edward S.
Adams, Captain J. F. C.
    See Ellis, Edward S.
Adams, Dale
    See Quinn, Elisabeth
Adams, Daniel
    See Nicole, Christopher (Robin)
Adams, Debra
    See Speregen, Devra Newberger
Adams, Diane 1960- 217
Adams, Douglas 1952-2001 116
    Obituary 128
Adams, Douglas Noel
    See Adams, Douglas
Adams, Edith
    See Shine, Deborah
Adams, Florence 1932- 61
Adams, Georgie 1945- 216
Adams, Harriet S(tratemeyer) 1892(?)-1982 .. 1
    Obituary 29
Adams, Harrison
    See Rathborne, St. George (Henry)
    and Stratemeyer, Edward L.
Adams, Hazard 1926- 6
Adams, Hazard Simeon
    See Adams, Hazard
Adams, John Anthony 1944- 67
Adams, Kathryn 224

Adams, Laurie 1941- 33
Adams, Lowell
  See Joseph, James (Herz)
Adams, Nicholas
  See Pine, Nicholas
Adams, Nicholas
  See Smith, Sherwood
Adams, Nicholas
  See Doyle, Debra
  and Macdonald, James D.
Adams, Pam 1919- 112
Adams, Pamela
  See Adams, Pam
Adams, Richard 1920- 69
  Earlier sketch in SATA 7
  See also CLR 121
Adams, Richard George
  See Adams, Richard
Adams, Ruth Joyce 14
Adams, Tricia
  See Kite, Pat
Adams, William Taylor 1822-1897 28
Adam Smith, Janet (Buchanan) 1905-1999 .. 63
Adamson, Gareth 1925-1982(?) 46
  Obituary 30
Adamson, George 1906-1989
  Obituary 63
Adamson, George (Worsley) 1913-2005 30
Adamson, Graham
  See Groom, Arthur William
Adamson, Joy(-Friederike Victoria)
  1910-1980 11
  Obituary 22
Adamson, Wendy Writson 1942- 22
Addasi, Maha 1968- 205
Addison, Kenneth 1949(?)-2005 187
Addison, Kenneth L.
  See Addison, Kenneth
Addona, Angelo F. 1925- 14
Addy, Sean 1976- 222
Addy, Sharon Hart 1943- 192
  Earlier sketch in SATA 108
Addy, Ted
  See Winterbotham, R(ussell) R(obert)
Adelberg, Doris
  See Orgel, Doris
Adelson, Leone 1908- 11
Adinolfi, JoAnn 176
Adkins, Jan 1944- 210
  Autobiography Feature 210
  Earlier sketches in SATA 8, 69, 144
  See also CLR 77
  See also SAAS 19
Adl, Shirin 1975- 225
Adler, C. S. 1932- 126
  Earlier sketches in SATA 26, 63, 102
  See also CLR 78
  See also SAAS 15
Adler, Carole Schwerdtfeger
  See Adler, C. S.
Adler, David A. 1947- 178
  Earlier sketches in SATA 14, 70, 106, 151
  See also CLR 108
Adler, Irene
  See Penzler, Otto
  and Storr, Catherine (Cole)
Adler, Irving 1913- 29
  Autobiography Feature 164
  Earlier sketch in SATA 1
  See also CLR 27
  See also SAAS 15
Adler, Larry 1939- 36
Adler, Peggy 22
Adler, Ruth 1915-1968 1
Adlerman, Daniel (Ezra) 1963- 163
  Earlier sketch in SATA 96
Adlerman, Kim
  See Adlerman, Kimberly M(arie)
Adlerman, Kimberly M(arie) 1964- 163
  Earlier sketch in SATA 96

Adoff, Arnold 1935- 96
  Earlier sketches in SATA 5, 57
  See also CLR 7
  See also SAAS 15
Adoff, Jaime 163
Adoff, Jaime Levi
  See Adoff, Jaime
Adorjan, Carol (Madden) 1934- 71
  Earlier sketch in SATA 10
Adrian, Frances
  See Polland, Madeleine A(ngela Cahill)
Adrian, Mary
  See Jorgensen, Mary Venn
Adshead, Gladys L(ucy) 1896-1985 3
Aesop 620(?)B.C.-560(?)B.C. 64
  See also CLR 14
Aesop, Abraham
  See Newbery, John
Affabee, Eric
  See Stine, R.L.
Agapida, Fray Antonio
  See Irving, Washington
Agard, John 1949- 223
  Earlier sketch in SATA 138
Agard, Nadema 1948- 18
Agarwal, Deepa 1947- 141
Agee, Jon 1960- 196
  Earlier sketches in SATA 116, 157
Agell, Charlotte 1959- 214
  Earlier sketches in SATA 99, 150
Agent Orange
  See Moseley, James W(illett)
Aghill, Gordon
  See Garrett, Randall
  and Silverberg, Robert
Agle, Nan Hayden 1905- 3
  See also SAAS 10
Agnew, Edith J(osephine) 1897-1988 11
Agnew, Lincoln 222
Agonito, Joseph 177
Agonito, Rosemary 1937- 177
Aguilar, David 214
Aguilar, David A.
  See Aguilar, David
Ahern, Margaret McCrohan 1921- 10
Ahl, Anna Maria 1926- 32
Ahlberg, Allan 1938- 214
  Brief entry 35
  Earlier sketches in SATA 68, 120, 165
  See also CLR 18
Ahlberg, Janet 1944-1994 120
  Brief entry 32
  Obituary 83
  Earlier sketch in SATA 68
  See also CLR 18
Aho, Julia Kay
  See Kay, Julia
Aichinger, Helga 1937- 4
Aiken, Clarissa (M.) Lorenz 1899-1992 12
  Obituary 109
Aiken, Conrad 1889-1973 30
  Earlier sketch in SATA 3
Aiken, Conrad Potter
  See Aiken, Conrad
Aiken, Joan (Delano) 1924-2004 73
  Autobiography Feature 109
  Obituary 152
  Earlier sketches in SATA 2, 30
  See also CLR 90
  See also SAAS 1
Aillaud, Cindy Lou 1955- 184
Ainsley, Alix
  See Steiner, Barbara A(nnette)
Ainsworth, Catherine Harris 1910- 56
Ainsworth, Norma 1911-1987 9
Ainsworth, Ruth (Gallard) 1908- 73
  Earlier sketch in SATA 7
Ainsworth, William Harrison 1805-1882 24
Aistrop, Jack 1916- 14
Aitken, Amy 1952- 54
  Brief entry 40

Aitken, Dorothy 1916- 10
Aitmatov, Chingiz 1928-2008 56
Aitmatov, Chingiz Torekulovich
  See Aitmatov, Chingiz
Ajhar, Brian 1957- 220
Akaba, Suekichi 1910- 46
Akers, Floyd
  See Baum, L. Frank
Akib, Jamel 181
Aks, Patricia 1926-1994 68
Alagoa, Ebiegberi Joe 1933- 108
Alain
  See Brustlein, Daniel
Alajalov, Constantin 1900-1987
  Obituary 53
Alalou, Ali 203
Alalou, Elizabeth 203
Alan, David
  See Horsfield, Alan
Alan, Robert
  See Silverstein, Robert Alan
Alarcon, Francisco X. 1954- 215
  Earlier sketch in SATA 104
Alarcon, Francisco Xavier
  See Alarcon, Francisco X.
Alarcon, Karen Beaumont
  See Beaumont, Karen
Albert, Burton 1936- 22
Albert, Louise 1928- 157
Albert, Michael 1966- 202
Albert, Richard E. 1909-1999 82
Albert, Susan Wittig 1940- 107
Alberts, Frances Jacobs 1907-1989 14
Albertson, Susan
  See Wojciechowski, Susan
Albion, Lee Smith 29
Alborough, Jez 1959- 149
  Earlier sketch in SATA 86
Albrecht, Lillie (Vanderveer H.)
  1894-1985 12
Albyn, Carole Lisa 1955- 83
Alchemy, Jack
  See Gershator, David
Alcock, Gudrun 1908- 56
  Brief entry 33
Alcock, Vivien (Dolores) 1924-2003 76
  Brief entry 38
  Obituary 148
  Earlier sketch in SATA 45
  See also CLR 26
Alcorn, John 1935- 31
  Brief entry 30
Alcorn, Stephen 1958- 207
  Earlier sketch in SATA 110
Alcott, Louisa May 1832-1888 100
  See also YABC 1
  See also CLR 109
Alda, Arlene 1933- 205
  Brief entry 36
  Earlier sketches in SATA 44, 106, 158
  See also CLR 93
Alden, Isabella (Macdonald) 1841-1930 115
  See also YABC 2
Alden, Sue
  See Francis, Dorothy
Alderman, Clifford Lindsey 1902-1988 3
Alderson, Sue Ann 1940- 59
  Brief entry 48
Alding, Peter
  See Jeffries, Roderic
Aldis, Dorothy (Keeley) 1896-1966 2
Aldiss, Brian W. 1925- 34
Aldiss, Brian Wilson
  See Aldiss, Brian W.
Aldon, Adair
  See Meigs, Cornelia Lynde
Aldous, Allan (Charles) 1911- 27
Aldrich, Ann
  See Meaker, Marijane
Aldrich, Bess Streeter 1881-1954
  See CLR 70

Aldrich, Thomas (Bailey) 1836-1907 .... *114*
　Earlier sketch in SATA *17*
Aldridge, (Harold Edward) James 1918- *87*
Aldridge, Josephine Haskell *14*
Aldridge, Sheila 1974- *192*
Aleas, Richard
　See Appelt, Kathi
Alegria, Malin 1974(?)- *190*
Alegria, Ricardo E(nrique) 1921- *6*
Aleksin, Anatolii Georgievich 1924- *36*
Alenov, Lydia 1948- *61*
Alex, Ben (a pseudonym) 1946- *45*
Alex, Marlee (a pseudonym) 1948- *45*
Alexander, Alma 1963- *217*
Alexander, Anna B(arbara Cooke) 1913- *1*
Alexander, Anne
　See Alexander, Anna B(arbara Cooke)
Alexander, Ellen 1938- *91*
Alexander, Frances (Laura) 1888-1979 .... *4*
Alexander, Janet 1907-1994 .... *97*
　Earlier sketch in SATA *1*
Alexander, Jill S. 1964- *223*
Alexander, Jill Shurbet
　See Alexander, Jill S.
Alexander, Jocelyn Anne Arundel 1930- *22*
Alexander, Linda 1935- *2*
Alexander, Lloyd 1924-2007 .... *135*
　Obituary *182*
　Earlier sketches in SATA *3, 49, 81, 129*
　See also CLR *48*
　See also SAAS *19*
Alexander, Lloyd Chudley
　See Alexander, Lloyd
Alexander, Marc 1929- *117*
Alexander, Martha 1920- *136*
　Earlier sketches in SATA *11, 70*
Alexander, Rae Pace
　See Alexander, Raymond Pace
Alexander, Raymond Pace 1898-1974 .... *22*
Alexander, Robert *200*
Alexander, Rod
　See Pellowski, Michael (Joseph)
Alexander, Sally Hobart 1943- *84*
Alexander, Sue 1933-2008 .... *136*
　Obituary *195*
　Earlier sketches in SATA *12, 89*
　See also SAAS *15*
Alexander, Vincent Arthur 1925-1980
　Obituary *23*
Alexeieff, Alexandre A. 1901-1979 .... *14*
Alger, Horatio, Jr.
　See Stratemeyer, Edward L.
Alger, Horatio, Jr. 1832-1899 .... *16*
　See also CLR *87*
Alger, Leclaire (Gowans) 1898-1969 .... *15*
Aliki
　See Brandenberg, Aliki
Alkema, Chester Jay 1932- *12*
Al-Khalili, Jim 1962- *124*
Alkiviades, Alkis 1953- *105*
Alko, Selina 1968- *218*
Alkouatli, Claire *186*
Allaby, John Michael
　See Allaby, Michael
Allaby, Michael 1933- *167*
Allamand, Pascale 1942- *12*
Allan, Mabel Esther 1915-1998 .... *75*
　Earlier sketches in SATA *5, 32*
　See also CLR *43*
　See also SAAS *11*
Allan, Nicholas 1956- *123*
　Earlier sketch in SATA *79*
Allan-Meyer, Kathleen 1918- *51*
　Brief entry *46*
Allard, Harry
　See Allard, Harry G., Jr.
Allard, Harry G.
　See Allard, Harry G., Jr.
Allard, Harry G., Jr. 1928- *216*
　Earlier sketches in SATA *42, 102*
　See also CLR *85*

Allee, Marjorie Hill 1890-1945 .... *17*
Allen, Adam
　See Epstein, Beryl
　and Epstein, Samuel
Allen, Alex B.
　See Heide, Florence Parry
Allen, Allyn
　See Eberle, Irmengarde
Allen, Betsy
　See Harrison, Elizabeth (Allen) Cavanna
Allen, Bob 1961- *76*
Allen, Gertrude E(lizabeth) 1888-1984 .... *9*
Allen, Grace
　See Hogarth, Grace (Weston Allen)
Allen, Jeffrey (Yale) 1948- *42*
Allen, John
　See Perry, Ritchie (John Allen)
Allen, Jonathan 1957- *177*
　Earlier sketch in SATA *131*
Allen, Jonathan Dean
　See Allen, Jonathan
Allen, Joy 1948- *217*
Allen, Judy (Christina) 1941- *124*
　Earlier sketch in SATA *80*
Allen, Kenneth S. 1913-1981 .... *56*
Allen, Leroy 1912- *11*
Allen, Linda 1925- *33*
Allen, Marjorie 1931- *22*
Allen, Maury 1932-2010 .... *26*
Allen, Merritt Parmelee 1892-1954 .... *22*
Allen, Nancy Kelly 1949- *171*
　Earlier sketch in SATA *127*
Allen, Nina (Stroemgren) 1935- *22*
Allen, Pamela (Kay) 1934- *123*
　Earlier sketches in SATA *50, 81*
　See also CLR *44*
Allen, Raul *205*
Allen, Rodney F. 1938-1999 .... *27*
Allen, Roger MacBride 1957- *105*
Allen, Ruth
　See Peterson, Esther (Allen)
Allen, Samuel W(ashington) 1917- *9*
Allen, T. D.
　See Allen, Terril Diener
Allen, Terril Diener 1908- *35*
Allen, Terry D.
　See Allen, Terril Diener
Allen, Thomas B. 1929- *193*
　Earlier sketches in SATA *45, 140*
Allen, Thomas Benton
　See Allen, Thomas B.
Allen, Tom
　See Allen, Thomas B.
Allende, Isabel 1942- *163*
　See also CLR *99*
Allerton, Mary
　See Govan, (Mary) Christine Noble
Alley, Robert W.
　See Alley, R.W.
Alley, R.W. *211*
　Earlier sketch in SATA *169*
Alley, Zoe B. *214*
Alleyn, Ellen
　See Rossetti, Christina
Allington, Richard L(loyd) 1947- *39*
　Brief entry *35*
Allison, Amy 1956- *138*
Allison, Bob *14*
Allison, Diane Worfolk *78*
Allison, Jennifer *173*
Allison, Linda 1948- *43*
Allison, Margaret
　See Klam, Cheryl
Allman, Barbara 1950- *137*
Allmendinger, David F(rederick), Jr. 1938- . *35*
Allred, Alexandra Powe 1965- *144*
Allred, Gordon T(hatcher) 1930- *10*
Allsop, Kenneth 1920-1973 .... *17*
Allsopp, Sophie *188*
Alma, Ann 1946- *201*

Almedingen, E. M.
　See Almedingen, Martha Edith von
Almedingen, Martha Edith von 1898-1971 .... *3*
Almon, Russell
　See Clevenger, William R.
　and Downing, David A(lmon)
Almond, David 1951- *158*
　Earlier sketch in SATA *114*
　See also CLR *85*
Almond, Linda Stevens 1881(?)-1987
　Obituary *50*
Almquist, Don 1929- *11*
Alonzo, Sandra *199*
Alphin, Elaine Marie 1955- *139*
　Autobiography Feature *139*
　Earlier sketches in SATA *80, 130*
Alsenas, Linas 1979- *186*
Alsop, Mary O'Hara 1885-1980 .... *34*
　Obituary *24*
　Earlier sketch in SATA *2*
Alter, Anna 1974- *206*
　Earlier sketch in SATA *135*
Alter, Judith 1938- *101*
　Earlier sketch in SATA *52*
Alter, Judith MacBain
　See Alter, Judith
Alter, Judy
　See Alter, Judith
Alter, Robert Edmond 1925-1965 .... *9*
Alter, Stephen 1956- *187*
Althea
　See Braithwaite, Althea
Altman, Linda Jacobs 1943- *21*
Altman, Suzanne
　See Orgel, Doris
　and Schecter, Ellen
Alton, Steve *169*
Altschuler, Franz 1923- *45*
Altsheler, Joseph A(lexander) 1862-1919
　See YABC *1*
Alvarez, John
　See del Rey, Lester
Alvarez, Joseph A. 1930- *18*
Alvarez, Julia 1950- *129*
al-Windawi, Thura
　See Windawi, Thura al-
Alyer, Philip A.
　See Stratemeyer, Edward L.
Amado, Elisa *193*
Amann, Janet 1951- *79*
Amato, Carol A. 1942- *92*
Amato, Mary 1961- *178*
　Earlier sketch in SATA *140*
Ambrose, Stephen E. 1936-2002 .... *138*
　Earlier sketch in SATA *40*
Ambrose, Stephen Edward
　See Ambrose, Stephen E.
Ambrus, Gyozo Laszlo 1935- *1*
　See also SAAS *4*
Ambrus, Victor G.
　See Ambrus, Gyozo Laszlo
Amend, Bill 1962- *147*
Amerman, Lockhart 1911-1969 .... *3*
Ames, Evelyn 1908-1990 .... *13*
　Obituary *64*
Ames, Gerald 1906-1993 .... *11*
　Obituary *74*
Ames, Lee J(udah) 1921- *151*
　Earlier sketch in SATA *3*
Ames, Mildred 1919-1994 .... *85*
　Earlier sketches in SATA *22, 81*
Amico, Tom 1960(?)- *176*
Amit, Ofra 1966- *205*
Ammon, Richard 1942- *124*
Amon, Aline 1928- *9*
Amory, Jay
　See Lovegrove, James
Amoss, Berthe 1925- *112*
　Earlier sketch in SATA *5*
Amstutz, Andre 1925- *214*

Anastasio, Dina 1941- *94*
  Brief entry *30*
  Earlier sketch in SATA *37*
Anaya, Rudolfo 1937-
  See CLR *129*
Anaya, Rudolfo A.
  See Anaya, Rudolfo
Anaya, Rudolpho Alfonso
  See Anaya, Rudolfo
Anckarsvard, Karin Inez Maria 1915-1969 .... *6*
Ancona, George 1929- *208*
  Autobiography Feature *208*
  Earlier sketches in SATA *12, 85, 145, 192*
  See also SAAS *18*
Anders, C. J.
  See Bennett, Cherie
Anders, Isabel 1946- *101*
Anders, Lou *176*
Andersdatter, Karla M. 1938- *34*
Andersen, Bethanne 1954- *191*
Andersen, Hans Christian 1805-1875 .... *100*
  See also YABC *1*
  See also CLR *113*
Andersen, Ted
  See Boyd, Waldo T.
Andersen, Yvonne 1932- *27*
Anderson, Bernice G(oudy) 1894-1997 .... *33*
Anderson, Bob 1944- *139*
  Earlier sketch in SATA *136*
Anderson, Brad 1924- *33*
  Brief entry *31*
Anderson, Bradley Jay
  See Anderson, Brad
Anderson, Brian 1974- *211*
Anderson, C. C.
  See Anderson, Catherine Corley
Anderson, C(larence) W(illiam) 1891-1971 . *11*
Anderson, Carolyn Dunn
  See Dunn, Carolyn
Anderson, Catherine C.
  See Anderson, Catherine Corley
Anderson, Catherine Corley 1909-2001 .... *72*
  See Lee, Cora
Anderson, Clifford
  See Gardner, Richard (M.)
Anderson, Daryl Shon 1963- *93*
Anderson, Dave
  See Anderson, David
Anderson, David 1929- *60*
Anderson, Derek 1969- *169*
Anderson, Eloise Adell 1927- *9*
Anderson, George
  See Groom, Arthur William
Anderson, Grace Fox 1932- *43*
Anderson, J(ohn) R(ichard) L(ane)
  1911-1981 .... *15*
  Obituary *27*
Anderson, Jessica Lee 1980- *224*
Anderson, Jodi Lynn *182*
Anderson, John David *197*
Anderson, John L. 1905- *2*
Anderson, Joy 1928- *1*
Anderson, Kevin J. 1962- *117*
  Earlier sketch in SATA *74*
Anderson, Kevin James
  See Anderson, Kevin J.
Anderson, Kirsty 1978- *108*
Anderson, K.J.
  See Moesta, Rebecca
Anderson, Laurie Halse 1961- *186*
  Earlier sketches in SATA *95, 132*
  See also CLR *138*
Anderson, LaVere Francis Shoenfelt
  1907-1998 .... *27*
Anderson, Leone Castell 1923- *53*
  Brief entry *49*
Anderson, Lisa G. 1963- *108*
Anderson, Lonzo
  See Anderson, John L.
Anderson, Lucia (Lewis) 1922- *10*
Anderson, Madelyn Klein 1926-2005 .... *28*

Anderson, Margaret J(ean) 1931- *27*
  See also SAAS *8*
Anderson, Marilyn D. 1943- *144*
Anderson, Mary 1939- *82*
  Earlier sketch in SATA *7*
  See also SAAS *23*
Anderson, Matthew Tobin
  See Anderson, M.T.
Anderson, Mona 1910-2004 .... *40*
Anderson, Mrs. Melvin
  See Anderson, Catherine Corley
Anderson, M.T. 1968- *182*
  Earlier sketches in SATA *97, 146*
Anderson, Norman Dean 1928- *22*
Anderson, Peggy Perry 1953- *179*
  Earlier sketch in SATA *84*
Anderson, Poul 1926-2001 .... *90*
  Autobiography Feature *106*
  Brief entry *39*
  See also CLR *58*
Anderson, Poul William
  See Anderson, Poul
Anderson, Rachel 1943- *86*
  Earlier sketch in SATA *34*
  See also SAAS *18*
Anderson, Rebecca J.
  See Anderson, R.J.
Anderson, Rebecca M.
  See Moesta, Rebecca
Anderson, Rebecca Moesta
  See Moesta, Rebecca
Anderson, Richard
  See Anderson, J(ohn) R(ichard) L(ane)
Anderson, R.J. 1970(?)- *216*
Anderson, Sara *173*
Anderson, Scoular *201*
Anderson, (Tom) Scoular *138*
Anderson, Stephanie 1976- *225*
Anderson, Susan 1952- *90*
Anderson, Thomas Scoular
  See Anderson, Scoular
Anderson, W. B.
  See Schultz, James Willard
Anderson, Wayne 1946- *202*
  Earlier sketches in SATA *56, 147*
Andersson, Kenneth 1970- *200*
Andre, Evelyn M. 1924- *27*
Andre, Evelyn Marie
  See Andre, Evelyn M.
Andreasen, Dan *186*
Andreassen, Karl
  See Boyd, Waldo T.
Andreassi, K. Robert
  See DeCandido, Keith R.A.
Andree, Louise
  See Coury, Louise Andree
Andrew, Ian 1962- *166*
  Earlier sketch in SATA *116*
Andrew, Ian Peter
  See Andrew, Ian
Andrew, Prudence (Hastings) 1924- *87*
Andrews, Benny 1930-2006 .... *31*
  Obituary *178*
Andrews, Eleanor Lattimore
  See Lattimore, Eleanor Frances
Andrews, Elton V.
  See Pohl, Frederik
Andrews, F(rank) Emerson 1902-1978 .... *22*
Andrews, J(ames) S(ydney) 1934- *4*
Andrews, Jan 1942- *167*
  Brief entry *49*
  Earlier sketches in SATA *58, 98*
Andrews, Julie 1935- *153*
  Earlier sketch in SATA *7*
  See also CLR *85*
Andrews, Laura
  See Coury, Louise Andree
Andrews, Roy Chapman 1884-1960 .... *19*
Andrews, Tamra 1959- *129*
Andrews, V(irginia) C(leo) 1924(?)-1986
  Obituary *50*

Andrews, Wendy
  See Sharmat, Marjorie Weinman
Andrews, William G. 1930- *74*
Andrews, William George
  See Andrews, William G.
Andrezel, Pierre
  See Blixen, Karen
Andriani, Renee
  See Williams-Andriani, Renee
Andriola, Alfred J. 1912-1983
  Obituary *34*
Andrist, Ralph K. 1914-2004 .... *45*
Andronik, Catherine M. *189*
Andryszewski, Tricia 1956- *148*
  Earlier sketch in SATA *88*
Anelli, Melissa 1979- *215*
Angel, Ann 1952- *192*
Angel, Carl *178*
Angel, Marie 1923- *47*
Angeles, Peter A. 1931- *40*
Angeletti, Roberta 1964- *124*
Angeli, Marguerite (Lofft) de
  See de Angeli, Marguerite (Lofft)
Angell, Judie 1937- *78*
  Earlier sketch in SATA *22*
  See also CLR *33*
Angell, Madeline 1919- *18*
Angelo, Valenti 1897- *14*
Angelou, Maya 1928- *136*
  Earlier sketch in SATA *49*
  See also CLR *53*
Angier, Bradford -1997 .... *12*
Angle, Kimberly Greene *203*
Angle, Paul M(cClelland) 1900-1975
  Obituary *20*
Anglund, Joan Walsh 1926- *2*
  See also CLR *94*
Ango, Fan D.
  See Longyear, Barry B(rookes)
Angrist, Stanley W(olff) 1933- *4*
Anholt, Catherine 1958- *131*
  Earlier sketch in SATA *74*
Anholt, Laurence 1959- *141*
  Earlier sketch in SATA *74*
Anita
  See Daniel, Anita
Anmar, Frank
  See Nolan, William F.
Annett, Cora
  See Scott, Cora Annett (Pipitone)
Annie-Jo
  See Blanchard, Patricia
  and Suhr, Joanne
Annixter, Jane
  See Sturtzel, Jane Levington
Annixter, Paul
  See Sturtzel, Howard A(llison)
Anno, Mitsumasa 1926- *157*
  Earlier sketches in SATA *5, 38, 77*
  See also CLR *122*
Anrooy, Francine Van
  See Van Anrooy, Francine
Ansary, Mir Tamim 1948- *140*
Anstey, Caroline 1958- *81*
Antell, Will D. 1935- *31*
Anthony, Barbara
  See Barber, Antonia
Anthony, C. L.
  See Smith, Dorothy Gladys
Anthony, Edward 1895-1971 .... *21*
Anthony, John
  See Beckett, Ronald Brymer
  and Ciardi, John (Anthony)
  and Sabini, John Anthony
Anthony, Joseph Patrick 1964- *103*
Anthony, Patricia 1947- *109*
Anthony, Piers 1934- *129*
  Autobiography Feature *129*
  Earlier sketch in SATA *84*
  See also CLR *118*
  See also SAAS *22*

Anthony, Susan C(arol) 1953- 87
Anticaglia, Elizabeth 1939- 12
Antieau, Kim 214
Antilles, Kem
    See Moesta, Rebecca
Antle, Nancy 1955- 102
Antolini, Margaret Fishback 1904-1985
    Obituary 45
Anton, Michael J(ames) 1940- 12
Antonacci, Robert J(oseph) 1916- 45
    Brief entry 37
Anvil, Christopher 1925-2009 102
Anzaldua, Gloria (Evanjelina) 1942-2004
    Obituary 154
Aoki, Hisako 1942- 45
Apfel, Necia H(alpern) 1930- 51
    Brief entry 41
Aphrodite, J.
    See Livingston, Carole
Apikuni
    See Schultz, James Willard
Apostolina, M. 184
Apostolina, Michael
    See Apostolina, M.
Apostolou, Christine Hale 1955- 179
    Earlier sketches in SATA *82, 128*
Appel, Allen (R.) 1945- 115
Appel, Benjamin 1907-1977 39
    Obituary 21
Appel, Martin 1948- 45
Appel, Martin Eliot
    See Appel, Martin
Appel, Marty
    See Appel, Martin
Appelbaum, Diana Muir Karter 1953- 132
Appelt, Kathi 1954- 190
    Earlier sketches in SATA *83, 129*
Apperley, Dawn 1969- 135
Appiah, Peggy 1921-2006 84
    Earlier sketch in SATA *15*
    See also SAAS *19*
Apple, Margot 214
    Brief entry 42
    Earlier sketches in SATA *64, 152*
Applebaum, Stan 1922- 45
Applegate, K.A.
    See Applegate, Katherine
Applegate, Katherine 1956- 196
    Earlier sketches in SATA *109, 162*
    See also CLR *90*
Applegate, Katherine Alice
    See Applegate, Katherine
Appleton, Victor
    See Barrett, Neal, Jr.
    and Doyle, Debra
    and Stratemeyer, Edward L.
    and Vardeman, Robert E.
Appollo 1969- 214
Appollodorus, Olivier
    See Appollo
Apsler, Alfred 1907-1982 10
Aragones, Sergio 1937- 48
    Brief entry 39
Araujo, Frank P. 1937- 86
Arbo, Cris 1950- 220
    Earlier sketch in SATA *103*
Arbuckle, Dorothy Fry 1910-1982
    Obituary 33
Arbuthnot, May Hill 1884-1969 2
Archambault, John 163
    Earlier sketches in SATA *67, 112*
Archambault, Matthew 1968- 219
Archbold, Rick 1950- 97
Archer, Colleen Rutherford 1949- 164
Archer, Frank
    See O'Connor, Richard
Archer, Jules 1915- 85
    Earlier sketch in SATA *4*
    See also SAAS *5*
Archer, Lily 1981- 193
Archer, Marion Fuller 1917- 11

Archer, Nathan
    See Watt-Evans, Lawrence
Archer, Peggy 1947- 199
Archibald, Joe
    See Archibald, Joseph S(topford)
Archibald, Joseph S(topford) 1898-1986 3
    Obituary 47
Ard, William
    See Jakes, John
Ardagh, Philip 1961- 154
Ardai, Charles 1969- 85
Arden, Barbi
    See Stoutenburg, Adrien (Pearl)
Arden, William
    See Lynds, Dennis
Ardizzone, Edward (Jeffrey Irving)
    1900-1979 28
    Obituary 21
    Earlier sketch in SATA *1*
    See also CLR *3*
Ardley, Neil 1937- 121
    Earlier sketch in SATA *43*
Ardley, Neil Richard
    See Ardley, Neil
Arehart-Treichel, Joan 1942- 22
Arena, Felice 1968- 151
Arenella, Roy 1939- 14
Argent, Kerry 1960- 138
Arguelles, Francisco Xavier
    See Stork, Francisco X.
Argueta, Jorge 179
Arihara, Shino 1973- 201
Arkin, Alan 1934- 59
    Brief entry 32
Arkin, Alan Wolf
    See Arkin, Alan
Arksey, Neil 158
Arlen, Leslie
    See Nicole, Christopher (Robin)
Arley, Robert
    See Jackson, Mike
Armer, Alberta (Roller) 1904-1986 9
Armer, Laura Adams 1874-1963 13
Armistead, John 1941- 130
Armitage, David 1943- 155
    Brief entry 38
    Earlier sketch in SATA *99*
Armitage, Frank
    See Carpenter, John
Armitage, Ronda (Jacqueline) 1943- 155
    Brief entry 38
    Earlier sketches in SATA *47, 99*
Armour, Richard (Willard) 1906-1989 14
    Obituary 61
Armstrong, Alan 1939- 172
Armstrong, Alan W.
    See Armstrong, Alan
Armstrong, George D. 1927- 10
Armstrong, Gerry (Breen) 1929- 10
Armstrong, Jeannette (C.) 1948- 102
Armstrong, Jennifer 1961- 165
    Autobiography Feature 120
    Earlier sketches in SATA *77, 111*
    See also CLR *66*
    See also SAAS *24*
Armstrong, Louise 43
    Brief entry 33
Armstrong, Martin Donisthorpe
    1882-1974 115
Armstrong, Matthew 1975- 188
Armstrong, Matthew S.
    See Armstrong, Matthew
Armstrong, Ralph Richard
    See Armstrong, Richard
Armstrong, Richard 1903-1986 11
Armstrong, Shelagh 1961- 224
Armstrong, William H(oward) 1914-1999 4
    Obituary 111
    See also CLR *117*
    See also SAAS *7*
Armstrong-Ellis, Carey (Fraser) 1956- 145

Armstrong-Hodgson, Shelagh
    See Armstrong, Shelagh
Arndt, Ursula (Martha H.) 56
    Brief entry 39
Arneson, D(on) J(on) 1935- 37
Arnett, Caroline
    See Cole, Lois Dwight
Arnett, Jack
    See Goulart, Ron
Arnette, Robert
    See Silverberg, Robert
Arno, Enrico 1913-1981 43
    Obituary 28
Arnold, Ann 1953(?)- 207
Arnold, Caroline 1944- 174
    Brief entry 34
    Earlier sketches in SATA *36, 85, 131*
    See also CLR *61*
    See also SAAS *23*
Arnold, Elizabeth 1944- 164
Arnold, Elliott 1912-1980 5
    Obituary 22
Arnold, Emily 1939- 210
    Autobiography Feature 134
    Earlier sketches in SATA *5, 50, 76, 110, 134*
    See also CLR *46*
    See also SAAS *7*
Arnold, Gillian Clare
    See Cross, Gillian
Arnold, Katya 1947- 168
    Earlier sketches in SATA *82, 115*
Arnold, Louise 175
Arnold, Louise Claire
    See Arnold, Louise
Arnold, Marsha Diane 1948- 147
    Earlier sketch in SATA *93*
Arnold, Nick 1961- 113
Arnold, Oren 1900-1980 4
Arnold, Susan (Riser) 1951- 58
Arnold, Tedd 1949- 208
    Earlier sketches in SATA *69, 116, 160*
Arnoldy, Julie
    See Bischoff, Julia Bristol
Arnosky, James Edward 1946- 189
    Earlier sketches in SATA *70, 118*
    See also CLR *93*
Arnosky, Jim
    See Arnosky, James Edward
Arnott, Kathleen 1914- 20
Arnov, Boris, Jr. 1926- 12
Arnow, Harriette (Louisa) Simpson
    1908-1986 42
    Obituary 47
Arnsteen, Katy Keck 1934- 68
Arnstein, Helene S(olomon) 1915- 12
Arntson, Herbert E(dward) 1911-1982 12
Aroner, Miriam 82
Aronin, Ben 1904-1980
    Obituary 25
Aronson, Marc 1950- 189
    Autobiography Feature 189
    Earlier sketches in SATA *126, 175*
Aronson, Marc Henry
    See Aronson, Marc
Aronson, Sarah 196
Aronson, Virginia 1954- 122
Arora, Shirley (Lease) 1930- 2
Arrasmith, Patrick 176
Arrick, Fran
    See Angell, Judie
Arrigan, Mary 1943- 142
Arrington, Aileen 183
Arrington, Stephen L. 1948- 97
Arrington, Stephen Lee
    See Arrington, Stephen L.
Arrley, Richmond
    See Delany, Samuel R., Jr.
Arrou-Vignod, Jean-Philippe 1958- 218
Arrowood, (McKendrick Lee) Clinton
    1939- 19
Arrowsmith, Pat 1930- 59

Arsenault, Isabelle 1978- 207
Artell, Mike 1948- 183
  Earlier sketches in SATA *89, 134*
Arthur, Robert (Andrew) 1909-1969
  See Arthur, Robert, (Jr.)
Arthur, Robert, (Jr.) 1909-1969 118
Arthur, Ruth M(abel) 1905-1979 26
  Earlier sketch in SATA *7*
Artis, Vicki Kimmel 1945- 12
Artzybasheff, Boris (Miklailovich)
  1899-1965 14
Aruego, Ariane
  See Dewey, Ariane
Aruego, Jose 1932- 178
  Earlier sketches in SATA *6, 68, 125*
  See also CLR *5*
Aruego, Jose Espiritu
  See Aruego, Jose
Arundel, Honor (Morfydd) 1919-1973 4
  Obituary 24
  See also CLR *35*
Arundel, Jocelyn
  See Alexander, Jocelyn Anne Arundel
Arvey, Michael 1948- 79
Arzoumanian, Alik 177
Asare, Meshack (Yaw) 1945- 139
  Earlier sketch in SATA *86*
Asaro, Catherine 1955- 165
  Earlier sketch in SATA *101*
Asaro, Catherine Ann 1955-
  See Asaro, Catherine
Asay, Donna Day 1945- 127
Asbjornsen, Peter Christen 1812-1885 15
  See also CLR *104*
Asch, Frank 1946- 154
  Earlier sketches in SATA *5, 66, 102*
Ash, Jutta 1942- 38
Ashabranner, Brent 1921- 166
  Earlier sketches in SATA *1, 67, 130*
  See also CLR *28*
  See also SAAS *14*
Ashabranner, Brent Kenneth
  See Ashabranner, Brent
Ashbless, William
  See Blaylock, James P.
  and Powers, Tim
Ashby, Gil 1958- 146
Ashby, Gwynneth 1922- 44
Ashby, Ruth 170
Ashby, Yvonne 1955- 121
Ashe, Arthur (Robert, Jr.) 1943-1993 65
  Obituary 87
Ashe, Geoffrey (Thomas) 1923- 17
  Autobiography Feature 125
Ashe, Mary Ann
  See Lewis, Mary
Asher, Bridget
  See Baggott, Julianna
Asher, Sandra Fenichel
  See Asher, Sandy
Asher, Sandy 1942- 71
  Autobiography Feature 158
  Brief entry 34
  Earlier sketch in SATA *36*
  See also SAAS *13*
Asheron, Sara
  See Moore, Lilian
Ashey, Bella
  See Breinburg, Petronella
Ashford, Daisy
  See Ashford, Margaret Mary
Ashford, Jeffrey
  See Jeffries, Roderic
Ashford, Margaret Mary 1881-1972 10
Ashland, Monk 1972- 207
Ashley, Bernard (John) 1935- 155
  Brief entry 39
  Earlier sketches in SATA *47, 79*
  See also CLR *4*
Ashley, Elizabeth
  See Salmon, Annie Elizabeth

Ashley, Ray
  See Abrashkin, Raymond
Ashman, Linda 1960- 203
  Earlier sketch in SATA *150*
Ashton, Lorayne
  See Gottfried, Theodore Mark
Ashton, Warren T.
  See Adams, William Taylor
Asimov, Isaac 1920-1992 74
  Earlier sketches in SATA *1, 26*
  See also CLR *79*
Asinof, Eliot 1919-2008 6
Asinof, Eliot Tager
  See Asinof, Eliot
Aska, Warabe
  See Masuda, Takeshi
Asprin, Robert 1946-2008 92
Asprin, Robert L.
  See Asprin, Robert
Asprin, Robert Lynn
  See Asprin, Robert
Asquith, Cynthia Mary Evelyn (Charteris)
  1887-1960 107
Asquith, Ros 153
Astley, Juliet
  See Lofts, Norah (Robinson)
Aston, Dianna Hutts 1964- 176
Aston, James
  See White, T(erence) H(anbury)
Ata, Te 1895-1995 119
Atene, Ann
  See Atene, (Rita) Anna
Atene, (Rita) Anna 1922- 12
Atheling, William, Jr.
  See Blish, James
Atkins, Catherine 160
Atkins, Jeannine 1953- 172
  Earlier sketch in SATA *113*
Atkinson, Allen G. 1953(?)-1987 60
  Brief entry 46
  Obituary 55
Atkinson, Elizabeth 215
Atkinson, M. E.
  See Frankau, Mary Evelyn Atkinson
Atkinson, Margaret Fleming 14
Atteberry, Kevan J. 186
Attema, Martha 1949- 156
  Earlier sketch in SATA *94*
Atticus
  See Davies, Hunter
  and Fleming, Ian
  and Pawle, Gerald Strachan
  and Wilson, (Thomas) Woodrow
Atwater, Florence (Hasseltine Carroll)
  1896-1979 66
  Earlier sketch in SATA *16*
  See also CLR *19*
Atwater, Montgomery Meigs 1904-1976 15
Atwater, Richard (Tupper) 1892-1948 66
  Brief entry 27
  Earlier sketch in SATA *54*
  See also CLR *19*
Atwater-Rhodes, Amelia 1984- 170
  Earlier sketch in SATA *124*
Atwell, Debby 1953- 150
  Earlier sketch in SATA *87*
Atwood, Ann (Margaret) 1913-1992 7
Atwood, Margaret 1939- 170
  Earlier sketch in SATA *50*
Atwood, Margaret Eleanor
  See Atwood, Margaret
Aubrey, Meg Kelleher 1963- 83
Aubry, Claude B. 1914-1984 29
  Obituary 40
Auch, Herm 173
Auch, Mary Jane 173
  Earlier sketch in SATA *138*
Auch, M.J.
  See Auch, Mary Jane
Auclair, Joan 1960- 68
Auel, Jean 1936- 91

Auel, Jean M.
  See Auel, Jean
Auel, Jean Marie
  See Auel, Jean
Auer, Martin 1951- 77
Augarde, Steve 1950- 210
  Earlier sketches in SATA *25, 159*
Augarde, Steven Andre
  See Augarde, Steve
Augelli, John P(at) 1921- 46
Augustine, Mildred
  See Benson, Mildred
Ault, Phil
  See Ault, Phillip H(alliday)
Ault, Phillip H(alliday) 1914- 23
Ault, Rosalie Sain 1942- 38
Ault, Roz
  See Ault, Rosalie Sain
Aung, (Maung) Htin 1909- 21
Auntie Deb
  See Coury, Louise Andree
Auntie Louise
  See Coury, Louise Andree
Aunt Weedy
  See Alcott, Louisa May
Auseon, Andrew 1976- 217
  Earlier sketch in SATA *166*
Austen, Carrie
  See Bennett, Cherie
Austen, Catherine 1965- 223
Austin, Carrie
  See Seuling, Barbara
Austin, Elizabeth S. 1907-1977 5
Austin, Harry
  See McInerny, Ralph
Austin, Margot 1909(?)-1990 11
  Obituary 66
Austin, Michael 178
Austin, Oliver L(uther), Jr. 1903-1988 7
  Obituary 59
Austin, Patricia 1950- 137
Austin, R. G.
  See Gelman, Rita Golden
  and Lamb, Nancy
Austin, Virginia 1951- 152
  Earlier sketch in SATA *80*
Auteur, Hillary
  See Gottfried, Theodore Mark
Auth, Tony
  See Auth, William Anthony, Jr.
Auth, William Anthony, Jr. 1942- 192
Autry, Gloria Diener
  See Allen, Terril Diener
Auvil, Peggy A 1954- 122
Auvil, Peggy Appleby
  See Auvil, Peggy A
Aveni, Anthony F. 1938- 181
Aveni, Anthony Francis
  See Aveni, Anthony F.
Averbeck, Jim 1963- 201
Averill, Esther (Holden) 1902-1992 28
  Obituary 72
  Earlier sketch in SATA *1*
Avery, A. A.
  See Montgomery, Rutherford George
Avery, Al
  See Montgomery, Rutherford George
Avery, Gillian 1926- 137
  Autobiography Feature 137
  Earlier sketches in SATA *7, 75*
  See also SAAS *6*
Avery, Gillian Elise
  See Avery, Gillian
Avery, Kay 1908- 5
Avery, Lorraine
  See Older, Effin
  and Older, Jules
Avery, Lynn
  See Cole, Lois Dwight

Avi 1937- *190*
 Earlier sketches in SATA *14, 71, 108, 156*
 See also CLR *68*
Aviles, Martha *218*
Avishai, Susan 1949- *82*
Avril, Francois 1961- *191*
Avril, Lynne
 See Cravath, Lynne W.
Awdry, Christopher Vere 1940- *67*
Awdry, Wilbert Vere 1911-1997 .... *94*
 See also CLR *23*
Axelrod, Amy *131*
Axelsen, Stephen 1953- *165*
Axton, David
 See Koontz, Dean
Ayars, James S(terling) 1898-1986 .... *4*
Aye, A. K.
 See Edwards, Hazel (Eileen)
Ayer, Eleanor H. 1947-1998 .... *121*
 Earlier sketch in SATA *78*
Ayer, Jacqueline 1930- *13*
Ayer, Margaret (?)-1981 .... *15*
Aylesworth, Jim 1943- *213*
 Earlier sketches in SATA *38, 89, 139*
 See also CLR *89*
Aylesworth, Thomas G(ibbons) 1927-1995 .. *88*
 Earlier sketch in SATA *4*
 See also CLR *6*
 See also SAAS *17*
Ayliffe, Alex *190*
Aylward, Marcus
 See Alexander, Marc
Aymar, Brandt 1911- *22*
Ayme, Marcel (Andre) 1902-1967 .... *91*
 See also CLR *25*
Ayres, Becky
 See Hickox, Rebecca (Ayres)
Ayres, Katherine 1947- *187*
Ayres, Pam 1947- *90*
Ayres, Patricia Miller 1923-1985
 Obituary *46*
Aytmatov, Chingiz
 See Aitmatov, Chingiz
Ayto, Russell 1960- *206*
 Earlier sketches in SATA *111, 166*
Azaid
 See Zaidenberg, Arthur
Azar, Penny 1952- *121*
Azarian, Mary 1940- *171*
 Earlier sketch in SATA *112*
Azore, Barbara 1934- *188*

B

Baasansuren, Bolormaa 1982- *216*
Baastad, Babbis Friis
 See Friis-Baastad, Babbis Ellinor
Bab
 See Gilbert, W(illiam) S(chwenck)
Babbis, Eleanor
 See Friis-Baastad, Babbis Ellinor
Babbitt, Lucy Cullyford 1960- *85*
Babbitt, Natalie 1932- *194*
 Earlier sketches in SATA *6, 68, 106*
 See also CLR *141*
 See also SAAS *5*
Babbitt, Natalie Zane Moore
 See Babbitt, Natalie
Babcock, Chris 1963- *83*
Babcock, Dennis 1948- *22*
Babcock, Dennis Arthur
 See Babcock, Dennis
Baber, Carolyn Stonnell 1936- *96*
Baboni, Elena *198*
Baca, Ana 1967- *191*
Baca, Maria 1951- *104*
Baccalario, Pierdomenico 1974- *222*

Bach, Alice (Hendricks) 1942- *93*
 Brief entry *27*
 Earlier sketch in SATA *30*
Bach, Bellamy
 See Windling, Terri
Bach, Mary 1960- *125*
Bach, Richard 1936- *13*
Bach, Richard David
 See Bach, Richard
Bache, Ellyn 1942- *124*
Bachel, Beverly K. 1957- *142*
Bachelet, Gilles 1952- *196*
Bachman, Fred 1949- *12*
Bachman, Richard
 See King, Stephen
Bachrach, Deborah *80*
Backus, James Gilmore 1913-1989
 Obituary *63*
Backus, Jim
 See Backus, James Gilmore
Bacmeister, Rhoda W(arner) 1893-1991 .... *11*
Bacon, Betty
 See Bacon, Elizabeth
Bacon, Elizabeth 1914-2001 .... *3*
 Obituary *131*
Bacon, Joan Chase
 See Bowden, Joan Chase
Bacon, Josephine Dodge (Daskam)
 1876-1961 .... *48*
Bacon, Margaret Frances
 See Bacon, Peggy
Bacon, Margaret Hope 1921- *6*
Bacon, Martha Sherman 1917-1981 .... *18*
 Obituary *27*
 See also CLR *3*
Bacon, Melvin 1950- *93*
Bacon, Melvin L.
 See Bacon, Melvin
Bacon, Peggy 1895-1987 .... *50*
Bacon, R(onald) L(eonard) 1924- *84*
 Earlier sketch in SATA *26*
Baddiel, Ivor 1963- *210*
Baden, Robert 1936- *70*
Baden-Powell, Robert (Stephenson Smyth)
 1857-1941 .... *16*
Badt, Karin L(uisa) 1963- *91*
Bae, Hyun-Joo *186*
Baehr, Kingsley M. 1937- *89*
Baehr, Patricia 1952- *65*
Baehr, Patricia Goehner
 See Baehr, Patricia
Baek, Matthew J. 1971- *202*
Baer, Jill
 See Gilbert, (Agnes) Joan (Sewell)
Baer, Judy 1951- *71*
Baer, Julie 1960- *161*
Baer-Block, Roxanna *172*
Baerg, Harry J(ohn) 1909-1996 .... *12*
Baeten, Lieve 1954- *83*
Bagert, Brod 1947- *191*
 Earlier sketch in SATA *80*
Baggette, Susan K. 1942- *126*
Baggott, Julianna 1969- *197*
Bagnold, Enid 1889-1981 .... *25*
 Earlier sketch in SATA *1*
Baguley, Elizabeth 1959- *199*
Bahlke, Valerie Worth -1994
 See Worth, Valerie
Bahous, Sally 1939- *86*
Bahr, Mary (Madelyn) 1946- *95*
Bahr, Robert 1940- *38*
Bahti, Tom 1926-1972 .... *57*
 Brief entry *31*
Bai, Durga *211*
Baicker-McKee, Carol 1958- *177*
Bailey, Alice Cooper 1890-1978 .... *12*
Bailey, Anne 1958- *71*
Bailey, Bernadine (Freeman) 1901-1995 ...... *14*
Bailey, Carolyn Sherwin 1875-1961 .... *14*
Bailey, Debbie 1954- *123*
Bailey, Donna (Veronica Anne) 1938- *68*

Bailey, Jane H(orton) 1916- *12*
Bailey, John (Robert) 1940- *52*
Bailey, Len *193*
Bailey, Linda 1948- *217*
 Earlier sketches in SATA *107, 182*
Bailey, Maralyn Collins (Harrison) 1941- *12*
Bailey, Matilda
 See Radford, Ruby L(orraine)
Bailey, Maurice Charles 1932- *12*
Bailey, Pearl (Mae) 1918-1990 .... *81*
Bailey, Peter 1946- *194*
Bailey, Ralph Edgar 1893-1982 .... *11*
Bailey, Sheila (Lucas) 1960- *155*
Baillie, Allan 1943- *151*
 Earlier sketch in SATA *87*
 See also CLR *49*
 See also SAAS *21*
Baillie, Allan Stuart
 See Baillie, Allan
Baines, John (David) 1943- *71*
Bains, Larry
 See Sabin, Louis
Baird, Alison 1963- *138*
Baird, Bil 1904-1987 .... *30*
 Obituary *52*
Baird, Thomas (P.) 1923-1990 .... *45*
 Brief entry *39*
 Obituary *64*
Baird, William Britton
 See Baird, Bil
Baity, Elizabeth Chesley 1907-1989 .... *1*
Baiul, Oksana 1977- *108*
Bajoria, Paul 1964- *187*
Bakeless, John (Edwin) 1894-1978 .... *9*
Bakeless, Katherine Little 1895-1992 .... *9*
Baker, Alan 1951- *146*
 Earlier sketches in SATA *22, 93*
Baker, Augusta 1911-1998 .... *3*
Baker, Barbara 1947- *192*
Baker, Betty Lou 1928-1987 .... *73*
 Obituary *54*
 Earlier sketch in SATA *5*
Baker, Carin Greenberg 1959- *79*
Baker, Charlotte 1910- *2*
Baker, Christina
 See Kline, Christina Baker
Baker, Christopher W. 1952- *144*
Baker, Deirdre 1955- *195*
Baker, E.D. *190*
Baker, (Mary) Elizabeth (Gillette) 1923- *7*
Baker, Gayle Cunningham 1950- *39*
Baker, James W. 1924- *65*
 Earlier sketch in SATA *22*
Baker, James W. 1926- *122*
Baker, Janice E(dla) 1941- *22*
Baker, Jeanette *178*
Baker, Jeannie 1950- *156*
 Earlier sketches in SATA *23, 88*
 See also CLR *28*
Baker, Jeffrey J(ohn) W(heeler) 1931- *5*
Baker, Jim
 See Baker, James W.
Baker, Keith 1953- *222*
 Earlier sketch in SATA *179*
Baker, Ken 1962- *133*
Baker, Laura Nelson 1911- *3*
Baker, Margaret 1890-1965 .... *4*
Baker, Margaret J(oyce) 1918- *12*
 See also SAAS *8*
Baker, Mary Gladys Steel 1892-1974 .... *12*
Baker, (Robert) Michael (Graham) 1938- *4*
Baker, Nina (Brown) 1888-1957 .... *15*
Baker, Pamela J. 1947- *66*
Baker, Rachel 1904-1978 .... *2*
 Obituary *26*
Baker, Roberta *206*
Baker, Rosalie F. 1945- *166*
Baker, Samm Sinclair 1909-1997 .... *12*
 Obituary *96*
Baker, Sharon Reiss 1962- *207*
Baker, Susan (Catherine) 1942-1991 .... *29*

Baker-Smith, Grahame *223*
Balaam
  See Lamb, G(eoffrey) F(rederick)
Balan, Bruce 1959- *113*
Balcavage, Dynise 1965- *137*
Balch, Glenn 1902-1989 .... *3*
  Obituary *83*
  See also SAAS *11*
Baldacci, David 1960- *184*
Baldacci, David G.
  See Baldacci, David
  and Baldacci, David
Balderose, Nancy Ward 1952- *93*
Balderson, Margaret 1935- *151*
Baldini, Michelle *205*
Baldry, Cherith 1947- *167*
  Earlier sketch in SATA *72*
Balducci, Carolyn 1946- *5*
Balducci, Carolyn Feleppa
  See Balducci, Carolyn
Baldwin, Alex
  See Griffin, W. E. B.
Baldwin, Anne Norris 1938- *5*
Baldwin, Clara *11*
Baldwin, Gordo
  See Baldwin, Gordon C(ortis)
Baldwin, Gordon C(ortis) 1908-1983 .... *12*
Baldwin, James 1841-1925 .... *24*
Baldwin, James 1924-1987 .... *9*
  Obituary *54*
Baldwin, Louis 1919- *110*
Baldwin, Margaret
  See Weis, Margaret
Baldwin, Stan(ley C.) 1929- *62*
  Brief entry *28*
Bales, Carol Ann 1940- *57*
  Brief entry *29*
Balet, Jan (Bernard) 1913- *11*
Balgassi, Haemi 1971- *131*
Balian, Lorna 1929- *91*
  Earlier sketch in SATA *9*
Balit, Christina 1961- *212*
  Earlier sketches in SATA *102, 159*
Ball, Duncan 1941- *73*
Ball, Zachary
  See Janas, Frankie-Lee
  and Masters, Kelly R(ay)
Ballantine, Lesley Frost
  See Frost, Lesley
Ballantyne, R(obert) M(ichael) 1825-1894 ... *24*
  See also CLR *137*
Ballard, James G.
  See Ballard, J.G.
Ballard, James Graham
  See Ballard, J.G.
Ballard, Jane
  See Gorman, Carol
Ballard, J.G. 1930-2009 .... *93*
  Obituary *203*
Ballard, Jim G.
  See Ballard, J.G.
Ballard, John 1945- *110*
Ballard, Lowell C(lyne) 1904-1986 .... *12*
  Obituary *49*
Ballard, (Charles) Martin 1929- *1*
Ballard, Mignon F. 1934- *64*
  Brief entry *49*
Ballard, Mignon Franklin
  See Ballard, Mignon F.
Ballard, Robert D(uane) 1942- *85*
  See also CLR *60*
Ballard, Robin 1965- *126*
Balliett, Blue 1955- *156*
Ballinger, Bryan 1968- *161*
Ballouhey, Pierre 1944- *90*
Balog, Cyn *221*
Balogh, Penelope 1916-1975 .... *1*
  Obituary *34*
Balouch, Kristen *176*
Balow, Tom 1931- *12*
Baltazzi, Evan S(erge) 1921- *90*

Balterman, Marcia Ridlon 1942- *22*
Baltimore, J.
  See Catherall, Arthur
Baltzer, Hans (Adolf) 1900- *40*
Balzano, Jeanne (Koppel) 1912- *7*
Bambara, Toni Cade 1939-1995 .... *112*
Bamfylde, Walter
  See Bevan, Tom
Bamman, Henry A. 1918- *12*
Banat, D. R.
  See Bradbury, Ray
Bancroft, Bronwyn 1958- *216*
Bancroft, Griffing 1907-1999 .... *6*
Bancroft, Laura
  See Baum, L. Frank
Bandel, Betty 1912- *47*
Baner, Skulda Vanadis 1897-1964 .... *10*
Banerjee, Anjali *174*
Banfill, A. Scott 1956- *98*
Bang, Betsy 1912- *48*
  Brief entry *37*
Bang, Garrett
  See Bang, Molly
Bang, Molly 1943- *215*
  Earlier sketches in SATA *24, 69, 111, 158*
  See also CLR *8*
Bang, Molly Garrett
  See Bang, Molly
Bang-Campbell, Monika 1975(?)- *195*
  Earlier sketch in SATA *140*
Banjo, The
  See Paterson, A(ndrew) B(arton)
Banke, Cecile de
  See de Banke, Cecile
Banks, Erin Bennett 1978- *211*
Banks, Kate 1960- *200*
  Earlier sketches in SATA *134, 172*
Banks, Laura Stockton Voorhees 1908(?)-1980
  Obituary *23*
Banks, Lynne Reid
  See Reid Banks, Lynne
Banks, Merry *197*
Banks, Michael A. 1951- *101*
Banks, Paul 1952- *174*
Banks, Sara
  See Harrell, Sara Gordon
Banks, Sara Jeanne Gordon Harrell
  See Harrell, Sara Gordon
Bannatyne-Cugnet, Elizabeth Jo-Anne
  See Bannatyne-Cugnet, Jo
Bannatyne-Cugnet, Jo 1951- *101*
Banner, Angela
  See Maddison, Angela Mary
Bannerman, Helen (Brodie Cowan Watson)
  1862(?)-1946 .... *19*
  See also CLR *144*
Banning, Evelyn I. 1903-1993 .... *36*
Bannon, Laura (?)-1963 .... *6*
Bannor, Brett 1959- *143*
Bansch, Helga 1957- *224*
Banta, Susan *181*
Bantock, Nick 1950(?)- *95*
Banyai, Istvan *193*
Barakat, Ibtisam 1963- *186*
Barasch, Lynne 1939- *186*
  Earlier sketches in SATA *74, 126*
Barbalet, Margaret 1949- *77*
Barbary, James
  See Baumann, Amy Beeching
  and Beeching, Jack
Barbash, Shepard 1957- *84*
Barbauld, Anna Laetitia 1743-1825
  See CLR *160*
Barbe, Walter Burke 1926- *45*
Barber, Alison *222*
Barber, Antonia 1932- *163*
  Earlier sketch in SATA *29*
Barber, Atiim Kiambu
  See Barber, Tiki
Barber, Lynda
  See Graham-Barber, Lynda

Barber, Lynda Graham
  See Graham-Barber, Lynda
Barber, Richard (William) 1941- *35*
Barber, Ronde 1975- *182*
Barber, Tiki 1975- *182*
Barbera, Joe 1911-2006 .... *51*
  Obituary *179*
Barbera, Joseph
  See Barbera, Joe
Barbera, Joseph Roland
  See Barbera, Joe
Barberis, Juan C(arlos) 1920- *61*
Barbour, Karen 1956- *170*
  Earlier sketches in SATA *63, 121*
Barbour, Ralph Henry 1870-1944 .... *16*
Barclay, Bill
  See Moorcock, Michael
Barclay, Isabel
  See Dobell, I(sabel) M(arian) B(arclay)
Barclay, William Ewert
  See Moorcock, Michael
Barclay, William Ewert
  See Moorcock, Michael
Bardhan-Quallen, Sudipta 1977- *214*
  Earlier sketch in SATA *168*
Bardoe, Cheryl *181*
Bare, Arnold Edwin 1920- *16*
Bare, Colleen Stanley *32*
Bar-el, Dan *199*
Barenholtz, Bernard 1914-1989
  Obituary *64*
Bargar, Gary W. 1947-1985 .... *63*
Barger, Jan 1948- *147*
Barish, Matthew 1907-2000 .... *12*
Barkan, Joanne *127*
  Earlier sketch in SATA *77*
Barker, Albert W. 1900- *8*
Barker, Carol (Minturn) 1938- *31*
Barker, Cicely Mary 1895-1973 .... *49*
  Brief entry *39*
  See also CLR *88*
Barker, Melvern 1907-1989 .... *11*
Barker, S. Omar 1894-1985 .... *10*
Barker, Squire Omar
  See Barker, S. Omar
Barker, Will 1913-1983 .... *8*
Barkin, Carol 1944- *52*
  Earlier sketch in SATA *42*
Barklem, Jill 1951- *96*
  See also CLR *31*
Barkley, Brad *178*
Barkley, James Edward 1941- *6*
Barks, Carl 1901-2000 .... *37*
Barley, Janet Crane 1934- *95*
Barlow, Steve 1952- *211*
Barnaby, Ralph S(tanton) 1893-1986 .... *9*
Barnard, A. M.
  See Alcott, Louisa May
Barnard, Bryn 1956- *169*
  Earlier sketch in SATA *115*
Barne, Kitty
  See Barne, Marion Catherine
Barne, Marion Catherine 1883-1957 .... *97*
Barneda, David *206*
Barner, Bob 1947- *136*
  Earlier sketch in SATA *29*
Barnes, Dawn 1957- *175*
Barnes, Derrick *191*
Barnes, Derrick D.
  See Barnes, Derrick
Barnes, (Frank) Eric Wollencott 1907-1962 . *22*
Barnes, Joyce Annette 1958- *85*
Barnes, Laura T. 1958- *119*
Barnes, Loutricia
  See Barnes-Svarney, Patricia L(ou)
Barnes, Malcolm 1909(?)-1984
  Obituary *41*
Barnes, Michael 1934- *55*
Barnes-Murphy, Frances 1951- *88*
Barnes-Murphy, Rowan 1952- *88*
Barnes-Svarney, Patricia L(ou) 1953- *67*

Barnet, Nancy 1954- 84
Barnett, Ivan 1947- 70
Barnett, Lincoln (Kinnear) 1909-1979 36
Barnett, Mac 223
Barnett, Moneta 1922-1976 33
Barnett, Naomi 1927- 40
Barney, Maginel Wright 1881(?)-1966 39
   Brief entry 32
Barnhart, Clarence L(ewis) 1900-1993 48
   Obituary 78
Barnhouse, Rebecca 1961- 225
Barnouw, Adriaan Jacob 1877-1968
   Obituary 27
Barnouw, Victor 1915-1989 43
   Brief entry 28
Barnstone, Willis 1927- 20
Barnum, Jay Hyde 1888(?)-1962 20
Barnum, P. T., Jr.
   See Stratemeyer, Edward L.
Barnum, Richard 67
   Earlier sketch in SATA 1
Barnum, Theodore
   See Stratemeyer, Edward L.
Barnwell, Ysaye M. 1946- 200
Baron, Kathy 1954- 90
Baron, Virginia Olsen 1931- 46
   Brief entry 28
Barr, Donald 1921-2004 20
   Obituary 152
Barr, George 1907-1992 2
Barr, Jene 1922-1985 16
   Obituary 42
Barr, Nevada 1952- 126
   Earlier sketch in SATA 115
Barragan, Paula 1963- 216
Barratt, Mark 1954- 224
Barrer, Gertrude
   See Barrer-Russell, Gertrude
Barrer-Russell, Gertrude 1921- 27
Barrett, Angela 1955- 223
Barrett, Angela (Jane) 1955- 145
   Earlier sketch in SATA 75
Barrett, Ethel 87
   Brief entry 44
Barrett, Joyce Durham 1943- 138
Barrett, Judi
   See Barrett, Judith
Barrett, Judith 1941- 204
   Earlier sketch in SATA 26
   See also CLR 98
Barrett, Robert T(heodore) 1949- 92
Barrett, Ron 1937- 14
Barrett, Susan (Mary) 1938- 113
Barrett, Tracy 1955- 207
   Earlier sketches in SATA 84, 115, 156
Barrett, William E(dmund) 1900-1986
   Obituary 49
Barretta, Gene 214
   Earlier sketch in SATA 176
Barretton, Grandall
   See Garrett, Randall
Barrie, Baronet
   See Barrie, J. M.
Barrie, J. M. 1860-1937 100
   See also YABC 1
   See also CLR 124
Barrie, James Matthew
   See Barrie, J. M.
Barringer, William 1940-1996 153
Barrington, Michael
   See Moorcock, Michael
Barris, George 1925- 47
Barrol, Grady
   See Bograd, Larry
Barron, Rex 1951- 84
Barron, T.A. 1952- 192
   Earlier sketches in SATA 83, 126
   See also CLR 86
Barron, Thomas Archibald
   See Barron, T.A.

Barron, Tom
   See Barron, T.A.
Barrow, Lloyd H. 1942- 73
Barrows, Annie 1962- 180
Barry, Dan 1958- 177
Barry, Dana (Marie Malloy) 1949- 139
Barry, James P(otvin) 1918- 14
Barry, Katharina Watjen 1936- 4
Barry, Robert 1931- 6
Barry, Robert Everett
   See Barry, Robert
Barry, Scott 1952- 32
Barry, Sheila Anne -2003 91
Barshaw, Ruth McNally 203
Bartell, Susan S. 175
Bartenbach, Jean 1918- 40
Barth, Edna 1914-1980 7
   Obituary 24
Barth, Kelly L. 1964- 152
Barthelme, Donald 1931-1989 7
   Obituary 62
Barth-Grozinger, Inge 1950- 185
Bartholomew, Barbara 1941- 86
   Brief entry 42
Bartholomew, Jean
   See Beatty, Patricia (Robbins)
Bartlett, Alison 153
Bartlett, Philip A. 1
Bartlett, Robert Merrill 1899-1995 12
Bartoletti, Susan Campbell 1958- 173
   Earlier sketches in SATA 88, 129, 135
Barton, Byron 1930- 126
   Earlier sketches in SATA 9, 90
Barton, Chris 224
Barton, Jill(ian) 1940- 75
Barton, May Hollis 67
   Earlier sketch in SATA 1
Barton, Pat
   See Arrowsmith, Pat
Bartos-Hoeppner, Barbara 1923- 5
Bartram, Simon 218
   Earlier sketch in SATA 156
Bartsch, Jochen 1906- 39
Baruch, Dorothy W(alter) 1899-1962 21
Barunga, Albert 1912(?)-1977 120
Baryshnikov, Mikhail 1948- 192
Bas, Rutger
   See Rutgers van der Loeff-Basenau, An(na)
   Maria Margaretha
Base, Graeme 1958- 162
   Earlier sketches in SATA 67, 101
   See also CLR 22
Base, Graeme Rowland
   See Base, Graeme
Baseman, Gary 1960- 174
Bash, Barbara 1948- 132
Bashevis, Isaac
   See Singer, Isaac Bashevis
Bashevis, Yitskhok
   See Singer, Isaac Bashevis
Bashista, Adrienne Ehlert 203
Basile, Gloria Vitanza 1929- 180
Baskin, Leonard 1922-2000 120
   Brief entry 27
   Earlier sketch in SATA 30
Baskin, Nora Raleigh 1961- 189
   Earlier sketch in SATA 129
Bason, Lillian 1913- 20
Bass, Hester 1956- 223
Bass, L. G.
   See Geringer, Laura
Bassett, Jeni 1959- 64
   Brief entry 43
Bassett, John Keith
   See Keating, Lawrence A.
Bassett, Lisa 1958- 61
Bassil, Andrea
   See Nilsen, Anna
Bastyra, Judy 108
Basye, Dale E. 205
Bataille, Marion 1963- 209

Bat-Ami, Miriam 1950- 150
   Autobiography Feature 150
   Earlier sketches in SATA 82, 122
Bate, Lucy 1939-1993 18
Bate, Norman (Arthur) 1916- 5
Bateman, Colin 1962- 172
Bateman, Donna M. 190
Bateman, Teresa 1957- 216
   Earlier sketches in SATA 112, 168
Bates, Amy June 189
Bates, Barbara S(nedeker) 1919- 12
Bates, Betty
   See Bates, Elizabeth
Bates, Dianne 1948- 147
Bates, Elizabeth 1921- 19
Bates, Ivan 175
Bates, Katharine Lee 1859-1929 113
Bates, Martine
   See Leavitt, Martine
Bateson, Catherine 1960- 197
   Earlier sketch in SATA 157
Batey, Tom 1946- 52
   Brief entry 41
Bath, Kevin P.
   See Bath, K.P.
Bath, K.P. 1959- 171
Batherman, Muriel
   See Sheldon, Muriel
Batson, Larry 1930- 35
Batt, Tanya Robyn 1970- 131
Battaglia, Aurelius 1910- 50
   Brief entry 33
Batten, H(arry) Mortimer 1888-1958 25
Batten, Mary 1937- 162
   Earlier sketches in SATA 5, 102
Batterberry, Ariane Ruskin 1935- 13
Batterberry, Michael Carver 1932-2010 32
Battle-Lavert, Gwendolyn 1951- 155
   Earlier sketches in SATA 85, 131
Battles, (Roxy) Edith 1921- 7
Baudouy, Michel-Aime 1909- 7
Bauer, A.C.E. 201
Bauer, Caroline Feller 1935- 98
   Brief entry 46
   Earlier sketch in SATA 52
   See also SAAS 24
Bauer, Fred 1934- 36
Bauer, Helen 1900-1988 2
Bauer, Joan 1951- 160
   Earlier sketch in SATA 117
Bauer, Jutta 1955- 150
Bauer, Marion Dane 1938- 192
   Autobiography Feature 144
   Earlier sketches in SATA 20, 69, 113, 144
   See also SAAS 9
Bauer, Michael Gerard 1955(?)- 167
Bauer, Steven 1948- 125
Bauerschmidt, Marjorie 1926- 15
Baughman, Dorothy 1940- 61
Baum, Allyn Z(elton) 1924-1997 98
   Earlier sketch in SATA 20
Baum, L. Frank
   See Thompson, Ruth Plumly
Baum, L. Frank 1856-1919 100
   Earlier sketch in SATA 18
   See also CLR 107
Baum, Louis 1948- 182
   Brief entry 52
   Earlier sketch in SATA 64
Baum, Louis F.
   See Baum, L. Frank
Baum, Lyman Frank
   See Baum, L. Frank
Baum, Maxie 188
Baum, Willi 1931- 4
Bauman, Beth Ann 1964- 220
Baumann, Amy Beeching 1922- 10
Baumann, Amy Brown Beeching
   See Baumann, Amy Beeching
Baumann, Hans 1914- 2
   See also CLR 35

Baumann, Kurt 1935- 21
Baumgartner, Barbara 1939- 86
Baurys, Flo 1938- 122
Baurys, Florence
    See Baurys, Flo
Bausum, Ann 173
Bawden, Nina 1925- 132
    Earlier sketches in SATA *4, 72*
    See also CLR *51*
    See also SAAS *16*
Bawden, Nina Mary Mabey
    See Bawden, Nina
Baxter, Andy
    See Dakin, Glenn
Baxter, Roberta 1952- 219
Baxter, Valerie
    See Meynell, Laurence Walter
Bay, Jeanette Graham 1928- 88
Bayer, Harold
    See Gregg, Andrew K.
Bayer, Jane E. (?)-1985
    Obituary 44
Bayley, Nicola 1949- 129
    Earlier sketches in SATA *41, 69*
Baylor, Byrd 1924- 136
    Earlier sketches in SATA *16, 69*
    See also CLR *3*
Baynes, Pauline 1922-2008 133
    Obituary 196
    Earlier sketches in SATA *19, 59*
Baynes, Pauline Diana
    See Baynes, Pauline
Bayoc, Cbabi 186
Bayrock, Fiona 215
BB
    See Watkins-Pitchford, Denys James
Beach, Charles
    See Reid, (Thomas) Mayne
Beach, Charles Amory 1
Beach, Edward L. 1918-2002 12
    Obituary 140
Beach, Edward Latimer
    See Beach, Edward L.
Beach, Lisa 1957- 111
Beach, Lynn
    See Lance, Kathryn
Beach, Stewart T(aft) 1899-1979 23
Beachcroft, Nina 1931- 18
Beagle, Peter S. 1939- 130
    Earlier sketch in SATA *60*
Beagle, Peter Soyer
    See Beagle, Peter S.
Beaglehole, Helen 1946- 117
Beake, Lesley 1949- 209
Beale, Fleur 107
Bealer, Alex W(inkler III) 1921-1980 8
    Obituary 22
Beales, Valerie 1915- 74
Beals, Carleton 1893-1979 12
Beals, Frank Lee 1881-1972
    Obituary 26
Beam, Matt 1970- 187
Beame, Rona 1934- 12
Beamer, Charles 1942- 43
Beamer, George Charles, Jr.
    See Beamer, Charles
Bean, Jonathan 1979- 194
Bean, Normal
    See Burroughs, Edgar Rice
Beaney, Jan
    See Udall, Jan Beaney
Beaney, Jane
    See Udall, Jan Beaney
Bear, Carolyn
    See Rayban, Chloe
Bear, Greg 1951- 105
    Earlier sketch in SATA *65*
Bear, Gregory Dale
    See Bear, Greg
Bearanger, Marie
    See Messier, Claire

Beard, Alex 1970- 222
Beard, Charles A(ustin) 1874-1948 18
Beard, Dan(iel Carter) 1850-1941 22
Beard, Darleen Bailey 1961- 96
Bearden, Romare (Howard) 1914(?)-1988 ... 22
    Obituary 56
Beardmore, Cedric
    See Beardmore, George
Beardmore, George 1908-1979 20
Beardshaw, Rosalind 1969- 225
    Earlier sketch in SATA *190*
Beardsley, Martyn R. 1957- 150
Bearman, Jane (Ruth) 1917- 29
Bearn, Emily 220
Beaton, Clare 1947- 220
    Earlier sketch in SATA *125*
Beatty, Elizabeth
    See Holloway, Teresa (Bragunier)
Beatty, Hetty Burlingame 1907-1971 5
Beatty, Jerome, Jr. 1918- 5
Beatty, John (Louis) 1922-1975 6
    Obituary 25
Beatty, Patricia (Robbins) 1922-1991 73
    Obituary 68
    Earlier sketches in SATA *1, 30*
    See also SAAS *4*
Beaty, Andrea 186
Beaty, Mary (T.) 1947- 146
Beaudoin, Sean 210
Beauford, Jhenne Tyler
    See Beauford, Tyler
Beauford, Tyler 1990- 225
Beaumont, Karen 1954- 204
Beavers, Ethen 1971- 225
Beccia, Carlyn 189
Bechard, Margaret 1953- 164
    Earlier sketch in SATA *85*
Bechtel, Louise Seaman 1894-1985 4
    Obituary 43
Bechtold, Lisze 208
Beck, Barbara L. 1927- 12
Beck, Ian 1947- 190
    Earlier sketch in SATA *138*
    See Beck, Ian Archibald
Beck, Peggy 1949- 171
Beck, Scott 197
Becker, Beril 1901-1999 11
Becker, Bonny 184
Becker, Deborah Zimmett 1955- 138
Becker, Helaine 1961- 142
Becker, John (Leonard) 1901- 12
Becker, John E(mil) 1942- 148
Becker, Joyce 1936- 39
Becker, May Lamberton 1873-1958 33
Becker, Neesa 1951- 123
Becker, Shari 174
Beckerman, Chad W. 198
Beckett, Sheilah 1913- 33
Beckhorn, Susan Williams 1953- 189
Beckles Willson, Robina 1930- 27
Beckman, Delores 1914-1994 51
Beckman, Gunnel 1910- 6
    See also CLR *25*
    See also SAAS *9*
Beckman, Kaj
    See Beckman, Karin
Beckman, Karin 1913- 45
Beckman, Per (Frithiof) 1913- 45
Bedard, Michael 1949- 154
    Earlier sketch in SATA *93*
    See also CLR *35*
Beddor, Frank 194
Beddows, Eric
    See Nutt, Ken
Bedford, A. N.
    See Watson, Jane Werner
Bedford, Annie North
    See Watson, Jane Werner
Bedford, David 224
    Earlier sketch in SATA *159*

Bedford, David J.
    See Bedford, David
Bedoukian, Kerop 1907-1981 53
Bee, Jay
    See Brainerd, John W(hiting)
Bee, William 188
Beebe, B. F.
    See Johnson, B. F.
Beebe, (Charles) William 1877-1962 19
Beeby, Betty 1923- 25
Beech, Mark 1971- 191
Beech, Webb
    See Griffin, W. E. B.
Beecham, Jahnna 161
Beechcroft, William
    See Hallstead, William F(inn III)
Beeching, Jack 1922- 14
Beeke, Tiphanie 219
    Earlier sketch in SATA *163*
Beeler, Janet
    See Shaw, Janet
Beeler, Nelson F(rederick) 1910-1978 13
Beere, Peter 1951- 97
Beers, Dorothy Sands 1917- 9
Beers, Lorna 1897-1989 14
Beers, V(ictor) Gilbert 1928- 130
    Earlier sketch in SATA *9*
Beeton, Max
    See Redding, Robert Hull
Begay, Shonto 1954- 137
Begaye, Lisa Shook
    See Beach, Lisa
Begin, Mary Jane 1963- 82
Begin-Callanan, Mary Jane
    See Begin, Mary Jane
Begley, Kathleen A. 1948- 21
Begley, Kathleen Anne
    See Begley, Kathleen A.
Beguine, Anna
    See Saintcrow, Lilith
Beha, Eileen 221
Beha, Philippe 211
Behan, Leslie
    See Gottfried, Theodore Mark
Behler, Deborah A. 1947- 145
Behler, John L. 1943-2006 145
    Obituary 173
Behler, John Luther
    See Behler, John L.
Behn, Harry 1898-1973 2
    Obituary 34
Behnke, Frances L. 8
Behr, Joyce 1929- 15
Behrens, June York 1925- 19
Behrman, Carol H(elen) 1925- 144
    Earlier sketch in SATA *14*
Beifuss, John, (Jr.) 1959- 92
Beil, Karen Magnuson 1950- 221
    Earlier sketch in SATA *124*
Beiler, Edna 1923- 61
Beingessner, Laura 1965- 220
Beinicke, Steve 1956- 69
Beirne, Barbara 1933- 71
Beiser, Arthur 1931- 22
Beiser, Germaine 1931- 11
Belair, Richard L. 1934- 45
Belaney, Archibald Stansfeld 1888-1938 24
    See also CLR *32*
Belasen, Amy 1983- 213
Belbin, David 1958- 164
    Earlier sketch in SATA *106*
Belden, Wilanne Schneider 1925- 56
Belfrage, Sally 1936-1994 65
    Obituary 79
Belknap, B. H.
    See Ellis, Edward S.
Belknap, Boynton
    See Ellis, Edward S.
Belknap, Boynton M.D.
    See Ellis, Edward S.

Bell, Anthea 1936- *148*
    Earlier sketch in SATA *88*
Bell, Cathleen Davitt 1971- *203*
Bell, Cece *202*
Bell, Clare (Louise) 1952- *99*
Bell, Corydon Whitten 1894-1980 .... *3*
Bell, David Owen 1949- *99*
Bell, Emerson
    See Stratemeyer, Edward L.
Bell, Emily Mary
    See Cason, Mabel Earp
Bell, Frank
    See Benson, Mildred
Bell, Gertrude (Wood) 1911-1987 .... *12*
Bell, Gina
    See Balzano, Jeanne (Koppel)
Bell, Hilari 1958- *197*
    Earlier sketch in SATA *151*
Bell, Jadrien
    See Golden, Christie
Bell, Janet
    See Clymer, Eleanor
Bell, Janet Cheatham 1937- *127*
Bell, Krista 1950- *215*
    Earlier sketch in SATA *126*
Bell, Krista Anne Blakeney
    See Bell, Krista
Bell, Margaret E(lizabeth) 1898-1990 .... *2*
Bell, Mary Reeves 1946- *88*
Bell, Norman (Edward) 1899- *11*
Bell, Raymond Martin 1907-1999 .... *13*
Bell, Siobhan *177*
Bell, Thelma Harrington 1896-1985 .... *3*
Bell, William 1945- *90*
    See also CLR *91*
Bellairs, John (Anthony) 1938-1991 .... *160*
    Obituary *66*
    Earlier sketches in SATA *2, 68*
    See also CLR *37*
Beller, Susan Provost 1949- *128*
    Earlier sketch in SATA *84*
    See also CLR *106*
Bellingham, Brenda 1931- *99*
    Brief entry *51*
Bello, Rosario de
    See De Bello, Rosario
Belloc, Hilaire 1870-1953 .... *112*
    See also YABC *1*
    See also CLR *102*
Belloc, Joseph Hilaire Pierre Sebastien Rene
    Swanton
    See Belloc, Hilaire
Belloc, Joseph Peter Rene Hilaire
    See Belloc, Hilaire
Belloc, Joseph Pierre Hilaire
    See Belloc, Hilaire
Belloli, Andrea P. A. 1947- *86*
Bell-Rehwoldt, Sheri 1962- *199*
Bellville, Cheryl Walsh 1944- *54*
    Brief entry *49*
Bell-Zano, Gina
    See Balzano, Jeanne (Koppel)
Belpre, Pura 1899-1982 .... *16*
    Obituary *30*
Belting, Natalia Maree 1915-1997 .... *6*
Belton, John Raynor 1931- *22*
Belton, Sandra 1939- *186*
    Earlier sketches in SATA *85, 134*
Belton, Sandra Yvonne
    See Belton, Sandra
Beltran, Alberto 1923- *43*
Beltran-Hernandez, Irene 1945- *74*
Belvedere, Lee
    See Grayland, Valerie (Merle Spanner)
Bemelmans, Ludwig 1898-1962 .... *100*
    Earlier sketch in SATA *15*
    See also CLR *93*
Benander, Carl D. 1941- *74*
Benary, Margot
    See Benary-Isbert, Margot

Benary-Isbert, Margot 1889-1979 .... *2*
    Obituary *21*
    See also CLR *12*
Benasutti, Marion 1908-1992 .... *6*
Benatar, Raquel 1955- *167*
Benchley, Nathaniel (Goddard) 1915-1981 .. *25*
    Obituary *28*
    Earlier sketch in SATA *3*
Benchley, Peter 1940-2006 .... *164*
    Earlier sketches in SATA *3, 89*
Benchley, Peter Bradford
    See Benchley, Peter
Bendall-Brunello, John *185*
Bender, Edna 1941- *92*
Bender, Esther 1942- *88*
Bender, Lucy Ellen 1942- *22*
Bender, Robert 1962- *160*
    Earlier sketch in SATA *79*
Bendick, Jeanne 1919- *135*
    Earlier sketches in SATA *2, 68*
    See also CLR *5*
    See also SAAS *4*
Bendick, Robert L(ouis) 1917- *11*
Benedetto, William R. 1928- *180*
Benedetto, William Ralph
    See Benedetto, William R.
Benedict, Andrew
    See Arthur, Robert, (Jr.)
Benedict, Dorothy Potter 1889-1979 .... *11*
    Obituary *23*
Benedict, Lois Trimble 1902-1967 .... *12*
Benedict, Rex 1920-1995 .... *8*
Benedict, Stewart H(urd) 1924- *26*
Beneduce, Ann Keay *128*
Benet, Laura 1884-1979 .... *3*
    Obituary *23*
Benet, Stephen Vincent 1898-1943
    See YABC *1*
Benet, Sula 1906-1982 .... *21*
    Obituary *33*
Ben-Ezer, Ehud 1936- *122*
Benezra, Barbara (Beardsley) 1921- *10*
Benham, Leslie 1922- *48*
Benham, Lois (Dakin) 1924- *48*
Benham, Mary Lile 1914-1991 .... *55*
Benjamin, E. M. J.
    See Bache, Ellyn
Benjamin, Floella 1949- *206*
Benjamin, Nora
    See Kubie, Nora Gottheil Benjamin
Benjamin, Saragail Katzman 1953- *86*
Benner, Cheryl 1962- *80*
Benner, Judith Ann 1942- *94*
Bennett, Alice
    See Ziner, Florence
Bennett, Cherie 1960- *158*
    Earlier sketch in SATA *97*
Bennett, Dorothea
    See Young, Dorothea Bennett
Bennett, Erin Susanne
    See Banks, Erin Bennett
Bennett, Holly 1957- *181*
Bennett, James (W.) 1942- *153*
    Autobiography Feature *153*
    Earlier sketches in SATA *93, 148*
Bennett, Jay 1912- *87*
    Brief entry *27*
    Earlier sketch in SATA *41*
    See also SAAS *4*
Bennett, Jill (Crawford) 1934- *41*
Bennett, John 1865-1956
    See YABC *1*
Bennett, Penelope (Agnes) 1938- *94*
Bennett, Rachel
    See Hill, Margaret (Ohler)
Bennett, Rainey 1907-1998 .... *15*
    Obituary *111*
Bennett, Richard 1899- *21*
Bennett, Russell H(oradley) 1896- *25*
Bennett, Veronica 1953- *178*
Bennett, William (John) 1943- *102*

Benning, Elizabeth
    See Rice, Bebe Faas
Benny, Mike 1964- *203*
Benson, Elizabeth P(olk) 1924- *65*
Benson, Kathleen 1947- *183*
    Earlier sketches in SATA *62, 111*
Benson, Linda M(aria) 1959- *84*
Benson, Mildred 1905-2002 .... *100*
    Obituary *135*
    Earlier sketches in SATA *1, 65, 67*
Benson, Mildred Augustine Wirt
    See Benson, Mildred
Benson, Mildred Wirt
    See Benson, Mildred
Benson, Millie
    See Benson, Mildred
Benson, Patrick 1956- *147*
Benson, Sally 1900-1972 .... *35*
    Obituary *27*
    Earlier sketch in SATA *1*
Bentley, Judith (McBride) 1945- *89*
    Earlier sketch in SATA *40*
Bentley, Karen
    See Taschek, Karen
Bentley, Nancy (L.) 1946- *78*
Bentley, Nicolas Clerihew 1907-1978
    Obituary *24*
Bentley, Phyllis Eleanor 1894-1977 .... *6*
    Obituary *25*
Bentley, Roy 1947- *46*
Bentley, William (George) 1916- *84*
Bently, Peter 1960- *221*
Benton, Jim 1963- *172*
ben Uzair, Salem
    See Horne, Richard Henry Hengist
Ben-Zvi, Rebeccca Tova
    See O'Connell, Rebecca
Bercaw, Edna Coe 1961- *124*
Berck, Judith 1960- *75*
Berelson, Howard 1940- *5*
Berends, Polly Berrien 1939- *50*
    Brief entry *38*
Berenstain, Jan 1923- *135*
    Earlier sketches in SATA *12, 64, 129*
    See also CLR *150*
    See also SAAS *20*
Berenstain, Janice
    See Berenstain, Jan
Berenstain, Michael 1951- *220*
    Earlier sketch in SATA *45*
Berenstain, Mike
    See Berenstain, Michael
Berenstain, Stan 1923-2005 .... *135*
    Obituary *169*
    Earlier sketches in SATA *12, 64, 129*
    See also CLR *150*
    See also SAAS *20*
Berenstain, Stanley
    See Berenstain, Stan
Berenzy, Alix 1957- *168*
    Earlier sketch in SATA *65*
Beresford, Elisabeth 1928-2010 .... *141*
    Earlier sketches in SATA *25, 86*
    See also SAAS *20*
Berg, Adriane G(ilda) 1948- *152*
Berg, Dave
    See Berg, David
Berg, David 1920-2002 .... *27*
    Obituary *137*
Berg, Elizabeth 1948- *104*
Berg, Jean Horton 1913-1995 .... *6*
Berg, Joan
    See Victor, Joan Berg
Berg, Ron 1952- *48*
Bergaust, Erik 1925-1978 .... *20*
Bergel, Colin J. 1963- *137*
Bergen, Joyce 1949- *95*
Berger, Barbara (Helen) 1945- *77*
Berger, Carin *185*
Berger, Gilda 1935- *88*
    Brief entry *42*

Berger, Joe 1970- *221*
Berger, Josef 1903-1971 .... *36*
Berger, Lou 1950- *213*
Berger, Melvin H. 1927- *158*
   Autobiography Feature *124*
   Earlier sketches in SATA *5, 88*
   See also CLR *32*
   See also SAAS *2*
Berger, Phil 1942-2001 .... *62*
Berger, Samantha 1969- *140*
Berger, Samantha Allison
   See Berger, Samantha
Berger, Terry 1933- *8*
Bergey, Alyce 1934- *45*
Bergey, Alyce Mae
   See Bergey, Alyce
Bergin, Mark 1961- *160*
   Earlier sketch in SATA *114*
Berglin, Ruth Marie 1970- *181*
Bergman, Donna 1934- *73*
Bergman, Mara 1956- *196*
Bergman, Tamar 1939- *95*
Bergren, Lisa T.
   See Bergren, Lisa Tawn
Bergren, Lisa Tawn *200*
Bergsma, Jody Lynn *163*
Bergstein, Rita M. *211*
Bergum, Constance R. 1952- *208*
   Earlier sketch in SATA *121*
Berk, Ari *208*
Berkebile, Fred D(onovan) 1900-1978
   Obituary *26*
Berkeley, Jon 1962- *204*
Berkes, Marianne *217*
   Earlier sketch in SATA *173*
Berkey, Barry Robert 1935- *24*
Berkowitz, Freda Pastor 1908-1994 .... *12*
Berkus, Clara Widess 1909- *78*
Berlan, Kathryn Hook 1946- *78*
Berlfein, Judy Reiss 1958- *79*
Berlin, Eric 1968- *195*
Berliner, Don 1930- *33*
Berliner, Franz 1930- *13*
Berlitz, Charles (L. Frambach) 1914-2003 ... *32*
   Obituary *151*
Berman, Linda 1948- *38*
Berman, Paul (Lawrence) 1949- *66*
Berman, Rachel 1946- *217*
Berna, Paul 1910-1994 .... *15*
   Obituary *78*
   See also CLR *19*
Bernadette
   See Watts, (Anna) Bernadette
Bernard, Bruce 1928-2000 .... *78*
   Obituary *124*
Bernard, George I. 1949- *39*
Bernard, Jacqueline (de Sieyes) 1921-1983 ... *8*
   Obituary *45*
Bernard, Patricia 1942- *181*
   Earlier sketch in SATA *106*
Bernard, Trish
   See Bernard, Patricia
Bernardin, James (B.) 1966- *112*
Bernardo, Anilu *184*
Bernards, Neal 1963- *71*
Bernasconi, Pablo 1973- *183*
Bernays, Anne 1930- *32*
Berner, Rotraut Susanne 1948- *214*
Bernhard, Durga T. 1961- *80*
Bernhard, Emery 1950- *80*
Bernheimer, Kate *201*
Bernier-Grand, Carmen T. 1947- *202*
Bernstein, Daryl (Evan) 1976- *81*
Bernstein, Joanne E(ckstein) 1943- *15*
Bernstein, Jonathan *217*
Bernstein, Margery 1933- *114*
Bernstein, Nina 1949- *180*
Bernstein, Theodore M(enline) 1904-1979 ... *12*
   Obituary *27*
Berrien, Edith Heal
   See Heal, Edith

Berrill, Jacquelyn (Batsel) 1905- *12*
Berrington, John
   See Brownjohn, Alan
Berry, B. J.
   See Berry, Barbara J.
Berry, Barbara J. 1937- *7*
Berry, Erick
   See Best, (Evangel) Allena Champlin
Berry, Holly 1957- *210*
Berry, James 1924- *110*
   Earlier sketch in SATA *67*
   See also CLR *143*
Berry, Jane Cobb 1915(?)-1979
   Obituary *22*
Berry, Joy 1944- *58*
   Brief entry *46*
Berry, Joy Wilt
   See Berry, Joy
Berry, Julie 1974- *218*
Berry, Lynne *190*
Berry, William D(avid) 1926- *14*
Bersani, Shennen 1961- *164*
Berson, Harold 1926- *4*
Bertagna, Julie 1962- *151*
Bertholf, Bret *189*
Bertin, Charles-Francois
   See Berlitz, Charles (L. Frambach)
Bertolet, Paul
   See McLaughlin, Frank
Berton, Pierre (Francis de Marigny) 1920-2004 .... *99*
   Obituary *158*
Bertrand, Cecile 1953- *76*
Bertrand, Diane Gonzales 1956- *177*
   Earlier sketch in SATA *106*
Bertrand, Lynne 1963- *164*
   Earlier sketch in SATA *81*
Beskow, Elsa (Maartman) 1874-1953 ...... *20*
   See also CLR *17*
Bess, Clayton
   See Locke, Robert
Besson, Luc 1959- *199*
Best, (Evangel) Allena Champlin 1892-1974 . *2*
   Obituary *25*
Best, Cari 1951- *200*
   Earlier sketches in SATA *107, 149*
Best, (Oswald) Herbert 1894-1980 .... *2*
Bestall, A(lfred) E(dmeades) 1892-1986 ...... *97*
   Obituary *48*
Betancourt, Jeanne 1941- *148*
   Brief entry *43*
   Earlier sketches in SATA *55, 96*
Beth, Mary
   See Miller, Mary Beth
Bethancourt, T. Ernesto
   See Paisley, Tom
Bethel, Dell 1929- *52*
Bethell, Jean (Frankenberry) 1922- *8*
Bethers, Ray 1902-1973 .... *6*
Bethke, Bruce Raymond 1955- *114*
Bethlen, T.D.
   See Silverberg, Robert
Bethune, J. G.
   See Ellis, Edward S.
Bethune, J. H.
   See Ellis, Edward S.
Betteridge, Anne
   See Potter, Margaret
Betteridge, Deirdre *214*
Bettina
   See Ehrlich, Bettina Bauer
Bettmann, Otto Ludwig 1903-1998 .... *46*
Bettoli, Delana *187*
Betts, James
   See Haynes, Betsy
Betz, Eva Kelly 1897-1968 .... *10*
Bevan, Tom 1868-1930(?)
   See YABC *2*
Bevis, Mary 1939- *202*
Bewick, Thomas 1753-1828 .... *16*
Beyer, Audrey White 1916- *9*

Beyer, Paul J. III 1950- *74*
Beynon, John
   See Harris, John (Wyndham Parkes Lucas) Beynon
Bezencon, Jacqueline (Buxcel) 1924- *48*
Bhatia, Jamunadevi 1919- *48*
Bhatia, June
   See Bhatia, Jamunadevi
Bial, Morrison David 1917- *62*
Bial, Raymond 1948- *225*
   Earlier sketches in SATA *76, 116, 165*
Biala
   See Brustlein, Janice Tworkov
Biale, Rachel 1952- *99*
Bialk, Elisa
   See Krautter, Elisa (Bialk)
Bianchi, John 1947- *91*
Bianchi, Robert S(teven) 1943- *92*
Bianco, Margery
   See Bianco, Margery Williams
Bianco, Margery Williams 1881-1944 .... *15*
   See also CLR *146*
Bianco, Pamela 1906- *28*
Bibby, Violet 1908-1996 .... *24*
Bible, Charles 1937- *13*
Bibo, Bobette
   See Gugliotta, Bobette
Bice, Clare 1909-1976 .... *22*
Bickerstaff, Isaac
   See Swift, Jonathan
Bidner, Jenni 1963- *193*
Biedrzycki, David 1955- *219*
Biegel, Paul 1925- *79*
   Earlier sketch in SATA *16*
   See also CLR *27*
   See also SAAS *18*
Biemiller, Carl L(udwig), Jr.) 1912-1979 ..... *40*
   Obituary *21*
Bienenfeld, Florence L(ucille) 1929- *39*
Bierhorst, John (William) 1936- *149*
   Autobiography Feature *149*
   Earlier sketches in SATA *6, 91*
   See also SAAS *10*
Biggar, Joan R. 1936- *120*
Biggar, Joan Rawlins
   See Biggar, Joan R.
Biggle, Lloyd, Jr. 1923-2002 .... *65*
Biggs, Brian 1968- *192*
Bilal, Abdel W(ahab) 1970- *92*
Bilbrough, Norman 1941- *111*
Bildner, Phil *173*
Bileck, Marvin 1920- *40*
Bilibin, Ivan (Iakolevich) 1876-1942 .... *61*
Bill, Alfred Hoyt 1879-1964 .... *44*
Billam, Rosemary 1952- *61*
Billings, Charlene W(interer) 1941- *41*
Billingsley, Franny 1954- *132*
Billington, Elizabeth T(hain) *50*
   Brief entry *43*
Billout, Guy (Rene) 1941- *144*
   Earlier sketch in SATA *10*
   See also CLR *33*
Bilson, Geoffrey 1938-1987 .... *99*
Binch, Caroline (Lesley) 1947- *140*
   Earlier sketch in SATA *81*
Bing, Christopher (H.) *126*
Bingham, Caroline 1962- *158*
Bingham, Jane M. 1941- *163*
Bingham, Jane Marie
   See Bingham, Jane M.
Bingham, Janet 1959- *200*
Bingham, Kelly 1967- *207*
Bingham, Sam 1944- *96*
Bingham, Samuel A.
   See Bingham, Sam
Bingley, Margaret (Jane Kirby) 1947- *72*
Binkley, Anne
   See Rand, Ann (Binkley)
Binzen, Bill
   See Binzen, William
Binzen, William *24*

Birch, David (W.) 1913-1996 89
Birch, Reginald B(athurst) 1856-1943 19
Birchman, David 1949- 72
Birchmore, Daniel A. 1951- 92
Bird, Carmel 1940- 124
Bird, E(lzy) J(ay) 1911- 58
Birdsall, Jeanne 1952(?)- 170
Birdseye, Tom 1951- 148
    Earlier sketches in SATA *66, 98*
Birenbaum, Barbara 1941- 65
Birmingham, Christian 1970- 220
Birmingham, Lloyd P(aul) 1924- 83
    Earlier sketch in SATA *12*
Birmingham, Ruth
    See Sorrells, Walter
Birney, Betty G. 1947- 169
    Earlier sketch in SATA *98*
Biro, B.
    See Biro, B. S.
Biro, B. S. 1921- *1*
    See also CLR *28*
    See also SAAS *13*
Biro, Val
    See Biro, B. S.
Bischoff, Julia Bristol 1899-1970 .... *12*
Bishop, Bonnie 1943- 37
Bishop, Claire Huchet 1899(?)-1993 .... *14*
    Obituary 74
    See also CLR *80*
Bishop, Courtney
    See Ruemmler, John D(avid)
Bishop, Curtis (Kent) 1912-1967 6
Bishop, Elizabeth 1911-1979
    Obituary 24
Bishop, Gavin 1946- 216
    Earlier sketches in SATA *97, 144*
Bishop, Kathleen Wong 1954- 120
Bishop, Kathy
    See Bishop, Kathleen Wong
Bishop, Nic 1955- 161
    Earlier sketch in SATA *107*
Bishop, Rudine Sims 224
Bisset, Donald 1910-1995 86
    Earlier sketch in SATA *7*
Bisson, Terry 1942- 99
Bisson, Terry Ballantine
    See Bisson, Terry
Bitter, Gary G(len) 1940- 22
Bixby, William (Courtney) 1920-1986 6
    Obituary 47
Bjoerk, Christina 1938- 99
    Earlier sketch in SATA *67*
    See also CLR *22*
Bjork, Christina
    See Bjoerk, Christina
Bjorklund, Lorence F. 1913-1978 35
    Brief entry 32
Bjorkman, Lauren 222
Bjorkman, Steve 223
    Earlier sketch in SATA *163*
Blabey, Aaron 1975(?)- 214
Black, Algernon David 1900-1993 .... *12*
    Obituary 76
Black, Holly 1971- 210
    Earlier sketch in SATA *147*
Black, Irma Simonton 1906-1972 .... *2*
    Obituary 25
Black, Joe 1959- 224
Black, Rabbi Joe
    See Black, Joe
Black, Kat 217
Black, Katherine
    See Black, Kat
Black, Mansell
    See Trevor, Elleston
Black, MaryAnn
    See Easley, MaryAnn
Black, Susan Adams 1953- 40
Blackall, Bernie 1956- 126
Blackall, Sophie 182

Blackburn, Claire
    See Altman, Linda Jacobs
Blackburn, John(ny) Brewton 1952- 15
Blackburn, Joyce Knight 1920- 29
Blacker, Terence 1948- 194
Blacker, Tina
    See Louise, Tina
Blackett, Veronica Heath 1927- 12
Blackie, Jean Cutler 1943- 79
Blacklin, Malcolm
    See Chambers, Aidan
Blacklock, Dyan 1951- 112
Blackman, Malorie 1962- 196
    Earlier sketches in SATA *83, 128*
Blackton, Peter
    See Wilson, Lionel
Blackwood, Alan 1932- 70
Blackwood, Freya 199
Blackwood, Gary
    See Blackwood, Gary L.
Blackwood, Gary L. 1945- 169
    Earlier sketches in SATA *72, 118*
Blade, Alexander
    See Garrett, Randall
    and Hamilton, Edmond
    and Silverberg, Robert
Blades, Ann (Sager) 1947- 69
    Earlier sketch in SATA *16*
    See also CLR *15*
Bladow, Suzanne Wilson 1937- 14
Blaine, Chris
    See Gardner, Craig Shaw
Blaine, John
    See Goodwin, Harold L(eland)
Blaine, Marge
    See Blaine, Margery Kay
Blaine, Margery Kay 1937- 11
Blair, Alison
    See Lerangis, Peter
Blair, Anne Denton 1914-1993 46
Blair, David Nelson 1954- 80
Blair, Eric
    See Orwell, George
Blair, Jay 1953- 45
Blair, Lucile
    See Yeakley, Marjory Hall
Blair, Margaret Whitman 1951- 124
Blair, Mary 1911-1978 195
Blair, Pauline Hunter
    See Clarke, Pauline
Blair, Ruth Van Ness 1912-1999 12
Blair, Shannon
    See Kaye, Marilyn
Blair, Walter 1900-1992 12
    Obituary 72
Blaisdell, Bob
    See Blaisdell, Robert
Blaisdell, Robert 1959- 105
Blake, Bronwyn 1940- 149
Blake, Francis 198
Blake, Jon 1954- 171
    Earlier sketch in SATA *78*
Blake, Olive
    See Supraner, Robyn
Blake, Quentin 1932- 211
    Earlier sketches in SATA *9, 52, 96, 125*
    See also CLR *31*
Blake, Robert 1949- 42
Blake, Robert J. 160
Blake, Walker E.
    See Griffin, W. E. B.
Blake, William 1757-1827 30
    See also CLR *52*
Blakely, Gloria 1950- 139
Blakely, Roger K. 1922- 82
Blakeney, Jay D.
    See Chester, Deborah
Blakeslee, Lys 1985- 218
Blakey, Nancy 1955- 94
Blanc, Esther S. 1913-1997 66

Blanc, Mel 1908-1989
    Obituary 64
Blanchard, Patricia 125
Blanchet, M(uriel) Wylie 1891-1961 106
Blanco, Richard L(idio) 1926- 63
Bland, E.
    See Nesbit, E.
Bland, Edith Nesbit
    See Nesbit, E.
Bland, Fabian
    See Nesbit, E.
Blane, Gertrude
    See Blumenthal, Gertrude
Blank, Clarissa Mabel 1915-1965 62
Blankenship, LeeAnn 1944- 181
Blassingame, Wyatt Rainey 1909-1985 34
    Obituary 41
    Earlier sketch in SATA *1*
Blatchford, Claire H. 1944- 94
Blauer, Ettagale 1940- 49
Bleck, Linda 207
Bledsoe, Glen L. 1951- 108
Bledsoe, Glen Leonard
    See Bledsoe, Glen L.
Bledsoe, Karen E. 1962- 167
    Earlier sketch in SATA *108*
Bledsoe, Karen Elizabeth
    See Bledsoe, Karen E.
Bledsoe, Lucy Jane 1957- 162
    Earlier sketch in SATA *97*
Bleeker, Sonia
    See Zim, Sonia Bleeker
Blegen, Daniel M. 1950- 92
Blegvad, Erik 1923- 132
    Earlier sketches in SATA *14, 66*
Blegvad, Lenore 1926- 176
    Earlier sketches in SATA *14, 66*
Blessing, Charlotte 223
Bley, Anette 1967- 188
Blish, James 1921-1975 66
Blish, James Benjamin
    See Blish, James
Blishen, Edward (William) 1920-1996 66
    Obituary 93
    Earlier sketch in SATA *8*
Bliss, Corinne Demas 1947- 203
    Earlier sketches in SATA *37, 131*
Bliss, Frederick
    See Card, Orson Scott
Bliss, Gillian
    See Paton Walsh, Jill
Bliss, Harry 1964- 196
    Earlier sketch in SATA *156*
Bliss, Reginald
    See Wells, H. G.
Bliss, Ronald G(ene) 1942- 12
Blitt, Barry 187
Bliven, Bruce, Jr. 1916-2002 2
Blixen, Karen 1885-1962 44
Blizzard, Gladys S. (?)-1992 79
Blobaum, Cindy 1966- 123
Bloch, Lucienne 1909-1999 10
Bloch, Marie Halun 1910-1998 6
    See also SAAS *9*
Bloch, Robert (Albert) 1917-1994 12
    Obituary 82
Bloch, Serge 1956- 213
Blochman, Lawrence G(oldtree)
    1900-1975 22
Block, Francesca Lia 1962- 213
    Earlier sketches in SATA *80, 116, 158*
    See also CLR *116*
    See also SAAS *21*
Block, Irvin 1917- 12
Blomgren, Jennifer (Alice) 1954- 136
Blonder, Terry Joyce
    See Golson, Terry
Blood, Charles Lewis 1929- 28
Bloom, Barbara Lee 1943- 146
Bloom, Freddy 1914-2000 37
    Obituary 121

Bloom, Lloyd 1947- *108*
   Brief entry *43*
Bloom, Suzanne 1950- *172*
Bloomfield, Michaela 1966- *70*
Bloor, Edward 1950- *201*
   Earlier sketches in SATA *98, 155*
Bloor, Edward William
   See Bloor, Edward
Blos, Joan W. 1928- *153*
   Autobiography Feature *153*
   Brief entry *27*
   Earlier sketches in SATA *33, 69, 109*
   See also CLR *18*
   See also SAAS *11*
Blos, Joan Winsor
   See Blos, Joan W.
Blough, Glenn O(rlando) 1907-1995 .... *1*
Blue, Rose 1931- *166*
   Autobiography Feature *117*
   Earlier sketches in SATA *5, 91, 93*
   See also SAAS *24*
Blue, Zachary
   See Stine, R.L.
Bluemle, Elizabeth *209*
Bluggage, Oranthy
   See Alcott, Louisa May
Blumberg, Leda 1956- *59*
Blumberg, Rhoda 1917- *123*
   Earlier sketches in SATA *35, 70*
   See also CLR *21*
Blume, Judy 1938- *195*
   Earlier sketches in SATA *2, 31, 79, 142*
   See also CLR *69*
Blume, Judy Sussman
   See Blume, Judy
Blume, Lesley M.M. 1975- *180*
Blumenthal, Deborah *204*
   Earlier sketch in SATA *161*
Blumenthal, Gertrude 1907-1971
   Obituary *27*
Blumenthal, Shirley 1943- *46*
Blutig, Eduard
   See Gorey, Edward (St. John)
Bly, Janet 1945- *43*
Bly, Janet Chester
   See Bly, Janet
Bly, Stephen A(rthur) 1944- *116*
   Earlier sketch in SATA *43*
Blyler, Allison Lee 1966- *74*
Blythe, Gary 1959- *185*
Blyton, Carey 1932-2002 .... *9*
   Obituary *138*
Blyton, Enid 1897-1968 .... *25*
   See also CLR *31*
Blyton, Enid Mary
   See Blyton, Enid
Bo, Ben
   See Richardson, V.A.
Boardman, Fon Wyman, Jr. 1911-2000 .... *6*
Boardman, Gwenn R.
   See Petersen, Gwenn Boardman
Boase, Wendy 1944-1999 .... *28*
   Obituary *110*
Boatner, Mark Mayo III 1921- *29*
Bobbe, Dorothie de Bear 1905-1975 .... *1*
   Obituary *25*
Bober, Natalie S. 1930- *134*
   Earlier sketch in SATA *87*
   See also SAAS *23*
Bobette, Bibo
   See Gugliotta, Bobette
Bobri, Vladimir V. 1898-1986 .... *47*
   Brief entry *32*
Bobritsky, Vladimir
   See Bobri, Vladimir V.
Bochak, Grayce 1956- *76*
Bock, Hal
   See Bock, Harold I.
Bock, Harold I. 1939- *10*
Bock, William Sauts Netamux'we 1939- *14*
Bodanis, David *179*

Bode, Janet 1943-1999 .... *96*
   Obituary *118*
   Earlier sketch in SATA *60*
Bode, N.E.
   See Baggott, Julianna
Bodecker, N(iels) M(ogens) 1922-1988 .... *73*
   Obituary *54*
   Earlier sketch in SATA *8*
Bodeen, S. A. 1965- *158*
   Earlier sketch in SATA *114*
Boden, Hilda
   See Bodenham, Hilda Morris
Bodenham, Hilda Morris 1901- *13*
Bodett, Thomas Edward 1955- *70*
Bodett, Tom
   See Bodett, Thomas Edward
Bodie, Idella F(allaw) 1925- *89*
   Earlier sketch in SATA *12*
Bodker, Cecil
   See Bodker, Cecil
Bodker, Cecil 1927- *133*
   Earlier sketch in SATA *14*
   See also CLR *23*
Bodsworth, (Charles) Fred(erick) 1918- *27*
Boeckman, Charles 1920- *12*
Boegehold, Betty (Doyle) 1913-1985
   Obituary *42*
Boelts, Maribeth 1964- *200*
   Earlier sketches in SATA *78, 163*
Boerst, William J. 1939- *170*
   Earlier sketch in SATA *121*
Boesch, Mark J(oseph) 1917- *12*
Boesen, Victor 1908- *16*
Bogacki, Tomek 1950- *214*
   Earlier sketch in SATA *138*
Bogaerts, Gert 1965- *80*
Bogan, Paulette 1960- *201*
   Earlier sketch in SATA *129*
Bogart, Jo Ellen 1945- *222*
   Earlier sketch in SATA *92*
   See also CLR *59*
Boggs, Ralph Steele 1901-1994 .... *7*
Bograd, Larry 1953- *89*
   Earlier sketch in SATA *33*
   See also SAAS *21*
Bogue, Gary 1938- *195*
Bogue, Gary L.
   See Bogue, Gary
Bohdal, Susi 1951- *101*
   Earlier sketch in SATA *22*
Bohlen, Nina 1931- *58*
Bohlmeijer, Arno 1956- *94*
Bohner, Charles (Henry) 1927- *62*
Bohnhoff, Maya Kaathryn 1954- *88*
Boie, Kirsten 1950- *221*
Boiger, Alexandra *178*
Boissard, Janine 1932- *59*
Bojunga, Lygia
   See Nunes, Lygia Bojunga
Bojunga-Nunes, Lygia
   See Nunes, Lygia Bojunga
Bok, Arthur
   See Bok, Chip
Bok, Chip 1952- *205*
Bolam, Emily 1969- *206*
Boland, Janice *98*
Bolden, Tonya 1959- *188*
   Earlier sketches in SATA *79, 138*
Bolden, Tonya Wilyce
   See Bolden, Tonya
Boles, Paul Darcy 1916-1984 .... *9*
   Obituary *38*
Bolian, Polly 1925- *4*
Bollen, Roger 1941(?)- *83*
   Brief entry *29*
Bolliger, Max 1929- *7*
Bollinger, Max 1929- *167*
Bollinger, Peter *172*
Bolognese, Don(ald Alan) 1934- *129*
   Earlier sketches in SATA *24, 71*
Bolognese, Elaine 1933- *23*

Bolotin, Norman (Phillip) 1951- *93*
Bolton, Carole 1926- *6*
Bolton, Elizabeth
   See St. John, Nicole
Bolton, Evelyn
   See Bunting, Eve
Bonar, Veronica
   See Bailey, Donna (Veronica Anne)
Bond, B. J.
   See Heneghan, James
Bond, Bruce 1939- *61*
Bond, Felicia 1954- *219*
   Earlier sketches in SATA *49, 126*
Bond, Gladys Baker 1912- *14*
Bond, Higgins 1951- *220*
   Earlier sketches in SATA *83, 177*
Bond, J. Harvey
   See Winterbotham, R(ussell) R(obert)
Bond, (Thomas) Michael 1926- *157*
   Earlier sketches in SATA *6, 58*
   See also CLR *95*
   See also SAAS *3*
Bond, Nancy 1945- *159*
   Autobiography Feature *159*
   Earlier sketches in SATA *22, 82*
   See also CLR *11*
   See also SAAS *13*
Bond, Nancy Barbara
   See Bond, Nancy
Bond, Rebecca 1972- *214*
   Earlier sketch in SATA *130*
Bond, Ruskin 1934- *87*
   Earlier sketch in SATA *14*
Bondie, J. D.
   See Cunningham, Chet
Bondoux, Anne-Laure 1971- *175*
Bone, Ian 1956- *158*
   Earlier sketch in SATA *117*
Bonehill, Captain Ralph
   See Stratemeyer, Edward L.
Bonestell, Chesley 1888-1986
   Obituary *48*
Bonham, Barbara Thomas 1926- *7*
Bonham, Frank 1914-1989 .... *49*
   Obituary *62*
   Earlier sketch in SATA *1*
   See also SAAS *3*
Boniface, William 1963- *182*
   Earlier sketch in SATA *102*
Bonino, Louise
   See Williams, Louise Bonino
Bonk, John J. *189*
Bonn, Pat
   See Bonn, Patricia Carolyn
Bonn, Patricia Carolyn 1948- *43*
Bonner, Hannah *197*
Bonner, Mary Graham 1890-1974 .... *19*
Bonner, Mike 1951- *121*
Bonners, Susan 1947- *85*
   Brief entry *48*
Bonnett-Rampersaud, Louise *173*
Bonning, Tony 1948- *169*
Bonsall, Crosby Barbara (Newell)
   1921-1995 .... *23*
   Obituary *84*
Bonsall, Joseph S. 1948- *119*
Bonsignore, Joan 1959- *140*
Bontemps, Arna 1902-1973 .... *44*
   Obituary *24*
   Earlier sketch in SATA *2*
   See also CLR *6*
Bontemps, Arnaud Wendell
   See Bontemps, Arna
Bonzon, Paul-Jacques 1908-1978 .... *22*
Boock, Paula 1964- *134*
Booher, Dianna Daniels 1948- *33*
Book, Rick 1949- *119*
Book, Rita
   See Holub, Joan
Bookman, Charlotte
   See Zolotow, Charlotte

Boon, Debbie 1960- *103*
Boon, Emilie (Laetitia) 1958- *86*
Boone, Charles Eugene
  See Boone, Pat
Boone, Pat 1934- *7*
Booraem, Ellen *211*
Boorman, Linda 1940- *46*
Boorman, Linda Kay
  See Boorman, Linda
Boorstin, Daniel J(oseph) 1914-2004 .... *52*
Boos, Ben 1971- *206*
Booth, Coe *187*
Booth, Ernest Sheldon 1915-1984 .... *43*
Booth, George 1926- *191*
Booth, Graham (Charles) 1935- *37*
Bootman, Colin *159*
Borden, Louise 1949- *190*
  Autobiography Feature *141*
  Earlier sketches in SATA *68, 104, 141*
Bordier, Georgette 1924- *16*
Borgman, James
  See Borgman, Jim
Borgman, James Mark
  See Borgman, Jim
Borgman, Jim 1954- *122*
Borgo, Lacy Finn 1972- *194*
Boring, Mel 1939- *168*
  Earlier sketch in SATA *35*
Borja, Corinne 1929- *22*
Borja, Robert 1923- *22*
Borland, Hal
  See Borland, Harold Glen
Borland, Harold Glen 1900-1978 .... *5*
  Obituary *24*
Borland, Kathryn Kilby 1916- *16*
Borlenghi, Patricia 1951- *79*
Born, Adolf 1930- *49*
Bornstein, Ruth Lercher
  See Bornstein-Lercher, Ruth
Bornstein-Lercher, Ruth 1927- *88*
  Autobiography Feature *107*
  Earlier sketch in SATA *14*
Borris, Albert *221*
Borski, Lucia Merecka *18*
Borten, Helen Jacobson 1930- *5*
Bortolotti, Dan 1969- *157*
Borton, Elizabeth
  See Trevino, Elizabeth B(orton) de
Borton, Lady 1942- *98*
Borton de Trevino, Elizabeth
  See Trevino, Elizabeth B(orton) de
Bortstein, Larry 1942-2010 .... *16*
Bortz, Alfred B(enjamin) 1944- *139*
  Earlier sketch in SATA *74*
Bortz, Fred
  See Bortz, Alfred B(enjamin)
Bosch, Pseudonymous *199*
Bosco, Jack
  See Holliday, Joseph
Bose, Mitali
  See Perkins, Mitali
Boshell, Gordon 1908-1991 .... *15*
Boshinski, Blanche 1922- *10*
Bosman, Paul 1929- *107*
Bosse, Malcolm (Joseph, Jr.) 1926-2002 .... *136*
  Earlier sketch in SATA *35*
Bosserman, Charles Phillip
  See Bosserman, Phillip
Bosserman, Phillip 1931- *84*
Bossley, Michele Martin 1969- *219*
Bossom, Naomi 1933- *35*
Bostock, Mike 1962- *114*
Boston, L(ucy) M(aria Wood) 1892-1990 .... *19*
  Obituary *64*
  See also CLR *3*
Bostrom, Kathleen (Susan) Long 1954- *139*
Bostrom, Kathy
  See Bostrom, Kathleen (Susan) Long
Boswell, Addie *208*
Boswell, Addie Kay
  See Boswell, Addie

Bosworth, J. Allan 1925- *19*
Bothwell, Jean (?)-1977 .... *2*
Botkin, B(enjamin) A(lbert) 1901-1975 .... *40*
Botsford, Ward 1927-2004 .... *66*
Botting, Douglas (Scott) 1934- *43*
Bottner, Barbara 1943- *170*
  Autobiography Feature *121*
  Earlier sketches in SATA *14, 93*
  See also SAAS *26*
Bottone, Frank G., Jr. 1969- *141*
Bouchard, David 1952- *213*
  Earlier sketch in SATA *117*
Boucher, (Clarence) Carter 1954- *129*
Boudelang, Bob
  See Pell, Ed(ward)
Boughton, Richard 1954- *75*
Boulet, Susan Seddon 1941- *50*
Boulle, Pierre (Francois Marie-Louis)
  1912-1994 .... *22*
  Obituary *78*
Boulton, Jane 1921- *91*
Bouma, Paddy 1947- *128*
Bour, Daniele 1939- *62*
Bourbonniere, Sylvie 1966- *182*
Bourdon, David 1934-1998 .... *46*
Bourgeois, Paulette 1951- *153*
Bourne, Lesley
  See Marshall, Evelyn
Bourne, Miriam Anne 1931-1989 .... *16*
  Obituary *63*
Boutavant, Marc 1970- *200*
Boutet de Monvel, (Louis) M(aurice)
  1850(?)-1913 .... *30*
  See also CLR *32*
Bouwman, Heather M.
  See Bouwman, H.M.
Bouwman, H.M. *209*
Bova, Ben 1932- *133*
  Earlier sketches in SATA *6, 68*
  See also CLR *96*
Bova, Benjamin William
  See Bova, Ben
Bovaird, Anne E(lizabeth) 1960- *90*
Bow, Patricia 1946- *168*
Bowden, Joan Chase 1925- *51*
  Brief entry *38*
Bowe, Julie 1962- *194*
Bowen, Alexandria Russell *97*
Bowen, Andy Russell
  See Bowen, Alexandria Russell
Bowen, Anne 1952- *202*
  Earlier sketch in SATA *170*
Bowen, Betty Morgan
  See West, Betty
Bowen, Catherine (Shober) Drinker
  1897-1973 .... *7*
Bowen, David
  See Bowen, Joshua David
Bowen, Fred 1953- *136*
Bowen, Joshua David 1930- *22*
Bowen, Rhys
  See Quin-Harkin, Janet
Bowen, Robert Sydney 1900-1977 .... *52*
  Obituary *21*
Bowermaster, Jon 1954- *135*
  Earlier sketch in SATA *77*
Bowers, Terrell L. 1945- *101*
Bowers, Terry
  See Bowers, Terrell L.
Bowers, Tim *218*
  Earlier sketch in SATA *185*
Bowie, C. W.
  See Old, Wendie C(orbin)
  and Wirths, Claudine (Turner) G(ibson)
Bowie, Jim
  See Norwood, Victor G(eorge) C(harles)
  and Stratemeyer, Edward L.
Bowkett, Stephen 1953- *67*
Bowler, Jan Brett
  See Brett, Jan

Bowler, Tim 1953- *209*
  Earlier sketch in SATA *149*
Bowman, Catherine
  See Smith, Cat Bowman
Bowman, Crystal 1951- *105*
Bowman, James Cloyd 1880-1961 .... *23*
Bowman, John S(tewart) 1931- *16*
Bowman, Kathleen (Gill) 1942- *52*
  Brief entry *40*
Bowman, Leslie
  See Bowman, Leslie W.
Bowman, Leslie W. *182*
Bowsher, Melodie *195*
Boxall, Ed *178*
Boyce, Frank Cottrell *182*
Boyce, George A(rthur) 1898- *19*
Boyd, Candy Dawson 1946- *72*
  See also CLR *50*
Boyd, Pauline
  See Schock, Pauline
Boyd, Selma
  See Acuff, Selma Boyd
Boyd, Waldo T. 1918- *18*
Boyden, Linda 1948- *143*
Boyer, Allen B. 1963- *153*
Boyer, Robert E(rnst) 1929- *22*
Boyes, Vivien 1952- *106*
Boyes, Vivien Elizabeth
  See Boyes, Vivien
Boyle, Ann (Peters) 1916- *10*
Boyle, Eleanor Vere (Gordon) 1825-1916 .... *28*
Boyle, Robert H. 1928- *65*
Boylston, Helen Dore 1895-1984 .... *23*
  Obituary *39*
Boyne, John 1971- *181*
Boynton, Sandra (Keith) 1953- *152*
  Brief entry *38*
  Earlier sketches in SATA *57, 107*
  See also CLR *105*
Boz
  See Dickens, Charles
Braasch, Gary *201*
Bracken, Charles
  See Pellowski, Michael (Joseph)
Brackers de Hugo, Pierre 1960- *115*
Brackett, Dolli Tingle 1911-1993 .... *137*
Brackett, Virginia 1950- *166*
  Earlier sketch in SATA *121*
Brackett, Virginia Roberts Meredith
  See Brackett, Virginia
Bradbury, Bianca (Ryley) 1908-1982 .... *56*
  Earlier sketch in SATA *3*
Bradbury, Edward P.
  See Moorcock, Michael
Bradbury, Ray 1920- *123*
  Earlier sketches in SATA *11, 64*
Bradbury, Ray Douglas
  See Bradbury, Ray
Bradby, Marie *161*
Bradfield, Carl 1942- *91*
Bradford, Ann (Liddell) 1917- *56*
  Brief entry *38*
Bradford, Barbara Taylor 1933- *66*
Bradford, Chris 1974- *215*
Bradford, Karleen 1936- *96*
  Earlier sketch in SATA *48*
Bradford, Lois J(ean) 1936- *36*
Bradford, Richard (Roark) 1932-2002 .... *59*
  Obituary *135*
Bradley, Duane
  See Sanborn, Duane
Bradley, Kimberly Brubaker 1967- *179*
Bradley, Marion Zimmer 1930-1999 .... *139*
  Obituary *116*
  Earlier sketch in SATA *90*
  See also CLR *158*
Bradley, Timothy J. *193*
Bradley, Virginia 1912- *23*
Bradley, Will
  See Strickland, Brad

Bradman, Tony 1954- *152*
  Earlier sketch in SATA *81*
Bradshaw, Gillian (Joan) 1949- *118*
Bradshaw, Gillian 1956- *127*
Bradshaw, Gillian Marucha
  See Bradshaw, Gillian
Bradstreet, T. J.
  See Thesman, Jean
Brady, Esther Wood 1905-1987 .... *31*
  Obituary *53*
Brady, Irene 1943- *4*
Brady, Kimberley S. 1953- *101*
Brady, Kimberley Smith
  See Brady, Kimberley S.
Brady, Lillian 1902- *28*
Bragdon, Elspeth MacDuffie 1897-1980 .... *6*
Bragdon, Lillian Jacot *24*
Brager, Bruce L. 1949- *146*
Bragg, Georgia *225*
Bragg, Mabel Caroline 1870-1945 .... *24*
Bragg, Michael 1948- *46*
Bragg, Ruth Gembicki 1943- *77*
Brahm, Sumishta 1954- *58*
Brailsford, Frances
  See Wosmek, Frances
Brainerd, John W(hiting) 1918- *65*
Braithwaite, Althea 1940- *23*
  Autobiography Feature *119*
  See also SAAS *24*
Bram, Elizabeth 1948- *30*
Brancato, Robin F. 1936- *97*
  See also CLR *32*
  See also SAAS *9*
Brancato, Robin Fidler
  See Brancato, Robin F.
Branch, Muriel Miller 1943- *152*
  Earlier sketch in SATA *94*
Brand, Christianna
  See Lewis, Mary
Brand, Rebecca
  See Charnas, Suzy McKee
Brande, Robin *194*
Brandel, Marc 1919- *71*
Brandenberg, Alexa (Demetria) 1966- *97*
Brandenberg, Aliki 1929- *157*
  Earlier sketches in SATA *2, 35, 75, 113*
  See also CLR *71*
Brandenberg, Franz 1932- *75*
  Earlier sketches in SATA *8, 35*
Brandenburg, Jim 1945- *87*
Brandhorst, Carl T(heodore) 1898-1988 .... *23*
Brandis, Marianne 1938- *149*
  Earlier sketches in SATA *59, 96*
Brandon, Brumsic, Jr. 1927- *9*
Brandon, Curt
  See Bishop, Curtis (Kent)
Brandreth, Gyles 1948- *28*
Brandreth, Gyles Daubeney
  See Brandreth, Gyles
Brandt, Catharine 1905-1997 .... *40*
Brandt, Keith
  See Sabin, Louis
Brandt, Sue R(eading) 1916- *59*
Branfield, John (Charles) 1931- *11*
Branford, Henrietta 1946-1999 .... *106*
Branley, Franklyn M(ansfield) 1915-2002 .. *136*
  Earlier sketches in SATA *4, 68*
  See also CLR *13*
  See also SAAS *16*
Brannen, Sarah S. *202*
Branscum, Robbie (Tilley) 1937-1997 .... *72*
  Obituary *96*
  Earlier sketch in SATA *23*
  See also SAAS *17*
Bransom, (John) Paul 1885-1979 .... *43*
Brashares, Ann 1967- *188*
  Earlier sketch in SATA *145*
  See also CLR *113*
Brassard, France 1963- *186*
Braswell, E.J.
  See Lynn, Tracy

Braswell, Elizabeth J.
  See Lynn, Tracy
Braswell, Liz
  See Lynn, Tracy
Bratton, Helen 1899-1986 .... *4*
Bratun, Katy 1950- *160*
  Earlier sketch in SATA *83*
Braude, Michael 1936- *23*
Braun, Lilian Jackson 1916(?)- *109*
Brautigan, Richard 1935-1984 .... *56*
Brautigan, Richard Gary
  See Brautigan, Richard
Bray, Libba *203*
  Earlier sketch in SATA *159*
Bray, Martha E.
  See Bray, Libba
Braymer, Marjorie Elizabeth 1911-1988 .... *6*
Brazil, Angela 1869(?)-1947
  See CLR *157*
Breathed, Berke 1957- *161*
  Earlier sketch in SATA *86*
Breathed, Berkeley
  See Breathed, Berke
Breathed, Guy Berkeley
  See Breathed, Berke
Brecht, Edith 1895-1975 .... *6*
  Obituary *25*
Breck, Vivian
  See Breckenfeld, Vivian Gurney
Breckenfeld, Vivian Gurney 1895-1992 .... *1*
Breda, Tjalmar
  See DeJong, David C(ornel)
Bredeson, Carmen 1944- *163*
  Earlier sketch in SATA *98*
Breen, M.E. *216*
Breen, Molly
  See Breen, M.E.
Breen, Steve 1970- *186*
Brcinburg, Petronella 1927- *11*
  See also CLR *31*
Breisky, William J(ohn) 1928- *22*
Brenaman, Miriam *172*
Brennan, Caitlin
  See Tarr, Judith
Brennan, Gale (Patrick) 1927- *64*
  Brief entry *53*
Brennan, Herbie 1940- *214*
  Autobiography Feature *214*
  Earlier sketches in SATA *140, 183*
Brennan, J. H.
  See Brennan, Herbie
Brennan, James Herbert
  See Brennan, Herbie
Brennan, Jan
  See Brennan, Herbie
Brennan, Joseph Lomas 1903-2000 .... *6*
Brennan, Linda Crotta 1952- *130*
Brennan, Sarah Rees 1983- *221*
Brennan, Tim
  See Conroy, John Wesley
Brennan-Nelson, Denise *203*
Brenner, Anita 1905-1974 .... *56*
Brenner, Barbara (Johnes) 1925- *124*
  Earlier sketches in SATA *4, 42, 76*
  See also SAAS *14*
Brenner, Fred 1920- *36*
  Brief entry *34*
Brent, Hope 1935(?)-1984
  Obituary *39*
Brent, Stuart 1912-2010 .... *14*
Breskin, Jane
  See Zalben, Jane Breskin
Breslin, Theresa *128*
  Autobiography Feature *128*
  Earlier sketch in SATA *70*
Breslow, Maurice 1935- *72*
Breslow, Maurice A
  See Breslow, Maurice
Breslow, Susan 1951- *69*
Brett, Bernard 1925- *22*
Brett, Grace N(eff) 1900-1975 .... *23*

Brett, Jan 1949- *171*
  Earlier sketches in SATA *42, 71, 130*
  See also CLR *27*
Brett, Jan Churchill
  See Brett, Jan
Brett Bowler, Jan
  See Brett, Jan
Brewer, Heather 1973- *196*
Brewer, James D. 1951- *108*
Brewer, Sally King 1947- *33*
Brewster, Benjamin
  See Folsom, Franklin (Brewster)
Brewster, Hugh 1950- *191*
  Earlier sketch in SATA *95*
Brewster, Patience 1952- *97*
Brewton, John E(dmund) 1898-1982 .... *5*
Breznak, Irene *218*
Brian, Janeen (Paulette) 1948- *141*
Briant, Ed *218*
  Earlier sketch in SATA *180*
Brick, John 1922-1973 .... *10*
Brickman, Robin D. 1954- *155*
Bride, Nadja
  See Nobisso, Josephine
Bridgers, Sue Ellen 1942- *90*
  Autobiography Feature *109*
  Earlier sketch in SATA *22*
  See also CLR *18*
  See also SAAS *1*
Bridges, Laurie
  See Bruck, Lorraine
Bridges, Ruby (Nell) 1954- *131*
Bridges, William (Andrew) 1901-1984 .... *5*
Bridwell, Norman (Ray) 1928- *138*
  Earlier sketches in SATA *4, 68*
  See also CLR *96*
Brier, Howard M(axwell) 1903-1969 .... *8*
Brierley, (Louise) 1958- *59*
Briggs, Katharine Mary 1898-1980 .... *101*
  Obituary *25*
Briggs, Peter 1921-1975 .... *39*
  Obituary *31*
Briggs, Raymond 1934- *184*
  Earlier sketches in SATA *23, 66, 131*
  See also CLR *10*
Briggs, Raymond Redvers
  See Briggs, Raymond
Bright, Paul 1949- *182*
Bright, Robert Sr.) 1902-1988 .... *63*
  Obituary *60*
  Earlier sketch in SATA *24*
Bright, Robert Douglas
  See Bright, Robert Sr.)
Bright, Sarah
  See Shine, Deborah
Brightfield, Richard 1927- *65*
  Brief entry *53*
Brightfield, Rick
  See Brightfield, Richard
Brighton, Catherine 1943- *206*
  Earlier sketches in SATA *65, 107*
Brill, Marlene Targ 1945- *124*
  Earlier sketch in SATA *77*
Brimberg, Stanlee 1947- *9*
Brimner, Larry Dane 1949- *170*
  Autobiography Feature *112*
  Earlier sketch in SATA *79*
Brin, David 1950- *65*
Brin, Ruth Firestone 1921- *22*
Brinckloe, Julie 1950- *13*
Brinckloe, Julie Lorraine
  See Brinckloe, Julie
Brindel, June (Rachuy) 1919- *7*
Brindle, Max
  See Fleischman, Sid
Brindze, Ruth 1903-1984 .... *23*
Brink, Carol Ryrie 1895-1981 .... *100*
  Obituary *27*
  Earlier sketches in SATA *1, 31*
  See also CLR *149*

Brinsmead, H. F(ay)
  See Brinsmead, H(esba) F(ay)
Brinsmead, H. F.
  See Brinsmead, H(esba) F(ay)
Brinsmead, H(esba) F(ay) 1922- 78
  Earlier sketch in SATA 18
  See also CLR 47
  See also SAAS 5
Briquebec, John
  See Rowland-Entwistle, (Arthur) Theodore
  (Henry)
Brisbane, Henry R.
  See Ellis, Edward S.
Brisco, P. A.
  See Matthews, Patricia
Brisco, Patty
  See Matthews, Patricia
  and Matthews, Clayton (Hartley)
Briscoe, Jill (Pauline) 1935- 56
  Brief entry 47
Brisley, Joyce Lankester 1896-1978 22
  Obituary 84
Brissenden, Connie
  See Brissenden, Constance
Brissenden, Constance 1947- 150
Brisson, Pat 1951- 177
  Autobiography Feature 133
  Earlier sketches in SATA 67, 128, 133
Britt, Albert 1874-1969
  Obituary 28
Britt, Dell 1934- 1
Brittain, Bill
  See Brittain, William
Brittain, C. Dale 1948- 82
Brittain, William 1930- 76
  Earlier sketch in SATA 36
  See also SAAS 7
Brittingham, Geoffrey (Hugh) 1959- 76
Brittney, L. 209
Britton, Kate
  See Stegeman, Janet Allais
Britton, Louisa
  See McGuire, Leslie (Sarah)
Britton, Rick 1952- 82
Bro, Margueritte (Harmon) 1894-1977 19
  Obituary 27
Broach, Elise 1963- 173
Broadhead, Helen Cross 1913- 25
Broadway, Hannah 208
Brochmann, Elizabeth 1938- 41
Brock, Betty (Carter) 1923-2003 4
  Obituary 150
Brock, C(harles) E(dmund) 1870-1938 42
  Brief entry 32
Brock, Delia
  See Ephron, Delia
Brock, Emma L(illian) 1886-1974 8
Brock, H(enry) M(atthew) 1875-1960 42
Brockett, Eleanor Hall 1913-1967 10
Brockman, C(hristian) Frank 1902-1985 26
Brockmeier, Kevin 1972- 176
Broda, Ron 1954- 209
Broderick, Dorothy M. 1929- 5
Brodeur, Ruth Wallace
  See Wallace-Brodeur, Ruth
Brodie, Sally
  See Cavin, Ruth
Brodsky, Beverly
  See McDermott, Beverly Brodsky
Brody, Wendy
  See Staub, Wendy Corsi
Broekel, Rainer Lothar
  See Broekel, Ray
Broekel, Ray 1923- 38
Broekstra, Lorette 1964- 189
  Earlier sketch in SATA 124
Brogden, Sherryl
  See Jordan, Sherryl
Broger, Achim
  See Broger, Achim
Broger, Achim 1944- 31

Broida, Marian 154
Brokamp, Marilyn 1920- 10
Broman, Fred
  See Moseley, James W(illett)
Bromhall, Winifred 26
Brommer, Gerald F(rederick) 1927- 28
Brondfield, Jerome 1913-1998 22
Brondfield, Jerry
  See Brondfield, Jerome
Bronner, Stephen Eric 1949- 101
Bronowski, Jacob 1908-1974 55
Bronson, Alice
  See Watkins, Dawn L.
Bronson, Linda 203
Bronson, Lynn
  See Lampman, Evelyn Sibley
Bronson, Wilfrid Swancourt 1894-1985
  Obituary 43
Brook, Judith (Penelope) 1926- 59
  Brief entry 51
Brook, Judy
  See Brook, Judith (Penelope)
Brooke, L(eonard) Leslie 1862-1940 17
  See also CLR 20
Brooke, William J. 1946- 139
Brooke-Haven, P.
  See Wodehouse, P. G.
Brooker, Kyrsten 199
Brookins, Dana 1931- 28
Brooks, Anita
  See Abramovitz, Anita (Zeltner Brooks)
Brooks, Bill 1939- 59
Brooks, Bruce 1950- 112
  Brief entry 53
  Earlier sketch in SATA 72
  See also CLR 25
Brooks, Caryl 1924- 84
Brooks, Charlotte K(endrick) 1918-1998 24
  Obituary 112
Brooks, Erik 1972- 182
  Earlier sketch in SATA 152
Brooks, George
  See Baum, L. Frank
Brooks, Gwendolyn 1917-2000 6
  Obituary 123
  See also CLR 27
Brooks, Gwendolyn Elizabeth
  See Brooks, Gwendolyn
Brooks, Jerome 1931- 23
Brooks, Kevin 1959- 197
  Earlier sketch in SATA 150
Brooks, Kevin M.
  See Brooks, Kevin
Brooks, Laurie 209
Brooks, Lester 1924- 7
Brooks, Martha 1944- 134
  Autobiography Feature 134
  Earlier sketches in SATA 68, 121
Brooks, Maurice (Graham) 1900- 45
Brooks, Polly Schoyer 1912- 12
Brooks, Ron 1948- 212
  Brief entry 33
  Earlier sketch in SATA 94
Brooks, Ronald George
  See Brooks, Ron
Brooks, Terry 1944- 60
Brooks, Walter R(ollin) 1886-1958 17
Brooks-Hill, Helen (Mason) 1908-1994 59
Broome, Errol 1937- 158
  Earlier sketch in SATA 105
Brophy, Nannette 1963- 73
Brosnan, James Patrick 1929- 14
Brosnan, Jim
  See Brosnan, James Patrick
Brostoff, Anita 1931- 132
Brothers Grimm
  See Grimm, Jacob Ludwig Karl
  and Grimm, Wilhelm Karl
Brothers Hildebrandt, The
  See Hildebrandt, Greg
  and Hildebrandt, Tim

Broun, Emily
  See Sterne, Emma Gelders
Brouwer, S. W.
  See Brouwer, Sigmund (W.)
Brouwer, Sigmund (W.) 1959- 109
Brow, Thea 1934- 60
Brower, Millicent 8
Brower, Pauline 1929- 22
Browin, Frances Williams 1898-1986 5
Brown, Alexis
  See Baumann, Amy Beeching
Brown, Anne Ensign 1937- 61
Brown, Beverly Swerdlow 97
Brown, Bill
  See Brown, William L(ouis)
Brown, Billye Walker
  See Cutchen, Billye Walker
Brown, Bob
  See Brown, Robert Joseph
Brown, Buck 1936- 45
Brown, Calef 217
  Earlier sketch in SATA 179
Brown, Cassie 1919-1986 55
Brown, Charlotte Lewis 181
Brown, Conrad 1922- 31
Brown, Craig 1947- 224
Brown, Craig 1947- 224
  Earlier sketch in SATA 73
Brown, Craig McFarland
  See Brown, Craig
Brown, David
  See Brown, David A(lan)
  and Myller, Rolf
Brown, Dee 1908-2002 110
  Obituary 141
  Earlier sketch in SATA 5
Brown, Dee Alexander
  See Brown, Dee
Brown, Don 1949- 200
  Earlier sketch in SATA 172
Brown, Drew T. III 1955- 83
Brown, Drollene P. 1939- 53
Brown, Elbrite 198
Brown, Eleanor Frances 1908-1987 3
Brown, Elizabeth Ferguson 1937- 153
Brown, Elizabeth M(yers) 1915- 43
Brown, Fern G. 1918- 34
Brown, (Robert) Fletch 1923- 42
Brown, Fornan 1901-1996 71
  Obituary 88
Brown, George Earl 1883-1964 11
Brown, George Mackay 1921-1996 35
Brown, Irene Bennett 1932- 3
Brown, Irving
  See Adams, William Taylor
Brown, Ivor (John Carnegie) 1891-1974 5
  Obituary 26
Brown, Jane Clark 1930- 81
Brown, Janet Mitsui 87
Brown, Jo 1964- 170
Brown, Joanne 1933- 147
Brown, Joe David 1915-1976 44
Brown, Joseph E(dward) 1929- 59
  Brief entry 51
Brown, Judith Gwyn 1933- 20
Brown, Kathryn 1955- 168
  Earlier sketch in SATA 98
Brown, Kathy
  See Brown, Kathryn
Brown, Ken (James) 129
Brown, Kevin 1960- 101
Brown, Laurene Krasny 1945- 99
  Earlier sketch in SATA 54
Brown, Laurie Krasny
  See Brown, Laurene Krasny
Brown, Leo 225
Brown, Lloyd Arnold 1907-1966 36
Brown, Mahlon A.
  See Ellis, Edward S.

Brown, Marc (Tolon) 1946- *145*
  Earlier sketches in SATA *10, 53, 80*
  See also CLR *29*
Brown, Marcia (Joan) 1918- *47*
  Earlier sketch in SATA *7*
  See also CLR *12*
Brown, Margaret Wise 1910-1952 .... *100*
  See also YABC *2*
  See also CLR *107*
Brown, Margery (Wheeler) *78*
  Earlier sketch in SATA *5*
Brown, Marion Marsh 1908-2001 .... *6*
Brown, Myra Berry 1918- *6*
Brown, Palmer 1919- *36*
Brown, Pamela (Beatrice) 1924-1989 .... *5*
  Obituary *61*
Brown, Paul 1942- *221*
Brown, Peter 1979- *178*
Brown, Rachel W.N. 1947- *203*
Brown, Reeve Lindbergh
  See Lindbergh, Reeve
Brown, Richard E. 1946- *61*
Brown, Robert Joseph 1907-1989 .... *14*
Brown, Roderick (Langmere) Haig-
  See Haig-Brown, Roderick (Langmere)
Brown, Rosalie
  See Moore, Rosalie (Gertrude)
Brown, Roswell
  See Webb, Jean Francis (III)
Brown, Roy (Frederick) 1921-1982 .... *51*
  Obituary *39*
Brown, Ruth 1941- *170*
  Earlier sketch in SATA *105*
Brown, Scott 1971- *134*
Brown, Sue Ellen 1954- *81*
Brown, Tricia 1954- *114*
Brown, Vinson 1912-1991 .... *19*
Brown, Walter R(eed) 1929- *19*
Brown, Will
  See Ainsworth, William Harrison
Brown, William L(ouis) 1910-1964 .... *5*
Browne, Anthony 1946- *163*
  Brief entry *44*
  Earlier sketches in SATA *45, 61, 105*
  See also CLR *156*
Browne, Anthony Edward Tudor
  See Browne, Anthony
Browne, Dik
  See Browne, Richard Arthur Allen
Browne, Hablot Knight 1815-1882 .... *21*
Browne, Matthew
  See Rands, William Brighty
Browne, Nicki M.
  See Browne, N.M.
Browne, Nicky Matthews
  See Browne, N.M.
Browne, N.M. 1960- *167*
Browne, Richard Arthur Allen 1917-1989 ... *67*
  Brief entry *38*
Browne, Vee F. 1956- *214*
  Earlier sketch in SATA *90*
Browning, Robert 1812-1889
  See YABC *1*
  See also CLR *97*
Brownjohn, Alan 1931- *6*
Brownlee, Walter 1930- *62*
Brownlie, Betty 1946- *159*
Brownlow, Kevin 1938- *65*
Brownlow, Mike *183*
Brownridge, William R(oy) 1932- *94*
Broyles, Anne 1953- *201*
Bruce, Dorita Fairlie 1885-1970
  Obituary *27*
Bruce, (William) Harry 1934- *77*
Bruce, Mary 1927- *1*
Bruchac, Joseph III
  See Bruchac, Joseph
Bruchac, Joseph 1942- *176*
  Autobiography Feature *176*
  Earlier sketches in SATA *42, 89, 131*
  See also CLR *46*

Bruchac, Margaret M.
  See Bruchac, Marge
Bruchac, Marge *181*
Bruck, Lorraine 1921- *55*
  Brief entry *46*
Bruel, Nick *205*
  Earlier sketch in SATA *166*
Bruel, Robert O. 1929-2002 .... *189*
Bruemmer, Fred 1929- *47*
Brugman, Alyssa (F.) 1974- *152*
Brumbeau, Jeff 1955- *157*
Bruna, Dick 1927- *76*
  Brief entry *30*
  Earlier sketch in SATA *43*
  See also CLR *7*
Brunhoff, Jean de 1899-1937 .... *24*
  See also CLR *116*
Brunhoff, Laurent de 1925- *150*
  Earlier sketches in SATA *24, 71*
  See also CLR *116*
Brunkus, Denise *204*
Bruno, Elsa Knight 1935-2009 .... *221*
Brunskill, Elizabeth Ann Flatt
  See Flatt, Lizann
Brush, Karen A(lexandra) 1960- *85*
Brussel-Smith, Bernard 1914- *58*
Brust, Steven 1955- *121*
  Earlier sketch in SATA *86*
Brust, Steven Karl Zoltan
  See Brust, Steven
Brustlein, Daniel 1904- *40*
Brustlein, Janice Tworkov -2000 .... *40*
  Obituary *126*
Brutschy, Jennifer 1960- *84*
Bryan, Ashley 1923- *178*
  Earlier sketches in SATA *31, 72, 132*
  See also CLR *66*
Bryan, Ashley F.
  See Bryan, Ashley
Bryan, Dorothy M. 1896(?)-1984
  Obituary *39*
Bryan, Jennifer *190*
Bryan, Sean *192*
Bryant, Bernice (Morgan) 1908-1976 .... *11*
Bryant, Jen 1960- *218*
  Earlier sketches in SATA *94, 175*
Bryant, Jennifer
  See Bryant, Jen
Bryant, Jennifer Fisher
  See Bryant, Jen
Bryant, Laura J. *176*
Brychta, Alex 1956- *21*
Brynie, Faith H. 1946- *113*
Brynie, Faith Hickman
  See Brynie, Faith H.
Bryson, Bernarda 1903-2004 .... *9*
Buba, Joy Flinsch 1904- *44*
Buchan, Bryan 1945- *36*
Buchan, John 1875-1940
  See YABC *2*
Buchan, Stuart 1942-1987
  Obituary *54*
Buchanan, Debby 1952- *82*
Buchanan, Deborah Leevonne
  See Buchanan, Debby
Buchanan, Jane 1956- *160*
Buchanan, Paul 1959- *116*
Buchanan, Sue 1939- *139*
Buchheimer, Naomi Barnett
  See Barnett, Naomi
Buchignani, Walter 1965- *84*
Buchmann, Stephen L. *194*
Buchwald, Art 1925-2007 .... *10*
Buchwald, Arthur
  See Buchwald, Art
Buchwald, Emilie 1935- *7*
Buck, Gisela 1941- *101*
Buck, Lewis 1925- *18*
Buck, Margaret Waring 1905-1997 .... *3*
Buck, Nola
  See Godwin, Laura

Buck, Pearl S. 1892-1973 .... *25*
  Earlier sketch in SATA *1*
Buck, Pearl Sydenstricker
  See Buck, Pearl S.
Buck, Siegfried 1941- *101*
Buckalew, Clare B.
  See Dunkle, Clare B.
Buckeridge, Anthony (Malcolm)
  1912-2004 .... *85*
  Earlier sketch in SATA *6*
Buckholtz, Eileen (Garber) 1949- *54*
  Brief entry *47*
Buckingham, Royce 1966- *210*
Buckingham, Royce Scott
  See Buckingham, Royce
Buckler, Ernest 1908-1984 .... *47*
Buckless, Andrea K. 1968- *117*
Buckley, Helen E(lizabeth) 1918- *90*
  Earlier sketch in SATA *2*
Buckley, James, Jr. 1963- *166*
  Earlier sketch in SATA *114*
Buckley, Michael *177*
Buckley, Susan *184*
Buckley, Susan Washburn
  See Buckley, Susan
Buckley-Archer, Linda *185*
Buckmaster, Henrietta
  See Stephens, Henrietta Henkle
Bucks, Brad
  See Holub, Joan
Budd, E. S.
  See Sirimarco, Elizabeth
Budd, Lillian (Peterson) 1897-1989 .... *7*
Budhos, Marina *173*
Buehler, Stephanie Jona 1956- *83*
Buehner, Caralyn 1963- *219*
  Earlier sketches in SATA *104, 159*
Buehner, Mark 1959- *221*
  Earlier sketches in SATA *104, 159*
Buehr, Walter Franklin 1897-1971 .... *3*
Buell, Ellen Lewis
  See Cash, Ellen Lewis Buell
Buell, Janet 1952- *185*
  Earlier sketch in SATA *106*
Buergel, Paul-Hermann H. 1949- *83*
Buettner, Dan 1960- *95*
Buff, Conrad 1886-1975 .... *19*
Buff, Mary (E. Marsh) 1890-1970 .... *19*
Buffett, Jimmy 1946- *110*
  Earlier sketch in SATA *76*
Buffie, Margaret 1945- *161*
  Earlier sketches in SATA *71, 107*
  See also CLR *39*
Bugbee, Emma 1888(?)-1981
  Obituary *29*
Bugni, Alice 1951- *122*
Buhhos, Marina Tamar
  See Budhos, Marina
Bujold, Lois McMaster 1949- *136*
Bulfinch, Thomas 1796-1867 .... *35*
Bulion, Leslie 1958- *209*
  Earlier sketch in SATA *161*
Bull, Angela (Mary) 1936- *45*
Bull, Emma 1954- *190*
  Autobiography Feature *103*
  Earlier sketch in SATA *99*
Bull, Norman John 1916- *41*
Bull, Peter (Cecil) 1912-1984
  Obituary *39*
Bull, Schuyler M. 1974- *138*
Bulla, Clyde R. 1914-2007 .... *139*
  Obituary *182*
  Earlier sketches in SATA *2, 41, 91*
  See also SAAS *6*
Bullard, Lisa 1961- *142*
Buller, Jon *205*
Bullock, Kathleen (Mary) 1946- *77*
Bullock, Robert (D.) 1947- *92*
Bulpin, (Barbara) Vicki *92*
Bulwer-Lytton, Edward 1803-1873 .... *23*

Bulwer-Lytton, Edward George Earle Lytton
  See Bulwer-Lytton, Edward
Bumstead, Kathleen Mary 1918-1987 .... *53*
Bundles, A'Lelia Perry 1952- *76*
Bunge, Daniela 1973- *207*
Bunin, Catherine 1967- *30*
Bunin, Sherry 1925- *30*
Bunkers, Suzanne L. 1950- *136*
Bunting, A.E.
  See Bunting, Eve
Bunting, Anne Evelyn
  See Bunting, Eve
Bunting, Eve 1928- *196*
  Earlier sketches in SATA *18, 64, 110, 158*
  See also CLR *82*
Bunting, Glenn (Davison) 1957- *22*
Bunyan, John 1628-1688
  See CLR *124*
Bupp, Walter
  See Garrett, Randall
Burack, Sylvia K. 1916-2003 .... *35*
  Obituary *143*
Burbank, Addison (Buswell) 1895-1961 ...... *37*
Burch, Joann J(ohansen) *75*
Burch, Robert J(oseph) 1925- *74*
  Earlier sketch in SATA *1*
  See also CLR *63*
Burchard, Peter Duncan 1921- *143*
  Earlier sketches in SATA *5, 74*
  See also SAAS *13*
Burchard, S. H.
  See Burchard, Sue
Burchard, Sue 1937- *22*
Burchardt, Nellie 1921- *7*
Burckhardt, Marc 1962- *196*
Burdett, Lois *117*
Burdick, Eugene (Leonard) 1918-1965 .... *22*
Burford, Eleanor
  See Hibbert, Eleanor Alice Burford
Burg, Ann E. 1954- *217*
Burg, Shana 1968- *204*
Burgan, Michael 1960- *167*
  Earlier sketch in SATA *118*
Burger, Carl 1888-1967 .... *9*
Burgess, Ann Marie
  See Gerson, Noel Bertram
Burgess, Barbara Hood 1926- *69*
Burgess, Em
  See Burgess, Mary Wyche
Burgess, (Frank) Gelett 1866-1951 .... *32*
  Brief entry *30*
Burgess, Mark *157*
Burgess, Mary Wyche 1916- *18*
Burgess, Melvin 1954- *198*
  Earlier sketches in SATA *96, 146*
Burgess, Michael
  See Gerson, Noel Bertram
Burgess, Robert F(orrest) 1927- *4*
Burgess, Starling
  See Tudor, Tasha
Burgess, Thornton Waldo 1874-1965 .... *17*
Burgess, Trevor
  See Trevor, Elleston
Burgwyn, Mebane Holoman 1914-1992 .... *7*
Burke, David 1927- *46*
Burke, Diana G.
  See Gallagher, Diana G.
Burke, Diana Gallagher
  See Gallagher, Diana G.
Burke, Dianne O'Quinn 1940- *89*
Burke, Janine 1952- *139*
Burke, Jim 1973- *179*
Burke, John
  See O'Connor, Richard
Burke, Katie 1953- *168*
Burke, Patrick 1958- *114*
Burke, Ralph
  See Garrett, Randall
  and Silverberg, Robert
Burkert, Nancy Ekholm 1933- *24*
  See also SAAS *14*

Burkett, D. Brent *194*
Burke-Weiner, Kimberly 1962- *95*
Burks, Brian 1955- *95*
Burland, Brian (Berkeley) 1931- *34*
Burland, C. A.
  See Burland, Cottie (Arthur)
Burland, Cottie (Arthur) 1905-1983 .... *5*
Burleigh, Robert 1936- *193*
  Earlier sketches in SATA *55, 98, 146*
Burlingame, (William) Roger 1889-1967 .... *2*
Burman, Alice Caddy 1896(?)-1977
  Obituary *24*
Burman, Ben Lucien 1896-1984 .... *6*
  Obituary *40*
Burn, Doris 1923- *1*
Burn, Ted
  See Burn, Thomas E.
Burn, Thomas E. 1940- *150*
Burnard, Damon 1963- *115*
Burnett, Constance Buel 1893-1975 .... *36*
Burnett, Frances Eliza Hodgson
  See Burnett, Frances Hodgson
Burnett, Frances Hodgson 1849-1924 .... *100*
  See also YABC *2*
  See also CLR *122*
Burnett, Lindy *210*
Burnett Bossi, Lisa *193*
Burney, Anton
  See Hopkins, (Hector) Kenneth
Burnford, Sheila (Philip Cochrane Every)
  1918-1984 .... *3*
  Obituary *38*
  See also CLR *2*
Burnham, Gretchen
  See Sprague, Gretchen
Burnham, Nicole 1970- *161*
Burnham, Niki
  See Burnham, Nicole
Burnham, Sophy 1936- *65*
Burningham, John 1936- *225*
  Earlier sketches in SATA *16, 59, 111, 160*
  See also CLR *9*
Burningham, Robin Yoko
  See Racoma, Robin Yoko
Burningham, Sarah O'Leary *216*
Burns, Diane L. 1950- *81*
  See also SAAS *24*
Burns, Eloise Wilkin
  See Wilkin, Eloise
Burns, Florence M. 1905-1988 .... *61*
Burns, Khephra 1950- *92*
Burns, Loree Griffin *193*
Burns, Marilyn 1941- *96*
  Brief entry *33*
Burns, Olive Ann 1924-1990 .... *65*
Burns, Paul C. *5*
Burns, Ray
  See Burns, Raymond (Howard)
Burns, Raymond (Howard) 1924- *9*
Burns, Theresa 1961- *84*
Burns, William A. 1909-1999 .... *5*
Burr, Dan 1951- *65*
Burr, Dan 1960- *219*
Burr, Lonnie 1943- *47*
Burrell, Roy E(ric) C(harles) 1923- *72*
Burroughs, Edgar Rice 1875-1950 .... *41*
  See also CLR *157*
Burroughs, Jean Mitchell 1908- *28*
Burroughs, Polly 1925- *2*
Burroway, Janet 1936- *23*
Burroway, Janet Gay
  See Burroway, Janet
Burstein, Chaya M(alamud) 1923- *64*
Burstein, Fred 1950- *83*
Burstein, John 1949- *54*
  Brief entry *40*
Burstein, Stanley M.
  See Burstein, Stanley Mayer
Burstein, Stanley Mayer 1941- *175*
Bursztynski, Sue 1953- *114*

Burt, Jesse Clifton 1921-1976 .... *46*
  Obituary *20*
Burt, Olive Woolley 1894-1981 .... *4*
Burtinshaw, Julie *185*
Burton, Gennett 1945- *95*
Burton, Hester (Wood-Hill) 1913-2000 .... *74*
  Earlier sketch in SATA *7*
  See also CLR *1*
  See also SAAS *8*
Burton, Leslie
  See McGuire, Leslie (Sarah)
Burton, Marilee Robin 1950- *82*
  Earlier sketch in SATA *46*
Burton, Maurice 1898-1992 .... *23*
Burton, Rebecca 1970- *183*
Burton, Robert (Wellesley) 1941- *22*
Burton, Virginia Lee 1909-1968 .... *100*
  Earlier sketch in SATA *2*
  See also CLR *11*
Burton, William H(enry) 1890-1964 .... *11*
Busby, Ailie *192*
Busby, Cylin 1970- *118*
Busby, Edith (A. Lake) (?)-1964
  Obituary *29*
Busby, John 1942- *209*
Buscaglia, (Felice) Leo(nardo) 1924-1998 ... *65*
Buscaglia, Leo F.
  See Buscaglia, (Felice) Leo(nardo)
Busch, Phyllis S. 1909- *30*
Bush, Anne Kelleher
  See Kelleher, Anne
Bush, Catherine 1961- *128*
Bush, Jenna 1981- *208*
Bush, Laura 1946- *208*
Bushmiller, Ernest Paul 1905-1982 .... *31*
Bushmiller, Ernie
  See Bushmiller, Ernest Paul
Bushnell, Jack 1952- *86*
Busoni, Rafaello 1900-1962 .... *16*
Buss, Helen M.
  See Clarke, Margaret
Busse, Sarah Martin *194*
Busselle, Rebecca 1941- *80*
Bustard, Anne 1951- *173*
Butcher, Kristin 1951- *140*
Butenko, Bohdan 1931- *90*
Butler, Beverly Kathleen 1932- *7*
Butler, Bill
  See Butler, William Vivian
  and Butler, Ernest Alton
  and Butler, William Huxford
Butler, Charles 1963- *175*
  Earlier sketch in SATA *121*
Butler, Charles Cadman
  See Butler, Charles
Butler, Dori Hillestad 1965- *207*
  Earlier sketch in SATA *164*
Butler, Dorothy 1925- *73*
Butler, Geoff 1945- *94*
Butler, John 1952- *225*
Butler, M. Christina 1934- *224*
  Earlier sketches in SATA *72, 170*
Butler, Octavia 1947-2006 .... *84*
  See also CLR *65*
Butler, Octavia E.
  See Butler, Octavia
Butler, Octavia Estelle
  See Butler, Octavia
Butler, Vivian
  See Butler, William Vivian
Butler, William
  See Butler, William Vivian
Butler, William Vivian 1927-1987 .... *79*
Butterfield, Moira 1960- *219*
Butters, Dorothy Gilman
  See Gilman, Dorothy
Butterworth, Emma Macalik 1928- *43*
Butterworth, Nick 1946- *149*
  Earlier sketch in SATA *106*
Butterworth, Oliver 1915-1990 .... *1*
  Obituary *66*

Butterworth, W. E.
  See Griffin, W. E. B.
Butterworth, William E.
  See Griffin, W. E. B.
Butterworth, William Edmund III
  See Griffin, W. E. B.
Butts, Ed 1951- *177*
Butts, Edward P.
  See Butts, Ed
Butts, Ellen R. 1942- *93*
Butts, Ellen Rubinstein
  See Butts, Ellen R.
Butzer, C. M. 1974- *212*
Buxton, Ralph
  See Silverstein, Alvin
  and Silverstein, Virginia B.
Buzzeo, Toni 1951- *215*
  Earlier sketch in SATA *135*
Byalick, Marcia 1947- *141*
  Earlier sketch in SATA *97*
Byard, Carole (Marie) 1941- *57*
Byars, Betsy 1928- *223*
  Autobiography Feature *108*
  Earlier sketches in SATA *4, 46, 80, 163*
  See also CLR *72*
  See also SAAS *1*
Byars, Betsy Cromer
  See Byars, Betsy
Byfield, Barbara Ninde 1930-1988 .... *8*
Byman, Jeremy 1944- *129*
Bynum, Janie *133*
Byrd, Elizabeth 1912-1989 .... *34*
Byrd, Nicole
  See Zach, Cheryl (Byrd)
Byrd, Robert (John) 1942- *158*
  Earlier sketches in SATA *33, 112*
Byrd, Tim 1964- *216*
Byrne, Gayle *218*
Byrne, Mary Gregg 1951- *162*

C

C. 3. 3.
  See Wilde, Oscar
C. E. M.
  See Mastrangelo, Charles E(lmer)
Cabaniss, J(ames) Allen 1911-1997 .... *5*
Cabat, Erni 1914- *74*
Cabban, Vanessa 1971- *176*
Cable, Mary 1920- *9*
Cabot, Meg 1967- *217*
  Earlier sketches in SATA *127, 175*
  See also CLR *85*
Cabot, Meggin
  See Cabot, Meg
Cabot, Meggin Patricia
  See Cabot, Meg
Cabot, Patricia
  See Cabot, Meg
Cabral, O. M.
  See Cabral, Olga
Cabral, Olga 1909- *46*
Cabrera, Cozbi A. 1963- *177*
Cabrera, Jane 1968- *182*
  Earlier sketches in SATA *103, 152*
Cabrera, Marcela 1966- *90*
Caddy, Alice
  See Burman, Alice Caddy
Cade, Toni
  See Bambara, Toni Cade
Cadena, Beth *222*
Cadmus and Harmonia
  See Buchan, John
Cadnum, Michael 1949- *225*
  Earlier sketches in SATA *87, 121, 165*
  See also CLR *78*
Caduto, Michael J. 1955- *103*
Cadwallader, Sharon 1936- *7*
Cady, (Walter) Harrison 1877(?)-1970 .... *19*

Caffey, Donna (J.) 1954- *110*
Cagle, Malcolm W(infield) 1918- *32*
Cahn, Rhoda 1922- *37*
Cahn, William 1912-1976 .... *37*
Cain, Arthur H(omer) 1913-1981 .... *3*
Cain, Christopher
  See Fleming, Thomas
Cain, Sheridan 1952- *186*
Caine, Geoffrey
  See Walker, Robert W.
Caines, Jeannette (Franklin) 1938- *78*
  Brief entry *43*
  See also CLR *24*
Cairns, Trevor 1922- *14*
Calabro, Marian 1954- *79*
Caldecott, Moyra 1927- *22*
Caldecott, Randolph (J.) 1846-1886 .... *100*
  Earlier sketch in SATA *17*
  See also CLR *110*
Calder, Charlotte 1952- *125*
Calder, David 1932-1997 .... *105*
Calder, Lyn
  See Calmenson, Stephanie
Calder, Marie D(onais) 1948- *96*
Calderone-Stewart, Lisa
  See Calderone-Stewart, Lisa-Marie
Calderone-Stewart, Lisa-Marie 1958- *123*
Caldwell, Doreen (Mary) 1942- *71*
Caldwell, John C(ope) 1913-1984 .... *7*
Caletti, Deb 1963- *221*
  Earlier sketch in SATA *171*
Calhoun, B. B. 1961- *98*
Calhoun, Chad
  See Barrett, Neal, Jr.
  and Cunningham, Chet
  and Goulart, Ron
Calhoun, Dia 1959- *183*
  Earlier sketch in SATA *129*
Calhoun, Mary
  See Wilkins, Mary Huiskamp
Calhoun, T.B.
  See Bisson, Terry
Cali, Davide 1972- *190*
Calif, Ruth 1922- *67*
Calkins, Franklin
  See Stratemeyer, Edward L.
Call, Greg *197*
Call, Hughie Florence 1890-1969 .... *1*
Callahan, Dorothy M. 1934- *39*
  Brief entry *35*
Callahan, Dorothy Monahan
  See Callahan, Dorothy M.
Callahan, Philip Serna 1923- *25*
Callahan, Sean 1965- *222*
Callan, Jamie 1954- *59*
Callan, Jim 1951- *181*
Callaway, Bernice (Anne) 1923- *48*
Callaway, Kathy 1943- *36*
Callen, Larry
  See Callen, Lawrence Willard, Jr.
Callen, Lawrence Willard, Jr. 1927- *19*
Calley, Karin 1965- *92*
Calmenson, Stephanie 1952- *211*
  Brief entry *37*
  Earlier sketches in SATA *51, 84, 139*
Calonita, Jen *216*
Calvert, Elinor H.
  See Lasell, Elinor H.
Calvert, John
  See Leaf, (Wilbur) Munro
Calvert, Pam 1966- *205*
Calvert, Patricia 1931- *132*
  Earlier sketches in SATA *45, 69*
  See also SAAS *17*
Camburn, Carol A.
  See Camburn-Bracalente, Carol A.
Camburn-Bracalente, Carol A. 1962- *118*
Cameron, Ann 1943- *129*
  Earlier sketches in SATA *27, 89*
  See also SAAS *20*
Cameron, Edna M. 1905-1999 .... *3*

Cameron, Eleanor (Frances) 1912-1996 .... *25*
  Obituary *93*
  Earlier sketch in SATA *1*
  See also CLR *72*
  See also SAAS *10*
Cameron, Elizabeth
  See Nowell, Elizabeth Cameron
Cameron, Elizabeth Jane 1910-1976 .... *32*
  Obituary *30*
Cameron, Ian
  See Payne, Donald Gordon
Cameron, M(alcolm) G(ordon) Graham
  See Graham-Cameron, M(alcolm) G(ordon)
Cameron, M. Graham
  See Graham-Cameron, M(alcolm) G(ordon)
Cameron, Mike Graham
  See Graham-Cameron, M(alcolm) G(ordon)
Cameron, Natalie Russell
  See Russell, Natalie
Cameron, Polly 1928- *2*
Cameron, Scott 1962- *84*
Camp, Charles L. 1893-1975
  Obituary *31*
Camp, Lindsay 1957- *133*
Camp, Madeleine L'Engle
  See L'Engle, Madeleine
Camp, Walter (Chauncey) 1859-1925
  See YABC *1*
Campbell, (Elizabeth) Andrea 1963- *50*
Campbell, Ann R. 1925- *11*
Campbell, Bill 1960- *89*
Campbell, Bruce
  See Epstein, Samuel
Campbell, Camilla 1905-1992 .... *26*
Campbell, Carole R. 1939- *125*
Campbell, Hope 1925- *20*
Campbell, Hugh 1930- *90*
Campbell, Jane
  See Edwards, Jane Campbell
Campbell, Julie
  See Tatham, Julie Campbell
Campbell, Patricia J(ean) 1930- *45*
Campbell, Patty
  See Campbell, Patricia J(ean)
Campbell, Peter A. 1948- *99*
Campbell, R. W.
  See Campbell, Rosemae Wells
Campbell, Robin
  See Strachan, Ian
Campbell, Rod 1945- *98*
  Brief entry *44*
  Earlier sketch in SATA *51*
Campbell, Rosemae Wells 1909- *1*
Campbell, Sarah C. 1966- *207*
Camper, Cathy 1956- *170*
Campion, Nardi Reeder 1917-2007 .... *22*
Campling, Elizabeth 1948- *53*
Campoy, F. Isabel 1946- *181*
  Earlier sketch in SATA *143*
Camps, Luis 1928- *66*
Canales, Viola 1957- *141*
Candell, Victor 1903-1977
  Obituary *24*
Canfield, Dorothea F.
  See Fisher, Dorothy (Frances) Canfield
Canfield, Dorothea Frances
  See Fisher, Dorothy (Frances) Canfield
Canfield, Dorothy
  See Fisher, Dorothy (Frances) Canfield
Canfield, Jack 1944- *164*
Canfield, Jane White 1897-1984 .... *32*
  Obituary *38*
Canfield, Muriel 1935- *94*
Canga, C.B. 1976- *216*
Canga, Chris
  See Canga, C.B.
Caniff, Milton 1907-1988
  Obituary *58*
Caniff, Milton Arthur Paul
  See Caniff, Milton

Cann, Helen 1969- *179*
  Earlier sketch in SATA *124*
Cann, Kate 1954- *152*
  Earlier sketch in SATA *103*
Cannan, Joanna
  See Pullein-Thompson, Joanna Maxwell
Cannell, Jon *196*
Cannell, Jonathan C.
  See Cannell, Jon
Cannon, A.E. *202*
  Earlier sketches in SATA *93, 163*
Cannon, Ann Edwards
  See Cannon, A.E.
Cannon, Bettie (Waddell) 1922- *59*
Cannon, Curt
  See Hunter, Evan
Cannon, Eileen E(mily) 1948- *119*
Cannon, Frank
  See Mayhar, Ardath
Cannon, Janell 1957- *128*
  Earlier sketch in SATA *78*
  See also CLR *120*
Cannon, Marian G. 1923- *85*
Cannon, Taffy
  See Cannon, Eileen E(mily)
Cantone, AnnaLaura *182*
Cantrell, Julie 1973- *217*
Canusi, Jose
  See Barker, S. Omar
Canyon, Christopher 1966- *150*
  Earlier sketch in SATA *104*
Caparo, Antonio
  See Caparo, Antonio Javier
Caparo, Antonio Javier *205*
Capek, Michael 1947- *142*
  Earlier sketch in SATA *96*
Capes, Bernard (Edward Joseph)
  1854-1918 .... *116*
Caple, Kathy *193*
Caple, Laurie 1958- *201*
Caplin, Alfred Gerald 1909-1979 .... *61*
  Obituary *21*
Caponigro, John Paul 1965- *84*
Capote, Truman 1924-1984 .... *91*
Capp, Al
  See Caplin, Alfred Gerald
Cappel, Constance 1936- *22*
Cappetta, Cynthia 1949- *125*
Cappo, Nan Willard 1955- *143*
Capps, Benjamin (Franklin) 1922- *9*
Cappy Dick
  See Cleveland, George
Captain Kangaroo
  See Keeshan, Robert J.
Captain Wheeler
  See Ellis, Edward S.
Captain Young of Yale
  See Stratemeyer, Edward L.
Capucilli, Alyssa Satin 1957- *203*
  Earlier sketches in SATA *115, 163*
Capucine
  See Mazille, Capucine
Carafoli, Marci
  See Balterman, Marcia Ridlon
Caraher, Kim(berley Elizabeth) 1961- *105*
Caraker, Mary 1929- *74*
Caras, Roger A(ndrew) 1928-2001 .... *12*
  Obituary *127*
Caravantes, Peggy 1935- *140*
Caraway, Caren 1939- *57*
Carbone, Elisa 1954- *173*
  Earlier sketches in SATA *81, 137*
Carbone, Elisa Lynn
  See Carbone, Elisa
Carbonnier, Jeanne 1894-1974 .... *3*
  Obituary *34*
Card, Orson Scott 1951- *127*
  Earlier sketch in SATA *83*
  See also CLR *116*
Care, Felicity
  See Coury, Louise Andree

Carew, Jan 1925- *51*
  Brief entry *40*
Carew, Jan Rynveld
  See Carew, Jan
Carey, Benedict 1960- *219*
Carey, Bonnie
  See Marshall, Bonnie C.
Carey, Charles W., Jr. 1951- *170*
Carey, Ernestine Gilbreth 1908-2006 .... *2*
  Obituary *177*
Carey, Janet Lee 1954(?)- *225*
  Earlier sketch in SATA *185*
Carey, Lisa *110*
Carey, M. V.
  See Carey, Mary V(irginia)
Carey, Mary V(irginia) 1925-1994 .... *44*
  Brief entry *39*
Carey, Peter 1943- *94*
Carey, Peter Philip
  See Carey, Peter
Carey, Valerie Scho 1949- *60*
Carheden, Goorel Kristina
  See Naaslund, Goorel Kristina
Carigiet, Alois 1902-1985 .... *24*
  Obituary *47*
  See also CLR *38*
Carini, Edward 1923- *9*
Carkeet, David 1946- *75*
Carle, Eric 1929- *163*
  Earlier sketches in SATA *4, 65, 120*
  See also CLR *72*
  See also SAAS *6*
Carleton, Captain L. C.
  See Ellis, Edward S.
Carleton, Captain Latham C.
  See Ellis, Edward S.
Carleton, Latham C.
  See Ellis, Edward S.
Carley, V(an Ness) Royal 1906-1976
  Obituary *20*
Carling, Amelia Lau 1949- *164*
  Earlier sketch in SATA *119*
Carlisle, Carolyn
  See Hawes, Louise
Carlisle, Clark
  See Holding, James (Clark Carlisle, Jr.)
Carlisle, Olga Andreyev 1930- *35*
Carlock, Miriam
  See Eyerly, Jeannette
Carls, Claudia 1978- *198*
Carlsen, G(eorge) Robert 1917- *30*
Carlsen, Ruth C(hristoffer) 1918- *2*
Carlson, Bernice Wells 1910- *8*
Carlson, Christopher C. *202*
Carlson, Dale (Bick) 1935- *1*
Carlson, Daniel (Bick) 1960- *27*
Carlson, Kirsten 1968- *192*
Carlson, Kirsten M.
  See Carlson, Kirsten
Carlson, Laurie 1952- *173*
  Earlier sketch in SATA *101*
Carlson, Laurie Winn
  See Carlson, Laurie
Carlson, Melody 1956- *171*
  Earlier sketch in SATA *113*
Carlson, Nancy 1953- *213*
  Brief entry *45*
  Earlier sketches in SATA *56, 90, 144*
Carlson, Nancy L.
  See Carlson, Nancy
Carlson, Natalie Savage 1906-1997 .... *68*
  Earlier sketch in SATA *2*
  See also SAAS *4*
Carlson, Susan Johnston 1953- *88*
Carlson, Vada F. 1897- *16*
Carlstrom, Nancy White 1948- *215*
  Brief entry *48*
  Earlier sketches in SATA *53, 92, 156*
Carlton, Keith
  See Robertson, Keith (Carlton)
Carlton, Susan 1960- *195*

Carlyon, Richard *55*
Carman, Bill
  See Carman, William
Carman, Patrick 1966- *197*
  Earlier sketch in SATA *161*
Carman, William *223*
Carmer, Carl (Lamson) 1893-1976 .... *37*
  Obituary *30*
Carmer, Elizabeth Black 1904- *24*
Carmi, Giora 1944- *149*
  Earlier sketch in SATA *79*
Carmichael, Carrie
  See Carmichael, Harriet
Carmichael, Clay *218*
Carmichael, Harriet *40*
Carmody, Isobelle 1958- *191*
  Earlier sketch in SATA *161*
Carmody, Isobelle Jane
  See Carmody, Isobelle
Carney, Elizabeth 1981- *199*
Carney, Jeff 1962- *196*
Carney, Mary Lou 1949- *170*
Carol, Bill J.
  See Knott, William C(ecil, Jr.)
Caron, Romi
  See Caron-Kyselkova', Romana
Caron-Kyselkova', Romana 1967- *94*
Caroselli, Remus F(rancis) 1916- *36*
Carpelan, Bo 1926- *8*
Carpelan, Bo Gustaf Bertelsson
  See Carpelan, Bo
Carpenter, (John) Allan 1917- *81*
  Earlier sketch in SATA *3*
Carpenter, Angelica Shirley 1945- *153*
  Earlier sketch in SATA *71*
Carpenter, Frances 1890-1972 .... *3*
  Obituary *27*
Carpenter, John 1948- *58*
Carpenter, John Howard
  See Carpenter, John
Carpenter, Johnny
  See Carpenter, John
Carpenter, Nancy *215*
Carpenter, Nancy Sippel
  See Carpenter, Nancy
Carpenter, Patricia (Healy Evans) 1920- *11*
Carr, Glyn
  See Styles, (Frank) Showell
Carr, Harriett H(elen) 1899-1977 .... *3*
Carr, Jan 1953- *132*
  Earlier sketch in SATA *89*
Carr, M. J.
  See Carr, Jan
Carr, Mary Jane 1899-1988 .... *2*
  Obituary *55*
Carr, Philippa
  See Hibbert, Eleanor Alice Burford
Carr, Roger Vaughan 1937- *95*
Carrel, Annette Felder 1929- *90*
Carrick, Carol (Hatfield) 1935- *118*
  Earlier sketches in SATA *7, 63*
  See also SAAS *18*
Carrick, Donald (F.) 1929-1989 .... *63*
  Earlier sketch in SATA *7*
Carrick, Malcolm 1945- *28*
Carrick, Paul 1972- *194*
Carrier, Lark 1947- *71*
  Brief entry *50*
Carrier, Roch 1937- *166*
  Earlier sketch in SATA *105*
Carrighar, Sally 1898-1985 .... *24*
Carrillo, Patricia S.
  See Carrillo, P.S.
Carrillo, P.S. *209*
Carrington, G. A.
  See Cunningham, Chet
Carrington, Marsha Gray 1954- *168*
  Earlier sketch in SATA *111*
Carris, Joan 1938- *182*
  Brief entry *42*
  Earlier sketch in SATA *44*

Carris, Joan Davenport
See Carris, Joan
Carroll, Curt
See Bishop, Curtis (Kent)
Carroll, Elizabeth
See Barkin, Carol
and James, Elizabeth
Carroll, Jaye
See Carroll, Michael
Carroll, Jenny
See Cabot, Meg
Carroll, (Archer) Latrobe 1894-1996 7
Carroll, Laura
See Parr, Lucy
Carroll, Lewis 1832-1898 100
See also YABC 2
See also CLR 108
Carroll, Michael 1966- 203
Carroll, Raymond 1924- 86
Brief entry 47
Carruth, Hayden 1921-2008 47
Obituary 197
Carryl, Charles E. 1841-1920 114
Carryl, Charles Edward
See Carryl, Charles E.
Carse, Robert 1902-1971 5
Carson, J(ohn) Franklin 1920-1981 1
Obituary 107
Carson, Mary Kay 1964- 200
Earlier sketch in SATA *150*
Carson, Rachel 1907-1964 23
Carson, Rachel Louise
See Carson, Rachel
Carson, Rosalind
See Chittenden, Margaret
Carson, S. M.
See Gorsline, (Sally) Marie
Carson, William C. 1928- 154
Carter, Abby 222
Earlier sketch in SATA *184*
Carter, Alden R 1947- 137
Earlier sketch in SATA *67*
See also CLR 22
See also SAAS 18
Carter, Alden Richardson
See Carter, Alden R
Carter, Andy 1948- 134
Carter, Angela 1940-1992 66
Obituary 70
Carter, Angela Olive
See Carter, Angela
Carter, Anne Laurel 1953- 209
Earlier sketch in SATA *135*
Carter, Asa Earl
See Carter, Forrest
Carter, Avis Murton
See Allen, Kenneth S.
Carter, Bruce
See Hough, Richard (Alexander)
Carter, Carol S(hadis) 1948- 124
Carter, David A. 1957- 170
Earlier sketch in SATA *114*
Carter, Don 1958- 192
Earlier sketch in SATA *124*
Carter, Dorothy Sharp 1921- 8
Carter, Forrest 1927(?)-1979 32
Carter, Helene 1887-1960 15
Carter, (William) Hodding, Jr. 1907-1972 2
Obituary 27
Carter, James Earl, Jr.
See Carter, Jimmy
Carter, Jimmy 1924- 79
Carter, Katharine J(ones) 1905-1984 2
Carter, Lin(wood Vrooman) 1930-1988 91
Carter, Mike 1936- 138

Carter, Nick
See Avallone, Michael (Angelo, Jr.)
and Ballard, (Willis) Todhunter
and Crider, Bill
and Cassiday, Bruce (Bingham)
and Chastain, Thomas
and Dey, Frederic (Merrill) Van Rensselaer
and Garside, Jack
and Hayes, Ralph E(ugene)
and Henderson, M(arilyn) R(uth)
and Lynds, Dennis
and Lynds, Gayle (Hallenbeck)
and Randisi, Robert J.
and Rasof, Henry
and Stratemeyer, Edward L.
and Smith, Martin Cruz
and Swain, Dwight V(reeland)
and Vardeman, Robert E.
and Wallmann, Jeffrey M(iner)
and White, Lionel
Carter, Peter 1929- 57
Carter, Phyllis Ann
See Eberle, Irmengarde
Carter, Samuel (Thomson) III 1904-1988 37
Obituary 60
Carter, Timothy 1972- 224
Carter, William E. 1926-1983 1
Obituary 35
Cartlidge, Michelle 1950- 96
Brief entry 37
Earlier sketch in SATA *49*
Cartner, William Carruthers 1910- 11
Cartwright, Ann 1940- 78
Cartwright, Reg(inald Ainsley) 1938- 64
Cartwright, Sally 1923- 9
Carusone, Al 1949- 89
Carvell, Marlene 172
Carver, John
See Gardner, Richard (M.)
Carwell, L'Ann
See McKissack, Patricia C.
Cary
See Cary, Louis F(avreau)
Cary, Barbara Knapp 1912(?)-1975
Obituary 31
Cary, Kate 1967(?)- 174
Cary, Louis F(avreau) 1915- 9
Caryl, Jean
See Kaplan, Jean Caryl Korn
Casanova, Mary 1957- 186
Earlier sketches in SATA *94, 136*
Cascone, A.G.
See Cascone, Annette
and Cascone, Gina
Cascone, Annette 1960- 103
Cascone, Gina 1955- 103
Case, Chris 1976- 209
Case, Marshal T(aylor) 1941- 9
Case, Michael
See Howard, Robert West
Caseley, Judith 1951- 159
Brief entry 53
Earlier sketch in SATA *87*
Casewit, Curtis W(erner) 1922-2002 4
Casey, Barbara (Louise) 1944- 147
Earlier sketch in SATA *79*
Casey, Brigid 1950- 9
Casey, Tina 1959- 141
Cash, Ellen Lewis Buell 1905-1989
Obituary 64
Cash, John Carter 1970- 218
Cash, Megan Montague 160
Cashore, Kristin 1976(?)- 206
Casilla, Robert 1959- 211
Earlier sketches in SATA *75, 146*
Cason, Mabel Earp 1892-1965 10
Cass, Joan E(velyn) 1
Cass-Beggs, Barbara 1904- 62
Cassedy, Patrice (Rinaldo) 1953- 149

Cassedy, Sylvia 1930-1989 77
Obituary 61
Earlier sketch in SATA 27
See also CLR 26
Cassel, Lili
See Wronker, Lili Cassel
Cassels, Jean 173
Cassidy, Anne 1952- 166
Cassidy, Anne Josephine
See Cassidy, Anne
Cassidy, Cathy 1962- 183
Casson, Hugh Maxwell 1910-1999 65
Obituary 115
Cassutt, Michael 1954- 78
Cassutt, Michael Joseph
See Cassutt, Michael
Castaldi, Elicia 194
Castaldo, Nancy Fusco 1962- 151
Earlier sketch in SATA *93*
Castaneda, Omar S. 1954- 71
Castell, Megan
See Williams, Jeanne
Castellanos, Jane Mollie Robinson
1913-2001 9
Castellon, Federico 1914-1971 48
Castellucci, Cecil 1969- 176
Castillo, Edmund L. 1924-2005 1
Obituary 167
Castillo, Lauren 195
Castle, Lee
See Ogan, George F.
and Ogan, Margaret E. (Nettles)
Castle, Paul
See Howard, Vernon (Linwood)
Castle, Robert
See Hamilton, Edmond
Castrovilla, Selene 1966- 186
Caswell, Brian 1954- 171
Earlier sketch in SATA 97
Caswell, Deanna 223
Caswell, Helen (Rayburn) 1923- 12
Catalano, Dominic 1956- 163
Earlier sketch in SATA *76*
Catalano, Grace (A.) 1961- 99
Catalanotto, Peter 1959- 195
Autobiography Feature 113
Earlier sketches in SATA *70, 114, 159*
See also CLR 68
See also SAAS 25
Catanese, P. W. 1961- 179
Cate, Annette LeBlanc 196
Cate, Dick
See Cate, Richard Edward Nelson
Cate, Richard Edward Nelson 1932- 28
Cather, Willa 1873-1947 30
See also CLR 98
Catherall, Arthur 1906-1980 74
Earlier sketches in SATA *3, 4*
Cathon, Laura E(lizabeth) 1908-1991 27
Catlett, Elizabeth 1919(?)- 82
Catlin, Wynelle 1930- 13
Catlow, Nikalas
See Catlow, Niki
Catlow, Niki 1975- 193
Cato, Heather 105
Cato, Sheila 114
Catran, Ken 1944- 190
Catrow, David
See Catrow, David J. III
Catrow, David J. III 206
Earlier sketch in SATA *152*
Catt, Louis
See French, Vivian
Cattell, James 1954- 123
Catton, (Charles) Bruce 1899-1978 2
Obituary 24
Catusanu, Mircea 222
Catz, Max
See Glaser, Milton
Caudell, Marian 1930- 52

Caudill, Rebecca 1899-1985 .... *1*
  Obituary *44*
Cauley, Lorinda Bryan 1951- *46*
  Brief entry *43*
Caulfield, Peggy F. 1926-1987
  Obituary *53*
Cauman, Samuel 1910-1971 .... *48*
Causley, Charles (Stanley) 1917-2003 .... *66*
  Obituary *149*
  Earlier sketch in SATA *3*
  See also CLR *30*
Cavallaro, Ann (Abelson) 1918- *62*
Cavallo, Diana 1931- *7*
Cavanagh, Helen (Carol) 1939- *98*
  Brief entry *37*
  Earlier sketch in SATA *48*
Cavanah, Frances 1899-1982 .... *31*
  Earlier sketch in SATA *1*
Cavanna, Betty
  See Harrison, Elizabeth (Allen) Cavanna
Cavanna, Elizabeth
  See Harrison, Elizabeth (Allen) Cavanna
Cave, Kathryn 1948- *123*
  Earlier sketch in SATA *76*
Cavendish, Peter
  See Horler, Sydney
Caveney, Philip 1951- *219*
Caveney, Philip Richard
  See Caveney, Philip
Cavin, Ruth 1918-2011 .... *38*
Cavin, Ruth Brodie
  See Cavin, Ruth
Cavoukian, Raffi 1948- *68*
Cawley, Winifred 1915- *13*
Cazeau, Charles J(ay) 1931- *65*
Cazet, Denys 1938- *191*
  Brief entry *41*
  Earlier sketches in SATA *52, 99, 163*
Cazzola, Gus 1934- *73*
Cebulash, Mel 1937- *91*
  Earlier sketch in SATA *10*
Ceccoli, Nicoletta *181*
Cecil, Randy 1968- *223*
  Earlier sketch in SATA *187*
Cecka, Melanie *199*
Ceder, Georgiana Dorcas -1985 .... *10*
Celenza, Anna Harwell *133*
Celestino, Martha Laing
  See Laing, Martha
Cepeda, Joe *215*
  Earlier sketch in SATA *159*
Cerf, Bennett (Alfred) 1898-1971 .... *7*
Cerf, Christopher (Bennett) 1941- *2*
Cermak, Martin
  See Duchacek, Ivo D(uka)
Cerullo, Mary M. 1949- *145*
  Earlier sketch in SATA *86*
Cervon, Jacqueline
  See Moussard, Jacqueline
Cetin, Frank Stanley 1921- *2*
Chabon, Michael 1963- *145*
Chabrian, Deborah
  See Chabrian, Deborah L.
Chabrian, Deborah L. *212*
Chaconas, D.J.
  See Chaconas, Dori
Chaconas, Dori 1938- *208*
  Earlier sketches in SATA *145, 175*
Chaconas, Doris J.
  See Chaconas, Dori
Chadda, Sarwat *224*
Chadwick, Lester *67*
  Earlier sketch in SATA *1*
Chaffee, Allen *3*
Chaffin, Lillie D(orton) 1925- *4*
Chaikin, Miriam 1924- *152*
  Earlier sketches in SATA *24, 102*
Chall, Marsha Wilson *150*
Challand, Helen J(ean) 1921- *64*
Challans, Mary
  See Renault, Mary

Chalmers, Mary (Eileen) 1927- *6*
  See also SAAS *14*
Chamberlain, Barbara A.
  See Azore, Barbara
Chamberlain, Margaret 1954- *212*
  Earlier sketch in SATA *46*
Chamberlin, Kate 1945- *105*
Chamberlin, Mary 1960- *177*
Chamberlin, Rich *177*
Chamberlin, Richard
  See Chamberlin, Rich
Chambers, Aidan 1934- *171*
  Earlier sketches in SATA *1, 69, 108*
  See also CLR *151*
  See also SAAS *12*
Chambers, Bradford 1922-1984
  Obituary *39*
Chambers, Catherine E.
  See St. John, Nicole
Chambers, John W. 1933- *57*
  Brief entry *46*
Chambers, Kate
  See St. John, Nicole
Chambers, Margaret Ada Eastwood 1911- *2*
Chambers, Peggy
  See Chambers, Margaret Ada Eastwood
Chambers, Robert W(illiam) 1865-1933 .... *107*
Chambliss, Maxie *186*
Champlin, Susan 1961- *225*
Chan, Gillian 1954- *147*
  Earlier sketch in SATA *102*
Chan, Peter 1980(?)- *207*
Chance, James T.
  See Carpenter, John
Chance, John T.
  See Carpenter, John
Chance, Stephen
  See Turner, Philip (William)
Chandler, Caroline A(ugusta) 1906-1979 ..... *22*
  Obituary *24*
Chandler, David P. 1933- *28*
Chandler, David Porter
  See Chandler, David P.
Chandler, Edna Walker 1908-1982 .... *11*
  Obituary *31*
Chandler, Jennifer
  See Westwood, Jennifer
Chandler, Karen 1959- *122*
Chandler, Linda S(mith) 1929- *39*
Chandler, Pauline *175*
Chandler, Robert 1953- *40*
Chandler, Ruth Forbes 1894-1978 .... *2*
  Obituary *26*
Chandonnet, Ann F. 1943- *92*
Chaney, Jill 1932- *87*
Chang, Chih-Wei 1966- *111*
Chang, Cindy 1968- *90*
Chang, Margaret 1941- *71*
Chang, Margaret Scrogin
  See Chang, Margaret
Chang, Raymond 1939- *142*
  Earlier sketches in SATA *71, 142 PEN*
Chanin, Michael 1952- *84*
Channel, A. R.
  See Catherall, Arthur
Chapian, Marie 1938- *29*
Chapin, Alene Olsen Dalton 1915(?)-1986
  Obituary *47*
Chapin, Tom 1945- *83*
Chapman, Allen *67*
  Earlier sketch in SATA *1*
Chapman, Cheryl O(rth) 1948- *80*
Chapman, (Constance) Elizabeth (Mann)
  1919- *10*
Chapman, Gaye 1970- *200*
Chapman, Gaye Coralie
  See Chapman, Gaye
Chapman, Gaynor 1935- *32*
Chapman, Gillian 1955- *120*
Chapman, Jane 1970- *212*
  Earlier sketches in SATA *122, 176*

Chapman, Jean *104*
  Earlier sketch in SATA *34*
  See also CLR *65*
Chapman, John Stanton Higham 1891-1972
  Obituary *27*
Chapman, Lee
  See Bradley, Marion Zimmer
Chapman, Linda 1969- *223*
Chapman, Lynne 1960- *197*
Chapman, Lynne F(erguson) 1963- *150*
  Earlier sketch in SATA *94*
Chapman, Maristan
  See Chapman, John Stanton Higham
Chapman, Vera (Ivy May) 1898-1996 .... *33*
Chapman, Walker
  See Silverberg, Robert
Chappell, Audrey 1954- *72*
Chappell, Crissa-Jean *198*
Chappell, Warren 1904-1991 .... *68*
  Obituary *67*
  Earlier sketch in SATA *6*
  See also SAAS *10*
Chapra, Mimi *182*
Charbonneau, Eileen 1951- *118*
  Earlier sketch in SATA *84*
Charbonnet, Gabrielle 1961- *81*
Chardiet, Bernice 1927(?)- *27*
Chardiet, Bernice Kroll
  See Chardiet, Bernice
Charest, Emily MacLachlan *198*
Charles, Donald
  See Meighan, Donald Charles
Charles, Louis
  See Stratemeyer, Edward L.
Charles, Nicholas
  See Kuskin, Karla
Charles, Nicholas J.
  See Kuskin, Karla
Charles, Norma *153*
Charles, Veronika Martenova *182*
Charlip, Remy 1929- *119*
  Earlier sketches in SATA *4, 68*
  See also CLR *8*
Charlot, Jean 1898-1979 .... *8*
  Obituary *31*
Charlot, Martin 1944- *64*
Charlot, Martin Day
  See Charlot, Martin
Charlton, Michael (Alan) 1923- *34*
Charlton-Trujillo, e.E. *189*
Charmatz, Bill 1925-2005 .... *7*
Charnas, Suzy McKee 1939- *110*
  Earlier sketch in SATA *61*
Charosh, Mannis 1906- *5*
Chartier, Normand L. 1945- *66*
Chase, Alice
  See McHargue, Georgess
Chase, Alyssa 1965- *92*
Chase, Andra 1942- *91*
Chase, Emily
  See Aks, Patricia
  and Garwood, Julie
  and Sachs, Judith
  and White, Carol
Chase, Mary (Coyle) 1907-1981 .... *17*
  Obituary *29*
Chase, Mary Ellen 1887-1973 .... *10*
Chase, Paula *214*
Chase, Richard 1904-1988 .... *64*
  Obituary *56*
Chase, Samantha
  See Glick, Ruth (Burtnick)
Chast, Roz 1954- *212*
  Earlier sketch in SATA *97*
Chastain, Madye Lee 1908-1989 .... *4*
Chataway, Carol 1955- *140*
Chatterjee, Debjani 1952- *83*
Chatterton, Martin 1961- *225*
Chauncy, Nan(cen Beryl Masterman)
  1900-1970 .... *6*
  See also CLR *6*

Chaundler, Christine 1887-1972 .... *1*
   Obituary 25
Chayka, Doug 196
Chbosky, Stephen 1972- 164
Cheaney, Janie B.
   See Cheaney, J.B.
Cheaney, J.B. 1950- 188
Chee, Cheng-Khee 1934- 79
Cheese, Chloe 1952- 118
Chekhonte, Antosha
   See Chekhov, Anton
Chekhov, Anton 1860-1904 90
Chekhov, Anton Pavlovich
   See Chekhov, Anton
Chelushkin, Kirill 1968- 186
Chen, Anthony 1929- 6
Chen, Chih-Yuan 1975- 216
   Earlier sketch in SATA *155*
Chen, Ju-Hong 1941- 78
Chen, Pauline 1966- 202
Chen, Sara
   See Odgers, Sally Farrell
Chen, Tony
   See Chen, Anthony
Chen, Yong 1963- 183
Chen, Yuan-tsung 1932- 65
Chen, Zhiyuan
   See Chen, Chih-Yuan
Chenault, Nell
   See Smith, Linell Nash
Chen Chih-Yuan
   See Chen, Chih-Yuan
Chenery, Janet (Dai) 1923- 25
Cheney, Cora 1916-1999 3
   Obituary 110
Cheney, Glenn (Alan) 1951- 99
Cheney, Lynne V. 1941- 152
Cheney, Lynne Vincent
   See Cheney, Lynne V.
Cheney, Ted
   See Cheney, Theodore Albert
Cheney, Theodore A. Rees
   See Cheney, Theodore Albert
Cheney, Theodore Albert 1928- *11*
Cheng, Andrea 1957- 205
   Earlier sketches in SATA *128, 172*
Cheng, Christopher 1959- 173
   Earlier sketch in SATA *106*
Cheng, Judith 1955- 36
Cheng, Shan
   See Jiang, Cheng An
Cheripko, Jan 1951- 155
   Earlier sketch in SATA *83*
Chermayeff, Ivan 1932- 47
Chernenko, Dan
   See Turtledove, Harry
Chernett, Dan 224
Chernoff, Dorothy A.
   See Ernst, (Lyman) John
Chernoff, Goldie Taub 1909- 10
Cherry, Carolyn Janice
   See Cherryh, C.J.
Cherry, Lynne 1952- 99
   Earlier sketch in SATA *34*
Cherryh, C.J. 1942- 172
   Earlier sketch in SATA *93*
Cherryholmes, Anne
   See Price, Olive
Cheshire, Simon 172
Chesler, Bernice 1932-2002 59
Chess, Victoria (Dickerson) 1939- 92
   Earlier sketch in SATA *33*
Chessa, Francesca 191
Chester, Deborah 1957- 85
Chester, Kate
   See Guccione, Leslie Davis
Chesterton, G. K. 1874-1936 27
Chesterton, Gilbert Keith
   See Chesterton, G. K.
Chesworth, Michael 207
   Earlier sketch in SATA *160*

Chetin, Helen 1922- 6
Chetwin, Grace 86
   Brief entry 50
Chevalier, Christa 1937- 35
Chevalier, Tracy 1962- 128
Chew, Ruth 1920-2010 7
Chichester Clark, Emma 1955- 209
   Earlier sketches in SATA *117, 156, 69*
Chidsey, Donald Barr 1902-1981 3
   Obituary 27
Chiefari, Janet D. 1942- 58
Chien, Catia 193
Chien-min, Lin
   See Rumford, James
Child, L. Maria
   See Child, Lydia Maria
Child, Lauren 1965- 183
   Earlier sketches in SATA *119, 160*
Child, Lincoln 1957- 113
Child, Lincoln B.
   See Child, Lincoln
Child, Lydia Maria 1802-1880 67
Child, Mrs.
   See Child, Lydia Maria
Child, Philip 1898-1978 47
Children's Shepherd, The
   See Westphal, Arnold Carl
Childress, Alice 1920-1994 81
   Earlier sketches in SATA *7, 48*
   See also CLR *14*
Childs, H(alla) Fay (Cochrane) 1890-1971 .... *1*
   Obituary 25
Chilton, Charles (Frederick William)
   1917- 102
Chima, Cinda Williams 192
Chimaera
   See Farjeon, Eleanor
Chin, Jason 1978- 218
Chin, Richard (M.) 1946- 52
Chinery, Michael 1938- 26
Chin-Lee, Cynthia 1958- 102
Chin-Lee D., Cynthia
   See Chin-Lee, Cynthia
Chippendale, Lisa A. 158
Chipperfield, Joseph Eugene 1912-1980(?) .. 87
   Earlier sketch in SATA *2*
Chisholm, P. F.
   See Finney, Patricia
Chislett, Gail (Elaine) 1948- 58
Chittenden, Elizabeth F. 1903-1999 9
Chittenden, Margaret 1935- 28
Chittum, Ida 1918- 7
Chitwood, Suzanne Tanner 1958- 160
Chmielarz, Sharon Lee 1940- 72
Choate, Judith (Newkirk) 1940- 30
Chocolate, Debbi 1954- 223
   Earlier sketch in SATA *96*
Chocolate, Deborah H. Newton
   See Chocolate, Debbi
Chodos-Irvine, Margaret 211
   Earlier sketch in SATA *152*
Choi, Sook Nyul 1937- 73
   Autobiography Feature 126
   See also CLR *53*
Choi, Yangsook 178
Choksi, Nishant 1975- 222
Choldenko, Gennifer 1957- 182
   Earlier sketch in SATA *135*
Chorao, Kay 1936- 215
Chorao, (Ann Mc)Kay (Sproat) 1936- 162
   Earlier sketches in SATA *8, 69*
Choron, Sandra (Zena Samelson) 1950- 146
Choung, Eun-hee 199
Chown, Marcus 1959- 137
Choyce, Lesley 1951- 165
   Earlier sketch in SATA *94*
Choyce, Lesley Willis
   See Choyce, Lesley
Chrisman, Arthur Bowie 1889-1953 124
   See also YABC *1*

Christelow, Eileen 1943- 184
   Autobiography Feature 120
   Brief entry 35
   Earlier sketches in SATA *38, 90*
Christensen, Bonnie 1951- 213
   Earlier sketches in SATA *110, 157*
Christensen, Gardell Dano 1907-1991 .... *1*
Christensen, Laurie
   See Steding, Laurie
Christesen, Barbara 1940- 40
Christgau, Alice Erickson 1902-1977 13
Christian, Mary Blount 1933- 9
Christiana, David 195
Christie, Agatha 1890-1976 36
Christie, Agatha Mary Clarissa
   See Christie, Agatha
Christie, Ann Philippa
   See Pearce, Philippa
Christie, Gregory
   See Christie, R. Gregory
Christie, Philippa
   See Pearce, Philippa
Christie, R. Gregory 1971- 225
   Earlier sketches in SATA *127, 185*
Christopher, John
   See Youd, Samuel
Christopher, Louise
   See Hale, Arlene
Christopher, Matt(hew Frederick)
   1917-1997 80
   Obituary 99
   Earlier sketches in SATA *2, 47*
   See also CLR *119*
   See also SAAS *9*
Christopher, Milbourne 1914(?)-1984 46
Christy, Howard Chandler 1873-1952 21
Chrustowski, Rick 176
Chrystie, Frances N(icholson) 1904-1986 60
Chu, Daniel 1933- 11
Chukovsky, Kornei (Ivanovich) 1882-1969 . 34
   Earlier sketch in SATA *5*
Church, Caroline Jayne 219
   Earlier sketch in SATA *179*
Church, Richard 1893-1972 3
Churchill, E(lmer) Richard 1937- 11
Churchill, Elizabeth
   See Hough, Richard (Alexander)
Chute, B(eatrice) J(oy) 1913-1987 2
   Obituary 53
Chute, Marchette (Gaylord) 1909-1994 .... *1*
Chwast, Jacqueline 1932- 6
Chwast, Seymour 1931- 146
   Earlier sketches in SATA *18, 96*
Ciardi, John (Anthony) 1916-1986 65
   Obituary 46
   Earlier sketch in SATA *1*
   See also CLR *19*
   See also SAAS *26*
Ciccone, Madonna Louise Veronica
   See Madonna
Ciddor, Anna 1957- 213
Ciment, James D. 1958- 140
Cirrone, Dorian 182
Cisneros, Sandra 1954-
   See CLR *123*
Citra, Becky 1954- 137
Citrin, Michael 1965(?)- 183
Claflin, Willy 1944- 208
Clair, Andree 19
Clampett, Bob 1914(?)-1985 44
   Obituary 38
Clampett, Robert
   See Clampett, Bob
Clapp, John 1968- 109
Clapp, Patricia 1912- 74
   Earlier sketch in SATA *4*
   See also SAAS *4*
Clare, Ellen
   See Sinclair, Olga
Clare, Helen
   See Clarke, Pauline

Claremont, Chris 1950- 87
Claremont, Christopher Simon
    See Claremont, Chris
Clark, Ann Nolan 1896-1995 82
    Obituary 87
    Earlier sketch in SATA *4*
    See also CLR *16*
    See also SAAS *16*
Clark, Champ 1923-2002 47
Clark, Christopher (Anthony) Stuart
    See Stuart-Clark, Christopher (Anthony)
Clark, Clara Gillow 1951- 154
    Earlier sketch in SATA *84*
Clark, David
    See Hardcastle, Michael
Clark, David Allen
    See Ernst, (Lyman) John
Clark, Emma Chichester
    See Chichester Clark, Emma
Clark, Frank J(ames) 1922- 18
Clark, Garel
    See Garelick, May
Clark, Halsey
    See Deming, Richard
Clark, Joan
    See Benson, Mildred
Clark, Joan 1934- 182
    Earlier sketches in SATA *59, 96*
Clark, Leonard 1905-1981 30
    Obituary 29
Clark, M. R.
    See Clark, Mavis Thorpe
Clark, Margaret (D.) 1943- 126
Clark, Margaret Goff 1913- 82
    Earlier sketch in SATA *8*
Clark, Mary Higgins 1929- 46
Clark, Mavis Thorpe 1909-1999 74
    Earlier sketch in SATA *8*
    See also CLR *30*
    See also SAAS *5*
Clark, Merle
    See Gessner, Lynne
Clark, Patricia Denise
    See Robins, Patricia
Clark, Patricia Finrow 1929- 11
Clark, Ronald Harry 1904-1999 193
Clark, Ronald William 1916-1987 2
    Obituary 52
Clark, Sherryl 1956- 149
Clark, Van D(eusen) 1909-1974 2
Clark, Virginia
    See Gray, Patricia (Clark)
Clark, Walter Van Tilburg 1909-1971 8
Clarke, Arthur
    See Clarke, Arthur C.
Clarke, Arthur C. 1917-2008 115
    Obituary 191
    Earlier sketches in SATA *13, 70*
    See also CLR *119*
Clarke, Arthur Charles
    See Clarke, Arthur C.
Clarke, Clorinda 1917- 7
Clarke, Elizabeth L. 1934- 103
Clarke, Greg 1959- 215
Clarke, Gus 1948- 134
Clarke, J.
    See Clarke, Judith
Clarke, James Hall
    See Rowland-Entwistle, (Arthur) Theodore
    (Henry)
Clarke, Joan B. 1921- 42
    Brief entry 27
Clarke, John
    See Laklan, Carli
    and Sontup, Dan(iel)
Clarke, Judith 1943- 164
    Earlier sketches in SATA *75, 110*
    See also CLR *61*
Clarke, Julia 1950- 138
Clarke, Kenneth 1957- 107

Clarke, Lea
    See Rowland-Entwistle, (Arthur) Theodore
    (Henry)
Clarke, Margaret 1941-
    See CLR *99*
Clarke, Mary Stetson 1911-1994 5
Clarke, Michael
    See Newlon, (Frank) Clarke
Clarke, Pauline 1921- 131
    Earlier sketch in SATA *3*
    See also CLR *28*
Clarkson, E(dith) Margaret 1915- 37
Clarkson, Ewan 1929- 9
Claudia, Susan
    See Goulart, Ron
    and Johnston, William
Claverie, Jean 1946- 38
Clay, Patrice 1947- 47
Clay, Wil 203
Clayman, Deborah Paula
    See Da Costa, Deborah
Claypool, Jane
    See Miner, Jane Claypool
Clayton, Elaine 1961- 209
    Earlier sketches in SATA *94, 159*
Clayton, Lawrence (Otto, Jr.) 1945- 75
Clayton, Sally Pomme 218
Clayton, Sandra 1951- 110
Cle, Troy 202
Clea, Super
    See Hantman, Clea
Cleary, Beverly 1916- 121
    Earlier sketches in SATA *2, 43, 79*
    See also CLR *72*
    See also SAAS *20*
Cleary, Beverly Atlee Bunn
    See Cleary, Beverly
Cleary, Brian P. 1959- 186
    Earlier sketches in SATA *93, 132*
Cleaver, Bill
    See Cleaver, William J.
Cleaver, Carole 1934- 6
Cleaver, Elizabeth (Ann Mrazik)
    1939-1985 23
    Obituary 43
    See also CLR *13*
Cleaver, Hylton Reginald 1891-1961 49
Cleaver, Vera 1919-1993 76
    Earlier sketch in SATA *22*
    See also CLR *6*
Cleaver, Vera Allen
    See Cleaver, Vera
Cleaver, William J. 1920-1981 22
    Obituary 27
    See also CLR *6*
Cleishbotham, Jebediah
    See Scott, Sir Walter
Cleland, Mabel
    See Widdemer, Mabel Cleland
Clem, Margaret H(ollingsworth) 1923- 90
Clemens, James
    See Rollins, James
Clemens, Samuel
    See Twain, Mark
Clemens, Samuel Langhorne
    See Twain, Mark
Clemens, Virginia Phelps 1941- 35
Clement, Gary 191
Clement, Janet 182
Clement, Nathan 1966- 200
Clement, Priscilla Ferguson 1942- 171
Clement, Rod 97
Clement-Moore, Rosemary 188
Clements, Andrew 1949- 203
    Earlier sketches in SATA *104, 158*
Clements, Bruce 1931- 178
    Earlier sketches in SATA *27, 94*
Clemesha, David 192
Cleminson, Katie 221
Clemons, Elizabeth
    See Nowell, Elizabeth Cameron

Clerk, N. W.
    See Lewis, C. S.
Cleveland, Bob
    See Cleveland, George
Cleveland, George 1903(?)-1985
    Obituary 43
Cleveland-Peck, Patricia 80
Cleven, Cathrine
    See Cleven, Kathryn Seward
Cleven, Kathryn Seward 2
Clevenger, William R. 1954- 84
Clevenger, William Russell
    See Clevenger, William R.
Clevin, Joergen 1920- 7
Clevin, Jorgen
    See Clevin, Joergen
Clewes, Dorothy (Mary) 1907-2003 86
    Obituary 138
    Earlier sketch in SATA *1*
Clifford, David
    See Rosenberg, Eth Clifford
Clifford, Eth
    See Rosenberg, Eth Clifford
Clifford, Harold B(urton) 1893-1988 10
Clifford, Margaret Cort 1929- 1
Clifford, Martin
    See Hamilton, Charles (Harold St. John)
Clifford, Mary Louise Beneway 1926- 23
Clifford, Peggy
    See Clifford, Margaret Cort
Clifford, Rachel Mark
    See Lewis, Brenda Ralph
Clifton, Lucille 1936-2010 128
    Earlier sketches in SATA *20, 69*
    See also CLR *5*
Clifton, Thelma Lucille
    See Clifton, Lucille
Climo, Shirley 1928- 166
    Autobiography Feature 110
    Brief entry 35
    Earlier sketches in SATA *39, 77*
    See also CLR *69*
Cline-Ransome, Lesa 201
Clinton, Catherine 1952- 203
Clinton, Cathryn 1957- 136
Clinton, Dirk
    See Silverberg, Robert
Clinton, Jon
    See Prince, J(ack) H(arvey)
Clippinger, Carol 193
Clish, (Lee) Marian 1946- 43
Clive, Clifford
    See Hamilton, Charles (Harold St. John)
Clokey, Art 1921- 59
Cloudsley-Thompson, J(ohn) L(eonard)
    1921- 19
Clouse, Nancy L. 1938- 78
Clover, Peter 1952- 215
    Earlier sketch in SATA *152*
Clutha, Janet
    See Frame, Janet
Clutha, Janet Paterson Frame
    See Frame, Janet
Clymer, Eleanor 1906-2001 85
    Obituary 126
    Earlier sketch in SATA *9*
    See also SAAS *17*
Clyne, Patricia (Edwards) 31
Cneut, Carll 1969- 197
Coalson, Glo 1946- 94
    Earlier sketch in SATA *26*
Coates, Anna 1958- 73
Coates, Belle 1896-1986 2
Coates, Ruth Allison 1915- 11
Coats, Alice M(argaret) 1905-1976 11
Coatsworth, Elizabeth (Jane) 1893-1986 100
    Obituary 49
    Earlier sketches in SATA *2, 56*
    See also CLR *2*
Cobalt, Martin
    See Mayne, William

Cobb, Jane
    See Berry, Jane Cobb
Cobb, Mary 1931- 88
Cobb, Vicki 1938- 136
    Autobiography Feature 136
    Earlier sketches in SATA *8, 69, 131*
    See also CLR *2*
    See also SAAS *6*
Cobbett, Richard
    See Pluckrose, Henry (Arthur)
Cober, Alan E(dwin) 1935-1998 7
    Obituary *101*
Cobham, Sir Alan
    See Hamilton, Charles (Harold St. John)
Coburn, Jake 1978- 155
Cocagnac, Augustin Maurice(-Jean) 1924- 7
Cocca-Leffler, Maryann 1958- 194
    Earlier sketches in SATA *80, 136*
Cochran, Bill 187
Cochran, Bobbye A. 1949- 11
Cochran, Josh 221
Cochran, Thomas 1955- 198
Cochrane, Hamilton E.
    See Cochrane, Mick
Cochrane, Mick 1956- 215
Cockcroft, Jason 217
Cockett, Mary 3
Cocks, Peter 204
Cocovini, Abby 202
Coddell, Esme Raji
    See Codell, Esme Raji
Codell, Esme Raji 1968- 160
Cody, C. S.
    See Waller, Leslie
Cody, Jess
    See Cunningham, Chet
Coe, Anne (E.) 1949- 95
Coe, Douglas
    See Epstein, Beryl
    and Epstein, Samuel
Coe, Lloyd 1899(?)-1976
    Obituary 30
Coen, Rena Neumann 1925- 20
Coerr, Eleanor (Beatrice) 1922- 67
    Earlier sketch in SATA *1*
Cofer, Judith Ortiz 1952- 164
    Earlier sketch in SATA *110*
Coffelt, Nancy 1961- 189
Coffey, Brian
    See Koontz, Dean
Coffin, Geoffrey
    See Mason, F(rancis) van Wyck
Coffin, M. T.
    See Stanley, George Edward
Coffman, Ramon Peyton 1896-1989 4
Cogan, Karen 1954- 125
Coggins, Jack (Banham) 1911-2006 2
Cohen, Barbara 1932-1992 77
    Obituary 74
    Earlier sketch in SATA *10*
    See also SAAS *7*
Cohen, Daniel (E.) 1936- 70
    Earlier sketch in SATA *8*
    See also CLR *43*
    See also SAAS *4*
Cohen, Deborah Bodin 1968- 180
Cohen, Jan Barger
    See Barger, Jan
Cohen, Jene Barr
    See Barr, Jene
Cohen, Joan Lebold 1932- 4
Cohen, Judith Love 1933- 78
Cohen, Lisa 1963- 225
Cohen, Miriam 1926-1955 155
    Earlier sketches in SATA *29, 106*
    See also SAAS *11*
Cohen, Nora 75
Cohen, Paul 1945- 58
Cohen, Paul S.
    See Cohen, Paul

Cohen, Peter Zachary 1931- 150
    Earlier sketch in SATA *4*
Cohen, Robert Carl 1930- 8
Cohen, Santiago 1954- 215
Cohen, Sholom 1951- 94
Cohn, Angelo 1914-1997 19
Cohn, Diana 194
Cohn, Rachel 1968- 161
Coit, Margaret Louise 1922-2003 2
    Obituary 142
Colasanti, Susane 1973- 214
Colato Lainez, Rene 1970- 176
Colbert, Anthony 1934-2007 15
Colbert, Nancy A. 1936- 139
Colby, C(arroll) B(urleigh) 1904-1977 35
    Earlier sketch in SATA *3*
Colby, Jean Poindexter 1909-1993 23
Cole, Annette
    See Steiner, Barbara A(nnette)
Cole, Babette 1949- 155
    Earlier sketches in SATA *61, 96*
Cole, Betsy 1940- 83
Cole, Brock 1938- 200
    Earlier sketches in SATA *72, 136*
    See also CLR *18*
Cole, Davis
    See Elting, Mary
Cole, Hannah 1954- 74
Cole, Henry 1955- 213
    Earlier sketch in SATA *181*
Cole, Jack -1974
    See Stewart, John
Cole, Jackson
    See Curry, Thomas Albert
    and Germano, Peter B.
    and Heckelmann, Charles N(ewman)
    and Newton, D(wight) B(ennett)
    and Schisgall, Oscar
Cole, Jennifer
    See Zach, Cheryl (Byrd)
Cole, Joanna 1944- 168
    Brief entry 37
    Earlier sketches in SATA *49, 81, 120*
    See also CLR *40*
Cole, Lois Dwight 1903-1979 10
    Obituary 26
Cole, Michael 1947- 59
Cole, Samantha
    See Cole, Stephen
Cole, Sheila 1939- 171
    Earlier sketches in SATA *24, 95*
Cole, Sheila R.
    See Cole, Sheila
Cole, Sheila Rotenberg
    See Cole, Sheila
Cole, Stephen 1971- 161
Cole, William (Rossa) 1919-2000 71
    Earlier sketch in SATA *9*
    See also SAAS *9*
Coleman, Andrew
    See Pine, Nicholas
Coleman, Clare
    See Bell, Clare (Louise)
    and Easton, M(alcolm) Coleman
Coleman, Janet Wyman 184
Coleman, Loren 1947- 164
Coleman, Loren Elwood, Jr.
    See Coleman, Loren
Coleman, Mary Ann 1928- 83
Coleman, Michael
    See Jones, Allan Frewin
Coleman, Michael 1946- 199
    Autobiography Feature 133
    Earlier sketches in SATA *108, 133*
Coleman, Rowan 187
Coleman, William L(eRoy) 1938- 49
    Brief entry 34
Coleman, Wim 1926- 212
Coles, Robert (Martin) 1929- 23

Colfer, Eoin 1965- 197
    Earlier sketch in SATA *148*
    See also CLR *112*
Colin, Ann
    See Ure, Jean
Collard, Sneed B. III 1959- 184
    Earlier sketches in SATA *84, 139*
Colledge, Anne 1939- 142
Colley, Jacqui 1965- 202
Collicott, Sharleen 1937- 143
    Earlier sketch in SATA *98*
Collier, Bryan 204
    Earlier sketches in SATA *126, 174*
Collier, Christopher 1930- 70
    Earlier sketch in SATA *16*
    See also CLR *126*
Collier, Ethel 1903-1999 22
Collier, James Lincoln 1928- 166
    Earlier sketches in SATA *8, 70*
    See also CLR *126*
    See also SAAS *21*
Collier, Jane
    See Collier, Zena
Collier, Kristi 182
Collier, Steven 1942- 61
Collier, Zena 1926- 23
Collings, Gillian 1939- 102
Collington, Peter 1948- 99
    Earlier sketch in SATA *59*
Collins, Ace 1953- 82
Collins, Andrew J.
    See Collins, Ace
Collins, B. R. 1981- 214
Collins, David R(aymond) 1940-2001 121
    Earlier sketch in SATA *7*
Collins, Heather 1946- 81
Collins, Hunt
    See Hunter, Evan
Collins, Michael
    See Lynds, Dennis
Collins, Michael 1930- 58
Collins, Pat Lowery 1932- 217
    Earlier sketches in SATA *31, 151*
Collins, Paul 1954- 126
Collins, Ross 1972- 200
Collins, Ruth Philpott 1890-1975
    Obituary 30
Collins, Suzanne 224
    Earlier sketch in SATA *180*
Collins, Yvonne 194
Collinson, A. S.
    See Collinson, Alan S.
Collinson, Alan S. 1934- 80
Collinson, Roger (Alfred) 1936- 133
Collison, Linda 1953- 185
Collodi, Carlo 1826-1890 100
    Earlier sketch in SATA *29*
    See also CLR *120*
Colloms, Brenda 1919- 40
Colman, Hila 1909-2008 53
    Earlier sketch in SATA *1*
    See also SAAS *14*
Colman, Morris 1899(?)-1981
    Obituary 25
Colman, Penny (Morgan) 1944- 160
    Autobiography Feature 160
    Earlier sketches in SATA *77, 114*
Colman, Warren (David) 1944- 67
Coloma, Cindy
    See Martinusen-Coloma, Cindy
Colombo, John Robert 1936- 50
Colon, Raul 156
Colon, Raul 1952- 202
Colonius, Lillian 1911-1992 3
Colorado, Antonio J.
    See Colorado (Capella), Antonio J(ulio)
Colorado (Capella), Antonio J(ulio)
    1903-1994 23
    Obituary 79
Colquhoun, Glenn 1964- 165
Colston, Fifi E. 1960- 150

Colt, Martin
  See Epstein, Beryl
  and Epstein, Samuel
Colum, Padraic 1881-1972 .... *15*
  See also CLR *36*
Columbus, Chris 1959- *97*
Columbus, Christopher
  See Columbus, Chris
Columella
  See Moore, Clement Clarke
Colver, Anne 1908- *7*
Colvin, James
  See Moorcock, Michael
Colwell, Eileen (Hilda) 1904-2002 .... *2*
Colwyn, Stewart
  See Pepper, Frank S.
Coman, Carolyn 1951- *197*
  Earlier sketch in SATA *127*
Combs, Lisa M.
  See McCourt, Lisa
Combs, Robert
  See Murray, John
Comfort, Jane Levington
  See Sturtzel, Jane Levington
Comfort, Mildred Houghton 1886-1976 .... *3*
Comins, Ethel M(ae) *11*
Comins, Jeremy 1933- *28*
Commager, Henry Steele 1902-1998 .... *23*
  Obituary *102*
Comora, Madeleine *190*
Compere, Mickie
  See Davidson, Margaret
Compestine, Ying Chang 1963- *187*
  Earlier sketch in SATA *140*
Comport, Sally Wern *190*
Compton, Patricia A. 1936- *75*
Comte, The Great
  See Hawkesworth, Eric
Comus
  See Ballantyne, R(obert) M(ichael)
Comyns, Nance
  See Comyns-Toohey, Nantz
Comyns-Toohey, Nantz 1956- *86*
Conahan, Carolyn
  See Conahan, Carolyn Digby
Conahan, Carolyn Digby 1961- *216*
Conan Doyle, Arthur
  See Doyle, Sir Arthur Conan
Condie, Ally *204*
Condie, Allyson B.
  See Condie, Ally
Condit, Martha Olson 1913- *28*
Condon, Bill 1949- *142*
Condon, Judith *83*
Condon, Ken *195*
Condy, Roy 1942- *96*
Cone, Ferne Geller 1921- *39*
Cone, Molly (Lamken) 1918- *151*
  Autobiography Feature *151*
  Earlier sketches in SATA *1, 28, 115*
  See also SAAS *11*
Cone, Patrick 1954- *89*
Coney, Michael G. 1932-2005 .... *61*
  Obituary *170*
Coney, Michael Greatrex
  See Coney, Michael G.
Coney, Mike
  See Coney, Michael G.
Conford, Ellen 1942- *162*
  Earlier sketches in SATA *6, 68, 110*
  See also CLR *71*
Conger, Lesley
  See Suttles, Shirley (Smith)
Conklin, Gladys Plemon 1903- *2*
Conklin, Paul S. 1929(?)-2003 .... *43*
  Brief entry *33*
  Obituary *147*
Conkling, Hilda 1910-1986 .... *23*
Conlan, Kathleen Elizabeth 1950- *145*
Conlan, Kathy
  See Conlan, Kathleen Elizabeth

Conley, Robyn 1963- *125*
Conley-Weaver, Robyn
  See Conley, Robyn
Conlon-McKenna, Marita 1956- *71*
Conly, Jane Leslie 1948- *164*
  Earlier sketches in SATA *80, 112*
Conly, Robert Leslie 1918(?)-1973 .... *23*
  See also CLR *2*
Connell, Kirk
  See Chapman, John Stanton Higham
Connell, Tom *206*
Connelly, Gwen 1952- *212*
Connelly, Marc(us Cook) 1890-1980
  Obituary *25*
Connolly, Jerome P(atrick) 1931- *8*
Connolly, Pat 1943- *74*
Connolly, Peter 1935- *105*
  Earlier sketch in SATA *47*
Conover, Chris 1950- *213*
  Earlier sketch in SATA *31*
Conquest, Owen
  See Hamilton, Charles (Harold St. John)
Conrad, Joseph 1857-1924 .... *27*
Conrad, Pam 1947-1996 .... *133*
  Brief entry *49*
  Obituary *90*
  Earlier sketches in SATA *52, 80*
  See also CLR *18*
  See also SAAS *19*
Conroy, Jack
  See Conroy, John Wesley
Conroy, John Wesley 1899-1990 .... *19*
  Obituary *65*
Conroy, Robert
  See Goldston, Robert (Conroy)
Constable, Kate 1966- *172*
Constant, Alberta Wilson 1908-1981 .... *22*
  Obituary *28*
Constantin, Pascale *185*
Conway, Celeste *210*
Conway, David 1970- *213*
Conway, Diana C. 1943- *91*
Conway, Diana Cohen
  See Conway, Diana C.
Conway, Gordon
  See Hamilton, Charles (Harold St. John)
Cook, Ande *192*
Cook, Bernadine 1924- *11*
Cook, Fred J(ames) 1911-2003 .... *2*
  Obituary *145*
Cook, Glen 1944- *171*
  Earlier sketch in SATA *108*
Cook, Glen Charles
  See Cook, Glen
Cook, Hugh 1956- *85*
Cook, Hugh, Walter Gilbert
  See Cook, Hugh
Cook, Jean Thor 1930- *94*
Cook, Joel 1934- *79*
Cook, Joseph Jay 1924- *8*
Cook, Lisa Broadie *157*
Cook, Lyn
  See Waddell, Evelyn Margaret
Cook, Roy
  See Silverberg, Robert
Cook, Sally *207*
Cook, Trish *175*
Cooke, Ann
  See Cole, Joanna
Cooke, Arthur
  See Lowndes, Robert A(ugustine) W(ard)
Cooke, Barbara
  See Alexander, Anna B(arbara Cooke)
Cooke, David Coxe 1917- *2*
Cooke, Donald Ewin 1916-1985 .... *2*
  Obituary *45*
Cooke, Frank E. 1920- *87*
Cooke, Jean (Isobel Esther) 1929- *74*
Cooke, John Estes
  See Baum, L. Frank
Cooke, Trish 1962- *129*

Cookson, Catherine (McMullen) 1906-1998 .. *9*
  Obituary *116*
Cooley, Beth *210*
Cooley, Elizabeth
  See Cooley, Beth
Cooley, Regina Francoise 1940- *177*
Coolidge, Olivia E(nsor) 1908- *26*
  Earlier sketch in SATA *1*
Cooling, Wendy *169*
  Earlier sketch in SATA *111*
Coombs, Charles I(ra) 1914-1994 .... *43*
  Earlier sketch in SATA *3*
  See also SAAS *15*
Coombs, Chick
  See Coombs, Charles I(ra)
Coombs, Jonathan *204*
Coombs, Kate *190*
Coombs, Patricia 1926- *51*
  Earlier sketch in SATA *3*
  See also SAAS *22*
Cooney, Barbara 1917-2000 .... *96*
  Obituary *123*
  Earlier sketches in SATA *6, 59*
  See also CLR *23*
Cooney, Caroline B. 1947- *218*
  Brief entry *41*
  Earlier sketches in SATA *48, 80, 113, 130,*
  179
Cooney, Doug *181*
Cooney, Nancy Evans 1932- *42*
Coontz, Otto 1946- *33*
Cooper, Ann (Catharine) 1939- *104*
Cooper, Dutch
  See Kuyper, Sjoerd
Cooper, Elisha 1971- *157*
  Earlier sketch in SATA *99*
Cooper, Elizabeth Keyser -1992 .... *47*
Cooper, Floyd *187*
  Earlier sketches in SATA *96, 144*
  See also CLR *60*
Cooper, Gordon 1932- *23*
Cooper, Helen 1963- *169*
  Earlier sketch in SATA *102*
Cooper, Henry S. F., Jr. 1933- *65*
Cooper, Henry Spotswood Fenimore, Jr.
  See Cooper, Henry S. F., Jr.
Cooper, Ilene 1948- *145*
  Earlier sketches in SATA *66, 97*
Cooper, James Fenimore 1789-1851 .... *19*
  See also CLR *105*
Cooper, John R. *1*
Cooper, Kay 1941- *11*
Cooper, Lee Pelham 1926- *5*
Cooper, Lester (Irving) 1919-1985 .... *32*
  Obituary *43*
Cooper, Lettice (Ulpha) 1897-1994 .... *35*
  Obituary *82*
Cooper, Louise 1952-2009 .... *152*
Cooper, M.E.
  See Davis, Maggie S.
Cooper, M.E.
  See Lerangis, Peter
Cooper, Melrose
  See Kroll, Virginia L.
Cooper, Michael L. 1950- *181*
  Earlier sketches in SATA *79, 117*
Cooper, Patrick 1949- *134*
Cooper, Susan 1935- *151*
  Earlier sketches in SATA *4, 64, 104*
  See also CLR *161*
  See also SAAS *6*
Cooper, Susan Mary
  See Cooper, Susan
Cope, Jane U(rsula) 1949- *108*
Copeland, Helen 1920- *4*
Copeland, Mark 1956- *180*
Copeland, Paul W. *23*
Coplans, Peta 1951- *84*
Copley (Diana) Heather Pickering 1918- *45*
Coppard, A(lfred) E(dgar) 1878-1957
  See YABC *1*

Copper, Melinda 1952- *172*
Copper, Melinda McConnaughey
　See Copper, Melinda
Corace, Jen *208*
Coralie
　See Anderson, Catherine Corley
Corbett, Grahame *43*
　Brief entry *36*
Corbett, Scott 1913- *42*
　Earlier sketch in SATA *2*
　See also CLR *1*
　See also SAAS *2*
Corbett, Sue *174*
Corbett, W(illiam) J(esse) 1938- *102*
　Brief entry *44*
　Earlier sketch in SATA *50*
　See also CLR *19*
Corbin, Sabra Lee
　See Malvern, Gladys
Corbin, William
　See McGraw, William Corbin
Corbman, Marjorie 1987- *179*
Corby, Dan
　See Catherall, Arthur
Corcoran, Barbara (Asenath) 1911-2003 ...... *77*
　Autobiography Feature *125*
　Earlier sketch in SATA *3*
　See also CLR *50*
　See also SAAS *20*
Corcos, Lucille 1908-1973 .... *10*
Cordell, Alexander
　See Graber, Alexander
Cordell, Matthew 1975- *199*
Corder, Zizou
　See Young, Louisa
Corella, Joseph
　See Odgers, Sally Farrell
Coren, Alan 1938-2007 .... *32*
　Obituary *187*
Corey, Dorothy *23*
Corey, Shana 1974- *219*
　Earlier sketch in SATA *133*
Corfe, Thomas Howell 1928- *27*
Corfe, Tom
　See Corfe, Thomas Howell
Corfield, Robin Bell 1952- *74*
Corke, Estelle 1969- *220*
Corlett, William 1938-2005 .... *46*
　Brief entry *39*
Cormack, M(argaret) Grant 1913- *11*
Cormack, Maribelle B. 1902-1984 .... *39*
Cormier, Robert 1925-2000 .... *83*
　Obituary *122*
　Earlier sketches in SATA *10, 45*
　See also CLR *55*
Cormier, Robert Edmund
　See Cormier, Robert
Cornelius, Carol 1942- *40*
Cornelius, Kay 1933- *157*
Cornell, J.
　See Cornell, Jeffrey
Cornell, James (Clayton, Jr.) 1938- *27*
Cornell, Jean Gay 1920- *23*
Cornell, Jeffrey 1945- *11*
Cornell, Laura *189*
Cornish, D.M. 1972- *185*
Cornish, Sam(uel James) 1935- *23*
Cornwall, Nellie
　See Sloggett, Nellie
Cornwell, Autumn *195*
Corr, Christopher 1955- *189*
Correy, Lee
　See Stine, G(eorge) Harry
Corrick, James A. 1945- *76*
Corrigan, (Helen) Adeline 1909- *23*
Corrigan, Barbara 1922- *8*
Corrigan, Eireann 1977- *163*
Corrin, Sara 1918- *86*
　Brief entry *48*
Corrin, Stephen *86*
　Brief entry *48*

Corsi, Wendy
　See Staub, Wendy Corsi
Cort, M. C.
　See Clifford, Margaret Cort
Cort, Margaret
　See Clifford, Margaret Cort
Corwin, Judith H(offman) 1946- *10*
Corwin, Oliver
　See Corwin, Oliver J.
Corwin, Oliver J. *206*
Cory, Rowena
　See Lindquist, Rowena Cory
Cosby, Bill 1937- *110*
　Earlier sketch in SATA *66*
Cosby, William Henry, Jr.
　See Cosby, Bill
　and Cosby, Bill
Cosentino, Ralph *169*
Cosgrave, John O'Hara II 1908-1968
　Obituary *21*
Cosgrove, Margaret (Leota) 1926- *47*
Cosgrove, Stephen E(dward) 1945- *53*
　Brief entry *40*
Coskey, Evelyn 1932- *7*
Cosner, Shaaron 1940- *43*
Cossi, Olga 1921- *216*
　Earlier sketches in SATA *67, 102*
Costabel, Eva Deutsch 1924- *45*
Costabel-Deutsch, Eva
　See Costabel, Eva Deutsch
Coste, Marion 1938- *183*
Costello, David *174*
Costello, David F(rancis) 1904-1990 .... *23*
Cte, Genevieve 1964- *184*
Cote, Nancy 1952- *182*
Cott, Jonathan 1942- *23*
Cottam, Clarence 1899-1974 .... *25*
Cotten, Cynthia *188*
Cottin, Menena 1950- *213*
Cottle, Joan 1960- *135*
Cottler, Joseph 1899-1996 .... *22*
Cottonwood, Joe 1947- *92*
Cottrell, Leonard 1913-1974 .... *24*
Cottringer, Anne 1952- *150*
　Earlier sketch in SATA *97*
Couch, Greg *199*
Coulman, Valerie 1969- *161*
Couloumbis, Akila 1932-2009 .... *225*
Couloumbis, Audrey *173*
Counsel, June 1926- *70*
Countryman, The
　See Whitlock, Ralph
Courlander, Harold 1908-1996 .... *6*
　Obituary *88*
Coursen, Valerie 1965(?)- *102*
Courtis, Stuart Appleton 1874-1969
　Obituary *29*
Courtland, Tyler
　See Stevens, Serita
Courtney, Dayle
　See Goldsmith, Howard
Coury, Louise Andree 1895(?)-1983
　Obituary *34*
Cousins, Linda 1946- *90*
Cousins, Lucy 1964- *205*
　Earlier sketch in SATA *172*
Cousins, Margaret 1905-1996 .... *2*
　Obituary *92*
Cousteau, Jacques 1910-1997 .... *98*
　Earlier sketch in SATA *38*
Cousteau, Jacques-Yves
　See Cousteau, Jacques
Couture, Christin 1951- *73*
Couvillon, Jacques *195*
Coverly, Dave 1964- *223*
Covert, Ralph 1968- *197*
Coville, Bruce 1950- *216*
　Autobiography Feature *155*
　Earlier sketches in SATA *32, 77, 118, 155*
Covington, Dennis *109*

Covington, Linda
　See Windsor, Linda
Cowan, Catherine *121*
Cowan, Rebecca M.
　See Moesta, Rebecca
Cowan, Rebecca Moesta
　See Moesta, Rebecca
Coward, Fiona 1963- *178*
Cowdrey, Richard 1959- *204*
Cowell, Cressida 1966- *140*
Cowen, Eve
　See Werner, Herma
Cowen, Ida 1898-1993 .... *64*
Cowie, Leonard W(allace) 1919- *4*
Cowles, Kathleen
　See Krull, Kathleen
Cowley, Cassia Joy
　See Cowley, Joy
Cowley, Joy 1936- *164*
　Autobiography Feature *118*
　Earlier sketches in SATA *4, 90*
　See also CLR *55*
　See also SAAS *26*
Cowley, Marjorie 1925- *111*
Cox, (Christopher) Barry 1931- *62*
Cox, Clinton 1934- *108*
　Earlier sketch in SATA *74*
Cox, David 1933- *56*
Cox, David Dundas
　See Cox, David
Cox, Donald William 1921- *23*
Cox, Jack
　See Cox, John Roberts
Cox, John Roberts 1915-1981 .... *9*
Cox, Judy 1954- *198*
　Earlier sketches in SATA *117, 160*
Cox, Marion Monroe 1898-1983
　Obituary *34*
Cox, Palmer 1840-1924 .... *24*
　See also CLR *24*
Cox, Vic 1942- *88*
Cox, Vicki 1945- *158*
Cox, Victoria 1945- *44*
Cox, Wallace 1924-1973 .... *25*
Cox, Wally
　See Cox, Wallace
Cox, William R(obert) 1901-1988 .... *46*
　Brief entry *31*
　Obituary *57*
Coxe, Molly 1959- *101*
　Earlier sketch in SATA *69*
Coxon, Michele 1950- *158*
　Earlier sketch in SATA *76*
Coy, Harold 1902-1986 .... *3*
Coy, John 1958- *171*
　Earlier sketch in SATA *120*
Craats, Rennay 1973- *131*
Crabtree, Judith 1928- *98*
　Earlier sketch in SATA *63*
Crabtree, Julie 1970- *214*
Cracker, Edward E.B.
　See Odgers, Sally Farrell
Craft, Elizabeth 1971(?)- *204*
Craft, K. Y.
　See Craft, Kinuko Y.
Craft, Kinuko Y. 1940- *127*
　Earlier sketch in SATA *65*
Craft, Kinuko Yamabe
　See Craft, Kinuko Y.
Craft, Ruth 1935- *87*
　Brief entry *31*
Craig, A. A.
　See Anderson, Poul
Craig, Alisa
　See MacLeod, Charlotte (Matilda)
Craig, David
　See James, Bill
Craig, Helen 1934- *213*
　Earlier sketches in SATA *46, 49, 94*
Craig, Joe 1979- *198*

Craig, Joe Alexander
  See Craig, Joe
Craig, John Eland
  See Chipperfield, Joseph Eugene
Craig, John Ernest 1921- 23
Craig, Kit
  See Reed, Kit
Craig, M. F.
  See Craig, Mary (Francis) Shura
Craig, M. Jean 17
Craig, M. S.
  See Craig, Mary (Francis) Shura
Craig, Margaret (Maze) 1911-1964 9
Craig, Mary
  See Craig, Mary (Francis) Shura
Craig, Mary Shura
  See Craig, Mary (Francis) Shura
Craig, Mary (Francis) Shura 1923-1991 86
  Obituary 65
  Earlier sketch in SATA 6
  See also SAAS 7
Craig, Ruth 1922- 95
Craik, Mrs.
  See Craik, Dinah Maria (Mulock)
Craik, Dinah Maria (Mulock) 1826-1887 34
Crandall, Court 1965- 175
Crandell, Rachel 1943- 152
Crane, Barbara (Joyce) 1934- 31
Crane, Caroline 1930- 11
Crane, Jordan 1973- 174
Crane, M. A.
  See Wartski, Maureen (Ann Crane)
Crane, Royston Campbell 1901-1977
  Obituary 22
Crane, Stephen 1871-1900
  See YABC 2
  See also CLR 132
Crane, Stephen Townley
  See Crane, Stephen
Crane, Walter 1845-1915 100
  Earlier sketch in SATA 18
  See also CLR 56
Crane, William D(wight) 1892-1976 1
Cranfield, Ingrid 1945- 74
Cranshaw, Stanley
  See Fisher, Dorothy (Frances) Canfield
Crary, Elizabeth (Ann) 1942- 99
  Brief entry 43
Crary, Margaret (Coleman) 1906-1986 9
Craste, Marc 201
Cravath, Lynne Avril
  See Cravath, Lynne W.
Cravath, Lynne W. 1951- 182
  Earlier sketches in SATA 98, 148
Craven, Thomas 1889-1969 22
Crawford, Brent 1975- 220
Crawford, Charles P. 1945- 28
Crawford, Deborah 1922- 6
Crawford, John E(dmund) 1904-1971 3
Crawford, K(aren) Michael 1959- 155
Crawford, Mel 1925- 44
  Brief entry 33
Crawford, Phyllis 1899- 3
Crawley, Dave 177
Cray, Roberta
  See Emerson, Ru
Crayder, Dorothy 7
Crayder, Teresa
  See Colman, Hila
Crayon, Geoffrey
  See Irving, Washington
Craz, Albert G. 1926- 24
Crebbin, June 1938- 169
  Earlier sketch in SATA 80
Crecy, Jeanne
  See Williams, Jeanne
Credle, Ellis 1902-1998 1
Creech, Sharon 1945- 172
  Earlier sketches in SATA 94, 139
  See also CLR 89
Creeden, Sharon 1938- 91

Creel, Ann Howard 1953- 187
Creighton, (Mary) Helen 1899-1989
  Obituary 64
Creighton, Jill 1949- 96
Crelin, Bob 1959(?)- 221
Crenson, Victoria 1952- 159
  Earlier sketch in SATA 88
Cresp, Gael 1954- 119
Crespo, George 1962- 82
Cresswell, Helen 1934-2005 79
  Obituary 168
  Earlier sketches in SATA 1, 48
  See also CLR 18
  See also SAAS 20
Cressy, Michael 1955- 124
Cressy, Mike
  See Cressy, Michael
Cretan, Gladys (Yessayan) 1921- 2
Cretzmeyer, Stacy (Megan) 1959- 124
Crew, Gary 1947- 163
  Earlier sketches in SATA 75, 110
  See also CLR 42
Crew, Helen (Cecilia) Coale 1866-1941
  See YABC 2
Crew, Linda (Jean) 1951- 137
  Earlier sketch in SATA 71
Crewe, Megan 1980- 225
Crews, Donald 1938- 76
  Brief entry 30
  Earlier sketch in SATA 32
  See also CLR 7
Crews, Nina 1963- 158
  Earlier sketch in SATA 97
Crichton, John Michael
  See Crichton, Michael
Crichton, Michael 1942-2008 88
  Obituary 199
  Earlier sketch in SATA 9
Crider, Allen Billy
  See Crider, Bill
Crider, Bill 1941- 99
Crilley, Mark 1966- 210
  Autobiography Feature 148
  Earlier sketches in SATA 120, 148
Crimi, Carolyn 1959- 219
  Earlier sketch in SATA 176
Cripps, Enid Margaret
  See Appiah, Peggy
Crisler, Curtis L. 188
Crisman, Ruth 1914- 73
Crisp, Marta Marie
  See Crisp, Marty
Crisp, Marty 1947- 128
Crispin, A(nn) C(arol) 1950- 86
Crist, James J. 1961- 168
Cristall, Barbara 79
Crist-Evans, Craig 1954- 153
Crocker, Carter 193
Crocker, Nancy 1956- 185
Crofford, Emily (Ardell) 1927- 61
Crofut, William E. III 1934- 23
Croggon, Alison 1962- 194
Croll, Carolyn 1945- 102
  Brief entry 52
  Earlier sketch in SATA 56
Croman, Dorothy Young
  See Rosenberg, Dorothy
Cromie, Alice Hamilton 1914-2000 24
Cromie, William J(oseph) 1930- 4
Crompton, Anne Eliot 1930- 73
  Earlier sketch in SATA 23
Crompton, Richmal
  See Lamburn, Richmal Crompton
Cronbach, Abraham 1882-1965 11
Crone, Ruth 1919-2003 4
Cronin, A(rchibald) J(oseph) 1896-1981 47
  Obituary 25
Cronin, Doreen (A.) 125
Cronin, Doreen 1966(?)- 178
  See also CLR 136

Cronin, Doreen A.
  See Cronin, Doreen
Cronn-Mills, Kirstin 1968- 224
Crook, Beverly Courtney 38
  Brief entry 35
Crook, Connie Brummel 1930- 168
  Earlier sketch in SATA 98
Crook, Constance
  See Crook, Connie Brummel
Crosby, Alexander L. 1906-1980 2
  Obituary 23
Crosby, Harry C.
  See Anvil, Christopher
Crosby, Margaret
  See Rathmann, Peggy
Crosher, G. R. 14
Cross, Gilbert B. 1939- 60
  Brief entry 51
Cross, Gillian 1945- 178
  Autobiography Feature 178
  Earlier sketches in SATA 38, 71, 110, 165
  See also CLR 28
Cross, Gillian Clare
  See Cross, Gillian
Cross, Helen Reeder
  See Broadhead, Helen Cross
Cross, Peter 1951- 95
Cross, Sarah 216
Cross, Shauna 1976(?)- 196
Cross, Tom 1954- 146
Cross, Verda 1914- 75
Cross, Wilbur Lucius III 1918- 2
Crossland, Caroline 1964- 83
Crossley-Holland, Kevin 1941- 165
  Earlier sketches in SATA 5, 74, 120
  See also CLR 84
  See also SAAS 20
Crossley-Holland, Kevin John William
  See Crossley-Holland, Kevin
Crossman, David A. 1951- 219
Crouch, Karen Hillard
  See Good, Karen Hillard
Crouch, Marcus 1913-1996 4
Crout, George C(lement) 1917- 11
Crow, Donna Fletcher 1941- 40
Crow, Francis Luther
  See Luther, Frank
Crow, Kristyn 208
Crowe, Andrew 111
Crowe, Carole 1943- 204
Crowe, Chris 206
Crowe, Ellie 203
Crowe, John
  See Lynds, Dennis
Crowe, (Bettina) Peter Lum 1911- 6
Crowell, Grace Noll 1877-1969 34
Crowell, Pers 1910-1990 2
Crowell, Robert Leland 1909-2001 63
Crowfield, Christopher
  See Stowe, Harriet Beecher
Crowley, Arthur 1945- 38
Crowley, Arthur McBlair
  See Crowley, Arthur
Crowley, John 1942- 140
  Earlier sketch in SATA 65
Crowley, Suzanne 1963- 196
Crowley, Suzanne Carlisle
  See Crowley, Suzanne
Crownfield, Gertrude 1867-1945
  See YABC 1
Crowther, James Gerald 1899-1983 14
Crowther, Kitty 1970- 220
Crowther, Robert 1948- 163
Cruikshank, George 1792-1878 22
  See also CLR 63
Cruise, Robin 1951- 179
Crum, Shutta 192
  Earlier sketch in SATA 134
Crummel, Susan Stevens 1949- 176
  Earlier sketch in SATA 130

Crump, Fred H., Jr. 1931- 76
  Earlier sketch in SATA 11
Crump, J(ames) Irving 1887-1979 57
  Obituary 21
Crump, William D(rake) 1949- 138
Crunden, Reginald
  See Cleaver, Hylton Reginald
Crunk, T.
  See Crunk, Tony
Crunk, Tony 1956- 130
Crutcher, Chris 1946- 196
  Earlier sketches in SATA 52, 99, 153
  See also CLR 159
Crutcher, Christopher C.
  See Crutcher, Chris
Cruz, Ray(mond) 1933- 6
Cruz Martinez, Alejandro (?)-1987 74
Crystal, Billy 1947- 154
Crystal, William
  See Crystal, Billy
Ctvrtek, Vaclav 1911-1976
  Obituary 27
Cuate, Melodie A. 219
Cuetara, Mittie 1957- 158
  Earlier sketch in SATA 106
Cuffari, Richard 1925-1978 66
  Obituary 25
  Earlier sketch in SATA 6
Cuffe-Perez, Mary 1946- 199
Cullen, Countee 1903-1946 18
Cullen, Lynn 190
Culliford, Pierre 1928-1992 40
  Obituary 74
Cullinan, Bernice E(llinger) 1926- 135
Culp, Louanna McNary 1901-1965 2
Culper, Felix
  See McCaughrean, Geraldine
Cumbaa, Stephen 1947- 72
Cumming, Peter 1951- 168
Cumming, Primrose Amy 1915- 24
Cumming, Robert 1945- 65
Cummings, Betty Sue 1918- 15
  See also SAAS 9
Cummings, John Michael 1963(?)- 216
Cummings, Mary 1951- 185
Cummings, Parke 1902-1987 2
  Obituary 53
Cummings, Pat 1950- 203
  Earlier sketches in SATA 42, 71, 107
  See also CLR 48
  See also SAAS 13
Cummings, Phil 1957- 123
  Earlier sketch in SATA 74
Cummings, Priscilla 1951- 170
  Earlier sketch in SATA 129
Cummings, Richard
  See Gardner, Richard (M.)
Cummins, Julie 200
Cummins, Maria Susanna 1827-1866
  See YABC 1
Cumpliano, Ina 207
Cuneo, Mary Louise -2001 85
Cunliffe, John Arthur 1933- 86
  Earlier sketch in SATA 11
Cunliffe, Marcus (Falkner) 1922-1990 37
  Obituary 66
Cunnane, Kelly 175
Cunningham, Bob
  See May, Julian
Cunningham, Captain Frank
  See Glick, Carl (Cannon)
Cunningham, Cathy
  See Cunningham, Chet
Cunningham, Chet 1928- 23
Cunningham, Dale S(peers) 1932- 11
Cunningham, Dru 91
Cunningham, E. V.
  See Fast, Howard
Cunningham, Julia (Woolfolk) 1916- 132
  Earlier sketches in SATA 1, 26
  See also SAAS 2

Cunningham, Lawrence J. 1943- 125
Cunningham, Virginia
  See Holmgren, Virginia C(unningham)
Cunxin, Li 1961- 220
Curiae, Amicus
  See Fuller, Edmund (Maybank)
Curie, Eve 1904-2007 1
  Obituary 188
Curlee, Lynn 1947- 190
  Earlier sketches in SATA 98, 141
Curley, Daniel 1918-1988 23
  Obituary 61
Curley, Marianne 1959- 175
  Earlier sketch in SATA 131
Currey, Anna 194
Currie, Robin 1948- 120
Currie, Stephen 1960- 132
  Earlier sketch in SATA 82
Curry, Ann (Gabrielle) 1934- 72
Curry, Jane L(ouise) 1932- 138
  Autobiography Feature 138
  Earlier sketches in SATA 1, 52, 90
  See also CLR 31
  See also SAAS 6
Curry, Peggy Simson 1911-1987 8
  Obituary 50
Curry, Tom 185
Curtis, Bruce (Richard) 1944- 30
Curtis, Chara M(ahar) 1950- 78
Curtis, Christopher Paul 1953- 187
  Earlier sketches in SATA 93, 140
  See also CLR 68
Curtis, Gavin 1965- 107
Curtis, Jamie Lee 1958- 144
  Earlier sketch in SATA 95
  See also CLR 88
Curtis, Jennifer Keats 185
Curtis, Marci 160
Curtis, Munzee
  See Caseley, Judith
Curtis, Neil 1950-2006 202
Curtis, Patricia 1921- 101
  Earlier sketch in SATA 23
Curtis, Peter
  See Lofts, Norah (Robinson)
Curtis, Philip (Delacourt) 1920- 62
Curtis, Richard 1937- 29
Curtis, Richard Alan
  See Curtis, Richard
Curtis, Richard Hale
  See Deming, Richard
  and Levinson, Leonard
  and Rothweiler, Paul Roger
Curtis, Stacy 205
Curtis, Wade
  See Pournelle, Jerry
Curtiss, A(rlene) B. 1934- 90
Cusack, Margaret 1945- 58
Cushman, Doug 1953- 210
  Earlier sketches in SATA 65, 101, 157
Cushman, Jerome 2
Cushman, Karen 1941- 147
  Earlier sketch in SATA 89
  See also CLR 55
Cusick, Richie Tankersley 1952- 140
  Earlier sketch in SATA 67
Cusimano, Maryann K.
  See Love, Maryann Cusimano
Cutbill, Andy 1972- 201
Cutchen, Billye Walker 1930- 15
Cutchins, Judy 1947- 59
Cutler, Daniel S. 1951- 78
Cutler, Daniel Solomon
  See Cutler, Daniel S.
Cutler, Ebbitt 1923- 9
Cutler, Ivor 1923-2006 24
  Obituary 174
Cutler, Jane 1936- 162
  Earlier sketches in SATA 75, 118
Cutler, May Ebbitt
  See Cutler, Ebbitt

Cutler, Samuel
  See Folsom, Franklin (Brewster)
Cutlip, Kimbra L(eigh-Ann) 1964- 128
Cutrate, Joe
  See Spiegelman, Art
Cutt, W(illiam) Towrie 1898-1981 16
  Obituary 85
Cuyler, Margery 1948- 195
  Earlier sketches in SATA 39, 99, 156
Cuyler, Margery Stuyvesant
  See Cuyler, Margery
Cuyler, Stephen
  See Bates, Barbara S(nedeker)
Cyrus, Kurt 1954- 179
  Earlier sketch in SATA 132
Czajkowski, James
  See Rollins, James
Czekaj, Jef 1969- 217
Czernecki, Stefan 1946- 178

D

Dabba Smith, Frank 174
Dabcovich, Lydia 99
  Brief entry 47
  Earlier sketch in SATA 58
Dace, Dolores B(oelens) 1929- 89
Da Costa, Deborah 193
Daddo, Andrew 1967- 198
Dadey, Debbie 1959- 217
  Earlier sketches in SATA 73, 136
Dahl, Borghild (Margrethe) 1890-1984 7
  Obituary 37
Dahl, Roald 1916-1990 73
  Obituary 65
  Earlier sketches in SATA 1, 26
  See also CLR 111
Dahlberg, Maurine F. 1951- 171
Dahlstedt, Marden (Stewart) 1921-1983 8
  Obituary 110
Dahme, Joanne 206
Dain, Martin J. 1924-2000 35
Dakin, Glenn 1960- 224
Dakos, Kalli 1950- 115
  Earlier sketch in SATA 80
Dale, Anna 1971- 170
Dale, Gary
  See Reece, Colleen L.
Dale, George E.
  See Asimov, Isaac
Dale, Jack
  See Holliday, Joseph
Dale, Kim 1957- 123
Dale, Margaret J(essy) Miller 1911- 39
Dale, Mitzi
  See Hemstock, Gillian
Dale, Norman
  See Denny, Norman (George)
Dale, Penny 1954- 151
  Earlier sketch in SATA 70
Daley, Michael J. 170
Dalgliesh, Alice 1893-1979 17
  Obituary 21
  See also CLR 62
Dalkey, Kara 1953- 132
Dalkey, Kara Mia
  See Dalkey, Kara
Dallas, Ruth 1919- 86
Dalmas, John
  See Jones, John R(obert)
Dalton, Alene
  See Chapin, Alene Olsen Dalton
Dalton, Annie 1948- 140
  Earlier sketch in SATA 40
Dalton, Kit
  See Cunningham, Chet
Dalton, Pamela
  See Johnson, Pamela

Dalton, Sean
   See Chester, Deborah
Dalton, Sheila 1949- 108
D'Aluisio, Faith 1957- 205
Daly, James 217
Daly, Jim
   See Stratemeyer, Edward L.
Daly, Jude 1951- 222
   Earlier sketch in SATA *177*
Daly, Kathleen N(orah) 124
   Brief entry 37
Daly, Maureen 1921-2006 129
   Obituary 176
   Earlier sketch in SATA *2*
   See also CLR *96*
   See also SAAS *1*
Daly, Nicholas
   See Daly, Niki
Daly, Niki 1946- 198
   Earlier sketches in SATA *37, 76, 114, 164*
   See also CLR *41*
   See also SAAS *21*
D'Amato, Alex 1919- 20
D'Amato, Janet (Potter) 1925- 9
Damerow, Gail 1944- 83
Damerow, Gail Jane
   See Damerow, Gail
D'Amico, Carmela 170
D'Amico, Steve 170
Damrell, Liz 1956- 77
Damrosch, Helen
   See Tee-Van, Helen Damrosch
Dana, Barbara 1940- 218
   Earlier sketch in SATA *22*
Dana, Richard Henry, Jr. 1815-1882 26
Danachair, Caoimhín O
   See Danaher, Kevin
Danaher, Kevin 1913-2002 22
Danakas, John 1963- 94
Dandi
   See Mackall, Dandi Daley
D'Andrea, Kate
   See Steiner, Barbara A(nnette)
Dangerfield, Balfour
   See McCloskey, (John) Robert
Daniel, Alan 1939- 76
   Brief entry 53
Daniel, Anita 1893(?)-1978 23
   Obituary 24
Daniel, Anne
   See Steiner, Barbara A(nnette)
Daniel, Becky 1947- 56
Daniel, Claire 1949- 164
Daniel, Colin
   See Windsor, Patricia
Daniel, Hawthorne 1890- 8
Daniel, (Donna) Lee 1944- 76
Daniel, Rebecca
   See Daniel, Becky
Daniels, Guy 1919-1989 11
   Obituary 62
Daniels, Kit
   See Diver, Lucienne
Daniels, Lucy
   See Oldfield, Jenny
Daniels, Max
   See Gellis, Roberta
Daniels, Olga
   See Sinclair, Olga
Daniels, Patricia 1955- 93
Daniels, Zoe
   See Laux, Constance
Dank, Gloria Rand 1955- 56
   Brief entry 46
Dank, Leonard D(ewey) 1929- 44
Dank, Milton 1920- 31
Dann, Max 1955- 62
Danneberg, Julie 1958- 173
Dantz, William R.
   See Philbrick, Rodman
Danzig, Dianne 213

Danziger, Paula 1944-2004 149
   Brief entry 30
   Obituary 155
   Earlier sketches in SATA *36, 63, 102*
   See also CLR *20*
Darby, Gene Kegley
   See Darby, Jean (Kegley)
Darby, J. N.
   See Govan, (Mary) Christine Noble
Darby, Jean (Kegley) 1921- 68
Darby, Patricia (Paulsen) 14
Darby, Ray(mond) 1912-1982 7
Darbyshire, Kristen 218
d'Arcy, Willard
   See Cox, William R(obert)
Dare, Geena
   See McNicoll, Sylvia (Marilyn)
D'arge, Mackie 218
Darian, Shea 1959- 97
Daringer, Helen Fern 1892-1986 1
Darke, Marjorie 1929- 87
   Earlier sketch in SATA *16*
Darley, F(elix) O(ctavius) C(arr)
   1822-1888 35
Darling, David J. 1953- 60
   Brief entry 44
Darling, Kathy
   See Darling, Mary Kathleen
Darling, Lois (MacIntyre) 1917-1989 3
   Obituary 64
Darling, Louis, (Jr.) 1916-1970 3
   Obituary 23
Darling, Mary Kathleen 1943- 124
   Earlier sketches in SATA *9, 79*
Darling, Sandra Louise Woodward
   See Day, Alexandra
Darnell, K(athryn) L(ynne) 1955- 150
Darroll, Sally
   See Odgers, Sally Farrell
Darrow, Sharon 181
Darrow, Whitney, (Jr.) 1909-1999 13
   Obituary 115
Darwin, Len
   See Darwin, Leonard
Darwin, Leonard 1916- 24
Dasent, Sir George Webbe 1817-1896 62
   Brief entry 29
Dash, Joan 1925- 142
Daskam, Josephine Dodge
   See Bacon, Josephine Dodge (Daskam)
D'ath, Justin 1953- 174
   Earlier sketch in SATA *106*
Dauer, Rosamond 1934- 23
Daugherty, Charles Michael 1914- 16
Daugherty, James (Henry) 1889-1974 13
   See also CLR *78*
Daugherty, Richard D(eo) 1922- 35
Daugherty, Sonia Medwedeff (?)-1971
   Obituary 27
d'Aulaire, Edgar Parin 1898-1986 66
   Obituary 47
   Earlier sketch in SATA *5*
   See also CLR *21*
d'Aulaire, Ingri 1904-1980 66
   Obituary 24
   Earlier sketch in SATA *5*
   See also CLR *21*
d'Aulaire, Ingri Mortenson Parin
   See d'Aulaire, Ingri
Dave, Dave
   See Berg, David
Daveluy, Paule Cloutier 1919- 11
Davenier, Christine 1961- 216
   Earlier sketches in SATA *127, 179*
Davenport, John 1960- 156
Daves, Michael 1938- 40
David, A. R.
   See David, A(nn) Rosalie
David, A(nn) Rosalie 1946- 103
David, Jonathan
   See Ames, Lee J(udah)

David, Lawrence 1963- 165
   Earlier sketch in SATA *111*
David, Peter 1956- 72
David, Peter Allen
   See David, Peter
David, Rosalie
   See David, A(nn) Rosalie
Davidson, Alice Joyce 1932- 54
   Brief entry 45
Davidson, Basil 1914-2010 13
Davidson, (Marie) Diane 1924- 91
Davidson, Hugh
   See Hamilton, Edmond
Davidson, Jessica 1915-1986 5
Davidson, Judith 1953- 40
Davidson, Lionel 1922-2009 87
Davidson, Margaret 1936- 5
Davidson, Marion
   See Garis, Howard R.
Davidson, Mary R. 1885-1973 9
Davidson, Mary S. 1940- 61
Davidson, Mickie
   See Davidson, Margaret
Davidson, Nicole
   See Jensen, Kathryn
Davidson, R.
   See Davidson, Raymond
Davidson, Raymond 1926- 32
Davidson, Rosalie 1921- 23
Davie, Helen K(ay) 1952- 148
   Earlier sketch in SATA *77*
Davies, Andrew (Wynford) 1936- 27
Davies, Andy Robert 200
Davies, Bettilu D(onna) 1942- 33
Davies, Hunter 1936- 55
   Brief entry 45
Davies, Jacqueline 1962- 186
   Earlier sketch in SATA *155*
Davies, Joan 1934- 50
   Brief entry 47
Davies, Nicola 1958- 182
   Earlier sketches in SATA *99, 150*
Davies, Peter J(oseph) 1937- 52
Davies, Sumiko 1942- 46
Davis, (A.) Aubrey 1949- 153
Davis, Barbara Steincrohn
   See Davis, Maggie S.
Davis, Bette J. 1923- 15
Davis, Burke 1913- 4
Davis, Christopher 1928- 6
Davis, D(elbert) Dwight 1908-1965 33
Davis, Daniel S(heldon) 1936- 12
Davis, David R. 1948- 106
Davis, Donald 1944- 169
   Earlier sketch in SATA *93*
Davis, Donald D.
   See Davis, Donald
Davis, Eleanor 1983(?)- 209
Davis, Emma
   See Davis, Maggie S.
Davis, Gibbs 1953- 102
   Brief entry 41
   Earlier sketch in SATA *46*
Davis, Grania 1943- 88
   Brief entry 50
Davis, H(arold) L(enoir) 1896-1960 114
Davis, Heather 1970- 221
Davis, Hubert J(ackson) 1904-1997 31
Davis, Jack E. 210
Davis, Jacky 204
Davis, James Robert 1945- 32
Davis, Jenny 1953- 74
Davis, Jim
   See Davis, James Robert
Davis, Julia 1900(?)-1993 6
   Obituary 75
Davis, Karen (Elizabeth) 1944- 109
Davis, Katie 1959(?)- 208
   Earlier sketch in SATA *152*
Davis, Lambert 176

Davis, Leslie
    See Guccione, Leslie Davis
Davis, Louise Littleton 1921- 25
Davis, Maggie S. 1943- 57
Davis, Marguerite 1889- 34
Davis, Mary L(ee) 1935- 9
Davis, Mary Octavia 1901-1976 6
Davis, Nelle 1958- 73
Davis, Ossie 1917-2005 81
    See also CLR 56
Davis, Paxton 1925-1994 16
Davis, Rich 1958- 206
Davis, Robert 1881-1949
    See YABC 1
Davis, Robin W(orks) 1962- 87
Davis, Russell Gerard 1922- 3
Davis, Tanita S. 212
Davis, Tim(othy N.) 1957- 94
Davis, Tony 1961- 222
Davis, Verne Theodore 1889-1973 6
Davis, Yvonne 1927- 115
Davol, Marguerite W. 1928- 146
    Earlier sketch in SATA 82
DaVolls, Andy (P.) 1967- 85
DaVolls, Linda 1966- 85
Davys, Sarah
    See Manning, Rosemary
Dawes, Claiborne 1935- 111
Dawson, Arthur L. 207
Dawson, Elmer A. 67
    Earlier sketch in SATA 1
Dawson, Imogen (Zoe) 1948- 126
    Earlier sketch in SATA 90
Dawson, Janine 1957- 196
Dawson, Mary 1919- 11
Dawson, Willow 1975- 208
Day, A(rthur) Grove 1904-1994 59
Day, Alexandra 1941- 197
    Autobiography Feature 197
    Earlier sketches in SATA 67, 97, 169
    See also CLR 22
    See also SAAS 19
Day, Beth (Feagles) 1924- 33
Day, Donna
    See Asay, Donna Day
Day, Edward C. 1932- 72
Day, Jon 1936(?)- 79
Day, Karen 187
Day, Larry 1956- 181
Day, Nancy 1953- 140
Day, Nancy Raines 1951- 148
    Earlier sketch in SATA 93
Day, Shirley 1962- 94
Day, Thomas 1748-1789
    See YABC 1
Day, Trevor 1955- 124
Dazey, Agnes J(ohnston) 2
Dazey, Frank M. 2
Deacon, Alexis 1978- 139
Deacon, Eileen
    See Geipel, Eileen
Deacon, Richard
    See McCormick, (George) Donald (King)
Deadman, Ronald 1919-1988(?)
    Obituary 56
Deak, Erzsi 1959- 152
Dean, Anabel 1915- 12
Dean, Carolee 1962- 148
Dean, Claire 215
Dean, David 1976- 192
Dean, Karen Strickler 1923- 49
Dean, Ruth (Brigham) 1947- 145
Dean, Zoey
    See Bennett, Cherie
de Angeli, Marguerite (Lofft) 1889-1987 ... 100
    Obituary 51
    Earlier sketches in SATA 1, 27
    See also CLR 1
Deans, Karen 195
Deans, Sis Boulos 1955- 136
    Earlier sketch in SATA 78

DeArmand, Frances Ullmann 1904(?)-1984 . 10
    Obituary 38
DeArmond, Dale 1914- 70
DeArmond, Dale Burlison
    See DeArmond, Dale
Deary, Terry 1946- 171
    Brief entry 41
    Earlier sketches in SATA 51, 101
Deaver, Julie Reece 1953- 68
de Banke, Cecile 1889-1965 11
De Bello, Rosario 1923- 89
Debon, Nicolas 186
    Earlier sketch in SATA 151
de Bono, Edward 1933- 66
de Brissac, Malcolm
    See Dickinson, Peter
de Brunhoff, Jean
    See Brunhoff, Jean de
De Brunhoff, Laurent
    See Brunhoff, Laurent de
De Bruyn, Monica G. 1952- 13
De Bruyn, Monica Jean Grembowicz
    See De Bruyn, Monica G.
DeBry, Roger K. 1942- 91
de Camp, Catherine Crook 1907-2000 83
    Earlier sketch in SATA 12
de Camp, L. Sprague 1907-2000 83
    Earlier sketch in SATA 9
de Camp, Lyon Sprague
    See de Camp, L. Sprague
DeCandido, Keith R.A. 112
Dechausay, Sonia E. 94
Decker, C.B. 172
Decker, Cynthia B.
    See Decker, C.B.
Decker, Duane 1910-1964 5
Decker, Timothy 1974- 197
DeClements, Barthe 1920- 131
    Earlier sketches in SATA 35, 71
    See also CLR 23
DeClements, Barthe Faith
    See DeClements, Barthe
de Clercq Zubli, Rita la Fontaine 1929- 199
de Conte, Sieur Louis
    See Twain, Mark
Dedman, Stephen 108
Dee, Barbara 1958- 220
Dee, Catherine 1964- 138
Dee, Ruby
    See Wallace, Ruby Ann
Deeble, Jason 1979- 221
Deedy, Carmen Agra 1960- 196
Deedy, John 1923- 24
Deegan, Paul Joseph 1937- 48
    Brief entry 38
Deem, James M. 1950- 191
    Autobiography Feature 191
    Earlier sketches in SATA 75, 134
Deem, James Morgan
    See Deem, James M.
Deeter, Catherine 1947- 137
DeFelice, Cynthia 1951- 165
    Earlier sketches in SATA 79, 121
DeFelice, Cynthia C.
    See DeFelice, Cynthia
Defoe, Daniel 1660(?)-1731 22
    See also CLR 61
de Fombelle, Timothee
    See Fombelle, Timothee de
DeFord, Deborah H. 123
deFrance, Anthony
    See DiFranco, Anthony (Mario)
Degen, Bruce 1945- 205
    Brief entry 47
    Earlier sketches in SATA 57, 97, 147
DeGering, Etta (Belle) Fowler 1898-1996 7
De Goldi, Kate 1959- 123
De Goldi, Kathleen Domenica
    See De Goldi, Kate
de Goursac, Olivier 1959- 184
De Grazia, Ettore 1909-1982 39

De Grazia, Ted
    See De Grazia, Ettore
deGroat, Diane 1947- 169
    Earlier sketches in SATA 31, 90
deGros, J. H.
    See Villiard, Paul
de Grummond, Lena Young 62
    Earlier sketch in SATA 6
de Hamel, Joan Littledale 1924- 86
De Haven, Tom 1949- 72
de Hugo, Pierre
    See Brackers de Hugo, Pierre
Deines, Brian 1955- 220
Deiss, Joseph Jay 1912-1999 12
de Jenkins, Lyll Becerra 1925-1997 102
DeJong, David C(ornel) 1905-1967 10
de Jong, Dola
    See de Jong, Dorothea Rosalie
de Jong, Dorothea Rosalie 1911-2003 7
    Obituary 149
DeJong, Meindert 1906-1991 2
    Obituary 68
    See also CLR 73
DeJonge, Joanne E. 1943- 56
Deka, Connie
    See Laux, Constance
de Kay, Ormonde (Jr.) 1923-1998 7
    Obituary 106
DeKeyser, Stacy 1959- 214
de Kiriline, Louise
    See Lawrence, Louise de Kiriline
Dekker, Carl
    See Laffin, John (Alfred Charles)
    and Lynds, Dennis
deKruif, Paul (Henry) 1890-1971 50
    Earlier sketch in SATA 5
Delacre, Lulu 1957- 209
    Earlier sketches in SATA 36, 156
DeLaCroix, Alice 1940- 195
    Earlier sketch in SATA 75
de la Cruz, Melissa 1971- 179
De la Garza, Phyllis 1942- 169
De Lage, Ida 1918- 11
de la Mare, Walter (John) 1873-1956 16
    See also CLR 148
Delaney, Harry 1932- 3
Delaney, Joseph 1945- 172
Delaney, M.C.
    See Delaney, Michael
Delaney, Michael 1955- 180
    Earlier sketch in SATA 96
Delaney, Michael Clark
    See Delaney, Michael
Delaney, Ned 1951- 28
Delaney, Thomas Nicholas III
    See Delaney, Ned
DeLange, Alex Pardo
    See Pardo DeLange, Alex
Delano, Hugh 1933- 20
Delano, Marfe Ferguson 215
Delany, Samuel R., Jr. 1942- 92
Delany, Samuel Ray
    See Delany, Samuel R., Jr.
de la Pena, Matt 205
De La Ramee, Marie Louise 1839-1908 20
de la Roche, Mazo 1879-1961 64
De La Roche Saint Andre, Anne 1950- 75
de Las Casas, Dianne 1970- 221
Delaune, (Jewel) Lynn (de Grummond) 7
DeLaurentis, Louise Budde 1920- 12
del Barco, Lucy Salamanca 1900(?)-1989
    Obituary 64
Delderfield, Eric R(aymond) 1909-1995 14
Delderfield, Ronald Frederick 1912-1972 20
DeLeeuw, Adele (Louise) 1899-1988 30
    Obituary 56
    Earlier sketch in SATA 1
De Leon, Nephtali 1945- 97

Delessert, Etienne 1941- 179
  Brief entry 27
  Earlier sketches in SATA 46, 130
  See also CLR 81
Delgado, James P. 1958- 122
de Lint, Charles 1951- 207
  Earlier sketches in SATA 115, 157
de Lint, Charles Henri Diederick Hofsmit
  See de Lint, Charles
Delmar, Roy
  See Wexler, Jerome (LeRoy)
Del Negro, Janice M. 197
Deloria, Vine, Jr. 1933-2005 21
  Obituary 171
Deloria, Vine Victor, Jr.
  See Deloria, Vine, Jr.
del Rey, Lester 1915-1993 22
  Obituary 76
Delrio, Martin
  See Doyle, Debra
  and Macdonald, James D.
Delton, Judy 1931-2001 77
  Obituary 130
  Earlier sketch in SATA 14
  See also SAAS 9
Delulio, John 1938- 15
Delving, Michael
  See Williams, Jay
de Marcken, Gail 186
Demarest, Chris L. 1951- 175
  Brief entry 44
  Earlier sketches in SATA 45, 82, 128
Demarest, Christopher Lynn
  See Demarest, Chris L.
Demarest, Doug
  See Barker, Will
De Mari, Silvana 1953- 193
Demas, Corinne
  See Bliss, Corinne Demas
Demas, Vida 1927- 9
Dematons, Charlotte 1957- 203
DeMatteis, J.M. 1953- 180
DeMatteis, John Marc
  See DeMatteis, J.M.
De Mejo, Oscar 1911-1992 40
Demers, Dominique 1956- 177
de Messieres, Nicole 1930- 39
Demi 1942- 210
  Earlier sketches in SATA 11, 66, 102, 152
  See also CLR 58
Demijohn, Thom
  See Disch, Thomas M.
  and Sladek, John
Deming, Richard 1915-1983 24
Deming, Sarah 191
de Monfreid, Dorothee 1973- 189
Demuth, Patricia Brennan 1948- 84
  Brief entry 51
De Muth, Roger 1948- 221
Dendinger, Roger E. 1952- 158
Denenberg, Barry 1940- 175
Dengler, Marianna (Herron) 1935- 103
Dengler, Sandy 1939- 54
  Brief entry 40
Denim, Sue
  See Pilkey, Dav
Denise, Anika 210
Denise, Christopher 1968- 193
  Earlier sketch in SATA 147
Denman, K.L. 1957- 186
Denmark, Harrison
  See Zelazny, Roger
Dennard, Deborah 1953- 136
  Earlier sketch in SATA 78
Denney, Diana 1910-2000 25
  Obituary 120
Dennis, Morgan 1891(?)-1960 18
Dennis, Wesley 1903-1966 18
Denniston, Elinore 1900-1978
  Obituary 24
Denny, Norman (George) 1901-1982 43

Denos, Julia 202
Denslow, Sharon Phillips 1947- 142
  Earlier sketch in SATA 68
Denslow, W(illiam) W(allace) 1856-1915 16
  See also CLR 15
Dent, Grace 1973- 187
Denton, Kady MacDonald 181
  Earlier sketches in SATA 66, 110
  See also CLR 71
Denton, Terry 1950- 186
Denver, Walt
  See Redding, Robert Hull
  and Sherman, Jory (Tecumseh)
Denzel, Justin F(rancis) 1917-1999 46
  Brief entry 38
Denzer, Ann Wiseman
  See Wiseman, Ann (Sayre)
DePalma, Mary Newell 1961- 185
  Earlier sketch in SATA 139
De Palma, Toni 199
dePaola, Thomas Anthony 1934- 200
  Earlier sketches in SATA 11, 59, 108, 155
  See also CLR 81
  See also SAAS 15
dePaola, Tomie
  See dePaola, Thomas Anthony
deParrie, Paul 1949- 74
DePauw, Linda Grant 1940- 24
De Pretto, Lorenzo 1966- 225
DeRan, David 1946- 76
Derby, Ken 1956- 181
Derby, Kenneth R.
  See Derby, Ken
Derby, Pat 1942- 172
Derby, Sally 1934- 189
  Earlier sketches in SATA 89, 132
de Regniers, Beatrice Schenk (Freedman)
  1914-2000 68
  Obituary 123
  Earlier sketch in SATA 2
  See also SAAS 6
Dereske, Jo 1947- 72
Deriso, Christine Hurley 1961- 210
Derleth, August (William) 1909-1971 5
Derman, Martha (Winn) 74
Derman, Sarah Audrey 1915- 11
DeRoberts, Lyndon
  See Silverstein, Robert Alan
Derom, Dirk 1980- 224
de Roo, Anne Louise 1931-1997 84
  Earlier sketch in SATA 25
  See also CLR 63
deRosa, Dee 70
Derrick, Lionel
  See Cunningham, Chet
Derrickson, Jim 1959- 141
Derry Down Derry
  See Lear, Edward
Dervaux, Isabelle 1961- 106
Derwent, Lavinia 14
Desai, Anita 1937- 126
  Earlier sketch in SATA 63
DeSaix, Deborah Durland 188
De Saulles, Tony 1958- 119
Desbarats, Peter 1933- 39
de Selincourt, Aubrey 1894-1962 14
de Seve, Peter 1958- 219
de Seve, Randall 198
Deshpande, Chris 1950- 69
Desimini, Lisa 1964- 216
  Earlier sketches in SATA 86, 148
Desjarlais, John 1953- 71
Desjarlais, John J.
  See Desjarlais, John
Desmoinaux, Christel 1967- 149
  Earlier sketch in SATA 103
Desmond, Adrian 1947- 51
Desmond, Adrian J.
  See Desmond, Adrian
Desmond, Adrian John
  See Desmond, Adrian

Desmond, Alice Curtis 1897-1990 8
Desnoettes, Caroline 183
DeSpain, Pleasant 1943- 87
Desputeaux, Helene 1959- 95
Dessen, Sarah 1970- 172
  Earlier sketch in SATA 120
Detine, Padre
  See Olsen, Ib Spang
de Trevino, Elizabeth B.
  See Trevino, Elizabeth B(orton) de
de Trevino, Elizabeth Borton
  See Trevino, Elizabeth B(orton) de
Detwiler, Susan Dill 1956- 58
Deuker, Carl 1950- 196
  Earlier sketches in SATA 82, 150
Deutsch, Babette 1895-1982 1
  Obituary 33
Deutsch, Eva Costabel
  See Costabel, Eva Deutsch
Deutsch, Helen 1906-1992 76
Deutsch, Kurt
  See Singer, Kurt D.
De Valera, Sinead 1879(?)-1975
  Obituary 30
Devaney, John 1926-1994 12
de Varennes, Monique 1947- 168
de Varona, Frank J. 1943- 83
Devereux, Frederick L(eonard), Jr.
  1914-1993 9
Devi, Nila
  See Woody, Regina Jones
deVinck, Christopher 1951- 85
DeVita, James 195
DeVito, Cara 1956- 80
Devlin, Dorothy Wende
  See Devlin, Wende
Devlin, Harry 1918-2001 136
  Earlier sketches in SATA 11, 74
Devlin, Wende 1918-2002 74
  Earlier sketch in SATA 11
Devon, Paddie 1953- 92
Devons, Sonia 1974- 72
Devorah-Leah 111
de Vos, Gail 1949- 122
de Vries, Anke 1936- 222
DeVries, Douglas 1933- 122
De Waard, E(lliott) John 1935- 7
Dewan, Ted 1961- 157
  Earlier sketch in SATA 108
Dewdney, Anna 184
Dewdney, Selwyn (Hanington) 1909-1979 ... 64
DeWeese, Gene
  See DeWeese, Thomas Eugene
DeWeese, Jean
  See DeWeese, Thomas Eugene
DeWeese, Thomas Eugene 1934- 46
  Brief entry 45
Dewey, Ariane 1937- 178
  Earlier sketches in SATA 7, 109
Dewey, Jennifer (Owings) 1941- 103
  Brief entry 48
  Earlier sketch in SATA 58
Dewey, Kenneth Francis 1940- 39
Dewin, Howie
  See Howie, Betsy
De Wire, Elinor 1953- 180
deWit, Dorothy (May Knowles) 1916-1980 . 39
  Obituary 28
Dexter, Alison 1966- 125
Dexter, John
  See Bradley, Marion Zimmer
Deyneka, Anita 1943- 24
Deyrup, Astrith Johnson 1923- 24
Dezern, Chad 201
de Zubizarreta, Alma
  See Ada, Alma Flor
Dhami, Narinder 1958- 152
Dhondy, Farrukh 1944- 152
  Earlier sketch in SATA 65
  See also CLR 41
Diakite, Baba Wague 1961- 174

Diakite, Penda 1993(?)- *174*
Diamond, Arthur 1957- *76*
Diamond, Donna 1950- *69*
　Brief entry *30*
　Earlier sketch in SATA *35*
Diamond, Petra
　See Sachs, Judith
Diamond, Rebecca
　See Sachs, Judith
Dias, Earl Joseph 1916- *41*
Dias, Ron 1937- *71*
Diaz, David 1959(?)- *189*
　Earlier sketches in SATA *96, 150*
　See also CLR *65*
di Bartolo, Jim *225*
Dibley, Glin *188*
DiCamillo, Kate 1964- *202*
　Earlier sketches in SATA *121, 163*
　See also CLR *117*
Di Certo, J(oseph) J(ohn) 1933- *60*
DiCianni, Ron 1952- *107*
Dick, Trella Lamson 1889-1974 .... *9*
Dickens, Charles 1812-1870 .... *15*
　See also CLR *162*
Dickens, Charles John Huffam
　See Dickens, Charles
Dickens, Frank
　See Huline-Dickens, Frank William
Dickens, Monica (Enid) 1915-1992 .... *4*
　Obituary *74*
Dickerson, Roy Ernest 1886-1965
　Obituary *26*
Dickinson, Emily 1830-1886 .... *29*
Dickinson, Emily Elizabeth
　See Dickinson, Emily
Dickinson, Mary 1949- *48*
　Brief entry *41*
Dickinson, Mary-Anne
　See Rodda, Emily
Dickinson, Peter 1927- *150*
　Earlier sketches in SATA *5, 62, 95*
　See also CLR *125*
Dickinson, Peter Malcolm de Brissac
　See Dickinson, Peter
Dickinson, Susan 1931- *8*
Dickinson, Terence 1943- *102*
Dickinson, W(illiam) Croft 1897-1963 .... *13*
Dickson, Gordon R. 1923-2001 .... *77*
Dickson, Gordon Rupert
　See Dickson, Gordon R.
Dickson, Helen
　See Reynolds, Helen Mary Greenwood Campbell
Dickson, Naida 1916- *8*
Diehn, Gwen 1943- *80*
Dierssen, Andreas 1962- *190*
Diesen, Deborah 1967- *200*
Dieterich, Michele M. 1962- *78*
Dietz, David H(enry) 1897-1984 .... *10*
　Obituary *41*
Dietz, Lew 1907-1997 .... *11*
　Obituary *95*
Diffily, Deborah *159*
Di Fiori, Larry
　See Di Fiori, Lawrence
Di Fiori, Lawrence 1934- *130*
DiFranco, Anthony (Mario) 1945- *42*
Digby, Anne 1935- *72*
Digges, Jeremiah
　See Berger, Josef
Digman, Kristina 1959- *176*
D'Ignazio, Fred 1949- *39*
　Brief entry *35*
D'Ignazio, Frederick
　See D'Ignazio, Fred
Di Grazia, Thomas (?)-1983 .... *32*
Dijkstra, Lida 1961- *195*
Dikty, Julian May
　See May, Julian
Dillard, Annie 1945- *140*
　Earlier sketch in SATA *10*

Dillard, Kristine 1964- *113*
Dillard, Polly Hargis 1916- *24*
Dillard, Sarah 1961- *217*
Diller, Harriett 1953- *78*
Dillon, Anna
　See Scott, Michael
Dillon, Barbara 1927- *44*
　Brief entry *39*
Dillon, Diane 1933- *194*
　Earlier sketches in SATA *15, 51, 106*
　See also CLR *44*
Dillon, Diane Claire
　See Dillon, Diane
Dillon, Eilis 1920-1994 .... *74*
　Autobiography Feature *105*
　Obituary *83*
　Earlier sketch in SATA *2*
　See also CLR *26*
Dillon, Jana (a pseudonym) 1952- *117*
Dillon, Leo 1933- *194*
　Earlier sketches in SATA *15, 51, 106*
　See also CLR *44*
Dillon, Sharon Saseen
　See Saseen, Sharon (Dillon)
Dils, Tracey E. 1958- *83*
Dilson, Jesse 1914-1988 .... *24*
Dinan, Carolyn *59*
　Brief entry *47*
Dines, Carol 1956- *175*
Dines, (Harry) Glen 1925-1996 .... *7*
Dinesen, Isak
　See Blixen, Karen
Dinessi, Alex
　See Schembri, Jim
Dinneen, Betty 1929- *61*
Dinnerstein, Harvey 1928- *42*
Dinsdale, Tim(othy Kay) 1924-1987 .... *11*
Dion, Nathalie 1964- *213*
Dionne, Erin 1975- *217*
Diop, Birago (Ismael) 1906-1989
　Obituary *64*
Diouf, Sylviane A. *168*
Diouf, Sylviane Anna
　See Diouf, Sylviane A.
DiPucchio, Kelly *204*
　Earlier sketch in SATA *159*
Dirk
　See Gringhuis, Richard H.
Dirks, Wilhelmina 1916- *59*
Dirks, Willy
　See Dirks, Wilhelmina
Dirtmeister
　See Tomecek, Steve
DiSalvo, DyAnne 1960- *144*
　Earlier sketch in SATA *59*
DiSalvo-Ryan, DyAnne
　See DiSalvo, DyAnne
Disch, Thomas M. 1940-2008 .... *92*
　Obituary *195*
　See also CLR *18*
　See also SAAS *15*
Disch, Thomas Michael
　See Disch, Thomas M.
Disch, Tom
　See Disch, Thomas M.
Disher, Garry 1949- *125*
　Earlier sketch in SATA *81*
Disney, Walt(er Elias) 1901-1966 .... *28*
　Brief entry *27*
Ditchfield, Christin 1973- *189*
DiTerlizzi, Tony 1969- *214*
　Earlier sketch in SATA *154*
DiTerlooney, Tiny
　See DiTerlizzi, Tony
Divakaruni, Chitra Banerjee 1956- *222*
　Earlier sketch in SATA *160*
Di Valentin, Maria (Amelia) Messuri
　1911-1985 .... *7*
Diver, Lucienne 1971- *218*
Divine, Arthur Durham 1904-1987
　Obituary *52*

Divine, David
　See Divine, Arthur Durham
Dixon, Ann 1954- *212*
　Earlier sketches in SATA *77, 127*
Dixon, Ann Renee
　See Dixon, Ann
Dixon, Dougal 1947- *190*
　Earlier sketches in SATA *45, 127*
Dixon, Franklin W.
　See Barrett, Neal, Jr.
　and Goulart, Ron
　and Lantz, Francess L(in)
　and Lerangis, Peter
　and McFarlane, Leslie
　and Stanley, George Edward
　and Stratemeyer, Edward L.
Dixon, Jeanne 1936- *31*
Dixon, Paige
　See Corcoran, Barbara (Asenath)
Dixon, Peter L(ee) 1931- *6*
Dixon, Rachel 1952- *74*
Djoleto, (Solomon Alexander) Amu 1929- ... *80*
d'lacey, Chris 1949- *165*
Doak, Annie
　See Dillard, Annie
Doane, Pelagie 1906-1966 .... *7*
Dob, Bob *207*
Dobell, I(sabel) M(arian) B(arclay)
　1909-1998 .... *11*
Dobie, J(ames) Frank 1888-1964 .... *43*
Dobkin, Alexander 1908-1975
　Obituary *30*
Dobler, Lavinia G. 1910- *6*
Dobrin, Arnold 1928- *4*
Dobson, Jill 1969- *140*
Dobson, Julia 1941- *48*
Dobson, Mary 1954- *117*
DoCampo, Valeria 1976- *217*
Docherty, James
　See Docherty, Jimmy
Docherty, Jimmy 1976- *204*
Docherty, Thomas 1955- *218*
Dockery, Wallene T. 1941- *27*
Dockray, Tracy 1962- *139*
Dockrey, Karen 1955- *103*
Doctor, Bernard
　See Doctor, Bernard Aquina
Doctor, Bernard Aquina 1950- *81*
Doctor X
　See Nourse, Alan E(dward)
Dodd, Ed(ward Benton) 1902-1991 .... *4*
　Obituary *68*
Dodd, Emma 1969- *203*
Dodd, Lynley (Stuart) 1941- *132*
　Earlier sketches in SATA *35, 86*
　See also CLR *62*
Dodd, Marty 1921- *142*
Dodd, Quentin 1972- *137*
Dodds, Bill 1952- *78*
Dodds, Dayle Ann 1952- *201*
　Earlier sketches in SATA *75, 150*
Doder, Josh 1968- *187*
Dodge, Bertha S(anford) 1902-1995 .... *8*
Dodge, Fremont
　See Grimes, Lee
Dodge, Gil
　See Hano, Arnold
Dodge, Mary (Elizabeth) Mapes
　1831(?)-1905 .... *100*
　Earlier sketch in SATA *21*
　See also CLR *62*
Dodgson, Charles Lutwidge
　See Carroll, Lewis
Dodson, Kenneth MacKenzie 1907-1999 ..... *11*
Dodson, Susan 1941- *50*
　Brief entry *40*
Doerrfeld, Cori 1964- *214*
Dogar, Sharon 1962- *211*
Dogyear, Drew
　See Gorey, Edward (St. John)

Doherty, Berlie 1943- *111*
  Earlier sketch in SATA 72
  See also CLR 21
  See also SAAS 16
Doherty, Charles Hugh 1913- *6*
Doherty, Craig A. 1951- *169*
  Earlier sketch in SATA 83
Doherty, Katherine M(ann) 1951- *83*
Doherty, Kieran 1945- *164*
Dokas, Dara 1968- *216*
Dokey, Cameron 1956- *97*
Dolan, Edward F(rancis), Jr. 1924- *94*
  Brief entry *31*
  Earlier sketch in SATA 45
Dolan, Ellen M(eara) 1929-1998 .... *88*
Dolan, Sean J. 1958- *74*
Dolce, J. Ellen 1948- *75*
Dolch, Edward William 1889-1961 .... *50*
Dolch, Marguerite Pierce 1891-1978 .... *50*
Dollar, Diane (Hills) 1933- *57*
Dolson, Hildegarde
  See Lockridge, Hildegarde (Dolson)
Domanska, Janina 1913(?)-1995 .... *68*
  Obituary *84*
  Earlier sketch in SATA 6
  See also CLR 40
  See also SAAS 18
Dominguez, Angel 1953- *76*
Dominguez, Angela N. 1982- *219*
Domino, John
  See Averill, Esther (Holden)
Domjan, Joseph (Spiri) 1907-1992 .... *25*
Domm, Jeffrey C. 1958- *84*
Donahue, Dorothy *178*
Donald, Rhonda Lucas 1962- *147*
Donalds, Gordon
  See Shirreffs, Gordon D(onald)
Donaldson, Bryna
  See Stevens, Bryna
Donaldson, Gordon 1913-1993 .... *64*
  Obituary *76*
Donaldson, Joan 1953- *78*
Donaldson, Julia 1948- *180*
  Earlier sketches in SATA 82, 132
Donaldson, Stephen R. 1947- *121*
Donaldson, Stephen Reeder
  See Donaldson, Stephen R.
Doner, Kim 1955- *208*
  Earlier sketch in SATA 91
Doney, Todd L. W. 1959- *104*
Dong-Sung, Kim 1970- *195*
Dong-Sung Kim
  See Dong-Sung, Kim
Donkin, Andrew *219*
Donkin, Nance (Clare) 1915- *95*
Donna, Natalie 1934-1979 .... *9*
Donnelly, Elfie 1950-
  See CLR 104
Donnelly, Jennifer 1963- *154*
Donnelly, Matt 1972- *148*
Donnio, Sylviane *188*
Donofrio, Beverly 1950- *209*
Donoghue, Emma 1969- *101*
Donohue, Moira Rose 1954- *201*
Donoughue, Carol 1935- *139*
Donovan, Frank (Robert) 1906-1975
  Obituary *30*
Donovan, Gail 1962- *217*
Donovan, John 1928-1992 .... *72*
  Brief entry *29*
  See also CLR 3
Donovan, Mary Lee 1961- *86*
Donovan, William
  See Berkebile, Fred D(onovan)
Donze, Mary Terese 1911- *89*
Doob, Leonard W(illiam) 1909-2000 .... *8*
Doodler, Todd H.
  See Goldman, Todd Harris
Dooley, Norah 1953- *74*
Dooling, Michael 1958- *220*
  Earlier sketch in SATA 105

Dor, Ana
  See Ceder, Georgiana Dorcas
Doran, Colleen 1963- *211*
Dore, (Louis Christophe Paul) Gustave
  1832-1883 .... *19*
Doremus, Robert 1913-2010 .... *30*
Doren, Marion (Walker) 1928- *57*
Dorenkamp, Michelle 1957- *89*
Dorflinger, Carolyn 1953- *91*
Dorfman, Joaquin 1979- *180*
Dorfman, Joaquin Emiliano
  See Dorfman, Joaquin
Dorian, Edith M(cEwen) 1900-1983 .... *5*
Dorian, Harry
  See Hamilton, Charles (Harold St. John)
Dorian, Marguerite *7*
Dorin, Patrick C(arberry) 1939- *59*
  Brief entry *52*
Dorman, Brandon *194*
Dorman, Michael 1932- *7*
Dorman, N. B. 1927- *39*
Dormer, Frank W. *200*
Dorris, Michael 1945-1997 .... *75*
  Obituary *94*
  See also CLR 58
Dorris, Michael A.
  See Dorris, Michael
Dorris, Michael Anthony
  See Dorris, Michael
Dorritt, Susan
  See Schlein, Miriam
Dorros, Alex 1991- *194*
Dorros, Arthur 1950- *168*
  Earlier sketches in SATA 78, 122
  See also CLR 42
  See also SAAS 20
Dorros, Arthur M.
  See Dorros, Arthur
Dorson, Richard M(ercer) 1916-1981 .... *30*
Doss, Helen (Grigsby) 1918- *20*
Doss, Margot Patterson *6*
dos Santos, Joyce Audy 1949- *57*
  Brief entry *42*
Dothers, Anne
  See Chess, Victoria (Dickerson)
Dotlich, Rebecca Kai 1951- *182*
Dottig
  See Grider, Dorothy
Dotts, Maryann J. 1933- *35*
Doty, Jean Slaughter 1929- *28*
Doty, Roy 1922- *28*
Doubtfire, Dianne (Abrams) 1918- *29*
Doucet, Sharon Arms 1951- *144*
  Autobiography Feature *144*
  Earlier sketch in SATA 125
Dougherty, Charles 1922- *18*
Dougherty, Terri (L.) 1964- *146*
Doughty, Rebecca 1955- *174*
Douglas, Allen *223*
Douglas, Blaise 1960- *101*
Douglas, Carole Nelson 1944- *73*
Douglas, Garry
  See Kilworth, Garry
Douglas, James McM.
  See Griffin, W. E. B.
Douglas, Kathryn
  See Ewing, Kathryn
Douglas, Leonard
  See Bradbury, Ray
Douglas, Lola
  See Zeises, Lara M.
Douglas, Marjory Stoneman 1890-1998 .... *10*
Douglas, Michael
  See Crichton, Michael
Douglas, Michael
  See Bright, Robert Sr.)
Douglas, Shirley Stewart
  See Tepper, Sheri S.
Douglass, Barbara 1930- *40*
Douglass, Frederick 1817(?)-1895 .... *29*

Douglass, Keith
  See Cunningham, Chet
Douty, Esther M(orris) 1909-1978 .... *8*
  Obituary *23*
Dow, Emily R. 1904-1987 .... *10*
Dow, Vicki
  See McVey, Vicki
Dowd, John David 1945- *78*
Dowd, Siobhan 1960-2007 .... *204*
Dowdell, Dorothy (Florence) Karns 1910- ... *12*
Dowden, Anne Ophelia Todd 1907-2007 .... *7*
  Obituary *180*
  See also SAAS 10
Dowdey, Landon Gerald 1923- *11*
Dowdy, Mrs. Regera
  See Gorey, Edward (St. John)
Dowell, Frances O'Roark 1964- *205*
  Earlier sketch in SATA 157
Dower, Laura 1967- *185*
Dowling, Terry 1947- *101*
Downard, Barry 1956- *202*
Downer, Ann 1960- *155*
Downer, Marion 1892(?)-1971 .... *25*
Downes, Belinda 1962- *180*
Downey, Fairfax D(avis) 1893-1990 .... *3*
  Obituary *66*
Downey, Lisa *214*
Downey, Lynn 1961- *185*
Downham, Jenny 1964- *192*
Downie, John 1931- *87*
Downie, Mary Alice 1934- *171*
  Earlier sketches in SATA 13, 87
Downie, Mary Alice Dawe
  See Downie, Mary Alice
Downing, David A(lmon) 1958- *84*
Downing, Johnette *184*
Downing, Julie 1956- *148*
  Earlier sketch in SATA 81
Downing, Paula E. 1951- *80*
Downing, Warwick
  See Downing, Wick
Downing, Wick 1931- *138*
Dowswell, Paul 1957- *184*
Doyle, A. Conan
  See Doyle, Sir Arthur Conan
Doyle, Sir Arthur Conan 1859-1930 .... *24*
  See also CLR 106
Doyle, Brian 1935- *156*
  Earlier sketches in SATA 67, 104
  See also CLR 22
  See also SAAS 16
Doyle, Charlotte 1937- *178*
  Earlier sketch in SATA 94
Doyle, Charlotte Lackner
  See Doyle, Charlotte
Doyle, Conan
  See Doyle, Sir Arthur Conan
Doyle, Debra 1952- *165*
  Earlier sketch in SATA 105
Doyle, Donovan
  See Boegehold, Betty (Doyle)
Doyle, Eugenie 1952- *225*
Doyle, John
  See Graves, Robert
Doyle, Malachy 1954- *165*
  Earlier sketch in SATA 120
  See also CLR 83
Doyle, Richard 1824-1883 .... *21*
Doyle, Sir A. Conan
  See Doyle, Sir Arthur Conan
Dr. A
  See Asimov, Isaac
  and Silverstein, Alvin
  and Silverstein, Virginia B.
Dr. Alphabet
  See Morice, Dave
Dr. Fred
  See Bortz, Alfred B(enjamin)
Dr. Laura
  See Schlessinger, Laura (Catherine)

Dr. Seuss 1904-1991 .... *100*
  Obituary *67*
  Earlier sketches in SATA *1, 28, 75*
  See also CLR *100*
Dr. Zed
  See Penrose, Gordon
Drabble, Margaret 1939- *48*
Drackett, Phil(ip Arthur) 1922- *53*
Draco, F.
  See Davis, Julia
Dracup, Angela 1943- *74*
Dragisic, Patricia *116*
Dragonwagon, Crescent 1952- *186*
  Autobiography Feature *186*
  Earlier sketches in SATA *11, 41, 75, 133*
  See also SAAS *14*
Drake, David 1945- *85*
Drake, David Allen
  See Drake, David
Drake, Frank
  See Hamilton, Charles (Harold St. John)
Drake, Jane 1954- *82*
Drake, Salamanda
  See Barlow, Steve
Drakeford, Dale B 1952- *113*
Drakeford, Dale Benjamin
  See Drakeford, Dale B
Draper, Hastings
  See Jeffries, Roderic
Draper, Sharon
  See Draper, Sharon M.
Draper, Sharon M. 1948- *195*
  Autobiography Feature *146*
  Earlier sketches in SATA *98, 146*
  See also CLR *57*
Draper, Sharon Mills
  See Draper, Sharon M.
Drapier, M. B.
  See Swift, Jonathan
Drawson, Blair 1943- *126*
  Earlier sketch in SATA *17*
Dray, Matt 1967- *177*
Dray, Matthew Frederick
  See Dray, Matt
Dresang, Eliza (Carolyn Timberlake) 1941- . *19*
Drescher, Henrik 1955- *172*
  Earlier sketches in SATA *67, 105*
  See also CLR *20*
Drescher, Joan E(lizabeth) 1939- *137*
  Earlier sketch in SATA *30*
Dressen-McQueen, Stacey *191*
Dreves, Veronica R. 1927-1986
  Obituary *50*
Drew, Patricia 1938- *15*
Drew, Patricia Mary
  See Drew, Patricia
Drewery, Mary 1918- *6*
Drewery, Melanie 1970- *165*
Drewry, Henry N(athaniel) 1924- *138*
Dreyer, Ellen *177*
Drial, J. E.
  See Laird, Jean E(louise)
Drimmer, Frederick 1916-2000 .... *60*
  Obituary *124*
Driskill, J. Lawrence 1920- *90*
Driskill, Larry
  See Driskill, J. Lawrence
Driving Hawk, Virginia
  See Sneve, Virginia Driving Hawk
Dron, Laura
  See Matthews, L. S.
Dronzek, Laura *199*
Drucker, Malka 1945- *214*
  Brief entry *29*
  Earlier sketches in SATA *39, 111*
Drucker, Olga Levy 1927- *79*
Druitt, Tobias
  See Purkiss, Diane
Drummond, Allan 1957- *209*
Drummond, Karona 1965- *220*
Drummond, V(iolet) H(ilda) 1911-2000 .... *6*

Drummond, Walter
  See Silverberg, Robert
Drury, Clare Marie
  See Hoskyns-Abrahall, Clare (Constance Drury)
Drury, Roger W(olcott) 1914-1996 .... *15*
Druse, Eleanor
  See King, Stephen
Dryden, Pamela
  See St. John, Nicole
D.T., Hughes
  See Hughes, Dean
Duane, Diane (Elizabeth) 1952- *145*
  Brief entry *46*
  Earlier sketches in SATA *58, 95*
Dubanevich, Arlene 1950- *56*
Dubelaar, Thea 1947- *60*
Dubin, Jill *205*
du Blane, Daphne
  See Groom, Arthur William
Duble, Kathleen Benner 1958- *164*
Dubois, Claude K. 1960- *196*
DuBois, Rochelle Holt 1946- *41*
Du Bois, Shirley Graham 1907(?)-1977 .... *24*
  See Graham, Shirley
Du Bois, W. E. B. 1868-1963 .... *42*
Du Bois, William Edward Burghardt
  See Du Bois, W. E. B.
du Bois, William Pene
  See Pene du Bois, William (Sherman)
Duboise, Novella 1911-1999 .... *88*
Dubosarsky, Ursula 1961- *193*
  Earlier sketches in SATA *107, 147*
DuBose, LaRocque (Russ) 1926- *2*
Dubrovin, Vivian 1931- *139*
  Earlier sketch in SATA *65*
DuBurke, Randy *224*
  Earlier sketch in SATA *172*
Ducey, Jean Sparks 1915- *93*
Duchacek, Ivo D(uka) 1913-1988
  Obituary *55*
Du Chaillu, Paul (Belloni) 1835(?)-1903 ..... *26*
Ducharme, Dede Fox
  See Ducharme, Lilian Fox
Ducharme, Lilian Fox 1950- *122*
Ducornet, Erica 1943- *7*
Ducornet, Rikki
  See Ducornet, Erica
Duddle, Jonny 1971(?)- *219*
Duden, Jane 1947- *136*
Duder, Tessa 1940- *117*
  Earlier sketch in SATA *80*
  See also CLR *43*
  See also SAAS *23*
Dudley, Helen
  See Hope Simpson, Jacynth
Dudley, Martha Ward 1909(?)-1985
  Obituary *45*
Dudley, Nancy
  See Cole, Lois Dwight
Dudley, Robert
  See Baldwin, James
Dudley, Ruth H(ubbell) 1905-2001 .... *11*
Dudley-Smith, T.
  See Trevor, Elleston
Due, Linnea A. 1948- *64*
Dueck, Adele 1955- *97*
Dueland, Joy V(ivian) *27*
Duerr, Gisela 1968- *89*
Duey, Kathleen 1950- *199*
  Earlier sketch in SATA *132*
Dufault, Joseph Ernest Nephtali
  See James, Will(iam Roderick)
Duff, Annis (James) 1904(?)-1986
  Obituary *49*
Duff, Maggie
  See Duff, Margaret K(app)
Duff, Margaret K(app) 1916-2003 .... *37*
  Obituary *144*
Duffey, Betsy (Byars) 1953- *131*
  Earlier sketch in SATA *80*

Duffie, Charles 1960- *144*
Duffield, Katy S. 1961- *147*
Duffy, Carol Ann 1955- *165*
  Earlier sketch in SATA *95*
Duffy Stone, Heather *217*
Dugan, Jack
  See Griffin, W. E. B.
Dugan, John Kevin
  See Griffin, W. E. B.
Dugan, Karen *202*
Dugan, Karen M.
  See Dugan, Karen
Dugan, Michael (Gray) 1947- *15*
Duggan, Alfred Leo 1903-1964 .... *25*
Duggan, Maurice 1922-1974 .... *40*
  Obituary *30*
Duggan, Maurice Noel
  See Duggan, Maurice
Dugger, Elizabeth L.
  See Kanell, Beth
Duggleby, John 1952- *94*
Dugin, Andrej 1955- *77*
Dugina, Olga 1964- *77*
du Jardin, Rosamond Neal 1902-1963 .... *2*
Duka, Ivo
  See Duchacek, Ivo D(uka)
Duke, Kate 1956- *192*
  Earlier sketches in SATA *90, 148*
  See also CLR *51*
Duke, Will
  See Gault, William Campbell
Dulac, Edmund 1882-1953 .... *19*
Dumas, Alexandre (pere) 1802-1870 .... *18*
  See also CLR *134*
Dumas, Jacqueline 1946- *55*
Dumas, Philippe 1940- *119*
  Earlier sketch in SATA *52*
du Maurier, Daphne 1907-1989 .... *27*
  Obituary *60*
Dumbleton, Mike 1948- *206*
  Earlier sketches in SATA *73, 124*
Dunbar, Fiona 1961- *167*
Dunbar, Joyce 1944- *213*
  Earlier sketches in SATA *76, 112, 162*
Dunbar, Paul Laurence 1872-1906 .... *34*
Dunbar, Polly 1980(?)- *211*
  Earlier sketch in SATA *181*
Dunbar, Robert E(verett) 1926- *32*
Duncan, Alexandra
  See Moore, Ishbel (Lindsay)
Duncan, Alice Faye 1967- *168*
  Earlier sketch in SATA *95*
Duncan, Gregory
  See McClintock, Marshall
Duncan, Jane
  See Cameron, Elizabeth Jane
Duncan, Julia K.
  See Benson, Mildred
Duncan, Lois 1934- *219*
  Autobiography Feature *141*
  Earlier sketches in SATA *1, 36, 75, 133, 141*
  See also CLR *129*
  See also SAAS *2*
Duncan, Norman 1871-1916
  See YABC *1*
Duncan, Terence
  See Nolan, William F.
Duncombe, Frances (Riker) 1900-1994 .... *25*
  Obituary *82*
Dungy, Anthony
  See Dungy, Tony
Dungy, Tony 1955- *206*
Dunham, Montrew 1919- *162*
Dunham, Montrew Goetz
  See Dunham, Montrew
Dunkle, Clare B. 1964- *223*
  Earlier sketch in SATA *155*
Dunlap, Julie 1958- *84*
Dunleavy, Deborah 1951- *133*
Dunlop, Agnes M. R. (?)-1982 .... *87*

Dunlop, Eileen (Rhona) 1938- 76
  Earlier sketch in SATA 24
  See also SAAS 12
Dunmore, Helen 1952- 201
Dunn, Anne M. 1940- 107
Dunn, Carolyn 1965- 208
Dunn, Harvey T(homas) 1884-1952 34
Dunn, Herb
  See Gutman, Dan
Dunn, John M. (III) 1949- 93
Dunn, Judy
  See Spangenberg, Judith Dunn
Dunn, Mary Lois 1930- 6
Dunnahoo, Terry Janson 1927- 7
Dunne, Jeanette 1952- 72
Dunne, Kathleen 1933- 126
Dunne, Marie
  See Clark, Ann Nolan
Dunne, Mary Collins 1914- 11
Dunne, Mary Jo
  See Dunne, Mary Collins
Dunnett, Kaitlyn
  See Emerson, Kathy Lynn
Dunnett, Margaret (Rosalind) 1909-1977 42
Dunnick, Regan 178
Dunphy, Madeleine 1962- 219
Dunrea, Olivier 1953- 160
  Brief entry 46
  Earlier sketches in SATA 59, 118
Dunrea, Olivier Jean-Paul Dominique
  See Dunrea, Olivier
Dunstan Muller, Rachel 221
Dunton, Dorothy 1912- 92
Dupasquier, Philippe 1955- 151
  Earlier sketch in SATA 86
duPont, Lindsay 207
duPont, Lindsay Harper
  See duPont, Lindsay
DuPrau, Jeanne 1944- 215
  Earlier sketch in SATA 144
Dupuy, T(revor) N(evitt) 1916-1995 4
  Obituary 86
DuQuette, Keith 1960- 155
  Earlier sketch in SATA 90
Duran, Gloria 1924- 171
Duran, Gloria Bradley
  See Duran, Gloria
Duranceau, Suzanne 1952- 162
Durand, Delphine 1971- 200
Durand, Hallie 1964(?)- 216
Durango, Julia 1967- 215
  Earlier sketch in SATA 173
Durant, Alan 1958- 214
  Earlier sketches in SATA 121, 165
Durant, John 1902- 27
Durbin, William 1951- 174
  Earlier sketch in SATA 143
Durell, Ann 1930- 66
Durkee, Sarah 173
Durney, Ryan 205
Durrant, Lynda 1954- 212
  Earlier sketches in SATA 96, 148
Durrant, Sabine 210
Durrell, Gerald (Malcolm) 1925-1995 8
  Obituary 84
Durrell, Julie 1955- 94
Durrett, Deanne 1940- 144
  Earlier sketch in SATA 92
Durst, Sarah Beth 1974- 203
Dusikova, Maja 1946- 223
Du Soe, Robert C. 1892-1958
  See YABC 2
Dussling, Jennifer 1970- 143
  Earlier sketch in SATA 96
DuTemple, Lesley A. 1952- 113
Dutton, Sandra 191
Dutz
  See Davis, Mary Octavia
Duval, Katherine
  See James, Elizabeth
Duval, Kathy 1946- 181

Duvall, Aimee
  See Thurlo, Aimee
  and Thurlo, David
Duvall, Evelyn Millis 1906- 9
Duvall, Jill D. 1932- 102
Duvall, Jill Donovan
  See Duvall, Jill D.
Duvoisin, Roger (Antoine) 1904-1980 30
  Obituary 23
  Earlier sketch in SATA 2
  See also CLR 23
Dwiggins, Don(ald J.) 1913-1988 4
  Obituary 60
Dwight, Allan
  See Cole, Lois Dwight
Dwyer, Deanna
  See Koontz, Dean
Dwyer, K.R.
  See Koontz, Dean
Dyck, Peter J. 1914- 75
Dyer, Alan 1953- 218
Dyer, James (Frederick) 1934- 37
Dyer, Jane 191
  Earlier sketch in SATA 147
Dyer, Sarah 1978- 212
Dyer, Sarah L.
  See Dyer, Sarah
Dyess, John (Foster) 1939- 76
Dygard, Thomas J. 1931-1996 97
  Obituary 92
  Earlier sketch in SATA 24
  See also SAAS 15
Dyke, John 1935- 35

E

E. V. L.
  See Lucas, E(dward) V(errall)
Eagar, Frances (Elisabeth Stuart)
  1940-1978 11
  Obituary 55
Eager, Edward (McMaken) 1911-1964 17
  See also CLR 43
Eager, George 1921- 56
Eager, George B.
  See Eager, George
Eagle, Ellen 1953- 61
Eagle, Kin
  See Adlerman, Daniel (Ezra)
  and Adlerman, Kimberly M(arie)
Eagle, Mike 1942- 11
Eamer, Claire 1947- 222
Earle, Olive L(ydia) 1888-1982 7
Earle, William
  See Johns, W(illiam) E(arle)
Earls, Nick 1963- 156
  Earlier sketch in SATA 95
Early, Jack
  See Scoppettone, Sandra
Early, Jon
  See Johns, W(illiam) E(arle)
Early, Margaret 1951- 72
Earnest, Peter 1934- 222
Earnshaw, Brian 1929- 17
Earnshaw, Micky 1939- 88
Earnshaw, Spencer Wright
  See Earnshaw, Micky
Easley, MaryAnn 94
Eason, Alethea 1957- 197
East, Jacqueline 224
Eastman, Charles A(lexander) 1858-1939
  See YABC 1
Eastman, P(hilip) D(ey) 1909-1986 33
  Obituary 46
Easton, Kelly 1960- 192
  Earlier sketch in SATA 141
Eastwick, Ivy (Ethel) O(live) 3
Eaton, Anne T(haxter) 1881-1971 32
Eaton, Anthony 1971- 167

Eaton, George L.
  See Verral, Charles Spain
Eaton, Janet
  See Givens, Janet E(aton)
Eaton, Jeanette 1886-1968 24
Eaton, Maxwell III 1981- 199
Eaton, Tom 1940- 22
Ebbeler, Jeff
  See Ebbeler, Jeffrey
Ebbeler, Jeffrey 1974- 206
Ebbitt, Carolyn Q. 1974(?)- 225
Ebel, Alex 1927- 11
Eber, Dorothy (Margaret) Harley 1930- 27
Eberhart, Sheri S.
  See Tepper, Sheri S.
Eberle, Irmengarde 1898-1979 2
  Obituary 23
Eble, Diane 1956- 74
Eboch, Chris 113
Eccles Williams, Ferelith 1920- 22
Echeverria-Bis, Olivia 217
Echeverria Gyorkos, Charmaine 216
Echlin, Kim 1955- 166
Eckblad, Edith Berven 1923- 23
Ecke, Wolfgang 1927-1983
  Obituary 37
Eckert, Allan W. 1931- 91
  Brief entry 27
  Earlier sketch in SATA 29
  See also SAAS 21
Eckert, Horst 1931- 72
  Earlier sketch in SATA 8
  See also CLR 26
Ecklar, Julia (Marie) 1964- 112
Eddings, David 1931-2009 91
Eddings, David Carroll
  See Eddings, David
Ede, Janina 1937- 33
Edell, Celeste 12
Edelman, Lily (Judith) 1915-1981 22
Edelson, Edward 1932- 51
Edens, Cooper 1945- 166
  Earlier sketches in SATA 49, 112
Edens, (Bishop) David 1926- 39
Edey, Maitland A(rmstrong) 1910-1992 25
  Obituary 71
Edgerton, Perky 196
Edgeworth, Maria 1768-1849 21
  See also CLR 153
Edgson, Alison 211
Edgy, Wardore
  See Gorey, Edward (St. John)
Edison, Theodore
  See Stratemeyer, Edward L.
Edler, Tim(othy) 1948- 56
Edmiston, Jim 1948- 80
Edmonds, I(vy) G(ordon) 1917- 8
Edmonds, Walter D(umaux) 1903-1998 27
  Obituary 99
  Earlier sketch in SATA 1
  See also SAAS 4
Edmund, Sean
  See Pringle, Laurence
Edsall, Marian (Stickney) 1920- 8
Edwards, Al
  See Nourse, Alan E(dward)
Edwards, Anne 1927- 35
Edwards, Audrey 1947- 52
  Brief entry 31
Edwards, Becky (Jane) 1966- 125
Edwards, Bertram
  See Edwards, Herbert Charles
Edwards, Bronwen Elizabeth
  See Rose, Wendy
Edwards, Cecile Pepin 1916- 25
Edwards, David 1962- 198
Edwards, Dorothy 1914-1982 88
  Obituary 31
  Earlier sketch in SATA 4
Edwards, F. E.
  See Nolan, William F.

Edwards, Frank B. 1952- 93
Edwards, Gunvor 32
Edwards, Harvey 1929- 5
Edwards, Hazel (Eileen) 1945- 135
Edwards, Herbert Charles 1912- 12
Edwards, Jane Campbell 1932- 10
Edwards, Julia
  See Stratemeyer, Edward L.
Edwards, Julie
  See Andrews, Julie
Edwards, Julie Andrews
  See Andrews, Julie
Edwards, June
  See Bhatia, Jamunadevi
Edwards, Linda Strauss 1948- 49
  Brief entry 42
Edwards, Margaret (Alexander) 1902-1988
  Obituary 56
Edwards, Michelle 1955- 152
  Earlier sketch in SATA 70
Edwards, Monica le Doux Newton
  1912-1998 12
Edwards, Olwen
  See Gater, Dilys
Edwards, Page (Lawrence, Jr.) 1941-1999 ... 59
Edwards, Pamela Duncan 189
Edwards, R. T.
  See Goulart, Ron
Edwards, Sally (Cary) 1929- 7
Edwards, Samuel
  See Gerson, Noel Bertram
Edwards, Wallace 1957(?)- 170
Edwardson, Debby Dahl 223
Eeckhout, Emmanuelle 1976- 208
Egan, E. W. 1922- 35
Egan, Edward Welstead
  See Egan, E. W.
Egan, Kerry 175
Egan, Lorraine Hopping 1960- 134
  Earlier sketch in SATA 91
Egan, Tim 1957- 191
  Earlier sketches in SATA 89, 155
Egermeier, Elsie E(milie) 1890-1986 65
Eggenberger, David 1918- 6
Eggleston, Edward 1837-1902 27
Egielski, Richard 1952- 220
  Earlier sketches in SATA 11, 49, 106, 163
Egypt, Ophelia Settle 1903-1984 16
  Obituary 38
Ehlert, Lois 1934- 172
  Earlier sketches in SATA 35, 69, 128
  See also CLR 28
Ehlert, Lois Jane
  See Ehlert, Lois
Ehling, Katalin Olah 1941- 93
Ehrenberg, Pamela 1972- 219
Ehrenfreund, Norbert 1921- 86
Ehrenhaft, Daniel 1970- 185
Ehrenhaft, Daniel Parker
  See Ehrenhaft, Daniel
Ehrhardt, Karen 1963- 184
Ehrlich, Amy 1942- 217
  Earlier sketches in SATA 25, 65, 96, 132
Ehrlich, Bettina Bauer 1903-1985 1
Ehrlich, Fred 205
Ehrlich, Fred M.D.
  See Ehrlich, Fred
Ehrlich, H. M.
  See Ziefert, Harriet
Eichenberg, Fritz 1901-1990 50
  Earlier sketch in SATA 9
Eichler, Margrit 1942- 35
Eichner, James A. 1927- 4
Eidson, Thomas 1944- 112
Eifert, Virginia (Louise) S(nider) 1911-1966 . 2
Eige, (Elizabeth) Lillian 1915- 65
Eiken, J. Melia 1967- 125
Einhorn, Edward 1970- 204
Einsel, Naiad 10
Einsel, Walter 1926- 10
Einzig, Susan 1922- 43

Eiseman, Alberta 1925- 15
Eisenberg, Azriel (Louis) 1903-1985 12
Eisenberg, Lisa 1949- 155
  Brief entry 50
  Earlier sketch in SATA 57
Eisenberg, Phyllis Rose 1924- 41
Eisner, Vivienne
  See Margolis, Vivienne
Eisner, Will 1917-2005 165
  Earlier sketch in SATA 31
Eisner, William Erwin
  See Eisner, Will
Eitzen, Allan 1928- 9
Eitzen, Ruth (Carper) 1924- 9
Ekwensi, C. O. D.
  See Ekwensi, Cyprian
Ekwensi, Cyprian 1921-2007 66
Ekwensi, Cyprian Odiatu Duaka
  See Ekwensi, Cyprian
Elam, Richard M(ace, Jr.) 1920- 9
Elborn, Andrew
  See Clements, Andrew
  and Clements, Andrew
Elboz, Stephen 1956- 152
Eldin, Peter 1939- 154
Eldon, Kathy 1946- 107
Eldridge, Marion 199
Eley, Robin 219
Elfman, Blossom 1925- 8
Elgin, Kathleen 1923- 39
Elia
  See Lamb, Charles
Eliot, A. D.
  See Jewett, Sarah Orne
Eliot, Alice
  See Jewett, Sarah Orne
Eliot, Anne
  See Cole, Lois Dwight
Eliot, Dan
  See Silverberg, Robert
Elish, Dan 1960- 204
  Earlier sketches in SATA 68, 129
Elisha, Ron 1951- 104
Elisofon, Eliot 1911-1973
  Obituary 21
Elkeles, Simone 1970- 187
Elkin, Benjamin 1911-1995 3
Elkins, Dov Peretz 1937- 5
Ellacott, S(amuel) E(rnest) 1911- 19
Elleman, Barbara 1934- 147
Ellen, Jaye
  See Nixon, Joan Lowery
Eller, Scott
  See Holinger, William (Jacques)
  and Shepard, Jim
Ellery, Amanda 216
Ellestad, Myrvin
  See Ellestad, Myrvin H.
Ellestad, Myrvin H. 1921- 120
Elliot, Bruce
  See Field, Edward
Elliot, David 1952- 208
  Earlier sketch in SATA 122
Elliott, Bruce
  See Field, Edward
Elliott, David 1947- 201
  Earlier sketch in SATA 163
Elliott, Don
  See Silverberg, Robert
Elliott, Elizabeth Shippen Green
  See Green, Elizabeth Shippen
Elliott, Janice 1931-1995 119
Elliott, Joey
  See Houk, Randy
Elliott, Laura Malone 1957- 197
Elliott, L.M.
  See Elliott, Laura Malone
Elliott, Louise 111
Elliott, Mark 1949- 210
Elliott, Odette 1939- 75
Elliott, Patricia 1946- 176

Elliott, Sarah M(cCarn) 1930- 14
Elliott, (Robert) Scott 1970- 153
Elliott, William
  See Bradbury, Ray
Elliott, Zetta 206
Ellis, (Mary) Amabel (Nassau Strachey)
  Williams
  See Williams-Ellis, (Mary) Amabel (Nassau
  Strachey)
Ellis, Ann Dee 210
Ellis, Anyon
  See Rowland-Entwistle, (Arthur) Theodore
  (Henry)
Ellis, Carson 1975- 190
Ellis, Carson Friedman
  See Ellis, Carson
Ellis, Deborah 1960- 187
  Earlier sketch in SATA 129
Ellis, E. S.
  See Ellis, Edward S.
Ellis, Edward S. 1840-1916
  See YABC 1
Ellis, Edward Sylvester
  See Ellis, Edward S.
Ellis, Ella Thorp 1928- 127
  Earlier sketch in SATA 7
  See also SAAS 9
Ellis, Harry Bearse 1921-2004 9
Ellis, Herbert
  See Wilson, Lionel
Ellis, Mel(vin Richard) 1912-1984 7
  Obituary 39
Ellis, Richard 1938- 130
Ellis, Sarah 1952- 179
  Earlier sketches in SATA 68, 131
  See also CLR 42
Ellison, Chris 196
Ellison, Elizabeth Stow 1970- 209
Ellison, Emily 114
Ellison, Lucile Watkins 1907(?)-1979 50
  Obituary 22
Ellison, Virginia H(owell) 1910- 4
Ellsberg, Edward 1891-1983 7
Ellsworth, Loretta 1954- 199
Ellsworth, Mary Ellen (Tressel) 1940- 146
Ellwand, David 1965(?)- 213
Elmer, Robert 1958- 154
  Earlier sketch in SATA 99
Elmore, (Carolyn) Patricia 1933- 38
  Brief entry 35
El-Moslimany, Ann P(axton) 1937- 90
Elschner, Geraldine 1954- 183
Elspeth
  See Bragdon, Elspeth MacDuffie
Elster, Jean Alicia 1953- 150
Elting, Mary 1906- 88
  Earlier sketch in SATA 2
  See also SAAS 20
Elvgren, Jennifer Riesmeyer 179
Elwart, Joan Potter 1927- 2
Elwell, Peter 220
Elwood, Ann 1931- 55
  Brief entry 52
Elwood, Roger 1943-2007 58
Ely, Lesley 212
Elya, Susan Middleton 1955- 202
  Earlier sketches in SATA 106, 159
Elzbieta 88
Ember, Kathi 190
Emberley, Barbara A. 1932- 146
  Earlier sketches in SATA 8, 70
  See also CLR 5
Emberley, Barbara Anne
  See Emberley, Barbara A.
Emberley, Ed 1931- 146
  Earlier sketches in SATA 8, 70
  See also CLR 81
Emberley, Edward Randolph
  See Emberley, Ed
Emberley, Michael 1960- 189
  Earlier sketches in SATA 34, 80, 119

Emberley, Rebecca 1958- 218
Embry, Margaret Jacob 1919-1975 5
Emecheta, Buchi 1944- 66
  See also CLR *158*
Emecheta, Florence Onye Buchi
  See Emecheta, Buchi
Emerson, Alice B.
  See Benson, Mildred
Emerson, Kate
  See Emerson, Kathy Lynn
Emerson, Kathy Lynn 1947- 63
Emerson, Kevin 209
Emerson, Ru 1944- 107
  Earlier sketch in SATA *70*
Emerson, Sally 1952- 111
Emerson, William K(eith) 1925- 25
Emert, Phyllis R. 1947- 93
Emert, Phyllis Raybin
  See Emert, Phyllis R.
Emery, Anne (McGuigan) 1907- 33
  Earlier sketch in SATA *1*
Emmens, Carol Ann 1944- 39
Emmett, Jonathan 1965- 188
  Earlier sketch in SATA *138*
Emmons, Della (Florence) Gould 1890-1983
  Obituary 39
Emory, Jerry 1957- 96
Emrich, Duncan (Black Macdonald)
  1908-1970(?) 11
Emshwiller, Carol 1921- 174
  Autobiography Feature 174
Emshwiller, Carol Fries
  See Emshwiller, Carol
Emslie, M. L.
  See Simpson, Myrtle L(illias)
Ende, Michael (Andreas Helmuth)
  1929-1995 130
  Brief entry 42
  Obituary 86
  Earlier sketch in SATA *61*
  See also CLR *138*
Enderle, Dotti 1954- 203
  Earlier sketch in SATA *145*
Enderle, Judith (Ann) Ross 1941- 89
  Autobiography Feature 114
  Earlier sketch in SATA *38*
  See also SAAS *26*
Endle, Kate 207
Enell, Trinka (Gochenour) 1951- 79
Enfield, Carrie
  See Smith, Susan Vernon
Engdahl, Sylvia Louise 1933- 4
  Autobiography Feature 122
  See also CLR *2*
  See also SAAS *5*
Engel, Diana 1947- 70
Engelbreit, Mary 1952- 169
Engelhart, Margaret S. 1924- 59
Engelmann, Kim (V.) 1959- 87
England, George Allan 1877-1936 102
Englart, Mindi Rose 1965- 146
Engle, Eloise
  See Paananen, Eloise (Katherine)
Engle, Margarita 1951- 193
Englebert, Victor 1933- 8
English, James W(ilson) 1915- 37
English, Karen 202
Engstrom, Elizabeth 1951- 110
Enright, D(ennis) J(oseph) 1920-2002 25
  Obituary 140
Enright, Dominique 194
Enright, Elizabeth (Wright) 1909-1968 9
  See also CLR *4*
Ensor, Barbara 180
Ensor, Robert (T.) 1922- 93
Enthoven, Sam 1974- 187
Entwistle, (Arthur) Theodore (Henry) Rowland
  See Rowland-Entwistle, (Arthur) Theodore
  (Henry)
Enys, Sarah L.
  See Sloggett, Nellie

Epanya, Christian A(rthur Kingue) 1956- 91
Ephraim, Shelly S(chonebaum) 1952- 97
Ephron, Delia 1944- 197
  Brief entry 50
  Earlier sketch in SATA *65*
Epler, Doris M. 1928- 73
Epp, Margaret A(gnes) 1913- 20
Eppenstein, Louise (Kohn) 1892-1987
  Obituary 54
Epple, Anne Orth 1927- 20
Epstein, Anne Merrick 1931- 20
Epstein, Beryl 1910- 31
  Earlier sketch in SATA *1*
  See also CLR *26*
  See also SAAS *17*
Epstein, Beryl M. Williams
  See Epstein, Beryl
Epstein, Perle S(herry) 1938- 27
Epstein, Rachel S. 1941- 102
Epstein, Samuel 1909-2000 31
  Earlier sketch in SATA *1*
  See also CLR *26*
  See also SAAS *17*
Erdman, Loula Grace 1905(?)-1976 1
Erdoes, Richard 1912- 33
  Brief entry 28
Erdogan, Buket 187
Erdrich, Karen Louise
  See Erdrich, Louise
Erdrich, Louise 1954- 141
  Earlier sketch in SATA *94*
Erickson, Betty J. 1923- 97
Erickson, Betty Jean
  See Erickson, Betty J.
Erickson, John R. 1943- 136
  Earlier sketch in SATA *70*
Erickson, Jon 1948- 141
Erickson, Phoebe 59
Erickson, Russell E(verett) 1932- 27
Erickson, Sabra Rollins 1912-1995 35
Erickson, Walter
  See Fast, Howard
Ericson, Walter
  See Fast, Howard
Ericsson, Jennifer A. 170
Erikson, Mel 1937- 31
Eriksson, Eva 1949- 207
Ering, Timothy Basil 176
Erlanger, Baba
  See Trahey, Jane
Erlbach, Arlene 1948- 160
  Earlier sketches in SATA *78, 115*
Erlbruch, Wolf 1948- 181
Erlich, Lillian (Feldman) 1910-1983 10
Erlings, Fridrik 1962- 196
Erlingsson, Friorik
  See Erlings, Fridrik
Ermatinger, James W. 1959- 170
Ernest, William
  See Berkebile, Fred D(onovan)
Ernst, Kathleen
  See Ernst, Kathleen A.
Ernst, Kathleen A. 1959- 162
Ernst, Kathryn (Fitzgerald) 1942- 25
Ernst, Lisa Campbell 1957- 212
  Brief entry 44
  Earlier sketches in SATA *55, 95, 154*
Erskine, Kathryn 193
Ervin, Janet Halliday 1923- 4
Erwin, Will
  See Eisner, Will
Esbaum, Jill 213
  Earlier sketch in SATA *174*
Esbensen, Barbara J(uster) 1925-1996 97
  Brief entry 53
  Earlier sketch in SATA *62*
Eschbacher, Roger 160
Eschmeyer, R. E. 1898-1989 29
Escriva, Vivi 182

Eseki, Bruno
  See Mphahlele, Es'kia
Esekie, Bruno
  See Mphahlele, Es'kia
Eshmeyer, Reinhart Ernst
  See Eschmeyer, R. E.
Eskridge, Ann E. 1949- 84
Espeland, Pamela (Lee) 1951- 128
  Brief entry 38
  Earlier sketch in SATA *52*
Espinosa, Laura 203
Espinosa, Leo 203
Espriella, Don Manuel Alvarez
  See Southey, Robert
Espy, Willard R(ichardson) 1910-1999 38
  Obituary 113
Essakalli, Julie Klear 200
Essrig, Harry 1912- 66
Estep, Irene Compton 5
Esterl, Arnica 1933- 77
Estes, Eleanor (Ruth) 1906-1988 91
  Obituary 56
  Earlier sketch in SATA *7*
  See also CLR *70*
Estoril, Jean
  See Allan, Mabel Esther
Estrada, Pau 1961- 200
  Earlier sketch in SATA *74*
Etchemendy, Nancy 1952- 166
  Earlier sketch in SATA *38*
Etchemendy, Nancy Elise Howell
  See Etchemendy, Nancy
Etchison, Birdie L(ee) 1937- 38
Etchison, Craig 1945- 133
Etherington, Frank 1945- 58
Eton, Robert
  See Meynell, Laurence Walter
Ets, Marie Hall 1893-1984 2
  See also CLR *33*
Ettlinger, Doris 1950- 173
Eugnia, Maria 222
Eunson, (John) Dale 1904-2002 5
  Obituary 132
Evan, Frances Y. 1951- 167
Evanoff, Vlad 1916- 59
Evans, Cambria 1981- 178
Evans, Douglas 1953- 144
  Earlier sketch in SATA *93*
Evans, Eva (Knox) 1905-1998 27
Evans, Freddi Williams 1957- 211
  Earlier sketch in SATA *134*
Evans, Greg 1947- 143
  Earlier sketch in SATA *73*
Evans, Hubert Reginald 1892-1986 118
  Obituary 48
Evans, Katherine (Floyd) 1901-1964 5
Evans, Larry
  See Evans, Laurence Chubb
Evans, Laurence Chubb 1939- 88
Evans, Lawrence Watt
  See Watt-Evans, Lawrence
Evans, Leslie 1953- 214
Evans, Lezlie 180
Evans, Mari 1923- 10
Evans, Mark 19
Evans, Nancy 1950- 65
Evans, Nate 201
Evans, Patricia Healy
  See Carpenter, Patricia (Healy Evans)
Evans, (Alice) Pearl 1927- 83
Evans, Shane W. 189
Evans, Shirlee 1931- 58
Evans, Tabor
  See Cameron, Lou
  and Knott, William C(ecil, Jr.)
  and Wallmann, Jeffrey M(iner)
  and Whittington, Harry (Benjamin)
Evarts, Esther
  See Benson, Sally
Evarts, Hal G., (Jr.) 1915-1989 6

Everett, Gail
    See Hale, Arlene
Evernden, Margery 1916- 5
Eversole, Robyn 1971- 74
Eversole, Robyn H.
    See Eversole, Robyn
Eversole, Robyn Harbert
    See Eversole, Robyn
Evslin, Bernard 1922-1993 83
    Brief entry 28
    Obituary 77
    Earlier sketch in SATA 45
Ewart, Claire 1958- 145
    Earlier sketch in SATA 76
Ewart, Franzeska G. 1950- 205
Ewen, David 1907-1985 4
    Obituary 47
Ewing, Juliana (Horatia Gatty) 1841-1885 ... 16
    See also CLR 78
Ewing, Kathryn 1921- 20
Eyerly, Jeannette 1908-2008 86
    Obituary 196
    Earlier sketch in SATA 4
    See also SAAS 10
Eyerly, Jeannette Hyde
    See Eyerly, Jeannette
Eyre, Dorothy
    See McGuire, Leslie (Sarah)
Eyre, Frank 1910-1988
    Obituary 62
Eyre, Katherine Wigmore 1901-1970 26
Ezzell, Marilyn 1937- 42
    Brief entry 38

F

Fabe, Maxene 1943- 15
Faber, Doris (Greenberg) 1924- 78
    Earlier sketch in SATA 3
Faber, Harold 1919-2010 5
Fabre, Jean Henri (Casimir) 1823-1915 22
Fabry, Glenn 1961- 205
Facklam, Margaret
    See Thomas, Peggy
Facklam, Margery (Metz) 1927- 132
    Earlier sketches in SATA 20, 85
Fadden, David Kanietakeron 196
Fadiman, Clifton (Paul) 1904-1999 11
    Obituary 115
Fagan, Cary 1957- 186
Fagan, Deva 220
Fahs, Sophia Blanche Lyon 1876-1978 102
Failing, Barbara Larmon 182
Fain, Sarah 1971- 204
Fair, David 1952- 96
Fair, Sylvia 1933- 13
Fairfax-Lucy, Brian (Fulke Cameron-Ramsay)
    1898-1974 6
    Obituary 26
Fairfield, Flora
    See Alcott, Louisa May
Fairlie, Gerard 1899-1983
    Obituary 34
Fairman, Joan A(lexandra) 1935- 10
Faithfull, Gail 1936- 8
Falcone, L(ucy) M. 1951- 155
Falconer, Ian 1959- 179
    Earlier sketch in SATA 125
    See also CLR 146
Falconer, James
    See Kirkup, James
Falconer, Lee N.
    See May, Julian
Falkner, Brian 1962- 206
Falkner, Leonard 1900-1977 12
Fall, Andrew
    See Arthur, Robert, (Jr.)
Fall, Thomas
    See Snow, Donald Clifford

Faller, Regis 1968- 187
Falls, C(harles) B(uckles) 1874-1960 38
    Brief entry 27
Falstein, Louis 1909-1995 37
Falvey, David 1982- 222
Falwell, Cathryn 1952- 196
Fancher, Lou 1960- 177
Fanelli, Sara 1969- 126
    Earlier sketch in SATA 89
Fanning, Leonard M(ulliken) 1888-1967 5
Fantaskey, Beth 1965- 217
Faralla, Dana 1909- 9
Faralla, Dorothy W.
    See Faralla, Dana
Farb, Peter 1929-1980 12
    Obituary 22
Farber, Norma 1909-1984 75
    Obituary 38
    Earlier sketch in SATA 25
Fardell, John 1967- 195
Fardell, John William
    See Fardell, John
Faria, Rosana 213
Farish, Terry 1947- 146
    Earlier sketch in SATA 82
Farjeon, (Eve) Annabel 1919-2004 11
    Obituary 153
Farjeon, Eleanor 1881-1965 2
    See also CLR 34
Farley, Carol (J.) 1936- 137
    Earlier sketch in SATA 4
Farley, Terri 165
Farley, Walter (Lorimer) 1915-1989 132
    Earlier sketches in SATA 2, 43
Farlow, James O(rville, Jr.) 1951- 75
Farmer, Jacqueline 210
Farmer, Nancy 1941- 161
    Earlier sketches in SATA 79, 117
Farmer, Patti 1948- 79
Farmer, Penelope (Jane) 1939- 105
    Brief entry 39
    Earlier sketch in SATA 40
    See also CLR 8
    See also SAAS 22
Farmer, Peter 1950- 38
Farmer, Philip Jose
    See Farmer, Philip Jose
Farmer, Philip Jose 1918-2009 93
    Obituary 201
Farmer, Philipe Jos
    See Farmer, Philip Jose
Farnham, Burt
    See Clifford, Harold B(urton)
Farnsworth, Bill 1958- 186
    Earlier sketches in SATA 84, 135
Farooqi, Musharraf Ali 1968- 207
Farquhar, Margaret C(utting) 1905-1988 13
Farquharson, Alexander 1944- 46
Farquharson, Martha
    See Finley, Martha
Farr, Diana 82
    Earlier sketch in SATA 3
Farr, Finis (King) 1904-1982 10
Farr, Richard 1960- 209
Farrar, Jill
    See Morris, Jill
Farrar, Susan Clement 1917- 33
Farrell, Ben
    See Cebulash, Mel
Farrell, John 1951- 204
Farrell, Patrick
    See Odgers, Sally Farrell
Farrell, Sally
    See Odgers, Sally Farrell
Farrer, Vashti 167
Farrington, Benjamin 1891-1974
    Obituary 20
Farrington, S(elwyn) Kip, Jr. 1904-1983 20
Farris, Christine King 1927- 206
Farshtey, Greg(ory T.) 1965- 148

Farthing, Alison 1936- 45
    Brief entry 36
Farthing-Knight, Catherine 1933- 92
Fassler, Joan (Grace) 1931- 11
Fast, Howard 1914-2003 7
    Autobiography Feature 107
Fast, Howard Melvin
    See Fast, Howard
Fasulo, Michael 1963- 83
Fatchen, Max 1920- 84
    Earlier sketch in SATA 20
    See also SAAS 20
Fate, Marilyn
    See Collins, Paul
Father Goose
    See Ghigna, Charles
Fatigati, Evelyn 1948- 24
Fatigati, Frances Evelyn
    See Fatigati, Evelyn
Fatio, Louise 1904-1993 6
Fatus, Sophie 1957- 182
Faulhaber, Martha 1926- 7
Faulkner, Anne Irvin 1906- 23
Faulkner, Frank
    See Ellis, Edward S.
Faulkner, Nancy
    See Faulkner, Anne Irvin
Faulknor, Cliff(ord Vernon) 1913- 86
Favole, Robert J(ames) 1950- 125
Fax, Elton Clay 1909-1993 25
Faxon, Lavinia
    See Russ, Lavinia (Faxon)
Feagles, Anita M.
    See Feagles, Anita MacRae
Feagles, Anita MacRae 1927- 9
Feagles, Elizabeth
    See Day, Beth (Feagles)
Feague, Mildred H. 1915- 14
Fearing, Mark 1968- 224
Fearnley, Jan 1965- 205
    Earlier sketch in SATA 153
Fearrington, Ann (Peyton) 1945- 146
Fecher, Constance
    See Heaven, Constance (Christina)
Feder, Chris Welles 1938- 81
Feder, Harriet K. 1928- 73
Feder, Paula (Kurzband) 1935- 26
Federici, Debbie 1965- 175
Federici, Debbie Tanner
    See Federici, Debbie
Feelings, Muriel 1938- 16
    See also CLR 5
    See also SAAS 8
Feelings, Muriel Lavita Grey
    See Feelings, Muriel
Feelings, Thomas 1933-2003 69
    Obituary 148
    Earlier sketch in SATA 8
    See also CLR 58
    See also SAAS 19
Feelings, Tom
    See Feelings, Thomas
Fehler, Gene 1940- 201
    Earlier sketch in SATA 74
Fehrenbach, T(heodore) R(eed, Jr.) 1925- 33
Feiffer, Jules 1929- 201
    Earlier sketches in SATA 8, 61, 111, 157
Feiffer, Jules Ralph
    See Feiffer, Jules
Feiffer, Kate 1964- 206
    Earlier sketch in SATA 170
Feig, Barbara Krane 1937- 34
Feig, Paul 221
Feikema, Feike
    See Manfred, Frederick (Feikema)
Feil, Hila 1942- 12
Feilen, John
    See May, Julian
Feinberg, Barbara Jane 1938- 123
    Earlier sketch in SATA 58

Feinberg, Barbara Silberdick
  See Feinberg, Barbara Jane
Feinstein, John 1956- 195
  Earlier sketch in SATA *163*
Feldman, Anne (Rodgers) 1939- 19
Feldman, Elane 79
Feldman, Eve B. 221
Feldman, Jody 200
Felin, M. Sindy 194
Felix
  See Vincent, Felix
Fell, Derek 1939- 167
Fell, Derek John
  See Fell, Derek
Fellowes, Julian 1950- 198
Fellows, Muriel H. 10
Fellows, Stan 1957- 177
Fellows, Stanley
  See Fellows, Stan
Felsen, Henry Gregor 1916-1995 1
  See also SAAS *2*
Felstead, Cathie 1954- 192
Feltenstein, Arlene 1934- 119
Feltenstine, Arlene H.
  See Feltenstein, Arlene
Felton, Harold William 1902-1991 1
Felton, Ronald Oliver 1909- 3
Felts, Shirley 1934- 33
Felts, Susannah 1973- 214
Fenderson, Lewis H., Jr. 1907-1983 47
  Obituary 37
Fenner, Carol (Elizabeth) 1929-2002 89
  Obituary 132
  Earlier sketch in SATA *7*
  See also SAAS *24*
Fenner, Phyllis R(eid) 1899-1982 1
  Obituary 29
Fensham, Elizabeth 169
Fenten, Barbara D(oris) 1935- 26
Fenten, D(onald) X. 1932- 4
Fenton, Carroll Lane 1900-1969 5
Fenton, Edward 1917-1995 7
  Obituary 89
Fenton, Joe 213
Fenton, Mildred Adams 1899-1995 21
Fenwick, Patti
  See Grider, Dorothy
Feravolo, Rocco Vincent 1922- 10
Ferber, Brenda A. 1967- 184
Ferber, Edna 1887-1968 7
Fergus, Charles 114
Ferguson, Alane 1957- 182
  Earlier sketch in SATA *85*
Ferguson, Bob
  See Ferguson, Robert Bruce
Ferguson, Cecil 1931- 45
Ferguson, Peter 1968- 199
Ferguson, Robert Bruce 1927-2001 13
Ferguson, Sarah 1959- 180
  Earlier sketches in SATA *66, 110*
Ferguson, Sarah Margaret
  See Ferguson, Sarah
Ferguson, Walter (W.) 1930- 34
Fergusson, Erna 1888-1964 5
Fermi, Laura 1907-1977 6
  Obituary 28
Fern, Eugene A. 1919-1987 10
  Obituary 54
Fern, Tracey E. 202
Fernandes, Eugenie 1943- 205
  Earlier sketches in SATA *77, 139*
Fernandez, Laura 1960- 171
Ferraiolo, Jack D. 208
Ferrari, Maria 123
Ferrari, Michael 223
Ferrari, Michael J.
  See Ferrari, Michael
Ferreiro, Carmen 1958- 158
Ferrell, Nancy Warren 1932- 70
Ferrer, Isabel
  See Riu, Isabel Ferrer

Ferri, Giuliano 1965- 197
Ferrier, Lucy
  See Penzler, Otto
Ferris, Helen Josephine 1890-1969 21
Ferris, James Cody
  See McFarlane, Leslie
Ferris, Jean 1939- 202
  Brief entry 50
  Earlier sketches in SATA *56, 105, 149*
Ferris, Jeri Chase 1937- 84
Ferry, Charles 1927- 92
  Earlier sketch in SATA *43*
  See also CLR *34*
  See also SAAS *20*
Fetz, Ingrid 1915- 30
Feydy, Anne Lindbergh
  See Sapieyevski, Anne Lindbergh
Fiammenghi, Gioia 1929- 66
  Earlier sketch in SATA *9*
Fiarotta, Noel
  See Ficarotta, Noel
Fiarotta, Phyllis
  See Ficarotta, Phyllis
Ficarotta, Noel 1944- 15
Ficarotta, Phyllis 1942- 15
Fichter, George S. 1922-1993 7
Ficocelli, Elizabeth 189
Fidler, Kathleen (Annie) 1899-1980 87
  Obituary 45
  Earlier sketch in SATA *3*
Fiedler, Jean(nette Feldman) 4
Fiedler, Joseph Daniel 159
Fiedler, Lisa 185
Field, Dorothy 1944- 97
Field, Edward 1924- 109
  Earlier sketch in SATA *8*
Field, Elinor Whitney 1889-1980
  Obituary 28
Field, Eugene 1850-1895 16
Field, Gans T.
  See Wellman, Manly Wade
Field, James 1959- 113
Field, Peter
  See Drago, Harry Sinclair
  and Dresser, Davis
  and Mann, E(dward) B(everly)
Field, Rachel (Lyman) 1894-1942 15
  See also CLR *21*
Fielding, Kate
  See Oldfield, Jenny
Fields, Bryan W. 1958(?)- 188
Fields, Lisa 1984(?)- 216
Fields, Terri 1948- 191
Fields, T.S.
  See Fields, Terri
Fienberg, Anna 1956- 183
  Earlier sketch in SATA *112*
Fiery, Ann
  See Barrows, Annie
Fife, Dale (Odile Hollerbach) 1901- 18
Fighter Pilot, A
  See Johnston, H(ugh) A(nthony) S(tephen)
Figler, Jeanie 1949- 123
Figley, Marty Rhodes 1948- 158
  Earlier sketch in SATA *88*
Figueredo, D(anilo) H. 1951- 155
Figueroa, Pablo 1938- 9
Fijan, Carol 1918- 12
Filderman, Diane E(lizabeth) 1959- 87
Files, Meg 1946- 107
Fillmore, Parker H(oysted) 1878-1944
  See YABC *1*
Filstrup, Chris
  See Filstrup, E(dward) Christian
Filstrup, E(dward) Christian 1942- 43
Filstrup, Janie
  See Merrill, Jane
Finbarr, Desmond
  See Zobel Nolan, Allia
Finchler, Judy 1943- 93

Finder, Martin
  See Salzmann, Siegmund
Findlay, Jamieson 1958- 169
Findon, Joanne 1957- 161
Fine, Anne 1947- 197
  Earlier sketches in SATA *29, 72, 111, 160*
  See also CLR *25*
  See also SAAS *15*
Fine, Edith Hope 169
Fine, Howard 1961- 181
Fine, Jane
  See Ziefert, Harriet
Finger, Charles J(oseph) 1869(?)-1941 42
Fink, William B(ertrand) 1916- 22
Finke, Blythe Foote 1922- 26
Finkel, George (Irvine) 1909-1975 8
Finkelstein, Norman H. 1941- 220
  Earlier sketches in SATA *73, 137*
Finkelstein, Norman Henry
  See Finkelstein, Norman H.
Finlay, Alice Sullivan 1946- 82
Finlay, Winifred Lindsay Crawford
  (McKissack) 1910-1989 23
Finlayson, Ann 1925- 8
Finley, Martha 1828-1909 43
  See also CLR *148*
Finley, Mary Peace 1942- 83
Finn, Mary 208
Finney, Jack 1911-1995 109
Finney, Patricia 1958- 163
Finney, Shan 1944- 65
Finney, Walter Braden
  See Finney, Jack
Firer, Ben Zion
  See Firer, Benzion
Firer, Benzion 1914- 64
Fireside, Bryna J. 1932- 73
Firmin, Charlotte 1954- 29
Firmin, Peter 1928- 58
  Earlier sketch in SATA *15*
Firth, Barbara 179
Fischbach, Julius 1894-1988 10
Fischer, John
  See Fluke, Joanne
Fischer, R.J.
  See Fluke, Joanne
Fischer, Scott M. 1971- 195
Fischer-Nagel, Andreas 1951- 56
Fischer-Nagel, Heiderose 1956- 56
Fischler, Shirley (Walton) 66
Fischler, Stan(ley I.) 66
  Brief entry 36
Fischtrom, Harvey 1933-1974 3
Fishback, Margaret
  See Antolini, Margaret Fishback
Fishbone, Greg R. 195
Fisher, Aileen (Lucia) 1906-2002 73
  Obituary 143
  Earlier sketches in SATA *1, 25*
  See also CLR *49*
Fisher, Barbara 1940- 44
  Brief entry 34
Fisher, Carolyn 1968- 154
Fisher, Catherine 1957- 155
Fisher, Chris 1958- 80
Fisher, Clavin C(argill) 1912- 24
Fisher, Cynthia 195
Fisher, Dorothy (Frances) Canfield 1879-1958
  See YABC *1*
  See also CLR *71*
Fisher, Gary L. 1949- 86
Fisher, John 1909-1996 15
Fisher, John Oswald Hamilton
  See Fisher, John
Fisher, Laura Harrison 1934- 5
Fisher, Leonard Everett 1924- 176
  Autobiography Feature 122
  Earlier sketches in SATA *4, 34, 73, 120*
  See also CLR *18*
  See also SAAS *1*

Fisher, Lois I. 1948- 38
  Brief entry 35
Fisher, Margery (Turner) 1913-1992 20
  Obituary 74
Fisher, Marshall Jon 1963- 113
Fisher, Nikki
  See Strachan, Ian
Fisher, Robert (Tempest) 1943- 47
Fisher, Suzanne
  See Staples, Suzanne Fisher
Fisher, Valorie 214
  Earlier sketch in SATA 177
Fishman, Cathy Goldberg 1951- 106
Fisk, Nicholas
  See Higginbottom, David
Fisk, Pauline 1948- 160
  Earlier sketch in SATA 66
Fiske, Tarleton
  See Bloch, Robert (Albert)
Fisscher, Catharina G. M. 1958- 142
Fisscher, Tiny
  See Fisscher, Catharina G. M.
Fitch, Clarke
  See Sinclair, Upton
Fitch, John IV
  See Cormier, Robert
Fitch, Sheree 1956- 178
  Earlier sketch in SATA 108
Fitschen, Dale 1937- 20
Fitzalan, Roger
  See Trevor, Elleston
Fitzgerald, Captain Hugh
  See Baum, L. Frank
FitzGerald, Cathleen 1932-1987
  Obituary 50
Fitzgerald, Dawn 175
Fitzgerald, Edward Earl 1919-2001 20
Fitzgerald, F(rancis) A(nthony) 1940- 15
Fitzgerald, Joanne 1956- 198
Fitzgerald, John D(ennis) 1907(?)-1988 20
  Obituary 56
  See also CLR 1
Fitzgerald, Merni Ingrassia 1955- 53
Fitzgibbon, Terry 1948- 121
Fitzhardinge, Joan Margaret 1912- 73
  Earlier sketch in SATA 2
  See also CLR 5
  See also SAAS 3
Fitzhugh, Louise (Perkins) 1928-1974 45
  Obituary 24
  Earlier sketch in SATA 1
  See also CLR 72
Fitzhugh, Percy Keese 1876-1950 65
Fitzmaurice, Kathryn 217
Fitzpatrick, Becca 1979- 224
Fitzpatrick, Marie-Louise 1962- 189
  Earlier sketch in SATA 125
FitzRalph, Matthew
  See McInerny, Ralph
Fitz-Randolph, Jane (Currens) 1915- 51
Fitzsimons, Cecilia 1952- 97
Fitzsimons, Cecilia A.L.
  See Fitzsimons, Cecilia
Flack, Marjorie 1897-1958 100
  See also YABC 2
  See also CLR 28
Flack, Naomi John White -1999 40
  Brief entry 35
Flake, Sharon G. 166
Flanagan, John 1944- 180
Flanagan, John Anthony
  See Flanagan, John
Flannery, Kate
  See De Goldi, Kate
Flatt, Lizann 1966- 88
Fleagle, Gail S(hatto) 1940- 117
Fleetwood, Jenni 1947- 80
Fleischer, Jane
  See Oppenheim, Joanne
Fleischhauer-Hardt, Helga 1936- 30

Fleischman, Albert Sidney
  See Fleischman, Sid
Fleischman, John 1948- 145
Fleischman, Paul 1952- 156
  Brief entry 32
  Earlier sketches in SATA 39, 72, 110
  See also CLR 66
  See also SAAS 20
Fleischman, Sid 1920-2010 185
  Earlier sketches in SATA 8, 59, 96, 148
  See also CLR 15
Fleischner, Jennifer 1956- 188
  Earlier sketch in SATA 93
Fleisher, Paul 1948- 132
  Earlier sketch in SATA 81
Fleisher, Robbin 1951-1977 52
  Brief entry 49
Fleishman, Seymour 1918- 66
  Brief entry 32
Fleming, A. A.
  See Arthur, Robert, (Jr.)
Fleming, Alice Mulcahey 1928- 9
Fleming, Candace 1962- 225
  Earlier sketches in SATA 94, 143, 190
Fleming, Denise 1950- 173
  Earlier sketches in SATA 81, 126
Fleming, Elizabeth P. 1888-1985
  Obituary 48
Fleming, Ian 1908-1964 9
Fleming, Ian Lancaster
  See Fleming, Ian
Fleming, Ronald Lee 1941- 56
Fleming, Sally
  See Walker, Sally M.
Fleming, Stuart
  See Knight, Damon (Francis)
Fleming, Susan 1932- 32
Fleming, Thomas 1927- 8
Fleming, Thomas James
  See Fleming, Thomas
Fleming, Virginia (Edwards) 1923- 84
Flesch, Y.
  See Flesch, Yolande
Flesch, Yolande 1950- 55
Flesch, Yolande Catarina
  See Flesch, Yolande
Fletcher, Charlie 220
Fletcher, Charlie May Hogue 1897-1977 3
Fletcher, Colin 1922-2007 28
Fletcher, Dirk
  See Cunningham, Chet
Fletcher, George U.
  See Pratt, (Murray) Fletcher
Fletcher, Helen Jill 1910- 13
Fletcher, Ralph 1953- 195
  Earlier sketches in SATA 105, 149
  See also CLR 104
Fletcher, Ralph J.
  See Fletcher, Ralph
Fletcher, Richard E. 1917(?)-1983
  Obituary 34
Fletcher, Rick
  See Fletcher, Richard E.
Fletcher, Susan 1951- 181
  Earlier sketches in SATA 70, 110
Fletcher, Susan Clemens
  See Fletcher, Susan
Fleur, Paul
  See Pohl, Frederik
Flexner, James Thomas 1908-2003 9
Flinn, Alex 1966- 198
  Earlier sketch in SATA 159
Flint, Helen 1952- 102
Flint, Russ 1944- 74
Flitner, David, Jr. 1949- 7
Flitner, David Perkins
  See Flitner, David, Jr.
Floca, Brian 190
  Earlier sketch in SATA 155
Floethe, Louise Lee 1913-1988 4
Floethe, Richard 1901-1998 4

Floherty, John Joseph 1882-1964 25
Flood, Bo
  See Flood, Nancy Bo
Flood, Nancy Bo 1945- 130
Flood, Pansie Hart 1964- 140
Flood, William 1942- 129
Flooglebuckle, Al
  See Spiegelman, Art
Flora, James (Royer) 1914-1998 30
  Obituary 103
  Earlier sketch in SATA 1
  See also SAAS 6
Flores-Galbis, Enrique 1952- 186
Florian, Douglas 1950- 177
  Earlier sketches in SATA 19, 83, 125
Flory, Jane Trescott 1917- 22
Flournoy, Valerie 1952- 95
Flournoy, Valerie Rose
  See Flournoy, Valerie
Flowerdew, Phyllis -1994 33
Flowers, Pam 1946- 136
Flowers, Sarah 1952- 98
Floyd, Gareth 1940- 62
  Brief entry 31
Fluchere, Henri 1914-1991 40
Fluke, Joanne 1943- 88
Flutsztejn-Gruda, Ilona 1930- 170
Flynn, Barbara 1928- 9
Flynn, Jackson
  See Bensen, Donald R.
  and Shirreffs, Gordon D(onald)
Flynn, Nicholas
  See Odgers, Sally Farrell
Flynn, Pat 1968- 214
Flynn, Patrick
  See Flynn, Pat
Flynn, Rachel 1953- 171
  Earlier sketch in SATA 109
Flynn, Warren (G.) 1950- 154
Fodor, R. V. 1944- 25
Fodor, Ronald Victor
  See Fodor, R. V.
Fogelin, Adrian 1951- 175
  Earlier sketch in SATA 129
Foley, (Anna) Bernice Williams 1902-1987 . 28
Foley, Greg E. 1969- 190
Foley, June 1944- 44
Foley, (Mary) Louise Munro 1933- 106
  Brief entry 40
  Earlier sketch in SATA 54
Foley, Rae
  See Denniston, Elinore
Folke, Will
  See Bloch, Robert (Albert)
Follett, Helen Thomas 1884(?)-1970
  Obituary 27
Folsom, Franklin (Brewster) 1907-1995 5
  Obituary 88
Folsom, Michael (Brewster) 1938-1990 40
  Obituary 88
Fombelle, Timothee de 1973- 218
Fontenot, Mary Alice 1910-2003 91
  Obituary 209
  Earlier sketch in SATA 34
Fontes, Justine 172
Fontes, Ron 1952- 183
Foon, Dennis 1951- 119
Fooner, Michael 22
Foote, Timothy (Gilson) 1926- 52
Forberg, Ati
  See Forberg, Beate Gropius
Forberg, Beate Gropius 1925- 22
Forbes, Anna 1954- 101
Forbes, Bryan 1926- 37
Forbes, Cabot L.
  See Hoyt, Edwin P(almer), Jr.
Forbes, Esther 1891-1967 100
  Earlier sketch in SATA 2
  See also CLR 147
Forbes, Graham B. 1

Forbes, Kathryn
   See McLean, Kathryn (Anderson)
Forbes, Robert
   See Arthur, Robert, (Jr.)
Ford, Albert Lee
   See Stratemeyer, Edward L.
Ford, Barbara 56
   Brief entry 34
Ford, Bernette 212
Ford, Bernette G.
   See Ford, Bernette
Ford, B.G.
   See Ford, Bernette
Ford, Brian J(ohn) 1939- 49
Ford, Carolyn 1938- 98
Ford, Carolyn Mott
   See Ford, Carolyn
Ford, Christine 1953- 176
Ford, David
   See Baldacci, David
   and Baldacci, David
Ford, David B.
   See Baldacci, David
Ford, David Baldacci
   See Baldacci, David
Ford, Elbur
   See Hibbert, Eleanor Alice Burford
Ford, Ellen 1949- 89
Ford, George (Jr.) 31
Ford, Hilary
   See Youd, Samuel
Ford, Hildegarde
   See Morrison, Velma Ford
Ford, Jerome W. 1949- 78
Ford, Jerry
   See Ford, Jerome W.
Ford, John C. 1971- 221
Ford, Juwanda G(ertrude) 1967- 102
Ford, Marcia
   See Radford, Ruby L(orraine)
Ford, Nancy K(effer) 1906-1961
   Obituary 29
Ford, Peter 1936- 59
Ford, S. M.
   See Uhlig, Susan
Forde, Catherine 1961- 170
Foreman, Mark 199
Foreman, Michael 1938- 216
   Earlier sketches in SATA *2, 73, 129, 135, 184*
   See also CLR *32*
   See also SAAS *21*
Foreman, Wilmoth 1939- 153
Forest, Antonia 1915-2003 29
   Obituary 149
Forest, Dial
   See Gault, William Campbell
Forest, Heather 1948- 185
   Earlier sketch in SATA *120*
Forester, C. S. 1899-1966 13
Forester, Cecil Scott
   See Forester, C. S.
Forester, Victoria 214
Forler, Nan 223
Forman, Brenda 1936- 4
Forman, James
   See Forman, James D.
Forman, James D. 1932-2009 70
   Earlier sketch in SATA *8*
Forman, James Douglas
   See Forman, James D.
Forman, Mark L.
   See Forman, M.L.
Forman, M.L. 1964- 215
Forman, Ruth 1970- 186
Forrest, Elizabeth
   See Salsitz, Rhondi Vilott
Forrest, Mary
   See Pausacker, Jenny
Forrest, Sybil
   See Markun, Patricia Maloney

Forrestal, Elaine 1941- 165
   Earlier sketch in SATA *117*
Forrester, Frank H. 1919(?)-1986
   Obituary 52
Forrester, Helen
   See Bhatia, Jamunadevi
Forrester, Jade
   See Pausacker, Jenny
Forrester, Marian
   See Schachtel, Roger
Forrester, Sandra 1949- 166
   Earlier sketch in SATA *90*
Forrester, Victoria 1940- 40
   Brief entry 35
Forsee, (Frances) Aylesa -1986 1
Forsey, Chris 1950- 59
Forshay-Lunsford, Cin 1965- 60
Forster, E. M. 1879-1970 57
Forster, Edward Morgan
   See Forster, E. M.
Forsyth, Kate 1966- 154
Fort, Paul
   See Stockton, Francis Richard
Forte, Maurizio 1961- 110
Fortey, Richard 1946- 109
Fortey, Richard A.
   See Fortey, Richard
Fortey, Richard Alan
   See Fortey, Richard
Forth, Melissa D(eal) 96
Fortnum, Peggy
   See Nuttall-Smith, Margaret Emily Noel
Fortune, Eric 182
Forward, Robert L(ull) 1932-2002 82
Foster, Alan Dean 1946- 70
Foster, Brad W. 1955- 34
Foster, Doris Van Liew 1899-1993 10
Foster, E(lizabeth) C(onnell) 1902- 9
Foster, Elizabeth 1902- 12
Foster, Elizabeth 1905-1963 10
Foster, F. Blanche 1919- 11
Foster, G(eorge) Allen 1907-1969 26
Foster, Genevieve (Stump) 1893-1979 2
   Obituary 23
   See also CLR *7*
Foster, Gerald L. 198
Foster, Hal
   See Foster, Harold
Foster, Harold 1892-1982 31
Foster, Jeanne
   See Williams, Jeanne
Foster, John
   See Foster, John L(ouis)
   and Furcolo, Foster
Foster, John (Thomas) 1925- 8
Foster, John L(ouis) 1941- 102
Foster, Juliana 196
Foster, Laura Louise (James) 1918- 6
Foster, Leila Merrell 1929- 73
Foster, Lynne 1937- 74
Foster, Margaret Lesser 1899(?)-1979
   Obituary 21
Foster, Marian Curtis 1909-1978 23
Foster, Mark 1961- 197
Foster, Sally 58
Fotheringham, Edwin 201
Foulds, E. V.
   See Foulds, Elfrida Vipont
Foulds, Elfrida Vipont 1902-1992 52
Fountas, Angela Jane 180
Fourie, Corlia 1944- 91
Fourth Brother, The
   See Aung, (Maung) Htin
Fowke, Edith (Margaret) 1913-1996 14
Fowles, John 1926-2005 22
   Obituary 171
Fowles, John Robert
   See Fowles, John
Fowles, Shelley 1956- 205
Fox, Aileen 1907-2005 58
   Obituary 170

Fox, Aileen Mary
   See Fox, Aileen
Fox, Annie 1950- 175
Fox, Charles Philip 1913-2003 12
   Obituary 150
Fox, Christyan 188
Fox, Diane 188
Fox, Eleanor
   See St. John, Wylly Folk
Fox, Fontaine Talbot, Jr. 1884-1964
   Obituary 23
Fox, Fred 1903(?)-1981
   Obituary 27
Fox, Freeman
   See Hamilton, Charles (Harold St. John)
Fox, Geoffrey 1941- 73
Fox, Grace
   See Anderson, Grace Fox
Fox, Helen 1962- 181
Fox, Larry 30
Fox, Lorraine 1922-1976 27
   Earlier sketch in SATA *11*
Fox, Louisa
   See Kroll, Virginia L.
Fox, Mary Virginia 1919- 152
   Brief entry 39
   Earlier sketches in SATA *44, 88*
Fox, Mem 1946- 211
   Earlier sketches in SATA *51, 103, 155*
   See also CLR *80*
Fox, Merrion Frances
   See Fox, Mem
Fox, Michael W(ilson) 1937- 15
Fox, Norma Diane
   See Mazer, Norma Fox
Fox, Paula 1923- 167
   Earlier sketches in SATA *17, 60, 120*
   See also CLR *96*
Fox, Robert J. 1927- 33
Fox, Robert Joseph
   See Fox, Robert J.
Fox-Davies, Sarah 1956- 199
Foyt, Victoria .... 187.
Fradin, Dennis
   See Fradin, Dennis Brindell
Fradin, Dennis Brindell 1945- 185
   Earlier sketches in SATA *29, 90, 135*
Fradin, Judith Bloom 1945- 185
   Earlier sketches in SATA *90, 152*
Frailey, Paige (Menefee) 1965- 82
Frame, Janet 1924-2004 119
Frame, Janet Paterson
   See Frame, Janet
Frame, Paul 1913-1994 60
   Brief entry 33
   Obituary 83
Frances, Miss
   See Horwich, Frances R(appaport)
Franchere, Ruth 18
Francis, Charles
   See Holme, Bryan
Francis, Dee
   See Haas, Dorothy F.
Francis, Dorothy 1926- 127
   Earlier sketch in SATA *10*
Francis, Dorothy B.
   See Francis, Dorothy
Francis, Dorothy Brenner
   See Francis, Dorothy
Francis, Guy 225
Francis, Jaye
   See Pausacker, Jenny
Francis, Pamela (Mary) 1926- 11
Franck, Eddie
   See Cooke, Frank E.
Franco, Betsy 223
   Earlier sketches in SATA *150, 188*
Franco, Eloise (Bauder) 1910- 62
Franco, Johan (Henri Gustave) 1908-1988 ... 62
Franco, Marjorie 38
Franco, Tom 224

Francois, Andre 1915-2005 25
Francoise
  See Seignobosc, Francoise
Frank, Anne 1929-1945 87
  Brief entry 42
  See also CLR *101*
Frank, Annelies Marie
  See Frank, Anne
Frank, Daniel B. 1956- 55
Frank, Emily R.
  See Frank, E.R.
Frank, E.R. 1967- 157
Frank, Helene
  See Vautier, Ghislaine
Frank, Hillary 1976- 148
Frank, John 199
Frank, Josette 1893-1989 10
  Obituary 63
Frank, Lucy 1947- 166
  Earlier sketch in SATA *94*
Frank, Mary 1933- 34
Frank, R., Jr.
  See Ross, Frank (Xavier), Jr.
Frankau, Mary Evelyn Atkinson 1899-1974 .. 4
Frankel, Alona 1937- 66
Frankel, Bernice 9
Frankel, Edward 1910- 44
Frankel, Ellen 1951- 78
Frankel, Julie 1947- 40
  Brief entry 34
Frankenberg, Robert 1911- 22
Frankland, David 207
Franklin, Cheryl J. 1955- 70
Franklin, Harold 1926- 13
Franklin, Kristine L. 1958- 124
  Earlier sketch in SATA *80*
Franklin, Lance
  See Lantz, Francess L(in)
Franklin, Madeleine
  See L'Engle, Madeleine
Franklin, Madeleine L'Engle
  See L'Engle, Madeleine
Franklin, Madeleine L'Engle Camp
  See L'Engle, Madeleine
Franklin, Max
  See Deming, Richard
Franklin, Steve
  See Stevens, Franklin
Franson, Leanne 1963- 223
  Earlier sketch in SATA *111*
Franson, Scott E. 1966- 192
Franzen, Nils-Olof 1916- 10
Frascino, Edward 48
  Brief entry 33
  See also SAAS *9*
Frasconi, Antonio 1919- 131
  Earlier sketches in SATA *6, 53*
  See also SAAS *11*
Fraser, Betty
  See Fraser, Elizabeth Marr
Fraser, Elizabeth Marr 1928- 31
Fraser, Eric (George) 1902-1983 38
Fraser, Mary Ann 1959- 214
  Earlier sketches in SATA *76, 137*
  See also SAAS *23*
Fraser, Wynnette (McFaddin) 1925- 90
Frasier, Debra 1953- 182
  Earlier sketches in SATA *69, 112*
Fraustino, Lisa Rowe 1961- 146
  Autobiography Feature 146
  Earlier sketch in SATA *84*
Frazee, Marla 1958- 225
  Earlier sketches in SATA *105, 151, 187*
Frazer, Megan 1977- 221
Frazetta, Frank 1928-2010 58
Frazier, Craig 1955- 221
  Earlier sketch in SATA *177*
Frazier, Neta (Osborn) Lohnes 1890-1990 7
Frazier, Sundee T. 1968- 198
Frazier, Sundee Tucker
  See Frazier, Sundee T.

Frederic, Mike
  See Cox, William R(obert)
Frederick, Heather Vogel 207
Fredericks, Anthony D. 1947- 113
Freed, Alvyn M. 1913-1993 22
Freedman, Benedict 1919- 27
Freedman, Claire 185
Freedman, Deborah 1960- 191
Freedman, Jeff 1953- 90
Freedman, Nancy 1920-2010 27
Freedman, Russell 1929- 175
  Earlier sketches in SATA *16, 71, 123*
  See also CLR *71*
Freedman, Russell Bruce
  See Freedman, Russell
Freeman, Barbara C. 1906-1999 28
Freeman, Barbara Constance
  See Freeman, Barbara C.
Freeman, Bill
  See Freeman, William Bradford
Freeman, Don 1908-1978 17
  See also CLR *90*
Freeman, Ira Maximilian 1905-1987 21
Freeman, Kimberley
  See Wilkins, Kim
Freeman, Laura 200
Freeman, Lucy (Greenbaum) 1916-2004 24
Freeman, Mae 1907-1985 25
Freeman, Mae Blacker
  See Freeman, Mae
Freeman, Marcia S. 1937- 102
Freeman, Marcia Sheehan
  See Freeman, Marcia S.
Freeman, Martha 1956- 201
  Earlier sketches in SATA *101, 152*
Freeman, Nancy 1932- 61
Freeman, Peter J.
  See Calvert, Patricia
Freeman, Sarah (Caroline) 1940- 66
Freeman, Tor 1977- 164
Freeman, VicToria
  See Freeman, Tor
Freeman, William Bradford 1938- 58
  Brief entry 48
Fregosi, Claudia (Anne Marie) 1946- 24
Freitas, Donna 1972- 205
French, Allen 1870-1946
  See YABC *1*
French, Dorothy Kayser 1926- 5
French, Fiona 1944- 132
  Earlier sketches in SATA *6, 75*
  See also CLR *37*
  See also SAAS *21*
French, Jackie 186
  Autobiography Feature 139
  Earlier sketches in SATA *108, 139*
  See French, Jackie Anne
  and French, Jacqueline Anne
French, Kathryn
  See Mosesson, Gloria R(ubin)
French, Martin 176
French, Michael 1944- 49
  Brief entry 38
French, Paul
  See Asimov, Isaac
French, S. Terrell 216
French, Simon 1957- 147
  Earlier sketch in SATA *86*
French, Vivian 209
  Earlier sketch in SATA *165*
Frenette, Liza 126
Freschet, Gina 1960- 175
  Earlier sketch in SATA *139*
Frewer, Glyn (M.) 1931- 11
Frey, Darcy 98
Freymann, Saxton 1958(?)- 178
Freymann-Weyr, Garret 1965- 145
Freymann-Weyr, Rhoda Garret Michaela
  See Freymann-Weyr, Garret
Frick, C. H.
  See Irwin, Constance (H.) Frick

Frick, Constance
  See Irwin, Constance (H.) Frick
Fricke, Aaron 1962- 89
Fridell, Ron 1943- 124
Fried, Janice 197
Friedlander, Joanne K(ohn) 1930- 9
Friedman, Aimee 1979- 189
Friedman, D. Dina 1957- 180
Friedman, Debra 1955- 150
Friedman, Estelle (Ehrenwald) 1920- 7
Friedman, Frieda 1905- 43
Friedman, Ina R(osen) 1926- 136
  Brief entry 41
  Earlier sketch in SATA *49*
Friedman, Jerrold David
  See Gerrold, David
Friedman, Judi 1935- 59
Friedman, Laurie 1964- 219
  Earlier sketches in SATA *138, 179*
Friedman, Marvin 1930- 42
  Brief entry 33
Friedman, Robin 1968- 219
  Earlier sketch in SATA *162*
Friedmann, Stan 1953- 80
Friedrich, Otto (Alva) 1929-1995 33
Friedrich, Priscilla 1927- 39
Friend, Catherine 1957(?)- 194
Friend, David Michael 1975- 195
Friend, Natasha 1972- 184
Friendlich, Dick
  See Friendlich, Richard J.
Friendlich, Richard J. 1909- 11
Friermood, Elisabeth Hamilton 1903-1992 5
Friesen, Bernice (Sarah Anne) 1966- 105
Friesen, Gayle 1960- 200
  Earlier sketch in SATA *109*
Friesen, Jonathan 1967(?)- 206
Friesner, Esther 1951- 207
  Earlier sketches in SATA *71, 168*
Friesner, Esther M.
  See Friesner, Esther
Friis-Baastad, Babbis Ellinor 1921-1970 7
Frimmer, Steven 1928- 31
Frischmuth, Barbara 1941- 114
Friskey, Margaret (Richards) 1901-1995 5
Fritts, Mary Bahr
  See Bahr, Mary (Madelyn)
Fritz, Jean (Guttery) 1915- 163
  Autobiography Feature 122
  Earlier sketches in SATA *1, 29, 72, 119*
  See also CLR *96*
  See also SAAS *2*
Froehlich, Margaret W(alden) 1930- 56
Frois, Jeanne 1953- 73
Froissart, Jean 1338(?)-1410(?) 28
Froman, Elizabeth Hull 1920-1975 10
Froman, Robert (Winslow) 1917- 8
Fromm, Lilo 1928- 29
Frommer, Harvey 1937- 41
Frost, A(rthur) B(urdett) 1851-1928 19
Frost, Elizabeth
  See Frost-Knappman, Elizabeth
Frost, Erica
  See Supraner, Robyn
Frost, Helen 1949- 194
  Autobiography Feature 194
  Earlier sketches in SATA *157, 183*
Frost, Helen Marie
  See Frost, Helen
Frost, Lesley 1899-1983 14
  Obituary 34
Frost, Robert 1874-1963 14
  See also CLR *67*
Frost, Robert Lee
  See Frost, Robert
Frost, Shelley 1960- 138
Frost-Knappman, Elizabeth 1943- 179
Froud, Brian 1947- 150
Fry, Annette R(iley) 89
Fry, Christopher 1907-2005 66
Fry, Edward Bernard 1925- 35

Fry, Rosalie Kingsmill 1911-1992 .... *3*
  See also SAAS *11*
Fry, Virginia Lynn 1952- *95*
Frye, Sally
  See Moore, Elaine
Fuchs, Bernie 1932- *162*
  Earlier sketch in SATA *95*
Fuchs, Erich 1916- *6*
Fuchshuber, Annegert 1940- *43*
Fucile, Tony *221*
Fuerst, Jeffrey B. 1956- *143*
Fuertes, Gloria 1918-1998 .... *115*
Fuge, Charles 1966- *144*
  Earlier sketch in SATA *74*
Fujikawa, Gyo 1908-1998 .... *76*
  Brief entry *30*
  Obituary *110*
  Earlier sketch in SATA *39*
  See also CLR *25*
  See also SAAS *16*
Fujita, Tamao 1905-1999 .... *7*
Fujiwara, Kim 1957- *81*
Fujiwara, Michiko 1946- *15*
Fuka, Vladimir 1926-1977
  Obituary *27*
Fulcher, Jennifer
  See Westwood, Jennifer
Fuller, Catherine Leuthold 1916- *9*
Fuller, Edmund (Maybank) 1914- *21*
Fuller, Iola
  See McCoy, Iola Fuller
Fuller, John G(rant, Jr.) 1913-1990 .... *65*
Fuller, Kathleen
  See Gottfried, Theodore Mark
Fuller, Lois Hamilton 1915- *11*
Fuller, Margaret 1810-1850 .... *25*
Fuller, Maud
  See Petersham, Maud
Fuller, Roy (Broadbent) 1912-1991 .... *87*
Fuller, Sarah Margaret
  See Fuller, Margaret
Fults, John Lee 1932- *33*
Funk, Thompson 1911- *7*
Funk, Tom
  See Funk, Thompson
Funke, Cornelia 1958- *209*
  Earlier sketches in SATA *154, 174*
  See also CLR *145*
Funke, Cornelia Caroline
  See Funke, Cornelia
Funke, Lewis 1912-1992 .... *11*
Fuqua, Jonathon Scott 1966- *141*
Furbee, Mary R.
  See Furbee, Mary Rodd
Furbee, Mary Rodd 1954- *138*
Furchgott, Terry 1948- *29*
Furlong, Monica (Mavis) 1930-2003 .... *86*
  Obituary *142*
Furlonger, Patricia
  See Wrightson, Patricia
Furman, Gertrude Lerner Kerman 1909- *21*
Furniss, Tim 1948- *49*
Furrow, Robert 1985- *172*
Furukawa, Toshi 1924- *24*
Fusillo, Archimede 1962- *137*
Futcher, Jane P. 1947- *76*
Futehali, Zahida
  See Whitaker, Zai
Fyleman, Rose (Amy) 1877-1957 .... *21*
Fyson, Jenny Grace
  See Fyson, J.G.
Fyson, J.G. 1904-1998 .... *42*

G

Gaan, Margaret 1914- *65*
Gaber, Susan 1956- *169*
  Earlier sketch in SATA *115*

Gaberman, Judie Angell
  See Angell, Judie
Gabhart, Ann
  See Gabhart, Ann H.
Gabhart, Ann H. 1947- *75*
Gable, Brian 1949- *195*
Gabler, Mirko 1951- *77*
Gabriel, Adriana
  See Rojany, Lisa
Gabrys, Ingrid Schubert
  See Schubert-Gabrys, Ingrid
Gackenbach, Dick 1927- *79*
  Brief entry *30*
  Earlier sketch in SATA *48*
Gadd, Jeremy 1949- *116*
Gaddis, Vincent H. 1913-1997 .... *35*
Gadler, Steve J. 1905-1985 .... *36*
Gaeddert, Lou Ann (Bigge) 1931- *103*
  Earlier sketch in SATA *20*
Gaeddert, Louann
  See Gaeddert, Lou Ann (Bigge)
Gaer, Joseph 1897-1969 .... *118*
Gaer, Yossef
  See Gaer, Joseph
Gaetz, Dayle Campbell 1947- *138*
Gaffney, Timothy R. 1951- *170*
  Earlier sketch in SATA *69*
Gaffron, Norma 1931- *97*
Gaffron, Norma Bondeson
  See Gaffron, Norma
Gag, Flavia 1907-1979
  Obituary *24*
Gag, Wanda (Hazel) 1893-1946 .... *100*
  See also YABC *1*
  See also CLR *150*
Gage, Brian *162*
Gage, Wilson
  See Steele, Mary Q(uintard Govan)
Gagliano, Eugene M. 1946- *150*
Gagliardo, Ruth Garver 1895(?)-1980
  Obituary *22*
Gagnon, Cecile 1936- *58*
Gaillard, Jason 1965- *200*
Gaiman, Neil 1960- *197*
  Earlier sketches in SATA *85, 146*
  See also CLR *109*
Gaiman, Neil Richard
  See Gaiman, Neil
Gainer, Cindy 1962- *74*
Gaines, Ernest J. 1933- *86*
  See also CLR *62*
Gaines, Ernest James
  See Gaines, Ernest J.
Gaither, Gloria 1942- *127*
Gal, Laszlo 1933- *96*
  Brief entry *32*
  Earlier sketch in SATA *52*
  See also CLR *61*
Galbraith, Ben 1980- *200*
Galbraith, Kathryn O. 1945- *219*
  Earlier sketch in SATA *85*
Galbraith, Kathryn Osebold
  See Galbraith, Kathryn O.
Galdone, Paul 1907(?)-1986 .... *66*
  Obituary *49*
  Earlier sketch in SATA *17*
  See also CLR *16*
Galindo, Claudia 1979- *203*
Galinsky, Ellen 1942- *23*
Gall, Chris 1961- *176*
Gallagher, Diana G. 1946- *153*
Gallagher, Lurlene Nora
  See McDaniel, Lurlene
Gallagher-Cole, Mernie 1958- *206*
Gallant, Roy A(rthur) 1924- *110*
  Earlier sketches in SATA *4, 68*
  See also CLR *30*
Gallardo, Evelyn 1948- *78*
Gallaz, Christophe 1948- *162*
  See also CLR *126*
Gallego Garcia, Laura 1977- *173*

Gallico, Paul 1897-1976 .... *13*
Gallico, Paul William
  See Gallico, Paul
Gallo, Donald R. 1938- *112*
  Autobiography Feature *104*
Gallo, Donald Robert
  See Gallo, Donald R.
Galloway, Owateka (S.) 1981- *121*
Galloway, Priscilla 1930- *112*
  Earlier sketch in SATA *66*
Gallup, Joan 1957- *128*
Galouchko, Annouchka Gravel 1960- *95*
Galt, Thomas Franklin, Jr. 1908-1989 .... *5*
Galt, Tom
  See Galt, Thomas Franklin, Jr.
Galvin, Matthew R. 1950- *93*
Galvin, Matthew Reppert
  See Galvin, Matthew R.
Gamble, Kim 1952- *183*
  Earlier sketches in SATA *81, 124*
Gambrell, Jamey *82*
Gamerman, Martha 1941- *15*
Gammell, Stephen 1943- *128*
  Earlier sketches in SATA *53, 81*
  See also CLR *83*
Ganly, Helen (Mary) 1940- *56*
Gannett, Ruth Chrisman (Arens)
  1896-1979 .... *33*
Gannett, Ruth Stiles 1923- *3*
Gannij, Joan *208*
Gannij, Joan Levine
  See Gannij, Joan
Gannon, Ned 1974- *205*
Gannon, Robert Haines 1931- *8*
Gano, Lila 1949- *76*
Gans, Roma 1894-1996 .... *45*
  Obituary *93*
Gant, Matthew
  See Hano, Arnold
Gantner, Susan (Verble) 1939- *63*
Gantos, Jack 1951- *169*
  Earlier sketches in SATA *20, 81, 119*
  See also CLR *85*
Gantos, John Bryan, Jr.
  See Gantos, Jack
Ganz, Yaffa 1938- *61*
  Brief entry *52*
Garafano, Marie 1942- *84*
Garant, Andre J. 1968- *123*
Garbe, Ruth Moore
  See Moore, Ruth (Ellen)
Garber, Esther
  See Lee, Tanith
Garcia, Cristina 1958- *208*
Garcia, Emma 1969- *198*
Garcia, Geronimo 1960- *222*
Garcia, Yolanda P. 1952- *113*
Garcia, Yolanda Pacheco
  See Garcia, Yolanda P.
Gard, Janice
  See Latham, Jean Lee
Gard, Joyce
  See Reeves, Joyce
Gard, Robert Edward 1910-1992 .... *18*
  Obituary *74*
Gard, (Sanford) Wayne 1899-1986
  Obituary *49*
Gardam, Jane 1928- *130*
  Brief entry *28*
  Earlier sketches in SATA *39, 76*
  See also CLR *12*
  See also SAAS *9*
Gardam, Jane Mary
  See Gardam, Jane
Gardella, Tricia 1944- *96*
Garden, Nancy 1938- *147*
  Autobiography Feature *147*
  Earlier sketches in SATA *12, 77, 114*
  See also CLR *51*
  See also SAAS *8*

Gardiner, John Reynolds 1944-2006 .... *64*
  Obituary *174*
Gardiner, Lindsey 1971- *144*
Gardner, Craig Shaw 1949- *99*
Gardner, Dic
  See Gardner, Richard (M.)
Gardner, Graham *159*
Gardner, Hugh 1910-1986
  Obituary *49*
Gardner, Jane Mylum 1946- *83*
Gardner, Jeanne LeMonnier 1925- *5*
Gardner, John, Jr. 1933-1982 .... *40*
  Obituary *31*
Gardner, John Champlin, Jr.
  See Gardner, John, Jr.
Gardner, John E(dward) 1917- *192*
Gardner, Lyn *192*
Gardner, Martin 1914-2010 .... *142*
  Earlier sketch in SATA *16*
Gardner, Miriam
  See Bradley, Marion Zimmer
Gardner, Richard (M.) 1931- *24*
Gardner, Richard A(lan) 1931-2003 .... *13*
  Obituary *144*
Gardner, Sally *177*
Gardner, Sandra 1940- *70*
Gardner, Scot 1968- *143*
Gardner, Sheldon 1934- *33*
Gardner, Ted
  See Gardner, Theodore Roosevelt II
Gardner, Theodore Roosevelt
  See Gardner, Theodore Roosevelt II
Gardner, Theodore Roosevelt II 1934- *84*
Garelick, May 1910-1989 .... *19*
Garfield, James B. 1881-1984 .... *6*
  Obituary *38*
Garfield, Leon 1921-1996 .... *76*
  Obituary *90*
  Earlier sketches in SATA *1, 32*
  See also CLR *21*
Garfinkle, Debra L.
  See Garfinkle, D.L.
Garfinkle, D.L. *187*
Garis, Howard R. 1873-1962 .... *13*
Garis, Howard Roger
  See Garis, Howard R.
Garland, Mark 1953- *79*
Garland, Mark A.
  See Garland, Mark
Garland, Michael 1952- *208*
  Earlier sketch in SATA *168*
Garland, Sarah 1944- *135*
  Earlier sketch in SATA *62*
Garland, Sherry 1948- *145*
  Autobiography Feature *145*
  Earlier sketches in SATA *73, 114*
Garner, Alan 1934- *69*
  Autobiography Feature *108*
  Earlier sketch in SATA *18*
  See also CLR *130*
Garner, David 1958- *78*
Garner, Eleanor Ramrath 1930- *122*
Garner, James Finn 1960(?)- *92*
Garnet, A. H.
  See Slote, Alfred
Garnett, Eve C. R. 1900-1991 .... *3*
  Obituary *70*
Garofoli, Viviana 1970- *186*
Garou, Louis P.
  See Bowkett, Stephen
Garraty, John A. 1920-2007 .... *23*
  Obituary *189*
Garraty, John Arthur
  See Garraty, John A.
Garren, Devorah-Leah
  See Devorah-Leah
Garret, Maxwell R. 1917- *39*
Garretson, Victoria Diane
  See Cox, Victoria
Garrett, Helen 1895- *21*
Garrett, Randall 1927-1987 .... *180*

Garrett, Richard 1920- *82*
Garrigue, Sheila 1931- *21*
Garrison, Barbara 1931- *163*
  Earlier sketch in SATA *19*
Garrison, Frederick
  See Sinclair, Upton
Garrison, Mary 1952- *146*
Garrison, Peter
  See Gardner, Craig Shaw
Garrison, Webb B(lack) 1919-2000 .... *25*
Garrity, Jennifer Johnson 1961- *124*
Garrity, Linda K. 1947- *128*
Garsee, Jeannine *199*
Garst, Doris Shannon 1894-1981 .... *1*
Garst, Shannon
  See Garst, Doris Shannon
Garth, Will
  See Hamilton, Edmond
  and Kuttner, Henry
Garthwaite, Marion H(ook) 1893-1981 .... *7*
Garton, Malinda D(ean) (?)-1976
  Obituary *26*
Garvie, Maureen 1944- *175*
Garvie, Maureen McCallum
  See Garvie, Maureen
Garza, Carmen Lomas 1948- *182*
Garza, Xavier *184*
Gascoigne, Bamber 1935- *62*
Gaskins, Pearl Fuyo 1957- *134*
Gasperini, Jim 1952- *54*
  Brief entry *49*
Gater, Dilys 1944- *41*
Gates, Doris 1901-1987 .... *34*
  Obituary *54*
  Earlier sketch in SATA *1*
  See also SAAS *1*
Gates, Frieda 1933- *26*
Gates, Susan 1950- *153*
Gates, Viola R. 1931- *101*
Gathorne-Hardy, Jonathan G. 1933- *124*
  Earlier sketch in SATA *26*
Gatti, Anne 1952- *103*
Gatty, Juliana Horatia
  See Ewing, Juliana (Horatia Gatty)
Gauch, Patricia Lee 1934- *80*
  Earlier sketch in SATA *26*
  See also CLR *56*
  See also SAAS *21*
Gauch, Sarah *223*
Gaudasinska, Elzbieta 1943- *190*
Gaul, Randy 1959- *63*
Gault, Clare 1925- *36*
Gault, Frank 1926-1982 .... *36*
  Brief entry *30*
Gault, William Campbell 1910-1995 .... *8*
Gauthier, Gail 1953- *203*
  Earlier sketches in SATA *118, 160*
Gaver, Becky
  See Gaver, Rebecca
Gaver, Rebecca 1952- *20*
Gavin, Jamila 1941- *223*
  Earlier sketches in SATA *96, 125*
Gay, Amelia
  See Hogarth, Grace (Weston Allen)
Gay, Francis
  See Gee, H(erbert) L(eslie)
Gay, Kathlyn 1930- *144*
  Earlier sketch in SATA *9*
Gay, Marie-Louise 1952- *179*
  Earlier sketches in SATA *68, 126*
  See also CLR *27*
  See also SAAS *21*
Gay, Michel 1947- *162*
Gay, Zhenya 1906-1978 .... *19*
Gaze, Gillian
  See Barklem, Jill
Gear, Kathleen M. O'Neal
  See Gear, Kathleen O'Neal
Gear, Kathleen O'Neal 1954- *224*
  Earlier sketches in SATA *71, 166*

Gear, W. Michael 1955- *224*
  Earlier sketches in SATA *71, 166*
Geary, Rick 1946- *142*
Geason, Susan 1946- *122*
Gedalof, Robin
  See McGrath, Robin
Gedge, Pauline (Alice) 1945- *101*
Gee, H(erbert) L(eslie) 1901-1977
  Obituary *26*
Gee, Maurice 1931- *101*
  Earlier sketch in SATA *46*
  See also CLR *56*
Gee, Maurice Gough
  See Gee, Maurice
Geehan, Wayne (E.) 1947- *107*
Geer, Charles 1922- *42*
  Brief entry *32*
Geeslin, Campbell 1925- *163*
  Earlier sketch in SATA *107*
Gehman, Mary W. 1923- *86*
Gehr, Mary 1910(?)-1997 .... *32*
  Obituary *99*
Geipel, Eileen 1932- *30*
Geis, Alissa Imre 1976- *189*
Geis, Darlene Stern 1918(?)-1999 .... *7*
  Obituary *111*
Geisel, Helen 1898-1967 .... *26*
Geisel, Theodor Seuss
  See Dr. Seuss
Geisert, Arthur 1941- *171*
  Brief entry *52*
  Earlier sketches in SATA *56, 92, 133*
  See also CLR *87*
  See also SAAS *23*
Geisert, Arthur Frederick
  See Geisert, Arthur
Geisert, Bonnie 1942- *165*
  Earlier sketch in SATA *92*
Geist, Ken *191*
Gelber, Lisa *210*
Geldart, William 1936- *15*
Gelinas, Paul J. 1904-1996 .... *10*
Gellis, Roberta 1927- *128*
Gellis, Roberta Leah Jacobs
  See Gellis, Roberta
Gellman, Marc *112*
Gelman, Amy 1961- *72*
Gelman, Jan 1963- *58*
Gelman, Rita Golden 1937- *131*
  Brief entry *51*
  Earlier sketch in SATA *84*
Gelman, Steve 1934- *3*
Gemignani, Tony 1973- *220*
Gemming, Elizabeth 1932- *11*
Gendel, Evelyn W. 1916(?)-1977
  Obituary *27*
Gennaro, Joseph F., Jr. 1924- *53*
Gennaro, Joseph Francis, Jr.
  See Gennaro, Joseph F., Jr.
Gentieu, Penny *204*
Gentile, Petrina 1969- *91*
Gentle, Mary 1956- *48*
Gentleman, David (William) 1930- *7*
Gentry, Marita *215*
Geoghegan, Adrienne 1962- *143*
George, Barbara
  See Katz, Bobbi
George, Emily
  See Katz, Bobbi
George, Gail
  See Katz, Bobbi
George, Jean
  See George, Jean Craighead
George, Jean C.
  See George, Jean Craighead
George, Jean Craighead 1919- *170*
  Earlier sketches in SATA *2, 68, 124*
  See also CLR *136*
George, Jessica Day 1976- *210*
George, John L(othar) 1916- *2*

George, Kristine O'Connell 1954- *156*
  Earlier sketch in SATA *110*
George, Lindsay Barrett 1952- *206*
  Earlier sketches in SATA *95, 155*
George, S. C. 1898- *11*
George, Sally
  See Orr, Wendy
George, Sidney Charles
  See George, S. C.
George, Twig C. 1950- *114*
George, W(illiam) Lloyd 1900(?)-1975
  Obituary *30*
Georgiou, Constantine 1927- *7*
Georgiou, Theo
  See Odgers, Sally Farrell
Geraghty, Paul 1959- *130*
Gerard, Jean Ignace Isidore 1803-1847 .... *45*
Geras, Adele 1944- *180*
  Autobiography Feature *180*
  Earlier sketches in SATA *23, 87, 129, 173*
  See also SAAS *21*
Geras, Adele Daphne Weston
  See Geras, Adele
Gerber, Carole 1947- *207*
Gerber, Linda *213*
Gerber, Merrill Joan 1938- *170*
  Autobiography Feature *170*
  Earlier sketches in SATA *64, 127*
Gerber, Perren 1933- *104*
Gerberg, Mort 1931- *64*
Gergely, Tibor 1900-1978 .... *54*
  Obituary *20*
Geringer, Laura 1948- *164*
  Earlier sketches in SATA *29, 94*
Gerler, William R(obert) 1917-1996 .... *47*
Gerrard, Jean 1933- *51*
Gerrard, Roy 1935-1997 .... *90*
  Brief entry *45*
  Obituary *99*
  Earlier sketch in SATA *47*
  See also CLR *23*
Gerritsen, Paula 1956- *177*
Gerrold, David 1944- *144*
  Earlier sketch in SATA *66*
Gershator, David 1937- *180*
Gershator, Phillis 1942- *188*
  Earlier sketches in SATA *90, 158*
Gershon, Dann 1955- *187*
Gershon, Gina 1962- *187*
Gerson, Corinne 1927- *37*
Gerson, Mary-Joan *136*
  Earlier sketch in SATA *79*
Gerson, Noel Bertram 1914-1988 .... *22*
  Obituary *60*
Gerstein, Mordicai 1935- *222*
  Brief entry *36*
  Earlier sketches in SATA *47, 81, 142, 178*
  See also CLR *102*
Gertridge, Allison 1967- *132*
Gervais, Bernadette 1959- *80*
Gervay, Susanne *183*
Gesner, Clark 1938-2002 .... *40*
  Obituary *143*
Gessner, Lynne 1919- *16*
Geter, Tyrone *150*
Getz, David 1957- *91*
Getzinger, Donna 1968- *128*
Geus, Mireille 1964- *207*
Gevirtz, Eliezer 1950- *49*
Gevry, Claudine *188*
Gewe, Raddory
  See Gorey, Edward (St. John)
Ghan, Linda (R.) 1947- *77*
Ghent, Natale 1962- *148*
Gherman, Beverly 1934- *123*
  Earlier sketch in SATA *68*
Ghigna, Charles 1946- *153*
  Earlier sketch in SATA *108*
Giacobbe, Beppe 1953- *174*
Giambastiani, Kurt R. A. 1958- *141*
Giannini, Enzo 1946- *68*

Gibala-Broxholm, Scott 1959(?)- *205*
Gibbons, Alan 1953- *198*
  Earlier sketch in SATA *124*
Gibbons, Faye 1938- *103*
  Earlier sketch in SATA *65*
Gibbons, Gail 1944- *201*
  Earlier sketches in SATA *23, 72, 104, 160*
  See also CLR *8*
  See also SAAS *12*
Gibbons, Gail Gretchen
  See Gibbons, Gail
Gibbons, Kaye 1960- *117*
Gibbs, Adrea 1960- *126*
Gibbs, Alonzo (Lawrence) 1915-1992 .... *5*
Gibbs, (Cecilia) May 1877-1969
  Obituary *27*
Gibbs, Tony
  See Gibbs, Wolcott, Jr.
Gibbs, Wolcott, Jr. 1935- *40*
Giblin, James Cross 1933- *197*
  Earlier sketches in SATA *33, 75, 122*
  See also CLR *29*
  See also SAAS *12*
Gibson, Andrew (William) 1949- *72*
Gibson, Barbara L. *205*
Gibson, Barbara Leonard
  See Gibson, Barbara L.
Gibson, Betty 1911- *75*
Gibson, Jo
  See Fluke, Joanne
Gibson, Josephine
  See Hine, Sesyle Joslin
  and Hine, Al(fred Blakelee)
Gibson, Marley 1966- *225*
Gibson, Sarah P. 1962- *211*
Gibson, William 1914-2008 .... *66*
  Obituary *199*
Gibson, William Ford
  See Gibson, William
Gidal, Nachum
  See Gidal, Tim Nachum
Gidal, Sonia (Epstein) 1922- *2*
Gidal, Tim Nachum 1909-1996 .... *2*
Gidalewitsch, Nachum
  See Gidal, Tim Nachum
Gideon, Melanie 1963- *175*
Giegling, John A(llan) 1935- *17*
Gifaldi, David 1950- *209*
  Earlier sketch in SATA *76*
Giff, Patricia Reilly 1935- *203*
  Earlier sketches in SATA *33, 70, 121, 160*
Giffard, Hannah 1962- *83*
Gifford, Carrie *224*
Gifford, Clive 1966- *198*
Gifford, Griselda 1931- *171*
  Earlier sketch in SATA *42*
Gifford, Kerri 1961- *91*
Gifford, Peggy 1952- *191*
Gilbert, Ann
  See Taylor, Ann
Gilbert, Anne Yvonne 1951- *185*
Gilbert, Barbara Snow 1954- *97*
Gilbert, Catherine
  See Murdock, Catherine Gilbert
Gilbert, Frances
  See Collings, Gillian
Gilbert, Harriett 1948- *30*
Gilbert, (Agnes) Joan (Sewell) 1931- *10*
Gilbert, John (Raphael) 1926- *36*
Gilbert, Nan
  See Gilbertson, Mildred Geiger
Gilbert, Roby Goodale 1966- *90*
Gilbert, Ruth Gallard Ainsworth
  See Ainsworth, Ruth (Gallard)
Gilbert, Sara (Dulaney) 1943- *82*
  Earlier sketch in SATA *11*
Gilbert, Sheri L. *157*
Gilbert, Suzie 1956- *97*
Gilbert, W(illiam) S(chwenck) 1836-1911 ... *36*
Gilbert, Yvonne
  See Gilbert, Anne Yvonne

Gilbertson, Mildred Geiger 1908-1988 .... *2*
Gilbreath, Alice 1921- *12*
Gilbreth, Frank B., Jr. 1911-2001 .... *2*
Gilbreth, Frank Bunker
  See Gilbreth, Frank B., Jr.
Gilchrist, Jan Spivey 1949- *130*
  Earlier sketch in SATA *72*
Gilden, Mel 1947- *97*
Giles, Gail *196*
  Earlier sketch in SATA *152*
Gilfond, Henry *2*
Gilge, Jeanette 1924- *22*
Gili, Phillida 1944- *70*
Gill, Derek (Lewis Theodore) 1919-1997 ...... *9*
Gill, Margery Jean 1925- *22*
Gill, Shelley *176*
Gill, Stephen 1932- *63*
Gillespie, Carol Ann 1951- *158*
Gillett, Mary (Bledsoe) *7*
Gillette, Henry Sampson 1915- *14*
Gillette, J. Lynett 1946- *103*
Gillette, Jan Lynett
  See Gillette, J. Lynett
Gilley, Jeremy 1969- *174*
Gillham, Bill
  See Gillham, W(illiam) E(dwin) C(harles)
Gillham, W(illiam) E(dwin) C(harles)
  1936- *42*
Gilliam, Stan 1946- *39*
  Brief entry *35*
Gilliland, Alexis A. 1931- *72*
Gilliland, Alexis Arnaldus
  See Gilliland, Alexis A.
Gilliland, (Cleburne) Hap 1918- *92*
Gilliland, Judith Heide *180*
Gillmor, Don 1954- *127*
Gilman, Dorothy 1923- *5*
Gilman, Esther 1925- *15*
Gilman, Laura Anne *178*
Gilman, Phoebe 1940-2002 .... *104*
  Obituary *141*
  Earlier sketch in SATA *58*
Gilmore, Iris 1900-1982 .... *22*
Gilmore, Kate 1931- *87*
Gilmore, Mary (Jean Cameron) 1865-1962 . *49*
Gilmore, Rachna 1953- *209*
Gilmore, Susan 1954- *59*
Gilpin, Stephen *213*
  Earlier sketch in SATA *177*
Gilroy, Beryl (Agatha) 1924- *80*
Gilson, Barbara
  See Gilson, Charles James Louis
Gilson, Charles James Louis 1878-1943
  See YABC *2*
Gilson, Jamie 1933- *176*
  Brief entry *34*
  Earlier sketches in SATA *37, 91*
Gimpel, Carolyn
  See Hart, Carolyn
Ginsberg, Blaze 1987- *222*
Ginsburg, Mirra 1909-2000 .... *92*
  Earlier sketch in SATA *6*
  See also CLR *45*
Giovanni, Nikki 1943- *208*
  Earlier sketches in SATA *24, 107*
  See also CLR *73*
Giovanni, Yolanda Cornelia
  See Giovanni, Nikki
Giovanni, Yolande Cornelia
  See Giovanni, Nikki
Giovanni, Yolande Cornelia, Jr.
  See Giovanni, Nikki
Giovanopoulos, Paul (Arthur) 1939- *7*
Gipson, Billie
  See Letts, Billie
Gipson, Fred(erick Benjamin) 1908-1973 ...... *2*
  Obituary *24*
Girard, Linda (Walvoord) 1942- *41*
Giraudon, David 1975- *215*

Girion, Barbara 1937- 78
  Earlier sketch in SATA 26
  See also SAAS 14
Girl, Nerdy
  See Castellucci, Cecil
Girouard, Patrick 1957- 155
Girzone, Joseph F. 1930- 76
Girzone, Joseph Francis
  See Girzone, Joseph F.
Gise, Joanne
  See Mattern, Joanne
Gist, E.M. 206
Gittings, Jo (Grenville) Manton 1919- 3
Gittings, Robert (William Victor) 1911-1992 . 6
  Obituary 70
Givens, Janet E(aton) 1932- 60
Givner, Joan 1936- 171
Givner, Joan Mary
  See Givner, Joan
Gladstone, Eve
  See Werner, Herma
Gladstone, Gary 1935- 12
Gladstone, M(yron) J. 1923- 37
Glanville, Brian (Lester) 1931- 42
Glanzman, Louis S. 1922- 36
Glaser, Byron 1954- 154
Glaser, Dianne E(lizabeth) 1937- 50
  Brief entry 31
Glaser, Isabel Joshlin 1929- 94
Glaser, Linda 225
Glaser, Milton 1929- 151
  Earlier sketch in SATA 11
Glaser, Shirley 151
Glaspell, Susan 1882(?)-1948
  See YABC 2
Glass, Andrew 1949- 223
  Brief entry 46
  Earlier sketches in SATA 90, 150
Glass, Linzi 175
Glass, Linzi Alex
  See Glass, Linzi
Glasscock, Amnesia
  See Steinbeck, John
Glassman, Bruce 1961- 76
Glatt, Lisa 1963- 217
Glauber, Uta (Heil) 1936- 17
Glazer, Thomas (Zachariah) 1914-2003 9
Glazer, Tom
  See Glazer, Thomas (Zachariah)
Gleasner, Diana (Cottle) 1936- 29
Gleason, Judith 1929- 24
Gleason, Katherine (A.) 1960- 104
Gleeson, Libby 1950- 142
  Autobiography Feature 142
  Earlier sketches in SATA 82, 118
Gleiter, Jan 1947- 111
Gleitzman, Morris 1953- 156
  Earlier sketch in SATA 88
  See also CLR 88
Glen, Maggie 1944- 88
Glendinning, Richard 1917-1988 24
Glendinning, Sally
  See Glendinning, Sara W(ilson)
Glendinning, Sara W(ilson) 1913-1993 24
Glenn, John W. 195
Glenn, Mel 1943- 93
  Brief entry 45
  Earlier sketch in SATA 51
  See also CLR 51
Glenn, Patricia Brown 1953- 86
Glenn, Sharlee 159
Glenn, Sharlee Mullins
  See Glenn, Sharlee
Glennon, Karen M. 1946- 85
Gles, Margaret Breitmaier 1940- 22
Glick, Carl (Cannon) 1890-1971 14
Glick, Ruth (Burtnick) 1942- 125
Glick, Virginia Kirkus 1893-1980
  Obituary 23
Gliewe, Unada (Grace) 1927- 3
Glimmerveen, Ulco 1958- 85

Glines, Carroll V(ane), Jr. 1920- 19
Gliori, Debi 1959- 189
  Earlier sketches in SATA 72, 138
Globe, Leah Ain 1900- 41
Glori Ann
  See Blakely, Gloria
Glovach, Linda 1947- 105
  Earlier sketch in SATA 7
Glover, Denis (James Matthews) 1912-1980 . 7
Glubok, Shirley (Astor) 146
  Autobiography Feature 146
  Earlier sketches in SATA 6, 68
  See also CLR 1
  See also SAAS 7
Gluck, Felix 1923-1981
  Obituary 25
Glyman, Caroline A. 1967- 103
Glynne-Jones, William 1907-1977 11
Gobbato, Imero 1923- 39
Gobbletree, Richard
  See Quackenbush, Robert M(ead)
Goble, Dorothy 26
Goble, Paul 1933- 131
  Earlier sketches in SATA 25, 69
  See also CLR 21
Goble, Warwick (?)-1943 46
Godden, (Margaret) Rumer 1907-1998 36
  Obituary 109
  Earlier sketch in SATA 3
  See also CLR 20
  See also SAAS 12
Gode, Alexander
  See Gode von Aesch, Alexander (Gottfried Friedrich)
Gode von Aesch, Alexander (Gottfried Friedrich) 1906-1970 14
Godfrey, Jane
  See Bowden, Joan Chase
Godfrey, Martyn
  See Godfrey, Martyn N.
  and Godfrey, Martyn N.
Godfrey, Martyn N. 1949-2000 95
  See also CLR 57
Godfrey, William
  See Youd, Samuel
Godkin, Celia 1948- 145
  Earlier sketch in SATA 66
Godkin, Celia Marilyn
  See Godkin, Celia
Godon, Ingrid 1958- 186
Godwin, Laura 1956- 179
Godwin, Sam
  See Pirotta, Saviour
Godwin, Sarah Massini
  See Massini, Sarah
Goede, Irene 1966- 208
Goedecke, Christopher (John) 1951- 81
Goekler, Susan
  See Wooley, Susan Frelick
Goembel, Ponder 204
Goertzen, Glenda 172
Goettel, Elinor 1930- 12
Goetz, Delia 1898-1996 22
  Obituary 91
Goffe, Toni 1936- 61
Goffstein, Brooke
  See Goffstein, Marilyn Brooke
Goffstein, M. B.
  See Goffstein, Marilyn Brooke
Goffstein, Marilyn Brooke 1940- 70
  Earlier sketch in SATA 8
  See also CLR 3
Goforth, Ellen
  See Francis, Dorothy
Gogol, Sara 1948-2004 80
Goh, Chan Hon 1969- 145
Going, Kelly L.
  See Going, K.L.
Going, Kelly Louise
  See Going, K.L.

Going, K.L. 199
  Earlier sketch in SATA 156
Golann, Cecil Paige 1921-1995 11
Golbin, Andree 1923- 15
Gold, Alison Leslie 1945- 104
Gold, August 1955- 215
Gold, Bernice 150
Gold, Phyllis
  See Goldberg, Phyllis
Gold, Robert S(tanley) 1924- 63
Gold, Sharlya 9
Gold, Susan
  See Gold, Susan Dudley
Gold, Susan Dudley 1949- 147
Goldbach, Veronica 1980- 220
Goldberg, Grace 1956- 78
Goldberg, Herbert S. 1926- 25
Goldberg, Jacob 1943- 94
Goldberg, Jake
  See Goldberg, Jacob
Goldberg, Myla 1972(?)- 210
Goldberg, Phyllis 1941- 21
Goldberg, Stan J. 1939- 26
Goldberg, Susan 1948- 71
Goldberg, Whoopi 1955- 119
Goldberger, Judith M. 1948- 80
Goldblatt, Stacey 1969(?)- 191
Golden, Christie 1963- 167
  Earlier sketch in SATA 116
Goldentyer, Debra 1960- 84
Goldfeder, Cheryl
  See Pahz, Cheryl Suzanne
Goldfeder, James
  See Pahz, James Alon
Goldfeder, Jim
  See Pahz, James Alon
Goldfinger, Jennifer P. 1963- 185
Goldfrank, Helen Colodny 1912- 6
Goldin, Augusta 1906-1999 13
Goldin, Barbara Diamond 1946- 129
  Autobiography Feature 129
  Earlier sketch in SATA 92
  See also SAAS 26
Goldin, David 1963- 101
Golding, Julia 1969- 188
Golding, Theresa Martin 1960- 150
Golding, William 1911-1993
  See CLR 130
Golding, William Gerald
  See Golding, William
Goldman, Alex J. 1917- 65
Goldman, E. M. 1943- 103
Goldman, Eleanor Maureen
  See Goldman, E. M.
Goldman, Elizabeth 1949- 90
Goldman, Judy 1955- 212
Goldman, Steven 1964- 207
Goldman, Todd Harris 221
Goldring, Ann 1937- 149
Goldsborough, June 1923- 19
Goldschmidt, Judy 202
Goldsmith, Connie 1945- 147
Goldsmith, Howard 1943- 108
  Earlier sketch in SATA 24
Goldsmith, John Herman Thorburn 1903-1987
  Obituary 52
Goldsmith, Oliver 1730(?)-1774 26
Goldsmith, Ruth M. 1919- 62
Goldstein, Nathan 1927- 47
Goldstein, Philip 1910-1997 23
Goldston, Robert (Conroy) 1927- 6
Goldstone, Bruce 183
Goldstone, Lawrence A.
  See Treat, Lawrence
Goldszmit, Henryk 1878-1942 65
  See also CLR 152
Golembe, Carla 1951- 79
Golenbock, Peter 1946- 99
Goll, Reinhold W(eimar) 1897-1993 26
Gollub, Matthew 1960- 134
  Earlier sketch in SATA 83

Golson, Terry 213
Golson, Terry Blonder
  See Golson, Terry
Gomes, Filomena 1965- 183
Gomez, Elena 191
Gomez, Elizabeth 133
Gomez-Freer, Elizabeth
  See Gomez, Elizabeth
Gomi, Taro 1945- 103
  Earlier sketch in SATA *64*
  See also CLR 57
Gondosch, Linda 1944- 58
Gonsalves, Rob 1959- 209
Gonyea, Mark 194
Gonzalez, Catherine Troxell 1917-2000 87
Gonzalez, Christina
  See Gonzalez, Maya Christina
Gonzalez, Gloria 1940- 23
Gonzalez, Julie 1958- 174
Gonzalez, Julie Sehers
  See Gonzalez, Julie
Gonzalez, Lucia M. 1957- 202
Gonzalez, Maya
  See Gonzalez, Maya Christina
Gonzalez, Maya Christina 1964- 175
  Earlier sketch in SATA *115*
Gonzalez, Rigoberto 1970- 147
Goobie, Beth 1959- 128
Good, Alice 1950- 73
Good, Clare
  See Romano, Clare
Good, Karen Hillard 214
Goodall, Daphne Machin
  See Machin Goodall, Daphne (Edith)
Goodall, Jane 1934- 111
Goodall, John S(trickland) 1908-1996 66
  Obituary 91
  Earlier sketch in SATA *4*
  See also CLR 25
Goodbody, Slim
  See Burstein, John
Goode, Diane 1949- 225
  Earlier sketches in SATA *15, 84, 114, 170*
Goode, Diane Capuozzo
  See Goode, Diane
Goode, Stephen Ray 1943- 55
  Brief entry 40
Goodenow, Earle 1913- 40
Goodhart, Pippa 1958- 196
  Earlier sketch in SATA *153*
Goodhue, Thomas W. 1949- 143
Goodin, Sallie (Brown) 1953- 74
Goodman, Alison 1966- 111
Goodman, Deborah Lerme 1956- 50
  Brief entry 49
Goodman, Elaine 1930- 9
Goodman, Emily 217
Goodman, Joan Elizabeth 1950- 162
  Earlier sketches in SATA *50, 94*
Goodman, Susan E. 1952- 181
Goodman, Walter 1927-2002 9
Goodman Koz, Paula 211
Goodrich, Carter 1959(?)- 221
Goodrich, Samuel Griswold 1793-1860 23
Goodsell, Jane Neuberger 1921(?)-1988
  Obituary 56
Goodweather, Hartley
  See King, Thomas
GoodWeather, Hartley
  See King, Thomas
Goodwin, Hal
  See Goodwin, Harold L(eland)
Goodwin, Harold L(eland) 1914-1990 51
  Obituary 65
  Earlier sketch in SATA *13*
Goodwin, William 1943- 117
Goor, Nancy (Ruth Miller) 1944- 39
  Brief entry 34
Goor, Ron(ald Stephen) 1940- 39
  Brief entry 34

Goossen, Agnes
  See Epp, Margaret A(gnes)
Goossens, Philippe 1963- 195
Gootman, Marilyn E. 1944- 179
Gopnik, Adam 1956- 171
Gorbachev, Valeri 1944- 222
  Autobiography Feature 143
  Earlier sketches in SATA *98, 143, 184*
Gordion, Mark
  See Turtledove, Harry
Gordon, Ad
  See Hano, Arnold
Gordon, Amy 1949- 197
  Earlier sketches in SATA *115, 156*
Gordon, Bernard Ludwig 1931-2010 27
Gordon, Colonel H. R.
  See Ellis, Edward S.
Gordon, David
  See Garrett, Randall
Gordon, Donald
  See Payne, Donald Gordon
Gordon, Dorothy 1893-1970 20
Gordon, Esther S(aranga) 1935- 10
Gordon, Frederick 1
Gordon, Gaelyn 1939-1997
  See CLR 75
Gordon, Garrett
  See Garrett, Randall
Gordon, Gary
  See Edmonds, I(vy) G(ordon)
Gordon, Hal
  See Goodwin, Harold L(eland)
Gordon, Jeffie Ross
  See Enderle, Judith (Ann) Ross
  and Gordon, Stephanie Jacob
Gordon, John
  See Gesner, Clark
Gordon, John (William) 1925- 84
Gordon, Lew
  See Baldwin, Gordon C(ortis)
Gordon, Margaret (Anna) 1939- 9
Gordon, Mike 1948- 101
Gordon, Mildred 1912-1979
  Obituary 24
Gordon, Selma
  See Lanes, Selma G.
Gordon, Sheila 1927- 88
  See also CLR 27
Gordon, Shirley 1921- 48
  Brief entry 41
Gordon, Sol 1923- 11
Gordon, Stephanie Jacob 1940- 89
  Autobiography Feature 114
  Earlier sketch in SATA *64*
  See also SAAS 26
Gordon, Stewart
  See Shirreffs, Gordon D(onald)
Gordons, The
  See Gordon, Mildred
  and Gordon, Gordon
Gore, Leonid 222
  Earlier sketch in SATA *185*
Gorelick, Molly C(hernow) 1920-2003 9
  Obituary 153
Gorey, Edward (St. John) 1925-2000 70
  Brief entry 27
  Obituary 118
  Earlier sketch in SATA *29*
  See also CLR 36
Gorham, Charles Orson 1868-1936 36
Gorham, Michael
  See Folsom, Franklin (Brewster)
Gorman, Carol 187
  Earlier sketch in SATA *150*
Gorman, Jacqueline Laks 1955- 148
Gorman, Mike 206
Gormley, Beatrice 1942- 202
  Brief entry 35
  Earlier sketches in SATA *39, 127*
Gorog, Judith (Katharine Allen) 1938- 75
  Earlier sketch in SATA *39*

Gorrell, Gena K. 1946- 170
Gorsline, Douglas (Warner) 1913-1985 11
  Obituary 43
Gorsline, (Sally) Marie 1928- 28
Gorsline, S. M.
  See Gorsline, (Sally) Marie
Gorton, Julia 218
Gorton, Kaitlyn
  See Emerson, Kathy Lynn
Gorton, Kathy Lynn
  See Emerson, Kathy Lynn
Goryan, Sirak
  See Saroyan, William
Goschke, Julia 1973- 208
Goscinny, Rene 1926-1977 47
  Brief entry 39
  See also CLR 37
Goss, Clay(ton E.) 1946- 82
Goss, Gary 1947- 124
Goss, Mini 1963- 186
Goto, Scott 203
Gott, Barry 197
Gottesman, S. D.
  See Kornbluth, C(yril) M.
  and Lowndes, Robert A(ugustine) W(ard)
  and Pohl, Frederik
Gottfried, Ted
  See Gottfried, Theodore Mark
Gottfried, Theodore Mark 1928- 150
  Earlier sketch in SATA *85*
Gottlieb, Gerald 1923- 7
Gottlieb, William P. 1917-2006 24
Gottlieb, William Paul
  See Gottlieb, William P.
Goudey, Alice E(dwards) 1898-1993 20
Goudge, Eileen 1950- 88
Goudge, Elizabeth (de Beauchamp)
  1900-1984 2
  Obituary 38
  See also CLR 94
Gough, Catherine
  See Mulgan, Catherine
Gough, Philip 1908-1986 45
Gough, Sue 1940- 106
Goulart, Ron 1933- 67
  Earlier sketch in SATA *1*
Goulart, Ronald Joseph
  See Goulart, Ron
Gould, Alberta 1945- 96
Gould, Chester 1900-1985 49
  Obituary 43
Gould, Jean R(osalind) 1909-1993 11
  Obituary 77
Gould, Lilian 6
Gould, Marilyn 1928- 76
  Earlier sketch in SATA *15*
Gould, Robert 154
Gould, Steven 1955- 95
Gould, Steven Charles
  See Gould, Steven
Gourley, Catherine 1950- 190
  Earlier sketch in SATA *95*
Gourse, Leslie 1939-2004 89
Govan, (Mary) Christine Noble 1898-1985 ... 9
Gove, Doris 1944- 72
Govenar, Alan 1952- 189
Govenar, Alan Bruce
  See Govenar, Alan
Govern, Elaine 1939- 26
Gowen, L. Kris 1968- 156
Graaf, Peter
  See Youd, Samuel
Graber, Alexander 1914-1997 98
  Earlier sketch in SATA *7*
Graber, George Alexander
  See Graber, Alexander
Graber, Janet 1942- 170
Graber, Richard (Fredrick) 1927- 26
Grabianski, Janusz 1928-1976 39
  Obituary 30
Graboff, Abner 1919-1986 35

Grace, Fran(ces Jane) 45
Grace, N.B.
    See Harper, Suzanne
Grace, Theresa
    See Mattern, Joanne
Gracza, Margaret Young 1928- 56
Graduate of Oxford, A
    See Ruskin, John
Grady, Denise 1952- 189
Graeber, Charlotte Towner 106
    Brief entry 44
    Earlier sketch in SATA 56
Graef, Renee 1956- 204
Graeme, Roderic
    See Jeffries, Roderic
Graf, Michael
    See Graf, Mike
Graf, Mike 1960- 164
Grafe, Max 198
Graff, Lisa 1981- 188
Graff, Polly Anne Colver
    See Colver, Anne
Graff, (S.) Stewart 1908-2009 9
Graham, Ada 1931- 11
Graham, Alastair 1945- 74
Graham, Arthur Kennon
    See Harrison, David L.
Graham, Bob 1942- 187
    Earlier sketches in SATA 63, 101, 151
    See also CLR 31
Graham, Brenda Knight 1942- 32
Graham, Charlotte
    See Bowden, Joan Chase
Graham, Christine 1952- 224
Graham, Eleanor 1896-1984 18
    Obituary 38
Graham, Ennis
    See Molesworth, Mary Louisa
Graham, Frank, Jr. 1925- 11
Graham, Georgia 1959- 190
Graham, Ian 1953- 112
Graham, John 1926-2007 11
Graham, Kennon
    See Harrison, David L.
Graham, Larry
    See Graham, Lawrence
Graham, Lawrence 1962- 63
Graham, Lawrence Otis
    See Graham, Lawrence
Graham, Linda
    See Graham-Barber, Lynda
Graham, Lorenz (Bell) 1902-1989 74
    Obituary 63
    Earlier sketch in SATA 2
    See also CLR 10
    See also SAAS 5
Graham, Margaret Bloy 1920- 11
Graham, Robin Lee 1949- 7
Graham, Shirley 1896(?)-1977
    See Du Bois, Shirley Graham
Graham-Barber, Lynda 1944- 159
    Earlier sketch in SATA 42
Graham-Cameron, M.
    See Graham-Cameron, M(alcolm) G(ordon)
Graham-Cameron, M(alcolm) G(ordon)
    1931- 53
    Brief entry 45
Graham-Cameron, Mike
    See Graham-Cameron, M(alcolm) G(ordon)
Grahame, Kenneth 1859-1932 100
    See also YABC 1
    See also CLR 135
Gralley, Jean 166
Gramatky, Hardie 1907-1979 30
    Obituary 23
    Earlier sketch in SATA 1
    See also CLR 22
Grambling, Lois G. 1927- 206
    Earlier sketches in SATA 71, 148
Grambo, Rebecca L(ynn) 1963- 109
Grammer, June Amos 1927- 58

Grand, Samuel 1912-1988 42
Grandits, John 1949- 192
GrandPre, Mary 1954- 184
Grandville, J. J.
    See Gerard, Jean Ignace Isidore
Grandville, Jean Ignace Isidore Gerard
    See Gerard, Jean Ignace Isidore
Granfield, Linda 1950- 160
    Earlier sketch in SATA 96
Grange, Peter
    See Nicole, Christopher (Robin)
Granger, Margaret Jane 1925(?)-1977
    Obituary 27
Granger, Michele 1949- 88
Granger, Peggy
    See Granger, Margaret Jane
Granowsky, Alvin 1936- 101
Granstaff, Bill 1925- 10
Granstrom, Brita 1969- 224
    Earlier sketches in SATA 111, 167
Grant, Bruce 1893-1977 5
    Obituary 25
Grant, Cynthia D. 1950- 147
    Earlier sketches in SATA 33, 77
Grant, Eva 1907-1996 7
Grant, Evva H. 1913-1977
    Obituary 27
Grant, Gordon 1875-1962 25
Grant, Gwen(doline Ellen) 1940- 47
Grant, Judyann Ackerman 211
Grant, Katie M.
    See Grant, K.M.
Grant, K.M. 175
Grant, (Alice) Leigh 1947- 10
Grant, Matthew G.
    See May, Julian
Grant, Maxwell
    See Gibson, Walter B(rown)
    and Lynds, Dennis
Grant, Melvyn 183
Grant, Myrna (Lois) 1934- 21
Grant, Neil 1938- 154
    Earlier sketch in SATA 14
Grant, Nicholas
    See Nicole, Christopher (Robin)
Grant, Richard 1948- 80
Grant, Skeeter
    See Spiegelman, Art
Grater, Michael 1923- 57
Gratz, Alan 1972- 212
Graullera, Fabiola
    See Graullera Ramirez, Fabiola
Graullera Ramirez, Fabiola 225
Gravel, Fern
    See Hall, James Norman
Gravelle, Karen 1942- 166
    Earlier sketch in SATA 78
Graves, Charles Parlin 1911-1972 4
Graves, Keith 191
    Earlier sketch in SATA 156
Graves, Robert 1895-1985 45
Graves, Robert von Ranke
    See Graves, Robert
Graves, Valerie
    See Bradley, Marion Zimmer
Gravett, Emily 1972(?)- 189
Gray, Betsy
    See Poole, Gray Johnson
Gray, Caroline
    See Nicole, Christopher (Robin)
Gray, Claudia 213
Gray, Dianne E. 183
Gray, Elizabeth Janet
    See Vining, Elizabeth Gray
Gray, Genevieve S(tuck) 1920-1995 4
Gray, Harold (Lincoln) 1894-1968 33
    Brief entry 32
Gray, Jenny
    See Gray, Genevieve S(tuck)
Gray, John Lee
    See Jakes, John

Gray, Judith A. 1949- 93
Gray, Judith Anne
    See Gray, Judith A.
Gray, Keith 151
Gray, Kes 1960- 153
Gray, Les 1929- 82
Gray, Libba Moore 1937- 83
Gray, Luli 1945- 149
    Earlier sketch in SATA 90
Gray, Marian
    See Pierce, Edith Gray
Gray, Nicholas Stuart 1922-1981 4
    Obituary 27
Gray, Nigel 1941- 104
    Earlier sketch in SATA 33
Gray, (Lucy) Noel (Clervaux) 1898-1983 47
Gray, Patricia (Clark) 7
Gray, Patsey
    See Gray, Patricia (Clark)
Gray, Rita 184
Graydon, Shari 1958- 158
Grayland, V. Merle
    See Grayland, Valerie (Merle Spanner)
Grayland, Valerie (Merle Spanner) 7
Grayson, Devin (Kalile) 1970- 119
Grayson, Kristine
    See Rusch, Kristine Kathryn
Grayson, Paul 1946- 79
Graystone, Lynn
    See Brennan, Joseph Lomas
Great Comte, The
    See Hawkesworth, Eric
Greaves, Margaret 1914-1995 87
    Earlier sketch in SATA 7
Greaves, Nick 1955- 77
Greban, Quentin 1977- 223
Gree, Alain 1936- 28
Green, Adam
    See Weisgard, Leonard (Joseph)
Green, Anne Canevari 1943- 62
Green, Brian
    See Card, Orson Scott
Green, Cliff(ord) 1934- 126
Green, Connie Jordan 1938- 80
Green, D.
    See Casewit, Curtis W(erner)
Green, Elizabeth Shippen 1871-1954 139
Green, Hannah
    See Greenberg, Joanne (Goldenberg)
Green, Jane 1937- 9
Green, Jessica 211
Green, John 1977(?)- 170
Green, Mary Moore 1906- 11
Green, Morton 1937- 8
Green, Norma B(erger) 1925- 11
Green, Phyllis 1932- 20
Green, Roger (Gilbert) Lancelyn 1918-1987 . 2
    Obituary 53
Green, (James Le)Roy 1948- 89
Green, Sheila Ellen 1934- 148
    Earlier sketches in SATA 8, 87
Green, Timothy 1953- 91
Greenaway, Kate 1846-1901 100
    See also YABC 2
    See also CLR 111
Greenbank, Anthony Hunt 1933- 39
Greenberg, David 1954- 171
Greenberg, David T.
    See Greenberg, David
Greenberg, Harvey R. 1935- 5
Greenberg, Jan 1942- 211
    Earlier sketches in SATA 61, 125
Greenberg, Joanne (Goldenberg) 1932- 25
Greenberg, Melanie Hope 1954- 214
    Earlier sketch in SATA 72
Greenberg, Polly 1932- 52
    Brief entry 43
Greenblat, Rodney Alan 1960- 106
Greenburg, Dan 1936- 175
    Earlier sketch in SATA 102

Greene, Bette 1934- *161*
   Earlier sketches in SATA *8, 102*
   See also CLR *140*
   See also SAAS *16*
Greene, Carla 1916- *67*
   Earlier sketch in SATA *1*
Greene, Carol *102*
   Brief entry *44*
   Earlier sketch in SATA *66*
Greene, Constance C(larke) 1924- *72*
   Earlier sketch in SATA *11*
   See also CLR *62*
   See also SAAS *11*
Greene, Edgar
   See Papademetriou, Lisa
Greene, Ellin 1927- *23*
Greene, Graham 1904-1991 .... *20*
Greene, Graham Henry
   See Greene, Graham
Greene, Jacqueline Dembar 1946- *212*
   Earlier sketches in SATA *76, 131*
Greene, Laura Offenhartz 1935- *38*
Greene, Meg
   See Malvasi, Meg Greene
Greene, Michele 1962- *178*
Greene, Michele Dominguez
   See Greene, Michele
Greene, Rhonda Gowler 1955- *160*
   Earlier sketch in SATA *101*
Greene, Stephanie 1950- *221*
   Earlier sketches in SATA *127, 173*
Greene, Wade 1933- *11*
Greene, Yvonne
   See Flesch, Yolande
Greenfeld, Howard (Scheinman) 1928- *140*
   Earlier sketch in SATA *19*
Greenfeld, Josh(ua Joseph) 1928- *62*
Greenfield, Eloise 1929- *155*
   Earlier sketches in SATA *19, 61, 105*
   See also CLR *38*
   See also SAAS *16*
Greenhaus, Thelma Nurenberg 1903-1984
   Obituary *45*
Greenhut, Josh
   See Mercer, Sienna
Greening, Hamilton
   See Hamilton, Charles (Harold St. John)
Greenlaw, M. Jean 1941- *107*
Greenleaf, Barbara Kaye 1942- *6*
Greenleaf, Peter 1910-1997 .... *33*
Greenlee, Sharon 1935- *77*
Greeno, Gayle 1949- *81*
Greenseid, Diane 1948- *178*
   Earlier sketch in SATA *93*
Greenspun, Adele Aron 1938- *142*
   Earlier sketch in SATA *76*
Greenstein, Elaine 1959- *150*
   Earlier sketch in SATA *82*
Greenwald, Sheila
   See Green, Sheila Ellen
Greenwood, Barbara 1940- *129*
   Earlier sketch in SATA *90*
Greenwood, Mark 1958- *202*
Greenwood, Pamela D. 1944- *115*
Greer, Richard
   See Garrett, Randall
   and Silverberg, Robert
Gregg, Andrew K. 1929- *81*
Gregg, Charles T(hornton) 1927- *65*
Gregg, Walter H(arold) 1919- *20*
Gregor, Arthur 1923- *36*
Gregor, Lee
   See Pohl, Frederik
Gregori, Leon 1919- *15*
Gregorian, Joyce Ballou 1946-1991 .... *30*
   Obituary *83*
Gregorich, Barbara 1943- *184*
   Earlier sketch in SATA *66*
Gregorowski, Christopher 1940- *30*
Gregory, Diana (Jean) 1933- *49*
   Brief entry *42*

Gregory, Harry
   See Gottfried, Theodore Mark
Gregory, Jean
   See Ure, Jean
Gregory, Kristiana 1951- *212*
   Earlier sketches in SATA *74, 136*
Gregory, Nan 1944- *192*
   Earlier sketch in SATA *148*
Gregory, Philippa 1954- *122*
Gregory, Stephen
   See Penzler, Otto
Gregory, Valiska 1940- *82*
Greif, Jean-Jacques 1944- *195*
Greisman, Joan Ruth 1937- *31*
Grendon, Stephen
   See Derleth, August (William)
Grenville, Pelham
   See Wodehouse, P. G.
Gretz, Susanna 1937- *7*
Gretzer, John *18*
Grewdead, Roy
   See Gorey, Edward (St. John)
Grey, Carol
   See Lowndes, Robert A(ugustine) W(ard)
Grey, Christopher *191*
Grey, Christopher Peter
   See Grey, Christopher
Grey, Jerry 1926- *11*
Grey, Mini *205*
   Earlier sketch in SATA *166*
Greybeard the Pirate
   See Macintosh, Brownie
Grey Owl
   See Belaney, Archibald Stansfeld
Gri
   See Denney, Diana
Gribbin, John 1946- *159*
Gribbin, John R.
   See Gribbin, John
Grice, Frederick 1910-1983 .... *6*
Grider, Dorothy 1915- *31*
Gridley, Marion E(leanor) 1906-1974 .... *35*
   Obituary *26*
Grieco-Tiso, Pina 1954- *108*
Grieder, Walter 1924- *9*
Griego, Tony A. 1955- *77*
Griese, Arnold A(lfred) 1921- *9*
Griessman, Annette 1962- *170*
   Earlier sketch in SATA *116*
Grieve, James 1934- *146*
Grifalconi, Ann 1929- *210*
   Earlier sketches in SATA *2, 66, 133*
   See also CLR *35*
   See also SAAS *16*
Griffin, Adele 1970- *195*
   Earlier sketches in SATA *105, 153*
Griffin, Elizabeth May 1985- *89*
Griffin, Gillett Good 1928- *26*
Griffin, Judith Berry *34*
Griffin, Kitty 1951- *137*
Griffin, Peni R. 1961- *193*
   Earlier sketches in SATA *67, 99*
Griffin, Steven A. 1953- *89*
Griffin, Steven Arthur
   See Griffin, Steven A.
Griffin, W. E. B. 1929- *5*
Griffith, Connie 1946- *89*
Griffith, Gershom 1960- *85*
Griffith, Helen V. 1934- *87*
   Autobiography Feature *107*
   Earlier sketch in SATA *39*
Griffith, Helen Virginia
   See Griffith, Helen V.
Griffith, Jeannette
   See Eyerly, Jeannette
Griffith, Saul 1974- *200*
Griffiths, Andy 1961- *196*
   Earlier sketch in SATA *152*
Griffiths, G(ordon) D(ouglas) 1910-1973
   Obituary *20*

Griffiths, Helen 1939- *86*
   Earlier sketch in SATA *5*
   See also CLR *75*
   See also SAAS *5*
Grigson, Jane (McIntire) 1928-1990 .... *63*
Grimes, Lee 1920- *68*
Grimes, Nikki 1950- *218*
   Earlier sketches in SATA *93, 136, 174*
   See also CLR *42*
Grimly, Gris *186*
Grimm, Jacob Ludwig Karl 1785-1863 .... *22*
   See also CLR *112*
Grimm, Wilhelm Karl 1786-1859 .... *22*
   See also CLR *112*
Grimm, William C(arey) 1907-1992 .... *14*
Grimm and Grim
   See Grimm, Jacob Ludwig Karl
   and Grimm, Wilhelm Karl
Grimm Brothers
   See Grimm, Jacob Ludwig Karl
   and Grimm, Wilhelm Karl
Grimsdell, Jeremy 1942- *83*
Grimshaw, Nigel (Gilroy) 1925- *23*
Grimsley, Gordon
   See Groom, Arthur William
Grindley, Jane Sally
   See Grindley, Sally
Grindley, Sally 1953- *148*
Gringhuis, Dirk
   See Gringhuis, Richard H.
Gringhuis, Richard H. 1918-1974 .... *6*
   Obituary *25*
Grinnell, David
   See Wollheim, Donald A(llen)
Grinnell, George Bird 1849-1938 .... *16*
Grinspoon, David
   See Grinspoon, David H.
Grinspoon, David H. 1959- *156*
Grinspoon, David Harry
   See Grinspoon, David H.
Gripe, Maria 1923- *74*
   Earlier sketch in SATA *2*
   See also CLR *5*
Gripe, Maria Kristina
   See Gripe, Maria
Gritton, Steve *223*
Grobler, Piet 1959- *201*
Groch, Judith (Goldstein) 1929- *25*
Grode, Redway
   See Gorey, Edward (St. John)
Groener, Carl
   See Lowndes, Robert A(ugustine) W(ard)
Groening, Matt 1954- *116*
   Earlier sketch in SATA *81*
Grohmann, Susan 1948- *84*
Grohskopf, Bernice *7*
Grol, Lini R(icharda) 1913- *9*
Grollman, Earl A. 1925- *22*
Groom, Arthur William 1898-1964 .... *10*
Grooms, Duffy 1964- *169*
Gross, Alan 1947- *54*
   Brief entry *43*
Gross, Ernie 1913- *67*
Gross, Philip 1952- *164*
   Earlier sketch in SATA *84*
Gross, Philip John
   See Gross, Philip
Gross, Ruth Belov 1929- *33*
Gross, Sarah Chokla 1906-1976 .... *9*
   Obituary *26*
Grosser, Morton 1931- *74*
Grosser, Vicky 1958- *83*
Grossman, Bill 1948- *126*
   Earlier sketch in SATA *72*
Grossman, Nancy 1940- *29*
Grossman, Patricia 1951- *73*
Grossman, Robert 1940- *11*
Grossmann-Hensel, Katharina 1973- *219*
Grote, JoAnn A. 1951- *113*
Groten, Dallas 1951- *64*

Groth, John (August) 1908-1988 21
Obituary 56
Groth-Fleming, Candace
See Fleming, Candace
Grove, Vicki 1948- 151
Autobiography Feature 151
Earlier sketch in SATA 122
Grover, Lorie Ann 1964- 168
Grover, Wayne 1934- 69
Groves, Georgina
See Symons, (Dorothy) Geraldine
Groves, Maketa 1950- 107
Groves, Seli 77
Grubb, Lisa 160
Gruber, Michael 1940- 173
Gruber, Terry (deRoy) 1953- 66
Gruelle, John 1880-1938 35
Brief entry 32
See also CLR 34
Gruelle, Johnny
See Gruelle, John
Gruenberg, Sidonie Matsner 1881-1974 2
Obituary 27
Gruhzit-Hoyt, Olga (Margaret) 1922- 127
Earlier sketch in SATA 16
Grummer, Arnold E(dward) 1923- 49
Grunewalt, Pine
See Kunhardt, Edith
Grunwell, Jeanne Marie 1971- 147
Grupper, Jonathan 137
Gryski, Camilla 1948- 72
Guarino, Dagmar
See Guarino, Deborah
Guarino, Deborah 1954- 68
Guay, Georgette (Marie Jeanne) 1952- 54
Guay, Rebecca 209
Guay-Mitchell, Rebecca
See Guay, Rebecca
Guback, Georgia 88
Guccione, Leslie Davis 1946- 111
Earlier sketch in SATA 72
Guck, Dorothy 1913-2002 27
Gudeon, Karla 212
Guerny, Gene
See Gurney, Gene
Guest, Elissa Haden 1953- 218
Earlier sketch in SATA 125
Guest, Jacqueline 1952- 135
Guevara, Susan 167
Earlier sketch in SATA 97
Gugler, Laurel Dee 95
Gugliotta, Bobette 1918-1994 7
Guianan, Eve 1965- 102
Guiberson, Brenda Z. 1946- 211
Earlier sketches in SATA 71, 124
Guibert, Emmanuel 1964- 181
Guile, Melanie 1949- 152
Earlier sketch in SATA 104
Guillaume, Jeanette G. Flierl 1899-1990 8
Guillot, Rene 1900-1969 7
See also CLR 22
Guisewite, Cathy 1950- 57
Guisewite, Cathy Lee
See Guisewite, Cathy
Gulbis, Stephen 1959- 142
Gulley, Judie 1942- 58
Gump, P. Q.
See Card, Orson Scott
Gundrey, Elizabeth 1924- 23
Gunn, James E. 1923- 35
Gunn, James Edwin
See Gunn, James E.
Gunn, Robin Jones 1955- 84
Gunnella 1956- 197
Gunning, Monica Olwen 1930- 161
Gunston, Bill
See Gunston, William Tudor
Gunston, William Tudor 1927- 9
Gunterman, Bertha Lisette 1886(?)-1975
Obituary 27
Gunther, John 1901-1970

Guravich, Dan 1918- 74
Gurko, Leo 1914- 9
Gurko, Miriam 1910(?)-1988 9
Obituary 58
Gurney, Gene 1924- 65
Gurney, James 1958- 120
Earlier sketch in SATA 76
Gurney, John Steven 1962- 143
Earlier sketch in SATA 75
Gustafson, Sarah R.
See Riedman, Sarah R(egal)
Gustafson, Scott 1956- 34
Gustavson, Adam 1974- 214
Earlier sketch in SATA 176
Guthrie, A(lfred) B(ertram), Jr. 1901-1991 .. 62
Obituary 67
Guthrie, Anne 1890-1979 28
Guthrie, Donna W. 1946- 105
Earlier sketch in SATA 63
Gutierrez, Akemi 172
Gutierrez, Rudy 203
Gutman, Bill 128
Brief entry 43
Earlier sketch in SATA 67
Gutman, Dan 1955- 221
Earlier sketches in SATA 77, 139, 188
Gutman, Naham 1899(?)-1981
Obituary 25
Gutmann, Bessie Pease 1876-1960 73
Guy, Geoffrey 1942- 153
Guy, Ginger Foglesong 1954- 171
Guy, Rosa 1925- 122
Earlier sketches in SATA 14, 62
See also CLR 137
Guy, Rosa Cuthbert
See Guy, Rosa
Guy, Susan 1948- 149
Guymer, (Wilhelmina) Mary 1909- 50
Guzman, Lila 1952- 168
Guzman, Rick 1957- 168
Gwaltney, Doris 1932- 181
Gwynne, Fred(erick Hubbard) 1926-1993 41
Brief entry 27
Obituary 75
Gwynne, Oscar A.
See Ellis, Edward S.
Gwynne, Oswald A.
See Ellis, Edward S.
Gyorkos, Charmaine Echeverria
See Echeverria Gyorkos, Charmaine

H

Haab, Sherri 1964- 169
Earlier sketch in SATA 91
Haar, Jaap ter
See ter Haar, Jaap
Haarsma, P.J. 183
Haas, Carolyn Buhai 1926- 43
Haas, Dan 1957- 105
Haas, Dorothy F. 46
Brief entry 43
See also SAAS 17
Haas, Irene 1929- 96
Earlier sketch in SATA 17
Haas, James E. 1943- 40
Haas, James Edward
See Haas, James E.
Haas, Jessie 1959- 215
Haas, (Katherine) Jessie 1959- 135
Autobiography Feature 135
Earlier sketch in SATA 98
Haas, Merle S. 1896(?)-1985
Obituary 41
Habenstreit, Barbara 1937- 5
Haber, Karen 1955- 78
Haber, Louis 1910-1988 12
Hacker, Randi 1951- 185

Hacker, Randi Dawn
See Hacker, Randi
Hackett, John Winthrop 1910-1997 65
Hacks, Peter 1928-2003
Obituary 151
Haddix, Margaret Peterson 1964- 224
Earlier sketches in SATA 94, 125, 187
Haddon, Mark 1962- 223
Earlier sketch in SATA 155
Hader, Berta (Hoerner) 1891(?)-1976 16
Hader, Elmer (Stanley) 1889-1973 16
Hadithi, Mwenye
See Hobson, Bruce
Hadley, Franklin
See Winterbotham, R(ussell) R(obert)
Hadley, Lee 1934-1995 89
Brief entry 38
Obituary 86
Earlier sketch in SATA 47
See also CLR 40
See also SAAS 14
Haeffele, Deborah 1954- 76
Haenel, Wolfram 1956- 89
See also CLR 64
Hafner, Marylin 1925- 179
Earlier sketches in SATA 7, 121
Haft, Erin
See Ehrenhaft, Daniel
Hager, Alan 1940- 176
Hager, Alice Rogers 1894-1969
Obituary 26
Hager, Betty 1923- 89
Hager, Jenna Bush
See Bush, Jenna
Hager, Sarah 171
Hager, Thomas 1953- 119
Hager, Tom
See Hager, Thomas
Hagerup, Klaus 1946- 186
Haggard, H(enry) Rider 1856-1925 16
Haggerty, James J(oseph) 1920- 5
Hagon, Priscilla
See Allan, Mabel Esther
Hague, Kathleen 1949- 49
Brief entry 45
Hague, Michael 1948- 185
Brief entry 32
Earlier sketches in SATA 48, 80, 129
Hague, Michael R.
See Hague, Michael
Hague, Susan Kathleen
See Hague, Kathleen
Hahn, Emily 1905-1997 3
Obituary 96
Hahn, Hannelore 8
Hahn, James (Sage) 1947- 9
Hahn, Lynn 1949- 9
Hahn, Mary Downing 1937- 208
Autobiography Feature 157
Brief entry 44
Earlier sketches in SATA 50, 81, 138, 157
See also SAAS 12
Hahn, Michael T. 1953- 92
Hahn, Mona Lynn
See Hahn, Lynn
Haig, Matt 1975- 221
Haig-Brown, Roderick (Langmere)
1908-1976 12
See also CLR 31
Haight, Anne Lyon 1895-1977
Obituary 30
Haight, Rip
See Carpenter, John
Haight, Sandy 1949- 79
Haij, Vera
See Jansson, Tove (Marika)
Hailstone, Ruth 219
Haines, Gail Kay 1943- 11
Haines, Margaret Ann Beck
See Beck, Peggy

Haining, Peter 1940-2007 .... *14*
  Obituary *188*
Haining, Peter Alexander
  See Haining, Peter
Hains, Harriet
  See Watson, Carol
Hajdusiewicz, Babs Bell *163*
Hakim, Joy 1931- *173*
  Earlier sketch in SATA *83*
Halacy, D. S., Jr. 1919-2002 .... *36*
  See also SAAS *8*
Halacy, Dan
  See Halacy, D. S., Jr.
Halam, Ann
  See Jones, Gwyneth A.
Haldane, Roger John 1945- *13*
Hale, Arlene 1924-1982 .... *49*
Hale, Bruce 1957- *203*
  Earlier sketch in SATA *123*
Hale, Christy
  See Apostolou, Christine Hale
Hale, Edward Everett 1822-1909 .... *16*
Hale, Glenn
  See Walker, Robert W.
Hale, Helen
  See Mulcahy, Lucille Burnett
Hale, Irina 1932- *26*
Hale, Kathleen 1898-2000 .... *66*
  Obituary *121*
  Earlier sketch in SATA *17*
Hale, Linda (Howe) 1929- *6*
Hale, Lucretia P.
  See Hale, Lucretia Peabody
Hale, Lucretia Peabody 1820-1900 .... *26*
  See also CLR *105*
Hale, Marian *194*
Hale, Nancy 1908-1988 .... *31*
  Obituary *57*
Hale, Nathan 1976- *210*
Hale, Shannon *200*
  Earlier sketch in SATA *158*
Haley, Amanda *205*
Haley, Gail E(inhart) 1939- *161*
  Autobiography Feature *161*
  Brief entry *28*
  Earlier sketches in SATA *43, 78, 136*
  See also CLR *21*
  See also SAAS *13*
Haley, Neale *52*
Halfmann, Janet 1944- *208*
Hall, Adam
  See Trevor, Elleston
Hall, Adele 1910- *7*
Hall, Anna Gertrude 1882-1967 .... *8*
Hall, August *207*
Hall, Barbara 1961- *68*
Hall, Becky 1950- *186*
Hall, Beverly B. 1918- *95*
Hall, Borden
  See Yates, Raymond F(rancis)
Hall, Brian P(atrick) 1935- *31*
Hall, Cameron
  See del Rey, Lester
Hall, Caryl
  See Hansen, Caryl (Hall)
Hall, Donald 1928- *97*
  Earlier sketch in SATA *23*
Hall, Donald Andrew, Jr.
  See Hall, Donald
Hall, Douglas 1931- *43*
Hall, Elizabeth 1929- *77*
Hall, Elvajean 1910-1984 .... *6*
Hall, Francie 1940- *166*
Hall, James Norman 1887-1951 .... *21*
Hall, Jesse
  See Boesen, Victor
Hall, Katy
  See McMullan, Kate
Hall, Kirsten Marie 1974- *67*

Hall, Lynn 1937- *79*
  Earlier sketches in SATA *2, 47*
  See also SAAS *4*
Hall, Malcolm 1945- *7*
Hall, Marcellus *203*
Hall, Marjory
  See Yeakley, Marjory Hall
Hall, Melanie W. 1949- *169*
  Earlier sketches in SATA *78, 116*
Hall, Patricia 1940- *136*
Hall, Rosalys Haskell 1914- *7*
Hall, Willis 1929-2005 .... *66*
Hallard, Peter
  See Catherall, Arthur
Hallas, Richard
  See Knight, Eric
Hall-Clarke, James
  See Rowland-Entwistle, (Arthur) Theodore
  (Henry)
Hallensleben, Georg 1958- *173*
Haller, Dorcas Woodbury 1946- *46*
Hallett, Mark 1947- *220*
  Earlier sketch in SATA *83*
Halliburton, Richard 1900-1939(?) *81*
Halliburton, Warren J. 1924- *19*
Halliday, Brett
  See Dresser, Davis
  and Johnson, (Walter) Ryerson
  and Terrall, Robert
Halliday, William R(oss) 1926- *52*
Hallin, Emily Watson 1916-1995 .... *6*
Hallinan, P. K. 1944- *39*
  Brief entry *37*
Hallinan, Patrick Kenneth
  See Hallinan, P. K.
Hallman, Ruth 1929- *43*
  Brief entry *28*
Hallowell, Tommy
  See Hill, Thomas
Hall-Quest, (Edna) Olga W(ilbourne)
  1899-1986 .... *11*
  Obituary *47*
Halls, Kelly Milner 1957- *220*
  Earlier sketch in SATA *131*
Hallstead, William F(inn III) 1924- *11*
Hallward, Michael 1889-1982 .... *12*
Halperin, Michael *156*
Halperin, Wendy Anderson 1952- *200*
  Earlier sketches in SATA *80, 125*
Halpern, Julie 1975- *198*
Halpin, Brendan 1968- *193*
Halpin, Marlene 1927- *88*
Halse, Laurie Beth
  See Anderson, Laurie Halse
Halsell, Grace (Eleanor) 1923-2000 .... *13*
Halsey, Megan *185*
Halsted, Anna Roosevelt 1906-1975
  Obituary *30*
Halter, Jon C(harles) 1941- *22*
Halverson, Deborah *202*
Halvorson, Adeline *218*
Halvorson, Marilyn 1948- *123*
Hamalian, Leo 1920- *41*
Hamberger, John 1934- *14*
Hamblin, Dora Jane 1920- *36*
Hambly, Barbara 1951- *108*
Hambly, Barbara Joan
  See Hambly, Barbara
Hamer, Martyn
  See Eldin, Peter
Hamerstrom, Frances 1907-1998 .... *24*
Hamil, Thomas Arthur 1928- *14*
Hamill, Ethel
  See Webb, Jean Francis (III)
Hamilton, (John) Alan 1943- *66*
Hamilton, Alice
  See Cromie, Alice Hamilton
Hamilton, Anita 1919- *92*
Hamilton, Buzz
  See Hemming, Roy G.
Hamilton, Carol (Jean Barber) 1935- *94*

Hamilton, Charles (Harold St. John)
  1876-1961 .... *13*
Hamilton, Charles 1913-1996 .... *65*
  Obituary *93*
Hamilton, Clive
  See Lewis, C. S.
Hamilton, Dorothy (Drumm) 1906-1983 ...... *12*
  Obituary *35*
Hamilton, Edith 1867-1963 .... *20*
Hamilton, Edmond 1904-1977 .... *118*
Hamilton, (Muriel) Elizabeth (Mollie)
  1906- *23*
Hamilton, Emma Walton 1962- *177*
Hamilton, Franklin
  See Silverberg, Robert
Hamilton, Gail
  See Corcoran, Barbara (Asenath)
  and Dodge, Mary Abigail
Hamilton, Kersten 1958- *204*
  Earlier sketch in SATA *134*
Hamilton, K.R.
  See Hamilton, Kersten
Hamilton, Martha 1953- *183*
  Earlier sketch in SATA *123*
Hamilton, Mary (E.) 1927- *55*
Hamilton, Mollie
  See Kaye, M.M.
Hamilton, Morse 1943-1998 .... *101*
  Earlier sketch in SATA *35*
Hamilton, Peter F. 1960- *109*
Hamilton, Priscilla
  See Gellis, Roberta
Hamilton, Ralph
  See Stratemeyer, Edward L.
Hamilton, Virginia 1936-2002 .... *123*
  Obituary *132*
  Earlier sketches in SATA *4, 56, 79*
  See also CLR *127*
Hamilton, Virginia Esther
  See Hamilton, Virginia
Hamilton-Paterson, James 1941- *82*
Hamlet, Ova
  See Lupoff, Richard A(llen)
Hamley, D. C.
  See Hamley, Dennis
Hamley, Dennis 1935- *69*
  Earlier sketch in SATA *39*
  See also CLR *47*
  See also SAAS *22*
Hamley, Dennis C.
  See Hamley, Dennis
Hamlin, Peter J. 1970- *84*
Hamm, Diane Johnston 1949- *78*
Hammer, Charles 1934- *58*
Hammer, Richard 1928- *6*
Hammerman, Gay M(orenus) 1926- *9*
Hammill, Matt 1982- *206*
Hammond, Andrew 1970- *181*
Hammond, Ralph
  See Hammond Innes, Ralph
Hammond, Winifred G(raham) 1899-1992 ... *29*
  Obituary *107*
Hammond Innes, Ralph 1913-1998 .... *116*
Hammontree, Marie (Gertrude) 1913- *13*
Hample, Zack 1977- *161*
Hampshire, Joyce Gregorian
  See Gregorian, Joyce Ballou
Hampshire, Susan 1942- *98*
Hampson, (Richard) Denman 1929- *15*
Hampson, Frank 1918(?)-1985
  Obituary *46*
Hampton, Wilborn 1940- *196*
  Earlier sketch in SATA *156*
Hamre, Leif 1914- *5*
Hamsa, Bobbie 1944- *52*
  Brief entry *38*
Han, Jenny 1981- *175*
Han, Lu
  See Stickler, Soma Han
Han, Soma
  See Stickler, Soma Han

Han, Suzanne Crowder 1953- *89*
Hancock, Mary A. 1923- *31*
Hancock, Sibyl 1940- *9*
Hand, Elizabeth 1957- *167*
    Earlier sketch in SATA *118*
Handford, Martin (John) 1956- *64*
    See also CLR *22*
Handforth, Thomas (Schofield) 1897-1948 .. *42*
Handleman, Philip 1951- *222*
Handler, Daniel
    See Snicket, Lemony
Handville, Robert (Tompkins) 1924- *45*
Hane, Roger 1940-1974
    Obituary *20*
Hanel, Wolfram
    See Haenel, Wolfram
Haney, Lynn 1941- *23*
Hanff, Helene 1916-1997 .... *97*
    Earlier sketch in SATA *11*
Hanft, Josh 1956- *197*
Hanft, Joshua E.
    See Hanft, Josh
Hanley, Boniface Francis 1924- *65*
Hanlon, Emily 1945- *15*
Hann, Jacquie 1951- *19*
Hann, Judith 1942- *77*
Hanna, Bill
    See Hanna, William (Denby)
Hanna, Cheryl 1951- *84*
Hanna, Dan *200*
Hanna, Jack (Bushnell) 1947- *74*
Hanna, Nell(ie L.) 1908- *55*
Hanna, Paul R(obert) 1902-1988 .... *9*
Hanna, William (Denby) 1910-2001 .... *51*
    Obituary *126*
Hannam, Charles 1925- *50*
Hannan, Peter 1954- *187*
Hannigan, Katherine *170*
Hannon, Ezra
    See Hunter, Evan
Hann-Syme, Marguerite *127*
Hano, Arnold 1922- *12*
Hano, Renee Roth
    See Roth-Hano, Renee
Hanover, Terri
    See Huff, Tanya
Hansen, Ann Larkin 1958- *96*
Hansen, Brooks 1965- *104*
Hansen, Caryl (Hall) 1929- *39*
Hansen, Ian V. 1929- *113*
Hansen, Jennifer 1972- *156*
Hansen, Joyce 1942- *172*
    Autobiography Feature *172*
    Brief entry *39*
    Earlier sketches in SATA *46, 101*
    See also CLR *21*
    See also SAAS *15*
Hansen, Joyce Viola
    See Hansen, Joyce
Hansen, Mark Victor *112*
Hansen, Ron 1947- *56*
Hansen, Ronald Thomas
    See Hansen, Ron
Hansen, Thore 1942- *224*
Hanser, Richard (Frederick) 1909-1981 .... *13*
Hanson, Joan 1938- *8*
Hanson, Joseph E. 1894(?)-1971
    Obituary *27*
Hanson, Mary Elizabeth *188*
Hanson, Warren 1949- *155*
Hansson, Gunilla 1939- *64*
Hantman, Clea *200*
Hapka, C.A.
    See Hapka, Catherine
Hapka, Catherine *223*
Hapka, Cathy
    See Hapka, Catherine
Harald, Eric
    See Boesen, Victor
Harazin, S. A. *210*
Harbour, Elizabeth 1968- *221*

Harcourt, Ellen Knowles 1890(?)-1984
    Obituary *36*
Hard, Charlotte (Ann) 1969- *98*
Hardcastle, Michael 1933- *216*
    Brief entry *38*
    Earlier sketch in SATA *47*
Harding, Lee 1937- *32*
    Brief entry *31*
Hardinge, Frances 1973- *210*
Hardt, Helga Fleischhauer
    See Fleischhauer-Hardt, Helga
Hardwick, Richard Holmes, Jr. 1923- *12*
Hardy, Alice Dale *67*
    Earlier sketch in SATA *1*
Hardy, David A(ndrews) 1936- *9*
Hardy, Janice *222*
Hardy, Jon 1958- *53*
Hardy, LeAnne 1951- *154*
Hardy, Stuart
    See Schisgall, Oscar
Hare, Norma Q(uarles) 1924- *46*
    Brief entry *41*
Harel, Nira 1936- *154*
Harford, Henry
    See Hudson, W(illiam) H(enry)
Hargis, Wes *219*
Hargrave, Leonie
    See Disch, Thomas M.
Hargreaves, (Charles) Roger 1935-1988
    Obituary *56*
Hargrove, James 1947- *57*
    Brief entry *50*
Hargrove, Jim
    See Hargrove, James
Harik, Elsa
    See Marston, Elsa
Harik, Elsa M.
    See Marston, Elsa
Harik, Elsa Marston
    See Marston, Elsa
Hariton, Anca I. 1955- *79*
Hark, Mildred
    See McQueen, Mildred Hark
Harkaway, Hal
    See Stratemeyer, Edward L.
Harkins, Philip 1912-1997 .... *6*
    Obituary *129*
Harlan, Elizabeth 1945- *41*
    Brief entry *35*
Harlan, Glen
    See Cebulash, Mel
Harlan, Judith 1949- *135*
    Earlier sketch in SATA *74*
    See also CLR *81*
Harland, Richard 1947- *152*
Harlee, J. V.
    See Leese, Jennifer L.B.
Harler, Ann
    See Van Steenwyk, Elizabeth (Ann)
Harley, Avis *183*
Harley, Bill 1954- *208*
    Earlier sketch in SATA *87*
Harlow, Joan Hiatt 1932- *157*
Harman, Fred 1902(?)-1982
    Obituary *30*
Harman, Hugh 1903-1982
    Obituary *33*
Harmelink, Barbara (Mary) *9*
Harmer, Mabel 1894-1992 .... *45*
Harmon, Dan
    See Harmon, Daniel E(lton)
Harmon, Daniel E(lton) 1949- *157*
Harmon, Margaret 1906- *20*
Harmon, Michael 1969- *189*
Harmon, Michael B.
    See Harmon, Michael
Harmon, William (Ruth) 1938- *65*
Harnan, Terry 1920- *12*
Harness, Cheryl 1951- *178*
    Earlier sketch in SATA *131*

Harnett, Cynthia (Mary) 1893-1981 .... *5*
    Obituary *32*
Harper, Anita 1943- *41*
Harper, Betty 1946- *126*
Harper, Charise
    See Harper, Charise Mericle
Harper, Charise Mericle *179*
Harper, Elaine
    See Hallin, Emily Watson
Harper, Ellen
    See Noble, Marty
Harper, Jamie *174*
Harper, Jessica 1949- *148*
Harper, Jo 1932- *169*
    Earlier sketch in SATA *97*
Harper, Lee *201*
Harper, Mary Wood
    See Dixon, Jeanne
Harper, Piers 1966- *161*
    Earlier sketch in SATA *105*
Harper, Suzanne *194*
Harper, Wilhelmina 1884-1973 .... *4*
    Obituary *26*
Harrah, Madge 1931- *154*
Harrah, Michael 1940- *41*
Harrah, Monique
    See Harrah, Madge
Harrar, George E. 1949- *124*
Harrell, Beatrice Orcutt 1943- *93*
Harrell, Janice 1945- *70*
Harrell, Sara Gordon 1940- *26*
Harrell, Sara Jeanne Gordon
    See Harrell, Sara Gordon
Harries, Joan 1922- *39*
Harrill, Ronald 1950- *90*
Harrington, Denis J(ames) 1932- *88*
Harrington, Evelyn Davis 1911- *5*
Harrington, Janice N. 1956- *187*
Harrington, Lyn
    See Harrington, Evelyn Davis
Harris, Alan 1944- *71*
Harris, Aurand 1915-1996 .... *37*
    Obituary *91*
Harris, Bob
    See Harris, Robert J.
Harris, Carol Flynn 1933- *135*
Harris, Catherine
    See Ainsworth, Catherine Harris
Harris, Christie
    See Harris, Christie (Lucy) Irwin
Harris, Christie (Lucy) Irwin 1907-2002 ...... *74*
    Autobiography Feature *116*
    Earlier sketch in SATA *6*
    See also CLR *47*
    See also SAAS *10*
Harris, Christine 1955- *105*
Harris, Colver
    See Colver, Anne
Harris, David 1942- *118*
Harris, David William
    See Harris, David
Harris, Dorothy Joan 1931- *153*
    Earlier sketch in SATA *13*
Harris, Geraldine 1951- *54*
Harris, Geraldine Rachel
    See Harris, Geraldine
Harris, Jacqueline L. 1929- *62*
Harris, Janet 1932-1979 .... *4*
    Obituary *23*
Harris, Jesse
    See Standiford, Natalie
Harris, Joan 1946- *146*
Harris, Joe 1928- *201*
Harris, Joel Chandler 1848-1908 .... *100*
    See also YABC *1*
    See also CLR *128*
Harris, John (Wyndham Parkes Lucas) Beynon
    1903-1969 .... *118*
Harris, Johnson
    See Harris, John (Wyndham Parkes Lucas)
    Beynon

Harris, Jonathan 1921-1997 52
Harris, Larry Vincent 1939- 59
Harris, Lavinia
  See St. John, Nicole
Harris, Leon A., Jr. 1926-2000 4
Harris, Lois V. 199
Harris, Lorle K(empe) 1912-2001 22
Harris, Marilyn
  See Springer, Marilyn Harris
Harris, Mark Jonathan 1941- 84
  Earlier sketch in SATA 32
Harris, Mary K(athleen) 1905-1966 119
Harris, Robert J. 1955- 195
Harris, Robie H. 1940- 203
  Brief entry 53
  Earlier sketches in SATA 90, 147
Harris, Robin
  See Shine, Deborah
Harris, Rosemary (Jeanne) 82
  Earlier sketch in SATA 4
  See also CLR 30
  See also SAAS 7
Harris, Ruth Elwin 1935- 164
Harris, Sherwood 1932-2009 25
Harris, Steven Michael 1957- 55
Harris, Trudy 1949- 191
  Earlier sketch in SATA 128
Harris-Filderman, Diane
  See Filderman, Diane E(lizabeth)
Harrison, C(hester) William 1913-1994 35
Harrison, Carol
  See Harrison, Carol Thompson
Harrison, Carol Thompson 113
Harrison, David L. 1937- 186
  Earlier sketches in SATA 26, 92, 150
Harrison, Deloris 1938- 9
Harrison, Edward Hardy 1926- 56
Harrison, Elizabeth (Allen) Cavanna
  1909-2001 30
  Earlier sketch in SATA 1
  See also SAAS 4
Harrison, Harry 1925- 4
Harrison, Harry Max
  See Harrison, Harry
Harrison, Mette Ivie 1970- 202
  Earlier sketch in SATA 149
Harrison, Michael 1939- 106
Harrison, Molly (Hodgett) 1909-2002 41
Harrison, Sarah 1946- 63
Harrison, Ted
  See Harrison, Edward Hardy
Harsh, Fred (T.) 1925- 72
Harshaw, Ruth H(etzel) 1890-1968 27
Harshman, Marc 1950- 109
  Earlier sketch in SATA 71
Hart, Alexandra 1939- 14
Hart, Alison
  See Leonhardt, Alice
Hart, Bruce 1938-2006 57
  Brief entry 39
Hart, Carole 1943- 57
  Brief entry 39
Hart, Carolyn 1936- 74
Hart, Carolyn G.
  See Hart, Carolyn
Hart, Carolyn Gimpel
  See Hart, Carolyn
Hart, Jan Siegel 1940- 79
Hart, Joyce 1954- 148
Hart, Karen 185
Hart, Lenore 171
Hart, Philip S. 1944- 180
Hart, Virginia 1949- 83
Harte, Bret 1836(?)-1902 26
Harte, Francis Brett
  See Harte, Bret
Harter, Debbie 1963- 107
Hartfield, Claire 1957- 147
Hartinger, Brent 1964- 217
  Earlier sketches in SATA 145, 174
Hartland, Jessie 171

Hartley, Ellen (Raphael) 1915-1980 23
Hartley, Fred Allan III 1953- 41
Hartley, William B(rown) 1913-1980 23
Hartling, Peter
  See Hartling, Peter
Hartling, Peter 1933- 66
  See also CLR 29
Hartman, Bob 1955- 224
Hartman, Cassie 202
Hartman, Dan 1955- 202
Hartman, Evert 1937- 38
  Brief entry 35
Hartman, Jane E. 1928- 47
Hartman, Jane Evangeline
  See Hartman, Jane E.
Hartman, Louis F(rancis) 1901-1970 22
Hartman, Rachel 174
Hartman, Victoria 1942- 91
Hartnett, Sonya 1968- 176
  Earlier sketches in SATA 93, 130
Hartry, Nancy 219
Hartshorn, Ruth M. 1928- 11
Hartung, Susan Kathleen 192
  Earlier sketch in SATA 150
Hartwig, Manfred 1950- 81
Harvey, Brett 1949- 61
Harvey, Edith 1908(?)-1972
  Obituary 27
Harvey, Gill 189
Harvey, Karen D. 1935- 88
Harvey, Roland 1945- 219
  Earlier sketches in SATA 71, 123, 179
Harvey-Fitzhenry, Alyxandra 1974- 189
Harwick, B. L.
  See Keller, Beverly L(ou)
Harwin, Brian
  See Henderson, LeGrand
Harwood, Pearl Augusta (Bragdon)
  1903-1998 9
Haseley, Dennis 1950- 221
  Brief entry 44
  Earlier sketches in SATA 57, 105, 157
Hashmi, Kerri 1955- 108
Haskell, Arnold L(ionel) 1903-1981(?) 6
Haskins, James
  See Haskins, James S.
Haskins, James S. 1941-2005 132
  Autobiography Feature 132
  Earlier sketches in SATA 9, 69, 105
  See also CLR 39
  See also SAAS 4
Haskins, Jim
  See Haskins, James S.
Hasler, Eveline 1933- 181
Hasler, Joan 1931- 28
Hass, Robert 1941- 94
Hassall, Joan 1906-1988 43
  Obituary 56
Hassett, Ann 1958- 162
Hassett, John 162
Hassler, Jon 1933-2008 19
  Obituary 191
Hassler, Jon Francis
  See Hassler, Jon
Hastings, Beverly
  See Barkin, Carol
  and James, Elizabeth
Hastings, Graham
  See Jeffries, Roderic
Hastings, Ian 1912- 62
Hastings, Victor
  See Disch, Thomas M.
Haszard, Patricia Moyes 1923-2000 63
Hatch, Lynda S. 1950- 90
Hathaway, Barbara 164
Hathorn, Elizabeth
  See Hathorn, Elizabeth Helen
Hathorn, Elizabeth Helen 1943- 156
  Autobiography Feature 156
  Earlier sketches in SATA 74, 120

Hathorn, Libby 1943-
  See Hathorn, Elizabeth Helen
Hatkoff, Craig 1954- 192
Hatlo, Jimmy 1898-1963
  Obituary 23
Hatton, Caroline 1957- 205
Hauff, Wilhelm 1802-1827
  See CLR 155
Haugaard, Erik Christian 1923- 68
  Earlier sketch in SATA 4
  See also CLR 11
  See also SAAS 12
Haugaard, Kay 117
Haugen, Hayley Mitchell 1968- 172
Haugen, Tormod 1945- 66
Hauman, Doris 1898-1984 32
Hauman, George 1890-1961 32
Hauptly, Denis J. 1945- 57
Hauptly, Denis James
  See Hauptly, Denis J.
Hauser, Jill Frankel 1950- 127
Hauser, Margaret L(ouise) 1909- 10
Hausherr, Rosmarie 1943- 86
Hausman, Gerald 1945- 180
  Earlier sketches in SATA 13, 90, 132
  See also CLR 89
Hausman, Gerry
  See Hausman, Gerald
Hauth, Katherine B. 1940- 99
Hautman, Pete 1952- 173
  Earlier sketches in SATA 82, 128
Hautman, Peter Murray
  See Hautman, Pete
Hautzig, Deborah 1956- 106
  Earlier sketch in SATA 31
Hautzig, Esther Rudomin 1930-2009 148
  Earlier sketches in SATA 4, 68
  See also CLR 22
  See also SAAS 15
Havel, Geoff 1955- 152
Havel, Jennifer
  See Havill, Juanita
Havelin, Kate 1961- 143
Haven, Paul 1971(?)- 213
Haverfield, Mary 225
Havighurst, Walter (Edwin) 1901-1994 1
  Obituary 79
Haviland, Virginia 1911-1988 6
  Obituary 54
Havill, Juanita 1949- 224
  Earlier sketches in SATA 74, 155
Hawes, Judy 1913- 4
Hawes, Louise 1943- 180
  Earlier sketch in SATA 60
Hawk, Fran 222
Hawke, Rosanne 1953- 165
  Earlier sketch in SATA 124
Hawke, Rosanne Joy
  See Hawke, Rosanne
Hawkes, Kevin 1959- 201
  Earlier sketches in SATA 78, 150
Hawkes, Nigel 1943- 119
Hawkesworth, Eric 1921- 13
Hawking, Lucy 1969- 197
Hawkins, Arthur 1903-1985 19
Hawkins, Colin 1945- 162
  Earlier sketch in SATA 112
Hawkins, Jacqui 162
  Earlier sketch in SATA 112
Hawkins, Jimmy 1941- 188
Hawkins, Laura 1951- 74
Hawkins, (Helena Ann) Quail 1905-2002 6
  Obituary 141
Hawkinson, John (Samuel) 1912-1994 4
Hawkinson, Lucy (Ozone) 1924-1971 21
Hawks, Robert 1961- 85
Hawley, Mabel C. 67
  Earlier sketch in SATA 1
Haworth, Danette 207
Haworth-Attard, Barbara 1953- 215

Hawthorne, Captain R. M.
　See Ellis, Edward S.
Hawthorne, Nathaniel 1804-1864
　See YABC 2
　See also CLR 163
Hay, Jeff T. 154
Hay, John 1915- 13
Hay, Samantha 213
Hay, Timothy
　See Brown, Margaret Wise
Hayashi, Leslie Ann 1954- 115
Hayashi, Nancy 1939- 186
　Earlier sketch in SATA 80
Haycak, Cara 1961- 180
Haycock, Kate 1962- 77
Haycraft, Howard 1905-1991 6
　Obituary 70
Haycraft, Molly Costain 1911- 6
Hayden, Gwendolen Lampshire 1904- 35
Hayden, Robert
　See Hayden, Robert Earl
Hayden, Robert C(arter), Jr. 1937- 47
　Brief entry 28
Hayden, Robert E.
　See Hayden, Robert Earl
Hayden, Robert Earl 1913-1980 19
　Obituary 26
Hayden, Torey L. 1951- 163
　Earlier sketch in SATA 65
Hayden, Torey Lynn
　See Hayden, Torey L.
Hayes, Carlton J(oseph) H(untley)
　1882-1964 11
Hayes, Daniel 1952- 109
　Earlier sketch in SATA 73
Hayes, Geoffrey 1947- 207
　Earlier sketches in SATA 26, 91
Hayes, Joe 1945- 131
　Earlier sketch in SATA 88
Hayes, John F. 1904-1980 11
Hayes, Karel 1949- 207
Hayes, Rosemary 158
Hayes, Sarah 1945- 208
Hayes, Sheila 1937- 51
　Brief entry 50
Hayes, Will 7
Hayes, William D(imitt) 1913-1976 8
Haynes, Betsy 1937- 94
　Brief entry 37
　Earlier sketch in SATA 48
　See also CLR 90
Haynes, David 1955- 97
Haynes, Linda
　See Swinford, Betty (June Wells)
Haynes, Mary 1938- 65
Haynes, Max 1956- 72
Hays, Anna Jane 214
Hays, H(offmann) R(eynolds) 1904-1980 26
Hays, Thomas A.
　See Hays, Tony
Hays, Thomas Anthony
　See Hays, Tony
Hays, Tony 1957- 84
Hays, Wilma Pitchford 1909- 28
　Earlier sketch in SATA 1
　See also CLR 59
　See also SAAS 3
Hayward, Linda 1943- 185
　Brief entry 39
　Earlier sketch in SATA 101
Haywood, Carolyn 1898-1990 75
　Obituary 64
　Earlier sketches in SATA 1, 29
　See also CLR 22
Hazelaar, Cor 217
Hazell, Rebecca (Eileen) 1947- 141
Hazen, Barbara Shook 1930- 178
　Earlier sketches in SATA 27, 90
Hazen, Lynn E. 202
Head, Gay
　See Hauser, Margaret L(ouise)

Head, Tom 1978- 167
Headley, Elizabeth
　See Harrison, Elizabeth (Allen) Cavanna
Headley, Justina Chen 1968- 176
Headstrom, (Birger) Richard 1902-1985 8
Heady, Eleanor B(utler) 1917-1979 8
Heagy, William D. 1964- 76
Heal, Edith 1903-1995 7
Heal, Gillian 1934- 89
Heale, Jay (Jeremy Peter Wingfield) 1937- .. 84
Healey, Brooks
　See Albert, Burton
Healey, Larry 1927- 44
　Brief entry 42
Heap, Sue 1954- 187
　Earlier sketch in SATA 150
Heaps, Willard A(llison) 1908-1987 26
Hearn, Diane Dawson 1952- 209
　Earlier sketch in SATA 79
Hearn, Emily
　See Valleau, Emily
Hearn, Julie 1958- 212
　Earlier sketch in SATA 152
Hearn, Lian
　See Rubinstein, Gillian
Hearn, Sneed
　See Gregg, Andrew K.
Hearne, Betsy 1942- 146
　Earlier sketches in SATA 38, 95
Heath, Charles D(ickinson) 1941- 46
Heath, Veronica
　See Blackett, Veronica Heath
Heaven, Constance (Christina) 1911- 7
Hebert-Collins, Sheila 1948- 111
Hecht, George J(oseph) 1895-1980
　Obituary 22
Hecht, Henri Joseph 1922- 9
Hechtkopf, Henryk 1910- 17
Heck, Bessie (Mildred) Holland 1911-1995 . 26
Heck, Ed 1963- 173
Heckert, Connie K(aye Delp) 1948- 82
Hector, Julian 205
Hedderwick, Mairi 1939- 145
　Earlier sketches in SATA 30, 77
Hedges, Sid(ney) G(eorge) 1897-1974 28
Hedrick, Irene Hope 1920- 175
Heelan, Jamee Riggio 1965- 146
Heerboth, Sharon
　See Leon, Sharon
Heffernan, John 1949- 168
　Earlier sketch in SATA 121
Heffron, Dorris 1944- 68
Hefter, Richard 1942- 31
Hegamin, Tonya C. 1975- 209
Hegarty, Reginald Beaton 1906-1973 10
Hehenberger, Shelly 1968- 126
Heidbreder, Robert 1947- 196
　Earlier sketch in SATA 130
Heidbreder, Robert K.
　See Heidbreder, Robert
Heide, Florence Parry 1919- 192
　Earlier sketches in SATA 32, 69, 118
　See also CLR 60
　See also SAAS 6
Heiderstadt, Dorothy 1907-2001 6
Heidi Louise
　See Erdrich, Louise
Heidler, David S(tephen) 1955- 132
Heidler, Jeanne T. 1956- 132
Heilbroner, Joan Knapp 1922- 63
Heilbrun, Lois Hussey 1922(?)-1987
　Obituary 54
Heiligman, Deborah 1958- 193
　Earlier sketches in SATA 90, 144
Heilman, Joan Rattner 50
Heimann, Rolf 1940- 164
　Earlier sketch in SATA 120
Hein, Lucille Eleanor 1915-1994 20
Heine, Helme 1941- 135
　Earlier sketch in SATA 67
　See also CLR 18

Heinlein, Robert A. 1907-1988 69
　Obituary 56
　Earlier sketch in SATA 9
　See also CLR 75
Heinlein, Robert Anson
　See Heinlein, Robert A.
Heins, Ethel L(eah) 1918-1997 101
Heins, Paul 1909- 13
Heintze, Carl 1922- 26
Heinz, Bill
　See Heinz, W. C.
Heinz, Brian J. 1946- 181
　Earlier sketch in SATA 95
Heinz, Brian James
　See Heinz, Brian J.
Heinz, W. C. 1915-2008 26
Heinz, Wilfred Charles
　See Heinz, W. C.
Heinzen, Mildred
　See Masters, Mildred
Heisel, Sharon E(laine) 1941- 125
　Earlier sketch in SATA 84
Heitzmann, William Ray 1948- 73
Heitzmann, Wm. Ray
　See Heitzmann, William Ray
Helakoski, Leslie 178
Helberg, Shirley Adelaide Holden 1919- ... 138
Helfer, Andrew 187
Helfer, Ralph 1937- 177
Helfman, Elizabeth S(eaver) 1911-2001 3
Helfman, Harry Carmozin 1910-1995 3
Helgerson, Joseph 1950- 181
Hellard, Susan 182
Hellberg, Hans-Eric 1927- 38
Heller, Linda 1944- 46
　Brief entry 40
Heller, Mike
　See Hano, Arnold
Heller, Ruth M. 1924- 112
　Earlier sketch in SATA 66
Hellman, Hal
　See Hellman, Harold
Hellman, Harold 1927- 4
Helman, Andrea (Jean) 1946- 160
　Earlier sketch in SATA 107
Helmer, Diana Star 1962- 86
Helmer, Marilyn 160
　Earlier sketch in SATA 112
Helps, Racey 1913-1971 2
　Obituary 25
Helquist, Brett 187
　Earlier sketch in SATA 146
Helweg, Hans H. 1917- 50
　Brief entry 33
Helyar, Jane Penelope Josephine 1933- 5
　Autobiography Feature 138
　See also SAAS 2
Hemingway, Edith M. 1950- 223
Hemingway, Edith Morris
　See Hemingway, Edith M.
Hemingway, Edward 1969(?)- 212
Hemmant, Lynette 1938- 69
Hemming, Roy G. 1928-1995 11
　Obituary 86
Hemphill, Helen 1955- 179
Hemphill, Kris (Harrison) 1963- 118
Hemphill, Martha Locke 1904-1973 37
Hemphill, Michael 220
Hemphill, Stephanie 190
Hemstock, Gillian 1956- 173
Henba, Bobbie 1926- 87
Henbest, Nigel 1951- 55
　Brief entry 52
Henderley, Brooks 1
Henderson, Aileen Kilgore 1921- 178
Henderson, Aileen Mary
　See Fox, Aileen
Henderson, Gordon 1950- 53
Henderson, Kathy 1949- 155
　Brief entry 53
　Earlier sketches in SATA 55, 95

Henderson, Lauren 1966- *201*
Henderson, LeGrand 1901-1965 .... *9*
Henderson, Nancy Wallace 1916- *22*
Henderson, Zenna (Chlarson) 1917-1983 .... *5*
Hendrickson, Walter Brookfield, Jr. 1936- *9*
Hendrix, John 1976- *208*
Hendry, Diana 1941- *213*
  Earlier sketches in SATA *68, 106*
Hendry, Frances Mary 1941- *171*
  Earlier sketch in SATA *110*
Hendry, Linda (Gail) 1961- *83*
Heneghan, James 1930- *160*
  Earlier sketches in SATA *53, 97*
Henkes, Kevin 1960- *207*
  Earlier sketches in SATA *43, 76, 108, 154*
  See also CLR *108*
Henn, Astrid *214*
Hennessy, Barbara G.
  See Hennessy, B.G.
Hennessy, Barbara Gulbrandsen
  See Hennessy, B.G.
Hennessy, B.G. 1951- *175*
Hennesy, Carolyn 1962- *221*
Henney, Carolee Wells 1928- *102*
Henriod, Lorraine 1925- *26*
Henriquez, Emile F. 1937- *170*
  Earlier sketch in SATA *89*
Henry, April 1959- *174*
Henry, Ernest 1948- *107*
Henry, Joanne Landers 1927- *6*
Henry, Maeve 1960- *75*
Henry, Marguerite 1902-1997 .... *100*
  Obituary *99*
  See also CLR *4*
  See also SAAS *7*
Henry, Marie H. 1935- *65*
Henry, Marilyn 1939- *117*
Henry, Marion
  See del Rey, Lester
Henry, O. 1862-1910
  See YABC *2*
Henry, Oliver
  See Henry, O.
Henry, Rohan *217*
Henry, T. E.
  See Rowland-Entwistle, (Arthur) Theodore
  (Henry)
Henschel, Elizabeth Georgie *56*
Henson, Heather *206*
Henson, James Maury
  See Henson, Jim
Henson, Jim 1936-1990 .... *43*
  Obituary *65*
Henstra, Friso 1928- *73*
  Earlier sketch in SATA *8*
  See also SAAS *14*
Hentoff, Nat(han Irving) 1925- *133*
  Brief entry *27*
  Earlier sketches in SATA *42, 69*
  See also CLR *52*
Henty, G(eorge) A(lfred) 1832-1902 .... *64*
  See also CLR *76*
Heo, Yumi 1964- *206*
  Earlier sketches in SATA *94, 146*
Hepler, Heather *177*
Herald, Kathleen
  See Peyton, Kathleen Wendy
Herb, Angela M. 1970- *92*
Herbert, Cecil
  See Hamilton, Charles (Harold St. John)
Herbert, Don 1917-2007 .... *2*
  Obituary *184*
Herbert, Donald Jeffrey
  See Herbert, Don
Herbert, Frank 1920-1986 .... *37*
  Obituary *47*
  Earlier sketch in SATA *9*
Herbert, Frank Patrick
  See Herbert, Frank
Herbert, Helen (Jean) 1947- *57*
Herbert, Janis 1956- *139*

Herbert, Wally 1934-2007 .... *23*
Herbert, Walter William
  See Herbert, Wally
Herbst, Judith 1947- *74*
Herda, D.J. 1948- *80*
Herge
  See Remi, Georges
Heritage, Martin
  See Horler, Sydney
Herkimer, L(awrence) R(ussell) 1925(?)- *42*
Herlihy, Dirlie Anne 1935- *73*
Herlong, Madaline
  See Herlong, M.H.
Herlong, M.H. *211*
Herman, Charlotte 1937- *203*
  Earlier sketches in SATA *20, 99*
Hermanson, Dennis (Everett) 1947- *10*
Hermes, Jules 1962- *92*
Hermes, Patricia 1936- *191*
  Earlier sketches in SATA *31, 78, 141*
Hermes, Patricia Mary
  See Hermes, Patricia
Hernandez, Natalie Nelson 1929- *123*
Herndon, Ernest *91*
Herold, Ann Bixby 1937- *72*
Herrera, Juan Felipe 1948- *127*
Herrick, Steven 1958- *209*
  Earlier sketches in SATA *103, 156*
Herriman, George (Joseph) 1880-1944 .... *140*
Herriot, James 1916-1995 .... *135*
  Brief entry *44*
  Earlier sketch in SATA *86*
  See also CLR *80*
Herrmanns, Ralph 1933- *11*
Herrold, Tracey
  See Dils, Tracey E.
Herron, Carolivia 1947- *203*
Herron, Edward A(lbert) 1912- *4*
Herschler, Mildred Barger *130*
Hersey, John 1914-1993 .... *25*
  Obituary *76*
Hersey, John Richard
  See Hersey, John
Hershberger, Priscilla (Gorman) 1951- *81*
Hershenhorn, Esther 1945- *151*
Hershey, Kathleen M. 1934- *80*
Hershey, Mary *173*
Hershey, Mary L.
  See Hershey, Mary
Hersom, Kathleen 1911- *73*
Hertz, Grete Janus 1915- *23*
Herxheimer, Sophie 1963- *220*
Herzig, Alison Cragin 1935- *87*
Herzog, Brad 1968- *131*
Heslewood, Juliet 1951- *82*
Hess, Lilo 1916- *4*
Hess, Paul 1961- *134*
Hesse, Hermann 1877-1962 .... *50*
Hesse, Karen 1952- *215*
  Autobiography Feature *113*
  Earlier sketches in SATA *74, 103, 158*
  See also CLR *141*
  See also SAAS *25*
Hest, Amy 1950- *193*
  Earlier sketches in SATA *55, 82, 129*
Heuer, Karsten 1968(?)- *202*
Heuer, Kenneth John 1927- *44*
Heuman, William 1912-1971 .... *21*
Heuston, Kimberley 1960- *167*
Heuston, Kimberley Burton
  See Heuston, Kimberley
Heuvel, Eric 1960- *224*
Hewes, Agnes Danforth 1874-1963 .... *35*
Hewett, Anita 1918-1989 .... *13*
Hewett, Joan 1930- *140*
  Earlier sketch in SATA *81*
Hewett, Richard 1929- *81*
Hewitson, Jennifer 1961- *97*
Hewitt, Margaret 1961- *84*
Hewitt, Sally 1949- *127*

Hext, Harrington
  See Phillpotts, Eden
Hey, Nigel S(tewart) 1936- *20*
Heyduck-Huth, Hilde 1929- *8*
Heyer, Carol 1950- *130*
  Earlier sketch in SATA *74*
Heyer, Marilee 1942- *102*
  Earlier sketch in SATA *64*
Heyerdahl, Thor 1914-2002 .... *52*
  Earlier sketch in SATA *2*
Heyes, (Nancy) Eileen 1956- *150*
  Earlier sketch in SATA *80*
Heyliger, William 1884-1955
  See YABC *1*
Heyman, Ken(neth Louis) 1930- *114*
  Earlier sketch in SATA *34*
Heyward, (Edwin) DuBose 1885-1940 .... *21*
Heywood, Karen 1946- *48*
Hezlep, William (Earl) 1936- *88*
Hiaasen, Carl 1953- *208*
Hibbert, Arthur Raymond
  See Hibbert, Christopher
Hibbert, Christopher 1924-2008 .... *4*
  Obituary *201*
Hibbert, Eleanor Alice Burford 1906-1993 .... *2*
  Obituary *74*
Hickman, Estella (Lee) 1942- *111*
Hickman, Janet 1940- *127*
  Earlier sketch in SATA *12*
Hickman, Martha Whitmore 1925- *26*
Hickman, Pamela 1958- *186*
  Earlier sketch in SATA *128*
Hickock, Will
  See Harrison, C(hester) William
Hickok, Lorena A. 1893-1968 .... *20*
Hickox, Rebecca (Ayres) *116*
Hicks, Barbara Jean 1953- *165*
Hicks, Betty *191*
Hicks, Clifford B. 1920- *50*
Hicks, Eleanor B.
  See Coerr, Eleanor (Beatrice)
Hicks, Harvey
  See Stratemeyer, Edward L.
Hicks, Peter 1952- *111*
Hicyilmaz, Gaye 1947- *157*
  Earlier sketch in SATA *77*
Hieatt, Constance B(artlett) 1928- *4*
Hiebert, Ray Eldon 1932- *13*
Hierstein, Judith *212*
Hierstein, Judy
  See Hierstein, Judith
Higdon, Hal 1931- *4*
Higginbottom, David 1923- *87*
  Earlier sketch in SATA *25*
Higginbottom, J(effrey) Winslow 1945- *29*
Higgins, Dalton *223*
Higgins, F.E. *219*
Higgins, Fiona
  See Higgins, F.E.
Higgins, Joanna 1945- *125*
Higgins, Simon (Richard) 1958- *105*
Higginsen, Vy *79*
High, Linda Oatman 1958- *188*
  Autobiography Feature *188*
  Earlier sketches in SATA *94, 145*
High, Philip E. 1914- *119*
High, Philip Empson
  See High, Philip E.
Higham, David 1949- *50*
Higham, David Michael
  See Higham, David
Higham, Jon Atlas
  See Higham, Jonathan Huw
Higham, Jonathan Huw 1960- *59*
Highet, Helen
  See MacInnes, Helen (Clark)
Hightman, Jason 1971(?)- *189*
Hightman, J.P.
  See Hightman, Jason
Hightower, Florence Cole 1916-1981 .... *4*
  Obituary *27*

Highwater, Jamake (Mamake)
    1942(?)-2001 69
    Brief entry 30
    Earlier sketch in SATA 32
    See also CLR 17
Hilb, Nora 1953- 178
Hildebrandt, Greg 1939- 172
    Brief entry 33
    Earlier sketch in SATA 55
Hildebrandt, Tim 1939-2006 55
    Brief entry 33
Hildebrandt, Timothy
    See Hildebrandt, Tim
Hildebrandts, The
    See Hildebrandt, Greg
    and Hildebrandt, Tim
Hilder, Rowland 1905-1993 36
    Obituary 77
Hildick, E. W.
    See Hildick, Wallace
Hildick, Wallace 1925-2001 68
    Earlier sketch in SATA 2
    See also SAAS 6
Hilgartner, Beth 1957- 58
Hill, Alexis
    See Craig, Mary (Francis) Shura
    and Glick, Ruth (Burtnick)
Hill, Anthony R. 1942- 164
    Earlier sketch in SATA 91
Hill, Anthony Robert
    See Hill, Anthony R.
Hill, David 1942- 152
    Earlier sketch in SATA 103
Hill, Donna (Marie) 1921- 124
    Earlier sketch in SATA 24
Hill, Douglas 1935-2007 78
    Earlier sketch in SATA 39
Hill, Douglas Arthur
    See Hill, Douglas
Hill, Elizabeth Starr 1925- 143
    Earlier sketch in SATA 24
Hill, Eric 1927- 133
    Brief entry 53
    Earlier sketch in SATA 66
    See also CLR 13
Hill, Gordon
    See Eldin, Peter
Hill, Grace Brooks 67
    Earlier sketch in SATA 1
Hill, Grace Livingston 1865-1947
    See YABC 2
Hill, Helen M(orey) 1915- 27
Hill, Isabel 225
Hill, Isabel T.
    See Hill, Isabel
Hill, John
    See Koontz, Dean
Hill, Johnson
    See Kunhardt, Edith
Hill, Judy I. R.
    See Roberts, Judy I.
Hill, Kathleen Louise 1917- 4
Hill, Kay
    See Hill, Kathleen Louise
Hill, Kirkpatrick 1938- 188
    Earlier sketches in SATA 72, 126
Hill, Laban
    See Hill, Laban Carrick
Hill, Laban Carrick 170
Hill, Lee Sullivan 1958- 96
Hill, Lorna 1902-1991 12
Hill, Margaret (Ohler) 1915- 36
Hill, Meg
    See Hill, Margaret (Ohler)
Hill, Meredith
    See Craig, Mary (Francis) Shura
Hill, Monica
    See Watson, Jane Werner
Hill, Pamela Smith 1954- 112
Hill, Ralph Nading 1917-1987 65

Hill, Robert W(hite) 1919-1982 12
    Obituary 31
Hill, Ruth A.
    See Viguers, Ruth Hill
Hill, Ruth Livingston
    See Munce, Ruth Hill
Hill, Stuart 1958- 186
Hill, Susan 1942- 183
Hill, Susan Elizabeth
    See Hill, Susan
Hill, Susanna Leonard 1965- 193
Hill, Thomas 1960- 82
Hillcourt, William 1900-1992 27
Hillenbrand, Will 1960- 210
    Earlier sketches in SATA 84, 147
Hiller, Ilo (Ann) 1938- 59
Hillerman, Anthony Grove
    See Hillerman, Tony
Hillerman, Tony 1925-2008 6
    Obituary 198
Hillert, Margaret 1920- 91
    Earlier sketch in SATA 8
Hilliard, Richard 183
Hillman, Ben 1957- 202
Hillman, Elizabeth 1942- 75
Hillman, John 1952- 120
Hillman, Martin
    See Hill, Douglas
Hillman, Priscilla 1940- 48
    Brief entry 39
Hillman, Shane 200
Hills, C.A.R. 1955- 39
Hills, Charles Albert Reis
    See Hills, C.A.R.
Hills, Tad 173
Hilton, Irene Pothus -1979 7
Hilton, James 1900-1954 34
Hilton, Margaret Lynette 1946- 105
    Earlier sketch in SATA 68
    See also CLR 25
    See also SAAS 21
Hilton, Nette
    See Hilton, Margaret Lynette
Hilton, Ralph 1907-1982 8
Hilton, Suzanne 1922- 4
Hilton-Bruce, Anne
    See Hilton, Margaret Lynette
Him, George 1937-1982
    Obituary 30
Himelblau, Linda -2005 179
Himelstein, Shmuel 1940- 83
Himler, Ann 1946- 8
Himler, Ronald 1937- 183
    Earlier sketches in SATA 6, 92, 137
Himler, Ronald Norbert
    See Himler, Ronald
Himmelman, John 1959- 221
    Earlier sketches in SATA 47, 94, 159
Himmelman, John C.
    See Himmelman, John
Hinckley, Helen
    See Jones, Helen Hinckley
Hind, Dolores (Ellen) 1931- 53
    Brief entry 49
Hindin, Nathan
    See Bloch, Robert (Albert)
Hindley, Judy 1940- 179
    Earlier sketch in SATA 120
Hinds, P. Mignon 98
Hinds, Patricia Mignon
    See Hinds, P. Mignon
Hine, Sesyle Joslin 1929- 2
Hines, Anna Grossnickle 1946- 209
    Brief entry 45
    Earlier sketches in SATA 51, 95, 141
    See also SAAS 16
Hines, Gary (Roger) 1944- 136
    Earlier sketch in SATA 74
Hinman, Bonnie 1950- 216
Hinojosa, Maria (de Lourdes) 1961- 88
Hinton, Nigel 1941- 166

Hinton, S. E. 1950- 160
    Earlier sketches in SATA 19, 58, 115
    See also CLR 23
Hinton, Sam 1917-2009 43
Hinton, Susan Eloise
    See Hinton, S. E.
Hintz, Martin 1945- 128
    Brief entry 39
    Earlier sketch in SATA 47
Hintz, Stephen V. 1975- 129
Hippopotamus, Eugene H.
    See Kraus, (Herman) Robert
Hirano, Cathy 1957- 68
Hirao, Amiko 203
Hirsch, Karen 1941- 61
Hirsch, Odo 157
    Earlier sketch in SATA 111
Hirsch, Phil 1926- 35
Hirsch, S. Carl 1913-1990 2
    See also SAAS 7
Hirschfelder, Arlene B. 1943- 138
    Earlier sketch in SATA 80
Hirschi, Ron 1948- 192
    Earlier sketches in SATA 56, 95
Hirschmann, Linda (Ann) 1941- 40
Hirsh, Marilyn 1944-1988 7
    Obituary 58
Hirshberg, Al(bert Simon) 1909-1973 38
Hiscock, Bruce 1940- 204
    Earlier sketches in SATA 57, 137
Hiser, Constance 1950- 71
Hiser, Iona Seibert -1998 4
Hislop, Julia Rose Catherine 1962- 74
Hissey, Jane 1952- 130
    Autobiography Feature 130
    Earlier sketches in SATA 58, 103
Hissey, Jane Elizabeth
    See Hissey, Jane
Hitchcock, Alfred (Joseph) 1899-1980 27
    Obituary 24
Hite, Sid 1954- 175
    Earlier sketches in SATA 75, 136
Hitte, Kathryn 1919- 16
Hitz, Demi
    See Demi
Hitzeroth, Deborah L. 1961- 78
Hnizdovsky, Jacques 1915- 32
Ho, Louise 185
Ho, Minfong 1951- 151
    Earlier sketches in SATA 15, 94
    See also CLR 28
Hoagland, Edward (Morley) 1932- 51
Hoare, Robert J(ohn) 1921-1975 38
Hoban, Julia 217
Hoban, Lillian 1925-1998 69
    Obituary 104
    Earlier sketch in SATA 22
    See also CLR 67
Hoban, Russell 1925- 136
    Earlier sketches in SATA 1, 40, 78
    See also CLR 139
Hoban, Russell Conwell
    See Hoban, Russell
Hoban, Tana 1917(?)-2006 104
    Obituary 173
    Earlier sketches in SATA 22, 70
    See also CLR 76
    See also SAAS 12
Hobart, Lois (Elaine) 7
Hobbie, Holly 1942- 225
    Earlier sketch in SATA 178
    See also CLR 88
Hobbie, Jocelyn 190
Hobbie, Nathaniel 196
Hobbs, Leigh 1953- 166
Hobbs, Valerie 1941- 193
    Autobiography Feature 145
    Earlier sketches in SATA 93, 145
    See also CLR 148

Hobbs, Will 1947- 177
  Autobiography Feature 127
  Earlier sketches in SATA 72, 110
  See also CLR 59
Hobbs, William Carl
  See Hobbs, Will
Hoberman, Mary Ann 1930- 158
  Earlier sketches in SATA 5, 72, 111
  See also CLR 22
  See also SAAS 18
Hobson, Bruce 1950- 62
Hobson, Burton (Harold) 1933- 28
Hobson, Laura Z(ametkin) 1900-1986 52
Hobson, Sally 1967- 172
  Earlier sketch in SATA 84
Hoce, Charley E. 174
Hochman, David 202
Hochschild, Arlie Russell 1940- 11
Hockaby, Stephen
  See Mitchell, Gladys (Maude Winifred)
Hockenberry, Hope
  See Newell, Hope Hockenberry
Hodge, Deborah 1954- 163
  Earlier sketch in SATA 122
Hodge, P. W.
  See Hodge, Paul W(illiam)
Hodge, Paul W(illiam) 1934- 12
Hodgell, P(atricia) C(hristine) 1951- 42
Hodges, C. Walter 1909-2004 2
  Obituary 158
Hodges, Carl G. 1902-1964 10
Hodges, Cyril Walter
  See Hodges, C. Walter
Hodges, Elizabeth Jamison 1
Hodges, Margaret 1911-2005 167
  Obituary 172
  Earlier sketches in SATA 1, 33, 75, 117
  See also SAAS 9
Hodges, Margaret Moore
  See Hodges, Margaret
Hodgetts, Blake Christopher 1967- 43
Hodgkins, Fran 1964- 199
Hodgkinson, Leigh 1975- 202
Hodgman, Ann 1956- 198
Hodgson, Harriet (W.) 1935- 84
Hoehne, Marcia 1951- 89
Hoellwarth, Cathryn Clinton
  See Clinton, Cathryn
Hoestlandt, Jo 1948- 221
  Earlier sketch in SATA 94
Hoestlandt, Jocelyne
  See Hoestlandt, Jo
Hoexter, Corinne K. 1927- 6
Hoeye, Michael 1947- 136
Hoff, Carol 1900-1979 11
Hoff, Mary (King) 1956- 157
  Earlier sketch in SATA 74
Hoff, Syd(ney) 1912-2004 138
  Obituary 154
  Earlier sketches in SATA 9, 72
  See also CLR 83
  See also SAAS 4
Hoffman, Edwin D. 49
Hoffman, Elizabeth P(arkinson) 1921-2003
  Obituary 153
Hoffman, Mary 1945- 211
  Earlier sketches in SATA 59, 97, 144
  See also SAAS 24
Hoffman, Mat 1972- 150
Hoffman, Nina Kiriki 1955- 160
Hoffman, Phyllis M. 1944- 4
Hoffman, Phyllis Miriam
  See Hoffman, Phyllis M.
Hoffman, Rosekrans 1926- 15
Hoffmann, E(rnst) T(heodor) A(madeus)
  1776-1822 27
  See also CLR 133
Hoffmann, Felix 1911-1975 9
Hoffmann, Heinrich 1809-1894
  See CLR 122
Hoffmann, Margaret Jones 1910- 48

Hoffmann, Peggy
  See Hoffmann, Margaret Jones
Hofher, Catherine Baxley 1954- 130
Hofher, Cathy
  See Hofher, Catherine Baxley
Hofmeyr, Dianne (Louise) 138
Hofsepian, Sylvia A. 1932- 74
Hofsinde, Robert 1902-1973 21
Hogan, Bernice Harris 1929- 12
Hogan, Inez 1895-1973 2
Hogan, James P. 1941-2010 81
Hogan, James Patrick
  See Hogan, James P.
Hogan, Jamie 192
Hogan, Linda 1947- 132
Hogan, Mary 1957- 210
Hogarth, Burne 1911-1996 89
  Earlier sketch in SATA 63
Hogarth, Grace (Weston Allen) 1905-1995 .. 91
Hogarth, Jr.
  See Kent, Rockwell
Hogarth, (Arthur) Paul 1917-2001 41
Hogg, Garry 1902-1976 2
Hogg, Gary 1957- 172
  Earlier sketch in SATA 105
Hogner, Dorothy Childs 4
Hogner, Nils 1893-1970 25
Hogrogian, Nonny 1932- 74
  Autobiography Feature 127
  Earlier sketch in SATA 7
  See also CLR 95
  See also SAAS 1
Hoh, Diane 1937- 102
  Brief entry 48
  Earlier sketch in SATA 52
Hoke, Helen
  See Watts, Helen L. Hoke
Hoke, Helen L.
  See Watts, Helen L. Hoke
Hoke, John 1925- 7
Hoke, John Lindsay
  See Hoke, John
Hokenson, Terry 1948- 193
Hol, Coby 1943- 126
Holabird, Katharine 1948- 213
  Earlier sketches in SATA 62, 135
Holaday, Bobbie 1922- 153
Holbeach, Henry
  See Rands, William Brighty
Holberg, Ruth L(angland) 1889-1984 1
Holbrook, Kathy 1963- 107
Holbrook, Peter
  See Glick, Carl (Cannon)
Holbrook, Sabra
  See Erickson, Sabra Rollins
Holbrook, Sara 131
Holbrook, Stewart Hall 1893-1964 2
Holcomb, Jerry (Leona) Kimble 1927- 113
Holcomb, Nan
  See McPhee, Norma H.
Holden, Elizabeth Rhoda
  See Lawrence, Louise
Holding, James (Clark Carlisle, Jr.)
  1907-1997 3
Hole, Stian 1969- 204
Holeman, Linda 1949- 136
  Autobiography Feature 136
  Earlier sketch in SATA 102
Holgate, Doug 225
Holinger, William (Jacques) 1944- 90
Holisher, Desider 1901-1972 6
Holl, Adelaide Hinkle 1910- 8
Holl, Kristi
  See Holl, Kristi D.
Holl, Kristi D. 1951- 51
Holl, Kristi Diane
  See Holl, Kristi D.
Holland, Gay W. 1941- 128

Holland, Isabelle (Christian) 1920-2002 70
  Autobiography Feature 103
  Obituary 132
  Earlier sketch in SATA 8
  See also CLR 57
Holland, Janice 1913-1962 18
Holland, John L(ewis) 1919- 20
Holland, Joyce
  See Morice, Dave
Holland, Julia 1954- 106
Holland, Lynda (H.) 1959- 77
Holland, Lys
  See Gater, Dilys
Holland, Marion 1908-1989 6
  Obituary 61
Holland, Richard 1976- 216
Holland, Trish 221
Hollander, John 1929- 13
Hollander, Nicole 1940(?)- 101
Hollander, Paul
  See Silverberg, Robert
Hollander, Phyllis 1928- 39
Hollander, Zander 1923- 63
Holldobler, Turid 1939- 26
Holliday, Joe
  See Holliday, Joseph
Holliday, Joseph 1910- 11
Holling, Holling C(lancy) 1900-1973 15
  Obituary 26
  See also CLR 50
Hollingsworth, Alvin C(arl) 1930- 39
Hollingsworth, Mary 1947- 166
  Earlier sketch in SATA 91
Holloway, Teresa (Bragunier) 1906- 26
Hollyer, Belinda 204
Holm, (Else) Anne (Lise) 1922-1998 1
  See also CLR 75
  See also SAAS 7
Holm, Jennifer L. 1968(?)- 183
  Earlier sketches in SATA 120, 163
Holm, Matthew 1974- 174
Holm, Sharon Lane 1955- 114
  Earlier sketch in SATA 78
Holman, Felice 1919- 82
  Earlier sketch in SATA 7
  See also SAAS 17
Holm and Hamel
  See Holm, Jennifer L.
Holmberg, Bo R. 1945- 203
Holme, Bryan 1913-1990 26
  Obituary 66
Holmes, Barbara Ware 1945- 127
  Earlier sketch in SATA 65
Holmes, Elizabeth 1957- 191
Holmes, Elizabeth Ann
  See Holmes, Elizabeth
Holmes, John
  See Souster, (Holmes) Raymond
Holmes, Marjorie (Rose) 1910-2002 43
Holmes, Martha 1961- 72
Holmes, Mary Tavener 1954- 199
Holmes, Mary Z(astrow) 1943- 80
Holmes, Oliver Wendell 1809-1894 34
Holmes, Peggy 1898- 60
Holmes, Raymond
  See Souster, (Holmes) Raymond
Holmes, Rick
  See Hardwick, Richard Holmes, Jr.
Holmes, Sara Lewis 186
Holmgren, Helen Jean 1930- 45
Holmgren, Sister George Ellen
  See Holmgren, Helen Jean
Holmgren, Virginia C(unningham) 1909- 26
Holmquist, Eve 1921- 11
Holt, K.A.
  See Roy, Kari Anne
Holt, Kimberly Willis 1960- 223
  Earlier sketch in SATA 122, 179
Holt, Margaret 1937- 4
Holt, Margaret Van Vechten (Saunders)
  1899-1963 32

Holt, Michael (Paul) 1929- 13
Holt, Rackham
　See Holt, Margaret Van Vechten (Saunders)
Holt, Rochelle L.
　See DuBois, Rochelle Holt
Holt, Stephen
　See Thompson, Harlan
Holt, Victoria
　See Hibbert, Eleanor Alice Burford
Holtei, Christa 1953- 214
Holton, Leonard
　See Wibberley, Leonard
Holtz, Thomas R., Jr. 1965- 203
Holtze, Sally Holmes 1952- 64
Holtzman, Jerome 1926-2008 57
　Obituary 194
Holub, Joan 1956- 149
　Earlier sketch in SATA 99
Holub, Josef 1926- 175
Holubitsky, Katherine 1955- 165
　Earlier sketch in SATA 121
Holyer, Erna Maria 1925- 22
Holyer, Ernie
　See Holyer, Erna Maria
Holz, Loretta 1943- 17
Holz, Loretta Marie
　See Holz, Loretta
Homel, David 1952- 97
Homze, Alma C. 1932- 17
Honey, Elizabeth 1947- 137
　Autobiography Feature 137
　Earlier sketch in SATA 112
Honeycutt, Natalie 1945- 97
Hong, Lily Toy 1958- 76
Hong, Maxine Ting Ting
　See Kingston, Maxine Hong
Honig, Donald 1931- 18
Honig, Donald Martin
　See Honig, Donald
Honness, Elizabeth H. 1904- 2
Hoobler, Dorothy 1941- 161
　Earlier sketches in SATA 28, 109
Hoobler, Thomas 161
　Earlier sketches in SATA 28, 109
Hood, Joseph F. 1925- 4
Hood, Robert E. 1926- 21
Hood, Sarah
　See Killough, (Karen) Lee
Hook, Brendan 1963- 105
Hook, Frances 1912-1983 27
Hook, Geoffrey R(aynor) 1928- 103
Hook, Jeff
　See Hook, Geoffrey R(aynor)
Hook, Martha 1936- 27
Hooker, Richard
　See Heinz, W. C.
Hooker, Ruth 1920-1998 21
hooks, bell 1952(?)- 170
　Earlier sketch in SATA 115
Hooks, William H(arris) 1921- 94
　Earlier sketch in SATA 16
Hoon, Patricia Easterly 1954- 90
Hooper, Byrd
　See St. Clair, Byrd Hooper
Hooper, Mary 1948- 205
　Earlier sketch in SATA 160
Hooper, Maureen Brett 1927- 76
Hooper, Meredith 1939- 159
　Earlier sketches in SATA 28, 101
Hooper, Meredith Jean
　See Hooper, Meredith
Hooper, Patricia 1941- 95
Hoopes, Lyn Littlefield 1953- 49
　Brief entry 44
Hoopes, Ned E(dward) 1932- 21
Hoopes, Roy 1922-2009 11
Hoose, Phillip 1947- 215
　Earlier sketch in SATA 137

Hoover, H(elen) M(ary) 1935- 132
　Brief entry 33
　Earlier sketches in SATA 44, 83
　See also SAAS 8
Hoover, Helen (Drusilla Blackburn)
　1910-1984 12
　Obituary 39
Hope, Christopher 1944- 62
Hope, Christopher David Tully
　See Hope, Christopher
Hope, Laura Lee
　See Goulart, Ron
　and Stanley, George Edward
Hope Simpson, Jacynth 1930- 12
Hopf, Alice (Martha) L(ightner) 1904-1988 ... 5
　Obituary 55
Hopgood, Tim 1961- 224
Hopkins, A. T.
　See Turngren, Annette
Hopkins, C. M.
　See Hopkins, Cathy
Hopkins, Cathy 1953- 165
Hopkins, Cathy M.
　See Hopkins, Cathy
Hopkins, Clark 1895-1976
　Obituary 34
Hopkins, Ellen 1955- 128
Hopkins, Ellen L.
　See Hopkins, Ellen
Hopkins, Jackie
　See Hopkins, Jackie Mims
Hopkins, Jackie Mims 1952- 178
　Earlier sketch in SATA 92
Hopkins, Joseph G(erard) E(dward) 1909- ... 11
Hopkins, (Hector) Kenneth 1914-1988
　Obituary 58
Hopkins, Lee Bennett 1938- 215
　Earlier sketches in SATA 3, 68, 125, 168
　See also CLR 44
　See also SAAS 4
Hopkins, Lyman
　See Folsom, Franklin (Brewster)
Hopkins, Marjorie 1911-1999 9
Hopkins, Mary R(ice) 1956- 97
Hopkinson, Amanda 1948- 84
Hopkinson, Deborah 1952- 216
　Autobiography Feature 180
　Earlier sketches in SATA 76, 108, 159, 180
　See also CLR 118
Hopman, Philip 1961- 177
Hoppe, Joanne 1932- 42
Hoppe, Matthias 1952- 76
Hoppe, Paul 209
Hopper, Nancy J. 1937- 38
　Brief entry 35
Hoppey, Tim 1958- 225
Hopping, Lorraine Jean
　See Egan, Lorraine Hopping
Horacek, Judy 1961- 211
Horaek, Petr 214
　Earlier sketch in SATA 163
Horenstein, Henry 1947- 108
Horgan, Paul (George Vincent O'Shaughnessy)
　1903-1995 13
　Obituary 84
Horlak, E.E.
　See Tepper, Sheri S.
Horler, Sydney 1888-1954 102
Horn, Sandra Ann 1944- 154
Hornblow, Arthur, Jr. 1893-1976 15
Hornblow, Leonora 1920-2005 18
　Obituary 171
Hornblow, Leonora Schinasi
　See Hornblow, Leonora
Horne, Constance 1927- 149
Horne, Richard 1960-2007 169
　Obituary 180
　Earlier sketch in SATA 111
Horne, Richard Henry Hengist
　1802(?)-1884 29
Horner, Althea (Jane) 1926- 36

Horner, Dave 1934- 12
Horner, Jack 1946- 106
Horner, John R.
　See Horner, Jack
Horner, John Robert
　See Horner, Jack
Hornik, Laurie Miller 159
Horniman, Joanne 1951- 167
　Earlier sketch in SATA 98
Hornos, Axel 1907-1994 20
Hornstein, Reuben Aaron 1912- 64
Horowitz, Anthony 1955- 195
　Earlier sketch in SATA 137
Horowitz, Dave 1970- 204
　Earlier sketch in SATA 172
Horowitz, Ruth 1957- 136
Horrocks, Anita 1958- 169
Horse, Harry
　See Horne, Richard
Horsfield, Alan 1939- 153
Horstman, Lisa 1964- 219
Hort, Lenny 179
Horton, James O. 1943- 173
Horton, James Oliver
　See Horton, James O.
Horton, Joan 217
Horton, Madelyn (Stacey) 1962- 77
Horvath, Betty 1927- 4
Horvath, David 1972(?)- 192
Horvath, Polly 1957- 194
　Earlier sketches in SATA 85, 140
　See also CLR 90
Horwich, Frances R(appaport) 1908-2001 11
　Obituary 130
Horwitz, Elinor Lander 45
　Brief entry 33
Horwood, William 1944- 85
Hosford, Dorothy (Grant) 1900-1952 22
Hosford, Jessie 1892-1990 5
Hoshi, Shin'ichi 1926- 101
Hoshino, Felicia 1968- 189
Hoskyns-Abrahall, Clare (Constance
　Drury) 13
Hosler, Danamarie 1978- 184
Hossack, Sylvia 1939- 83
Hossack, Sylvie Adams
　See Hossack, Sylvia
Hosseini, Khaled 1965- 156
Hossell, Karen Price
　See Price, Karen
Hosta, Dar 192
Hostetler, Marian 1932- 91
Houck, Carter 1924- 22
Hough, Charlotte 1924-2008 9
　Obituary 202
Hough, Helen Charlotte
　See Hough, Charlotte
Hough, Judy Taylor 1932- 63
　Brief entry 51
　Earlier sketch in SATA 56
Hough, Richard (Alexander) 1922-1999 17
Houghton, Eric 1930- 7
Houk, Randy 1944- 97
Houlehen, Robert J. 1918- 18
Houlton, Peggy Mann 1925(?)-1990 6
Household, Geoffrey 1900-1988 14
　Obituary 59
Housman, Laurence 1865-1959 25
Houston, Dick 1943- 74
Houston, Gloria 138
　Autobiography Feature 138
　Earlier sketch in SATA 81
Houston, James A(rchibald) 1921-2005 74
　Obituary 163
　Earlier sketch in SATA 13
　See also CLR 3
　See also SAAS 17
Houston, James D. 1933-2009 78
　Obituary 203
Houston, James Dudley
　See Houston, James D.

Houston, James Dudley
  See Houston, James D.
Houston, Jeanne Toyo Wakatsuki
  See Houston, Jeanne Wakatsuki
Houston, Jeanne Wakatsuki 1934- *168*
  Autobiography Feature *168*
  Earlier sketch in SATA *78*
Houston, Juanita C. 1921- *129*
Houton, Kathleen
  See Kilgore, Kathleen
Houts, Amy F. *164*
Houts, Michelle *219*
Hovey, Kate *158*
Howard, Alan 1922- *45*
Howard, Alyssa
  See Buckholtz, Eileen (Garber)
  and Glick, Ruth (Burtnick)
  and Titchener, Louise
Howard, Arthur 1948- *212*
  Earlier sketch in SATA *165*
Howard, Arthur Charles
  See Howard, Arthur
Howard, Elizabeth Fitzgerald 1927- *119*
  Earlier sketch in SATA *74*
Howard, Ellen 1943- *184*
  Earlier sketches in SATA *67, 99*
Howard, Jane R(uble) 1924- *87*
Howard, Norman Barry 1949- *90*
Howard, P. M.
  See Howard, Pauline Rodriguez
Howard, Paul 1967- *190*
  Earlier sketch in SATA *118*
Howard, Pauline Rodriguez 1951- *124*
Howard, Prosper
  See Hamilton, Charles (Harold St. John)
Howard, Robert West 1908-1988 .... *5*
Howard, Todd 1964- *135*
Howard, Tristan
  See Currie, Stephen
Howard, Vernon (Linwood) 1918-1992 .... *40*
  Obituary *73*
Howard, Warren F.
  See Pohl, Frederik
Howarth, Daniel *222*
  Earlier sketch in SATA *188*
Howarth, David (Armine) 1912-1991 .... *6*
  Obituary *68*
Howarth, Lesley 1952- *94*
Howe, Deborah 1946-1978 .... *29*
Howe, James 1946- *224*
  Earlier sketches in SATA *29, 71, 111, 161*
  See also CLR *9*
Howe, John F. 1957- *79*
Howe, Norma 1930- *126*
Howe, Peter 1942- *214*
Howell, Pat 1947- *15*
Howell, S.
  See Styles, (Frank) Showell
Howell, Simmone 1971- *214*
Howell, Virginia
  See Ellison, Virginia H(owell)
Howes, Barbara 1914-1996 .... *5*
Howie, Betsy 1962- *215*
Howie, Diana 1945- *122*
Howie, Diana Melson
  See Howie, Diana
Howker, Janni 1957- *72*
  Brief entry *46*
  See also CLR *14*
  See also SAAS *13*
Howland, Ethan 1963- *131*
Hoy, Linda 1946- *65*
Hoy, Nina
  See Roth, Arthur J(oseph)
Hoyle, Geoffrey 1942- *18*
Hoyt, Ard *190*
Hoyt, Edwin P(almer), Jr. 1923- *28*
Hoyt, Erich 1950- *140*
  Earlier sketch in SATA *65*
Hoyt, Olga
  See Gruhzit-Hoyt, Olga (Margaret)

Hrdlitschka, Shelley 1956- *167*
  Earlier sketch in SATA *111*
Hrdlitschka, Shelley Joanne
  See Hrdlitschka, Shelley
Hromic, Alma A.
  See Alexander, Alma
Htin Aung, U.
  See Aung, (Maung) Htin
Hu, Ying-Hwa *173*
Huang, Benrei 1959- *86*
Hubalek, Linda K. 1954- *111*
Hubbard, Crystal *209*
Hubbard, Margaret Ann
  See Priley, Margaret (Ann) Hubbard
Hubbard, Michelle Calabro 1953- *122*
Hubbard, Patricia 1945- *124*
Hubbard, Woodleigh Marx *160*
  Earlier sketch in SATA *98*
Hubbell, Patricia 1928- *186*
  Earlier sketches in SATA *8, 132*
Hubery, Julia *195*
Hubley, Faith Elliot 1924-2001 .... *48*
  Obituary *133*
Hubley, John 1914-1977 .... *48*
  Obituary *24*
Huck, Charlotte S. 1922- *136*
  Earlier sketch in SATA *82*
Hucke, Johannes 1966- *218*
Hudak, Michal 1956- *143*
Hudson, Cheryl Willis 1948- *160*
  Earlier sketch in SATA *81*
Hudson, Jan 1954-1990 .... *77*
  See also CLR *40*
Hudson, Jeffery
  See Crichton, Michael
Hudson, Jeffrey
  See Crichton, Michael
Hudson, (Margaret) Kirsty 1947- *32*
Hudson, Margaret
  See Shuter, Jane (Margaret)
Hudson, W(illiam) H(enry) 1841-1922 .... *35*
Hudson, Wade 1946- *162*
  Earlier sketch in SATA *74*
Huelsmann, Eva 1928- *16*
Huerlimann, Bettina 1909-1983 .... *39*
  Obituary *34*
Huerlimann, Ruth 1939- *32*
  Brief entry *31*
Huff, Barbara A. 1929- *67*
Huff, Tanya 1957- *171*
  Earlier sketch in SATA *85*
Huff, Tanya Sue
  See Huff, Tanya
Huff, T.S.
  See Huff, Tanya
Huff, Vivian 1948- *59*
Huffaker, Sandy 1943- *10*
Huffman, Tom *24*
Huggins, Nathan Irvin 1927-1989 .... *63*
Huggins, Peter 1951- *178*
Hughes, Carol 1955- *217*
  Earlier sketch in SATA *108*
Hughes, Dean 1943- *139*
  Earlier sketches in SATA *33, 77*
  See also CLR *76*
Hughes, Eden
  See Griffin, W. E. B.
Hughes, Edward James
  See Hughes, Ted
Hughes, James Langston
  See Hughes, Langston
Hughes, Langston 1902-1967 .... *33*
  Earlier sketch in SATA *4*
  See also CLR *17*
Hughes, Libby *71*
Hughes, Matilda
  See MacLeod, Charlotte (Matilda)
Hughes, Monica 1925-2003 .... *162*
  Earlier sketches in SATA *15, 70, 119*
  See also CLR *60*
  See also SAAS *11*

Hughes, Monica Ince
  See Hughes, Monica
Hughes, Pat *197*
Hughes, Richard (Arthur Warren)
  1900-1976 .... *8*
  Obituary *25*
Hughes, Sara
  See Saunders, Susan
Hughes, Shirley 1927- *159*
  Earlier sketches in SATA *16, 70, 110*
  See also CLR *15*
Hughes, Susan 1960- *216*
Hughes, Ted 1930-1998 .... *49*
  Brief entry *27*
  Obituary *107*
  See also CLR *131*
Hughes, Thomas 1822-1896 .... *31*
  See also CLR *160*
Hughes, Virginia
  See Campbell, Hope
Hughes, Walter (Llewellyn) 1910-1993 .... *26*
Hughey, Roberta 1942- *61*
Hugo, Pierre Brackers de
  See Brackers de Hugo, Pierre
Hugo, Victor 1802-1885 .... *47*
Hugo, Victor Marie
  See Hugo, Victor
Huline-Dickens, Frank William 1931- *34*
Huling, Jan *172*
Huliska-Beith, Laura *175*
Hull, Eleanor (Means) 1913- *21*
Hull, Eric Traviss
  See Harnan, Terry
Hull, H. Braxton
  See Jacobs, Helen Hull
Hull, Jesse Redding
  See Hull, Jessie Redding
Hull, Jessie Redding 1932- *51*
Hull, Katharine 1921-1977 .... *23*
Hull, Lise (E.) 1954- *148*
Hull, Maureen 1949- *142*
Hulme, Joy N. 1922- *161*
  Earlier sketches in SATA *74, 112*
Hults, Dorothy Niebrugge 1898-2000 .... *6*
Humble, Richard 1945- *60*
Hume, Lachie *189*
Hume, Lotta Carswell *7*
Hume, Ruth Fox 1922-1980 .... *26*
  Obituary *22*
Hume, Stephen Eaton 1947- *136*
Hummel, Berta 1909-1946 .... *43*
Hummel, Sister Maria Innocentia
  See Hummel, Berta
Hummon, Marcus 1960- *213*
Humphrey, Carol Sue 1956- *167*
Humphrey, Henry (III) 1930- *16*
Humphrey, Kate
  See Forsyth, Kate
Humphrey, Sandra McLeod 1936- *95*
Humphreys, Martha 1943- *71*
Humphreys, Susan L.
  See Lowell, Susan
Hundal, Nancy 1957- *128*
Huneck, Stephen 1949- *183*
  Earlier sketch in SATA *129*
Hungerford, Hesba Fay
  See Brinsmead, H(esba) F(ay)
Hungerford, Pixie
  See Brinsmead, H(esba) F(ay)
Hunkin, Tim 1950- *53*
Hunkin, Timothy Mark Trelawney
  See Hunkin, Tim
Hunt, Angela Elwell 1957- *159*
  Earlier sketch in SATA *75*
Hunt, Bernice 1920- *4*
Hunt, Charlotte Dumaresq
  See Demi
Hunt, Francesca
  See Holland, Isabelle (Christian)

Hunt, Irene 1907-2001 91
  Earlier sketch in SATA 2
  See also CLR 1
Hunt, Janie Louise 1963- 102
Hunt, Jonathan 1966- 84
Hunt, Joyce 1927- 31
Hunt, Linda 1940- 39
Hunt, Lisa B(ehnke) 1967- 84
Hunt, Mabel Leigh 1892-1971 1
  Obituary 26
Hunt, Morton M(agill) 1920- 22
Hunt, Nigel
  See Greenbank, Anthony Hunt
Hunt, Peter (Leonard) 1945- 76
Hunter, Anne B. 1966- 118
Hunter, Bernice Thurman 1922-2002 85
  Brief entry 45
Hunter, Bobbi Dooley 1945- 89
Hunter, Captain Marcy
  See Ellis, Edward S.
Hunter, Chris
  See Fluke, Joanne
Hunter, Clingham M.D.
  See Adams, William Taylor
Hunter, Edith Fisher 1919- 31
Hunter, Erin
  See Cary, Kate
Hunter, Evan 1926-2005 25
  Obituary 167
Hunter, George E.
  See Ellis, Edward S.
Hunter, Hilda 1921- 7
Hunter, Jana
  See Hunter, Jana Novotny
Hunter, Jana Novotny 190
Hunter, Jim 1939- 65
Hunter, Kristin
  See Lattany, Kristin Hunter
Hunter, Leigh
  See Etchison, Birdie L(ee)
Hunter, Lieutenant Ned
  See Ellis, Edward S.
Hunter, Mel 1927-2004 39
Hunter, Mollie 1922- 139
  Autobiography Feature 139
  Earlier sketches in SATA 2, 54, 106
  See also CLR 25
  See also SAAS 7
Hunter, Ned
  See Ellis, Edward S.
Hunter, Norman (George Lorimer)
  1899-1995 84
  Earlier sketch in SATA 26
Hunter, Ryan Ann
  See Greenwood, Pamela D.
  and Macalaster, Elizabeth G.
Hunter, Sara Hoagland 1954- 98
Hunter Blair, Pauline
  See Clarke, Pauline
Huntington, Amy 1956- 180
  Earlier sketch in SATA 138
Huntington, Geoffrey 145
Huntington, Harriet E(lizabeth) 1909- 1
Huntley, Amy 225
Huntsberry, William E(mery) 1916- 5
Hurd, Clement (G.) 1908-1988 64
  Obituary 54
  Earlier sketch in SATA 2
  See also CLR 49
Hurd, Edith Thacher 1910-1997 64
  Obituary 95
  Earlier sketch in SATA 2
  See also CLR 49
  See also SAAS 13
Hurd, John Thacher
  See Hurd, Thacher
Hurd, Thacher 1949- 219
  Autobiography Feature 123
  Brief entry 45
  Earlier sketches in SATA 46, 94

Hurley, Jo
  See Dower, Laura
Hurley, Tonya 207
Hurlimann, Bettina
  See Huerlimann, Bettina
Hurlimann, Ruth
  See Huerlimann, Ruth
Hurmence, Belinda 1921- 77
  See also CLR 25
  See also SAAS 20
Hurst, Carol Otis 1933-2007 185
  Earlier sketch in SATA 130
Hurt-Newton, Tania 1968- 84
Hurwin, Davida Wills 1950- 180
Hurwitz, Johanna 1937- 175
  Earlier sketches in SATA 20, 71, 113
  See also SAAS 18
Hurwood, Bernhardt J. 1926-1987 12
  Obituary 50
Husain, Shahrukh 1950- 108
Huser, Glen 1943- 151
Hutchens, Paul 1902-1977 31
Hutchins, Carleen M.
  See Hutchins, Carleen Maley
Hutchins, Carleen Maley 1911-2009 9
  Obituary 206
Hutchins, Hazel J. 1952- 175
  Brief entry 51
  Earlier sketches in SATA 81, 135
  See also SAAS 24
Hutchins, Pat 1942- 178
  Earlier sketches in SATA 15, 70, 111
  See also CLR 20
  See also SAAS 16
Hutchins, Ross Elliott 1906- 4
Hutchison, Linda 1942- 152
Huthmacher, J. Joseph 1929- 5
Hutto, Nelson (Allen) 1904-1985 20
Hutton, Kathryn 1915- 89
Hutton, Sam
  See Jones, Allan Frewin
Hutton, Warwick 1939-1994 20
  Obituary 83
  See also SAAS 17
Huxley, Aldous 1894-1963 63
  See also CLR 151
Huxley, Aldous Leonard
  See Huxley, Aldous
Huxley, Elspeth (Josceline Grant)
  1907-1997 62
  Obituary 95
Hyde, Catherine R.
  See Hyde, Catherine Ryan
Hyde, Catherine Ryan 1955- 224
  Earlier sketch in SATA 141
Hyde, Dayton O(gden) 9
Hyde, Hawk
  See Hyde, Dayton O(gden)
Hyde, Jeannette
  See Eyerly, Jeannette
Hyde, Margaret O. 1917- 139
  Earlier sketches in SATA 1, 42, 76
  See also CLR 23
  See also SAAS 8
Hyde, Margaret Oldroyd
  See Hyde, Margaret O.
Hyde, Shelley
  See Reed, Kit
Hyde, Wayne Frederick 1922- 7
Hylander, Clarence J(ohn) 1897-1964 7
Hyman, Miles 1962- 210
Hyman, Paula Chase
  See Chase, Paula
Hyman, Robin 1931- 12
Hyman, Robin Phiilip
  See Hyman, Robin
Hyman, Trina Schart 1939-2004 95
  Obituary 158
  Earlier sketches in SATA 7, 46
  See also CLR 50
Hymes, Lucia M(anley) 1907-1998 7

Hyndman, Jane Andrews Lee 1912-1978 46
  Obituary 23
  Earlier sketch in SATA 1
Hyndman, Robert Utley 1906-1973 18
Hynes, Pat 98

                    I

Iannone, Jeanne
  See Balzano, Jeanne (Koppel)
Ibatoulline, Bagram 1965(?)- 225
  Earlier sketch in SATA 174
Ibbitson, John Perrie 1955- 102
Ibbotson, Eva 1925-2010 221
  Earlier sketches in SATA 13, 103, 156
Ibbotson, M. C(hristine) 1930- 5
Icenoggle, Jodi 1967- 168
Icenoggle, Jodi O.
  See Icenoggle, Jodi
Ichikawa, Satomi 1949- 208
  Brief entry 36
  Earlier sketches in SATA 47, 78, 146
  See also CLR 62
Idle, Molly Schaar 223
Iggulden, Hal 1972- 196
Ignoffo, Matthew 1945- 92
Igus, Toyomi 1953- 112
  Earlier sketch in SATA 76
Ihimaera, Witi (Tame) 1944- 148
Ikeda, Daisaku 1928- 77
Ilowite, Sheldon A. 1931- 27
Ilsey, Dent
  See Chapman, John Stanton Higham
Ilsley, Dent
  See Chapman, John Stanton Higham
Ilsley, Velma (Elizabeth) 1918- 12
Imai, Ayano 1980- 190
Imai, Miko 1963- 90
Imershein, Betsy 1953- 62
Immel, Mary Blair 1930- 28
Immell, Myra H. 1941- 92
Impey, Rose 1947- 223
  Earlier sketches in SATA 69, 152
Ingelow, Jean 1820-1897 33
Ingermanson, Randall 1958- 134
Ingermanson, Randy
  See Ingermanson, Randall
Ingersoll, Norman 1928- 79
Ingham, Colonel Frederic
  See Hale, Edward Everett
Ingman, Bruce 1963- 182
  Earlier sketch in SATA 134
Ingman, Nicholas 1948- 52
Ingold, Jeanette 128
Ingpen, Robert 1936- 166
  Earlier sketch in SATA 109
Ingpen, Robert Roger
  See Ingpen, Robert
Ingraham, Erick 1950- 145
Ingraham, Leonard W(illiam) 1913-2003 4
Ingram, Scott 1948- 167
  Earlier sketch in SATA 92
Ingram, W. Scott
  See Ingram, Scott
Ingrams, Doreen 1906-1997 97
  Earlier sketch in SATA 20
Ingrid, Charles
  See Salsitz, Rhondi Vilott
Ingves, Gunilla 1939- 101
Ingves, Gunilla Anna Maria Folkesdotter
  See Ingves, Gunilla
Inkpen, Mick 1952- 154
  Earlier sketch in SATA 99
Innes, (Ralph) Hammond
  See Hammond Innes, Ralph
Innes, Ralph Hammond
  See Hammond Innes, Ralph
Innes, Stephanie 220

Innocenti, Roberto 1940- *159*
    Earlier sketch in SATA *96*
    See also CLR *126*
Innocenti and Gallaz
    See Gallaz, Christophe
    and Innocenti, Roberto
Inns, Chris *212*
Inyart, Gene
    See Namovicz, Gene Inyart
Ionesco, Eugene 1909-1994 .... *7*
    Obituary *79*
Ipcar, Dahlov (Zorach) 1917- *147*
    Autobiography Feature *147*
    Earlier sketches in SATA *1, 49*
    See also SAAS *8*
Ireland, Karin *151*
    Earlier sketch in SATA *101*
Ironside, Jetske 1940- *60*
Irvin, Fred 1914- *15*
Irvine, Georgeanne 1955- *72*
Irvine, Joan 1951- *80*
Irving, Alexander
    See Hume, Ruth Fox
Irving, Robert
    See Adler, Irving
Irving, Washington 1783-1859
    See YABC *2*
    See also CLR *97*
Irwin, Ann(abelle Bowen) 1915-1998 .... *89*
    Brief entry *38*
    Obituary *106*
    Earlier sketch in SATA *44*
    See also CLR *40*
    See also SAAS *14*
Irwin, Constance (H.) Frick 1913-1995 .... *6*
Irwin, Hadley
    See Hadley, Lee
    and Irwin, Ann(abelle Bowen)
Irwin, Keith Gordon 1885-1964 .... *11*
Isaac, Joanne 1934- *21*
Isaacs, Anne 1949- *185*
    Earlier sketch in SATA *90*
Isaacs, Jacob
    See Kranzler, George G(ershon)
Isaacson, Philip M(arshal) 1924- *87*
Isadora, Rachel 1953(?)- *204*
    Brief entry *32*
    Earlier sketches in SATA *54, 79, 121, 165*
    See also CLR *7*
Isbell, Rebecca T(emple) 1942- *125*
Isham, Charlotte H(ickock) 1912- *21*
Ishida, Jui *176*
Ish-Kishor, Judith 1892-1972 .... *11*
Ish-Kishor, Sulamith 1896-1977 .... *17*
Ishmael, Woodi 1914-1995 .... *31*
    Obituary *109*
Isle, Sue 1963- *105*
Isol 1972- *220*
Israel, Elaine 1945- *12*
Israel, Marion Louise 1882-1973
    Obituary *26*
Iterson, S(iny) R(ose) Van
    See Van Iterson, S(iny) R(ose)
Ivanko, John D. 1966- *111*
Ivanko, John Duane
    See Ivanko, John D.
Iversen, Jeremy 1980(?)- *174*
Iversen, Jeremy Watt
    See Iversen, Jeremy
Iverson, Carol (L.) 1941- *145*
Iverson, Diane 1950- *122*
Iverson, Eric G.
    See Turtledove, Harry
Ivery, Martha M. 1948- *124*
Ives, David 1951- *173*
Ives, Morgan
    See Bradley, Marion Zimmer
Ives, Penny 1956- *215*
Iwai, Melissa *183*

Iwamatsu, Jun Atsushi 1908-1994 .... *81*
    Earlier sketch in SATA *14*
    See also CLR *4*
Iwamura, Kazuo 1939- *213*
Iwasaki (Matsumoto), Chihiro 1918-1974
    See CLR *18*
Iyengar, Malathi Michelle 1954- *220*

J

Jabar, Cynthia *210*
Jablonski, Carla *184*
Jac, Lee
    See Morton, Lee Jack, Jr.
Jacka, Martin 1943- *72*
Jackson, Alison 1953- *160*
    Earlier sketches in SATA *73, 108*
Jackson, Anne 1896(?)-1984
    Obituary *37*
Jackson, Barry
    See Jackson, Barry E.
Jackson, Barry E. *200*
Jackson, C(aary) Paul 1902-1991 .... *6*
Jackson, Caary
    See Jackson, C(aary) Paul
Jackson, Charlotte E. (Cobden) 1903(?)-1989
    Obituary *62*
Jackson, Dave
    See Jackson, J. David
Jackson, Donna M. 1959- *206*
Jackson, Ellen 1943- *214*
    Earlier sketches in SATA *75, 115, 167*
Jackson, Ellen B.
    See Jackson, Ellen
Jackson, Garnet Nelson 1944- *87*
Jackson, Geoffrey (Holt Seymour) 1915-1987
    Obituary *53*
Jackson, Gina
    See Fluke, Joanne
Jackson, Guida M. 1930- *71*
Jackson, J. David 1944- *91*
Jackson, Jacqueline 1928- *65*
Jackson, Jacqueline Dougan
    See Jackson, Jacqueline
Jackson, Jesse 1908-1983 .... *29*
    Obituary *48*
    Earlier sketch in SATA *2*
    See also CLR *28*
Jackson, Marjorie 1928- *127*
Jackson, Melanie 1956- *141*
Jackson, Mike 1946- *91*
Jackson, Neta J. 1944- *91*
Jackson, O. B.
    See Jackson, C(aary) Paul
Jackson, Rob 1961- *176*
Jackson, Robert B(lake) 1926- *8*
Jackson, Robert Bradley
    See Jackson, Rob
Jackson, Sally
    See Kellogg, Jean (Defrees)
Jackson, Shirley 1919-1965 .... *2*
Jackson, Woody 1948- *92*
Jackson Issa, Kai *205*
Jacob, Helen Pierce 1927- *21*
Jacobin
    See Bisson, Terry
Jacobs, Deborah Lynn *187*
Jacobs, Flora Gill 1918-2006 .... *5*
    Obituary *178*
Jacobs, Francine 1935- *150*
    Brief entry *42*
    Earlier sketch in SATA *43*
Jacobs, Frank 1929- *30*
Jacobs, Helen Hull 1908-1997 .... *12*
Jacobs, Joseph 1854-1916 .... *25*
Jacobs, Judy 1952- *69*
Jacobs, Laurie A. 1956- *89*
Jacobs, Leah
    See Gellis, Roberta

Jacobs, Lee
    See Stone, Tanya Lee
Jacobs, Leland Blair 1907-1992 .... *20*
    Obituary *71*
Jacobs, Linda
    See Altman, Linda Jacobs
Jacobs, Lou(is), Jr. 1921- *2*
Jacobs, Shannon K. 1947- *77*
Jacobs, Susan
    See Quinn, Susan
Jacobs, William Jay 1933- *89*
    Earlier sketch in SATA *28*
Jacobsen, Laura *177*
Jacobson, Daniel 1923- *12*
Jacobson, Jennifer
    See Jacobson, Jennifer Richard
Jacobson, Jennifer Richard 1958- *170*
Jacobson, Morris K(arl) 1906- *21*
Jacobson, Rick *170*
Jacopetti, Alexandra
    See Hart, Alexandra
Jacques, Brian 1939-2011 .... *176*
    Earlier sketches in SATA *62, 95, 138*
    See also CLR *21*
Jacques, Robin 1920-1995 .... *32*
    Brief entry *30*
    Obituary *86*
    See also SAAS *5*
Jaekel, Susan M. 1948- *89*
Jaffe, Michele *179*
Jaffe, Michele Sharon
    See Jaffe, Michele
Jaffee, Al(lan) 1921- *66*
    Earlier sketch in SATA *37*
Jagendorf, Moritz (Adolf) 1888-1981 .... *2*
    Obituary *24*
Jago 1979- *216*
Jahn, Joseph Michael
    See Jahn, Michael
Jahn, Michael 1943- *28*
Jahn, Mike
    See Jahn, Michael
Jahn-Clough, Lisa 1967- *193*
    Earlier sketches in SATA *88, 152*
Jahsmann, Allan Hart 1916- *28*
Jakes, John 1932- *62*
Jakes, John William
    See Jakes, John
James, Andrew
    See Kirkup, James
James, Ann 1952- *168*
    Earlier sketches in SATA *82, 117*
James, Betsy *183*
James, Bill 1929- *205*
James, B.J.
    See James, Brian
James, Brian 1976- *212*
    Earlier sketch in SATA *140*
James, Bronte
    See Nash, Renea Denise
James, Captain Lew
    See Stratemeyer, Edward L.
James, Charlie 1961- *185*
James, Curtis E. *182*
James, Dynely
    See Mayne, William
James, Edwin
    See Gunn, James E.
James, Elizabeth 1942- *97*
    Earlier sketches in SATA *39, 45, 52*
James, Emily
    See Standiford, Natalie
James, Gordon C. 1973- *195*
James, Harry Clebourne 1896-1978 .... *11*
James, J. Alison 1962- *146*
    Earlier sketch in SATA *83*
James, Josephine
    See Sterne, Emma Gelders
James, Mary
    See Meaker, Marijane
James, Matt *201*

James, Philip
  See del Rey, Lester
  and Moorcock, Michael
James, Robin 1953- 50
James, Robin Irene
  See James, Robin
James, Simon 1961- 202
James, T. F.
  See Fleming, Thomas
James, Tegan
  See Odgers, Sally Farrell
James, Will(iam Roderick) 1892-1942 19
Jameson, W. C. 1942- 93
Jamieson, Ian R.
  See Goulart, Ron
Jamieson, Victoria 218
Jamiolkowski, Raymond M. 1953- 81
Jane, Mary Childs 1909-1991 6
Jane, Pamela 158
Janeczko, Paul B(ryan) 1945- 155
  Earlier sketches in SATA *53, 98*
  See also CLR *47*
  See also SAAS *18*
Janes, Edward C. 1908-1984 25
Janes, Edward Clarence
  See Janes, Edward C.
Janes, J(oseph) Robert 1935- 148
  Brief entry 50
  Earlier sketch in SATA *101*
Janeway, Elizabeth (Hall) 1913-2005 19
Janger, Kathleen N. 1940- 66
Jango-Cohen, Judith 1955- 208
Janice
  See Brustlein, Janice Tworkov
Janisch, Heinz 1960- 181
Janosch
  See Eckert, Horst
Janover, Caroline (Davis) 1943- 141
  Earlier sketch in SATA *89*
Janovitz, Marilyn 194
Jansen, Jared
  See Cebulash, Mel
Janson, Dora Jane (Heineberg) 1916- 31
Janson, H(orst) W(oldemar) 1913-1982 9
Jansson, Tove (Marika) 1914-2001 41
  Earlier sketch in SATA *3*
  See also CLR *125*
Janus, Grete
  See Hertz, Grete Janus
Jaques, Faith 1923-1997 97
  Earlier sketches in SATA *21, 69*
Jaquith, Priscilla 1908- 51
Jaramillo, Mari-Luci 1928- 139
Jarka, Jeff 221
Jarman, Julia 1946- 198
  Earlier sketch in SATA *133*
Jarman, Rosemary Hawley 1935- 7
Jarrell, Mary Von Schrader 1914- 35
Jarrell, Randall 1914-1965 7
  See also CLR *111*
Jarrett, Clare 1952- 201
Jarrett, Roxanne
  See Werner, Herma
Jarrie, Martin 1953- 219
Jarrow, Gail 1952- 185
  Earlier sketch in SATA *84*
Jarvis, E.K.
  See Ellison, Harlan
  and Silverberg, Robert
Jarvis, Robin 1963- 181
Jaskol, Julie 1958- 127
Jasner, W. K.
  See Watson, Jane Werner
Jassem, Kate
  See Oppenheim, Joanne
Jauss, Anne Marie 1902(?)-1991 10
  Obituary 69
Javernick, Ellen 1938- 217
  Earlier sketch in SATA *89*
Javins, Marie 1966- 212
Jay, Alison 196

Jayne, Lieutenant R. H.
  See Ellis, Edward S.
Jaynes, Clare
  See Mayer, Jane Rothschild
Jeake, Samuel, Jr.
  See Aiken, Conrad
Jean-Bart, Leslie 1954- 121
Jeapes, Ben 1965- 174
Jecan, Gavriel 1962- 200
Jefferds, Vincent H(arris) 1916- 59
  Brief entry 49
Jefferies, (John) Richard 1848-1887 16
Jeffers, Dawn 189
Jeffers, Oliver 1977- 213
  Earlier sketch in SATA *175*
Jeffers, Susan 1942- 202
  Earlier sketches in SATA *17, 70, 129, 137*
  See also CLR *30*
Jefferson, Sarah
  See Farjeon, (Eve) Annabel
Jeffries, Roderic 1926- 4
Jeffries, Roderic Graeme
  See Jeffries, Roderic
Jenkin-Pearce, Susie 1943- 80
Jenkins, A. M. 1961- 174
Jenkins, Amanda McRaney
  See Jenkins, A. M.
Jenkins, Debra Reid
  See Reid Jenkins, Debra
Jenkins, Emily 1967- 174
  Earlier sketch in SATA *144*
Jenkins, Jean 98
Jenkins, Jerry B. 1949- 149
Jenkins, Jerry Bruce
  See Jenkins, Jerry B.
Jenkins, Leonard 189
Jenkins, Marie M(agdalen) 1909- 7
Jenkins, Martin 1959- 216
Jenkins, M.D.
  See Jenkins, Martin
Jenkins, Patrick 1955- 72
Jenkins, Steve 1952- 218
  Earlier sketches in SATA *154, 188*
Jenkins, William A(twell) 1922-1998 9
Jenkyns, Chris 1924- 51
Jennewein, James 215
Jennewein, Jim
  See Jennewein, James
Jennings, Christopher S. 1971(?)- 201
Jennings, Coleman A(lonzo) 1933- 64
Jennings, C.S.
  See Jennings, Christopher S.
Jennings, Dana Andrew 1957- 93
Jennings, Elizabeth (Joan) 1926-2001 66
Jennings, Gary 1928-1999 9
  Obituary 117
Jennings, Gary Gayne
  See Jennings, Gary
Jennings, Linda 1937- 211
Jennings, Linda M.
  See Jennings, Linda
Jennings, Patrick 1962- 205
  Earlier sketches in SATA *96, 160*
Jennings, Paul 1943- 165
  Earlier sketch in SATA *88*
  See also CLR *40*
Jennings, Richard W. 1945- 185
  Earlier sketch in SATA *136*
Jennings, Robert
  See Hamilton, Charles (Harold St. John)
Jennings, S. M.
  See Meyer, Jerome Sydney
Jennings, Sharon 1954- 95
Jennings, Sharon Elizabeth
  See Jennings, Sharon
Jennison, C. S.
  See Starbird, Kaye
Jennison, Keith Warren 1911-1995 14
Jensen, Kathryn 1949- 81
Jensen, Kristine Mary 1961- 78
Jensen, Niels 1927- 25

Jensen, Vickie (Dee) 1946- 81
Jensen, Virginia Allen 1927- 8
Jenson-Elliott, Cynthia L(ouise) 1962- 143
Jeram, Anita 1965- 219
  Earlier sketches in SATA *71, 102, 154*
Jerman, Jerry 1949- 89
Jernigan, E. Wesley 1940- 85
Jernigan, Gisela (Evelyn) 1948- 85
Jeschke, Susan 1942- 42
  Brief entry 27
Jessel, Camilla (Ruth) 1937- 143
  Earlier sketch in SATA *29*
Jessell, Tim 225
  Earlier sketch in SATA *177*
Jessey, Cornelia
  See Sussman, Cornelia Silver
Jewel
  See Kilcher, Jewel
Jewell, Nancy 1940- 109
  Brief entry 41
Jewett, Eleanore Myers 1890-1967 5
Jewett, Sarah Orne 1849-1909 15
Jewett, Theodora Sarah Orne
  See Jewett, Sarah Orne
Jezard, Alison 1919- 57
  Brief entry 34
Jiang, Cheng An 1943- 109
Jiang, Ji-li 1954- 101
Jiang, Zheng An
  See Jiang, Cheng An
Jiler, John 1946- 42
  Brief entry 35
Jimenez, Francisco 1943- 219
  Earlier sketch in SATA *108*
Jinks, Catherine 1963- 207
  Earlier sketches in SATA *94, 155*
Jobb, Jamie 1945- 29
Jobling, Curtis 131
Jocelyn, Ann Henning 1948- 92
Jocelyn, Marthe 1956- 198
  Earlier sketches in SATA *118, 163*
Joerns, Consuelo 44
  Brief entry 33
Joey D
  See Macaulay, Teresa
Johansen, Krista V.
  See Johansen, K.V.
Johansen, K.V 1968- 186
Johansen, K.V. 1968- 186
  Earlier sketch in SATA *129*
Johansson, Philip 163
John, Antony 1972- 206
John, Joyce 59
Johns, Avery
  See Cousins, Margaret
Johns, Elizabeth 1943- 88
Johns, Janetta
  See Quin-Harkin, Janet
Johns, Linda 1945- 173
Johns, W(illiam) E(arle) 1893-1968 55
Johns, Captain W. E.
  See Johns, W(illiam) E(arle)
Johnson, A.
  See Johnson, Annabell
Johnson, A. E.
  See Johnson, Annabell
  and Johnson, Edgar (Raymond)
Johnson, Angela 1961- 188
  Earlier sketches in SATA *69, 102, 150*
  See also CLR *33*
Johnson, Annabel
  See Johnson, Annabell
Johnson, Annabell 1921- 72
  Earlier sketch in SATA *2*
Johnson, Art 1946- 123
Johnson, B. F. 1920- 1
Johnson, Benjamin F., of Boone
  See Riley, James Whitcomb
Johnson, Bettye 1858-1919
  See Rogers, Bettye

Johnson, Caryn
    See Goldberg, Whoopi
Johnson, Caryn E.
    See Goldberg, Whoopi
Johnson, Caryn Elaine
    See Goldberg, Whoopi
Johnson, Charles R. 1925- *11*
Johnson, Charlotte Buel
    See von Wodtke, Charlotte Buel Johnson
Johnson, Chuck
    See Johnson, Charles R.
Johnson, Crockett
    See Leisk, David (Johnson)
Johnson, D(ana) William 1945- *23*
Johnson, Daniel Shahid 1954- *73*
Johnson, David
    See Johnson, David A.
Johnson, David A. 1951- *191*
Johnson, D.B. 1944- *183*
    Earlier sketch in SATA *146*
Johnson, Dianne 1960- *130*
Johnson, Dinah
    See Johnson, Dianne
Johnson, Dolores 1949- *69*
Johnson, Donald B.
    See Johnson, D.B.
Johnson, Dorothy M(arie) 1905-1984 .... *6*
    Obituary *40*
Johnson, E(ugene) Harper *44*
Johnson, Edgar (Raymond) 1912-1990 .... *72*
    Earlier sketch in SATA *2*
Johnson, Eleanor Murdock 1892-1987
    Obituary *54*
Johnson, Elizabeth 1911-1984 .... *7*
    Obituary *39*
Johnson, Eric W(arner) 1918-1994 ....
    Obituary *82*
    Earlier sketch in SATA *8*
Johnson, Evelyne 1922- *20*
Johnson, Fred 19(?)-1982 .... *63*
Johnson, Gaylord 1884-1972 .... *7*
Johnson, Gerald White 1890-1980 .... *19*
    Obituary *28*
Johnson, Gillian 1963- *215*
Johnson, Harper
    See Johnson, E(ugene) Harper
Johnson, Harriett 1908-1987
    Obituary *53*
Johnson, James Ralph 1922- *1*
Johnson, James Weldon 1871-1938 .... *31*
    See also CLR *32*
Johnson, Jane 1951- *48*
Johnson, Joan J. 1942- *59*
Johnson, John E(mil) 1929- *34*
Johnson, Johnny 1901-1995
    See Johnson, (Walter) Ryerson
Johnson, Kathleen Jeffrie 1950- *186*
Johnson, La Verne B(ravo) 1925- *13*
Johnson, Layne *222*
    Earlier sketch in SATA *187*
Johnson, Lee Kaiser 1962- *78*
Johnson, Lissa H(alls) 1955- *65*
Johnson, Lois Smith 1894-1993 .... *6*
Johnson, Lois Walfrid 1936- *130*
    Earlier sketches in SATA *22, 91*
Johnson, Margaret S(weet) 1893-1964 .... *35*
Johnson, Marguerite Annie
    See Angelou, Maya
Johnson, Mary Frances K. 1929(?)-1979
    Obituary *27*
Johnson, Maud Battle 1918(?)-1985
    Obituary *46*
Johnson, Maureen 1973- *200*
Johnson, Meredith Merrell 1952- *104*
Johnson, Milton 1932- *31*
Johnson, Neil 1954- *135*
    Earlier sketch in SATA *73*
Johnson, Pamela 1949- *71*
Johnson, Patricia Polin 1956- *84*
Johnson, Paul Brett 1947- *132*
    Earlier sketch in SATA *83*

Johnson, Rebecca L. 1956- *147*
    Earlier sketch in SATA *67*
Johnson, Rick L. 1954- *79*
Johnson, (Walter) Ryerson 1901-1995 .... *10*
    Obituary *106*
Johnson, Scott 1952- *119*
    Earlier sketch in SATA *76*
Johnson, Sherrie 1948- *87*
Johnson, Shirley K(ing) 1927- *10*
Johnson, Siddie Joe 1905-1977
    Obituary *20*
Johnson, Spencer 1938- *145*
    Brief entry *38*
Johnson, Stacie
    See Myers, Walter Dean
Johnson, Stephen T. 1964- *189*
    Earlier sketches in SATA *84, 141*
Johnson, Steve 1960- *177*
Johnson, Sue Kaiser 1963- *78*
Johnson, Sylvia A. *166*
    Brief entry *52*
    Earlier sketch in SATA *104*
Johnson, William R. *38*
Johnson, William Weber 1909-1992 .... *7*
Johnson-Feelings, Dianne
    See Johnson, Dianne
Johnston, Agnes Christine
    See Dazey, Agnes J(ohnston)
Johnston, Annie Fellows 1863-1931 .... *37*
Johnston, Dorothy Grunbock 1915-1979 ...... *54*
Johnston, Ginny 1946- *60*
Johnston, H(ugh) A(nthony) S(tephen)
    1913-1967 .... *14*
Johnston, Janet 1944- *71*
Johnston, Jeffry W. *188*
Johnston, Johanna 1914(?)-1982 .... *12*
    Obituary *33*
Johnston, Julie 1941- *110*
    Autobiography Feature *128*
    Earlier sketch in SATA *78*
    See also CLR *41*
    See also SAAS *24*
Johnston, Lynn 1947- *216*
    Earlier sketch in SATA *118*
Johnston, Lynn Beverley
    See Johnston, Lynn
Johnston, Mark *194*
Johnston, Norma
    See St. John, Nicole
Johnston, Portia
    See Takakjian, Portia
Johnston, Susan Taylor 1942- *180*
    Earlier sketches in SATA *8, 83, 128*
Johnston, Tim(othy Patrick) 1962- *146*
Johnston, Tony
    See Johnston, Susan Taylor
Joinson, Carla *160*
Jolin, Paula *186*
Jolivet, Joelle 1965- *221*
Jonas, Ann 1932- *135*
    Brief entry *42*
    Earlier sketch in SATA *50*
    See also CLR *74*
Jonell, Lynne 1956- *196*
    Earlier sketch in SATA *109*
Jones, Adrienne 1915-2000 .... *82*
    Earlier sketch in SATA *7*
    See also SAAS *10*
Jones, Allan Frewin 1954- *204*
Jones, Annabel
    See Lewis, Mary
Jones, Betty Millsaps 1940- *54*
Jones, Carol 1942- *153*
    Earlier sketch in SATA *79*
Jones, Carrie 1971- *191*
Jones, Charles M.
    See Jones, Chuck
Jones, Charlotte Foltz 1945- *122*
    Earlier sketch in SATA *77*
Jones, Chuck 1912-2002 .... *53*
    Obituary *133*

Jones, Constance *112*
Jones, Constance A.
    See Jones, Constance
Jones, David 1956- *202*
Jones, Diana Wynne 1934- *160*
    Earlier sketches in SATA *9, 70, 108*
    See also CLR *120*
    See also SAAS *7*
Jones, Douglas B. *202*
Jones, Douglas C(lyde) 1924-1998 .... *52*
Jones, Elizabeth McDavid *155*
Jones, Elizabeth Orton 1910-2005 .... *18*
    Obituary *164*
Jones, Evan 1915-1996 .... *3*
Jones, Frewin
    See Jones, Allan Frewin
Jones, Geraldine
    See McCaughrean, Geraldine
Jones, Gillingham
    See Hamilton, Charles (Harold St. John)
Jones, Gwyneth A. 1952- *159*
Jones, Gwyneth Ann
    See Jones, Gwyneth A.
Jones, Harold 1904-1992 .... *14*
    Obituary *72*
Jones, Helen Hinckley 1903-1991 .... *26*
Jones, Helen L(ouise) 1903-1973
    Obituary *22*
Jones, Hettie 1934- *42*
    Brief entry *27*
Jones, Hortense P. 1918- *9*
Jones, J. Sydney 1948- *101*
Jones, Jasmine
    See Papademetriou, Lisa
Jones, Jennifer (Berry) 1947- *90*
Jones, Jessie Mae Orton 1887(?)-1983
    Obituary *37*
Jones, John R(obert) 1926- *76*
Jones, Jon Sydney
    See Jones, J. Sydney
Jones, Judith
    See James, Bill
Jones, Kimberly K. 1957- *187*
Jones, Marcia Thornton 1958- *217*
    Earlier sketches in SATA *73, 115*
Jones, Martha T(annery) 1931- *130*
Jones, Mary Alice 1898(?)-1980 .... *6*
Jones, McClure *34*
Jones, Noah Z. *182*
Jones, Patrick 1961- *210*
    Earlier sketch in SATA *136*
Jones, Penelope 1938- *31*
Jones, Rebecca C(astaldi) 1947- *99*
    Earlier sketch in SATA *33*
Jones, Robin D(orothy) 1959- *80*
Jones, Sanford W.
    See Thorn, John
Jones, Sylvie *185*
Jones, Sylvie Michelle
    See Jones, Sylvie
Jones, Terence Graham Parry 1942- *127*
    Brief entry *51*
    Earlier sketch in SATA *67*
Jones, Terry
    See Jones, Terence Graham Parry
Jones, Tim Wynne
    See Wynne-Jones, Tim
Jones, Traci L. *186*
Jones, V. M. 1958- *147*
Jones, Veda Boyd 1948- *119*
Jones, Victoria Mary
    See Jones, V. M.
Jones, Volcano
    See Mitchell, Adrian
Jones, Weyman (B.) 1928- *4*
    See also SAAS *11*
Jones, William Glynne
    See Glynne-Jones, William
Jonk, Clarence 1906-1987 .... *10*
Jonsberg, Barry 1951- *168*
Joos, Francoise 1956- *78*

Joos, Frederic 1953- *78*
Joosse, Barbara 1949- *220*
  Earlier sketches in SATA *52, 96, 164*
Joosse, Barbara M.
  See Joosse, Barbara
Joosse, Barbara Monnot
  See Joosse, Barbara
Jordan, Alexis Hill
  See Glick, Ruth (Burtnick)
  and Titchener, Louise
Jordan, Anne Devereaux 1943- *80*
Jordan, Chris
  See Philbrick, Rodman
Jordan, Deloris *191*
Jordan, Devin *221*
Jordan, Don
  See Howard, Vernon (Linwood)
Jordan, Hope Dahle 1905-1995 .... *15*
Jordan, Jael (Michal) 1949- *30*
Jordan, June 1936-2002 .... *136*
  Earlier sketch in SATA *4*
  See also CLR *10*
Jordan, June Meyer
  See Jordan, June
Jordan, Lee
  See Scholefield, Alan
Jordan, Martin George 1944- *84*
Jordan, Robert 1948-2007 .... *95*
Jordan, Robert K.
  See Jordan, Robert
Jordan, Rosa 1939- *191*
Jordan, Roslyn M. *189*
Jordan, Sherryl 1949- *122*
  Earlier sketch in SATA *71*
  See also SAAS *23*
Jordan, Shirley 1930- *154*
Jordan, Tanis 1946- *84*
Jorgensen, Ivar
  See Ellison, Harlan
  and Garrett, Randall
Jorgensen, Mary Venn -1995 .... *36*
Jorgensen, Norman 1954- *157*
Jorgenson, Ivar
  See Silverberg, Robert
Jorisch, Stephane *178*
Joseph, Anne
  See Coates, Anna
Joseph, James (Herz) 1924- *53*
Joseph, Joan 1939- *34*
Joseph, Joseph M(aron) 1903-1979 .... *22*
Joseph, Patrick
  See O'Malley, Kevin
Josephs, Rebecca
  See Talbot, Toby
Josephson, Judith Pinkerton 1943- *198*
Josh
  See Twain, Mark
Joshua, Peter
  See Stone, Peter
Joslin, Mary 1953- *176*
Joslin, Sesyle
  See Hine, Sesyle Joslin
Joubert, Beverly 1957- *204*
Joubert, Dereck *204*
Journet, Mireille
  See Marokvia, Mireille
Joyce, Bill
  See Joyce, William
Joyce, J(ames) Avery 1902-1987 .... *11*
  Obituary *50*
Joyce, Peter 1937- *127*
Joyce, William 1957- *118*
  Brief entry *46*
  Earlier sketch in SATA *72*
  See also CLR *26*
Joyner, Jerry 1938- *34*
Juan, Ana 1961- *179*
Jubb, Sophie *210*
Jubert, Herve *185*
Juby, Susan 1969- *202*
  Earlier sketch in SATA *156*

Jucker, Sita 1921- *5*
Judah, Aaron 1923- *118*
Judd, Cyril
  See Kornbluth, C(yril) M.
  and Merril, Judith
  and Pohl, Frederik
Judd, Denis (O'Nan) 1938- *33*
Judd, Frances K.
  See Benson, Mildred
Jude, Conny *81*
Judge, Lita *192*
Judson, Clara Ingram 1879-1960 .... *38*
  Brief entry *27*
Judy, Stephen
  See Tchudi, Stephen N.
Judy, Stephen N.
  See Tchudi, Stephen N.
Juhasz, Victor 1954- *177*
Jukes, Mavis 1947- *219*
  Brief entry *43*
  Earlier sketches in SATA *72, 111*
  See also SAAS *12*
Jules, Jacqueline 1956- *218*
  Earlier sketches in SATA *148, 183*
Julesberg, Elizabeth Rider Montgomery
  1902-1985 .... *34*
  Obituary *41*
  Earlier sketch in SATA *3*
Julian, Jane
  See Wiseman, David
Jumpp, Hugo
  See MacPeek, Walter G.
Junco, Martha Aviles
  See Aviles, Martha
Jungman, Ann *165*
Jupo, Frank J. 1904-1981 .... *7*
Jurmain, Suzanne 1945- *169*
  Earlier sketch in SATA *72*
Jurmain, Suzanne Tripp
  See Jurmain, Suzanne
Juster, Norton 1929- *220*
  Earlier sketches in SATA *3, 132*
  See also CLR *112*
Justus, May 1898-1989 .... *1*
  Obituary *106*
Juvenilia
  See Taylor, Ann

K

Kaaberbol, Lene
  See Kaaberbol, Lene
Kaaberbol, Lene 1960- *159*
Kabdebo, Tamas
  See Kabdebo, Thomas
Kabdebo, Thomas 1934- *10*
Kabibble, Osh
  See Jobb, Jamie
Kacer, Kathy 1954- *184*
  Earlier sketch in SATA *142*
Kaczman, James *156*
Kadair, Deborah Ousley *184*
Kadefors, Sara 1965- *218*
Kadesch, Robert R(udstone) 1922- *31*
Kadohata, Cynthia 1956(?)- *180*
  Earlier sketch in SATA *155*
  See also CLR *121*
Kadohata, Cynthia L.
  See Kadohata, Cynthia
Kaempfert, Wade
  See del Rey, Lester
Kaestner, Erich 1899-1974 .... *14*
  See also CLR *153*
Kahl, Jonathan (D.) 1959- *77*
Kahl, M(arvin) P(hilip) 1934- *37*
Kahl, Virginia (Caroline) 1919-2004 .... *48*
  Brief entry *38*
  Obituary *158*

Kahn, Joan 1914-1994 .... *48*
  Obituary *82*
Kahn, Katherine Janus 1942- *220*
  Earlier sketches in SATA *90, 167*
Kahn, Peggy
  See Katz, Bobbi
Kahn, Roger 1927- *37*
Kahukiwa, Robyn 1940- *134*
Kains, Josephine
  See Goulart, Ron
Kaizuki, Kiyonori 1950- *72*
Kajikawa, Kimiko *212*
Kakimoto, Kozo 1915- *11*
Kalashnikoff, Nicholas 1888-1961 .... *16*
Kalb, Jonah 1926- *23*
Kalbacken, Joan 1925- *96*
Kalechofsky, Roberta 1931- *92*
Kaler, James Otis 1848-1912 .... *15*
Kalis, Jennifer *207*
Kallen, Stuart A. 1955- *126*
  Earlier sketch in SATA *86*
Kallen, Stuart Arnold
  See Kallen, Stuart A.
Kallevig, Christine Petrell 1955- *164*
Kalman, Bobbie 1947- *63*
Kalman, Maira 1949- *137*
  Earlier sketch in SATA *96*
  See also CLR *32*
Kalnay, Francis 1899-1992 .... *7*
Kaloustian, Rosanne 1955- *93*
Kalow, Gisela 1946- *32*
Kalstein, Dave *175*
Kamara, Mariatu *214*
Kamen, Gloria 1923- *98*
  Earlier sketch in SATA *9*
Kamerman, Sylvia E.
  See Burack, Sylvia K.
Kamm, Josephine (Hart) 1905-1989 .... *24*
Kammerman, Sylvia K.
  See Burack, Sylvia K.
Kandel, Michael 1941- *93*
Kandell, Alice S. 1938- *35*
Kane, Bob 1916-1998 .... *120*
Kane, Henry Bugbee 1902-1971 .... *14*
Kane, Kim 1973(?)- *221*
Kane, L. A.
  See Mannetti, Lisa
Kane, Robert W. 1910- *18*
Kane, Wilson
  See Bloch, Robert (Albert)
Kanefield, Teri 1960- *135*
Kanell, Beth *215*
Kaner, Etta 1947- *198*
  Earlier sketch in SATA *126*
Kanetzke, Howard W(illiam) 1932- *38*
Kangas, Juli 1958- *200*
Kann, Elizabeth *180*
Kann, Victoria *180*
Kanninen, Barbara *196*
Kanninen, Barbara J.
  See Kanninen, Barbara
Kanoza, Muriel Canfield
  See Canfield, Muriel
Kantner, Seth 1965- *179*
Kanzawa, Toshiko
  See Furukawa, Toshi
Kanzler, John 1963- *188*
Kaplan, Andrew 1960- *78*
Kaplan, Anne Bernays
  See Bernays, Anne
Kaplan, Bess 1927- *22*
Kaplan, Boche 1926- *24*
Kaplan, Elizabeth 1956- *83*
Kaplan, Elizabeth A.
  See Kaplan, Elizabeth
Kaplan, Irma 1900- *10*
Kaplan, Jean Caryl Korn 1926- *10*
Kaplow, Robert 1954- *70*
Karageorge, Michael
  See Anderson, Poul

Karas, G. Brian 1957- 222
  Earlier sketch in SATA *178*
Karas, George Brian
  See Karas, G. Brian
Karasz, Ilonka 1896-1981
  Obituary 29
Karen, Ruth 1922-1987 9
  Obituary 54
Kark, Nina Mary
  See Bawden, Nina
Karl, Herb 1938- 73
Karl, Jean E(dna) 1927-2000 122
  Earlier sketch in SATA *34*
  See also SAAS *10*
Karlin, Bernie 1927- 68
Karlin, Eugene 1918- 10
Karlin, Nurit 103
  Earlier sketch in SATA *63*
Karlins, Mark 1947- 219
Karnes, Frances A. 1937- 110
Karp, Naomi J. 1926- 16
Karpinski, J. Rick
  See Karpinski, John Eric
Karpinski, John Eric 1952- 81
Karpinski, Rick
  See Karpinski, John Eric
Karr, Kathleen 1946- 212
  Earlier sketches in SATA *82, 127*
Karr, Phyllis Ann 1944- 119
Karwoski, Gail 1949- 127
Karwoski, Gail Langer
  See Karwoski, Gail
Kashiwagi, Isami 1925- 10
Kaslik, Ibi
  See Kaslik, Ibolya Emma
Kaslik, Ibolya Emma 1973- 185
Kassem, Lou 1931- 62
  Brief entry 51
Kastel, Warren
  See Silverberg, Robert
Kastner, Erich
  See Kaestner, Erich
Kastner, Jill (Marie) 1964- 117
  Earlier sketch in SATA *70*
Kasuya, Masahiro 1937- 51
Kasza, Keiko 1951- 191
  Earlier sketch in SATA *124*
Kataphusin
  See Ruskin, John
Katchen, Carole 1944- 9
Katcher, Brian 1975- 203
Kathryn
  See Searle, Kathryn Adrienne
Kato, Aya 1982- 202
Katona, Robert 1949- 21
Katsarakis, Joan Harries
  See Harries, Joan
Katz, Alan 185
Katz, Avi 1949- 199
Katz, Avner 1939- 103
Katz, Bobbi 1933- 217
  Earlier sketches in SATA *12, 179*
Katz, Fred(eric Phillip) 1938- 6
Katz, Jane B(resler) 1934- 33
Katz, Karen 1947- 195
  Earlier sketch in SATA *158*
Katz, Marjorie P.
  See Weiser, Marjorie P(hillis) K(atz)
Katz, Susan 1945- 156
Katz, Welwyn Wilton 1948- 96
  Autobiography Feature 118
  Earlier sketch in SATA *62*
  See also CLR *45*
Katz, William 1940- 98
Katz, William Loren 1927- 13
Kaufman, Bel 57
Kaufman, Jeff 1955- 84
Kaufman, Joe 1911-2001 33
Kaufman, Joseph
  See Kaufman, Joe
Kaufman, Mervyn D. 1932- 4

Kaufmann, Angelika 1935- 15
Kaufmann, John 1931- 18
Kaula, Edna Mason 1906-1987 13
Kaur Khalsa, Dayal
  See Khalsa, Dayal Kaur
Kavaler, Lucy 1930- 23
Kavanagh, Jack 1920- 85
Kavanagh, P(atrick) J(oseph Gregory)
  1931- 122
Kavanaugh, Ian
  See Webb, Jean Francis (III)
Kay, Alan N. 1965- 144
Kay, Elizabeth 1949- 165
Kay, Guy Gavriel 1954- 167
  Earlier sketch in SATA *121*
Kay, Helen
  See Goldfrank, Helen Colodny
Kay, Jackie 1961- 165
  Earlier sketch in SATA *97*
Kay, Jacqueline Margaret
  See Kay, Jackie
Kay, Julia 205
Kay, Mara 13
Kay, Verla 1946- 210
  Earlier sketch in SATA *120*
Kaye, Danny 1913-1987
  Obituary 50
Kaye, Geraldine (Hughesdon) 1925- 85
  Earlier sketch in SATA *10*
Kaye, Judy
  See Baer, Judy
Kaye, Marilyn 1949- 110
  Earlier sketch in SATA *56*
Kaye, Mary Margaret
  See Kaye, M.M.
Kaye, M.M. 1908-2004 62
  Obituary 152
Kaye, Mollie
  See Kaye, M.M.
Kaye, Peggy 1948- 143
Keach, James P. 1950- 125
Keams, Geri 1951- 117
Keane, Bil 1922- 4
Keane, Dave 1965- 216
Keaney, Brian 1954- 188
  Earlier sketch in SATA *106*
Kearney, Meg 1964- 178
Kearny, Jillian
  See Goulart, Ron
Keat, Nawuth 1964- 222
Keating, Bern
  See Keating, Leo Bernard
Keating, Frank 1944- 143
Keating, Lawrence A. 1903-1966 23
Keating, Leo Bernard 1915- 10
Keats, Emma 1899(?)-1979(?) 68
Keats, Ezra Jack 1916-1983 57
  Obituary 34
  Earlier sketch in SATA *14*
  See also CLR *35*
Keefer, Catherine
  See Ogan, George F.
  and Ogan, Margaret E. (Nettles)
Keefer, Janice Kulyk
  See Kulyk Keefer, Janice
Keegan, Marcia 1943- 104
  Earlier sketch in SATA *9*
Keehn, Sally M. 1947- 165
  Earlier sketch in SATA *87*
Keel, Frank
  See Keeler, Ronald F(ranklin)
Keeler, Patricia 183
Keeler, Patricia A.
  See Keeler, Patricia
Keeler, Ronald F(ranklin) 1913-1983 47
Keely, Jack 1951- 119
Keen, Martin L. 1913-1992 4
Keenan, Sheila 1953- 95
Keene, Ann T. 1940- 86
Keene, Ann Todd
  See Keene, Ann T.

Keene, Carolyn
  See Benson, Mildred
  and Goulart, Ron
  and Lerangis, Peter
  and McFarlane, Leslie
  and Stanley, George Edward
  and Stratemeyer, Edward L.
Keens-Douglas, Richardo 1953- 154
  Earlier sketch in SATA *95*
Keep, Linda Lowery
  See Lowery, Linda
Keep, Richard 1949- 170
Keep, Richard Cleminson
  See Keep, Richard
Keeping, Charles (William James)
  1924-1988 69
  Obituary 56
  Earlier sketch in SATA *9*
  See also CLR *34*
Keeshan, Robert J. 1927-2004 32
  Obituary 151
Kehlenbeck, Angela 1959- 186
Kehoe, Tim 1970- 224
Kehret, Peg 1936- 212
  Autobiography Feature 149
  Earlier sketches in SATA *73, 108, 149*
Keillor, Garrison 1942- 58
Keillor, Gary Edward
  See Keillor, Garrison
Keir, Christine
  See Pullein-Thompson, Christine
Keiser, Paige 220
Keister, Douglas 1948- 88
Keith, Doug 1952- 81
Keith, Eros 1942- 52
Keith, Hal 1934- 36
Keith, Harold (Verne) 1903-1998 74
  Earlier sketch in SATA *2*
Keith, Robert
  See Applebaum, Stan
Keleinikov, Andrei 1924- 65
Kelemen, Julie 1959- 78
Kelen, Emery 1896-1978 13
  Obituary 26
Kelleam, Joseph E(veridge) 1913-1975 31
Kelleher, Anne 1959- 97
Kelleher, Annette 1950- 122
Kelleher, Daria Valerian 1955- 79
Kelleher, Victor (Michael Kitchener)
  1939- 129
  Brief entry 52
  Earlier sketch in SATA *75*
  See also CLR *36*
Keller, Beverly L(ou) 91
  Earlier sketch in SATA *13*
Keller, Charles 1942- 82
  Earlier sketch in SATA *8*
Keller, Debra 1958- 94
Keller, Dick 1923- 36
Keller, Emily 96
Keller, Gail Faithfull
  See Faithfull, Gail
Keller, Holly 1942- 216
  Brief entry 42
  Earlier sketches in SATA *76, 108, 157*
  See also CLR *45*
Keller, Irene (Barron) 1927-2002 36
  Obituary 139
Keller, Laurie 1961(?)- 196
Kelley, Ann 1941- 217
Kelley, Ellen A. 185
Kelley, Ellen Chavez
  See Kelley, Ellen A.
Kelley, Gary 1945- 217
  Earlier sketch in SATA *183*
Kelley, Leo P(atrick) 1928- 32
  Brief entry 31
Kelley, Marty 1971- 211
Kelley, Patrick (G.) 1963- 129
Kelley, Patte 1947- 93
Kelley, True 1946- 179

Kelley, True (Adelaide) 1946- 130
  Brief entry 39
  Earlier sketches in SATA 41, 92
Kelley, True Adelaide
  See Kelley, True
Kellin, Sally Moffet 1932- 9
Kelling, Furn L. 1914-2000 37
Kellogg, Gene
  See Kellogg, Jean (Defrees)
Kellogg, Jean (Defrees) 1916-1978 10
Kellogg, Steven 1941- 177
  Earlier sketches in SATA 8, 57, 130
  See also CLR 6
Kellogg, Steven Castle
  See Kellogg, Steven
Kellow, Kathleen
  See Hibbert, Eleanor Alice Burford
Kelly, C. M. O.
  See Gibbs, (Cecilia) May
Kelly, Clint 1950- 140
Kelly, Eric P(hilbrook) 1884-1960
  See YABC 1
Kelly, Fiona
  See Coleman, Michael
  and Hendry, Frances Mary
  and Jones, Allan Frewin
  and Oldfield, Jenny
  and Welford, Sue
Kelly, Irene 1957- 210
  Earlier sketch in SATA 147
Kelly, Jacqueline 216
Kelly, Jeff
  See Kelly, Jeffrey
Kelly, Jeffrey 1946- 65
Kelly, Joanne (W.) 1934- 87
Kelly, Kate 1958- 91
Kelly, Kathleen M. 1964- 71
Kelly, Katy 1955- 215
  Earlier sketch in SATA 169
Kelly, Lauren
  See Oates, Joyce Carol
Kelly, Laurene 1954- 123
Kelly, Martha Rose 1914-1983 37
Kelly, Marty
  See Kelly, Martha Rose
Kelly, Mij 166
Kelly, Ralph
  See Geis, Darlene Stern
Kelly, Regina Z(immerman) 1898-1986 5
Kelly, Rosalie (Ruth) 43
Kelly, Tom 1961- 191
Kelly, Walt(er Crawford) 1913-1973 18
Kelsey, Alice Geer 1896-1982 1
Kelsey, Elin 1961- 159
Kelsey, Marybeth 216
Kemly, Kathleen 1958- 197
Kemnitz, Thomas Milton, Jr. 1984- 152
Kemnitz, Tom, Jr.
  See Kemnitz, Thomas Milton, Jr.
Kemp, Gene 1926- 75
  Earlier sketch in SATA 25
  See also CLR 29
Kempner, Mary Jean 1913-1969 10
Kempter, Christa 1945- 187
Kempton, Jean Welch 1914- 10
Kenah, Katharine 1949- 182
Kenda, Margaret 1942- 71
Kendall, Carol (Seeger) 1917- 74
  Earlier sketch in SATA 11
  See also SAAS 7
Kendall, Gideon 1966- 215
Kendall, Katherine
  See Applegate, Katherine
Kendall, Lace
  See Stoutenburg, Adrien (Pearl)
Kendall, Martha E. 87
Kendall, Russ 1957- 83
Kenealy, James P. 1927- 52
  Brief entry 29
Kenealy, Jim
  See Kenealy, James P.

Kennaway, Adrienne 1945- 171
  Earlier sketch in SATA 60
Kennedy, Anne 1955- 198
Kennedy, Anne Vittur
  See Kennedy, Anne
Kennedy, Brendan 1970- 57
Kennedy, Dana Forrest 1917- 74
Kennedy, Dorothy M(intzlaff) 1931- 53
Kennedy, Doug 1963- 189
  Earlier sketch in SATA 122
Kennedy, Frances 1937- 192
Kennedy, James 214
Kennedy, John F. 1917-1963 11
Kennedy, John Fitzgerald
  See Kennedy, John F.
Kennedy, Joseph Charles
  See Kennedy, X. J.
Kennedy, Kim 189
Kennedy, Marlane 1962- 210
Kennedy, Pamela (J.) 1946- 87
Kennedy, Paul E(dward) 1929- 113
  Earlier sketch in SATA 33
Kennedy, Richard (Pitt) 1910-1989
  Obituary 60
Kennedy, (Jerome) Richard 1932- 22
Kennedy, Robert 1938- 63
Kennedy, T.A. 1953- 42
  Brief entry 35
Kennedy, Teresa
  See Kennedy, T.A.
Kennedy, Teresa A.
  See Kennedy, T.A.
Kennedy, William 1928- 57
Kennedy, William Joseph
  See Kennedy, William
Kennedy, X. J. 1929- 130
  Autobiography Feature 130
  Earlier sketches in SATA 14, 86
  See also CLR 27
  See also SAAS 22
Kennell, Ruth Epperson 1893-1977 6
  Obituary 25
Kennemore, Tim 1957- 220
  Earlier sketch in SATA 133
Kennen, Ally 190
Kennett, David 1959- 206
  Earlier sketch in SATA 121
Kennison, Ruth 202
Kenny, Ellsworth Newcomb 1909-1971
  Obituary 26
Kenny, Herbert Andrew 1912-2002 13
Kenny, Jude
  See Daly, Jude
Kenny, Kathryn
  See Bowden, Joan Chase
  and Krull, Kathleen
  and Sanderlin, Owenita (Harrah)
  and Stack, Nicolete Meredith
Kenny, Kevin
  See Krull, Kathleen
Kensinger, George
  See Fichter, George S.
Kensington, Kathryn Wesley
  See Rusch, Kristine Kathryn
Kent, Alexander
  See Reeman, Douglas Edward
Kent, David
  See Lambert, David
Kent, Deborah Ann 1948- 155
  Brief entry 41
  Earlier sketches in SATA 47, 104
Kent, Jack
  See Kent, John Wellington
Kent, John Wellington 1920-1985 24
  Obituary 45
Kent, Lisa 1942- 90
Kent, Mallory
  See Lowndes, Robert A(ugustine) W(ard)
Kent, Margaret 1894- 2
Kent, Rockwell 1882-1971 6
Kent, Rose 188

Kent, Sherman 1903-1986 20
  Obituary 47
Kenward, Jean 1920- 42
Kenworthy, Leonard S. 1912-1991 6
Kenyon, Karen (Smith) 1938- 145
Kenyon, Kate
  See Adorjan, Carol (Madden)
  and Ransom, Candice
Kenyon, Ley 1913-1990 6
Keown, Elizabeth 78
Kepes, Juliet A(ppleby) 1919-1999 13
Kephart, Beth 1960- 196
Kerby, Mona 1951- 202
  Earlier sketch in SATA 75
Kerigan, Florence 1896-1984 12
Kerley, Barbara 1960- 191
  Earlier sketch in SATA 138
Kerman, Gertrude
  See Furman, Gertrude Lerner Kerman
Kerns, Thelma 1929- 116
Kerr, Anne Louise
  See Mackey, Weezie Kerr
Kerr, Bob 1951- 120
Kerr, Jessica 1901-1991 13
Kerr, (Anne-)Judith 1923-1970 24
Kerr, M. E.
  See Meaker, Marijane
Kerr, P.B.
  See Kerr, Philip
Kerr, Philip 1956- 168
Kerr, Phyllis Forbes 1942- 72
Kerr, Tom 1950- 77
Kerrin, Jessica Scott 174
Kerry, Frances
  See Kerigan, Florence
Kerry, Lois
  See Duncan, Lois
Kershen, (L.) Michael 1982- 82
Kerven, Rosalind 1954- 83
Ker Wilson, Barbara 1929- 121
  Earlier sketches in SATA 20, 70
  See also SAAS 18
Kerz, Anna 1947- 220
Keselman, Gabriela 1953- 128
Kesey, Ken 1935-2001 66
  Obituary 131
Kesey, Ken Elton
  See Kesey, Ken
Kesler, Jay 1935- 65
Kessel, Joyce Karen 1937- 41
Kessler, Cristina 190
Kessler, Ethel 1922- 44
  Brief entry 37
Kessler, Leonard P. 1921- 14
Kessler, Liz 1966- 206
Kest, Kristin 1967- 168
  Earlier sketch in SATA 118
Kesteven, G. R.
  See Crosher, G. R.
Ketcham, Hank
  See Ketcham, Henry King
Ketcham, Henry King 1920-2001 28
  Brief entry 27
  Obituary 128
Ketcham, Sallie 1963- 124
Ketchum, Liza 1946- 132
  Earlier sketch in SATA 78
Ketner, Mary Grace 1946- 75
Kettelkamp, Larry (Dale) 1933- 2
  See also SAAS 3
Ketteman, Helen 1945- 223
  Earlier sketches in SATA 73, 115, 167
Kettle, Peter
  See Glover, Denis (James Matthews)
Kevles, Bettyann Holtzmann 1938- 23
Key, Alexander (Hill) 1904-1979 8
  Obituary 23
Key, Samuel M.
  See de Lint, Charles
Key, Watt 1970- 189
Keyes, Daniel 1927- 37

Keyes, Diane 207
Keyes, Fenton 1915-1999 34
Keyes, Greg 1963- 116
Keyes, J. Gregory
    See Keyes, Greg
Keyser, Marcia 1933- 42
Keyser, Sarah
    See McGuire, Leslie (Sarah)
Khalid, Mohamed Nor
    See Lat
Khalsa, Dayal Kaur 1943-1989 62
    See also CLR 30
Khan, Hena 214
Khan, Rukhsana 1962- 165
    Earlier sketch in SATA *118*
Khanshendel, Chiron
    See Rose, Wendy
Kheirabadi, Masoud 1951- 158
Khemir, Sabiha 87
Kherdian, David 1931- 74
    Autobiography Feature 125
    Earlier sketch in SATA *16*
    See also CLR 24
Khing, T.T. 1933- 192
Kibbe, Pat (Hosley) 60
Kidd, Diana 1933-2000 150
Kidd, Richard 1952-2008 152
    Obituary 194
Kidd, Ronald 1948- 173
    Earlier sketches in SATA *42, 92*
Kiddell, John 1922- 3
Kiddell-Monroe, Joan 1908-1972 55
Kidwell, Carl 1910- 43
Kiefer, Irene 1926- 21
Kiefer, Kathleen Balmes 1957- 142
Kiepper, Shirley Morgan 1933- 10
Kierstead, Vera M.
    See Kierstead-Farber, Vera M.
Kierstead-Farber, Vera M. 1913- 121
Kierstead-Farber, Vera May
    See Kierstead-Farber, Vera M.
Kiesel, Stanley 1925- 35
Kiesler, Kate (A.) 1971- 152
    Earlier sketch in SATA *90*
Kihn, Greg 1952- 110
Kikukawa, Cecily H(arder) 1919- 44
    Brief entry 35
Kilaka, John 1966- 223
Kilcher, Jewel 1974- 109
Kile, Joan 1940- 78
Kilgore, Kathleen 1946- 42
Kilian, Crawford 1941- 35
Killdeer, John
    See Mayhar, Ardath
Killien, Christi 1956- 73
Killilea, Marie (Lyons) 1913-1991 2
Killingback, Julia 1944- 63
Killough, (Karen) Lee 1942- 64
Kilpatrick, Don 206
Kilreon, Beth
    See Walker, Barbara (Jeanne) K(erlin)
Kilworth, Garry 1941- 216
    Earlier sketch in SATA *94*
Kilworth, Garry D.
    See Kilworth, Garry
Kilworth, Garry Douglas
    See Kilworth, Garry
Kim, David 1977- 201
Kim, Dong-hwa 1950- 225
Kim, Helen 1899-1970 98
Kim, Joung Un 1970- 205
Kimball, Gayle 1943- 90
Kimball, Violet T(ew) 1932- 126
Kimball, Yeffe 1914-1978 37
Kimber, Murray 1964- 171
Kimble, Warren 176
Kimbrough, Emily 1899-1989 2
    Obituary 59
Kimeldorf, Martin 1948- 121
Kimeldorf, Martin R.
    See Kimeldorf, Martin

Kimenye, Barbara 1940(?)- 121
Kimmel, Elizabeth Cody 209
    Earlier sketch in SATA *170*
Kimmel, Eric A. 1946- 208
    Earlier sketches in SATA *13, 80, 125, 176*
Kimmel, Margaret Mary 1938- 43
    Brief entry 33
Kimmelman, Burt 1947- 180
Kimmelman, Leslie 1958- 211
    Earlier sketches in SATA *85, 156*
Kincaid, Jamaica 1949-
    See CLR 63
Kincher, Jonni 1949- 79
Kindl, Patrice 1951- 128
    Earlier sketch in SATA *82*
    See also CLR 132
Kindred, Wendy (Good) 1937- 7
Kinerk, Robert 199
Kines, Pat Decker 1937- 12
King, Adam
    See Hoare, Robert J(ohn)
King, Alison
    See Martini, Teri
King, (Maria) Anna 1964- 72
King, A.S. 1970- 217
King, Billie Jean 1943- 12
King, Christine
    See Farris, Christine King
King, Christopher (L.) 1945- 84
King, (David) Clive 1924- 144
    Earlier sketch in SATA *28*
King, Colin 1943- 76
King, Cynthia 1925- 7
King, Daniel (John) 1963- 130
King, Daren 1972- 197
King, Elizabeth 1953- 83
King, Frank O. 1883-1969
    Obituary 22
King, Frank R. 1904-1999 127
King, Jane
    See Currie, Stephen
King, Jeanette (Margaret) 1959- 105
King, Larry L. 1929- 66
King, Laurie R. 1952- 88
King, Marian 1900(?)-1986 23
    Obituary 47
King, Martin Luther, Jr. 1929-1968 14
King, Mary Ellen 1958- 93
King, Paul
    See Drackett, Phil(ip Arthur)
King, Paula
    See Downing, Paula E.
King, Stephen 1947- 161
    Earlier sketches in SATA *9, 55*
    See also CLR 124
King, Stephen Edwin
    See King, Stephen
King, Stephen Michael 218
    Earlier sketch in SATA *157*
King, Steve
    See King, Stephen
King, Thomas 1943- 96
King, Thomas Hunt
    See King, Thomas
King, Tony 1947- 39
King, Willie Christine
    See Farris, Christine King
Kingfisher, Rupert 209
Kingman, Dong (Moy Shu) 1911-2000 44
Kingman, Lee
    See Natti, Lee
Kingsbury, Evan
    See Walker, Robert W.
Kingsland, Leslie William 1912- 13
Kingsley, Charles 1819-1875
    See YABC 2
    See also CLR 77
Kingsley, Emily Perl 1940- 33
Kingsley, Kaza 193

King-Smith, Dick 1922-2011 192
    Brief entry 38
    Earlier sketches in SATA *47, 80, 135*
    See also CLR 40
Kingston, Maxine Hong 1940- 53
Kingston, Maxine Ting Ting Hong
    See Kingston, Maxine Hong
Kinney, C. Cle(land) 1915- 6
Kinney, Harrison 1921- 13
Kinney, Jean Stout 1912- 12
Kinney, Jeff 1971- 187
Kinsey, Elizabeth
    See Clymer, Eleanor
Kinsey, Helen 1948- 82
Kinsey-Warnock, Natalie 1956- 167
    Earlier sketches in SATA *71, 116*
Kinzel, Dorothy 1950- 57
Kinzel, Dottie
    See Kinzel, Dorothy
Kipling, Joseph Rudyard
    See Kipling, Rudyard
Kipling, Rudyard 1865-1936 100
    See also YABC 2
    See also CLR 65
Kippax, Frank
    See Needle, Jan
Kirby, David 1944- 78
Kirby, David K.
    See Kirby, David
Kirby, David Kirk
    See Kirby, David
Kirby, Margaret
    See Bingley, Margaret (Jane Kirby)
Kirby, Pamela F. 1952- 220
Kirby, Susan E. 1949- 62
Kirk, Connie Ann 1957- 167
Kirk, Daniel 1952- 196
    Earlier sketches in SATA *107, 153*
Kirk, David 1955- 161
    Earlier sketch in SATA *117*
Kirk, Heather 1949- 166
Kirk, Ruth (Kratz) 1925- 5
Kirkham, Dinah
    See Card, Orson Scott
Kirkland, Will
    See Hale, Arlene
Kirkpatrick, Katherine (Anne) 1964- 113
Kirkup, James 1918-2009 12
Kirkus, Virginia
    See Glick, Virginia Kirkus
Kirkwood, Kathryn
    See Fluke, Joanne
Kirsch, Vincent X. 211
Kirshenbaum, Binnie 79
Kirshner, David S. 1958- 123
Kirtland, G. B.
    See Hine, Sesyle Joslin
    and Hine, Al(fred Blakelee)
Kirwan, Wednesday 198
Kish, Eleanor M(ary) 1924- 73
Kish, Ely
    See Kish, Eleanor M(ary)
Kishida, Eriko 1929- 12
Kisinger, Grace Gelvin (Maze) 1913-1965 .. 10
Kissel, Richard 209
Kissin, Eva H. 1923- 10
Kissinger, Rosemary K.
    See Updyke, Rosemary K.
Kistler, John M. 1967- 160
Kitamura, Satoshi 1956- 201
    Earlier sketches in SATA *62, 98, 143*
    See also CLR 60
Kitchen, Bert
    See Kitchen, Herbert Thomas
Kitchen, Herbert Thomas 1940- 70
Kite, L. Patricia
    See Kite, Pat
Kite, Pat 1940- 78
Kitt, Tamara
    See de Regniers, Beatrice Schenk (Freedman)

Kittinger, Jo S(usenbach) 1955- *148*
Earlier sketch in SATA *96*
Kituomba
See Odaga, Asenath (Bole)
Kitzinger, Sheila 1929- *57*
Kiwak, Barbara 1966- *103*
Kjelgaard, James Arthur 1910-1959 .... *17*
See also CLR *81*
Kjelgaard, Jim
See Kjelgaard, James Arthur
Kjelle, Marylou Morano 1954- *146*
Klages, Ellen 1954- *196*
Klagsbrun, Francine (Lifton) *36*
Klaits, Barrie 1944- *52*
Klam, Cheryl *191*
Klaperman, Gilbert 1921- *33*
Klaperman, Libby Mindlin 1921-1982 .... *33*
Obituary *31*
Klass, David 1960- *207*
Earlier sketches in SATA *88, 142*
Klass, Morton 1927-2001 .... *11*
Klass, Sheila Solomon 1927- *219*
Autobiography Feature *126*
Earlier sketches in SATA *45, 99*
See also SAAS *26*
Klause, Annette Curtis 1953- *175*
Earlier sketch in SATA *79*
See also CLR *104*
Klaveness, Jan O'Donnell 1939- *86*
Kleberger, Ilse 1921- *5*
Kleeberg, Irene (Flitner) Cumming 1932- *65*
Klein, Aaron E. 1930-1998 .... *45*
Brief entry *28*
Klein, Bill 1945- *89*
Klein, David 1919-2001 .... *59*
Klein, Frederick C. 1938- *154*
Klein, Gerda Weissmann 1924- *44*
Klein, H(erbert) Arthur *8*
Klein, James 1932- *115*
Klein, Leonore (Glotzer) 1916- *6*
Klein, Lisa 1958- *211*
Klein, Lisa M.
See Klein, Lisa
Klein, Mina C(ooper) 1906-1979 .... *8*
Klein, Norma 1938-1989 .... *57*
Earlier sketch in SATA *7*
See also CLR *162*
See also SAAS *1*
Klein, Rachel S. 1953- *105*
Klein, Robin 1936- *164*
Brief entry *45*
Earlier sketches in SATA *55, 80*
See also CLR *21*
Klemin, Diana *65*
Klemm, Barry 1945- *104*
Klemm, Edward G., Jr. 1910-2001 .... *30*
Klemm, Roberta K(ohnhorst) 1884-1975 ..... *30*
Kleven, Elisa 1958- *217*
Earlier sketches in SATA *76, 173*
See also CLR *85*
Klevin, Jill Ross 1935- *39*
Brief entry *38*
Kliban, B(ernard) 1935-1990 .... *35*
Obituary *66*
Klier, Kimberly Wagner *208*
Klimo, Kate *214*
Klimowicz, Barbara 1927- *10*
Kline, Christina Baker 1964- *101*
Kline, James
See Klein, James
Kline, Jim
See Kline, Jim
Kline, Lisa Williams 1954- *143*
Kline, Suzy 1943- *193*
Autobiography Feature *193*
Brief entry *48*
Earlier sketches in SATA *67, 99, 152*
Kliros, Thea 1935- *106*
Klise, Kate *221*
Earlier sketch in SATA *181*

Klise, M. Sarah 1961- *180*
Earlier sketch in SATA *128*
Klots, Alexander Barrett 1903-1989
Obituary *62*
Klug, Ron(ald) 1939- *31*
Knaak, Richard A. 1961- *166*
Earlier sketch in SATA *86*
Knaak, Richard Allen
See Knaak, Richard A.
Knapman, Timothy *200*
Knapp, Edward
See Kunhardt, Edith
Knapp, Ron 1952- *34*
Knebel, Fletcher 1911-1993 .... *36*
Obituary *75*
Kneeland, Linda Clarke 1947- *94*
Kneen, Maggie 1957- *221*
Knickerbocker, Diedrich
See Irving, Washington
Knifesmith
See Cutler, Ivor
Knigge, Robert (R.) 1921(?)-1987 .... *50*
Knight, Anne (Katherine) 1946- *34*
Knight, Brenda *112*
Knight, Christopher G. 1943- *96*
Knight, Damon (Francis) 1922-2002 .... *9*
Obituary *139*
Knight, David C(arpenter) 1925-1984 .... *14*
See also CLR *38*
Knight, Eric 1897-1943 .... *18*
Knight, Eric Mowbray
See Knight, Eric
Knight, Francis Edgar 1905- *14*
Knight, Frank
See Knight, Francis Edgar
Knight, Hilary 1926- *132*
Earlier sketches in SATA *15, 69*
Knight, Joan
See Knight, Joan (MacPhail)
Knight, Joan (MacPhail) *159*
Earlier sketch in SATA *82*
Knight, Kathryn Lasky
See Lasky, Kathryn
Knight, Mallory T.
See Hurwood, Bernhardt J.
Knight, Ruth Adams 1898-1974
Obituary *20*
Knight, Theodore O. 1946- *77*
Knobloch, Dorothea 1951- *88*
Knoepfle, John (Ignatius) 1923- *66*
Knorr, Laura 1971- *200*
Knott, Bill
See Knott, William C(ecil, Jr.)
Knott, William C(ecil, Jr.) 1927- *3*
Knotts, Howard (Clayton, Jr.) 1922- *25*
Knowles, Anne 1933- *37*
Knowles, Jo 1970- *197*
Knowles, Johanna Beth
See Knowles, Jo
Knowles, John 1926-2001 .... *89*
Obituary *134*
Earlier sketch in SATA *8*
See also CLR *98*
Knox, Calvin M.
See Silverberg, Robert
Knox, (Mary) Eleanor Jessie 1909-2000 ...... *59*
Earlier sketch in SATA *30*
Knox, Elizabeth 1959- *176*
Knox, Elizabeth Fiona
See Knox, Elizabeth
Knox, James
See Brittain, William
Knox, Jolyne 1937- *76*
Knudsen, James 1950- *42*
Knudsen, Michelle 1974- *220*
Earlier sketch in SATA *171*
Knudson, Mike 1965- *209*
Knudson, R. R.
See Knudson, Rozanne
Knudson, Richard L(ewis) 1930- *34*

Knudson, Rozanne 1932-2008 .... *79*
Earlier sketch in SATA *7*
See also SAAS *18*
Knutson, Barbara 1959-2005 .... *166*
Knutson, Kimberley *115*
Knye, Cassandra
See Disch, Thomas M.
Kobayashi, Masako Matsuno 1935- *6*
Kober, Shahar 1979- *213*
Koch, Dorothy Clarke 1924- *6*
Koch, Kenneth 1925-2002 .... *65*
Koch, Kenneth Jay
See Koch, Kenneth
Koch, Phyllis (Mae) McCallum 1911- *10*
Kochalka, James 1967- *196*
Kocsis, J. C.
See Paul, James
Koda-Callan, Elizabeth 1944- *140*
Earlier sketch in SATA *67*
Kodera, Craig 1956- *222*
Kodman, Stanislawa *201*
Koehler, Phoebe 1955- *85*
Koehler-Pentacoff, Elizabeth 1957- *160*
Earlier sketch in SATA *96*
Koehn, Ilse
See Van Zwienen, Ilse Charlotte Koehn
Koeller, Carol *192*
Koenig, Viviane 1950- *80*
Koering, Ursula 1921-1976 .... *64*
Koerner, W(illiam) H(enry) D(avid)
1878-1938 .... *21*
Koertge, Ron 1940- *209*
Earlier sketches in SATA *53, 92, 131*
Koestler-Grack, Rachel A. 1973- *156*
Koff, Richard Myram 1926- *62*
Koffinke, Carol 1949- *82*
Kogan, Deborah
See Kogan Ray, Deborah
Kogan Ray, Deborah 1940- *203*
Earlier sketches in SATA *8, 50, 161*
Kogawa, Joy 1935- *99*
Kogawa, Joy Nozomi
See Kogawa, Joy
Kogler, Jennie
See Kogler, Jennifer Anne
Kogler, Jennifer Anne 1982(?)- *174*
Kohara, Kazuno *207*
Kohl, Herbert 1937- *47*
Kohl, Herbert R.
See Kohl, Herbert
Kohl, MaryAnn F(aubion) 1947- *144*
Earlier sketch in SATA *74*
Kohler, Julilly H(ouse) 1908-1976
Obituary *20*
Kohn, Bernice
See Hunt, Bernice
Kohn, Rita (T.) 1933- *89*
Kohner, Frederick 1905-1986 .... *10*
Obituary *48*
Koide, Tan 1938-1986 .... *50*
Koike, Kay 1940- *72*
Koja, Kathe 1960- *199*
Earlier sketch in SATA *155*
Koja, Stephan *198*
Kolar, Bob 1960(?)- *206*
Kolb, Larry J. 1953- *175*
Kolba, St. Tamara *22*
Kolibalova, Marketa
See Kolibalova, Marketa
Kolibalova, Marketa 1953- *126*
Koller, Jackie French 1948- *157*
Earlier sketches in SATA *72, 109*
See also CLR *68*
Kolodny, Nancy J. 1946- *76*
Kolosov, Jacqueline 1967- *199*
Komaiko, Leah 1954- *164*
Earlier sketch in SATA *97*
Komisar, Lucy 1942- *9*
Komoda, Beverly 1939- *25*
Komoda, Kiyo 1937- *9*
Kompaneyets, Marc 1974- *169*

Komroff, Manuel 1890-1974 2
Obituary 20
Konigsberg, Bill 1970- 207
Konigsburg, E.L. 1930- 194
Earlier sketches in SATA 4, 48, 94, 126
See also CLR 81
Konigsburg, Elaine Lobl
See Konigsburg, E.L.
Koning, Hans 1921-2007 5
Obituary 182
Koningsberger, Hans
See Koning, Hans
Konkle, Janet Everest 1917- 12
Kono, Erin Eitter 1973- 177
Konrad, Marla Stewart 218
Konzak, Burt 1946- 151
Koob, Theodora (J. Foth) 1918- 23
Kooiker, Leonie
See Kooyker-Romijn, Johanna Maria
Koons, James
See Pernu, Dennis
Koontz, Dean 1945- 165
Earlier sketch in SATA 92
See Koontz, Dean R.
Koontz, Dean R. 225
See Koontz, Dean
Koontz, Dean Ray
See Koontz, Dean
Koontz, Robin Michal 1954- 136
Earlier sketch in SATA 70
Kooyker, Leonie
See Kooyker-Romijn, Johanna Maria
Kooyker-Romijn, Johanna Maria 1927- 48
Kooyker-Romyn, Johanna Maria
See Kooyker-Romijn, Johanna Maria
Kopelke, Lisa 1963- 154
Kopper, Lisa 1950- 105
Brief entry 51
Kopper, Lisa Esther
See Kopper, Lisa
Koppes, Steven N. 1957- 169
Koppes, Steven Nelson
See Koppes, Steven N.
Korach, Mimi 1922- 9
Koralek, Jenny 1934- 215
Earlier sketches in SATA 71, 140
Korczak, Janusz
See Goldszmit, Henryk
Koren, Edward (Benjamin) 1935- 148
Earlier sketch in SATA 5
Koren, Edward 1935- 206
Korinets, Iurii Iosifovich
See Korinetz, Yuri (Iosifovich)
Korinetz, Yuri (Iosifovich) 1923- 9
See also CLR 4
Korman, Bernice 1937- 78
Korman, Gordon 1963- 167
Brief entry 41
Earlier sketches in SATA 49, 81, 119
See also CLR 25
Korman, Gordon Richard
See Korman, Gordon
Korman, Justine 1958- 70
Kornblatt, Marc 1954- 147
Earlier sketch in SATA 84
Kornprobst, Jacques 1937- 177
Korte, Gene J. 1950- 74
Korthues, Barbara 1971- 203
Korty, Carol 1937- 15
Koscielniak, Bruce 1947- 153
Earlier sketches in SATA 67, 99
Koshin, Alexander (A.) 1952- 86
Kositsky, Lynne 1947- 158
Koskenmaki, Rosalie
See Maggio, Rosalie
Koss, Amy Goldman 1954- 158
Earlier sketch in SATA 115
Kossin, Sandy (Sanford) 1926- 10
Kossman, Nina 1959- 84
Kostecki-Shaw, Jenny Sue 203
Kostick, Conor 1964- 186

Kotzwinkle, William 1938- 146
Earlier sketches in SATA 24, 70
See also CLR 6
Kouhi, Elizabeth 1917- 54
Brief entry 49
Kouts, Anne 1945- 8
Koutsky, Jan Dale 1955- 146
Kovacs, Deborah 1954- 132
Earlier sketch in SATA 79
Kovalski, Maryann 1951- 175
Earlier sketches in SATA 58, 97
See also CLR 34
See also SAAS 21
Kowalski, Kathiann M. 1955- 151
Earlier sketch in SATA 96
Koz, Paula G.
See Goodman Koz, Paula
Kozjan, Drazen 209
Kraft, Betsy Harvey 1937- 157
Kraft, Erik P. 193
Krahn, Fernando 1935- 49
Brief entry 31
See also CLR 3
Krakauer, Hoong Yee Lee 1955- 86
Krakauer, Jon 1954- 108
Krall, Dan 1970- 218
Kramer, George
See Heuman, William
Kramer, Nora 1896(?)-1984 26
Obituary 39
Kramer, Remi (Thomas) 1935- 90
Krantz, Hazel (Newman) 12
Kranzler, George G(ershon) 1916- 28
Kranzler, Gershon
See Kranzler, George G(ershon)
Krasilovsky, Phyllis 1926- 38
Earlier sketch in SATA 1
See also CLR 83
See also SAAS 5
Krasne, Betty
See Levine, Betty K(rasne)
Krasner, Steven 1953- 154
Krasnesky, Thad 1969(?)- 224
Krasno, Rena 1923- 104
Kratman, Tom 175
Kraus, Joanna Halpert 1937- 87
Kraus, (Herman) Robert 1925-2001 93
Obituary 130
Earlier sketches in SATA 4, 65
See also SAAS 11
Krauss, Ruth 1911-1993 30
Obituary 75
Earlier sketch in SATA 1
See also CLR 42
Krauss, Ruth Ida
See Krauss, Ruth
Krautter, Elisa (Bialk) 1912(?)-1990 1
Obituary 65
Krautwurst, Terry 1946- 79
Kray, Robert Clement 1930- 82
Krech, Bob 1956- 185
Krech, Robert
See Krech, Bob
Kredel, Fritz 1900-1973 17
Kreikemeier, Gregory Scott 1965- 85
Kreloff, Elliot 189
Krementz, Jill 1940- 134
Earlier sketches in SATA 17, 71
See also CLR 5
See also SAAS 8
Kremer, Marcie
See Sorenson, Margo
Krenina, Katya 1968- 221
Earlier sketch in SATA 101
Krensky, Stephen 1953- 188
Brief entry 41
Earlier sketches in SATA 47, 93, 136
Krensky, Stephen Alan
See Krensky, Stephen
Kresh, Paul 1919-1997 61
Obituary 94

Kress, Nancy 1948- 147
Autobiography Feature 147
Earlier sketch in SATA 85
Kricher, John C. 1944- 113
Krieger, Melanie 96
Krinitz, Esther Nisenthal 1927-2001 194
Kripke, Dorothy Karp 30
Krisher, Trudy 1946- 160
Earlier sketch in SATA 86
Krisher, Trudy B.
See Krisher, Trudy
Krishnaswami, Uma 1956- 182
Earlier sketch in SATA 144
Kristiansen, Teddy 1964- 210
Kristiansen, Teddy H.
See Kristiansen, Teddy
Kristof, Jane 1932- 8
Kroeber, Theodora (Kracaw) 1897-1979 1
Kroeger, Mary Kay 1950- 92
Krohn, Katherine E(lizabeth) 1961- 125
Earlier sketch in SATA 84
Kroll, Francis Lynde 1904-1973 10
Kroll, Steven 1941- 212
Autobiography Feature 135
Earlier sketches in SATA 19, 66, 125, 135
See also SAAS 7
Kroll, Virginia L. 1948- 225
Earlier sketches in SATA 76, 114, 168
Kroll, Virginia Louisa
See Kroll, Virginia L.
Kromhout, Rindert 1958- 189
Krommes, Beth 1956- 208
Earlier sketches in SATA 128, 181
Kronenwetter, Michael 1943- 62
Kroniuk, Lisa
See Berton, Pierre (Francis de Marigny)
Kropp, Paul 1948- 38
Brief entry 34
See also CLR 96
Kropp, Paul Stephan
See Kropp, Paul
Krosoczka, Jarrett J. 1977- 200
Earlier sketch in SATA 155
Krovatin, Christopher 1985- 171
Krudop, Walter
See Krudop, Walter Lyon
Krudop, Walter Lyon 1966- 210
Kruess, James
See Kruss, James
Kruglik, Gerald 187
Krull, Kathleen 1952- 184
Autobiography Feature 106
Brief entry 39
Earlier sketches in SATA 52, 80, 149
See also CLR 44
Krumgold, Joseph (Quincy) 1908-1980 48
Obituary 23
Earlier sketch in SATA 1
Krupinski, Loretta 1940- 161
Earlier sketches in SATA 67, 102
Krupnick, Karen 1947- 89
Krupp, E. C. 1944- 123
Earlier sketch in SATA 53
Krupp, Edwin Charles
See Krupp, E. C.
Krupp, Robin Rector 1946- 53
Krush, Beth 1918- 18
Krush, Joe 1918-
See Krush, Joseph P.
Krush, Joseph P. 1918- 18
Kruss, James 1926-1997 8
See also CLR 9
Kruusval, Catarina 1951- 201
Krykorka, Vladyana 1945- 96
Krystoforski, Andrej 1943- 196
Kubick, Dana 212
Kubie, Eleanor Gottheil
See Kubie, Nora Gottheil Benjamin
Kubie, Nora Benjamin
See Kubie, Nora Gottheil Benjamin

Kubie, Nora Gottheil Benjamin 1899-1988 . *39*
  Obituary *59*
Kubinyi, Laszlo 1937- *94*
  Earlier sketch in SATA *17*
Kudlinski, Kathleen V. 1950- *213*
  Earlier sketch in SATA *150*
Kuehnert, Stephanie 1979- *205*
Kuenstler, Morton 1927- *10*
Kuh, Charlotte 1892(?)-1985
  Obituary *43*
Kuharski, Janice 1947- *128*
Kuhn, Dwight *199*
Kuijer, Guus 1942- *179*
Kujoth, Jean Spealman 1935-1975
  Obituary *30*
Kuklin, Susan 1941- *163*
  Earlier sketches in SATA *63, 95*
  See also CLR *51*
Kulak, Jeff 1984(?)- *223*
Kulikov, Boris 1966- *205*
  Earlier sketch in SATA *170*
Kulka, Joe *188*
Kulling, Monica 1952- *89*
Kullman, Harry 1919-1982 .... *35*
Kulyk Keefer, Janice 1952- *132*
Kumin, Maxine 1925- *12*
Kumin, Maxine Winokur
  See Kumin, Maxine
Kunhardt, Dorothy (Meserve) 1901-1979 .... *53*
  Obituary *22*
Kunhardt, Edith 1937- *67*
Kunjufu, Jawanza 1953- *73*
Kunstler, Morton
  See Kuenstler, Morton
Kuntz, J(ohn) L. 1947- *91*
Kuntz, Jerry 1956- *133*
Kupferberg, Herbert 1918-2001 .... *19*
Kuratomi, Chizuko 1939- *12*
  See also CLR *32*
Kurczok, Belinda 1978- *121*
Kurelek, William 1927-1977 .... *8*
  Obituary *27*
  See also CLR *2*
Kurian, George 1928- *65*
Kurjian, Judi(th M.) 1944- *127*
Kurland, Gerald 1942- *13*
Kurland, Michael 1938- *118*
  Earlier sketch in SATA *48*
Kurland, Michael Joseph
  See Kurland, Michael
Kuroi, Ken 1947- *120*
Kurokawa, Mitsuhiro 1954- *88*
Kurten, Bjorn (Olof) 1924-1988 .... *64*
Kurtz, Jane 1952- *139*
  Earlier sketch in SATA *91*
  See also CLR *123*
Kurtz, Katherine 1944- *182*
  Earlier sketches in SATA *76, 126*
Kurtz, Katherine Irene
  See Kurtz, Katherine
Kurz, Rudolf 1952- *95*
Kushner, Donn (J.) 1927- *52*
  See also CLR *55*
Kushner, Ellen 1955- *202*
  Earlier sketch in SATA *98*
Kushner, Ellen Ruth
  See Kushner, Ellen
Kushner, Jill Menkes 1951- *62*
Kushner, Lawrence 1943- *169*
  Earlier sketch in SATA *83*
Kushner, Tony 1956- *160*
Kuskin, Karla 1932-2009 .... *164*
  Obituary *206*
  Earlier sketches in SATA *2, 68, 111*
  See also CLR *4*
  See also SAAS *3*
Kuskin, Karla Seidman
  See Kuskin, Karla
Kusugak, Michael 1948- *143*
Kusugak, Michael Arvaarluk
  See Kusugak, Michael

Kutner, Merrily 1948- *196*
Kuttner, Paul 1922- *18*
Kuyper, Sjoerd 1952- *177*
Kuzma, Kay 1941- *39*
Kvale, Velma R(uth) 1898-1979 .... *8*
Kvasnosky, Laura McGee 1951- *182*
  Earlier sketches in SATA *93, 142*
Kwasney, Michelle D. 1960- *162*
Kyle, Benjamin
  See Gottfried, Theodore Mark
Kyle, Elisabeth
  See Dunlop, Agnes M. R.
Kyte, Kathy S. 1946- *50*
  Brief entry *44*

L

L., Barry
  See Longyear, Barry B(rookes)
L., Tommy
  See Lorkowski, Thomas V(incent)
Labatt, Mary 1944- *215*
Labouisse, Eve Curie
  See Curie, Eve
Labouisse, Eve Denise
  See Curie, Eve
Lace, William W. 1942- *126*
Lacey, Joshua
  See Doder, Josh
Lachenmeyer, Nathaniel 1969- *221*
Lachner, Dorothea
  See Knobloch, Dorothea
Lachtman, Ofelia Dumas 1919- *179*
Lackey, Mercedes
  See Lackey, Mercedes R.
Lackey, Mercedes R. 1950- *127*
  Earlier sketch in SATA *81*
Lackey, Mercedes Ritchie
  See Lackey, Mercedes R.
Lacoe, Addie *78*
Lacombe, Benjamin 1982- *198*
Lacome, Julie 1961- *174*
  Earlier sketch in SATA *80*
LaCour, Nina 1982- *222*
Lacy, Leslie Alexander 1937- *6*
Ladd, Cheryl (Jean) 1951- *113*
Ladd, London 1972(?)- *206*
Ladd, Louise 1943- *97*
Ladd, Veronica
  See Miner, Jane Claypool
Laden, Nina 1962- *148*
  Earlier sketch in SATA *85*
Lader, Lawrence 1919-2006 .... *6*
  Obituary *178*
LaDoux, Rita C. 1951- *74*
Ladwig, Tim 1952- *223*
Ladwig, Timothy
  See Ladwig, Tim
Lady, A
  See Taylor, Ann
Lady Mears
  See Tempest, Margaret Mary
Lady of Quality, A
  See Bagnold, Enid
La Farge, Oliver 1901-1963 .... *19*
La Farge, Oliver Hazard Perry
  See La Farge, Oliver
La Farge, Phyllis *14*
LaFave, Kim *196*
LaFaye, A. 1970- *220*
  Earlier sketches in SATA *105, 156*
LaFaye, Alexandria R.T.
  See LaFaye, A.
LaFevers, R.L. *191*
LaFevers, Robin L.
  See LaFevers, R.L.
Laffin, John (Alfred Charles) 1922- *31*
LaFleur, Suzanne 1983- *221*

LaFontaine, Bruce 1948- *176*
  Earlier sketch in SATA *114*
La Fontaine, Jean de 1621-1695 .... *18*
Lafrance, Marie 1955- *197*
Lager, Claude
  See Lapp, Christiane (Germain)
Lager, Marilyn 1939- *52*
Lagercrantz, Rose (Elsa) 1947- *39*
Lagerloef, Selma
  See Lagerlof, Selma
Lagerlof, Selma 1858-1940 .... *15*
  See also CLR 7
Laguna, Sofie 1968- *158*
LaHaye, Tim 1926- *149*
LaHaye, Timothy F.
  See LaHaye, Tim
Laidlaw, Rob *205*
Laiken, Deirdre S. 1948- *48*
  Brief entry *40*
Laiken, Deirdre Susan
  See Laiken, Deirdre S.
Laimgruber, Monika 1946- *11*
Lain, Anna
  See Lamb, Nancy
Laing, Alexander (Kinnan) 1903-1976 .... *117*
Laing, Martha 1951- *39*
Laird, Christa 1944- *108*
  Autobiography Feature *120*
  See also SAAS *26*
Laird, Elizabeth 1943- *159*
  Earlier sketches in SATA *77, 114*
  See also CLR *65*
Laird, Elizabeth Mary Risk
  See Laird, Elizabeth
Laird, Jean E(louise) 1930- *38*
Laite, Gordon 1925- *31*
Lake, Harriet
  See Taylor, Paula (Wright)
Lakeman, Victoria
  See Forester, Victoria
Lakin, Patricia 1944- *190*
Laklan, Carli 1907-1988 .... *5*
Laliberte, Louise-Andree 1958- *169*
Lalicki, Barbara *61*
Lalicki, Tom 1949- *186*
Lally, Soinbhe 1945- *119*
LaMarche, Jim *162*
Lamb, Albert *187*
Lamb, Beatrice Pitney 1904-1997 .... *21*
Lamb, Charles 1775-1834 .... *17*
Lamb, Elizabeth Searle 1917- *31*
Lamb, G(eoffrey) F(rederick) *10*
Lamb, Harold (Albert) 1892-1962 .... *53*
Lamb, Lynton (Harold) 1907-1977 .... *10*
Lamb, Mary Ann 1764-1847 .... *17*
Lamb, Nancy 1939- *80*
Lamb, Robert (Boyden) 1941- *13*
Lamba, Marie *195*
Lambert, David 1932- *84*
  Brief entry *49*
Lambert, David Compton
  See Lambert, David
Lambert, Janet 1895(?)-1973 .... *25*
Lambert, Martha L. *113*
Lambert, Saul 1928- *23*
Lambert, Stephen *174*
Lamburn, Richmal Crompton 1890-1969 .... *5*
Lamensdorf, Len 1930- *120*
Lamensdorf, Leonard
  See Lamensdorf, Len
Laminack, Lester L. 1956- *163*
  Earlier sketch in SATA *120*
Lammle, Leslie 1965- *213*
Lamont, Priscilla *200*
Lamorisse, Albert (Emmanuel) 1922-1970 ... *23*
Lampert, Emily 1951- *52*
  Brief entry *49*
Lamplugh, Lois 1921- *17*
Lampman, Evelyn Sibley 1907-1980 .... *87*
  Obituary *23*
  Earlier sketch in SATA *4*

Lamprey, Louise 1869-1951
  See YABC 2
Lampton, Chris
  See Lampton, Christopher F.
Lampton, Christopher
  See Lampton, Christopher F.
Lampton, Christopher F. 67
  Brief entry 47
Lamstein, Sarah 1943- 174
  Earlier sketch in SATA *126*
Lamstein, Sarah Marwil
  See Lamstein, Sarah
Lanagan, Margo 1960- 201
  Earlier sketch in SATA *163*
Lancaster, Bruce 1896-1963 9
Lancaster, Matthew 1973(?)-1983
  Obituary 45
Lance, Kathryn 1943- 76
Land, Barbara (Neblett) 1923- 16
Land, Jane
  See Borland, Kathryn Kilby
  and Speicher, Helen Ross S(mith)
Land, Myrick (Ebben) 1922-1998 15
Land, Ross
  See Borland, Kathryn Kilby
  and Speicher, Helen Ross S(mith)
Landa, Norbert 1952- 218
Landau, Elaine 1948- 141
  Earlier sketches in SATA *10, 94*
Landau, Jacob 1917- 38
Landeck, Beatrice 1904-1978 15
Landin, Les 1923- 2
Landis, J. D. 1942- 60
  Brief entry 52
Landis, James D.
  See Landis, J. D.
Landis, James David
  See Landis, J. D.
Landis, Jill Marie 1948- 101
Landman, Tanya 207
Landmann, Bimba 1968- 176
Landon, Dena 1978(?)- 168
Landon, Lucinda 1950- 56
  Brief entry 51
Landon, Margaret (Dorothea Mortenson)
  1903-1993 50
Landowne, Youme 1970- 211
Landry, Leo 202
Landshoff, Ursula 1908-1989 13
Landstrom, Lena 1943- 206
  Earlier sketch in SATA *146*
Landstrom, Olof 1943- 146
Landy, Derek 1974- 210
Lane, Alison Hoffman 215
Lane, Carolyn 1926-1993 10
Lane, Connie
  See Laux, Constance
Lane, Dakota 1959- 166
  Earlier sketch in SATA *105*
Lane, Jerry
  See Martin, Patricia Miles
Lane, John (Richard) 1932- 15
Lane, Leena 199
Lane, Margaret 1907-1994 65
  Brief entry 38
  Obituary 79
Lane, Rose Wilder 1887-1968 29
  Brief entry 28
Lanes, Selma G. 1929- 3
Lanes, Selma Gordon
  See Lanes, Selma G.
Lanfredi, Judy 1964- 83
Lang, Andrew 1844-1912 16
  See also CLR *101*
Lang, Aubrey 169
Lang, Glenna 1951- 221
Lang, Lang 1982- 208
Lang, Paul 1948- 83
Lang, Susan S. 1950- 68
Lang, T.T.
  See Taylor, Theodore

Langart, Darrell T.
  See Garrett, Randall
Langdo, Bryan 1973- 191
  Earlier sketch in SATA *138*
Lange, John
  See Crichton, Michael
Lange, Karen E. 190
Lange, Suzanne 1945- 5
Langley, Andrew 1949- 166
  Earlier sketch in SATA *104*
Langley, Charles P(itman) III 1949- 103
Langley, Jonathan 1952- 122
Langley, Noel 1911-1980
  Obituary 25
Langley, Wanda 173
Langner, Nola
  See Malone, Nola Langner
Langone, John (Michael) 1929- 46
  Brief entry 38
Langreuter, Jutta 1944- 122
Langrish, Katherine 177
Langsen, Richard C. 1953- 95
Langstaff, John 1920-2005 68
  Obituary 172
  Earlier sketch in SATA *6*
  See also CLR *3*
Langstaff, John Meredith
  See Langstaff, John
Langstaff, Launcelot
  See Irving, Washington
Langston, Laura 1958- 186
Langton, Jane 1922- 200
  Autobiography Feature 140
  Earlier sketches in SATA *3, 68, 129, 140*
  See also CLR *33*
  See also SAAS *5*
Lanier, Sidney 1842-1881 18
Lanier, Sterling E. 1927-2007 109
Lanier, Sterling Edmund
  See Lanier, Sterling E.
Lanino, Deborah 1964- 123
Lankford, Mary D. 1932- 112
  Earlier sketch in SATA *77*
Lannin, Joanne 1951- 121
Lannin, Joanne A.
  See Lannin, Joanne
Lansdale, Joe R. 1951- 116
Lansdale, Joe Richard
  See Lansdale, Joe R.
Lansing, Alfred 1921-1975 35
Lansing, Karen E. 1954- 71
Lansky, Vicki 1942- 177
Lanthier, Jennifer 1964- 204
Lantier-Sampon, Patricia 1952- 92
Lantz, Fran
  See Lantz, Francess L(in)
Lantz, Francess L(in) 1952-2004 153
  Autobiography Feature 153
  Obituary 159
  Earlier sketches in SATA *63, 109*
Lantz, Paul 1908- 45
Lantz, Walter 1900-1994 37
  Obituary 79
Lanza, Barbara 1945- 101
Lapp, Christiane (Germain) 1948- 74
Lappin, Peter 1911-1999 32
Larbalestier, Justine 178
Lardy, Philippe 1963- 168
LaReau, Jenna 181
LaReau, Kara 181
Larios, Julie 1949- 178
Larios, Julie Hofstrand
  See Larios, Julie
Larkin, Amy
  See Burns, Olive Ann
Larkin, Maia
  See Wojciechowska, Maia (Teresa)
Larkspur, Penelope
  See Wyatt, Valerie
Laroche, Giles 1956- 221
  Earlier sketches in SATA *71, 126*

LaRochelle, David 1960- 171
  Earlier sketch in SATA *115*
Larom, Henry V. 1903(?)-1975
  Obituary 30
LaRose, Linda 125
Larrabee, Lisa 1947- 84
Larrecq, John M(aurice) 1926-1980 44
  Obituary 25
Larrick (Crosby), Nancy 1910-2004 4
Larsen, Anita 1942- 78
Larsen, Egon 1904- 14
Larsen, Rebecca 1944- 54
Larson, Eve
  See St. John, Wylly Folk
Larson, Gary 1950- 57
Larson, Hope 1982- 205
Larson, Ingrid D(ana) 1965- 92
Larson, Jean Russell 1930- 121
Larson, Kirby 1954- 181
  Earlier sketch in SATA *96*
Larson, Norita D. 1944- 29
Larson, Norita Dittberner
  See Larson, Norita D.
Larson, William H. 1938- 10
Larsson, Carl (Olof) 1853-1919 35
LaSalle, Charles A.
  See Ellis, Edward S.
LaSalle, Charles E.
  See Ellis, Edward S.
Lasell, Elinor H. 1929- 19
Lasell, Fen H.
  See Lasell, Elinor H.
Lasenby, Jack 1931- 172
  Earlier sketches in SATA *65, 103*
Laser, Michael 1954- 117
Lash, Joseph P. 1909-1987 43
Lasher, Faith B. 1921- 12
Lasker, David 1950- 38
Lasker, Joe
  See Lasker, Joseph Leon
Lasker, Joseph Leon 1919- 83
  Earlier sketch in SATA *9*
  See also SAAS *17*
Laski, Marghanita 1915-1988 55
Laskin, Pamela L. 1954- 75
Lasky, Kathryn 1944- 210
  Earlier sketches in SATA *13, 69, 112, 157*
  See also CLR *140*
Lasky Knight, Kathryn
  See Lasky, Kathryn
Lass, Bonnie 131
Lassalle, C. E.
  See Ellis, Edward S.
Lassiter, Mary
  See Hoffman, Mary
Lassiter, Rhiannon 1977- 157
Lat 1951- 196
Latham, Barbara 1896- 16
Latham, Frank B(rown) 1910-2000 6
Latham, Jean Lee 1902-1995 68
  Earlier sketch in SATA *2*
  See also CLR *50*
Latham, Mavis
  See Clark, Mavis Thorpe
Latham, Philip
  See Richardson, Robert S(hirley)
Lathrop, Dorothy P(ulis) 1891-1980 14
  Obituary 24
Lathrop, Francis
  See Leiber, Fritz (Reuter, Jr.)
Latimer, Jim 1943- 80
Latta, Rich
  See Latta, Richard
Latta, Richard 1946- 113
Latta, Sara L. 1960- 174
Lattany, Kristin
  See Lattany, Kristin Hunter
Lattany, Kristin (Eggleston) Hunter 1931- . 154
  Autobiography Feature 154
  Earlier sketch in SATA *132*

Lattany, Kristin Hunter 1931-2008 .... *132*
  Earlier sketch in SATA *12*
  See also CLR *3*
  See also SAAS *10*
Lattimore, Eleanor Frances 1904-1986 .... *7*
  Obituary *48*
Lattin, Ann
  See Cole, Lois Dwight
Lauber, Patricia (Grace) 1924- *138*
  Earlier sketches in SATA *1, 33, 75*
  See also CLR *16*
Laugesen, Malene *207*
Laugesen, Malene Reynolds
  See Laugesen, Malene
Laugesen, Mary E(akin) 1906-1995 .... *5*
Laughbaum, Steve 1945- *12*
Laughlin, Florence Young 1910-2001 .... *3*
Laughlin, Rosemary 1941- *123*
Launder, Sally *206*
Laure, Ettagale
  See Blauer, Ettagale
Laure, Jason 1940- *50*
  Brief entry *44*
Laurence, Ester Hauser 1935- *7*
Laurence, Jean Margaret Wemyss
  See Laurence, Margaret
Laurence, Margaret 1926-1987
  Obituary *50*
Laurie, Rona 1916- *55*
Laurie, Victoria *218*
Laurin, Anne
  See McLaurin, Anne
Lauritzen, Jonreed 1902-1979 .... *13*
Lauscher, Hermann
  See Hesse, Hermann
Lauture, Denize 1946- *86*
Laux, Connie
  See Laux, Constance
Laux, Constance 1952- *97*
Laux, Dorothy 1920- *49*
Lavallee, Barbara 1941- *166*
  Earlier sketch in SATA *74*
Lavender, David (Sievert) 1910-2003 .... *97*
  Obituary *145*
  Earlier sketch in SATA *64*
Lavender, William D. 1921- *143*
Laverne, Christine *175*
Lavert, Gwendolyn Battle 1951-
  See Battle-Lavert, Gwendolyn
Laverty, Donald
  See Blish, James
  and Knight, Damon (Francis)
Lavigne, Louis-Dominique *107*
Lavine, David 1928- *31*
Lavine, Sigmund Arnold 1908-1986 .... *82*
  Earlier sketch in SATA *3*
  See also CLR *35*
Lavis, Steve *225*
Lavond, Paul Dennis
  See Kornbluth, C(yril) M.
  and Lowndes, Robert A(ugustine) W(ard)
  and Pohl, Frederik
Law, Stephen *225*
Law, Stephen
  See Law, Stephen
Lawford, Paula Jane 1960- *57*
  Brief entry *53*
Lawhead, Stephen R. 1950- *109*
Lawhead, Steve
  See Lawhead, Stephen R.
Lawler, Janet *222*
Lawlor, Laurie 1953- *137*
  Earlier sketch in SATA *80*
Lawlor, William
  See Lawlor, William T.
Lawlor, William T. 1951- *183*
Lawrence, Ann (Margaret) 1942-1987 .... *41*
  Obituary *54*
Lawrence, Caroline 1954- *203*
Lawrence, Iain 1955- *183*
  Earlier sketch in SATA *135*

Lawrence, J. T.
  See Rowland-Entwistle, (Arthur) Theodore
  (Henry)
Lawrence, Jerome 1915-2004 .... *65*
Lawrence, John 1933- *30*
Lawrence, Josephine 1890(?)-1978
  Obituary *24*
Lawrence, Louise 1943- *119*
  Earlier sketches in SATA *38, 78*
Lawrence, Louise de Kiriline 1894-1992 ..... *13*
Lawrence, Lynn
  See Garland, Sherry
Lawrence, Margery H. 1889-1969 .... *120*
Lawrence, Michael 1943- *132*
Lawrence, Mildred Elwood 1907-1997 .... *3*
Lawrence, R(onald) D(ouglas) 1921- *55*
Lawrinson, Julia 1969- *141*
Lawson, Amy
  See Gordon, Amy
Lawson, Carol (Antell) 1946- *42*
Lawson, Don(ald Elmer) 1917-1990 .... *9*
Lawson, Joan 1906- *55*
Lawson, Julie 1947- *126*
  Earlier sketch in SATA *79*
  See also CLR *89*
Lawson, Marion Tubbs 1896-1994 .... *22*
Lawson, Robert 1892-1957 .... *100*
  See also YABC *2*
  See also CLR *73*
Lawton, Clive A. 1951- *145*
Laxdal, Vivienne 1962- *112*
Laybourn, Emma *193*
Laycock, George (Edwin) 1921- *5*
Layne, Laura
  See Knott, William C(ecil, Jr.)
Layne, Steven L. *171*
Layson, Annelex Hofstra 1938(?)- *211*
Layton, Neal 1971- *187*
  Earlier sketch in SATA *152*
Layton, Neal Andrew
  See Layton, Neal
Lazare, Gerald John 1927- *44*
Lazare, Jerry
  See Lazare, Gerald John
Lazarevich, Mila 1942- *17*
Lazarus, Keo Felker 1913-1993 .... *21*
  Obituary *129*
Lea, Alec 1907- *19*
Lea, Bob 1952- *203*
Lea, Joan
  See Neufeld, John (Arthur)
Leach, Maria 1892-1977 .... *39*
  Brief entry *28*
Leacock, Elspeth 1946- *131*
Leacroft, Helen (Mabel Beal) 1919- *6*
Leacroft, Richard (Vallance Becher) 1914- *6*
Leaf, Margaret P. 1909(?)-1988
  Obituary *55*
Leaf, (Wilbur) Munro 1905-1976 .... *20*
  See also CLR *25*
Leaf, VaDonna Jean 1929- *26*
Leah, Devorah
  See Devorah-Leah
Leakey, Richard E(rskine Frere) 1944- *42*
Leal, Ann Haywood *216*
Leander, Ed
  See Richelson, Geraldine
Lear, Edward 1812-1888 .... *100*
  Earlier sketch in SATA *18*
  See also CLR *75*
Lears, Laurie 1955- *127*
Leasor, James 1923-2007 .... *54*
Leasor, Thomas James
  See Leasor, James
Leavitt, Jerome E(dward) 1916- *23*
Leavitt, Martine 1953- *170*
LeBar, Mary E(velyn) 1910-1982 .... *35*
LeBlanc, Annette M. 1965- *68*
LeBlanc, L(ee) 1913- *54*
LeBox, Annette 1943- *145*
Lebrun, Claude 1929- *66*

Le Cain, Errol (John) 1941-1989 .... *68*
  Obituary *60*
  Earlier sketch in SATA *6*
Lechner, Jack *201*
Lechner, John 1966- *200*
Lecourt, Nancy (Hoyt) 1951- *73*
Ledbetter, Suzann 1953- *119*
Leder, Jane Mersky 1945- *61*
  Brief entry *51*
Lederer, Muriel 1929- *48*
Lederer, William J. 1912-2009 .... *62*
Lederer, William Julius
  See Lederer, William J.
Lee, Amanda
  See Baggett, Nancy
  and Buckholtz, Eileen (Garber)
  and Glick, Ruth (Burtnick)
Lee, Benjamin 1921- *27*
Lee, Betsy 1949- *37*
Lee, Carol
  See Fletcher, Helen Jill
Lee, Carol Ann 1969- *185*
Lee, Chinlun *182*
Lee, Cora *223*
  See Anderson, Catherine Corley
Lee, Dennis (Beynon) 1939- *102*
  Earlier sketch in SATA *14*
  See also CLR *3*
Lee, Dom 1959- *146*
  Autobiography Feature *121*
  Earlier sketch in SATA *83*
  See also SAAS *26*
Lee, Doris Emrick 1905-1983 .... *44*
  Obituary *35*
Lee, Edward
  See Lee, J. Edward
Lee, Elizabeth Rogers 1940- *90*
Lee, Harper 1926- *11*
Lee, Hector Viveros 1962- *115*
Lee, Howard N.
  See Goulart, Ron
Lee, Huy Voun 1969- *217*
  Earlier sketch in SATA *129*
Lee, Insu *213*
Lee, J. Edward 1953- *130*
Lee, Jared 1943- *215*
Lee, Jared D.
  See Lee, Jared
Lee, Jeanne M. 1943- *138*
Lee, John R(obert) 1923-1976 .... *27*
Lee, Jordan
  See Scholefield, Alan
Lee, Joseph Edward
  See Lee, J. Edward
Lee, Julian
  See Latham, Jean Lee
Lee, Linda
  See Eyerly, Jeannette
Lee, Liz
  See Lee, Elizabeth Rogers
Lee, Lucy
  See Talbot, Charlene Joy
Lee, Lyn 1953- *128*
Lee, Manning de Villeneuve 1894-1980 ...... *37*
  Obituary *22*
Lee, Marian
  See Clish, (Lee) Marian
Lee, Marie G. 1964- *178*
  Earlier sketches in SATA *81, 130*
Lee, Marie Myung-Ok
  See Lee, Marie G.
Lee, Mary Price 1934- *82*
  Earlier sketch in SATA *8*
Lee, Mildred
  See Scudder, Mildred Lee
Lee, Nelle Harper
  See Lee, Harper
Lee, Richard S. 1927- *82*
Lee, Robert C. 1931- *20*
Lee, Robert Edwin 1918-1994 .... *65*
  Obituary *82*

Lee, Robert J. 1921- *10*
Lee, Roy
  See Hopkins, Clark
Lee, Sally 1943- *67*
Lee, Suzy *193*
Lee, Tammie
  See Townsend, Thomas L.
Lee, Tanith 1947- *185*
  Earlier sketches in SATA *8, 88, 134*
Lee, Virginia 1976- *208*
Leech, Ben
  See Bowkett, Stephen
Leeds, Contance *188*
Leedy, Loreen 1959- *175*
  Brief entry *50*
  Earlier sketches in SATA *54, 84, 128*
Leedy, Loreen Janelle
  See Leedy, Loreen
Lee-Hostetler, Jeri 1940- *63*
Leekley, Thomas B(riggs) 1910-2001 .... *23*
Leeming, Jo Ann
  See Leeming, Joseph
Leeming, Joseph 1897-1968 .... *26*
Leemis, Ralph B. 1954- *72*
Leese, Jennifer L.B. 1970- *163*
Leeson, Muriel 1920- *54*
Leeson, R. A.
  See Leeson, Robert (Arthur)
Leeson, Robert (Arthur) 1928- *76*
  Earlier sketch in SATA *42*
Lee Tae-Jun 1904-1956(?) *194*
Lee-Tai, Amy 1964- *189*
Leffland, Ella 1931- *65*
Leffler, Silke *197*
Lefler, Irene (Whitney) 1917- *12*
LeFrak, Karen *182*
Le Gallienne, Eva 1899-1991 .... *9*
  Obituary *68*
Legg, Gerald 1947- *143*
Legg, Sarah Martha Ross Bruggeman (?)-1982
  Obituary *40*
LeGrand
  See Henderson, LeGrand
Le Guin, Ursula K. 1929- *194*
  Earlier sketches in SATA *4, 52, 99, 149*
  See also CLR *91*
Le Guin, Ursula Kroeber
  See Le Guin, Ursula K.
Legum, Colin 1919-2003 .... *10*
Lehman, Barbara 1963- *170*
  Earlier sketch in SATA *115*
Lehman, Bob *91*
Lehman, Elaine *91*
Lehmann, Debra Lynn
  See Vanasse, Deb
Lehman-Wilzig, Tami 1950- *224*
Lehn, Cornelia 1920- *46*
Lehne, Judith Logan 1947- *93*
Lehr, Delores 1920- *10*
Lehr, Norma 1930- *71*
Leiber, Fritz (Reuter, Jr.) 1910-1992 .... *45*
  Obituary *73*
Leibold, Jay 1957- *57*
  Brief entry *52*
Leichman, Seymour 1933- *5*
Leick, Bonnie *205*
Leigh, Nila K. 1981- *81*
Leigh, Tom 1947- *46*
Leigh-Pemberton, John 1911-1997 .... *35*
Leighton, Clare (Veronica Hope)
  1899-1989 .... *37*
Leighton, Margaret (Carver) 1896-1987 .... *1*
  Obituary *52*
Leijten, Aileen *216*
Leiner, Al(an) 1938- *83*
Leiner, Katherine 1949- *93*
Leipold, L. Edmond 1902-1983 .... *16*
Leisk, David (Johnson) 1906-1975 .... *30*
  Obituary *26*
  Earlier sketch in SATA *1*
  See also CLR *98*

Leister, Mary 1917- *29*
Leitch, Patricia 1933- *98*
  Earlier sketch in SATA *11*
Leitner, Isabella 1924- *86*
Lekich, John *202*
Leland, Bob 1956- *92*
Leland, Robert E.
  See Leland, Bob
Lematre, Pascal 1967- *225*
  Earlier sketch in SATA *176*
Lember, Barbara Hirsch 1941- *92*
LeMieux, A.C. 1954- *125*
  Earlier sketch in SATA *90*
LeMieux, Anne
  See LeMieux, A.C.
LeMieux, Anne Connelly
  See LeMieux, A.C.
Lemieux, Michele 1955- *139*
Lemke, Horst 1922- *38*
Lemna, Don 1936- *216*
Lenain, Thierry 1959- *201*
Lenanton, Carola Mary Anima Oman
  See Oman, Carola (Mary Anima)
Lenard, Alexander 1910-1972
  Obituary *21*
Lendroth, Susan *207*
L'Engle, Madeleine 1918-2007 .... *128*
  Obituary *186*
  Earlier sketches in SATA *1, 27, 75*
  See also CLR *57*
  See also SAAS *15*
L'Engle, Madeleine Camp Franklin
  See L'Engle, Madeleine
Lengyel, Cornel Adam 1915- *27*
Lengyel, Emil 1895-1985 .... *3*
  Obituary *42*
Lennon, John 1940-1980 .... *114*
Lennon, John Ono
  See Lennon, John
Leno, Jay 1950- *154*
LeNoir, Janice 1941- *89*
Lens, Sidney 1912-1986 .... *13*
  Obituary *48*
Lenski, Lois 1893-1974 .... *100*
  Earlier sketches in SATA *1, 26*
  See also CLR *26*
Lent, Blair 1930-2009 .... *133*
  Obituary *200*
  Earlier sketch in SATA *2*
Lent, Henry Bolles 1901-1973 .... *17*
Lent, John 1948- *108*
Leodhas, Sorche Nic
  See Alger, Leclaire (Gowans)
Leokum, Arkady 1916(?)- *45*
Leon, Carol Boyd *212*
Leon, Sharon 1959- *79*
Leonard, Alison 1944- *70*
Leonard, Anna
  See Gilman, Laura Anne
Leonard, Constance (Brink) 1923- *42*
  Brief entry *40*
Leonard, Dutch
  See Leonard, Elmore
Leonard, Elmore 1925- *163*
Leonard, Elmore John, Jr.
  See Leonard, Elmore
Leonard, Jonathan N(orton) 1903-1975 .... *36*
Leonard, Laura 1923- *75*
Leonard, Tom 1955- *207*
Leonetti, Mike 1958- *202*
Leong, Gor Yun
  See Ellison, Virginia H(owell)
Leonhard, Herb *217*
Leonhardt, Alice 1950- *152*
Lerangis, Peter 1955- *171*
  Earlier sketch in SATA *72*
Lerman, Josh *215*
Lerner, Aaron 1920-2007 .... *35*
  Obituary *179*
Lerner, Aaron Bunsen
  See Lerner, Aaron

Lerner, Carol 1927- *86*
  Earlier sketch in SATA *33*
  See also CLR *34*
  See also SAAS *12*
Lerner, Gerda 1920- *65*
Lerner, Harriet 1944- *101*
Lerner, Marguerite Rush 1924-1987 .... *11*
  Obituary *51*
Lerner, Sharon (Ruth) 1938-1982 .... *11*
  Obituary *29*
Leroe, Ellen 1949- *99*
  Brief entry *51*
  Earlier sketch in SATA *61*
Leroe, Ellen W.
  See Leroe, Ellen
Leroe, Ellen Whitney
  See Leroe, Ellen
Leroux, Gaston 1868-1927 .... *65*
Leroux-Hugon, Helene 1955- *132*
LeRoy, Gen *52*
  Brief entry *36*
Lerrigo, Marion Olive 1898-1968
  Obituary *29*
LeShan, Eda J(oan) 1922-2002 .... *21*
  See also CLR *6*
Leshem, Yossi 1947- *222*
LeSieg, Theo.
  See Dr. Seuss
Lesinski, Jeanne M. 1960- *120*
Leslie, Robert Franklin 1911-1990 .... *7*
Leslie, Roger 1961- *168*
Leslie, Roger James
  See Leslie, Roger
Leslie, Sarah
  See McGuire, Leslie (Sarah)
LeSourd, Catherine
  See Marshall, (Sarah) Catherine (Wood)
Lessac, Frane
  See Lessac, Frane
Lessac, Frane 1954- *209*
  Earlier sketches in SATA *61, 148*
Lessem, Dino Don
  See Lessem, Don
Lessem, Don 1951- *182*
  Earlier sketches in SATA *97, 155*
Lesser, Margaret 1899(?)-1979
  Obituary *22*
Lesser, Rika 1953- *53*
Lester, Alison 1952- *218*
  Earlier sketches in SATA *50, 90, 129*
Lester, Helen 1936- *189*
  Earlier sketches in SATA *46, 92, 145*
Lester, Julius 1939- *157*
  Earlier sketches in SATA *12, 74, 112*
  See also CLR *143*
Lester, Julius Bernard
  See Lester, Julius
Lester, Mike 1955- *206*
  Earlier sketch in SATA *131*
Le Sueur, Meridel 1900-1996 .... *6*
Leszczynski, Diana *211*
Lethcoe, Jason *191*
Le Tord, Bijou 1945- *95*
  Earlier sketch in SATA *49*
Letts, Billie 1938- *121*
Letts, Elizabeth
  See Alalou, Elizabeth
Leuck, Laura 1962- *192*
  Earlier sketches in SATA *85, 146*
Leung, Hilary 1975- *225*
Leutscher, Alfred (George) 1913- *23*
Levai, Blaise 1919- *39*
Levchuk, Lisa *215*
Levenkron, Steven 1941- *86*
Leverich, Kathleen 1948- *103*
LeVert, John 1946- *55*
Levert, Mireille 1956- *211*
LeVert, William John
  See LeVert, John
Levete, Sarah 1961- *153*

Levin, Betty 1927- *201*
  Earlier sketches in SATA *19, 84, 137*
  See also SAAS *11*
Levin, Ira 1929-2007 .... *66*
  Obituary *187*
Levin, Ira Marvin
  See Levin, Ira
Levin, Marcia Obrasky 1918- *13*
Levin, Meyer 1905-1981 .... *21*
  Obituary *27*
Levin, Miriam (Ramsfelder) 1962- *97*
Levine, Abby 1943- *54*
  Brief entry *52*
Levine, Anna *212*
Levine, Betty K(rasne) 1933- *66*
Levine, David 1926-2009 .... *43*
  Brief entry *35*
Levine, Edna S(imon) *35*
Levine, Ellen 1939- *190*
Levine, Evan 1962- *77*
  Earlier sketch in SATA *74*
Levine, Gail Carson 1947- *195*
  Earlier sketches in SATA *98, 161*
  See also CLR *85*
Levine, I(srael) E. 1923-2003 .... *12*
  Obituary *146*
Levine, Joan Goldman *11*
Levine, Joseph 1910- *33*
Levine, Kristin 1974- *213*
Levine, Marge 1934- *81*
Levine, Rhoda *14*
Levine, Sarah 1970- *57*
Levine, Shar 1953- *131*
Levine-Freidus, Gail
  See Provost, Gail Levine
Levinson, Nancy Smiler 1938- *211*
  Earlier sketches in SATA *33, 80, 140*
Levinson, Riki *99*
  Brief entry *49*
  Earlier sketch in SATA *52*
Levithan, David 1972- *166*
Levitin, Sonia 1934- *192*
  Autobiography Feature *131*
  Earlier sketches in SATA *4, 68, 119, 131*
  See also CLR *53*
  See also SAAS *2*
Levitt, Sidney (Mark) 1947- *68*
Levon, O. U.
  See Kesey, Ken
Levoy, Myron 1930- *49*
  Brief entry *37*
Levy, Barrie *112*
Levy, Constance 1931- *140*
  Earlier sketch in SATA *73*
  See also SAAS *22*
Levy, Elizabeth 1942- *169*
  Earlier sketches in SATA *31, 69, 107*
  See also SAAS *18*
Levy, Janice *172*
Levy, Marilyn 1937- *67*
Levy, Nathan 1945- *63*
Levy, Robert 1945- *82*
Lewees, John
  See Stockton, Francis Richard
Lewin, Betsy 1937- *222*
  Autobiography Feature *115*
  Earlier sketches in SATA *32, 90, 169*
Lewin, Hugh 1939- *72*
  Brief entry *40*
  See also CLR *9*
Lewin, Ted 1935- *195*
  Autobiography Feature *115*
  Earlier sketches in SATA *21, 76, 119, 165*
Lewis, Alice C. 1936- *46*
Lewis, Alice Hudson 1895(?)-1971
  Obituary *29*
Lewis, Amanda 1955- *80*
Lewis, Anthony 1927- *27*
Lewis, Anthony 1966- *120*
Lewis, Barbara A. 1943- *73*
Lewis, Beverly 1949- *80*

Lewis, Brenda Ralph 1932- *72*
Lewis, Brian 1963- *128*
Lewis, C. S. 1898-1963 .... *100*
  Earlier sketch in SATA *13*
  See also CLR *109*
Lewis, Claudia (Louise) 1907-2001 .... *5*
Lewis, Clive Staples
  See Lewis, C. S.
Lewis, Cynthia Copeland 1960- *111*
Lewis, E. M. *123*
  Earlier sketch in SATA *20*
Lewis, Earl Bradley
  See Lewis, E.B.
Lewis, E.B. 1956- *211*
  Earlier sketches in SATA *93, 124, 168*
Lewis, Elizabeth Foreman 1892-1958 .... *121*
  See also YABC *2*
Lewis, Francine
  See Wells, Helen
Lewis, Harry Sinclair
  See Lewis, Sinclair
Lewis, Hilda (Winifred) 1896-1974
  Obituary *20*
Lewis, J. Patrick 1942- *205*
  Earlier sketches in SATA *69, 104, 162*
Lewis, Jack P(earl) 1919- *65*
Lewis, Jean 1924- *61*
Lewis, Jon Samuel
  See Lewis, J.S.
Lewis, Joseph Anthony
  See Lewis, Anthony
Lewis, J.S. 1972- *203*
Lewis, Julinda
  See Lewis-Ferguson, Julinda
Lewis, Kevin *173*
Lewis, Kim 1951- *217*
  Earlier sketches in SATA *84, 136*
Lewis, Linda (Joy) 1946- *67*
Lewis, Lucia Z.
  See Anderson, Lucia (Lewis)
Lewis, Marjorie 1929- *40*
  Brief entry *35*
Lewis, Mary 1907(?)-1988 .... *64*
  Obituary *56*
Lewis, Mervyn
  See Frewer, Glyn (M.)
Lewis, Michael
  See Untermeyer, Louis
Lewis, Naomi 1911-2009 .... *144*
  Earlier sketch in SATA *76*
Lewis, Paeony 1960- *173*
Lewis, Paul
  See Gerson, Noel Bertram
Lewis, Richard 1935- *3*
Lewis, Richard 1956- *209*
Lewis, Rob 1962- *72*
Lewis, Roger
  See Zarchy, Harry
Lewis, Rose *209*
Lewis, Rose A.
  See Lewis, Rose
Lewis, Shannon
  See Llwyelyn, Morgan
Lewis, Shari 1934-1998 .... *35*
  Brief entry *30*
  Obituary *104*
Lewis, Sylvan R.
  See Aronson, Virginia
Lewis, Thomas P(arker) 1936- *27*
Lewis, Wendy A. 1966- *150*
Lewis-Ferguson, Julinda 1955- *85*
Lewison, Wendy Cheyette *177*
Lewiton, Mina 1904-1970 .... *2*
Lew-Vriethoff, Joanne *186*
Lexau, Joan M. *130*
  Earlier sketches in SATA *1, 36*
Ley, Willy 1906-1969 .... *2*
Leydon, Rita (Floden) 1949- *21*
Leyland, Eric (Arthur) 1911- *37*
L'Hommedieu, Dorothy Keasley 1885-1961
  Obituary *29*

Li, Xiao Jun 1952- *86*
Liao, Jimmy 1958- *202*
Liatsos, Sandra Olson 1942- *103*
Libby, Alisa M. *189*
Libby, Barbara M. *153*
Libby, Bill
  See Libby, William M.
Libby, William M. 1927-1984 .... *5*
  Obituary *39*
Liberty, Gene 1924- *3*
Lichtenheld, Tom *208*
  Earlier sketch in SATA *152*
Lichtman, Wendy 1946- *193*
Liddell, Kenneth 1912-1975 .... *63*
Liddiment, Carol *224*
Lidz, Jane *120*
Lieb, Josh 1972- *224*
Lieberman, E(dwin) James 1934- *62*
Liebers, Arthur 1913-1984 .... *12*
Lieblich, Irene 1923- *22*
Liers, Emil E(rnest) 1890-1975 .... *37*
Lies, Brian 1963- *190*
  Earlier sketch in SATA *131*
Lieshout, Elle van
  See van Lieshout, Elle
Liestman, Vicki 1961- *72*
Lietz, Gerald S. 1918- *11*
Liew, Sonny 1974- *219*
Life, Kay (Guinn) 1930- *83*
Lifton, Betty Jean 1926-2010 .... *118*
  Earlier sketch in SATA *6*
Lifton, Robert Jay 1926- *66*
Lightburn, Ron 1954- *91*
Lightburn, Sandra 1955- *91*
Lightner, A. M.
  See Hopf, Alice (Martha) L(ightner)
Lightner, Alice
  See Hopf, Alice (Martha) L(ightner)
Lignell, Lois 1911- *37*
Liles, Maurine Walpole 1935- *81*
Lillegard, Dee *184*
Lilley, Stephen R. 1950- *97*
Lilley, Stephen Ray
  See Lilley, Stephen R.
Lillington, Kenneth (James) 1916-1998 .... *39*
Lilly, Nate *182*
Lilly, Ray
  See Curtis, Richard
Lim, John 1932- *43*
Liman, Ellen (Fogelson) 1936- *22*
Limb, Sue 1946- *203*
  Earlier sketch in SATA *158*
Limburg, Peter R(ichard) 1929- *13*
Lin, Grace 1974- *198*
  Earlier sketches in SATA *111, 162*
Lincoln, C(harles) Eric 1924-2000 .... *5*
Lincoln, Christopher 1952- *208*
Lincoln, Hazel *187*
Lincoln, James
  See Bates, Katharine Lee
Lindbergh, Anne
  See Sapieyevski, Anne Lindbergh
Lindbergh, Anne Morrow 1906-2001 .... *33*
  Obituary *125*
Lindbergh, Anne Spencer Morrow
  See Lindbergh, Anne Morrow
Lindbergh, Charles A(ugustus, Jr.)
  1902-1974 .... *33*
Lindbergh, Reeve 1945- *163*
  Earlier sketch in SATA *116*
Lindblom, Steven (Winther) 1946- *94*
  Brief entry *39*
  Earlier sketch in SATA *42*
Linde, Gunnel 1924- *5*
Lindenbaum, Pija 1955- *183*
  Earlier sketches in SATA *77, 144*
Lindgren, Astrid (Anna Emilia Ericsson)
  1907-2002 .... *38*
  Obituary *128*
  Earlier sketch in SATA *2*
  See also CLR *119*

Lindgren, Barbro 1937- 207
Brief entry 46
Earlier sketches in SATA 63, 120
See also CLR 86
Lindman, Maj (Jan) 1886-1972 43
Lindo, Elvira 1962- 219
Lindop, Edmund 1925- 5
Lindquist, Jennie Dorothea 1899-1977 13
Lindquist, Rowena Cory 1958- 98
Lindquist, Willis 1908-1988 20
Lindsay, Nicholas Vachel
See Lindsay, Vachel
Lindsay, Norman Alfred William
1879-1969 67
See also CLR 8
Lindsay, Vachel 1879-1931 40
Lindsey, Kathleen D(orothy) 1949- 153
Line, David
See Davidson, Lionel
Line, Les 1935-2010 27
Lines, Kathleen Mary 1902-1988
Obituary 61
Linfield, Esther 40
Lingard, Joan (Amelia) 1932- 130
Autobiography Feature 130
Earlier sketches in SATA 8, 74, 114
See also CLR 89
See also SAAS 5
Link, Martin 1934- 28
Linn, Margot
See Ziefert, Harriet
Linnea, Sharon 1956- 82
Lion, Melissa 1976- 176
Lionni, Leo(nard) 1910-1999 72
Obituary 118
Earlier sketch in SATA 8
See also CLR 71
Lipinsky de Orlov, Lino S. 1908- 22
Lipkind, William 1904-1974 15
Lipman, David 1931-2008 21
Lipman, Matthew 1923-2010 14
Lipp, Frederick 204
Lippincott, Bertram 1898(?)-1985
Obituary 42
Lippincott, Gary A. 1953- 220
Earlier sketches in SATA 73, 119
Lippincott, Joseph W(harton) 1887-1976 17
Lippincott, Sarah Lee 1920- 22
Lippman, Peter J. 1936- 31
Lipsyte, Robert 1938- 198
Earlier sketches in SATA 5, 68, 113, 161
See also CLR 76
Lipsyte, Robert Michael
See Lipsyte, Robert
Lisandrelli, Elaine Slivinski 1951- 94
Lisker, Sonia O. 1933- 44
Lisle, Holly 1960- 208
Earlier sketch in SATA 98
Lisle, Janet Taylor 1947- 150
Brief entry 47
Earlier sketches in SATA 59, 96
See also SAAS 14
Lisle, Rebecca 162
Lisle, Seward D.
See Ellis, Edward S.
Lisowski, Gabriel 1946- 47
Brief entry 31
Liss, Howard 1922-1995 4
Obituary 84
Lissiat, Amy
See Thompson, Colin
Lisson, Deborah 1941- 110
Earlier sketch in SATA 71
List, Ilka Katherine 1935- 6
Liston, Robert A. 1927- 5
Litchfield, Ada B(assett) 1916-1999 5
Litchfield, Jo 1973- 116
Lithgow, John 1945- 145
Lithgow, John Arthur
See Lithgow, John
Litowinsky, Olga 1936- 26

Litowinsky, Olga Jean
See Litowinsky, Olga
Littke, Lael J. 1929- 140
Earlier sketches in SATA 51, 83
Little, A. Edward
See Klein, Aaron E.
Little, Douglas 1942- 96
Little, (Flora) Jean 1932- 149
Earlier sketches in SATA 2, 68, 106
See also CLR 4
See also SAAS 17
Little, Lessie Jones 1906-1986 60
Obituary 50
Little, Mary E. 1912-1999 28
Littlechild, George 1958- 85
Littledale, Freya (Lota) 1929-1992 74
Earlier sketch in SATA 2
Littlefield, Bill 1948- 83
Littlefield, Holly 1963- 97
Littlesugar, Amy 1953- 176
Earlier sketch in SATA 122
Littleton, Mark R. 1950- 142
Earlier sketch in SATA 89
Littlewood, Karin 211
Littman, Sarah Darer 221
Earlier sketch in SATA 175
Litty, Julie 1971- 181
Litzinger, Rosanne 1948- 196
Liu, Cynthea 221
Lively, Penelope 1933- 164
Earlier sketches in SATA 7, 60, 101
See also CLR 159
Lively, Penelope Margaret
See Lively, Penelope
Liverakos, L. A.
See Gilman, Laura Anne
Liversidge, (Henry) Douglas 1913- 8
Livesey, Claire (Warner) 1927- 127
Livingston, Carole 1941- 42
Livingston, (M.) Irene 1932- 150
Livingston, Myra Cohn 1926-1996 68
Obituary 92
Earlier sketch in SATA 5
See also CLR 7
See also SAAS 1
Livingston, Richard R(oland) 1922- 8
Livo, Norma J. 1929- 76
Liwska, Renata 199
Ljungkvist, Laura 180
Llerena Aguirre, Carlos 1952- 19
Llerena Aguirre, Carlos Antonio
See Llerena Aguirre, Carlos
Llewellyn, Claire 1954- 196
Earlier sketches in SATA 77, 143
Llewellyn, Grace 1964- 110
Llewellyn, Richard
See Llewellyn Lloyd, Richard Dafydd Vivian
Llewellyn, Sam 1948- 185
Earlier sketch in SATA 95
Llewellyn Lloyd, Richard Dafydd Vivian
1906-1983 11
Obituary 37
Llewelyn, T. Harcourt
See Hamilton, Charles (Harold St. John)
Lloyd, Alan
See Lloyd, A.R.
Lloyd, Alan Richard
See Lloyd, A.R.
Lloyd, A.R. 1927- 168
Earlier sketch in SATA 97
Lloyd, David
See Lloyd, David T.
Lloyd, David T. 1954- 167
Lloyd, E. James
See James, Elizabeth
Lloyd, Errol 1943- 22
Lloyd, Hugh
See Fitzhugh, Percy Keese
Lloyd, James
See James, Elizabeth

Lloyd, Megan 1958- 189
Earlier sketches in SATA 77, 117
Lloyd, Norman 1909-1980
Obituary 23
Lloyd, (Mary) Norris 1908-1993 10
Obituary 75
Lloyd, Saci 1967- 220
Lloyd, Sam 183
Lloyd-Jones, Sally 1960- 179
Lloyd Webber, Andrew 1948- 56
Llywelyn, Morgan 1937- 109
Lo, Ginnie 165
Lo, Malinda 1974- 222
Lo, Virginia M.
See Lo, Ginnie
Lobato, Jose Bento Monteiro 1882-1948 ... 114
Lobel, Anita (Kempler) 1934- 162
Earlier sketches in SATA 6, 55, 96
Lobel, Arnold (Stark) 1933-1987 55
Obituary 54
Earlier sketch in SATA 6
See also CLR 5
Lobel, Gillian 181
Lobsenz, Amelia 12
Lobsenz, Norman M(itchell) 1919- 6
Lochak, Michele 1936- 39
Lochlons, Colin
See Jackson, C(aary) Paul
Locke, Clinton W. 1
Locke, Elsie (Violet) 1912-2001 87
Locke, Gary 1963- 197
Locke, Lucie 1904-1989 10
Locke, Robert 1944- 63
See also CLR 39
Locker, Thomas 1937- 109
Earlier sketch in SATA 59
See also CLR 14
Lockhart, E.
See Jenkins, Emily
Lockridge, Hildegarde (Dolson)
1908-1981 121
Earlier sketch in SATA 5
Lockwood, Mary
See Spelman, Mary
Lodge, Bernard 1933- 215
Earlier sketches in SATA 33, 107
Lodge, Jo 1966- 173
Earlier sketch in SATA 112
Loeb, Jeffrey 1946- 57
Loeb, Robert H., Jr. 1917- 21
Loefgren, Ulf 1931- 3
Loehfelm, Bill 1969- 153
Loehr, Mallory 184
Loehr, Patrick 1968(?)- 194
Loeper, John J(oseph) 1929- 118
Earlier sketch in SATA 10
Loescher, Ann Dull 1942- 20
Loescher, Gil 1945- 20
Loescher, Gilburt Damian
See Loescher, Gil
Loewer, Jean Jenkins
See Jenkins, Jean
Loewer, (Henry) Peter 1934- 98
LoFaro, Jerry 1959- 77
Lofo
See Heimann, Rolf
Lofthouse, Liz 199
Lofting, Hugh (John) 1886-1947 100
Earlier sketch in SATA 15
See also CLR 143
Lofts, Norah (Robinson) 1904-1983 8
Obituary 36
Logan, Jake
See Knott, William C(ecil, Jr.)
and Krepps, Robert W(ilson)
and Pearl, Jacques Bain
and Riefe, Alan
and Rifkin, Shepard
and Smith, Martin Cruz
Logan, Mark
See Nicole, Christopher (Robin)

Logan, Rochelle 1954- *169*
Logsted, Greg *221*
Logston, Anne 1962- *112*
Logue, Christopher 1926- *23*
Logue, Mary 1952- *161*
  Earlier sketch in SATA *112*
Logue, Mary Louise
  See Logue, Mary
Loh, Morag 1935- *73*
Lohans, Alison 1949- *101*
Loizeaux, William *185*
Loken, Newton Clayton 1919- *26*
Lomas, Steve
  See Brennan, Joseph Lomas
Lomask, Milton (Nachman) 1909-1991 .... *20*
Lombard, Jenny *178*
Lombino, Salvatore
  See Hunter, Evan
LoMonaco, Palmyra 1932- *102*
London, Jack 1876-1916 .... *18*
  See also CLR *108*
London, Jane
  See Geis, Darlene Stern
London, John Griffith
  See London, Jack
London, Jonathan 1947- *221*
  Earlier sketches in SATA *74, 113, 157*
Lonergan, (Pauline) Joy (MacLean) 1909- ... *10*
Lonette, Reisie (Dominee) 1924- *43*
Long, Cathryn J. 1946- *89*
Long, Earlene (Roberta) 1938- *50*
Long, Emmett
  See Leonard, Elmore
Long, Ethan 1968(?)- *223*
  Earlier sketch in SATA *182*
Long, Helen Beecher *1*
Long, Judith Elaine 1953- *20*
Long, Judy
  See Long, Judith Elaine
Long, Kim 1949- *69*
Long, Laura Mooney 1892-1967
  Obituary *29*
Long, Laurel *203*
Long, Loren 1966(?)- *188*
  Earlier sketch in SATA *151*
Long, Melinda 1960- *152*
Long, Sylvia 1948- *179*
  Earlier sketch in SATA *120*
Longbeard, Frederick
  See Longyear, Barry B(rookes)
Longfellow, Henry Wadsworth 1807-1882 ... *19*
  See also CLR *99*
Longfellow, Layne 1937- *102*
Longfellow, Layne A.
  See Longfellow, Layne
Longman, Harold S. 1919- *5*
Longsworth, Polly 1933- *28*
Longtemps, Kenneth 1933- *17*
Longway, A. Hugh
  See Lang, Andrew
Longyear, Barry B(rookes) 1942- *117*
Look, Lenore *180*
Loomans, Diane 1955- *90*
Loomis, Christine *160*
  Earlier sketch in SATA *113*
Loomis, Jennifer A. 1942- *101*
Loomis, Robert D. *5*
Lopez, Angelo (Cayas) 1967- *83*
Lopez, Barry 1945- *67*
Lopez, Barry Holstun
  See Lopez, Barry
Lopez, Jack 1950- *178*
Lopez, Loretta 1963- *190*
Lopez, Lorraine 1956- *181*
Lopez, Lorraine M.
  See Lopez, Lorraine
Lopez, Rafael 1961(?)- *198*
Lopshire, Robert M(artin) 1927- *6*
Loraine, Connie
  See Reece, Colleen L.

Lorbiecki, Marybeth 1959- *172*
  Earlier sketch in SATA *121*
Lord, Athena V. 1932- *39*
Lord, Beman 1924-1991 .... *5*
  Obituary *69*
Lord, Bette Bao 1938- *58*
  See also CLR *151*
Lord, Cynthia *182*
Lord, Doreen Mildred Douglas
  See Lord, Douglas
Lord, Douglas 1904-1992 .... *12*
Lord, Janet *204*
Lord, John Vernon 1939- *21*
Lord, Michele *201*
Lord, Nancy J.
  See Titus, Eve
Lord, Patricia C. 1927-1988
  Obituary *58*
Lord, Walter 1917-2002 .... *3*
Lorde, Diana
  See Reno, Dawn E(laine)
Lorenz, Albert 1941- *115*
Lorenzini, Carlo
  See Collodi, Carlo
Lorey, Dean 1967- *193*
Lorimer, Janet 1941- *60*
Loring, Emilie (Baker) 1864(?)-1951 .... *51*
Lorkowski, Thomas V(incent) 1950- *92*
Lorkowski, Tom
  See Lorkowski, Thomas V(incent)
Lorraine, Walter (Henry) 1929- *16*
Lorrimer, Claire
  See Robins, Patricia
Loss, Joan 1933- *11*
Lothrop, Harriet Mulford Stone 1844-1924 . *20*
Lottridge, Celia Barker 1936- *157*
  Earlier sketch in SATA *112*
LoTurco, Laura 1963- *84*
Lotz, Wolfgang 1912-1981 .... *65*
Loughridge, Stuart 1978- *214*
Louie, Ai-Ling 1949- *40*
  Brief entry *34*
Louis, Catherine 1963- *186*
Louis, Pat
  See Francis, Dorothy
Louisburgh, Sheila Burnford
  See Burnford, Sheila (Philip Cochrane Every)
Louise, Anita
  See Riggio, Anita
Louise, Tina 1934- *191*
Lourie, Helen
  See Storr, Catherine (Cole)
Lourie, Peter 1952- *183*
  Earlier sketches in SATA *82, 142*
Lourie, Peter King
  See Lourie, Peter
Love, Ann 1947- *168*
  Earlier sketch in SATA *79*
Love, D. Anne 1949- *180*
  Earlier sketches in SATA *96, 145*
Love, Douglas 1967- *92*
Love, Judith Dufour
  See Love, Judy
Love, Judy *188*
Love, Katherine (Isabel) 1907- *3*
Love, Kathleen Ann
  See Love, Ann
Love, Maryann Cusimano *223*
Love, Sandra (Weller) 1940- *26*
Lovegrove, James 1965- *216*
Lovegrove, J.M.H.
  See Lovegrove, James
Lovejoy, Jack 1937- *116*
Lovelace, Delos Wheeler 1894-1967 .... *7*
Lovelace, Maud Hart 1892-1980 .... *2*
  Obituary *23*
Lovell, Ingraham
  See Bacon, Josephine Dodge (Daskam)
Lovelock, Brian 1956- *214*
Loverseed, Amanda (Jane) 1965- *75*
Lovett, Margaret (Rose) 1915- *22*

Low, Alice 1926- *156*
  Earlier sketches in SATA *11, 76*
Low, Elizabeth Hammond 1898-1991 .... *5*
Low, Joseph 1911-2007 .... *14*
Low, Penelope Margaret
  See Lively, Penelope
Low, William *177*
Lowe, Helen 1961- *206*
Lowe, Jay, Jr.
  See Loeper, John J(oseph)
Lowell, Pamela *187*
Lowell, Susan 1950- *206*
  Earlier sketches in SATA *81, 127*
Lowenstein, Dyno 1914-1996 .... *6*
Lowenstein, Sallie 1949- *116*
Lowery, Linda 1949- *151*
  Earlier sketch in SATA *74*
Lowitz, Anson C. 1901(?)-1978 .... *18*
Lowitz, Sadyebeth Heath 1901-1969 .... *17*
Lowndes, Robert A(ugustine) W(ard)
  1916-1998 .... *117*
Lowrey, Janette Sebring 1892-1986 .... *43*
Lowry, Lois 1937- *177*
  Autobiography Feature *127*
  Earlier sketches in SATA *23, 70, 111*
  See also CLR *72*
  See also SAAS *3*
Lowry, Lois Hammersberg
  See Lowry, Lois
Lowry, Peter 1953- *7*
Lowther, George F. 1913-1975
  Obituary *30*
Loyie, Larry 1933- *150*
Lozansky, Edward D. 1941- *62*
Lozier, Herbert 1915- *26*
Lubar, David 1954- *190*
  Earlier sketch in SATA *133*
Lubell, Cecil 1912-2000 .... *6*
Lubell, Winifred (A. Milius) 1914- *6*
Lubin, Leonard
  See Lubin, Leonard B.
Lubin, Leonard B. 1943-1994 .... *45*
  Brief entry *37*
Lubka, S. Ruth 1948- *154*
Lubner, Susan *185*
Luby, Thia 1954- *124*
Lucado, Max (Lee) 1955- *104*
Lucas, Cedric 1962- *101*
Lucas, David 1966- *208*
Lucas, E(dward) V(errall) 1868-1938 .... *20*
Lucas, Eileen 1956- *113*
  Earlier sketch in SATA *76*
Lucas, George 1944- *56*
Lucas, Jerry 1940- *33*
Lucas, Margeaux *186*
Lucas, Victoria
  See Plath, Sylvia
Lucashenko, Melissa 1967- *104*
Luccarelli, Vincent 1923- *90*
Luce, Celia (Geneva Larsen) 1914- *38*
Luce, Willard (Ray) 1914-1990 .... *38*
Lucht, Irmgard 1937- *82*
Lucke, Deb *202*
Luckett, Dave 1951- *220*
  Earlier sketches in SATA *106, 167*
Luckhardt, Mildred Corell 1898-1990 .... *5*
Ludden, Allen (Ellsworth) 1918(?)-1981
  Obituary *27*
Ludel, Jacqueline 1945- *64*
Ludlow, Geoffrey
  See Meynell, Laurence Walter
Ludlum, Mabel Cleland
  See Widdemer, Mabel Cleland
Ludwig, Helen *33*
Ludwig, Lyndell 1923- *63*
Ludwig, Trudy 1959- *209*
  Earlier sketch in SATA *166*
Luebs, Robin 1949- *212*
Lueders, Edward (George) 1923- *14*
Luenn, Nancy 1954- *79*
  Earlier sketch in SATA *51*

Lufkin, Raymond H. 1897- *38*
Lugard, Flora Louisa Shaw 1852-1929 .... *21*
Luger, Harriett Mandelay 1914- *23*
Luhrmann, Winifred B(ruce) 1934- *11*
Luis, Earlene W. 1929- *11*
Lujan, Jorge *201*
Luke, Pauline *178*
Luke, Pauline R.
    See Luke, Pauline
Lum, Peter
    See Crowe, (Bettina) Peter Lum
Lumry, Amanda (R.) *159*
Lund, Deb *157*
Lund, Doris Herold 1919- *12*
Lunde, Darrin *202*
Lundebrek, Amy 1975- *213*
Lung, Chang
    See Jordan, Robert
Lunge-Larsen, Lise 1955- *184*
    Earlier sketch in SATA *138*
Lunn, Carolyn (Kowalczyk) 1960- *67*
Lunn, Janet (Louise Swoboda) 1928- *110*
    Earlier sketches in SATA *4, 68*
    See also CLR *18*
    See also SAAS *12*
Lunsford, Cin Forshay
    See Forshay-Lunsford, Cin
Lupica, Michael
    See Lupica, Mike
Lupica, Michael Thomas
    See Lupica, Mike
Lupica, Mike 1952- *177*
Lupoff, Dick
    See Lupoff, Richard A(llen)
Lupoff, Richard A(llen) 1935- *60*
Lurie, Alison 1926- *112*
    Earlier sketch in SATA *46*
Lurie, Morris 1938- *72*
Lussert, Anneliese 1929- *101*
Lusted, Marcia Amidon 1962- *143*
Lustig, Arnost 1926-2011 .... *56*
Lustig, Loretta 1944- *46*
Lutes, Jason 1967- *210*
Luthardt, Kevin 1973- *172*
Luther, Frank 1905-1980
    Obituary *25*
Luther, Rebekah (Lyn) S(tiles) 1960- *90*
Luttmann, Gail
    See Damerow, Gail
Luttrell, Guy L. 1938- *22*
Luttrell, Ida (Alleene) 1934- *91*
    Brief entry *35*
    Earlier sketch in SATA *40*
Luttrell, William (J. III) 1954- *149*
Lutz, John 1939- *180*
Lutz, John Thomas
    See Lutz, John
Lutz, Norma Jean 1943- *122*
Lutzeier, Elizabeth 1952- *72*
Lutzker, Edythe 1904-1991 .... *5*
Luxbacher, Irene 1970- *219*
    Earlier sketch in SATA *153*
Luzadder, Patrick 1954- *89*
Luzzati, Emanuele 1921-2007 .... *7*
Luzzatto, Paola Caboara 1938- *38*
Ly, Many 1977- *208*
Lybbert, Tyler 1970- *88*
Lydon, Michael 1942- *11*
Lyfick, Warren
    See Reeves, Lawrence F.
Lyle, Katie Letcher 1938- *8*
Lynch, Chris 1962- *209*
    Earlier sketches in SATA *95, 131, 171*
    See also CLR *58*
Lynch, Janet Nichols 1952- *221*
Lynch, Jay 1945- *204*
Lynch, Lorenzo 1932- *7*
Lynch, Marietta 1947- *29*
Lynch, Patricia (Nora) 1898-1972 .... *9*
Lynch, Patrick James
    See Lynch, P.J.

Lynch, P.J. 1962- *213*
    Earlier sketches in SATA *79, 122*
Lynds, Dennis 1924-2005 .... *47*
    Brief entry *37*
Lyne, Alison Davis *188*
Lyngseth, Joan
    See Davies, Joan
Lynn, Elizabeth A(nne) 1946- *99*
Lynn, Mary
    See Brokamp, Marilyn
Lynn, Patricia
    See Watts, Mabel Pizzey
Lynn, Tracy *175*
Lyon, Elinor 1921-2008 .... *6*
    Obituary *192*
Lyon, Elinor Bruce
    See Lyon, Elinor
Lyon, George Ella 1949- *207*
    Autobiography Feature *148*
    Earlier sketches in SATA *68, 119, 148*
Lyon, Lea 1945- *212*
Lyon, Lyman R.
    See de Camp, L. Sprague
Lyons, Dorothy M(arawee) 1907-1997 .... *3*
Lyons, Grant 1941- *30*
Lyons, Marcus
    See Blish, James
Lyons, Mary E. 1947- *195*
    Autobiography Feature *195*
    Earlier sketches in SATA *93, 142*
Lyons, Mary Evelyn
    See Lyons, Mary E.
Lystad, Mary (Hanemann) 1928- *11*
Lytle, Elizabeth Stewart 1949- *79*
Lytle, Robert A. 1944- *119*
Lyttle, Richard B(ard) 1927- *23*
Lytton, Deborah 1966- *218*
Lytton, Edward G.E.L. Bulwer-Lytton Baron
    See Bulwer-Lytton, Edward
Lytton of Knebworth, Baron
    See Bulwer-Lytton, Edward

                            M

Ma, Wenhai 1954- *84*
Maar, Leonard (Frank, Jr.) 1927- *30*
Maartens, Maretha 1945- *73*
Maas, Selve -1997 .... *14*
Maass, Robert *195*
Mabie, Grace
    See Mattern, Joanne
Mac
    See MacManus, Seumas
    and Maccari, Ruggero
Macalaster, Elizabeth G. 1951- *115*
MacAlister, Katie *159*
MacAlister, V. A.
    See McKernan, Victoria
MacAllan, Andrew
    See Leasor, James
MacAodhagain, Eamon
    See Egan, E. W.
MacArthur-Onslow, Annette Rosemary
    1933- *26*
Macaulay, David (Alexander) 1946- *137*
    Brief entry *27*
    Earlier sketches in SATA *46, 72*
    See also CLR *14*
Macaulay, Teresa 1947- *95*
Macauley, Theresa E.
    See Macaulay, Teresa
Macavinta, Courtney *176*
MacBeth, George (Mann) 1932-1992 .... *4*
    Obituary *70*
MacBride, Roger Lea 1929-1995 .... *85*
MacCarter, Don 1944- *91*
MacClintock, Dorcas 1932- *8*
MacCready, Robin Merrow 1959(?)- *190*
MacCullough, Carolyn *174*

MacDonald, Alan 1958- *192*
MacDonald, Amy 1951- *156*
    Autobiography Feature *156*
    Earlier sketches in SATA *76, 136*
MacDonald, Anne Elizabeth Campbell Bard
    -1958
    See MacDonald, Betty
MacDonald, Anne Louise 1955- *217*
MacDonald, Anson
    See Heinlein, Robert A.
MacDonald, Betty 1908-1958
    See YABC *1*
Macdonald, Blackie
    See Emrich, Duncan (Black Macdonald)
Macdonald, Caroline 1948- *86*
    Obituary *111*
    See also CLR *60*
Macdonald, Dwight 1906-1982 .... *29*
    Obituary *33*
MacDonald, George 1824-1905 .... *100*
    Earlier sketch in SATA *33*
    See also CLR *67*
MacDonald, Golden
    See Brown, Margaret Wise
Macdonald, Guy *195*
Macdonald, James D. 1954- *67*
    Earlier sketches in SATA *81, 114, 165, 1*
Macdonald, Marcia
    See Hill, Grace Livingston
MacDonald, Margaret Read 1940- *194*
    Earlier sketches in SATA *94, 164*
Macdonald, Marianne 1934- *113*
Macdonald, Mary
    See Gifford, Griselda
Macdonald, Maryann 1947- *189*
    Earlier sketch in SATA *72*
MacDonald, Ross 1957- *201*
Macdonald, Shelagh 1937- *25*
MacDonald, Suse 1940- *193*
    Brief entry *52*
    Earlier sketches in SATA *54, 109*
Macdonald, Wendy *217*
Macdonald, Wendy M.
    See Macdonald, Wendy
Macdonald, Zillah K(atherine) 1885-1979 ... *11*
MacDonnell, Megan
    See Stevens, Serita
MacDougal, John
    See Blish, James
Mace, Elisabeth 1933- *27*
Mace, Varian 1938- *49*
MacEachern, Stephen *206*
MacEwen, Gwendolyn (Margaret)
    1941-1987 .... *50*
    Obituary *55*
Macfarlan, Allan A. 1892-1982 .... *35*
MacFarlane, Iris 1922- *11*
MacGill-Callahan, Sheila 1926-2000 .... *78*
MacGregor, Carol Lynn *153*
MacGregor, Ellen 1906-1954 .... *39*
    Brief entry *27*
MacGregor-Hastie, Roy (Alasdhair Niall)
    1929- *3*
MacGrory, Yvonne 1948- *142*
Machado, Ana Maria 1941- *150*
MacHale, D.J. 1956- *175*
MacHale, Donald James
    See MacHale, D.J.
Machetanz, Frederick 1908- *34*
Machin, Sue
    See Williams, Sue
Machin Goodall, Daphne (Edith) *37*
Macht, Norm
    See Macht, Norman L.
Macht, Norman L. 1929- *122*
Macht, Norman Lee
    See Macht, Norman L.
Macht, Norman Lee
    See Macht, Norman L.
MacInnes, Helen (Clark) 1907-1985 .... *22*
    Obituary *44*

Macintosh, Brownie 1950- 98
MacIntyre, Elisabeth 1916- 17
MacIntyre, Rod
    See MacIntyre, R.P.
MacIntyre, R.P. 1947- 203
MacIntyre, R.P. 1947- 203
MacIntyre, Wendy 1947- 196
Mack, Jeff 194
Mack, L.V.
    See Kimmelman, Burt
Mack, Stan(ley) 17
Mack, Todd 168
Mack, Tracy 1968- 183
    Earlier sketch in SATA *128*
Mackall, Dandi D.
    See Mackall, Dandi Daley
Mackall, Dandi Daley 1949- 218
    Earlier sketches in SATA *118, 177, 182*
Mackay, Claire 1930- 97
    Autobiography Feature 124
    Earlier sketch in SATA *40*
    See also CLR *43*
Mackay, Constance D'Arcy (?)-1966 125
Mackay, Donald 1914-2005 81
    Obituary 173
Mackay, Donald Alexander
    See Mackay, Donald
MacKaye, Percy (Wallace) 1875-1956 32
Mackel, Kathryn 1950- 162
Mackel, Kathy
    See Mackel, Kathryn
MacKellar, William 1914- 4
Macken, JoAnn Early 1953- 201
Macken, Walter 1915-1967 36
Mackenzie, Anna 1963- 212
MacKenzie, Jill (Kelly) 1947- 75
Mackenzie, Robert 1974- 204
Mackey, Ernan
    See McInerny, Ralph
Mackey, Weezie Kerr 188
Mackie, Maron
    See McNeely, Jeannette
Mackin, Edward
    See McInerny, Ralph
MacKinnon, Bernie 1957- 69
MacKinnon Groomer, Vera 1915- 57
MacKinstry, Elizabeth 1879-1956 42
Mackler, Carolyn 1973- 156
MacLachlan, Emily
    See Charest, Emily MacLachlan
MacLachlan, Patricia 1938- 168
    Brief entry 42
    Earlier sketches in SATA *62, 107*
    See also CLR *14*
MacLane, Jack
    See Crider, Bill
MacLean, Alistair 1922(?)-1987 23
    Obituary 50
MacLean, Alistair Stuart
    See MacLean, Alistair
Maclean, Art
    See Shirreffs, Gordon D(onald)
MacLean, Christine Kole 1962- 177
MacLean, Glynne 1964- 150
MacLean, Jill 1941- 211
MacLeod, Beatrice 1910- 162
    Earlier sketch in SATA *10*
MacLeod, Beatrice Beach
    See MacLeod, Beatrice
MacLeod, Charlotte (Matilda) 1922-2005 28
    Obituary 160
MacLeod, Doug 1959- 201
    Earlier sketch in SATA *60*
MacLeod, Elizabeth 184
    Earlier sketch in SATA *158*
MacLeod, Ellen Jane (Anderson) 1916- 14
MacManus, James
    See MacManus, Seumas
MacManus, Seumas 1869-1960 25
MacMaster, Eve (Ruth) B(owers) 1942- 46

MacMillan, Annabelle
    See Quick, Annabelle
MacMillan, Dianne M(arie) 1943- 125
    Earlier sketch in SATA *84*
Macnaughton, Tina 218
    Earlier sketch in SATA *182*
Macneill, Janet
    See McNeely, Jeannette
MacPeek, Walter G. 1902-1973 4
    Obituary 25
MacPhail, Catherine 1946- 197
    Earlier sketch in SATA *130*
MacPherson, Margaret 1908-2001 9
    See also SAAS *4*
MacPherson, Thomas George 1915-1976
    Obituary 30
MacPherson, Winnie 1930- 107
MacRae, Tom 1980- 181
Macrae, Travis
    See Feagles, Anita MacRae
MacRaois, Cormac 1944- 72
Macumber, Mari
    See Sandoz, Mari(e Susette)
Macy, Sue 1954- 134
    Earlier sketch in SATA *88*
Madaras, Lynda 1947- 151
Madden, Don 1927- 3
Madden, Kerry 1961- 168
Madden-Lunsford, Kerry
    See Madden, Kerry
Maddern, Eric 1950- 166
Maddigan, Beth 1967- 174
Maddison, Angela Mary 1923- 10
    See also CLR *24*
Maddock, Reginald (Bertram) 1912-1994 15
Madenski, Melissa (Ann) 1949- 77
Madian, Jon 1941- 9
Madigan, Lisa Kay
    See Madigan, L.K.
Madigan, L.K. (?)-2011 224
Madison, Alan 182
Madison, Arnold 1937- 6
Madison, Bennett 220
Madison, Winifred 5
Madonna 1958- 149
Madsen, Gunnar 171
Madsen, Jim 1964- 202
Madsen, Ross Martin 1946- 82
Madsen, Susan A. 1954- 90
Madsen, Susan Arrington
    See Madsen, Susan A.
Maehlqvist, Stefan 1943- 30
Maestro, Betsy (Crippen) 1944- 106
    Brief entry 30
    Earlier sketch in SATA *59*
    See also CLR *45*
Maestro, Giulio 1942- 106
    Earlier sketches in SATA *8, 59*
    See also CLR *45*
Maeterlinck, Maurice 1862-1949 66
Magee, Doug 1947- 78
Magee, Wes 1939- 64
Maggio, Rosalie 1943- 69
Magid, Ken(neth Marshall) 65
Magnus, Erica 1946- 77
Magoon, Kekla 1980- 213
Magoon, Scott 222
    Earlier sketch in SATA *182*
Magorian, James 1942- 92
    Earlier sketch in SATA *32*
Magorian, Michelle 1947- 128
    Earlier sketch in SATA *67*
Magorian, Michelle Jane
    See Magorian, Michelle
Magovern, Peg 103
Magsamen, Sandra 1959- 213
Maguire, Anne
    See Nearing, Penny

Maguire, Gregory 1954- 200
    Autobiography Feature 200
    Earlier sketches in SATA *28, 84, 129*
    See also SAAS *22*
Maguire, Gregory Peter
    See Maguire, Gregory
Maguire, Jack 1920-2000 74
Maguire, Jesse
    See Smith, Sherwood
Maguire, Jessie
    See Smith, Sherwood
Maher, Ramona 1934- 13
Mahlqvist, Stefan
    See Maehlqvist, Stefan
Mahon, Julia C(unha) 1916- 11
Mahony, Elizabeth Winthrop
    See Winthrop, Elizabeth
Mahood, Kenneth 1930- 24
Mahy, Margaret 1936- 171
    Earlier sketches in SATA *14, 69, 119*
    See also CLR *155*
Mahy, Margaret May
    See Mahy, Margaret
Maiden, Cecil (Edward) 1902-1981 52
Maidoff, Ilka
    See List, Ilka Katherine
Maifair, Linda Lee 1947- 83
Maik, Henri
    See Hecht, Henri Joseph
Maillu, David G(ian) 1939- 111
Maine, Trevor
    See Catherall, Arthur
Mains, Randolph P. 1946- 80
Maione, Heather 189
Maiorano, Robert 1946- 43
Maisner, Heather 1947- 89
Maison, Della
    See Katz, Bobbi
Maitland, Antony Jasper 1935- 25
Maitland, Barbara 102
Mai-Wyss, Tatjana 1972- 187
Maizels, Jennie 210
Major, Kevin (Gerald) 1949- 134
    Earlier sketches in SATA *32, 82*
    See also CLR *11*
Majure, Janet 1954- 96
Makhijani, Pooja 188
Makie, Pam 1943- 37
Makowski, Silk
    See Sullivan, Silky
Makowski, Silvia Ann
    See Sullivan, Silky
Malam, John 1957- 152
    Earlier sketch in SATA *89*
Maland, Nick 195
Malaspina, Ann 1957- 222
Malcolm, Dan
    See Silverberg, Robert
Malcolm, Jahnna N.
    See Beecham, Jahnna
Malcolmson, Anne
    See von Storch, Anne B.
Malcolmson, David 1899-1978 6
Maletta, Dr. Arlene
    See Feltenstein, Arlene
Maley, Carleen
    See Hutchins, Carleen Maley
Mali, Jane Lawrence 1937-1995 51
    Brief entry 44
    Obituary 86
Malkin, Nina 1959(?)- 179
Mallett, Jerry J. 1939- 76
Malley, Gemma 198
Malley, G.R.
    See Malley, Gemma
Mallory, Kenneth 1945- 185
    Earlier sketch in SATA *128*
Mallowan, Agatha Christie
    See Christie, Agatha
Malmberg, Carl 1904-1979 9
Malmgren, Dallin 1949- 65

Author Index

Malo, John W. 1911-2000 4
Malone, James Hiram 1930- 84
Malone, Nola Langner 1930-2003 8
    Obituary 151
Malone, Patricia 1932- 155
Malone, Peter 1953- 191
Maloney, Pat
    See Markun, Patricia Maloney
Malory, Sir Thomas 1410(?)-1471(?) 59
    Brief entry 33
Maltese, Michael 1909(?)-1981
    Obituary 24
Malvasi, Meg Greene 143
Malvern, Corinne 1905-1956 34
Malvern, Gladys (?)-1962 23
Mama G.
    See Davis, Grania
Mammano, Julie 1962- 202
    Earlier sketch in SATA *107*
Mamonova, Tatyana 1943- 93
Manchel, Frank 1935- 10
Manchess, Gregory 1955- 203
Manchester, William (Raymond)
    1922-2004 65
Mandabach, Brian 1962(?)- 197
Mandel, Brett H. 1969- 108
Mandel, Peter 1957- 87
Mandel, Sally (Elizabeth) 1944- 64
Mandell, Muriel (Hortense Levin) 1921- 63
Manders, John 1957- 219
    Earlier sketch in SATA *175*
Manes, Stephen 1949- 99
    Brief entry 40
    Earlier sketch in SATA *42*
Manfred, Frederick (Feikema) 1912-1994 30
Mangin, Marie France 1940- 59
Mangione, Gerlando 1909-1998 6
    Obituary 104
Mangione, Jerre
    See Mangione, Gerlando
Mango, Karin N. 1936- 52
Mangurian, David 1938- 14
Mania, Cathy 1950- 102
Mania, Robert 1952- 102
Mania, Robert C., Jr.
    See Mania, Robert
Maniatty, Taramesha 1978- 92
Maniscalco, Joseph 1926- 10
Manley, Deborah 1932- 28
Manley, Seon 1921- 15
    See also CLR *3*
    See also SAAS *2*
Mann, Elizabeth 1948- 153
Mann, Josephine
    See Pullein-Thompson, Josephine (Mary
        Wedderburn)
Mann, Kenny 1946- 91
Mann, Pamela 1946- 91
Mann, Patrick
    See Waller, Leslie
Mann, Peggy
    See Houlton, Peggy Mann
Mannetti, Lisa 1953- 57
    Brief entry 51
Mannheim, Grete (Salomon) 1909-1986 10
Manniche, Lise 1943- 31
Manning, Jane K. 185
Manning, Maurie
    See Manning, Maurie J.
Manning, Maurie J. 211
Manning, Maurie Jo
    See Manning, Maurie J.
Manning, Mick 1959- 176
Manning, Rosemary 1911-1988 10
Manning, Sarra 162
Manning-Sanders, Ruth (Vernon)
    1895(?)-1988 73
    Obituary 57
    Earlier sketch in SATA *15*
Mannion, Diane
    See Paterson, Diane

Mannis, Celeste Davidson 173
Mannon, Warwick
    See Hopkins, (Hector) Kenneth
Manos, Helen 199
Mansir, A. Richard 1932- 170
Manson, Ainslie Kertland 1938- 115
Manson, Beverlie 1945- 57
    Brief entry 44
Mantchev, Lisa 221
Mantha, John 1960- 217
Manthorpe, Helen 1958- 122
Mantinband, Gerda (B.) 1917- 74
Manton, Jo
    See Gittings, Jo (Grenville) Manton
Manuel, Lynn 1948- 179
    Earlier sketch in SATA *99*
Manushkin, Fran 1942- 205
    Earlier sketches in SATA *7, 54, 93, 166*
Manushkin, Frances
    See Manushkin, Fran
Man Without a Spleen, A
    See Chekhov, Anton
Many, Paul 1947- 210
Many, Paul A.
    See Many, Paul
Manzano, Sonia 1950- 167
Mapes, Mary A.
    See Ellison, Virginia H(owell)
Maple, Marilyn 1931- 80
Mappin, Strephyn 1956- 109
Mara, Barney
    See Roth, Arthur J(oseph)
Mara, Jeanette
    See Cebulash, Mel
Mara, Rachna
    See Gilmore, Rachna
Marais, Josef 1905-1978
    Obituary 24
Marasmus, Seymour
    See Rivoli, Mario
Marbach, Ethel
    See Pochocki, Ethel (Frances)
Marcal, Annette B.
    See Callaway, Bernice (Anne)
Marcelino
    See Agnew, Edith J(osephine)
Marcellino, Fred 1939-2001 118
    Obituary 127
    Earlier sketch in SATA *68*
March, Carl
    See Fleischman, Sid
Marchant, Bessie 1862-1941
    See YABC *2*
Marchant, Catherine
    See Cookson, Catherine (McMullen)
Marcher, Marion Walden 1890-1987 10
Marchesi, Stephen 1951- 114
Marchesi, Steve
    See Marchesi, Stephen
    and Older, Effin
    and Older, Jules
Marchetta, Melina 1965- 170
Marciano, John Bemelmans 1970- 167
    Earlier sketch in SATA *118*
    See also CLR *93*
Marco, Lou
    See Gottfried, Theodore Mark
Marcus, Leonard S. 1950- 187
    Earlier sketch in SATA *133*
Marcus, Paul 1953- 82
Marcus, Rebecca B(rian) 1907- 9
Marcuse, Aida E. 1934- 89
Marek, Margot L. 1934(?)-1987
    Obituary 54
Maren, Julie 1970- 199
Margaret, Karla
    See Andersdatter, Karla M.
Margolin, Harriet
    See Ziefert, Harriet
Margolis, Jeffrey A. 1948- 108
Margolis, Leslie 187

Margolis, Richard J(ules) 1929-1991 86
    Obituary 67
    Earlier sketch in SATA *4*
Margolis, Vivienne 1922- 46
Mariana
    See Foster, Marian Curtis
Marie, Geraldine 1949- 61
Mariner, Scott
    See Pohl, Frederik
Marino, Dorothy Bronson 1912- 14
Marino, Jan 1936- 114
Marino, Nan 216
Marino, Nick
    See Deming, Richard
Marino, Peter 1960- 179
Mario, Anna
    See Odgers, Sally Farrell
Marion, Henry
    See del Rey, Lester
Maris, Ron 71
    Brief entry 45
Mark, Jan 1943-2006 164
    Obituary 173
    Earlier sketches in SATA *22, 69, 114*
    See also CLR *11*
Mark, Janet Marjorie
    See Mark, Jan
Mark, Joan T. 1937- 122
Mark, Pauline (Dahlin) 1913-1997 14
Mark, Polly
    See Mark, Pauline (Dahlin)
Mark, Ted
    See Gottfried, Theodore Mark
Markel, Michelle 169
Marker, Sherry 1941- 76
Markert, Jennifer 1965- 83
Markert, Jenny
    See Markert, Jennifer
Markey, Kevin 1965- 215
Markham, Lynne 1947- 102
Markham, Marion M. 1929- 60
Markham, Wendy
    See Staub, Wendy Corsi
Markins, W. S.
    See Jenkins, Marie M(agdalen)
Markle, Sandra 1946- 218
    Brief entry 41
    Earlier sketches in SATA *57, 92, 148, 185*
Markle, Sandra L.
    See Markle, Sandra
Marklew, Gilly 211
Marko, Katherine D(olores) 28
Markoosie
    See Patsauq, Markoosie
Marks, Alan 1957- 187
    Earlier sketches in SATA *77, 151*
Marks, Burton 1930- 47
    Brief entry 43
Marks, Graham 158
Marks, Hannah K.
    See Trivelpiece, Laurel
Marks, J.
    See Highwater, Jamake (Mamake)
Marks, J(ames) M(acdonald) 1921- 13
Marks, Laurie J. 1957- 68
Marks, Margaret L. 1911(?)-1980
    Obituary 23
Marks, Mickey Klar -1986 12
Marks, Peter
    See Smith, Robert Kimmel
Marks, Rita 1938- 47
Marks, Stan(ley) 14
Marks-Highwater, J.
    See Highwater, Jamake (Mamake)
Markun, Patricia Maloney 1924- 15
Markusen, Bruce (Stanley Rodriguez)
    1965- 141
Marley, Louise 1952- 173
    Earlier sketch in SATA *120*
Marlin, Hilda
    See Van Stockum, Hilda

Marlow, Layne *204*
Marlow, Max
   See Nicole, Christopher (Robin)
Marlow, Susan K. 1953- *178*
Marlowe, Amy Bell *67*
   Earlier sketch in SATA *1*
Marlowe, Jack
   See Deary, Terry
Marlowe, Tess
   See Glick, Ruth (Burtnick)
Marney, Dean 1952- *90*
Marokvia, Artur 1909- *31*
Marokvia, Mireille 1908-2008 .... *5*
   Obituary *197*
Marokvia, Mireille Journet
   See Marokvia, Mireille
Marol, Jean-Claude 1946- *125*
Marr, John S(tuart) 1940- *48*
Marr, Melissa 1972- *189*
Marric, J. J.
   See Butler, William Vivian
   and Creasey, John
Marrin, Albert 1936- *193*
   Brief entry *43*
   Earlier sketches in SATA *53, 90, 126*
   See also CLR *53*
Marriott, Alice Lee 1910-1992 .... *31*
   Obituary *71*
Marriott, Janice 1946- *134*
Marriott, Pat(ricia) 1920- *35*
Marriott, Zoe 1982- *216*
Marriott, Zoe Davina
   See Marriott, Zoe
Marroquin, Patricio
   See Markun, Patricia Maloney
Mars, W. T.
   See Mars, Witold Tadeusz J.
Mars, Witold Tadeusz J. 1912-1985 .... *3*
Marsden, Carolyn 1950- *212*
   Autobiography Feature *212*
   Earlier sketches in SATA *140, 175*
Marsden, John 1950- *146*
   Earlier sketches in SATA *66, 97*
   See also CLR *34*
   See also SAAS *22*
Marsh, Carole 1946- *127*
Marsh, Dave 1950- *66*
Marsh, J. E.
   See Marshall, Evelyn
Marsh, James 1946- *73*
Marsh, Jean
   See Marshall, Evelyn
Marsh, Joan F. 1923- *83*
Marsh, Katherine 1974- *220*
Marsh, Paul
   See Hopkins, (Hector) Kenneth
Marsh, Valerie 1954- *89*
Marshall, Anthony D(ryden) 1924- *18*
Marshall, Bonnie C. 1941- *141*
   Earlier sketch in SATA *18*
Marshall, Bridget M(ary) 1974- *103*
Marshall, (Sarah) Catherine (Wood)
   1914-1983 .... *2*
   Obituary *34*
Marshall, Douglas
   See McClintock, Marshall
Marshall, Edmund
   See Hopkins, (Hector) Kenneth
Marshall, Edward
   See Marshall, James
Marshall, Evelyn 1897-1991 .... *11*
Marshall, Felicity 1950- *116*
Marshall, Garry 1934- *60*
Marshall, H. H.
   See Jahn, Michael
Marshall, James 1942-1992 .... *75*
   Earlier sketches in SATA *6, 51*
   See also CLR *21*
Marshall, James Edward
   See Marshall, James

Marshall, James Vance
   See Payne, Donald Gordon
Marshall, Janet (Perry) 1938- *97*
Marshall, Jeff
   See Laycock, George (Edwin)
Marshall, Kim
   See Marshall, Michael (Kimbrough)
Marshall, Michael (Kimbrough) 1948- *37*
Marshall, Percy
   See Young, Percy M(arshall)
Marshall, S(amuel) L(yman) A(twood)
   1900-1977 .... *21*
Marsoli, Lisa Ann 1958- *101*
   Brief entry *53*
Marsten, Richard
   See Hunter, Evan
Marston, Elsa 1933- *156*
Marston, Hope Irvin 1935- *127*
   Earlier sketch in SATA *31*
Marszalek, John F. 1939- *167*
Marszalek, John Francis, Jr.
   See Marszalek, John F.
Marszalek, John Francis 1939-
   See Marszalek, John F.
Martchenko, Michael 1942- *154*
   Earlier sketches in SATA *50, 95*
Martel, Aimee
   See Thurlo, Aimee
   and Thurlo, David
Martel, Suzanne 1924- *99*
Martignoni, Margaret E. 1908(?)-1974
   Obituary *27*
Martin, Ann M. 1955- *192*
   Brief entry *41*
   Earlier sketches in SATA *44, 70, 126*
   See also CLR *32*
Martin, Bill, Jr. 1916-2004 .... *145*
   Brief entry *40*
   Earlier sketches in SATA *40, 67*
   See also CLR *97*
Martin, Charles E(lmer)
   See Mastrangelo, Charles E(lmer)
Martin, Christopher
   See Hoyt, Edwin P(almer), Jr.
Martin, C.K. Kelly *207*
Martin, Claire 1933- *76*
Martin, Courtney Autumn 1984- *205*
Martin, David Stone 1913-1992 .... *39*
Martin, Donald
   See Honig, Donald
Martin, Dorothy 1921- *47*
Martin, Dorothy McKay
   See Martin, Dorothy
Martin, Eugene *1*
Martin, Eva M. 1939- *65*
Martin, Frances M(cEntee) 1906-1998 .... *36*
Martin, Francesca 1947- *101*
Martin, Fred 1948- *119*
Martin, Fredric
   See Christopher, Matt(hew Frederick)
Martin, George Raymond Richard
   See Martin, George R.R.
Martin, George R.R. 1948- *118*
Martin, J(ohn) P(ercival) 1880(?)-1966 .... *15*
Martin, Jacqueline Briggs 1945- *188*
   Earlier sketches in SATA *98, 149*
Martin, Jane Read 1957- *84*
Martin, Jeremy
   See Levin, Marcia Obrasky
Martin, Les
   See Schulman, L(ester) M(artin)
Martin, Linda 1961- *82*
Martin, Lynne 1923- *21*
Martin, Marcia
   See Levin, Marcia Obrasky
Martin, Marvin 1926- *126*
Martin, Melanie
   See Pellowski, Michael (Joseph)
Martin, Nancy
   See Salmon, Annie Elizabeth
Martin, Patricia *200*

Martin, Patricia A.
   See Martin, Patricia
Martin, Patricia Miles 1899-1986 .... *43*
   Obituary *48*
   Earlier sketch in SATA *1*
Martin, Peter
   See Chaundler, Christine
Martin, Rafe 1946- *175*
Martin, Rene 1891-1977 .... *42*
   Obituary *20*
Martin, Rupert (Claude) 1905- *31*
Martin, S. R.
   See Mappin, Strephyn
Martin, Stefan 1936- *32*
Martin, Vicky
   See Storey, Victoria Carolyn
Martin, Webber
   See Silverberg, Robert
Martin, Wendy
   See Martini, Teri
Martin, William Ivan, Jr.
   See Martin, Bill, Jr.
Martineau, Diane 1940- *178*
Martineau, Harriet 1802-1876
   See YABC *2*
Martinet, Jeanne 1958- *80*
Martinez, Agnes *167*
Martinez, Arturo O. 1933- *192*
Martinez, Claudia Guadalupe 1978- *214*
Martinez, Ed(ward) 1954- *98*
Martinez, Elizabeth Coonrod 1954- *85*
Martinez, Victor 1954- *95*
Martini, Angela 1972(?)- *223*
Martini, Teri 1930- *3*
Martini, Therese
   See Martini, Teri
Martino, Alfred C. 1964- *174*
Martinson, Janis
   See Herbert, Janis
Martinusen, Cindy
   See Martinusen-Coloma, Cindy
Martinusen, Cindy McCormick
   See Martinusen-Coloma, Cindy
Martinusen-Coloma, Cindy 1970- *218*
Marton, Jirina 1946- *144*
   Earlier sketch in SATA *95*
Marton, Pierre
   See Stone, Peter
Martson, Del
   See Lupoff, Richard A(llen)
Martyr, Paula (Jane)
   See Lawford, Paula Jane
Maruki, Toshi 1912-2000 .... *112*
   See also CLR *19*
Marvin, Isabel R(idout) 1924- *84*
Marx, Patricia Windschill
   See Marx, Trish
Marx, Robert F(rank) 1936- *24*
Marx, Trish 1948- *202*
   Earlier sketches in SATA *112, 160*
Marzani, Carl (Aldo) 1912-1994 .... *12*
Marzollo, Jean 1942- *190*
   Autobiography Feature *190*
   Earlier sketches in SATA *29, 77, 130*
   See also SAAS *15*
Masefield, John (Edward) 1878-1967 .... *19*
Masiello, Ralph 1961- *214*
Masoff, Joy 1951- *118*
Mason, Adrienne 1962- *163*
Mason, Cherie *170*
Mason, Edwin A. 1905-1979
   Obituary *32*
Mason, Ernst
   See Pohl, Frederik
Mason, F(rancis) van Wyck 1901-1978 .... *3*
   Obituary *26*
Mason, Frank W.
   See Mason, F(rancis) van Wyck
Mason, George Frederick 1904-2000 .... *14*
Mason, Miriam E(vangeline) 1900-1973 .... *2*
   Obituary *26*

Mason, Prue 195
Mason, Simon 1962- 178
Mason, Tally
  See Derleth, August (William)
Mason, Van Wyck
  See Mason, F(rancis) van Wyck
Mass, Wendy 1967- 196
  Earlier sketch in SATA *158*
Mass, William
  See Gibson, William
Masse, Josee 221
Masselman, George 1897-1971 19
Massey, Misty 212
Massie, Dianne Redfield 1938- 125
  Earlier sketch in SATA *16*
Massie, Elizabeth 108
Massini, Sarah 213
Masson, Sophie 1959- 179
  Earlier sketch in SATA *133*
Masters, Anthony (Richard) 1940-2003 112
  Obituary 145
Masters, Kelly R(ay) 1897-1987 3
Masters, Mildred 1932- 42
Masters, William
  See Cousins, Margaret
Masters, Zeke
  See Bensen, Donald R.
  and Goulart, Ron
Mastrangelo, Charles E(lmer) 1910-1995 70
  Earlier sketch in SATA *69*
Masuda, Takeshi 1944- 56
Matas, Carol 1949- 194
  Autobiography Feature 112
  Earlier sketch in SATA *93*
  See also CLR *52*
Matchette, Katharine E. 1941- 38
Math, Irwin 1940- 42
Mathabane, Mark 1960- 123
Mather, Kirtley F(letcher) 1888-1978 65
Mathers, Petra 1945- 176
  Earlier sketch in SATA *119*
  See also CLR *76*
Matheson, Richard (Christian) 1953- 119
Matheson, Shirlee Smith 1942- 155
Mathews, Eleanor
  See Mathews, Ellie
Mathews, Ellie 1946(?)- 193
Mathews, Janet 1914-1992 41
Mathews, Judith
  See Goldberger, Judith M.
Mathews, Louise
  See Tooke, Louise Mathews
Mathiesen, Egon 1907-1976
  Obituary 28
Mathieu, Joe 1949- 185
  Brief entry 36
  Earlier sketches in SATA *43, 94*
Mathieu, Joseph P.
  See Mathieu, Joe
Mathis, Sharon Bell 1937- 58
  Earlier sketch in SATA *7*
  See also CLR *147*
  See also SAAS *3*
Matlin, Marlee 1965- 181
Matlin, Marlee Beth
  See Matlin, Marlee
Matloff, Gregory 1945- 73
Matott, Justin 1961- 109
Matranga, Frances Carfi 1922- 78
Matray, James I. 1948- 161
Matray, James Irving
  See Matray, James I.
Matson, Emerson N(els) 1926- 12
Matsui, Tadashi 1926- 8
Matsuno, Masako
  See Kobayashi, Masako Matsuno
Matsuoka, Mei 1981- 192
Matte, (Encarnacion) L'Enc 1936- 22
Mattern, Joanne 1963- 122
Mattheson, Jenny 180

Matthew, James
  See Barrie, J. M.
Matthews, Aline
  See De Wire, Elinor
Matthews, Andrew 1948- 138
Matthews, Caitlin 1952- 122
Matthews, Cecily 1945- 221
Matthews, Downs 1925- 71
Matthews, Elizabeth 1978- 194
Matthews, Ellen
  See Bache, Ellyn
Matthews, Ellen 1950- 28
Matthews, Harold Downs
  See Matthews, Downs
Matthews, Jacklyn Meek
  See Meek, Jacklyn O'Hanlon
Matthews, John (Kentigern) 1948- 116
Matthews, L. S. 183
Matthews, Laura S.
  See Matthews, L. S.
Matthews, Liz
  See Pellowski, Michael (Joseph)
Matthews, Morgan
  See Pellowski, Michael (Joseph)
Matthews, Nicola
  See Browne, N.M.
Matthews, Patricia 1927-2006 28
Matthews, Patricia Anne
  See Matthews, Patricia
Matthews, Tina 1961- 190
Matthews, Tom L.
  See Lalicki, Tom
Matthews, William Henry III 1919- 45
  Brief entry 28
Matthiessen, Peter 1927- 27
Mattingley, Christobel (Rosemary) 1931- 85
  Earlier sketch in SATA *37*
  See also CLR *24*
  See also SAAS *18*
Matulay, Laszlo 1912- 43
Matus, Greta 1938- 12
Matzigkeit, Philip 220
Maugham, W. S.
  See Maugham, W. Somerset
Maugham, W. Somerset 1874-1965 54
Maugham, William S.
  See Maugham, W. Somerset
Maugham, William Somerset
  See Maugham, W. Somerset
Maurer, Diane Philippoff
  See Maurer-Mathison, Diane V(ogel)
Maurer, Diane Vogel
  See Maurer-Mathison, Diane V(ogel)
Maurer-Mathison, Diane V(ogel) 1944- 89
Mauser, Pat Rhoads
  See McCord, Patricia
Mauser, Patricia Rhoads
  See McCord, Patricia
Maves, Mary Carolyn 1916- 10
Maves, Paul B(enjamin) 1913-1994 10
Mavor, Salley 1955- 125
Mawicke, Tran 1911- 15
Max 1906-1989
  See Diop, Birago (Ismael)
Max, Peter 1939- 45
Maxon, Anne
  See Best, (Evangel) Allena Champlin
Maxwell, Arthur S. 1896-1970 11
Maxwell, B.E. 1957- 211
Maxwell, Bruce E.
  See Maxwell, B.E.
Maxwell, Edith 1923- 7
Maxwell, Gavin 1914-1969 65
Maxwell, Katie
  See MacAlister, Katie
Maxwell, William (Keepers, Jr.) 1908-2000
  Obituary 128
Maxwell-Hyslop, Miranda 1968- 154
May, Charles Paul 1920- 4
May, Elaine Tyler 1947- 120

May, J. C.
  See May, Julian
May, Julian 1931- 11
May, Katie 225
May, Robert Lewis 1905-1976
  Obituary 27
May, Robert Stephen 1929-1996 46
May, Robin
  See May, Robert Stephen
Mayall, Beth 171
Mayberry, Florence V(irginia) Wilson 10
Maybury, Richard J. 1946- 72
Maybury, Rick
  See Maybury, Richard J.
Maydak, Michael S. 1952- 220
Mayer, Agatha
  See Maher, Ramona
Mayer, Albert Ignatius, Jr. 1906-1994
  Obituary 29
Mayer, Ann M(argaret) 1938- 14
Mayer, Bill 200
Mayer, Danuta 1958- 117
Mayer, Hannelore Valencak 1929- 42
Mayer, Jane Rothschild 1903-2001 38
Mayer, Marianna 1945- 132
  Earlier sketches in SATA *32, 83*
Mayer, Mercer 1943- 137
  Earlier sketches in SATA *16, 32, 73, 129*
  See also CLR *11*
Mayerson, Charlotte Leon 36
Mayerson, Evelyn Wilde 1935- 55
Mayfield, Katherine 1958- 118
Mayfield, Sue 1963- 146
  Earlier sketch in SATA *72*
Mayhar, Ardath 1930- 38
Mayhew, James 1964- 204
  Earlier sketches in SATA *85, 149*
Maynard, Olga 1920- 40
Mayne, William 1928-2010 122
  Earlier sketches in SATA *6, 68*
  See also CLR *123*
  See also SAAS *11*
Mayne, William James Carter
  See Mayne, William
Maynes, J. O. Rocky, Jr.
  See Maynes, J. Oscar, Jr.
Maynes, J. Oscar, Jr. 1929- 38
Mayo, Gretchen Will 1936- 163
  Earlier sketch in SATA *84*
Mayo, Margaret 1935- 165
  Earlier sketches in SATA *38, 96*
Mayo, Margaret Mary
  See Mayo, Margaret
Mayr, Diane 1949- 197
Mays, Lucinda L(a Bella) 1924- 49
Mays, (Lewis) Victor (Jr.) 1927- 5
Mazellan, Ron 210
Mazer, Anne 1953- 192
  Earlier sketches in SATA *67, 105*
Mazer, Harry 1925- 167
  Earlier sketches in SATA *31, 67, 105*
  See also CLR *16*
  See also SAAS *11*
Mazer, Norma Fox 1931-2009 198
  Earlier sketches in SATA *24, 67, 105, 168*
  See also CLR *23*
  See also SAAS *1*
Mazille, Capucine 1953- 96
Mazo, Michael 223
Mazza, Adriana 1928- 19
Mazzio, Joann 1926- 74
Mbugua, Kioi Wa 1962- 83
McAfee, Carol 1955- 81
McAllister, Amanda
  See Dowdell, Dorothy (Florence) Karns
  and Hager, Jean
  and Meaker, Eloise
McAllister, Angela 225
  Earlier sketch in SATA *182*
McAllister, Margaret I. 1956- 169
  Earlier sketch in SATA *117*

McAllister, M.I.
  See McAllister, Margaret I.
McArdle, Paula 1971- 198
McArthur, Nancy 96
McAvoy, Jim 1972- 142
McBain, Ed
  See Hunter, Evan
McBain, Georgina 189
McBratney, Sam 1943- 203
  Earlier sketches in SATA 89, 164
  See also CLR 44
McBrier, Michael
  See Older, Effin
  and Older, Jules
McCafferty, Jim 1954- 84
McCaffery, Janet 1936- 38
McCaffrey, Anne 1926- 152
  Autobiography Feature 152
  Earlier sketches in SATA 8, 70, 116
  See also CLR 130
  See also SAAS 11
McCaffrey, Anne Inez
  See McCaffrey, Anne
McCaffrey, Mary
  See Szudek, Agnes S(usan) P(hilomena)
McCain, Becky Ray 1954- 138
McCain, Murray (David, Jr.) 1926-1981 7
  Obituary 29
McCall, Bruce 1935(?)- 209
McCall, Edith (Sansom) 1911- 6
McCall, Virginia Nielsen 1909-2000 13
McCall, Wendell
  See Pearson, Ridley
McCall Smith, Alexander
  See Smith, Alexander McCall
McCallum, Phyllis
  See Koch, Phyllis (Mae) McCallum
McCallum, Stephen 1960- 91
McCampbell, Darlene Z. 1942- 83
McCann, Edson
  See del Rey, Lester
  and Pohl, Frederik
McCann, Gerald 1916- 41
McCann, Helen 1948- 75
McCannon, Dindga 41
McCants, William D. 1961- 82
McCarter, Neely Dixon 1929- 47
McCarthy, Agnes 1933- 4
McCarthy, Colin (John) 1951- 77
McCarthy, Mary 1951- 203
McCarthy, Meghan 199
  Earlier sketch in SATA 168
McCarthy, Ralph F. 1950- 139
McCarthy-Tucker, Sherri N. 1958- 83
McCarty, Peter 1966- 182
McCarty, Rega Kramer 1904-1986 10
McCaslin, Nellie 1914-2005 12
McCaughrean, Geraldine 1951- 173
  Earlier sketches in SATA 87, 139
  See also CLR 38
McCaughren, Tom 1936- 75
McCauley, Adam 1965- 209
  Earlier sketch in SATA 128
McCay, (Zenas) Winsor 1869-1934 134
  Earlier sketch in SATA 41
McClafferty, Carla Killough 1958- 137
McClary, Jane Stevenson 1919-1990
  Obituary 64
McCleery, Patsy R. 1925- 133
  Earlier sketch in SATA 88
McClelland, Susan 214
McClements, George 196
McClintock, Barbara 1955- 213
  Earlier sketches in SATA 57, 95, 146
McClintock, Marshall 1906-1967 3
McClintock, May Garelick
  See Garelick, May
McClintock, Mike
  See McClintock, Marshall
McClintock, Norah 178
McClintock, Theodore 1902-1971 14

McClinton, Leon 1933- 11
McCloskey, Kevin 1951- 79
McCloskey, (John) Robert 1914-2003 100
  Obituary 146
  Earlier sketches in SATA 2, 39
  See also CLR 7
McCloy, James F(loyd) 1941- 59
McClung, Robert M(arshall) 1916- 135
  Earlier sketches in SATA 2, 68
  See also CLR 11
  See also SAAS 15
McClure, Gillian Mary 1948- 31
McClure, Nikki 218
McColley, Kevin 1961- 80
  See also SAAS 23
McConduit, Denise Walter 1950- 89
McConnell, James Douglas Rutherford
  1915-1988 40
  Obituary 56
McCord, Anne 1942- 41
McCord, David (Thompson Watson)
  1897-1997 18
  Obituary 96
  See also CLR 9
McCord, Jean 1924- 34
McCord, Pat Mauser
  See McCord, Patricia
McCord, Patricia 1943- 159
  Earlier sketch in SATA 37
McCord, Patricia Sue Rhoads Mauser
  See McCord, Patricia
McCormack, Caren McNelly 217
McCormick, Brooks
  See Adams, William Taylor
McCormick, Dell J. 1892-1949 19
McCormick, (George) Donald (King)
  1911-1998 14
McCormick, Edith (Joan) 1934- 30
McCormick, Kimberly A. 1960- 153
McCormick, Patricia 1956- 181
  Earlier sketch in SATA 128
McCourt, Edward (Alexander) 1907-1972
  Obituary 28
McCourt, Lisa 1964- 214
  Earlier sketches in SATA 117, 159
McCourt, Malachy 1931- 126
McCoy, Glenn 1965- 212
McCoy, Iola Fuller 3
McCoy, J(oseph) J(erome) 1917- 8
McCoy, Karen Kawamoto 1953- 82
McCoy, Lois (Rich) 1941- 38
McCrady, Lady 1951- 16
McCrea, James (Craig, Jr.) 1920- 3
McCrea, Ruth (Pirman) 1921- 3
McCreigh, James
  See Pohl, Frederik
McCrumb, Sharyn 1948- 109
McCue, Lisa 1959- 212
  Earlier sketches in SATA 65, 177
McCue, Lisa Emiline
  See McCue, Lisa
McCullen, Andrew
  See Arthur, Robert, (Jr.)
McCullers, Carson 1917-1967 27
McCullers, Lula Carson Smith
  See McCullers, Carson
McCulloch, Derek (Ivor Breashur) 1897-1967
  Obituary 29
McCulloch, John Tyler
  See Burroughs, Edgar Rice
McCulloch, Sarah
  See Ure, Jean
McCullough, David 1933- 62
McCullough, David Gaub
  See McCullough, David
McCullough, Frances Monson 1938- 8
McCullough, Sharon Pierce 1943- 131
McCully, Emily Arnold
  See Arnold, Emily
McCune, Dan
  See Haas, Dorothy F.

McCunn, Ruthanne Lum 1946- 63
McCurdy, Michael (Charles) 1942- 147
  Earlier sketches in SATA 13, 82
McCusker, Paul 1958- 220
McCutcheon, Elsie (Mary Jackson) 1937- ... 60
McCutcheon, John 1952- 97
McDaniel, Becky Bring 1953- 61
McDaniel, Lurlene 1944- 218
  Earlier sketches in SATA 71, 146
McDaniels, Pellom III 1968- 121
McDaniels, Preston 1952- 192
McDearmon, Kay 20
McDermott, Beverly Brodsky 1941- 11
McDermott, Eleni 156
McDermott, Gerald (Edward) 1941- 163
  Earlier sketches in SATA 16, 74
  See also CLR 9
McDermott, Michael 1962- 76
McDevitt, Jack 1935- 155
  Earlier sketch in SATA 94
McDevitt, John Charles
  See McDevitt, Jack
McDole, Carol
  See Farley, Carol (J.)
McDonald, Candice Hartsough 1982- 225
McDonald, Collin 1943- 79
McDonald, Gerald D(oan) 1905-1970 3
McDonald, Jamie
  See Heide, Florence Parry
McDonald, Janet 1953-2007 204
  Earlier sketch in SATA 148
McDonald, Jill (Masefield) 1927-1982 13
  Obituary 29
McDonald, Joyce 1946- 164
  Earlier sketch in SATA 101
McDonald, Lucile Saunders 1898-1992 10
McDonald, Mary Ann 1956- 84
McDonald, Megan 1958- 202
  Autobiography Feature 151
  Earlier sketches in SATA 67, 99, 148, 151
  See also CLR 94
McDonald, Meme 1954- 112
McDonald, Mercedes 1956- 169
  Earlier sketch in SATA 97
McDonald, Rae A. 1952- 201
McDonell, Chris 1960- 138
McDonnell, Christine 1949- 225
  Earlier sketches in SATA 34, 115
McDonnell, Flora (Mary) 1963- 146
  Earlier sketch in SATA 90
McDonnell, Kathleen 1947- 186
McDonnell, Lois Eddy 1914-2001 10
McDonnell, Patrick 1956- 221
  Earlier sketch in SATA 179
McDonough, Yona Zeldis 1957- 73
McDowell, Marilyn Taylor 217
McElligott, Matt 1968- 196
  Earlier sketch in SATA 135
McElligott, Matthew
  See McElligott, Matt
McElmeel, Sharron L. 1942- 128
McElmurry, Jill 198
  Earlier sketch in SATA 159
McElrath, William N. 1932- 65
McElrath-Eslick, Lori 1960- 204
  Earlier sketch in SATA 96
McEntee, Dorothy (Layng) 1902- 37
McEvoy, Anne 214
McEwen, Katherine 183
McEwen, Robert (Lindley) 1926-1980
  Obituary 23
McFadden, Kevin Christopher
  See Pike, Christopher
McFall, Christie 1918- 12
McFall, Gardner 1952- 183
McFarlan, Donald M(aitland) 1915- 59
McFarland, Henry "Hammer"
  See McFarland, Henry O.
McFarland, Henry O. 1934- 143
McFarland, Kenton D(ean) 1920- 11

McFarland, Martha
    See Smith-Ankrom, M. E.
McFarlane, Leslie 1902-1977 100
    Earlier sketches in SATA *31, 1, 65, 67*
    See also CLR *118*
McFarlane, Leslie Charles
    See McFarlane, Leslie
McFarlane, Peter 1940- 95
McFarlane, Peter William
    See McFarlane, Peter
McFarlane, Sheryl P. 1954- 86
McFarlane, Todd 1961- 117
McGaw, Jessie Brewer 1913-1997 10
McGee, Barbara 1943- 6
McGee, Marni 163
McGhee, Alison 1960- 196
McGhee, Alison R.
    See McGhee, Alison
McGhee, Holly M.
    See Durand, Hallie
McGiffin, (Lewis) Lee (Shaffer) 1908-1978 ... 1
McGill, Alice 159
McGill, Marci
    See Balterman, Marcia Ridlon
McGill, Marci Ridlon
    See Balterman, Marcia Ridlon
McGill, Ormond 1913- 92
McGinley, Jerry 1948- 116
McGinley, Phyllis 1905-1978 44
    Obituary 24
    Earlier sketch in SATA *2*
McGinnis, Lila S(prague) 1924- 44
McGinty, Alice B. 1963- 202
    Earlier sketch in SATA *134*
McGivern, Justin 1985- 129
McGivern, Maureen Daly
    See Daly, Maureen
McGivern, Maureen Patricia Daly
    See Daly, Maureen
McGough, Elizabeth (Hemmes) 1934- 33
McGovern, Ann 1930- 132
    Earlier sketches in SATA *8, 69, 70*
    See also CLR *50*
    See also SAAS *17*
McGowen, Thomas E. 1927- 109
    Earlier sketch in SATA *2*
McGowen, Tom
    See McGowen, Thomas E.
McGrady, Mike 1933- 6
McGrath, Barbara Barbieri 1953- 169
    Earlier sketch in SATA *108*
McGrath, Robin 1949- 121
McGrath, Thomas (Matthew) 1916-1990 41
    Obituary 66
McGraw, Eloise Jarvis 1915-2000 67
    Obituary 123
    Earlier sketch in SATA *1*
    See also SAAS *6*
McGraw, William Corbin 1916-1999 3
McGreal, Elizabeth
    See Yates, Elizabeth
McGregor, Barbara 1959- 82
McGregor, Craig 1933- 8
McGregor, Iona 1929- 25
McGrory, Anik 193
McGuffey, Alexander Hamilton 1816-1896 . 60
McGuigan, Mary Ann 1949- 106
McGuire, Edna 1899- 13
McGuire, Leslie (Sarah) 1945- 94
    Brief entry 45
    Earlier sketch in SATA *52*
McGuire, Robert 187
McGuirk, Leslie (A.) 1960- 152
McGurk, Slater
    See Roth, Arthur J(oseph)
McHargue, Georgess 1941- 77
    Earlier sketch in SATA *4*
    See also CLR *2*
    See also SAAS *5*
McHenry, E.B. 1963(?)- 193

McHugh, (Berit) Elisabet 1941- 55
    Brief entry 44
McIlvaine, Jane
    See McClary, Jane Stevenson
McIlwraith, Maureen Mollie Hunter
    See Hunter, Mollie
McInerney, Judith W(hitelock) 1945- 49
    Brief entry 46
McInerny, Ralph 1929-2010 93
McInerny, Ralph Matthew
    See McInerny, Ralph
McKaughan, Larry (Scott) 1941- 75
McKay, Donald 1895- 45
McKay, Hilary 1959- 208
    Earlier sketches in SATA *92, 145*
    See also SAAS *23*
McKay, Hilary Jane
    See McKay, Hilary
McKay, Lawrence, Jr. 1948- 114
McKay, Robert W. 1921- 15
McKay, Sharon E. 1954- 165
McKay, Simon
    See Nicole, Christopher (Robin)
McKean, Dave 1963- 197
McKean, David Jeff
    See McKean, Dave
McKeating, Eileen 1957- 81
McKee, David (John) 1935- 158
    Earlier sketches in SATA *70, 107*
    See also CLR *38*
McKee, Tim 1970- 111
McKeever, Marcia
    See Laird, Jean E(louise)
McKellar, Danica 1975- 213
McKelvey, Carole A. 1942- 78
McKelvy, Charles 1950- 124
McKendrick, Melveena (Christine) 1941- 55
McKendry, Joe 1972- 170
McKenna, Colleen O'Shaughnessy 1948- .. 136
    Earlier sketch in SATA *76*
McKenzie, Dorothy Clayton 1910-1981
    Obituary 28
McKenzie, Ellen Kindt 1928- 80
McKernan, Victoria 1957- 171
McKie, Robin 112
McKillip, Patricia A. 1948- 174
    Earlier sketches in SATA *30, 80, 126*
McKillip, Patricia Anne
    See McKillip, Patricia A.
McKim, Audrey Margaret 1909-1999 47
McKimmie, Chris 194
McKinley, Jennifer Carolyn Robin
    See McKinley, Robin
McKinley, Robin 1952- 195
    Brief entry 32
    Earlier sketches in SATA *50, 89, 130*
    See also CLR *127*
McKinney, Barbara Shaw 1951- 116
McKinney, Nadine 1938- 91
McKinty, Adrian 186
McKissack, Fredrick L. 1939- 162
    Brief entry 53
    Earlier sketches in SATA *73, 117*
    See also CLR *55*
McKissack, Fredrick Lemuel
    See McKissack, Fredrick L.
McKissack, Patricia C. 1944- 195
    Earlier sketches in SATA *51, 73, 117, 162*
    See also CLR *129*
McKissack, Patricia L'Ann Carwell
    See McKissack, Patricia C.
McKissack and McKissack
    See McKissack, Fredrick L.
    and McKissack, Patricia C.
McKown, Robin (?)-1976 6
McKy, Katie 1956- 184
McLaren, Chesley 213
McLaren, Clemence 1938- 158
    Earlier sketch in SATA *105*
McLaughlin, Frank 1934- 73
McLaughlin, Lauren 209

McLaurin, Anne 1953- 27
McLean, Andrew 1946- 172
    Earlier sketch in SATA *113*
McLean, J. Sloan
    See Gillette, Virginia M(ary)
    and Wunsch, Josephine (McLean)
McLean, Jacqueline
    See Kolosov, Jacqueline
McLean, Janet 1946- 113
McLean, Kathryn (Anderson) 1909-1966 9
McLean, Virginia Overton 1946- 90
McLean-Carr, Carol 1948- 122
McLeish, Kenneth 1940-1997 35
McLenighan, Valjean 1947- 46
    Brief entry 40
McLennan, Connie 171
McLennan, Will
    See Wisler, G(ary) Clifton
McLeod, Bob 1951- 173
McLeod, Chum 1955- 95
McLeod, Emilie Warren 1926-1982 23
    Obituary 31
McLeod, Kirsty
    See Hudson, (Margaret) Kirsty
McLeod, Margaret Vail
    See Holloway, Teresa (Bragunier)
McLerran, Alice 1933- 137
    Earlier sketch in SATA *68*
McLimans, David 1949- 182
McLoughlin, John C. 1949- 47
McMahon, Bob 1956- 208
McManus, Patrick F. 1933- 46
McManus, Patrick Francis
    See McManus, Patrick F.
McMeekin, Clark
    See McMeekin, Isabel McLennan
McMeekin, Isabel McLennan 1895-1973 3
McMenemy, Sarah 1965- 156
McMillan, Bruce 1947- 192
    Earlier sketches in SATA *22, 70, 129*
    See also CLR *47*
McMillan, Naomi
    See Grimes, Nikki
McMorey, James L.
    See Moyer, Terry J.
McMorrow, Annalisa 1969- 104
McMullan, Jim 1934- 150
    Earlier sketch in SATA *87*
McMullan, K. H.
    See McMullan, Kate
McMullan, Kate 1947- 189
    Brief entry 48
    Earlier sketches in SATA *52, 87, 132*
McMullan, Kate Hall
    See McMullan, Kate
McMullan, Margaret 1960- 203
McMurtrey, Martin A(loysias) 1921- 21
McNabb, Linda 1963- 147
McNair, Kate 3
McNair, Sylvia 1924-2002 74
McNamara, Margaret C(raig) 1915-1981
    Obituary 24
McNaught, Harry 32
McNaughton, Colin 1951- 211
    Earlier sketches in SATA *39, 92, 134*
    See also CLR *54*
McNaughton, Janet 1953- 162
    Earlier sketch in SATA *110*
McNeal, Laura 194
McNeal, Tom 194
McNeely, Jeannette 1918- 25
McNeer, May (Yonge) 1902-1994 81
    Earlier sketch in SATA *1*
McNeese, Tim 1953- 139
McNeill, Janet
    See Alexander, Janet
McNicholas, Shelagh 191
McNickle, D'Arcy 1904-1977
    Obituary 22
McNickle, William D'Arcy
    See McNickle, D'Arcy

McNicoll, Sylvia (Marilyn) 1954- *113*
See also CLR 99
McNulty, Faith 1918-2005 .... *168*
Earlier sketches in SATA *12, 84, 139*
McPhail, David 1940- *219*
Brief entry *32*
Earlier sketches in SATA *47, 81, 140, 183*
McPhail, David M.
See McPhail, David
McPhail, David Michael
See McPhail, David
McPhee, Norma H. 1928- *95*
McPhee, Peter 1957- *214*
McPhee, Richard B(yron) 1934- *41*
McPherson, James M. 1936- *141*
Earlier sketch in SATA *16*
McPherson, James Munro
See McPherson, James M.
McQueen, Lucinda 1950- *58*
Brief entry *48*
McQueen, Mildred Hark 1908-1978 .... *12*
McQuillan, Mary *200*
McRae, Russell (William) 1934- *63*
McShean, Gordon 1936- *41*
Mc Swigan, Marie 1907-1962 .... *24*
McTavish, Sandy
See Eyerly, Jeannette
McVeity, Jen *148*
McVey, Vicki 1946- *80*
McVicker, Charles (Taggart) 1930- *39*
McVicker, Chuck
See McVicker, Charles (Taggart)
McVoy, Terra Elan *220*
McWhirter, A(lan) Ross 1925-1975 .... *37*
Obituary *31*
McWhirter, Norris (Dewar) 1925-2004 .... *37*
McWilliam, Howard 1977- *219*
McWilliams, Karen 1943- *65*
Mdurvwa, Hajara E. 1962- *92*
Meacham, Margaret 1952- *203*
Earlier sketch in SATA *95*
Meachum, Virginia 1918- *133*
Earlier sketch in SATA *87*
Mead, Alice 1952- *146*
Earlier sketch in SATA *94*
Mead, Margaret 1901-1978
Obituary *20*
Mead, Russell (M., Jr.) 1935- *10*
Mead, Stella (?)-1981
Obituary *27*
Meade, Elizabeth Thomasina 1854(?)-1914(?)
See CLR *163*
Meade, Ellen
See Roddick, Ellen
Meade, Holly *207*
Meade, L. T.
See Meade, Elizabeth Thomasina
Meade, Marion 1934- *127*
Earlier sketch in SATA *23*
Meader, Stephen W(arren) 1892-1977 .... *1*
Meadmore, Susan
See Sallis, Susan (Diana)
Meadow, Charles T(roub) 1929- *23*
Meadowcroft, Enid LaMonte
See Wright, Enid Meadowcroft (LaMonte)
Meadows, Daisy
See Chapman, Linda
Meadows, Graham (W.) 1934- *161*
Meadows, Michelle *202*
Meaker, M. J.
See Meaker, Marijane
Meaker, Marijane 1927- *160*
Autobiography Feature *111*
Earlier sketches in SATA *20, 61, 99*
See also CLR *29*
See also SAAS *1*
Meaker, Marijane Agnes
See Meaker, Marijane
Means, Florence Crannell 1891-1980 .... *1*
Obituary *25*
See also CLR *56*

Mearian, Judy Frank 1936- *49*
Mebus, Scott 1974- *216*
Mecca, Judy Truesdell 1955- *127*
Mechling, Lauren 1978(?)- *194*
Mechling, Lauren 1978(?)- *194*
Mechner, Jordan 1964- *205*
Medary, Marjorie 1890-1980 .... *14*
Meddaugh, Susan 1944- *176*
Earlier sketches in SATA *29, 84, 125*
Medearis, Angela Shelf 1956- *123*
Earlier sketch in SATA *72*
Medearis, Mary 1915- *5*
Medina, Jane 1953- *167*
Earlier sketch in SATA *122*
Medina, Meg 1963- *212*
Medina, Nico 1982- *193*
Medlicott, Mary 1946- *88*
Mee, Charles L., Jr. 1938- *72*
Earlier sketch in SATA *8*
Meehan, Kierin *218*
Meehl, Brian *204*
Meek, Jacklyn O'Hanlon 1933- *51*
Brief entry *34*
Meek, S(terner St.) P(aul) 1894-1972
Obituary *28*
Meeker, Clare Hodgson 1952- *96*
Meeker, Oden 1919(?)-1976 .... *14*
Meeker, Richard
See Brown, Fornan
Meeks, Esther MacBain *1*
Meggs, Libby Phillips 1943- *130*
Mehdevi, Alexander (Sinclair) 1947- *7*
Mehdevi, Anne (Marie) Sinclair 1947- *8*
Meidell, Sherry 1951- *73*
Meier, Minta 1906- *55*
Meighan, Donald Charles 1929- *30*
Meigs, Cornelia Lynde 1884-1973 .... *6*
See also CLR *55*
Meilach, Dona Z(weigoron) 1926- *34*
Meilman, Philip W(arren) 1951- *79*
Meinstereifel, Ronald L. 1960- *134*
Meisel, Paul *224*
Earlier sketch in SATA *184*
Meister, Cari *204*
Melanson, Luc *198*
Melcher, Daniel 1912-1985
Obituary *43*
Melcher, Frederic Gershom 1879-1963
Obituary *22*
Melcher, Marguerite Fellows 1879-1969 ...... *10*
Meldrum, Christina *206*
Melendez, Francisco 1964- *72*
Melhuish, Eva *199*
Melin, Grace Hathaway 1892-1973 .... *10*
Mellersh, H(arold) E(dward) L(eslie)
1897- *10*
Melling, David *186*
Melmed, Laura Krauss *212*
Melmoth, Sebastian
See Wilde, Oscar
Melnikoff, Pamela (Rita) *97*
Meltzer, Amy 1968- *202*
Meltzer, Milton 1915-2009 .... *201*
Autobiography Feature *124*
Earlier sketches in SATA *1, 50, 80, 128*
See also CLR *13*
See also SAAS *1*
Melville, Anne
See Potter, Margaret
Melville, Herman 1819-1891 .... *59*
Melwood, Mary
See Lewis, E. M.
Melzack, Ronald 1929- *5*
Memling, Carl 1918-1969 .... *6*
Menchin, Scott *188*
Mendel, Jo
See Bond, Gladys Baker
and Gilbertson, Mildred Geiger
Mendelson, Steven T. 1958-1995 .... *86*
Mendelson-Stevens, Serita Deborah
See Stevens, Serita

Mendes, Valerie 1939- *157*
Mendez, Raymond A. 1947- *66*
Mendez, Simon 1975- *215*
Mendonca, Susan
See Smith, Susan Vernon
Mendoza, George 1934- *41*
Brief entry *39*
See also SAAS *7*
Menendez, Shirley (C.) 1937- *146*
Meng, Cece *194*
Meng, Heinz (Karl) 1924- *13*
Mennen, Ingrid 1954- *85*
Menotti, Gian Carlo 1911-2007 .... *29*
Obituary *180*
Menuhin, Sir Yehudi 1916-1999 .... *40*
Obituary *113*
Menville, Douglas 1935- *64*
Menzel, Barbara Jean 1946- *63*
Menzel, Peter 1948- *207*
Mercati, Cynthia *164*
Mercati, Cynthia J.
See Mercati, Cynthia
Mercer, Charles (Edward) 1917-1988 .... *16*
Obituary *61*
Mercer, Jessie *21*
Mercer, Sienna *192*
Meredith, Arnold
See Hopkins, (Hector) Kenneth
Meredith, David William
See Miers, Earl Schenck
Meringoff, Laurene Krasny
See Brown, Laurene Krasny
Meriwether, Louise 1923- *52*
Brief entry *31*
Merlin, Arthur
See Blish, James
Merlin, Christina
See Heaven, Constance (Christina)
Merrell, Billy 1982- *222*
Merriam, Eve 1916-1992 .... *73*
Earlier sketches in SATA *3, 40*
See also CLR *14*
Merrill, Jane 1946- *42*
Merrill, Jane Merrill
See Merrill, Jane
Merrill, Jean (Fairbanks) 1923- *82*
Earlier sketch in SATA *1*
See also CLR *52*
Merrill, Phil
See Merrill, Jane
Merriman, Alex
See Silverberg, Robert
Merriman, Rachel 1971- *149*
Earlier sketch in SATA *98*
Merrit, Elizabeth
See Goudge, Eileen
Merski, Patricia K.
See Merski, P.K.
Merski, P.K. *172*
Mertz, Barbara
See Peters, Elizabeth
Mertz, Barbara Gross
See Peters, Elizabeth
Merveille, David *200*
Merz, Jennifer J. *196*
Meschel, Susan V. 1936- *83*
Meserve, Jessica *211*
Messenger, Charles (Rynd Milles) 1942- *59*
Messick, Dale 1906-2005 .... *64*
Brief entry *48*
Messier, Claire 1956- *103*
Messieres, Nicole de
See de Messieres, Nicole
Messinger, Carla *198*
Messmer, Otto 1892(?)-1983 .... *37*
Messner, Kate *224*
Mesta, Gabriel
See Moesta, Rebecca
Metaxas, Eric 1963- *211*
Metcalf, Doris H(unter) *91*

Metcalf, Suzanne
  See Baum, L. Frank
Metos, Thomas H(arry) 1932- 37
Metter, Bert(ram Milton) 1927- 56
Metzenthen, David 1958- 167
  Earlier sketch in SATA *106*
Meunier, Brian 1954- 195
Meyer, Barbara 1939- 77
Meyer, Carolyn 1935- 142
  Autobiography Feature 142
  Earlier sketches in SATA *9, 70, 118*
  See also SAAS *9*
Meyer, Carolyn Mae
  See Meyer, Carolyn
Meyer, Edith Patterson 1895-1993 5
Meyer, F(ranklyn) E(dward) 1932- 9
Meyer, Jean Shepherd 11
Meyer, Jerome Sydney 1895-1975 3
  Obituary 25
Meyer, June
  See Jordan, June
Meyer, Kerstin 1966- 190
Meyer, L.A. 1942- 221
  Earlier sketches in SATA *12, 144*
Meyer, Louis A.
  See Meyer, L.A.
Meyer, Renate 1930- 6
Meyer, Stephenie 1973- 193
  See also CLR *142*
Meyer, Susan E. 1940- 64
Meyerhoff, Jenny 1972- 208
Meyers, Susan 1942- 164
  Earlier sketches in SATA *19, 108*
Meynell, Laurence Walter 1899-1989
  Obituary 61
Meynier, Yvonne (Pollet) 1908- 14
Mezey, Robert 1935- 33
Micale, Albert 1913- 22
Michael, James
  See Scagnetti, Jack
Michael, Jan 1947- 216
Michael, Livi 1960- 172
Michael, Manfred
  See Winterfeld, Henry
Michael, Olivia
  See Michael, Livi
Michaelis, Antonia 1979- 215
Michaels, Barbara
  See Peters, Elizabeth
Michaels, Jamie 195
Michaels, Joanne Louise
  See Teitelbaum, Michael
Michaels, Kristin
  See Williams, Jeanne
Michaels, Molly
  See Untermeyer, Louis
Michaels, Neal
  See Teitelbaum, Michael
Michaels, Rune 194
Michaels, Ski
  See Pellowski, Michael (Joseph)
Michaels, Steve 1955- 71
Michaels, William M. 1917- 77
Michalak, Jamie 1973- 217
Michel, Anna 1943- 49
  Brief entry 40
Michel, Francois 1948- 82
Michelin, Linda 183
Michelson, Richard 198
  Earlier sketch in SATA *173*
Micich, Paul 74
Mickelson, Scott 1963- 213
Micklish, Rita 1931- 12
Micklos, John, Jr. 1956- 173
  Earlier sketch in SATA *129*
Micklos J., John, Jr. 1956-
  See Micklos, John, Jr.
Micucci, Charles (Patrick, Jr.) 1959- 144
  Earlier sketch in SATA *82*
Middleton, Haydn 1955- 152
  Earlier sketch in SATA *85*

Miers, Earl Schenck 1910-1972 .... *1*
  Obituary 26
Migdale, Lawrence 1951- 89
Miglio, Paige 1966- 201
Mikaelsen, Ben 1958- 173
  Earlier sketches in SATA *73, 107*
Mikaelsen, Benjamin John
  See Mikaelsen, Ben
Miklowitz, Gloria D. 1927- 129
  Earlier sketches in SATA *4, 68*
  See also SAAS *17*
Mikolaycak, Charles 1937-1993 78
  Obituary 75
  Earlier sketch in SATA *9*
  See also SAAS *4*
Mild, Warren (Paul) 1922- 41
Milelli, Pascal 1965- 135
Miles, Betty 1928- 78
  Earlier sketch in SATA *8*
  See also SAAS *9*
Miles, Miska
  See Martin, Patricia Miles
Miles, (Mary) Patricia 1930- 29
Miles, Patricia A.
  See Martin, Patricia Miles
Miles, Victoria 1966- 188
Milgrim, David 223
  Earlier sketches in SATA *158, 187*
Milgrom, Harry 1912-1978 25
Milhous, Katherine 1894-1977 15
Milich, Zoran 174
Milios, Rita 1949- 79
Militant
  See Sandburg, Carl
Millais, Raoul 1901- 77
Millar, Barbara F. 1924- 12
Millar, Margaret (Ellis Sturm) 1915-1994 61
  Obituary 79
Millard, Glenda 203
Millard, Kerry 204
Millbank, Captain H. R.
  See Ellis, Edward S.
Millen, C(ynthia) M. 1955- *114*
Miller, Albert G(riffith) 1905-1982 12
  Obituary 31
Miller, Alice Ann 1958- 150
Miller, Alice P(atricia McCarthy) 22
Miller, Allan 1978- 216
Miller, Christopher 1976- 215
Miller, Debbie 1951- 160
  Earlier sketch in SATA *103*
Miller, Debbie S.
  See Miller, Debbie
Miller, Deborah Uchill 1944- 61
Miller, Don 1923- 15
Miller, Doris R.
  See Mosesson, Gloria R(ubin)
Miller, Eddie
  See Miller, Edward
Miller, Edna Anita 1920- 29
Miller, Edward 1905-1974 8
Miller, Edward 1964- 218
  Earlier sketch in SATA *183*
Miller, Elizabeth 1933- 41
Miller, Ellanita 1957- 87
Miller, Eugene 1925- 33
Miller, Frances A. 1937- 52
  Brief entry 46
Miller, Heather Lynn 1971- 214
Miller, Helen M(arkley) -1984 5
Miller, Helen Topping 1884-1960
  Obituary 29
Miller, Jane (Judith) 1925-1989 15
Miller, Jewel 1956- 73
Miller, John
  See Samachson, Joseph
Miller, Judi 117
Miller, Karen 1949- 210
Miller, Karen Hokanson
  See Miller, Karen
Miller, Kate 1948- 193

Miller, Kirsten 1973- 185
Miller, Louise (Rolfe) 1940- 76
Miller, M. L. 85
Miller, Madge 1918- 63
Miller, Margaret J.
  See Dale, Margaret J(essy) Miller
Miller, Marilyn (Jean) 1925- 33
Miller, Marvin 65
Miller, Mary
  See Northcott, (William) Cecil
Miller, Mary Beth 1942- 9
Miller, Mary Beth 1964- 185
Miller, Maryann 1943- 73
Miller, Natalie 1917-1976 35
Miller, Pat 1951- 214
Miller, Robert H. 1944- 91
Miller, Ron 1947- 185
Miller, Ruth White
  See White, Ruth
Miller, Sandra
  See Miller, Sandy
Miller, Sandra Peden
  See Miller, Sandy
Miller, Sandy 1948- 41
  Brief entry 35
Miller, Sarah 1969- 175
Miller, Virginia
  See Austin, Virginia
Miller, William R. 1959- 116
Miller Brothers
  See Miller, Allan
Milligan, Bryce 1953- 170
Milligan, Spike
  See Milligan, Terence Alan
Milligan, Terence Alan 1918-2002 29
  Obituary 134
  See also CLR *92*
Millington, Ada
  See Deyneka, Anita
Millman, Isaac 1933- 140
Mills, Adam
  See Stanley, George Edward
Mills, Claudia 1954- 191
  Brief entry 41
  Earlier sketches in SATA *44, 89, 145*
Mills, Elaine (Rosemary) 1941- 72
Mills, G. Riley 196
Mills, Joyce C. 1944- 102
Mills, Judith Christine 1956- 130
Mills, Yaroslava Surmach 1925-2008 35
Millspaugh, Ben P. 1936- 77
Millstead, Thomas E. 30
Millward, Gwen 202
Milne, A. A. 1882-1956 100
  See also YABC *1*
  See also CLR *108*
Milne, Alan Alexander
  See Milne, A. A.
Milne, Lorus J. 5
  See also CLR *22*
  See also SAAS *18*
Milne, Margery 5
  See also CLR *22*
  See also SAAS *18*
Milne, Terry
  See Milne, Theresa Ann
Milne, Theresa Ann 1964- 84
Milnes, Irma McDonough 1924- 101
Milonas, Rolf
  See Myller, Rolf
Milone, Karen
  See Dugan, Karen
Milone-Dugan, Karen
  See Dugan, Karen
Milord, Susan 1954- 200
  Earlier sketches in SATA *74, 147*
Milotte, Alfred G(eorge) 1904-1989 11
  Obituary 62
Milstein, Linda 1954- 80
Milton, Ann 134
Milton, Hilary (Herbert) 1920- 23

Milton, John R(onald) 1924- 24
Milton, Joyce 1946- *101*
  Brief entry *41*
  Earlier sketch in SATA *52*
Milusich, Janice *216*
Milverton, Charles A.
  See Penzler, Otto
Milway, Alex 1978- *215*
Milway, Katie Smith 1960- *203*
Minahan, John A. 1956- *92*
Minar, Barbra (Goodyear) 1940- *79*
Minard, Rosemary 1939- *63*
Minarik, Else Holmelund 1920- *127*
  Earlier sketch in SATA *15*
  See also CLR *33*
Miner, Jane Claypool 1933- *103*
  Brief entry *37*
  Earlier sketch in SATA *38*
Miner, Lewis S. 1909-1971 .... *11*
Mines, Jeanette 1948- *61*
Mines, Jeanette Marie
  See Mines, Jeanette
Minier, Nelson
  See Stoutenburg, Adrien (Pearl)
Minnitt, Ronda Jacqueline
  See Armitage, David
Minor, Wendell 1944- *199*
  Earlier sketches in SATA *78, 109, 164*
Minter, Daniel 1961- *176*
Mintonye, Grace *4*
Miranda, Anne 1954- *109*
  Earlier sketch in SATA *71*
Miranda, Inaki 1983(?)- *207*
Mirocha, Paul *192*
Mirsky, Jeannette 1903-1987 .... *8*
  Obituary *51*
Mirsky, Reba Paeff 1902-1966 .... *1*
Misako Rocks! *192*
Misenta, Marisol
  See Innes, Stephanie
Mishica, Clare 1960- *91*
Miskovits, Christine 1939- *10*
Miss Frances
  See Horwich, Frances R(appaport)
Miss Read
  See Saint, Dora Jessie
Mister Rogers
  See Rogers, Fred McFeely
Mitchard, Jacquelyn 1956- *219*
  Earlier sketches in SATA *98, 168*
Mitchell, Adrian 1932-2008 .... *166*
  Obituary *200*
  Earlier sketch in SATA *104*
Mitchell, Allison
  See Griffin, W. E. B.
Mitchell, Betty Jo
  See Mitchell, B.J.
Mitchell, B.J. 1931- *120*
Mitchell, Clyde
  See Ellison, Harlan
  and Silverberg, Robert
Mitchell, Cynthia 1922- *29*
Mitchell, (Sibyl) Elyne (Keith) 1913- *10*
Mitchell, Gladys (Maude Winifred)
  1901-1983 .... *46*
  Obituary *35*
Mitchell, Jay
  See Roberson, Jennifer
Mitchell, Joyce Slayton 1933- *142*
  Brief entry *43*
  Earlier sketch in SATA *46*
Mitchell, K. L.
  See Lamb, Elizabeth Searle
Mitchell, Kathy 1948- *59*
Mitchell, Lori 1961- *128*
Mitchell, Margaree King 1953- *84*
Mitchell, Marianne 1947- *145*
Mitchell, Rhonda *89*
Mitchell, Saundra 1974(?)- *217*
Mitchell, Stephen 1943- *199*

Mitchell, Susan
  See Mitchell, Susan K.
Mitchell, Susan K. 1972- *210*
Mitchell, Todd 1974- *191*
Mitchell, Yvonne 1925-1979
  Obituary *24*
Mitchelson, Mitch
  See Mitchelson, Peter Richard
Mitchelson, Peter Richard 1950- *104*
Mitchison, Naomi (Margaret Haldane)
  1897-1999 .... *24*
  Obituary *112*
Mitchnik, Helen 1901-1982 .... *41*
  Brief entry *35*
Mitchum, Hank
  See Knott, William C(ecil, Jr.)
  and Murray, Stuart A. P.
  and Newton, D(wight) B(ennett)
  and Sherman, Jory (Tecumseh)
Mitgutsch, Ali 1935- *76*
Mitsuhashi, Yoko *45*
  Brief entry *33*
Mitton, Jacqueline 1948- *162*
  Earlier sketches in SATA *66, 115*
Mitton, Simon 1946- *66*
Mitton, Tony 1951- *203*
  Earlier sketches in SATA *104, 149*
Miura, Taro 1968- *181*
Mizner, Elizabeth Howard 1907- *27*
Mizumura, Kazue *18*
Mlynowski, Sarah 1977(?)- *180*
Mobin-Uddin, Asma *216*
  Earlier sketch in SATA *172*
Mobley, Joe A. 1945- *91*
Moche, Dinah (Rachel) L(evine) 1936- *44*
  Brief entry *40*
Mochi, Ugo (A.) 1889-1977 .... *38*
Mochizuki, Ken 1954- *146*
  Earlier sketch in SATA *81*
  See also SAAS *22*
Modarressi, Mitra 1967- *200*
  Earlier sketch in SATA *126*
Modell, Frank B. 1917- *39*
  Brief entry *36*
Modesitt, Jeanne 1953- *217*
  Earlier sketches in SATA *92, 143*
Modesitt, L.E., Jr. 1943- *164*
  Earlier sketch in SATA *91*
Modesitt, Leland Exton, Jr.
  See Modesitt, L.E., Jr.
Modrell, Dolores 1933- *72*
Moe, Barbara 1937- *20*
Moe, Jorgen (Ingebretsen) 1813-1882
  See CLR *104*
Moed-Kass, Pnina *169*
Moerbeek, Kees 1955- *98*
Moeri, Louise 1924- *93*
  Earlier sketch in SATA *24*
  See also SAAS *10*
Moesta, Rebecca 1956- *182*
Moffett, Jami 1952- *84*
Moffett, Mark W. 1957(?)- *203*
Moffett, Martha (Leatherwood) 1934- *8*
Mogensen, Suzanne A(ncher) 1946- *129*
Mohammed, Khadra *197*
Mohanty, Raja *223*
Mohn, Peter B(urnet) 1934- *28*
Mohn, Viola Kohl 1914- *8*
Mohr, Nicholasa 1938- *97*
  Autobiography Feature *113*
  Earlier sketch in SATA *8*
  See also CLR *22*
  See also SAAS *8*
Mok, Esther 1953- *93*
Molan, Christine 1943- *84*
Molarsky, Osmond 1909- *16*
Moldon, Peter L(eonard) 1937- *49*
Mole, John 1941- *103*
  Earlier sketch in SATA *36*
  See also CLR *61*
Molesworth, Mary Louisa 1839-1921 .... *98*

Molin, Charles
  See Mayne, William
Molina, Silvia 1946- *97*
Molk, Laurel 1957- *162*
  Earlier sketch in SATA *92*
Mollel, Tololwa M. 1952- *88*
Molloy, Anne Baker 1907-1999 .... *32*
Molloy, Michael (John) 1940- *162*
Molloy, Paul (George) 1924- *5*
Moloney, James 1954- *202*
  Autobiography Feature *144*
  Earlier sketches in SATA *94, 144*
Molski, Carol *215*
Momaday, N. Scott 1934- *48*
  Brief entry *30*
Momaday, Navarre Scott
  See Momaday, N. Scott
Monaco, Octavia 1963- *169*
Monagle, Bernie 1957- *121*
Moncure, Jane Belk 1926- *23*
Monjo, F(erdinand) N(icholas III)
  1924-1978 .... *16*
  See also CLR *2*
Monk, Isabell 1952- *136*
Monks, Lydia *189*
Monroe, Chris 1962- *219*
Monroe, Christine
  See Monroe, Chris
Monroe, Lyle
  See Heinlein, Robert A.
Monroe, Marion
  See Cox, Marion Monroe
Monroy, Manuel 1970- *196*
Monsell, Helen Albee 1895-1971 .... *24*
Monson-Burton, Marianne 1975- *139*
Montana, Bob 1920-1975
  Obituary *21*
Montanari, Eva 1977- *209*
Montecalvo, Janet *177*
Montenegro, Laura Nyman 1953- *95*
Montero, Gloria 1933- *109*
Montes, Marisa 1951- *144*
Montgomerie, Norah (Mary) 1913- *26*
Montgomery, Constance
  See Cappel, Constance
Montgomery, Elizabeth
  See Julesberg, Elizabeth Rider Montgomery
Montgomery, Elizabeth Rider
  See Julesberg, Elizabeth Rider Montgomery
Montgomery, Hugh (Edward) 1962- *146*
Montgomery, L. M. 1874-1942 .... *100*
  See also YABC *1*
  See also CLR *145*
Montgomery, Lucy Maud
  See Montgomery, L. M.
Montgomery, Michael G. 1952- *208*
Montgomery, Raymond A. (Jr.) 1936- *39*
Montgomery, Rutherford George 1894-1985 . *3*
Montgomery, Sy 1958- *184*
  Autobiography Feature *132*
  Earlier sketches in SATA *114, 132*
Montgomery, Vivian *36*
Monthei, Betty *179*
Montijo, Rhode *179*
Montileaux, Donald F. 1948- *183*
Montpetit, Charles 1958- *101*
Montresor, Beni 1926-2001 .... *38*
  Earlier sketch in SATA *3*
  See also SAAS *4*
Montserrat, Pep *181*
Monty Python
  See Chapman, Graham
  and Cleese, John (Marwood)
  and Gilliam, Terry
  and Idle, Eric
  and Jones, Terence Graham Parry
  and Palin, Michael
Moodie, Craig 1956- *172*
Moodie, Fiona 1952- *133*
Moody, Minerva
  See Alcott, Louisa May

Moody, Ralph Owen 1898-1982 .... *1*
Moon, Carl 1879(?)-1948 .... *25*
Moon, Grace (Purdie) 1877(?)-1947 .... *25*
Moon, Lily
  See Warnes, Tim
Moon, Nicola 1952- *147*
  Earlier sketch in SATA *96*
Moon, Pat 1946- *113*
Moon, Sheila 1910-1991 .... *5*
  Obituary *114*
Moon, Sheila Elizabeth
  See Moon, Sheila
Mooney, Bel 1946- *95*
Mooney, Bill 1936- *122*
Mooney, Elizabeth C(omstock) 1918-1986
  Obituary *48*
Mooney, William
  See Mooney, Bill
Moor, Emily
  See Deming, Richard
Moorcock, Michael 1939- *166*
  Earlier sketch in SATA *93*
Moorcock, Michael John
  See Moorcock, Michael
Moorcock, Michael John
  See Moorcock, Michael
Moore, Anne Carroll 1871-1961 .... *13*
Moore, Cheri
  See Ladd, Cheryl (Jean)
Moore, Clement Clarke 1779-1863 .... *18*
Moore, Cyd 1957- *186*
  Earlier sketches in SATA *83, 133*
Moore, Don W. 1905(?)-1986
  Obituary *48*
Moore, Elaine 1944- *86*
Moore, Eva 1942- *103*
  Earlier sketch in SATA *20*
Moore, Ishbel (Lindsay) 1954- *140*
Moore, Jack (William) 1941- *46*
  Brief entry *32*
Moore, Janet Gaylord 1905-1992 .... *18*
Moore, Jim 1946- *42*
Moore, John Travers 1908- *12*
Moore, Lilian 1909-2004 .... *137*
  Obituary *155*
  Earlier sketch in SATA *52*
  See also CLR *15*
Moore, Liz
  See Moore, M. Elizabeth
Moore, M. Elizabeth 1959- *156*
Moore, Margaret R(umberger) 1903- *12*
Moore, Margie *224*
  Earlier sketch in SATA *176*
Moore, Marianne 1887-1972 .... *20*
Moore, Marianne Craig
  See Moore, Marianne
Moore, Patrick (Alfred Caldwell) 1923- *49*
  Brief entry *39*
  See also SAAS *8*
Moore, Patrick 1959- *184*
Moore, Perry 1971-2011 .... *193*
Moore, Peter 1963- *175*
Moore, Peter G.
  See Moore, Peter
Moore, Raina 1970- *212*
Moore, Ray (S.) 1905(?)-1984
  Obituary *37*
Moore, Regina
  See Dunne, Mary Collins
Moore, Rosalie (Gertrude) 1910-2001 .... *9*
Moore, Ruth (Ellen) 1908-1989 .... *23*
Moore, Ruth Nulton 1923- *38*
Moore, S(arah) E. *23*
Moore, Sarah Margaret
  See Hodges, Margaret
Moore, Stephanie Perry 1969(?)- *214*
Moore, Tara 1950- *61*
Moore, Yvette 1958- *154*
  Earlier sketches in SATA *69, 70*
Moores, Dick
  See Moores, Richard (Arnold)

Moores, Richard (Arnold) 1909-1986
  Obituary *48*
Mooser, Stephen 1941- *75*
  Earlier sketch in SATA *28*
Mora, Francisco X(avier) 1952- *90*
Mora, Pat 1942- *186*
  Earlier sketches in SATA *92, 134*
  See also CLR *58*
Mora, Patricia
  See Mora, Pat
Morais, Flavio *207*
Morales, Magaly *225*
Morales, Yuyi *180*
  Earlier sketch in SATA *154*
Moran, Tom 1943- *60*
Moranville, Sharelle Byars *196*
  Earlier sketch in SATA *152*
Moray Williams, Ursula 1911-2006 .... *3*
  Obituary *177*
  See also SAAS *9*
Mordecai, Martin *220*
Morden, Simon 1966(?)- *211*
Mordhorst, Heidi 1964- *222*
Mordvinoff, Nicolas 1911-1973 .... *17*
More, Caroline
  See Cone, Molly (Lamken)
  and Strachan, Margaret Pitcairn
Moreau, Jean-Pierre
  See Jarrie, Martin
Moreno, Rene King *190*
Moreton, Andrew Esq.
  See Defoe, Daniel
Morey, Charles
  See Fletcher, Helen Jill
Morey, Walt(er Nelson) 1907-1992 .... *51*
  Obituary *70*
  Earlier sketch in SATA *3*
  See also SAAS *9*
Morgan, Alfred P(owell) 1889-1972 .... *33*
Morgan, Alison (Mary) 1930- *85*
  Earlier sketch in SATA *30*
Morgan, Anne 1954- *121*
Morgan, Christopher 1956- *199*
Morgan, Clay 1950- *198*
Morgan, Douglas
  See Macdonald, James D.
Morgan, Ellen
  See Bumstead, Kathleen Mary
Morgan, Geoffrey 1916- *46*
Morgan, Helen (Gertrude Louise)
  1921-1990 .... *29*
Morgan, Jane
  See Cooper, James Fenimore
  and Franklin, Jane (Morgan)
  and Moren, Sally M(oore)
Morgan, Lenore H. 1908-1976 .... *8*
Morgan, Mary 1957- *213*
  Earlier sketches in SATA *81, 114*
Morgan, McKayla
  See Basile, Gloria Vitanza
Morgan, Michaela
  See Basile, Gloria Vitanza
Morgan, Nicola 1961- *161*
Morgan, Nina 1953- *110*
Morgan, Pierr 1952- *122*
  Earlier sketch in SATA *77*
Morgan, Robin (Evonne) 1941- *80*
Morgan, Roxanne
  See Gentle, Mary
Morgan, Sarah (Nicola) 1959- *68*
Morgan, Shirley
  See Kiepper, Shirley Morgan
Morgan, Stacy T(owle) 1959- *104*
Morgan, Stevie
  See Davies, Nicola
Morgan, Tom 1942- *42*
Morgan, Wendy
  See Staub, Wendy Corsi
Morgan-Vanroyen, Mary
  See Morgan, Mary
Morgenstern, Susie Hoch 1945- *133*

Mori, Hana 1909-1990(?) *88*
Mori, Kyoko 1957- *122*
  Autobiography Feature *126*
  See also CLR *64*
  See also SAAS *26*
Moriarty, Jaclyn 1968- *162*
Moriarty, William J. 1930- *127*
Morice, Dave 1946- *93*
Morin, Isobel V. 1928- *110*
Morine, Hoder
  See Conroy, John Wesley
Morley, Taia *199*
Morley, Wilfred Owen
  See Lowndes, Robert A(ugustine) W(ard)
Morningstar, Mildred (Whaley) 1912-1997 .. *61*
  Obituary *114*
Morozumi, Atsuko *217*
  Earlier sketch in SATA *110*
Morpurgo, Michael 1943- *225*
  Earlier sketches in SATA *93, 143, 184*
  See also CLR *51*
Morrah, Dave
  See Morrah, David Wardlaw, Jr.
Morrah, David Wardlaw, Jr. 1914-1991 .... *10*
Morreale-de la Garza, Phyllis
  See De la Garza, Phyllis
Morressy, John 1930-2006 .... *23*
Morrill, Leslie H(olt) 1934-2003 .... *48*
  Brief entry *33*
  Obituary *148*
  See also SAAS *22*
Morris, Carla *210*
Morris, Carla D.
  See Morris, Carla
Morris, Chris(topher Crosby) 1946- *66*
Morris, Deborah 1956- *91*
Morris, Desmond 1928- *14*
Morris, Desmond John
  See Morris, Desmond
Morris, Don 1954- *83*
Morris, Gerald 1963- *207*
  Earlier sketches in SATA *107, 150*
Morris, Gerald Paul
  See Morris, Gerald
Morris, Gilbert (Leslie) 1929- *104*
Morris, Jackie *202*
  Earlier sketch in SATA *151*
Morris, Janet (Ellen) 1946- *66*
Morris, Jay
  See Tatham, Julie Campbell
Morris, (Margaret) Jean 1924- *98*
Morris, Jeffrey
  See Morris, Jeffrey Brandon
Morris, Jeffrey B.
  See Morris, Jeffrey Brandon
Morris, Jeffrey Brandon 1941- *92*
Morris, Jennifer E. 1969- *179*
Morris, Jill 1936- *165*
  Earlier sketch in SATA *119*
Morris, Juddi *85*
Morris, Judy K. 1936- *61*
Morris, Oradel Nolen *128*
Morris, Richard 1969- *224*
Morris, Robert A(da) 1933- *7*
Morris, William 1913-1994 .... *29*
Morrison, Angela *218*
Morrison, Bill 1935- *66*
  Brief entry *37*
Morrison, Chloe Anthony Wofford
  See Morrison, Toni
Morrison, Dorothy Nafus *29*
Morrison, Frank 1971- *185*
Morrison, Gordon 1944- *183*
  Earlier sketches in SATA *87, 128*
Morrison, Joan 1922- *65*
Morrison, Lillian 1917- *108*
  Earlier sketch in SATA *3*
Morrison, Lucile Phillips 1896- *17*
Morrison, Martha A. 1948- *77*
Morrison, Meighan 1966- *90*
Morrison, P.R. *196*

Morrison, Richard
　See Lowndes, Robert A(ugustine) W(ard)
Morrison, Robert
　See Lowndes, Robert A(ugustine) W(ard)
Morrison, Roberta
　See Webb, Jean Francis (III)
Morrison, Susan Dudley
　See Gold, Susan Dudley
Morrison, Taylor 1971- 187
　Earlier sketches in SATA *95, 159*
Morrison, Toni 1931- 144
　Earlier sketch in SATA *57*
　See also CLR *99*
Morrison, Velma Ford 1909- 21
Morrison, Wilbur Howard 1915- 64
Morrison, William
　See Samachson, Joseph
Morriss, James E(dward) 1932- 8
Morrissey, Dean 183
Morrow, Barbara Olenyik 1952- 167
Morrow, Betty
　See Bacon, Elizabeth
Morrow, Sue Anne 1966- 218
Morse, C. Scott
　See Morse, Scott
Morse, Carol
　See Yeakley, Marjory Hall
Morse, C.S.
　See Morse, Scott
Morse, Dorothy B(ayley) 1906-1979
　Obituary 24
Morse, Flo 1921- 30
Morse, Scott 1973- 200
Morse, Tony 1953- 129
Mort, Vivian
　See Cromie, Alice Hamilton
Mortensen, Denise Dowling 179
Mortensen, Lori 1955- 221
Mortimer, Anne 1958- 206
　Earlier sketch in SATA *116*
Mortimer, Mary H.
　See Coury, Louise Andree
Morton, Alexandra (Hubbard) 1957- 144
Morton, Anthony
　See Arthur, Robert, (Jr.)
Morton, Christine
　See Morton-Shaw, Christine
Morton, Jane 1931- 50
Morton, Joseph C. 1932- 156
Morton, Lee Jack, Jr. 1928- 32
Morton, Miriam 1918(?)-1985 9
　Obituary 46
Morton-Shaw, Christine 1957- 211
Mosatche, Harriet 1949- 122
Mosatche, Harriet S.
　See Mosatche, Harriet
Moscow, Alvin 1925- 3
Mosel, Arlene (Tichy) 1921-1996 7
Moseley, James W(illett) 1931- 139
Moseng, Elisabeth 1967- 90
Moser, Barry 1940- 185
　Earlier sketches in SATA *56, 79, 138*
　See also CLR *49*
　See also SAAS *15*
Moser, Don(ald Bruce) 1932- 31
Moser, Laura 194
Moser, Lisa 192
Moses, Sheila P. 1961- 168
Moses, Will 1956- 178
　Earlier sketch in SATA *120*
Mosesson, Gloria R(ubin) 24
Mosher, Richard 1949- 120
Moskin, Marietta D(unston) 1928- 23
Moskof, Martin Stephen 1930- 27
Mosley, Francis 1957- 57
Moss, Don(ald) 1920- 11
Moss, Elaine (Dora) 1924- 57
　Brief entry 31
Moss, Jeff(rey) 1942-1998 73
　Obituary 106

Moss, Marissa 1959- 216
　Earlier sketches in SATA *71, 104, 163*
　See also CLR *134*
Moss, Miriam 1955- 202
　Earlier sketches in SATA *76, 140*
Moss, Thylias 1954- 108
Moss, Thylias Rebecca Brasier
　See Moss, Thylias
Most, Bernard 1937- 134
　Brief entry 40
　Earlier sketches in SATA *48, 91*
Mosz, Gosia 1972- 194
Mott, Evelyn Clarke 1962- 133
　Earlier sketch in SATA *75*
Motz, Lloyd 1909-2004 20
Mould, Chris 205
Mould, Edwin
　See Whitlock, Ralph
Moulton, Mark Kimball 212
Mouly, Francoise 155
Mountain, Robert
　See Montgomery, Raymond A. (Jr.)
Mountfield, David
　See Grant, Neil
Mourlevat, Jean-Claude 1952- 187
Mourning, Tuesday 206
Moussard, Jacqueline 1924- 24
Mowat, Claire 1933- 123
Mowat, Claire Angel Wheeler
　See Mowat, Claire
Mowat, Farley 1921- 55
　Earlier sketch in SATA *3*
　See also CLR *20*
Mowat, Farley McGill
　See Mowat, Farley
Mowll, Joshua 1970(?)- 188
Mowry, Jess 1960- 131
　Autobiography Feature 131
　Earlier sketch in SATA *109*
　See also CLR *65*
Moxley, Sheila 1966- 96
Moyer, Terry J. 1937- 94
Moyes, Patricia
　See Haszard, Patricia Moyes
Moyler, Alan (Frank Powell) 1926- 36
Mozelle, Shirley 179
Mozley, Charles 1915- 43
　Brief entry 32
Mphahlele, Es'kia 1919-2008 119
　Obituary 198
Mphahlele, Ezekiel
　See Mphahlele, Es'kia
Mphahlele, Zeke
　See Mphahlele, Es'kia
Mr. McGillicuddy
　See Abisch, Roslyn Kroop
Mr. Sniff
　See Abisch, Roslyn Kroop
Mr. Tivil
　See Lorkowski, Thomas V(incent)
Mr. Wizard
　See Herbert, Don
Mraz, David 1947- 219
Mrs. Fairstar
　See Horne, Richard Henry Hengist
Muchamore, Robert 1972- 175
Muchmore, Jo Ann 1937- 103
Mude, O.
　See Gorey, Edward (St. John)
Mudgeon, Apeman
　See Mitchell, Adrian
Mueller, Jorg 1942- 67
　See also CLR *43*
Mueller, Miranda R. 201
Mueller, Virginia 1924- 28
Muggs
　See Watkins, Lois
Muir, Diana
　See Appelbaum, Diana Muir Karter
Muir, Frank (Herbert) 1920-1998 30
Muir, Helen 1937- 65

Muirhead, Margaret 220
Mukerji, Dhan Gopal 1890-1936 40
　See also CLR *10*
Mulcahy, Lucille Burnett 12
Mulford, Philippa G. 1948- 112
　Earlier sketch in SATA *43*
Mulford, Philippa Greene
　See Mulford, Philippa G.
Mulgan, Catherine 1931- 24
Mulila, Vigad G.
　See Maillu, David G(ian)
Mull, Brandon 1974- 190
Mullen, Michael 1937- 122
Muller, Billex
　See Ellis, Edward S.
Muller, Birte 1973- 214
Muller, Jorg
　See Mueller, Jorg
Muller, (Lester) Robin 1953- 86
Mullin, Caryl Cude 1969- 130
Mullins, Edward S(wift) 1922- 10
Mullins, Hilary 1962- 84
Mulock, Dinah Maria
　See Craik, Dinah Maria (Mulock)
Mulvihill, William Patrick 1923- 8
Mumford, Ruth
　See Dallas, Ruth
Mumy, Bill 1954- 112
Mun
　See Leaf, (Wilbur) Munro
Munari, Bruno 1907-1998 15
　See also CLR *9*
Munce, Ruth Hill 1898- 12
Mundy, Simon 1954- 64
Mundy, Simon Andrew James Hainault
　See Mundy, Simon
Munger, Nancy 170
Munowitz, Ken 1935-1977 14
Munoz, Claudio 208
Munoz, William 1949- 92
　Earlier sketch in SATA *42*
Munro, Alice 1931- 29
Munro, Alice Anne
　See Munro, Alice
Munro, Eleanor 1928- 37
Munro, Roxie 1945- 223
　Earlier sketches in SATA *58, 136, 184*
Munsch, Bob
　See Munsch, Robert (Norman)
Munsch, Robert (Norman) 1945- 120
　Brief entry 48
　Earlier sketches in SATA *50, 83*
　See also CLR *19*
Munsinger, Lynn 1951- 221
　Earlier sketches in SATA *33, 94, 177*
Munson, Derek 1970- 139
Munson, R. W.
　See Karl, Jean E(dna)
Munson-Benson, Tunie 1946- 15
Munsterberg, Peggy 1921- 102
Muntean, Michaela 182
Munthe, Nelly 1947- 53
Munves, James (Albert) 1922- 30
Munzer, Martha E. 1899-1999 4
Murawski, Darlyne A. 193
Murch, Mel
　See Manes, Stephen
Murdoch, David H(amilton) 1937- 96
Murdoch, Patricia 1957- 192
Murdock, Catherine Gilbert 185
Murhall, J(acqueline) J(ane) 1964- 143
Murphy, Barbara Beasley 1933- 130
　Earlier sketch in SATA *5*
Murphy, Claire Rudolf 1951- 137
　Earlier sketch in SATA *76*
Murphy, E(mmett) Jefferson 1926- 4
Murphy, Elizabeth Ann Maureen
　See Murphy, Liz
Murphy, Jill 1949- 214
　Earlier sketches in SATA *37, 70, 142*
　See also CLR *39*

Murphy, Jill Frances
  See Murphy, Jill
Murphy, Jim 1947- 224
  Brief entry 32
  Earlier sketches in SATA *37, 77, 124, 185*
  See also CLR *53*
Murphy, Joseph E., Jr. 1930- 65
Murphy, Kelly 1977- 190
  Earlier sketch in SATA *143*
Murphy, Liz 1964- 210
Murphy, Louise 1943- 155
Murphy, Mary 1961- 196
Murphy, Pat
  See Murphy, E(mmett) Jefferson
Murphy, Patricia J. 1963- 132
Murphy, Rita 180
Murphy, Robert (William) 1902-1971 10
Murphy, Shirley Rousseau 1928- 126
  Earlier sketches in SATA *36, 71*
  See also SAAS *18*
Murphy, Stuart J. 1942- 157
  Earlier sketch in SATA *115*
Murphy, Thomas Basil, Jr. 1935- 191
Murphy, Tim
  See Murphy, Jim
Murphy, Tom
  See Murphy, Thomas Basil, Jr.
Murray, John 1923- 39
Murray, Kirsty 1960- 165
  Earlier sketch in SATA *108*
Murray, Marguerite 1917- 63
Murray, Marian 5
Murray, Martine 1965- 125
Murray, (Judith) Michele (Freedman)
  1933-1974 7
Murray, Ossie 1938- 43
Murray, Peter
  See Hautman, Pete
Murrow, Liza Ketchum
  See Ketchum, Liza
Musgrave, Florence 1902-1999 3
Musgrove, Margaret W(ynkoop) 1943- 124
  Earlier sketch in SATA *26*
Musgrove, Marianne 207
Mussey, Virginia Howell
  See Ellison, Virginia H(owell)
Mussey, Virginia T.H.
  See Ellison, Virginia H(owell)
Mussi, Sarah 206
Mutel, Cornelia F. 1947- 74
Muth, Jon J. 206
  Earlier sketch in SATA *165*
Mutz
  See Kuenstler, Morton
Mwangi, Meja 1948- 174
My Brother's Brother
  See Chekhov, Anton
Myers, Anna 220
  Earlier sketch in SATA *160*
Myers, Arthur 1917- 91
  Earlier sketch in SATA *35*
Myers, Bernice 81
  Earlier sketch in SATA *9*
Myers, Caroline Elizabeth Clark
  1887-1980 28
Myers, Christopher 1975- 183
  See also CLR *97*
Myers, Edward 1950- 172
  Earlier sketch in SATA *96*
Myers, Elisabeth P(erkins) 1918- 36
Myers, (Mary) Hortense (Powner)
  1913-1987 10
Myers, Jack 1913-2006 83
  Obituary 178
Myers, Jack Edgar
  See Myers, Jack
Myers, Lou 1915-2005 81
  Obituary 171
Myers, Louis
  See Myers, Lou
Myers, R.E. 1924- 119

Myers, Robert Eugene
  See Myers, R.E.
Myers, Tim 1953- 176
  Earlier sketch in SATA *147*
Myers, Timothy Joseph
  See Myers, Tim
Myers, Walter Dean 1937- 193
  Brief entry 27
  Earlier sketches in SATA *41, 71, 109, 157*
  See also CLR *110*
  See also SAAS *2*
Myers, Walter M.
  See Myers, Walter Dean
Myller, Rolf 1926-2006 27
  Obituary 175
Myra, Harold L(awrence) 1939- 46
  Brief entry 42
Myracle, Lauren 1969- 204
  Earlier sketch in SATA *162*
Myrus, Donald (Richard) 1927- 23
Mysterious Traveler, The
  See Arthur, Robert, (Jr.)

N

Na, An 149
Naaslund, Goorel Kristina 1940- 170
Nadel, Laurie 1948- 74
Naden, Corinne J. 1930- 166
  Earlier sketch in SATA *79*
Nadimi, Suzan 188
Nagda, Ann Whitehead 199
Nagel, Andreas Fischer
  See Fischer-Nagel, Andreas
Nagel, Heiderose Fischer
  See Fischer-Nagel, Heiderose
Nagle, Shane 176
Nahoko, Uehashi
  See Uehashi, Nahoko
Naidoo, Beverley 1943- 180
  Earlier sketches in SATA *63, 135*
  See also CLR *29*
Nails, Jennifer 213
Nakae, Noriko 1940- 59
Nakata, Hiroe 205
Nakatani, Chiyoko 1930-1981 55
  Brief entry 40
  See also CLR *30*
Nally, Susan W. 1947- 90
Namioka, Lensey 1929- 157
  Autobiography Feature 116
  Earlier sketches in SATA *27, 89*
  See also CLR *48*
  See also SAAS *24*
Namovicz, Gene Inyart 1927- 6
Nance, Andrew 210
Nanji, Shenaaz 1954- 204
  Earlier sketch in SATA *131*
Nanogak Agnes 1925- 61
Napier, Mark
  See Laffin, John (Alfred Charles)
Napoli, Donna Jo 1948- 190
  Earlier sketches in SATA *92, 137*
  See also CLR *51*
  See also SAAS *23*
Napp, Daniel 1974- 204
Narahashi, Keiko 1959- 115
  Earlier sketch in SATA *79*
Narayan, R. K. 1906-2001 62
Narayan, Rasipuram Krishnaswami
  See Narayan, R. K.
Nascimbene, Yan 1949- 173
  Earlier sketch in SATA *133*
Nash, Bruce M(itchell) 1947- 34
Nash, Fredric Ogden
  See Nash, Ogden
Nash, Linell
  See Smith, Linell Nash
Nash, Mary (Hughes) 1925- 41

Nash, Ogden 1902-1971 46
  Earlier sketch in SATA *2*
Nash, Renea Denise 1963- 81
Nast, Elsa Ruth
  See Watson, Jane Werner
Nast, Thomas 1840-1902 51
  Brief entry 33
Nastick, Sharon 1954- 41
Natale, Vince 196
Natalini, Sandro 1970- 222
Natarajan, Srividya 187
Nathan, Adele (Gutman) 1900(?)-1986
  Obituary 48
Nathan, Amy 155
  Earlier sketch in SATA *104*
Nathan, Dorothy (Goldeen) (?)-1966 15
Nathan, Robert (Gruntal) 1894-1985 6
  Obituary 43
Nathanson, Laura Walther 1941- 57
Nation, Kaleb 1988- 222
Natti, Lee 1919- 67
  Earlier sketch in SATA *1*
  See also SAAS *3*
Natti, Susanna 1948- 125
  Earlier sketch in SATA *32*
Nau, Thomas 186
Naughtie, Eleanor
  See Updale, Eleanor
Naughton, Bill
  See Naughton, William John (Francis)
Naughton, James Franklin 1957- 85
Naughton, Jim
  See Naughton, James Franklin
Naughton, William John (Francis)
  1910-1992 86
Navarra, John Gabriel 1927- 8
Naylor, Penelope 1941- 10
Naylor, Phyllis 1933-
  See Naylor, Phyllis Reynolds
Naylor, Phyllis Reynolds 1933- 209
  Autobiography Feature 152
  See also CLR *135*
  See also SAAS *10*
Nazarian, Nikki
  See Nichols, Cecilia Fawn
Nazaroff, Alexander I(vanovich) 1898-1981 .. 4
Nazoa, Aquiles 1920-1976 198
Neal, Harry Edward 1906-1993 5
  Obituary 76
Neal, Michael
  See Teitelbaum, Michael
Nearing, Penny 1916- 47
  Brief entry 42
Nebel, Gustave E. 45
  Brief entry 33
Nebel, Mimouca
  See Nebel, Gustave E.
Nee, Kay Bonner 10
Needham, Kate 1962- 95
Needle, Jan 1943- 98
  Earlier sketch in SATA *30*
  See also CLR *43*
  See also SAAS *23*
Needleman, Jacob 1934- 6
Neel, David 1960- 82
Neel, Preston 1959- 93
Neff, Henry H. 1973- 221
Negri, Rocco 1932- 12
Negrin, Fabian 1963- 189
Neidigh, Sherry 1956- 204
Neier, Aryeh 1937- 59
Neigoff, Anne 13
Neigoff, Mike 1920- 13
Neilan, Eujin Kim 1969- 200
Neilson, Frances Fullerton (Jones)
  1910-2001 14
Neimark, Anne E. 1935- 145
  Earlier sketch in SATA *4*
Neimark, Paul G. 1934- 80
  Brief entry 37

Neitzel, Shirley 1941- *134*
  Earlier sketch in SATA 77
Nell
  See Hanna, Nell(ie L.)
Nelscott, Kris
  See Rusch, Kristine Kathryn
Nelson, Blake 1960- *177*
Nelson, Catherine Chadwick 1926- *87*
Nelson, Cordner 1918-2009 .... *54*
  Brief entry *29*
Nelson, Cordner Bruce
  See Nelson, Cordner
Nelson, D.A. 1970- *215*
Nelson, Dawn Ann
  See Nelson, D.A.
Nelson, Drew 1952- *77*
Nelson, Esther L. 1928- *13*
Nelson, Jim A.
  See Stotter, Mike
Nelson, Julie L. 1970- *117*
Nelson, Kadir *213*
  Earlier sketches in SATA *154, 181*
Nelson, Kris
  See Rusch, Kristine Kathryn
Nelson, Lawrence E(rnest) 1928-1977
  Obituary *28*
Nelson, Marilyn 1946- *60*
  Autobiography Feature *180*
Nelson, Mary Carroll 1929- *23*
Nelson, O. Terry 1941- *62*
Nelson, Peter 1953- *73*
Nelson, Peter N.
  See Nelson, Peter
Nelson, R. A. *197*
Nelson, Richard K(ing) 1941- *65*
Nelson, Robin Laura 1971- *141*
Nelson, Roy Paul 1923- *59*
Nelson, S.D. *181*
Nelson, Sharlene (P.) 1933- *96*
Nelson, Suzanne 1976- *184*
Nelson, Ted (W.) 1931- *96*
Nelson, Theresa 1948- *143*
  Autobiography Feature *143*
  Earlier sketch in SATA 79
Nelson, Vaunda Micheaux 1953- *220*
Nemeth, Sally *187*
Neri, G. *197*
Neri, Greg
  See Neri, G.
Neri, Gregory
  See Neri, G.
Nerlove, Miriam 1959- *53*
  Brief entry *49*
Nesbit, E. 1858-1924 .... *100*
  See also YABC *1*
  See also CLR *70*
Nesbit, Edith
  See Nesbit, E.
Nesbit, Troy
  See Folsom, Franklin (Brewster)
Nespojohn, Katherine V(eronica) 1912-1975 . *7*
Ness, Evaline (Michelow) 1911-1986 .... *26*
  Obituary *49*
  Earlier sketch in SATA *1*
  See also CLR *6*
  See also SAAS *1*
Ness, Patrick 1971- *207*
Nestor, Larry 1940- *149*
Nestor, William P(rodromos) 1947- *49*
Nethery, Mary *93*
Neubecker, Robert *214*
  Earlier sketch in SATA *170*
Neuberger, Julia (Babette Sarah) 1950- *142*
  Earlier sketch in SATA 78
Neufeld, John (Arthur) 1938- *131*
  Autobiography Feature *131*
  Earlier sketches in SATA 6, *81*
  See also CLR *52*
  See also SAAS *3*
Neuhaus, David 1958- *83*
Neumeyer, Peter F(lorian) 1929- *13*

Neurath, Marie (Reidemeister) 1898-1986 ..... *1*
Neuschwander, Cindy 1953- *157*
  Earlier sketch in SATA *107*
Neusner, Jacob 1932- *38*
Neville, Charles
  See Bodsworth, (Charles) Fred(erick)
Neville, Emily Cheney 1919- *1*
  See also SAAS 2
Neville, Mary
  See Woodrich, Mary Neville
Nevins, Albert (Francis) J(erome)
  1915-1997 .... *20*
Nevius, Carol 1955- *186*
Newberger, Devra
  See Speregen, Devra Newberger
Newberry, Clare Turlay 1903-1970 .... *1*
  Obituary *26*
Newbery, John 1713-1767 .... *20*
  See also CLR *147*
Newbery, Linda 1952- *184*
  Earlier sketch in SATA *142*
Newbigging, Martha *198*
Newbold, Greg *199*
Newcomb, Ellsworth
  See Kenny, Ellsworth Newcomb
Newcombe, Eugene A. 1923-1990 .... *45*
  Brief entry *33*
Newcombe, Jack
  See Newcombe, Eugene A.
Newcome, Robert 1955- *91*
Newcome, Zita 1959- *88*
Newell, Crosby
  See Bonsall, Crosby Barbara (Newell)
Newell, Edythe W(eatherford) 1910-1989 .... *11*
Newell, Hope Hockenberry 1896-1965 .... *24*
Newfeld, Frank 1928- *26*
Newgarden, Mark 1959- *194*
Newland, Gillian *220*
Newlon, (Frank) Clarke 1905(?)-1982 .... *6*
  Obituary *33*
Newman, Barbara Johansen *191*
Newman, C.J.
  See Newman, Coleman J.
Newman, Coleman J. 1935- *82*
Newman, Daisy 1904-1994 .... *27*
  Obituary *78*
Newman, Gerald 1939- *46*
  Brief entry *42*
Newman, Jerry
  See Newman, Coleman J.
Newman, Leslea 1955- *134*
  Earlier sketches in SATA *71, 128*
Newman, Margaret
  See Potter, Margaret
Newman, Marjorie *146*
Newman, Matthew (Harrison) 1955- *56*
Newman, Nanette 1934- *162*
Newman, Robert (Howard) 1909-1988 .... *87*
  Obituary *60*
  Earlier sketch in SATA 4
Newman, Shirlee P(etkin) *144*
  Earlier sketches in SATA *10, 90*
Newsom, Carol 1948- *92*
  Earlier sketch in SATA *40*
Newsom, Tom 1944- *80*
Newth, Mette 1942- *140*
Newton, David E(dward) 1933- *67*
Newton, James R(obert) 1935- *23*
Newton, Jill 1964- *200*
Newton, Robert 1965- *191*
Newton, Suzanne 1936- *77*
  Earlier sketch in SATA 5
Newton, Vanessa
  See Newton, Vanessa Brantley
Newton, Vanessa Brantley 1962(?)- *206*
Ney, John 1923- *43*
  Brief entry *33*
Nez, John *218*
  Earlier sketch in SATA *155*
Nez, John Abbott
  See Nez, John

Ng, Franklin *82*
Nguyen, Vincent *187*
Nichol, B(arrie) P(hillip) 1944-1988 .... *66*
Nicholas, Louise D.
  See Watkins, Dawn L.
Nicholls, Judith (Ann) 1941- *61*
Nicholls, Sally 1983- *209*
Nichols, Cecilia Fawn 1906-1987 .... *12*
Nichols, Grace 1950- *164*
  Earlier sketch in SATA 98
Nichols, Janet (Louise) 1952- *67*
Nichols, Judy 1947- *124*
Nichols, Leigh
  See Koontz, Dean
Nichols, Michael 1952- *215*
Nichols, Nick
  See Nichols, Michael
Nichols, Paul
  See Hawks, Robert
Nichols, Peter
  See Youd, Samuel
Nichols, (Joanna) Ruth 1948- *15*
  See also CLR *149*
Nichols, Travis *206*
Nicholson, C. R.
  See Nicole, Christopher (Robin)
Nicholson, Christina
  See Nicole, Christopher (Robin)
Nicholson, Joyce Thorpe 1919-2011 .... *35*
Nicholson, Lois P. 1949- *88*
Nicholson, Robin
  See Nicole, Christopher (Robin)
Nicholson, William *180*
Nicholson, William 1872-1949
  See CLR *76*
Nickel, Barbara 1966- *188*
Nickell, Joe 1944- *167*
  Earlier sketch in SATA 73
Nickelsburg, Janet 1893-1983 .... *11*
Nickerson, Betty 1922- *14*
Nickerson, Elizabeth
  See Nickerson, Betty
Nickl, Barbara (Elisabeth) 1939- *56*
Nicklaus, Carol *62*
  Brief entry *33*
Nickle, John *181*
Nickless, Will 1902-1979(?) *66*
Nic Leodhas, Sorche
  See Alger, Leclaire (Gowans)
Nicol, Ann
  See Turnbull, Ann
Nicolas
  See Mordvinoff, Nicolas
Nicolay, Helen 1866-1954
  See YABC *1*
Nicole, Christopher (Robin) 1930- *5*
Nicoll, Helen 1937- *87*
Nicolson, Cynthia Pratt 1949- *141*
Ni Dhuibhne, Eilis 1954- *91*
Niehaus, Paddy Bouma
  See Bouma, Paddy
Nields, Nerissa 1967- *166*
Nielsen, Kay (Rasmus) 1886-1957 .... *16*
  See also CLR *16*
Nielsen, Laura F. 1960- *93*
Nielsen, Laura Farnsworth
  See Nielsen, Laura F.
Nielsen, Nancy J. 1951- *77*
Nielsen, Susin 1964- *195*
Nielsen, Virginia
  See McCall, Virginia Nielsen
Nielsen-Fernlund, Susin
  See Nielsen, Susin
Niemann, Christoph 1970- *191*
Nieuwsma, Milton J(ohn) 1941- *142*
Nightingale, Sandy 1953- *76*
Nikolajeva, Maria 1952- *127*
Nikola-Lisa, W. 1951- *180*
  Earlier sketch in SATA 71
Niland, Deborah 1951- *172*
  Earlier sketch in SATA 27

Niland, Kilmeny 75
Nilsen, Anna 1948- 174
  Earlier sketch in SATA 96
Nilsson, Eleanor 1939- 117
  Earlier sketch in SATA 81
  See also SAAS 23
Nilsson, Per 1954- 159
Nimmo, Jenny 1944- 144
  Earlier sketch in SATA 87
  See also CLR 44
Nishimura, Kae 196
Niven, Larry 1938- 171
  Earlier sketch in SATA 95
Niven, Laurence Van Cott
  See Niven, Larry
Niven, Laurence VanCott
  See Niven, Larry
Nivola, Claire A. 1947- 208
  Earlier sketches in SATA 84, 140
Nix, Garth 1963- 210
  Earlier sketches in SATA 97, 143
  See also CLR 68
Nixon, Hershell Howard 1923- 42
Nixon, Joan Lowery 1927-2003 115
  Obituary 146
  Earlier sketches in SATA 8, 44, 78
  See also CLR 24
  See also SAAS 9
Nixon, K.
  See Nixon, Kathleen Irene (Blundell)
Nixon, Kathleen Irene (Blundell)
  1894-1988(?) 14
  Obituary 59
Nobati, Eugenia 1968- 201
Nobisso, Josephine 1953- 121
  Earlier sketch in SATA 78
Noble, Iris (Davis) 1922-1986 5
  Obituary 49
Noble, Marty 1947- 125
  Earlier sketch in SATA 97
Noble, Trinka Hakes 1944- 197
  Brief entry 37
  Earlier sketch in SATA 123
Nobleman, Marc Tyler 1972- 203
Noda, Takayo 1961- 168
Nodelman, Perry 1942- 101
Nodset, Joan L.
  See Lexau, Joan M.
Noel Hume, Ivor 1927- 65
Noestlinger, Christine
  See Nostlinger, Christine
Noguere, Suzanne 1947- 34
Nolan, Dennis 1945- 166
  Brief entry 34
  Earlier sketches in SATA 42, 92
Nolan, Han 1956- 157
  Earlier sketch in SATA 109
Nolan, Janet 1956- 191
  Earlier sketch in SATA 145
Nolan, Jeannette Covert 1897-1974 2
  Obituary 27
Nolan, Lucy 215
Nolan, Paul T(homas) 1919- 48
Nolan, William F. 1928- 88
  Brief entry 28
Nolan, William Francis
  See Nolan, William F.
Nolen, Jerdine 1953- 157
  Earlier sketch in SATA 105
Noll, Amanda 219
Noll, Sally 1946- 82
Noonan, Brandon 1979- 184
Noonan, Diana 1960- 146
Noonan, Julia 1946- 148
  Earlier sketches in SATA 4, 95
Norac, Carl 1960- 166
Norcross, John
  See Conroy, John Wesley
Nordan, Robert W(arren) 1934-2004 133
Nordhoff, Charles Bernard 1887-1947 23
Nordlicht, Lillian 29

Nordstrom, Ursula 1910-1988 3
  Obituary 57
Nordtvedt, Matilda 1926- 67
Norling, Beth 1969- 149
Norman, Charles 1904-1996 38
  Obituary 92
Norman, Geoffrey 223
Norman, Howard
  See Norman, Howard A.
Norman, Howard A. 1949- 81
Norman, James
  See Schmidt, James Norman
Norman, Jay
  See Arthur, Robert, (Jr.)
Norman, Lilith 1927- 120
  Earlier sketch in SATA 86
Norman, Mary 1931- 36
Norman, Steve
  See Pashko, Stanley
Norment, Lisa 1966- 91
Norris, Gunilla Brodde 1939- 20
North, Andrew
  See Norton, Andre
North, Anthony
  See Koontz, Dean
North, Captain George
  See Stevenson, Robert Louis
North, Captain George
  See Stevenson, Robert Louis
North, Howard
  See Trevor, Elleston
North, Joan 1920- 16
North, Milou
  See Erdrich, Louise
North, Robert
  See Withers, Carl A.
North, Sara
  See Bonham, Barbara Thomas
  and Hager, Jean
North, Sherry 201
North, Sterling 1906-1974 45
  Obituary 26
  Earlier sketch in SATA 1
Northcott, (William) Cecil 1902-1987
  Obituary 55
Northeast, Brenda V(ictoria) 1948- 106
Northmore, Elizabeth Florence 1906-1974 . 122
Norton, Alice Mary
  See Norton, Andre
Norton, Andre 1912-2005 91
  Earlier sketches in SATA 1, 43
  See also CLR 50
Norton, Browning
  See Norton, Frank R. B(rowning)
Norton, Frank R. B(rowning) 1909-1989 10
Norton, Mary 1903-1992 60
  Obituary 72
  Earlier sketch in SATA 18
  See also CLR 140
Nosredna, Trebor
  See Anderson, Bob
Nostlinger, Christine 1936- 162
  Brief entry 37
  Earlier sketch in SATA 64
  See also CLR 12
Nourse, Alan E(dward) 1928-1992 48
  See also CLR 33
Novak, Matt 1962- 204
  Brief entry 52
  Earlier sketches in SATA 60, 104, 165
Novelli, Luca 1947- 61
Novgorodoff, Danica 1982(?)- 215
Nowell, Elizabeth Cameron 12
Noyes, Deborah 1965- 194
  Earlier sketch in SATA 145
Nugent, Cynthia 1954- 205
Nugent, Nicholas 1949- 73
Numberman, Neil 1981(?)- 220
Numeroff, Laura 1953- 206
  Earlier sketches in SATA 28, 90, 142
  See also CLR 85

Numeroff Joffe, Laura
  See Numeroff, Laura
Nunes, Lygia Bojunga 1932- 154
  Earlier sketch in SATA 75
Nunn, Laura (Donna) Silverstein 1968- 124
Nurenberg, Thelma
  See Greenhaus, Thelma Nurenberg
Nurnberg, Maxwell 1897-1984 27
  Obituary 41
Nussbaumer, Paul (Edmund) 1934- 16
Nutt, Ken 1951- 163
  Earlier sketch in SATA 97
Nuttall-Smith, Margaret Emily Noel 1919- .. 26
Nuygen, Mathieu 1967- 80
Nuzum, K. A. 195
Nuzum, Kathy A.
  See Nuzum, K. A.
Nwapa, Flora (Nwanzuruaha) 1931-1993
  See CLR 162
Nyberg, (Everett Wayne) Morgan 1944- 87
Nyce, (Nellie) Helene von Strecker
  1885-1969 19
Nyce, Vera 1862-1925 19
Nye, Naomi Shihab 1952- 198
  Earlier sketches in SATA 86, 147
  See also CLR 59
Nye, Robert 1939- 6
Nyeu, Tao 206
Nyikos, Stacy A. 1969- 164
Nystrom, Carolyn 1940- 130
  Earlier sketch in SATA 67

O

O. Henry
  See Henry, O.
Oakes, Elizabeth H. 1964- 132
Oakes, Vanya 1909-1983 6
  Obituary 37
Oakley, Don(ald G.) 1927- 8
Oakley, Graham 1929- 84
  Earlier sketch in SATA 30
  See also CLR 7
Oakley, Helen (McKelvey) 1906- 10
Oaks, J. Adams 220
Oana, Katherine 1929- 53
  Brief entry 37
Oates, Eddie H. 1943- 88
Oates, Joyce Carol 1938- 159
Oates, Stephen B(aery) 1936- 59
Obed, Ellen Bryan 1944- 74
Oberle, Joseph 1958- 69
Oberman, Sheldon 1949-2004 85
  Autobiography Feature 114
  Obituary 153
  See also CLR 54
  See also SAAS 26
Obligado, Lilian (Isabel) 1931- 61
  Brief entry 45
Obrant, Susan 1946- 11
O'Brian, E.G.
  See Clarke, Arthur C.
O'Brien, Anne Sibley 1952- 213
  Brief entry 48
  Earlier sketches in SATA 53, 80
O'Brien, E.G.
  See Clarke, Arthur C.
O'Brien, Esse Forrester 1895(?)-1975
  Obituary 30
O'Brien, Johnny 222
O'Brien, Patrick 1960- 193
O'Brien, Robert C.
  See Conly, Robert Leslie
O'Brien, Thomas C. 1938-2010 29
O'Brien, Thomas Clement
  See O'Brien, Thomas C.
O'Callaghan, Julie 1954- 113
O'Callahan, Jay 1938- 88

O'Carroll, Ryan
    See Markun, Patricia Maloney
Ochiltree, Dianne 1953- 117
Ockham, Joan Price
    See Price, Joan
O'Connell, Margaret F(orster) 1935-1977 30
    Obituary 30
O'Connell, Peg
    See Ahern, Margaret McCrohan
O'Connell, Rebecca 1968- 212
    Earlier sketch in SATA *130*
O'Connor, Barbara 1950- 193
    Earlier sketch in SATA *154*
O'Connor, Francine M(arie) 1930- 90
O'Connor, Genevieve A. 1914- 75
O'Connor, George 183
O'Connor, Ian 1965- 188
O'Connor, Jane 1947- 186
    Brief entry 47
    Earlier sketches in SATA *59, 103, 150*
O'Connor, Karen 1938- 89
    Earlier sketch in SATA *34*
O'Connor, Patrick
    See Wibberley, Leonard
O'Connor, Richard 1915-1975
    Obituary 21
O'Conor, Jane 1958- 78
Odaga, Asenath (Bole) 1937- 130
    Earlier sketch in SATA *67*
    See also SAAS *19*
O Danachair, Caoimhin
    See Danaher, Kevin
Odanaka, Barbara 159
O'Daniel, Janet 1921- 24
O'Day, Cathy
    See Crane, Barbara (Joyce)
O'Dell, Scott 1898-1989 134
    Earlier sketches in SATA *12, 60*
    See also CLR *126*
Odenwald, Robert P(aul) 1899-1965 11
Odgers, Sally
    See Odgers, Sally Farrell
Odgers, Sally Farrell 1957- 139
    Earlier sketch in SATA *72*
Odone, Jamison 1980- 209
O'Donnell, Dick
    See Lupoff, Richard A(llen)
    and Thompson, Don(ald Arthur)
O'Donnell, Liam 1970- 209
Odriozola, Elena 186
Oechsli, Kelly 1918-1999 5
Oesterle, Virginia Rorby
    See Rorby, Ginny
Ofek, Uriel 1926- 36
    See also CLR *28*
Ofer, Avi 1975- 207
Offenbacher, Ami 1958- 91
Offill, Jenny 1968- 211
Offit, Sidney 1928- 10
Ofosu-Appiah, L(awrence) H(enry) 1920- ... 13
Ogan, George F. 1912-1983 13
Ogan, M. G.
    See Ogan, George F.
    and Ogan, Margaret E. (Nettles)
Ogan, Margaret E. (Nettles) 1923-1979 13
Ogburn, Charlton (Jr.) 1911-1998 3
    Obituary 109
Ogburn, Jacqueline K. 162
Ogilvie, Elisabeth May 1917-2006 40
    Brief entry 29
    Obituary 176
Ogilvy, Gavin
    See Barrie, J. M.
Ogilvy, Ian 1943- 177
Ogilvy, Ian Raymond
    See Ogilvy, Ian
Ogle, Lucille Edith 1904-1988
    Obituary 59
Ogletree, Charles J. 1952- 175
O'Green, Jennifer
    See Roberson, Jennifer

O'Green, Jennifer Roberson
    See Roberson, Jennifer
O'Hagan, Caroline 1946- 38
O'Hanlon, Jacklyn
    See Meek, Jacklyn O'Hanlon
O'Hara, Elizabeth
    See Ni Dhuibhne, Eilis
O'Hara, Kenneth
    See Morris, (Margaret) Jean
O'Hara, Mary
    See Alsop, Mary O'Hara
O'Hara (Alsop), Mary
    See Alsop, Mary O'Hara
O'Hare, Jeff(rey A.) 1958- 105
O'hearn, Kate 225
Ohi, Ruth 1964- 95
Ohiyesa
    See Eastman, Charles A(lexander)
Ohlsson, Ib 1935- 7
Ohmi, Ayano 1959- 115
Ohtomo, Yasuo 1946- 37
o huigin, sean 1942- 138
    See also CLR *75*
Oiseau
    See Moseley, James W(illett)
Oke, Janette 1935- 97
O'Keefe, Susan Heyboer 176
    Earlier sketch in SATA *133*
O'Keeffe, Frank 1938- 99
O'Kelley, Mattie Lou 1908-1997 97
    Earlier sketch in SATA *36*
Okimoto, Jean Davies 1942- 103
    Earlier sketch in SATA *34*
Okomfo, Amasewa
    See Cousins, Linda
olafsdottir, Gudrun Elin
    See Gunnella
Olaleye, Isaac O. 1941- 96
    See also SAAS *23*
Olcott, Frances Jenkins 1872(?)-1963 19
Old, Wendie C(orbin) 1943- 154
Old Boy
    See Hughes, Thomas
Oldenburg, E(gbert) William 1936-1974 35
Older, Effin 1942- 114
Older, Jules 1940- 156
    Earlier sketch in SATA *114*
Oldfield, Jenny 1949- 140
Oldfield, Margaret J(ean) 1932- 56
Oldfield, Pamela 1931- 86
Oldham, June 70
Oldham, Mary 1944- 65
Oldland, Nicholas 1972- 223
Olds, Elizabeth 1896-1991 3
    Obituary 66
Olds, Helen Diehl 1895-1981 9
    Obituary 25
Oldstyle, Jonathan
    See Irving, Washington
O'Leary, Brian (Todd) 1940- 6
O'Leary, Chris 208
O'Leary, Patsy B. 1937- 97
O'Leary, Patsy Baker
    See O'Leary, Patsy B.
Oleynikov, Igor 1953- 202
Oliphant, B.J.
    See Tepper, Sheri S.
Oliver, Burton
    See Burt, Olive Woolley
Oliver, Chad
    See Oliver, Symmes C.
Oliver, John Edward 1933- 21
Oliver, Lin 202
Oliver, Marilyn Tower 1935- 89
Oliver, Mark 1960- 214
Oliver, Narelle 1960- 197
    Earlier sketch in SATA *152*
Oliver, Shirley (Louise Dawkins) 1958- 74
Oliver, Symmes C. 1928-1993 101
Oliviero, Jamie 1950- 84
Olmsted, Lorena Ann 1890-1989 13

Olney, Ross R. 1929- 13
Olschewski, Alfred (Erich) 1920- 7
Olsen, Barbara 148
Olsen, Carol 1945- 89
Olsen, Ib Spang 1921- 81
    Earlier sketch in SATA 6
Olsen, Violet (Mae) 1922-1991 58
Olson, Arielle North 1932- 67
Olson, David J. 1974- 198
Olson, Gene 1922- 32
Olson, Gretchen 187
Olson, Helen Kronberg 48
Olson, Kay Melchisedech 1948- 175
Olson, Marianne
    See Mitchell, Marianne
Olson-Brown, Ellen 1967- 183
Olten, Manuela 1970- 197
Olugebefola, Ademole 1941- 15
Oluonye, Mary N(kechi) 1955- 111
Om
    See Gorey, Edward (St. John)
O'Malley, Donough 208
O'Malley, Kevin 1961- 191
    Earlier sketch in SATA *157*
Oman, Carola (Mary Anima) 1897-1978 35
O'Mara, Carmel 1965- 166
O'Mara-Horwitz, Carmel
    See O'Mara, Carmel
O'Meara, Walter (Andrew) 1897-1989 65
Ommanney, F(rancis) D(ownes) 1903-1980 . 23
Omololu, Cynthia Jaynes 222
O Mude
    See Gorey, Edward (St. John)
Oneal, Elizabeth 1934- 82
    Earlier sketch in SATA *30*
    See also CLR *13*
O'Neal, Katherine Pebley 1957- 204
O'Neal, Reagan
    See Jordan, Robert
O'Neal, Regan
    See Jordan, Robert
Oneal, Zibby
    See Oneal, Elizabeth
O'neill, Alexis 1949- 220
O'Neill, Amanda 1951- 111
O'Neill, Catharine 203
O'Neill, Gerard K(itchen) 1927-1992 65
O'Neill, Judith (Beatrice) 1930- 34
O'Neill, Mary L(e Duc) 1908(?)-1990 2
    Obituary 64
O'Neill, Reagan
    See Jordan, Robert
Onslow, Annette Rosemary MacArthur
    See MacArthur-Onslow, Annette Rosemary
Onslow, John 1906-1985
    Obituary 47
Onyefulu, Ifeoma 1959- 157
    Earlier sketches in SATA *81, 115*
Opie, Iona (Margaret Balfour) 1923- 118
    Earlier sketches in SATA *3, 63*
    See also SAAS *6*
Opie, Peter (Mason) 1918-1982 118
    Obituary 28
    Earlier sketches in SATA *3, 63*
Oppel, Kenneth 1967- 199
    Earlier sketches in SATA *99, 153*
Oppel, Kenneth Kerry
    See Oppel, Kenneth
Oppenheim, Joanne 1934- 174
    Earlier sketches in SATA *5, 82, 136*
Oppenheim, Shulamith Levey 1928- 177
Oppenheimer, Joan L(etson) 1925- 28
Oppong, Joseph Ransford 1953- 160
Optic, Oliver
    See Adams, William Taylor
    and Stratemeyer, Edward L.
Oram, Hiawyn 1946- 101
    Earlier sketch in SATA *56*
Orbach, Ruth Gary 1941- 21
Orback, Craig 197

Orczy, Emma
  See Orczy, Baroness Emmuska
Orczy, Emma Magdalena Rosalia Maria Josefa
  See Orczy, Baroness Emmuska
Orczy, Emmuska
  See Orczy, Baroness Emmuska
Orczy, Baroness Emmuska 1865-1947 40
Orde, A.J.
  See Tepper, Sheri S.
O'Reilly, Jackson
  See Jordan, Robert
Orenstein, Denise Gosliner 1950- 157
Orgad, Dorit 1936- 199
Orgel, Doris 1929- 148
  Earlier sketches in SATA 7, 85
  See also CLR 48
  See also SAAS 19
Orgill, Roxane 198
Oriolo, Joe
  See Oriolo, Joseph D.
Oriolo, Joseph D. 1913-1985
  Obituary 46
Orlean, Susan 1955- 209
Orleans, Ilo 1897-1962 10
Orlev, Uri 1931- 135
  Earlier sketch in SATA 58
  See also CLR 30
  See also SAAS 19
Ormai, Stella 57
  Brief entry 48
Ormerod, Jan 1946- 210
  Brief entry 44
  Earlier sketches in SATA 55, 70, 132
  See also CLR 20
Ormerod, Janette Louise
  See Ormerod, Jan
Ormes, Jackie
  See Ormes, Zelda J.
Ormes, Zelda J. 1914-1986
  Obituary 47
Ormondroyd, Edward 1925- 14
Ormsby, Virginia H(aire) 1906-1990 11
Orona-Ramirez, Kristy 1964- 189
Orozco, Jose-Luis 1948- 179
Orr, Katherine S(helley) 1950- 72
Orr, Wendy 1953- 206
  Earlier sketches in SATA 90, 141
Orris
  See Ingelow, Jean
Orth, Richard
  See Gardner, Richard (M.)
Ortiz Cofer, Judith
  See Cofer, Judith Ortiz
Orwell, George 1903-1950 29
  See also CLR 68
Orwin, Joanna 1944- 141
Os, Eric van
  See van Os, Erik
Osborn, Elinor 1939- 145
Osborn, Jacob 1981(?)- 215
Osborn, Kathy 1955(?)- 199
Osborn, Lois D(orothy) 1915- 61
Osborne, Charles 1927- 59
Osborne, Chester G(orham) 1915-1987 11
Osborne, David
  See Silverberg, Robert
Osborne, George
  See Silverberg, Robert
Osborne, Leone Neal 1914-1996 2
Osborne, Linda Barrett 1949- 215
Osborne, Mary Pope 1949- 144
  Earlier sketches in SATA 41, 55, 98
  See also CLR 88
Osceola
  See Blixen, Karen
Osgood, William E(dward) 1926- 37
O'Shaughnessy, Darren
  See Shan, Darren
O'Shaughnessy, Ellen Cassels 1937- 78
O'shaughnessy, Tam 1951- 221

O'Shea, Catherine Patricia Shiels
  See O'Shea, Pat
O'Shea, Pat 1931-2007 87
  See also CLR 18
Osmond, Edward 1900- 10
Ossoli, Sarah Margaret
  See Fuller, Margaret
Ostendorf, (Arthur) Lloyd, (Jr.) 1921-2000 .. 65
  Obituary 125
Osterweil, Adam 1972- 217
Ostow, Micol 1976- 223
  Earlier sketch in SATA 170
Otfinoski, Steven 1949- 116
  Earlier sketch in SATA 56
Otis, James
  See Kaler, James Otis
O'Toole, Thomas 1941- 71
O'Trigger, Sir Lucius
  See Horne, Richard Henry Hengist
Otten, Charlotte
  See Otten, Charlotte F.
Otten, Charlotte F. 1926- 98
Otten, Charlotte Fennema
  See Otten, Charlotte F.
Ottley, Matt 1962- 171
  Earlier sketch in SATA 102
Ottley, Reginald Leslie 1909-1985 26
  See also CLR 16
Otto, Margaret Glover 1909-1976
  Obituary 30
Otto, Svend
  See Soerensen, Svend Otto
Ouellet, Debbie 1954- 219
Oughton, Jerrie (Preston) 1937- 131
  Earlier sketch in SATA 76
Oughton, (William) Taylor 1925- 104
Ouida
  See De La Ramee, Marie Louise
Ousley, Odille 1896-1976 10
Outcalt, Todd 1960- 123
Overmyer, James E. 1946- 88
Overton, Jenny (Margaret Mary) 1942- 52
  Brief entry 36
Owen, Ann
  See Qualey, Marsha
Owen, Annie 1949- 75
Owen, Caroline Dale
  See Snedeker, Caroline Dale (Parke)
Owen, Clifford
  See Hamilton, Charles (Harold St. John)
Owen, Dilys
  See Gater, Dilys
Owen, (Benjamin) Evan 1918-1984 38
Owen, (John) Gareth 1936-2002 162
  Earlier sketch in SATA 83
  See also CLR 31
  See also SAAS 14
Owen, James A. 185
Owens, Bryant 1968- 116
Owens, Dana Elaine
  See Queen Latifah
Owens, Gail 1939- 54
Owens, Mary Beth 191
Owens, Thomas S(heldon) 1960- 86
Owens, Tom
  See Owens, Thomas S(heldon)
Oxenbury, Helen 1938- 149
  Earlier sketches in SATA 3, 68
  See also CLR 70
Oxendine, Bess Holland 1933- 90
Oz, Frank (Richard) 1944- 60
Ozer, Jerome S. 1927- 59

P

Paananen, Eloise (Katherine) 1923-1993 9
Pace, Lorenzo 1943- 131
Pace, Mildred Mastin 1907- 46
  Brief entry 29

Pachter, Hedwig (?)-1988 63
Pack, Janet 1952- 77
Pack, Robert 1929- 118
Packard, Edward 1931- 148
  Earlier sketches in SATA 47, 90
Packer, Kenneth L. 1946- 116
Packer, Vin
  See Meaker, Marijane
Pad, Peter
  See Stratemeyer, Edward L.
Page, Eileen
  See Heal, Edith
Page, Eleanor
  See Coerr, Eleanor (Beatrice)
Page, Gail 1950- 205
Page, Jake 1936- 81
Page, James Keena, Jr.
  See Page, Jake
Page, Lou Williams 1912-1997 38
Page, Mary
  See Heal, Edith
Page, Robin 1943- 154
Pagliarulo, Antonio 1977(?)- 212
Pagnucci, Susan 1944- 90
Pahlen, Kurt 1907-2003
  Obituary 147
Pahz, Cheryl
  See Pahz, Cheryl Suzanne
Pahz, Cheryl Suzanne 1949- 11
Pahz, James Alon 1943- 11
Paice, Margaret 1920- 10
Paige, Harry W(orthington) 1922- 41
  Brief entry 35
Paige, Richard
  See Koontz, Dean
Paige, Robin
  See Albert, Susan Wittig
Paine, Penelope Colville 1946- 87
Paine, Roberta M. 1925- 13
Paisley, Tom 1932- 11
  See also CLR 3
Palatini, Margie 207
  Earlier sketches in SATA 134, 174
Palazzo, Anthony D.
  See Palazzo, Tony
Palazzo, Tony 1905-1970 3
Palder, Edward L. 1922- 5
Palecek, Josef 1932- 56
Palecek, Libuse 1937- 89
Palen, Debbie 195
Palin, Michael 1943- 67
Palin, Michael Edward
  See Palin, Michael
Palladini, David (Mario) 1946- 40
  Brief entry 32
Pallas, Norvin 1918-1983 23
Pallister, John C(lare) 1891-1980
  Obituary 26
Pallotta, Gerard Larry
  See Pallotta, Jerry
Pallotta, Jerry 1953- 186
Pallotta-Chiarolli, Maria 1960- 117
Palmer, Bernard (Alvin) 1914-1998 26
Palmer, C. Everard 1930- 14
Palmer, (Ruth) Candida 1926- 11
Palmer, Cyril Everard
  See Palmer, C. Everard
Palmer, Don
  See Benson, Mildred
Palmer, Hap 1942- 68
Palmer, Heidi 1948- 15
Palmer, Helen Marion
  See Geisel, Helen
Palmer, Jessica 1953- 120
Palmer, Judd 1972- 153
Palmer, Juliette 1930- 15
Palmer, Kate Salley 1946- 97
Palmer, Maria
  See Strachan, Ian
Palmer, Maria
  See Brennan, Herbie

Palmer, Robin 1909-2000 .... *43*
Palmero Caceres, Ana *198*
Palmisciano, Diane *202*
Paltrowitz, Donna 1950- *61*
   Brief entry *50*
Paltrowitz, Donna Milman
   See Paltrowitz, Donna
Paltrowitz, Stuart 1946- *61*
   Brief entry *50*
Pamela, Todd 1950- *124*
Pamintuan, Macky *214*
   Earlier sketch in SATA *178*
Panagopoulos, Janie Lynn *149*
Panati, Charles 1943- *65*
Panchyk, Richard 1970- *138*
Panetta, George 1915-1969 .... *15*
Panetta, Joseph N. 1953- *96*
Pang, YaWen Ariel *206*
Panik, Sharon 1952- *82*
Panowski, Eileen Thompson 1920- *49*
Pansy
   See Alden, Isabella (Macdonald)
Pantell, Dora (Fuchs) *39*
Panter, Carol 1936- *9*
Paolini, Christopher 1983- *157*
   See also CLR *102*
Papademetriou, Lisa *175*
Paparone, Pam *185*
Paparone, Pamela
   See Paparone, Pam
Papas, Bill
   See Papas, William
Papas, William 1927-2000 .... *50*
Papashvily, George 1898-1978 .... *17*
Papashvily, Helen (Waite) 1906-1996 .... *17*
Pape, D. L.
   See Pape, Donna (Lugg)
Pape, Donna (Lugg) 1930- *82*
   Earlier sketch in SATA *2*
Paperny, Myra (Green) 1932- *51*
   Brief entry *33*
Papineau, Lucie 1962- *224*
Papp, Robert 1967- *205*
Paradis, Adrian A(lexis) 1912- *67*
   Earlier sketch in SATA *1*
   See also SAAS *8*
Paradis, Marjorie Bartholomew
   1886(?)-1970 .... *17*
Paradiz, Valerie 1963- *176*
Paratore, Coleen
   See Paratore, Coleen Murtagh
Paratore, Coleen Murtagh 1958- *200*
Pardo DeLange, Alex *211*
Parenteau, Shirley 1935- *199*
   Brief entry *40*
   Earlier sketch in SATA *47*
Parish, Margaret 1927-1988 .... *73*
   Obituary *59*
   Earlier sketch in SATA *17*
   See also CLR *22*
Parish, Margaret Holt
   See Holt, Margaret
Parish, Peggy
   See Parish, Margaret
Park, Barbara 1947- *123*
   Brief entry *35*
   Earlier sketches in SATA *40, 78*
   See also CLR *34*
Park, Bill
   See Park, W(illiam) B(ryan)
Park, Frances 1955- *171*
Park, Ginger *173*
Park, Janie Jaehyun *150*
Park, Jordan
   See Kornbluth, C(yril) M.
   and Pohl, Frederik
Park, Linda Sue 1960- *200*
   Earlier sketches in SATA *127, 173*
   See also CLR *84*
Park, Nick 1958- *113*

Park, Rosina Ruth Lucia
   See Park, Ruth
Park, Ruth 1917(?)-2010 .... *93*
   Earlier sketch in SATA *25*
   See also CLR *51*
Park, W(illiam) B(ryan) 1936- *22*
Parke, Marilyn 1928- *82*
Parker, Barbara Keevil 1938- *157*
Parker, Daniel
   See Ehrenhaft, Daniel
Parker, Elinor Milnor 1906- *3*
Parker, Julie F. 1961- *92*
Parker, Kim 1963- *174*
Parker, Kristy 1957- *59*
Parker, Lois M(ay) 1912-1996 .... *30*
Parker, Margot M. 1937- *52*
Parker, Marjorie Blain 1960- *205*
   Earlier sketch in SATA *145*
Parker, Mary Jessie 1948- *71*
Parker, Nancy Winslow 1930- *132*
   Earlier sketches in SATA *10, 69*
   See also SAAS *20*
Parker, Richard 1915-1990 .... *14*
Parker, Robert
   See Boyd, Waldo T.
   and Parker, Robert Andrew
Parker, Robert Andrew 1927- *200*
Parker, Steve 1954- *213*
Parker, Tom S. *215*
Parker, Toni Trent 1947-2005 .... *142*
   Obituary *169*
Parker-Rees, Guy *193*
Parker-Rock, Michelle *214*
Parkes, Lucas
   See Harris, John (Wyndham Parkes Lucas)
   Beynon
Parkhill, John
   See Cox, William R(obert)
Parkins, David 1955- *218*
   Earlier sketch in SATA *176*
Parkinson, Curtis *219*
Parkinson, Ethelyn M(inerva) 1906-1999 .... *11*
Parkinson, Kathryn N. 1954- *71*
Parkinson, Kathy
   See Parkinson, Kathryn N.
Parkinson, Siobhan
   See Parkinson, Siobhan
Parkinson, Siobhan 1954- *178*
Parks, Deborah A. 1948- *133*
   Earlier sketch in SATA *91*
Parks, Edd Winfield 1906-1968 .... *10*
Parks, Gordon 1912-2006 .... *108*
   Obituary *175*
   Earlier sketch in SATA *8*
Parks, Gordon Roger Alexander
   See Parks, Gordon
Parks, Peggy J. 1951- *143*
Parks, PJ
   See Parks, Peggy J.
Parks, Rosa 1913-2005 .... *83*
   Obituary *169*
Parks, Rosa Louise Lee
   See Parks, Rosa
Parks, Van Dyke 1943- *62*
Parlato, Stephen 1954- *222*
Parley, Peter
   See Goodrich, Samuel Griswold
Parlin, John
   See Graves, Charles Parlin
Parme, Fabrice 1966- *191*
Parnall, Peter 1936- *69*
   Earlier sketch in SATA *16*
   See also SAAS *11*
Paros, Jennifer *210*
Parotti, Phillip (Elliott) 1941- *109*
Parr, Ann 1943- *144*
Parr, Danny
   See Parr, Ann
Parr, Letitia (Evelyn) 1906-1985(?) *37*
Parr, Lucy 1924- *10*

Parr, Todd *179*
   Earlier sketch in SATA *134*
Parra, John 1972- *225*
Parrish, Anne 1888-1957 .... *27*
Parrish, Mary
   See Cousins, Margaret
Parrish, Maxfield
   See Parrish, (Frederick) Maxfield
Parrish, (Frederick) Maxfield 1870-1966 .... *14*
Parry, Marian 1924- *13*
Parry, Rosanne *212*
Parson Lot
   See Kingsley, Charles
Parsons, Alexandra 1947- *92*
Parsons, Ellen
   See Dragonwagon, Crescent
Parsons, Garry *197*
Parsons, Martin 1951- *116*
Parsons, Martin Leslie
   See Parsons, Martin
Parsons, Tom
   See MacPherson, Thomas George
Parsons-Yazzi, Evangeline *172*
Partch, Virgil Franklin II 1916-1984 .... *39*
   Obituary *39*
Parton, Dolly 1946- *94*
Parton, Dolly Rebecca
   See Parton, Dolly
Partridge, Benjamin W., Jr. 1915-2005 .... *28*
   Obituary *163*
Partridge, Benjamin Waring, Jr.
   See Partridge, Benjamin W., Jr.
Partridge, Cora Cheney
   See Cheney, Cora
Partridge, Elizabeth *216*
   Earlier sketch in SATA *134*
Partridge, Jenny (Lilian) 1947- *52*
   Brief entry *37*
Pasachoff, Naomi 1947- *147*
Pascal, David 1918- *14*
Pascal, Francine 1938- *143*
   Brief entry *37*
   Earlier sketches in SATA *51, 80*
   See also CLR *25*
Paschal, Nancy
   See Trotter, Grace V(iolet)
Paschkis, Julie 1957- *220*
   Earlier sketch in SATA *177*
Pascudniak, Pascal
   See Lupoff, Richard A(llen)
Pashko, Stanley 1913-1982 .... *29*
Passailaigue, Thomas E.
   See Paisley, Tom
Pastel, Elyse *201*
Pateman, Robert 1954- *84*
Patent, Dorothy Hinshaw 1940- *162*
   Autobiography Feature *162*
   Earlier sketches in SATA *22, 69, 120*
   See also CLR *19*
   See also SAAS *13*
Paterson, A(ndrew) B(arton) 1864-1941 .... *97*
Paterson, Banjo
   See Paterson, A(ndrew) B(arton)
Paterson, Diane 1946- *177*
   Brief entry *33*
   Earlier sketch in SATA *59*
Paterson, John (Barstow) 1932- *114*
Paterson, Katherine 1932- *204*
   Earlier sketches in SATA *13, 53, 92, 133*
   See also CLR *127*
Paterson, Katherine Womeldorf
   See Paterson, Katherine
Patience, John 1949- *90*
Patneaude, David 1944- *159*
   Earlier sketch in SATA *85*
Paton, Alan 1903-1988 .... *11*
   Obituary *56*
Paton, Alan Stewart
   See Paton, Alan
Paton, Jane (Elizabeth) 1934- *35*
Paton, Priscilla 1952- *98*

Paton Walsh, Gillian
See Paton Walsh, Jill
Paton Walsh, Jill 1937- *190*
Autobiography Feature *190*
Earlier sketches in SATA *4, 72, 109*
See also CLR *128*
See also SAAS *3*
Patricelli, Leslie *207*
Patrick, Susan
See Robins, Patricia
Patron, Susan 1948- *182*
Earlier sketch in SATA *76*
Patsauq, Markoosie 1942-
See CLR *23*
Patschke, Steve 1955- *125*
Patten, Brian 1946- *152*
Earlier sketch in SATA *29*
Patterson, Charles 1935- *59*
Patterson, Geoffrey 1943- *54*
Brief entry *44*
Patterson, James 1947- *197*
Earlier sketch in SATA *164*
Patterson, James B.
See Patterson, James
Patterson, Lillie G. -1999 .... *88*
Earlier sketch in SATA *14*
Patterson, Nancy Ruth 1944- *148*
Earlier sketch in SATA *72*
Patterson, Valerie O. *223*
Pattison, Darcy (S.) 1954- *126*
Earlier sketch in SATA *72*
Pattou, Edith *164*
Patz (Blaustein), Nancy *154*
Paul, Aileen 1917- *12*
Paul, Alison *196*
Paul, Ann Whitford 1941- *209*
Earlier sketches in SATA *76, 110, 168*
Paul, Chris 1985- *224*
Paul, David (Tyler) 1934-1988
Obituary *56*
Paul, Dominique 1973- *184*
Paul, Elizabeth
See Crow, Donna Fletcher
Paul, Hamish Vigne Christie 1951- *151*
See also CLR *87*
Paul, James 1936- *23*
Paul, Korky
See Paul, Hamish Vigne Christie
Paul, Robert
See Roberts, John G(aither)
Paul, Tessa 1944- *103*
Pauley, Kimberly 1973- *208*
Pauli, Hertha (Ernestine) 1909-1973 ...... *3*
Obituary *26*
Paull, Grace A. 1898- *24*
Paulsen, Gary 1939- *189*
Earlier sketches in SATA *22, 50, 54, 79, 111, 158*
See also CLR *82*
Paulson, Jack
See Jackson, C(aary) Paul
Pauquet, Gina Ruck
See Ruck-Pauquet, Gina
Pausacker, Jenny 1948- *72*
See also SAAS *23*
Pausewang, Gudrun 1928- *165*
Earlier sketch in SATA *104*
Pavel, Frances 1907- *10*
Paver, Michelle *215*
Earlier sketch in SATA *170*
Paxton
See Barr, Nevada
Paxton, Thomas R. 1937- *70*
Paxton, Tom
See Paxton, Thomas R.
Paye, Won-Ldy *185*
Payne, Alan
See Jakes, John
Payne, Bernal C., Jr. 1941- *60*
Payne, C. Douglas
See Payne, C.D.

Payne, C.D. 1949- *133*
Payne, C.F. 1956- *179*
Payne, Chris Fox
See Payne, C.F.
Payne, Donald Gordon 1924- *37*
Payne, Emmy
See West, Emily Govan
Payne, Nina *135*
Payne, Rachel Ann
See Jakes, John
Payson, Dale 1943- *9*
Payzant, Charles *18*
Paz, A.
See Pahz, James Alon
Paz, Natalia Toledo
See Toledo, Natalia
Paz, Zan
See Pahz, Cheryl Suzanne
Peace, Mary
See Finley, Mary Peace
Peacock, Mary *210*
Peacock, Shane 1957- *192*
Peake, Mervyn 1911-1968 .... *23*
Peale, Norman Vincent 1898-1993 ...... *20*
Obituary *78*
Pearce, Ann Philippa
See Pearce, Philippa
Pearce, Emily Smith 1975- *199*
Pearce, Jacqueline 1962- *146*
Pearce, Margaret *104*
Pearce, Philippa 1920-2006 .... *129*
Obituary *179*
Earlier sketches in SATA *1, 67*
See also CLR *9*
Peare, Catherine Owens 1911- *9*
Pearle, Ida *207*
Pearsall, Shelley 1966- *190*
Pearson, Gayle 1947- *119*
Earlier sketch in SATA *53*
Pearson, Jean Mary
See Gardam, Jane
Pearson, Kit 1947- *77*
Autobiography Feature *117*
See also CLR *26*
Pearson, Mary E. 1955- *211*
Earlier sketch in SATA *134*
Pearson, Ridley 1953- *182*
Pearson, Susan 1946- *166*
Brief entry *27*
Earlier sketches in SATA *39, 91*
Pearson, Tracey Campbell 1956- *219*
Earlier sketches in SATA *64, 155*
Pease, (Clarence) Howard 1894-1974 ...... *2*
Obituary *25*
Peavy, Linda 1943- *54*
Peck, Anne Merriman 1884-1976 ...... *18*
Peck, Beth 1957- *190*
Earlier sketch in SATA *79*
Peck, Jan *159*
Peck, Jeanie J. 1967- *147*
Peck, Marshall III 1951- *92*
Peck, Richard 1934- *190*
Autobiography Feature *110*
Earlier sketches in SATA *18, 55, 97, 110, 158*
See also CLR *142*
See also SAAS *2*
Peck, Richard Wayne
See Peck, Richard
Peck, Robert Newton 1928- *156*
Autobiography Feature *108*
Earlier sketches in SATA *21, 62, 111*
See also CLR *163*
See also SAAS *1*
Peck, Sylvia 1953- *133*
Peck-Whiting, Jeanie J.
See Peck, Jeanie J.
Peddicord, Jane Ann *199*
Pedersen, Janet *193*
Pederson, Sharleen
See Collicott, Sharleen
Pedler, Caroline *197*

Peebles, Anne
See Galloway, Priscilla
Peek, Merle 1938- *39*
Peel, John 1954- *79*
Peel, Norman Lemon
See Hirsch, Phil
Peeples, Edwin A(ugustus, Jr.) 1915-1994 ..... *6*
Peers, Judi 1956- *119*
Peers, Judith May West
See Peers, Judi
Peet, Bill
See Peet, William Bartlett
Peet, Creighton B. 1899-1977 ...... *30*
Peet, Mal *171*
Peet, Malcolm
See Peet, Mal
Peet, William Bartlett 1915-2002 ...... *78*
Obituary *137*
Earlier sketches in SATA *2, 41*
See also CLR *12*
Peguero, Leone *116*
Pelaez, Jill 1924- *12*
Pelham, David 1938- *70*
Pelikan, Judy 1941- *219*
Pell, Ed(ward) 1950- *157*
Pelletier, Andrew T. *195*
Pelletier, Andrew Thomas
See Pelletier, Andrew T.
Pellowski, Anne 1933- *20*
Pellowski, Michael (Joseph) 1949- *151*
Brief entry *48*
Earlier sketch in SATA *88*
Pellowski, Michael Morgan
See Pellowski, Michael (Joseph)
Pelta, Kathy 1928- *18*
Peltier, Leslie C(opus) 1900-1980 ..... *13*
Pemberton, Bonnie *191*
Pemberton, John Leigh
See Leigh-Pemberton, John
Pembury, Bill
See Groom, Arthur William
Pemsteen, Hans
See Manes, Stephen
Pendennis, Arthur Esquir
See Thackeray, William Makepeace
Pender, Lydia Podger 1907- *61*
Pendery, Rosemary (Schmitz) *7*
Pendle, Alexy 1943- *29*
Pendle, George 1906-1977
Obituary *28*
Pendleton, Don
See Cunningham, Chet
and Garside, Jack
and Jagninski, Tom
and Krauzer, Steven M(ark)
and Obstfeld, Raymond
Pendleton, Thomas 1965- *206*
Pendziwol, Jean E. 1965- *177*
Pene du Bois, William (Sherman) 1916-1993 ...... *68*
Obituary *74*
Earlier sketch in SATA *4*
See also CLR *1*
Penn, Audrey 1947- *212*
Penn, Audrey 1950- *22*
Penn, Ruth Bonn
See Rosenberg, Eth Clifford
Pennac, Daniel 1944- *155*
Pennage, E. M.
See Finkel, George (Irvine)
Penner, Fred 1946- *169*
Earlier sketch in SATA *67*
Penner, Frederick Ralph Cornelius
See Penner, Fred
Penney, Grace Jackson 1904-2000 ...... *35*
Penney, Ian 1960- *76*
Penney, Sue 1957- *152*
Earlier sketch in SATA *102*
Pennington, Eunice 1923- *27*
Pennington, Lillian Boyer 1904-2003 ...... *45*
Pennypacker, Sara 1951- *187*

Penrose, Gordon 1925- 66
Penson, Mary E. 1917- 78
Penzler, Otto 1942- 38
Pepe, Phil 1935- 20
Pepe, Philip
    See Pepe, Phil
Peppe, Rodney (Darrell) 1934- 74
    Earlier sketch in SATA 4
    See also SAAS 10
Pepper, Frank S. 1910-1988
    Obituary 61
Percy, Charles Henry
    See Smith, Dorothy Gladys
Percy, Rachel 1930- 63
Perdrizet, Marie-Pierre 1952- 79
Perenyi, Constance 1954- 93
Perenyi, Constance Marie
    See Perenyi, Constance
Perera, Hilda 1926- 105
Perera, Thomas Biddle 1938- 13
Peretti, Frank E. 1951- 141
    Earlier sketch in SATA 80
Perez, L. King 1940- 199
Perez, Lana
    See Perez, Marlene
Perez, Lucia Angela 1973- 182
Perez, Marlene 170
Pericoli, Matteo 1968- 178
Perkins, Al(bert Rogers) 1904-1975 30
Perkins, Dan
    See Tomorrow, Tom
Perkins, Lucy Fitch 1865-1937 72
Perkins, Lynne Rae 1956- 212
    Earlier sketches in SATA 131, 172
Perkins, (Richard) Marlin 1905-1986 21
    Obituary 48
Perkins, Mitali 1963- 188
    Earlier sketch in SATA 88
Perks, Anne-Marie 1955- 122
Perl, Erica S. 222
    Earlier sketch in SATA 188
Perl, Lila 72
    Earlier sketch in SATA 6
Perl, Susan 1922-1983 22
    Obituary 34
Perlman, Janet 1954- 222
Perlman, Rhea 1948- 183
Perlmutter, O(scar) William 1920-1975 8
Pernu, Dennis 1970- 87
Perrault, Charles 1628-1703 25
    See also CLR 134
Perret, Delphine 1980- 190
Perret, Gene (Richard) 1937- 76
Perriman, Cole
    See Perrin, Pat
Perriman, Cole
    See Coleman, Wim
Perrin, Pat 212
Perrine, Mary 1913-1976 2
Perrins, Lesley 1953- 56
Perrow, Angeli 1954- 121
Perry, Andrea 1956- 190
    Earlier sketch in SATA 148
Perry, Barbara Fisher
    See Fisher, Barbara
Perry, Elizabeth 1959- 174
Perry, Elizabeth Goodwin
    See Perry, Elizabeth
Perry, John 1967- 223
Perry, Marie Fritz 165
Perry, Patricia 1949- 30
Perry, Phyllis J(ean) 1933- 152
    Earlier sketches in SATA 60, 101
Perry, Ritchie (John Allen) 1942- 105
Perry, Roger 1933- 27
Perry, Steve(n Carl) 1947- 76
Pershall, Mary K. 1951- 172
    Earlier sketch in SATA 70
Pershing, Marie
    See Schultz, Pearle Henriksen
Perske, Robert 1927- 57

Persun, Morgan Reed
    See Watkins, Dawn L.
Perversi, Margaret 213
Petach, Heidi 149
Peter
    See Stratemeyer, Edward L.
Peters, Alexander
    See Hollander, Zander
Peters, Andrew Fusek 1965- 169
    Earlier sketch in SATA 107
Peters, Bernadette 1948- 212
Peters, Caroline
    See Betz, Eva Kelly
Peters, David
    See David, Peter
Peters, Elizabeth 1927- 49
Peters, Emma
    See Price, Karen
Peters, Gabriel
    See Matott, Justin
Peters, Julie Anne 1952- 197
    Earlier sketches in SATA 82, 128
Peters, Linda
    See Catherall, Arthur
Peters, Lisa Westberg 1951- 161
    Earlier sketches in SATA 74, 115
Peters, Patricia 1953- 84
Peters, Russell M. 1929- 78
Peters, S. H.
    See Henry, O.
    and Proffitt, Nicholas
Peters, Stephanie True 1965- 224
Petersen, David 1946- 109
    Earlier sketch in SATA 62
Petersen, Gwenn Boardman 1924- 12
Petersen, P(eter) J(ames) 1941- 118
    Brief entry 43
    Earlier sketches in SATA 48, 83
Petersen, Palle 1943- 85
Petersham, Maud 1890-1971 17
    See also CLR 24
Petersham, Maud Sylvia Fuller
    See Petersham, Maud
Petersham, Miska 1888-1960 17
    See also CLR 24
Peterson, Cris 1952- 174
    Earlier sketches in SATA 84, 145
Peterson, Dawn 1934- 86
Peterson, Esther (Allen) 1934- 35
Peterson, Hans 1922- 8
Peterson, Harold L(eslie) 1922-1978 8
Peterson, Helen Stone 1910- 8
Peterson, Jean Sunde 1941- 108
Peterson, Jeanne Whitehouse 1939- 159
    Earlier sketch in SATA 29
Peterson, Kathleen B. 1951- 119
Peterson, Lorraine 1940- 56
    Brief entry 44
Peterson, Mary 215
Peterson, Shelley 1952- 146
Peterson, Will
    See Cocks, Peter
Petie, Haris
    See Petty, Roberta
Petricic, Dusan 1946- 176
Petrides, Heidrun 1944- 19
Petrie, Catherine 1947- 52
    Brief entry 41
Petrone, Valeria 186
Petrosino, Tamara 193
Petroski, Catherine (Ann Groom) 1939- 48
Petrovich, Michael B(oro) 1922- 40
Petrovskaya, Kyra
    See Wayne, Kyra Petrovskaya
Petruccio, Steven James 1961- 67
Petrucha, Stefan 1959- 213
Petry, Ann 1908-1997 5
    Obituary 94
    See also CLR 12
Petry, Ann Lane
    See Petry, Ann

Pettit, Jayne 1932- 108
Petty, J.T. 1977- 189
Petty, Kate 1951-2007 204
Petty, Roberta 1915- 10
Pevsner, Stella 131
    Earlier sketches in SATA 8, 77
    See also SAAS 14
Peyo
    See Culliford, Pierre
Peyton, K. M.
    See Peyton, Kathleen Wendy
Peyton, Kathleen Wendy 1929- 157
    Earlier sketches in SATA 15, 62
    See also CLR 3
    See also SAAS 17
Pfanner, (Anne) Louise 1955- 68
Pfeffer, Susan Beth 1948- 180
    Earlier sketches in SATA 4, 83
    See also CLR 11
    See also SAAS 17
Pfeffer, Wendy 1929- 204
    Earlier sketches in SATA 78, 142
Pfeiffer, Janet (B.) 1949- 96
Pfister, Marcus 207
    Earlier sketches in SATA 83, 150
    See also CLR 42
Pfitsch, Patricia Curtis 1948- 148
Pfitzenmaier, Audrey 1959- 220
Pflieger, Pat 1955- 84
Pham, LeUyen 1973- 201
    Earlier sketch in SATA 175
Phelan, Mary Kay 1914- 3
Phelan, Matt 1970- 215
    Earlier sketch in SATA 172
Phelan, Terry Wolfe 1941- 56
Phelps, Ethel Johnston 1914-1984 35
Philbrick, Rodman 1951- 163
Philbrick, W. Rodman
    See Philbrick, Rodman
Philbrick, W.R.
    See Philbrick, Rodman
Philbrook, Clem(ent E.) 1917- 24
Phillipps, J.C. 218
Phillipps, Julie Christine
    See Phillipps, J.C.
Phillips, Aileen Paul
    See Paul, Aileen
Phillips, Betty Lou
    See Phillips, Elizabeth Louise
Phillips, Bob 1940- 95
Phillips, Douglas A. 1949- 161
Phillips, Elizabeth Louise 58
    Brief entry 48
Phillips, Gary R. 225
Phillips, Irv(ing W.) 1905-2000 11
    Obituary 125
Phillips, Jack
    See Sandburg, Carl
Phillips, Leon
    See Gerson, Noel Bertram
Phillips, Loretta (Hosey) 1893-1987 10
Phillips, Louis 1942- 102
    Earlier sketch in SATA 8
Phillips, Mark
    See Garrett, Randall
    and Janifer, Laurence M(ark)
Phillips, Mary Geisler 1881-1964 10
Phillips, Michael
    See Nolan, William F.
Phillips, (Woodward) Prentice 1894-1981 10
Phillpotts, Eden 1862-1960 24
Phin
    See Thayer, Ernest Lawrence
Phipson, Joan
    See Fitzhardinge, Joan Margaret
Phiz
    See Browne, Hablot Knight
Phleger, Fred B. 1909-1993 34
Phleger, Marjorie Temple 1908(?)-1986 1
    Obituary 47

Piaget, Jean 1896-1980
  Obituary 23
Piatti, Celestino 1922- 16
Picard, Barbara Leonie 1917- 89
  Earlier sketch in SATA 2
  See also SAAS 10
Pichon, Liz 174
Pickard, Charles 1932- 36
Pickering, James Sayre 1897-1969 36
  Obituary 28
Pickering, Jimmy 195
Pickering, Robert B. 1950- 93
Pielichaty, Helena 1955- 142
Pien, Lark 222
Pienkowski, Jan (Michal) 1936- 131
  Earlier sketches in SATA 6, 58
  See also CLR 6
Pierce, Edith Gray 1893-1977 45
Pierce, Katherine
  See St. John, Wylly Folk
Pierce, Meredith Ann 1958- 127
  Brief entry 48
  Earlier sketch in SATA 67
  See also CLR 20
Pierce, Ruth (Ireland) 1936- 5
Pierce, Sharon
  See McCullough, Sharon Pierce
Pierce, Tamora 1954- 187
  Brief entry 49
  Earlier sketches in SATA 51, 96, 153
Pierce, Terry 178
Pierik, Robert 1921- 13
Piernas-Davenport, Gail 199
Piers, Robert
  See Anthony, Piers
Pig, Edward
  See Gorey, Edward (St. John)
Pignataro, Anna 1965- 223
Pike, Aprilynne 218
Pike, Bob
  See Pike, Robert W.
Pike, Christopher 1954(?)- 156
  Earlier sketch in SATA 68
  See also CLR 29
Pike, Deborah 1951- 89
Pike, E(dgar) Royston 1896-1980 22
  Obituary 56
Pike, R. William 1956- 92
Pike, Robert
  See Pike, Robert W.
Pike, Robert W. 1931- 102
Pike, Robert Wilson
  See Pike, Robert W.
Pilarski, Laura 1926- 13
Pilgrim, Anne
  See Allan, Mabel Esther
Pilkey, Dav 1966- 166
  Earlier sketches in SATA 68, 115
  See also CLR 160
Pilkey, David Murray, Jr.
  See Pilkey, Dav
Pilkington, Francis Meredyth 1907-1993 4
Pilkington, Roger (Windle) 1915-2003 10
  Obituary 144
Pilutti, Deb 208
Pin, Isabel 1975- 183
Pinchot, David 1914(?)-1983
  Obituary 34
Pincus, Harriet 1938- 27
Pinczes, Elinor J(ane) 1940- 81
Pine, Nicholas 1951- 91
Pine, Tillie S(chloss) 1896-1999 13
Pini, Richard (Alan) 1950- 89
Pini, Wendy 1951- 89
Pinkerton, Kathrene Sutherland (Gedney)
  1887-1967
  Obituary 26
Pinkett, Jada
  See Smith, Jada Pinkett
Pinkney, Andrea Davis 1963- 160
  Earlier sketch in SATA 113

Pinkney, Brian 1961- 206
  Earlier sketches in SATA 74, 148
  See also CLR 54
Pinkney, Gloria Jean 1941- 212
  Earlier sketch in SATA 85
Pinkney, J. Brian
  See Pinkney, Brian
Pinkney, Jerry 1939- 198
  Autobiography Feature 198
  Brief entry 32
  Earlier sketches in SATA 41, 71, 107, 151
  See also CLR 43
  See also SAAS 12
Pinkney, John 97
Pinkney, Sandra L. 193
  Earlier sketch in SATA 128
Pinkwater, D. Manus
  See Pinkwater, Daniel
Pinkwater, Daniel 1941- 210
  Earlier sketches in SATA 8, 46, 76, 114, 158
  See also CLR 4
  See also SAAS 3
Pinkwater, Daniel M.
  See Pinkwater, Daniel
Pinkwater, Daniel Manus
  See Pinkwater, Daniel
Pinkwater, Jill 188
Pinkwater, Manus
  See Pinkwater, Daniel
Pinner, Joma
  See Werner, Herma
Pinto, Sara 200
Pioneer
  See Yates, Raymond F(rancis)
Piowaty, Kim Kennelly 1957- 49
Piper, Roger
  See Fisher, John
Pirner, Connie White 1955- 72
Piro, Richard 1934- 7
Pirot, Alison Lohans
  See Lohans, Alison
Pirotta, Saviour 184
Pirsig, Robert M(aynard) 1928- 39
Pita
  See Rendon, Maria
Pitcher, C.
  See Pitcher, Caroline
Pitcher, Caroline 1948- 214
  Earlier sketch in SATA 128
Pitcher, Caroline Nell
  See Pitcher, Caroline
Pitman, (Isaac) James 1901-1985
  Obituary 46
Pitre, Felix 1949- 84
Pitrone, Jean Maddern 1920- 4
Pittman, Helena Clare 1945- 71
Pitz, Henry C(larence) 1895-1976 4
  Obituary 24
Pitzer, Susanna 1958- 181
Piven, Hanoch 1963- 173
Pixley, Marcella 194
Pizer, Vernon 1918- 21
Place, Marian T(empleton) 1910- 3
Place, Robin (Mary) 1926- 71
Plaidy, Jean
  See Hibbert, Eleanor Alice Burford
Plain, Belva 1919-2010 62
Plaine, Alfred R. 1898(?)-1981
  Obituary 29
Plant, Andrew 214
Plath, Sylvia 1932-1963 96
Platt, Chris 1959- 185
Platt, Kin 1911- 86
  Earlier sketch in SATA 21
  See also SAAS 17
Platt, Randall 1948- 95
Platt, Randall Beth
  See Platt, Randall
Platt, Richard 1953- 218
  Earlier sketches in SATA 120, 166

Playfellow, Robin
  See Ellis, Edward S.
Playsted, James
  See Wood, James Playsted
Plecas, Jennifer 1966- 149
  Earlier sketch in SATA 84
Plimpton, George 1927-2003 10
  Obituary 150
Plimpton, George Ames
  See Plimpton, George
Plomer, William Charles Franklin
  1903-1973 24
Plotz, Helen Ratnoff 1913-2000 38
Plourde, Lynn 1955- 218
  Earlier sketches in SATA 122, 168
Plowden, David 1932- 52
Plowden, Martha Ward 1948- 98
Plowhead, Ruth Gipson 1877-1967 43
Plowman, Stephanie 1922- 6
Pluckrose, Henry (Arthur) 1931- 141
  Earlier sketch in SATA 13
Plum, J.
  See Wodehouse, P. G.
Plum, Jennifer
  See Kurland, Michael
Plumb, Charles P. 1900(?)-1982
  Obituary 29
Plume, Ilse 170
  Brief entry 43
Plumme, Don E.
  See Katz, Bobbi
Plummer, Margaret 1911- 2
Plum-Ucci, Carol 184
Poblocki, Dan 1981- 224
Pochocki, Ethel (Frances) 1925- 76
Podendorf, Illa (E.) 1903(?)-1983 18
  Obituary 35
Podwal, Mark 1945- 224
  Earlier sketches in SATA 101, 160
Podwal, Mark H.
  See Podwal, Mark
Poe, Edgar Allan 1809-1849 23
Poe, Ty (Christopher) 1975- 94
Pogany, William Andrew 1882-1955 44
  Brief entry 30
Pogany, Willy
  See Pogany, William Andrew
Pogue, Carolyn 1948- 223
Pohl, Frederik 1919- 24
Pohlmann, Lillian (Grenfell) 1902-1997 11
Pohrt, Tom 1953- 195
  Earlier sketches in SATA 67, 152
Pointon, Robert
  See Rooke, Daphne
Points, Larry G. 1945- 177
  Earlier sketch in SATA 133
Points, Larry Gene
  See Points, Larry G.
Pokeberry, P.J.
  See Mitchell, B.J.
POLA
  See Watson, Pauline
Polacco, Patricia 1944- 212
  Earlier sketches in SATA 74, 123, 180
  See also CLR 40
Polacco, Patricia Ann
  See Polacco, Patricia
Polak, Monique 1960- 178
Polatnick, Florence T. 1923- 5
Polcovar, Jane 1948- 211
Polder, Markus
  See Kruss, James
Polenghi, Evan 1961- 225
Polese, Carolyn 1947- 58
Polese, James 1914- 87
Polette, Nancy (Jane) 1930- 42
Polhamus, Jean Burt 1928- 21
Polhemus, Coleman 210
Policoff, Stephen Phillip 1948- 77
Polikoff, Barbara G. 1929- 162
  Earlier sketch in SATA 77

Polikoff, Barbara Garland
  See Polikoff, Barbara G.
Polisar, Barry Louis 1954- *134*
  Earlier sketch in SATA 77
Politi, Leo 1908-1996 .... *47*
  Obituary *88*
  Earlier sketch in SATA *1*
  See also CLR 29
Polking, Kirk 1925- *5*
Pollack, Jill S. 1963- *88*
Pollack, Merrill S. 1924-1988
  Obituary *55*
Polland, Barbara K(ay) 1939- *44*
Polland, Madeleine A(ngela Cahill) 1918- ... *68*
  Earlier sketch in SATA 6
  See also SAAS 8
Pollema-Cahill, Phyllis 1958- *123*
Pollock, Bruce 1945- *46*
Pollock, Mary
  See Blyton, Enid
Pollock, Penny 1935- *137*
  Brief entry *42*
  Earlier sketch in SATA 44
Pollowitz, Melinda Kilborn 1944- *26*
Polner, Murray 1928- *64*
Polonsky, Arthur 1925- *34*
Polseno, Jo *17*
Pomaska, Anna 1946- *117*
Pomerantz, Charlotte 1930- *177*
  Earlier sketches in SATA 20, 80
Pomeroy, Pete
  See Roth, Arthur J(oseph)
Pon, Cindy 1973- *216*
Pond, Alonzo W(illiam) 1894-1986 .... *5*
Pontiflet, Ted 1932- *32*
Poole, Gray Johnson 1906- *1*
Poole, Josephine
  See Helyar, Jane Penelope Josephine
Poole, (Jane Penelope) Josephine
  See Helyar, Jane Penelope Josephine
Poole, Lynn 1910-1969 .... *1*
Poole, Peggy 1925- *39*
Poortvliet, Rien 1932- *65*
  Brief entry *37*
Pope, Elizabeth Marie 1917-1992 .... *38*
  Brief entry *36*
Pope, Kevin 1958- *183*
Popescu, Christine
  See Pullein-Thompson, Christine
Poploff, Michelle 1956- *67*
Popp, K. Wendy *91*
Poppel, Hans 1942- *71*
Porfirio, Guy 1958- *197*
Portal, Colette 1936- *6*
Porte, Barbara Ann 1943- *152*
  Brief entry *45*
  Earlier sketches in SATA 57, 93
Porter, A(nthony) P(eyton) 1945- *68*
Porter, Connie (Rose) 1959(?)- *129*
  Earlier sketch in SATA 81
Porter, Donald Clayton
  See Gerson, Noel Bertram
Porter, Eleanor H(odgman) 1868-1920
  See CLR *110*
Porter, Gene Stratton
  See Stratton-Porter, Gene
Porter, Janice Lee 1953- *108*
  Earlier sketch in SATA 68
Porter, Katherine Anne 1890-1980 .... *39*
  Obituary *23*
Porter, Kathryn
  See Swinford, Betty (June Wells)
Porter, Pamela 1956- *193*
Porter, Sheena 1935- *24*
  See also SAAS 10
Porter, Sue
  See Limb, Sue
Porter, Sue 1951- *213*
  Earlier sketch in SATA 76
Porter, Tracey *191*

Porter, William Sydney
  See Henry, O.
Portis, Antoinette *189*
Porto, Tony 1960- *153*
Portteus, Eleanora Marie Manthei (?)-1983
  Obituary *36*
Posada, Mia *187*
Posell, Elsa Z(eigerman) -1995 .... *3*
Posesorski, Sherie *216*
Posten, Margaret L(ois) 1915- *10*
Postgate, Daniel 1964- *216*
Posthuma, Sieb 1960- *150*
Postier, Jim 1965- *202*
Potok, Chaim 1929-2002 .... *106*
  Obituary *134*
  Earlier sketch in SATA 33
  See also CLR 92
Potok, Herbert Harold
  See Potok, Chaim
Potok, Herman Harold
  See Potok, Chaim
Potter, Alicia *216*
Potter, Beatrix 1866-1943 .... *132*
  Earlier sketch in SATA 100
  See also YABC *1*
  See also CLR 73
Potter, Ellen 1973- *218*
Potter, Giselle *187*
  Earlier sketch in SATA 150
Potter, Helen Beatrix
  See Potter, Beatrix
Potter, Katherine *217*
Potter, Margaret 1926-1998 .... *21*
  Obituary *104*
Potter, Marian 1915- *9*
Potter, Miriam Clark 1886-1965 .... *3*
Poulin, Stephane 1961- *98*
  See also CLR 28
Poulton, Kimberly 1957(?)- *136*
Pournelle, Jerry 1933- *161*
  Earlier sketches in SATA 26, 91
Pournelle, Jerry Eugene
  See Pournelle, Jerry
Povelite, Kay 1955- *102*
Pow, Tom 1950- *163*
Powe-Allred, Alexandra
  See Allred, Alexandra Powe
Powell, A. M.
  See Morgan, Alfred P(owell)
Powell, Consie *174*
Powell, E. Sandy 1947- *72*
Powell, E.S.
  See Powell, E. Sandy
Powell, Pamela 1960- *78*
Powell, Patricia Hruby 1951- *136*
Powell, Randy 1956- *118*
Powell, Richard Stillman
  See Barbour, Ralph Henry
Powell, Robert (Stephenson Smyth) Baden
  See Baden-Powell, Robert (Stephenson Smyth)
Powell, Stephanie 1953- *93*
Power, Margaret (M.) 1945- *125*
  Earlier sketch in SATA 75
Powers, Anne
  See Schwartz, Anne Powers
Powers, Bill 1931- *52*
  Brief entry *31*
Powers, Daniel 1959- *164*
Powers, J. L. *195*
Powers, Jessica
  See Powers, J. L.
Powers, Jessica Lynn
  See Powers, J. L.
Powers, Margaret
  See Heal, Edith
Powers, Tim 1952- *107*
Powers, Timothy Thomas
  See Powers, Tim
Powledge, Fred 1935- *37*
Poydar, Nancy *190*

Poynter, Margaret 1927- *27*
Prachaticka, Marketa
  See Kolibalova, Marketa
Prachatika, Marketa
  See Kolibalova, Marketa
Prager, Arthur *44*
Prager, Ellen J. 1962- *136*
Prange, Beckie *172*
Prap, Lila 1955- *177*
Praprotnik-Zupancic, Lilijana
  See Prap, Lila
Pratchett, Terence David John
  See Pratchett, Terry
Pratchett, Terry 1948- *185*
  Earlier sketches in SATA 82, 139
  See also CLR 64
Prater, John 1947- *149*
  Earlier sketches in SATA 72, 103
Prato, Rodica *184*
Pratt, Christine Joy *214*
Pratt, (Murray) Fletcher 1897-1956 .... *102*
Pratt, Kristin Joy 1976- *87*
Pratt, Pierre 1962- *208*
  Earlier sketches in SATA 95, 166
Preiss, Byron 1953-2005 .... *166*
  Brief entry *42*
  Earlier sketch in SATA 47
Preiss, Byron Cary
  See Preiss, Byron
Preller, James 1961- *209*
  Earlier sketch in SATA 88
Prelutsky, Jack 1940- *171*
  Earlier sketches in SATA 22, 66, 118
  See also CLR 115
Prentice, Amy
  See Kaler, James Otis
Prescott, Casey
  See Morris, Chris(topher Crosby)
Presnall, Judith (Ann) Janda 1943- *96*
Pressler, Mirjam 1940- *155*
Preston, Douglas 1956- *113*
Preston, Edna Mitchell *40*
Preston, Lillian Elvira 1918- *47*
Preus, Margi *209*
Preussler, Otfried 1923- *24*
Prevert, Jacques 1900-1977
  Obituary *30*
Prevert, Jacques Henri Marie
  See Prevert, Jacques
Prevost, Guillaume 1964- *192*
Prevost, Mikela *203*
Price, Beverley Joan 1931- *98*
Price, Charlie *187*
Price, Christine (Hilda) 1928-1980 .... *3*
  Obituary *23*
Price, Garrett 1896-1979
  Obituary *22*
Price, Jennifer
  See Hoover, Helen (Drusilla Blackburn)
Price, Joan 1931- *124*
Price, Jonathan (Reeve) 1941- *46*
Price, Karen 1957- *125*
Price, Kathy Z. 1957- *172*
Price, Lucie Locke
  See Locke, Lucie
Price, Olive 1903-1991 .... *8*
Price, Susan 1955- *128*
  Earlier sketches in SATA 25, 85
Price, Willard 1887-1983 .... *48*
  Brief entry *38*
Price-Groff, Claire *127*
Priceman, Marjorie 1958- *168*
  Earlier sketches in SATA 81, 120
Prichard, Katharine Susannah 1883-1969 ..... *66*
Prideaux, Tom 1908-1993 .... *37*
  Obituary *76*
Priestley, Alice 1962- *95*
Priestley, Chris 1958- *198*
Priestley, Lee (Shore) 1904-1999 .... *27*
Priestly, Doug 1954- *122*

Author Index

Priestly, Douglas Michael
 See Priestly, Doug
Prieto, Mariana Beeching 1912-1999 8
Priley, Margaret (Ann) Hubbard 1909-1992
 Obituary 130
Primavera, Elise 1954- 185
 Brief entry 48
 Earlier sketches in SATA 58, 109
Prime, Derek (James) 1931- 34
Prince, Alison (Mary) 1931- 86
 Earlier sketch in SATA 28
Prince, April Jones 1975- 180
Prince, J(ack) H(arvey) 1908- 17
Prince, Joshua 188
Prince, Maggie 102
Prineas, Sarah 204
Pringle, Eric 138
Pringle, Laurence 1935- 201
 Autobiography Feature 201
 Earlier sketches in SATA 4, 68, 104, 154
 See also CLR 57
 See also SAAS 6
Pringle, Laurence Patrick
 See Pringle, Laurence
Prinz, Yvonne 1960- 175
Prior, Natalie Jane 1963- 106
Pritchett, Elaine H(illyer) 1920- 36
Pritchett, Laura 1971- 178
Pritchett, Laura Rose
 See Pritchett, Laura
Pritts, Kim Derek 1953- 83
Prochazkova, Iva 1953- 68
Proctor, Everitt
 See Montgomery, Rutherford George
Proeysen, Alf 1914-1970 67
 See also CLR 24
Professor Scribbler
 See Hollingsworth, Mary
Proimos, James 1955- 217
 Earlier sketch in SATA 173
Prose, Francine 1947- 198
 Earlier sketches in SATA 101, 149
Prosek, James 1975- 216
Protopopescu, Orel 186
Protopopescu, Orel Odinov
 See Protopopescu, Orel
Provensen, Alice 1918- 147
 Earlier sketches in SATA 9, 70
 See also CLR 11
Provensen, Martin 1916-1987 70
 Obituary 51
 Earlier sketch in SATA 9
 See also CLR 11
Provensen, Martin Elias
 See Provensen, Martin
Provenzo, Eugene (F., Jr.) 1949- 142
 Earlier sketch in SATA 78
Provist, d'Alain 1906-1989
 See Diop, Birago (Ismael)
Provost, Gail Levine 1944- 65
Provost, Gary (Richard) 1944-1995 66
Proysen, Alf
 See Proeysen, Alf
Pruett, Candace (J.) 1968- 157
Pryor, Bonnie H. 1942- 69
Pryor, Boori (Monty) 1950- 112
Pryor, Helen Brenton 1897-1972 4
Pryor, Michael 1957- 153
Pucci, Albert John 1920- 44
Pudney, John (Sleigh) 1909-1977 24
Pugh, Ellen (Tiffany) 1920- 7
Pullein-Thompson, Christine 1925-2005 82
 Obituary 172
 Earlier sketch in SATA 3

Pullein-Thompson, Diana
 See Farr, Diana
Pullein-Thompson, Joanna Maxwell
 1898-1961 82
Pullein-Thompson, Josephine (Mary
 Wedderburn) 82
 Earlier sketch in SATA 3
Pullen, Zachary 189
Pullman, Philip 1946- 198
 Earlier sketches in SATA 65, 103, 150
 See also CLR 84
 See also SAAS 17
Pullman, Philip Nicholas
 See Pullman, Philip
Pulver, Harry, Jr. 1960- 129
Pulver, Robin 1945- 208
 Earlier sketches in SATA 76, 133
Puner, Helen W(alker) 1915-1989 37
 Obituary 63
Purdy, Carol 1943- 120
 Earlier sketch in SATA 66
Purdy, Susan G(old) 1939- 8
Purkiss, Diane 1961- 194
Purmell, Ann 1953- 206
 Earlier sketch in SATA 147
Purnell, Idella 1901-1982 120
Purscell, Phyllis 1934- 7
Purtill, Richard L. 1931- 53
Pushker, Gloria 1927- 162
 Earlier sketch in SATA 75
Pushker, Gloria Teles
 See Pushker, Gloria
Pushkin, Aleksandr Sergeevich
 See Pushkin, Alexander
Pushkin, Alexander 1799-1837 61
Putnam, Alice 1916- 61
Putnam, Arthur Lee
 See Alger, Horatio, Jr.
Putnam, Peter B(rock) 1920-1998 30
 Obituary 106
Puttapipat, Niroot 199
Puttock, Simon 178
Puvilland, Alex 205
Puvilland, Alexandre
 See Puvilland, Alex
Puybaret, Eric 1976- 195
Pyle, Howard 1853-1911 100
 Earlier sketch in SATA 16
 See also CLR 117
Pyle, Katharine 1863-1938 66
Pyne, Mable Mandeville 1903-1969 9
Pyrnelle, Louise-Clarke 1850-1907 114

Q

Quackenbush, Robert M(ead) 1929- 133
 Autobiography Feature 133
 Earlier sketches in SATA 7, 70
 See also CLR 122
 See also SAAS 7
Qualey, Marsha 1953- 124
 Earlier sketch in SATA 79
Qualls, Sean 177
Quammen, David 1948- 7
Quark, Jason
 See Eldin, Peter
Quarles, Benjamin 1904-1996 12
Quarles, Benjamin Arthur
 See Quarles, Benjamin
Quatermass, Martin
 See Carpenter, John
Quattlebaum, Mary 1958- 185
 Earlier sketches in SATA 88, 134

Quay, Emma 173
 Earlier sketch in SATA 119
Queen, Ellery
 See Deming, Richard
 and Dannay, Frederic
 and Davidson, Avram (James)
 and Fairman, Paul W.
 and Flora, Fletcher
 and Holding, James (Clark Carlisle, Jr.)
 and Hoch, Edward D.
 and Kane, Henry
 and Lee, Manfred B.
 and Marlowe, Stephen
 and Powell, (Oval) Talmage
 and Sheldon, Walter J(ames)
 and Sturgeon, Theodore (Hamilton)
 and Tracy, Don(ald Fiske)
 and Vance, Jack
Queen Latifah 1970- 185
Quennell, Marjorie Courtney 1884-1972 29
Quentin
 See Sheldon, David
Quentin, Brad
 See Bisson, Terry
Quest, (Edna) Olga W(ilbourne) Hall
 See Hall-Quest, (Edna) Olga W(ilbourne)
Quick, Annabelle 1922-1986 2
Quigg, Jane (Hulda) (?)-1986
 Obituary 49
Quigley, Sarah 1976- 220
Quill, Monica
 See McInerny, Ralph
Quin-Harkin, Janet 1941- 165
 Earlier sketches in SATA 18, 90, 119
Quin-Harkin, Janet Elizabeth
 See Quin-Harkin, Janet
Quinlan, Susan E. 1954- 88
Quinlan, Susan Elizabeth
 See Quinlan, Susan E.
Quinn, Elisabeth 1881-1962 22
Quinn, Pat 1947- 130
Quinn, Patrick 1950- 73
Quinn, Rob 1972- 138
Quinn, Susan 1940- 30
Quinn, Susan Taft
 See Quinn, Susan
Quinn, Theodora K.
 See Kroeber, Theodora (Kracaw)
Quinn, Vernon
 See Quinn, Elisabeth
Quirk, Anne (E.) 1956- 99
Quixley, Jim 1931- 56
Quyth, Gabriel
 See Jennings, Gary

R

Ra, Carol F. 1939- 76
Raab, Evelyn 1951- 129
Rabb, Margo 1972- 188
Rabb, M.E.
 See Rabb, Margo
Rabe, Berniece (Louise) 1928- 148
 Autobiography Feature 148
 Earlier sketches in SATA 7, 77
 See also SAAS 10
Rabe, Olive H(anson) (?)-1968 13
Rabin, Staton 1958- 162
 Earlier sketch in SATA 84
Rabinowich, Ellen 1946- 29
Rabinowitz, Sandy 1954- 52
 Brief entry 39
Rachlin, Carol K(ing) 1919- 64
Rachlin, Harvey 1951- 47

Author Index

Rachlin, Harvey Brant
  See Rachlin, Harvey
Rachlin, Nahid 64
Rachlis, Eugene (Jacob) 1920-1986
  Obituary 50
Rackham, Arthur 1867-1939 100
  Earlier sketch in SATA 15
  See also CLR 57
Racoma, Robin Yoko 1953- 207
Raczka, Bob 1963- 191
  Earlier sketch in SATA 163
Radencich, Marguerite C. 1952-1998 79
Rader, Laura 197
Radford, Ruby L(orraine) 1891-1971 6
Radin, Ruth Yaffe 1938- 107
  Brief entry 52
  Earlier sketch in SATA 56
Radlauer, David 1952- 28
Radlauer, Edward 1921- 15
Radlauer, Ruth Shaw 1926- 98
  Earlier sketch in SATA 15
Radley, Gail 1951- 112
  Earlier sketch in SATA 25
Radunsky, Vladimir 177
Radzinski, Kandy 1948- 212
Rae, Gwynedd 1892-1977 37
Raebeck, Lois 1921- 5
Rael, Elsa Okon 1927-
  See CLR 84
Raffi
  See Cavoukian, Raffi
Raftery, Gerald (Bransfield) 1905-1986 11
Ragan-Reid, Gale 1956- 90
Rahaman, Vashanti 1953- 98
Rahn, Joan Elma 1929- 27
Rai, Bali 1971- 152
Raible, Alton (Robert) 1918- 35
Raiff, Stan 1930- 11
Raines, Shirley C(arol) 1945- 128
Rainey, W. B.
  See Blassingame, Wyatt Rainey
Rake, Jody 1961- 157
Rallison, Janette 1966- 183
Ralston, Jan
  See Dunlop, Agnes M. R.
Rama, Sue 190
Ramal, Walter
  See de la Mare, Walter (John)
Ramanujan, A(ttipat) K(rishnaswami)
  1929-1993 86
Rame, David
  See Divine, Arthur Durham
Ramirez, Jose 1967- 198
Ramirez, Orlando L. 1972- 194
Ramos, Jorge 1958- 205
Ramstad, Ralph L. 1919- 115
Ramthun, Bonnie 214
Rana, Indi
  See Rana, Indira Higham
Rana, Indira Higham 1944- 82
Rana, J.
  See Bhatia, Jamunadevi
Ranadive, Gail 1944- 10
Rand, Ann (Binkley) 30
Rand, Gloria 1925- 156
  Earlier sketch in SATA 101
Rand, Paul 1914-1996 6
Randall, Carrie
  See Ransom, Candice
Randall, David 1972- 167
Randall, Florence Engel 1917-1997 5
Randall, Janet
  See Young, Janet Randall
  and Young, Robert W(illiam)
Randall, Robert
  See Garrett, Randall
  and Silverberg, Robert
Randall, Ruth (Elaine) Painter 1892-1971 3
Randell, Beverley
  See Price, Beverley Joan

Randle, Kristen D. 1952- 92
  Autobiography Feature 119
  See also SAAS 24
Randle, Kristen Downey
  See Randle, Kristen D.
Randolph, Boynton M.D.
  See Ellis, Edward S.
Randolph, Ellen
  See Rawn, Melanie
Randolph, Geoffrey
  See Ellis, Edward S.
Randolph, J. H.
  See Ellis, Edward S.
Randolph, Lieutenant J. H.
  See Ellis, Edward S.
Rands, William Brighty 1823-1882 17
Raney, Ken 1953- 74
Rankin, Joan 1940- 212
  Earlier sketches in SATA 88, 148
Rankin, Laura 1953(?)- 176
Ranney, Agnes V. 1916-1985 6
Ransom, Candice 1952- 222
  Brief entry 49
  Earlier sketches in SATA 52, 89, 135, 183
Ransom, Jeanie Franz 1957- 187
Ransome, Arthur (Michell) 1884-1967 22
  See also CLR 8
Ransome, James E. 1961- 178
  Earlier sketches in SATA 76, 123
  See also CLR 86
Rant, Tol E.
  See Longyear, Barry B(rookes)
Rao, Rohitash 218
Raphael, Elaine
  See Bolognese, Elaine
Raposo, Joseph Guilherme 1938-1989
  Obituary 61
Rapp, Adam 1968- 148
Rappaport, Doreen 211
  Earlier sketch in SATA 151
Rappaport, Eva 1924- 6
Rappoport, Ken 1935- 167
  Earlier sketch in SATA 89
Rarick, Carrie 1911-2002 41
Raschka, Chris 1959- 207
  Earlier sketches in SATA 80, 117, 166
Raschka, Christopher
  See Raschka, Chris
Rascol, Sabina I. 159
Rash, Andy 219
  Earlier sketch in SATA 162
Raskin, Edith Lefkowitz 1908-1987 9
Raskin, Ellen 1928-1984 139
  Earlier sketches in SATA 2, 38
  See also CLR 12
Raskin, Joseph 1897-1982 12
  Obituary 29
Rathjen, Carl Henry 1909-1984 11
Rathmann, Peggy 1953- 157
  Earlier sketch in SATA 94
  See also CLR 77
Ratliff, Thomas M. 1948- 118
Ratner, Sue Lynn
  See Alexander, Sue
Rattigan, Jama Kim 1951- 99
Ratto, Linda Lee 1952- 79
Rattray, Simon
  See Trevor, Elleston
Ratz de Tagyos, Paul 1958- 198
  Earlier sketch in SATA 76
Rau, Dana Meachen 1971- 218
  Earlier sketches in SATA 94, 167
Rau, Margaret 1913- 168
  Earlier sketch in SATA 9
  See also CLR 8
Rauch, Mabel Thompson 1888-1972
  Obituary 26
Raucher, Herman 1928- 8
Raude, Karina 199
Rauh, Sherry
  See North, Sherry

Raum, Elizabeth 1949- 155
Raut, Radhashyam 222
Raven, Margot Theis 184
RavenWolf, Silver 1956- 155
Ravielli, Anthony 1916-1997 3
  Obituary 95
Ravilious, Robin 1944- 77
Ravishankar, Anushka 1961- 200
Rawding, F(rederick) W(illiam) 1930- 55
Rawlings, Marjorie Kinnan 1896-1953 100
  See also YABC 1
  See also CLR 63
Rawlins, Donna 1956- 206
Rawlinson, Julia 212
  Earlier sketch in SATA 175
Rawls, (Woodrow) Wilson 1913-1984 22
  See also CLR 81
Rawlyk, George Alexander 1935- 64
Rawn, Melanie 1954- 98
Rawn, Melanie Robin
  See Rawn, Melanie
Rawson, Katherine 1955- 190
Ray, Carl 1943-1978 63
Ray, Deborah
  See Kogan Ray, Deborah
Ray, Delia 1963- 179
  Earlier sketch in SATA 70
Ray, Irene
  See Sutton, Margaret Beebe
Ray, Jane 1960- 196
  Earlier sketches in SATA 72, 152
Ray, JoAnne 1935- 9
Ray, Mary (Eva Pedder) 1932- 127
  Earlier sketch in SATA 2
Ray, Mary Lyn 1946- 154
  Earlier sketch in SATA 90
Rayban, Chloe 1944- 167
Rayevsky, Robert 1955- 190
  Earlier sketch in SATA 81
Raymond, James Crossley 1917-1981
  Obituary 29
Raymond, Robert
  See Alter, Robert Edmond
Rayner, Catherine 204
Rayner, Hugh 151
Rayner, Mary 1933- 87
  Earlier sketch in SATA 22
  See also CLR 41
Rayner, Shoo
  See Rayner, Hugh
Rayner, William 1929- 55
  Brief entry 36
Raynor, Dorka 28
Raynor, Gemma 1985- 216
Rayson, Steven 1932- 30
Rayyan, Omar 1968- 216
Razzell, Arthur (George) 1925- 11
Razzell, Mary (Catherine) 1930- 102
Razzi, James 1931- 10
Read, Elfreida 1920- 2
Read, Nicholas 1956- 146
Read, Piers Paul 1941- 21
Reade, Deborah 1949- 69
Reader, Dennis 1929- 71
Reading, Richard P(atrick) 1962- 161
Readman, Jo 1958- 89
Ready, Kirk L(ewis) 1943- 39
Reaney, James 1926-2008 43
Reaney, James Crerar
  See Reaney, James
Reardon, Joyce
  See Pearson, Ridley
Reaver, Chap 1935-1993 69
  Obituary 77
Reaver, Herbert R.
  See Reaver, Chap
Reaves, J. Michael
  See Reaves, (James) Michael
Reaves, (James) Michael 1950- 99
Reber, Deborah 189
Recorvits, Helen 191

Redding, Robert Hull 1919- 2
Redekopp, Elsa 61
Redlich, Ben 1977- 181
Redsand, Anna 1948- 184
Redway, Ralph
See Hamilton, Charles (Harold St. John)
Redway, Ridley
See Hamilton, Charles (Harold St. John)
Reece, Colleen L. 1935- 116
Reece, Gabrielle 1970- 108
Reed, Amy 1979- 223
Reed, Betty Jane 1921- 4
Reed, Dallas
See Pendleton, Thomas
Reed, E.
See Evans, Mari
Reed, Gwendolyn E(lizabeth) 1932- 21
Reed, Kit 1932- 184
Autobiography Feature 184
Earlier sketches in SATA 34, 116
Reed, Lynn Rowe 215
Earlier sketch in SATA 171
Reed, Mike 1951- 211
Reed, Neil 1961- 99
Reed, Talbot Baines 1852-1893
See CLR 76
Reed, Thomas (James) 1947- 34
Reed, William Maxwell 1871-1962 15
Reeder, Carolyn 1937- 97
Earlier sketch in SATA 66
See also CLR 69
Reeder, Colin (Dawson) 1938- 74
Reeder, Colonel Red
See Reeder, Russell P(otter), Jr.
Reeder, Russell P(otter), Jr. 1902-1998 4
Obituary 101
Reeder, Stephanie Owen 1951- 102
Reed-Jones, Carol 1955- 112
Reef, Catherine 1951- 223
Earlier sketches in SATA 73, 128, 189
Reekie, Jocelyn (Margaret) 1947- 145
Reeman, Douglas Edward 1924- 63
Brief entry 28
Rees, Celia 1949- 124
Rees, David (Bartlett) 1936-1993 69
Obituary 76
Earlier sketch in SATA 36
See also SAAS 5
Rees, Douglas 1947- 169
Rees, Ennis (Samuel, Jr.) 1925-2009 3
Rees, (George) Leslie (Clarence)
1905-2000 105
Obituary 135
Reese, Bob
See Reese, Robert A.
Reese, Carolyn Johnson 1938- 64
Reese, Della 1931(?)- 114
Reese, Lyn
See Reese, Carolyn Johnson
Reese, Robert A. 1938- 60
Brief entry 53
Reese, (John) Terence 1913-1996 59
Reeve, Joel
See Cox, William R(obert)
Reeve, Kirk 1934- 117
Reeve, Philip 201
Earlier sketch in SATA 170
Reeve, Rosie 188
Earlier sketch in SATA 186
Reeves, Faye Couch 1953- 76
Reeves, James
See Reeves, John Morris
Reeves, Jeni 1947- 111
Reeves, John Morris 1909-1978 87
Earlier sketch in SATA 15
Reeves, Joyce 1911- 17
Reeves, Lawrence F. 1926- 29
Reeves, Ruth Ellen
See Ranney, Agnes V.

Regan, Dian Curtis 1950- 224
Autobiography Feature 149
Earlier sketches in SATA 75, 133, 149
Regehr, Lydia 1903-1991 37
Reger, James P. 1952- 106
Reggiani, Renee 1925- 18
Rehm, Karl M. 1935- 72
Reibstein, Mark 211
Reich, Ali
See Katz, Bobbi
Reich, Susanna 1954- 214
Earlier sketch in SATA 113
Reiche, Dietlof 1941- 159
Reichert, Edwin C(lark) 1909-1988
Obituary 57
Reichert, Mickey Zucker
See Reichert, Miriam Zucker
Reichert, Miriam Zucker 1962- 85
Reichert, Renee 172
Reichhold, Jane(t E.) 1937- 147
Reid, Alastair 1926- 46
Reid, Barbara 1922- 21
Reid, Barbara (Jane) 1957- 93
See also CLR 64
Reid, Desmond
See Moorcock, Michael
and McNeilly, Wilfred (Glassford)
Reid, Eugenie Chazal 1924- 12
Reid, John Calvin 21
Reid, (Thomas) Mayne 1818-1883 24
Reid, Meta Mayne 1905-1991 58
Brief entry 36
Reid, Robin (Nicole) 1969- 145
Reid Banks, Lynne 1929- 165
Earlier sketches in SATA 22, 75, 111
See also CLR 86
Reider, Katja 1960- 126
Reid Jenkins, Debra 1955- 87
Reiff, Stephanie Ann 1948- 47
Brief entry 28
Reig, June 1933- 30
Reigot, Betty Polisar 1924- 55
Brief entry 41
Reilly, Joan 195
Reim, Melanie (K.) 1956- 104
Reinach, Jacquelyn (Krasne) 1930-2000 28
Reiner, Carl 1922- 151
Reiner, William B(uck) 1910-1976 46
Obituary 30
Reinfeld, Fred 1910-1964 3
Reinhardt, Dana 1971- 175
Reinhart, Matthew 1971- 197
Earlier sketch in SATA 161
Reiniger, Lotte 1899-1981 40
Obituary 33
Reinsma, Carol 1949- 91
Reinstedt, Randall A. 1935- 101
Reinstedt, Randy
See Reinstedt, Randall A.
Reisberg, Mira 1955- 82
Reisberg, Veg
See Reisberg, Mira
Reiser, Lynn 1944- 180
Earlier sketches in SATA 81, 138
Reiser, Lynn Whisnant
See Reiser, Lynn
Reisgies, Teresa (Maria) 1966- 74
Reiss, Johanna 1929(?)- 18
See also CLR 19
Reiss, Johanna de Leeuw
See Reiss, Johanna
Reiss, John J. 23
Reiss, Kathryn 1957- 144
Earlier sketch in SATA 76
Reit, Seymour Victory 1918-2001 21
Obituary 133
Reit, Sy
See Reit, Seymour Victory
Relf, Patricia 1954- 134
Earlier sketch in SATA 71

Remark, Erich Paul
See Remarque, Erich Maria
Remarque, Erich Maria 1898-1970
See CLR 159
Remi, Georges 1907-1983 13
Obituary 32
See also CLR 114
Remington, Frederic S(ackrider)
1861-1909 41
Remkiewicz, Frank 1939- 217
Earlier sketches in SATA 77, 152
Rempt, Fiona 1973- 198
Remy, Georges
See Remi, Georges
Renaud, Anne 1957- 211
Renaud, Bernadette 1945- 66
Renault, Mary 1905-1983 23
Obituary 36
Rendell, Joan 28
Rendina, Laura (Jones) Cooper 1902- 10
Rendon, Marcie R. 1952- 97
Rendon, Maria 1965- 116
Renee, Janina 1956- 140
Renfro, Ed 1924- 79
Renick, Marion (Lewis) 1905-1983 1
Renier, Aaron 1977- 202
Renken, Aleda 1907- 27
Renlie, Frank H. 1936- 11
Rennert, Laura Joy 224
Rennert, Richard Scott 1956- 67
Rennison, Louise 1951- 149
Reno, Dawn E(laine) 1953- 130
Rensie, Willis
See Eisner, Will
Renton, Cam
See Armstrong, Richard
Renvoize, Jean 5
Resau, Laura 1973- 190
Resciniti, Angelo G. 1952- 75
Resnick, Michael David
See Resnick, Mike
Resnick, Mike 1942- 159
Earlier sketches in SATA 38, 106
Resnick, Seymour 1920- 23
Retla, Robert
See Alter, Robert Edmond
Rettig, Liz 199
Rettstatt, Chris
See Ashland, Monk
Reuter, Bjarne (B.) 1950- 142
Earlier sketch in SATA 68
Reuter, Carol (Joan) 1931- 2
Revena
See Wright, Betty Ren
Revsbech, Vicki
See Liestman, Vicki
Rex, Adam 225
Earlier sketch in SATA 186
Rex, Michael 191
Rey, H. A. 1898-1977 100
Earlier sketches in SATA 1, 26, 69
See also CLR 93
Rey, Hans Augusto
See Rey, H. A.
Rey, Luis V. 1955- 201
Rey, Margret 1906-1996 86
Obituary 93
Earlier sketch in SATA 26
See also CLR 93
Rey, Margret Elisabeth
See Rey, Margret
Reyher, Becky
See Reyher, Rebecca Hourwich
Reyher, Rebecca Hourwich 1897-1987 18
Obituary 50
Reynish, Jenny 222
Reynold, Ann
See Bernardo, Anilu
Reynolds, Aaron 1970- 197
Reynolds, Adrian 1963- 192
Reynolds, C. Buck 1957- 107

Reynolds, Dickson
    See Reynolds, Helen Mary Greenwood Campbell
Reynolds, Helen Mary Greenwood Campbell
    1884-1969
    Obituary 26
Reynolds, Jan 1956- 180
Reynolds, John
    See Whitlock, Ralph
Reynolds, Madge
    See Whitlock, Ralph
Reynolds, Malvina 1900-1978 44
    Obituary 24
Reynolds, Marilyn 1935- 121
    See also SAAS 23
Reynolds, Marilyn M.
    See Reynolds, Marilyn
Reynolds, Marilynn 1940- 141
    Earlier sketch in SATA 80
Reynolds, Pamela 1923- 34
Reynolds, Peter H. 1961- 128
Reynolds, Peter J. 1961- 179
Reynolds, Susan 179
Rhine, Richard
    See Silverstein, Alvin
    and Silverstein, Virginia B.
Rhoades, Diane 1952- 90
Rhodes, Bennie (Loran) 1927- 35
Rhodes, Donna McKee 1962- 87
Rhodes, Frank Harold Trevor 1926- 37
Rhue, Morton
    See Strasser, Todd
Rhyne, Nancy 1926- 66
Rhynes, Martha E. 1939- 141
Ribbons, Ian 1924- 37
    Brief entry 30
    See also SAAS 3
Ricciuti, Edward R(aphael) 1938- 10
Rice, Alice (Caldwell) Hegan 1870-1942 63
Rice, Bebe Faas 1932- 89
Rice, Charles D(uane) 1910-1971
    Obituary 27
Rice, Dale R. 1948- 42
Rice, Dale Richard
    See Rice, Dale R.
Rice, Dick
    See Rice, R. Hugh
Rice, Earle (Wilmont), Jr. 1928- 151
    Earlier sketch in SATA 92
Rice, Edward 1918-2001 47
    Brief entry 42
Rice, Elizabeth 1913-1976 2
Rice, Eve 1951- 91
    Earlier sketch in SATA 34
Rice, Eve Hart
    See Rice, Eve
Rice, Inez 1907- 13
Rice, James 1934- 93
    Earlier sketch in SATA 22
Rice, John F. 1958- 82
Rice, R. Hugh 1929- 115
Rice, Richard H.
    See Rice, R. Hugh
Rich, Anna 1956- 212
Rich, Barbara
    See Graves, Robert
Rich, Elaine Sommers 1926- 6
Rich, Josephine Bouchard 1912- 10
Rich, Louise Dickinson 1903-1991 54
    Obituary 67
Rich, Naomi 217
Richard, Adrienne 1921- 5
    See also SAAS 9
Richard, James Robert
    See Bowen, Robert Sydney
Richards, Chuck 1957- 170
Richards, Frank
    See Hamilton, Charles (Harold St. John)
Richards, Hilda
    See Hamilton, Charles (Harold St. John)
Richards, Jackie 1925- 102

Richards, Jean 1940- 135
Richards, Justin 169
Richards, Kay
    See Baker, Susan (Catherine)
Richards, Laura E(lizabeth Howe) 1850-1943
    See YABC 1
    See also CLR 54
Richards, Leigh
    See King, Laurie R.
Richards, Marlee
    See Brill, Marlene Targ
Richards, Norman 1932- 48
Richards, R(onald) C(harles) W(illiam)
    1923- 59
    Brief entry 43
Richards, Walter Alden (Jr.) 1907-1988
    Obituary 56
Richardson, Andrew (William) 1986- 120
Richardson, Carol 1932- 58
Richardson, Frank Howard 1882-1970
    Obituary 27
Richardson, Grace Lee
    See Dickson, Naida
Richardson, Jean (Mary) 59
Richardson, Judith Benet 1941- 77
Richardson, Nigel 1957- 187
Richardson, Robert S(hirley) 1902-1981 8
Richardson, Sandy 1949- 116
Richardson, V.A. 189
Richardson, Willis 1889-1977 60
Richelson, Geraldine 1922- 29
Richemont, Enid 1940- 82
Richler, Mordecai 1931-2001 98
    Brief entry 27
    Earlier sketch in SATA 44
    See also CLR 17
Richman, Sophia 1941- 142
Rich-McCoy, Lois
    See McCoy, Lois (Rich)
Richmond, Robin 1951- 75
Richoux, Pat(ricia) 1927- 7
Richter, Alice 1941- 30
Richter, Conrad (Michael) 1890-1968 3
Richter, Hans Peter 1925-1993 6
    See also CLR 21
    See also SAAS 11
Richter, Jutta 1955- 184
Rickard, Graham 1949- 71
Rico, Don(ato) 1917-1985
    Obituary 43
Riddell, Chris 1962- 219
    Earlier sketches in SATA 114, 166
Riddell, Christopher Barry
    See Riddell, Chris
Riddell, Edwina 1955- 82
Ridden, Brian 1934- 123
    See Ridden, Brian John
Riddle, Tohby 1965- 223
    Earlier sketches in SATA 74, 151
Riddleburger, Sam 202
Riddles, Libby 1956- 140
Ride, Sally 1951- 219
Ride, Sally Kristen
    See Ride, Sally
Rideout, Sandy 194
Ridge, Antonia (Florence) (?)-1981 7
    Obituary 27
Ridge, Martin 1923-2003 43
Ridley, Philip 171
    Earlier sketch in SATA 88
Ridlon, Marci
    See Balterman, Marcia Ridlon
Riedman, Sarah R(egal) 1902-1995 1
Riehecky, Janet 1953- 164
Ries, Lori 185
Riesenberg, Felix, Jr. 1913-1962 23
Rieu, E(mile) V(ictor) 1887-1972 46
    Obituary 26
Riffenburgh, Beau 1955- 175
Rigg, Sharon
    See Creech, Sharon

Riggenbach, Holly
    See Black, Holly
Riggio, Anita 1952- 148
    Earlier sketch in SATA 73
Riggs, Shannon 190
Riggs, Sidney Noyes 1892-1975
    Obituary 28
Riggs, Stephanie 1964- 138
Riglietti, Serena 1969- 189
Rigney, James Oliver, Jr.
    See Jordan, Robert
Rikhoff, Jean 1928- 9
Rikki
    See Ducornet, Erica
Riley, James A. 1939- 97
Riley, James Whitcomb 1849-1916 17
Riley, Jocelyn 1949- 60
    Brief entry 50
Riley, Jocelyn Carol
    See Riley, Jocelyn
Riley, Linda Capus 1950- 85
Riley, Martin 1948- 81
Rim, Sujean 225
Rimbauer, Steven
    See Pearson, Ridley
Rimes, (Margaret) LeAnn 1982- 154
Rinaldi, Ann 1934- 202
    Brief entry 50
    Earlier sketches in SATA 51, 78, 117, 161
    See also CLR 46
Rinard, Judith E(llen) 1947- 140
    Earlier sketch in SATA 44
Rinck, Maranke 1976- 214
Rinder, Lenore 1949- 92
Ring, Elizabeth 1920- 79
Ringdahl, Mark
    See Longyear, Barry B(rookes)
Ringgold, Faith 1930- 187
    Earlier sketches in SATA 71, 114
    See also CLR 30
Ringi, Kjell (Arne Soerensen) 1939- 12
Rinkoff, Barbara Jean (Rich) 1923-1975 4
    Obituary 27
Rinn, Miriam 1946- 127
Riordan, James 1936- 95
Riordan, Rick 208
    Earlier sketch in SATA 174
Rios, Tere
    See Versace, Marie Teresa Rios
Ripken, Cal, Jr. 1960- 215
    Earlier sketch in SATA 114
Ripken, Calvin Edward, Jr.
    See Ripken, Cal, Jr.
Ripley, Catherine 1957- 82
Ripley, Elizabeth Blake 1906-1969 5
Ripper, Charles L(ewis) 1929- 3
Ripper, Chuck
    See Ripper, Charles L(ewis)
Rippin, Sally 220
Riq
    See Atwater, Richard (Tupper)
Rish, David 1955- 110
Riskind, Mary 1944- 60
Rissinger, Matt 1956- 93
Rissman, Art
    See Sussman, Susan
Rissman, Susan
    See Sussman, Susan
Ritchie, Barbara Gibbons 14
Ritchie, Scot 1954- 217
Ritter, Felix
    See Kruss, James
Ritter, John H. 1951- 215
    Earlier sketches in SATA 129, 137
Ritter, Lawrence S(tanley) 1922-2004 58
    Obituary 152
Ritthaler, Shelly 1955- 91
Ritts, Paul 1920(?)-1980
    Obituary 25
Ritz, Karen 1957- 202
    Earlier sketch in SATA 80

Riu, Isabel Ferrer 1969- 222
Rivera, Geraldo (Miguel) 1943- *54*
   Brief entry 28
Rivera, Guadalupe
   See Rivera Marin, Guadalupe
Rivera Marin, Guadalupe 1924- 224
Rivers, Elfrida
   See Bradley, Marion Zimmer
Rivers, Karen 1970- 131
Riverside, John
   See Heinlein, Robert A.
Rivkin, Ann 1920- 41
Rivoli, Mario 1943- *10*
Roach, Marilynne K. 1946- 9
Roach, Marilynne Kathleen
   See Roach, Marilynne K.
Roach, Portia
   See Takakjian, Portia
Robb, Don 1937- 194
Robb, Laura 1937- 95
Robberecht, Thierry 1960- 182
Robbins, Frank 1917-1994(?) 42
   Brief entry 32
Robbins, Jacqui 221
Robbins, Ken 1945- 219
   Brief entry 53
   Earlier sketches in SATA *94, 147*
Robbins, Raleigh
   See Hamilton, Charles (Harold St. John)
Robbins, Ruth 1917(?)- 14
Robbins, Tony
   See Pashko, Stanley
Robbins, Wayne
   See Cox, William R(obert)
Robel, S. L.
   See Fraustino, Lisa Rowe
Roberson, Jennifer 1953- 72
Roberson, John R(oyster) 1930- 53
Robert, Adrian
   See St. John, Nicole
Roberts, Bethany 202
   Earlier sketch in SATA *133*
Roberts, Bruce (Stuart) 1930- 47
   Brief entry 39
Roberts, Charles G(eorge) D(ouglas)
   1860-1943 88
   Brief entry 29
   See also CLR *33*
Roberts, David
   See Cox, John Roberts
Roberts, David 1970- 191
Roberts, Diane 1937- 184
Roberts, Elizabeth 1944- 80
Roberts, Elizabeth Madox 1886-1941 33
   Brief entry 27
   See also CLR *100*
Roberts, Jim
   See Bates, Barbara S(nedeker)
Roberts, Jody 218
Roberts, John G(aither) 1913-1993 27
Roberts, Judy I. 1957- 93
Roberts, Katherine 1962- 152
Roberts, Ken 223
   See Lake, Kenneth R(obert)
Roberts, M. L.
   See Mattern, Joanne
Roberts, Marion 1966- 212
Roberts, Nancy Correll 1924- 52
   Brief entry 28
Roberts, Priscilla 1955- 184
Roberts, Terence
   See Sanderson, Ivan T(erence)
Roberts, Willo Davis 1928-2004 .... *150*
   Autobiography Feature *150*
   Obituary *160*
   Earlier sketches in SATA *21, 70, 133*
   See also CLR *95*
   See also SAAS *8*
Robertson, Barbara (Anne) 1931- *12*
Robertson, Don 1929-1999 .... *8*
   Obituary *113*

Robertson, Dorothy Lewis 1912- *12*
Robertson, Ellis
   See Ellison, Harlan
   and Silverberg, Robert
Robertson, James I., Jr. 1930- *182*
Robertson, James Irvin
   See Robertson, James I., Jr.
Robertson, Janet (E.) 1935- 68
Robertson, Jennifer Sinclair 1942-1998 .... *12*
Robertson, Jenny
   See Robertson, Jennifer Sinclair
Robertson, Keith (Carlton) 1914-1991 85
   Obituary 69
   Earlier sketch in SATA *1*
   See also SAAS *15*
Robertson, Mark
   See Robertson, M.P.
Robertson, M.P. 1965- *197*
Robertson, Stephen
   See Walker, Robert W.
Robertus, Polly M. 1948- *212*
   Earlier sketch in SATA *73*
Robeson, Kenneth
   See Dent, Lester
   and Goulart, Ron
Robeson, Kenneth
   See Johnson, (Walter) Ryerson
Robinet, Harriette Gillem 1931- *104*
   Earlier sketch in SATA *27*
   See also CLR *64*
Robins, Deri 1958- *166*
   Earlier sketch in SATA *117*
Robins, Patricia 1921- *117*
Robins, Rollo, Jr.
   See Ellis, Edward S.
Robins, Seelin
   See Ellis, Edward S.
Robinson, Adjai 1932- 8
Robinson, Aminah Brenda Lynn 1940- *159*
   Earlier sketch in SATA *77*
Robinson, Barbara (Webb) 1927- 84
   Earlier sketch in SATA *8*
Robinson, C(harles) A(lexander), Jr.
   1900-1965 36
Robinson, Charles 1870-1937 .... *17*
Robinson, Charles 1931- 6
Robinson, Dorothy W. 1929- 54
Robinson, Elizabeth Keeler 1959- *204*
Robinson, Eve
   See Tanselle, Eve
Robinson, Fiona 1965- *225*
Robinson, Glen 1953- 92
Robinson, Glendal P.
   See Robinson, Glen
Robinson, Jan M. 1933- 6
Robinson, Jean O. 1934- 7
Robinson, Joan (Mary) G(ale Thomas)
   1910-1988 7
Robinson, Kim Stanley 1952- *109*
Robinson, Lee 1948- *110*
Robinson, Lloyd
   See Silverberg, Robert
Robinson, Lynda S(uzanne) 1951- *107*
Robinson, Marileta 1942- 32
Robinson, Maudie Millian Oller 1914- *11*
Robinson, Maurice R(ichard) 1895-1982
   Obituary 29
Robinson, Nancy K(onheim) 1942-1994 91
   Brief entry 31
   Obituary 79
   Earlier sketch in SATA *32*
Robinson, Ray 1920- 23
Robinson, Raymond Kenneth
   See Robinson, Ray
Robinson, Shari
   See McGuire, Leslie (Sarah)
Robinson, Sharon 1950- *197*
   Earlier sketch in SATA *162*
Robinson, Spider 1948- *118*
Robinson, Sue
   See Robinson, Susan Maria

Robinson, Susan Maria 1955- *105*
Robinson, Susan Patricia
   See Gates, Susan
Robinson, Suzanne
   See Robinson, Lynda S(uzanne)
Robinson, T(homas) H(eath) 1869-1950 ...... *17*
Robinson, Tim 1963- *205*
Robinson, (Wanda) Veronica 1926- 30
Robinson, W(illiam) Heath 1872-1944 .... *17*
Robison, Bonnie 1924- *12*
Robison, Nancy L(ouise) 1934- 32
Robles, Harold E. 1948- 87
Robottom, John 1934- 7
Robson, Eric 1939- 82
Roca, Francois 1971- *200*
Rocco, John 1967- *188*
Roche, A. K.
   See Abisch, Roslyn Kroop
   and Kaplan, Boche
Roche, Denis 1967- *196*
   Earlier sketch in SATA *99*
Roche, Denis Mary
   See Roche, Denis
Roche, Luane 1937- *170*
Roche, P(atricia) K. 1935- 57
   Brief entry 34
Roche, Terry
   See Poole, Peggy
Rochman, Hazel 1938- *105*
Rock, Lois
   See Joslin, Mary
Rock, Maxine 1940- *108*
Rocker, Fermin 1907- 40
Rockliff, Mara 224
Rocklin, Joanne 1946- *134*
   Earlier sketch in SATA *86*
Rockwell, Anne F. 1934- *194*
   Earlier sketches in SATA *33, 71, 114, 162*
   See also SAAS *19*
Rockwell, Anne Foote
   See Rockwell, Anne F.
Rockwell, Bart
   See Pellowski, Michael (Joseph)
Rockwell, Harlow 1910-1988 33
   Obituary 56
Rockwell, Lizzy 1961- *185*
Rockwell, Norman (Percevel) 1894-1978 23
Rockwell, Thomas 1933- 70
   Earlier sketch in SATA *7*
   See also CLR *6*
Rockwood, Joyce 1947- 39
Rockwood, Roy
   See McFarlane, Leslie
   and Stratemeyer, Edward L.
Rodanas, Kristina 1952- *155*
Rodari, Gianni 1920-1980
   See CLR *24*
Rodd, Kathleen Tennant
   See Rodd, Kylie Tennant
Rodd, Kylie Tennant 1912-1988 57
   Obituary 55
   Earlier sketch in SATA *6*
Rodda, Emily 1948- *146*
   Earlier sketch in SATA *97*
   See also CLR *32*
Roddenberry, Eugene Wesley 1921-1991 45
   Obituary 69
Roddenberry, Gene
   See Roddenberry, Eugene Wesley
Roddick, Ellen 1936- 5
Roddie, Shen *153*
Roddy, Lee 1921- 57
Rodenas, Paula 73
Rodgers, Frank 1944- 69
Rodgers, Mary 1931- *130*
   Earlier sketch in SATA *8*
   See also CLR *20*
Rodman, Emerson
   See Ellis, Edward S.
Rodman, Eric
   See Silverberg, Robert

Rodman, Maia
    See Wojciechowska, Maia (Teresa)
Rodman, Mary Ann 185
Rodman, (Cary) Selden 1909-2002 9
Rodowsky, Colby 1932- 164
    Earlier sketches in SATA 21, 77, 120
    See also SAAS 22
Rodowsky, Colby F.
    See Rodowsky, Colby
Rodriguez, Alejo 1941- 83
Rodriguez, Alex 1975- 189
Rodriguez, Christina 1981- 177
Rodriguez, Edel 1971- 196
Rodriguez, Luis J. 1954- 125
Rodriguez, Rachel 180
Rodriguez, Rachel Victoria
    See Rodriguez, Rachel
Roeder, Virginia Marsh 1926- 98
Roehrig, Catharine H. 1949- 67
Roennfeldt, Robert 1953- 78
Roessel-Waugh, C. C.
    See Waugh, Carol-Lynn Rossel
    and Waugh, Charles G(ordon)
Roets, Lois F. 1937- 91
Roever, J(oan) M(arilyn) 1935- 26
Rofes, Eric 1954-2006 52
Rofes, Eric Edward 1954-2006
    See Rofes, Eric
Roffey, Maureen 1936- 33
Rogak, Lisa 1962- 80
Rogak, Lisa Angowski
    See Rogak, Lisa
Rogan, S. Jones 199
Rogan, Sally Jones
    See Rogan, S. Jones
Rogasky, Barbara 1933- 144
    Earlier sketch in SATA 86
Rogers, (Thomas) Alan (Stinchcombe)
    1937- 81
    Earlier sketch in SATA 2
Rogers, Bettye 1858-1919 103
Rogers, Cindy 1950- 89
Rogers, Emma 1951- 74
Rogers, Frances 1888-1974 10
Rogers, Fred McFeely 1928-2003 33
    Obituary 138
Rogers, Gregory 1957- 211
Rogers, Hal
    See Sirimarco, Elizabeth
Rogers, Jacqueline 1958- 213
Rogers, Jean 1919- 55
    Brief entry 47
Rogers, Matilda 1894-1976 5
    Obituary 34
Rogers, Pamela 1927- 9
Rogers, Paul 1950- 98
    Earlier sketch in SATA 54
Rogers, Robert
    See Hamilton, Charles (Harold St. John)
Rogers, Sherry 193
Rogers, W(illiam) G(arland) 1896-1978 23
Rohan, M. S.
    See Rohan, Michael Scott
Rohan, Michael Scott 1951- 98
Rohan, Mike Scott
    See Rohan, Michael Scott
Rohmann, Eric 1957- 171
    See also CLR 100
Rohmer, Harriet 1938- 56
Rohrer, Doug 1962- 89
Rojan
    See Rojankovsky, Feodor (Stepanovich)
Rojankovsky, Feodor (Stepanovich)
    1891-1970 21
Rojany, Lisa 94
Rokeby-Thomas, Anna E(lma) 1911- 15
Roland, Albert 1925-2002 11
Roland, Mary
    See Lewis, Mary
Roleff, Tamara L. 1959- 143
Rolerson, Darrell A(llen) 1946- 8

Roll, Winifred 1909-1998 6
Rollins, Charlemae Hill 1897-1979 3
    Obituary 26
Rollins, James 1961- 216
Rollock, Barbara T(herese) 1924- 64
Rolston, Steve 1978- 209
Romack, Janice Reed
    See LeNoir, Janice
Romain, Trevor 134
Romanenko, Vitaliy 1962- 101
Romano, Christy
    See Romano, Christy Carlson
Romano, Christy Carlson 1984- 210
Romano, Clare 1922- 111
    Earlier sketch in SATA 48
Romano, Louis G. 1921- 35
Romano, Melora A. 1966- 118
Romano, Ray 1957- 170
Romano, Raymond
    See Romano, Ray
Romijn, Johanna Maria Kooyker
    See Kooyker-Romijn, Johanna Maria
Romyn, Johanna Maria Kooyker
    See Kooyker-Romijn, Johanna Maria
Rong, Yu 1970- 174
Rongen, Bjoern 1906- 10
Rongen, Bjorn
    See Rongen, Bjoern
Ronson, Mark
    See Alexander, Marc
Rood, Ronald (N.) 1920- 12
Rook, Sebastian
    See Jeapes, Ben
Rooke, Daphne 1914-2009 12
Rooke, Daphne Marie
    See Rooke, Daphne
Rooney, Ronnie 1970- 212
Roop, Connie 1951- 167
    Brief entry 49
    Earlier sketches in SATA 54, 116
Roop, Constance Betzer
    See Roop, Connie
Roop, Peter 1951- 167
    Brief entry 49
    Earlier sketches in SATA 54, 116
Roop, Peter G.
    See Roop, Peter
Roop, Peter Geiger
    See Roop, Peter
Roos, Maryn 225
Roos, Stephen 1945- 128
    Brief entry 41
    Earlier sketches in SATA 47, 77
Roosa, Karen 1961- 218
Roose-Evans, James 1927- 65
Roosevelt, Eleanor 1884-1962 50
Root, Barry 182
Root, Betty 84
Root, Kimberly Bulcken 192
Root, Phyllis 1949- 224
    Brief entry 48
    Earlier sketches in SATA 55, 94, 145, 184
Root, Shelton L., Jr. 1923-1986
    Obituary 51
Roper, Laura (Newbold) Wood 1911-2003 .. 34
    Obituary 150
Roper, Robert 1946- 142
    Earlier sketch in SATA 78
Roraback, Robin (Ellan) 1964- 111
Rorby, Ginny 1944- 94
Rorer, Abigail 1949- 85
Rosaler, Maxine 208
Rosamel, Godeleine de 1968- 151
Roscoe, D(onald) T(homas) 1934- 42
Rose, Anne 8
Rose, Deborah Lee 1955- 185
    Earlier sketches in SATA 71, 124
Rose, Elizabeth (Jane Pretty) 1933- 68
    Brief entry 28
Rose, Florella
    See Carlson, Vada F.

Rose, Gerald (Hembdon Seymour) 1935- 68
    Brief entry 30
Rose, Malcolm 1953- 168
    Earlier sketch in SATA 107
Rose, Nancy A.
    See Sweetland, Nancy A(nn)
Rose, Ted 1940- 93
Rose, Wendy 1948- 12
Rosen, Elizabeth 1961- 205
Rosen, Lillian (Diamond) 1928- 63
Rosen, Marvin 1933- 161
Rosen, Michael 1946- 181
    Brief entry 40
    Earlier sketches in SATA 48, 84, 137
    See also CLR 45
Rosen, Michael J. 1954- 199
    Earlier sketch in SATA 86
Rosen, Michael Wayne
    See Rosen, Michael
Rosen, Sidney 1916- 1
Rosen, Winifred 1943- 8
Rosenbaum, Maurice 1907-1987 6
Rosenberg, Amye 1950- 74
Rosenberg, Dorothy 1906- 40
Rosenberg, Eth Clifford 1915- 92
    See also SAAS 22
Rosenberg, Jane 1949- 58
Rosenberg, Liz 1958- 129
    Earlier sketch in SATA 75
Rosenberg, Maxine B(erta) 1939- 93
    Brief entry 47
    Earlier sketch in SATA 55
Rosenberg, Nancy (Sherman) 1931- 4
    See Sherman, Nancy
Rosenberg, Sharon 1942- 8
Rosenberry, Vera 1948- 219
    Earlier sketches in SATA 83, 144
Rosenblatt, Arthur
    See Rosenblatt, Arthur S.
Rosenblatt, Arthur S. 1938- 68
    Brief entry 45
Rosenblatt, Lily 1956- 90
Rosenbloom, Joseph 1928- 21
Rosenblum, Richard 1928- 11
Rosenburg, John M. 1918- 6
Rosenfeld, Dina 1962- 99
Rosenstiehl, Agnes 1941- 203
Rosenthal, Amy Krouse 1965- 222
    Earlier sketch in SATA 177
Rosenthal, Betsy R. 1957- 178
Rosenthal, Harold 1914-1999 35
Rosenthal, M(acha) L(ouis) 1917-1996 59
Rosenthal, Marc 1949- 193
Rosenthal, Mark A(lan) 1946- 64
Rosing, Norbert 1953- 196
Rosman, Steven M 1956- 81
Rosman, Steven Michael
    See Rosman, Steven M
Rosoff, Meg 1956- 209
    Earlier sketch in SATA 160
Ross, Alan
    See Warwick, Alan R(oss)
Ross, Christine 1950- 172
    Earlier sketch in SATA 83
Ross, Clare
    See Romano, Clare
Ross, Dana Fuller
    See Cockrell, Amanda
    and Gerson, Noel Bertram
Ross, Dave
    See Ross, David
Ross, David 1896-1975 49
    Obituary 20
Ross, David 1949- 133
    Earlier sketch in SATA 32
Ross, Deborah J.
    See Wheeler, Deborah
Ross, Diana
    See Denney, Diana
Ross, Edward S(hearman) 1915- 85
Ross, Eileen 1950- 115

Ross, Frank (Xavier), Jr. 1914- 28
Ross, Jane 1961- 79
Ross, John 1921- 45
Ross, Judy 1942- 54
Ross, Katharine Reynolds
   See Ross, Kathy
Ross, Kathy 1948- 169
   Earlier sketch in SATA 89
Ross, Kent 1956- 91
Ross, Lillian Hammer 1925- 72
Ross, Michael Elsohn 1952- 170
   Earlier sketches in SATA 80, 127
Ross, Pat(ricia Kienzle) 1943- 53
   Brief entry 48
Ross, Ramon R(oyal) 1930- 62
Ross, Stewart 1947- 134
   Earlier sketch in SATA 92
   See also SAAS 23
Ross, Tom 1958- 84
Ross, Tony 1938- 225
   Earlier sketches in SATA 17, 65, 130, 176
Ross, Wilda 1915- 51
   Brief entry 39
Rossel, Seymour 1945- 28
Rossell, Judith 1953- 187
Rossel-Waugh, C. C.
   See Waugh, Carol-Lynn Rossel
Rossetti, Christina 1830-1894 20
   See also CLR 115
Rossetti, Christina Georgina
   See Rossetti, Christina
Rossi, Joyce 1943- 116
Rossotti, Hazel Swaine 1930- 95
Rostkowski, Margaret I. 1945- 59
Roth, Arnold 1929- 21
Roth, Arthur J(oseph) 1925-1993 43
   Brief entry 28
   Obituary 75
   See also SAAS 11
Roth, Carol 222
Roth, David 1940- 36
Roth, Julie Jersild 180
Roth, Matthue 1978(?)- 174
Roth, Roger 190
Roth, Ruby 1983(?)- 216
Roth, Stephanie 202
Roth, Susan L. 181
   Earlier sketch in SATA 134
Rothberg, Abraham 1922- 59
Roth-Hano, Renee 1931- 85
Rothkopf, Carol Z. 1929- 4
Rothman, Joel 1938- 7
Rotner, Shelley 1951- 169
   Earlier sketch in SATA 76
Rottman, S.L. 1970- 157
   Earlier sketch in SATA 106
Rottman, Susan Lynn
   See Rottman, S.L.
Roueche, Berton 1911-1994 28
Roughsey, Dick 1921(?)-1985 35
   See also CLR 41
Roughsey, Goobalathaldin
   See Roughsey, Dick
Rounds, Glen (Harold) 1906-2002 112
   Obituary 141
   Earlier sketches in SATA 8, 70
Rourke, Constance Mayfield 1885-1941
   See YABC 1
Rouss, Sylvia 211
Rovetch, Gerda 1925(?)- 202
Rovetch, L. Bob
   See Rovetch, Lissa
Rovetch, Lissa 201
Rowan, Deirdre
   See Williams, Jeanne
Rowe, Jennifer
   See Rodda, Emily
Rowe, John A. 1949- 198
   Earlier sketch in SATA 146
Rowe, Viola Carson 1903-1969
   Obituary 26

Rowh, Mark 1952- 90
Rowland, Florence Wightman 1900-1997 8
   Obituary 108
Rowland-Entwistle, (Arthur) Theodore (Henry)
   1925- 94
   Earlier sketch in SATA 31
Rowling, J.K. 1965- 174
   Earlier sketch in SATA 109
   See also CLR 112
Rowling, Joanne Kathleen
   See Rowling, J.K.
Rowsome, Frank (Howard), Jr. 1914-1983 .. 36
Roy, Gabrielle 1909-1983 104
Roy, Jacqueline 1954- 74
Roy, James 1968- 218
Roy, Jennifer
   See Roy, Jennifer Rozines
Roy, Jennifer Rozines 1967- 178
Roy, Jessie Hailstalk 1895-1986
   Obituary 51
Roy, Kari Anne 1977(?)- 221
Roy, Liam
   See Scarry, Patricia (Murphy)
Roy, Ron(ald) 1940- 110
   Brief entry 35
   Earlier sketch in SATA 40
Roybal, Laura 1956- 85
Roybal, Laura Husby
   See Roybal, Laura
Royds, Caroline 1953- 55
Royston, Angela 1945- 169
   Earlier sketch in SATA 120
Rozakis, Laurie E. 1952- 84
Rozen, Anna 1960- 206
Rubbino, Salvatore 1970- 220
Rubel, David 1961- 223
Rubel, Nicole 1953- 181
   Earlier sketches in SATA 18, 95, 135
Rubin, Eva Johanna 1925- 38
Rubin, Susan Goldman 1939- 182
   Earlier sketches in SATA 84, 132
Rubin, Vicky 1964- 193
Rubinetti, Donald 1947- 92
Rubinger, Ami 1953- 225
Rubinstein, Gillian 1942- 158
   Autobiography Feature 116
   Earlier sketches in SATA 68, 105
   See also CLR 35
   See also SAAS 25
Rubinstein, Gillian Margaret
   See Rubinstein, Gillian
Rubinstein, Patricia -2003
   See Forest, Antonia
Rubinstein, Patricia Giulia Caulfield Kate
   See Forest, Antonia
Rubinstein, Robert E(dward) 1943- 49
Rublowsky, John M(artin) 1928- 62
Rubright, Lynn 1936- 171
Ruby, Laura 181
   Earlier sketch in SATA 155
Ruby, Lois 1942- 184
   Autobiography Feature 105
   Brief entry 34
   Earlier sketches in SATA 35, 95
Ruby, Lois F.
   See Ruby, Lois
Ruchlis, Hy(man) 1913-1992 3
   Obituary 72
Ruckdeschel, Liz 214
Rucker, Mike 1940- 91
Ruckman, Ivy 1931- 93
   Earlier sketch in SATA 37
Ruck-Pauquet, Gina 1931- 40
   Brief entry 37
Ruddell, Deborah 1949- 210
Ruditis, Paul 190
Rudley, Stephen 1946- 30
Rudolph, Marguerita 1908- 21
Rudomin, Esther
   See Hautzig, Esther Rudomin

Rue, Leonard Lee III 1926- 142
   Earlier sketch in SATA 37
Rueda, Claudia 183
Ruedi, Norma Paul
   See Ainsworth, Norma
Ruelle, Karen Gray 1957- 209
   Earlier sketches in SATA 84, 126
Ruemmler, John D(avid) 1948- 78
Ruepp, Krista 1947- 143
Ruffell, Ann 1941- 30
Ruffins, Reynold 1930- 125
   Earlier sketch in SATA 41
Rugg, Jim 206
Ruggles, Lucy
   See Williams, Kathryn
Rugoff, Milton 1913- 30
Ruhen, Olaf 1911-1989 17
Rui, Paolo 1962- 217
Rukeyser, Muriel 1913-1980
   Obituary 22
Rumbaut, Hendle 1949- 84
Rumford, James 1948- 193
   Earlier sketch in SATA 116
Rumsey, Marian (Barritt) 1928- 16
Rumstuckle, Cornelius
   See Brennan, Herbie
Runholt, Susan 216
Runnerstroem, Bengt Arne 1944- 75
Runyan, John
   See Palmer, Bernard (Alvin)
Runyon, Brent 217
Runyon, Catherine 1947- 62
Ruoff, A. LaVonne Brown 1930- 76
Rupp, Rebecca 185
Rusch, Elizabeth 1966- 198
Rusch, Kris
   See Rusch, Kristine Kathryn
Rusch, Kristine Kathryn 1960- 113
Rush, Alison 1951- 41
Rush, Peter 1937- 32
Rushdie, Ahmed Salman
   See Rushdie, Salman
Rushdie, Salman 1947-
   See CLR 125
Rushford, Patricia H(elen) 1943- 134
Rushmore, Helen 1898-1994 3
Rushmore, Robert (William) 1926-1986 8
   Obituary 49
Ruskin, Ariane
   See Batterberry, Ariane Ruskin
Ruskin, John 1819-1900 24
Russ, Lavinia (Faxon) 1904-1992 74
Russell, Charlotte
   See Rathjen, Carl Henry
Russell, Ching Yeung 1946- 107
Russell, Don(ald Bert) 1899-1986
   Obituary 47
Russell, Franklin (Alexander) 1926- 11
Russell, Gertrude Barrer
   See Barrer-Russell, Gertrude
Russell, Helen Ross 1915- 8
Russell, James 1933- 53
Russell, Jim
   See Russell, James
Russell, Joan Plummer 1930- 139
Russell, Natalie 1972- 218
Russell, P(hilip) Craig 1951- 162
   Earlier sketch in SATA 80
Russell, Patrick
   See Sammis, John
Russell, Paul (Gary) 1942- 57
Russell, Sarah
   See Laski, Marghanita
Russell, Sharman Apt 1954- 123
Russell, Solveig Paulson 1904-1985 3
Russo, Marisabina 1950- 188
   Earlier sketches in SATA 106, 151
Russo, Monica J. 1950- 83
Russo, Susan 1947- 30
Russon, Penni 1974- 179

Rutgers van der Loeff, An
    See Rutgers van der Loeff-Basenau, An(na)
    Maria Margaretha
Rutgers van der Loeff-Basenau, An(na) Maria
    Margaretha 1910- 22
Ruth, Rod 1912-1987 9
Rutherford, Douglas
    See McConnell, James Douglas Rutherford
Rutherford, Meg 1932- 34
Ruthin, Margaret
    See Catherall, Arthur
Rutkoski, Marie 1977- 219
Rutledge, Jill Zimmerman 1951- 155
Rutz, Viola Larkin 1932- 12
Ruurs, Margriet 1952- 215
    Earlier sketches in SATA 97, 147
Ruzicka, Rudolph 1883-1978
    Obituary 24
Ruzzier, Sergio 1966- 210
    Earlier sketch in SATA 159
Ryan, Betsy
    See Ryan, Elizabeth (Anne)
Ryan, Cheli Duran 20
Ryan, Darlene 1958- 176
Ryan, Elizabeth (Anne) 1943- 30
Ryan, Jeanette
    See Mines, Jeanette
Ryan, John 1921-2009 22
Ryan, John Gerald Christopher
    See Ryan, John
Ryan, Margaret 1950- 166
    Earlier sketch in SATA 78
Ryan, Mary E. 1953- 61
Ryan, Mary Elizabeth
    See Ryan, Mary E.
Ryan, Pam Munoz 1951- 197
    Earlier sketch in SATA 134
Ryan, Patrick 1957- 138
Ryan, Peter (Charles) 1939- 15
Ryan-Lush, Geraldine 1949- 89
Rybakov, Anatoli (Naumovich) 1911-1998 .. 79
    Obituary 108
Rybakov, Anatolii (Naumovich)
    See Rybakov, Anatoli (Naumovich)
Rybolt, Thomas R. 1954- 62
Rybolt, Thomas Roy
    See Rybolt, Thomas R.
Rybolt, Tom
    See Rybolt, Thomas R.
Rydberg, Ernest E(mil) 1901-1993 21
Rydberg, Lou(isa Hampton) 1908- 27
Rydell, Katy 1942- 91
Rydell, Wendell
    See Rydell, Wendy
Rydell, Wendy 4
Ryden, Hope 91
    Earlier sketch in SATA 8
Ryder, Joanne (Rose) 1946- 163
    Brief entry 34
    Earlier sketches in SATA 65, 122
    See also CLR 37
Ryder, Pamela
    See Lamb, Nancy
Rye, Anthony
    See Youd, Samuel
Rylant, Cynthia 1954- 195
    Brief entry 44
    Earlier sketches in SATA 50, 76, 112, 160
    See also CLR 86
    See also SAAS 13
Rymer, Alta May 1925- 34
Rymond, Lynda Gene 199

S

S. L. C.
    See Twain, Mark
S., Svend Otto
    See Soerensen, Svend Otto

Saaf, Donald W(illiam) 1961- 124
Saal, Jocelyn
    See Sachs, Judith
Sabbeth, Carol (Landstrom) 1957- 125
Saberhagen, Fred 1930-2007 89
    Obituary 184
    Earlier sketch in SATA 37
Saberhagen, Fred T.
    See Saberhagen, Fred
Saberhagen, Fred Thomas
    See Saberhagen, Fred
Saberhagen, Frederick Thomas
    See Saberhagen, Fred
Sabin, Edwin L(egrand) 1870-1952
    See YABC 2
Sabin, Francene 27
Sabin, Lou
    See Sabin, Louis
Sabin, Louis 1930- 27
Sabre, Dirk
    See Laffin, John (Alfred Charles)
Sabuda, Robert (James) 1965- 120
    Earlier sketch in SATA 81
Sabuda, Robert 1965- 170
Sabuda, Robert James
    See Sabuda, Robert
Sachar, Louis 1954- 154
    Brief entry 50
    Earlier sketches in SATA 63, 104
    See also CLR 161
Sachs, Elizabeth-Ann 1946- 48
Sachs, Judith 1947- 52
    Brief entry 51
Sachs, Marilyn 1927- 164
    Autobiography Feature 110
    Earlier sketches in SATA 3, 68
    See also CLR 2
    See also SAAS 2
Sachs, Marilyn Stickle
    See Sachs, Marilyn
Sackett, S(amuel) J(ohn) 1928- 12
Sackson, Sid 1920- 16
Sacre, Antonio 1968- 152
Saddler, Allen
    See Richards, R(onald) C(harles) W(illiam)
Saddler, K. Allen
    See Richards, R(onald) C(harles) W(illiam)
Sadie, Stanley 1930-2005 14
Sadie, Stanley John
    See Sadie, Stanley
Sadiq, Nazneen
    See Sheikh, Nazneen
Sadler, Catherine Edwards 1952- 60
    Brief entry 45
Sadler, Marilyn (June) 1950- 79
Sadler, Mark
    See Lynds, Dennis
Saffer, Barbara 144
Sagan, Carl 1934-1996 58
    Obituary 94
Sagan, Carl Edward
    See Sagan, Carl
Sage, Angie 1952- 197
Sage, Juniper
    See Brown, Margaret Wise
    and Hurd, Edith Thacher
Sagsoorian, Paul 1923- 12
Said, S.F. 1967- 174
Saidman, Anne 1952- 75
Saint, Dora Jessie 1913- 10
St. Anthony, Jane 175
St. Antoine, Sara L. 1966- 84
St. Clair, Byrd Hooper 1905-1976
    Obituary 28
St. Crow, Lili
    See Saintcrow, Lilith
Saintcrow, Lilith 1976- 221
Saint-Exupery, Antoine de 1900-1944 20
    See also CLR 142

Saint-Exupery, Antoine Jean Baptiste Marie
    Roger de
    See Saint-Exupery, Antoine de
St. George, Judith 1931- 161
    Earlier sketches in SATA 13, 99
    See also CLR 57
    See also SAAS 12
St. George, Judith Alexander
    See St. George, Judith
St. James, Blakely
    See Gottfried, Theodore Mark
    and Platt, Charles
St. James, Blakely
    See Griffin, W. E. B.
St. James, Sierra
    See Rallison, Janette
Saint James, Synthia 1949- 152
    Earlier sketch in SATA 84
St. John, Lauren 1966- 214
St. John, Nicole 143
    Autobiography Feature 143
    Earlier sketches in SATA 29, 89
    See also CLR 46
    See also SAAS 7
St. John, Patricia Mary 1919-1993
    Obituary 79
St. John, Philip
    See del Rey, Lester
St. John, Wylly Folk 1908-1985 10
    Obituary 45
St. Max, E. S.
    See Ellis, Edward S.
St. Meyer, Ned
    See Stratemeyer, Edward L.
St. Mox, E. A.
    See Ellis, Edward S.
St. Myer, Ned
    See Stratemeyer, Edward L.
St. Tamara
    See Kolba, St. Tamara
Saito, Michiko
    See Fujiwara, Michiko
Sakai, Komako 1966- 213
Sakaki, Ichiro 1969- 192
Sakamoto, Miki 198
Sakers, Don 1958- 72
Sakharnov, S.
    See Sakharnov, Svyatoslav
Sakharnov, Svyatoslav 1923- 65
Sakharnov, Svyatoslav Vladimirovich
    See Sakharnov, Svyatoslav
Saksena, Kate 148
Sakurai, Gail 1952- 153
    Earlier sketch in SATA 87
Salamanca, Lucy
    See del Barco, Lucy Salamanca
Salas, Laura Purdie 1966- 216
Salassi, Otto R(ussell) 1939-1993 38
    Obituary 77
Salat, Cristina 82
Saldana, Rene, Jr. 186
Saldutti, Denise 1953- 39
Sale, Tim 1956- 153
Salem, Kay 1952- 92
Salerno, Steven 176
Salinger, J.D. 1919-2010 67
    See also CLR 18
Salinger, Jerome David
    See Salinger, J.D.
Salisbury, Graham 1944- 195
    Earlier sketches in SATA 76, 108, 161
Salisbury, Joyce E(llen) 1944- 138
Salkey, (Felix) Andrew (Alexander)
    1928-1995 118
    Earlier sketch in SATA 35
Salley, Coleen 166
Sallis, Susan (Diana) 1929- 55
Salmieri, Daniel 1983- 208
Salmon, Annie Elizabeth 1899- 13
Salmon, Dena K. 1959(?)- 219
Salonen, Roxane Beauclair 1968- 184

Salsi, Lynn 1947- *130*
Salsitz, R. A. V.
　See Salsitz, Rhondi Vilott
Salsitz, Rhondi Vilott *115*
Salten, Felix
　See Salzmann, Siegmund
Salter, Cedric
　See Knight, Francis Edgar
Salter, Sydney *220*
Saltman, Judith 1947- *64*
Saltzberg, Barney 1955- *194*
　Earlier sketch in SATA *135*
Saltzman, David (Charles Laertes)
　1967-1990 .... *86*
Salvadori, Mario (George) 1907-1997 .... *97*
　Earlier sketch in SATA *40*
Salwood, F.K.
　See Kilworth, Garry
Salzer, L. E.
　See Wilson, Lionel
Salzman, Marian 1959- *77*
Salzmann, Siegmund 1869-1945 .... *25*
Samachson, Dorothy (Mirkin) 1914-1997 ...... *3*
Samachson, Joseph 1906-1980 .... *3*
　Obituary *52*
Sammis, John 1942- *4*
Sampson, Emma (Keats) Speed 1868-1947 . *68*
Sampson, Fay (Elizabeth) 1935- *151*
　Brief entry *40*
　Earlier sketch in SATA *42*
Sampson, Michael 1952- *143*
　Earlier sketch in SATA *95*
Samson, Anne S(tringer) 1933- *2*
Samson, Joan 1937-1976 .... *13*
Samson, Suzanne M. 1959- *91*
Samuels, Barbara *199*
Samuels, Charles 1902-1982 .... *12*
Samuels, Cynthia K(alish) 1946- *79*
Samuels, Gertrude 1910(?)-2003 .... *17*
　Obituary *147*
Sanborn, Duane 1914-1996 .... *38*
Sancha, Sheila 1924- *38*
Sanchez, Alex 1957- *151*
Sanchez, Anita 1956- *209*
Sanchez, Sonia 1934- *136*
　Earlier sketch in SATA *22*
　See also CLR *18*
Sanchez-Silva, Jose Maria 1911- *132*
　Earlier sketch in SATA *16*
　See also CLR *12*
Sand, George X. *45*
Sandak, Cass R(obert) 1950-2001 .... *51*
　Brief entry *37*
Sandberg, (Karin) Inger 1930- *15*
Sandberg, Karl C. 1931- *35*
Sandberg, Lasse (E. M.) 1924- *15*
Sandburg, Carl 1878-1967 .... *8*
　See also CLR *67*
Sandburg, Carl August
　See Sandburg, Carl
Sandburg, Charles
　See Sandburg, Carl
Sandburg, Charles A.
　See Sandburg, Carl
Sandburg, Helga 1918- *3*
　See also SAAS *10*
Sandell, Lisa Ann 1977- *175*
Sandemose, Iben 1950- *211*
Sander, Heather L. 1947- *157*
Sanderlin, George 1915- *4*
Sanderlin, Owenita (Harrah) 1916- *11*
Sanders, Betty Jane
　See Monthei, Betty
Sanders, Nancy I. 1960- *141*
　Earlier sketch in SATA *90*
Sanders, Scott Russell 1945- *109*
　Earlier sketch in SATA *56*
Sanders, Winston P.
　See Anderson, Poul
Sanderson, Irma 1912- *66*
Sanderson, Ivan T(erence) 1911-1973 .... *6*

Sanderson, Margaret Love
　See Keats, Emma
　and Sampson, Emma (Keats) Speed
Sanderson, Ruth 1951- *224*
　Earlier sketches in SATA *41, 109, 172*
Sanderson, Ruth L.
　See Sanderson, Ruth
Sanders-Wells, Linda *220*
Sand-Eveland, Cyndi *211*
Sandin, Joan 1942- *197*
　Earlier sketches in SATA *12, 94, 153*
Sandison, Janet
　See Cameron, Elizabeth Jane
Sandler, Martin W. *216*
　Earlier sketch in SATA *160*
Sandom, J. Gregory
　See Welsh, T.K.
Sandom, J.G.
　See Welsh, T.K.
Sandoz, Mari(e Susette) 1900-1966 .... *5*
Sanford, Agnes (White) 1897-1976 .... *61*
Sanford, Doris 1937- *69*
Sanford, Rose
　See Simmonds, Posy
Sanger, Amy Wilson 1967- *205*
Sanger, Marjory Bartlett 1920- *8*
San Jose, Christine 1929- *167*
Sankey, Alice (Ann-Susan) 1910- *27*
San Souci, Daniel *192*
　Earlier sketch in SATA *96*
San Souci, Robert D. 1946- *220*
　Earlier sketches in SATA *40, 81, 117, 158*
　See also CLR *43*
Santamaria, Benjamin 1955- *184*
Santat, Dan *224*
　Earlier sketch in SATA *188*
Santesson, Hans Stefan 1914(?)-1975
　Obituary *30*
Santiago, Esmeralda 1948- *129*
Santopolo, Jill *214*
Santore, Charles 1935- *200*
Santoro, C.
　See Santoro, Christopher
Santoro, Christopher *218*
Santos, Helen
　See Griffiths, Helen
Santrey, Louis
　See Sabin, Louis
Santucci, Barbara 1948- *130*
Sapergia, Barbara 1943- *181*
Sapet, Kerrily 1972- *214*
Sapieyevski, Anne Lindbergh 1940-1993 ..... *81*
　Brief entry *32*
　Earlier sketches in SATA *35, 78*
Saport, Linda 1954- *123*
Sapp, Allen 1929- *151*
Sarac, Roger
　See Caras, Roger A(ndrew)
Sarah, Duchess of York
　See Ferguson, Sarah
Sarasin, Jennifer
　See Sachs, Judith
Sarcone-Roach, Julia *215*
Sardinha, Rick *192*
Sarg, Anthony Frederick
　See Sarg, Tony
Sarg, Tony 1882-1942
　See YABC *1*
Sargent, Pamela 1948- *78*
　Earlier sketch in SATA *29*
Sargent, Robert 1933- *2*
Sargent, Sarah 1937- *44*
　Brief entry *41*
Sargent, Shirley 1927-2004 .... *11*
Sarnoff, Jane 1937- *10*
Saroff, Phyllis V. *202*
Saroyan, William 1908-1981 .... *23*
　Obituary *24*
Sarton, Eleanor May
　See Sarton, May

Sarton, May 1912-1995 .... *36*
　Obituary *86*
Sasaki, Chris *182*
Sasaki, Ellen Joy *206*
Saseen, Sharon (Dillon) 1949- *59*
Sasek, Miroslav 1916-1980 .... *16*
　Obituary *23*
　See also CLR *4*
Sasso, Sandy Eisenberg 1947- *162*
　Earlier sketches in SATA *86, 116*
Sathre, Vivian 1952- *133*
　Earlier sketch in SATA *79*
Satterfield, Charles
　See del Rey, Lester
　and Pohl, Frederik
Sattgast, L. J.
　See Sattgast, Linda J.
Sattgast, Linda J. 1953- *91*
Sattler, Helen Roney 1921-1992 .... *74*
　Earlier sketch in SATA *4*
　See also CLR *24*
Sattler, Jennifer
　See Sattler, Jennifer Gordon
Sattler, Jennifer Gordon *218*
Sauer, Julia Lina 1891-1983 .... *32*
　Obituary *36*
Sauer, Tammi 1972- *223*
Sauerwein, Leigh 1944- *155*
Saul, Carol P. 1947- *117*
　Earlier sketch in SATA *78*
Saul, John III
　See Saul, John
Saul, John 1942- *98*
Saul, John W.
　See Saul, John
Saul, John W. III
　See Saul, John
Saul, John Woodruff III
　See Saul, John
Saul, (Ellen) Wendy 1946- *42*
Saulnier, Karen Luczak 1940- *80*
Saunders, Caleb
　See Heinlein, Robert A.
Saunders, Dave 1939- *85*
Saunders, Julie 1939- *85*
Saunders, (William) Keith 1910-1994 .... *12*
Saunders, Rubie (Agnes) 1929- *21*
Saunders, Steven
　See Jones, Allan Frewin
Saunders, Susan 1945- *96*
　Brief entry *41*
　Earlier sketch in SATA *46*
Saunders-Smith, Gail 1952- *169*
Sauvain, Philip Arthur 1933- *111*
Savadier, Elivia 1950- *164*
　Earlier sketch in SATA *79*
Savage, Alan
　See Nicole, Christopher (Robin)
Savage, Blake
　See Goodwin, Harold L(eland)
Savage, Candace 1949- *142*
Savage, Deborah 1955- *76*
Savage, Jeff 1961- *97*
Savage, Katharine James 1905-1989
　Obituary *61*
Savage, Stephen 1965- *194*
Savage, Thomas 1915-2003
　Obituary *147*
Savageau, Cheryl 1950- *96*
Savery, Constance (Winifred) 1897-1999 .... *1*
Saville, Andrew
　See Taylor, Andrew
Saville, (Leonard) Malcolm 1901-1982 .... *23*
　Obituary *31*
Saviozzi, Adriana
　See Mazza, Adriana
Savitt, Sam 1917-2000 .... *8*
　Obituary *126*
Savitz, Harriet May 1933-2008 .... *72*
　Earlier sketch in SATA *5*
　See also SAAS *26*

Sawicki, Mary 1950- 90
Sawyer, (Frederick) Don(ald) 1947- 72
Sawyer, Kem Knapp 1953- 84
Sawyer, Robert J. 1960- 149
    Earlier sketch in SATA 81
Sawyer, Robert James
    See Sawyer, Robert J.
Sawyer, Ruth 1880-1970 17
    See also CLR 36
Saxby, H.M.
    See Saxby, (Henry) Maurice
Saxby, (Henry) Maurice 1924- 71
Saxon, Andrew
    See Arthur, Robert, (Jr.)
Saxon, Antonia
    See Sachs, Judith
Say, Allen 1937- 161
    Earlier sketches in SATA 28, 69, 110
    See also CLR 135
Sayers, Frances Clarke 1897-1989 3
    Obituary 62
Sayles, Elizabeth 1956- 220
    Earlier sketches in SATA 108, 163
Saylor-Marchant, Linda 1963- 82
Sayre, April Pulley 1966- 191
    Earlier sketches in SATA 88, 131
Sazer, Nina 1949- 13
Scabrini, Janet 1953- 13
Scagell, Robin 1946- 107
Scagnetti, Jack 1924- 7
Scaletta, Kurtis 1968- 215
Scalora, Suza 224
Scamander, Newt
    See Rowling, J.K.
Scamell, Ragnhild 1940- 180
    Earlier sketch in SATA 77
Scanlon, Marion Stephany 11
Scannel, John Vernon
    See Scannell, Vernon
Scannell, Vernon 1922-2007 59
    Obituary 188
Scarborough, Elizabeth
    See Scarborough, Elizabeth Ann
Scarborough, Elizabeth Ann 1947- 171
    Earlier sketch in SATA 98
Scarf, Maggi
    See Scarf, Maggie
Scarf, Maggie 1932- 5
Scariano, Margaret M. 1924- 86
Scarlett, Susan
    See Streatfeild, Noel
Scarry, Huck
    See Scarry, Richard McClure, Jr.
Scarry, Patricia (Murphy) 1924- 2
Scarry, Patsy
    See Scarry, Patricia (Murphy)
Scarry, Richard (McClure) 1919-1994 75
    Obituary 90
    Earlier sketches in SATA 2, 35
    See also CLR 41
Scarry, Richard McClure, Jr. 1953- 35
Schachner, Judith Byron 1951- 178
    Earlier sketch in SATA 88
Schachner, Judy
    See Schachner, Judith Byron
Schachtel, Roger 1949- 38
Schachtel, Roger Bernard
    See Schachtel, Roger
Schade, Susan 189
Schaedler, Sally 116
Schaefer, Carole Lexa 173
Schaefer, Jack (Warner) 1907-1991 66
    Obituary 65
    Earlier sketch in SATA 3
Schaefer, Lola M. 1950- 183
    Earlier sketches in SATA 91, 144
Schaeffer, Mead 1898- 21
Schaeffer, Susan Fromberg 1941- 22
Schaer, Brigitte 1958- 112
Schallau, Daniel 1966- 222

Schaller, George
    See Schaller, George B.
Schaller, George B. 1933- 30
Schaller, George Beals
    See Schaller, George B.
Schanzer, Rosalyn (Good) 1942- 138
    Earlier sketch in SATA 77
Schatell, Brian 66
    Brief entry 47
Schechter, Betty (Goodstein) 1921- 5
Schechter, Simone
    See Elkeles, Simone
Schecter, Ellen 1944- 85
Scheeder, Louis 1946- 141
Scheer, Julian (Weisel) 1926-2001 8
Scheffer, Victor B(lanchard) 1906- 6
Scheffler, Axel 1957- 180
Scheffler, Ursel 1938- 81
Scheffrin-Falk, Gladys 1928- 76
Scheidl, Gerda Marie 1913- 85
Scheier, Michael 1943- 40
    Brief entry 36
Schell, Mildred 1922- 41
Schell, Orville (Hickok) 1940- 10
Scheller, Melanie 1953- 77
Schellie, Don 1932- 29
Schembri, Jim 1962- 124
Schembri, Pamela 1969- 195
Schemm, Mildred Walker 1905-1998 21
    Obituary 103
Schenker, Dona 1947- 133
    Earlier sketch in SATA 68
Scher, Paula 1948- 47
Scherer, Jeffrey 194
Scherf, Margaret 1908-1979 10
Schermer, Judith (Denise) 1941- 30
Schertle, Alice 1941- 192
    Earlier sketches in SATA 36, 90, 145
Schick, Alice 1946- 27
Schick, Eleanor 1942- 144
    Earlier sketches in SATA 9, 82
Schick, Joel 1945- 31
    Brief entry 30
Schields, Gretchen 1948- 75
Schiff, Ken(neth Roy) 1942- 7
Schiller, Andrew 1919- 21
Schiller, Barbara (Heyman) 1928- 21
Schiller, Pamela (Byrne) 127
Schindel, John 1955- 213
    Earlier sketches in SATA 77, 115
Schindelman, Joseph 1923- 67
    Brief entry 32
Schindler, S.D. 1952- 198
    Brief entry 50
    Earlier sketches in SATA 75, 118, 171
Schindler, Steven D.
    See Schindler, S.D.
Schinto, Jeanne 1951- 93
Schisgall, Oscar 1901-1984 12
    Obituary 38
Schlaepfer, Gloria G. 1931- 154
Schlee, Ann 1934- 44
    Brief entry 36
Schleichert, Elizabeth 1945- 77
Schlein, Miriam 1926-2004 130
    Obituary 159
    Earlier sketches in SATA 2, 87
    See also CLR 41
Schlesinger, Arthur M., Jr. 1917-2007 61
    Obituary 181
    See Schlesinger, Arthur Meier
Schlesinger, Arthur Meier 1888-1965
Schlessinger, Laura (Catherine) 1947- 160
    Earlier sketch in SATA 110
Schlitz, Laura Amy 184
Schloat, G. Warren, Jr. 1914-2000 4
Schlossberg, Elisabeth 221
Schmatz, Pat 197
Schmid, Eleonore 1939- 126
    Earlier sketches in SATA 12, 84
Schmid, Susan Maupin 208

Schmiderer, Dorothy 1940- 19
Schmidt, Annie M. G. 1911-1995 67
    Obituary 91
    See also CLR 22
Schmidt, C.A. 196
Schmidt, Diane 1953- 70
Schmidt, Elizabeth 1915- 15
Schmidt, Gary D. 1957- 193
    Earlier sketches in SATA 93, 135
Schmidt, James Norman 1912-1983 21
Schmidt, Karen Lee 1953- 185
    Earlier sketch in SATA 94
Schmidt, Lynette 1952- 76
Schmitz, Tamara 207
Schneider, Antonie 1954- 167
    Earlier sketch in SATA 89
Schneider, Christine M. 1972(?)- 171
    Earlier sketch in SATA 120
Schneider, Dick
    See Schneider, Richard H.
Schneider, Elisa
    See Kleven, Elisa
Schneider, Herman 1905-2003 7
    Obituary 148
Schneider, Howie -2007 181
Schneider, Josh 1980- 196
Schneider, Laurie
    See Adams, Laurie
Schneider, Nina 1913-2007 2
    Obituary 186
Schneider, Nina Zimet
    See Schneider, Nina
Schneider, Rex 1937- 44
Schneider, Richard H. 1922- 171
Schneider, Richard Henry
    See Schneider, Richard H.
Schneider, Robyn 1986- 187
Schnirel, James R. 1931- 14
Schnitter, Jane T. 1958- 88
Schnitzlein, Danny 134
Schnur, Steven 1952- 144
    Earlier sketch in SATA 95
Schnurre, Wolfdietrich 1920-1989
    Obituary 63
Schoberle, Cecile 1949- 80
Schock, Pauline 1928- 45
Schoell, William 1951- 160
Schoen, Barbara (Taylor) 1924-1993 13
Schoenherr, Ian 177
Schoenherr, John 1935-2010 66
    Earlier sketch in SATA 37
    See also SAAS 13
Schoenherr, John Carl
    See Schoenherr, John
Schofield, Sandy
    See Rusch, Kristine Kathryn
Scholastica, Sister Mary
    See Jenkins, Marie M(agdalen)
Scholefield, A. T.
    See Scholefield, Alan
Scholefield, Alan 1931- 66
Scholefield, Edmund O.
    See Griffin, W. E. B.
Scholey, Arthur 1932- 28
Scholz, Jackson Volney 1897-1986
    Obituary 49
Schon, Nick 1955- 223
Schone, Virginia 22
Schongut, Emanuel 1936- 184
    Brief entry 36
    Earlier sketch in SATA 52
Schoonover, Frank (Earle) 1877-1972 24
Schoor, Gene 1921- 3
Schories, Pat 1952- 164
    Earlier sketch in SATA 116
Schorr, Melissa 1972- 194
Schorr, Melissa Robin
    See Schorr, Melissa
Schott, Jane A. 1946- 172
Schotter, Roni 190
    Earlier sketches in SATA 105, 149

Schrader, Dave 1967(?)- 225
Schraff, Anne E(laine) 1939- 92
    Earlier sketch in SATA 27
Schram, Penninah 1934- 219
    Earlier sketch in SATA 119
Schrank, Joseph 1900-1984
    Obituary 38
Schrecengost, Maity 1938- 118
Schrecengost, S. Maitland
    See Schrecengost, Maity
Schreck, Karen
    See Schreck, Karen Halvorsen
Schreck, Karen Halvorsen 1962- 185
Schrecker, Judie 1954- 90
Schreiber, Elizabeth Anne (Ferguson)
    1947- 13
Schreiber, Ralph W(alter) 1942- 13
Schreiner, Samuel A(gnew), Jr. 1921- 70
Schroades, John 214
Schroeder, Alan 1961- 98
    Earlier sketch in SATA 66
Schroeder, Binette
    See Nickl, Barbara (Elisabeth)
Schroeder, Russell (K.) 1943- 146
Schroeder, Ted 1931(?)-1973
    Obituary 20
Schubert, Dieter 1947- 217
    Earlier sketches in SATA 62, 101
Schubert, Ingrid 1953- 217
Schubert, Leda 1950(?)- 181
Schubert-Gabrys, Ingrid 1953- 101
    Earlier sketch in SATA 62
Schuelein-Steel, Danielle
    See Steel, Danielle
Schuelein-Steel, Danielle Fernande
    See Steel, Danielle
Schuerger, Michele R. 110
Schuett, Stacey 1960- 168
    Earlier sketch in SATA 75
Schulke, Flip Phelps Graeme 1930- 57
Schulman, Arlene 1961- 105
Schulman, Janet 1933- 208
    Earlier sketches in SATA 22, 137
Schulman, L(ester) M(artin) 1934- 13
Schulte, Elaine L(ouise) 1934- 36
Schultz, Betty K(epka) 1932- 125
Schultz, Gwendolyn 21
Schultz, James Willard 1859-1947
    See YABC 1
Schultz, Pearle Henriksen 1918- 21
Schulz, Charles M. 1922-2000 10
    Obituary 118
Schulz, Charles Monroe
    See Schulz, Charles M.
Schumacher, Julie 1958- 191
Schumaker, Ward 1943- 96
Schuman, Michael A. 1953- 134
    Earlier sketch in SATA 85
Schur, Maxine
    See Schur, Maxine Rose
Schur, Maxine Rose 1948- 135
    Autobiography Feature 135
    Brief entry 49
    Earlier sketches in SATA 53, 98
Schurfranz, Vivian 1925- 13
Schutzer, A. I. 1922- 13
Schuyler, Pamela R. 1948- 30
Schwabach, Karen 185
Schwager, Tina 1964- 110
Schwandt, Stephen (William) 1947- 61
Schwark, Mary Beth 1954- 51
Schwartz, Alvin 1927-1992 56
    Obituary 71
    Earlier sketch in SATA 4
    See also CLR 89
Schwartz, Amy 1954- 189
    Brief entry 41
    Earlier sketches in SATA 47, 83, 131
    See also CLR 25
    See also SAAS 18
Schwartz, Anne Powers 1913-1987 10

Schwartz, Carol 1954- 77
Schwartz, Charles W(alsh) 1914- 8
Schwartz, David M. 1951- 110
    Earlier sketch in SATA 59
Schwartz, David Martin
    See Schwartz, David M.
Schwartz, Elizabeth Reeder 1912- 8
Schwartz, Ellen 1949- 117
Schwartz, Jerome L.
    See Lawrence, Jerome
Schwartz, Joanne 1960- 220
Schwartz, Joel L. 1940- 54
    Brief entry 51
Schwartz, Joyce R. 1950- 93
Schwartz, Julius 1907-2004 45
Schwartz, Perry 1942- 75
Schwartz, Sheila (Ruth) 1929- 27
Schwartz, Stephen (Lawrence) 1948- 19
Schwartz, Virginia Frances 1950- 184
    Earlier sketch in SATA 131
Schwarz, Silvia Tessa Viviane
    See Schwarz, Viviane
Schwarz, Viviane 1977- 204
Schwarz, (Silvia Tessa) Viviane 1977- 141
Schweitzer, Byrd Baylor
    See Baylor, Byrd
Schweitzer, Iris 59
    Brief entry 36
Schweninger, Ann 1951- 168
    Earlier sketches in SATA 29, 98
Schwerin, Doris H(alpern) 1922- 64
Schy, Yael 197
Scieszka, Jon 1954- 199
    Earlier sketches in SATA 68, 105, 160
    See also CLR 107
Scillian, Devin 199
    Earlier sketch in SATA 128
Scioscia, Mary (Hershey) 1926- 63
Sciurba, Katie 1957- 196
Scofield, Penrod 1933- 62
    Obituary 78
Scoggin, Margaret C(lara) 1905-1968 47
    Brief entry 28
Scoltock, Jack 1942- 141
    Earlier sketch in SATA 72
Scoppettone, Sandra 1936- 92
    Earlier sketch in SATA 9
Scot, Michael
    See Rohan, Michael Scott
Scot-Bernard, P.
    See Bernard, Patricia
Scotland, Jay
    See Jakes, John
Scott, Alastair
    See Allen, Kenneth S.
Scott, Ann Herbert 1926- 140
    Autobiography Feature 140
    Brief entry 29
    Earlier sketches in SATA 56, 94
Scott, Bill
    See Scott, William N(eville)
Scott, Bill 1920(?)-1985
    Obituary 46
Scott, Cora Annett (Pipitone) 1931- 11
Scott, Dan
    See Barker, S. Omar
Scott, Elaine 1940- 198
    Earlier sketches in SATA 36, 90, 164
Scott, Elizabeth 1972- 194
Scott, Jack Denton 1915-1995 83
    Earlier sketch in SATA 31
    See also CLR 20
    See also SAAS 14
Scott, Jane (Harrington) 1931- 55
Scott, Jessica
    See De Wire, Elinor
Scott, John 1912-1976 14
Scott, John Anthony 1916- 23
Scott, John M(artin) 1913- 12
Scott, Mary
    See Mattern, Joanne

Scott, Melissa 1960- 109
Scott, Michael 1959- 211
Scott, Michael Peter
    See Scott, Michael
Scott, Mike
    See Scott, Michael
Scott, Richard
    See Rennert, Richard Scott
Scott, Roney
    See Gault, William Campbell
Scott, Sally 1909-1978 43
Scott, Sally 1948- 44
Scott, Sally Elisabeth
    See Scott, Sally
Scott, W. N.
    See Scott, William N(eville)
Scott, Sir Walter 1771-1832
    See YABC 2
    See also CLR 154
Scott, Warwick
    See Trevor, Elleston
Scott, William N(eville) 1923- 87
Scotti, Anna
    See Coates, Anna
Scotton, Rob 1960- 214
    Earlier sketch in SATA 177
Scribner, Charles, Jr. 1921-1995 13
    Obituary 87
Scribner, Joanne L. 1949- 33
Scribner, Kimball 1917- 63
Scrimger, Richard 1957- 164
    Earlier sketch in SATA 119
Scrimsher, Lila Gravatt 1897-1974
    Obituary 28
Scroder, Walter K. 1928- 82
Scroggs, Kirk 187
Scruggs, Sandy 1961- 89
Scudder, Brooke 1959- 154
Scudder, Mildred Lee 1908- 6
    See also SAAS 12
Scull, Marie-Louise 1943-1993 77
Scuro, Vincent 1951- 21
Seabrooke, Brenda 1941- 148
    Earlier sketches in SATA 30, 88
Seagraves, D.B.
    See Seagraves, Donny Bailey
Seagraves, Donny
    See Seagraves, Donny Bailey
Seagraves, Donny Bailey 1951- 224
Seaman, Augusta Huiell 1879-1950 31
Seamands, Ruth 1916- 9
Searcy, Margaret Zehmer 1926- 54
    Brief entry 39
Searight, Mary W(illiams) 1918- 17
Searle, Kathryn Adrienne 1942- 10
Searle, Ronald (William Fordham) 1920- 70
    Earlier sketch in SATA 42
Sears, Stephen W. 1932- 4
Seaskull, Cecil
    See Castellucci, Cecil
Sebastian, Lee
    See Silverberg, Robert
Sebestyen, Igen
    See Sebestyen, Ouida
Sebestyen, Ouida 1924- 140
    Earlier sketch in SATA 39
    See also CLR 17
    See also SAAS 10
Sebrey, Mary Ann 1951- 62
Sechrist, Elizabeth Hough 1903-1991 2
Sederman, Marty 211
Sedges, John
    See Buck, Pearl S.
Sedgwick, Marcus 1968- 197
    Earlier sketch in SATA 160
Seed, Cecile Eugenie 1930- 86
    Earlier sketch in SATA 8
    See also CLR 76
Seed, Jenny
    See Seed, Cecile Eugenie

Seed, Sheila Turner 1937(?)-1979
  Obituary 23
Seeger, Elizabeth 1889-1973
  Obituary 20
Seeger, Laura Vaccaro 200
  Earlier sketch in SATA 172
Seeger, Pete 1919- 139
  Earlier sketch in SATA 13
Seeger, Peter R.
  See Seeger, Pete
Seeley, Laura L. 1958- 71
Seever, R.
  See Reeves, Lawrence F.
Sefozo, Mary 1925- 82
Sefton, Catherine
  See Waddell, Martin
Segal, John 178
Segal, Joyce 1940- 35
Segal, Lore 1928- 163
  Earlier sketches in SATA 4, 66
  See also SAAS 11
Segal, Lore Groszmann
  See Segal, Lore
Segar, E(lzie) C(risler) 1894-1938 61
Segovia, Andres 1893(?)-1987
  Obituary 52
Seguin, Marilyn W(eymouth) 1951- 91
Seguin-Fontes, Marthe 1924- 109
Seibold, J. Otto 1960- 196
  Earlier sketches in SATA 83, 149
  See also SAAS 22
Seidel, Ross 95
Seidelman, James Edward 1926- 6
Seiden, Art(hur) 107
  Brief entry 42
Seidensticker, John 1944- 200
Seidler, Ann (G.) 1925- 131
Seidler, Tor 1952- 149
  Brief entry 46
  Earlier sketches in SATA 52, 98
Seidman, Karla
  See Kuskin, Karla
Seidman, Laurence Ivan 1925- 15
Seigel, Kalman 1917-1998 12
  Obituary 103
Seignobosc, Francoise 1897-1961 21
Seinfeld, Jerry 1954- 146
Seitz, Jacqueline 1931- 50
Seixas, Judith S. 1922- 17
Sejima, Yoshimasa 1913- 8
Selberg, Ingrid (Maria) 1950- 68
Selden, George
  See Thompson, George Selden
Selden, Neil R(oy) 1931- 61
Self, Margaret Cabell 1902-1996 24
Selfors, Suzanne 1963- 193
Selick, Henry 1952- 183
Selig, Sylvie 1942- 13
Selkirk, Jane
  See Chapman, John Stanton Higham
Sellers, Naomi
  See Flack, Naomi John White
Sellier, Marie 1953- 212
Selman, LaRue W. 1927- 55
Selsam, Millicent E(llis) 1912-1996 29
  Obituary 92
  Earlier sketch in SATA 1
  See also CLR 1
Seltzer, Meyer 1932- 17
Seltzer, Richard 1946- 41
Seltzer, Richard Warren, Jr.
  See Seltzer, Richard
Selvadurai, Shyam 1965(?)- 171
Selway, Martina 1940- 169
  Earlier sketch in SATA 74
Selzer, Adam 1980- 192
Selznick, Brian 1966- 210
  Earlier sketches in SATA 79, 117, 171
Semel, Nava 1954- 107
Semloh
  See Holmes, Peggy

Sendak, Jack 1924(?)-1995 28
Sendak, Maurice 1928- 165
  Earlier sketches in SATA 1, 27, 113
  See also CLR 131
Sendak, Maurice Bernard
  See Sendak, Maurice
Sender, Ruth M(insky) 1926- 62
Sengler, Johanna 1924- 18
Senisi, Ellen B. 1951- 116
Senisi, Ellen Babinec
  See Senisi, Ellen B.
Senn, J(oyce) A(nn) 1941- 115
Senn, Steve 1950- 60
  Brief entry 48
Sensel, Joni 1962- 204
Serafini, Frank 201
Serage, Nancy 1924- 10
Seredy, Kate 1899-1975 1
  Obituary 24
  See also CLR 10
Serfozo, Mary 1925- 194
Seroff, Victor I(ilyitch) 1902-1979 12
  Obituary 26
Serra, Sebastia 1966- 202
Serraillier, Ian (Lucien) 1912-1994 73
  Obituary 83
  Earlier sketch in SATA 1
  See also CLR 2
  See also SAAS 3
Serros, Michele 175
Serros, Michele M.
  See Serros, Michele
Servello, Joe 1932- 10
Service, Pamela F. 1945- 222
  Earlier sketch in SATA 64
Service, Robert
  See Service, Robert W.
Service, Robert W. 1874(?)-1958 20
Serwadda, W(illiam) Moses 1931- 27
Serwer-Bernstein, Blanche L(uria)
  1910-1997 10
Sescoe, Vincent E. 1938- 123
Seskin, Steve 1953- 211
Seth, Mary
  See Lexau, Joan M.
Seton, Anya 1904(?)-1990 3
  Obituary 66
Seton, Ernest (Evan) Thompson 1860-1946 . 18
  See also CLR 59
Seton-Thompson, Ernest
  See Seton, Ernest (Evan) Thompson
Seuling, Barbara 1937- 220
  Autobiography Feature 220
  Earlier sketches in SATA 10, 98, 145, 193
  See also SAAS 24
Seuss, Dr.
  See Dr. Seuss
Severn, Bill
  See Severn, William Irving
Severn, David
  See Unwin, David S.
Severn, William Irving 1914- 1
Sewall, Marcia 1935- 119
  Earlier sketches in SATA 37, 69
Seward, Prudence 1926- 16
Sewell, Anna 1820-1878 100
  Earlier sketch in SATA 24
  See also CLR 17
Sewell, Helen (Moore) 1896-1957 38
Sexton, Anne 1928-1974 10
Sexton, Anne Harvey
  See Sexton, Anne
Seymour, Alta Halverson 10
Seymour, Jane 1951- 139
Seymour, Tres 1966- 164
  Earlier sketch in SATA 82
Sfar, Joann 1971- 182
Shachtman, Tom 1942- 49
Shackleton, C.C.
  See Aldiss, Brian W.

Shader, Rachel
  See Sofer, Barbara
Shadow, Jak
  See Sutherland, Jon
Shadyland, Sal
  See Cooper, Louise
Shafer, Audrey 183
Shafer, Robert E(ugene) 1925- 9
Shaffer, Terea 1968- 79
Shahan, Sherry 1949- 216
  Earlier sketches in SATA 92, 134
Shahn, Ben(jamin) 1898-1969
  Obituary 21
Shahn, Bernarda Bryson
  See Bryson, Bernarda
Shaik, Fatima 114
Shalant, Phyllis 1949- 150
Shan, Darren 1972- 199
  Earlier sketches in SATA 129, 168
Shan, D.B.
  See Shan, Darren
Shanahan, Lisa 199
Shanberg, Karen
  See Shragg, Karen (I.)
Shane, Harold Gray 1914-1993 36
  Obituary 76
Shange, Ntozake 1948- 157
Shanks, Ann Zane (Kushner) 10
Shannon, David 1959- 152
  Earlier sketch in SATA 107
  See also CLR 87
Shannon, George 1952- 202
  Earlier sketches in SATA 35, 94, 143
Shannon, George William Bones
  See Shannon, George
Shannon, Jacqueline 63
Shannon, Margaret
  See Silverwood, Margaret Shannon
Shannon, Monica 1905(?)-1965 28
Shannon, Terry
  See Mercer, Jessie
Shannon, Terry Miller 1951- 148
Shapiro, Irwin 1911-1981 32
Shapiro, Jody Fickes 1940- 193
Shapiro, Karen Jo 1964- 186
Shapiro, Michelle 1961- 196
Shapiro, Milton J. 1926- 32
Shapiro, Tricia
  See Andryszewski, Tricia
Shapiro, Zachary 1970- 213
Shapp, Charles M(orris) 1906-1989
  Obituary 61
Shapp, Martha Glauber 1910- 3
Sharenow, Robert 193
Sharfman, Amalie 14
Sharkey, Niamh 213
Sharma, Partap 1939- 15
Sharma, Rashmi
  See Singh, Rashmi Sharma
Sharman, Alison
  See Leonard, Alison
Sharmat, Marjorie Weinman 1928- 133
  Earlier sketches in SATA 4, 33, 74
Sharmat, Mitchell 1927- 127
  Earlier sketch in SATA 33
Sharp, Anne Wallace 1947- 144
Sharp, Luke
  See Alkiviades, Alkis
Sharp, Margery 1905-1991 29
  Obituary 67
  Earlier sketch in SATA 1
  See also CLR 27
Sharp, Zerna A. 1889-1981
  Obituary 27
Sharpe, Jon
  See Duncan, Alice
  and Knott, William C(ecil, Jr.)
  and Messman, Jon
Sharpe, Mitchell R(aymond) 1924- 12
Sharpe, Susan 1946- 71

Sharratt, Nick 1962- 199
　Earlier sketches in SATA *104, 153*
Shasha, Mark 1961- 80
Shattuck, Roger 1923-2005 64
　Obituary 174
Shattuck, Roger Whitney
　See Shattuck, Roger
Shaw, Arnold 1909-1989 4
　Obituary 63
Shaw, Carolyn V. 1934- 91
Shaw, Charles (Green) 1892-1974 13
Shaw, Evelyn S. 1927- 28
Shaw, Flora Louisa
　See Lugard, Flora Louisa Shaw
Shaw, Janet 1937- 146
　Earlier sketch in SATA *61*
　See also CLR *96*
Shaw, Janet Beeler
　See Shaw, Janet
Shaw, Liane 1959- 222
Shaw, Lisa
　See Rogak, Lisa
Shaw, Margret 1940- 68
Shaw, Mary 1965- 180
Shaw, Nancy 1946- 162
　Earlier sketch in SATA *71*
Shaw, Ray 7
Shaw, Richard 1923- 12
Shawn, Frank S.
　See Goulart, Ron
Shay, Art
　See Shay, Arthur
Shay, Arthur 1922- 4
Shay, Lacey
　See Shebar, Sharon Sigmond
Shea, Bob 188
Shea, George 1940- 54
　Brief entry 42
Shea, Pegi Deitz 1960- 172
　Earlier sketches in SATA *77, 137*
Shearer, Alex 1949- 204
Shearer, John 1947- 43
　Brief entry 27
　See also CLR *34*
Shearer, Ted 1919- 43
Shearing, Leonie 1972- 184
Sheban, Chris 182
Shebar, Sharon Sigmond 1945- 36
Shecter, Ben 1935- 16
Shedd, Warner 1934- 147
　Earlier sketch in SATA *87*
Sheedy, Alexandra Elizabeth 1962- 39
　Earlier sketch in SATA *19*
Sheehan, Ethna 1908-2000 9
Sheehan, Patty 1945- 77
Sheehan, Sean 1951- 154
　Earlier sketch in SATA *86*
Sheen, Barbara 1949- 143
Shefelman, Janice 1930- 205
　Earlier sketches in SATA *58, 129*
Shefelman, Janice Jordan
　See Shefelman, Janice
Shefelman, Tom 1927- 204
　Earlier sketch in SATA *58*
Sheffer, H. R.
　See Abels, Harriette S(heffer)
Sheffield, Charles 1935-2002 109
Sheffield, Janet N. 1926- 26
Sheikh, Nazneen 1944- 101
Sheinkin, Steve 1968- 204
Sheinmel, Courtney 1977- 211
Shekerjian, Regina Tor 16
Shelby, Anne 1948- 85
　Autobiography Feature 121
　See also SAAS *26*
Sheldon, Ann
　See Antle, Nancy
Sheldon, Ann 67
　Earlier sketch in SATA *1*
Sheldon, Aure 1917-1976 12
Sheldon, David 185

Sheldon, Deyan 181
Sheldon, John
　See Bloch, Robert (Albert)
Sheldon, Muriel 1926- 45
　Brief entry 39
Shell, Barry 1951- 176
Shelley, Frances
　See Wees, Frances Shelley
Shelley, John 1959- 202
Shelley, Mary
　See Shelley, Mary Wollstonecraft
Shelley, Mary Wollstonecraft 1797-1851 29
　See also CLR *133*
Shelton, William Roy 1919-1995 5
　Obituary 129
Shemie, Bonnie (Jean Brenner) 1949- 96
Shemin, Margaretha (Hoeneveld) 1928- 4
Shen, Michele 1953- 173
Shenker, Michele
　See Shen, Michele
Shenton, Edward 1895-1977 45
Shepard, Aaron 1950- 187
　Earlier sketches in SATA *75, 113*
Shepard, Ernest Howard 1879-1976 100
　Obituary 24
　Earlier sketches in SATA *3, 33*
　See also CLR *27*
Shepard, James R.
　See Shepard, Jim
Shepard, Jim 1956- 164
　Earlier sketch in SATA *90*
Shepard, Mary
　See Knox, (Mary) Eleanor Jessie
Shephard, Esther 1891-1975 5
　Obituary 26
Shepherd, Amanda 201
Shepherd, Donna Walsh
　See Walsh Shepherd, Donna
Shepherd, Elizabeth 4
Shepherd, Irana 173
Shepherd, Roni
　See Shepherd, Irana
Sheppard, Kate 195
Shepperson, Rob 178
Sherburne, Zoa (Lillian Morin) 1912-1995 3
　See also SAAS *18*
Sherk-Savage, Candace
　See Savage, Candace
Sherlock, Patti 71
Sherman, D(enis) R(onald) 1934- 48
　Brief entry 29
Sherman, Diane (Finn) 1928- 12
Sherman, Elizabeth
　See Friskey, Margaret (Richards)
Sherman, Harold (Morrow) 1898-1987 37
　Obituary 137
Sherman, Josepha 163
　Earlier sketch in SATA *75*
Sherman, Michael
　See Lowndes, Robert A(ugustine) W(ard)
Sherman, Nancy
　See Rosenberg, Nancy (Sherman)
Sherman, Pat 174
Sherman, Peter Michael
　See Lowndes, Robert A(ugustine) W(ard)
Sherrard, Valerie (Anne) 1957- 141
Sherrod, Jane
　See Singer, Jane Sherrod
Sherry, Clifford J. 1943- 84
Sherry, (Dulcie) Sylvia 1932- 122
　Earlier sketch in SATA *8*
Sherwan, Earl 1917- 3
Sherwood, Jonathan
　See London, Jonathan
Sheth, Kashmira 186
Shetterly, Will 1955- 78
　Autobiography Feature 106
Shetterly, William Howard
　See Shetterly, Will
Shiefman, Vicky 1942- 22

Shields, Brenda Desmond (Armstrong)
　1914- 37
Shields, Carol Diggory 174
Shields, Charles 1944- 10
Shields, Gillian 203
Shiels, Barbara
　See Adams, Barbara Johnston
Shiffman, Lena 1957- 101
Shiina, Makoto 1944- 83
Shimin, Symeon 1902-1984 13
Shimko, Bonnie 1941- 191
Shine, Andrea 1955- 104
Shine, Deborah 1932- 71
Shinn, Everett 1876-1953 21
Shinn, Sharon 1957- 164
　Earlier sketch in SATA *110*
Shippen, Katherine B(inney) 1892-1980 1
　Obituary 23
　See also CLR *36*
Shippey, T. A. 1943- 143
Shippey, Thomas Alan
　See Shippey, T. A.
Shipton, Eric Earle 1907-1977 10
Shipton, Jonathan 1948- 215
Shipton, Paul 1963- 196
Shiraz, Yasmin 173
Shirer, William L(awrence) 1904-1993 45
　Obituary 78
Shirley, Debra 203
Shirley, Gayle C 1955- 96
Shirley, Gayle Corbett
　See Shirley, Gayle C
Shirley, Jean 1919- 70
Shirreffs, Gordon D(onald) 1914-1996 11
Shirts, Morris A(lpine) 1922- 63
Shlichta, Joe 1968- 84
Shmurak, Carole B. 1944- 118
Sholokhov, Mikhail 1905-1984
　Obituary 36
Sholokhov, Mikhail Aleksandrovich
　See Sholokhov, Mikhail
Shore, Diane Z. 215
　Earlier sketch in SATA *179*
Shore, Diane ZuHone
　See Shore, Diane Z.
Shore, June Lewis 30
Shore, Nancy 1960- 124
Shore, Robert 1924- 39
Short, Michael 1937- 65
Short, Roger
　See Arkin, Alan
Shortall, Leonard W. 19
Shortt, Tim(othy Donald) 1961- 96
Shotwell, Louisa Rossiter 1902-1993 3
Shoulders, Michael 1954- 216
Shoup, Barbara 1947- 156
　Earlier sketch in SATA *86*
　See also SAAS *24*
Shoveller, Herb 184
Showalter, Jean B(reckinridge) 12
Showell, Ellen Harvey 1934- 33
Showers, Paul C. 1910-1999 92
　Obituary 114
　Earlier sketch in SATA *21*
　See also CLR *6*
　See also SAAS *7*
Shpakow, Tanya 1959(?)- 94
Shpitalnik, Vladimir 1964- 83
Shragg, Karen (I.) 1954- 142
Shreeve, Elizabeth 1956- 156
Shreve, Susan
　See Shreve, Susan Richards
Shreve, Susan Richards 1939- 152
　Brief entry 41
　Earlier sketches in SATA *46, 95*
Shriver, Jean Adair 1932- 75
Shriver, Maria 1955- 134
Shriver, Maria Owings
　See Shriver, Maria
Shrode, Mary
　See Hollingsworth, Mary

Shtainmets, Leon 32
Shub, Elizabeth 1915(?)-2004 5
Shuken, Julia 1948- 84
Shulevitz, Uri 1935- 165
    Earlier sketches in SATA 3, 50, 106
    See also CLR 61
Shulman, Alix Kates 1932- 7
Shulman, Dee 1957- 146
Shulman, Irving 1913-1995 13
Shulman, Lisa 202
Shulman, Mark 1962- 184
Shulman, Max 1919-1988
    Obituary 59
Shulman, Milton 1913-2004
    Obituary 154
Shulman, Neil B(arnett) 1945- 89
Shumsky, Zena
    See Collier, Zena
Shura, Mary Francis
    See Craig, Mary (Francis) Shura
Shusterman, Neal 1962- 201
    Autobiography Feature 140
    Earlier sketches in SATA 85, 121, 140
Shuter, Jane (Margaret) 1955- 151
    Earlier sketch in SATA 90
Shuttlesworth, Dorothy Edwards 3
Shwartz, Susan (Martha) 1949- 94
Shyer, Christopher 1961- 98
Shyer, Marlene Fanta 13
Siberell, Anne 29
Sibley, Don 1922- 12
Siburt, Ruth 1951- 121
Siculan, Daniel 1922- 12
Siddon, Barbara
    See Bradford, Barbara Taylor
Sidgwick, Ethel 1877-1970 116
Sidjakov, Nicolas 1924- 18
Sidman, Joyce 1956- 181
    Earlier sketch in SATA 145
Sidney, Frank
    See Warwick, Alan R(oss)
Sidney, Margaret
    See Lothrop, Harriet Mulford Stone
Siebert, Diane 1948- 189
Siegal, Aranka 1930- 88
    Brief entry 37
Siegel, Beatrice 36
Siegel, Helen
    See Siegl, Helen
Siegel, Robert 1939- 39
Siegel, Robert Harold
    See Siegel, Robert
Siegel, Siena Cherson 1967(?)- 185
Siegelson, Kim L. 1962- 114
Sieger, Ted 1958- 189
Siegl, Helen 1924- 34
Siepmann, Mary Aline
    See Wesley, Mary (Aline)
Sierra, Judy 1945- 195
    Earlier sketches in SATA 104, 162
Sieswerda, Paul L. 1942- 147
Sievert, Terri
    See Dougherty, Terri (L.)
Sigsawa, Keiichi 1972- 211
Silas
    See McCay, (Zenas) Winsor
Silcock, Sara Lesley 1947- 12
Silin-Palmer, Pamela 184
Sill, Cathryn 1953- 221
    Earlier sketches in SATA 74, 141
Sill, John 1947- 222
    Earlier sketches in SATA 74, 140
Sillitoe, Alan 1928-2010 61
Sills, Leslie (Elka) 1948- 129
Silly, E. S.
    See Kraus, (Herman) Robert
Silsbe, Brenda 1953- 73
Silva, Joseph
    See Goulart, Ron
Silvano, Wendi 1962- 223

Silver, Jago
    See Jago
Silver, Maggie 216
Silver, Ruth
    See Chew, Ruth
Silverberg, Robert 1935- 91
    Autobiography Feature 104
    Earlier sketch in SATA 13
    See also CLR 59
Silverman, Erica 1955- 222
    Earlier sketches in SATA 78, 112, 165
Silverman, Janis L. 1946- 127
Silverman, Mel(vin Frank) 1931-1966 9
Silverman, Robin L. 1954- 96
Silverman, Robin Landew
    See Silverman, Robin L.
Silverstein, Alvin 1933- 124
    Earlier sketches in SATA 8, 69
    See also CLR 25
Silverstein, Herma 1945- 106
Silverstein, Robert Alan 1959- 124
    Earlier sketch in SATA 77
Silverstein, Shel 1932-1999 92
    Brief entry 27
    Obituary 116
    Earlier sketch in SATA 33
    See also CLR 96
Silverstein, Sheldon Allan
    See Silverstein, Shel
Silverstein, Virginia B. 1937- 124
    Earlier sketches in SATA 8, 69
    See also CLR 25
Silverstein, Virginia Barbara Opshelor
    See Silverstein, Virginia B.
Silverthorne, Elizabeth 1930- 35
Silverwood, Margaret Shannon 1966- 137
    Earlier sketch in SATA 83
Silvey, Diane F. 1946- 135
Sim, David 1953- 162
Sim, Dorrith M. 1931- 96
Simak, Clifford D(onald) 1904-1988
    Obituary 56
Simard, Remy 1959- 168
Siminovich, Lorena 1976(?)- 219
Simmie, Lois (Ann) 1932- 106
Simmonds, Posy 1945- 130
    See also CLR 23
Simmonds, Rosemary Elizabeth
    See Simmonds, Posy
Simmons, Andra 1939- 141
Simmons, Elly 1955- 134
Simmons, Michael 1970- 185
Simms, Laura 1947- 117
Sinner, Janni Lee 113
Simon, Charlie May
    See Fletcher, Charlie May Hogue
Simon, Francesca 1955- 111
Simon, Gabriel 1972- 118
Simon, Hilda Rita 1921- 28
    See also CLR 39
Simon, Howard 1903-1979 32
    Obituary 21
Simon, Joe
    See Simon, Joseph H.
Simon, Joseph H. 1913- 7
Simon, Martin P(aul William) 1903-1969 12
Simon, Mina Lewiton
    See Lewiton, Mina
Simon, Norma (Feldstein) 1927- 129
    Earlier sketches in SATA 3, 68
Simon, Seymour 1931- 202
    Earlier sketches in SATA 4, 73, 138
    See also CLR 63
Simon, Shirley (Schwartz) 1921- 11
Simon, Solomon 1895-1970 40
Simonetta, Linda 1948- 14
Simonetta, Sam 1936- 14
Simons, Barbara B(rooks) 1934- 41
Simont, Marc 1915- 126
    Earlier sketches in SATA 9, 73
Simpson, Colin 1908-1983 14

Simpson, Harriette
    See Arnow, Harriette (Louisa) Simpson
Simpson, Jacynth Hope
    See Hope Simpson, Jacynth
Simpson, Lesley 1963- 150
Simpson, Margaret 1943- 128
Simpson, Myrtle L(illias) 1931- 14
Sims, Blanche 168
    Earlier sketch in SATA 75
Sims, Blanche L.
    See Sims, Blanche
Sims, Rudine
    See Bishop, Rudine Sims
Simundsson, Elva 1950- 63
Sinclair, Clover
    See Gater, Dilys
Sinclair, Emil
    See Hesse, Hermann
Sinclair, Jeff 1958- 77
Sinclair, Olga 1923- 121
Sinclair, Rose
    See Smith, Susan Vernon
Sinclair, Upton 1878-1968 9
Sinclair, Upton Beall
    See Sinclair, Upton
Singer, A.L.
    See Lerangis, Peter
Singer, Arthur 1917-1990 64
Singer, Isaac
    See Singer, Isaac Bashevis
Singer, Isaac Bashevis 1904-1991 27
    Obituary 68
    Earlier sketch in SATA 3
    See also CLR 1
Singer, Jane Sherrod 1917-1985 4
    Obituary 42
Singer, Julia 1917- 28
Singer, Kurt D. 1911-2005 38
    Obituary 172
Singer, Marilyn 1948- 201
    Autobiography Feature 158
    Brief entry 38
    Earlier sketches in SATA 48, 80, 125, 158
    See also CLR 48
    See also SAAS 13
Singer, Muff 1942-2005 104
    Obituary 160
Singer, Nicky 1956- 194
Singer, Susan (Mahler) 1941- 9
Singh, Rashmi Sharma 1952- 90
Singleton, Linda Joy 1957- 166
    Earlier sketch in SATA 88
Singleton, L.J.
    See Singleton, Linda Joy
Singleton, Sarah 1966- 214
Sinykin, Sheri
    See Sinykin, Sheri Cooper
Sinykin, Sheri Cooper 1950- 142
    Autobiography Feature 142
    Earlier sketches in SATA 72, 133
Sinykin, Sheril Terri Cooper
    See Sinykin, Sheri Cooper
Siomades, Lorianne 217
Sipiera, Paul P., (Jr.) 1948- 144
    Earlier sketch in SATA 89
Siracusa, Catherine (Jane) 1947- 82
Sirett, Dawn (Karen) 1966- 88
Sirimarco, Elizabeth 1966- 158
Sirof, Harriet 1930- 94
    Earlier sketch in SATA 37
Sirois, Allen L. 1950- 76
Sirvaitis (Chernyaev), Karen (Ann) 1961- ... 79
Sis, Peter 1949- 192
    Earlier sketch in SATA 149
    See also CLR 110
Sisson, Rosemary Anne 1923- 11
Sister Mary Terese
    See Donze, Mary Terese
Sita, Lisa 1962- 87
Sitarski, Anita 200
Sitomer, Alan Lawrence 174

Sitomer, Harry 1903-1985 .... *31*
Sitomer, Mindel 1903-1987 .... *31*
Sittenfeld, Curtis 1975(?)- *164*
Sive, Helen R(obinson) 1951- *30*
Sivulich, Sandra (Jeanne) Stroner 1941- *9*
Siy, Alexandra *193*
Skarmeta, Antonio 1940- *57*
Skeers, Linda 1958- *207*
Skelly, James R(ichard) 1927- *17*
Skelton, Matthew 1971- *185*
Skinner, Constance Lindsay 1877-1939
    See YABC *1*
Skinner, Cornelia Otis 1901-1979 .... *2*
Skipper, G. C. 1939- *46*
    Brief entry *38*
Sklansky, Amy E(dgar) 1971- *145*
Sklansky, Amy E. 1971- *204*
Skofield, James *95*
    Brief entry *44*
Skold, Betty Westrom 1923- *41*
Skorpen, Liesel Moak 1935- *3*
Skott, Maria
    See Nikolajeva, Maria
Skrypuch, Marsha Forchuk 1954- *134*
Skultety, Nancy Laney 1960- *175*
Skurzynski, Gloria 1930- *145*
    Autobiography Feature *145*
    Earlier sketches in SATA *8, 74, 122*
    See also SAAS *9*
Skurzynski, Gloria Joan
    See Skurzynski, Gloria
Skutch, Robert 1925- *89*
Skye, Maggie
    See Werner, Herma
Skye, Obert *200*
    Earlier sketch in SATA *170*
Slack, Michael 1969- *189*
Slackman, Charles B. 1934- *12*
Slade, Arthur G. 1967- *221*
    Earlier sketches in SATA *106, 149*
Slade, Arthur Gregory
    See Slade, Arthur G.
Slade, Christian 1974- *193*
Slade, Richard 1910-1971 .... *9*
Slangerup, Erik Jon 1969- *130*
Slate, Joseph 1928- *174*
    Earlier sketches in SATA *38, 122*
Slate, Joseph Frank
    See Slate, Joseph
Slater, Dashka 1963- *179*
Slater, David Michael 1970- *212*
Slater, Ray
    See Lansdale, Joe R.
Slaughter, Hope 1940- *84*
Slaughter, Jean
    See Doty, Jean Slaughter
Slaughter, Tom 1955- *152*
Slavicek, Louise Chipley 1956- *144*
Slavin, Bill 1959- *199*
    Earlier sketches in SATA *76, 148*
Slaymaker, Melissa Eskridge 1958- *158*
Slayton, Fran Cannon *221*
Sleator, William 1945- *208*
    Earlier sketches in SATA *3, 68, 118, 161*
    See also CLR *128*
Sleator, William Warner III
    See Sleator, William
Slegers, Liesbet 1975- *154*
Sleigh, Barbara 1906-1982 .... *86*
    Obituary *30*
    Earlier sketch in SATA *3*
Slepian, Jan 1921- *85*
    Brief entry *45*
    Earlier sketch in SATA *51*
    See also SAAS *8*
Slepian, Janice B.
    See Slepian, Jan
Slicer, Margaret O. 1920- *4*
Slier, Debby
    See Shine, Deborah
Sloan, Brian 1966- *172*

Sloan, Carolyn 1937- *116*
    Earlier sketch in SATA *58*
Sloan, Glenna 1930- *120*
Sloan, Glenna Davis
    See Sloan, Glenna
Sloane, Eric 1910(?)-1985 .... *52*
    Obituary *42*
Sloane, Todd 1955- *88*
Sloat, Teri 1948- *164*
    Earlier sketch in SATA *70, 106*
Slobodkin, Florence Gersh 1905-1994 .... *5*
    Obituary *107*
Slobodkin, Louis 1903-1975 .... *26*
    Earlier sketch in SATA *1*
Slobodkina, Esphyr 1908-2002 .... *1*
    Obituary *135*
    See also SAAS *8*
Sloggett, Nellie 1851-1923 .... *44*
Slonim, David 1966- *207*
Sloss, Lesley Lord 1965- *72*
Slote, Alfred 1926- *72*
    Earlier sketch in SATA *8*
    See also CLR *4*
    See also SAAS *21*
Slote, Elizabeth 1956- *80*
Small, Charlie
    See Ward, Nick
Small, David 1945- *216*
    Brief entry *46*
    Earlier sketches in SATA *50, 95, 126, 183*
    See also CLR *53*
Small, Ernest
    See Lent, Blair
Small, Mary 1932- *165*
Small, Terry 1942- *75*
Smallcomb, Pam 1954- *159*
Smallman, Steve *197*
Smalls, Irene
    See Smalls-Hector, Irene
Smalls-Hector, Irene 1950- *146*
    Earlier sketch in SATA *73*
    See also CLR *103*
Smallwood, Norah (Evelyn) 1910(?)-1984
    Obituary *41*
Smaridge, Norah (Antoinette) 1903-1994 ...... *6*
Smath, Jerry 1933- *198*
Smee, Nicola 1948- *167*
    Earlier sketch in SATA *76*
Smiley, Virginia Kester 1923- *2*
Smit, Noelle 1972- *199*
Smith, Alexander McCall 1948- *179*
    Earlier sketch in SATA *73*
Smith, Andrew 1959- *209*
Smith, Andrew Anselmo
    See Smith, Andrew
Smith, Andy J. 1975- *207*
Smith, Anne Warren 1938- *41*
    Brief entry *34*
Smith, Barry (Edward Jervis) 1943- *75*
Smith, Beatrice S(chillinger) *12*
Smith, Betsy Covington 1937- *55*
    Earlier sketch in SATA *43*
Smith, Betty (Wehner) 1904-1972 .... *6*
Smith, Bradford 1909-1964 .... *5*
Smith, Brenda 1946- *82*
Smith, C. Pritchard
    See Hoyt, Edwin P(almer), Jr.
Smith, Caesar
    See Trevor, Elleston
Smith, Cat Bowman 1939- *201*
Smith, Charles R., Jr. 1969- *203*
    Earlier sketch in SATA *159*
Smith, Craig 1955- *172*
    Earlier sketches in SATA *81, 117*
Smith, Cynthia Leitich 1967- *215*
    Earlier sketch in SATA *152*
Smith, D. James 1955- *176*
Smith, Danna *216*
Smith, Danna Kessimakis
    See Smith, Danna

Smith, Datus C(lifford), Jr. 1907-1999 .... *13*
    Obituary *116*
Smith, Debra 1955- *89*
Smith, Derek 1943- *141*
Smith, Dick King
    See King-Smith, Dick
Smith, D.J.
    See Smith, D. James
Smith, Dodie
    See Smith, Dorothy Gladys
Smith, Doris Buchanan 1934-2002 .... *75*
    Obituary *140*
    Earlier sketch in SATA *28*
    See also SAAS *10*
Smith, Dorothy Gladys 1896-1990 .... *82*
    Obituary *65*
Smith, Dorothy Stafford 1905- *6*
Smith, Duane 1974- *202*
Smith, E(lmer) Boyd 1860-1943
    See YABC *1*
Smith, E(dric) Brooks 1917- *40*
Smith, Elwood H. 1941- *203*
Smith, Emily Wing 1980- *215*
Smith, Emma 1923- *52*
    Brief entry *36*
Smith, (Katherine) Eunice (Young)
    1902-1993 .... *5*
Smith, Frances C(hristine) 1904-1986 .... *3*
Smith, Gary R. 1932- *14*
Smith, Geof 1969- *102*
Smith, George Harmon 1920- *5*
Smith, Gordon 1951- *184*
Smith, Greg Leitich *152*
Smith, H(arry) Allen 1907-1976
    Obituary *20*
Smith, Helene 1937- *142*
Smith, Hope Anita *202*
Smith, Howard E(verett), Jr. 1927- *12*
Smith, Hugh L(etcher) 1921-1968 .... *5*
Smith, Imogene Henderson 1922- *12*
Smith, Jacqueline B. 1937- *39*
Smith, Jada Pinkett 1971- *161*
Smith, James Noel 1950- *193*
Smith, Janet (Buchanan) Adam
    See Adam Smith, Janet (Buchanan)
Smith, Janice Lee 1949- *155*
    Earlier sketch in SATA *54*
Smith, Jean
    See Smith, Frances C(hristine)
Smith, Jean Pajot 1945- *10*
Smith, Jeff 1958- *161*
    Earlier sketch in SATA *93*
Smith, Jeff Allen
    See Smith, Jeff
Smith, Jeffrey Alan
    See Smith, Jeff
Smith, Jenny 1963- *90*
Smith, Jessie
    See Kunhardt, Edith
Smith, Jessie Willcox 1863-1935 .... *21*
    See also CLR *59*
Smith, Joan (Mary) 1933- *54*
    Brief entry *46*
Smith, Johnston
    See Crane, Stephen
Smith, Jos A. 1936- *181*
    Earlier sketches in SATA *73, 120*
Smith, Joseph Arthur
    See Smith, Jos A.
Smith, Judie R. 1936- *80*
Smith, Kirsten 1970- *210*
Smith, Lafayette
    See Higdon, Hal
Smith, Lane 1959- *224*
    Earlier sketches in SATA *76, 131, 179*
    See also CLR *47*
Smith, Lee
    See Albion, Lee Smith
Smith, Lendon H(oward) 1921- *64*
Smith, Lillian H(elena) 1887-1983
    Obituary *32*

Smith, Linda 1949- 177
Smith, Linell Nash 1932- 2
Smith, Lucia B. 1943- 30
Smith, Maggie 1965- 190
Smith, Margaret Emily Noel Nuttall
  See Nuttall-Smith, Margaret Emily Noel
Smith, Marion Hagens 1913- 12
Smith, Marion Jaques 1899-1987 13
Smith, Mary Ellen 10
Smith, Marya 1945- 78
Smith, Mike
  See Smith, Mary Ellen
Smith, Nancy Covert 1935- 12
Smith, Norman F. 1920- 70
  Earlier sketch in SATA 5
Smith, Patricia Clark 1943- 96
Smith, Pauline C.
  See Arthur, Robert, (Jr.)
Smith, Pauline C(oggeshall) 1908-1994 27
Smith, Philip Warren 1936- 46
Smith, R. Alexander McCall
  See Smith, Alexander McCall
Smith, Rebecca 1946- 123
Smith, Robert Kimmel 1930- 77
  Earlier sketch in SATA 12
Smith, Robert Paul 1915-1977 52
  Obituary 30
Smith, Roland 1951- 193
  Earlier sketches in SATA 115, 161
Smith, Rosamond
  See Oates, Joyce Carol
Smith, Ruth Leslie 1902- 2
Smith, Samantha 1972-1985
  Obituary 45
Smith, Sandra Lee 1945- 75
Smith, Sarah Stafford
  See Smith, Dorothy Stafford
Smith, Sharon 1947- 82
Smith, Sherri L. 1971- 156
Smith, Sherwood 1951- 206
  Autobiography Feature 206
  Earlier sketches in SATA 82, 140
Smith, Shirley Raines
  See Raines, Shirley C(arol)
Smith, Susan Carlton 1923- 12
Smith, Susan Mathias 1950- 43
  Brief entry 35
Smith, Susan Vernon 1950- 48
  Brief entry 45
Smith, Tim(othy R.) 1945- 151
Smith, Ursula 1934- 54
Smith, Vian (Crocker) 1920-1969 11
Smith, Wanda VanHoy 1926- 65
Smith, Ward
  See Goldsmith, Howard
Smith, William A. 1918- 10
Smith, William Jay 1918- 154
  Autobiography Feature 154
  Earlier sketches in SATA 2, 68
  See also SAAS 22
Smith, Winsome 1935- 45
Smith, Z.Z.
  See Westheimer, David
Smith-Ankrom, M. E. 1942- 130
Smith-Griswold, Wendy 1955- 88
Smith-Rex, Susan J. 1950- 94
Smithsen, Richard
  See Pellowski, Michael (Joseph)
Smithson, Ryan 1985- 216
Smits, Teo
  See Smits, Theodore R(ichard)
Smits, Theodore R(ichard) 1905-1996 45
  Brief entry 28
Smolinski, Dick 1932- 86
Smothers, Ethel Footman 1944- 149
  Earlier sketch in SATA 76
Smucker, Anna Egan 1948- 209
Smucker, Barbara 1915-2003 130
  Earlier sketches in SATA 29, 76
  See also CLR 10
  See also SAAS 11

Smucker, Barbara Claassen
  See Smucker, Barbara
Smyth, Iain 1959- 105
Snedeker, Caroline Dale (Parke) 1871-1956
  See YABC 2
Sneed, Brad 191
Sneider, Marian 1932-2005 197
Snell, Nigel (Edward Creagh) 1936- 57
  Brief entry 40
Snellgrove, L(aurence) E(rnest) 1928- 53
Snelling, Dennis (Wayne) 1958- 84
Sneve, Virginia Driving Hawk 1933- 95
  Earlier sketch in SATA 8
  See also CLR 2
Snicket, Lemony 1970- 215
  Earlier sketches in SATA 126, 187
  See also CLR 79
Sniegoski, Thomas E. 195
Sniegoski, Tom
  See Sniegoski, Thomas E.
Snir, Eleyor 225
Snodgrass, Mary Ellen 1944- 75
Snodgrass, Quentin Curtius
  See Twain, Mark
Snodgrass, Thomas Jefferson
  See Twain, Mark
Snook, Barbara (Lillian) 1913-1976 34
Snow, Alan 1959- 190
Snow, Carol 1965- 208
Snow, Donald Clifford 1917-1979 16
Snow, Dorothea J(ohnston) 1909- 9
Snow, Richard F(olger) 1947- 52
  Brief entry 37
Snyder, Anne 1922-2001 4
  Obituary 125
Snyder, Bernadette McCarver 1930- 97
Snyder, Carol 1941- 35
Snyder, Gerald S(eymour) 1933- 48
  Brief entry 34
Snyder, Jerome 1916-1976
  Obituary 20
Snyder, Laurel 1974- 209
Snyder, Midori 1954- 106
Snyder, Paul A. 1946- 125
Snyder, Zilpha Keatley 1927- 163
  Autobiography Feature 163
  Earlier sketches in SATA 1, 28, 75, 110
  See also CLR 121
  See also SAAS 2
Snyderman, Reuven K. 1922- 5
So, Meilo 162
Sobel, June 1950- 149
Soble, Jennie
  See Cavin, Ruth
Sobol, Donald J. 1924- 132
  Earlier sketches in SATA 1, 31, 73
  See also CLR 4
Sobol, Harriet Langsam 1936- 47
  Brief entry 34
Sobol, Richard 211
Sobol, Rose 1931- 76
Sobott-Mogwe, Gaele 1956- 97
Soderlind, Arthur E(dwin) 1920- 14
Soentpiet, Chris K. 1970- 159
  Earlier sketch in SATA 97
Soerensen, Svend Otto 1916- 67
Sofer, Barbara 1949- 109
Sofer, Rachel
  See Sofer, Barbara
Softly, Barbara Frewin 1924- 12
Sogabe, Aki 207
Soglow, Otto 1900-1975
  Obituary 30
Sohl, Frederic J(ohn) 1916- 10
Sohr, Daniel 1973- 190
Sokol, Bill
  See Sokol, William
Sokol, William 1923- 37
Sokolov, Kirill 1930- 34
Solbert, Romaine G. 1925- 2

Solbert, Ronni
  See Solbert, Romaine G.
Solheim, James 133
Solomon, Heather M. 188
Solomon, Joan 1930- 51
  Brief entry 40
Solomons, Ikey Esquir
  See Thackeray, William Makepeace
Solonevich, George 1915-2003 15
Solot, Mary Lynn 1939- 12
Solov'ev, Mikhail
  See Soloviov, Michael
Soloviov, Michael 1972- 222
Soman, David 1965- 200
Somerlott, Robert 1928-2001 62
Somers, Kevin 205
Somervill, Barbara A(nn) 1948- 140
Sommer, Angela
  See Sommer-Bodenburg, Angela
Sommer, Carl 1930- 175
  Earlier sketch in SATA 126
Sommer, Elyse 1929- 7
Sommer, Robert 1929- 12
Sommer-Bodenburg, Angela 1948- 113
  Earlier sketch in SATA 63
Sommerdorf, Norma 1926- 131
Sommerdorf, Norma Jean
  See Sommerdorf, Norma
Sommerfelt, Aimee 1892-1975 5
Son, John 160
Sones, Sonya 131
Sonneborn, Ruth (Cantor) 1899-1974 4
  Obituary 27
Sonnenblick, Jordan 1969- 223
  Earlier sketch in SATA 185
  See also CLR 144
Sonnenmark, Laura A. 1958- 73
Soo, Kean 201
Sopko, Eugen 1949- 58
Sorel, Edward 1929- 126
  Brief entry 37
  Earlier sketch in SATA 65
Sorensen, Henri 1950- 115
  Earlier sketch in SATA 77
Sorensen, Svend Otto
  See Soerensen, Svend Otto
Sorensen, Virginia 1912-1991 2
  Obituary 72
  See also SAAS 15
Sorenson, Jane 1926- 63
Sorenson, Margo 1946- 96
Sorley Walker, Kathrine 41
Sorra, Kristin 185
Sorrells, Walter 177
Sorrentino, Joseph N. 1937- 6
Sortor, June Elizabeth 1939- 12
Sortor, Toni
  See Sortor, June Elizabeth
Sosa, Hernan 1977- 203
Soskin, V. H.
  See Ellison, Virginia H(owell)
Soto, Gary 1952- 174
  Earlier sketches in SATA 80, 120
  See also CLR 38
Sotomayor, Antonio 1902-1985 11
Souci, Robert D. San
  See San Souci, Robert D.
Soudley, Henry
  See Wood, James Playsted
Souhami, Jessica 176
Soule, Gardner (Bosworth) 1913-2000 14
Soule, Jean Conder 1919- 10
Souster, (Holmes) Raymond 1921- 63
South, Sheri Cobb 1959- 82
Southall, Ivan 1921-2008 134
  Autobiography Feature 134
  Earlier sketches in SATA 3, 68
  See also CLR 2
  See also SAAS 3
Southall, Ivan Francis
  See Southall, Ivan

Southey, Robert 1774-1843 .... *54*
Southgate, Vera *54*
Souza, Janet
    See Tashjian, Janet
Sovak, Jan 1953- *115*
Sowden, Celeste
    See Walters, Celeste
Sowter, Nita *69*
Spafford, Suzy 1945- *160*
Spagnoli, Cathy 1950- *134*
    Earlier sketch in SATA *79*
Spain, Sahara Sunday 1991- *133*
Spain, Susan Rosson *185*
Spalding, Andrea 1944- *150*
    Earlier sketch in SATA *101*
Spalenka, Greg 1958- *198*
Spanfeller, James J. 1930- *19*
    See also SAAS *8*
Spanfeller, Jim
    See Spanfeller, James J.
Spangenberg, Judith Dunn 1942- *5*
Spangler, Brie *212*
Spanyol, Jessica 1965- *206*
    Earlier sketch in SATA *137*
Spar, Jerome 1918- *10*
Sparks, Barbara 1942- *78*
Sparks, Beatrice (Mathews) 1918- *44*
    Brief entry *28*
    See also CLR *139*
Sparks, Mary W. 1920- *15*
Spaulding, Douglas
    See Bradbury, Ray
Spaulding, Leonard
    See Bradbury, Ray
Spaulding, Norma *107*
Speare, Elizabeth George 1908-1994 .... *62*
    Obituary *83*
    Earlier sketch in SATA *5*
    See also CLR *8*
Spearing, Judith (Mary Harlow) 1922- *9*
Spears, Rick *182*
Speck, Katie *196*
Speck, Nancy 1959- *104*
Specking, Inez 1890-1960(?) *11*
Speed, Nell
    See Keats, Emma
    and Sampson, Emma (Keats) Speed
Speed, Nell (Ewing) 1878-1913 .... *68*
Speer, Bonnie Stahlman 1929- *113*
Speer-Lyon, Tammie L. 1965- *89*
Speicher, Helen Ross S(mith) 1915- *8*
Speir, Nancy 1958- *210*
    Earlier sketch in SATA *81*
Spellman, John W(illard) 1934- *14*
Spellman, Roger G.
    See Cox, William R(obert)
Spelman, Cornelia Maude 1946- *144*
    Earlier sketch in SATA *96*
Spelman, Mary 1934- *28*
Spelvin, George
    See Lerangis, Peter
    and Phillips, David Atlee
Spence, Cynthia
    See Eble, Diane
Spence, Eleanor (Rachel) 1928- *21*
    See also CLR *26*
Spence, Geraldine 1931- *47*
Spence, Ann 1918- *10*
Spencer, Britt *206*
Spencer, Cornelia
    See Yaukey, Grace S(ydenstricker)
Spencer, Donald D(ean) 1931- *41*
Spencer, Elizabeth 1921- *14*
Spencer, Leonard G.
    See Garrett, Randall
    and Silverberg, Robert
Spencer, William 1922- *9*
Spencer, Zane A(nn) 1935- *35*
Spengler, Margaret *223*
Sper, Emily 1957- *142*
Speregen, Devra Newberger 1964- *84*

Sperling, Dan(iel Lee) 1949- *65*
Sperry, Armstrong W. 1897-1976 .... *1*
    Obituary *27*
Sperry, Raymond
    See Garis, Howard R.
Sperry, Raymond, Jr. *1*
Spetter, Jung-Hee 1969- *134*
Spicer, Dorothy Gladys -1975 .... *32*
Spiegel, Beth *184*
Spiegelman, Art 1948- *158*
    Earlier sketch in SATA *109*
Spiegelman, Judith M. *5*
Spielberg, Steven 1947- *32*
Spier, Peter (Edward) 1927- *54*
    Earlier sketch in SATA *4*
    See also CLR *5*
Spilhaus, Athelstan (Frederick) 1911-1998 .. *13*
    Obituary *102*
Spilka, Arnold 1917- *6*
Spillane, Frank Morrison
    See Spillane, Mickey
Spillane, Mickey 1918-2006 .... *66*
    Obituary *176*
Spillebeen, Geert 1956- *225*
Spinelli, Eileen 1942- *225*
    Earlier sketches in SATA *38, 101, 150, 186*
Spinelli, Jerry 1941- *195*
    Earlier sketches in SATA *39, 71, 110, 158*
    See also CLR *82*
Spink, Reginald (William) 1905-1994 .... *11*
Spinka, Penina Keen 1945- *72*
Spinner, Stephanie 1943- *132*
    Earlier sketches in SATA *38, 91*
Spinossimus
    See White, William, Jr.
Spiotta-DiMare, Loren *173*
Spires, Ashley 1978- *183*
Spires, Elizabeth 1952- *215*
    Earlier sketches in SATA *71, 111*
Spiridellis, Gregg 1971(?)- *199*
Spirin, Gennadii
    See Spirin, Gennady
Spirin, Gennadij
    See Spirin, Gennady
Spirin, Gennady 1948- *204*
    Earlier sketches in SATA *95, 134*
    See also CLR *88*
Spiro, Ruth *208*
Spivak, Dawnine *101*
Spizman, Robyn Freedman *194*
Spohn, David 1948- *72*
Spohn, Kate 1962- *147*
    Earlier sketch in SATA *87*
Spollen, Christopher 1952- *12*
Spooner, Michael (Tim) 1954- *92*
Spoor, Mike *218*
Spowart, Robin 1947- *177*
    Earlier sketch in SATA *82*
Spradlin, Michael P. *204*
Sprague, Gretchen 1926-2003 .... *27*
Spranger, Nina 1969- *203*
Sprengel, Artie
    See Lerangis, Peter
Sprigge, Elizabeth (Miriam Squire)
    1900-1974 .... *10*
Spring, (Robert) Howard 1889-1965 .... *28*
Springer, Margaret 1941- *78*
Springer, Marilyn Harris 1931- *47*
Springer, Nancy 1948- *222*
    Earlier sketches in SATA *65, 110, 172*
Springstubb, Tricia 1950- *78*
    Brief entry *40*
    Earlier sketch in SATA *46*
Spudvilas, Anne 1951- *199*
    Earlier sketch in SATA *94*
Spurll, Barbara 1952- *78*
Spurr, Elizabeth *172*
Spykman, E(lizabeth) C(hoate) 1896-1965 .. *10*
    See also CLR *35*

Spyri, Johanna (Heusser) 1827-1901 .... *100*
    Earlier sketch in SATA *19*
    See also CLR *115*
Squires, Janet *215*
Squires, Phil
    See Barker, S. Omar
Srba, Lynne *98*
Sreenivasan, Jyotsna 1964- *101*
S-Ringi, Kjell
    See Ringi, Kjell (Arne Soerensen)
Staake, Bob 1957- *209*
Stacey, Cherylyn 1945- *96*
Stacy, Donald
    See Pohl, Frederik
Stadler, John *204*
Stadtler, Bea 1921- *17*
Stafford, Jean 1915-1979
    Obituary *22*
Stafford, Liliana 1950- *141*
Stafford, Paul 1966- *116*
Stahl, Ben(jamin) 1910-1987 .... *5*
    Obituary *54*
Stahl, Hilda 1938-1993 .... *48*
    Obituary *77*
Stahler, David, Jr. *218*
    Earlier sketch in SATA *162*
Staines, Bill 1949- *213*
Stainton, Sue *187*
Stair, Gobin (John) 1912- *35*
Stalder, Valerie *27*
Stamaty, Mark Alan 1947- *12*
Stambler, Irwin 1924- *5*
Stamp, Jorgen 1969- *225*
Stampler, Ann Redisch *209*
Standiford, Natalie 1961- *169*
    Earlier sketch in SATA *81*
Stanek, Lou Willett 1931- *63*
Stang, Judit 1921-1977 .... *29*
Stang, Judy
    See Stang, Judit
Stangl, (Mary) Jean 1928- *67*
Stanhope, Eric
    See Hamilton, Charles (Harold St. John)
Stankevich, Boris 1928- *2*
Stanley, Diane 1943- *213*
    Brief entry *32*
    Earlier sketches in SATA *37, 80, 115, 164*
    See also CLR *46*
    See also SAAS *15*
Stanley, Elizabeth 1947- *206*
Stanley, George Edward 1942- *67*
    Earlier sketches in SATA *53, 111, 157, 1*
Stanley, Jerry 1941- *127*
    Earlier sketch in SATA *79*
Stanley, Mandy *165*
Stanley, Robert
    See Hamilton, Charles (Harold St. John)
Stanley, Sanna 1962- *145*
Stanli, Sue
    See Meilach, Dona Z(weigoron)
Stanstead, John
    See Groom, Arthur William
Stanton, Karen 1960- *190*
Stanton, Schuyler
    See Baum, L. Frank
Staples, Suzanne Fisher 1945- *207*
    Earlier sketches in SATA *70, 105, 151*
    See also CLR *137*
Stapleton, Marjorie (Winifred) 1932- *28*
Stapp, Arthur D(onald) 1906-1972 .... *4*
Starbird, Kaye 1916- *6*
    See also CLR *60*
Stark, Evan 1942- *78*
Stark, James
    See Goldston, Robert (Conroy)
Stark, Ken 1943- *199*
Stark, Ulf 1944- *124*
Starke, Ruth (Elaine) 1946- *129*
Starkey, Marion L(ena) 1901-1991 .... *13*
Starr, Ward
    See Manes, Stephen

Starret, William
  See McClintock, Marshall
Starr Taylor, Bridget 1959- 99
Stasiak, Krystyna 49
Staub, Frank 1949- 116
Staub, Frank Jacob
  See Staub, Frank
Staub, Wendy Corsi 1964- 114
Stauffacher, Sue 1961- 199
  Earlier sketch in SATA 155
Stauffer, Don
  See Berkebile, Fred D(onovan)
Staunton, Schuyler
  See Baum, L. Frank
Staunton, Ted 1956- 167
  Earlier sketch in SATA 112
Stead, Judy 210
Stead, Philip C.
  See Stringer, Helen
Stead, Philip Christian 225
Stead, Rebecca 1968(?)- 188
Steadman, Ralph 1936- 123
  Earlier sketch in SATA 32
Steadman, Ralph Idris
  See Steadman, Ralph
Stearman, Kaye 1951- 118
Stearn, Ted 1961- 218
Stearns, Monroe (Mather) 1913-1987 5
  Obituary 55
Steckler, Arthur 1921-1985 65
Steding, Laurie 1953- 119
Steel, Danielle 1947- 66
Steel, Danielle Fernande
  See Steel, Danielle
Steele, Addison II
  See Lupoff, Richard A(llen)
Steele, Alexander 1958- 116
Steele, Henry Maxwell
  See Steele, Max
Steele, Mary 1930- 94
Steele, Mary Q(uintard Govan) 1922-1992 .. 51
  Obituary 72
  Earlier sketch in SATA 3
Steele, Max 1922-2005 168
  Earlier sketch in SATA 10
Steele, Philip 1948- 140
  Earlier sketch in SATA 81
Steele, William O(wen) 1917-1979 51
  Obituary 27
  Earlier sketch in SATA 1
Steelhammer, Ilona 1952- 98
Steelsmith, Shari 1962- 72
Stefanik, Alfred T. 1939- 55
Steffanson, Con
  See Cassiday, Bruce (Bingham)
  and Goulart, Ron
Steffens, Bradley 1955- 166
  Earlier sketch in SATA 77
Steffensmeier, Alexander 1977- 195
Stegeman, Janet Allais 1923- 49
  Brief entry 49
Steggall, Susan 1967- 182
Steig, William 1907-2003 111
  Obituary 149
  Earlier sketches in SATA 18, 70
  See also CLR 103
Steig, William H.
  See Steig, William
Stein, David Ezra 211
  Earlier sketch in SATA 180
Stein, Janet 1955- 218
Stein, M(eyer) L(ewis) 1920- 6
Stein, Mathilde 1969- 195
Stein, Mini 2
Stein, R(ichard) Conrad 1937- 154
  Earlier sketches in SATA 31, 82
Stein, Wendy 1951- 77
Steinbeck, John 1902-1968 9
Steinbeck, John Ernst
  See Steinbeck, John
Steinberg, Alfred 1917-1995 9

Steinberg, David 1962- 200
Steinberg, D.J.
  See Steinberg, David
Steinberg, Fannie 1899-1990 43
Steinberg, Fred J. 1933- 4
Steinberg, Phillip Orso 1921- 34
Steinberg, Rafael (Mark) 1927- 45
Steinberg, Saul 1914-1999 67
Steincrohn, Maggie
  See Davis, Maggie S.
Steiner, Barbara A(nnette) 1934- 83
  Earlier sketch in SATA 13
  See also SAAS 13
Steiner, Charlotte 1900-1981 45
Steiner, George 1929- 62
Steiner, Joan 199
  Earlier sketch in SATA 110
Steiner, Jorg
  See Steiner, Jorg
Steiner, Jorg 1930- 35
Steiner, K. Leslie
  See Delany, Samuel R., Jr.
Steiner, Stan(ley) 1925-1987 14
  Obituary 50
Steins, Richard 1942- 79
Stem, Jacqueline 1931- 110
Stemple, Heidi E.Y. 1966- 214
Stemple, Jason 179
Steneman, Shep 1945- 132
Stengel, Joyce A. 1938- 158
Stephanie, Gordon
  See Gordon, Stephanie Jacob
Stephens, Alice Barber 1858-1932 66
Stephens, Casey
  See Wagner, Sharon B.
Stephens, Henrietta Henkle 1909-1993 6
Stephens, J.B.
  See Lynn, Tracy
Stephens, Mary Jo 1935- 8
Stephens, Rebecca 1961- 141
Stephens, Reed
  See Donaldson, Stephen R.
Stephens, Suzanne
  See Kirby, Susan E.
Stephens, William M(cLain) 1925- 21
Stephensen, A. M.
  See Manes, Stephen
Stephenson, Kristina 224
Stephenson, Lynda 1941- 179
Stephenson, Lynda A.
  See Stephenson, Lynda
Stepp, Ann 1935- 29
Stepto, Michele 1946- 61
Steptoe, Javaka 1971- 213
  Earlier sketch in SATA 151
Steptoe, John (Lewis) 1950-1989 63
  Earlier sketch in SATA 8
  See also CLR 12
Sterling, Brett
  See Bradbury, Ray
  and Hamilton, Edmond
  and Samachson, Joseph
Sterling, Dorothy 1913-2008 83
  Autobiography Feature 127
  Obituary 200
  Earlier sketch in SATA 1
  See also CLR 1
  See also SAAS 2
Sterling, Helen
  See Watts, Helen L. Hoke
Sterling, Philip 1907-1989 8
  Obituary 63
Sterling, Shirley (Anne) 1948- 101
Stern, Ellen Norman 1927- 26
Stern, Judith M. 1951- 75
Stern, Madeleine
  See Stern, Madeleine B.
Stern, Madeleine B. 1912-2007 14
Stern, Madeleine Bettina
  See Stern, Madeleine B.
Stern, Maggie 1953- 156

Stern, Philip Van Doren 1900-1984 13
  Obituary 39
Stern, Simon 1943- 15
Sterne, Emma Gelders 1894- 6
Steurt, Marjorie Rankin 1888-1978 10
Stevens, April 1963- 208
Stevens, Bryna 1924- 65
Stevens, Carla M(cBride) 1928- 13
Stevens, Chambers 1968- 128
Stevens, Diane 1939- 94
Stevens, Franklin 1933- 6
Stevens, Greg
  See Cook, Glen
Stevens, Gwendolyn 1944- 33
Stevens, Helen 209
Stevens, Jan Romero 1953- 95
Stevens, Janet 1953- 193
  Earlier sketches in SATA 90, 148
Stevens, Kathleen 1936- 49
Stevens, Leonard A. 1920- 67
Stevens, Lucile Vernon 1899-1994 59
Stevens, Margaret Dean
  See Aldrich, Bess Streeter
Stevens, Patricia Bunning 1931- 27
Stevens, Peter
  See Geis, Darlene Stern
Stevens, Serita 1949- 70
Stevens, Serita Deborah
  See Stevens, Serita
Stevens, Serita Mendelson
  See Stevens, Serita
Stevens, Shira
  See Stevens, Serita
Stevenson, Anna (M.) 1905- 12
Stevenson, Augusta 1869(?)-1976 2
  Obituary 26
Stevenson, Burton Egbert 1872-1962 25
Stevenson, Drew 1947- 60
Stevenson, Emma 207
Stevenson, Harvey 1960- 148
  Earlier sketch in SATA 80
Stevenson, James 1929- 195
  Brief entry 34
  Earlier sketches in SATA 42, 71, 113, 161
  See also CLR 17
Stevenson, Janet 1913- 8
Stevenson, Robert Louis 1850-1894 100
  See also YABC 2
  See also CLR 107
Stevenson, Robert Louis Balfour
  See Stevenson, Robert Louis
Stevenson, Sucie
  See Stevenson, Sucie
Stevenson, Sucie 1956- 194
  Earlier sketch in SATA 104
Stewart, A(gnes) C(harlotte) 15
Stewart, Amber 181
Stewart, Chantal 1945- 173
  Earlier sketch in SATA 121
Stewart, Charles
  See Zurhorst, Charles (Stewart, Jr.)
Stewart, Eleanor
  See Porter, Eleanor H(odgman)
Stewart, Elisabeth J(ane) 1927- 93
Stewart, Elizabeth Laing 1907- 6
Stewart, Gail B. 1949- 141
Stewart, George Rippey 1895-1980 3
  Obituary 23
Stewart, Jennifer J. 1960- 128
Stewart, Jennifer Jenkins
  See Stewart, Jennifer J.
Stewart, Joel 211
  Earlier sketch in SATA 151
Stewart, John 1920- 14
Stewart, Mary (Florence Elinor) 1916- 12
Stewart, Mary Rainbow
  See Stewart, Mary (Florence Elinor)
Stewart, Melissa 1968- 209
  Earlier sketches in SATA 111, 167
Stewart, Paul 1955- 199
  Earlier sketches in SATA 114, 163

Stewart, Robert Neil 1891-1972 7
Stewart, Sarah 143
Stewart, Scott
  See Zaffo, George J.
Stewart, Trenton Lee 1970- 216
Stewart, W(alter) P. 1924- 53
Stewart, Whitney 1959- 167
  Earlier sketch in SATA 92
Stewig, John Warren 1937- 162
  Earlier sketches in SATA 26, 110
Stickler, Soma Han 1942- 128
Stidworthy, John 1943- 63
Stiegemeyer, Julie 180
Stier, Catherine 198
Stiles, Martha Bennett 108
  Earlier sketch in SATA 6
Still, James 1906-2001 29
  Obituary 127
Stille, Darlene R. 1942- 170
  Earlier sketch in SATA 126
Stille, Darlene Ruth
  See Stille, Darlene R.
Stillerman, Marci 104
Stillerman, Robbie 1947- 12
Stilley, Frank 1918- 29
Stilton, Geronimo 158
Stimpson, Gerald
  See Mitchell, Adrian
Stimson, James 1964- 213
Stine, Catherine 165
Stine, G(eorge) Harry 1928-1997 136
  Earlier sketch in SATA 10
Stine, Jovial Bob
  See Stine, R.L.
Stine, R.L. 1943- 194
  Earlier sketches in SATA 31, 76, 129
  See also CLR 111
Stine, Robert Lawrence
  See Stine, R.L.
Stinetorf, Louise (Allender) 1900-1992 10
Stinson, Kathy 1952- 98
Stirling, Arthur
  See Sinclair, Upton
Stirling, Ian 1941- 77
Stirling, Nora B(romley) 1900-1997 3
Stirnweis, Shannon 1931- 10
Stobbs, William 1914-2000 17
  Obituary 120
Stock, Carolmarie 1951- 75
Stock, Catherine 1952- 214
  Earlier sketches in SATA 65, 114, 158
Stockdale, Susan 1954- 206
  Earlier sketch in SATA 98
Stockham, Peter (Alan) 1928- 57
Stockton, Francis Richard 1834-1902 44
  Brief entry 32
Stockton, Frank R.
  See Stockton, Francis Richard
Stockwell-Moniz, Marc J. 1954- 164
Stoddard, Edward G. 1923- 10
Stoddard, Hope 1900-1987 6
Stoddard, Sandol 1927- 98
  Earlier sketch in SATA 14
Stoehr, Shelley 1969- 107
Stoeke, Janet Morgan 1957- 202
  Earlier sketches in SATA 90, 136
Stohner, Anu 1952- 179
Stoiko, Michael 1919- 14
Stojic, Manya 1967- 156
Stoker, Abraham
  See Stoker, Bram
Stoker, Bram 1847-1912 29
Stokes, Cedric
  See Beardmore, George
Stokes, Jack (Tilden) 1923- 13
Stokes, Olivia Pearl 1916- 32
Stolarz, Laurie Faria 1972- 203
Stolz, Mary 1920-2006 133
  Obituary 180
  Earlier sketches in SATA 10, 71
  See also SAAS 3

Stolz, Mary Slattery
  See Stolz, Mary
Stone, Alan
  See Svenson, Andrew E(dward)
Stone, David K(arl) 1922- 9
Stone, David Lee 1978- 166
Stone, Eugenia 1879-1971 7
Stone, Gene
  See Stone, Eugenia
Stone, Helen V(irginia) 6
Stone, Idella Purnell
  See Purnell, Idella
Stone, Ikey
  See Purnell, Idella
Stone, Irving 1903-1989 3
  Obituary 64
Stone, Jeff 178
Stone, Jon 1931-1997 39
  Obituary 95
Stone, Josephine Rector
  See Dixon, Jeanne
Stone, Kyle M. 1972- 202
Stone, Lesley
  See Trevor, Elleston
Stone, Peter 1930-2003 65
  Obituary 143
Stone, Phoebe 205
  Earlier sketch in SATA 134
Stone, Raymond 1
Stone, Rosetta
  See Dr. Seuss
Stone, Tanya Lee 1965- 217
  Earlier sketch in SATA 182
Stonehouse, Bernard 1926- 140
  Earlier sketches in SATA 13, 80
Stones, (Cyril) Anthony 1934- 72
Stong, Phil(ip Duffield) 1899-1957 32
Stoops, Erik D(aniel) 1966- 142
  Earlier sketch in SATA 78
Stoppelmoore, Cheryl Jean
  See Ladd, Cheryl (Jean)
Stops, Sue 1936- 86
Storace, Patricia 193
Storad, Conrad J. 1957- 119
Storey, Margaret 1926- 9
Storey, Victoria Carolyn 1945- 16
Stork, Francisco
  See Stork, Francisco X.
Stork, Francisco X. 1953- 210
Storme, Peter
  See Stern, Philip Van Doren
Storms, Patricia 1963- 217
Storr, Catherine (Cole) 1913-2001 87
  Obituary 122
  Earlier sketch in SATA 9
Story, Josephine
  See Loring, Emilie (Baker)
Stotko, Mary-Ann 1960- 154
Stott, Ann 219
Stott, Dorothy (M.) 1958- 99
  Earlier sketch in SATA 67
Stott, Dot
  See Stott, Dorothy (M.)
Stotter, Mike 1957- 108
Stout, William 1949- 132
Stoutenburg, Adrien (Pearl) 1916-1982 3
Stoutland, Allison 1963- 130
Stover, Allan C(arl) 1938- 14
Stover, Jill (Griffin) 1958- 82
Stover, Marjorie Filley 1914- 9
Stowe, Harriet Beecher 1811-1896
  See YABC 1
  See also CLR 131
Stowe, Harriet Elizabeth Beecher
  See Stowe, Harriet Beecher
Stowe, Leland 1899-1994 60
  Obituary 78
Stowe, Rosetta
  See Ogan, George F.
  and Ogan, Margaret E. (Nettles)
Stower, Adam 195

Strachan, Bruce 1959- 205
Strachan, Ian 1938- 85
Strachan, Linda 167
Strachan, Margaret Pitcairn 1908-1998 14
Strahinich, H. C.
  See Strahinich, Helen C.
Strahinich, Helen C. 1949- 78
Strait, Treva Adams 1909-2002 35
Strand, Mark 1934- 41
Strange, Philippa
  See Coury, Louise Andree
Stranger, Joyce
  See Wilson, Joyce M.
Strangis, Joel 1948- 124
Strannigan, Shawn 1956- 93
Strannigan, Shawn Alyne
  See Strannigan, Shawn
Strasnick, Lauren 222
Strasser, Todd 1950- 215
  Earlier sketches in SATA 41, 45, 71, 107, 153
  See also CLR 11
Stratemeyer, Edward L. 1862-1930 100
  Earlier sketches in SATA 1, 67
  See Adams, Harrison
Stratford, Philip 1927- 47
Stratton, Allan 1951- 178
Stratton, J. M.
  See Whitlock, Ralph
Stratton, Thomas
  See Coulson, Robert S(tratton)
  and DeWeese, Thomas Eugene
Stratton-Porter, Gene 1863-1924 15
  See also CLR 87
Strauss, Gwen 1963- 77
Strauss, Joyce 1936- 53
Strauss, Linda Leopold 1942- 127
Strauss, Susan (Elizabeth) 1954- 75
Strayer, E. Ward
  See Stratemeyer, Edward L.
Streano, Vince(nt Catello) 1945- 20
Streatfeild, Mary Noel
  See Streatfeild, Noel
Streatfeild, Noel 1897(?)-1986 20
  Obituary 48
  See also CLR 83
Street, Janet Travell 1959- 84
Street, Julia Montgomery 1898-1993 11
Streissguth, Thomas 1958- 116
Strelkoff, Tatiana 1957- 89
Stren, Patti 1949- 88
  Brief entry 41
  See also CLR 5
Strete, Craig Kee 1950- 96
  Earlier sketch in SATA 44
Stretton, Barbara (Humphrey) 1936- 43
  Brief entry 35
Strickland, Brad 1947- 200
  Earlier sketches in SATA 83, 137, 142
Strickland, Craig (A.) 1956- 102
Strickland, Dorothy S(alley) 1933- 89
Strickland, Michael R. 1965- 144
  Earlier sketch in SATA 83
Strickland, Shadra 209
Strickland, Tessa 173
Strickland, William Bradley
  See Strickland, Brad
Striegel, Jana 1955- 140
Striegel-Wilson, Jana
  See Striegel, Jana
Striker, Lee
  See Clark, Margaret (D.)
Striker, Susan 1942- 63
Stringer, Helen 225
Stringer, Lauren 1957- 183
  Earlier sketch in SATA 129
Stroeyer, Poul 1923- 13
Stromoski, Rick 1958- 111
Strong, Charles
  See Epstein, Beryl
  and Epstein, Samuel

Strong, David
    See McGuire, Leslie (Sarah)
Strong, Jeremy 1949- 175
    Earlier sketches in SATA *36, 105*
Strong, J.J.
    See Strong, Jeremy
Strong, Pat
    See Hough, Richard (Alexander)
Strong, Stacie 1965- 74
Stroud, Bettye 1939- 165
    Earlier sketch in SATA *96*
Stroud, Jonathan 1970- 213
    Earlier sketches in SATA *102, 159*
    See also CLR *134*
Stroyer, Poul
    See Stroeyer, Poul
Strug, Kerri 1977- 108
Stryer, Andrea Stenn 1938- 192
Stryker, Daniel
    See Morris, Chris(topher Crosby)
    and Stump, Jane Barr
Stuart, David
    See Hoyt, Edwin P(almer), Jr.
Stuart, Derek
    See Foster, John L(ouis)
Stuart, Forbes 1924- 13
Stuart, Ian
    See MacLean, Alistair
Stuart, Jesse (Hilton) 1906-1984 2
    Obituary 36
Stuart, Ruth McEnery 1849(?)-1917 116
Stuart, Sheila
    See Baker, Mary Gladys Steel
Stuart-Clark, Christopher (Anthony) 1940- .. 32
Stubis, Talivaldis 1926- 5
Stubley, Trevor (Hugh) 1932- 22
Stuchner, Joan Betty 209
Stucky, Naomi R. 1922- 72
Stucley, Elizabeth
    See Northmore, Elizabeth Florence
Stultifer, Morton
    See Curtis, Richard
Sture-Vasa, Mary
    See Alsop, Mary O'Hara
Sturges, Philemon 174
Sturtevant, Katherine 1950- 180
    Earlier sketch in SATA *130*
Sturton, Hugh
    See Johnston, H(ugh) A(nthony) S(tephen)
Sturtzel, Howard A(llison) 1894-1985 1
Sturtzel, Jane Levington 1903-1996 1
Stutley, D(oris) J(ean) 1959- 142
Stutson, Caroline 1940- 104
Stuve-Bodeen, Stephanie
    See Bodeen, S. A.
Stux, Erica 1929- 140
Styles, (Frank) Showell 1908- 10
Stynes, Barbara White 133
Suarez, Maribel 1952- 201
Suba, Susanne 4
Suber, Melissa 213
Subond, Valerie
    See Grayland, Valerie (Merle Spanner)
Sudbery, Rodie 1943- 42
Sudyka, Diana 208
Sue, Majella Lue 209
Suen, Anastasia 1956(?)- 157
Sufrin, Mark 1925- 76
Sugarman, Joan G. 1917- 64
Sugarman, Tracy 1921- 37
Sugita, Yutaka 1930- 36
Suhl, Yuri (Menachem) 1908-1986 8
    Obituary 50
    See also CLR *2*
    See also SAAS *1*
Suhr, Joanne 129
Suid, Murray 1942- 27
Sullivan, Edward T. 206
Sullivan, George (Edward) 1927- 147
    Earlier sketches in SATA *4, 89*
Sullivan, Jacqueline Levering 203

Sullivan, Jody
    See Rake, Jody
Sullivan, Kathryn A. 1954- 141
Sullivan, Mary Ann 1954- 63
Sullivan, Mary W(ilson) 1907- 13
Sullivan, Pat
    See Messmer, Otto
Sullivan, Paul 1939- 106
Sullivan, Sarah G. 1953- 179
Sullivan, Silky 1940- 101
Sullivan, Sue
    See Sullivan, Susan E.
Sullivan, Susan E. 1962- 123
Sullivan, Thomas Joseph, Jr. 1947- 16
Sullivan, Tom
    See Sullivan, Thomas Joseph, Jr.
Sully, Tom 1959- 104
Suma, Nova Ren 223
Sumichrast, Jozef 1948- 29
Sumiko
    See Davies, Sumiko
Summerforest, Ivy B.
    See Kirkup, James
Summers, Barbara 1944- 182
Summers, Cassia Joy
    See Cowley, Joy
Summers, James L(evingston) 1910-1973 57
    Brief entry 28
Summertree, Katonah
    See Windsor, Patricia
Summy, Barrie 208
Sun, Chyng Feng 1959- 90
Sunderlin, Sylvia (S.) 1911-1997 28
    Obituary 99
Sung, Betty Lee 26
Supeene, Shelagh Lynne 1952- 153
Supplee, Suzanne 204
Supraner, Robyn 1930- 101
    Earlier sketch in SATA *20*
Supree, Burt(on) 1941-1992 73
Surface, Mary Hall 1958- 126
Surge, Frank 1931- 13
Susac, Andrew 1929- 5
Susi, Geraldine Lee 1942- 98
Sussman, Cornelia Silver 1914-1999 59
Sussman, Irving 1908-1996 59
Sussman, Michael 1953- 217
Sussman, Michael B.
    See Sussman, Michael
Sussman, Susan 1942- 48
Sutcliff, Rosemary 1920-1992 78
    Obituary 73
    Earlier sketches in SATA *6, 44*
    See also CLR *138*
Sutcliffe, Jane 1957- 138
Sutherland, Colleen 1944- 79
Sutherland, Efua (Theodora Morgue)
    1924-1996 25
Sutherland, Jon 1958- 167
Sutherland, Jonathan D.
    See Sutherland, Jon
Sutherland, Jonathan David
    See Sutherland, Jon
Sutherland, Margaret 1941- 15
Sutherland, Zena Bailey 1915-2002 37
    Obituary 137
Suttles, Shirley (Smith) 1922- 21
Sutton, Ann (Livesay) 1923- 31
Sutton, Eve(lyn Mary) 1906-1992 26
Sutton, Felix 1910(?)-1973 31
Sutton, Jane 1950- 52
    Brief entry 43
Sutton, Larry M(atthew) 1931- 29
Sutton, Margaret Beebe 1903-2001 1
    Obituary 131
Sutton, Myron Daniel 1925- 31
Sutton, Roger 1956- 93
Sutton, Sally 1973- 214

Suzanne, Jamie
    See Hawes, Louise
    and Lantz, Francess L(in)
    and Singleton, Linda Joy
    and Zach, Cheryl (Byrd)
Suzuki, David 1936- 138
Suzuki, David Takayoshi
    See Suzuki, David
Svendsen, Mark 1962- 181
    Earlier sketch in SATA *120*
Svendsen, Mark Nestor
    See Svendsen, Mark
Svenson, Andrew E(dward) 1910-1975 2
    Obituary 26
Swaab, Neil 1978- 191
Swaim, Jessica 1950- 202
Swain, Carol 1962- 172
Swain, Gwenyth 1961- 134
    Earlier sketch in SATA *84*
Swain, Ruth
    See Swain, Ruth Freeman
Swain, Ruth Freeman 1951- 161
    Earlier sketch in SATA *119*
Swain, Su Zan (Noguchi) 1916- 21
Swain, Wilson 1976- 225
Swallow, Pamela Curtis 178
Swamp, Jake 1941- 98
Swan, Susan 1944- 108
    Earlier sketch in SATA *22*
Swann, Brian (Stanley Frank) 1940- 116
Swann, E.L.
    See Lasky, Kathryn
Swann, Ruth Rice 1920- 84
Swanson, Diane 1944- 203
Swanson, Helen M(cKendry) 1919- 94
Swanson, June 1931- 76
Swanson, Susan Marie 209
Swanson, Wayne 1942- 167
Swarner, Kristina 1965- 215
Swarthout, Glendon (Fred) 1918-1992 26
Swarthout, Kathryn 1919- 7
Swayne, Sam(uel F.) 1907- 53
Swayne, Zoa (Lourana) 1905- 53
Swearingen, Greg 1976- 225
Sweat, Lynn 1934- 168
    Earlier sketch in SATA *57*
Swede, George 1940- 67
Sweeney, James B(artholomew) 1910-1999 . 21
Sweeney, Joyce 1955- 167
    Earlier sketches in SATA *65, 68, 108*
Sweeney, Joyce Kay
    See Sweeney, Joyce
Sweeney, Karen O'Connor
    See O'Connor, Karen
Sweeney, Matthew (Gerard) 1952- 156
Sweet, Melissa 1956- 211
    Earlier sketch in SATA *172*
Sweet, Sarah C.
    See Jewett, Sarah Orne
Sweetland, Nancy A(nn) 1934- 48
Swenson, Allan A(rmstrong) 1933- 21
Swenson, May 1919-1989 15
Swentzell, Rina 1939- 79
Swiatkowska, Gabi 1971(?)- 180
Swift, Bryan
    See Knott, William C(ecil, Jr.)
Swift, David
    See Kaufmann, John
Swift, Hildegarde Hoyt 1890(?)-1977
    Obituary 20
Swift, Jonathan 1667-1745 19
    See also CLR *161*
Swift, Merlin
    See Leeming, Joseph
Swiger, Elinor Porter 1927- 8
Swinburne, Laurence (Joseph) 1924- 9
Swinburne, Stephen R. 1952- 188
    Earlier sketch in SATA *150*
Swinburne, Steve
    See Swinburne, Stephen R.

Swindells, Robert (Edward) 1939- *150*
  Brief entry *34*
  Earlier sketches in SATA *50, 80*
  See also SAAS *14*
Swinford, Betty (June Wells) 1927- *58*
Swinford, Bob
  See Swinford, Betty (June Wells)
Swithen, John
  See King, Stephen
Switzer, Ellen 1923- *48*
Swope, Sam *156*
Swope, Samuel
  See Swope, Sam
Sybesma, Jetske
  See Ironside, Jetske
Sydney, Frank
  See Warwick, Alan R(oss)
Sydor, Colleen 1960- *207*
Sykes, Julie 1963- *202*
Sylvada, Peter 1964- *202*
Sylvester, Natalie G(abry) 1922- *22*
Syme, (Neville) Ronald 1913-1992 .... *87*
  Earlier sketch in SATA *2*
Symes, R. F. *77*
Symes, Ruth Louise 1962- *179*
Symons, (Dorothy) Geraldine 1909- *33*
Symons, Stuart
  See Stanley, George Edward
Symnykywicz, Jeffrey B. 1954- *87*
Symnykywicz, Jeffrey Bruce
  See Symnykywicz, Jeffrey B.
Synge, (Phyllis) Ursula 1930- *9*
Sypher, Lucy Johnston 1907- *7*
Szasz, Suzanne (Shorr) 1915-1997 .... *13*
  Obituary *99*
Szekeres, Cyndy 1933- *157*
  Autobiography Feature *157*
  Earlier sketches in SATA *5, 60, 131*
  See also SAAS *13*
Szekessy, Tanja *98*
Szpura, Beata 1961- *93*
Szuc, Jeff 1975- *220*
Szudek, Agnes S(usan) P(hilomena) *57*
  Brief entry *49*
Szulc, Tad 1926-2001 .... *26*
Szydlow, Jarl
  See Szydlowski, Mary Vigliante
Szydlowski, Mary Vigliante 1946- *94*
Szymanski, Lois 1957- *91*

T

Taback, Simms 1932- *170*
  Brief entry *36*
  Earlier sketches in SATA *40, 104*
  See also CLR *100*
Taber, Gladys (Bagg) 1899-1980
  Obituary *22*
Tabor, Nancy Maria Grande 1949- *161*
  Earlier sketch in SATA *89*
Tabrah, Ruth Milander 1921- *14*
Tacang, Brian *213*
Tackach, James 1953- *123*
Tackach, James M.
  See Tackach, James
Tadgell, Nicole 1969- *220*
  Earlier sketch in SATA *177*
Tafolla, Carmen 1951- *220*
Tafolla, Mary Carmen
  See Tafolla, Carmen
Tafuri, Nancy 1946- *192*
  Autobiography Feature *192*
  Earlier sketches in SATA *39, 75, 130*
  See also CLR *74*
  See also SAAS *14*
Tagg, Christine Elizabeth 1962- *138*
Tagliaferro, Linda *173*
Taha, Karen T(erry) 1942- *156*
  Earlier sketch in SATA *71*

Tai, Sharon O. 1963- *153*
Tait, Douglas 1944- *12*
Takabayashi, Mari 1960- *156*
  Earlier sketch in SATA *115*
Takahashi, Hideko *209*
Takahashi, Rumiko 1957- *163*
Takakjian, Portia 1930- *15*
Takashima, Misako
  See Misako Rocks!
Takashima, Shizuye 1928- *13*
Takayama, Sandi 1962- *106*
Takeda, Pete(r M.) 1964- *148*
Tal, Eve 1947- *176*
Talbert, Marc (Alan) 1953- *154*
  Autobiography Feature *154*
  Earlier sketches in SATA *68, 99*
Talbot, Charlene Joy 1928- *10*
Talbot, Toby 1928- *14*
Talbott, Hudson 1949- *212*
  Earlier sketches in SATA *84, 131*
Talifero, Gerald 1950- *75*
Talker, T.
  See Rands, William Brighty
Tallarico, Tony 1933- *116*
Tallcott, Emogene *10*
Tallec, Olivier 1970- *197*
Tallis, Robyn
  See Smith, Sherwood
Tallon, Robert 1939- *43*
  Brief entry *28*
Talmadge, Marian *14*
Tamaki, Jillian 1980- *201*
Tamar, Erika 1934- *150*
  Earlier sketches in SATA *62, 101*
Tamarin, Alfred H. 1913-1980 .... *13*
Tamburine, Jean 1930- *12*
Tames, Richard (Lawrence) 1946- *102*
  Earlier sketch in SATA *67*
Tamminga, Frederick W(illiam) 1934- *66*
Tammuz, Benjamin 1919-1989
  Obituary *63*
Tan, Amy 1952- *75*
Tan, Amy Ruth
  See Tan, Amy
Tan, Shaun 1974- *198*
Tanaka, Beatrice 1932- *76*
Tanaka, Shelley *214*
  Earlier sketch in SATA *136*
Tanaka, Yoko 1947- *215*
Tang, Charles 1948- *81*
Tang, Greg *172*
Tang, You-Shan 1946- *53*
Tania B.
  See Blixen, Karen
Tankard, Jeremy 1973- *191*
Tannen, Mary 1943- *37*
Tannenbaum, Beulah Goldstein 1916- *3*
Tannenbaum, D(onald) Leb 1948- *42*
Tanner, Jane 1946- *74*
Tanner, Louise S(tickney) 1922-2000 .... *9*
Tanobe, Miyuki 1937- *23*
Tanselle, Eve 1933- *125*
Tapio, Pat Decker
  See Kines, Pat Decker
Tapp, Kathy Kennedy 1949- *88*
  Brief entry *50*
Tarbescu, Edith 1939- *107*
Tarkington, (Newton) Booth 1869-1946 .... *17*
Tarpley, Natasha A(nastasia) 1971- *147*
Tarr, Judith 1955- *149*
  Earlier sketch in SATA *64*
Tarry, Ellen 1906-2008 .... *16*
  See also CLR *26*
  See also SAAS *16*
Tarshis, Jerome 1936- *9*
Tarshis, Lauren *187*
Tarsky, Sue 1946- *41*
Taschek, Karen 1956- *185*
Tashjian, Janet 1956- *151*
  Earlier sketch in SATA *102*
Tashjian, Virginia A. 1921-2008 .... *3*

Tasker, James 1908- *9*
Tate, Don(ald E.) *159*
Tate, Eleanora E. 1948- *191*
  Earlier sketches in SATA *38, 94*
  See also CLR *37*
Tate, Eleanora Elaine
  See Tate, Eleanora E.
Tate, Ellalice
  See Hibbert, Eleanor Alice Burford
Tate, Joan 1922- *86*
  Earlier sketch in SATA *9*
  See also SAAS *20*
Tate, Mary Anne
  See Hale, Arlene
Tate, Nikki *134*
Tate, Richard
  See Masters, Anthony (Richard)
Tate, Suzanne 1930- *91*
Tatham, Betty *142*
Tatham, Campbell
  See Elting, Mary
Tatham, Julie
  See Tatham, Julie Campbell
Tatham, Julie Campbell 1908-1999 .... *80*
Tavares, Matt *198*
  Earlier sketch in SATA *159*
Tavares, Victor 1971- *176*
Taves, Isabella 1915- *27*
Tayleur, Karen 1961- *213*
Taylor, Alastair 1959- *130*
Taylor, Andrew 1951- *70*
Taylor, Andrew John Robert
  See Taylor, Andrew
Taylor, Ann 1782-1866 .... *41*
  Brief entry *35*
Taylor, Audilee Boyd 1931- *59*
Taylor, Barbara J. 1927- *10*
Taylor, Ben
  See Strachan, Ian
Taylor, Brooke *205*
Taylor, Carl 1937-2010 .... *14*
Taylor, Carrie-Jo
  See Taylor, C.J.
Taylor, Cheryl Munro 1957- *96*
Taylor, C.J. 1952- *224*
Taylor, Cora (Lorraine) 1936- *103*
  Earlier sketch in SATA *64*
  See also CLR *63*
Taylor, Dave 1948- *78*
Taylor, David
  See Taylor, Dave
Taylor, David 1900-1965 .... *10*
Taylor, Debbie A. 1955- *169*
Taylor, Eleanor 1969- *206*
Taylor, Elizabeth 1912-1975 .... *13*
Taylor, Florance Walton *9*
Taylor, Florence M(arian Tompkins)
  1892-1983 .... *9*
Taylor, Gage 1942-2000 .... *87*
Taylor, Geoff 1946- *204*
Taylor, G.P. 1958(?)- *216*
  Earlier sketch in SATA *156*
Taylor, Graham Peter
  See Taylor, G.P.
Taylor, Greg 1951- *221*
Taylor, Herb(ert Norman, Jr.) 1942-1987 ..... *22*
  Obituary *54*
Taylor, J. David
  See Taylor, Dave
Taylor, Jane 1783-1824 .... *41*
  Brief entry *35*
Taylor, Jerry D(uncan) 1938- *47*
Taylor, John Robert
  See Taylor, Andrew
Taylor, Judy
  See Hough, Judy Taylor
Taylor, Kenneth N. 1917-2005 .... *26*
Taylor, Kenneth Nathaniel
  See Taylor, Kenneth N.
Taylor, Kim *180*
Taylor, L(ester) B(arbour), Jr. 1932- *27*

Taylor, Lois Dwight Cole
See Cole, Lois Dwight
Taylor, Louise Todd 1939- *47*
Taylor, Margaret 1950- *106*
Taylor, Mark 1927- *32*
Brief entry *28*
Taylor, Mildred D. 1943- *135*
See also CLR *144*
See also SAAS *5*
Taylor, Mildred Delois
See Taylor, Mildred D.
Taylor, Paula (Wright) 1942- *48*
Brief entry *33*
Taylor, Peter Lane *210*
Taylor, Robert Lewis 1912-1998 .... *10*
Taylor, Sean 1965- *192*
Taylor, Susan Champlin
See Champlin, Susan
Taylor, Sydney (Brenner) 1904(?)-1978 .... *28*
Obituary *26*
Earlier sketch in SATA *1*
Taylor, Theodore 1921-2006 .... *128*
Obituary *177*
Earlier sketches in SATA *5, 54, 83*
See also CLR *30*
See also SAAS *4*
Taylor, William 1938- *164*
Earlier sketches in SATA *78, 113*
See also CLR *63*
Taylor-Butler, Christine 1959- *218*
Tazewell, Charles 1900-1972 .... *74*
Tchana, Katrin
See Tchana, Katrin Hyman
Tchana, Katrin H.
See Tchana, Katrin Hyman
Tchana, Katrin Hyman 1963- *177*
Earlier sketch in SATA *125*
Tchekhov, Anton
See Chekhov, Anton
Tchen, Richard *120*
Tchudi, Stephen N. 1942- *55*
Teague, Bob
See Teague, Robert
Teague, Mark 1963- *205*
Earlier sketches in SATA *68, 99, 170*
Teague, Mark Christopher
See Teague, Mark
Teague, Robert 1929- *32*
Brief entry *31*
Teal, Val 1902-1997 .... *10*
Obituary *114*
Teal, Valentine M.
See Teal, Val
Teale, Edwin Way 1899-1980 .... *7*
Obituary *25*
Teasdale, Sara 1884-1933 .... *32*
Tebbel, John (William) 1912-2004 .... *26*
Teckentrup, Britta 1969- *200*
Tedesco, P.R.
See Naylor, Phyllis Reynolds
Teensma, Lynne Bertrand
See Bertrand, Lynne
Tee-Van, Helen Damrosch 1893-1976 .... *10*
Obituary *27*
Teevee, Ningeokuluk 1963- *223*
Tegner, Bruce 1928- *62*
Teitelbaum, Michael 1953- *116*
Earlier sketch in SATA *59*
Tejima
See Tejima, Keizaburo
Tejima, Keizaburo 1931- *139*
See also CLR *20*
Telander, Todd (G.) 1967- *88*
Teleki, Geza 1943- *45*
Telemaque, Eleanor Wong 1934- *43*
Telescope, Tom
See Newbery, John
Tellis, Annabel 1967- *191*
Temkin, Sara Anne Schlossberg 1913-1996 . *26*
Temko, Florence *13*

Tempest, Margaret Mary 1892-1982
Obituary *33*
Templar, Maurice
See Groom, Arthur William
Temple, Arthur
See Northcott, (William) Cecil
Temple, Charles 1947- *79*
Temple, Frances (Nolting) 1945-1995 .... *85*
Temple, Herbert 1919- *45*
Temple, Paul
See McConnell, James Douglas Rutherford
Temple, William F(rederick) 1914-1989 .... *107*
Tenggren, Gustaf 1896-1970 .... *18*
Obituary *26*
Tennant, Kylie
See Rodd, Kylie Tennant
Tennant, Veronica 1947- *36*
Tenneshaw, S.M.
See Beaumont, Charles
and Garrett, Randall
and Silverberg, Robert
Tenniel, John 1820-1914 .... *74*
Brief entry *27*
See also CLR *146*
Tepper, Sheri S. 1929- *113*
Terada, Alice M. 1928- *90*
Terban, Marvin 1940- *54*
Brief entry *45*
Teresi, Judith M.
See Goldberger, Judith M.
ter Haar, Jaap 1922- *6*
See also CLR *15*
Terhune, Albert Payson 1872-1942 .... *15*
Terkel, Susan N(eiburg) 1948- *103*
Earlier sketch in SATA *59*
Terlouw, Jan (Cornelis) 1931- *30*
Terrazzini, Daniela Jaglenka *218*
Terrell, John Upton 1900-1988
Obituary *60*
Terrill, Beth *198*
Terrill, Elizabeth
See Terrill, Beth
Terris, Susan 1937- *77*
Earlier sketch in SATA *3*
Terry, Luther L(eonidas) 1911-1985 .... *11*
Obituary *42*
Terry, Margaret
See Dunnahoo, Terry Janson
Terry, Walter 1913-1982 .... *14*
Terry, Will 1966- *205*
Terzian, James P. 1915- *14*
Tessendorf, K(enneth) C(harles) 1925-2003 . *75*
Obituary *142*
Tessler, Manya *200*
Tessler, Stephanie Gordon
See Gordon, Stephanie Jacob
Testa, Dom *208*
Tester, Sylvia Root 1939- *64*
Brief entry *37*
Tether, (Cynthia) Graham 1950- *46*
Brief entry *36*
Tetzner, Lisa 1894-1963 .... *169*
Thach, James Otis 1969- *195*
Thacher, Mary McGrath 1933- *9*
Thackeray, William Makepeace 1811-1863 .. *23*
Thaler, Michael C.
See Thaler, Mike
Thaler, Mike 1936- *215*
Brief entry *47*
Earlier sketches in SATA *56, 93*
Thaler, Shmuel 1958- *126*
Earlier sketch in SATA *72*
Thamer, Katie 1955- *42*
Thane, Elswyth 1900-1984(?) *32*
Tharp, Louise (Marshall) Hall 1898-1992 ...... *3*
Obituary *129*
Tharp, Tim 1957- *189*
Thayer, Ernest Lawrence 1863-1940 .... *60*
Thayer, Jane
See Woolley, Catherine

Thayer, Marjorie 1908-1992 .... *74*
Brief entry *37*
Thayer, Peter
See Wyler, Rose
Thelwell, Norman 1923-2004 .... *14*
Themerson, Stefan 1910-1988 .... *65*
Thermes, Jennifer 1966- *155*
Theroux, Paul 1941- *109*
Earlier sketch in SATA *44*
Theroux, Paul Edward
See Theroux, Paul
Thesman, Jean *124*
Earlier sketch in SATA *74*
The Tjong-Khing
See Khing, T.T.
Thieda, Shirley Ann 1943- *13*
Thiele, Colin 1920-2006 .... *125*
Earlier sketches in SATA *14, 72*
See also CLR *27*
See also SAAS *2*
Thiele, Colin Milton
See Thiele, Colin
Thiesing, Lisa 1958- *159*
Earlier sketch in SATA *95*
Thimmesh, Catherine *189*
Thiry, Joan (Marie) 1926- *45*
Thisdale, Francois 1964- *222*
Thistlethwaite, Miles 1945- *12*
Thollander, Earl 1922- *22*
Thomas, Abigail 1941- *112*
Thomas, Andrea
See Hill, Margaret (Ohler)
Thomas, Art(hur Lawrence) 1952- *48*
Brief entry *38*
Thomas, Carroll
See Ratliff, Thomas M.
and Shmurak, Carole B.
Thomas, Dylan 1914-1953 .... *60*
Thomas, Dylan Marlais
See Thomas, Dylan
Thomas, Egbert S.
See Ellis, Edward S.
Thomas, Estelle Webb 1899-1982 .... *26*
Thomas, Frances 1943- *171*
Earlier sketch in SATA *92*
Thomas, Garen *213*
Thomas, H. C.
See Keating, Lawrence A.
Thomas, Ianthe 1951- *139*
Brief entry *42*
See also CLR *8*
Thomas, J. F.
See Fleming, Thomas
Thomas, Jan 1958- *197*
Thomas, Jane Resh 1936- *171*
Earlier sketches in SATA *38, 90*
Thomas, Jerry D. 1959- *91*
Thomas, Joan Gale
See Robinson, Joan (Mary) G(ale Thomas)
Thomas, Joyce Carol 1938- *210*
Autobiography Feature *137*
Earlier sketches in SATA *40, 78, 123, 137*
See also CLR *19*
See also SAAS *7*
Thomas, Lee
See Floren, Lee
and Pendleton, Thomas
Thomas, Lowell Jackson, Jr. 1923- *15*
Thomas, Margaret
See Thomas, Peggy
Thomas, Meredith 1963- *119*
Thomas, Michael
See Wilks, Michael Thomas
Thomas, Middy 1931- *191*
Thomas, Patricia 1934- *199*
Earlier sketch in SATA *51*
Thomas, Peggy *174*
Thomas, Rob 1965- *97*
Thomas, Scott 1959- *147*
Thomas, Velma Maia 1955- *171*
Thomas, Vernon (Arthur) 1934- *56*

Thomas, Victoria
  See DeWeese, Thomas Eugene
  and Kugi, Constance Todd
Thomasma, Kenneth R. 1930- *90*
Thomason, Mark *215*
Thomassie, Tynia 1959- *92*
Thompson, Alicia 1984- *224*
Thompson, Brenda 1935- *34*
Thompson, Carol 1951- *189*
  Earlier sketch in SATA *85*
Thompson, China
  See Lewis, Mary
Thompson, Colin 1942- *198*
  Earlier sketches in SATA *95, 163*
Thompson, David H(ugh) 1941- *17*
Thompson, Eileen
  See Panowski, Eileen Thompson
Thompson, George Selden 1929-1989 .... *73*
  Obituary *63*
  Earlier sketch in SATA *4*
  See also CLR *8*
Thompson, Harlan 1894-1987 .... *10*
  Obituary *53*
Thompson, Hilary 1943- *56*
  Brief entry *49*
Thompson, Joanna Maxwell Pullein
  See Pullein-Thompson, Joanna Maxwell
Thompson, Julian F(rancis) 1927- *155*
  Brief entry *40*
  Earlier sketches in SATA *55, 99*
  See also CLR *24*
  See also SAAS *13*
Thompson, K(athryn Carolyn) Dyble
  1952- *82*
Thompson, Kate 1956- *204*
Thompson, Kay 1912(?)-1998 .... *16*
  See also CLR *22*
Thompson, Lauren 1962- *200*
  Earlier sketches in SATA *132, 174*
Thompson, Lauren Stevens
  See Thompson, Lauren
Thompson, Megan Lloyd
  See Lloyd, Megan
Thompson, Richard 1951- *184*
Thompson, Ruth Plumly 1891-1976 .... *66*
Thompson, Sharon 1952- *119*
Thompson, Sharon Elaine
  See Thompson, Sharon
Thompson, Stith 1885-1976 .... *57*
  Obituary *20*
Thompson, Vivian L(aubach) 1911- *3*
Thomson, Bill 1963- *187*
Thomson, Celia
  See Lynn, Tracy
Thomson, David (Robert Alexander)
  1914-1988 .... *40*
  Obituary *55*
Thomson, Melissa 1979- *205*
Thomson, Pat 1939- *122*
  Earlier sketch in SATA *77*
Thomson, Peggy 1922- *31*
Thomson, Sarah L. *212*
  Earlier sketch in SATA *178*
Thon, Melanie Rae 1957- *132*
Thong, Roseanne *174*
Thor, Annika 1950- *222*
Thorburn, John
  See Goldsmith, John Herman Thorburn
Thorn, John 1947- *59*
Thorndyke, Helen Louise
  See Benson, Mildred
Thorne, Ian
  See May, Julian
Thorne, Jean Wright
  See May, Julian
Thornhill, Jan 1955- *148*
  Earlier sketch in SATA *77*
Thornton, Hall
  See Silverberg, Robert
Thornton, W. B.
  See Burgess, Thornton Waldo

Thornton, Yvonne S. 1947- *96*
Thornton, Yvonne Shirley
  See Thornton, Yvonne S.
Thorpe, E(ustace) G(eorge) 1916- *21*
Thorpe, J. K.
  See Nathanson, Laura Walther
Thorvall, Kerstin 1925- *13*
Thorvall-Falk, Kerstin
  See Thorvall, Kerstin
Thrasher, Crystal (Faye) 1921- *27*
Threadgall, Colin 1941- *77*
Three Little Pigs
  See Lantz, Francess L(in)
Thum, Gladys 1920- *26*
Thum, Marcella *28*
  Earlier sketch in SATA *3*
Thundercloud, Katherine
  See Witt, Shirley Hill
Thurber, James 1894-1961 .... *13*
Thurber, James Grover
  See Thurber, James
Thurlo, Aimee *161*
Thurlo, David *161*
Thurman, Judith 1946- *33*
Thurman, Mark (Gordon Ian) 1948- *63*
Thwaite, Ann (Barbara Harrop) 1932- *14*
Tibbetts, Peggy *127*
Tibbles, Jean-Paul 1958- *115*
Tibo, Gilles 1951- *107*
  Earlier sketch in SATA *67*
Tiburzi, Bonnie 1948- *65*
Ticheburn, Cheviot
  See Ainsworth, William Harrison
Tichenor, Tom 1923-1992 .... *14*
Tichnor, Richard 1959- *90*
Tichy, William 1924- *31*
Tickle, Jack
  See Chapman, Jane
Tidholm, Anna-Clara 1946- *223*
Tiegreen, Alan F. 1935- *94*
  Brief entry *36*
Tierney, Frank M. 1930- *54*
Tierney, Tom 1928- *113*
Tiffault, Benette W. 1955- *77*
Tildes, Phyllis Limbacher 1945- *210*
Tiller, Ruth L. 1949- *83*
Tilley, Debbie *190*
Tillman, Nancy *211*
Tillotson, Katherine *224*
Tilly, Nancy 1935- *62*
Tilton, Madonna Elaine 1929- *41*
Tilton, Rafael
  See Tilton, Madonna Elaine
Timberlake, Amy *156*
Timberlake, Carolyn
  See Dresang, Eliza (Carolyn Timberlake)
Timmers, Leo 1970- *190*
Timmins, William F(rederick) *10*
Tinbergen, Niko(laas) 1907-1988
  Obituary *60*
Tincknell, Cathy *194*
Tiner, John Hudson 1944- *32*
Tingle, Dolli (?)-
  See Brackett, Dolli Tingle
Tingle, Rebecca *174*
Tingle, Tim *208*
Tingum, Janice 1958- *91*
Tinkelman, Murray 1933- *12*
Tinkham, Kelly A. *188*
Tinkle, (Julien) Lon 1906-1980 .... *36*
Tinling, Marion (Rose) 1904- *140*
Tipene, Tim 1972- *141*
Tippett, James S(terling) 1885-1958 .... *66*
Tirone Smith, Mary-Ann 1944- *143*
Titlebaum, Ellen *195*
Titler, Dale M(ilton) 1926- *35*
  Brief entry *28*
Titmarsh, Michael Angelo
  See Thackeray, William Makepeace
Titus, Eve 1922- *2*
Tjia, Sherwin 1975- *204*

Tjong Khing, The 1933- *76*
Tobias, Katherine
  See Gottfried, Theodore Mark
Tobias, Tobi 1938- *82*
  Earlier sketch in SATA *5*
  See also CLR *4*
Tocci, C. Lee 1958- *220*
Tocci, Cynthia Lee
  See Tocci, C. Lee
Todd, Anne Ophelia
  See Dowden, Anne Ophelia Todd
Todd, Barbara 1961- *173*
Todd, Barbara K(eith) 1917- *10*
Todd, Chuck *195*
Todd, H(erbert) E(atton) 1908-1988 .... *84*
  Earlier sketch in SATA *11*
Todd, Loreto 1942- *30*
Todd, Pamela *212*
Todd, Peter
  See Hamilton, Charles (Harold St. John)
Toews, Miriam 1964- *165*
Tofel, Richard J. 1957- *140*
Toft, Kim Michelle 1960- *170*
Tokunbo, Dimitrea *187*
Tolan, Stephanie S. 1942- *142*
  Earlier sketches in SATA *38, 78*
Toland, John (Willard) 1912-2004 .... *38*
Tolbert, Steve 1944- *143*
Toledo, Francisco 1940- *198*
Toledo, Natalia 1967- *197*
Tolkien, J. R. R. 1892-1973 .... *100*
  Obituary *24*
  Earlier sketches in SATA *2, 32*
  See also CLR *152*
Tolkien, John Ronald Reuel
  See Tolkien, J. R. R.
Toll, Emily
  See Cannon, Eileen E(mily)
Toll, Nelly S. 1935- *78*
Tolland, W. R.
  See Heitzmann, William Ray
Tolles, Martha 1921- *76*
  Earlier sketch in SATA *8*
Tolliver, Ruby C(hangos) 1922- *110*
  Brief entry *41*
  Earlier sketch in SATA *55*
Tolmie, Kenneth Donald 1941- *15*
Tolstoi, Lev
  See Tolstoy, Leo
Tolstoy, Leo 1828-1910 .... *26*
Tolstoy, Count Leo
  See Tolstoy, Leo
Tolstoy, Leo Nikolaevich
  See Tolstoy, Leo
Tomalin, Ruth *29*
Tomaselli, Rosa
  See Pausacker, Jenny
Tomecek, Steve *172*
Tomes, Margot (Ladd) 1917-1991 .... *70*
  Brief entry *27*
  Obituary *69*
  Earlier sketch in SATA *36*
Tomey, Ingrid 1943- *77*
Tomfool
  See Farjeon, Eleanor
Tomic, Tomislav 1977- *202*
Tomkins, Jasper
  See Batey, Tom
Tomline, F. Latour
  See Gilbert, W(illiam) S(chwenck)
Tomlinson, Heather *192*
Tomlinson, Jill 1931-1976 .... *3*
  Obituary *24*
Tomlinson, Reginald R(obert) 1885-1979(?)
  Obituary *27*
Tomlinson, Theresa 1946- *165*
  Earlier sketch in SATA *103*
  See also CLR *60*
Tommaso, Rich 1970(?)- *200*
Tomorrow, Tom 1961- *223*

Tompert, Ann 1918- *139*
  Earlier sketches in SATA *14, 89*
Tompkins, Troy
  See Cle, Troy
Toner, Raymond John 1908-1986 .... *10*
Tong, Gary S. 1942- *66*
Tong, Paul *188*
Took, Belladonna
  See Chapman, Vera (Ivy May)
Tooke, Louise Mathews 1950- *38*
Tooke, Susan *173*
Toonder, Martin
  See Groom, Arthur William
Toothaker, Roy Eugene 1928- *18*
Tooze, Ruth (Anderson) 1892-1972 .... *4*
Topaz, Ksenia *212*
Topek, Susan Remick 1955- *78*
Topping, Audrey R(onning) 1928- *14*
Tor, Regina
  See Shekerjian, Regina Tor
Torbert, Floyd James 1922- *22*
Torgersen, Don Arthur 1934- *55*
  Brief entry *41*
Torley, Luke
  See Blish, James
Torrecilla, Pablo 1967- *206*
Torres, Andres Segovia
  See Segovia, Andres
Torres, Daniel 1958- *102*
Torres, John A. 1965- *163*
  Earlier sketch in SATA *94*
Torres, John Albert
  See Torres, John A.
Torres, Laura 1967- *146*
  Earlier sketch in SATA *87*
Torres, Leyla 1960- *155*
Torrey, Rich
  See Torrey, Richard
Torrey, Richard *189*
Torrie, Malcolm
  See Mitchell, Gladys (Maude Winifred)
Toten, Teresa 1955- *99*
Totham, Mary
  See Breinburg, Petronella
Touponce, William F. 1948- *114*
Tournier, Michel 1924- *23*
Tournier, Michel Edouard
  See Tournier, Michel
Towle, Wendy 1963- *79*
Towne, Mary
  See Spelman, Mary
Townley, Rod
  See Townley, Roderick
Townley, Roderick 1942- *177*
Townsend, Brad W. 1962- *91*
Townsend, John Rowe 1922- *132*
  Autobiography Feature *132*
  Earlier sketches in SATA *4, 68*
  See also CLR *2*
  See also SAAS *2*
Townsend, Michael 1981- *194*
Townsend, Sue 1946- *93*
  Brief entry *48*
  Earlier sketch in SATA *55*
Townsend, Susan Lilian
  See Townsend, Sue
Townsend, Thomas L. 1944- *59*
Townsend, Tom
  See Townsend, Thomas L.
Townsend, Wendy 1962- *201*
Townson, Hazel *134*
Toye, William Eldred 1926- *8*
Traherne, Michael
  See Watkins-Pitchford, Denys James
Trahey, Jane 1923-2000 .... *36*
  Obituary *120*
Trapani, Iza 1954- *214*
  Earlier sketches in SATA *80, 116*
Trapp, Maria Augusta von
  See von Trapp, Maria Augusta

Travers, P(amela) L(yndon) 1899-1996 ...... *100*
  Obituary *90*
  Earlier sketches in SATA *4, 54*
  See also CLR *93*
  See also SAAS *2*
Travis, Lucille *133*
  Earlier sketch in SATA *88*
Treadgold, Mary 1910-2005 .... *49*
Trease, (Robert) Geoffrey 1909-1998 .... *60*
  Obituary *101*
  Earlier sketch in SATA *2*
  See also CLR *42*
  See also SAAS *6*
Treat, Lawrence 1903-1998 .... *59*
Tredez, Alain 1926- *17*
Tredez, Denise 1930- *50*
Treece, Henry 1912-1966 .... *2*
  See also CLR *2*
Tregarthen, Enys
  See Sloggett, Nellie
Tregaskis, Richard 1916-1973 .... *3*
  Obituary *26*
Treherne, Katie Thamer 1955- *76*
Trell, Max 1900-1996 .... *14*
  Obituary *108*
Tremain, Ruthven 1922- *17*
Trembath, Don 1963- *168*
  Earlier sketch in SATA *96*
Tremens, Del
  See MacDonald, Amy
Trent, Robbie 1894-1988 .... *26*
Trent, Timothy
  See Malmberg, Carl
Treseder, Terry Walton 1956- *68*
Tresilian, (Cecil) Stuart 1891-(?) *40*
Tresselt, Alvin 1916-2000 .... *7*
  See also CLR *30*
Trevino, Elizabeth B(orton) de 1904- *29*
  Earlier sketch in SATA *1*
  See also SAAS *5*
Trevor, Elleston 1920-1995 .... *28*
Trevor, Frances
  See Teasdale, Sara
Trevor, Glen
  See Hilton, James
Trevor, (Lucy) Meriol 1919-2000 .... *113*
  Obituary *122*
  Earlier sketch in SATA *10*
Trewellard, J.M. *195*
Trewellard, Juliet
  See Trewellard, J.M.
Trez, Alain
  See Tredez, Alain
Trez, Denise
  See Tredez, Denise
Trezise, Percy 1923-
  See CLR *41*
Trezise, Percy James
  See Trezise, Percy
Triggs, Tony D. 1946- *70*
Trimble, Marshall I(ra) 1939- *93*
Trimby, Elisa 1948- *47*
  Brief entry *40*
Tring, A. Stephen
  See Meynell, Laurence Walter
Tripp, Eleanor B(aldwin) 1936- *4*
Tripp, Janet 1942- *108*
Tripp, Jenny *188*
Tripp, John
  See Moore, John Travers
Tripp, Nathaniel 1944- *101*
Tripp, Paul 1916-2002 .... *8*
  Obituary *139*
Tripp, Valerie 1951- *168*
  Earlier sketch in SATA *78*
Tripp, Wallace (Whitney) 1940- *31*
Trivelpiece, Laurel 1926- *56*
  Brief entry *46*
Trivett, Daphne Harwood 1940- *22*
Trivizas, Eugene 1946- *84*

Trnka, Jiri 1912-1969 .... *43*
  Brief entry *32*
Trollope, Anthony 1815-1882 .... *22*
Trost, Lucille W(ood) 1938- *149*
  Earlier sketch in SATA *12*
Trott, Betty 1933- *91*
Trotter, Deborah W. *184*
Trotter, Grace V(iolet) 1900-1991 .... *10*
Trottier, Maxine 1950- *175*
  Earlier sketch in SATA *131*
Troughton, Joanna (Margaret) 1947- *37*
Trout, Kilgore
  See Farmer, Philip Jose
Trout, Richard E. *123*
Trudeau, Garretson Beekman
  See Trudeau, G.B.
Trudeau, Garry
  See Trudeau, G.B.
Trudeau, Garry B.
  See Trudeau, G.B.
Trudeau, G.B. 1948- *168*
  Earlier sketch in SATA *35*
Trueit, Trudi
  See Trueit, Trudi Strain
Trueit, Trudi Strain 1963- *179*
Trueman, Matthew *183*
Trueman, Terry 1947- *178*
  Earlier sketch in SATA *132*
Truesdell, Judy
  See Mecca, Judy Truesdell
Truesdell, Sue
  See Truesdell, Susan G.
Truesdell, Susan G. *212*
  Brief entry *45*
  Earlier sketch in SATA *108*
Trumbauer, Lisa (Trutkoff) 1963- *149*
Truss, Jan 1925- *35*
Truss, Lynne 1955(?)- *194*
Tryon, Leslie *194*
  Earlier sketch in SATA *139*
Tubb, Jonathan N. 1951- *78*
Tubb, Kristin O'Donnell 1971- *209*
Tubby, I. M.
  See Kraus, (Herman) Robert
Tucker, Allan James
  See James, Bill
Tucker, Caroline
  See Nolan, Jeannette Covert
Tucker, James
  See James, Bill
Tudor, Edward
  See Browne, Anthony
Tudor, Tasha 1915-2008 .... *160*
  Obituary *205*
  Earlier sketches in SATA *20, 69*
  See also CLR *13*
Tuerk, Hanne 1951- *71*
Tugeau, Jeremy *199*
Tulloch, Richard 1949- *180*
  Earlier sketch in SATA *76*
Tulloch, Richard George
  See Tulloch, Richard
Tulloch, Shirley *169*
Tully, John (Kimberley) 1923- *14*
Tumanov, Vladimir A. 1961- *138*
Tung, Angela 1972- *109*
Tunis, Edwin (Burdett) 1897-1973 .... *28*
  Obituary *24*
  Earlier sketch in SATA *1*
  See also CLR *2*
Tunis, John R(oberts) 1889-1975 .... *37*
  Brief entry *30*
Tunnell, Michael
  See Tunnell, Michael O.
Tunnell, Michael O. 1950- *157*
  Earlier sketch in SATA *103*
Tunnell, Michael O'Grady
  See Tunnell, Michael O.
Tunnicliffe, C(harles) F(rederick)
  1901-1979 .... *62*
Turck, Mary C. 1950- *144*

Turk, Hanne
    See Tuerk, Hanne
Turk, Ruth 1917- 82
Turkle, Brinton 1915- 79
    Earlier sketch in SATA 2
Turlington, Bayly 1919-1977 5
    Obituary 52
Turnbull, Agnes Sligh 1888-1982 14
Turnbull, Ann 1943- 160
    Earlier sketch in SATA 18
Turnbull, Ann Christine
    See Turnbull, Ann
Turnbull, Susan 222
Turner, Alice K. 1940- 10
Turner, Ann 1945- 188
    Autobiography Feature 188
    Earlier sketches in SATA 14, 77, 113, 178
Turner, Ann Warren
    See Turner, Ann
Turner, Bonnie 1932- 75
Turner, Elizabeth 1774-1846
    See YABC 2
Turner, Glennette Tilley 1933- 183
    Earlier sketch in SATA 71
Turner, Josie
    See Crawford, Phyllis
Turner, Megan Whalen 1965- 174
    Earlier sketch in SATA 94
Turner, Pamela S. 1957- 211
Turner, Philip (William) 1925- 83
    Earlier sketch in SATA 11
    See also CLR 89
    See also SAAS 6
Turner, Robyn 1947- 77
Turner, Sheila R.
    See Seed, Sheila Turner
Turngren, Annette 1902(?)-1980
    Obituary 23
Turngren, Ellen (?)-1964 3
Turska, Krystyna (Zofia) 1933- 31
    Brief entry 27
Turteltaub, H. N.
    See Turtledove, Harry
Turtledove, Harry 1949- 166
    Earlier sketch in SATA 116
Turtledove, Harry Norman
    See Turtledove, Harry
Tusa, Tricia 1960- 207
    Earlier sketches in SATA 72, 111
Tusiani, Joseph 1924- 45
Twain, Mark 1835-1910 100
    See also YABC 2
    See also CLR 156
Tweit, Susan J 1956- 94
Tweit, Susan Joan
    See Tweit, Susan J
Tweton, D. Jerome 1933- 48
Twinem, Neecy 1958- 92
Twohill, Maggie
    See Angell, Judie
Tworkov, Jack 1900-1982 47
    Obituary 31
Tyche
    See Papademetriou, Lisa
Tyers, Jenny 1969- 89
Tyers, Kathy 1952- 82
Tyler, Anne 1941- 173
    Earlier sketches in SATA 7, 90
Tyler, Linda
    See Tyler, Linda W(agner)
Tyler, Linda W(agner) 1952- 65
Tyler, Vicki 1952- 64
Tyne, Joel
    See Schembri, Jim
Tyrrell, Frances 1959- 107

U

Ubell, Earl 1926-2007 4
    Obituary 182
Uchida, Yoshiko 1921-1992 53
    Obituary 72
    Earlier sketch in SATA 1
    See also CLR 56
    See also SAAS 1
Udall, Jan Beaney 1938- 10
Uden, (Bernard Gilbert) Grant 1910- 26
Uderzo, Albert 1927-
    See CLR 37
Udovic, David 1950- 189
Udovic, Jane Morris 1947- 224
Udry, Janice May 1928- 152
    Earlier sketch in SATA 4
Uegaki, Chieri 1969- 211
    Earlier sketch in SATA 153
Uehashi, Nahoko 1962- 215
Ueno, Noriko
    See Nakae, Noriko
Ugliano, Natascia 196
Uhlberg, Myron 174
Uhlig, Richard 1970- 195
Uhlig, Susan 1955- 129
Ulam, S(tanislaw) M(arcin) 1909-1984 51
Ullman, Barb Bentler 210
Ullman, James Ramsey 1907-1971 7
Ulm, Robert 1934-1977 17
Ulmer, Louise 1943- 53
Ulmer, Wendy K. 1950- 201
Ulrich, Maureen 1958- 206
Ulriksen, Mark 1957- 210
Ulyatt, Kenneth 1920- 14
Umansky, Kaye 1946- 224
    Earlier sketches in SATA 158, 188
Unada
    See Gliewe, Unada (Grace)
Uncle Carter
    See Boucher, (Clarence) Carter
Uncle Eric
    See Maybury, Richard J.
Uncle Gus
    See Rey, H. A.
Uncle Mac
    See McCulloch, Derek (Ivor Breashur)
Uncle Ray
    See Coffman, Ramon Peyton
Uncle Shelby
    See Silverstein, Shel
Underhill, Alice Mertie (Waterman)
    1900-1971 10
Underhill, Liz 1948- 53
    Brief entry 49
Underwood, Deborah 1962- 206
Unger, Harlow G. 1931- 75
Unger, Harlow Giles
    See Unger, Harlow G.
Unger, Jim 1937- 67
Ungerer, (Jean) Thomas 1931- 106
    Earlier sketches in SATA 5, 33
    See also CLR 77
Ungerer, Tomi 1931-
    See Ungerer, (Jean) Thomas
Unkelbach, Kurt 1913-1992 4
Unnerstad, Edith (Totterman) 1900-1982 3
    See also CLR 36
Unobagha, Uzo 139
Unrau, Ruth 1922- 9
Unstead, R(obert) J(ohn) 1915-1988 12
    Obituary 56
Unsworth, Walt(er) 1928- 4
Untermeyer, Bryna Ivens 1909-1985 61
Untermeyer, Louis 1885-1977 37
    Obituary 26
    Earlier sketch in SATA 2
Unwin, David S. 1918-2010 14
Unwin, David Storr
    See Unwin, David S.

Unwin, Nora S(picer) 1907-1982 3
    Obituary 49
Unzner, Christa 1958- 141
    Earlier sketch in SATA 80
Unzner-Fischer, Christa
    See Unzner, Christa
Updale, Eleanor 1953- 175
Updyke, Rosemary K. 1924- 103
Upitis, Alvis 109
Urbain, Cat 1956- 211
Urbain, Catherine
    See Urbain, Cat
Urban, Helle (Denise) 1957- 149
Urban, Linda 199
Urbanovic, Jackie 189
Urberuaga, Emilio 1954- 219
Urbigkit, Cat 1965- 196
Urdahl, Catherine 215
Ure, Jean 1943- 192
    Autobiography Feature 192
    Earlier sketches in SATA 48, 78, 129
    See also CLR 34
    See also SAAS 14
U'Ren, Andrea 1968- 213
    Earlier sketch in SATA 142
Uris, Leon 1924-2003 49
    Obituary 146
Uris, Leon Marcus
    See Uris, Leon
Ursu, Anne 177
Ury, Allen B. 1954- 98
Uschan, Michael V. 1948- 129
Usher, Margo Scegge
    See McHargue, Georgess
Usher, Mark David
    See Usher, M.D.
Usher, M.D. 1966- 221
Uslan, Michael E. 1951- 169
Uston, Ken(neth Senzo) 1935-1987 65
Uttley, Alice Jane 1884-1976 88
    Obituary 26
    Earlier sketch in SATA 3
Uttley, Alison
    See Uttley, Alice Jane
Utz, Lois (Marie) 1932-1986 5
    Obituary 50

V

Vaeth, J. Gordon 1921- 17
Vaeth, Joseph Gordon
    See Vaeth, J. Gordon
Vagin, Vladimir (Vasilevich) 1937- 142
Vail, Rachel 1966- 201
    Earlier sketches in SATA 94, 163
Vainio, Pirkko 1957- 123
    Earlier sketch in SATA 76
Valen, Nanine 1950- 21
Valencak, Hannelore
    See Mayer, Hannelore Valencak
Valens, Amy 1946- 70
Valens, E(vans) G(ladstone), Jr. 1920-1992 ... 1
Valentine, Johnny 72
Valerio, Geraldo 1970- 180
Valgardson, W. D. 1939- 151
    Earlier sketch in SATA 101
Valgardson, William Dempsey
    See Valgardson, W. D.
Valleau, Emily 1925- 51
Vamos, Samantha R. 215
Van Abbe, Salaman 1883-1955 18
Van Allsburg, Chris 1949- 156
    Earlier sketches in SATA 37, 53, 105
    See also CLR 113
Van Anrooy, Francine 1924- 2
Van Anrooy, Frans
    See Van Anrooy, Francine
Vanasse, Deb 1957- 170
Van Buren, David 203

Van Camp, Katie 1981- 222
Vance, Cynthia 207
Vance, Eleanor Graham 1908-1985 11
Vance, Gerald
    See Garrett, Randall
    and Silverberg, Robert
Vance, Marguerite 1889-1965 29
Vance-Abrams, Cynthia
    See Vance, Cynthia
VanCleave, Janice 1942- 116
    Autobiography Feature 123
    Earlier sketch in SATA 75
Vandenburg, Mary Lou 1943- 17
Vander Boom, Mae M. 14
Vander-Els, Betty 1936- 63
van der Heide, Iris 1970- 183
van der Linde, Laurel 1952- 78
van der Linden, Martijn 1979- 214
van der Meer, Ron 1945- 98
van de Ruit, John 1975- 199
Van der Veer, Judy 1912-1982 4
    Obituary 33
Vanderwal, Andrew H. 1956- 219
Vanderwerff, Corrine 1939- 117
Vander Zee, Ruth 199
    Earlier sketch in SATA 159
Vande Velde, Vivian 1951- 211
    Earlier sketches in SATA 62, 95, 141
    See also CLR 145
Vandivert, Rita (Andre) 1905-1986 21
Van Draanen, Wendelin 207
    Earlier sketch in SATA 122
Van Dusen, Chris 173
Van Duyn, Janet 1910- 18
Van Dyne, Edith
    See Baum, L. Frank
    and Sampson, Emma (Keats) Speed
    and van Zantwijk, Rudolf (Alexander
    Marinus)
Vane, Mitch
    See Vane, Mitchelle
Vane, Mitchelle 176
van Frankenhuyzen, Gijsbert 1951- 132
Van Genechten, Guido 1957- 165
van Haeringen, Annemarie 193
Van Hook, Beverly 1941- 99
Van Hook, Beverly H.
    See Van Hook, Beverly
Van Hook, Beverly Hennen
    See Van Hook, Beverly
Van Horn, William 1939- 43
van Hout, Mies 1962- 178
Van Iterson, S(iny) R(ose) 26
Van Kampen, Vlasta 1943- 163
    Earlier sketch in SATA 54
Van Laan, Nancy 1939- 214
    Earlier sketch in SATA 105
van Lawick-Goodall, Jane
    See Goodall, Jane
Van Leeuwen, Jean 1937- 211
    Autobiography Feature 141
    Earlier sketches in SATA 6, 82, 132, 141
    See also SAAS 8
van Lhin, Erik
    See del Rey, Lester
van Lieshout, Elle 1963- 217
van Lieshout, Maria 201
Van Loon, Hendrik Willem 1882-1944 18
van Ommen, Sylvia 1978- 186
VanOosting, James 1951- 170
Van Orden, M(erton) D(ick) 1921- 4
van Os, Erik 1963- 217
Van Patter, Bruce 183
Van Reek, Wouter 204
Van Rensselaer, Alexander (Taylor Mason)
    1892-1962 14
Van Riper, Guernsey, Jr. 1909-1995 3
van Rossum, Heleen 1962- 174
Van Rynbach, Iris 1952- 102
Vansant, Rhonda Joy Edwards 1950- 92

Van Steenwyk, Elizabeth (Ann) 1928- 89
    Earlier sketch in SATA 34
Van Stockum, Hilda 1908-2006 5
    Obituary 179
van Straaten, Harmen 1961- 218
    Earlier sketch in SATA 195
Van Tuyl, Barbara 1940- 11
van Vogt, A(lfred) E(lton) 1912-2000 14
    Obituary 124
Van Wassenhove, Sue 1951- 202
Van Woerkom, Dorothy (O'Brien)
    1924-1996 21
Van Wormer, Joe
    See Van Wormer, Joseph Edward
Van Wormer, Joseph Edward 1913-1998 35
Van Wright, Cornelius 173
Van Zwienen, Ilse Charlotte Koehn
    1929-1991 34
    Brief entry 28
    Obituary 67
Van Zyle, Jon 1942- 176
    Earlier sketch in SATA 84
Varela, Barry 180
Varga, Judy
    See Stang, Judit
Varley, Dimitry V. 1906-1984 10
Varley, Susan 1961- 134
    Earlier sketch in SATA 63
Varon, Sara 195
Vasileva, Tatiana
    See Wassiljewa, Tatjana
Vasiliev, Valery 1949- 80
Vasilieva, Tatiana
    See Wassiljewa, Tatjana
Vasiliu, Mircea 1920- 2
Vass, George 1927- 57
    Brief entry 31
Vaughan, Carter A.
    See Gerson, Noel Bertram
Vaughan, Harold Cecil 1923- 14
Vaughan, Marcia (K.) 1951- 159
    Earlier sketches in SATA 60, 95
Vaughan, Richard 1947- 87
Vaughan, Sam(uel) 1928- 14
Vaughn, Ruth 1935- 14
Vaught, Susan 1965- 195
Vaupel, Robin 198
Vautier, Ghislaine 1932- 53
Vavra, Robert James 1935- 8
Vecsey, George Spencer 1939- 9
Vedral, Joyce L(auretta) 1943- 65
Vega, Denise 216
    Earlier sketch in SATA 174
Vega, Denise B.
    See Vega, Denise
Vega, Diego
    See Adkins, Jan
Veglahn, Nancy (Crary) 1937- 5
Vejjajiva, Jane 1963- 189
Velasquez, Eric 192
Velasquez, Gloria 1949- 113
Velasquez, Gloria 1949-
    See Velasquez, Gloria
Velthuijs, Max 1923-2005 110
    Obituary 160
    Earlier sketch in SATA 53
Venable, Alan (Hudson) 1944- 8
Venezia, Mike 1945- 150
Ventura, Anthony
    See Pellowski, Michael (Joseph)
Ventura, Piero (Luigi) 1937- 61
    Brief entry 43
    See also CLR 16
Vequin, Capini
    See Quinn, Elisabeth
Verba, Joan Marie 1953- 78
Verboven, Agnes 1951- 103
verDorn, Bethea (Stewart) 1952- 76
Vere, Ed 197
Verissimo, Erico (Lopes) 1905-1975 113

Verne, Jules 1828-1905 21
    See also CLR 88
Verne, Jules Gabriel
    See Verne, Jules
Verner, Gerald 1897(?)-1980
    Obituary 25
Verney, John 1913-1993 14
    Obituary 75
Verniero, Joan C. 1949- 181
Vernon, (Elda) Louise A(nderson) 1914- 14
Vernon, Rosemary
    See Smith, Susan Vernon
Vernon, Ursula 204
Vernor, D.
    See Casewit, Curtis W(erner)
Verr, Harry Coe
    See Kunhardt, Edith
Verral, Charles Spain 1904-1990 11
    Obituary 65
Verrillo, Erica 1953- 199
Verrillo, Erica F.
    See Verrillo, Erica
Verroken, Sarah 1982- 223
Verrone, Robert J. 1935(?)-1984
    Obituary 39
Versace, Marie Teresa Rios 1917- 2
Vertreace, Martha M(odena) 1945- 78
Vesey, A(manda) 1939- 62
Vesey, Mark (David) 1958- 123
Vesey, Paul
    See Allen, Samuel W(ashington)
Vess, Charles 1951- 215
Vestergaard, Hope 178
Vestly, Anne-Cath(arina) 1920-2008 14
    See also CLR 99
Vevers, (Henry) Gwynne 1916-1988 45
    Obituary 57
Viator, Vacuus
    See Hughes, Thomas
Viau, Nancy 208
Vicar, Henry
    See Felsen, Henry Gregor
Vick, Helen Hughes 1950- 88
Vicker, Angus
    See Felsen, Henry Gregor
Vickers, Sheena 1960- 94
Vickery, Kate
    See Kennedy, T.A.
Victor, Edward 1914- 3
Victor, Joan Berg 1942- 30
Vidrine, Beverly Barras 1938- 188
    Earlier sketch in SATA 103
Vieceli, Emma 1979- 210
Viereck, Ellen K. 1928- 14
Viereck, Phillip 1925- 3
Viertel, Janet 1915- 10
Vigliante, Mary
    See Szydlowski, Mary Vigliante
Vigna, Judith 1936- 102
    Earlier sketch in SATA 15
Viguers, Ruth Hill 1903-1971 6
Vila, Laura 207
Vilela, Fernando 1973- 216
Villareal, Ray 187
Villasenor, Edmund
    See Villasenor, Victor E.
Villasenor, Edmundo
    See Villasenor, Victor E.
Villasenor, Victor
    See Villasenor, Victor E.
Villasenor, Victor E. 1940- 171
Villasenor, Victor Edmundo
    See Villasenor, Victor E.
Villiard, Paul 1910-1974 51
    Obituary 20
Villiers, Alan (John) 1903-1982 10
Vilott, Rhondi
    See Salsitz, Rhondi Vilott
Vincent, Amy
    See Gray, Claudia
Vincent, Eric Douglas 1953- 40

Vincent, Erin 1969- 188
Vincent, Felix 1946- 41
Vincent, Gabrielle 1928-2000 121
  Earlier sketch in SATA 61
  See also CLR 13
Vincent, Mary Keith
  See St. John, Wylly Folk
Vincent, Rachel 1978- 222
Vincent, William R.
  See Heitzmann, William Ray
Vinegar, Tom
  See Gregg, Andrew K.
Vinest, Shaw
  See Longyear, Barry B(rookes)
Vinge, Joan (Carol) D(ennison) 1948- 113
  Earlier sketch in SATA 36
Vining, Elizabeth Gray 1902-1999 6
  Obituary 117
Vinson, Kathryn 1911-1995 21
Vinton, Iris 1906(?)-1988 24
  Obituary 55
Viola, Herman J(oseph) 1938- 126
Viorst, Judith 1931- 172
  Earlier sketches in SATA 7, 70, 123
  See also CLR 90
Vip
  See Partch, Virgil Franklin II
Vipont, Charles
  See Foulds, Elfrida Vipont
Vipont, Elfrida
  See Foulds, Elfrida Vipont
Viramontes, Helena Maria 1954-
  See CLR 285
Viscott, David S(teven) 1938-1996 65
Visser, W(illem) F(rederik) H(endrik)
  1900-1968 10
Vitale, Stefano 1958- 225
  Earlier sketches in SATA 114, 180
Vivas, Julie 1947- 96
Vivelo, Jackie 1943- 63
Vivelo, Jacqueline J.
  See Vivelo, Jackie
Vivelo, Jacqueline Jean
  See Vivelo, Jackie
Vivian, Siobhan 1979(?)- 215
Vizzini, Ned 1981- 179
  Earlier sketch in SATA 125
Vlahos, Olivia 1924- 31
Vlasic, Bob
  See Hirsch, Phil
Voake, Charlotte 180
  Earlier sketch in SATA 114
Voake, Steve 1961- 178
Vo-Dinh, Mai 1933- 16
Vogel, Carole Garbuny 1951- 105
  Earlier sketch in SATA 70
Vogel, Ilse-Margret 1918- 14
Vogel, John H., Jr. 1950- 18
Vogt, Esther Loewen 1915-1999 14
Vogt, Gregory L. 94
Vogt, Marie Bollinger 1921- 45
Vohwinkel, Astrid 1969- 207
Voight, Virginia Frances 1909-1989 8
Voigt, Cynthia 1942- 160
  Brief entry 33
  Earlier sketches in SATA 48, 79, 116
  See also CLR 141
Voigt, Erna 1925- 35
Voigt-Rother, Erna
  See Voigt, Erna
Vojtech, Anna 1946- 108
  Earlier sketch in SATA 42
Vollstadt, Elizabeth Weiss 1942- 121
Volponi, Paul 175
Volting, Dr. R.E.
  See Lerangis, Peter
Von Ahnen, Katherine 1922- 93
von Buhler, Cynthia 185
Vondra, J. Gert
  See Vondra, Josef
Vondra, Josef 1941- 121

Vondra, Josef Gert
  See Vondra, Josef
Von Gunden, Kenneth 1946- 113
Von Hagen, Victor Wolfgang 1908-1985 29
von Klopp, Vahrah
  See Malvern, Gladys
von Schmidt, Eric 1931-2007 50
  Brief entry 36
  Obituary 181
von Storch, Anne B. 1910- 1
von Trapp, Maria Augusta 1905-1987 16
von Wodtke, Charlotte Buel Johnson
  1918-1982 46
von Ziegesar, Cecily 1970- 161
Vos, Ida 1931-2006 121
  Earlier sketch in SATA 69
  See also CLR 85
Vosburgh, Leonard (W.) 1912- 15
Votaw, Carol 1961- 201
Voyle, Mary
  See Manning, Rosemary
Vrettos, Adrienne Maria 187
Vriens, Jacques 1946- 151
Vugteveen, Verna Aardema
  See Aardema, Verna
Vulture, Elizabeth T.
  See Gilbert, Suzie
Vuong, Lynette Dyer 1938- 110
  Earlier sketch in SATA 60

                           W

Waas, Uli
  See Waas-Pommer, Ulrike
Waas-Pommer, Ulrike 1949- 85
Waber, Bernard 1924- 155
  Brief entry 40
  Earlier sketches in SATA 47, 95
  See also CLR 55
Wachtel, Shirley Russak 1951- 88
Wachter, Oralee (Roberts) 1935- 61
  Brief entry 51
Waddell, Evelyn Margaret 1918- 10
Waddell, Martin 1941- 129
  Autobiography Feature 129
  Earlier sketches in SATA 43, 81, 127
  See also CLR 31
  See also SAAS 15
Waddy, Lawrence 1912-2010 91
Waddy, Lawrence Heber
  See Waddy, Lawrence
Wade, Mary Dodson 1930- 151
  Earlier sketch in SATA 79
Wade, Suzanne
  See Kirby, Susan E.
Wade, Theodore E., Jr. 1936- 37
Wademan, Peter John 1946- 122
Wademan, Spike
  See Wademan, Peter John
Wadsworth, Ginger 1945- 223
  Earlier sketches in SATA 103, 157
Wagenheim, Kal 1935- 21
Wagner, Michele R. 1975- 157
Wagner, Sharon B. 1936- 4
Wagoner, David (Russell) 1926- 14
Wahl, Jan (Boyer) 1933- 132
  Earlier sketches in SATA 2, 34, 73
  See also SAAS 3
Wahl, Mats 1945- 186
Wahman, Wendy 218
Waide, Jan 1952- 29
Wainscott, John Milton 1910-1981 53
Wainwright, Debra 218
Wainwright, Richard M. 1935- 91
Wainwright, Ruth
  See Symes, Ruth Louise
Wait, Lea 1946- 137
Waite, Judy 174

Waite, Judy Bernard
  See Bernard, Patricia
Waite, Michael
  See Waite, Michael P.
Waite, Michael P. 1960- 101
Waite, P(eter) B(usby) 1922- 64
Waites, Joan C. 187
Waitley, Douglas 1927- 30
Wakefield, Jean L.
  See Laird, Jean E(louise)
Wakin, Daniel (Joseph) 1961- 84
Wakin, Edward 1927- 37
Wakiyama, Hanako 1966- 192
Walck, Henry Z. 1908(?)-1984
  Obituary 40
Walden, Amelia Elizabeth 3
Walden, Mark 188
Waldherr, Kris 1963- 76
Waldman, Bruce 1949- 15
Waldman, Neil 1947- 203
  Earlier sketches in SATA 51, 94, 142
Waldrep, Richard 198
Waldron, Ann Wood 1924-2010 16
Waldron, Kathleen Cook 176
Wales, Dirk 1931- 205
Walgren, Judy 1963- 118
Walker, Addison
  See Walker, Mort
Walker, Addison Mort
  See Walker, Mort
Walker, Alice 1944- 31
Walker, Alice Malsenior
  See Walker, Alice
Walker, Anna 223
Walker, Barbara (Jeanne) K(erlin) 1921- 80
  Earlier sketch in SATA 4
Walker, Barbara M(uhs) 1928- 57
Walker, (James) Braz(elton) 1934-1983 45
Walker, David 1965- 197
Walker, David G(ordon) 1926- 60
Walker, David Harry 1911-1992 8
  Obituary 71
Walker, Diana 1925- 9
Walker, Diane Marie Catherine
  See Walker, Kate
Walker, Dick
  See Pellowski, Michael (Joseph)
Walker, Frank 1931-2000 36
Walker, Holly Beth
  See Bond, Gladys Baker
Walker, Kate 1950- 165
  Earlier sketch in SATA 82
Walker, Kathrine Sorley
  See Sorley Walker, Kathrine
Walker, Lou Ann 1952- 66
  Brief entry 53
Walker, Louise Jean 1891-1976
  Obituary 35
Walker, Mary Alexander 1927- 61
Walker, Mildred
  See Schemm, Mildred Walker
Walker, Mort 1923- 8
Walker, Pamela 1948- 142
  Earlier sketch in SATA 24
Walker, Paul Robert 1953- 154
Walker, Robert W. 1948- 66
Walker, Robert Wayne
  See Walker, Robert W.
Walker, Sally M. 1954- 221
  Earlier sketch in SATA 135
Walker, Stephen J. 1951- 12
Walker-Blondell, Becky 1951- 89
Wallace, Barbara Brooks 1922- 136
  Earlier sketches in SATA 4, 78
  See also CLR 150
  See also SAAS 17
Wallace, Beverly Dobrin 1921- 19
Wallace, Bill 1947- 169
  Brief entry 47
  Earlier sketches in SATA 53, 101
Wallace, Carol 1948- 218

Wallace, Daisy
  See Cuyler, Margery
Wallace, Ian 1950- 219
  Earlier sketches in SATA *53, 56, 141*
  See also CLR *37*
Wallace, John 1966- 155
  Earlier sketch in SATA *105*
Wallace, John A(dam) 1915-2004 .... *3*
  Obituary 155
Wallace, Karen 1951- 188
  Earlier sketches in SATA *83, 139*
Wallace, Nancy Elizabeth 1948- 222
  Earlier sketches in SATA *141, 186*
Wallace, Nigel
  See Hamilton, Charles (Harold St. John)
Wallace, Paula S. 153
Wallace, Rich 1957- 196
  Earlier sketches in SATA *117, 158*
Wallace, Robert 1932-1999 47
  Brief entry 37
Wallace, Ruby Ann 1923(?)- 77
Wallace, William Keith
  See Wallace, Bill
Wallace-Brodeur, Ruth 1941- 169
  Brief entry 41
  Earlier sketches in SATA *51, 88*
Wallenta, Adam 1974- 123
Waller, Leslie 1923-2007 20
Walley, Byron
  See Card, Orson Scott
Wallis, Diz 1949- 77
Wallis, G. McDonald
  See Campbell, Hope
Wallner, Alexandra 1946- 156
  Brief entry 41
  Earlier sketches in SATA *51, 98*
Wallner, John C. 1945- 133
  Earlier sketches in SATA *10, 51*
Wallower, Lucille *11*
Walrod, Amy 1973(?)- 182
Walsh, Ann 1942- 176
  Earlier sketch in SATA *62*
Walsh, Ellen Stoll 1942- 194
  Earlier sketches in SATA *49, 99, 147*
Walsh, George Johnston 1889-1981 53
Walsh, Gillian Paton
  See Paton Walsh, Jill
Walsh, Jill Paton
  See Paton Walsh, Jill
Walsh, Joanna 1970- 182
Walsh, Lawrence 1942- 170
Walsh, Marissa 1972- 195
Walsh, Mary Caswell 1949- 118
Walsh, Mitzy
  See Walsh, Marissa
Walsh, Rebecca 217
Walsh, Suella 170
Walsh, V. L.
  See Walsh, Vivian
Walsh, Vivian 1960- 120
Walsh Shepherd, Donna 1948- 78
Walter, Frances V. 1923- 71
Walter, Mildred Pitts 1922- 133
  Brief entry 45
  Earlier sketch in SATA *69*
  See also CLR *61*
  See also SAAS *12*
Walter, Villiam Christian
  See Andersen, Hans Christian
Walter, Virginia
  See Walter, Virginia A.
Walter, Virginia A. 134
Walters, Audrey 1929- 18
Walters, Celeste 1938- 126
Walters, Eric 1957- 205
  Earlier sketches in SATA *99, 155*
Walters, Eric Robert
  See Walters, Eric
Walters, Gregory 1964- 213
Walters, Helen B. (?)-1987
  Obituary 50

Walters, Hugh
  See Hughes, Walter (Llewellyn)
Walther, Thomas A. 1950- *31*
Walther, Tom
  See Walther, Thomas A.
Waltner, Elma 1912-1987 40
Waltner, Willard H. 1909- 40
Walton, Darwin McBeth 1926- *119*
Walton, Fiona L. M. 1959- 89
Walton, Richard J. 1928- *4*
Walton, Rick 1957- 204
  Earlier sketches in SATA *101, 151*
Waltrip, Lela (Kingston) 1904-1995 9
Waltrip, Mildred 1911- 37
Waltrip, Rufus (Charles) 1898-1988 9
Walworth, Nancy Zinsser 1917- 14
Wang, Gabrielle 212
Wang, Lin 1973- 221
Wang, Shaoli 216
Wangerin, Walter, Jr. 1944- 98
  Brief entry 37
  Earlier sketch in SATA *45*
Waniek, Marilyn Nelson 1946-
  See Nelson, Marilyn
Wannamaker, Bruce
  See Moncure, Jane Belk
Warbler, J. M.
  See Cocagnac, Augustin Maurice(-Jean)
Warburg, Sandol Stoddard
  See Stoddard, Sandol
Warburton, Tom 1968(?)- 218
Ward, David 1967- 213
Ward, E. D.
  See Gorey, Edward (St. John)
  and Lucas, E(dward) V(errall)
Ward, Ed
  See Stratemeyer, Edward L.
Ward, Helen 1962- 206
  Earlier sketches in SATA *72, 144*
Ward, Jay 1920-1989
  Obituary 63
Ward, Jennifer 1963- 146
Ward, John (Stanton) 1917- 42
Ward, Jonas
  See Ard, William
  and Cox, William R(obert)
  and Garfield, Brian (Francis Wynne)
Ward, Lynd (Kendall) 1905-1985 36
  Obituary 42
  Earlier sketch in SATA *2*
Ward, Martha (Eads) 5
Ward, Melanie
  See Curtis, Richard
  and Lynch, Marilyn
Ward, Nicholas John
  See Ward, Nick
Ward, Nick 1955- 190
Ward, Tom
  See Stratemeyer, Edward L.
Wardell, Dean
  See Prince, J(ack) H(arvey)
Wardlaw, Lee 1955- 115
  Earlier sketch in SATA *79*
Ware, Cheryl 1963- 101
Ware, Chris 1967- 140
Ware, Leon (Vernon) 1909-1976 4
Wargin, Kathy-jo 1964- 210
  Earlier sketch in SATA *145*
Warhola, James 1955- 187
Warman, Jessica 1981- 225
Warner, Frank A. 67
  Earlier sketch in SATA *1*
Warner, Gertrude Chandler 1890-1979 9
  Obituary 73
Warner, J(ohn) F. 1929- 75
Warner, Lucille Schulberg 30
Warner, Matt
  See Fichter, George S.
Warner, Oliver (Martin Wilson) 1903-1976 . 29
Warner, Sally 1946- 214
  Earlier sketch in SATA *131*

Warner, Sunny (B.) 1931- 108
Warnes, Tim 1971- 216
  Earlier sketches in SATA *116, 166*
Warnes, Timothy
  See Warnes, Tim
Warnick, Elsa 1942- 113
Warren, Andrea 1946- 98
Warren, Betsy
  See Warren, Elizabeth Avery
Warren, Billy
  See Warren, William Stephen
Warren, Cathy 1951- 62
  Brief entry 46
Warren, Elizabeth
  See Supraner, Robyn
Warren, Elizabeth Avery 1916- 46
  Brief entry 38
Warren, Jackie M. 1953- *135*
Warren, Joshua P(aul) 1976- 107
Warren, Joyce W(illiams) 1935- 18
Warren, Mary Phraner 1929- 10
Warren, Robert Penn 1905-1989 46
  Obituary 63
Warren, Scott S. 1957- 79
Warren, William Stephen 1882-1968 9
Warrick, Patricia Scott 1925- 35
Warriner, John 1907(?)-1987
  Obituary 53
Warsh
  See Warshaw, Jerry
Warshaw, Jerry 1929- 30
Warshaw, Mary 1931- 89
Warshofsky, Fred 1931- 24
Warshofsky, Isaac
  See Singer, Isaac Bashevis
Wartski, Maureen (Ann Crane) 1940- 50
  Brief entry 37
Warwick, Alan R(oss) 1900-1973 42
Wa-sha-quon-asin
  See Belaney, Archibald Stansfeld
Wa-Sha-Quon-Asin
  See Belaney, Archibald Stansfeld
Washburn, Bradford 1910-2007 38
  Obituary 181
Washburn, Henry Bradford, Jr.
  See Washburn, Bradford
Washburn, Jan(ice) 1926- 63
Washburn, Lucia 193
Washburne, Carolyn Kott 1944- 86
Washburne, Heluiz Chandler 1892-1970 10
  Obituary 26
Washington, Booker T. 1856-1915 28
Washington, Donna L. 1967- 159
  Earlier sketch in SATA *98*
Wasserman, Robin 1978- 207
Wasserstein, Wendy 1950-2006 94
  Obituary 174
Wassiljewa, Tatjana 1928- 106
Watanabe, Etsuko 1968- 219
Watanabe, Shigeo 1928- 131
  Brief entry 32
  Earlier sketch in SATA *39*
  See also CLR *8*
Waters, John F(rederick) 1930- 4
Waters, Summer
  See Sykes, Julie
Waters, Tony 1958- 75
Waterton, Betty 1923- 99
  Brief entry 34
  Earlier sketch in SATA *37*
Waterton, Betty Marie
  See Waterton, Betty
Watkins, Dawn L. 126
Watkins, Gloria Jean
  See hooks, bell
Watkins, Lis
  See Watkins, Liselotte
Watkins, Liselotte 1971- 215
Watkins, Lois 1930- 88
Watkins, Peter 1934- 66
Watkins, Yoko Kawashima 1933- 93

Watkins-Pitchford, Denys James
1905-1990 87
  Obituary 66
  Earlier sketch in SATA 6
  See also SAAS 4
Watling, James 1933- 117
  Earlier sketch in SATA 67
Watson, Aldren A(uld) 1917- 42
  Brief entry 36
Watson, Amy Zakrzewski 1965- 76
Watson, B. S.
  See Teitelbaum, Michael
Watson, Carol 1949- 78
Watson, C.G. 193
Watson, Clyde 1947- 68
  Earlier sketch in SATA 5
  See also CLR 3
Watson, Helen Orr 1892-1978
  Obituary 24
Watson, James 1936- 106
  Earlier sketch in SATA 10
Watson, Jane Werner 1915- 54
  Earlier sketch in SATA 3
Watson, Jesse Joshua 199
Watson, John H.
  See Farmer, Philip Jose
Watson, Mary 1953- 117
Watson, N. Cameron 1955- 81
Watson, Nancy Dingman 32
Watson, Pauline 1925- 14
Watson, Richard F.
  See Silverberg, Robert
Watson, Richard Jesse 1951- 211
  Earlier sketch in SATA 62
Watson, Sally (Lou) 1924- 3
Watson, Sasha 211
Watson, Wendy (McLeod) 1942- 142
  Earlier sketches in SATA 5, 74
Watson Taylor, Elizabeth 1915- 41
Watt, Melanie 1975- 193
  Earlier sketch in SATA 136
Watt, Thomas 1935- 4
Wattenberg, Jane 174
Watterson, Bill 1958- 66
Watt-Evans, Lawrence 1954- 121
Watts, (Anna) Bernadette 1942- 103
  Earlier sketch in SATA 4
Watts, Ephraim
  See Horne, Richard Henry Hengist
Watts, Franklin (Mowry) 1904-1978 46
  Obituary 21
Watts, Helen L. Hoke 1903-1990
  Obituary 65
Watts, Irene N(aemi) 1931- 111
  Earlier sketch in SATA 56
Watts, Isaac 1674-1748 52
Watts, James K(ennedy) M(offitt) 1955- 59
Watts, Jeri Hanel 1957- 170
Watts, Julia 1969- 103
Watts, Leander 1956- 146
Watts, Leslie Elizabeth 1961- 168
Watts, Mabel Pizzey 1906-1994 11
Watts, Nigel 1957-1999 121
Waugh, C. C. Roessel
  See Waugh, Carol-Lynn Rossel
  and Waugh, Charles G(ordon)
Waugh, Carol-Lynn Rossel 1947- 41
Waugh, Dorothy -1996 11
Waugh, Sylvia 1935- 169
Waugh, Virginia
  See Sorensen, Virginia
Wax, Wendy A. 1963- 219
  Earlier sketches in SATA 73, 163
Wayland, April Halprin 1954- 143
  Earlier sketch in SATA 78
  See also SAAS 26
Wayland, Patrick
  See O'Connor, Richard
Wayne, (Anne) Jenifer 1917-1982 32
Wayne, Kyra Petrovskaya 1918- 8

Wayne, Richard
  See Decker, Duane
Wayshak, Deborah Noyes
  See Noyes, Deborah
Waystaff, Simon
  See Swift, Jonathan
Weales, Gerald (Clifford) 1925- 11
Weary, Ogdred
  See Gorey, Edward (St. John)
Weatherford, Carole Boston 1956- 181
  Earlier sketch in SATA 138
Weatherill, Cat 203
Weatherly, Lee 1967- 192
Weatherly, Myra 1926- 130
Weatherly, Myra S.
  See Weatherly, Myra
Weaver, Brian M.
  See Numberman, Neil
Weaver, Harriett E. 1908-1993 65
Weaver, John L. 1949- 42
Weaver, Robyn
  See Conley, Robyn
Weaver, Robyn M.
  See Conley, Robyn
Weaver, Tess 197
Weaver, Ward
  See Mason, F(rancis) van Wyck
Weaver, Will 1950- 217
  Earlier sketches in SATA 88, 109, 161
Weaver, William Weller
  See Weaver, Will
Weaver-Gelzer, Charlotte 1950- 79
Webb, Christopher
  See Wibberley, Leonard
Webb, Jacqueline
  See Pearce, Margaret
Webb, Jacquelyn
  See Pearce, Margaret
  and Pearce, Margaret
Webb, Jean Francis (III) 1910-1991 35
Webb, Kaye 1914- 60
Webb, Lois Sinaiko 1922- 82
Webb, Margot 1934- 67
Webb, Sharon 1936-2010 41
Webb, Sophie 1958- 135
Webber, Andrew Lloyd
  See Lloyd Webber, Andrew
Webber, Desiree Morrison 1956- 170
Webber, Irma E(leanor Schmidt)
  1904-1995 14
Weber, Alfons 1921- 8
Weber, Bruce 1942- 120
  Earlier sketch in SATA 73
Weber, Debora 1955- 58
Weber, EdNah New Rider 1919(?)- 168
Weber, Elka 1968- 219
Weber, Jill 1950- 209
  Earlier sketch in SATA 127
Weber, Judith E(ichler) 1938- 64
Weber, Ken(neth J.) 1940- 90
Weber, Lenora Mattingly 1895-1971 2
  Obituary 26
Weber, Lisa K. 217
Weber, Lori 1959- 220
Weber, Michael 1945- 87
Weber, Sandra 1961- 158
Weber, William J(ohn) 1927- 14
Webster, Alice Jane Chandler 1876-1916 17
Webster, David 1930- 11
Webster, Frank V. 67
  Earlier sketch in SATA 1
Webster, Gary
  See Garrison, Webb B(lack)
Webster, James 1925-1981 17
  Obituary 27
Webster, Jean
  See Webster, Alice Jane Chandler
Wechsler, Doug 189
Wechsler, Herman J. 1904-1976
  Obituary 20

Wechter, Nell (Carolyn) Wise 1913-1989 .. 127
  Earlier sketch in SATA 60
Weck, Thomas L. 1942- 62
Wedd, Kate
  See Gregory, Philippa
Weddle, Ethel Harshbarger 1897-1996 11
Wedekind, Annie 204
Weeks, Sarah 194
  Earlier sketch in SATA 158
Weems, David B(urnola) 1922- 80
Wees, Frances Shelley 1902-1982 58
Weevers, Peter 1944- 59
Wegen, Ronald 1946-1985 99
Wegman, William (George) 1943- 135
  Earlier sketches in SATA 78, 129
Wegner, Fritz 1924- 20
Wehrman, Vicki 223
Weidhorn, Manfred 1931- 60
Weidt, Maryann N. 1944- 85
Weigel, Jeff 1958- 170
Weigelt, Udo 1960- 201
  Earlier sketch in SATA 168
Weihs, Erika 1917-2010 107
  Earlier sketch in SATA 15
Weik, Mary Hays 1898(?)-1979 3
  Obituary 23
Weil, Ann Yezner 1908-1969 9
Weil, Lisl 1910- 7
Weilerstein, Sadie Rose 1894-1993 3
  Obituary 75
Weill, Cynthia 1959- 167
Wein, Elizabeth E. 1964- 151
  Earlier sketch in SATA 82
Wein, Elizabeth Eve
  See Wein, Elizabeth E.
Wein, Hallie
  See Zobel Nolan, Allia
Weinberg, Larry
  See Weinberg, Lawrence (E.)
Weinberg, Lawrence (E.) 92
  Brief entry 48
Weinberger, Tanya 1939- 84
Weiner, Sandra 1922- 14
Weingarten, Lynn 217
Weingarten, Violet (Brown) 1915-1976 3
  Obituary 27
Weingartner, Charles 1922- 5
Weinheimer, Beckie 1958- 186
Weinstein, Bruce 1960- 220
Weinstein, Bruce M.
  See Weinstein, Bruce
Weinstein, Ellen Slusky 1959- 200
Weinstein, Muriel Harris 215
Weinstein, Nina 1951- 73
Weinstock, Robert 1967- 204
Weir, Bob 1947- 76
Weir, Diana (R.) Loiewski 1958- 111
Weir, Joan S(herman) 1928- 99
Weir, LaVada 2
Weir, Rosemary (Green) 1905-1994 21
Weir, Wendy 1949- 76
Weis, Margaret 1948- 164
  Earlier sketches in SATA 38, 92
Weisberger, Bernard A(llen) 1922- 21
Weisburd, Stefi 1957- 202
Weiser, Marjorie P(hillis) K(atz) 1934- 33
Weisgard, Leonard (Joseph) 1916-2000 85
  Obituary 122
  Earlier sketches in SATA 2, 30
  See also SAAS 19
Weiss, Adelle 1920- 18
Weiss, Ann E(dwards) 1943- 69
  Earlier sketch in SATA 30
  See also SAAS 13
Weiss, Edna
  See Barth, Edna
Weiss, Ellen 1953- 44
Weiss, Harvey 1922- 76
  Earlier sketches in SATA 1, 27
  See also CLR 4
  See also SAAS 19

Weiss, Jaqueline Shachter 1926- 65
Weiss, Malcolm E. 1928- 3
Weiss, Margaret Edith
　See Weis, Margaret
Weiss, Miriam
　See Schlein, Miriam
Weiss, Mitch 1951- 183
　Earlier sketch in SATA 123
Weiss, Nicki 1954- 86
　Earlier sketch in SATA 33
Weiss, Renee Karol 1923- 5
Weissberger, Ela 1930- 181
Weissberger, Ela Stein
　See Weissberger, Ela
Weissenborn, Hellmuth 1898-1982
　Obituary 31
Weissman, Elissa Brent 217
Weitzman, David L. 1936- 172
　Earlier sketch in SATA 122
Wekesser, Carol A. 1963- 76
Welber, Robert 26
Welch, Amanda (Jane) 1945- 75
Welch, D'Alte Aldridge 1907-1970
　Obituary 27
Welch, Holly 206
Welch, Jean-Louise
　See Kempton, Jean Welch
Welch, Pauline
　See Bodenham, Hilda Morris
Welch, Ronald
　See Felton, Ronald Oliver
Welch, Sheila Kelly 1945- 130
Welch, Willy 1952- 93
Weldin, Frauke 1969- 188
Welford, Sue 1942- 75
Weller, George 1907-2002 31
　Obituary 140
Weller, George Anthony
　See Weller, George
Welling, Peter J. 1947- 135
Wellington, Monica 1957- 222
　Earlier sketches in SATA 67, 99, 157
Wellman, Alice 1900-1984 51
　Brief entry 36
Wellman, Manly Wade 1903-1986 6
　Obituary 47
Wellman, Paul I. 1898-1966 3
Wellman, Paul Iselin
　See Wellman, Paul I.
Wellman, Sam 1939- 122
Wellman, Samuel
　See Wellman, Sam
Wells, H. G. 1866-1946 20
　See also CLR 133
Wells, Helen
　See Campbell, Hope
Wells, Helen 1910-1986 49
　Earlier sketch in SATA 2
Wells, Herbert George
　See Wells, H. G.
Wells, J. Wellington
　See de Camp, L. Sprague
Wells, June
　See Swinford, Betty (June Wells)
Wells, Robert
　See Welsch, Roger L(ee)
Wells, Robert E. 184
Wells, Rosemary 1943- 207
　Earlier sketches in SATA 18, 69, 114, 156
　See also CLR 69
　See also SAAS 1
Wells, Susan (Mary) 1951- 78
Wels, Byron G(erald) 1924-1993 9
Welsbacher, Anne 1955- 89
Welsch, Roger L(ee) 1936- 82
Welsh, David
　See Hills, C.A.R.
Welsh, Mary Flynn 1910(?)-1984
　Obituary 38
Welsh, T.K. 1956- 184
Weltner, Linda R(iverly) 1938- 38

Welton, Jude 1955- 143
　Earlier sketch in SATA 79
Welty, S. F.
　See Welty, Susan F.
Welty, Susan F. 1905- 9
Wemmlinger, Raymond 190
Wendelin, Rudolph 1910-2000 23
Weninger, Brigitte 1960- 189
Wentworth, Robert
　See Hamilton, Edmond
Werlin, Nancy 1961- 161
　Earlier sketches in SATA 87, 119
Werner, Elsa Jane
　See Watson, Jane Werner
Werner, Herma 1926- 47
　Brief entry 41
Werner, Jane
　See Watson, Jane Werner
Werner, K.
　See Casewit, Curtis W(erner)
Wersba, Barbara 1932- 58
　Autobiography Feature 103
　Earlier sketch in SATA 1
　See also CLR 78
　See also SAAS 2
Werstein, Irving 1914(?)-1971 14
Werth, Kurt 1896-1983 20
Wesley, Alison
　See Barnes, Michael
Wesley, Kathryn
　See Rusch, Kristine Kathryn
Wesley, Mary (Aline) 1912-2002 66
Wesley, Valerie Wilson 1947- 168
　Earlier sketch in SATA 106
West, Andrew
　See Arthur, Robert, (Jr.)
West, Anna 1938- 40
West, Barbara
　See Price, Olive
West, Betty 1921- 11
West, Bruce 1951- 63
West, C. P.
　See Wodehouse, P. G.
West, Dorothy
　See Benson, Mildred
West, Emily Govan 1919- 38
West, Emmy
　See West, Emily Govan
West, James
　See Withers, Carl A.
West, Jerry
　See Svenson, Andrew E(dward)
West, (Mary) Jessamyn 1902-1984
　Obituary 37
West, John
　See Arthur, Robert, (Jr.)
West, Owen
　See Koontz, Dean
West, Ward
　See Borland, Harold Glen
Westall, Robert (Atkinson) 1929-1993 69
　Obituary 75
　Earlier sketch in SATA 23
　See also CLR 13
　See also SAAS 2
Westaway, Jane 1948- 121
Westcott, Nadine Bernard 1949- 130
Westera, Marleen 1962- 187
Westerberg, Christine 1950- 29
Westerduin, Anne 1945- 105
Westerfeld, Scott 1963- 161
Westervelt, Virginia Veeder 1914-2005 10
Westheimer, David 1917-2005 14
　Obituary 170
Westheimer, David Kaplan
　See Westheimer, David
Westmacott, Mary
　See Christie, Agatha
Westman, Barbara 70
Westman, Paul (Wendell) 1956- 39
Westmoreland, William C. 1914-2005 63

Westmoreland, William Childs
　See Westmoreland, William C.
Weston, Allen
　See Hogarth, Grace (Weston Allen)
　and Norton, Andre
Weston, Carol 1956- 135
Weston, Carrie 190
Weston, John (Harrison) 1932- 21
Weston, Martha 1947- 119
　Earlier sketch in SATA 53
Weston, Robert Paul 209
Westphal, Arnold Carl 1897- 57
Westrup, Hugh 102
Westwood, Jennifer 1940-2008 10
　Obituary 192
Wexler, Jerome (LeRoy) 1923- 14
Weyland, Jack 1940- 81
Weyn, Suzanne 1955- 220
　Earlier sketches in SATA 63, 101, 164
Weyr, Garret
　See Freymann-Weyr, Garret
Wezyk, Joanna 1966- 82
Whaley, Joyce Irene 1923- 61
Whalin, W. Terry 1953- 93
Whamond, Dave 222
Wharf, Michael
　See Weller, George
Wharmby, Margot 63
Wharton, Edith 1862-1937
　See CLR 136
Wharton, Edith Newbold Jones
　See Wharton, Edith
Wharton, Thomas 1963- 223
Whatley, Bruce 1954- 213
　Earlier sketch in SATA 177
Wheatley, Arabelle 1921- 16
Wheatley, Nadia 1949- 147
Wheeler, Cindy 1955- 49
　Brief entry 40
Wheeler, Deborah 1947- 83
Wheeler, Janet D. 1
Wheeler, Jill C. 1964- 136
　Earlier sketch in SATA 86
Wheeler, Jody 1952- 148
　Earlier sketch in SATA 84
Wheeler, Lisa 1963- 200
　Earlier sketch in SATA 162
Wheeler, Opal 1898- 23
Whelan, Elizabeth M(urphy) 1943- 14
Whelan, Gloria 1923- 224
　Earlier sketches in SATA 85, 128, 178
　See also CLR 90
Whelan, Gloria Ann
　See Whelan, Gloria
Whinnem, Reade Scott 224
Whipple, A(ddison) B(eecher) C(olvin)
　1918- 64
Whipple, Cal
　See Whipple, A(ddison) B(eecher) C(olvin)
Whisp, Kennilworthy
　See Rowling, J.K.
Whistler, Reginald John 1905-1944 30
Whistler, Rex
　See Whistler, Reginald John
Whitaker, Zai 183
Whitcher, Susan (Godsil) 1952- 96
Whitcomb, Jon 1906-1988 10
　Obituary 56
Whitcomb, Laura 1958- 214
　Earlier sketch in SATA 171
White, Anne Terry 1896-1980 2
White, Bessie (Felstiner) 1892(?)-1986
　Obituary 50
White, Carolyn 1948- 130
White, Dale
　See Place, Marian T(empleton)
White, Dori 1919- 10
White, E. B. 1899-1985 100
　Obituary 44
　Earlier sketches in SATA 2, 29
　See also CLR 107

White, Eliza Orne 1856-1947
   See YABC 2
White, Elwyn Brooks
   See White, E. B.
White, Florence M(eiman) 1910- *14*
White, Laurence B(arton), Jr. 1935- *10*
White, Lee *223*
   Earlier sketch in SATA *176*
White, Martin 1943- *51*
White, Nancy 1942- *126*
White, Ramy Allison *67*
   Earlier sketch in SATA *1*
White, Robb 1909-1990 .... *83*
   Earlier sketch in SATA *1*
   See also CLR *3*
   See also SAAS *1*
White, Ruth 1942- *186*
   Autobiography Feature *186*
   Earlier sketches in SATA *39, 117, 165*
White, Ruth C.
   See White, Ruth
White, T(erence) H(anbury) 1906-1964 .... *12*
   See also CLR *139*
White, Tekla N. 1934- *115*
White, Timothy (Thomas Anthony)
   1952-2002 .... *60*
White, Tom 1923- *148*
White, William, Jr. 1934- *16*
Whitehead, Don(ald) F. 1908-1981 .... *4*
Whitehead, Jenny 1964- *191*
Whitehead, Kathy 1957- *176*
Whitehouse, Arch
   See Whitehouse, Arthur George Joseph
Whitehouse, Arthur George Joseph
   1895-1979 .... *14*
   Obituary *23*
Whitehouse, Elizabeth S(cott) 1893-1968 .... *35*
Whitehouse, Jeanne
   See Peterson, Jeanne Whitehouse
Whitelaw, Nancy 1933- *166*
   Earlier sketch in SATA *76*
Whitesel, Cheryl Aylward *162*
Whiting, Sue 1960- *205*
Whiting, Susan Allana
   See Whiting, Sue
Whitinger, R. D.
   See Place, Marian T(empleton)
Whitley, David 1984- *225*
Whitley, Mary Ann
   See Sebrey, Mary Ann
Whitley, Peggy 1938- *140*
Whitlock, Pamela 1921(?)-1982
   Obituary *31*
Whitlock, Ralph 1914-1995 .... *35*
Whitman, Alice
   See Marker, Sherry
Whitman, Candace 1958- *208*
Whitman, Sylvia (Choate) 1961- *135*
   Earlier sketch in SATA *85*
Whitman, Walt 1819-1892 .... *20*
Whitman, Walter
   See Whitman, Walt
Whitmore, Arvella 1922- *125*
Whitmore, Benette 1955- *203*
Whitney, Alex(andra) 1922- *14*
Whitney, David C(harles) 1921- *48*
   Brief entry *29*
Whitney, Kim Ablon *162*
Whitney, Phyllis A. 1903-2008 .... *30*
   Obituary *189*
   Earlier sketch in SATA *1*
   See also CLR *59*
Whitney, Phyllis Ayame
   See Whitney, Phyllis A.
Whitney, Sharon 1937- *63*
Whitney, Thomas P. 1917-2007 .... *25*
   Obituary *189*
Whitney, Thomas Porter
   See Whitney, Thomas P.
Whittington, Mary K(athrine) 1941- *75*
Whitworth, John 1945- *123*

Whybrow, Ian *202*
   Earlier sketch in SATA *132*
Whyte, Mal(colm Kenneth, Jr.) 1933- *62*
Whyte, Mary 1953- *148*
   Earlier sketch in SATA *94*
Whyte, Ron 1942(?)-1989
   Obituary *63*
Whytock, Cherry *177*
Wiater, Stanley 1953- *84*
Wibbelsman, Charles J(oseph) 1945- *59*
Wibberley, Leonard 1915-1983 .... *45*
   Obituary *36*
   Earlier sketch in SATA *2*
   See also CLR *3*
Wibberley, Leonard Patrick O'Connor
   See Wibberley, Leonard
Wiberg, Harald (Albin) 1908- *93*
   Brief entry *40*
Wick, Walter 1953- *148*
Wickberg, Susan
   See Rottman, S.L.
Wickens, Elaine *86*
Wicker, Ireene 1905(?)-1987
   Obituary *55*
Wickstrom, Sylvie 1960- *169*
Wickstrom, Thor 1960- *200*
Widdemer, Mabel Cleland 1902-1964 .... *5*
Widener, Terry 1950- *209*
   Earlier sketch in SATA *105*
Widerberg, Siv 1931- *10*
Wiebe, Rudy 1934- *156*
Wiebe, Rudy Henry
   See Wiebe, Rudy
Wieler, Diana (Jean) 1961- *109*
Wiener, Lori 1956- *84*
Wier, Ester (Alberti) 1910-2000 .... *3*
Wiese, Kurt 1887-1974 .... *36*
   Obituary *24*
   Earlier sketch in SATA *3*
   See also CLR *86*
Wiesel, Elie 1928- *56*
Wiesel, Eliezer
   See Wiesel, Elie
Wiesner, David 1956- *181*
   Earlier sketches in SATA *72, 117, 139*
   See also CLR *84*
Wiesner, Portia
   See Takakjian, Portia
Wiesner, William 1899-1984 .... *5*
Wiggers, Raymond 1952- *82*
Wiggin, Eric E. 1939- *167*
   Earlier sketch in SATA *88*
Wiggin, Eric Ellsworth 1939-
   See Wiggin, Eric E.
Wiggin (Riggs), Kate Douglas (Smith)
   1856-1923
   See YABC *1*
   See also CLR *52*
Wiggins, VeraLee (Chesnut) 1928-1995 .... *89*
Wight, Eric 1974- *218*
Wight, James Alfred
   See Herriot, James
Wignell, Edel 1936- *69*
Wijnberg, Ellen *85*
Wikland, Ilon 1930- *93*
   Brief entry *32*
Wikler, Madeline 1943- *114*
Wilber, Donald N(ewton) 1907-1997 .... *35*
Wilbur, C. Keith 1923- *27*
Wilbur, Frances 1921- *107*
Wilbur, Helen L. 1948- *204*
Wilbur, Richard 1921- *108*
   Earlier sketch in SATA *9*
Wilbur, Richard Purdy
   See Wilbur, Richard
Wilburn, Kathy 1948- *68*
Wilcox, Charlotte 1948- *72*
Wilcox, Leah 1975(?)- *207*
Wilcox, R(uth) Turner 1888-1970 .... *36*
Wilcox, Roger
   See Collins, Paul

Wild, Jocelyn 1941- *46*
Wild, Kate 1954- *192*
Wild, Margaret 1948- *197*
   Earlier sketch in SATA *151*
Wild, Robin (Evans) 1936- *46*
Wild, Robyn 1947- *117*
Wilde, D. Gunther
   See Hurwood, Bernhardt J.
Wilde, Oscar 1854(?)-1900 .... *24*
   See also CLR *114*
Wilde, Oscar Fingal O'Flahertie Willis
   See Wilde, Oscar
Wilder, Buck
   See Smith, Tim(othy R.)
Wilder, Laura Elizabeth Ingalls
   See Wilder, Laura Ingalls
Wilder, Laura Ingalls 1867-1957 .... *100*
   Earlier sketches in SATA *15, 29*
   See also CLR *111*
Wildsmith, Brian 1930- *124*
   Earlier sketches in SATA *16, 69*
   See also CLR *52*
   See also SAAS *5*
Wiles, Deborah *171*
Wilhelm, Doug 1952- *190*
Wilhelm, Hans 1945- *196*
   Autobiography Feature *196*
   Earlier sketches in SATA *58, 135*
   See also CLR *46*
   See also SAAS *21*
Wilkie, Katharine E(lliott) 1904-1980 .... *31*
Wilkin, Eloise 1904-1987 .... *49*
   Obituary *54*
Wilkins, Frances 1923- *14*
Wilkins, Kim *147*
Wilkins, Marilyn (Ruth) 1926- *30*
Wilkins, Marne
   See Wilkins, Marilyn (Ruth)
Wilkins, Mary Huiskamp 1926- *2*
   See also CLR *42*
Wilkins, Mary Huiskamp Calhoun
   See Wilkins, Mary Huiskamp
Wilkins, Rose *180*
Wilkinson, (Thomas) Barry 1923- *50*
   Brief entry *32*
Wilkinson, Beth 1925- *80*
Wilkinson, Brenda 1946- *91*
   Earlier sketch in SATA *14*
   See also CLR *20*
Wilkinson, (John) Burke 1913-2000 .... *4*
Wilkinson, Carole 1950- *210*
Wilkinson, Sylvia 1940- *56*
   Brief entry *39*
Wilkon, Jozef 1930- *133*
   Earlier sketches in SATA *31, 71*
Wilkowski, Sue *193*
Wilks, Michael Thomas 1947- *44*
   See Wilks, Mike
Wilks, Mike *224*
   See Wilks, Michael Thomas
Will
   See Lipkind, William
Willard, Barbara (Mary) 1909-1994 .... *74*
   Earlier sketch in SATA *17*
   See also CLR *2*
   See also SAAS *5*
Willard, Elizabeth Kimmel
   See Kimmel, Elizabeth Cody
Willard, Mildred Wilds 1911-1978 .... *14*
Willard, Nancy 1936- *191*
   Brief entry *30*
   Earlier sketches in SATA *37, 71, 127*
   See also CLR *5*
Willcox, Isobel 1907-1996 .... *42*
Willems, Mo *180*
   Earlier sketch in SATA *154*
   See also CLR *114*
Willett, Edward 1959- *115*
Willett, Edward C.
   See Willett, Edward
Willey, Bee *184*

Willey, Margaret 1950- 86
Willey, Robert
 See Ley, Willy
Willhoite, Michael A. 1946- 71
William, Kate
 See Armstrong, Jennifer
Williams, Alex 1969- 209
Williams, Arlene 171
Williams, Barbara 1925- 107
 Earlier sketch in SATA *11*
 See also CLR *48*
 See also SAAS *16*
Williams, Barbara 1937- 62
Williams, Beryl
 See Epstein, Beryl
Williams, Brian (Peter) 1943- 54
Williams, Carol Lynch 1959- 212
 Earlier sketch in SATA *110*
Williams, Charles
 See Collier, James Lincoln
Williams, Clyde C. 1881-1974 8
 Obituary 27
Williams, Coe
 See Harrison, C(hester) William
Williams, Colleen Madonna Flood 1963- .. 156
Williams, Cynthia G. 1958- 123
Williams, Dar 1967- 168
Williams, Donna Reilly 1945- 83
Williams, Dorothy
 See Williams, Marcia
Williams, Dorothy Snowden
 See Williams, Dar
Williams, Eric (Ernest) 1911-1983 14
 Obituary 38
Williams, Ferelith Eccles
 See Eccles Williams, Ferelith
Williams, Frances B.
 See Browin, Frances Williams
Williams, Garth (Montgomery) 1912-1996 .. 66
 Obituary 90
 Earlier sketch in SATA *18*
 See also CLR *57*
 See also SAAS *7*
Williams, Guy R(ichard) 1920- 11
Williams, Hawley
 See Heyliger, William
Williams, Helen 1948- 77
Williams, J. R.
 See Williams, Jeanne
Williams, J. Walker
 See Wodehouse, P. G.
Williams, Jay 1914-1978 41
 Obituary 24
 Earlier sketch in SATA *3*
 See also CLR *8*
Williams, Jeanne 1930- 5
Williams, Jenny 1939- 60
Williams, Karen Lynn 1952- 224
 Earlier sketches in SATA *66, 99*
Williams, Kathryn 1981- 222
Williams, Kit 1946(?)- 44
 See also CLR *4*
Williams, L. E.
 See Williams, Laura E.
Williams, Laura E.
 See Williams, Laura Ellen
Williams, Laura Ellen 180
Williams, Leslie 1941- 42
Williams, Linda 1948- 59
Williams, Louise Bonino 1904(?)-1984
 Obituary 39
Williams, Lynn
 See Hale, Arlene
Williams, Marcia 1945- 159
 Earlier sketches in SATA *71, 97*
Williams, Marcia Dorothy
 See Williams, Marcia
Williams, Margery
 See Bianco, Margery Williams
Williams, Mark
 See Arthur, Robert, (Jr.)

Williams, Mark London 1959- 140
Williams, Maureen 1951- 12
Williams, Michael
 See St. John, Wylly Folk
Williams, Patrick J.
 See Griffin, W. E. B.
Williams, Paulette Linda
 See Shange, Ntozake
Williams, Pete
 See Faulknor, Cliff(ord Vernon)
Williams, S. P.
 See Hart, Virginia
Williams, Sam 177
 Earlier sketch in SATA *124*
Williams, Selma R(uth) 1925- 14
Williams, Sherley Anne 1944-1999 78
 Obituary 116
Williams, Sheron 1955- 77
Williams, Shirley
 See Williams, Sherley Anne
Williams, Slim
 See Williams, Clyde C.
Williams, Sophy 1965- 135
Williams, Sue 1948-2007 208
Williams, Susan
 See Beckhorn, Susan Williams
Williams, Suzanne
 See Williams, Suzanne Morgan
Williams, Suzanne 1953- 202
 Earlier sketch in SATA *71*
Williams, Suzanne M.
 See Williams, Suzanne Morgan
Williams, Suzanne Morgan 1949- 207
Williams, Ursula Moray
 See Moray Williams, Ursula
Williams, Vera B(aker) 1927- 102
 Brief entry 33
 Earlier sketch in SATA *53*
 See also CLR *9*
Williams-Andriani, Renee 1963- 98
Williams-Ellis, (Mary) Amabel (Nassau
 Strachey) 1894-1984 29
 Obituary 41
Williams-Garcia, Rita 1957- 160
 Earlier sketch in SATA *98*
 See also CLR *36*
Williamson, Gwyneth 1965- 109
Williamson, Henry (William) 1895-1977 37
 Obituary 30
Williamson, Joanne S(mall) 1926- 122
 Earlier sketch in SATA *3*
Williamson, Kate T. 1979- 215
Williamson, Melanie 196
Willis, Charles
 See Clarke, Arthur C.
Willis, Connie 1945- 110
 See also CLR *66*
Willis, Cynthia Chapman 215
Willis, Jeanne 1959- 195
 Earlier sketches in SATA *61, 123*
Willis, Jeanne Mary
 See Willis, Jeanne
Willis, Meredith Sue 1946- 101
Willis, Nancy Carol 1952- 139
 Earlier sketch in SATA *93*
Willis, Paul J. 1955- 113
Willms, Russ 95
Willoughby, Lee Davis
 See Avallone, Michael (Angelo, Jr.)
 and Brandner, Gary (Phil)
 and Deming, Richard
 and DeAndrea, William L(ouis)
 and Laymon, Richard (Carl)
 and Streib, Dan(iel Thomas)
 and Toombs, John
 and Webb, Jean Francis (III)
Willson, Robina Beckles
 See Beckles Willson, Robina
Wilma, Dana
 See Faralla, Dana
Wilsdorf, Anne 1954- 191

Wilson, Anne 1974- 224
Wilson, April 80
Wilson, Barbara Ker
 See Ker Wilson, Barbara
Wilson, Beth P(ierre) 8
Wilson, Budge 1927- 55
 Brief entry 51
Wilson, Carletta 1951- 81
Wilson, Carter 1941- 6
Wilson, Charles Morrow 1905-1977 30
Wilson, Christopher B. 1910(?)-1985
 Obituary 46
Wilson, Darryl B(abe) 1939- 90
Wilson, Diane Lee 172
Wilson, Dirk
 See Pohl, Frederik
Wilson, Dorothy Clarke 1904-2003 16
Wilson, Edward A(rthur) 1886-1970 38
Wilson, Ellen (Janet Cameron) (?)-1976 9
 Obituary 26
Wilson, Eric (H.) 1940- 34
 Brief entry 32
Wilson, Erica 51
Wilson, Forrest 1918- 27
Wilson, Gahan 1930- 35
 Brief entry 27
Wilson, Gina 1943- 85
 Brief entry 34
 Earlier sketch in SATA *36*
Wilson, (Leslie) Granville 1912- 14
Wilson, Hazel (Hutchins) 1898-1992 3
 Obituary 73
Wilson, J(erry) M. 1964- 121
Wilson, Jacqueline 1945- 199
 Brief entry 52
 Earlier sketches in SATA *61, 102, 153*
Wilson, John 1922- 22
Wilson, John 1951- 182
Wilson, John Alexander
 See Wilson, John
Wilson, Johnniece Marshall 1944- 75
Wilson, Jonathan 1950- 181
Wilson, Joyce M. 84
 Earlier sketch in SATA *21*
 See also SAAS *24*
Wilson, Karma 221
 Earlier sketch in SATA *174*
Wilson, Leslie 1952- 166
Wilson, Linda Miller 1936- 116
Wilson, Lionel 1924-2003 33
 Brief entry 31
 Obituary 144
Wilson, Marjorie
 See Wilson, Budge
Wilson, Martin 1973- 205
Wilson, Maurice (Charles John) 1914- 46
Wilson, Nancy Hope 1947- 138
 Earlier sketch in SATA *81*
Wilson, Nathan D.
 See Wilson, N.D.
Wilson, N.D. 1978- 194
Wilson, Nick
 See Ellis, Edward S.
Wilson, Phil 1948- 181
Wilson, Ron(ald William) 1941- 38
Wilson, Sarah 1934- 208
 Earlier sketches in SATA *50, 142*
Wilson, Tom 1931- 33
 Brief entry 30
Wilson, Troy 1970- 169
Wilson, Walt(er N.) 1939- 14
Wilson-Max, Ken 1965- 170
 Earlier sketch in SATA *93*
Wilton, Elizabeth 1937- 14
Wilton, Hal
 See Pepper, Frank S.
Wilwerding, Walter Joseph 1891-1966 9
Wimmer, Mike 1961- 194
 Earlier sketch in SATA *70*
Winborn, Marsha (Lynn) 1947- 75

Winch, John 1944- 165
Earlier sketch in SATA *117*
Winchester, James H(ugh) 1917-1985 30
Obituary 45
Winchester, Stanley
See Youd, Samuel
Windawi, Thura al- 1983(?)- 165
Winders, Gertrude Hecker -1987 3
Windham, Basil
See Wodehouse, P. G.
Windham, Kathryn T(ucker) 1918- 14
Windham, Sophie 184
Windling, Terri 1958- 151
Windrow, Martin
See Windrow, Martin Clive
Windrow, Martin C.
See Windrow, Martin Clive
Windrow, Martin Clive 1944- 68
Windsor, Claire
See Hamerstrom, Frances
Windsor, Linda 1950- 124
Windsor, Patricia 1938- 78
Earlier sketch in SATA *30*
See also SAAS *19*
Wineman-Marcus, Irene 1952- 81
Winer, Yvonne 1934- 120
Winerip, Michael 175
Winfield, Arthur M.
See Stratemeyer, Edward L.
Winfield, Edna
See Stratemeyer, Edward L.
Winfield, Julia
See Armstrong, Jennifer
Wing, Natasha 1960- 200
Earlier sketch in SATA *82*
Wingerter, Linda S. 1973(?)- 207
Winget, Susan 211
Winick, Judd 1970- 124
Winks, Robin William 1930-2003 61
Winn, Alison
See Wharmby, Margot
Winn, Chris 1952- 42
Winn, Janet Bruce 1928- 43
Winn, Marie 1936(?)- 38
Winnick, Karen B. 1946- 211
Winnick, Karen B(eth) B(inkoff) 1946- 51
Winn-Lederer, Ilene 198
Winslow, Barbara 1947- 91
Winstead, Rosie 180
Winston, Clara 1921-1983 54
Obituary 39
Winston, Richard 1917-1979 54
Winston, Sherri 1964(?)- 201
Winter, Janet 1926- 126
Winter, Jeanette 1939- 184
Earlier sketch in SATA *151*
Winter, Jonah 1962- 225
Earlier sketch in SATA *179*
Winter, Milo (Kendall) 1888-1956 21
Winter, Paula Cecelia 1929- 48
Winter, R. R.
See Winterbotham, R(ussell) R(obert)
Winter, Susan 182
Winterbotham, R(ussell) R(obert)
1904-1971 10
Winterbotham, Russ
See Winterbotham, R(ussell) R(obert)
Winterfeld, Henry 1901-1990 55
Winters, J. C.
See Cross, Gilbert B.
Winters, Jon
See Cross, Gilbert B.
Winters, Katherine
See Winters, Kay
Winters, Kay 1936- 153
Earlier sketch in SATA *103*
Winters, Nina 1944- 62
Winters, Paul A. 1965- 106
Winterson, Jeanette 1959- 190
Winterton, Gayle
See Adams, William Taylor

Winthrop, Elizabeth 1948- 164
Autobiography Feature 116
Earlier sketches in SATA *8, 76*
See also CLR *89*
Winton, Ian (Kenneth) 1960- 76
Winton, Tim 1960- 98
Wintz-Litty, Julie
See Litty, Julie
Wirt, Ann
See Benson, Mildred
Wirt, Mildred A.
See Benson, Mildred
Wirtenberg, Patricia Z. 1932-2007 10
Wirtenberg, Patricia Zarrella
See Wirtenberg, Patricia Z.
Wirth, Beverly 1938- 63
Wirths, Claudine (Turner) G(ibson)
1926-2000 104
Earlier sketch in SATA *64*
Wise, Bill 1958- 191
Wise, Lenny
See Wise, Leonard
Wise, Leonard 1940- 167
Wise, Leonard A.
See Wise, Leonard
Wise, Leonard Allan
See Wise, Leonard
Wise, William 1923- 163
Earlier sketch in SATA *4*
Wise, Winifred E. 2
Wiseman, Ann (Sayre) 1926- 31
Wiseman, B(ernard) 1922-1995 4
Wiseman, David 1916- 43
Brief entry 40
Wiseman, Eva 1947- 210
Wishinsky, Frieda 1948- 166
Earlier sketches in SATA *70, 112*
Wisler, G(ary) Clifton 1950- 103
Brief entry 46
Earlier sketch in SATA *58*
Wismer, Donald (Richard) 1946- 59
Wisner, Bill
See Wisner, William L.
Wisner, William L. 1914(?)-1983 42
Wisnewski, David 1953-2002
See Wisniewski, David
Wisniewski, David 1953-2002 95
Obituary 139
See also CLR *51*
Wister, Owen 1860-1938 62
Witham, (Phillip) Ross 1917- 37
Withers, Carl A. 1900-1970 14
Withers, Pam 1956- 182
Withrow, Sarah 1966- 199
Earlier sketch in SATA *124*
Witt, Dick 1948- 80
Witt, Shirley Hill 1934- 17
Wittanen, Etolin 1907- 55
Wittels, Harriet Joan 1938- 31
Wittig, Susan
See Albert, Susan Wittig
Wittlinger, Ellen 1948- 189
Autobiography Feature 128
Earlier sketches in SATA *83, 122*
Wittman, Sally (Anne Christensen) 1941- 30
Witty, Paul 1898-1976 50
Obituary 30
Wodehouse, P. G. 1881-1975 22
Wodehouse, Pelham Grenville
See Wodehouse, P. G.
Wodge, Dreary
See Gorey, Edward (St. John)
Woelfle, Gretchen 1945- 145
Wohlberg, Meg 1905-1990 41
Obituary 66
Wohlrabe, Raymond A. 1900-1977 4
Wohnoutka, Mike 195

Wojciechowska, Maia (Teresa) 1927-2002 ... 83
Autobiography Feature 104
Obituary 134
Earlier sketches in SATA *1, 28*
See also CLR *1*
See also SAAS *1*
Wojciechowski, Susan 126
Earlier sketch in SATA *78*
Wojnarowski, Adrian 1970- 190
Wojtusik, Elizabeth 208
Wolcott, Patty 1929- 14
Wold, Allen L. 1943- 64
Wold, Jo Anne 1938- 30
Woldin, Beth Weiner 1955- 34
Wolf, Allan 1963- 192
Wolf, Bernard 1930- 102
Brief entry 37
Wolf, Erica (Van Varick) 1978- 156
Wolf, Gita 1956- 101
Wolf, J. M.
See Wolf, Joan M.
Wolf, Janet 1957- 78
Wolf, Joan M. 1966- 193
Wolf, Sallie 1950- 205
Earlier sketch in SATA *80*
Wolfe, Art 1952- 76
Wolfe, Burton H. 1932- 5
Wolfe, Frances 216
Wolfe, Gene 1931- 165
Earlier sketch in SATA *118*
Wolfe, Gene Rodman
See Wolfe, Gene
Wolfe, Gillian 199
Wolfe, Louis 1905-1985 8
Obituary 133
Wolfe, Rinna (Evelyn) 1925- 38
Wolfenden, George
See Beardmore, George
Wolfer, Dianne 1961- 167
Autobiography Feature 117
Earlier sketch in SATA *104*
Wolff, Alexander (Nikolaus) 1957- 137
Earlier sketch in SATA *63*
Wolff, Ashley 1956- 203
Earlier sketches in SATA *50, 81, 155*
Wolff, Diane 1945- 27
Wolff, Ferida 1946- 164
Earlier sketch in SATA *79*
Wolff, Jason 1972- 213
Wolff, Jennifer Ashley
See Wolff, Ashley
Wolff, Nancy 202
Wolff, Robert Jay 1905-1977 10
Wolff, Sonia
See Levitin, Sonia
Wolff, Virginia Euwer 1937- 137
Earlier sketch in SATA *78*
See also CLR *62*
Wolfman, Judy 1933- 138
Wolfson, Evelyn 1937- 62
Wolitzer, Hilma 1930- 31
Wolkoff, Judie (Edwards) 93
Brief entry 37
Wolkstein, Diane 1942- 138
Earlier sketches in SATA *7, 82*
Wollheim, Donald A(llen) 1914-1990
Obituary 69
Wolny, P.
See Janeczko, Paul B(ryan)
Wolters, Richard A. 1920-1993 35
Wondriska, William 1931- 6
Wong, Jade Snow 1922-2006 112
Obituary 175
Wong, Janet S. 1962- 210
Earlier sketches in SATA *98, 148*
See also CLR *94*
Wong, Nicole 214
Woo, Howie 1974- 207
Wood, Addie Robinson
See Wiggin, Eric E.
Wood, Anne (Savage) 1937- 64

Wood, Audrey 198
  Brief entry 44
  Earlier sketches in SATA 50, 81, 139
  See also CLR 26
Wood, Catherine
  See Etchison, Birdie L(ee)
Wood, David 1944- 212
  Earlier sketch in SATA 87
Wood, Don 1945- 50
  Brief entry 44
  See also CLR 26
Wood, Douglas 1951- 180
  Earlier sketches in SATA 81, 132
Wood, Douglas Eric
  See Wood, Douglas
Wood, Edgar A(llardyce) 1907-1998 14
Wood, Esther
  See Brady, Esther Wood
Wood, Frances Elizabeth 34
Wood, Frances M. 1951- 97
Wood, Jacqueline
  See Wood, Jakki
Wood, Jakki 1957- 211
Wood, James Playsted 1905- 1
Wood, Jenny 1955- 88
Wood, John Norris 1930- 85
Wood, June Rae 1946- 120
  Earlier sketch in SATA 79
  See also CLR 82
Wood, Kerry
  See Wood, Edgar A(llardyce)
Wood, Kim Marie 134
Wood, Laura N.
  See Roper, Laura (Newbold) Wood
Wood, Linda C(arol) 1945- 59
Wood, Marcia 1956- 80
Wood, Marcia Mae
  See Wood, Marcia
Wood, Nancy
  See Wood, Nancy C.
Wood, Nancy C. 1936- 178
  Earlier sketch in SATA 6
Wood, Nuria
  See Nobisso, Josephine
Wood, Owen 1929- 64
Wood, Phyllis Anderson 1923- 33
  Brief entry 30
Wood, Richard 1949- 110
Wood, Tim(othy William Russell) 1946- 88
Wood, Wallace 1927-1981
  Obituary 33
Woodard, Carol 1929- 14
Woodburn, John Henry 1914- 11
Woodbury, David Oakes 1896-1981 62
Woodford, Peggy 1937- 25
Woodhouse, Barbara (Blackburn)
  1910-1988 63
Woodhull, Ann Love 194
Wooding, Chris 1977- 166
Wooding, Sharon
  See Wooding, Sharon L(ouise)
Wooding, Sharon L(ouise) 1943- 66
Woodman, Allen 1954- 76
Woodrich, Mary Neville 1915- 2
Woodruff, Elvira 1951- 211
  Earlier sketches in SATA 70, 106, 162
Woodruff, Joan Leslie 1953- 104
Woodruff, Liza 1971(?)- 182
Woodruff, Marian
  See Goudge, Eileen
Woodruff, Noah 1977- 86
Woods, George A(llan) 1926-1988 30
  Obituary 57
Woods, Geraldine 1948- 111
  Brief entry 42
  Earlier sketch in SATA 56
Woods, Harold 1945- 56
  Brief entry 42
Woods, Lawrence
  See Lowndes, Robert A(ugustine) W(ard)
Woods, Margaret 1921- 2

Woods, Nat
  See Stratemeyer, Edward L.
Woods, Titania
  See Weatherly, Lee
Woodson, Jack
  See Woodson, John Waddie Jr.
Woodson, Jacqueline 1964- 189
  Earlier sketches in SATA 94, 139
  See also CLR 49
Woodson, Jacqueline Amanda
  See Woodson, Jacqueline
Woodson, John Waddie Jr. 1913- 10
Woodtor, Dee
  See Woodtor, Delores Parmer
Woodtor, Dee Parmer 1945(?)-2002
  See Woodtor, Delores Parmer
Woodtor, Delores Parmer 1945-2002 93
Wood-Trost, Lucille
  See Trost, Lucille W(ood)
Woodward, (Landon) Cleveland 1900-1986 . 10
  Obituary 48
Woodworth, Chris 1957- 168
Woodworth, Viki 1952- 127
Woody, Regina Jones 1894-1983 3
Woodyadd, Charlotte
  See Hough, Charlotte
Woog, Adam 1953- 125
  Earlier sketch in SATA 84
Wooldridge, Connie Nordhielm 1950- 143
  Earlier sketch in SATA 92
Wooldridge, Frosty 1947- 140
Wooldridge, Rhoda 1906-1988 22
Wooley, Susan Frelick 1945- 113
Woolf, Paula 1950- 104
Woolfe, Angela 1976- 169
Woolley, Catherine 1904-2005 3
  Obituary 166
Woolman, Steven 1969-2004 163
  Earlier sketch in SATA 90
Woolsey, Janette 1904-1989 3
  Obituary 131
Worcester, Donald E(mmet) 1915- 18
Word, Reagan 1944- 103
Work, Virginia 1946- 57
  Brief entry 45
Worline, Bonnie Bess 1914- 14
Wormell, Christopher 1955- 154
  Earlier sketch in SATA 103
Wormell, Mary 1959- 96
Wormser, Richard 1933- 106
  Autobiography Feature 118
  See also SAAS 26
Wormser, Sophie 1897-1979 22
Worth, Richard
  See Wiggin, Eric E.
Worth, Richard 1945- 59
  Brief entry 46
Worth, Valerie 1933-1994 81
  Earlier sketches in SATA 8, 70
  See also CLR 21
Worthington, Leonie 1956- 200
Wortis, Avi
  See Avi
Wortis, Edward Irving
  See Avi
Wosmek, Frances 1917- 29
Woychuk, Denis 1953- 71
Wrede, Patricia C(ollins) 1953- 146
  Earlier sketch in SATA 67
Wriggins, Sally Hovey 1922- 17
Wright, Alexandra 1979- 103
Wright, Betty Ren 1927- 109
  Brief entry 48
  Earlier sketch in SATA 63
Wright, Cliff 1963- 168
  Earlier sketch in SATA 76
Wright, Courtni
  See Wright, Courtni C(rump)
Wright, Courtni C(rump) 1950- 84
Wright, Courtni Crump
  See Wright, Courtni C(rump)

Wright, Dare 1914(?)-2001 21
  Obituary 124
Wright, David K. 1943- 112
  Earlier sketch in SATA 73
Wright, Elinor
  See Lyon, Elinor
Wright, Enid Meadowcroft (LaMonte)
  1898-1966 3
Wright, Esmond 1915-2003 10
Wright, Frances Fitzpatrick 1897-1982 10
Wright, J. B.
  See Barkan, Joanne
Wright, Johanna 220
Wright, Judith 1915-2000 14
  Obituary 121
Wright, Judith Arundell
  See Wright, Judith
Wright, Katrina
  See Gater, Dilys
Wright, Kenneth
  See del Rey, Lester
Wright, Kit 1944- 87
Wright, Leslie B(ailey) 1959- 91
Wright, Michael 1954- 198
Wright, Nancy Means 38
Wright, R(obert) H(amilton) 1906- 6
Wright, Rachel 220
  Earlier sketch in SATA 134
Wright, Susan Kimmel 1950- 97
Wrightfrierson
  See Wright-Frierson, Virginia (Marguerite)
Wright-Frierson, Virginia (Marguerite)
  1949- 110
  Earlier sketch in SATA 58
Wrightson, Alice Patricia
  See Wrightson, Patricia
Wrightson, Patricia 1921-2010 112
  Obituary 215
  Earlier sketches in SATA 8, 66
  See also CLR 154
  See also SAAS 4
Wroble, Lisa A. 1963- 134
Wrongo, I.B.
  See Katz, Alan
Wronker, Lili
  See Wronker, Lili Cassel
Wronker, Lili Cassel 1924- 10
Wryde, Dogear
  See Gorey, Edward (St. John)
Wu, Donald 212
Wu, Elizabeth
  See Wu, Liz
Wu, Liz 184
Wu, Norbert 1961- 155
  Earlier sketch in SATA 101
Wulf, Linda Press 205
Wulffson, Don 1943- 155
  Earlier sketches in SATA 32, 88
Wulffson, Don L.
  See Wulffson, Don
Wummer, Amy 1955- 201
Wunderli, Stephen 1958- 79
Wunsch, Josephine (McLean) 1914- 64
Wunsch, Marjory 1942- 220
  Earlier sketch in SATA 82
Wuorio, Eva-Lis 1918- 34
  Brief entry 28
Wurts, Janny 1953- 98
Wyatt, B. D.
  See Robinson, Spider
Wyatt, David 1968- 185
Wyatt, Jane
  See Bradbury, Bianca (Ryley)
Wyatt, Melissa 1963- 177
Wyatt, Valerie 209
Wyeth, Betsy James 1921- 41
Wyeth, N(ewell) C(onvers) 1882-1945 17
  See also CLR 106
Wyler, Rose 1909-2000 18
  Obituary 121
Wylie, Betty Jane 48

Wylie, Laura
　See Matthews, Patricia
Wylie, Laurie
　See Matthews, Patricia
Wyllie, Stephen 86
Wyman, Andrea 75
Wyman, Carolyn 1956- 83
Wymer, Norman (George) 1911- 25
Wynard, Talbot
　See Hamilton, Charles (Harold St. John)
Wyndham, John
　See Harris, John (Wyndham Parkes Lucas)
　Beynon
Wyndham, Lee
　See Hyndman, Jane Andrews Lee
Wyndham, Robert
　See Hyndman, Robert Utley
Wynne, Patricia J. 210
Wynne-Jones, Tim 1948- 186
　Autobiography Feature 136
　Earlier sketches in SATA 67, 96, 136
　See also CLR 58
Wynne-Jones, Timothy
　See Wynne-Jones, Tim
Wynter, Edward (John) 1914- 14
Wynyard, Talbot
　See Hamilton, Charles (Harold St. John)
Wyss, Johann David Von 1743-1818 29
　Brief entry 27
　See also CLR 92
Wyss, Thelma Hatch 1934- 202
　Earlier sketches in SATA 10, 140

X

Xavier, Father
　See Hurwood, Bernhardt J.
Xuan, YongSheng 1952- 116
　Autobiography Feature 119

Y

Yaccarino, Dan 192
　Earlier sketch in SATA 141
Yadin, (Rav-Aloof) Yigael 1917-1984 55
Yaffe, Alan
　See Yorinks, Arthur
Yagher, Kevin 1962- 143
Yakovetic, (Joseph Sandy) 1952- 59
Yakovetic, Joe
　See Yakovetic, (Joseph Sandy)
Yamada, Utako 1963- 188
Yamaguchi, Marianne (Illenberger) 1936- 7
Yamaka, Sara 1978- 92
Yamanaka, Lois-Ann 1961- 166
Yamasaki, Katie 206
Yancey, Diane 1951- 138
　Earlier sketch in SATA 81
Yancey, Richard 193
Yancey, Rick
　See Yancey, Richard
Yang, Belle 1960- 170
Yang, James 1960- 190
Yang, Jay 1941- 12
Yang, Mingyi 1943- 72
Yarbrough, Camille 1938- 79
　See also CLR 29
Yarbrough, Ira 1910(?)-1983
　Obituary 35
Yaroslava
　See Mills, Yaroslava Surmach
Yarrow, Peter 1938- 195
Yashima, Taro
　See Iwamatsu, Jun Atsushi
Yates, Elizabeth 1905-2001 68
　Obituary 128
　Earlier sketch in SATA 4
　See also SAAS 6

Yates, Janelle K(aye) 1957- 77
Yates, John 1939- 74
Yates, Kelly 1971- 208
Yates, Louise 1983(?)- 218
Yates, Philip 1956- 212
　Earlier sketches in SATA 92, 149
Yates, Raymond F(rancis) 1895-1966 31
Yaukey, Grace S(ydenstricker) 1899-1994 ... 80
　Earlier sketch in SATA 5
Yazzie, Johnson 1946- 205
Ye, Ting-xing 1952- 106
Yeahpau, Thomas M. 1975- 187
Yeakley, Marjory Hall 1908- 21
Yeatman, Linda 1938- 42
Yeatts, Tabatha 1970- 215
Yee, Brenda Shannon 133
Yee, Lisa 1959- 218
　Earlier sketch in SATA 160
Yee, Paul 1956- 211
　Earlier sketches in SATA 67, 96, 143
　See also CLR 44
Yee, Tammy 206
Yee, Wong Herbert 1953- 172
　Earlier sketches in SATA 78, 115
Yeh, Chun-Chan 1914- 79
Ye Junjian
　See Yeh, Chun-Chan
Yelchin, Eugene 1956- 196
Yenawine, Philip 1942- 85
Yensid, Retlaw
　See Disney, Walt(er Elias)
Yeo, Wilma (Lethem) 1918-1994 81
　Earlier sketch in SATA 24
Yeoman, John 1934- 80
　Earlier sketch in SATA 28
　See also CLR 46
Yep, Kathleen S. 203
Yep, Laurence 1948- 213
　Earlier sketches in SATA 7, 69, 123, 176
　See also CLR 132
Yep, Laurence Michael
　See Yep, Laurence
Yepsen, Roger B(ennet), Jr. 1947- 59
Yerian, Cameron John 21
Yerian, Margaret A. 21
Yerxa, Leo 1947- 181
Yetska
　See Ironside, Jetske
Yezerski, Thomas F. 1969- 190
Yin 194
Ylvisaker, Anne 1965(?)- 172
Yoder, Carolyn P. 1953- 149
Yoder, Carolyn Patricia
　See Yoder, Carolyn P.
Yoder, Dorothy Meenen 1921- 96
Yoder, Dot
　See Yoder, Dorothy Meenen
Yoder, Walter D. 1933- 88
Yohalem, Eve 219
Yolen, Jane 1939- 194
　Autobiography Feature 111
　Earlier sketches in SATA 4, 40, 75, 112, 158
　See also CLR 149
　See also SAAS 1
Yolen, Jane Hyatt
　See Yolen, Jane
Yonezu, Yusuke 196
Yonge, Charlotte 1823-1901 17
Yonge, Charlotte Mary
　See Yonge, Charlotte
Yoo, Paula 1969(?)- 174
Yoo, Taeeun 191
Yoon, Salina 1972- 204
Yorinks, Adrienne 1956- 171
Yorinks, Arthur 1953- 200
　Earlier sketches in SATA 33, 49, 85, 144
　See also CLR 20
York, Alison
　See Nicole, Christopher (Robin)
York, Andrew
　See Nicole, Christopher (Robin)

York, Carol Beach 1928- 77
　Earlier sketch in SATA 6
York, Rebecca
　See Buckholtz, Eileen (Garber)
　and Glick, Ruth (Burtnick)
York, Simon
　See Heinlein, Robert A.
Yoshida, Toshi 1911- 77
Yoshikawa, Sachiko 181
Yost, Edna 1889-1971
　Obituary 26
Youd, C. S.
　See Youd, Samuel
Youd, Samuel 1922- 135
　Brief entry 30
　Earlier sketch in SATA 47
　See also CLR 2
　See also SAAS 6
Youme
　See Landowne, Youme
Young, Amy L. 185
Young, Anne Mortimer
　See Mortimer, Anne
Young, Bob
　See Young, Robert W(illiam)
　and Young, James Robert
Young, Carol 1945- 102
Young, Catherine
　See Olds, Helen Diehl
Young, Clarence
　See Garis, Howard R.
　and Stratemeyer, Edward L.
Young, Collier
　See Bloch, Robert (Albert)
Young, Dan 1952- 126
Young, Dianne 1959- 88
Young, Dorothea Bennett 1924- 31
Young, Ed 1931- 211
　Earlier sketches in SATA 10, 74, 122, 173
　See also CLR 27
Young, Ed Tse-chun
　See Young, Ed
Young, Edward
　See Reinfeld, Fred
Young, E.L. 1973- 219
Young, Elaine L.
　See Schulte, Elaine L(ouise)
Young, Emma L.
　See Young, E.L.
Young, James
　See Graham, Ian
Young, Jan
　See Young, Janet Randall
Young, Janet 1957- 188
Young, Janet Randall 1919-1994 3
Young, Janet Ruth
　See Young, Janet
Young, Jeff C. 1948- 132
Young, John
　See Macintosh, Brownie
Young, Judy 1956- 207
　Earlier sketch in SATA 155
Young, Judy (Elaine) Dockrey 1949- 72
Young, Karen Romano 1959- 168
　Earlier sketch in SATA 116
Young, Ken 1956- 86
Young, Lois Horton 1911-1981 26
Young, Louisa 161
Young, Louise B. 1919- 64
Young, Margaret B. 1922-2009 2
Young, Margaret Buckner
　See Young, Margaret B.
Young, Mary 1940- 89
Young, Miriam 1913-1974 7
Young, Noela 1930- 89
Young, (Rodney Lee) Patrick (Jr.) 1937- 22
Young, Percy M(arshall) 1912-2004 31
　Obituary 154
Young, Richard Alan 1946- 72
Young, Robert W(illiam) 1916-1969 3
Young, Ross B. 1955- 150

Young, Ruth 1946- 67
Young, Sara
  See Pennypacker, Sara
Young, Scott A. 1918-2005 5
Young, Scott Alexander
  See Young, Scott A.
Young, Selina 1971-2006 201
Young, Vivien
  See Gater, Dilys
Younger, Barbara 1954- 108
Youngs, Betty 1934-1985 53
  Obituary 42
Younkin, Paula 1942- 77
Yount, Lisa (Ann) 1944- 124
  Earlier sketch in SATA 74
Yourgrau, Barry 179
Yuditskaya, Tatyana 1964- 75
Yum, Hyewon 211
Yumoto, Kazumi 1959- 153

                    Z

Zach, Cheryl (Byrd) 1947- 98
  Brief entry 51
  Earlier sketch in SATA 58
  See also SAAS 24
Zacharias, Gary L. 1946- 153
Zadoff, Allen 1967- 224
Zaffo, George J. (?)-1984 42
Zagarenski, Pamela 1969(?)- 183
Zagwyn, Deborah Turney 1953- 138
  Earlier sketch in SATA 78
Zahares, Wade 193
Zahn, Timothy 1951- 156
  Earlier sketch in SATA 91
Zaid, Barry 1938- 51
Zaidenberg, Arthur 1908(?)-1990 34
  Obituary 66
Zalben, Jane Breskin 1950- 170
  Earlier sketches in SATA 7, 79, 120
  See also CLR 84
Zallinger, Jean (Day) 1918- 115
  Earlier sketches in SATA 14, 80
Zallinger, Peter Franz 1943- 49
Zambreno, Mary Frances 1954- 140
  Earlier sketch in SATA 75
Zanderbergen, George
  See May, Julian
Zappa, Ahmet 1974- 180
Zappa, Ahmet Emuukha Rodan
  See Zappa, Ahmet
Zappler, Lisbeth 1930- 10
Zarchy, Harry 1912-1987 34
Zarin, Cynthia 1959- 192
  Earlier sketch in SATA 108
Zaring, Jane (Thomas) 1936- 40
Zarins, Joyce Audy
  See dos Santos, Joyce Audy
Zaslavsky, Claudia 1917- 36
Zaugg, Sandra L. 1938- 118
Zaugg, Sandy
  See Zaugg, Sandra L.
Zaunders, Bo 1939- 137
Zawadzki, Marek 1958- 97
Zebra, A.
  See Scoltock, Jack
Zebrowski, George 1945- 67
Zebrowski, George T.
  See Zebrowski, George
Zecca, Katherine 207
Zeck, Gerald Anthony 1939- 40
Zeck, Gerry
  See Zeck, Gerald Anthony

Zed, Dr.
  See Penrose, Gordon
Zei, Alki 1925- 24
  See also CLR 6
Zeier, Joan T(heresa) 1931- 81
Zeinert, Karen 1942-2002 137
  Earlier sketch in SATA 79
Zeises, Lara M. 1976- 184
  Earlier sketch in SATA 145
Zelazny, Roger 1937-1995 57
  Brief entry 39
Zelazny, Roger Joseph
  See Zelazny, Roger
Zeldis, Malcah 1931- 146
  Earlier sketch in SATA 86
Zelinsky, Paul O. 1953- 154
  Brief entry 33
  Earlier sketches in SATA 49, 102
  See also CLR 55
Zellan, Audrey Penn
  See Penn, Audrey
Zemach, Harve
  See Fischtrom, Harvey
Zemach, Kaethe 1958- 149
  Brief entry 39
  Earlier sketch in SATA 49
Zemach, Margot 1931-1989 70
  Obituary 59
  Earlier sketch in SATA 21
Zemach-Bersin, Kaethe
  See Zemach, Kaethe
Zeman, Ludmila 1947- 153
Zepeda, Gwendolyn 1971- 206
Zephaniah, Benjamin 1958- 189
  Earlier sketches in SATA 86, 140
Zephaniah, Benjamin Obadiah Iqbal
  See Zephaniah, Benjamin
Zephaniah, Benjamin Pbadiah Iqubal
  See Zephaniah, Benjamin
Zerman, Melvyn Bernard 1930-2010 46
Zettner, Pat 1940- 70
Zevin, Gabrielle 176
Zhang, Christopher Zhong-Yuan 1954- 91
Zhang, Song Nan 1942- 170
  Earlier sketch in SATA 85
Ziefert, Harriet 1941- 205
  Earlier sketches in SATA 101, 154
Ziegler, Jack (Denmore) 1942- 60
Ziemienski, Dennis (Theodore) 1947- 10
Ziliox, Marc
  See Fichter, George S.
Zillah
  See Macdonald, Zillah K(atherine)
Zim, Herbert S(pencer) 1909-1994 30
  Obituary 85
  Earlier sketch in SATA 1
  See also CLR 2
  See also SAAS 2
Zim, Sonia Bleeker 1909-1971 2
  Obituary 26
Zima, Gordon 1920- 90
Zimelman, Nathan 1921- 65
  Brief entry 37
Zimmer, Dirk 1943- 147
  Earlier sketch in SATA 65
Zimmer, Tracie Vaughn 169
Zimmerman, Andrea 1950- 192
  Earlier sketch in SATA 123
Zimmerman, Andrea Griffing
  See Zimmerman, Andrea
Zimmerman, H. Werner 1951- 101
Zimmerman, Heinz Werner
  See Zimmerman, H. Werner
Zimmerman, Naoma 1914-2004 10
Zimmermann, Arnold E. 1909- 58
Zimmermann, Karl 1943- 211

Zimmermann, Karl R.
  See Zimmermann, Karl
Zimmett, Debbie
  See Becker, Deborah Zimmett
Zimmy
  See Stratemeyer, Edward L.
Zimnik, Reiner 1930- 36
  See also CLR 3
Zindel, Bonnie 1943- 34
Zindel, Lizabeth 187
Zindel, Paul 1936-2003 102
  Obituary 142
  Earlier sketches in SATA 16, 58
  See also CLR 85
Ziner, Feenie
  See Ziner, Florence
Ziner, Florence 1921- 5
Zingara, Professor
  See Leeming, Joseph
Zinger, Yitskhok
  See Singer, Isaac Bashevis
Zink, Michelle 1969- 220
Zion, Eugene 1913-1975 18
Zion, Gene
  See Zion, Eugene
Zobel, Allia
  See Zobel Nolan, Allia
Zobel Nolan, Allia 218
Zoehfeld, Kathleen Weidner 1954- 193
Zohorsky, Janet R. 1958- 148
Zolkower, Edie Stoltz 171
Zolkowski, Cathy (A.) 1969- 121
Zollars, Jaime 191
Zolotow, Charlotte 1915- 138
  Earlier sketches in SATA 1, 35, 78
  See also CLR 77
Zolotow, Charlotte Gertrude Shapiro
  See Zolotow, Charlotte
Zolotow, Ellen
  See Dragonwagon, Crescent
Zonderman, Jon 1957- 92
Zonia, Dhimitri 1921- 20
Zonta, Pat 1951- 143
Zubrowski, Bernard 1939- 90
  Earlier sketch in SATA 35
Zubrowski, Bernie
  See Zubrowski, Bernard
Zucker, Miriam S.
  See Reichert, Miriam Zucker
Zuckerman, Amy 217
Zuckerman, Andrew 1977- 224
Zuckerman, Linda 190
Zudeck, Darryl 1961- 61
Zug, Mark 204
Zulkey, Claire 1979- 225
Zupa, G. Anthony
  See Zeck, Gerald Anthony
Zupancic, Lilijana Praprotnik
  See Prap, Lila
Zurbo, Matt(hew) 1967- 98
Zurhorst, Charles (Stewart, Jr.) 1913-1989 .. 12
Zurlo, Tony 1941- 145
Zuromskis, Diane
  See Stanley, Diane
Zuromskis, Diane Stanley
  See Stanley, Diane
Zusak, Markus 1975- 149
Zwahlen, Diana 1947- 88
Zweifel, Frances W. 1931- 14
Zwerger, Lisbeth 1954- 194
  Earlier sketches in SATA 66, 130
  See also CLR 46
  See also SAAS 13
Zwinger, Ann (H.) 1925- 46
Zymet, Cathy Alter 1965- 121